BASIC STATISTICS

AF644654

BASIC STATISTICS

EIGHTH EDITION

B L AGARWAL
Formerly-Professor & University Head
Department of Statistics and Mathematics
Rajasthan Agricultural University
RCA, Udaipur
India

Committed to Educate the Nation

NEW AGE

Publishing Globally

IN INDIA

NEW AGE INTERNATIONAL (P) LIMITED, PUBLISHERS

LONDON • NEW DELHI

Bangalore • Chennai • Cochin • Guwahati • Hyderabad • Kolkata • Mumbai

Visit us at **www.newagepublishers.com**

Copyright © 2024, 2022, 2013, 2009, 2005, 1996, 1991, 1988, New Age International (P) Ltd., Publishers
Published by New Age International (P) Ltd., Publishers
First Edition: 1988
Eighth Edition: 2024
Reprint: 2026

All rights reserved.
No part of this book may be reproduced in any form, by photostat, microfilm, xerography, or any other means, or incorporated into any information retrieval system, electronic or mechanical, without the written permission of the publisher.

GLOBAL OFFICES

- **New Delhi** **NEW AGE INTERNATIONAL (P) LIMITED, PUBLISHERS**
  7/30 A, Daryaganj, New Delhi-110002, (INDIA), **Tel.:** (011) 23253472, 23253771, **Mob.:** 9315905300
  E-mail: contactus@newagepublishers.com • Visit us at www.newagepublishers.com

- **London** **NEW AGE INTERNATIONAL (UK) LTD.**
  27 Old Gloucester Street, London, WC1N 3AX, UK
  E-mail: info@newacademicscience.co.uk • Visit us at www.newacademicscience.co.uk

BRANCHES

- **Bangalore** 37/10, 8th Cross (Near Hanuman Temple), Azad Nagar, Chamarajpet, Bangalore- 560 018
  Tel.: (080) 26756823, **Mob.:** 9315905288, **E-mail: bangalore@newagepublishers.com**

- **Chennai** 26, Damodaran Street, T. Nagar, Chennai-600 017, **Tel.:** (044) 24353401, **Mob.:** 9315905309
  E-mail: chennai@newagepublishers.com

- **Cochin** CC-39/1016, Carrier Station Road, Ernakulam South, Cochin-682 016
  Tel.: (0484) 4051304, **Mob.:** 9315905289, **E-mail: cochin@newagepublishers.com**

- **Guwahati** Hemsen Complex, Mohd. Shah Road, Paltan Bazar, Near Starline Hotel
  Guwahati-781 008, **Tel.:** (0361) 2513881, **Mob.:** 9315905296, **E-mail: guwahati@newagepublishers.com**

- **Hyderabad** 105, 1st Floor, Madhiray Kaveri Tower, 3-2-19, Azam Jahi Road, Near Kumar Theater
  Nimboliadda Kachiguda, Hyderabad-500 027, **Tel.:** (040) 24652456, **Mob.:** 9315905326
  E-mail: hyderabad@newagepublishers.com

- **Kolkata** RDB Chambers (Formerly Lotus Cinema) 106A, 1st Floor, S N Banerjee Road
  Kolkata-700 014, **Tel.:** (033) 22273773, **Mob.:** 9315905319, **E-mail: kolkata@newagepublishers.com**

- **Mumbai** 142C, Victor House, Ground Floor, N.M. Joshi Marg, Lower Parel, Mumbai-400 013
  Tel.: (022) 24927869, 24915415, **Mob.:** 9315905282, **E-mail: mumbai@newagepublishers.com**

- **New Delhi** 22, Golden House, Daryaganj, New Delhi-110 002, **Tel.:** (011) 23262368, 23262370
  Mob.: 9315905300, **E-mail: sales@newagepublishers.com**

C-26-03-15413

Printed in India at R. K Printers, Delhi.
Typeset at In-house, Delhi.

NEW AGE INTERNATIONAL (P) LIMITED, PUBLISHERS
7/30 A, Daryaganj, New Delhi - 110002
Visit us at **www.newagepublishers.com**
(CIN: U74899DL1966PTC004618)

Preface to the Eighth Edition

There is a continuous growth in the application of statistical methods. The book entitled *Basic Statistics* fulfils the requirement of students, teachers and researchers of all faculties like Commerce, Humanities, Agricultural Sciences, Business Management, Biological Sciences, Professional Courses, Education, etc.

This book emphasises on conceptual understanding and proper application of statistical tools that are beneficial in all sciences. To fulfill the requirements of the present day courses, an Appendix on **Some Important Terms** has been added in this book. This edition is totally updated with latest developments in statistical methods and all the corrections left inadvertently in the previous edition have been duly rectified. An effort has been made to make this book error-free. This will instil greater confidence in inquisitive minds. Smoothness in readability has also been enhanced. On the whole, the eighth edition will prove to be the best book for success in various examinations. Researchers will find it as the best research guide to carry out their research by collecting the data in a proper statistical manner and analysing it manually or using SPSS package as per procedure expatiated in the appendices of a number of relevant chapters.

As per the feedback from the users, the author finds that the matter contained in this book is sufficient for all courses taught in various universities. Researchers will also be able to apply statistical methods in the analysis of data with the help of this book.

BASIC STATISTICS IS A READER–FRIENDLY BOOK AND KEY TO ASSURED SUCCESS.

Basant Lal Agarwal

Preface to the First Edition

Statistics is considered to be a tough subject, particularly by the students of humanities and commerce, since they do not have much background and interest in mathematics. Keeping in view these constraints, I have ventured to write the present book–*Basic Statistics*–which comprehensively covers the curriculum of M.Com., M.A. (Eco.), I.C.W.A. and C.A. I am confident that this book will not only meet the academic needs of students but will also rank them in good stead in the competitive examinations. Some of the salient features of this book are as follows:

(*a*) Each chapter provides stepwise historical development with the names of pioneer workers in the respective field and discusses the use and importance of each topic under reference.

(*b*) The matter has been gradually developed in logical and methodical manner involving as little mathematics as possible.

(*c*) The theory part has been explicated in lucid and unambiguous manner. Standard terminology and notations have been used throughout the book.

(*d*) The implications and applications of theory have been illustrated through examples from the applied fields. Numerical problems have been taken from the areas which seemed germane to me. Data chosen for the problems mostly related to the fields of economics and commerce. An effort has been made to create better understanding through real numerical examples rather than using imaginary and fictitious data. Such examples reflect real variability occurring in various situations and the inferences drawn are more sound and meaningful.

(*e*) The latest information and developments on each topic have been adequately discussed keeping in view, of course, the limitations of prescribed course work.

(*f*) Every effort has been made to make the language simple and easily understandable which conforms to definitions and explanations.

(*g*) Every kind of repetition and parallel examples have been avoided.

(*h*) Each chapter ends with a number of exercises which include objective, short essay, essay type questions and numerical problems. These questions will instill confidence in the students.

In addition to the above points, the inquisitive minds will find many more useful features dealt with in this book.

I would be grateful to the readers, for pointing out any shortcomings, mistakes and for sending their valued suggestions to bring about further improvements in this book.

I will be failing in my duty if I do not pay my thanks to those who have helped and encouraged me in the writing of this book. I am grateful to my brother Dr. S.P. Agarwal, Professor of Animal Physiology, College of Vety. Sciences, HAU, Hissar, for encouragement and guidelines provided to me. I pay my hearty thanks to Shri R.V. Singh, Asstt. Director, Sukhadia University for giving a thorough reading of all the chapters from language point of view.

I thank my friends and many others who have helped me in anyway in the completion of this book.

I gratefully acknowledge the valued opinion given by Dr. D.D. Joshi, Professor of Statistics and Director, Institute of Social Sciences, Agra University, Agra, Dr. R.B.L. Agarwal, Professor and Head, Department of Commerce, Sukhadia University, Udaipur and to Dr. R.D. Agarwal, Director, Department of Business Management, Devi Ahilya Vishwavidyalaya, Indore.

I am indebted to the Biometrika Trustees for permission to reproduce few statistical tables from, "Biometrika Tables for Statisticians", Vol. 1, 3rd ed., 1996.

I am grateful to the Literary Executor of the Late Sir Ronald A. Fisher, F.R.S., Dr. Frank Yates, F.R.S. and Longman Group Limited, London for permission to reproduce tables from their book, "Statistical Tables for Biological, Agricultural and Medical Research" 6th ed., 1974.

The author is highly thankful to the American Society for Testing and Materials for permission to reproduce the table, B_2 from ASTM, STP, ISC.

I am indebted to the authors and to the American Statistical Association for their permission to copy the tables from the Journal of American Statistical Association and include them in my book.

I wish to convey my hearty thanks to the authors and executives for academic affairs and provost to reproduce extended tables for the Mann-Whitney statistics published in the bulletin of the Institute of Educational Research at Indian University, Vol. 1, No. 2, 1953.

I gratefully acknowledge the permission of the American Cyanamid Company and the authors to include material from some Rapid Appropriate Statistical Procedures originally published in the bulletin.

I wish to express my sincere thanks to– The Managing Editor, Institute of Mathematical Statistics, California, for reproducing a few tables from their journal, Annals of Mathematical Statistics.

At last I thank my wife Mrs. Kanak Agarwal and my children for their sustenance and patience during the writing of the book.

Basant Lal Agarwal

Acknowledgements

First and foremost I am grateful to Dr. Nityesh Bhatt, Associate Professor, Pacific Institute of Management, Udaipur and presently at Nirma Institute of Management, Ahmedabad for prompting me to introduce an element of computer based data analysis. Dr. Bhatt not only suggested but provided full guidance in what way can this aspect be covered. The author thanks to Dr. Bhawna Agarwal, Lecturer, IILM, New Delhi, for exposure of SPSS windows and solve examples through SPSS package given in this book for verification and demonstration. I also thank Dr. B.R. Ranwah, Associate Professor, R.C.A., Udaipur for succour. I thank my grandson Tarun Goyal, a Medical Student for his help in computer work.

Ultimately, the credit for all this improvement goes to Shri Saumya Gupta, Managing Director, New Age International (P) Ltd., Publishers, New Delhi who reposed confidence in me and encouraged to revise the fifth edition in such a way that this book can make a place in international market. My hearty thanks to Mr. Saumya Gupta.

Basant Lal Agarwal

Symbols and Notations

A

A	Average
α	Probability of Type I error
α_3	Pearson's measure of skewness
α_4	Pearson's measure of kurtosis

B

β	Probability of Type II error
β_1	Coefficient of skewness
β_2	Coefficient of kurtosis
β_{yx} or b_{yx}	Regression coefficient of y on x
β_{xy} or b_{xy}	Regression coefficient of x on y
$\beta_{xy.z}$ or $b_{xy.z}$	Partial regression coefficient of x on y eliminating the effect of z.

C

χ^2	Chi-square

D

D_i	i-th decile
d	Precision required
$\overline{d}$ or $\overline{D}$	Mean of differences
Δ^i_y	i-th order difference used in interpolation

E

e	Error
E	Event
$\overline{E}$ or E^C	Complementary event
E_{12}	Efficiency of design 1 over 2

F

f	Frequency
$f_x(x)$	Frequency distribution of x
F	Snedecor's F-statistic
$F_x(x)$	Distribution function of x

G

G	Geometric mean
γ_1	Fisher's coefficient of skewness
γ_2	Fisher's coefficient of kurtosis

H

H	Harmonic mean

I

I or i	Class interval
I.R.	Interquartile range
I_{01}	Unweighted price index

L

L	Largest value
l_0 or L_0	Lower limit of a class interval
L_{01}	Laspeyre's price index

M

μ	Population mean
M_d	Median
M_o	Mode
μ_r	r-th central moment
μ'_r	r-th raw moment
μ^a_r	r-th moment about a
$m_x(t)$	Moment generating function

N

n	Sample size
N	Population size
$\binom{N}{n}$	Number of combination
$N(\mu, \sigma^2)$	Normal distribution with mean μ and variance σ^2

P

P_{01}	Paasche's price index
P_i	i-th percentile
P	Probability
ϕ	Null set
$\phi_x(t)$	Characteristic function of x
$P(B \mid A)$	Conditional probability of B
%	Per cent
$P_x(x)$	Probability function of x
‰	Per thousand

Q

Q_i	i-th quartile
Q	Coefficient of association

R

R	Range
r_s	Spearman's rank correlation
R	Multiple correlation
r^2	Coefficient of determination
ρ_{xy}	Population correlation coefficient between X and Y
r_{xy}	Sample correlation coefficient between X and Y
$r_{ij.k}$	Partial correlation coefficient

S

s	Sample standard deviation
s^2	Sample variance
S^2	Modified σ^2
σ^2	Population variance
S	Smallest value
σ	Population standard deviation
s_p	Pooled standard deviation
σ^2_{12}	Two groups pooled variance
σ_{12}	Two groups pooled standard deviation
σ_{xy} or s_{xy}	Covariance between X and Y
s^2_e	Mean squared error
s_r	Standard error of r
S^2_b	Variance between clusters
S^2_w	Variance within clusters

T

t	Student's t-statistic

U

U_R	Statistic value of reliability R

X

$\overline{X}$	Population mean
$\bar{x}$	Sample mean
$\bar{x}_{12}$	Two groups pooled mean

Y

Y	Coefficient of colligation

Z

Z	Standard normal variate

Abbreviations and Acronyms Used in the Book

A.E. Absolute Error
AIDS Acquired Immune Deficiency Syndrome
A.M. Arithmetic Mean
ANOVA Analysis of Variance
A.O.Q.L. Average Outgoing Quality Limit
A.Q.L. Acceptance Quality Level
ASFR Age Specific Fertility Rate
ASI Annual Survey of Industries
ASMFR Age Specific Marital Fertility Rate
ASN Average Sample Number

CATI Computer Assisted Telephone Interview
C.D.R Crude Death Rate
C.F. Characteristic Function
C.F. Correction Factor
C.I. Confidence Interval
C.L. Confidence Limits
CMFRI Central Marine Fisheries Research Institute
CSIR Council of Scientific and Industrial Research
CSO Central Statistical Office
CSO Central Statistical Organization
C.V. Coefficient of Variation

DCIS Directorate of Commercial Intelligence and Statistics
DCSSI Development Commissioner Small Scale Industries
DES Directorate of Economics and Statistics
DET Directorate of Employment and Training
DGMS Director General of Mines Safety

DIS	Department of Intelligence and Statistics
DMI	Directorate of Mining and Inspection
e.g.	For Example
EMV	Expected Monetary Value
EOL	Expected Opportunity Loss
EVPI	Expected Value of Perfect Information
EVUC	Expected Value Under Certainty
FAO	Food and Agricultural Organization
FOD	Field Operation Division
FPC (fpc)	Finite Population Correction
GDI	Gross Domestic Income
GDP	Gross Domestic Product
GFR	General Fertility Rate
G.M.	Geometric Mean
GMFR	General Marital Fertility Rate
GNI	Gross National Income
GRR	Gross Reproduction Rate
H.M.	Harmonic Mean
I	Instrumentation
IASRI	Indian Agricultural Statistics Research Institute
IBM	Indian Bureau of Mines
ICI	Imperial Chemical Industries
I.D.R.	Index Death Rate
i.e.	That is
IFA	Indian Factories Act
ILO	International Labor Organization
IMF	International Monetary Fund
LABSTAT	Bureau of Labor Statistics
LCL	Lower Control Limit
Lim	Limit
log	Logarithm
lsd	Least Significant Difference
L.T.P.D.	Lot Tolerance Percentage Defective
M.D.	Mean Deviation
M.G.F.	Moment Generating Function

M.S.	Mean Sum of Squares
M.S.E.	Mean Squared Error
MTE	Main Testing Effect
MYE	Mid-year Estimate
NAS	National Accounts Statistics
NDP	Net Domestic Product
NIC	National Income Committee
NIU	National Income Unit
NRR	Net Reproduction Rate
NSSO	National Sample Survey Organization
O.C.	Operating Characteristics
PGDHTP	Post Graduate Degree Holders and Technical Personnel
Q.D.	Quartile Deviation
SC	Schedule Caste
SB	Selection Bias
S.D.	Standard Deviation
S.D.R.	Specific Death Rate
S_T.D.R.	Standard Death Rate
S.E.	Standard Error
SFD	State Fisheries Department
S.N.D.	Standard Normal Deviate
S.O.C.	Standard Occupational Classification
S.P.R.T.	Sequential Probability Ratio Test
S.Q.C.	Sequential Quality Control
SR	Statistical Regression
srs	Simple random sampling
S.S.	Sum of Squares
ST	Schedule Tribes
swr	Selection with replacement
swor	Selection without replacement
TFR	Total Fertility Rate
TMFR	Total Marital Fertility Rate
U.C.L.	Upper Control Limit
U.N.O.	United Nations Organization
U.S.A.	United States of America

5. It should not be subjected to complicated and tedious calculations, though the advent of electronic calculators and computers has made it possible to overlook this aspect.
6. It should be capable of further algebraic treatment. By algebraic treatment, we mean that these measures can be used further in the formulation of other formulae. For instance, a mean can be used to calculate the pooled mean of two or more series.
7. It should be stable with regard to sampling. This means that if a number of samples of the same size are drawn from a population, the measure of central tendency having the minimum variation among the different calculated values should be preferred.

MEAN

There are three types of mean which are suitable for a particular type of data. They are,

(*a*) Arithmetic mean or Average
(*b*) Geometric mean
(*c*) Harmonic mean.

Arithmetic Mean (A.M.)

It is also popularly known as average. If mean is mentioned, it implies arithmetic mean, as the other means are identified by their full names. It is the most commonly used measure of central tendency.

Definition. Sum of the observed values of a set divided by the number of observations in the set is called a mean or an average.

If $X_1, X_2, ..., X_N$ are N observed values, the mean or average is given as,

$$\mu \text{ or } A = \frac{X_1 + X_2 + ... + X_N}{N} \quad ...(3.1)$$

$$= \frac{1}{N} \Sigma_i X_i \quad ...(3.1.1)$$

for $i = 1, 2, . . . N$

Population[1] mean is usually denoted by μ or $\overline{X}$ whereas the sample[2] mean is denoted by $\bar{x}$ (small letter).

When the data are arranged or given in the form of frequency distribution *i.e.*, there are k variate values such that a value X_i has a frequency f_i $(i = 1, 2, ..., k)$, the formula for the mean is,

$$\mu = \frac{f_1X_1 + f_2X_2 + ... + f_kX_k}{f_1 + f_2 + ... + f_k} \quad ...(3.2)$$

$$= \frac{\Sigma_i f_i X_i}{\Sigma_i f_i} \qquad i = 1, 2, ..., k \quad ...(3.2.1)$$

$$= \frac{1}{N} \Sigma_i f_i X_i \quad ...(3.2.2)$$

where $N = f_1 + f_2 + ... + f_k = \Sigma_i f_i$

1. See definition of population in Chapter 7.
2. See definition of sample in Chapter 7.

If the data are given with k class intervals *i.e.*, the data are in the form as follows:

Class interval	*Frequency*
$X_1 - X_2$	f_1
$X_2 - X_3$	f_2
$X_3 - X_4$	f_3
$\vdots$	$\vdots$
$X_k - X_{k+1}$	f_k

The arithmetic mean

$$\mu = \frac{f_1Y_1 + f_2Y_2 + ... + f_kY_k}{f_1 + f_2 + ... + f_k} \qquad ...(3.3)$$

$$= \frac{1}{N}\Sigma_i f_i Y_i \qquad ...(3.3.1)$$

where Y_i is the mid-point of the class interval X_i–X_{i+1} and is given as,

$$Y_i = \frac{X_i + X_{i+1}}{2} \qquad i = 1, 2, ..., k$$

In this situation the values in the interval are considered to be centered at the mid-point of the interval.

Weighted Mean

In case, k variate values $X_1, X_2, ..., X_k$ have known weights $\omega_1, \omega_2, ...\omega_k$ respectively, then the weighted mean is,

$$\mu = \frac{\omega_1X_1 + \omega_2X_2 + ... + \omega_kX_k}{\omega_1 + \omega_2 + ... + \omega_k} \qquad ...(3.4)$$

$$= \frac{1}{\omega}\Sigma_i \omega_i X_i \qquad ...(3.4.1)$$

where $\omega = \Sigma_i \omega_i$, $\qquad i = 1, 2, ..., k$

Weighted mean is commonly used in the construction of index numbers.

Note: If the sample values $x_1, x_2, ..., x_n$ are given, in the formulae given above, capital X will be changed to small x and N to n. The sample mean will be denoted by $\overline{x}$ *e.g.*, the formula (3.1) will be changed to

$$\overline{x} = \frac{x_1 + x_2 + ... + x_n}{n} \qquad ...(3.5)$$

$$= \frac{1}{n}\Sigma_i x_i \qquad ...(3.5.1)$$

$$i = 1, 2, ..., n$$

Similarly all other formulae will be changed to sample values. Since most of the studies are based on samples in practice, we use formulae for sample values.

Merits and Demerits

1. Algebraic sum of the deviations of the given values from their arithmetic mean is always zero, *i.e.*, $\Sigma_i(X_i - \overline{X}) = 0$.

2. The sum of the squares of the deviations of the given values from their A.M. is minimum, *i.e.*, $\Sigma_i (X_i - \overline{X})^2$.
3. An average possesses all the characteristics of a central value given earlier except no. 2, which is greatly affected by the extreme values.
4. In case of grouped data if any class interval is open, arithmetic mean cannot be calculated, *e.g.*, the classes are less than five in the beginning or more than 70 at the end of the distribution or both.

***Example* 3.1.** Daily cash earnings of 15 workers working in different industries are as follows:

Average daily earning (Rs)

11.63,	8.22,	12.56,	12.14,	29.23,	18.23,	11.49,	11.30,
17.00,	9.16,	8.64,	27.56,	8.23,	19.77	12.81	

Average daily earning of a worker can be calculated by the formula (3.1)

$$A = \frac{1}{15}(11.63 + 8.22 + ... + 12.81)$$
$$= \frac{217.97}{15}$$
$$= 14.53$$

The average daily earning of a worker is Rs. 14.53.

***Example* 3.2.** The distribution of age at first marriage of 130 males was as given below.

Age in years (X) :	18,	19,	20,	21,	22,	23,	24,	25,	26,	27,	28,	29,
No. of males (f) :	2,	1,	4,	8,	10,	12,	17,	19,	18,	14,	13,	12,

The average age can be computed by the formula (3.2).

$$A = \frac{18 \times 2 + 19 \times 1 + ... + 29 \times 12}{2 + 1 + ... + 12}$$
$$= \frac{3240}{130}$$
$$= 24.92 \text{ years.}$$

The mean age of males at first marriage is 24.92 years.

***Example* 3.3.** The distribution of size of holdings of cultivated land, in an area, was as follows:

Size of holdings (hectares)	*Mid-points (y)*	*No. of holdings (f)*
0 – 2	1	48
2 – 4	3	19
4 – 6	5	10
6 – 8	7	14
8 – 10	9	11
10 – 20	15	9
20 – 40	30	2
40 – 60	50	1

Average size of holding in the area can be calculated with the help of the formula (3.3). Mid-points of the class intervals are shown in the middle column along with the data. Hence,

$$\text{A.M.} = \frac{1\times48+3\times19+...+50\times1}{48+19+...+1}$$

$$= \frac{597}{114}$$

$$= 5.237$$

The average size of holding is 5.237 hectares.

***Example* 3.4.** The life of eighty condensers obtained in a life testing experiment has been presented below in the form of "less than" type of distribution.

Life of condensers (Years)	*No. of condensers*
Less than 1	3
,, ,, 2	12
,, ,, 3	14
,, ,, 4	22
,, ,, 5	33
,, ,, 6	46
,, ,, 7	58
,, ,, 8	66
,, ,, 9	75
,, ,, 10	80

The given distribution with regular class intervals and their mid-values can be written as,

Years	*Mid-values* (*y*)	*No. of condensers* (*f*)
0 – 1	0.5	3
1 – 2	1.5	9
2 – 3	2.5	2
3 – 4	3.5	8
4 – 5	4.5	11
5 – 6	5.5	13
6 – 7	6.5	12
7 – 8	7.5	8
8 – 9	8.5	9
9 – 10	9.5	5

The average life of a condenser can be calculated by the formula (3.3) as,

$$\overline{X} = \frac{3\times0.5+9\times1.5+...+5\times9.5}{3+9+...+5}$$

$$= \frac{431}{80}$$

$$= 5.39 \text{ years.}$$

***Example* 3.5.** The table below presents the total expenditure in the form of "more than" type frequency distribution. We know that the expenditure cannot exceed Rs. 2250 crores.

Expenditure (Rs crores)	*No. of banks*
More than 2000	1
,, ,, 1750	2
,, ,, 1500	4
,, ,, 1250	7
,, ,, 1000	13
,, ,, 750	18
,, ,, 550	28
,, ,, 250	40

To find the average expenditure, we rewrite the given cumulative frequency distribution, with regular class intervals, as given below. Mid-values of the classes are also shown in the middle column.

Expenditure (Rs crores)	*Mid-values*	*No. of banks*
2000 – 2250	2125	1
1750 – 2000	1875	2 – 1 = 1
1500 – 1750	1625	4 – 2 = 2
1250 – 1500	1375	7 – 4 = 3
1000 – 1250	1125	13 – 7 = 6
750 – 1000	875	18 – 13 = 5
500 – 750	625	28 – 18 = 10
250 – 500	375	40 – 28 = 12

On an average the expenditure per bank is,

$$\overline{X} = \frac{2125\times1+1875\times1+...+375\times12}{1+1+...+12}$$

$$= \frac{33250}{40}$$

$$= \text{Rs. } 831.25 \text{ crores}$$

CODING OF DATA

A linear transformation of data may be regarded as coding. In coding, we shift the origin and change the scale. A change can involve either a change of origin or a change of scale or change of both, origin and scale together. The effect of coding on mean is given below.

1. If we subtract an arbitrary constant from each of the observation, the mean is also reduced by the constant value.
2. If we divide each observation of a set by an arbitrary constant, the mean is reduced as many times as the constant divisor.

(**Note:** In case of addition or multiplication, the word 'reduced' should be replaced by 'increased' in the above statements. The above two operations cut short the calculation. But the availability of electronic calculators and computers has diminished the importance of coding of data. Anyhow, it can be used whenever needed.)

Let $X_1, X_2, ..., X_N$ be N observations. An arbitrary constant a is subtracted from each of the observation and the reduced observation is divided by a constant c. Suppose the transformed observations are denoted by $X'_1, X'_2, ..., X'_N$, where $X'_i = \frac{X_i - a}{c}$. The arithmetic mean of the original data with the help of coded observations is given as,

$$\overline{X} = a + \frac{\Sigma_i X'_i}{N} \times c \qquad ...(3.6)$$

for $i = 1, 2, ..., N$.

In case of frequency distribution with coding of data,

$$\overline{X} = a + \frac{\Sigma_i f_i X'_i}{N} \times c \qquad ...(3.7)$$

where $N = \Sigma_i f_i$.

In the case of group data, generally the central mid-value of the classes is subtracted from each of the mid-value and the reduced observation is divided by the constant class interval. If the class interval is not same for all classes, any suitable value may be chosen as divisor.

***Example* 3.6.** The production of pig iron and ferro-alloys in India from 1969 to 1975 is as given below.

Years :	1969	1970	1971	1972	1973	1974	1975
Production : (*Metric Tonnes*)	624,000	602,000	582,000	615,000	626,000	620,000	712,000

Average production of pig iron and ferro-alloys by coding of data can be calculated in the following manner.

From each observation, we subtract 5,80,000 and divide each subtracted value by 1000.

The coded values are,

$$X'_1 = \frac{624000 - 580000}{1000} = 44$$

$$X'_2 = \frac{602000 - 580000}{1000} = 22$$

Similarly, all other coded values are calculated. Thus, the coded observations are,

X' : 44, 22, 2, 35, 46, 40, 132

$$\Sigma_i X'_i = (44 + 22 + ... + 132)$$
$$= 321$$

The average production of the original observations with the help of coded values by the formula (3.6) is

$$\overline{X} = 580000 + \frac{321}{7} \times 1000$$
$$= 625857.14 \text{ metric tonnes.}$$

***Example* 3.7.** The distribution of the marks of commerce students of a college in Business Statistics was as follows:

Class intervals of marks	*No. of students*
20–30	2
30–40	5
40–50	22
50–60	34
60–70	9
70–80	3
80–100	1

The average marks earned by a student can be calculated by coding method. For this, the following table is prepared.

Class intervals	*Mid-values*	*Frequency (f)*	$X' = \frac{X-55}{10}$	fX'
20–30	25	2	–3	–6
30–40	35	5	–2	–10
40–50	45	22	–1	–22
50–60	55	34	0	00
60–70	65	9	1	9
70–80	75	3	2	6
80–100	90	1	3.5	3.5
Total		76		–19.5

In the above coding process, we have chosen $a = 55$ and $c = 10$. The average marks calculated by the formula (3.7) are,

$$\overline{X} = 55 + \frac{(-19.5)}{76} \times 10$$
$$= 55 - 2.57$$
$$= 52.43 \text{ marks.}$$

Pooled or Combined Mean

If we have arithmetic means $\overline{X}_1$ and $\overline{X}_2$ of two groups (having the same unit of measurement of a variable), based on N_1 and N_2 observations respectively, we can compute the mean $\overline{X}_{12}$ of the variate values of the groups taken together from the individual means by the formula,

$$\overline{X}_{12} = \frac{N_1\overline{X}_1 + N_2\overline{X}_2}{N_1 + N_2} \quad ...(3.8)$$

The advantage of this formula is that we do not have to do the entire calculations for the mean of the combined set of observations again. Moreover, the formula for two groups can be extended to any number of groups.

Geometric Mean (G.M.)

In algebra, geometric mean is calculated in case of geometric progression, but in statistics we need not bother about the progression. Here, it is the particular type of data for which the geometric mean is of importance because it gives a good mean value. If the variate values are measured as ratios, proportions or percentages, geometric mean gives a better measure of central tendency than other means.

Definition: Geometric mean of N variate values is the Nth root of their product. Like arithmetic mean it also depends on all observations. It is affected by the extreme values but not to the extent of average. However, there is one great drawback with it, that it cannot be calculated if any one or more values are zero or negative. In case an even number of observations are negative, an absurd value of geometric mean will be available from a practical point of view. Hence, if there is a zero or negative value in the set of variate values, it should not be used.

Suppose $X_1, X_2, ..., X_N$ are N variate values, then the geometric mean is given as,

$$G = \sqrt[N]{X_1 X_2 ... X_N} \qquad ...(3.9)$$

In case $X_1, X_2, ..., X_k$ have the corresponding frequencies $f_1, f_2, ..., f_k$ then

$$G = \sqrt[N]{X_1^{f_1} X_2^{f_2} ... X_k^{f_k}} \qquad ...(3.10)$$

where $N = \Sigma_i f_i$ for $i = 1, 2, ..., k$.

Formulae (3.9) and (3.10) are exactly similar in the sense that instead of multiplying X_i, f_i times in (3.9) X_i is raised to the power f_i in the formula (3.10). Moreover, when each f_i is unity, formula (3.10) reduces to (3.9). In case of grouped data, mid-values of the class intervals are considered as X_i and the formula (3.9) can be used as such.

Though, some standard techniques are available to find out square root and cube root, yet for large value of N, Nth root is not easy to compute. To overcome this difficulty, geometric mean is computed through logarithm. Hence, some people even call it *logarithmic mean.* For logarithmic values of X' s, it becomes average of $\log X_i$ values and the formula for geometric mean is

$$\log G = \frac{1}{N} \Sigma_i (\log_{10} X_i) \qquad ...(3.11)$$

for $i = 1, 2, ..., N$.

In case of frequency distribution where each of X_i occurs f_i times ($i = 1, 2, ..., k$).

$$\log G = \frac{1}{N} \Sigma_i \{f_i \log_{10} X_i\} \qquad ...(3.12)$$

where $N = \Sigma_i f_i$ for $i = 1, 2, ..., k$.

Taking antilog of both sides in (3.11) and (3.12), we obtain G.M. Geometric mean is usually calculated when the growth rate or increase in production etc. are given for a number of years or periods.

***Example* 3.8.** Decadal percentage growth of urban population in India (excluding Assam and J & K) from 1921 to 1981 is given below.

Years	1921	1931	1941	1951	1961	1971	1981
Decadal per- cent increase	8.25	19.08	32.09	41.49	25.85	37.91	46.02

Average per cent growth rate of urban population with the last seven decades can be obtained by calculating the geometric mean by the formula (3.11).

$$\log_{10}(G) = \frac{1}{7}(\log_{10} 8.25 + \log_{10} 19.08 + \log_{10} 32.09 + \log_{10} 41.49 + \log_{10} 25.85 + \log_{10} 37.91 + \log_{10} 46.02)$$

$$= \frac{1}{7}(0.9165 + 1.2806 + 1.5063 + 1.6179 + 1.4125 + 1.5787 + 1.6630)$$

$$= \frac{9.9755}{7} = 1.4251$$

Taking antilog of both sides, we get the geometric mean

$$G = 26.62$$

Harmonic Mean (H.M.)

In algebra, harmonic mean is found out in the case of harmonic progression only. But in statistics harmonic mean is a suitable measure of central tendency when the data pertains to speed, rates and time.

Definition. Harmonic mean is the inverse of the arithmetic mean of the reciprocals of the observations of a set.

Let $X_1, X_2, ..., X_N$ be N variate values in a set, then the harmonic mean,

$$H = \frac{1}{\frac{1}{N}\Sigma_i\left(\frac{1}{X_i}\right)} \quad ...(3.13)$$

for $i = 1, 2, ..., N$.

If the data are arranged in the form of a frequency distribution in which an observation X_i has frequency f_i $(i = 1, 2, ..., k)$, the harmonic mean is given by,

$$H = \frac{N}{f_1/X_1 + f_2/X_2 + ... + f_k/X_k} \quad ...(3.14)$$

$$H = \frac{1}{\frac{1}{N}\Sigma_i(f_i/X_i)} \quad ...(3.14.1)$$

where $N = \Sigma_i f_i$ for $i = 1, 2, ..., k$.

It fulfills almost all properties of a good measure of central tendency, except when any observation is zero, it cannot be calculated. Its main advantage is that it gives more weightage to small values and less weightage to large values.

Lemma 1. If x_1 and x_2 are two observed values, the geometric mean of their arithmetic mean and harmonic mean is equal to the geometric mean of the numbers x_1 and x_2.

We know, $A = \frac{x_1 + x_2}{2}$

$$G = \sqrt{x_1 x_2}$$

and $H = 1\big/\tfrac{1}{2}\left(\frac{1}{x_1} + \frac{1}{x_2}\right) = \frac{2x_1 x_2}{x_1 + x_2}$

$$\sqrt{\text{A.H.}} = \sqrt{\frac{x_1 + x_2}{2} \times \frac{2x_1 x_2}{x_1 + x_2}} = \sqrt{x_1 x_2} = G$$

Hence proved.

Lemma 2. If *A*, *G* and *H* stand for A.M., G.M. and H.M. respectively, the relation

$$A \geq G \geq H.$$

holds.

Here this lemma is proved in the case of two observed values only. Let x_1 and x_2 be two non-negative values of a variable. We know,

$$A = \frac{x_1 + x_2}{2} \quad G = \sqrt{x_1 x_2} \quad H = \frac{2x_1 x_2}{x_1 + x_2}$$

Consider two situations (*i*) $x_1 = x_2$, (*ii*) $x_1 \neq x_2$.

(*i*) suppose $x_1 = x_2 = x$.

$$A = \frac{2x}{2} = x \quad G = \sqrt{x.x} = x \quad H = \frac{2.x.x}{x + x} = x$$

In this situation $A = G = H$. ...(1)

(*ii*) when $x_1 \neq x_2, x_1 - x_2$ is a real quantity and hence $\sqrt{x_1} - \sqrt{x_2}$ will also be a real quantity.

$$\therefore \quad (\sqrt{x_1} - \sqrt{x_2})^2 \geq 0$$

$$x_1 + x_2 - 2\sqrt{x_1 x_2} \geq 0$$

$$\frac{x_1 + x_2}{2} \geq \sqrt{x_1 x_2}$$

i.e., $A \geq G$. ...(2)

Again, $x_1 + x_2 \geq 2\sqrt{x_1 x_2}$

or $(x_1 + x_2)\sqrt{x_1 x_2} \geq 2\sqrt{x_1 x_2}\sqrt{x_1 x_2}$

$$\sqrt{x_1 x_2} \geq \frac{2x_1 x_2}{x_1 + x_2}$$

$G \geq H$. ... (3)

Combining the results (2) and (3), we get,

$$A \geq G \geq H.$$

***Example* 3.9.** A man travels from Jaipur to Agra by a car and takes four hours to cover the whole distance. In the first hour he maintains a speed of 50 km/h, in the second hour his speed remains 64 km/h, in the third 80 km/h and in the fourth hour he travels at the speed of 55 km/h. The average speed of the motorist can be known by calculating the harmonic mean.

$$H = 1/\frac{1}{4}\left(\frac{1}{50}+\frac{1}{65}+\frac{1}{80}+\frac{1}{55}\right) = \frac{4}{0.02+0.0154+0.0125+0.0182}$$

$$= \frac{4}{0.0661} = 60.5 \text{ km/hr.}$$

***Example* 3.10.** The arithmetic mean of two numbers is 13 and their geometric mean is 12. Find (*i*) the numbers (*ii*) H.M.

Let the two numbers are x_1 and x_2.

(*i*) Given that,

$$\frac{x_1+x_2}{2} = 13$$

or $\quad x_1 + x_2 = 26$

and $\quad x_1x_2 = 144$

Also $\quad (x_1 - x_2)^2 = (x_1+x_2)^2 - 4x_1x_2$

$$= (26)^2 - 4\times 144$$

$$= 676 - 576$$

$$= 100$$

$\therefore \quad x_1 - x_2 = \pm 10$

Taking $\quad x_1 - x_2 = 10 \quad$ ...(1)

Also $\quad x_1 + x_2 = 26 \quad$ ...(2)

From equations (1) and (2), we get,

$$2x_1 = 36$$

or $\quad x_1 = 18$

Putting the value of x_1 in either of the equations we get, $x_2 = 8$.

Hence, the two numbers are $x_1 = 18$ and $x_2 = 8$.

Taking $x_1 - x_2 = -10$ and solving the equations we get $x_1 = 8$ and $x_2 = 18$.

(*ii*) We know

$$A \times H = G^2$$

Substituting the value of A and G, we get,

$$13 \times H = (12)^2$$

$$H = \frac{144}{13}$$

$$= 11.077$$

MEDIAN

It has been pointed out that mean cannot be calculated whenever there is frequency distribution with open end intervals. Also the mean to a great extent affected by the extreme values of the set of observations. Hence in such cases, there has been a search for some better measure of central tendency. For instance, there are eight persons getting salaries as Rs. 150, 225, 240, 260, 275, 290, 300 and 1500. The mean salary of the persons involved is Rs.405. This value is not a good measure of central tendency because out of the eight people, seven get Rs. 300 or less. Hence, some better measure is preferable and median is one of them.

Definitions

(*i*) In a distribution, median is the value of the variable which divides it into two equal halves.

(*ii*) In an ordered series of data, median is an observation lying exactly in the middle of the series.

(*iii*) In a set of observations, median is the value of a variable that have half of the number of observations below it and remaining half above it.

The median for a set of observations can easily be found out after arranging them in ascending or descending order.

Let $X_1, X_2, ..., X_N$ be N ordered observations. Now two possibilities are there: (*a*) N is odd, say, $N = 2p + 1$ where p is an integer. In this case $(p + 1)$th observation will be the median value; (*b*) if N is even, $N = 2p$, then the average of pth and $(p + 1)$th observations will be the median value.

Consider the case where the data are arranged in the form of frequency distribution. Suppose the ordered values $X_1, X_2, ..., X_k$ have their corresponding frequencies $f_1, f_2, ..., f_k$, the median for it can be worked out in the following manner.

1. Find the cumulative frequencies.
2. Find $N/2$ where $N = \Sigma_i f_i$ for $i = 1, 2, ..., k$.
3. Search for the smallest cumulative frequency which contains this value N/2. The variate value corresponding to this cumulative frequency is the median.

Median for Grouped Data

If the data are given with class intervals as,

Class intervals	*Frequency*	*Cumulative frequency*
Less than X_2	f_1	F_1
$X_2 - X_3$	f_2	F_2
⋮	⋮	⋮
$X_p - X_{p+1}$	f_p	F_p
⋮	⋮	⋮
$X_k - X_{k+1}$	f_k	F_k

where $F_k = N = \Sigma_i f_i$ for $i = 1, 2, ..., k$, we can calculate median by the procedure given here. Find $N/2$ and see in which minimum of the cumulative frequency, $N/2$ is contained. Suppose $N/2$ is contained in the minimum cumulative frequency F_p, then obviously the median class is $X_p - X_{p+1}$. To find the unique median value, we take the help of the interpolation. In this approach, it is assumed that the frequency of a class is uniformly distributed over the class interval. Let the cumulative frequency for the class just above the median class be c. Thus $(N/2 - c)$ is the frequency for the interval between the median and lower limit of the median class. The length of the interval for $(N/2 - c)$ is $\frac{1}{f}(N/2 - c) \times I$ where f—frequency of the median class, I—class interval of the median class and say L_0—lower limit of the median class.

Hence the median,

$$M_d = L_0 + \frac{N/2 - c}{f} \times I \qquad ...(3.15)$$

Properties

1. Median is a positional average and hence it is not influenced by the extreme values.
2. Median can be calculated even in the case of open end intervals.
3. Median can be located even if the data are incomplete.
4. It is not a good representative of data if the number of items is small.
5. It is not amenable to further algebraic treatment.
6. It is susceptible to sampling fluctuations.

***Example* 3.11.** Actual waiting time for the first job on the selected sample of nine people having different field of specialisations was as given below.

Waiting time (in months): 11.6, 11.3, 10.7, 18.0, 3.3, 9.2, 8.3, 3.8, 6.8

The median waiting time can be calculated by arranging the data first in ascending order and then taking the mid-value.

3.3, 3.8, 6.8, 8.3, 9.2, 10.7, 11.3, 11.6, 18.0

Hence $N = 9$, $\therefore p = 4$.

Hence 5th value is the median value that is 9.2 months.

***Example* 3.12.** The export of agricultural products in million dollars from a country during eight quarters in 1974 and 1975 was,

29.7, 16.6, 2.3, 14.1, 36.6, 18.7, 3.5, 21.3.

To find the median of the given set of values, we arrange the data in descending order

36.6, 29.7, 21.3, 18.7, 16.6, 14.1, 3.5, 2.3

Here $N = 8$, $\therefore p = 4$

The mean of 4th and 5th values will be median value.

4th value = 18.7 and 5th value = 16.6

$$\text{Median} = \frac{18.7 + 16.6}{2}$$

$$= 17.65 \text{ million dollars}$$

Example **3.13.** Given the distribution of income of different occupational groups for the families in a region as:

Professional groups	*Income per year ('000 Rs)*	*Number of families*	*Cu.fr.*
Manager	169.1	82	82
Professional	136.3	62	144
Middle management	79.1	235	379
Manual work	35.7	179	558
Shopkeeper	34.0	96	654
Self-employed	24.9	195	849
Small farmer	19.2	714	1563
Farm labour	14.4	147	1710

The data are written in descending order and the cumulative frequencies are shown in the last column.

$$N = 1710 \text{ and } N/2 = 1710/2 = 855$$

The number 855 is contained in the smallest cumulative frequency 1563. Hence the corresponding value, 19.2 is the median value. It means that the median income is Rs. 19.2 thousand per year.

MODE

It is another measure of central tendency. Mode is a value of a particular type of items which occur most frequently. For instance if shoe size No. 7 has maximum demand, size No. 7 is the modal value of shoe sizes.

Definition. Mode is a variate value which occurs most frequently in a set of values.

In case of discrete distribution, one can find mode by inspection. The variate value having the maximum frequency is the modal value. For instance, consider the discrete distribution.

Variate value (X)	:	3	4	7	8	9	11	12
Frequency (f)	:	2	6	5	14	10	6	3

Clearly $x = 8$ has maximum frequency 14. Hence 8 is the modal value.

Remark: If in a set of observed values, all values occur once or equal number of times, there is no mode.

In cases where maximum frequency is repeated for more than one variate value or occurs for extreme values, the variate value should not be taken as modal value.

In case of frequency distributions in which the maximum frequency differs minutely from its adjoining class frequencies, the modal value or class cannot be correctly adjudged and hence the variate value or class corresponding to largest frequency should not be accepted as modal value or modal class merely by inspection.

If there is an irregular distribution, that is, if the trend of frequency changes all of a sudden for certain value(s), the variate value or class corresponding to the maximum frequency should not be accepted as mode.

***Example* 3.14.** The distribution of marks of 174 students out of 25 marks is,

Marks (X) :	3	4	6	7	9	10	13	15	18	20
Frequency (f):	4	8	15	20	32	16	14	35	10	6

The given distribution is an irregular distribution because the frequencies are increasing up to the value of $X = 9$ and then gradually decreasing except for $X = 15$ corresponding to which $f = 35$. This frequency is not consistent with the trend of data. Hence to consider $X = 15$ as mode is not proper.

In all the above three situations, mode obtained by mere inspection is not the correct value due to certain vagaries in sampling. Moreover, a measure of central tendency is considered good, provided most of the variate values cluster around it. Therefore, a better modal value can be worked out by the *method of grouping*. Various steps involved in the method of grouping are:

(*i*) Write the variate values, in order, in column (1) and the frequencies corresponding to them in column (2).

(*ii*) Add frequencies in pairs starting from the first and place them in a position between the two frequencies in column (3).

(*iii*) Omit the first frequency and repeat the step (*ii*) and place the added frequencies in column (4).

(*iv*) Again group the frequencies in three's starting from the first and place the sum of each group against the mid-frequency in column (5).

(*v*) Leave first frequency and repeat step (*iv*) creating column (6).

(*vi*) Again leave first two frequencies and repeat step (*iv*) placing the added values in column (7). Draw brackets in each column against added frequencies for two's or three's.

(*vii*) Parenthesise the maximum frequency of each column. The end frequencies which are not used in grouping are left out. For any distribution, the above mentioned seven columns are to be created.

Marks	*Freq.*	*Added frequencies*				
(1)	(2)	(3)	(4)	(5)	(6)	(7)
3	4					
		12				
4	8			27		
			23			
6	15				43	
		35				
7	20					(67)
			(52)			
9	32			(68)		
		48			(62)	
10	16					
			30			65
13	14					
		(49)		59		
15	(35)					
			45		51	
18	10					
		16				
20	6					

Once the frequency table is prepared, another table known as *analysis table* has to be prepared. In this table, the variate values are written in the caption (column heads) and column numbers along the sub-head. In the body of the table, give value 1 to each of the variate value which has been summed up in constituting the maximum frequency. Total 1's of each column of the analysis table. The variate value having the maximum column total is the mode.

Note: In case of tie, choose the variate value or class having maximum frequency.

Analysis table

Columns	*Marks (X)*									
	3	4	6	7	9	10	13	15	18	20
(2)								1		
(3)							1	1		
(4)				1	1					
(5)				1	1	1				
(6)					1	1	1			
(7)			1	1	1					
Total			1	3	4	2	2	2		

In the above table for $X = 9$, the maximum sum of 1's is 4, hence the modal value is 9.

Remarks:

(1) It is worth pointing out that by inspection one would have concluded that the mode is 15 as it has maximum frequency 35, however this is not correct, as revealed by the analysis table.

(2) The given distribution is *unimodal* as it has only one modal value. There may be two or more columns having equal maximum frequency in the analysis table, in such case, each corresponding variate value would have been taken as mode. The distribution having two modes is known as *biomodal* and with more than two modes is known as *multimodal*.

Mode of a Continuous Distribution

If the distribution is with continuous class intervals, mode can be easily calculated in the manner described here. One must take care that the distribution is continuous and in order (ascending or descending). The class intervals for all the classes are equal. If they are unequal, they should be made equal presuming that the frequencies are uniformly distributed throughout the class interval.

Let the grouped frequency distribution be as follows:

Classes	*Frequency*
$X_1 - X_2$	f_1
$X_2 - X_3$	f_2
$X_3 - X_4$	f_3
$\vdots$	$\vdots$
$X_{p-1} - X_p$	f_{p-1}
$X_p - X_{p+1}$	f_p
$X_{p+1} - X_{p+2}$	f_{p+1}
$\vdots$	$\vdots$
$X_k - X_{k+1}$	f_k

Assume that the distribution is in order and the maximum frequency is f_p. Then, the modal class is X_p–X_{p+1}. The exact value of mode can be found out by the interpolation formula,

$$M_0 = X_p + \frac{f_p - f_{p-1}}{(f_p - f_{p-1}) + (f_p - f_{p+1})}(X_{p+1} - X_p) \quad ...(3.16)$$

If we denote the lower limit of the modal class by L_0, the maximum frequency by f, the frequency preceding f by f_{-1} and following f by f_{+1} and the class interval by I, the formula (3.16) can be written as,

$$M_0 = L_0 + \frac{f - f_{-1}}{(f - f_{-1}) + (f - f_{+1})} \times I \quad ...(3.16.1)$$

Putting $f - f_{-1} = \Delta_1$, $f - f_{+1} = \Delta_2$, the formula for mode is

$$M_0 = L_0 + \frac{\Delta_1}{\Delta_1 + \Delta_2} \times I \quad ...(3.16.2)$$

***Example* 3.15.** We find the mode for the frequency distribution given in example 2.5. The distribution is,

Classes (wt. in kg.)	*Number of children*
2.0 – 2.4	5
2.4 – 2.8	5
2.8 – 3.2	9
3.2 – 3.6	4
3.6 – 4.0	4
4.0 – 4.4	3

Obviously by inspection the modal class is (2.8–3.2). We calculate mode by the formula (3.16.2). In this case,

$$L_0 = 2.8,\ \Delta_1 = 9 - 5 = 4,\ \Delta_2 = 9 - 4 = 5,$$
$$I = 3.2 - 2.8 = 0.4$$

Hence,
$$M_0 = 2.8 + \frac{4}{4+5} \times 0.4$$
$$= 2.8 + 0.178$$
$$= 2.978 \text{ kg.}$$

In case the frequency distribution is such that the modal class cannot be ascertained merely by inspection, the method of grouping should be adapted.

Many frequency distributions have more than one mode. But, we are interested in a single central value and hence for such distributions mode is considered as an ill-defined measure of central tendency. For a moderately skewed[3] or asymmetrical frequency distribution, mode can be calculated by Karl Pearson's empirical formula,

$$\text{Mean} - \text{Mode} = 3\,(\text{Mean} - \text{Median}) \quad ...(3.17)$$

3. Skew distribution is discussed in Chapter 4.

$$\text{Mode} = 3 \text{ Median} - 2 \text{ Mean} \qquad ...(3.17.1)$$

In case where mode is ill-defined, formula (3.17) can be used to determine the modal value.

Graphical Method of Finding Mode

If we draw a histogram for the given distribution, naturally the highest bar will possess the modal value. To find the exact modal value consider only three bars namely, the highest bar and the bars adjacent to it on both the sides. In the middle bar draw two diagonal lines joining the point A of the preceding bar to D and B of the following bar to C as shown in Fig. 3.1. Suppose these diagonals AD and BC intersect each other at the point L. Draw a perpendicular line from L on the axis of X which meets it at the point M_0. The distance of M_0 from origin on the aforesaid scale is the modal value.

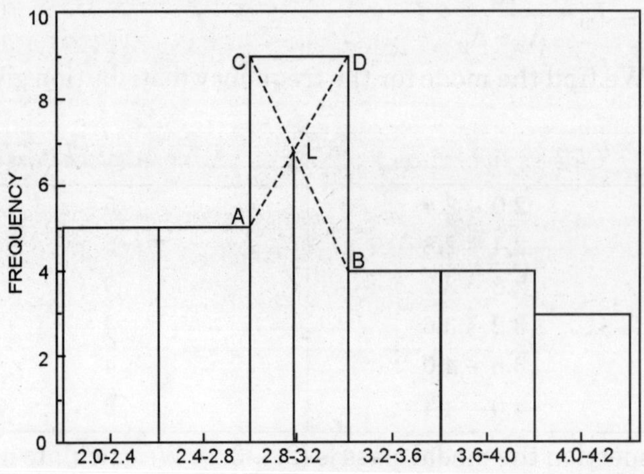

Figure 3.1 Mode by Graphical Method

Merits and Demerits

1. It is not affected by extreme values of a set of observations.
2. It can be calculated for distributions with open end classes.
3. The main drawback of mode is that often it does not exist.
4. Often its value is not unique.
5. It does not fulfil most of the requirements of a good measure of central tendency.

Remark:

After going through the details of the three measures of central tendency namely, the mean, median and mode, it is apparent that no measure is absolutely good. All these measures have some good and bad points. The choice of the measure depends more upon the purpose of information and the situation in which that average value is to be used. Therefore, a measure should be used judiciously.

***Example* 3.16.** Given the number of families in a locality according to their monthly per capita expenditure classes in rupees as, the modal per capita expenditure can be determined by the graphical method as depicted below.

Monthly per capita expenditure classes (Rs)	*Number of families*
140 – 150	17
150 – 160	29
160 – 170	42
170 – 180	72
180 – 190	84
190 – 200	107
200 – 210	49
210 – 220	34
220 – 230	31
230 – 240	16
240 – 250	12

Clearly the modal class is 190 – 200 as it has maximum frequency 107. We draw the following diagram and determine the modal value.

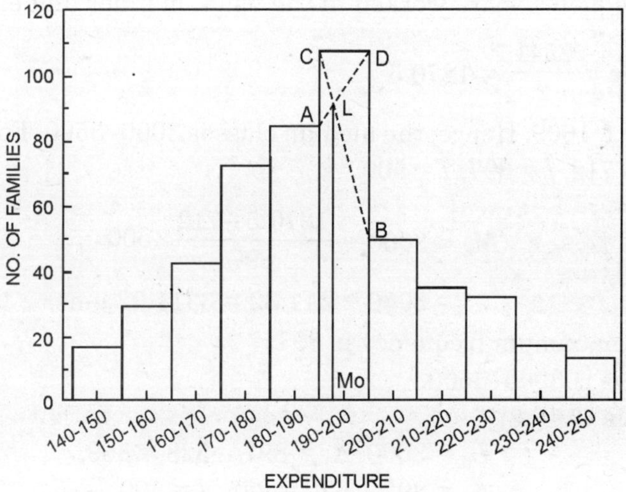

Fig. 3.2 Modal Expenditure by Graph

The value of M_0 on X-axis is 193. Hence, mode = 193.

(**Note :** It can be verified that the value of mode by the formula (3.16.2) is 192.84 which is almost equal to the value obtained by graph).

***Example* 3.17.** Demographic and health survey conducted in Dominican Republic in 1991 yielded the following information regarding birth weights and percentage of children. Total number of children was 2541 about whom the information was gathered.

(i) Birth weights in gms (x)	(ii) Percentage of children (p)	(iii) Number of children (f)	(iv) Cu. number of children (c.f.)
< 500	0.2	5	5
500 – 1000	0.1	3	8
1000 – 1500	0.9	23	31
1500 – 2000	1.6	41	72
2000 – 2500	4.4	112	184
2500 – 3000	20.8	528	712
3000 – 3500	35.3	897	1609
3500 – 4000	24.5	622	2231
4000 – 4500	9.9	252	2483
4500 +	2.3	58	2541

The class frequencies given in col. (iii) are calculated by the formula,

$$f = \frac{2541}{100} \times p$$

Median and modal birth weights in Dominican Republic are calculated by the formulae (3.15) and (3.16.2) respectively.

Cumulative frequencies are worked in the usual manner and entered in col. (iv).

For median, $\frac{N}{2} = \frac{2541}{2} = 1270.5$

1270.5 lies in c.f. 1609. Hence, the median class is 3000–3500. For the formula (3.15), $L_o = 3000$, $C = 712$, $f = 897$, $I = 500$

Thus,
$$M_d = 3000 + \frac{1270.5 - 712}{897} \times 500$$
$$= 3000 + 311.32 = 3311.32 \text{ gms.}$$

For mode, the maximum frequency is 897.

The modal class is 3000–3500.

For the formula (3.16.2),

$$L_0 = 3000, \Delta_1 = 897 - 528 = 369,$$
$$\Delta_2 = 897 - 622 = 275, I = 500$$

$\therefore$
$$M_0 = 3000 + \frac{369}{369 + 275} \times 500$$
$$= 3000 + 286.49 = 3286.49 \text{ gms.}$$

FRACTILES

α-fractile of a continuous distribution of a random variable X is a point, X_α, such that for the distribution of X, the random variable has probability α of being less than or equal to

X_a. For a discrete distribution, fractile may be defined as that variate value which has α -proportion of items up to this value for an increasing ordered set of values. Some people use the term *quartile* in place of fractile. For instance, 1/4-fractile is called first quartile, 1/2-fractile is known as second quartile and 3/4-fractile is called third quartile and are denoted by Q_1, Q_2 and Q_3, respectively. Similarly 1/10-fractile is known as first decile, 2/10-fractile is the second decile and so on. In all we have nine deciles which are denoted by D_i (i = 1, 2, ..., 9). In the same manner, the multiples of 1/100-fractile are called percentiles and are denoted by P_i (i = 1, 2, ..., 99).

Quartiles

From the definition of fractile, it is apparent that three variate values of the variable X which divide the series into four equal parts are called quartiles for the corresponding distribution of X. Hence Q_1 is a value which has 25% items which are less than or equal to Q_1. Similarly Q_2 has 50% items with values less than or equal to Q_2 and Q_3 has 75% items whose values are less than or equal to Q_3.

For discrete data it is simple to locate the fractiles. Arrange the data in order if they are not and work out the cumulative frequencies. To find out Q_1 calculate $(N + 1)/4$ where N is the total number of observations. Search for the minimum cumulative frequency in which $(N + 1)/4$ is contained. The variate value against this cumulative frequency is the value of Q_1. For Q_2, find $(N +1)/2$ and search for the minimum cumulative frequency in which $(N + 1)/2$ is contained. The variate value corresponding to this cumulative frequency is the second quartile Q_2. Calculate $3\,(N + 1)/4$ and locate Q_3 in the same manner as Q_1 and Q_2.

To find the decile D_i (i = 1, 2, ..., 9) we calculate the value $i\,(N + 1)/10$ and search for the minimum cumulative frequency which contains the value $i\,(N + 1)/10$. The variate value corresponding to this cumulative frequency is the ith decile. In a similar manner, calculate $i(N + 1)/100$ (i = 1, 2, ..., 99) for percentiles and proceeding on as for quartiles and deciles, the percentiles are located.

Continuous Distribution Case

Let the observations, arranged in order, in the form of a continuous distribution be as given below.

Classes	*Frequency*	*Cu.frequency*
$X_1 - X_2$	f_1	$F_1 = f_1$
$X_2 - X_3$	f_2	F_2
$X_3 - X_4$	f_3	F_3
⋮	⋮	⋮
$X_p - X_{P+1}$	f_P	F_p
⋮	⋮	⋮
$X_k - X_{k+1}$	f_k	$F_k = N$

To locate the quartile class, calculate $iN/4$ instead of $i(N+1)/4$ and proceed as we do for discrete distribution, *i.e.*, search that minimum cumulative frequency in which $iN/4$ is contained. The class corresponding to this cumulative frequency is called *quartile class.* The unique value of the i th quartile is calculated by the formula,

$$Q_i = l_0 + \frac{iN/4 - c}{f} \times I \qquad \text{...(3.18)}$$

where $i = 1, 2, 3$

Q_i — i th quartile which is to be worked out

l_0 — lower limit of the i th quartile class

N — total of all the frequencies

c — cumulative frequency for the class just above the quartile class

f — frequency of the quartile class

I — class interval

Deciles

The procedure for locating the i th decile class is to calculate $iN/10$ and search that minimum cumulative frequency in which this value is contained. The class corresponding to this cumulative frequency is i th decile class. The unique value of i th decile can be calculated by the formula,

$$D_i = l_0 + \frac{iN/10 - c}{f} \times I \qquad \text{...(3.19)}$$

where $i = 1, 2, ..., 9$.

All the terms in (3.19) can be decoded as explained in (3.18) by changing the word quartile class by decile class.

Percentiles

To locate i th percentile class, calculate $iN/100$ $(i = 1, 2, ..., 99)$ and find that minimum cumulative frequency which contains this value. The class corresponding to this minimum cumulative frequency is the percentile class. Unique value of i th percentile can be calculated by the formula,

$$P_i = l_0 + \frac{iN/100 - c}{f} \times I \qquad \text{...(3.20)}$$

where $(i = 1, 2, ..., 99)$.

All the terms in (3.20) are decoded as in (3.18) simply by replacing the word quartile class by percentile class.

Note that Q_2, D_5 and P_{50} are equivalent to the median of the given distribution.

***Example* 3.18.** Consider again the continuous distribution given in example 3.16 and calculate (*i*) all the quartiles, (*ii*) 70th decile and (*iii*) 90th percentile.

The frequency distribution and the cumulative frequencies in the last column are presented below.

Monthly per capita expenditure classes (Rs.)	*No. of families*	*Cumulative frequency*
140–150	17	17
150–160	29	46
160–170	42	88
170–180	72	160

180–190	84	244
190–200	107	351
200–210	49	400
210–220	34	434
220–230	31	465
230–240	16	481
240–250	12	493

(*i*) For Q_1, $\frac{N}{4} = \frac{493}{4} = 123.25$

The number 123.25 is contained in the minimum cu. freq., 160. Hence the class 170–180 is the first quartile class. By the formula (3.18) we have,

$$Q_1 = 170 + \frac{123.25 - 88}{72} \times 10$$
$$= 170 + 4.90$$
$$= \text{Rs. } 174.90$$

Similarly for Q_2, $\frac{2N}{4} = \frac{2 \times 493}{4} = 246.50$

The number 246.50 is contained in the minimum cu. freq. 351. Hence the class 190–200 is the second quartile class. Thus, by the formula (3.18),

$$Q_2 = 190 + \frac{246.50 - 244}{107} \times 10$$
$$= 190 + 0.23$$
$$= \text{Rs. } 190.23$$

Again for Q_3, $\frac{3N}{4} = \frac{3 \times 493}{4} = 369.75$

The number 369.75 is contained in the minimum cu. fr. 400.

Hence, the class 200–210 is the third quartile class. By the formula (3.18),

$$Q_3 = 200 + \frac{369.75 - 351}{49} \times 10$$
$$= 200 + 3.83$$
$$= \text{Rs. } 203.83$$

(*ii*) For D_7, $\frac{7N}{10} = \frac{7 \times 493}{10} = 345.1$

The number 345.1 is contained in the minimum cu. fr. 351. Hence the class 190–200 is the 7th decile class. By formula (3.19) we have,

$$D_7 = 190 + \frac{345.1 - 244}{107} \times 10$$
$$= 190 + 9.45$$
$$= \text{Rs. } 199.45$$

(*iii*) For P_{90}, $\frac{90N}{100} = \frac{90 \times 493}{100} = 443.70$

The number 443.70 is contained in the minimum cu. fr. 465. Hence, the 90th percentile class is 220–230. By formula (3.20) we have,

$$P_{90} = 220 + \frac{443.70 - 434}{31} \times 10$$
$$= 220 + 3.13$$
$$= \text{Rs. } 223.13$$

Concluding Remarks

Different measures of central tendency and fractiles (quantiles) have been discussed in this chapter. Out of mean, median and mode, the mean (average) is the most commonly used measure of central tendency. But the other two namely, the median and mode are not any less important. Median is a largely used central measure in psychology, education and other social sciences. It is a suitable average for qualitative information like the attitude towards disabled people, beauty or intelligence of certain individuals, etc. Mode is a useful measure for manufacturers.

Note: For SPSS window guide, see Appendix Chapter-4.

QUESTIONS AND EXERCISES

1. What do you understand by a measure of central tendency? Explain with examples.
2. What are the desirable properties which an average should possess? Which of the average to your mind possesses most of these properties and why?
3. Under what circumstances, would you use the following instead of any other measure of central tendency?
   (*a*) Mode.
   (*b*) Geometric mean.
   (*c*) Median.
4. In what respect is the weighted mean superior to the simple average?
5. Which type of average is most suitable for the following problems and why?
   (*a*) Average income per month in a year of an advocate.
   (*b*) Normal size of shirts for a readymade garment's manufacturer.
   (*c*) Consumption per head in a family consisting of 7 men, 4 women and 9 children.
   (*d*) The average marks of a mediocre student in a class.
   (*e*) Average speed of a plane in flight from Delhi to New York.
6. Name different kinds of averages and discuss their merits and demerits.
7. Explain the meaning of a fractile and give its uses. What information do we obtain by quartiles, deciles and percentiles?
8. What are the considerations will you weigh in choosing a suitable average for studying a phenomenon? Give a few typical cases in which your choice will fall on any average other than the arithmetic mean. (*C.A. 1965*)

9. How will you find (*a*) the average marks of a class of students to show the level of intelligence, (*b*) the average cost of goods purchased in different lots to determine the selling prices, (*c*) the average size of groups of items for the purpose of classification and (*d*) the average rate of increase in prices when the prices increase at different rates during successive periods. Explain why you adopt a particular method in each case?

(B.Com. Agra and Raj., 1948)

10. What is the effect of reducing each observation of a decreasing series by 10 on the following:
    (*a*) the average
    (*b*) the median
    (*c*) the mode
    (*d*) the quartiles.
11. Prove that
    (*a*) H.M. $\leq$ G.M. $\leq$ A.M.
    (*b*) $\sqrt{A.M. \times H.M.} = G.M.$
    where A.M., G.M. and H.M. are the usual abbreviations.
12. Define the following and give one appropriate example on your own for the use of each.
    (*a*) Mode.
    (*b*) Third quartile.
    (*c*) Geometric mean.
    (*d*) Median.
    (*e*) Average.
13. Additional irrigation utilisation from major and medium schemes at the end of various plans in India is,

Additional irrigation (Lakh hectares)

97,	110,	130,	152,	168,	187,	22,	266,	226.

Find the average additional irrigation utilisation during this period.

14. Following are the percentages of literates in six villages situated at six different distances from the district headquarters.
    Percentage of literates: 52.22, 46.59, 21.36, 30.17, 22.87, 17.77
    Find the mean percentage of literates.
15. The distribution of Labrum length of workers of Apis cerena measured in millimetre is as given below.

Labrum length (mm)	*No. of workers*
0.30	8
0.31	4
0.32	2
0.33	2
0.34	3
0.35	2
0.36	3
0.37	3
0.38	1
0.40	5

Find the average Labrum length of workers and the mode.

16. The distribution of the age of patients visiting an outdoor patients' department in a dispensary on Sunday is as follows:

Age (years)	*No. of patients*
More than 10	152
,, ,, 20	128
,, ,, 30	113
,, ,, 40	77
,, ,, 50	36
,, ,, 60	22
,, ,, 70	5
and up to 80	

Calculate (*i*) mean age of persons visiting the dispensary, (*ii*) median age and (*iii*) modal age.

17. The distribution of age of males at the time of marriage was as follows:

Age (years)	*No. of males*
18 – 20	5
20 – 22	18
22 – 24	28
24 – 26	37
26 – 28	24
28 – 30	22

Find at the time of marriage (*i*) the average age, (*ii*) the modal age, (*iii*) the median age, (*iv*) third quartile, (*v*) sixth decile and (*vi*) nintieth percentile.

18. The earnings of five nationalised banks in crore rupees are as given below:

217.40,	330.50,	682.55,	1263.59,	2249.63

Find the average earning of banks by using a suitable method.

19. The prices of wheat, dal, rice, vanaspati, ghee, milk, sugar and their weights are as given below.

Prices (Rs. per kg) :	1.57	5.77	3.94	17.00	3.50	4.50
Weights :	34	6	4	9	24	23

Find the weighted average of prices of the commodities.

20. In a factory a mechanic takes 15 days to fabricate a machine, the second mechanic takes 18 days, the third mechanic takes 30 days and the fourth mechanic takes 90 days. Find the average number of days taken by the workers to fabricate the machine.
[**Hint**: Find the harmonic mean]

21. Find out the arithmetic mean, mode and median for the following distribution.

Mid-points (weight in lbs)	*No. of students*
95	4
105	2
115	18
125	22
135	21
145	19
155	10
165	3
175	2

(*M.A. Econ., Meerut, 1983*)

22. Find the average rate of increase in population which in the first decade has increased 20%, in the next 30% and in the third 45%. *(B.Com., Agra, 1960)*

23. The following table gives the monthly income of twelve families in a town.

S.No :	1	2	3	4	5	6	7	8	9	10	11	12
	280	180	96	98	104	75	80	94	100	75	600	200

Calculate the arithmetic average, the median and the mode of the above incomes. Which average would represent the above series, the best? *(M.A., Lucknow, 1967)*

24. Find out the median and the mode from the following:

Less than :	5	10	15	20	25	30	35	40	45
No.of students :	29	224	465	582	634	644	650	653	655

(C.A., 1965; B.Com., Lucknow, 1968)

25. A limited company wants to pay bonus to the members of its staff. The bonus is to be paid as under.

Monthly salary	*Bonus*
100 and not exceeding 120	50
120 ,, ,, ,, 140	60
140 ,, ,, ,, 160	70
160 ,, ,, ,, 180	80
180 ,, ,, ,, 200	90
200 ,, ,, ,, 220	100
220 and above	110

Actual salaries of the members of the staff are given as under:

Rupees : 200, 180, 185, 195, 218, 187, 160, 250, 198
190, 168, 170, 178, 175, 140, 120, 148, 165,
155, 145, 125, 110, 162, 130 and 150.

What is the total bonus? What is the average bonus paid per member of the staff? *(B.Com., Gujarat, 1957)*

26. From the figures given below, find the mode, median and quartiles. What information do you deduce from them?

Age :	20–25	25–30	30–35	35–40	40–45	45–50	50–55	55–60
Persons :	50	70	100	180	150	120	70	59

(B.Com. Vikram, 1964)

27. Draw an ogive for the following distribution. Read the median and verify the result by calculation. How many workers earn monthly wages between 60 rupees and 72 rupees?

Monthly wages :	50–55	55–60	60–65	65–70	70–75	75–80	80–100
No. of workers :	6	10	22	30	16	12	15

(M.Com., Delhi, 1967)

28. (*a*) A man travels from Lucknow to Delhi at an average speed of 30 m.p.h and returns along the same route at an average speed of 60 m.p.h. Find the average speed for the entire trip.

(*b*) The national income of India has registered increase of 2.6, 1.9, 5.0 and 7.7 per cent respectively during the first four years of the third plan. What was the average rate of growth of national income during the period? (*M.A., Meerut, 1968*)

29. Find mode of the following frequency distribution.

Size :	5,	6,	7,	8,	9,	10,	11,	12,	13,	14,	15,	16,	17,	18,	19
Frequency :	48,	52,	56,	60,	63,	57,	55,	50,	52,	41,	57,	63,	52,	48,	40

[Translated from Hindi version] (*M.A. Sociology, Meerut, 1977*)

30. Following table presents the male population of a region of USA. Find the median age.

Age groups (yrs)	*Males*
0 – 5	2850
5 – 10	3737
10 – 15	4620
15 – 20	5200
20 – 25	7250
25 – 30	620
30 – 35	297
35 – 40	355

[Translated from Hindi version] (*M.A. Sociology, Meerut, 1978*)

31. Calculate the number and percentage of students whose marks are less than 45 marks.

Mark	*No. of students*
30 – 40	31
40 – 50	42
50 – 60	51
60 – 70	35
70 – 80	31

(*M.Com. Meerut, 1979*)

32. The arithmetic mean of two observations is 127.5 and their geometric mean is 60. Find (*i*) their harmonic mean and (*ii*) the two observations.

(*I.C.W.A., June, 1983*)

33. Calculate the median and mode of the following:

Annual sales (Rs. '000)	*Frequency*
Less than 10	4
Less than 20	20
Less than 30	35
Less than 40	55
Less than 50	62
Less than 60	67

Is it possible to calculate the arithmetic mean? If possible, calculate it.

(*M.A., Econ., Meerut, 1983*)

34. Calculate the mode and 75th percentile from the following distribution of marks.

Marks	*Frequency*
20–21	2
18–19	1
16–17	0
14–15	0
12–13	2
10–11	0
8–9	0
6–7	2
4–5	1
2–3	1
0–1	1

[Translated from Hindi version] (*M.A. Psychology, Agra, 1983*)

35. There are two branches of an establishment employing 100 and 80 persons respectively. If the arithmetic means of monthly salaries paid by two branches are Rs.275 and Rs.225 respectively, find the arithmetic mean of the salaries of the employees of the establishment as a whole. (*C.A., Nov., 1963*)

36. The median and mode of the following distribution are known to be 27 and 26 respectively. Find the values of a and b.

Values :	0–10	10–20	20–30	30–40	40–50
Frequency :	3	a	20	12	b

(*I.C.W.A., Dec., 1985*)

37. Draw a histogram for the following distribution and find the modal wage.

Wages per day (in Rs.):	10–15	15–20	20–25	25–30	30–35	35–40	40–45
No. of wage earners:	60	140	110	150	120	100	90

(*B.Com. I Yr. Andhra, 1988*)

38. Compute the geometric mean of the following:

2000, 200, 20, 12, 8, 0.8

39. Find the median and lower & upper quartiles for the following table:

Marks	*No. of students*
Below 10	15
,, 20	35
,, 30	60
,, 40	84
,, 50	106
,, 60	120
,, 70	125

(*I.C.W.A., June, 1984*)

40. From the following data, plot 'less than' and 'more than' types of ogives and find the value of median.

Marks :	10–20	20–30	30–40	40–50	50–60	60–70	70–80
No. of students :	4	6	10	15	12	7	6

(*B.Com. I Yr. Andhra, 1989*)

41. The first quartile of the following data is 21.5.

Classes :	10–15	15–20	20–25	25–30	
Frequency :	24	–	90	122	
	30–35	35–40	40–45	45–50	Total
	–	56	20	33	460

Find the missing frequencies and hence find the value of mode.

42. The number of employees in two branches, say A and B of a company are 80 and 65 respectively. Average salary of employees in branches A is Rs. 875 per month and in B is 1260 per month. Give the formula and calculate the combined average salary of the two branches.

(*C.A. PE-I, Nov. 2004*)

43. What are the properties of a good measure of central tendency ? Also discuss specifically the merits and demerits of arithmetic mean.

(*B.Sc.(Ag.) Hons. Pt.IV, RAU, 1997*)

44. From the following frequency distribution, calculate the missing frequency x when the value of median is 86.

Classes:	40–50	50–60	60–70	70–80	80–90	90–100	100–110
Frequency:	2	1	6	6	x	12	5

45. The mean annual salary of all employees in a company is Rs.25,000. The mean salary of male and female is Rs.27,000 and Rs.17,000 respectively. Find the percentage of males and females employed by the company.

(*C.A., Foundation, Nov.,1995*)

SUGGESTED READING

Baker, S. (2001). *Complete Idiots Guide to Business Statistics*, Alpha Books.

Elzey, Freeman F. (1985). *Elementary Statistical Techniques*, Brooks/Cole, Monterey.

Frederick J. Gravetter (2004). *Essential of Statistics for the Behavioral Sciences*, Thomson Wadsworth.

Freund, J.E. (1981). *Modern Elementary Statistics,* Prentice Hall of India, New Delhi.

Goon, A.M., M.K. Gupta and B. Dasgupta (1977). *Fundamentals of Statistics, Vol. I.*, The World Press, Calcutta.

Gupta, S.C. and V.K. Kapoor (1980). *Fundamentals of Mathematical Statistics,* Sultan Chand & Sons, Delhi, 7th. ed.

Hoel, P.G. and R.J. Jessen (1982). *Basic Statistics for Business and Economics,* John Wiley, New York.

Joseph, F. Healey. (2004). *Statistics*, Thomson Wadsworth.

Lee C.F., John C. Lee and Lee (1998). *Statistics for Business and Financial Economics,* World Scientific.

Meter, J., W. Wasserman, and G.A. Whitmore (1982). *Applied Statistics,* Allyn and Bacon, London.

Perry R. Hinton (1995). *Statistics Explained*, Routledge, U.K.

Sellers, G.R., and S.B. Vardeman (1982). *Elementary Statistics,* Saunders College Publishing, New York.

Stephen Bernstein and Ruth Bernstein (1999). *Schaum's Outline Theory and Problems of Elements of Statistics*, McGraw Hill Professional.

4

Chapter

Measures of Dispersion

In the third chapter, we concentrated upon a central value, which gives an idea of the whole mass that is a complete set of variate values. However, the information so obtained is neither exhaustive nor comprehensive, as the mean does not lead us to know whether the observations are close to each other or far apart. Median is a positional average and has nothing to do with the variability of the observations in the series. Mode is the largest occurring value independent of other values of the set. This leads us to conclude that a measure of central tendency alone is not enough to have a clear idea about the data unless all observations are almost the same. Moreover, two or more sets may have the same mean and/or median but they may be quite different. To clear this point consider the three sets as follows:

Set A	30	30	30	30	30
Set B	28	29	30	31	32
Set C	3	5	30	37	75

All the three sets *A, B* and *C* have mean 30 and median is also 30. But by inspection, it is apparent that the three sets differ remarkably from one another. Thus to have a clear picture of data, one needs to have a measure of dispersion or variability (scatteredness) amongst observations in the set. Commonly used measures of dispersion are:

1. Range
2. Interquartile range and Quartile deviation
3. Mean deviation
4. Variance
5. Standard deviation
6. Coefficient of variation.

Before giving the details of various measures of dispersion, it is worthwhile to enucleate the purposes of these measures and enunciate the properties of a good measure of dispersion.

PURPOSES OF MEASURES OF DISPERSION

Various measures of dispersion are calculated with the following purposes:

1. To have an idea about the reliability of central value

In a way, it is the measure of degree of scatteredness. If scatter is large, an average is less reliable. If the value of dispersion is small, it indicates that a central value is a good representative of all the values in the set.

2. To compare two or more sets of values with regard to their variability

Two or more sets can be compared by calculating the same measure of dispersion having the same unit of measure. A set with smaller value possess lesser variability.

3. To provide information about the structure of a series

A value of measure of dispersion gives an idea about the spread of the observations. Further one can surmise about limits of expansion of values in a set.

4. To control the variation

In many situations a measure of dispersion provides the basis for controlling the causes which lead to greater variation. For instance, one tries to have minimum error variance in experiments by controlling nuisance variables. In an industry, a production manager will like to maintain his product having negligible variability. If it is more, he will find ways to check it.

5. Gateway to other statistical measures

Measures of dispersion, especially variance and standard deviation lead to many statistical techniques like correlation, regression, analysis of variance, etc.

PROPERTIES OF A GOOD MEASURE OF DISPERSION

There are certain requisites of a good measure of dispersion in general. The same are expounded below:

1. It should be based on all values of a series.
2. It should not be susceptible to fluctuations of sampling.
3. It should be capable of further algebraic treatment.
4. It should be rigidly defined *i.e.*, each investigator should arrive at the same value for the same set of data.
5. It is preferable that the unit of measurement of dispersion should be same as the unit of measurement of observations.
6. It should be calculable with reasonable ease *i.e.*, the formula should be such that it does not complicate the computation of a measure of dispersion.
7. It should be least affected by extreme values.

Each of the measures of dispersion is adequately elucidated in the subsequent discussion.

RANGE

Definition. It is the difference between the largest and the smallest observation in a set.

If we denote the largest observation by L and the smallest observation by S, the formula is,

$$\text{Range} \quad R = L - S \qquad \ldots(4.1)$$

A relative measure known as *coefficient of range* is given as,

$$\text{Coeff. of range} = \frac{L-S}{L+S} \qquad \ldots(4.2)$$

Lesser the range or coefficient of range, better the result.

Properties

1. It is the simplest measure and can easily be understood.
2. Besides the above merit, it hardly satisfies any property of a good measure of dispersion *e.g.*, it is based on two extreme values only, ignoring the others. It is not liable to further algebraic treatment.

Example **4.1** The population in eighteen election wards of a district is as given below.

Population ('000 number)

77,	76,	83,	68,	57,	107,	80,	75,	95
100,	113,	119,	121,	121,	83,	87,	46,	74

We can find the range by the formula (4.1)

$$L = 121 \text{ and } S = 46$$

The range,

$$R = 121 - 46 = 75$$

Some people also write the range as i.e. 46 – 121.

Also,

$$\text{Coeff. of Range} = \frac{121-46}{121+46} = \frac{75}{167} = 0.449$$

INTERQUARTILE RANGE (I.R.)

Definition. The difference between the third quartile and first quartile is called interquartile range. Symbolically,

$$\text{I.R.} = Q_3 - Q_1 \qquad ...(4.3)$$

QUARTILE DEVIATION (Q.D.)

This is half of the interquartile range, *i.e.*,

$$\text{Q.D.} = \frac{Q_3 - Q_1}{2} \qquad ...(4.4)$$

Also the coefficient of quartile deviation is given by the formula,

$$\text{Coeff. of Q.D.} = \frac{Q_3 - Q_1}{Q_3 + Q_1} \qquad ...(4.5)$$

Coefficient of quartile deviation is an absolute quantity (unitless) and is useful to compare the variability among the middle 50% observations.

Properties

1. It is a better measure of dispersion than range in the sense that it involves 50% of the mid-values of a series of data rather than only two extreme values of a series.
2. Since it excludes the lowest and highest 25% values, it is not affected by the extreme values.

3. It can be calculated for the grouped data with open end intervals.
4. It is not capable of further algebraic treatment.
5. It is susceptible to sampling fluctuations.
6. This measure does not take into account the individual values occurring between Q_1 and Q_3. It means that no idea about the variation of even 50% mid values are available from this measure. Anyhow, it provides some idea if the values are uniformly distributed between Q_1 and Q_3.
7. It is not considered a good measure of dispersion as it does not show the scattering of the central value. In fact, it is a measure of partitioning of distribution. Hence, it is not commonly used.

***Example* 4.2.** The values of Q_1, Q_2 and Q_3 as worked out in example 3.18 are,

$$Q_1 = 174.90,\ Q_2 = 190.23,\ Q_3 = 203.83$$

Interquartile range, I.R. = 203.83 – 174.90 = 28.93

$$\text{Quartile deviation, Q.D.} = \frac{203.83 - 174.90}{2} = \frac{28.93}{2} = 14.465$$

$$\text{Coeff. of Q.D.} = \frac{203.83 - 174.90}{203.83 + 174.90} = \frac{28.93}{378.73} = 0.076$$

MEAN DEVIATION (M.D.)

The measures of dispersion discussed so far are not satisfactory in the sense that they lack most of the requirements of a good measure. Mean deviation is a better measure than range and Q.D.

Definition. It is the average of the absolute deviations taken from a central value, generally the mean or median.

Consider a set of N observations $X_1, X_2, ..., X_N$. Then the mean deviation,

$$\text{M.D.} = \frac{1}{N}\Sigma_i |X_i - A| \quad ...(4.6)$$

for $i = 1, 2, ..., N$ where A is a central value.

Let $|X_i - A| = d_i$,

Then, $$\text{M.D.} = \frac{1}{N}\Sigma_i d_i \quad ...(4.6.1)$$

In case of data given in the form of a frequency distribution where the variate values $X_1, X_2, ..., X_k$ occur $f_1, f_2, ..., f_k$ times respectively, the formula for mean deviation is,

$$\text{M.D.} = \frac{1}{N}\Sigma_i f_i |X_i - A| \quad ...(4.7)$$

where $\Sigma_i f_i = N$ for $i = 1, 2, ..., k$.

In case of grouped data, the mid-point of each class interval is treated as X_i and we can use formula (4.7).

Properties

1. Mean deviation removes one main objection of the earlier measures, that it involves each value of the set.

2. It is not affected much by extreme values.
3. Its main drawback is that algebraic negative signs of the deviations are ignored which is mathematically unsound.
4. Mean deviation is minimum when the deviations are taken from median.

Note : If the deviations are taken from mean and the signs of the deviations are taken into consideration, the sum of the deviations is zero *i.e.,* $\Sigma_i(X_i - \overline{X}) = 0$.

Example **4.3.** The production of all crops in India from 1971 to 1978 is given below:

Production (Million tonnes)							
111.5,	111.2,	102.3,	112.4,	108.8,	125.3,	116.5,	132.7

Mean deviation, taking deviations from the mean and also from the median has been calculated.

(*i*) Mean $= \frac{1}{8}(111.5 + 111.2 + ... + 132.7) = \frac{920.7}{8} = 115.09$

Mean deviation taking deviations from the mean using the formula (4.6) is,

$$\text{M.D.} = \frac{1}{8}(|111.5 - 115.09| + |111.2 - 115.09| + ... + |132.7 - 115.09|)$$

$$= \frac{1}{8}\ (3.59 + 3.89 + 12.79 + 2.69 + 6.29 + 10.21 + 1.41 + 17.61)$$

$$= \frac{58.48}{8} = 7.31 \text{ million tonnes.}$$

(*ii*) Now calculate the mean deviation taking the deviations from the median. For finding out the median, arrange the data in ascending order.

102.3, 108.8, 111.2, 111.5, 112.4, 116.5, 125.3, 132.7

$$\text{Median} = \frac{111.5 + 112.4}{2} = \frac{223.9}{2} = 111.95$$

Mean deviation taking deviations from the median by the formula (4.6) is,

$$\text{M.D.} = \frac{1}{8}\ (|102.3 - 111.95| + |108.8 - 111.95| + ... + |132.7 - 111.95|)$$

$$= \frac{1}{8}(9.65 + 3.15 + 0.75 + 0.45 + 0.45 + 4.55 + 13.35 + 20.75)$$

$$= \frac{53.1}{8} = 6.64 \text{ million tonnes.}$$

The mean deviation about median is less than the mean deviation about mean. This further substantiates the statement that mean deviation about median is minimum.

Example **4.4.** The distribution of age at the marriage of grooms with brides of age group 15–39 is displayed here.

Age groups : (years)	15–19	19–23	23–27	27–31	31–35	35–39
No. of grooms:	8	59	47	23	6	4

Mean deviation taking deviations from the mean has been calculated. The calculations are shown in the table given below.

Class intervals	*Midpoints* (*X*)	*Frequency* (*f*)	*f X*	$\lvert X-\overline{X}\rvert$	$f\lvert X-\overline{X}\rvert$
15–19	17	8	136	7.24	57.92
19–23	21	59	1239	3.24	191.16
23–27	25	47	1175	0.76	35.72
27–31	29	23	667	4.76	109.48
31–35	33	6	198	8.76	52.56
35–39	37	4	148	12.76	51.04
Total		147	3563		497.88

where $\overline{X} = \dfrac{3563}{147} = 24.24$

Mean deviation about mean by the formula (4.7) is,

$$\text{M.D.} = \frac{497.88}{147} = 3.39 \text{ years}$$

VARIANCE

The main objection of mean deviation, that the negative signs are ignored, is removed by taking the square of the deviations from the mean.

Definition. The variance is the average of the squares of the deviations taken from mean.

Let $X_1, X_2, ..., X_N$ be the measurements on N population units, the population variance,

$$\sigma^2 = \frac{1}{N}\Sigma_i (X_i - \overline{X})^2 \qquad ...(4.8)$$

for $i = 1, 2, 3, ..., N$.

$$\sigma^2 = \frac{1}{N}\{\Sigma_i X_i^2 - (\Sigma_i X_i)^2 / N\} \qquad ...(4.8.1)$$

where $\overline{X}$ is the population mean.

If the data are given in the form of frequency distribution in which the variate value X_i has its corresponding frequency f_i ($i = 1, 2, ..., k$), the variance,

$$\sigma^2 = \frac{1}{N}\Sigma_i f_i (X_i - \overline{X})^2 \qquad ...(4.9)$$

for $i = 1, 2, ... k$.

where $N = \Sigma_i f_i$ and $\overline{X} = \dfrac{1}{N}\Sigma_i f_i X_i$.

$$\sigma^2 = \frac{1}{N}\{\Sigma_i f_i X_i^2 - (\Sigma_i f_i X_i)^2 / N) \qquad (4.9.1)$$

In case of grouped data, mid-values of the classes are considered as X_i and consequently we can make use of the formula (4.9).

The sample variance of the set $x_1, x_2, ..., x_n$ of n observations is given by the formula,

$$s^2 = \frac{1}{n-1}\Sigma_i(x_i - \bar{x})^2 \qquad ...(4.10)$$

$$= \frac{1}{n-1}\{\Sigma_i x_i^2 - (\Sigma_i x_i)^2/n\} \qquad ...(4.10.1)$$

for $i = 1, 2, ..., n$.

where $\bar{x} = \frac{1}{n}\Sigma_i x_i$.

If the observation x_i occurs f_i times for $i = 1, 2, ..., k$, then the sample variance,

$$s^2 = \frac{1}{n-1}\Sigma_i f_i(x_i - \bar{x})^2 \qquad ...(4.11)$$

$$= \frac{1}{n-1}\{\Sigma_i f_i x_i^2 - (\Sigma_i f_i x_i)^2/n\} \qquad ...(4.11.1)$$

where $n = \Sigma_i f_i$.

***Example* 4.5.** The following nine measurements are the heights in inches in a sample of nine soldiers.

Height (*X*):	69,	66,	67,	69,	64,	63,	65,	68,	72

The sample variance of height of soldiers can be computed by formula (4.10).

$$\sum_{i=1}^{9} x_i = 69 + 66 + ... + 72 = 603$$

$$\bar{x} = \frac{603}{9} = 67 \text{ inches}$$

$$(x - \bar{x}): \; 2, \; -1, \; 0, \; 2, \; -3, \; -4, \; -2, \; 1, \; 5$$

$$(x - \bar{x})^2: \; 4, \; 1, \; 0, \; 4, \; 9, \; 16, \; 4, \; 1, \; 25$$

$$\sum_{i=1}^{9}(x_i - \bar{x})^2 = 4 + 1 + 0 + 4 + 9 + 16 + 4 + 1 + 25$$

$$= 64$$

$$s^2 = \frac{64}{8}$$

$$= 8 \text{ inches}^2$$

CODING OF DATA

If the values in a series or mid-values of the classes are large enough, coding of values is a good device to simplify the calculations. In coding subtract a constant A (generally the middle X_i value of the series) from each value or mid-value in case of grouped data and then divide the reduced values by a suitable constant 'C' ($C \neq 0$), generally the class interval in case of grouped data.

Thus, the coded value,

$$X' = \frac{X - A}{C}$$

We present elaborately the method of calculating the variance for the grouped data because it will automatically cover the case of ungrouped frequency distribution.

Classes	*Frequency*	*Mid-values*	$X' = \dfrac{X-A}{C}$	fX'	fX'^2
$Y_1 - Y_2$	f_1	X_1	$X'_1 = \dfrac{X_1 - A}{C}$	$f_1X'_1$	$f_1X_1'^2$
$Y_2 - Y_3$	f_2	X_2	$X'_2 = \dfrac{X_2 - A}{C}$	$f_2X'_2$	$f_2X_2'^2$
$\vdots$	$\vdots$	$\vdots$	$\vdots$	$\vdots$	$\vdots$
$Y_p - Y_{p+1}$	f_p	X_p	$X'_p = \dfrac{X_p - A}{C}$	$f_pX'_p$	$f_pX_p'^2$
$\vdots$	$\vdots$	$\vdots$	$\vdots$	$\vdots$	$\vdots$
$Y_k - Y_{k+1}$	f_k	X_k	$X'_k = \dfrac{X_k - A}{C}$	$f_kX'_k$	$f_kX_k'^2$
Total	N			$\Sigma_i f_i X'_i$	$\Sigma_i f_i X_i'^2$

for $i = 1, 2, .., k$.

Here the mean of uncoded data in terms of coded data can be obtained as,

$$\overline{X'} = \frac{1}{N}\Sigma_i f_i X'_i = \frac{1}{N}\Sigma_i f_i\left(\frac{X_i - A}{C}\right)$$

$$= \frac{1}{CN}\Sigma_i f_i X_i - \frac{1}{CN}\Sigma_i f_i A = \frac{1}{C}\overline{X} - \frac{A}{C}$$

Since $\qquad \dfrac{1}{N}\Sigma_i f_i X_i = \overline{X}$ and $\Sigma_i f_i = N$

or
$$\overline{X} = A + C\overline{X'} \qquad ...(4.12)$$

Variance of uncoded data 'σ^2' in terms of variance of coded data 'σ'^2' will be obtained as,

$$\sigma'^2 = \frac{1}{N}\Sigma_i f_i (X'_i - \overline{X}')^2 \qquad ...(4.13)$$

$$= \frac{1}{N}\Sigma_i f_i\left(\frac{X_i - A}{C} - \frac{\overline{X} - A}{C}\right)^2 = \frac{1}{N}\Sigma_i f_i\left(\frac{X_i}{C} - \frac{\overline{X}}{C}\right)^2$$

or
$$C^2\sigma'^2 = \frac{1}{N}\Sigma_i f_i (X_i - \overline{X})^2 = \sigma^2 \qquad ...(4.13.1)$$

Also we can write

$$\sigma^2 = C^2\frac{1}{N}\{\Sigma_i f_i X_i'^2 - (\Sigma_i f_i X'_i)^2 / N\} \qquad ...(4.13.2)$$

when each $f_i = 1$, the variance,

$$\sigma^2 = C^2 \frac{1}{N}\{\Sigma_i X_i'^2 - (\Sigma_i X'_i)^2 / N\} = C^2 \sigma'^2 \quad ...(4.13.3)$$

From (4.12) it is easily inferred that the mean is affected by the shift of origin, and also by the change of scale. Hence on subtracting A from each observation and then dividing by C, the mean of the coded data is to be multiplied by C, and then added to the constant A to get the mean of the uncoded data.

The relation (4.13.1) does not involve A. It means that the variance is not affected by the shift of origin, but the change of scale does affect it, as the relation involves C. Moreover, if the variance of coded variable is multiplied by the square of the scale constant C, the variance of the uncoded variable is obtained. In most of the situations coding makes the calculations simple if A and C are properly chosen.

Properties

1. The variance has mostly removed the lacunae which are present in the measures of dispersion given before it.
2. The main demerit of variance is, that its unit is the square of the unit of measurement of variate values. For clarity, say, the variable X is measured in cms, the unit of variance is cm^2. Generally, this value is large and makes it difficult to decide about the magnitude of variation.
3. The variance gives more weightage to the extreme values as compared to those which are near to mean value, because the difference is squared in variance.

STANDARD DEVIATION (S.D.)

The drawbacks of variance are overcome in this measure of dispersion.

Definition. The positive square root of the variance is called standard deviation.

$$\text{S.D.} = \sqrt{\sigma^2} = \sigma \quad ...(4.14)$$

For a sample,

$$\text{S.D.} = \sqrt{s^2} = s \quad ...(4.14.1)$$

In simple words, we can say that standard deviation explains the average amount of variation on either side of the mean.

Properties

1. Standard deviation is considered to be the best measure of dispersion and is used widely.
2. There is however one difficulty with it. If the unit of measurement of variables of two series is not the same, then their variability cannot be compared by comparing the values of standard deviation.
3. An empirical relation between Q.D., M. D. and S.D. is,

   $$6 \text{ Q.D.} = 5 \text{ M.D.} = 4 \text{ S.D.} \quad ...(4.15)$$

Measures Q.D., M.D. and S.D. are classified as methods of averaging deviations.

COEFFICIENT OF VARIATION (C.V.)

All the measures of dispersion discussed so far have units. If two series differ in their units of measurement, their variability cannot be compared by any measure given so far. Also, the size of measures of dispersion depends upon the size of values. Hence in situations where either the two series have different units of measurements, or their means differ sufficiently in size, the coefficient of variation should be used as a measure of dispersion. It is unitless measure of dispersion and also takes into account the size of the means of the two series. It is the best measure to compare the variability of two series or sets of observations. A series with less coefficient of variation is considered more consistent or stable.

Definition. Coefficient of variation of a series of variate values is the ratio of the standard deviation to the mean multiplied by 100.

If σ is the standard deviation and $\overline{X}$ is the mean of the set of values, the coefficient of variation is,

$$\text{C.V.} = \frac{\sigma}{\overline{X}} \times 100 \qquad \ldots(4.16)$$

This measure was given by Professor Karl Pearson.

Note: In case of sample studies, we use, the sample S.D. and $\bar{x}$, the sample mean instead of σ and $\overline{X}$ respectively.

Properties

1. It is one of the most widely used measure of dispersion because of its virtues.
2. Smaller the value of C.V., more consistent are the data and vice versa. Hence, a series with smaller C.V. than the C.V. of other series is more consistent, *i.e.*, it possesses less variability.
3. For field experiments, C.V. is generally reported. If C.V. is low, it indicates more reliability of experimental findings.
4. It is a relative measure of variability.

***Example* 4.6.** The following figures give the crude birth rate per 1000 people in Switzerland from 1968 to 1980.

Crude birth rate (*X*):	17.1,	16.5,	15.8,	15.2,	14.3,	13.6,	12.9,	12.3
	11.7,	11.5,	11.3,	11.3,	11.6			

The variance, standard deviation and coefficient of variation for birth rate are computed below.

We calculate the quantities,

$$\sum_{i=1}^{13} X_i = (17.1 + 16.5 + \ldots + 11.6) = 175.1$$

$$\overline{X} = \frac{175.1}{13} = 13.47$$

$$\sum_{i=1}^{13} X_i^2 = (17.1^2 + 16.5^2 + \ldots + 11.6^2) = 2411.57$$

Variance by the formula (4.8.1) is,

$$\sigma^2 = \frac{1}{13}\{2411.57-(175.1)^2/13\} = \frac{53.1077}{13} = 4.085$$

Standard deviation by the formula (4.14) is,

$$\sigma = \sqrt{4.085} = 2.021$$

Coefficient of variation by the formula (4.16) is,

$$\text{C.V.} = \frac{2.021}{13.47}\times 100 = 15.005 \text{ per cent}$$

Note: For calculation on computer, see Appendix, Chapter-4.

***Example* 4.7.** The prices of wheat at different centres were found to be as follows:

Prices of wheat (Rs./Kg)	*No. of centres*
1.75	3
1.72	2
1.73	4
1.76	5
1.71	6
1.80	2
1.87	7
2.34	1

We can measure the variation in prices of wheat by calculating the standard deviation. The computations are shown in the table below:

Prices of wheat (*X*)	*No. of centres* (*f*)	*f X*	$X-\overline{X}$	$f(X-\overline{X})$	$f(X-\overline{X})^2$
1.75	3	5.25	–.04	–.12	.0048
1.72	2	3.44	–.07	–.14	.0098
1.73	4	6.92	–.06	–.24	.0144
1.76	5	8.80	–.03	–.15	.0045
1.71	6	10.26	–.08	–.48	.0384
1.80	2	3.60	.01	.02	.0002
1.87	7	13.09	.08	.56	.0448
2.34	1	2.34	.55	.55	.3025
Total	30	53.70		00	.4194

$$\overline{X} = \frac{53.70}{30} = 1.79$$

The variance of prices by formula (4.9) is,

$$\sigma^2 = \frac{0.4194}{30} = 0.01398$$

$$\sigma = 0.1182$$

Example **4.8.** Following table gives the expenditure per month on food items per family of six persons in ten regions:

Regions :	1	2	3	4	5	6	7	8	9	10
Expenditure (*X*) : (*Rs.*)	1090	1270	1260	1200	1170	1080	1000	1310	1210	1130

The variance of above set of observations will be calculated with the help of coding. Subtract 1000 from each value and divide by 10 *i.e.*, take $A = 1000$ and $C = 10$.

We show the computation in the following table.

X	$X - 1000$	$X' = \dfrac{X-1000}{10}$	X'^2
1090	90	9	81
1270	270	27	729
1260	260	26	676
1200	200	20	400
1170	170	17	289
1080	80	8	64
1000	00	0	00
1310	310	31	961
1210	210	21	441
1130	130	13	169
Total		172	3810

The variance of the (coded) variable X' by formula (4.8.1) is

$$\sigma'^2 = \frac{1}{10}\{3810-(172)^2/10\} = \frac{851.6}{10} = 85.16$$

The variance of the uncoded variable by the relation (4.13.3) is

$$\sigma^2 = (10)^2 \times 85.16 = 8516$$

Example **4.9.** Monthly wages of employees in a factory are distributed as given below.

Wages (Rs.)	*No. of employees*
300 – 400	15
400 – 500	22
500 – 600	18
600 – 700	14
700 – 800	9
800 – 900	7
900 – 1000	5
1000 – 1100	4

We show the calculation of variance of the given distribution with and without coding. The method of computation is shown in the following table. For coding, we have chosen $A = 650$ and $C = 100$.

Wage (Rs.)	Mid-points (X)	Freq. (f)	fX	fX^2	$X' = \frac{X-650}{100}$	fX'	fX'^2
300 – 400	350	15	5250	1837500	–3	–45	135
400 – 500	450	22	9900	4455000	–2	–44	88
500 – 600	550	18	9900	5445000	–1	–18	18
600 – 700	650	14	9100	5915000	0	00	00
700 – 800	750	9	6750	5062500	1	9	9
800 – 900	850	7	5950	5057500	2	14	28
900 – 1000	950	5	4750	4512500	3	15	45
1000 – 1100	1050	4	4200	4410000	4	16	64
Total		94	55800	36695000		–53	387

The variance of the uncoded variable X by formula (4.9.1) is,

$$\sigma^2 = \frac{1}{94}\{36695000 - (55800)^2/94\}$$

$$= \frac{1}{94}\{36695000 - 33123829.79\}$$

$$= \frac{3571170.21}{94}$$

$$= 37991.17$$

Now the variance of the coded variable by formula (4.9.1) is,

$$\sigma'^2 = \frac{1}{94}\{387 - (-53)^2/94\}$$

$$= \frac{357.11702}{94}$$

$$= 3.7991172$$

The variance of the uncoded variable by relation (4.13.1) is,

$$\sigma^2 = (100)^2 \times 3.7991172$$

$$= 37991.17$$

This example throws light on two points:

1. The result obtained by the method of coding is same as one gets without coding the variable.
2. This shows how much labour is saved through the procedure of coding.

***Example* 4.10.** Find the number of items lying within the interval, mean ± S.D. of the following distribution.

Class intervals :	10–12	13–15	16–18	19–21	22–24	25–27	28–30	31–33	34–36
Frequency :	24	44	65	27	19	14	8	5	4

To find out the number of items within the interval, mean ± S.D., we calculate the mean and S.D. using the method of coding. Take $A = 23$ and $C = 3$.

Class intervals	*Continuous intervals*	*Mid-values*	$X' = \frac{X-23}{3}$	f	fX'	fX'^2
10–12	9.5–12.5	11	–4	24	–96	384
13–15	12.5–15.5	14	–3	44	–132	396
16–18	15.5–18.5	17	–2	65	–130	260
19–21	18.5–21.5	20	–1	27	–27	27
22–24	21.5–24.5	23	0	19	00	00
25–27	24.5–27.5	26	1	14	14	14
28–30	27.5–30.5	29	2	8	16	32
31–33	30.5–33.5	32	3	5	15	45
34–36	33.5–36.5	35	4	4	16	64
Total			0	210	–324	1222

The mean by formula (3.7) is

$$\overline{X} = 23 + \frac{(-324)}{210} \times 3$$

$$= 23 - 4.628 = 18.372$$

The variance by formula (4.13.2) is,

$$\sigma^2 = 3^2 \times \frac{1}{210}\left\{1222 - \frac{(-324)^2}{210}\right\}$$

$$= \frac{9}{210}\{1222 - 499.886\}$$

$$= \frac{9 \times 722.11}{210} = \frac{6499.03}{210} = 30.95$$

$$\sigma = 5.56$$

$$\overline{X} - \sigma = 18.372 - 5.56 = 12.81$$

$$\overline{X} + \sigma = 18.372 + 5.56 = 23.93$$

The number of items which spread between 12.5 and 15.4 is 44.

Number of items per unit length of interval = 44/3.

The number of items lying between 12.81 and 15.5.

$$= \frac{15.5 - 12.81}{3} \times 44 = \frac{118.36}{3} = 39.45$$

The number of items lying between 21.5 and 24.5 is 19.

Number of items lying between 21.5 and 23.93.

$$= \frac{23.93 - 21.5}{3} \times 19 = \frac{46.17}{3} = 15.39$$

Hence, the number of items lying between 12.81 and 23.93 is equal to sum of items lying between 12.81 to 15.5, 15.5 to 21.5 and 21.5 to 23.93 *i.e.*,

$$= 39.45 + (65 + 27) + 15.39 = 146.84$$
$$= 147$$

***Example* 4.11.** For the frequency distribution of birth weight given in Ex. 3.17, the standard deviation of birth weight in Dominican Republic is calculated using coding of data.

Table required to calculate the variance of birth weights by the formula (4.13.3) is given below without explanation as it is evident. In the following table open end classes are converted into equal interval classes.

Class intervals	*Mid-points*	$X' = \frac{X - 2250}{500}$	*f*	*fx'*	*fx'*^{2}
0 – 500	250	–4	5	–20	80
500 – 1000	750	–3	3	–9	27
1000 – 1500	1250	–2	23	–46	92
1500 – 2000	1750	–1	41	–41	41
2000 – 2500	2250	0	112	00	00
2500 – 3000	2750	1	528	528	528
3000 – 3500	3250	2	897	1794	3588
3500 – 4000	3750	3	622	1866	5598
4000 – 4500	4250	4	252	1008	4032
4500 – 5000	4750	5	58	290	1450
Total			2541	5370	15436

In the above table A is assumed to be 2250 and C is equal to 500.

Thus, $A = 2250$ and $C = 500$.

By the formula (4.13.3),

$$\sigma^2 = (500)^2 \times \frac{1}{2541}\left[15436 - \frac{(5370)^2}{2541}\right]$$

$$= \frac{250000}{2541} \times 4087.36$$

$$= 250000 \times 1.6086$$

$$= 402150 \text{ gm}^2$$

Thus, the standard deviation,

$$\sigma = \sqrt{402150}$$

$$= 634.15 \text{ gm}$$

POOLED OR COMBINED VARIANCE

By the combined variance of two groups, we mean the variance of the observations of the two groups taken together. Let us consider two groups consisting of N_1 and N_2 observations respectively. Suppose the means of the groups are $\overline{X}_1$ and $\overline{X}_2$, and the variances are σ_1^2 and σ_2^2 respectively. We know by formula (3.8) that the pooled mean of both the groups is,

$$\overline{X}_{12} = \frac{N_1\overline{X}_1 + N_2\overline{X}_2}{N_1 + N_2}$$

The combined variance of the two groups is given by the formula,

$$\sigma_{12}^2 = \frac{N_1\{\sigma_1^2 + (\overline{X}_1 - \overline{X}_{12})^2\} + N_2\{\sigma_2^2 + (\overline{X}_2 - \overline{X}_{12})^2\}}{N_1 + N_2} \quad ...(4.17)$$

$$= [N_1(\sigma_1^2 + d_1^2) + N_2(\sigma_2^2 + d_2^2)]/(N_1 + N_2) \quad ...(4.17.1)$$

where $d_1 = \left(\overline{X}_1 - \overline{X}_{12}\right)$ and $d_2 = (\overline{X}_2 - \overline{X}_{12})$.

The advantage of the formula of combined variance is that once we know the individual mean and variance of each group, we can calculate the variance of the combined groups without redoing the entire calculation.

Obviously the combined standard deviation can be found by taking the square root of the combined variance.

Formula (4.17) can be extended for more than two groups easily.

***Example* 4.12.** The mean and variance of scores earned by two groups, one of the boys and the other of the girls, on computation yielded the following results:

$N_1 = 62$ $\quad \overline{X}_1 = 108.2$ $\quad \sigma_1^2 = 524.41$

$N_2 = 45$ $\quad \overline{X}_2 = 105.4$ $\quad \sigma_2^2 = 355.32$

The variance of scores earned by boys and girls taken as one group of students can be calculated by the formula (4.17).

Pooled mean by formula (3.8) is

$$\overline{X}_{12} = \frac{62 \times 108.2 + 45 \times 105.4}{62 + 45} = \frac{11451.4}{107} = 107.02$$

Pooled variance,

$$\sigma_{12}^2 = \frac{62 \times \{524.41 + (108.2 - 107.02)^2\} + 45 \times \{355.32 + (105.4 - 107.02)^2\}}{62 + 45}$$

$$= \frac{62 \times \{524.41 + 1.3924\} + \{355.32 + 2.6244\} \times 45}{107}$$

$$= \frac{48707.24}{107} = 455.21$$

Combined standard deviation,

$$\sigma_{12} = 21.34$$

CONCLUDING REMARKS

A measure of dispersion, specially the variance, is the backbone of statistics. As a matter of fact, statistics involves variance almost in every study in one way or the other. Most of the surveys or experiments are considered as a study of sample units. Hence, the formulae for sampling are mostly used. In cases, where no inference has to be drawn for a larger group other than the observations under study, we should use the formulae given for the population. Moreover, all the formulae except variance are not affected whether we consider a population or a sample. Of course, the interpretation of values has to be made accordingly. Readers will come across the use of variance vis-a-vis the standard deviation in the chapters ahead.

QUESTIONS AND EXERCISES

1. What does dispersion indicate about the data? Why is this of great importance?
2. Which measure of dispersion do you consider the best and why?
3. Range gives very little information about data, still used widely, why?
4. In what respects is the coefficient of variation superior to other measures of dispersion?
5. Define and discuss the following terms:
   (*a*) Quartile deviation.
   (*b*) Mean deviation.
   (*c*) Variance.
   (*d*) Coefficient of variation.
6. What are the requirements of a good measure of dispersion?
7. Explain why standard deviation is considered superior to other measures of dispersion.
8. What is the effect of subtracting 25 from each observation and dividing the result of each observation by 5 on the following:
   (*a*) Mean deviation
   (*b*) Range
   (*c*) Standard deviation
   (*d*) Coefficient of variation
9. Distinguish between absolute and relative measures of dispersion.
10. Fill in the blanks:
    (*a*) Mean deviation is minimum about ________________.
    (*b*) Variance is zero when________________.
    (*c*) Range is zero when________________.
    (*d*) Coefficient of variation is infinity when________________.
    (*e*) Coefficient of variation is zero when________________.
11. Discuss the relative merits of range, standard deviation and mean deviation.
    (*M.Com. Saugar, 1963*)
12. What is meant by dispersion? What are the methods of computing measures of dispersion? Illustrate the practical utility of these methods.
    (*M.Com., Alld., 1956; B.Com., Agra, 1958; M.A., Vikram, 1961*)
13. Define 'mean deviation'. How does it differ from standard deviation? (*C.A., 1968*)

14. Following figures give the production of non-fatty dry milk during the twelve months of 1975.

Months:	Jan.	Feb.	Mar.	Apr.	May	June	July	Aug.	Sept.	Oct.	Nov.	Dec.
Production (million Lbs.):	83.5	81.6	95.8	111.5	131.4	126.5	98.7	76.2	53.2	50.3	49.3	67.1

Calculate (*i*) range, (*ii*) mean deviation about mean, (*iii*) variance and (*iv*) coefficient of variation.

15. The following table gives the number of branches and number of plants in a patch of field.

No. of branches (*X*)	*No. of plants* (*f*)
2	16
3	13
4	19
5	12
6	5
7	4

Calculate the mean deviation about median and variance of the number of branches.

16. The following table gives the distribution of monthly expenditure per head of the residents of a village.

Monthly expenditure (*Rs.*)	*No. of persons*
75–71	20
70–66	17
65–61	15
60–56	14
55–51	13
50–46	12
45–41	14
40–36	15
35–31	10

For the given distribution, calculate (*i*) quartile deviation, (*ii*) mean deviation about mean and (*iii*) standard deviation.

17. Two persons participated in five shooting competitions and were able to hit the target correctly out of fifteen shots as given below:

Competitor A	*Competitor B*
6	12
12	15
12	7
10	7
7	4

Find which of the competitor is more consistent in shooting performance.

18. The mean and variance of marks of a group of 120 students are 38.7 and 510.76, respectively. The mean and variance of marks of another group of 100 students are 54.4 and 412.09, respectively. Calculate the standard deviation of both the groups taken together.
19. Following table gives the distribution of the age of lady teachers of a school as revealed by records.

Age groups (years)	*No. of lady teachers*
15–19	3
20–24	13
25–29	21
30–34	15
35–39	5
40–44	4
45–49	2

Compute (*i*) quartile deviation, (*ii*) mean deviation about mean, (*iii*) coefficient of variation and (*iv*) number of teachers between the age of 26 and 33 years.

20. From the data given below, giving arithmetic average and standard deviation of four sub-groups, calculate the average and standard deviation of the whole group.

Sub-group	*No. of men*	*Average wages per month (Rs.)*	*Standard deviation of wages (Rs.)*
A	50	61.0	8.0
B	100	70.0	9.0
C	120	80.5	10.0
D	30	83.5	11.0

(*P.C.S., 1961; M.A., Raj., 1962*)

21. Goals scored by two teams A and B in a football season were as follows:

No. of goals scored in a match	*No. of matches*	
	A	*B*
0	27	17
1	9	9
2	8	6
3	5	5
4	4	3

Find which team may be considered more consistent in its performance.
(*I.A.S., 1954; B. Com., B.H.U., 1952; Saugar, 1958; P.C.S., 1962., B. Com., Raj., 1963*)

22. A group of 100 selected students average 163.8 cm in height with a coefficient of variation of 3.2%, what was the standard deviation of their height? (*M.A., B.H.U., 1961*)
23. A scientist reported that a sample of nine male albino rats had iron content under nine different diets as given below.

Iron determined (mg per kg)								
83.2,	87.2,	89.6,	20.4,	21.6,	20.0,	2.0,	2.0,	2.0

Calculate the sample variance from the given data.

24. The mean and standard deviation of a sample of 100 observations were calculated as 40 and 5.1 respectively by a student who took by mistake 50 instead of 40 for one observation. Calculate the correct mean and standard deviation.

25. Find the standard deviation of the following distribution:

Item :	6	7	8	9	10	11	12
Frequency:	3	6	9	13	8	5	4

(*M.A., Jodhpur, 1969*)

26. Three independent distributions each of 100 members and S.D. 4.5 units are located with their arithmetic means at 12.1, 17.1 and 22.1 units, respectively. Find the standard deviation of the distribution obtained by combining the three distributions. (*M.A., Delhi, 1961; M.Com., B.H.U., 1962*)

27. A purchasing agent receives samples of Manila envelopes from two suppliers. He had the samples tested in his own laboratory for tearing weight with the following results:

Tearing weight (in lbs)	*Samples from company A*	*Samples from company B*
50–60	3	10
60–70	42	16
70–80	22	36
80–90	3	8
	70	70

(*i*) Which company's envelope has higher tearing weight?

(*ii*) Which company's envelope is more variable in quality? (*C.A., 1963*)

28. The following is a random sample from a given population. Compute the arithmetic mean and coefficient of variation.

Lower class boundary	*Upper class boundary*	*Frequency*
9.5	14.5	1
14.5	19.5	7
19.5	24.5	5
24.5	29.5	5
29.5	34.5	2

(*M.Com., B.H.U., 1956*)

29. After change of origin and scale, a frequency distribution of a continuous variate takes the form as under:

Step deviation (u):	–3	–2	–1	0	1	2	3
Frequency (f):	10	15	25	25	10	10	5

If the mean and variance of the distribution are, respectively 31 and 254, find the original frequency distribution. (*I.C.W.A., Dec., 1985*)

30. (*a*) What are the important measures of locations and scatter of a random variable? Compare their relative merits and demerits.

(*b*) The average and standard deviation of the heights of two groups of students, numbering 100 and 250 respectively, are given below. What is the average and standard deviation of the heights of all the 350 students taken together?

	Group I	*Group II*
Average (*cm*):	150	165
S.D. (*cm*):	8	10

31. The first of the two groups has 100 items with mean 45 and variance 49. If the combined group has 250 items with mean 51 and variance 130, find the mean and the standard deviation of the second group. (*I.C.W.A., June, 1984*)

32. Weights of the students in kgs. are recorded by a machine as under:

50 55, 57, 49, 54, 61, 64, 59, 58, 56

If the weighing machine shows weight less by 5 kg, find correct values of range, standard deviation and coefficient of variation without calculating the correct weights.

(*I.C.W.A. June, 1984*)

33. The following table gives the result of three centres of a public examination.

Centre	*No. of examinees*	*Mean score*	*Standard deviation*
A	200	25	3
B	250	10	4
C	300	15	5

Calculate the mean and the standard deviation of the combined scores of the three centres.

(*I.C.W.A. (Inter); Dec., 1992*)

34. Explain the procedure of calculating the mean deviation from grouped frequency distribution. How standard deviation is superior than mean deviation?

(*B.Sc.(Ag), Hons. Pt. I, RAU 2001*)

35. The number of employees, average wages per weak, per employee and variance of the wage per employee for two factories are given below:

	Factory A	*Factory B*
No. of employees	100	200
Average wage for employee (Rs)	120	200
Variance of the wage per employee (Rs.)	16	25

In which factory is there greater variation in the distribution of wages per employee?

(*C.A. Foundation, Nov., 2000*)

36. (*a*) Distinguish between absolute and relative measure of dispersion.

(*b*) Find the range and coefficient of range for the following observations.

65, 70, 82, 59, 81, 76, 57, 60, 55 and 50 (*C.A. PE–I, Nov., 2003*)

37. (*a*) "Measures of central tendency, dispersion and skewness are, complementary to each other in understanding the characteristics of a frequency distribution." Elucidate.

(*b*) A factory produces two types of electric lamps, A and B. In an experiment relating to their life, the following results were obtained.

Length of life (in hours)	*No. of lamps (A)*	*No. of lamps (B)*
500–700	50	40
700–900	110	300
900–1100	260	120
1100–1300	100	80
1300–1500	80	60

Using your knowledge of average and dispersion, list your conclusions.

(*M.B.A. Part–II, MLSU, Udaipur, 2001*)

38. "Mean and Standard Deviation are necessary and sufficient parameters to describe any set of data." Comment on this statement.

(*M.B.A., Part–I, MLSU, Udaipur, 2002*)

SUGGESTED READING

Colin Rose and D.S. Murray (2002). *Mathematical Statistics with Mathematica*, Springer.

Douglas A. Downing and Jeffrey Clark (2003). *Business Statistics*, Barron's Educational Series.

Freund, J.E. (1981). *Modern Elementary Statistics*, Prentice-Hall of India, New Delhi.

Goon, A.M., M.K. Gupta and B.K. Dasgupta (1977). *Fundamentals of Statistics*, Vol. I, The World Press, Calcutta.

Gupta, S.C. and V.K. Kapoor (1980). *Fundamentals of Mathematical Statistics*, 7th ed., Sultan Chand & Sons, Delhi.

Hoel, P.G. and R.J. Jessen (1982). *Basic Statistics for Business and Economics*, John Wiley, New York.

John A., Rafter, Martha L. Abell and Tames P. Braseltton (2002). *Statistics with Maple*, Elsevier.

Meter J., W. Wasserman and G.A. Whitmore (1982). *Applied Statistics*, Allyn and Bacon, London.

Murray, R. Spiegel (1998). *Schaum's Outline of Statistics*, McGraw Hill Professional.

Richard, G. Lomax (2001). *An Introduction to Statistical Concepts for Educational and Behavioral Sciences*, Lawrence Erlbaum Associates.

Sellers, G.R. and S.B. Vardeman (1982). *Elementary Statistics*, Saunders College Publishing, New York.

APPENDIX

(SPSS Window Guide for Mean and Variance)

PROCEDURE OF OBTAINING VARIANCE IN SPSS V.11. 5

1. Click on Analyze in menu bar followed by Descriptive Statistics & Descriptives as given below:

Example 4.6

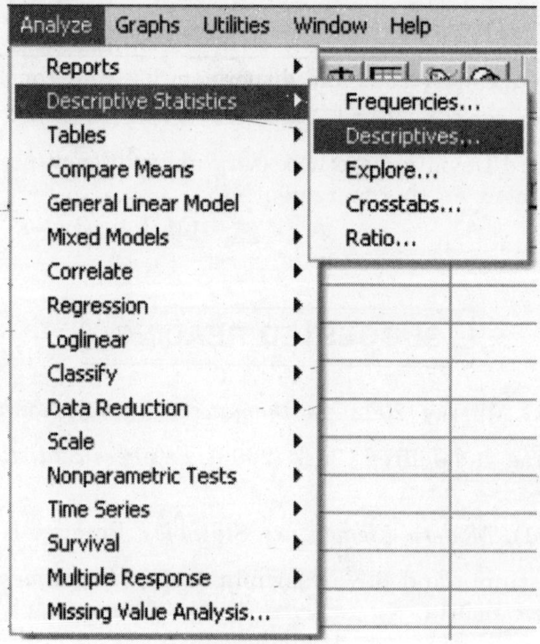

2. In the second step, select the variable birthrt and click on arrow button. When you click on OK button, you get another window given below. Here, you can select any measure by clicking on check box. Press OK button to get the following window.

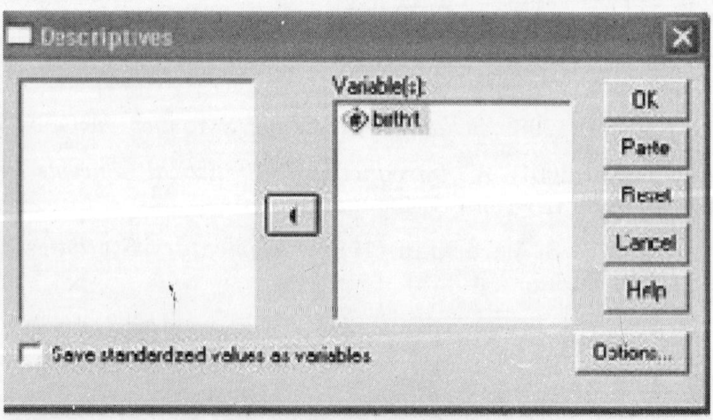

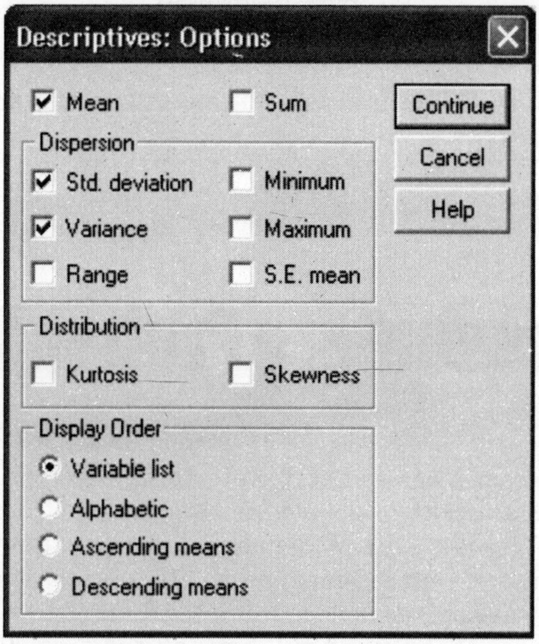

Descriptive Statistics

	N	*Mean*	*Std. deviation*	*Variance*
BIRTHRT	13	13.4692	2.10372	4.426
Valid N (listwise)	13			

5

Chapter

Elementary Probability

In day-to-day life, one comes across many statements which create doubt about certain happenings and one may want to determine the chance of occurrence of a particular happening, *e.g.*, if one desires to know the chance of rain based on some meteorological observations. In the case of coin tossing, one wants to know what will be the chance of winning if a person always stakes for head in a fixed number of tossings; in the game of bridge what is the chance that a hand will have all the aces. For a production unit one wants to know what would be the chance of a defective item being manufactured. There can be innumerable such queries which one would like to make and meanwhile evaluate mathematically the chance of the occurrence of such possibilities. This invoked the need of probability theory. The theory of probability came into existence when problems of games were referred to mathematicians like Karl Pearson, Laplace and others. Later, the credit of conceptual development of theory of probability goes to R.A. Fisher and R. von Mises. The idea of sample space was innovated by von Mises in 1931 and axiomatic approach of probability was originated by A. Kolmogorov in 1933. Complicated applications involving advanced theory of probability and axiomatic approach of probability are not dealt with in this book.

The calculation of probability, on the basis of observational phenomenon, needs some basic ideas on random experiments, sample space and event etc. These are explained and followed by an explanation of probability theory.

RANDOM EXPERIMENT

If an experiment or trial can be repeated any number of times under similar conditions and it is possible to enumerate the total number of outcomes, but an individual outcome is not predictable, such an experiment is called a random experiment. For instance, if a fair coin is tossed three times, it is possible to enumerate all the possible eight sequences of head (H) and tail (T). But, it is not possible to predict which sequence will occur at any occasion. This is one example of a random experiment. Many more can be thought of.

SAMPLE SPACE

Each conceivable outcome of a random experiment under consideration is said to be a *sample point*. The totality of all conceivable sample point is called a sample space. Sample space of a trial conducted by three tossings of a coin is, *HHH, HHT, HTH, HTT, THH, THT,TTH, TTT*.

In the above experiment it is simple to note that any one sequence of *H* and/or *T* is a sample point whereas all the possible eight sample points constitute the sample space.

EVENT

Any subset of the sample space is an event. In other words, the set of sample points which satisfy certain requirement(s) is called an event.

For example, in the event, that there are exactly two heads in three tossings of a coin, it would consist of three points *HTH, HHT* and *THH*.

Complementary Event

The complement of an event *A*, means non-occurrence of *A* and is denoted by $\overline{A}$ or A^c, $\overline{A}$ contains those points of the sample space which do not belong to *A*.

Elementary Event

An event having only one sample point is called an *elementary event or simple event.*

Mutually Exclusive Events

Two events E_1 and E_2 are said to be mutually exclusive if the occurrence of E_1 precludes the occurrence of E_2 and vice versa. In other words if there is no sample point in E_1 which is common to the sample points in E_2, *i.e.*, $E_1 \cap E_2 = \phi$, the events E_1 and E_2 are said to be mutually exclusive. *For example*, if we flip a fair coin, the coin will display either head or tail. Hence, the two events that the coin displays head E_1 or tail E_2 are mutually exclusive. Further, in a city a dealer has scooters of three models namely, Bajaj, Priya and Chetak, and another dealer has four models of scooters namely, Lambretta, Cento, Lamby and Mac 175. Let us denote the event E_1 as Bajaj, Priya and Chetak and event E_2 as Lambretta, Cento, Lamby and Mac 175. It is obvious that a buyer will select a scooter either from E_1 or E_2. Hence, the two events E_1 and E_2 are mutually exclusive.

Independent Events

Two events E_1 and E_2 are said to be independent if the occurrence of E_1 has no bearing on the occurrence of E_2 i.e., the knowledge that the event E_1 has occurred gives no information about the occurrence of the event E_2. Formally, two events E_1 and E_2 are independent if and only if,

$$P(E_1 \cap E_2) = P(E_1)P(E_2) \qquad ...(5.1)$$

The intersection, $(E_1 \cap E_2)$, between two events E_1 and E_2 is known as *joint event. For example*, a bag contains balls of two different colours say, red and white. The two balls are drawn successively. First a ball is drawn from one bag and replaced after noting its colour. Let us presume that it is white and is denoted by the event E_1. Another ball is drawn from the same bag and its colour is noted. Let this event be denoted by the event E_2. The result of the second draw is independent of the first draw. Hence the events E_1 and E_2 are independent. Let us consider another example. A State Director declares that each lottery ticket will have the chance of winning prizes at two draws at the intervals of one month. The event that a ticket wins a prize at the first draw is denoted by E_1, and the event that a ticket wins a prize at the second draw is denoted by E_2. It is obvious that the winning of a prize of any ticket at the first draw has no bearing on any ticket that wins a prize at the second draw. Hence, the events E_1 and E_2 are independent.

MATHEMATICAL OR CLASSICAL DEFINITION OF PROBABILITY

This definition of probability is credited to Laplace. If there are N mutually exclusive and equally likely outcomes of a random experiment, and out of these N outcomes, only n are favourable to an attribute *i.e.*, n sample points constitute an event E under consideration, the probability of the event E is,

$$P(E) = \frac{n}{N} \quad ...(5.2)$$

In the trial of tossing a coin three times, $N = 8$ and for the event E that there are exactly two heads, $n = 3$. It means that there are only three points favourable to E. Thus, the probability of event E is 3/8. Similarly if for the event E_1 is there are atleast two heads, $n = 4$. The probability of the event E_1 is 4/8 *i.e.*, 1/2. Students will come across a number of examples later in this chapter.

The above definition of probability is widely used, but it cannot be applied under the following situations:

(*i*) If it is not possible to enumerate all the possible outcomes for an experiment.

(*ii*) If the sample points (outcomes) are not mutually independent.

(*iii*) If the total number of outcomes is infinite.

(*iv*) If each and every outcome is not equally likely.

It is clear that the above drawbacks of a classical approach restrict its use in practical problems. Yet this is still widely used for problems concerning the flipping of coin(s), throwing of dice, games of cards and roulette wheel etc. The probability by classical approach cannot be discovered in the situations like an electric bulb will fuse before it is used for 100 hours, a patient will die if operated for an ailment, a student will fail in a particular examination. Some of the drawbacks of a classical probability are removed in another definition given below.

STATISTICAL DEFINITION OF PROBABILITY

If out of a large number of trials, only n of them are conducted and out of these n outcomes under each trial, only k outcomes are favourable to an event E, then the probability of E is,

$$P(E) = \lim_{n \to \infty} \left(\frac{k}{n} \right) \quad ...(5.3)$$

The above definition of probability involves a concept which has a long term consequence. This approach was initiated by von Mises. Moreover n is not equal to infinity. Thus, in this case, the probability is the limit of relative frequency. Whether such a limit always exists, is not definite. Hence, statistical definition of probability is also not very sound. The probability calculated by conducting an actual experiment is called a posteriori probability, whereas the probability specified by logic or based on some prior information is called a priori probability.

Basic Properties of Probability

1. The probability of an event E lies between 0 and 1 *i.e.*, $0 \leq P(E) \leq 1$. If an event is certain not to occur, its probability is zero and if it is certain to occur, its probability is one.
2. The assignment of probability to each outcome of an experiment is a rule to assign a non-negative number such that the sum of these numbers to all possible outcomes 'Ω' is unity, *i.e.*, $P(\Omega) = 1$.
3. Any two equivalent events will be assigned the same probability.
4. If two events E_1 and E_2 are mutually exclusive, the probability of occurrence of either E_1 or E_2 *i.e.*, of $(E_1 \cup E_2)$ is given as the sum of the individual probabilities, symbolically,

$$P(E_1 \cup E_2) = P(E_1) + P(E_2) \qquad ...(5.4)$$

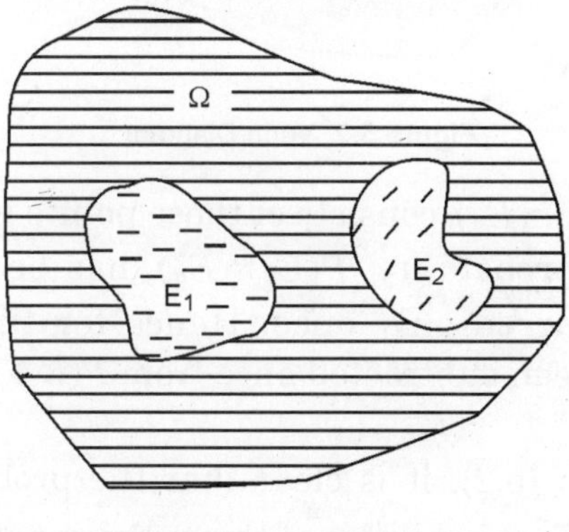

Figure 5.1 Venn Diagram

Venn diagram (5.1) shows the mutually exclusive events E_1 and E_2. This property of probability is known as *general additive property* of probability or addition law. This theorem may be extended to any number of mutually exclusive events. If E_1, E_2, ... E_k are k mutually exclusive events, the probability.

$$P(E_1 \cup E_2 \cup ... \cup E_k) = P(E_1) + P(E_2) + ... + P(E_k) \qquad ...(5.5)$$

***Example* 5.1.** If a person draws a card from a pack, what is the probability that the card is either ace or a king?

The events that the card drawn is either an ace or a king are mutually exclusive. Let the event of the ace card drawn be denoted by E_1 and the king card drawn be denoted by E_2. A pack consisting of 52 cards will have 4 aces and 4 kings, hence,

$$P(E_1) = \frac{4}{52} \text{ and } P(E_2) = \frac{4}{52}$$

$$P(E_1 \cup E_2) = P(E_1) + P(E_2)$$

$$= \frac{4}{52} + \frac{4}{52} = \frac{2}{13}$$

Readers will come across many other problems in which the additive property will be used.

Consider the case where two events, E_1 and E_2 are *not mutually exclusive.* The probability of the event that either E_1 or E_2 or both occur is given as,

$$P(E_1 \cup E_2) = P(E_1) + P(E_2) - P(E_1 \cap E_2) \qquad ...(5.6)$$

Venn diagram 5.2 depicts the non-mutually exclusive events.

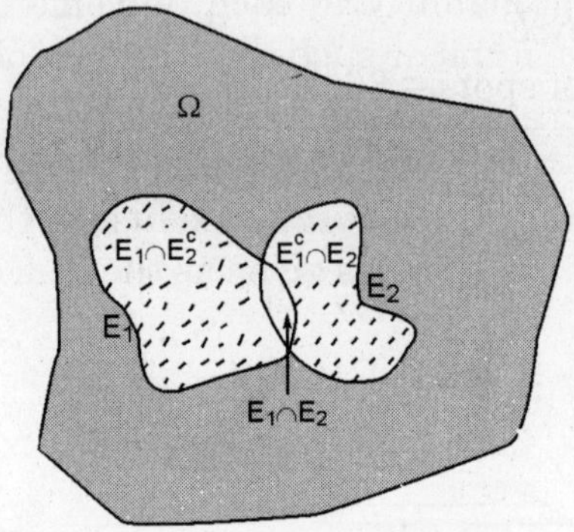

Figure 5.2 Venn Diagram

In Fig. 5.2, the event $(E_1 \cap E_2)$ consists of those points which are common to E_1 and E_2. In $\{P(E_1) + P(E_2)\}$, the probability $P(E_1 \cap E_2)$ has been included twice while in $(E_1 \cup E_2), (E_1 \cap E_2)$ has occurred only once. Hence for finding out $P(E_1 \cup E_2)$, the probability $P(E_1 \cap E_2)$ has been subtracted once from $P(E_1) + P(E_2)$.

Proof of addition law

From the Venn diagram (5.2), it is clear that the probability of the union of two events E_1 and E_2 is the sum of probabilities of three disjoint events $E_1 \cap E_2^c$, $E_1 \cap E_2$ and $E_1^c \cap E_2$ *i.e.,*

$$P(E_1 \cup E_2) = P(E_1 \cap E_2^c) + P(E_1 \cap E_2) + P(E_1^c \cap E_2) \qquad ...(1)$$

Also,

$$P(E_1) = P(E_1 \cap E_2^c) + P(E_1 \cap E_2)$$

or $$P(E_1 \cap E_2^c) = P(E_1) - P(E_1 \cap E_2) \qquad ...(2)$$

$$P(E_2) = P(E_1 \cap E_2) + P(E_1^c \cap E_2)$$

or $$P(E_1^c \cap E_2) = P(E_2) - P(E_1 \cap E_2) \qquad ...(3)$$

Substituting the values of $P(E_1 \cap E_2^c)$ and $P(E_1^c \cap E_2)$ in (1), we get

$$P(E_1 \cup E_2) = P(E_1) - P(E_1 \cap E_2) + P(E_1 \cap E_2) + P(E_2) - P(E_1 \cap E_2)$$

$$P(E_1 \cup E_2) = P(E_1) + P(E_2) - P(E_1 \cap E_2) \qquad ...(4)$$

This completes the proof of the theorem.

In the like manner, the formula for probability of the union of three mutually non-exclusive events E_1, E_2 and E_3 is,

$$P(E_1 \cup E_2 \cup E_3) = P(E_1) + P(E_2) + P(E_3) - P(E_1 \cap E_2) - P(E_1 \cap E_3) - P(E_2 \cap E_3) + P(E_1 \cap E_2 \cap E_3) \qquad ...(5.7)$$

By induction, formula (5.7) can be extended to any number of mutually non-exclusive events.

***Example* 5.2.** A die is thrown twice. The probability that the sum of the spots on the die at two throws is divisible by 2 or 3 can be calculated in the following manner. Let the event be, that the sum of the spots on the die is divisible by 2, denoted by E_1 and the sum is divisible by 3 is denoted by E_2.

Total number of pairs of spots = 36, which are:

1,1	1,2	1,3	1,4	1,5	1,6
2,1	2,2	2,3	2,4	2,5	2,6
3,1	3,2	3,3	3,4	3,5	3,6
4,1	4,2	4,3	4,4	4,5	4,6
5,1	5,2	5,3	5,4	5,5	5,6
6,1	6,2	6,3	6,4	6,5	6,6

E_1:	(1.1),	(1,3),	(1,5),	(2,2),	(2,4),	(2,6),	(3,1),	(3,3),	(3,5),
	(4,2),	(4,4),	(4,6),	(5,1),	(5,3),	(5,5),	(6,2),	(6,4),	(6,6),
E_2:	(1,2),	(1,5),	(2,1),	(2,4),	(3,3),	(3,6),	(4,2),	(4,5),	(5,1),
	(5,4),	(6,3),	(6,6).						

The points common to the events E_1 and E_2, are,

$$E_1 \cap E_2\text{: } (1,5), (2,4), (3,3), (4,2), (5,1), (6,6)$$

Obviously the events E_1 and E_2 are not mutually exclusive. Hence, the probability of the event $(E_1 \cup E_2)$ *i.e.*, the sum of the spots is divisible by 2 and 3 is,

$$P(E_1 \cup E_2) = P(E_1) + P(E_2) - P(E_1 \cap E_2)$$

where

$$P(E_1) = \frac{18}{36} = \frac{1}{2}; P(E_2) = \frac{12}{36} = \frac{1}{3}; P(E_1 \cap E_2) = \frac{6}{36} = \frac{1}{6}$$

Thus, $$P(E_1 \cup E_2) = \frac{1}{2} + \frac{1}{3} - \frac{1}{6} = \frac{2}{3} = 0.667$$

5. Two events E_1 and E_2 defined over a sample space Ω are said to be independent if and only if,

$$P(E_1 \cap E_2) = P(E_1)P(E_2)$$

The above rule may be extended to any number of events. Let E_1, E_2, ..., E_k be k events defined over the sample space, Ω, the events E_i's (i = 1, 2, ..., k) are said to be independent if and only if

$$P(E_1 \cap E_2 \cap ... \cap E_k) = P(E_1)P(E_2)...P(E_k) \quad ...(5.8)$$

or

$$P\left(\bigcap_{i=1}^{k} E_i\right) = \prod_{i=1}^{k} P(E_i) \quad ...(5.8.1)$$

The above rule is known as *multiplicative law of probability*.

Probability by De-Morgan's Laws

It $E_1, E_2, \dots E_k$ are k independent events such that the probability of the event E_i is p_i *i.e.*, $P(E_i) = p_i$ and $P(E_i^c) = 1 - p_i$, then the probability of happening of at least one of these k events can be found out by using the De-Morgan's laws.

Event $\quad (E_1 \cup E_2 \cup \dots \cup E_k)^c = (E_1^c \cap E_2^c \cap \dots \cap E_k^c) \quad$ ...(I)

Event $\quad (E_1 \cap E_2 \cap \dots \cap E_k)^c = E_1^c \cup E_2^c \cup \dots \cup E_k^c \quad$ ...(II)

$$\begin{aligned} P(E_1 \cup E_2 \cup \dots \cup E_k) &= 1 - P(E_1 \cup E_2 \cup \dots \cup E_k)^c \\ &= 1 - P(E_1^c \cap E_2^c \cap \dots \cap E_k^c) \\ &= 1 - P(E_1^c)P(E_2^c) \dots P(E_k^c) \\ &= 1 - (1-p_1)(1-p_2) \dots (1-p_k) \\ &= \sum_{i=1}^{k} p_i - \sum_{\substack{i,j=1 \\ i<j}}^{k} p_i p_j + \sum_{\substack{i,j,u=1 \\ i<j<u}}^{k} p_i p_j p_k \\ &\quad + \dots + (-1)^{k-1}(p_1 p_2 \dots p_k) \end{aligned} \quad \text{...(5.9)}$$

Hence,

$$P(E_1^c \cup E_2^c) = P(E_1 \cap E_2)^c = 1 - P(E_1 \cap E_2)$$

$$P(E_1^c \cap E_2^c) = P(E_1 \cup E_2)^c = 1 - P(E_1 \cup E_2)$$

For three events E_1, E_2 and E_3, some important relations are:

(1) $\quad P(E_1 \cup E_2 \mid E_3) = P(E_1 \mid E_3) + P(E_2 \mid E_3) + (E_1 \cap E_2 \mid E_3) \quad$ ...(5.10)

(2) $\quad P[(E_1 \cap E_3) \cup (E_2 \cap E_3)] = P(E_1 \cap E_3) + P(E_2 \cap E_3) - P(E_1 \cap E_2 \cap E_3) \quad$ ...(5.11)

(3) $\quad P[(E_1 \cup E_2) \mid E_3] = P(E_1 \mid E_3) + P(E_2 \mid E_3) - P(E_1 \cap E_2 \mid E_3) \quad$ ...(5.12)

***Example* 5.3.** A bag contains 8 white balls and 4 red balls. One ball is drawn from the bag and it is replaced after noting its colour. In the second draw again one ball is drawn and its colour is noted. The probability of the event that both the balls drawn are of different colours can be found out as follows:

Let the events that the ball at first draw is of white colour and at the second draw is of red colour be denoted by E_1 and E_2 respectively.

Total number of ways in which a ball can be drawn = $\binom{12}{1} = 12$

Number of ways in which a white ball can be drawn = $\binom{8}{1} = 8$

Number of ways in which a red ball can be drawn = $\binom{4}{1} = 4$

Hence,

$$P(E_1) = \frac{8}{12} = \frac{2}{3}$$

$$P(E_2) = \frac{4}{12} = \frac{1}{3}$$

Since the events E_1 and E_2 are independent,

$$P(E_1 \cap E_2) = P(E_1)P(E_2)$$

$$= \frac{2}{3} \times \frac{1}{3} = \frac{2}{9} = 0.22$$

Now, consider the situation when a unit selected is not replaced. In this case, the number of points in the sample are reduced by the number of units selected. Hence, the total number of sample points at each subsequent draw would change. The probability at any draw can be calculated as per the rules discussed so far. Now we consider an example for this situation.

***Example* 5.4.** Consider again the example 5.3 with the modification that the ball selected at the first draw is not replaced. We calculate the probability of the event E that the two balls selected at two successive draws are of different colours. The balls can be selected in two ways.

Case (*i*) If the ball at the first draw, white and at the second draw, red is represented by the event A.

As in example 5.3, $P(E_1) = \frac{2}{3}$

At the time of the second draw, total number of balls in the bag is 11 and the number of red balls is 4. The prob. of selection of a red ball = $\binom{4}{1} \Big/ \binom{11}{1} = \frac{4}{11}$.

Thus, the prob. of the event A

$$P(A) = \frac{2}{3} \times \frac{4}{11} = \frac{8}{33}$$

Case (*ii*) If the ball drawn at the first draw, red and at the second draw, white is represented by the event B.

Prob. of a red ball selected at first draw

$$= \binom{4}{1} \Big/ \binom{12}{1} = \frac{4}{12} = \frac{1}{3}$$

Prob. of a white ball selected at second draw

$$= \binom{8}{1} \Big/ \binom{11}{1} = \frac{8}{11}$$

Prob. of the event $B = \frac{1}{3} \times \frac{8}{11} = \frac{8}{33}$

Since, the two cases are mutually exclusive, their probabilities will be added.

Thus, $\quad P(E) = P(A) + P(B)$

$$= \frac{8}{33} + \frac{8}{33} = \frac{16}{33} = 0.485$$

More examples are given to create a better understanding of the matter discussed so far.

***Example* 5.5.** A sheet containing 10 riddles is given to three graduate students of three different subjects. It is considered that a mathematics' student can solve 60% riddles, a Physics' student can solve 40% riddles and that of economics 30% riddles. The probability of an event 'E' that a riddle chosen from the sheet will be solved by all the three students is calculable as given below.

Prob. of solving the riddle by a Maths student = 0.6

Prob. of solving the riddle by a Physics' student = 0.4

Prob. of solving the riddle by an Economics' student = 0.3

Solving of a riddle by a student is independent of solving the riddle by the other student.

Hence the probability,

$$P(E) = 0.6 \times 0.4 \times 0.3 = 0.072$$

***Example* 5.6.** A stockist has 20 items in a lot. Out of which, 12 are non-defective and 8 defective. A customer selects 3 items from the lot.

(*i*) What is the probability that all the three items are non-defective?

(*ii*) What is the probability that out of these three items, two are non-defective and one is defective?

The probability in the two cases is calculable in the following manner.

Case (*i*) Let the event, that all the three items are non-defective, be denoted by E_1.

There are 12 non-defective items and out of them 3 can be selected in $\binom{12}{3}$ ways.

Total number of ways in which 3 items can be selected are $\binom{20}{3}$.

Hence the probability,

$$P(E_1) = \binom{12}{3} \Big/ \binom{20}{3} = \frac{12 \times 11 \times 10}{20 \times 19 \times 18} = 0.193$$

Case (*ii*) Let the event, that two items are non-defective and one is defective, be denoted by E_2.

Two non-defective items out of 12 non-defective items can be selected in $\binom{12}{2}$ ways and one item out of 8 defective items can be selected in $\binom{8}{1}$ ways. Thus, the total number of favourable ways to $E_2 = \binom{12}{2}\binom{8}{1}$ The probability,

$$P(E_2) = \binom{12}{2}\binom{8}{1} \Big/ \binom{20}{3} = \frac{12 \times 11 \times 8 \times 3}{20 \times 19 \times 18} = 0.463$$

***Example* 5.7.** A fair dic is thrown twice. The probability that the sum of spots at two throws is more than nine can be calculated in the manner given below.

The sum of spots being more than nine means that it can be 10, 11 or 12. Let the three events be denoted by E_1, E_2 and E_3, respectively.

In two throws, total number of sample points = 36

The sample points in E_1 are : (4,6), (5,5), (6,4)

The sample points in E_2 are: (5,6), (6,5)

The sample point in E_3 is: (6,6)

Let the event that sum of spots at two throws is more than nine is denoted by E.

The events E_1, E_2 and E_3 are mutually exclusive. Hence the probability,

$$P(E) = P(E_1)+P(E_2)+P(E_3)$$

$$= \frac{3}{36}+\frac{2}{36}+\frac{1}{36}=\frac{1}{6}$$

***Example* 5.8.** There are three radio stations A, B and C which can be received in a city of 2000 families. The following information is available on the basis of a survey:

(*a*) 1200 families listen to radio station A.

(*b*) 1100 families listen to radio station B.

(*c*) 800 families listen to radio station C.

(*d*) 865 families listen to the radio stations A and B.

(*e*) 450 families listen to the radio stations A and C.

(*f*) 400 families listen to the radio stations B and C.

(*g*) 100 families listen to the radio stations A, B and C.

The probability that a family selected at random listens at least to one radio station can be calculated as follows. We first define the events.

A family listens to radio station $A = E_1$

A family listens to radio station $B = E_2$

A family listens to radio station $C = E_3$

We can define the events that a family listens to any two radio stations be $E_1 \cap E_2$, $E_1 \cap E_3$ and $E_2 \cap E_3$. The event that a family listens to all the three stations is given by $E_1 \cap E_2 \cap E_3$. The event that a family listens to at least one radio station is equivalent to $E_1 \cup E_2 \cup E_3$. The probability of the event $E_1 \cup E_2 \cup E_3$ is obtained by formula (5.7).

Total number of families = 2000

Number of favourable ways to different events are from data in (a) to (g).

Hence the probability,

$$P(E_1 \cup E_2 \cup E_3) = P(E_1)+P(E_2)+P(E_3)-P(E_1 \cap E_2)$$

$$-P(E_1 \cap E_3)-P(E_2 \cap E_3)+P(E_1 \cap E_2 \cap E_3)$$

$$= \frac{1200}{2000}+\frac{1100}{2000}+\frac{800}{2000}-\frac{865}{2000}-\frac{450}{2000}-\frac{400}{2000}+\frac{100}{2000}$$

$$= \frac{1485}{2000} = 0.742$$

There is around 74% chance that a family selected at random listens to one or more radio stations.

***Example* 5.9.** A traveller has a choice of travelling by car, train and plane. He has been given the option of using more than one mode of conveyance. The probability that the traveller may use two modes of conveyance can be calculated by a classical approach.

Let C, T and P correspond to the travelling by car, train and plane respectively. Since the traveller can travel by one or more modes of conveyance, the sample space will consist of the following points.

Sample space : C, T, P, CT, CP, TP and CTP *i.e.*, 7 points.

Let the event that the traveller may use two modes of conveyance be denoted by E. The sample points favourable to E are,

E: CT, CP, TP.

Hence the probability,

$$P(E) = \frac{3}{7} = 0.43$$

***Example* 5.10.** A traveller wants to go from a city A to city B by car. There are various routes to go from A to B which pass through the cities P, Q and R. The routes and the cities are as shown in the Fig. 5.3.

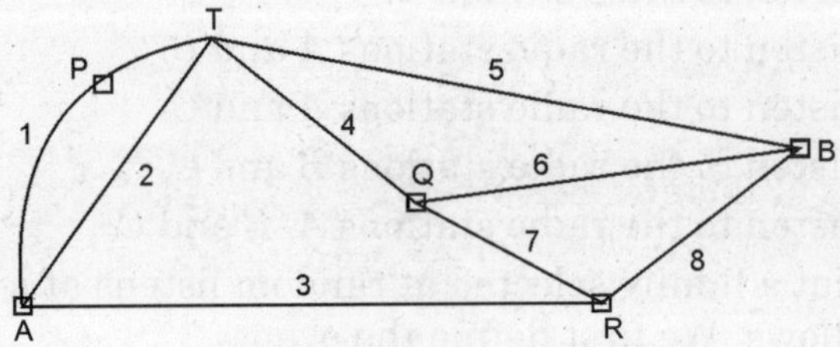

Figure 5.3 Routes Map

In Fig. 5.3, A is the starting city, T is a bifurcating point, P, Q and R are three cities and numerals show the route numbers. It is assumed that the traveller does not turn back.

The probability of the event E that the traveller passes through the two cities can be calculated in the following manner. To go from city A to B, following routes are possible which constitute the sample space.

Sample space:

15, 146, 1478, 25, 246, 2478, 38, 376, 3745, *i.e.*, 9 sample points

The sample points favourable to the event E are,

E: 146, 2478, 376, 3745, *i.e.*, 4 sample points.

Hence, the probability $P(E) = 4/9 = 0.44$

CONDITIONAL PROBABILITY

In many situations we have the information about the occurrence of an event A and are required to find out the probability of the occurrence of another event B. This is denoted by $P(B \mid A)$. *For example*, if we know that a card drawn from a pack is black and we want to calculate the probability that it is the ace of spade.

Let us take the problem of throwing a fair die twice. Suppose, the same number of spots do not appear in both the throws and we are required to find out the probability that the sum of the number of spots in both the throws is six.

Let us consider a biometrical problem, a patient comes to a doctor with his family history that his elders suffered from high blood pressure. He wants to know the probability of the event that he will also suffer from high blood pressure.

Now we consider an industrial problem. There are two lots of certain finished machine parts, lot A and lot B. Each lot has some defective machine parts. If we flip a coin and if it turns up with head upside, select lot A and if it turns with tail up, then select the lot B. We are interested to know the probability of the event, that a part selected from the lot obtained in this manner is defective.

Any number of examples in various disciplines can be cited. The readers themselves can think of problems relevant to the conditional probability pertaining to their own sphere of activity.

Definition. Let A and B be two events. The *conditional probability* of event B, if an event A has occurred, is defined by the relation,

$$P(B \mid A) = \frac{P(B \cap A)}{P(A)} \text{ iff } P(A) > 0 \qquad \text{...(5.13)}$$

In case when $P(A) = 0$, $P(B \mid A)$ is not defined because $P(B \cap A) = 0$ and $P(B \mid A) = 0/0$ which is an indeterminate quantity.

The conditional probability concept can be extended to the case where $B_1, B_2, \ldots, B_k$ is a sequence of mutually exclusive events given that an event A has occurred. The probability of the event $\overset{k}{\underset{i=1}{\cup}} B_i$, when the event A has occurred is,

$$P\left(\bigcup_{i=1}^{k} B_i \mid A\right) = \frac{P\left(\bigcup_{i=1}^{k} B_i \cap A\right)}{P(A)} \qquad \text{...(5.14)}$$

$$= \frac{\sum_{i=1}^{k} P(B_i \cap A)}{P(A)} \qquad \text{...(5.14.1)}$$

iff $P(A) > 0$

Generalization of Multiplicative law of probability

If $E_1, E_2, \ldots, E_k$ are k events, then the probability of the intersection of these k events can be calculated by the multiplicative formula developed in terms of conditional probabilities.

$$P(E_1 \cap E_2 \cap \text{--} \cap E_k) = P(E_1)P(E_2 \mid E_1)P(E_3 \mid E_1 \cap E_2)$$
$$\text{--}P(E_k \mid E_1 \cap E_2 \text{--} \cap E_{k-1}) \qquad \text{...(5.15)}$$

As a particular case, when $k = 3$,

$$P(E_1 \cap E_2 \cap E_3) = P(E_1)P(E_2 \mid E_1)P(E_3 \mid E_1 \cap E_2) \qquad \text{...(5.16)}$$

***Example* 5.11.** If a card drawn from a pack of cards is black, represented by the event A, the probability of the event B that the card drawn is ace of spade, can be calculated by formula (5.13).

The number of cards in the pack = 52.

Out of 52 cards, the number of black cards = 26

Prob. of drawing a black card *i.e.*, $P(A) = 26/52 = 1/2$

Out of 26 black cards, only one is an ace of spade.

The event $B \cap A$ contains only one point and thus,

$$P(B \cap A) = 1/52$$

Now the probability,

$$P(B \mid A) = \frac{P(B \cap A)}{P(A)}$$

$$= \frac{1/52}{1/2} = \frac{1}{26}$$

***Example* 5.12.** An experiment is conducted by throwing a fair die twice. Suppose the event that the same number of spots do not turn up in two throws is denoted by A, and the event that the sum of spots in two throws is 6, is denoted by B.

The probability of the event $(B \mid A)$ can be worked out as follows:

There can be in all 36 pairs of spots which are:

1,1	1,2	1,3	1,4	1,5	1,6
2,1	2,2	2,3	2,4	2,5	2,6
3,1	3,2	3,3	3,4	3,5	3,6
4,1	4,2	4,3	4,4	4,5	4,6
5,1	5,2	5,3	5,4	5,5	5,6
6,1	6,2	6,3	6,4	6,5	6,6

Out of these 36 pairs, 30 are favourable to the event A. It means that in A, the pairs (1,1), (2,2), (3,3), (4,4), (5,5) and (6,6) are excluded.

$$P(A) = 30/36 = 5/6$$

The points favourable to event B are:

(1,5), (2,4), (3,3), (4,2) and (5,1)

Points common to the events A and B *i.e.*, $B \cap A$ are:

(1,5), (2,4), (4,2) and (5,1)

Hence the probability,

$$P(B \cap A) = 4/36$$

Thus, the required probability,

$$P(B \mid A) = \frac{4/36}{30/36} = \frac{4}{30} = 0.133$$

***Example* 5.13.** The information at hand reveals that 10% of the patients feel they suffer from tuberculosis (T.B.) and are really suffering from it, 30% feel that they suffer from T.B. but they don't suffer from this disease, 25% don't feel it but are suffering from

T.B. The remaining 35% neither feel nor suffer from T.B. Then the probability of the four events,

E_1: A person who has T.B. and feels he suffers from T.B.

E_2: The person who has T.B. and does not feel it.

E_3: The person who feels that he has T.B. and does not suffer from T.B.

E_4: A person who feels that he has T.B. and has T.B.

is calculated in the manner given below.

Let us define the events as follows:

The person who feels that he has T.B.: A

The person who suffers from T.B.: B

The complementary events to A and B are denoted by $\overline{A}$ and $\overline{B}$ respectively. Now

$A \cap B$: The person who feels he suffers from T.B. and does suffer from it.

Thus, $P(A \cap B) = 0.10$

Similarly,

$$P(A \cap \overline{B}) = 0.30, \; P(\overline{A} \cap B) = 0.25 \text{ and } P(\overline{A} \cap \overline{B}) = 0.35$$

We can write,

$$P(A) = P(A \cap B) + P(A \cap \overline{B}) = 0.10 + 0.30 = 0.40$$
$$P(B) = P(A \cap B) + P(\overline{A} \cap B) = 0.10 + 0.25 = 0.35$$
$$P(\overline{A}) = P(\overline{A} \cap B) + P(\overline{A} \cap \overline{B}) = 0.25 + 0.35 = 0.60$$
$$P(\overline{B}) = P(A \cap \overline{B}) + P(\overline{A} \cap \overline{B}) = 0.30 + 0.35 = 0.65$$

Now the probabilities of the events E_1, E_2, E_3, and E_4 are given below straight way.

(*i*) $$P(E_1) = P(B \mid A) = \frac{P(B \cap A)}{P(A)} = \frac{0.10}{0.40} = \frac{1}{4} = 0.25$$

(*ii*) $$P(E_2) = P(B \mid \overline{A}) = \frac{P(B \cap \overline{A})}{P(\overline{A})} = \frac{0.25}{0.60} = \frac{5}{12} = 0.417$$

(*iii*) $$P(E_3) = P(A \mid \overline{B}) = \frac{P(A \cap \overline{B})}{P(\overline{B})} = \frac{0.30}{0.65} = \frac{6}{13} = 0.462$$

(*iv*) $$P(E_4) = P(A \mid B) = \frac{P(A \cap B)}{P(B)} = \frac{0.10}{0.35} = \frac{2}{7} = 0.286$$

***Example* 5.14.** There are two lots of a manufactured item. Lot one contains 40 pieces whereas lot two contains 50 pieces. It is known that the former lot contains 25 per cent defective pieces and the later one 10 per cent. We flip a coin and select a piece from lot one if it turns with head up otherwise we select a piece from lot two. The probability of the event that the selected piece will be defective is calculable in the following manner. Define the events as follows:

The piece is selected from lot 1: A

The selected piece is defective: B

Since the probability of turning head up = 1/2, we have

$$P(A) = \frac{1}{2} \text{ and } P(\overline{A}) = \frac{1}{2}$$

Lot 1 has 10 defective and 30 non-defective pieces.
Lot 2 has 5 defective and 45 non-defective pieces.
Given that,

$$P(B \mid A) = \frac{1}{4} \text{ and } P(B \mid \bar{A}) = \frac{1}{10}$$

From relation (5.13) we have,

$$P(A \cap B) = P(B \mid A)P(A) = \frac{1}{4}.\frac{1}{2} = \frac{1}{8}$$

$$P(\bar{A} \cap B) = P(B \mid \bar{A})P(\bar{A}) = \frac{1}{10}.\frac{1}{2} = \frac{1}{20}$$

The probability that the selected piece is defective

$$= P(A \cap B) + P(\bar{A} \cap B)$$

$$= \frac{1}{8} + \frac{1}{20} = \frac{7}{40} = 0.175$$

BAYES' PROBABILITIES

The principle given by Thomas Bayes in 1763 was reprinted in *Biometrika* (1958). His contention was that in absence of any idea about the prior probability of an event occurring, out of all possible events, one may assume that all the values of the probabilities are equal. Then on the basis of the experimental results (outcomes), one modifies his equally likely probabilities giving the posteriori probabilities. Briefly, assuming certain a priori probabilities, the posteriori probabilities are obtained. That is why Bayes probabilities are also called *posteriori probabilities*.

Suppose $E_1, E_2, ..., E_k$ are k mutually exclusive events defined in B (a collection of events) each being a subset of the sample space Ω such that $\overset{k}{\underset{i=1}{\cup}} E_i = \Omega$ and $P(E_i) > 0$ for $i = 1, 2, 3, ..., k$. Then for some arbitrary event B, which is associated with E_i's such that $P(B) > 0$, we can find out the probabilities

$$P(B \mid E_1), P(B \mid E_2) ... P(B \mid E_k).$$

In Bayes' approach we want to find out the posterior probability of an event E_i given that B has occurred, *i.e.*, $P(E_i \mid B)$.

By formula (5.13), we know

$$P(E_i \mid B) = \frac{P(E_i \cap B)}{P(B)} \quad ...(5.17)$$

We know B is also a set in Ω and hence $B \cap \Omega = B$ or in the other form,

$$B = B \cap (E_1 \cup E_2 \cup ... \cup E_k)$$

since $\overset{k}{\underset{i=1}{\cup}} E_i = \Omega$ and E_i's are disjoint.

or

$$B = (B \cap E_1) \cup (B \cap E_2) \cup \cdots \cup (B \cap E_k)$$

Thus,

$$P(B) = \sum_{i=1}^{k} P(B \cap E_i) \quad ...(5.18)$$

From (5.17),

$$P(B \cap E_i) = P(E_i \mid B)P(B) \qquad ...(5.19)$$

From (5.13),

$$P(B \cap E_i) = P(B \mid E_i)P(E_i) \qquad ...(5.20)$$

Putting the value of $P(B \cap E_i)$ from (5.20) in (5.18), we get

$$P(B) = \sum_{i=1}^{k} P(B \mid E_i)P(E_i) \qquad ...(5.21)$$

Substituting the value of $P(B \cap E_i)$ from (5.20) and $P(B)$ from (5.21) in (5.17) we obtain,

$$P(E_i \mid B) = \frac{P(B \mid E_i)P(E_i)}{\sum_{i=1}^{k} P(B \mid E_i)P(E_i)} \qquad ...(5.22)$$

Formula (5.22) is known as Bayes' formula. It is used to obtain the posteriori probability of E_i when the event B has occurred. To elucidate the theoretical concepts further, we give two examples.

***Example* 5.15.** On the basis of certain information it is known that the judgement given by a judge is correct in 90 per cent of the cases. Also let us suppose that 40 per cent of the criminals produced before the court are actually innocent. The probability of the event that an innocent person produced before the court has been declared innocent, can be worked out in the following manner.

Let the event that the person is innocent = I.

The event that the judge declares him innocent = J.

We have to evaluate $P(I/J)$.

Given that,

$$P(I) = 0.40 \text{ and } P(\bar{I}) = 0.60$$

$$P(J/I) = 0.90 \text{ and } P(\bar{J} \mid \bar{I}) = 0.90$$

$$P(J \mid \bar{I}) = 0.10 \text{ and } P(\bar{J} \mid I) = 0.10$$

Using formula (5.22) we get.

$$P(I \mid J) = \frac{P(J \mid I)P(I)}{P(J \mid I)P(I) + P(J \mid \bar{I})P(\bar{I})}$$

$$= \frac{(0.90)(0.40)}{(0.90)(0.40) + (0.10)(0.60)} = 0.857$$

***Example* 5.16.** In a city there are three stores each having 20 pieces of an item. Let these stores be denoted by S_1, S_2, and S_3. The stores S_1, S_2 and S_3 have 10%, 20% and 30% defective items, respectively. A customer first chooses a store randomly and then selects an item randomly from the store. The probability of an event that the selected item is defective can be calculated as follows: Let E_i denote the event that the store S_i ($i = 1, 2, 3$) is selected. Then,

$$P(E_i) = 1/3$$

Let B denotes the event that a selected item is defective. Given that $10i\%$ items in store i are defective where $i = 1, 2, 3$. Hence,

$$P(B \mid E_i) = \frac{10i}{100} = \frac{i}{10}$$

Now using formula (5.21), the probability of a selected item being defective is,

$$P(B) = \sum_{i=1}^{3} P(B \mid E_i)P(E_i) = \frac{1}{10}.\frac{1}{3} + \frac{2}{10}.\frac{1}{3} + \frac{3}{10}.\frac{1}{3} = \frac{1}{5}$$

If we find that the item selected is defective, the probability that it has come from store S_2 is,

$$P(E_2 \mid B) = \frac{P(B \mid E_2)P(E_2)}{\sum_{i=1}^{3} P(B \mid E_i)P(E_i)} = \frac{\frac{2}{10} \times \frac{1}{3}}{1/5} = \frac{1}{3}$$

Similarly $\quad P(E_1 \mid B) = \frac{1}{6}$ and $P(E_3 \mid B) = \frac{1}{2}$.

Check. A defective selected item belongs definitely to one of the stores. Hence the probability,

$$\sum_{i=1}^{3} P(E_i \mid B) = \frac{1}{6} + \frac{1}{3} + \frac{1}{2} = 1$$

An experiment with only two types of outcomes, either success or failure is termed as binomial experiment. In other words, the outcome of a binomial experiment is dichotomous. The probability of events in the case of dichotomous results of an experiment has been dealt with in Chapter 6. Hence, the readers are advised to go through binomial distribution given in Chapter 6.

It is noteworthy that the subject-matter embodied in this chapter requires the knowledge of permutations and combinations. It also needs basic understanding of the set theory, the reason is that a correspondence between the sets and events can always be established. Hence, the events are expressed through sets. Here it is presumed that the students possess a basic knowledge of permutations and combinations as it is taught in classes X to XII. Elementary set theory is also taught in class X. Anyway, if the students have either not studied them or is not in touch with the same topics, Appendix A can be used to attain basic understanding. For further details they may read any book on these topics.

Probability is the backbone of Statistics. It has vast applications in the theory of distributions, estimation and testing of hypothesis. Advance probability theory is quite complicated and exhaustive. But the matter covered in this chapter is in accordance with the syllabi.

QUESTIONS AND EXERCISES

1. Discuss the importance of probability in science and industry.
2. Let A, B and C be three events in a sample space. Find the expressions as union and/or intersection of A, B and C for the following events:

(a) At least one of the events, A, B or C occurs.
(b) Not more than two events occur simultaneously.
(c) A occurs with either B or C.
(d) All three events occur together.
(e) A and B occur but not C.

3. Discuss and give two examples of each of the following.
(a) Probability of an event.
(b) Complementary event.
(c) Mutually exclusive event.
(d) Elementary event.
(e) Conditional probability.

4. Given the following sample points of space Ω, form the following events where,

$$\Omega: 1, 2, 3, 4, 5, 6, 7, 8, 9, 10, 11, 12$$

(a) A : the set of numbers not divisible by 3.
(b) B : the set of even numbers.
(c) C : the set of odd numbers.

Give the sample points belonging to the following events and calculate their probabilities also. (a) $A \cap B$ (b) $A \cup \overline{C}$ (c) $A \cup B \cup \overline{C}$ (d) $\overline{A} \cap B$ (e) $A \cap B \cup C$.

5. In an experiment two fair dice of different colours are rolled. Let the four events E_1, E_2, E_3 and E_4 be defined as follows:
E_1: the sum of the number of spots on the dice is even.
E_2: the sum of the number of spots on the dice is divisible by 3.
E_3: the sum of the number of spots on the dice is divisible by 4.
E_4: the square root of the sum of number of spots on the dice is a whole number.
Compute the probabilities of the events E_1, E_2, E_3, E_4, $E_1 \cap E_2$, $E_1 \cup E_2$, and $E_2 \cup E_3 \cup E_4$.

6. From a well-shuffled deck of 52 cards, three cards are drawn with replacement. What is the probability of the events (*i*) all the three cards are clubs, (*ii*) the three cards are Jack, Queen and King and (*iii*) selected cards are higher than Ten?

7. A repair workshop has 6 Fiat cars and 10 Ambassador cars on a particular day. But only six cars can be serviced in a day. He chooses 6 cars randomly out of 16 cars. What is the probability that out of the six selected cars, two are fiat and four are Ambassador cars?

8. Three trains leave from Jaipur to Delhi, a passenger train, an express train and the Pink City Express (a superfast train). Experience tells that the passenger train reaches Delhi late on 80% of the days, the express train reaches late on 40% of the days and Pink City superfast train reaches late on 10% of the days. On a particular day a passenger chooses randomly one train out of three and travels by it.
(a) What is the probability that the passenger selects the express train and reaches Delhi late?
(b) What is the probability that the passenger reaches Delhi late?
(c) If the passenger reaches late, what is the probability that he has chosen the passenger train?
[*Hint*: Part *c* will use the probability obtained in part *b*.]

9. The table below presents the probabilities pertaining to the relationship of the educational standards and liking to the types of books. Let us denote Literates = *L*, Certificate

holders = C and Graduates = G. The types of books are denoted as, Romantic = R, Social = S and Educational = E.

		Edu. Standard			
		L	C	G	
	R	.10	.10	.05	.25
Liking	S	.20	.15	.10	.45
	E	.10	.10	.10	.30
		.40	.35	.25	

Compute the probabilities of the following events:

(i) $P(R \mid G)$ (ii) $P\{(L \cup G) \mid E\}$ (iii) $P(L \mid \overline{S})$

[*Hint*: For part (*iii*), use the relation $P(L) = P(S)P(L \mid S) + P(\overline{S})P(L \mid \overline{S})$

10. A bag contains 12 balls, of which 3 are red. If 5 balls are drawn together, determine the probability that all the three red balls are among these 5. (*M.A., Agra, 1974, B.Sc., Meerut, 1974*)
11. What is the probability of getting 3 white balls in a draw of 3 balls from a box containing 5 white and 4 black balls? (*C.A., May 1976*)
12. A committee of 5 is to be formed out of a group of 8 boys and 7 girls. Find the probability that in the committee, (*i*) there will be 3 boys and 2 girls and (*ii*) at least one girl. (*B.Com., Bombay, 1973*)
13. A problem in statistics is given to three students A, B and C whose chances of solving it are $\frac{1}{2}$, $\frac{1}{3}$ and $\frac{1}{4}$ respectively. What is the probability that the problem will be solved? (*M.A., Jiwaji, 1974*)
14. Three houses of the same type were advertised to be let in a locality. Three men made separate application for a house. What is the probability that
    (*i*) all the three made applications for the same house.
    (*ii*) each of the three applied for the same house.
    (*iii*) two of them applied for the same house and third for one of the other houses? (*M.Com., Delhi, 1975*)
15. Two cards are randomly drawn from a pack of 52 cards and thrown away. What is the probability of drawing an ace in a single draw from the remaining 50 cards? (*M.Com., Meerut, 1975*)
16. A university has to select an examiner from a list of 50 persons, 20 of them are women and 30 are men; 10 of them know Hindi and 40 do not; 15 of them being teachers and the remaining 35 are not. What is the probability of the university selecting a Hindi-knowing woman teacher? (*M.Com., Allahabad, 1974*)
17. If E_1 and E_2 are two mutually exclusive events and given that $P(E_2) = .5$ and $P(E_1 \cup E_2) = .7$, compute the probability $P(E_1)$.
18. There are three urns. Urn I contains three black balls, urn II contains two white and one black ball and urn III contains two black and one white ball. A ball is selected randomly from each urn. What is the probability that all the three balls will be of the same colour.

19. A declarer in the game of bridge knows that the opponents have five trump cards. What is the probability that there is a three-two split of trump cards among the opponents?

20. There are eight electric bulbs in the stock of a shop, out of which three are defective. A customer demands two bulbs. The shopkeeper picks up two bulbs randomly. What is the probability that both these bulbs are defective?

21. Five men in a company of 20 are graduates. If 3 men are picked out of 20 at random. What is the probability that they are all graduates? What is the probability of at least one graduate? *(I.C.W.A., 1965)*

22. Four coins are tossed simultaneously. What is the probability of getting 2 heads and 2 tails? *(C.A., May, 1977)*

23. The probability that a bomb dropped from an aeroplane will strike certain target is 1/5. If six bombs are dropped, find the chance that (*a*) exactly 2 will strike the target (*b*) none will strike the target. *(M.Com., Meerut, 1973)*

24. An article manufactured by a company consists of two parts *A* and *B*. In the process of manufacture of part *A*, 9 out of 100 are likely to be defective. Similarly 5 out of 100 are likely to be defective in the manufacture of part *B*.
Calculate the probability that the assembled part will not be defective.
(C.A., Nov., 1976)

25. A husband and wife appear in an interview for two vacancies in the same post. The probability of husband's selection is 1/7 and that of wife's selection is 1/5. What is the probability that (*a*) both of them will be selected, (*b*) only one of them will be selected, and (*c*) none of them will be selected. *(B.Com., Punjab, 1980)*

26. The probability that a contractor will get a plumbing contract is 2/3, and the probability that he will not get an electric contract is 5/9. If the probability of getting at least one contract is 4/5, what is the probability that he will get both.
(M.Com., Meerut, 1983)

27. Mention the correct answer noted against each of the following.
   (*i*) When two perfect coins are tossed simultaneously, the probability of getting at least one head is,
   $\frac{1}{2}, \frac{1}{4}, \frac{3}{4}, 1$
   (*ii*) Out of 120 tickets numbered consecutively from 1 to 120, one is drawn at random. What is the probability of getting a number which is a multiple of 5?
   $\frac{1}{24}, \frac{1}{8}, \frac{1}{5}, \frac{1}{16}$ *(C.A., May, 1981)*

28. The chance of drawing a white ball in the first draw and again a white ball in the second draw without replacement of the ball in the first draw from a bag containing 6 white and 4 red balls is (*a*) 2/10 (*b*) 6/10 (*c*) 36/100 (*d*) 1/3. *(C.A., May, 1983)*

29. Two dice were thrown and the sums of the numbers on the faces up are added. The probability of this sum being 2 is: $\frac{1}{6}, \frac{1}{36}, \frac{1}{18}$, none of these. *(C.A., May, 1982)*

30. A die is thrown two times, and the sum of numbers on the faces up is noted. The probability of this sum being 11 is:
$\frac{1}{6}, \frac{1}{36}, \frac{1}{18}$, none of these. *(C.A., Nov., 1982)*

31.

(*a*) In certain examination a total number of 200 students appeared out of which 120 are from university A and rest are from university B, university A is better than university B in the sense that 70% of its students got pass marks where as the percentage is only 50% for university B. Given that a student got pass marks, what is the probability that he is from university A?

(*b*) When are two events called independent?

(*c*) The percentages of families having a radio set and a television set or both kind of sets are respectively 87%, 36% and 29%. Is the family ownership of a radio set independent of the family ownership of a television set?

(*d*) Check the consistency of the following (any one).

(*i*) If two events A and B are independent then,

$$P(A \mid B) = P(B \mid A)$$

(*ii*) The probability of getting the first success at 6th trial is q^5p (p is the probability of success and q is the probability of failure, $p + q = 1$).

(*e*) If A is independent of B and B is independent of C then A is not necessarily independent of C. Give an example to justify this statement. (*M.Com., Kolkata, 1984*)

32.

(*a*) A salesman has a 65 per cent chance of making a sale to each customer. The behaviour of successive customers are independent. If two customers A and B enter, what is the probability that the salesman will make a sale to A and B both.

(*b*) Two sets of candidates are competing for the positions of the Board of Directors of a company. The probability that the first and second sets will win are 0.6 and 0.4 respectively. If the first set wins, the probability of introducing a new product is 0.08 and the corresponding probability if the second set wins is 0.3. What is the probability that the product will be introduced?

(*c*) Write down the Bayes' theorem for conditional probability.

(*d*) Answer any one of the following:

(*i*) Show that

$$P(A \mid B) = \frac{P(A)}{P(B)} P(B \mid A)$$

(*ii*) For two events A and B, let $P(A) = 0.4$, $P(A+B) = 0.58$ and $P(B) = 0.3$, check whether A and B are independent or not. (*M.Com., Kolkata, 1985*)

33. A, B and C are three mutually exclusive and exhaustive events. Find P (B), if

$$\frac{1}{3}P(C) = \frac{1}{2}P(A) = P(B)$$ (*I.C.W.A. June, 1987*)

34. (*a*) Let A, B, and C be three events. Write down the following events in the usual set theoretic notations:

(*i*) A and B occur together.

(*ii*) both A and B occurs but not C.

(*iii*) all the three events occur.

(*iv*) at least one event occurs and,

(*v*) at least two events occur.

(*b*) Two urns contain respectively 10 white, 5 red and 9 black balls and 3 white, 7 red and 15 black balls. One ball is drawn from each urn. Find the probability that:

(*i*) both balls are red, and (*ii*) both balls are of same colour.

(*I.C.W.A. June, 1989*)

35. (*a*) The independent probabilities that the three sections of a costing department will encounter a computer error are 0.1, 0.3, 0.3 each week respectively. Calculate the probability that there will be,

(*i*) at least one computer error and (*ii*) one and only one computer error encountered by the costing department next week.

(*b*) Experience has shown that, on the average, 2% of an airline flights suffer a minor equipment failure—in an aircraft. Estimate the probability the number of minor equipment failures in the next 50 flights will be (*i*) zero, (*ii*) at least two.

(*M.Com., Kolkata, 1985*)

36. State Baye's theorem of conditional probability. In a study made to find the relationship between I.Q. of a person and his academic achievements, the following results were obtained.

(*i*) Proportion of graduates: 0.7.

(*ii*) Proportion of persons with I.Q. above 115 among graduate: 0.3.

(*iii*) Proportion of persons with I.Q. above 115 among non-graduates: 0.2. Given that a person has I.Q. above 115, what is the probability that he is not a graduate.

(*M.Com., Kolkata, 1985*)

37. Two distinct fair dice marked as I and II are thrown at a time. Find the probability of obtaining a pair of numbers in which the number of the first die exceeds the number of the second die.

38. It is 10 to 6 against a person who is 55 years living till he is 70 and 9 to 7 against a person who is 65 living till he is 80. What is the probability that (*i*) at least one of them and (*ii*) only one of them, will remain alive after 15 years. [*C.A.* (*Inter*), May, *1993*]

39. If a die is thrown six times, calculate the probability that:

(*i*) a score of 3 or less occurs on exactly 2 throws;

(*ii*) a score of more than 2 occurs on exactly 3 throws;

(*iii*) a score of 5 or less occurs at least once;

(*iv*) a score of 2 or less occurs on at least 5 occasions. [*I.C.W.A.* (*Inter*), *June, 1991*]

40. Two persons X and Y appear in an interview for two vacancies in the same post. The probability of X's selection is $\frac{2}{11}$ and that of Y's selection is $\frac{1}{7}$. What is the probability that:

(*i*) both of them will be selected.

(*ii*) only one of them will be selected, and

(*iii*) none of them will be selected. (*M.B.A. I-Yr., MLSU, Udaipur, 2003*)

41. Let A and B be two events such that $P(A) = \frac{1}{2}$, $P(B) = \frac{1}{3}$ and $P(A \cap B) = \frac{1}{4}$. Obtain the probabilities $P(A | B)$, $P(A \cup B)$ and $P(\bar{A} \cap \bar{B})$ (*C.A., Foundation, May, 2001*)

42. (*a*) There are four clerks and 30 officers in a Bank. A committee of 3 is to be formed at random. Find the probability that at least one clerk and at least one officer are included in the committee.

(*b*) Urn 1 contains 4 red and 6 black balls and urn 2 contains 6 red and 4 black balls, one urn is chosen at random and a ball is drawn from it. The colour of the ball drawn is black. What is the probability that it has been drawn from urn 1.

(*I.C.W.A., Inter, Dec., 2004*)

43. A person is known to hit a target in 5 out of 8 shots, whereas another person is known to hit in 3 out of 5 shots. Find the probability that the target is hit at all when they both try. *(C.A., P.E.-I, Nov., 2004)*

44. A travel club has 1200 members, out of which 60% are males. 45% of these members pay by credit card when they travel including 210 females. If a member enters the travel club at random, what is the probability that:
    (*a*) The member is female.
    (*b*) The member is a male and pays by cash.
    (*c*) The member is a female or a credit card user.
    (*d*) The member pays cash if we know that the member is a female.
    (*e*) Are the sex of the member and the mode of payment independent.

45. The probability that a man will be alive in 25 years is $\frac{3}{5}$, and the probability that his wife will be alive in 25 years is $\frac{2}{3}$. Find the probability that:
    (*i*) both will be alive.
    (*ii*) only one will be alive.
    (*iii*) only man will be alive.
    (*iv*) at least one of them will be alive. *(C.A., P.E.-I, May, 2003)*

46. A pair of dice is rolled. If the sum of spots on two dice is 8, find the probability that one of the dice showed 3.

47. A security analyst feels that the chances are 40% that the prices of shares of company A would rise next week, and 10% that the prices of shares of company B would rise. The two prices are independent of each other. Find the probability that in the next week:
    (*i*) both prices would increase.
    (*ii*) only one company's share price would increase.
    (*iii*) neither would increase. *(M.B.A., Part–II, MLSU, Udaipur, 2001)*

48. (*a*) Two dice are thrown simultaneously and the points on the face of the dice are multiplied together. The probability that the product is 4, is

    (*i*) $\frac{1}{36}$, (*ii*) $\frac{2}{36}$, (*iii*) $\frac{1}{12}$, (*iv*) $\frac{1}{6}$

    (*b*) A card is drawn from a well-shuffled pack of 52 cards. What is the probability of the card being black or an ace?

    (*i*) $\frac{7}{13}$, (*ii*) $\frac{3}{7}$, (*iii*) $\frac{1}{26}$, (*iv*) none of these.

SUGGESTED READING

Albert Shiryaev and Albert N. Shiryaev (1995). *Probability*, Springer.

Bhat, B.R. (1985). *Modern Probability Theory*, New Age International Publishers, New Delhi, (2nd ed.).

Burr, I.W. (1974). *Applied Statistical Methods,* Academic Press, New York.

David, Stirzaker (2003). *Elementary Probability*, Cambridge University Press.

DeGroot, M.H. (1986). *Probability and Statistics*, 2nd ed., Addison Wesley.

Edward, Nelson (1987). *Radically Elementary Probability Theory*, Princeton University Press.

Feller, W. (1966). *An Introduction to Probability Theory and its Applications*, Vol. I & II, John Wiley, New York.

Finetti, B.D. (1974). *Theory of Probability*, Translated by Antonio Machi and Adrian Smith, John Wiley, New York.

Gottinger, H.W. (1980). *Elements of Statistical Analysis*, Water de Gruyter, Berlin.

Haight, F.A. (1981). *Applied Probability*, Plenum Press, New York.

Ian, Hacking (2001). *An Introduction to Probability and Inductive Logic*, Cambridge University Press.

Kai Lai Chung, John Lai Stillwell and Farid Aitsatilia (2003). *Elementary Probability Theory*, Springer.

Kathleen Subrahmaniam (1990). *A Primer in Probability*, Marcel Dekker.

Loe've, M.(1968). *Probability Theory and Mathematical Statistics*, John Wiley, New York.

Mises, R.V. (1957). *Probability, Statistics and Truth*, George Allen and Unwin, New York.

Parzen, E. (1960). *Modern Probability Theory and its Applications*, John Wiley, New York.

Rohatgi, V.K. (1993). *An Introduction to Probability Theory and Mathematical Statistics*, New Age International Publishers, New Delhi, (5th reprint).

Uspensky, J.V. (1965). *Introduction to Mathematical Probability*, Tata McGraw-Hill, Delhi.

6

Chapter

Random Variable and Probability Distributions

It has been a general notion that if an experiment is conducted under identical conditions, values so obtained would be similar. But the experiences of people have dispelled this belief. Observations are always taken about a factor or character under study, which can take different values, and the factor or character is termed as variable. The observations may be the number of certain items or objects or their measurements. These observations vary even though the experiment is conducted under identical conditions. Hence, we have a set of outcomes (sample points) of a random experiment. A rule that assigns a real number to each outcome (sample points) is called *random variable*. The rule is nothing but a function of the variable, say, X, that assigns a unique value to each sample point of the sample space.

From the above discussion it is clear that there is a value for each outcome, which it takes with certain probability. Hence a list of values of a random variable together with their corresponding probabilities of occurrence, is termed as *probability distribution*. As a tradition, probability distribution is used to denote the probability mass or probability density, of either a discontinuous or a continuous variable. The formal definitions of random variable and certain operations on random variable are given in this chapter prior to the details of probability distributions.

RANDOM VARIABLE (R.V.)

A random variable X is a real valued function, $X(x)$, of the elements of the sample space Ω where x is an element of the sample space. It should be noted that the range of the random variable will be a set of real numbers.

Generally, a random variable is denoted by capital letters like $X, Y, Z, U, V, \ldots$, whereas the values of the random variable are denoted by the corresponding small letters like $x, y, z, u, v, \ldots$.

Illustration (*i*): If we flip a coin and denote the head by 1 and tail by 0, then the random variable X takes only two values 1 and 0. Symbolically, the random variable,

$$X(x) = \{x : x = (1,0) \in \Omega\}$$

where $\in$ is a connotation for 'belongs to'.

Illustration (*ii*): If we measure the height of people, the random variable,

$$X(x) = \{ x : x \text{ is any real positive number}\}$$

Random variables are of two types: (*i*) Discrete random variable and (*ii*) Continuous random variable.

Discrete Random Variable

A random variable *X*, which can take only a finite number of values in an interval of the domain, is called discrete random variable. A few examples are: (*i*) If we throw two dice at a time and note the sum of spots which turn up on the upper face, the discrete r.v.,

$$X(x) = \{x : x = (x_1 + x_2) = 2, 3, ..., 12\}$$

where x_1 is the number of spots on the upper face of one die and x_2 is the number of spots on the other die.

(*ii*) The random variable denoting the number of students in a class is,

$$X(x) = \{ x : x \text{ is any positive integer}\}$$

Continuous Random Variable

A random variable *X*, which can take any value in the domain, or when its range '*R*' is an interval or the union of intervals on the real line, is called a continuous random variable.

Note that the probability of any single *x*, a value of *X*, is zero, *i.e.*,

$$P(X = x) = 0$$

Example (i). The height of students in India lies between 3 and 6 feet. The continuous r.v.

$$X(x) = \{x : 3 \le x \le 6\}$$

(ii). The maximum life of electric bulbs is 2000 hours. The continuous r.v.,

$$X(x) = \{x : 0 \le x \le 2000\}.$$

DISTRIBUTION FUNCTION

The distribution of a random variable *X* is a function $F_x(x)$ for a real value *x* which is the probability of the event $(X \le x)$, *i.e.*,

$$F_X(x) = P(X \le x) \qquad ...(6.1)$$

It is evident from the expression that the distribution function is the probability that *X* takes a value in the interval $(-\infty, x)$.

Discrete Probability Distribution

If a random variable is discrete, its distribution will also be discrete, except in some exceptional situations. For a discrete random variable *X*, the distribution function or cumulative distribution is given by *P*(*x*) and is same as given by (6.1) *i.e.*,

$$P(x) = P(X \le x) \qquad ...(6.2)$$

Discrete Probability Function

The probability function is the probability of a discrete random variable *X*, which takes the value *x* and is denoted by *p*(*x*) *i.e.*,

$$p(x) = P(X = x) \qquad ...(6.3)$$

The probability function always possesses the following properties:

(i) $p(x) \geq 0$ for all x in sample space Ω

(ii) $\sum_{all\,x} p(x) = 1$

Mathematical Expectation

The expected value of a random variable X is given as,

$$E(X) = \sum_{all\,x} x\,p(x) \qquad ...(6.4)$$

$E(X)$ is also known as theoretical average value. In general, the expected value of a function $H(X)$ of a discrete random variable X is given as,

$$E\{H(X)\} = \sum_{all\,x} H(x)p(x) \qquad ...(6.5)$$

Some Results on Expectation. If X and Y are two variates defined over the same sample space and if $E(X)$ and $E(Y)$ exist, then

$$E(X+Y) = E(X)+E(Y) \qquad ...(6.6)$$

Also if X and Y are independent, then

$$E(XY) = E(X)E(Y) \qquad ...(6.7)$$

Consider a variable X and a constant C. The expected values of X in relation to C are as follows.

$$E(C) = C \qquad ...(6.8)$$

$$E(CX) = CE(X) \qquad ...(6.9)$$

$$E(X+C) = E(X) + C \qquad ...(6.10)$$

If X and Y are two variables and C_1 and C_2 are any constants, then

$$E(C_1X + C_2Y) = C_1E(X)+C_2E(Y) \qquad ...(6.11)$$

If $X \leq Y$, then

$$E(X) \leq E(Y) \qquad ...(6.12)$$

The operations given from (6.8) to (6.12) are also true for functions of X and Y.

MOMENTS

The rth moment of a random variable X is defined as the expected value of X' where r is an integer *i.e.*, $r = 1, 2, ...$ The rth moment $E(X^r)$, about the origin (zero), is known as the rth *raw moment* and is generally denoted by μ_r'. Thus,

$$\mu_r' = E(X^r) \qquad ...(6.13)$$

Similarly the rth moment of a random variable X about the mean μ of a frequency distribution, is given by the formula,

$$\mu_r = E\{(X-\mu)^r\} \qquad ...(6.14)$$

where μ_r is symbolically known as the rth *central moment* of a random variable X.

Note: The expectation for discrete random variable can easily be worked out by the formula (6.5).

The first raw moment (about origin) is the mean of the distribution, *i.e.*,

$$E(X) = \sum_{all\,x} xp(x) = \frac{1}{N}\sum_{all\,x} x = \mu \qquad ...(6.15)$$

where $p(x) = 1/N$ for all x, and the first central moment about mean is zero, *i.e.*,

$$E(X-\mu) = \sum_{all\,x}(x-\mu)p(x)$$

$$= \frac{1}{N}\sum_{all\,x}(X-\mu) = \frac{1}{N}\sum_{all\,x} x - \mu = \mu - \mu = 0 \qquad ...(6.16)$$

Also,

$$E(X) - E(\mu) = 0 \text{ or } \mu_1' = \mu \qquad ...(6.16.1)$$

The second raw moment,

$$\mu_2' = E(X^2) = \sum_{all\,x} x^2 p(x)$$

The third raw moment,

$$\mu_3' = E(X^3) = \sum_{all\,x} x^3 p(x)$$

and so on.

The second central moment is,

$$\mu_2 = E\{(X-\mu)^2\}$$
$$= E\{(X^2 - 2\mu X + \mu^2)\}$$
$$= E(X^2) - 2\mu E(X) + \mu^2$$
$$= \mu_2' - 2\mu.\mu_1' + \mu'^2$$
$$= \mu_2' - \mu_1'^2 \text{ Since } \mu_1' = \mu. \qquad ...(6.17)$$

The second central moment is also known as the variance.

Similarly,

$$\mu_3 = E\{X-\mu)^3\} = E(X^3 - 3\mu X^2 + 3\mu^2 X - \mu^3)$$
$$= E(X^3) - 3\mu E(X^2) + 3\mu^2 E(X) - \mu^3$$

Using the relation (6.16.1), we get

$$\mu_3 = \mu_3' - 3\mu_2'\mu_1' + 3\mu_1'^3 - \mu_1'^3 = \mu_3' - 3\mu_2'\mu_1' + 2\mu_1'^3 \qquad ...(6.18)$$

In the same manner, we can get,

$$\mu_4 = \mu_4' - 4\mu_3'\mu_1' + 6\mu_2'\mu_1'^2 - 3\mu_1'^4 \qquad ...(6.19)$$

Now it will not be difficult for the readers to derive the relationship between the central moments and raw moments of any order.

The probability function or probability density function of any random variable, generally involves one or two parameters, particularly the mean and variance. But, still the importance and need for higher moments cannot be ruled out. The third and fourth moments are extremely useful for determining the shape of a frequency curve.

Sometimes the moments about an arbitrary constant a are found out. In that case, the rth moment about a is,

$$\mu_r^a = E\{(X-a)^r\} \qquad ...(6.20)$$

The first moment about 'a' is,

$$\mu_1^a = E(X-a) = E(X) - E(a) = \mu_1' - a \quad ...(6.21)$$

The second moment about 'a' is,

$$\begin{aligned}\mu_2^a &= E\{(X-a)^2\} = E(X^2 - 2aX + a^2)\\ &= E(X^2) - 2aE(X) + E(a^2)\\ &= \mu_2' - 2a\mu_1' + a^2 \quad ...(6.22)\end{aligned}$$

Similarly,

$$\mu_3^a = \mu_3' - 3a\mu_2' + 3a^2\mu_1' - a^3 \quad ...(6.23)$$

and

$$\mu_4^a = \mu_4' - 4a\mu_3' + 6a^2\mu_2' - 4a^3\mu_1' + a^4 \quad ...(6.24)$$

In general,

$$\mu_r^a = \mu_r' - \binom{r}{1} a\mu'_{r-1} + \binom{r}{2} a^2\mu'_{r-2} - ... + (-1)^r a^r \quad ...(6.25)$$

Using these relations we can find out the moments about the mean 0. Utilizing further the relationships between raw moments and central moments, the latter can be obtained.

Factorial Moments. In case of a discrete random variable X, which takes values at unit intervals, the rth factorial moment is given as,

$$\mu_r = E\{X(X-1)(X-2)...(X-r+1)\} = \sum_i (X_i)_r\, p(x_r) \quad ...(6.26)$$

where $(X_i)_r = X_i(X_i - 1)(X_i - 2)...(X_i - r + 1)$.

For example, if we throw a die, the possible outcomes will be 1, 2, 3, 4, 5, and 6 which are at unit intervals. Hence, in this case,

$$\mu_1' = \sum_i X_i p(x) = \frac{1}{6}(1+2+...+6) = \frac{21}{6}$$

$$\begin{aligned}\mu_2' &= \sum_i X_i(X_i - 1)p(x)\\ &= \frac{1}{6}\{1\times0 + 2\times1 + 3\times2 + 4\times3 + 5\times4 + 6\times5\}\\ &= \frac{1}{6}\{0+2+6+12+20+30\} = \frac{70}{6}\end{aligned}$$

Similarly,

$$\mu_3' = \sum_i X_i(X_i-1)(X_i-2)p(x) = \frac{210}{6}$$

and so on.

MOMENT GENERATING FUNCTION (M.G.F.)

From the discussion of moments, it is apparent that moments play an important role in the characterization of various distributions. Hence, to know the distribution, we need to find out the moments. For this, the moment generating function is a good device. The moment generating function is a special form of mathematical expectation, and is very useful in deriving the moments of a probability distribution.

Definition. If X is a random variable, then the expected value of e^{tx} is known as the moment generating function, provided the expected value exists for every value of t in an interval, $-h < t < h$ where h is some positive real value. The moment generating function which is denoted as $m_x(t)$ for a discrete random variable is,

$$m_x(t) = E(e^{tx}) = \sum_{all\,x} e^{t(x)} p_x(x) \quad \text{...(6.27)}$$

$$= \sum_{all\,x}\left(1+tx+\frac{t^2x^2}{2!}+\frac{t^3x^3}{3!}+...\right)p_x(x)$$

$$= 1+t\mu_1'+\frac{t^2}{2!}\mu_2'+\frac{t^3}{3!}\mu_3'... = \sum_{r=0}^{\infty}\frac{t^r}{r!}\mu_r' \quad \text{...(6.27.1)}$$

The convergence of the above sum is assumed here. In the above expression, the rth raw moment is the coefficient of $\frac{t^r}{r!}$ in the above expanded sum.

The main use of the moment generating function is that, if it exists, it can uniquely determine the distribution. But many distribution functions are known for which the moment generating functions do not exist.

The moment generating function is also useful for finding out the moments of a distribution. The technique for it is to differentiate the moment generating function with respect to (w.r.t) t once, twice, thrice, ... and put $t = 0$ in the first, second and third... derivatives to obtain the first, second, third, ... moments. From the resulting expressions we get 1st, 2nd, 3rd, ... raw moments about the origin. The central moments are obtained by using the relationship between raw moments and central moments.

CHARACTERISTIC FUNCTION (C.F.)

The moment generating function does not exist for every distribution. Hence, another function, which always exists for all the distributions, is known as characteristic function. It is the expected value of e^{itx}, where $i = \sqrt{-1}$ and t is a real valued continuous variable. Let the characteristic function of a random variable X be denoted by $\phi_X(t)$, then

$$\phi_X(t) = E(e^{itx}) \quad \text{...(6.28)}$$

For a discrete variable X having the probability function $p(x)$, the characteristic function.

$$\phi_X(t) = \sum_{all\,x} e^{itx} p(x) \quad \text{...(6.29)}$$

and for a continuous variable X having density function f(x), such that $a < X \le b$, the characteristic function,

$$\phi_X(t) = \int_a^b e^{itx} f(x)\,dx \quad \text{...(6.30)}$$

It is easy to prove that $\phi_X(0) = 1$.

Here are two important theorems without proof.

Uniqueness Theorem

Two distribution functions are identical if their characteristic functions are identical.

Inversion Theorem

Let F be a distribution function and $\phi_X(t)$ be its characteristic function. If a and b are any two points on a real line such that $a < b$, then we have,

$$F(b) - F(a) = \lim_{T \to \infty} \frac{1}{2\pi} \int_{-T}^{T} \frac{e^{-iat} - e^{-ibt}}{it} \phi_X(t)\, dt$$

CUMULANTS

The idea of cumulants was given by Thieles. Just like moments, cumulants are equally important as descriptive constants of a distribution to specify it. If the rth moment μ_r' of a random variable X exists, then from Maclaurin's theorem the characteristic function $\phi_x(t)$, in the neighbourhood of $t = 0$, can be expanded as follows:

$$\phi(t) = \sum_{j=1}^{r} \frac{(it)^j}{j!} \mu_j + 0(t^r) \qquad \text{...(6.31)}$$

If expression (6.31) is feasible, we can also expand $\log_e \phi(t)$ as

$$\log_e \phi(t) = \sum_{j=0}^{r} \frac{(it)^j}{j!} k_j + 0(t^r) \qquad \text{...(6.32)}$$

The quantity k_j in (6.32) is called the j th cumulant of the distribution function F. The r th cumulant k_r is the coefficient of $(it)^r/r!$ in the expansion of $\log_e \phi(t)$, whereas μ_r', the r th raw moment is the coefficient of $(it)^r/r!$ in the expansion of $\phi(t)$ given by (6.31). The following relations between raw moments and cumulants are evident.

$$\mu_1 = k_1$$

$$\mu_2' = k_2 + k_1^2$$

$$\mu_3' = k_2 + 3k_2k_1 + k_1^3$$

and so on.

MEASURES THROUGH INTEGRAL FORMULAE

Various measures in case of continuous distributions can be obtained with the help of integral formulae as given below.

Let $f(x)$ be the probability density function (p.d.f.) of a random variable X. Then we know that the area under the frequency curve within its full range say $[l, u]$ *i.e.*, $l < x \leq u$, is always equal to unity *i.e.*, 1. We know, for any two values of x say a and b, the integral $\int_a^b f(x)\, dx$ gives the area under the frequency curve which is equal to the probability of any value lying in the range a to b.

Integral formulae for different measures for a p.d.f., $f(x)$ defined over the range a to b are :

(*i*) $$\text{A.M.} = \int_a^b x f(x) dx \qquad \text{...(6.33)}$$

(*ii*) Log (G.M.) = $\int_a^b \log x\, f(x)\, dx$ ...(6.34)

(*iii*) $\dfrac{1}{\text{H.M.}} = \int_a^b \dfrac{1}{x} f(x)dx$ ...(6.35)

(*iv*) *r*th moment about the origin,

$$\mu_r' = \int_a^b x^r f(x)dx \quad \text{...(6.36)}$$

$$\text{Mean,} \quad \mu_1' = \int_a^b x f(x)dx = \mu \quad \text{...(6.37)}$$

$$\mu_2' = \int_a^b x^2 f(x)dx \quad \text{...(6.38)}$$

$$\text{Variance,} \quad \mu_2 = \mu_2' - (\mu_1')^2 \quad \text{...(6.39)}$$

Median (M_d) is obtained by solving either of the following equations. Also $M_d = Q_2$.

(*v*) $\int_a^{M_d} f(x)dx = \dfrac{1}{2}$ or $\int_{M_d}^b f(x)dx = \dfrac{1}{2}$ ...(6.40)

(*vi*) Mean deviation about any central value *A* is,

$$\text{M.D.} = \int_a^b |X - A| f(x)dx \quad \text{...(6.41)}$$

where A may be mean, median or mode. Quartiles Q_1 and Q_3 can be obtained by solving the following equations respectively.

(*vii*) $\int_a^{Q_1} f(x)dx = \dfrac{1}{4}$ and $\int_a^{Q_3} f(x)dx = \dfrac{3}{4}$ ...(6.42)

(*viii*) Decile D_i for $i = 1, 2, ..., 9$ is available as a solution of the equation,

$$\int_a^{D_i} f(x)dx = \frac{i}{10} \quad \text{...(6.43)}$$

(*ix*) Mode of a continuous distribution is obtained with the help of differentiation by the principle of maxima and minima.

The solution of the equation,

$$f'(x) = 0 \quad \text{...(6.44)}$$

where $f'(x)$ the first derivative provides a value of x which maximizes $f(x)$ provided $f''(x) < 0$ (negative). Of course, it lies within the range $[a, b]$.

SKEWNESS

The frequency curve or the probability density curve is obtained by smoothening of a frequency polygon. The shape of the curve is adjudged on the basis of the length of its tails and its peakedness. If both the tails (left and right) of the curve are not equally distributed, the curve is *asymmetric* and is called a *skewed curve.* The lack of symmetry of tails of a frequency curve is called *skewness.*

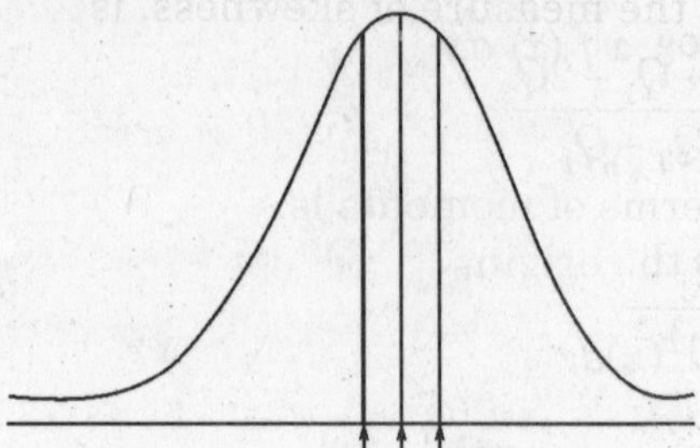

Figure 6.1 Negative Skew Curve

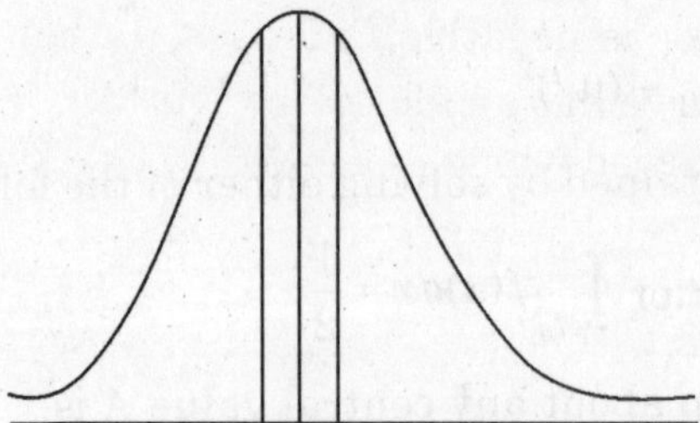

Figure 6.2 Positive Skew Curve

If the left tail of the frequency curve is longer than the right tail, the curve is said to be negatively skewed as shown in Fig. 6.1. In this case mean and median are pulled away from mode to the left.

On the other hand, if the right tail is more elongated than the left tail, the curve is said to be positively skewed as shown in Fig. 6.2. The mean and median are pulled away from mode towards right hand side. In the case where we are given some frequency distribution, the idea of skewness can be perceived through a frequency curve. The measure of skewness is an indicator of lack of symmetry. This also gives an idea as to whether dispersal of observations about a central value is symmetrical or not. The curve can give some vague idea but the numerical measurement of skewness gives an exact idea of distribution. Different formulae for the measure of skewness, denoted by α_3, are as follows:

Karl Pearson's method of measurement of skewness is based on the assumption that in an asymmetrical distribution, mean and mode never coincide. Thus, the difference between mean and mode gives some idea about the degree of asymmetry of a frequency distribution. Instead of giving an absolute measure, Pearson preferred a relative measure expressed in terms of standard deviation. Hence, Karl Pearson's measure of skewness,

$$\alpha_3 = \frac{\text{mean} - \text{mode}}{\text{S.D.}} \qquad \text{...(6.45)}$$

Obviously formula (6.45) is good when it is easy to find out the mean, mode and standard deviation.

A.L. Bowley gave a measure of skewness on the assumption that in an asymmetrical distribution, the second quartile is not equidistant from the first and the third quartile.

Thus, Bowley's formula for the measure of skewness, is

$$\alpha_3 = \frac{Q_3 + Q_1 - 2Q_2}{Q_3 - Q_1} \quad ...(6.46)$$

Another formula for α_3 in terms of moments is,

$$\alpha_3 = \frac{\mu_3}{(\mu_2)^{3/2}} \quad ...(6.47)$$

$$= \frac{\mu_3}{\sigma^3} \quad ...(6.47.1)$$

Value of α_3 by any formula is a pure number, *i.e.*, α_3 has no physical unit. For a symmetrical curve $\alpha_3 = 0$. If $\alpha_3 = 0$, mean, median and mode coincide. The sign of α_3 is same as that of μ_3. If α_3 is negative *i.e.*, $\alpha_3 < 0$, then the curve is negatively skewed which means that the curve has an elongated left tail. If α_3 is positive, *i.e.*, $\alpha_3 > 0$, then the curve is positively skewed which indicates that the right tail of the frequency curve is longer than the left tail.

Some other coefficients of skewness based on moments are Beta coefficient and Gamma coefficient. Their relation with each other is also given below:

$$\beta_1 = \frac{\mu_3^2}{\mu_2^3} \quad ...(6.48)$$

or

$$\sqrt{\beta_1} = \frac{\mu_3}{\mu_2^{3/2}} = \alpha_3 \quad ...(6.48.1)$$

Also,

$$\gamma_1 = \sqrt{\beta_1} = \alpha_3 \quad ...(6.49)$$

Karl Pearson introduced the concept of Beta Coefficients which are known as Pearsonian coefficients. Gamma notations were introduced by R.A. Fisher. The interpretation of γ_1 remains the same as that of α_3. It is a fact that median always lies between mean and mode in an asymmetrical distribution. Hence, the following relation between mean, median and mode based on experience and intuition holds good for a moderately asymmetrical distribution.

$$\text{Mean} - \text{Mode} = 3\,(\text{Mean} - \text{Median}) \quad ...(6.50)$$

or

$$\text{Mode} = 3\,\text{Median} - 2\,\text{Mean} \quad ...(6.50.1)$$

KURTOSIS

As already mentioned, the other criterion for determining the shape of a unimodal frequency curve is its peakedness. Kurtosis is a Greek word and it means bulginess. The term 'kurtosis' was introduced by Karl Pearson in 1906. If the frequency curve is highly peaked, a large number of observations have same values. Again, if curve is flat, a large number of observations have low frequency and are spread in the mid of interval. In both these situations, the curve is said to be a *kurtic curve,* If a frequency curve is more peaked than normal, it is called a *Leptokurtic curve.* If it is less peaked (flat) than normal, it is called a *Platykurtic curve.* If a curve is properly peaked, it is called a *Mesokurtic curve.* The three types of curves are shown in Fig. 6.3.

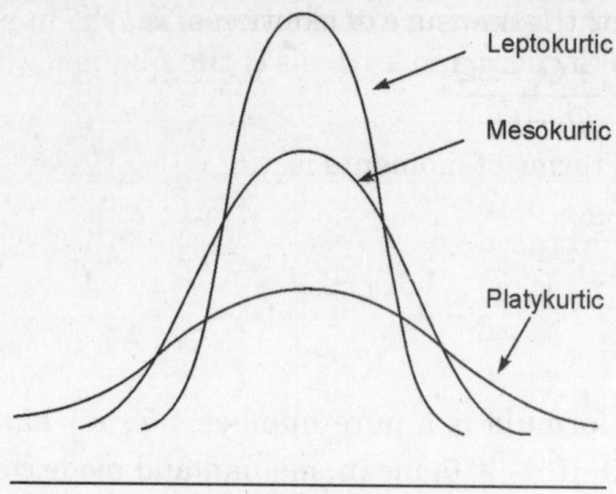

Figure 6.3 Kurtic Curves

Peakedness can vaguely be adjudged by the curve but it can be better ascertained by the mathematical measure known as the measure of kurtosis. The formula for the measure of kurtosis is,

$$\alpha_4 = \frac{\mu_4}{\mu_2^2} \quad \text{...(6.51)}$$

$$= \frac{\mu_4}{\sigma^4} \quad \text{...(6.51.1)}$$

It is apparent from (6.51) that α_4 is always positive, as it is the ratio of two positive quantities. α_4 has no physical unit. For leptokurtic curve, $\alpha_4 > 3$ and for a platykurtic curve $\alpha_4 < 3$. If $\alpha_4 = 3$, the curve is a mesokurtic. The quantity $(\alpha_4 - 3)$ is called the excess of kurtosis. α_3 and α_4 give an exact idea only if the population constants (moments) are known or the size of the sample is substantially large.

Note: In case moments and other population constants are not known, then their estimated values are substituted to get an idea of the shape of frequency curve.

As in the case of skewness, the measure of kurtosis in term of Beta and Gamma coefficients are also given. These coefficients are the expressions in terms of moment ratios and are given below. Inter-relationship between them have also been given.

$$\beta_2 = \frac{\mu_4}{\mu_2^2} = \alpha_4 \quad \text{...(6.52)}$$

$$\gamma_2 = (\beta_2 - 3) \quad \text{...(6.53)}$$

$$= \frac{\mu_4 - 3\mu_2^2}{\mu_2^2} \quad \text{...(6.53.1)}$$

Different values of γ_2 give information about the peakedness of the frequency curve.

If $\gamma_2 = 0$, the curve is properly peaked *i.e.,* mesokurtic curve.

If $\gamma_2 > 0$, the curve is more peaked than normal *i.e.,* leptokurtic curve.

If $\gamma_2 < 0$, the curve is less peaked than normal, *i.e.,* platykurtic curve. For a normal curve, $\gamma_1 = 0$ and $\gamma_2 = 0$.

***Example* 6.1.** Given the following distribution of marks in physics of 60 students of undergraduate class, the skewness and kurtosis of the frequency curve can be determined as follows:

Marks	*Frequency*
0–10	2
10–20	3
20–30	12
30–40	8
40–50	10
50–60	17
60–70	4
70–80	3
80–90	1

To clarify the method of calculation, the skewness has been calculated by all the three formulae, and kurtosis by the method of moments.

First prepare the following table:

Marks	*Mid values* (*X*)	$d = \frac{(X-45)}{10}$	*freq.* (*f*)	*cu. freq.*	*fd*	fd^2	fd^3	fd^4
0–10	5	–4	2	2	–8	32	–128	512
10–20	15	–3	3	5	–9	27	–81	243
20–30	25	–2	12	17	–24	48	–96	192
30–40	35	–1	8	25	–8	8	–8	8
40–50	45	0	10	35	0	0	0	0
50–60	55	1	17	52	17	17	17	17
60–70	65	2	4	56	8	16	32	64
70–80	75	3	3	59	9	27	81	243
80–90	85	4	1	60	4	16	64	256
		0	60		–11	191	–119	1535

(*i*) To find out the coefficient of kurtosis, first the mean, mode and standard deviation are calculated. We know,

$$\mu = A + \frac{\Sigma_i f_i d_i}{N} \times I$$

for $i = 1, 2, ..., 9$

Here we have taken $A = 45, I = 10.$

Also $N = 60$ and $\Sigma_i f_i d_i = -11$

Therefore, $$\mu = 45 + \frac{-11}{60} \times 10 = 43.17$$

$$\text{Mode} = l_0 + \frac{\Delta_1}{\Delta_1 + \Delta_2} \times I$$

In the given distribution modal class is (50–60),

$$\Delta_1 = 7,\ \Delta_2 = 13 \text{ and } I = 10$$

Therefore

$$\text{Mode} = 50 + \frac{7}{7+13} \times 10 = 53.5$$

We know

$$\sigma = \sqrt{\frac{1}{N}\left\{\Sigma_i f_i d_i^2 - \frac{(\Sigma_i f_i d_i)^2}{N}\right\}} \times I$$

In the above table $\Sigma_i f_i d_i^2 = 191$

Therefore, $$\sigma = \sqrt{\frac{1}{60}\left\{191 - \frac{(-11)^2}{60}\right\}} \times 10 = 17.75$$

$$\alpha_3 = \frac{\text{Mean} - \text{Mode}}{\text{S.D.}} = \frac{43.17 - 53.5}{17.75} = -0.58$$

(*ii*) Now, for Bowley's formula, three quartiles Q_1, Q_2, and Q_3 are calculated.

For $Q_1, \frac{N}{4} = \frac{60}{4} = 15,$

Thus, Q_1 lies in the class (20–30)

$$Q_1 = l_0 + \frac{1}{f}\left(\frac{N}{4} - c\right) \times I$$

$$= 20 + \frac{1}{12}(15 - 5) \times 10 = 28.33$$

For $Q_2, \frac{N}{2} = \frac{60}{2} = 30$

Thus, Q_2 lies in the class (40–50).

$$Q_2 = l_0 + \frac{1}{f}\left(\frac{N}{2} - C\right) \times I$$

$$= 40 + \frac{1}{10}(30 - 25) \times 10 = 45.00$$

Similarly for $Q_3, \frac{3N}{4} = \frac{3 \times 60}{4} = 45$

Hence, Q_3 lies in class (50–60)

$$Q_3 = l_0 + \frac{1}{f}\left(\frac{3N}{4} - c\right) \times I$$

$$= 50 + \frac{1}{17}(45 - 35) \times 10 = 55.88$$

Bowley's formula for measure of skewness is

$$\alpha_3 = \frac{Q_3 + Q_1 - 2Q_2}{Q_3 - Q_1}$$

$$\alpha_3 = \frac{55.88 + 28.33 - 2\times 45}{55.88 - 28.33} = -\frac{5.79}{27.55} = -0.21$$

Measure of skewness from moments can be calculated by the formula,

$$\alpha_3 = \frac{\mu_3}{\sigma^3}$$

We know,

$$\mu_3 = \frac{1}{N}\Sigma_i f_i (X_i - \overline{X})^3 \text{ for } i = 1, 2, \ldots, 9$$

$$= \frac{1}{N}\left\{\Sigma_i f_i (d_i - \bar{d})^3\right\} \times I^3$$

$$= \left[\left\{\frac{1}{N}(\Sigma_i f_i d_i^3 - 3\bar{d}\Sigma_i f_i d_i^2 + 3\bar{d}^2\Sigma_i f_i d_i - \bar{d}^3\right\}\times I^3\right]$$

where

$$\bar{d} = \Sigma_i f_i d_i / N$$

$$= \left[\frac{1}{60}\left\{(-119) - 3\left(\frac{-11}{60}\right)\times 191 + 3\left(\frac{-11}{60}\right)^2(-11) - \left(\frac{-11}{60}\right)^3\right\}\right]\times 10^3$$

$$= \left\{\frac{1}{60}(-119 + 105.05 - 1.11 + 0.006)\right\}\times 10^3$$

$$= -\,0.2509 \times 1000 = -\,250.90$$

$$\sigma^3 = (17.75)^3 = 5592.36$$

Thus,

$$\alpha_3 = \frac{-250.90}{5592.36} = -0.045$$

It is apparent from the values of α_3 obtained from the three formulae, that the distribution of marks is slightly negatively skewed.

Now to calculate the measure of kurtosis α_4, we have to calculate μ_4.

$$\mu_4 = \left[\frac{1}{N}\Sigma_i f_i (d_i - \bar{d})^4\right]\times I^4$$

$$= \left[\frac{1}{N}\left\{\Sigma_i f_i d_i^4 - 4\bar{d}\Sigma_i f_i d_i^3 + 6\bar{d}^2\Sigma_i f_i d_i^2 - 4\bar{d}^3\Sigma_i f_i d_i + \bar{d}^4\right\}\right]\times I^4$$

$$= \left[\frac{1}{60}\left\{1535 - 4\left(\frac{-11}{60}\right)(-119) + 6\left(\frac{-11}{60}\right)^2\times 191 - 4\left(\frac{-11}{60}\right)^3(-11) + \left(\frac{-11}{60}\right)^4\right\}\right]\times 10^4$$

$$= \left[\frac{1}{60}\{1535 - 87.27 + 38.52 - 0.27 + 0.001\}\right]\times 10^4$$

$$= 24.7664 \times 10000 = 247664$$

Also, $\sigma^4 = (17.75)^4 = 99264.38$

We know,

$$\alpha_4 = \frac{\mu_4}{\sigma^4} = \frac{247664.00}{99264.38} = 2.495$$

Since the value of α_4 is a little less than 3, the frequency curve is slightly platykurtic.

BINOMIAL DISTRIBUTION

It is one of the most popular discrete distributions. The origin of binomial distribution lies in Bernoulli's trails. A Bernoulli's trial is an experiment having only two possible outcomes, that is, success or failure. In other words, the results of the trial are always dichotomous. *For example,* if we flip a coin, it will show either head or tail on the upper face. The sex of an expected baby will either be male or female (excluding exceptions). A manufactured item will either be defective or non-defective. A person will either be healthy or sick.

Since a Bernoulli's trial has been considered, certain conditions for the application of binomial distribution are obvious. For clarity, (*i*) the probability of a success (or failure) remains same in each trial, (*ii*) trials must be independent, (*iii*) number of trials must be finite, (*iv*) the sum of probabilities of success and failure is one, (*v*) the probability of success vis-a-vis failure is not very low. A dichotomous variable X, which has the probability function,

$$P_X(x) = \binom{n}{x} p^x q^{n-x} \quad \text{for } x = 1, 2, ..., n \qquad ...(6.54)$$

$$= 0 \quad \text{otherwise}$$

is said to have binomial distribution. In the binomial function (6.54),
n = number of trials; p = probability of a success; q = probability of a failure and $P_X(x)$ = probability of getting exactly x successes in n trials.

The distribution given by (6.54) is called binomial distribution since it is the $(x + 1)$th term in the binomial expansion of $(q + p)^n$.

Properties of Binomial Distribution

1. Binomial distribution has two parameters, n and p (or q)
2. The mean of the binomial distribution is np and variance is npq.
3. The moment generating function is $(q + pe^t)^n$.
4. The characteristic function is $(q + pe^{it})^n$.
5. Binomial distribution tends to normal distribution as n increases. The normal approximation is correct enough if the mean np is greater than 15 for $p = 1/2$.

***Example* 6.2.** Consider a simple trial of tossing a perfectly round and balanced coin six times. Then the probability of getting (*i*) E_1: exactly three heads, (*ii*) E_2: at least three heads and (*iii*) E_3: not more than two heads, can be calculated by binomial distribution as follows:

***Solution*:** For the given example, $n = 6$, $p = q = 1/2$

(*i*) $$P(E_1) = \binom{6}{3}\left(\frac{1}{2}\right)^3\left(\frac{1}{2}\right)^{6-3} = \frac{6!}{3!(6-3)!}\cdot\frac{1}{2^6} = \frac{5}{16}$$

(ii) $$P(E_2) = \sum_{x=3}^{6} p_X(x)$$

$$= \binom{6}{3}\left(\frac{1}{2}\right)^3\left(\frac{1}{2}\right)^{6-3} + \binom{6}{4}\left(\frac{1}{2}\right)^4\left(\frac{1}{2}\right)^{6-4} + \binom{6}{5}\left(\frac{1}{2}\right)^5\left(\frac{1}{2}\right)^{6-5} + \binom{6}{6}\left(\frac{1}{2}\right)^6$$

$$= \frac{1}{2^6}\left\{\binom{6}{3}+\binom{6}{4}+\binom{6}{5}+\binom{6}{6}\right\}$$

$$= \frac{1}{64}\left\{\frac{6\times5\times4}{3\times2\times1}+\frac{6\times5}{2\times1}+6+1\right\} = \frac{21}{32}$$

(iii) $$P(E_3) = \sum_{x=0}^{2} p_X(x)$$

$$= \binom{6}{0}\left(\frac{1}{2}\right)^0\left(\frac{1}{2}\right)^6 + \binom{6}{1}\left(\frac{1}{2}\right)\left(\frac{1}{2}\right)^{6-1} + \binom{6}{2}\left(\frac{1}{2}\right)^2\left(\frac{1}{2}\right)^{6-2}$$

$$= \frac{1}{2^6}\left\{\binom{6}{0}+\binom{6}{1}+\binom{6}{2}\right\} = \frac{11}{32}$$

***Theorem* 6.1.** If r_1 and r_2 are two independent binomial variates whose parameters are (n_1, p) and (n_2, p) respectively, the distribution of $(r_1 + r_2)$ is also binomial.

Proof. The characteristic function of $(r_1 + r_2)$ is

$$\phi(r_1 + r_2)(t) = E\{e^{it(r_1+r_2)}\} = E(e^{itr_1})E(e^{itr_2})$$

(since r_1 and r_2 are independent)

$$= (q + pe^{it})^{n_1}(q + pe^{it})^{n_2} = (q + pe^{it})^{n_1+n_2}$$

The right hand expression is the characteristic function of a binomial variate whose parameters are $(n_1 + n_2)$ and p. Hence by the uniqueness theorem, the distribution of $(r_1 + r_2)$ is also binomial. This theorem may be extended to any finite number of binomial variates.

BERNOULLI'S THEOREM

If the number of successes of n trials is r, and the probability of a success is p, then the probability that the difference of r/n from p is greater than or equal to an infinitesimal small quantity ε, tends to zero as n tends to infinity. Symbolically,

$$\lim_{n\to\infty} P\left(\left|\frac{r}{n} - p\right| \geq \varepsilon\right) = 0 \qquad ...(6.55)$$

In other words, if a trial is repeated a large number of times under the same conditions, the sample proportion of successes, $\overline{X}_n (\overline{X}_n = r/n)$ in n Bernoullian trials converges in probability to p, the probability of a success, *i.e.*, $\overline{X}_n \xrightarrow{P} p$. This is also known as the *Weak Law of Large Numbers* (WLLN).

***Example* 6.3.** Let the probability of an item, to be defective, produced by a factory be 0.10. A sample of 10 items has been inspected. Then the probability of an event E that the sample has two defective item is,

$$P(E) = \binom{10}{2}(.1)^2(.9)^{10-2} = \frac{10\times 9}{2\times 1}\frac{1}{10^2}\left(\frac{9}{10}\right)^8 = \frac{1}{2}\left(\frac{9}{10}\right)^9$$

RELATION BETWEEN THE PROBABILITIES OF X AND (X+1) SUCCESSES IN BINOMIAL DISTRIBUTION

We know,

$$p(X = x) = \binom{n}{x}p^x q^{n-x} = \frac{n!}{x!(n-x)!}p^x q^{n-x}$$

and

$$p(X = x+1) = \binom{n}{x+1}p^{x+1}q^{n-x-1}$$

$$= \frac{n!}{(x+1)!(n-x-1)!}p^x q^{n-x}.\frac{p}{q}$$

$$= \frac{n!(n-x)}{x!(n-x)!(x+1)}.p^x q^{n-x}.\frac{p}{q}$$

$$= p(X = x).\frac{n-x}{x+1}.\frac{p}{q} \quad ...(6.56)$$

Relation (6.56) helps in calculating term by term probabilities.

POISSON DISTRIBUTION

Before we know the distribution, it becomes necessary to understand what is a Poisson random variable. A variable which can take only one discrete value in an interval of time, howsoever small, is known as Poisson variable. Some of the well known examples of Poisson variable are:

(*i*) number of mistakes in a typed page;

(*ii*) number of cars parked at a place in an hour, say between 10:00 a.m. and 11:00 a.m.;

(*iii*) number of defects in the insulation of a fifty metre length of wire;

(*iv*) number of suicides in a certain period in a city or town etc.

If we consider a Poisson's process for an unit length of interval (time, length, space etc.), the number of occurrences are a random variable which follow Poisson distribution. It has been named after its inventor, Simeon D. Poisson, a French probabilist of nineteenth century. It is one of the most important discrete distributions. Poisson distribution is a classical approximation to binomial distribution, in which case n, the number of trials, is comparatively large and p, the probability of an occurrence, is small.

Let X be the number of occurrences in a Poisson process and μ be the actual average number of occurrences of an event in an unit length of interval, the probability function for Poisson distribution is,

$$p_X(x) = \frac{e^{-\mu}\mu^x}{x!} \quad \text{for } x = 0, 1, 2, \ldots \qquad \ldots(6.57)$$
$$= 0 \text{ otherwise.}$$

If one considers the length of interval as d instead of unit length, the average number of occurrences in d length of interval is μd. Thus, the probability function in this situation is

$$P_X(x) = \frac{e^{-\mu d}(\mu d)^x}{x!} \quad \text{for } x = 0, 1, 2, \ldots \qquad \ldots(6.58)$$
$$= 0 \text{ otherwise.}$$

Properties of Poisson Distribution

1. Poisson distribution as given by (6.57) has mean μ and its variance is also μ. It is the only distribution known so far, of which the mean and variance are equal.
2. Poisson distribution possesses only one parameter (μ).
3. The moment generating function of a Poisson variate or equivalently the Poisson distribution is $e^{\mu(e^t-1)}$.
4. The characteristic function of Poisson distribution is $e^{\mu(e^{it}-1)}$.

***Theorem* 6.2.** If a number of independent Poisson random variables $r_1, r_2, \ldots, r_k$ (where k is an integer) are distributed with mean $\mu_1, \mu_2, \ldots, \mu_k$ respectively, then their sum $(r_1 + r_2 + \ldots + r_k)$ has also Poisson distribution with mean $(\mu_1 + \mu_2 + \ldots + \mu_k)$.

$$\phi_{r_1+r_2+\ldots+r_k}(t) = E\{e^{it(r_1+r_2+\ldots+r_k)}\}$$
$$= E(e^{itr_1})E(e^{itr_2})\ldots E(e^{itr_k})$$

since all r_i's are independent

$$= e^{\mu_1(e^{it}-1)}.e^{\mu_2(e^{it}-1)}\ldots e^{\mu_k(e^{it}-1)}$$
$$= e^{(\mu_1+\mu_2+\ldots+\mu_k)(e^{it}-1)}$$

The right-hand expression is the characteristic function for a Poisson variate whose mean is $(\mu_1 + \mu_2 + \ldots + \mu_k)$. Hence, by uniqueness theorem, the variable $(r_1 + r_2 + \ldots + r_k)$ has Poisson distribution whose mean is $(\mu_1 + \mu_2 + \ldots + \mu_k)$.

Notes: 1. It has been said that for Poisson variate the number of trials n is large and the probability of the so called success is small. Now the question arises what value of n is to be considered as large and what value of p as small. There is no hard-and-fast rule for this, but as a tradition if $n \geq 20$, it may be taken as large and $p = 0.05$ may be taken as small. Otherwise, the discrete variable with only two possibilities is generally taken to follow binomial distribution.

2. The value of $e^{-\mu}$ should either be seen from the Table III or may be calculated with the help of logarithm.

***Example* 6.4.** Suppose at a particular place, the average number of cars parked per hour is 3. Under Poisson's model, the probability of 5 cars parked in a particular hour can be calculated as under.

$$P(x = 5) = \frac{e^{-3}3^5}{5!}$$

Knowing that $e^{-3} = 0.050$, the probability,

$$P(x=5) = \frac{0.050 \times 3^5}{5!} = 0.101$$

***Example* 6.5.** The number of mistakes counted in one hundred typed pages of a typist revealed that he made 2.8 mistakes on an average per page. The probability, that in a page typed by him, (*i*) there is no mistake (*ii*) there are two or less mistakes, can be calculated as under.

Given that $\mu = 2.8$

(*i*) The probability, $P(X=0) = \dfrac{e^{-2.8}(2.8)^0}{0!}$

From Table III, $e^{-2.8} = 0.061$, the probability

$$P(X=0) = e^{-2.8} = 0.061$$

(*ii*) The probability, $P(X \le 2) = \sum_{x=0}^{2} \dfrac{e^{-2.8}(2.8)^x}{x!}$

$$= e^{-2.8}\left\{\frac{(2.8)^0}{0!} + \frac{(2.8)^1}{1!} + \frac{(2.8)^2}{2!}\right\}$$

From Table III, $e^{-2.8} = 0.061$, the probability,

$$P(X \le 2) = 0.061\,(1 + 2.8 + 3.92) = 0.471$$

***Example* 6.6.** It is known that the average number of suicides per week in Delhi is 1.5. Let X be the number of suicides which occur in a month. The probability, that there will be five or more suicides in a month, is obtained in the following manner. The distribution of X will be a Poisson distribution. In this problem,

$$d = 4,\ \mu = 1.5 \text{ and hence}$$

$$\mu d = 1.5 \times 4 = 6$$

The probability that there are five or more suicides in a month can be calculated with the help of (6.58). Thus, the probability.

$$P(X \ge 5) = \sum_{x=5}^{\infty} \frac{e^{-6}(6)^x}{x!}$$

It is difficult to evaluate $P(X \ge 5)$ from the above expression. But we can easily calculate $P(X \le 4)$ and then to find $P(X \ge 5)$, we use the relation,

$$P(X \ge 5) = 1 - P(X \le 4)$$

Again,

$$P(X \le 4) = \sum_{x=0}^{4} \frac{e^{-6}(6)^x}{x!}$$

From Table III, $e^{-6} = 0.002$, the probability

$$P(X \le 4) = e^{-6}\left(\frac{6^0}{0!} + \frac{6^1}{1!} + \frac{6^2}{2!} + \frac{6^3}{3!} + \frac{6^4}{4!}\right)$$

$$= 0.002\,(1 + 6 + 18 + 36 + 54)$$
$$= 0.230$$

Now, the probability,

$$P(X \geq 5) = 1 - 0.230 = 0.77$$

***Example* 6.7.** The number of calls arriving on in internal switchboard of an office is 90 per hour. The probability of 1 to 3 calls in a minute on the board is calculable as follows. Let X denotes the number of calls per minute. Obviously, X will follow Poisson distribution.

Average number of calls per minute, $\mu = \frac{90}{60} = 1.5.$

Now the probability,

$$\sum_{x=1}^{3} P_X(x) = \sum_{x=1}^{3} \frac{e^{-1.5}(1.5)^x}{x!}$$

From Table III, $e^{-1.5} = 0.223$, the probability,

$$\sum_{x=1}^{3} P_X(x) = e^{-1.5}\left\{\frac{1.5}{1!} + \frac{(1.5)^2}{2!} + \frac{(1.5)^3}{3!}\right\}$$
$$= 0.223\,(1.5 + 1.125 + 0.562)$$
$$= 0.711$$

***Example* 6.8.** It is known that the number of breaks in a coil of 100 metres insulated electric wire, on an average, is two. Let X denotes the number of breaks in a 100 metre insulated wire. The independence of these breaks in non-overlapping intervals is assumed. Then the probability of exactly 4 breaks in 100 metre wire will be,

$$P(X = 4) = \frac{e^{-2}(2)^4}{4!} \quad \text{since } \mu = 2.$$

From Table III, $e^{-2} = 0.135$

$$P(X = 4) = \frac{0.135 \times 16}{24} = 0.09$$

FOR POISSON VARIATE *X*, RELATIONSHIP BETWEEN THE PROBABILITIES, *P*(X = x) AND *P*(X = x + 1)

We know that for a Poisson random variable X having the mean μ, the probability,

$$P(X = x) = \frac{e^{-\mu}\mu^x}{x!}$$

and
$$P(X = x+1) = \frac{e^{-\mu}\mu^{x+1}}{(x+1)!}$$
$$= \frac{e^{-\mu}.\mu^x}{x!}\,\frac{\mu}{(x+1)} \qquad \text{...(6.59)}$$

***Example* 6.9.** If a Poisson random variable X is such that $P(X = 1) = P(X = 2)$, then the probability $P(X = 3)$ can be found out as under.

Using the relation (6.59),

$$P(X = 2) = P(X = 1).\frac{\mu}{2}$$

Since $$P(X = 1) = P(X = 2)$$

$$\frac{\mu}{2} = 1 \text{ or } \mu = 2$$

Hence, $$P(X = 3) = \frac{e^{-2}.2^3}{3!}$$

From Table III, $e^{-2} = 0.135$,

$$P(X = 3) = \frac{0.135 \times 8}{6} = 0.180$$

HYPERGEOMETRIC DISTRIBUTION

Consider a finite population of N individuals, where each individual may be categorized as success (S) and failure (F), and there are K successes (S) in the population. A random sample of size n is drawn from this population. If x is the number of S's in n randomly selected individuals from a population of K S's and $(N - K)$ F's, the probability function of X, known as *hypergeometric distribution,* is given by

$$P(X = x) = \frac{\binom{K}{x}\binom{N-K}{n-x}}{\binom{N}{n}} \quad \text{...(6.60)}$$

for $x = 0, 1, ..., n$, where $n \leq K$.

It is a discrete distribution with mean np and variance $\frac{(N-n)}{(N-1)} Npq$,

where $p = \frac{K}{N}$ and $q = 1 - p$.

NEGATIVE BINOMIAL DISTRIBUTION

A random variable X, the number of failures before the rth success occurs in a random experiment, which results in either a success or a failure, is called a *negative binomial random variable* and its probability function with probability p of a success is given by

$$P_X\{nb(x)\} = \binom{x+r-1}{r-1} p^r q^x \quad \text{...(6.61)}$$

for $x = 0, 1, 2, ...,$ where $r \geq 0$, $0 \leq p \leq 1$ and $q = 1 - p$.

Probability function (6.61) can also be written as,

$$P_X\{nb(x)\} = \binom{-r}{x} p^r (-q)^x \quad \text{...(6.61.1)}$$

$$\left[\text{Since}\binom{x+r-1}{r-1}=(-1)^x\binom{-r}{x}\right]$$

The distribution given by (6.61.1) is also called Pascal's distribution. The salient feature of this distribution is that the number of successes is fixed and the number of trials is random. It is a discrete distribution with mean $r\,(1-p)/p$ and variance $r\,(1-p)/p^2$.

NORMAL DISTRIBUTION

Normal distribution is the most popular and commonly used distribution. It was discovered by De Moivre in 1733, about twenty years after Bernoulli gave binomial distribution. A random variable X is said to follow normal distribution, if and only if, its probability density function (p.d.f.) is

$$f_X(x) = \frac{1}{\sigma\sqrt{2\pi}}e^{\frac{-1}{2\sigma^2}(x-\mu)^2} \qquad ...(6.62)$$

where x is the real value of X, *i.e.*, $-\infty < X < \infty$.

The variable X is said to be distributed normally with mean μ and variance σ^2, *i.e.* $X{\sim}N(\mu, \sigma^2)$.

The density function given by (6.62) has two parameters, namely μ and σ. Here μ can take any real value in the range $-\infty$ to ∞, where σ is any positive real value, *i.e.*, $\sigma > 0$.

Since the probability can never be negative,

$$f_X(x) \geq 0 \text{ for all } x.$$

In case $\mu = 0$, $\sigma = 1$, the density function for X is

$$f_X(x) = \frac{1}{\sqrt{2\pi}}e^{-\frac{1}{2}x^2} \qquad ...(6.63)$$

where $-\infty < X < \infty$. Notationally, $X \sim N(0, 1)$.

In this situation the variable X is called the *standardized normal variate and the distribution given by* (6.63) *is called the standardized normal distribution.*

Properties of Normal Distribution

1. If we plot the curve for the values of the standard normal variate X and the corresponding probabilities, it is of the shape given in Fig. 6.4.

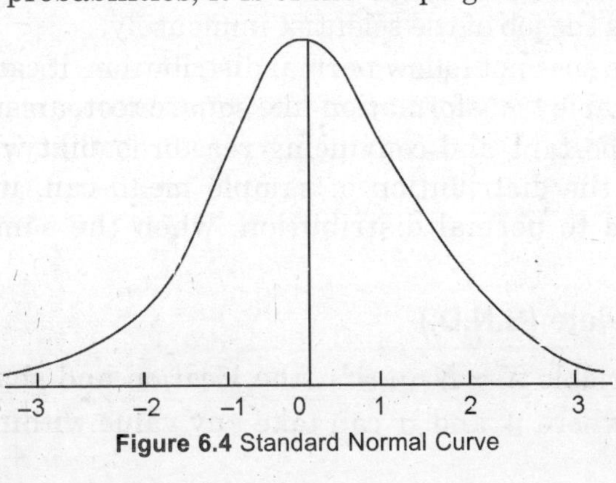

Figure 6.4 Standard Normal Curve

The curve is bell-shaped and symmetrical about the vertical line at $x = 0$. For the random variable $X \sim N(\mu, \sigma^2)$, the curve is symmetrical about the mean μ. Symmetry implies $f_X(x) = f_X(-x)$.

2. The vertical line at $x = 0$ cuts the curve at its highest point *i.e.*, $f_X(x)$ at $x = 0$ is maximum. The value of $f_X(x)$ decreases as the value of x is other than zero (or the mean μ).
3. The area under the normal curve within the limits $-\infty$ to ∞ is unity, *i.e.*,

$$\frac{1}{\sigma\sqrt{2\pi}}\int_{-\infty}^{\infty} e^{-\frac{1}{2\sigma^2}(x-\mu)^2}\, dx = 1$$

If $\mu = 0$, $\sigma = 1$, then

$$\frac{1}{\sqrt{2\pi}}\int_{-\infty}^{\infty} e^{-\frac{1}{2}x^2} = 1$$

4. On either side of the mean μ, the frequency decreases more rapidly within the range $(\mu \pm \sigma)$ and gets slower and slower as it goes away from the mean. The frequencies are extremely small beyond the distance of $\pm 3\sigma$. As a matter of fact 99.73 per cent units of the population lie within the range $\mu \pm 3\sigma$.
5. Theoretically the curve never touches the X-axis.
6. As the value of σ increases, the curve becomes more and more flat and vice versa.
7. The moment generating function of the general normal distribution is,

$$m_X(t) = e^{(\mu t + \frac{1}{2}\sigma^2 t^2)}$$

8. All central moments of odd order are zero.
9. The characteristic function of the general normal distribution is

$$\phi_X(t) = e^{(\mu it - \frac{1}{2}\sigma^2 t^2)}$$

Normal distribution is most widely used in statistics despite the fact that theoretically a population hardly follows the exact normal distribution. This is due to various reasons which are as follows:

(*i*) Convenience is a strong support for its use in statistics. Extensive tables have been prepared and provided for ordinates and area under the normal curve. This has facilitated the job of the scientist immensely.

(*ii*) If the variable does not follow normal distribution, it can be made to follow after making a suitable transformation like square root, arcsine, logarithm etc.

(*iii*) The most important and convincing reason is that whatever be the original distribution, the distribution of sample mean can, in most of the cases, be approximated to normal distribution, when the sample size is sufficiently increased.

Standard Normal Deviate (S.N.D.)

For a random variable $X \sim N(\mu, \sigma^2)$, the location and shape of the normal curve depends on μ and σ where μ and σ can take any value within their range. Hence, no master table for the area under the curve can be prepared. This difficulty is very well overcome by consideration of a variable Z where $Z = (X - \mu)/\sigma$. The variable Z is always distributed with mean zero and variance unity, *i.e.*, $Z \sim N(0, 1)$.

In this way, whatever be the parameters, the normal distribution of Z has parameters 0 and 1. Hence, only one table for area or ordinates of the normal curve is sufficient. Remember that normal curve is a symmetric curve and the area on either side of the ordinate at the origin is 0.5, since the total area under the curve is unity. The area as a matter of fact gives the probability for an event that Z takes certain values. These probabilities (areas) can always be found with the help of Table IV given in the appendix B.

For better understanding, consider the following situations.

(*i*) $P(Z \leq Z_0) = 0.5 - A$.

If Z_0 is a negative real value where A is the area between ordinates at $x = 0$ and $x = Z_0$. See (Fig. 6.5.)

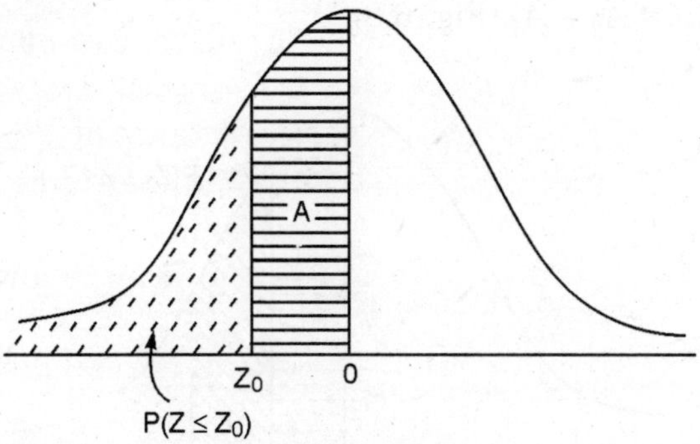

Figure 6.5

(*ii*) If Z_0 is a positive real number, then

$P(Z \leq Z_0) = 0.5 + A$

where A is the area between the ordinates at $x = 0$ and $x = Z_0$. (Fig. 6.6).

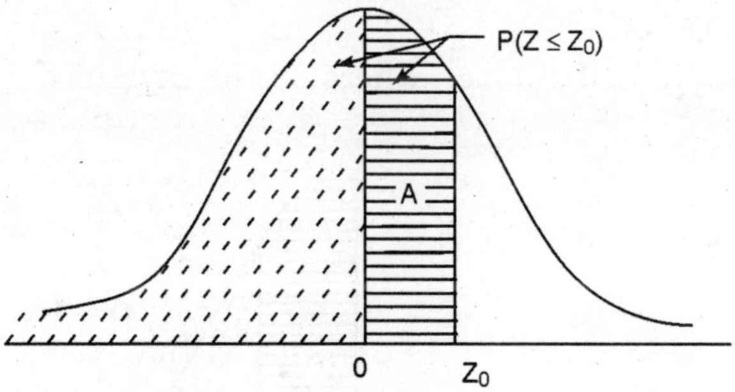

Figure 6.6

(*iii*) $P(Z_1 \leq Z \leq Z_2) = A_1 + A_2$

If Z_1 is negative and Z_2 is positive where A_1 is the area between ordinates at $x = 0$ and $x = Z_1$ and A_2 is the area between the ordinates at $x = 0$ and $x = Z_2$ (Fig. 6.7).

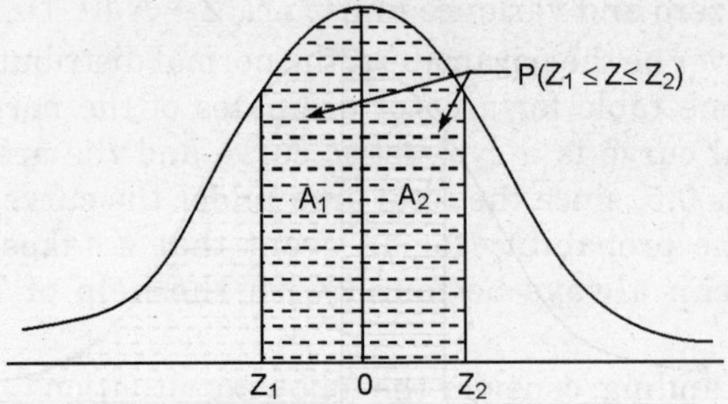

Figure 6.7

If Z_1 and Z_2 are both positive, the probability

$P(Z_1 \leq Z \leq Z_2) = A_2 - A_1$ (Fig. 6.8)

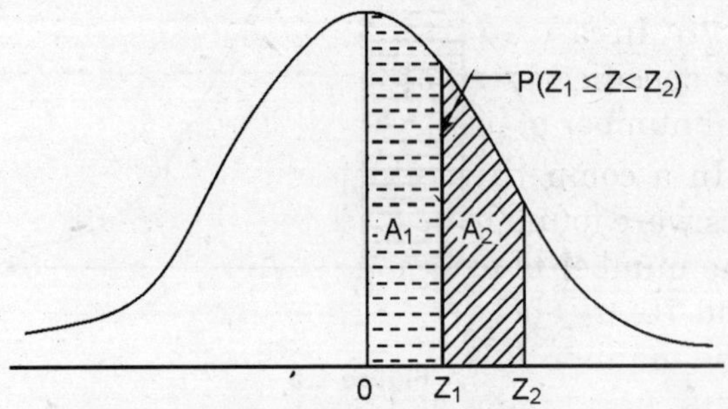

Figure 6.8

In case Z_1 and Z_2 are negative, the areas A_2 and A_1 will be to the left of the ordinate of the point zero.

(*iv*) $P(Z \geq Z_0) = 0.5 - A$.

If Z_0 is a positive real number, where A is as explained earlier (Fig. 6.9).

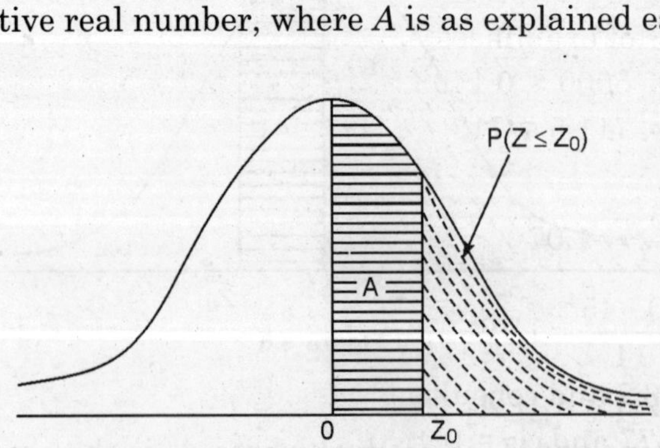

Figure 6.9

(*v*) $P(Z \geq Z_0) = 0.5 + A$,
If Z_0 is a negative real number, where A is as explained earlier (Fig. 6.10).

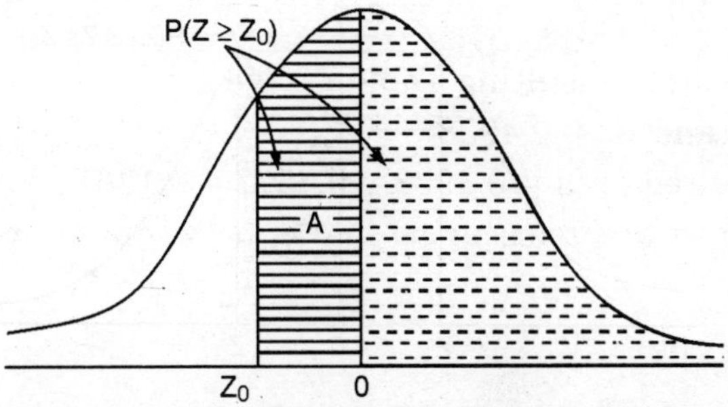

Figure 6.10

From the above description of probabilities, one can easily understand the approach of finding the required area under the standard normal curve. Wherever the values of X are not given for standard normal variable, they should be standardized by the transformation $(X - \mu)/\sigma$. In case we are interested in finding out the number of individuals or units lying in some specified interval, we should find out the required area and then multiply it by the total number of units of population.

***Example* 6.10.** In a competitive examination of 5000 students, the marks of the examinees in statistics were found to be distributed normally with mean 45 and standard deviation 14. Then the number of examinees whose marks out of 100 were: (*i*) less than 30, (*ii*) between 30 and 70, (*iii*) between 60 and 80, (*iv*) more than 60, (*v*) more than 40, can be found out in the manner described above with the help of Table IV.

Given that, $\mu = 45$, $\sigma = 14$ and $N = 5000$.

(*i*) $X = 30,\ Z = \dfrac{30-45}{14} = -1.07$

Using Fig. 6.5, the required area $A_1 = 0.5 - A$

From Table IV, $A = 0.3577$

$A_1 = 0.5 - 0.3577 = 0.1423$

The number of examinees having marks 30 or less

$= 5000 \times 0.1423$

$= 711.5 = 712$

Similarly,

(*ii*) $Z_1 = \dfrac{30-45}{14} = -1.07$

and $Z_2 = \dfrac{70-45}{14} = 1.79$

Using Fig. 6.7 and consulting Table IV,

$A_1 = 0.3577$ and $A_2 = 0.4633$

Thus, the required area $= 0.3577 + 0.4633 = 0.8210$

The number of examinees having marks between 30 and 70 $= 5000 \times 0.8210 = 4105$

(*iii*) $Z_1 = \dfrac{60-45}{14} = 1.07$

$Z_2 = \dfrac{80-45}{14} = 2.5$

Using Fig. 6.8 and consulting Table IV, we get

$A_1 = 0.3577$ and $A_2 = 0.4938$

Thus, the required area = 0.4938 – 0.3577 = 0.1361

The number of students securing marks between 60 and 80 = 5000 × 0.1361 = 680.5 = 680

(*iv*) $Z_0 = \dfrac{60-45}{14} = 1.07$

Using Fig. 6.9 and from Table IV,

$A_1 = 0.3577$

Hence the required area = 0.5 – 0.3577 = 0.1423

The number of examinees having marks more than 60 = 5000 × 0.1423 = 711.5 = 712

(*v*) $Z_0 = \dfrac{40-45}{14} = -0.36$

Using Fig. 6.10 and from Table IV,

$A_1 = 0.1406$

Hence the required area = 0.5 + 0.1406 = 0.6406

The number of examinees have marks more than 40

= 5000 × 0.6406 = 3203

Besides the most widely used normal distribution, there are numerous other continuous distributions. Some of the popular distributions are given below in brief.

LOGNORMAL DISTRIBUTION

A continuous r.v. X is said to follow a *lognormal distribution* if the distribution of $\log_e(X)$ is normal. The p.d.f. of $\log_e(X)$ with parameters μ and σ^2 is

$$f_X(x,\mu,\sigma^2) = \frac{1}{\sqrt{2\pi}\sigma x} e^{-\frac{1}{2\sigma^2}(\log_e x-\mu)^2} \quad \text{...(6.64)}$$

for $X > 0$.

The mean of lognormal distribution is $e^{\mu+\sigma^2/2}$ and variance is $e^{2\mu+\sigma^2} e^{\sigma^2-1}$. The hourly median power of received radio signals transmitted between two places follows lognormal distribution.

RECTANGULAR DISTRIBUTION

A r.v. X is said to follow rectangular distribution in the finite range (α, β) if the p.d.f. of X is

$$f_X(x,\alpha,\beta) = \frac{1}{\beta-\alpha} \quad \text{...(6.65)}$$

for $\alpha < x < \beta$.

The mean of rectangular distribution is $(\beta+\alpha)/2$ and variance is $(\beta-\alpha)^2/12$. In this distribution, the probability density for all the values throughout the range of X is the same.

CAUCHY'S DISTRIBUTION

A continuous r.v. X is said to follow *Cauchy's distribution* with parameters α, β if its p.d.f. is

$$f_X(x,\alpha,\beta) = \frac{1}{\pi\beta\left\{1+\left(\frac{x-\alpha}{\beta}\right)^2\right\}} \quad ...(6.66)$$

for $-\infty < x < \infty$ and where $-\infty < \alpha < \infty$ and $\beta > 0$.

The mean and variance of Cauchy's distribution do not exist.

BETA DISTRIBUTION

A continuous r.v. X is said to have beta distribution with parameters α and β if the p.d.f. of X is

$$f_X(x,\alpha,\beta) = \frac{1}{\beta(\alpha,\beta)} x^{\alpha-1}(1-x)^{\beta-1} \quad ...(6.67)$$

for $0 < X < 1$.

The mean of beta distribution is $\alpha/(\alpha+\beta)$ and variance is $\alpha\beta/\{(\alpha+\beta)^2(\alpha+\beta+1)\}$. The time X necessary for laying the foundation of a building follows beta distribution.

GAMMA DISTRIBUTION

A continuous r.v. X is said to follow a *gamma distribution* with parameters n and α if the p.d.f. of X is

$$f_X(x,n,\alpha) = \frac{1}{\alpha^n \Gamma n} x^{n-1} e^{-x/\alpha} \quad ...(6.68)$$

for $x \geq 0$ and where $n > 0$, $\alpha > 0$.

The mean of the gamma distribution is $n\alpha$ and variance is $n\alpha^2$. It is a highly skewed distribution.

EXPONENTIAL DISTRIBUTION

A r.v. X is said to follow an exponential distribution with parameter λ if the p.d.f. of X is

$$f_X(x,\lambda) = \lambda e^{-\lambda x} \quad ...(6.69)$$

for $\lambda > 0$.

The mean of exponential distribution is $1/\lambda$ and its variance is $1/\lambda^2$. The lapse of time between any two successive events follows exponential distribution. The elapsed time between calls into a telephone switch board is one example.

WEIBULL DISTRIBUTION

A r.v. X is said to follow *Weibull distribution* with parameters α and β if the p.d.f. of X is

$$f_X(x,\alpha,\beta) = \frac{\alpha}{\beta^\alpha} x^{\alpha-1} e^{-(x/\beta)^\alpha} \quad ...(6.70)$$

for $X > 0$ and α, $\beta > 0$.

This distribution was introduced by Swedish physicist Waloddi Weibull in 1939. The mean of Weibull distribution is $\beta\Gamma\left(1+\frac{1}{\alpha}\right)$ and variance is $\beta^2\left[\Gamma\left(1+\frac{2}{\alpha}\right)-\left\{\Gamma\left(1+\frac{1}{\alpha}\right)\right\}^2\right]$.

Corrosion weight loss of an alloy, tensile strength of a metal usually follow this distribution.

Besides the theoretical distributions discussed in this chapter, there are many more distributions. Logistic, Pareto, Gumbell, double exponential are a few to name. They are not included here as they are not so commonly used. Moreover, they do not form the part of the course work for which the book is meant.

It is felt that the given discussion of distribution theory and some well-known distributions will make the basic ideas clear about discrete and continuous distributions.

QUESTIONS AND EXERCISES

1. In the case of a normal distribution, mark √ sign on the statement which is true.
   (*a*) Standard deviation is a measure of central tendency.
   (*b*) Mean and mode coincide but not the median.
   (*c*) Standard deviation and mean are equal.
   (*d*) Q_1 and Q_3 are equidistant from Q_2.
   (*e*) Mean, median and mode coincide.
   (*f*) Coefficient of kurtosis is equal to zero and coefficient of skewness is equal to three.
2. When the number of trials is very large, then
   (*a*) Binomial distribution tends to ____________
   (*b*) Poisson distribution tends to ____________
3. The true value of the measure of kurtosis for a normal distribution is,
   (*a*) $\alpha_4 \geq 2$
   (*b*) $\alpha_4 = 2$
   (*c*) $\alpha_4 = 3$
   (*d*) $\alpha_4 < 3$
   (*e*) $\alpha_4 = 0$
4. Mark the distribution in which the mean and variance are the same.
   (*a*) Binomial distribution
   (*b*) Normal distribution
   (*c*) Poisson distribution
   (*d*) Exponential distribution
   (*e*) Cauchy distribution

5. Define the standard normal deviate and state its importance.
6. Why is the normal distribution so important and so frequently used?
7. Find the mean and variance of Bernoulli's distribution.
8. State uniqueness theorem and its utility in the distribution theory.
9. Which value of the measure of skewness holds true for a negatively skewed curve.
   (*a*) < 1
   (*b*) < 0
   (*c*) > 0
   (*d*) $= 3$
10. Name the distribution which the following variables are likely to follow:
    (*a*) Height of persons.
    (*b*) Number of defectives in a lot of manufactured items.
    (*c*) Success of a student in the examination.
    (*d*) Loss of weight of iron per month due to rusting.
11. Name the following graphs:

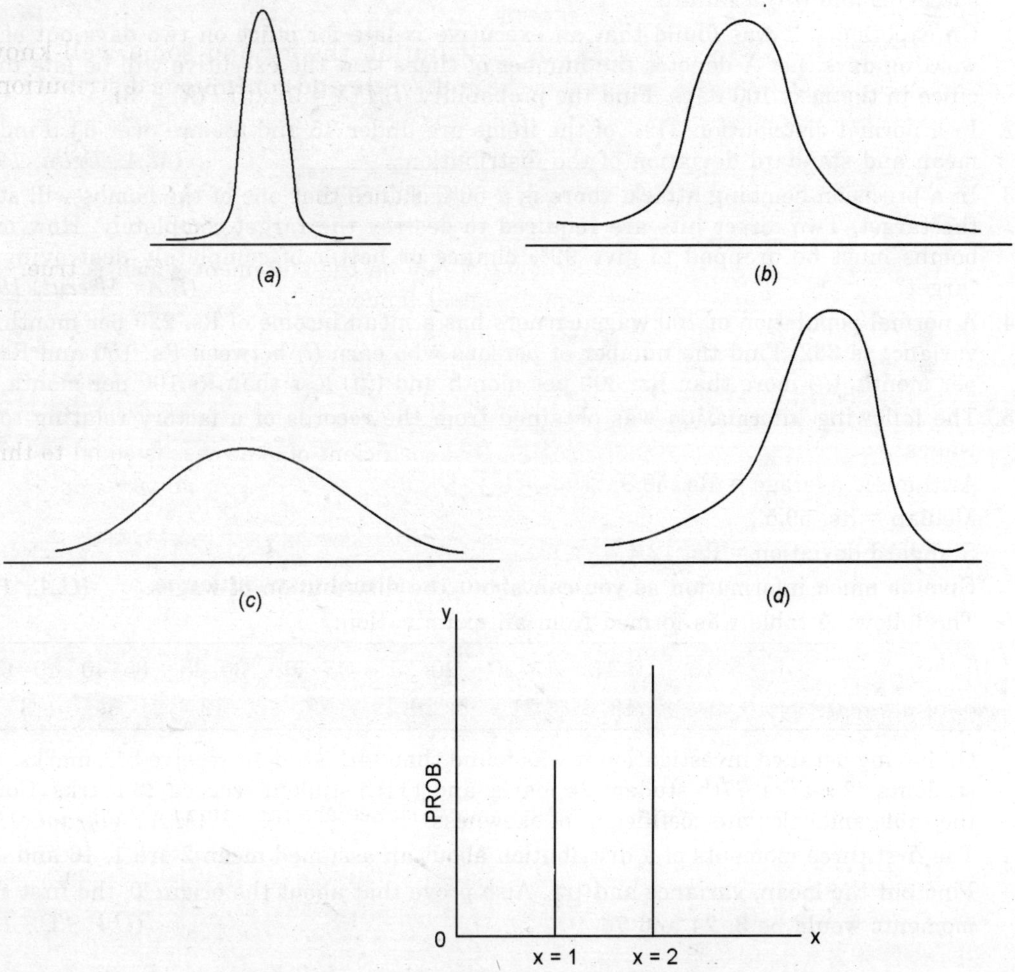

12. Explain a random variable. Also give three examples of discrete and continuous variables.
13. Differentiate between distribution function and density function.
14. Throw light on the importance of moment generating function and characteristic function.
15. Can we get the binomial distribution from the poisson distribution and vice-versa. Justify your answer.
16. (*a*) Define and discuss mathematical expectation.
    (*b*) Show that the mean of a binomial distribution is *np* and variance is *npq*.
17. If X_1, X_2 and X_3 are three independent Poisson variables, show that their sum has also Poisson distribution.
18. Given that the mean of a binomial distribution is 6 and variance is 4. Find the probability of a success.
19. A student answered that the mean of a binomial distribution is 18 and variance is equal to 12. Test whether the answer of the student is correct or not.
20. A die is thrown six times. If 1 to 3 spots appear on the upper face, then it is considered a failure. If 4 to 6 spots appear on the upper face of the die, then it is considered a success. What is the probability of (*i*) four successes out of six trials, (*ii*) at least four successes and (*iii*) a failure.
21. On experience it was found that an executive is late for office on two days out of 100 working days. Let X denotes the number of times that the executive will be late to the office in the next 100 days. Find the probability (*i*) $P(X = 0)$, (*ii*) $P(X \leq 3)$.
22. In a normal distribution 31% of the items are under 45 and 8% are over 64. Find the mean and standard deviation of the distribution. (*M.A., Delhi, 1967*)
23. In a precision bombing attack, there is a 50% chance that one of the bombs will strike the target. Two direct hits are required to destroy the target completely. How many bombs must be dropped to give 99% chance or better of completely destroying the target? (*B.A., Meerut, 1975*)
24. A normal population of 700 wage earners has a mean income of Rs. 220 per month and variance is 332. Find the number of persons who earn (*i*) between Rs. 150 and Rs.200 per month, (*ii*) more than Rs. 300 per month and (*iii*) less than Rs.100 per month.
25. The following information was obtained from the records of a factory relating to the wages.

    Arithmetic average = Rs. 58.8

    Median = Rs. 59.5

    Standard deviation = Rs. 12.4

    Give as much information as you can about the distribution of wages. (*C.A., 1966*)
26. The following table was formed from an examination.

Marks:	0–5	5–10	10–15	15–20	20–25	25–30	30–35	35–40	40–45
No. of students:	5	9	13	21	29	22	12	6	3

On having detailed investigation it was found that 14th student received 11 marks, 48th students 32 marks, 77th student 26 marks and 111th student secured 38 marks. Correct the table and calculate coeffficient of skewness. (*M.A., Vikram, 1971*).

27. The first three moments of a distribution about an assumed mean 2 are 1, 16 and – 40. Find out the mean, variance and μ_3. Also prove that about the origin '0' the first three moments would be 3, 24 and 76. (*U.P.S.C., 1972*)

28. Sketch a normal curve of a variable X that has mean $\mu = 5$ and S.D., $\sigma = 2.2$. What is the height of the normal curve at $X = 7$?

29. A coaching school claims that 50 per cent of its students succeed in a competitive examination. Five students take admission in this school. What is the probability that (*i*) at least 3 students will be selected, (*ii*) exactly 3 students will be selected and (*iii*) less than 3 students will be selected.

30. Given the following distribution of income of workers of a big concern:

(*a*) Find the number of workers who earn (*i*) more than Rs. 325 per month, (*ii*) between Rs. 425 and 525 and (*iii*) less than Rs. 375 per month.

Income groups (Rs. per month)	*No. of persons*
100–150	2
150–200	3
200–250	5
250–300	11
300–350	15
350–400	20
400–450	26
450–500	20
500–550	29
550–600	18
600–650	27
650–700	25
700–750	13

31. A sample of size 30 is drawn from a normal population having the mean 17.5 and variance 42.4. What will be the distribution of the sample mean?

32. It is known that 40 per cent tuberculosis patients die every year. Six patients are admitted in a hospital suffering from tuberculosis. What is the probability that (*i*) three patients will die, (*ii*) at least five patients will die, (*iii*) all patients will be cured and (*iv*) no patient will be saved.

33. Following table gives the number of effective working hours per month of 60 workers in a production unit.

100,	165,	123,	111,	128,	187,	185,	83,	146,	77,
120,	145,	115,	138,	155,	172,	134,	106,	109,	87,
46,	59,	120,	128,	174,	153,	114,	67,	53,	104,
35,	44,	88,	152,	124,	128,	158,	118,	106,	145,
121,	96,	74,	65,	89,	104,	170,	108,	171,	87,
105,	126,	137,	144,	129,	114,	98,	66,	157,	132

Write down the frequency distribution taking equal class intervals of 30 hours and find the measure of skewness.

34. A sample of 100 dry battery cells tested to find the length of life produced the following results:

$\overline{x} = 12$ hours, $\sigma = 3$ hours.

Assuming that the data are normally distributed, what percentage of battery cells are expected to have life.

(i) more than 15 hours.
(ii) less than 6 hours.
(iii) between 10 and 14 hours.

[Given

Z	2.5	2	1	0.67
area	0.4938	0.4772	0.3413	0.2487

]

(C.A. Final, 1979)

35. In a frequency distribution, Karl Pearson's coefficient of skewness revealed that the distribution was skewed to the left to an extent of 0.6. Its mean value was less than its modal value by 4.8. What is the standard deviation? *(I.C.W.A. 1982)*

36. Name the distribution which holds the following property:
   (a) Mean and standard deviation are equal.
   (b) Mean and variance are equal.
   (c) Variance is $1/\lambda$ times its mean.
   (d) Mean and variance do not exist.

37. Give the probability density function of any three continuous distributions and write their properties.

38. Define the following and give their uses.
   (a) Factorial moments
   (b) Characteristic function
   (c) Inversion theorem
   (d) Cumulants
   (e) Bernoulli's theorem.

39. Differentiate between discrete and continuous random variables.

40. In a sample of 120 workers in a factory the mean and standard deviation of daily wages were Rs.11.35 and Rs. 3.03 respectively. Find the percentage of workers getting wages between Rs.9.00 and Rs.17.00 in the whole factory assuming that the wages are normally distributed. *(C.A., May, 1981)*

41. In a certain examination the percentage of passes and distinctions were 46 and 9 respectively. Estimate the average marks obtained by the candidates, the minimum pass and distinction marks being 40 and 75 respectively. Assume the distribution of marks to be normal.

$\phi(0.1) = .5368,\ \phi(1.34) = .9099$ *(M.Com. Kolkata, 1984)*

[Hint: $\phi(Z)$ is the area under the normal curve for $X \leq Z$]

42. Calculate Karl Pearson's coefficient of skewness from the data given below:

Monthly Income (Rs.):	300–400	400–500	500–600	600–700	700–800	800–900
No. of families:	15	25	40	60	35	35

(B.Com. I Yr. Andhra, 1989)

43. Calculate coefficient of skewness based on quartiles and median from the following data:

Variable:	0–10	10–20	20–30	30–40	40–50	50–60	60–70	70–80
Frequency:	12	16	26	38	22	15	7	4

(B.Com. I Yr. Andhra, 1988)

44. In a given distribution,
Arithmetic Mean = 35, Median = 36. What is the mode?
(B.Com. I Yr. Andhra, 1988)

45. In a business, it is assumed that the average daily sales in (Rs.) follow normal distribution. It is given that probability of average daily sales less than Rs.124 is .0287 and the probability it exceeds Rs.270 is .4599. Find the mean and s.d. of the distribution.
(M.Com. Kolkata, 1985)

46. In calculating the moments of a frequency distribution based on 100 observations, the following results were obtained;
Mean = 9, Variance = 18
$\frac{m_3^2}{m_2^3} = 0.8$, where m_2 and m_3 represent the second and third moments respectively.
But later it was noticed that one observation 12 was read as 21. Obtain the correct value of the first three moments about zero. *(I.C.W.A., Dec., 1988)*

47. Marks obtained by a number of students are assumed to be normally distributed with mean 65 and variance 25. If 3 students are taken at random, what is the probability that exactly two of them will have marks over 70?
[Given $\int_0^1 \phi(z)\, dz = 0.34$, where $\phi(z)$ is $N(0,1)$] *(I.C.W.A., Dec., 1986)*

48. (*a*) Write down the p.d.f. $f(x)$ for a normal variable X with mean μ and s.d. s, hence show that it is symmetric about the mean μ.
(*b*) Assuming that the height distribution of a group of 450 students is normal with mean 164.734 cm and s.d. 5.472 cm. Calculate the expected frequency of heights within the class interval 149.55 cm to 154.55 cm.
(*c*) Calculate the mean of normal distribution whose s.d. is 9 and only 2% of its values are less than 117.
[$\phi(2.775) = .9972396$, $\phi(1.861) = .9686273$, $\phi(2.054) = .98$]
(M.Com., Calcutta, 1986)

49. The weekly wages of 2000 workers in a factory are normally distributed with a mean of Rs. 200 and a variance of Rs. 400. Estimate the lowest weekly wages of the 197 highest paid workers and the highest weekly wages of the 197 lowest paid workers.
(C.A. (Inter), May, 1993)

50. If a random variable X follows a normal distribution with mean 18 and variance 625, find: (*i*) $P(-31 < x < 67)$ (*ii*) $P(x < 67\ x > 18)$.

51. For a normal distribution with mean 3 and variance 16, find the value of y of the variate such that the probability of the variate lying in the interval (3, y) is 0.4772.
[You are given, $P(Z \leq 2) = 0.9772$]. *[I.C.W.A. (Inter); June, 1991]*

52. A player tosses 3 fair coins. He wins Rs.10 if 3 heads appear, Rs. 6 if 2 heads appear and Rs. 2 if one head appears. On the other hand he looses Rs. 25 if 3 tails appear. Find the expected gain of the player. *[I.C.W.A. (Inter), Dec., 1990]*

53. A man runs an ice cream parlour in a holiday resort. If the summer is mild he can sell 2,500 cups of ice cream; if it is hot, he can sell 4,000 cups; if it is very hot, he can sell

5,000 cups. It is known that the probability of any year the summer to be mild is $\frac{1}{7}$ and hot is $\frac{4}{7}$. A cup of ice cream costs Rs. 2 and sold for Rs. 3.50. What is his expectation?

[I.C.W.A. (Inter); June, 1990]

54. Fit a binomial distribution in the following data.

x	:	0	1	2	3	4
f	:	28	62	46	10	4

(I.C.W.A., Inter, Dec. 2004)

55. The annual incomes of a group of 10,000 persons were found to be normally distributed with mean equal to Rs.5200 and standard deviation equal to Rs.600. Find:
The number of persons having income between Rs. 4000 and Rs.5500.

(M.B.A., Part–II, MLSU, Udaipur, 2001)

56. (*a*) A fair coin is tossed three times. Let X be the number of tails appearing. Find probability distribution of X. Calculate the expected value of X. Find also its variance.

(*b*) If $P(x) = \begin{cases} 0.1x, & x = 1, 2, 3, 4 \\ 0, & \text{otherwise} \end{cases}$

Find (*i*) $P(x = 1 \text{ or } 2)$

(*ii*) $P\left\{\frac{1}{2} < x < \frac{5}{2} \middle| x > 1\right\}$ *(I.C.W.A., Inter, June, 2002)*

57. (*a*) The number of accidents in a year attributed to taxi drivers in a city follows Poisson distribution with mean 3. Out of 1000 taxi drivers, find the number of drivers with (*i*) no accident in a year and (*ii*) at least 3 accidents in a year. $[e^{-3} = 0.0498]$

(*b*) Write down the probability function of the variable X which follows a normal distribution. Give the salient features of normal probability distribution.

(C.A., P.E.–I, May, 2004)

58. Let X be a random variable assuming values x_1, x_2 and x_3. Then the function denoted by $f(x_i) = P(X = x_i)$ is given by:

X	:	-3	6	9
$P(X = x_i)$	:	$\frac{1}{6}$	$\frac{1}{2}$	$\frac{1}{3}$

Find $E(X)$, $E(X^2)$ and $E(2X + 1)^2$ *(C.A., P.E.–I, Nov., 2003)*

59. A random variable has the following probability distribution :

Value of X	:	-2	-1	0	1	2	3
$P(X=x)$	:	0.1	k	0.2	$2k$	.3	k

(*i*) Find the value of k.
(*ii*) Find the expected value and variance of x. *(C.A. Foundation, Nov., 1999)*

60. The probability density function of a continuous random variable is given by,

$$f(x) = kx(x-2), \quad 0 \le x \le 2$$
$$= 0 \quad \text{elsewhere}$$

Calculate the value of constant K and $E(X)$. *(I.C.W.A., Inter, June, 2004)*

61. Fit a Poisson distribution to the following data and calculate the theoretical frequencies.

x	:	0	1	2	3	4
Frequency	:	122	60	15	2	1

(Given that $e^{-0.5} = 0.61$) *(I.C.W.A., Inter, Dec., 2003)*

62. What probability model is appropriate to describe a situation where 100 misprints are distributed randomly throughout 100 pages of a book ? For this model, what is the probability that a page observed at random will contain at least three misprints. *(M.B.A., Part–I, MLSU, Udaipur, 2002)*

63. Find the value of K for which

$$f(x) = \begin{cases} x, & 0 \le x \le 1 \\ K - x, & 1 \le x \le 2 \\ 0, & \text{otherwise} \end{cases}$$

is a probability density function of a random variable X. Find $P\left(\frac{1}{2} < x \le \frac{3}{2}\right)$ and $E(x)$. *(I.C.W.A., Inter, June, 2001)*

64. A number is chosen at random from the set 10, 11, 12, ..., 109 and another number is chosen at random from the set 12, 13, 14, ..., 61. What are the expected values of sum and product of them? *(I.C.W.A., Inter, June, 2000)*

65. What is the purpose of measuring skewness and kurtosis and how can they be measured? *(RS–II, 1998)*

SUGGESTED READING

Hogg, R.V. and Craig, A.T. (1972). *Introduction to Mathematical Statistics*, 3rd ed., Amerind Publishing Co., New Delhi.

Johnson, N.L. and S.M. Kotz (1970). *Discrete Distributions,* John Wiley, New York.

Johnson, N.L. and S.M. Kotz (1970).*Continuous Univariate Distributions*-1, 2, John Wiley, New York.

Mood, A.M., F.A. Graybill and D.C. Boes (1974). *Introduction to the Theory of Statistics,* (International Student Edition), McGraw Hill, Koga Kusha, Tokyo.

Rao, C.R. (1974). *Linear Statistical Inference and its Applications,* Wiley Eastern, New Delhi.

Streater R.F. (1995). *Statistical Dynamics*, Imperial College Press.

Szulga, S. and Jerzy Szulga (1998). *Introduction to Random Chaos,* CRC Press.

Vladimir Rotar (1998). *Probability Theory,* World Scientific.

Chapter 7

Sampling and Its Uses

Sampling in statistics is as common and important as salt in the food. The origin of sampling is as old as our civilisation. The use of sampling in day-to-day life has been illustrated through certain examples. In homes, ladies take out one or two rice grains (any other food item) from the cooking pan and test so that they are able to decide whether the food in the pan is fully cooked or not. In medical sciences a few drops of blood are taken and tested microscopically or chemically to know whether the blood contains some abnormalities or not. Whatever is observed in the few drops is true for the blood of the whole body. In a bulb manufacturing factory, one tests the life of few bulbs and comes to a conclusion about the average life of bulbs in the whole lot. In the grain market, a person takes a handful of grain, judges its quality and decides about the quality of grain in the heap on the basis of this handful of grain. All these examples clearly reveal that sampling has been an age old practice.

Nowadays, sampling methods are extensively used in socio-economic surveys to know the living condition, cost of living index etc. of a class of people In biological studies, experiments are conducted on some units (persons, animals or plants) and inferences are drawn about the breed or variety to which the units belong. In the industries, sampling procedures are predominantly used for quality control.

DEFINITIONS

From the discussion so far, it is apparent that in sampling process we have to consider a complete set of objects or things known as *population* and a fraction of population selected in any manner is known as a *sample*. It will be appropriate to define and discuss these terms adequately.

Population

In statistics, the term 'population' is used in an altogether different sense from its literary sense. Population may consist of the animates or inanimates. In literature, population means the number of inhabitants in a well-defined area. But in statistics, "*It is the totality of persons, objects, items or anything conceivable pertaining to certain characteristics.*"

As per statistical dictionary by Kendall and Buckland (1975), the population is defined as, "*In statistical usage, the term population is applied to any finite or infinite collection of individuals.*"

For example, the population of students in a University. It means anybody who is enrolled in a University belongs to this population. The number of plants in a field, persons suffering from cancer, workers in textile industry, persons in army services in India, are some other examples of population in statistical sense.

From the definition it is evident that population can be finite as well as infinite. Obviously, the finite population consists of individuals or items which are finite in number. An infinite population is one which either possesses the infinite property through some limiting process or is non-enumerable. The population of all real numbers between 0 and 1, the population of all integers are examples of infinite population. In case of random sampling with replacement (discussed later), any population is always infinite. Without going too deep in the matter, we may say that a population consisting of a large number of units or items may be deemed to possess the properties of an infinite population.

From the above discussion it is evident that every population consists of individuals or items which are known as *sampling units.* The formal definition of sampling unit is given below.

Sampling Unit

The population may be regarded as consisting of units which are to be used for the purpose of sampling. Each unit is regarded as individual and indivisible when the selection is made. Such a unit is known as a sampling unit. A sampling unit may be specified on some natural basis or any other criterion fixed for it. The criteria for it depend on the purpose of the survey and the sampling scheme to be followed. A person, an animal, a household, an orchard, a factory or a village are few examples of sampling units.

Sample

A finite part of a population or a subset of a set of sampling units, selected by some process, usually by deliberate selection with the object of investigating the properties of the parent population or set, is called a sample. For example, if we select five students from a class of forty students, five selected students constitute a sample. We select fifty bulbs to test the life of bulbs, from a lot of bulbs manufactured by a factory in a week. Fifty selected bulbs constitute a sample.

Sampling is a device which makes one able to draw inferences about the whole population simply by observing or measuring a few of the sampling units. However, this creates many doubts like (*a*) whether the conclusions drawn on the basis of sample observations really hold good for the whole population or the whole mass? (*b*) would the results not be unreliable? Such questions always surface in the mind of applied scientists. But the fact remains that the sampling has served the purpose of all the scientists to a great extent. Many arguments can be put forth in its support. A few of them are as given below:

1. It is difficult to handle a population which usually consists of a large number of units.

2. Too much time is required to study the whole population and often the study becomes outdated by the time it is complete.
3. Finances required to cover the whole population can hardly be made available.
4. In a study where individuals are killed or perished under observation, studying the population serves no purpose. To clarify this point further we give an example. If all the battery cells of a manufacturing concern are put to life testing, nothing will be left for use.
5. In case, the population is infinite or consists of uncountable number of units, its study is impossible.

Some people also think that complete enumeration yields better results than the sampling studies. However, this is not correct because complete enumeration (census studies) adds many errors which are reduced or eliminated by sampling. Hence, in many cases sample studies yield better results than population studies. The reliability of results depends more on the quality of the sample. If the sample is a true representative of the population, the results obtained from it are very near to the true value. In the view of mathematicians, a 'random sample' can always be deemed as a true representative of the population. To a great extent it is correct. But the moment one starts identifying various sampling units belonging to a population, one resorts to thinking of various sampling schemes. The use of a particular type of sampling scheme depends on; (*i*) type of population, (*ii*) information available about sampling units, (*iii*) object of the study, (*iv*) availability of resources like sampling frame, time, money and trained personnel, and (*v*) last but not the least, the knowledge and experience of the person selecting the sample.

Errors in Surveys

In any survey two types of errors are likely to occur (*i*) sampling errors and (*ii*) non-sampling errors.

Sampling Errors. The errors which are introduced due to errors in selection of a sample or the discrepancies between population parameters and estimates which are derived from a random sample. This discrepancy generally decreases as the sample size increases, but gradually the decrease in error becomes negligible with increasing sample size. Hence a sample of optimum size must be obtained for a study. In this way we can minimize the error or keep the error as small as desired and at the same time minimizing the cost of the survey. To determine the optimum sample size, a tolerable amount of error is prefixed and the smallest sample size is determined to keep the error within tolerable limit.

Non-Sampling Error. An error in sample estimates cannot be attributed to sampling fluctuations. It is experienced that the studies based on complete enumeration do not yield similar results in repeated enumerations. Such a discrepancy occurs due to many errors which are termed as non-sampling errors. Various sources of such errors which may be visualized are,

(*i*) *Observational error or response error* : If the observations are taken repeatedly on the same unit, the observed values generally differ or otherwise even the same respondent is asked the same question repeatedly, his response may differ.

(*ii*) Lack of preciseness of definition also adds to the non-sampling errors. For example, in judging the loss of crop due to a disease like wilt or rust, will be subject to error due to definitions of what we call severely diseased, moderately diseased and a low intensity of disease. Moreover this measure of intensity will vary from person to person depending on the maturity, qualifications and training, the person has.

(*iii*) Errors are also introduced in *editing and tabulation of data*. Since the population data are large, the chances of errors in complete enumeration are more compared to a sample data.

Some better ways of minimising the sampling errors are the choice of an appropriate sampling scheme, selecting a sample of optimum size and the use of standard techniques of estimation. Whereas the non-sampling errors can be minimized through superior management of survey or investigation, employing befitting personnel and by using modern computational aids.

Here we define a few more terms which will be used often in this chapter and elsewhere.

Parameter

Any population constant is called a parameter. For example, population mean (μ) and population variance (σ^2) etc. are parameters. To obtain a parameter value, the observations are taken on each and every unit of the population and a value of a constant pertaining to a characteristic is calculated from those observations. This constant value is termed as parameter. Such constant measure(s) of a population characterise a population.

Estimator

An estimator is a rule or method of estimating a population parameter. It is generally expressed as a function of sample variates. An estimator is itself a random variable.

Estimate

A particular value of an estimator obtained from a set of values of a random sample is known as estimate. As an explanation, generally few units are selected from a population and then observations are taken on these selected units. The constant for a characteristic is calculated from these sample observations. The constant, so obtained, is known as an estimate and stands for a population parameter. For example the sample mean $\bar{x}$ is an estimate of population mean μ and sample variance s^2 is an estimate of population variance σ^2.

Statistic

A statistic is a function of observable random variables and does not involve any unknown parameter. All the more, the function itself is a random variable. But a statistic is not necessarily an estimator of some population parameter. For example, $\frac{1}{n}\Sigma_i X_i$ ($i = 1, 2, \ldots, n$) is a statistic, student-*t* i.e. $\sqrt{n}(\bar{X} - \mu) / s$ is a statistic etc.

Selection with Replacement (SWR)

In this case, a unit is selected from a population with a known probability and the unit is returned to the population before the next selection is made (after recording its characteristic(s)). Thus, in this method at each selection, the population size remains constant and the probability at each selection or draw remains the same. Under this sampling plan, a unit has chances of being selected more than once. For example, a card is randomly drawn from a pack of cards and placed back in the pack, after noting its face value before the next card is drawn. As another example from an urn containing balls of different colours, a ball is drawn, its colour is noted and kept back in the urn before another ball is drawn. Such a sampling method is known as sampling with replacement. There are N^n possible samples of size n from a population of N units in case of sampling with replacement.

Sampling without Replacement (SWOR)

In this selection procedure, if a unit from a population of size N is selected, it is not returned to the population. Thus, for any subsequent selection, the population size is reduced by one. Obviously, at the time of the first selection, the population size is N and the probability of a unit being selected randomly is $1/N$; for the second unit to be randomly selected, the population size is $(N - 1)$ and the probability of selection of any one of the remaining sampling unit is $1/(N - 1)$, similarly at the third draw, the probability of selection is $1/(N - 2)$ and so on.

If we consider the limiting case that N is very large $N \to \infty$, the probabilities $\frac{1}{N}, \frac{1}{N-1}, \frac{1}{N-2}, \ldots$, become constant and in the limiting situation, the selection procedures with replacement and without replacement become equivalent. Whereas in the case of small population, the values $\frac{1}{N}, \frac{1}{N-1}, \frac{1}{N-2}, \ldots, \frac{1}{N-n+1}$ differ considerably. The sampling from small and large populations is generally expressed as sampling from finite and infinite populations respectively. There are $\binom{N}{n}$ possible samples, in case of sampling without replacement.

Size of a Sample

The size of a sample is the number of sampling units which are selected from a population by a random method. The problem that arises is how to decide what should actually be the number of sampling units to be selected from a population. As a matter of fact, the sample size depends on a number of consideration which are as follows:

1. The purpose for which the sample is drawn.
2. The type of population from which the sample is to be drawn. That is, if the sampling units constituting the population are highly variable, then a large sample is required and conversely, if the population comprises of less variable units, then a small sample is good enough. For a perfectly homogeneous population, a single unit is sufficient to get the correct results for the whole population. For example, the blood of a person is perfectly homogeneous and hence a drop of blood taken for investigation gives the true picture of blood constitution in the body.
3. Availability of technical people or equipment needed.
4. Resources allotted for the study in terms of time and money.
5. Precision required: If we want to detect very minute differences, most probably a

large sample will be required and vice-versa. The mathematical formula for determining sample size is as given below.

$$d = u_R \frac{\hat{s}_x}{\sqrt{n}} \qquad ...(7.1)$$

or

$$n = \frac{(u_R \hat{s}_x)^2}{d^2} \qquad ...(7.1.1)$$

where d is the precision required to detect the differences to the extent of d; u_R—the value of statistic for the required level of reliability R, which is generally in terms of probability. The value of u_R is obtained from the table of the probability distribution which the data follow. For example, if the data are selected from a normal distribution, then for a 95 per cent level of confidence $u_R = 1.96$ and $\hat{s}_x$ – the standard deviation of x. Its value is substituted from experience or is based on the information obtained from some earlier study.

From (7.1.1) it is evident that if d is small i.e., greater precision is required, we will have to select a large sample. Also, if $\hat{s}_x$ is large, n is to be large. Moreover, as the level of reliability increases, n also increases.

SAMPLING METHODS

In the selection of a sample, always the effort is to make the sample a true representative of the population. A large number of schemes have been worked out to achieve this objective. In general, we do probability sampling which is free from human bias. But in some situations, judgement sampling or purposive sampling is preferred to probability sampling. For example, if we want a sample of persons who are suffering from cancer, we have to select cancer patients who happen to come to the hospital(s). But, in general, probability sampling is in use, which enables the investigator to control sampling errors and avoid human bias. Probability sampling scheme leads to two types of samples: (*i*) Unrestricted random samples, (*ii*) Restricted random samples.

UNRESTRICTED RANDOM SAMPLING

If from a population, selection of sampling units is done in such a manner that each and every unit in the population has the same probability (chance) of being selected, such a probability sampling plan is called random sampling. Suppose there are N sampling units in a population, the probability of selection of any unit is $1/N$.

Simple Random Sampling (SRS)

In this type of sampling, n units from a population of N units are selected, without replacement, in such a way that the probability of selection of any one sample, out of $\binom{N}{n}$ possible samples is same i.e. $1\Big/\binom{N}{n}$. In practice, the units are drawn one by one from the population numbered from 0 to (N – 1). This process gives an equal chance of being selected to all units not previously selected. A random number table is always helpful in selecting a simple random sample.

Method of Selection

A random sample may be selected either by drawing the chits or by the use of random numbers. The *chit method* is a random method and is subjected to many human biases as people can identify chits in many ways. The Roulette wheel is another device for drawing numbers randomly. It is more prevalent in lotteries. Two type is used in Indian subcontinent. But the best of all is the use of random numbers given by Fisher and Yates – known as Fisher and Yates random numbers. The random number table is also given by Tippett. This is known as Tippett's random number table. But Fisher and Yates random number tables are more popular. Which random number tables one uses, does not matter in any way. For selecting a random sample from a population of size N, each sampling unit is numbered from 0 to $(N-1)$. If N is a two-digit figure, the units can be numbered as 00, 01, 02, ... up to the maximum of 98. In case N is a three-digit figure, the units can be numbered as 000, 001, 002, ... up to the maximum of 998 and so on. In this way, the list of serially numbered sampling units is known as the *sampling frame.* Sometimes, a sampling frame is a map showing the position of sampling units with identification marks. Once the sampling frame is ready, a sample of size n can be selected in the following manner. Let N be a d-digit number. Make use of a d-digit random number table. Now read numbers one by one from the random number table. If this observed number, say K, is less than or equal to $(N-1)$, then select Kth unit. If the observed number is equal to N, select the unit at serial number 00. In case, K is greater than N, ($K > N$), divide K by N and get the remainder 'R'. Now the Rth unit is selected. This process continues till n sampling units are selected.

The sample may be selected with replacement or without replacement. In the case of sampling with replacement, a number occurring more than once is accepted. A unit is repeated as many times as a random number occurs. But in the case of sampling without replacement, if a random number directly or by way of a remainder occurs more than once is omitted at any subsequent stage. In the above selection procedure numbering of units from 00 onwards and making use of remainders have an advantage, as no random number is being wasted during the selection procedure. This saves time and labour.

To explain the selection procedure further consider an example where a population consists of 18 units and a sample of size 5 is to be selected from this population.

Since 18 is a two-digit figure, units are numbered as 00, 01, ..., 17. Five random numbers are obtained from a two digit random number table.

They are as given below:

65, 43, 62, 54, 46.

On dividing 65 by 18, the remainder is 11, hence select the unit on serial No. 11. Similarly dividing 43, 62, 54 and 46 by 18, the respective remainders are 7, 8, 0 and 10. Hence, select units at serial numbers, 11, 07, 08, 00 and 10 and these selected units constitute the sample.

ESTIMATION OF POPULATION PARAMETERS

Let $X_1, X_2, ..., X_n$ be a random sample of size n from a population of N units and $x_1, x_2, ..., x_n$ be the corresponding observed values. The values of the known parameter(s) should be estimated from the set of these sample observations. These estimates are often single valued which are known as point estimates. Also, many times an interval is to be estimated in which the parameter is expected to lie with a certain level of confidence. Here we will not pursue the estimation theory and hence the formulae for sample mean, sample variance, etc. are given directly.

Some properties of estimates are also discussed in this chapter. Formulae are presented in terms of x_i (i = 1, 2, ... n), the actual observed value corresponding to X_i.

Formulae for Mean and Variance

Let $U_1, U_2, ..., U_N$ be N population units. A random sample of n units is selected. Suppose the observations on the sampled units are $x_1, x_2, ..., x_n$. The sample mean,

$$\bar{x} = \frac{x_1 + x_2 + ... + x_n}{n} \quad ...(7.2)$$

$$= \frac{1}{n} \sum_i x_i \quad ...(7.2.1)$$

for i = 1, 2, ..., n.

The sample variance,

$$s^2 = \frac{1}{(n-1)} \sum_i (x_i - \bar{x})^2 \quad ...(7.3)$$

$$= \frac{1}{(n-1)} \{\Sigma x_i^2 - n\bar{x}^2\} \quad ...(7.3.1)$$

$$= \frac{1}{(n-1)} \left\{ \sum_i x_i^2 - \frac{\left(\sum_i x_i\right)^2}{n} \right\} \quad ...(7.3.2)$$

Let the population mean be μ and variance be σ^2. $\bar{x}$ is an estimated value of μ and s^2 is an estimated value of σ^2. Formulae for μ and σ^2 are given by (3.1) and (4.8).

Now, we define a special term S^2, which is slightly different from σ^2 and is given as,

$$S^2 = \frac{1}{(N-1)} \sum_i (X_i - \mu)^2 \quad ...(7.4)$$

$$= \frac{1}{(N-1)} \left\{ \sum_i X_i^2 - N\mu^2 \right\} \quad ...(7.4.1)$$

where i = 1, 2, ..., N.

PROPERTIES OF ESTIMATES

Unbiasedness An estimate is said to be unbiased if its expected value is equal to its parameter value. For example, if $\bar{x}$ is an estimate of μ, $\bar{x}$ will be an unbiased estimate if and only if

$$E(\bar{x}) = \mu \quad ...(7.5)$$

The expectation may well be understood with this example. If from a population, we take all possible samples of size n and take the mean of all samples, the mean of the estimates is known as the expected value. It can theoretically be proved that $\bar{x}$ is an unbiased estimate of μ. In formula (7.3) for s^2, the divisor is $(n-1)$ instead of n. The reason for this is that using the divisor $(n - 1)$ makes s^2 an unbiased estimate of S^2, i.e.,

$$E(s^2) = S^2 \qquad ...(7.6)$$

Mathematical proofs are avoided in this book. Hence, the above conjecture of unbiasedness will be shown through an example.

***Example* 7.1.** A population of five units has the observations

7, 6, 8, 4, 10

Random samples of three units are drawn such that no unit is repeated in a sample and the order of selection does not matter. Out of the 5 units, there can be 10 samples each consisting of 3 units.

Possible samples, their means and variances are given in the following table.

Sample Nos.	1	2	3	4	5
Observations	7, 6, 8	7, 6, 4	7, 6, 10	7, 8, 4	7, 8, 10
$\bar{x}$	7	17/3	23/3	19/3	25/3
s^2	1	7/3	13/3	13/3	7/3
	6	7	8	9	10
	7, 4, 10	6, 8, 4	6, 8, 10	6, 4, 10	8, 4, 10
	7	6	8	20/3	22/3
	9	4	4	28/3	28/3

$$\text{Mean of } \bar{x}\text{'s} = \frac{1}{10}\left(7+\frac{17}{3}+\frac{23}{3}+\frac{19}{3}+\frac{25}{3}+7+6+8+\frac{20}{3}+\frac{22}{3}\right)$$

$$= \frac{210}{30} = 7$$

Similarly, mean of s^2, $\bar{s}^2 = \frac{50}{10} = 5.0$

Population mean $\mu = \frac{35}{5} = 7$

and variance

$$S^2 = \frac{1}{4}\{(7-7)^2+(6-7)^2+(8-7)^2+(4-7)^2+(10-7)^2\}$$

$$= \frac{20}{4} = 5.0$$

The above calculations verify the statement that the sample mean is an unbiased estimate of population mean whereas, s^2 is an unbiased estimate of S^2.

Simple Consistency

The notion of consistency is mainly concerned with infinite population. If T_n is an estimator of a parameter θ where T_n is based on a random sample $X_1, X_2 ..., X_n$ such that $T_n = t_n(X_1, X_2, ... X_n)$ then the sequence $\{T_n\}$ is said to be a consistent estimator of θ if for every $\varepsilon > 0$, the following condition holds:

$$\lim_{n\to\infty} P\{\theta - \varepsilon < T_n < \theta + \varepsilon\} = 1 \qquad ...(7.7)$$

or $$\lim_{n \to \infty} P\{|T_n - \theta| > \varepsilon\} = 0 \qquad ...(7.7.1)$$

Mean Squared Error (M.S.E.)

If $T_n = t_n (X_1, X_2. ......, X_n)$ be an estimator of a parameter θ, then $E\{(T_n - \theta)^2\}$ is said to be the mean-squared error of the estimator T_n. The sequence of estimators $\{T_n\}$ is said to be a *mean squared error consistency* if the following condition holds

$$\lim_{n \to \infty} E\{(T_n - \theta)^2\} = 0 \qquad ...(7.8)$$

Note : When the observed values $x_1, x_2, ...x_n$ for $X_1, X_2, ..., X_n$ are substituted in the estimator, we get the estimated value.

Standard Error (S.E.)

Standard deviation has been discussed in Chapter 4 as a measure of variability. Another measure is standard error, which is the standard deviation of the sampling distribution of an estimator. The idea is that if we draw a number of repeated samples of fixed size n from a population having a mean μ and variance σ^2, each sample mean, say $\bar{x}$, will have a different value. Here $\bar{x}$ itself is a random variable and hence it has a distribution. The standard deviation of $\bar{x}$ is called *standard error.* It has been proved that the standard error '$\sigma_{\bar{x}}$' of the mean $\bar{x}$ based on a sample of size n is,

$$\sigma_{\bar{x}} = \frac{\sigma}{\sqrt{n}} \qquad ...(7.9)$$

From formula (7.9), it is obvious that the larger the sample size, the smaller the standard error and vice-versa. The advantage of considering standard error instead of a standard deviation is that this measure is not influenced by the extreme values present in a population under consideration. Moreover, it upholds all the virtues of standard deviation.

In practice we avoid studying or surveying the whole population. The process of drawing repeated samples is still more cumbersome. Hence, in reality neither we use σ to calculate the standard error of $\bar{x}$ nor we take more than one sample. As a matter of fact, what we do is, that we select only one sample, find its standard deviation s and use the following formula to find out the standard error of $\bar{x}$ i.e.,

$$\text{S.E.}(\bar{x}) = \frac{s}{\sqrt{n}} \qquad ....(7.10)$$

Standard error is commonly used in testing of hypothesis and interval estimation. Many distributions, which are originally not normally distributed, have been taken as normal by considering the distribution of mean $\bar{x}$ for a large n. This result follows from a most celebrated theorem known as *central limit theorem.* This theorem has been stated below.

CENTRAL LIMIT THEOREM

If $X_1, X_2, ..., X_n$ are n identically and independently distributed random variables with mean $\bar{X}_n$ and variance σ_x^2, the standardized variable $\{\bar{X}_n - E(\bar{X}_n)\}/\frac{\sigma_x}{\sqrt{n}}$ approaches a standard normal distribution as n approaches infinity.

Remark. The standard error may be considered as the key to the sampling theory.

Standard Error of Mean

Suppose a simple random sample of size n is drawn from a normal population of N units. The variance of the sample mean is,

$$V(\bar{x}) = \left(\frac{1}{n} - \frac{1}{N}\right)S^2 \quad \text{...(7.11)}$$

$$= \frac{N-n}{N} \cdot \frac{S^2}{n} \quad \text{...(7.11.1)}$$

An unbiased estimate of $V(\bar{x})$ is

$$s_{\bar{x}}^2 = \left(\frac{1}{n} - \frac{1}{N}\right)s^2 \quad \text{...(7.12)}$$

where s^2 is given by (7.3). If $1/N$ is negligible, we obtain

$$s_{\bar{x}}^2 = \frac{s^2}{n} \quad \text{...(7.13)}$$

or

$$s_{\bar{x}} = \frac{s}{\sqrt{n}} \quad \text{...(7.13.1)}$$

Finite Population Correction (FPC)

The quantity $\left(\frac{N-n}{N}\right)$ appears in (7.11.1) and other formulae only if N is finite. In case N is large (tending to infinity), the quantity $\left(\frac{N-n}{N}\right) = \left(1 - \frac{n}{N}\right)$ reduces to 1 in the limiting case since n/N becomes negligible. The quantity n/N is known as the *sampling fraction*. Though there is no rule governing the value n/N to be taken as small, even then as a tradition, n/N is taken as negligible if its value is equal to or less than 0.05 $\left(\frac{n}{N} \le 0.05\right)$. In this situation, the factor $\left(\frac{N-n}{N}\right)$ disappears from the formulae.

Often we estimate population total instead of population mean. Let $\hat{X}$ be the estimate of population total $X = \sum_{i=1}^{N} x_i$. The formula for $\hat{X}$ is,

$$\hat{X} = N\bar{x} \quad \text{...(7.14)}$$

The variance of $\hat{X}$ is given by the formula,

$$V(\hat{X}) = N^2 V(\bar{x}) \quad \text{...(7.15)}$$

$$= N^2\left(\frac{1}{n} - \frac{1}{N}\right)S^2 \quad \text{...(7.16)}$$

$$= N\left(\frac{N-n}{n}\right)S^2 \quad \text{...(7.16.1)}$$

The estimate of $V(\hat{X})$ is obtained when we replace S^2 by its unbiased estimate s^2.

Thus the estimated variance of $\hat{X}$ is,

$$S_{\hat{x}}^2 = N\left(\frac{N-n}{n}\right)s^2 \qquad ...(7.17)$$

Mean and Variance for Proportions

In many studies, the investigators want to know the proportions of units belonging to either of the two categories. For example, the number of people in favour of a plan and the number against it, the proportion of people in a specified area suffering from leprosy or the proportion of defective items produced in a factory etc. In such type of studies observations are not based on measurements but on the number in the two categories, classes or groups. Let the classes be c_1 and c_2. Let the units falling in class c_1 be N_1 and in class c_2 be N_2, out of the total number of units N. Also assume that P denotes the proportion of units in class c_1, i.e. $P = N_1/N$ and the proportion of units in class c_2 denoted by Q will be N_2/N. Since there are only two classes, any unit will belong to either of the classes and hence $P + Q = 1$. Instead of studying the whole population, let a simple random sample of size n be drawn and the study be made. Out of n, suppose n_1 units fall in c_1 and $n_2 = (n - n_1)$ units fall in c_2. Let the sample proportion in c_1 be denoted by p and in c_2 by q. Also suppose our observations are coded in the manner in which if an unit belongs to c_1, it is given the value 1 and if an unit belongs to c_2 it is given the value 0. The mean and variance for proportions in the case of population and in the case of sample are as given below.

Population	*Sample*
$\mu = \frac{1}{N}\sum_{i=1}^{N} x_i = \frac{N_1}{N} - P$ (7.18)	$\bar{x} = \frac{1}{n}\sum_{i=1}^{n} x_i = \frac{n_1}{n} = p$ ...(7.20)
Since $x_i = 1$ if $x_i \in c_1$ $= 0$ if $x_i \in c_2$	Since $x_i = 1$ if $x_i \in c_1$ $= 0$ if $x_i \in c_2$
or $N_1 = NP$ ...(7.18.1)	$n_1 = np$ ...(7.20.1)
$\sum_{i=1}^{N} x_i^2 = N_1 = NP$	$\sum_{i=1}^{n} x_i^2 = n_1 = np$
Hence, $S_p^2 = \frac{1}{N-1}\left\{\sum_{i-1}^{N} x_i^2 - N\mu^2\right\}$	Hence, $s_p^2 = \frac{1}{n-1}\left\{\sum_{i=1}^{n} x_i^2 - n\bar{x}^2\right\}$
$= \frac{1}{N-1}(NP - NP^2)$	$= \frac{1}{n-1}(np - np^2)$
$= \frac{N}{N-1}P(1-P)$	$= \frac{n}{n-1}p(1-p)$
$= \frac{N}{N-1}PQ$ ...(7.19)	$= \frac{n}{n-1}pq$ ...(7.21)

It is trivial to prove that p is an unbiased estimate of P.

Variance of p

$$V(p) = E(p-P)^2 = \frac{N-n}{N}.\frac{S_p^2}{n}$$

$$= \frac{N-n}{N}.\frac{N}{N-1}.\frac{PQ}{n} = \frac{N-n}{N-1}\frac{PQ}{n} \quad ...(7.22)$$

Taking the square root of $V(p)$, we get the standard error of p.

Estimated Value of N_1 and its Variance

Estimated value of total units in class c_1 is,

$$\hat{N}_1 = Np \quad ...(7.23)$$

Now the variance of $\hat{N}_1$ is given as,

$$V(\hat{N}_1) = V(Np) = N^2\, V(p)$$

$$= N^2.\frac{N-n}{N-1}\frac{PQ}{n} \quad ...(7.24)$$

Estimated variance of p is given as,

$$v(p) = v(\bar{x}) = \frac{N-n}{N}.\frac{s_p^2}{n}$$

$$= \frac{N-n}{N}.\frac{n}{n-1}.\frac{pq}{n} = \frac{N-n}{N(n-1)}.pq \quad ...(7.25)$$

If the sampling fraction n/N is negligible, then

$$v(p) = \frac{1}{n-1}pq \quad ...(7.25.1)$$

The square root of $v(p)$ gives the standard error of p.

***Example* 7.2.** A consignment of 2000 transistors was received by a manufacturing concern. The concerned person drew a random sample of 60 transistors from the lot and tested them to find the number of defective pieces. It was found that 7 transistors out of the 60 were out of order. In this case the estimated variance of p can be calculated as,

$$p = \frac{7}{60} \text{ and } q = 1 - \frac{7}{60} = \frac{53}{60}$$

In this case $\frac{n}{N} = \frac{60}{2000} = 0.03$, which is negligible. Hence, the estimated variance of p will be calculated from (7.25.1) i.e.

$$v(p) = \frac{1}{n-1}pq = \frac{1}{59}\times\frac{7}{60}\times\frac{53}{60} = 0.0017$$

whereas the standard deviation of p is equal to $\sqrt{0.0017}$, i.e. 0.0412.

RESTRICTED SAMPLING

Stratified Random Sampling

In the introductory part under the heading 'sampling methods', it has been mentioned that a sample is good, if it is a true representative of the population. The moment one starts identifying various sampling units, one is able to think of various sampling schemes. Stratified sampling is one of them. In this type of sampling plan, the whole population is divided into a number of homogeneous groups or *strata* on the basis of certain characteristic(s) of the sampling units. For example, a city is divided into groups according to wards. If the sampling unit is a household, then the households may be divided into homogeneous groups according to the income per family. In an opinion survey, persons may be divided into homogeneous groups according to their qualifications, age, sex, size of family etc. Each homogeneous group is known as *stratum*. From each stratum a random sample of required size is selected.

It is apparent from the preceding para that in this type of sampling plan, we need information about each and every sampling unit. If such prior information can be made available, stratified sampling proves to be very good. But generally such minute detail about each and every unit of a population is not available. Hence, the strata are based on some broad basis, e.g. different zones in a regional survey, nearby areas in a district serve as strata for estimation purposes. In short stratified sampling is suitable only when the population is known to have heterogeneity with regard to some factors and those factors are used for stratification. All the more, stratified sampling have the following advantages:

1. If the admissible error is given, we need a small sample resulting into a cut in the expenditure.
2. In the case where the cost of the survey is fixed, there is reduction in error.
3. It helps in determining the estimates for various groups, zones etc. i.e. for each stratum separately.
4. Stratified sampling is convenient from the organisation point of view. Linguistic zones are often formed and each zone serves as a stratum.
5. Sometimes various sampling schemes may be used to draw samples from different strata. But this creates problems in getting the overall estimates. Besides the above-mentioned advantages, many problems remain to be solved are:
   (*i*) What should be the criterion for stratification?
   (*ii*) How many strata can be formed?
   (*iii*) How does one find the points of demarcation between the strata?
   (*iv*) What should the sample size for each stratum be?
   (*v*) What should the method of sampling be for each stratum?
   (*vi*) How does one get the estimates from each stratum and how does one pool them to get the population estimates?

All the above points are dealt with briefly in this chapter taking them one by one.

Stratification and Estimation

(*i*) The variable or criterion for stratification depends on the purpose of the survey and the information available. As already indicated, strata are formed on the basis of administrative zones, socio-economic conditions or any other factor found suitable. Strata should be formed in such a way that they are as homogeneous as possible, especially in respect of the characteristic, factor or variable, which is likely to influence the results of the survey.

(*ii*) We should form as many strata as required so that they are homogeneous; in fact, more the number of strata, better the result. Some formulation has also been done to decide the number of strata. But keeping in view the requirements of this book, they have been kept out.

(*iii*) Points of demarcation of the strata should be clearcut so that no two strata overlap each other. For mathematical formulae, the readers are advised to read an advance book on sampling theory.

(*iv*) The problem of deciding the sample size for each stratum is known as the allocation problem. We know that the size of the sample directly influences the estimates. Hence, a sample of optimum size has to be chosen. Only formulae for optimum sample size are given in the following discussion.

(*v*) Generally, a random sample is drawn from each stratum. Any other sampling scheme, like selection of units with probability proportional to size (pps), may be adopted if the situation demands it.

(*vi*) Various formulae for mean and variance are given ahead, considering that a simple random sample is selected from each stratum.

First we have to clarify the notations which will commonly be used in all the formulae.

Population size → N units

Total number of strata → K

Size of the jth stratum → N_j for $j = 1, 2, ..., K$

such that $\sum_j N_j = N$

Sample size = n

Sample size in jth stratum = n_j

such that $\sum_j n_j = n$

Suppose x_{ij} denotes ith observation belonging to jth stratum.

We give formulae for means and variances.

The mean of the jth stratum, $$\overline{X}_j = \frac{1}{N_j}\sum_{i=1}^{N_j} x_{ij} \quad ...(7.26)$$

and its estimated mean, $$\overline{x}_j = \frac{1}{n_j}\sum_{i=1}^{n_j} x_{ij} \quad ...(7.27)$$

Variance for the jth stratum, $$S_j^2 = \frac{1}{N_j - 1}\sum_{i=1}^{N_j}(x_{ij} - \overline{X}_j)^2 \quad ...(7.28)$$

jth stratum sample variance, $$s_j^2 = \frac{1}{n_j - 1}\sum_{i=1}^{n_j}(x_{ij} - \overline{x}_j)^2 \quad ...(7.29)$$

Suppose μ is the population mean. An unbiased estimate of μ under stratified sampling is,

$$\overline{x}_{st} = \frac{1}{N}\sum_{j=1}^{k} N_j \overline{x}_j \quad ...(7.30)$$

Variance of stratified sample mean $\overline{x}_{st}$ is,

$$V(\overline{x}_{st}) = \frac{1}{N^2}\sum_{j=1}^{k} N_j(N_j - n_j)\frac{S_j^2}{n_j} \quad ...(7.31)$$

$$= \sum_{j=1}^{k} \frac{N_j^2}{N^2}\left(1-\frac{n_j}{N_j}\right)\frac{S_j^2}{n_j} \quad ...(7.31.1)$$

Putting $N_j / N = W_j$, we obtain

$$V(\overline{x}_{st}) = \sum_{j=1}^{k} W_j^2\left(1-\frac{n_j}{N_j}\right)\frac{S_j^2}{n_j} \quad ...(7.31.2)$$

If the sampling fraction n_j / N_j for each stratum is negligible, then

$$V(\overline{x}_{st}) = \sum_{j=1}^{k} \frac{W_j^2 S_j^2}{n_j} \quad ...(7.31.3)$$

Replacing S_j^2 by its estimate s_j^2, we get the estimate of $V(\overline{x}_{st})$, say $v(\overline{x}_{st})$. Thus,

$$v(\overline{x}_{st}) = \sum_{j=1}^{k} \frac{W_j^2 s_j^2}{n_j} \quad ...(7.32)$$

Mean and Variance for Proportions in Stratified Sampling

As in the case of simple random sampling, there are only two classes say c_1 and c_2. A unit under study falls in either of the classes. If it belongs to c_1; it receives the coded value 1 and if it belongs to the other class it receives the value 0. Let the number of units belonging to c_1 in the jth stratum be M_j and in the sample of size n_j from jth stratum, the number of units belonging to c_1 be m_j. Denoting the proportion of units in c_1 for the population, the jth stratum and sample from the jth stratum by P, P_j and p_j respectively, various formulae for means and variance are as follows:

$$P_j = \frac{M_j}{N_j} \text{ and } p_j = \frac{m_j}{n_j} \quad ...(7.33)$$

and

$$P = \Sigma_j \frac{N_j}{N} P_j = \Sigma_j W_j P_j \quad ...(7.34)$$

for $j = 1, 2, ..., k$.

The estimated proportion p_{st} under stratified sampling for the units belonging to c_1 is

$$p_{st} = \Sigma_j W_j p_j \quad ...(7.35)$$

and variance of p_{st} is,

$$V(p_{st}) = \frac{1}{N^2}\Sigma_j \frac{N_j^2(N_j - n_j)}{(N_j - 1)}\frac{P_j Q_j}{n_j} \quad ...(7.36)$$

where $Q_j = (1 - P_j)$.

If N_j is large enough to consider $1/N_j$ as negligible, formula for $V(p_{st})$ reduces to,

$$V(p_{st}) = \frac{1}{N^2}\Sigma_j N_j(N_j - n_j)\frac{P_jQ_j}{n_j} \qquad ...(7.36.1)$$

and if n_j/N_j is negligible,

$$V(p_{st}) = \Sigma_j W_j^2 \frac{P_jQ_j}{n_j} \qquad ...(7.36.2)$$

An unbiased estimate $v(p_{st})$ of V (p_{st}) is given as

$$v(p_{st}) = \frac{1}{N^2}\Sigma_j N_j \frac{(N_j - n_j)}{(n_j - 1)} p_j q_j \qquad ...(7.37)$$

Where $q_j = 1 - p_j$. When the sampling fraction n_j/N_j for each stratum is negligible, the formula for $v(p_{st})$ reduces to

$$v(p_{st}) = \Sigma_j W_j^2 \frac{p_j q_j}{(n_j - 1)} \qquad ...(7.37.1)$$

Allocation Problem

The problem of deciding the sample size in different strata is known as *allocation problem*. It is evident from the formula for variance of $\overline{x}_{st}$ that it depends on n_j. Hence the problem arises, what optimum value of n_j ($j = 1, 2, ..., k$) can be chosen out of n so that the variance is as small as possible. Two types of allocations are considered here: (*a*) proportional allocation and (*b*) optimum allocation.

(*a*) *Proportional Allocation* As its name indicates, proportional allocation means that we select a small sample from a small stratum and a large sample from a large stratum. The sample size in each stratum is fixed in such a way that for all the strata, the ratio n_j/N_j is equal to n/N, i.e.

$$\frac{n_j}{N_j} = \frac{n}{N} \qquad ...(7.38)$$

or

$$n_j = \frac{n}{N}N_j = nW_j \qquad ...(7.38.1)$$

Thus substituting the values of n_j and n_j/N_j as nW_j and n/N respectively in (7.31) through (7.31.3), we get

$$V(\overline{x}_{st}) = \left(1 - \frac{n}{N}\right)\Sigma_j \frac{W_jS_j^2}{n} \qquad ...(7.39)$$

In case the sampling fraction n/N is negligible,

$$V(\overline{x}_{st}) = \Sigma_j \frac{W_jS_j^2}{n} \qquad ...(7.39.1)$$

Proportional allocation is easy to apply because by simple arithmetic, one has to divide n into k parts such that $\frac{n_1}{N_1} = \frac{n_2}{N_2} = ... = \frac{n_k}{N_k} = \frac{n}{N}$.

(b) *Optimum Allocation* As discussed, variance of estimated mean depends on n_j which can arbitrarily be fixed. The cost of the survey also influences the variance of estimated mean and hence the cost factor is none the less important. The allocation problem is two-fold: (1) we attain maximum precision for the fixed cost of the survey and (2) we attain the desired degree of precision for the minimum cost. Thus the allocation of sample size in various strata, in accordance with these two objectives, is known as optimum allocation. Here we consider both these cases one by one.

It is easy to imagine that the cost of survey per sampling unit in different strata cannot be the same. That is, in one stratum the cost of transport may be different from the other. As far as crop cutting experiments are concerned, in one stratum the labour may be cheaper than the other. Hence it would not be wrong to fix the cost of the survey in each stratum differently. Let c_j be the cost per unit of survey in the jth stratum from which a sample of size n_j is stipulated. Also suppose c_0 as the overhead fixed cost of the survey. In this way the total cost c of the survey comes out to be

$$c = c_0 + \Sigma_j\ c_j\, n_j \quad \text{...(7.40)}$$

c_0 and c_j are beyond our control. Hence we will determine the optimum value of n_j which minimizes the variance of $\bar{x}_{st}$. For this, we use the method of Lagrange's multiplier λ. The function ϕ which is to be minimized is as follows. For ease, the variance $V(\bar{x}_{st})$ has been taken as in 7.31.3. Thus,

$$\phi = \Sigma_j \frac{W_j^2 S_j^2}{n_j} - \lambda(c - c_0 - \Sigma_j c_j n_j) \quad \text{...(7.41)}$$

Differentiating ϕ partially with respect to n_j and equating it to zero, we get the optimum value of n_j. For clarity a few steps are given here;

$$-\frac{W_j^2 S_j^2}{n_j^2} + \lambda c_j = 0$$

or
$$n_j = \frac{1}{\sqrt{\lambda}} \frac{W_j S_j}{\sqrt{c_j}} \quad \text{...(7.42)}$$

Since λ is an unknown quantity, it has to be determined in terms of known values. So we take the sum over all j's in (7.42) and thus obtain,

$$n = \frac{1}{\sqrt{\lambda}} \Sigma_j (W_j S_j / \sqrt{c_j})$$

or
$$\sqrt{\lambda} = \frac{1}{n} \Sigma_j (W_j S_j / \sqrt{c_j}) \quad \text{...(7.42.1)}$$

Substituting the value of $\sqrt{\lambda}$ we get the value of n_j as

$$n_j = n\, \frac{(W_j S_j / \sqrt{c_j})}{\Sigma_j (W_j S_j / \sqrt{c_j})} \quad \text{...(7.43)}$$

Formula (7.43) for n_j reveals that one must choose a large n_j if,

(i) n is large.

(ii) S_j is large, i.e. stratum is more heterogeneous.

(iii) c_j is small.

The result (7.43) was first given by Tchuprow (1923) which became popular only when Neyman in 1934 independently derived it. That is why such an allocation is known as *Neyman allocation.* On using the optimum value of n_j from (7.43) and putting it in (7.31.2), the variance of $\bar{x}_{st}$ under Neyman's allocation is given as,

$$V_{Ney}(\bar{x}_{st}) = \frac{1}{n}(\Sigma_j W_j S_j \sqrt{c_j})\left(\Sigma_j \frac{W_j S_j}{\sqrt{c_j}}\right) - \frac{1}{N}\Sigma_j W_j S_j^2 \quad ...(7.44)$$

In case c_j is the same for all the units, i.e., say $c_j = c$, the variance

$$V_{Ney}(\bar{x}_{st}) = \frac{1}{n}(\Sigma_j W_j S_j)^2 - \frac{1}{N}\Sigma_j W_j S_j^2 \quad ...(7.44.1)$$

Case 1 : When the cost of the survey is fixed. In this situation we obtain the value of n_j for each stratum so that $V(\bar{x}_{st})$ is minimum. Since c and c_0 are fixed quantities, we take $c_1 = c - c_0$. Therefore, from (7.40) we get,

$$c_1 = \Sigma_j \; c_j \, n_j \quad ...(7.45)$$

Now, substituting the optimum value of n_j from (7.43) in (7.45) we obtain the optimum sample size n in terms of c_1 as follows,

$$c_1 = \Sigma_j c_j n \frac{(W_j S_j / \sqrt{c_j})}{\Sigma_j (W_j S_j / \sqrt{c_j})}$$

or

$$n_{opt} = c_1 \frac{\Sigma_j (W_j S_j / \sqrt{c_j})}{\Sigma_j (W_j S_j \sqrt{c_j})} \quad ...(7.46)$$

Case 2 : If the variance $V(\bar{x}_{st})$ is fixed, and its value is V_0, then substituting the optimum value of n_j from (7.43) in (7.44), we obtain the optimum sample size n in terms of V_0 as follows:

$$n_{opt} = \frac{(\Sigma_j W_j S_j \sqrt{c_j})(\Sigma_j W_j S_j / \sqrt{c_j})}{V_0 + \frac{1}{N}\Sigma_j W_j S_j^2} \quad ...(7.47)$$

From the usage point of view, stratified sampling may be considered next to simple random sampling. The reasons for this are: increased precision, administrative convenience and many other reasons discussed in the running matter. It can easily be seen that variance of mean under random sampling is greater than the variance under proportional allocation in stratified sampling. Whereas out of the three, the variance of mean under Neyman allocation is minimum. These results can be written as

$$V_{ran} \geq V_{prop} \geq V_{Ney} \quad ...(7.48)$$

A lot of research work has been done on stratified sampling and for further details, readers are advised to study an advanced book on the theory of sampling.

SYSTEMATIC SAMPLING

Often we have to obtain the information from cards or registers which are in serial order. Sometimes we might need the sample of trees from a forest or houses in a city. In such a case, a sampling plan known as *systematic sampling* often works better than the simple random sampling. In order to draw a systematic sample of size n, divide the population into n equal parts. Supposing each part to consist of k units, draw a random number from 1 to k. Let the selected number be j. Then select j, $(j + k)$, $(j + 2k)$,..., $(j + \overline{n-1}\,k)$-th units. This constitutes a systematic sample of size n. For example, if there are 100 units in a population serially numbered from 1 to 100 and we want to draw a sample of 5 units. Draw a random number from 1 to 20 since $k = 20$ and let the selected number be 7, *i.e.* $j = 7$. Then select units in serial numbers 7, 27, 47, 67 and 87. These units constitute a systematic sample of 5 units. Further details will be given later.

Systematic sample has some advantages as well as disadvantages. Some of the advantages are:

1. The method of selection is very simple and is not very expensive.
2. The sample is evenly distributed over the whole population and hence all contiguous parts of the population are represented in the sample.
3. It has an advantage over other sampling plans because it has managerial control of field work.

The disadvantages are:

1. If the variation in units is periodic *i.e.,* the units at regular intervals are correlated, then the sample becomes highly biased. For example, if the houses are in blocks and if a corner house is selected at random then all other houses selected in the sample will be corner ones and this definitely gives a biased sample.
2. No single reliable formula for estimating standard error of sample mean is available. A formula is good enough, if the population is of the type it has been assumed to be. This is, of course, a great drawback.

Methods of Selection

Linear Systematic Sampling Though this selection procedure has already been given in the general discussion briefly, we will discuss it in detail now. Suppose a population consists of N units and from this a systematic sample of n units is to be selected. Also, assume that N is a multiple of n, i.e., let $N = nk$. The procedure is to select a random number, say j, such that $1 \leq j \leq k$ and then select the jth and every subsequent $j+k, j+2k,...,j+\overline{n-1}\,k$ th positional units. This sampling plan is known as *linear systematic sampling.* But the situation that N is a multiple of n does not always hold. In this situation it is just possible that we get a sample of $(n - 1)$ units instead of n. For example, if $N = 13$ and $n = 4$, then k has to be taken as 4. Now select a random number from 1 to 4, say it is 3. Then, the remaining three units to be selected are at positions 7, 11, 15. There is no unit in the population at serial number 15. Hence, we can select only a sample of size 3 in this situation. To cope with this situation, a sampling plan known as circular systematic sampling is used.

Circular Systematic Sampling This is applied when $N \neq nk$. This type of sampling was first used by D.B. Lahri (1952) in national sample surveys. Here we take N/n as k by rounding of N/n to the nearest integer. Select a random number from 1 to N. Let this number be m. Now select every $(m + jk)$ th unit when $m + jk < N$ and select every $(m + jk - N)$ th unit when $m + jk > N$ putting $j = 1, 2, 3, \ldots$ till n units are selected. By this method we always get a sample of size n. Suppose for the example given in the previous section with $N = 13$, $n = 4$ and $k = 3$, the randomly selected number from 1 to 13 is 8 and later the 11th, 1st, 4th and 7th units are selected. When $N = nk$, the linear and circular systematic plans become identical. For example, if $N = 12$, $n = 4$, $k = 3$ and the selected unit from 1 to 3 is 3 and from 1 to 12 is either of the numbers 3, 6, 9 and 12, then, under both the sampling schemes, the selected units will be those bearing serial numbers 3, 6, 9 and 12. Also, if the selected number from 1 to 3 is 2 and from 1 to 12 is any one of the 2, 5, 8 or 11, the selected units will be those bearing the serial numbers 2, 5, 8 and 11. This example shows the equivalence between two selection plans.

Mean and Variance of Systematic Sampling Let the observation on selected units be $x_1, x_2, \ldots, x_n$. Then the sample mean $\bar{x}_{sy}$ of the systematic sample is

$$\bar{x}_{sy} = \frac{1}{n}\Sigma_i x_i \qquad \ldots(7.49)$$

for $i = 1, 2, \ldots, n$ and variance of $\bar{x}_{sy}$ when $N = nk$ is

$$V(\bar{x}_{sy}) = \frac{N-1}{N}S^2 - \frac{k(n-1)}{N}S^2_{wsy} \qquad \ldots(7.50)$$

As we have noticed that for every random number selected from 1 to k, a separate systematic sample will be obtained. Let x_{ij} represent the i th observation in the jth systematic sample which is obtained when a random number $j = 1, 2, \ldots\, k$ is selected. Thus, in (7.50), the variance between systematic samples is,

$$S^2 = \frac{1}{N-1}\Sigma_j\Sigma_i(x_{ij} - \mu)^2 \qquad \ldots(7.51)$$

for $j = 1, 2, \ldots k$; and $i = 1, 2, \ldots n$.

Also,
$$\frac{N-1}{N}S^2 = \sigma^2 \qquad \ldots(7.52)$$

and the variance S^2_{wsy} within the systematic sample is,

$$S^2_{wsy} = \frac{1}{k(n-1)}\Sigma_j\Sigma_i(x_{ij} - \bar{x}_j)^2 \qquad \ldots(7.53)$$

and
$$\frac{k(n-1)}{N}S^2_{wsy} = \frac{1}{N}\Sigma_j\Sigma_i(x_{ij} - \bar{x}_j)^2 = \sigma^2_w \qquad \ldots(7.54)$$

Thus, formula (7.50) reduces to,

$$V(\bar{x}_{sy}) = (\sigma^2 - \sigma^2_w) \qquad \ldots(7.55)$$

σ^2, the population variance is a constant quantity and σ_w^2 is the variance within the systematic sample which is being subtracted from σ^2 to get $V(\overline{x}_{sy})$. Hence, the greater the heterogeneity among units within the sample, the better it is. We would like to remind readers that if the units at equal intervals are more alike, then the systematic sample is not a good sampling scheme.

Another point that may strike the mind is that systematic sampling in some sense resembles stratified sampling where k units form a stratum. But it differs widely in the sense that no independent sample is selected from each of the k units, which may be considered a stratum of contiguous units. Other arguments are trivial to think of. Hence systematic sampling can be used when no cyclic trend is evident.

CLUSTER SAMPLING

In the discussion so far we have been considering the smallest well-identifiable unit of the population known as elementary unit. The observations have been taken on these elementary units. But in some cases it is not possible to take a sample of these elementary units. Even if it is possible it is very costly, time consuming, less precise and inconspicuous. Various reasons, that cause problems in the selection of a sample of elementary units, are elucidated below:

(*i*) The sampling frame may not be available or may be too costly in terms of money, time and labour. For example, a list of fields and their owners in a state, a list of households in a big city etc.

(*ii*) The elementary units are situated far apart from one another and if selected it consumes a lot of time and money to survey them. If we select farmers in a state, the selected farmers will generally be at long distances. This, of course, increases the cost of the survey.

(*iii*) The elementary units may not be well identifiable and easily locatable. For instance, the population consisting of shepherds, the animals of a particular species in the forests of a country etc. In general, the migratory elementary units of a population are not easily identifiable and locatable.

Thus, to cope with the above problems, in sampling of elementary units, a sampling plan known as *cluster sampling* or *area sampling* yields satisfactory results. In cluster sampling, groups of elementary units are formed generally on location, class or area basis. When the whole of area constituting the population is divided into smaller area segments and these segments are being sampled, then it is called area sampling, otherwise cluster sampling. The clusters or segments are called the *primary units*. For example, cluster may be consisting of all households in a ward and hence there are as many clusters as the number of wards in a city. In area sampling it is easy to select a village as a whole rather than the individual farms of a district. Hence, all the farms in a village may be thought of as a cluster. Certain precautions should necessarily be taken for cluster sampling which are as given below:

(*i*) Each elementary unit should belong to one and only one cluster, area or segment.

(*ii*) The clusters constituting the population should include each and every elementary unit belonging to the population.

(*iii*) All clusters should be distinct, meaning that there should neither be overlapping nor omission of units.

Generally a simple random sample of clusters is selected from a population. Here we have considered the case when all clusters consist of unequal numbers of elementary units. First we define various notations and then give the formulae for various estimates.

Number of clusters = N

Number of elementary units in the jth cluster = M_j

Number of elementary units in the population, $M = \Sigma_j M_j$ where $j = 1, 2, ..., N$.

Sample size = n

Number of elementary units in the sample = $\Sigma_j M_j$ where $j = 1, 2, ..., n$.

Let x_{ij} denote the i th observation in the jth cluster.

Thus, the mean of jth cluster,

$$\bar{x}_j = \frac{1}{M_j}\sum_{i=1}^{M_j} x_{ij} \qquad ...(7.56)$$

for $j = 1, 2, ..., N$ and $i = 1, 2, ..., M_j$ and population mean.

$$\bar{X}_c = \Sigma_j \Sigma_i x_{ij} / \Sigma_j M_j \qquad ...(7.57)$$

$$= \frac{1}{M}\Sigma_j M_j \bar{x}_j \qquad ...(7.57.1)$$

where $M = \Sigma_j M_j$ for $j = 1, 2, ..., N$.

An estimate $\bar{x}_c$ of population mean $\bar{X}_c$ which is unbiased but not consistent is given as,

$$\bar{x}_c = \frac{1}{n}\Sigma_j M_j \bar{x}_j / \bar{M} \qquad ...(7.58)$$

where $\bar{M} = \frac{M}{N}$.

Let S_b^2 and S_w^2 denote the variance between and within clusters respectively. Now the population variance.

$$\sigma^2 = \frac{1}{NM-1}\Sigma_j \Sigma_i (x_{ij} - \bar{X}_c)^2 \qquad ...(7.59)$$

$$S_b^2 = \frac{1}{N-1}\Sigma_j (\bar{x}_j - \bar{X}_c)^2 \qquad ...(7.60)$$

and

$$S_w^2 = \frac{1}{N(M-1)}\Sigma_j \Sigma_i (x_{ij} - \bar{x}_j)^2 \qquad ...(7.61)$$

An unbiased estimate of the variance of $\bar{x}_c$ is given as,

$$v(\bar{x}_c) = \frac{N-n}{Nn} S_b^2 \qquad ...(7.62)$$

where $$S_b^2 = \frac{1}{n-1}\Sigma_j(M_j\bar{x}_j - \bar{x}_c)^2; \quad j = 1, 2, ..., n.$$

Also, an estimate of S_w^2 is,

$$S_w^2 = \frac{1}{n(M-1)}\Sigma_j\Sigma_i(x_{ij} - \bar{x}_j)^2 \quad ...(7.63)$$

where $j = 1, 2, ..., n$ and $i = 1, 2, ..., M_j$.

An intuition of a statistician came true when the variation within the cluster was proved less than the variation between clusters, i.e., $S_w^2 \leq S_b^2$ because the units within a cluster are more homogeneous than the units in different clusters.

Efficiency The *information* of a sampling design is equal to inverse of its variance and the *efficiency* of a sampling design, as compared to the other one, is the ratio of the inverse of their variances. If the variance of two sampling designs are V_1 and V_2 respectively, then the efficiency of sampling design-1 as compared to sampling design-2 is,

$$E_{12} = \frac{1/V_1}{1/V_2} = \frac{V_2}{V_1} \quad ...(7.64)$$

Using the above approach, the efficiency of cluster sampling as compared to random sampling is,

$$E = \frac{\frac{NM - nM}{NM}\frac{S^2}{nM}}{\frac{N-n}{N}\frac{S_b^2}{n}} \quad ...(7.65)$$

$$= \frac{S^2}{MS_b^2} \quad ...(7.65.1)$$

Likewise, we can find the efficiency of a design as compared to any other design. Moreover, from (7.65.1) it is apparent that the efficiency of cluster sampling increases as the cluster size decreases. Hence one should take clusters of as small size as possible, provided the set norms are not vitiated. Another point worth noting is that, in most respects, cluster sampling resembles stratified sampling. The salient difference is that in stratified sampling we take a sample from each stratum (cluster) whereas in cluster sampling all the sampling units are included. In large scale surveys, cluster sampling is often helpful and efficient.

MULTISTAGE SAMPLING

As already pointed out, a survey has certain limitations, mainly budget and time. Hence to survey too many elementary units is often not possible. In stratified sampling, a sample of optimum size is drawn from each stratum. In cluster sampling, a sample of clusters is selected in which each and every elementary unit of the selected clusters has to be studied. This is also costly in terms of time and money. In case the selected units (clusters) are homogeneous, i.e., the elements of the selected units give same response, it is advisable not to study the whole cluster or unit as it increases the cost and the time of the survey. Hence, if the cluster is homogeneous and basically each unit in the population is divisible into a number of smaller units or elements, a new sampling scheme known as multistage sampling or sub-sampling is extremely helpful. When large scale surveys on district, state or national level are to be conducted, it is one of the most suitable sampling plan. For example, if the government or some other agency wants to collect information about the tax payer households in a city, it is better to select a sample of various localities (wards) before selecting a sample of households from these selected localities. In this way, the localities are *first stage units* and households are *second stage units.* Such a sampling procedure on the whole is known as *two-stage sampling.* Again if a survey is conducted to estimate the crop production of a district, it is preferable to select villages as *first stage units,* sample of farms in selected villages as *second stage units,* and select a sample of plots from each selected farms as *third stage units.* In this case, the selection procedure is known as *three-stage sampling.* Selection procedure may be extended to any number of stages. Hence the sampling in various stages in general is known as *multi-stage sampling.*

Once the sampling has been completed in various stages and the observations are taken, we have to find out the mean and the variance. In this chapter, we confine the formulae only to two-stage sampling. These formulae may be extended to more than two-stage sampling. In this type of sampling on any subsequent stage, preceding stage units are just like strata from which a random sample is drawn. So the extension of formulae is trivial. Here we give formulae where the first stage units are of unequal size. In theory, we often come across the formulae where first stage units are taken to be of equal size but we take it as unconceivable thinking. Moreover, even if this happens, the formulae given here are easily applicable but the other way round it is not possible. First, we explain the notations and then give the formulae for mean and variance.

Total number of first stage units = N

Sample size of first stage units = n

Number of second stage units in i th first stage unit = M_i

Number of second stage units in the sample from ith first stage unit = m_i

Observation on the jth second stage unit belonging to ith first stage unit = x_{ij}

Mean of the ith first stage unit on the basis of per second stage unit = $\overline{X}_i$

The estimate of $\overline{X}_i = \overline{x}_i$

Overall sample mean on the basis of each second-stage unit when subsampling has been done = $\overline{x}_s$.

Total number of second stage units,

$$M = \Sigma_i M_i \text{ for } i = 1, 2, ..., N$$

Total number of second stage units in the sample,

$$m = \Sigma_i m_i \text{ for } i = 1, 2, ..., n$$

The first stage unit mean,

$$\overline{X}_i = \frac{1}{M_i}\Sigma_j x_{ij} \text{ for } j = 1, 2, ..., M_i \quad ...(7.66)$$

and its estimated mean,

$$\overline{x}_i = \frac{1}{m_i}\Sigma_j x_{ij} \qquad \text{for } j = 1, 2, ..., m_i \quad ...(7.67)$$

The population mean per second stage unit,

$$\overline{X}_s = \Sigma_i M_i \overline{X}_i / \Sigma_i M_i \qquad \text{for } i = 1, 2, ...N \qquad ...(7.68)$$

$$= \Sigma_i M_i \overline{X}_i / N\overline{M} \qquad ...(7.68.1)$$

where $\overline{M} = \frac{1}{N}\Sigma_i M_i$

or $$\Sigma_i M_i = N\overline{M} \qquad ...(7.69)$$

An unbiased estimate of $\overline{X}_s$ *i.e.* $\overline{x}_s$ is given as

$$\overline{x}_s = \frac{1}{n\overline{M}}\Sigma_i M_i \overline{x}_i \qquad ...(7.70)$$

The estimated variance of $\overline{x}_s$,

$$v(\overline{x}_s) = \left(\frac{1}{n} - \frac{1}{N}\right) S_b^2 + \frac{1}{nN}\Sigma_i \frac{M_i^2}{\overline{M}^2}\left(\frac{1}{m_i} - \frac{1}{M_i}\right) S_{wi}^2 \qquad ...(7.71)$$

for $i = 1, 2, ..., n,$ where

$$S_b^2 = \frac{1}{n-1}\Sigma_i\left(\frac{M_i}{M}\overline{x}_i - \overline{x}_s\right)^2 \qquad ...(7.72)$$

and $$S_{wi}^2 = \frac{1}{m_i - 1}\Sigma_i (x_{ij} - \overline{x}_i)^2 \qquad ...(7.73)$$

Here it is remarked, without proof, that the two-stage sampling design will generally be found to be less efficient than single stage sampling unless the correlation between the second stage units within a first stage unit is highly negative. But in some cases, particularly in field surveys, two or multistage sampling is still desirable keeping in view the cost and operational convenience of the survey. Hence, while choosing this sampling design, a balance between efficiency and operational cost must be maintained.

SAMPLING OF ACCOUNTING INFORMATION

It has already been mentioned in the beginning that, the moment, we start identifying the sampling units of a population to be sampled, we are worried about the sampling procedure most suited for it. Sampling of accounting records, falls in this category and hence a special consideration has to be made for it. As we know, accounting records are mostly available either in the form of invoices, or in the ledgers. Registers are generally used for inventories. Now the question arises, which method of sampling will yield good results ? No new method is given for the sampling of accounting records. Commonly used sampling methods are:

(*i*) Judgement sampling.

(*ii*) Systematic sampling.

(*iii*) Random sampling.

Judgement Sampling

It is one of the most used methods for checking accounting records by auditors. Under this approach, the auditor picks up an invoice as he likes and checks it. It is convenient but suffers from drawbacks also. Since this method does not involve any set procedure, one cannot draw any inferences about the whole population. Thus, the results confine only to the sample. It means that if any fault is found in an invoice, it cannot be said that it will pertain to other units of the population also. The greatest drawback of judgement sampling is that it is subject to unknown potential biases, and hence the inferences drawn may be highly misleading. Under judgement sampling, the whole of the population is rarely represented.

Systematic Sampling

This sampling procedure has already been discussed adequately in this chapter. As described earlier, this sampling plan is suitable when the information is on cards or in register. Hence, it is one of the potential method for sampling of accounting records. It is preferred because of its easiness and discarded because of the ambiguity of its results. Moreover, if the invoices are not arranged randomly, this method gives extremely poor results. Hence, systematic sampling may be as good as judgement sampling when the population is not in random order.

Random Sampling

This procedure has been dealt within detail as the first sampling procedure. Here we would like to give some special features of random selection with special reference to accounting records as we already know that in random sampling, a correspondence is established between the units of the population to be selected, and the random numbers. The units are selected as per procedure. If the number of units is less than the number of random numbers taken into consideration, then it is known as incomplete correspondence. For example, if the number of units in the population is 81 and two-digit random number table is taken for selecting units, any number from 00 to 99 can occur in the table but there is no unit numbered from 82 to 99. Hence, if any of these numbers occurs, it has to be rejected. Commonly the number 00 is taken to select the 100th serial number unit. If the numbering has been started from 00, then it is the first unit of the population.

Sampling from Un-numbered Accounting Records

So far, we have been considering the case where each item is assigned a number. Now let us consider the information in registers where only the pages are numbered and the entries or items are not. For example, there is a register having 96 pages and the entries on a page are from 15-50. To take a sample of entries, select a four-digit random number. Out of this four-digit number, assign the last two digits to the page and first two for the item on that selected page. Count digits from unit digit to next. If the selected random number is 6823, then select 23rd item on page number 68. If the selected random number is such that it does not fall in the range of pages assigned or the number of items on the page, then reject this number and select a new one. This procedure cuts short the labour of numbering each and every item which is sometimes very large.

For further details of sampling methods, the reader should consult the books, listed under 'Suggested Reading'.

QUESTIONS AND EXERCISES

1. Define and discuss a random sample from a finite population.
2. Is sampling always better than complete enumeration? Justify your answer with the help of suitable examples.
3. Discuss sampling and non-sampling errors. Also suggest ways of minimizing them.
4. Write short notes on the following:
   (*a*) Population.
   (*b*) Sample.
   (*c*) Optimum allocation.
   (*d*) Finite population correction.
   (*e*) Sampling frame.
   (*f*) Consistent estimator.
5. Give the criteria which help in determining the size of a sample.
6. Give the variance of sample mean in case of simple random sampling. How will you estimate the total population?
7. Why is stratified sampling known as restricted sampling?
8. In what respect does circular systematic sampling differ from linear systematic sampling? When are these two types of systematic sampling equivalent?
9. How would you determine sample size for each stratum under (*i*) proportional allocation and (*ii*) Neyman allocation.
10. Distinguish between sampling with replacement and sampling without replacement. Also give the formulae for standard deviation of mean in the two cases.
11. Enunciate circumstances under which multistage sampling is preferable over others.
12. Define efficiency of one sampling design as compared to the other. Also derive expression for efficiency of cluster sampling over simple random sampling.
13. Under what condition, does an estimator become consistent.
14. From a locality of 950 households, a simple random sample of 48 households was drawn. The number of persons in 48 houses were as follows:

4	7	5	6	9	3	2	4	8	6	5	3
8	4	3	2	2	1	5	6	8	11	8	6
5	4	3	5	6	7	8	5	7	2	4	5
6	3	4	7	2	4	5	3	1	6	3	4

   Estimate the total number of persons in the locality. Also find the estimated varian of the mean.
15. A population consists of 12 units which are divided into three strata. The first stratum consists of observed values 1, 3, 4, the second stratum has values 7, 9, 12, 10 and third stratum has values 18, 21, 20, 23, 24. From each of the first and second stratum draw a sample of two units and from the third stratum draw a sample of three units. On the basis of sampled observations, find the mean of the stratified sample and calculate its variance, $V(\overline{x}_{st})$.
16. What do you understand by census and sample methods of study? Also discuss their merits and demerits. (*C.A., May, 1983*)
17. (*a*) What is the standard error of a statistic and what is its utility?
    (*b*) What is the estimator for population mean in case of stratified sampling?

(c) Consider a population of 6 units with values 1, 2, 3, 4, 5 and 6. Write down all possible samples of size 2 (without replacement) from this population and verify that the sample mean is an unbiased estimator of the population mean.
Also calculate its sampling variance and verify that
(i) it agrees with the formula for the variance of the sample mean and
(ii) its variance is less than the variance obtained from sampling with replacement.
(M.Com., Kolkata, 1984)

18. (a) State briefly the relative advantage of sampling over complete enumeration.
(b) Define statistic and S.E. Give expressions for S.E. of the sample mean in case of simple random sampling with replacement and without replacement.
(c) The values of a characteristic x of the population containing 5 units are 7, 2, 3, 4, 1. Take all possible samples of size 2 (without replacement) and verify that the mean of the population is exactly equal to the mean of the sample means.
(M.Com., Kolkata, 1985)

19. A simple random sample of size 2 is drawn with replacement from a population of 4 values 50, 60, 64, 70. Find the sampling distribution of the sample mean ($\overline{x}$) and verify that E ($\overline{x}$) = population mean and v ($\overline{x}$) = 1/2 the population variance.
(I.C.W.A, Inter, Dec. 1996)

20. Differentiate between purposive sampling and random sampling.
(C.A., P.E.-I, Nov., 2004)

21. A simple random sample with replacement (SRSWR) and a simple random sample without replacement (SRSWOR), each of size n are drawn from finite population of size 28. If the number of defective units in the population is 7, find n such that standard error of proportion of defectives of SRSWOR is two-third that of SRSWR. Also determine the standard error of the said proportion in SRSWR.
(I.C.W.A., Inter, June 2000)

22. Define simple random sampling. Differentiate sampling with replacement and without replacement. *(B.Sc. (Ag.) Hons. Part-I, RAU, 2001)*

23. From a population of 5 numbers, 3, 6, 9, 12, 15, draw all possible simple random samples of size 3 without replacement. Obtain the sampling distribution of sample mean and from it calculate expectation of sample mean. *(I.C.W.A., Inter, Dec. 2000)*

24. A population consists of 5 units and the values of a characteristic for these units are 2, 4, 3, 6, 7. Take all possible samples each of size 3 from the population and verify that the mean of sample means is exactly equal to population mean, the sampling being done without replacement. *(I.C.W.A., Inter, June 1998)*

25. Describe various sampling methods which you are aware of. Also describe the differences among these methods. To conduct a national opinion poll which sampling method would you suggest and why? *(M.B.A., Part-II, MLSU, 2002)*

SUGGESTED READING

Adcock, C. (1997). Sample size determination: A review, *The Statistician*, 46(2), pp. 261-283.

Akin, H. (1984). *Handbook of Sampling for Auditing and Accounting,* McGraw-Hill Book Co., New York.

Burstein, H. (1971). *Attribute Sampling,* McGraw-Hill Book Co., New York.

Cochran, W.G. (1959). Sampling Techniques, Asia Publishing House, Mumbai.

Des Raj (1968). Sampling Theory, Tata McGraw-Hill Publishing Co., Mumbai.

Des Raj and P. Chandhok (1998). *Sample Survey Theory*, Narosa Publishing House.

Henry, George T. (1990). *Practical Sampling*, Sage, Newbury Park.

John, J.H. and H.J. Heldt (1998). *Quality Sampling and Reliability*, CRC Press.

Kelton, G. (1983). *Introduction to Survey Sampling,* Sage Publications, Beverley Hills.

Murthy, M.N. (1967). *Sampling Theory and Methods,* Statistical Publishing Society, Kolkata.

Namboodiri, N.K. (1978). *Survey Sampling and Measurement,* Academic Press, New York.

Sudman, S. (1976). *Applied Sampling,* Academic Press, New York.

Sukhatme, P.V., V.B. Sukhatme and C. Ashok (1970). *Sampling Theory of Surveys with Applications,* Indian Society of Agricultural Statistics, New Delhi.

Wilburn, A.J. (1984). *Practical Statistical Sampling for Auditors,* Marcel Dekker, New York.

8
Chapter

Some Sampling Distributions

In Chapter 7 we have studied the samples and estimates, which represent the corresponding population specified by the respective parameters. It means that the sample and its parent population are related to each other. Hence our study can always be two-fold, i.e. (*i*) what we can derive from the population regarding the sample(s) to be taken from it, and (*ii*) what kind of information can be gathered from a sample or a series of samples about the population from which they have been drawn. The first point has been covered to a great extent in Chapter 7. Therefore, we shall concentrate on the second point in this chapter. Here the objective is to know the manner in which a statistic or a series of statistics vary from one sample to another.

Statistic

A statistic is a function of one or more random variables not involving any unknown parameter, *e.g.*, $\Sigma_i X_i / n$, *i.e.*, $\overline{X}, \Sigma_i (X_i - \overline{X})^2 / (n-1)$, i.e., s^2, s and $\overline{X}/s$ etc. Moreover, a statistic itself is a random variable and follows some distribution.

Generally, we draw a random sample from a population and calculate its mean, range, median, variance and standard deviation. We know that there are $\binom{N}{n}$ possible samples of size n from a population of N units. One way is to draw all possible samples and then calculate for each sample, the mean $\overline{X}$, S.D.. s, etc., and find their frequency distribution. But this is possible only for small populations. Another approach is to draw a large number of samples and collect information on the sample distribution of various statistics. The studies from this approach have become easier with the help of electronic computers. But this technique is not always feasible because of the cost and ambiguity of results involved with it. Moreover, it is not an exact approach as we are concerned with the theoretical sampling distribution of various statistics.

Definition

Sampling distribution describes the way in which a statistic or a function of statistics, which is/are the function(s) of the random variables X_1, X_2, ..., X_n, will vary from one sample to another sample of the same size. Such sampling distributions have given a fillip to the number of test statistics for hypothesis testing[1]. Hence, some important sampling distributions are discussed in this chapter.

STUDENT'S *t*-DISTRIBUTION

This has been discussed in Chapter 7, under the heading 'Standard Error', that if a random sample $X_1, X_2, ..., X_n$ of size n, with observed values $x_1, x_2, ..., x_n$ is drawn from a normal population having mean μ and S.D. σ, the mean $\bar{x}$ is distributed normally with mean μ and S.D. $\sigma/\sqrt{n}$ i.e., $\bar{x} \sim N(\mu, \sigma/\sqrt{n})$.

Also the variable Z, where

$$Z = \frac{\bar{x}-\mu}{\sigma/\sqrt{n}} \qquad ...(8.1)$$

is a normal variate with mean 0 and standard deviation 1, i.e. $Z \sim N(0, 1)$.

In practice, the standard deviation σ is not known and in such a situation the only alternative left is to use s, the sample estimate of standard deviation σ. Thus the variate $\sqrt{n}(\bar{x}-\mu)/s$ is approximately normal provided n is sufficiently large. If n is not sufficiently large, the variate $\sqrt{n}(\bar{x}-\mu)/s$ is distributed as t and hence

$$t = \frac{\bar{x}-\mu}{s/\sqrt{n}} \qquad ...(8.2)$$

where $$s^2 = \frac{1}{n-1}\Sigma_i(x_1-\bar{x})^2$$

t is a widely used variable and the distribution of t is called student's t-distribution. This distribution was discovered by W.S. Gosset in 1908. The statistician Gosset is better known by the pseudonym 'student' and hence t-distribution is called student's t-distribution. He derived the distribution of $\bar{x}/s_{\bar{x}}$ (where $s_{\bar{x}} = s/\sqrt{n}$) to find an exact test of a mean by making use of estimated standard deviation s, based on a random sample of size n. R.A. Fisher in 1925 published that t-distribution can also be applied to the test of regression coefficient and other practical problems. Here, we give the density function and properties of t-distribution without derivation. The readers interested in the derivation should consult a book on mathematical statistics. The density function of variable t with $k = n-1$ degrees of freedom[2] is,

$$f_k(t) = \frac{1}{\sqrt{k}\,B\left(\frac{1}{2},\frac{k}{2}\right)} \frac{1}{\left(1+\frac{t^2}{k}\right)^{(k+1)/2}} \qquad -\infty < t < \infty \qquad ...(8.3)$$

$$B\left(\frac{1}{2},\frac{k}{2}\right) = \frac{\Gamma\left(\frac{1}{2}\right)\Gamma\left(\frac{k}{2}\right)}{\Gamma\left(\frac{k+1}{2}\right)} = \frac{\sqrt{\pi}\,\Gamma\left(\frac{k}{2}\right)}{\Gamma\left(\frac{k+1}{2}\right)}$$

1. It has been discussed in Chapters 10 and 15.
2. Degree of freedom are the number of independent observations in a set of observations.

Therefore,

$$f_k(t) = \frac{\Gamma(k+1)/2}{\sqrt{k\pi}\,\Gamma\left|\frac{k}{2}\right.}\left(1+\frac{t^2}{k}\right)^{\frac{-(k+1)}{2}} \qquad \text{...(8.3.1)}$$

Properties of *t*-Distribution

1. *t*-distribution is an unimodal distribution.
2. The probability distribution curve is symmetrical about the line $t = 0$.
3. It is a bell-shaped curve just like a normal curve with its tails a little higher above the abscissa than the normal curve. Its spread increases as degrees of freedom '*k*' decreases. This means that for the same value of *t*-variate and *x*, the normal variate, the area beyond *t* is larger than the area beyond *x*.

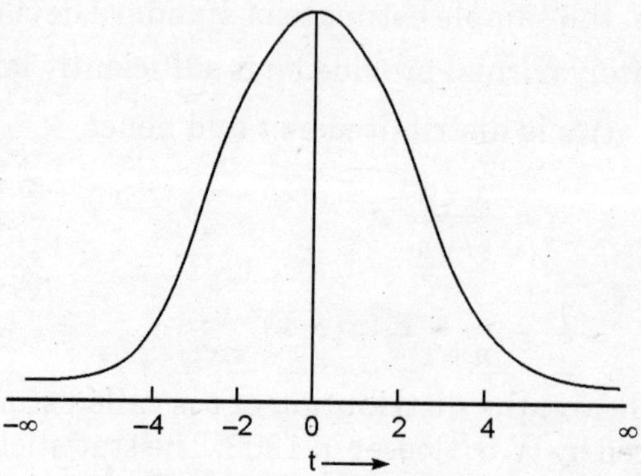

Figure 8.1 *t*–distribution Curve

4. *t*-distribution has only one parameter *k*, the degrees of freedom equal to $(n–1)$.
5. The constants of *t*-distribution are as follows:

(Mean) $\mu = 0$ for $k \geq 2$.

(Variance) $\sigma^2 = \dfrac{k}{k-2}$ for $k \geq 3$.

(Skewness) $\alpha_3 = 0$ for $k \geq 4$.

(Kurtosis) $\alpha_4 = \dfrac{3(k-2)}{(k-4)}$ for $k \geq 5$.

6. The area under *t*-distribution curve for $t < t'$ is determined by the equation,

$$F_k(t') = p(t < t') = \int_{-\infty}^{t'} f(t)\,dt \qquad \text{...(8.4)}$$

Students and other readers need not integrate actually for the area as the tables of area under the curve for different values of *t* are available and vice versa.

Equation (8.4) is given to acquaint the reader with the know-how of getting the area if t is given and the value of t if area is given.

7. t-distribution tends to normal distribution as k increases. For practical purposes, t is taken as equivalent to the normal distribution provided $k \geq 30$.
8. Moment generating function for t-distribution does not exist.

t-distribution has tremendous utility in testing of hypothesis about one population mean or about equality of two population means when standard deviation is not known. Other uses of t-distribution will be known to the readers in the chapters ahead. t-distribution table has been provided in Appendix B.

CHI-SQUARE DISTRIBUTION

So far, we have been discussing the distribution of mean obtained from all possible samples, or a large number of samples drawn from a normal population, distributed with mean μ and variance σ^2/n. Now we are interested in knowing the distribution, of sample variances s^2 of these samples. Consider a random sample $X_1, X_2,...., X_n$ of size n. Let the observations of this sample be denoted by $x_1, x_2,..., x_n$. We know that the variance,

$$s^2 = \frac{1}{n-1}\Sigma_i (x_i - \overline{x})^2 \text{ for } i = 1, 2, \ldots, n.$$

or $$\Sigma_i (x_i - \overline{x})^2 = (n-1)\, s^2 = ks^2 \qquad ...(8.5)$$

where $k = (n - 1)$.

A quantity ks^2/σ^2, which is a variable, is defined as χ^2_k. Now we will give the distribution of the random variable χ^2_k, which was first discovered by Helmert in 1876 and later independently given by Karl Pearson in 1900. Another way to understand chi-square is: if $X_1, X_2, ...X_n$ are n independent normal variates with mean zero and variance unity, the sum of squares of these variates is distributed as chi-square with n d.f. The chi-square distribution was discovered mainly as a measure of goodness of fit in case of frequency distribution, i.e., whether the observed frequencies follow a postulated distribution or not. The probability density function (p.d.f.) of χ^2-variate is,

$$f_k(\chi^2) = \frac{1}{2^{k/2}\Gamma(k/2)}(\chi^2)^{\frac{1}{2}k-1} e^{-\frac{1}{2}\chi^2} \qquad ...(8.6)$$

Properties of Chi-square Distribution

1. The whole chi-square distribution curve lies in the first quadrant since the range of χ^2 is from 0 to ∞.
2. From the density function given by (8.6), it is evident that χ^2-distribution has only one parameter k, the degrees of freedom for χ^2.

   Thus, the shape of the probability density curve mainly depends on the parameter k. The shape of the curves for four different degrees of freedom say, $k = 2$, $k = 7$,

$k = 12$, $k = 20$ are given below:

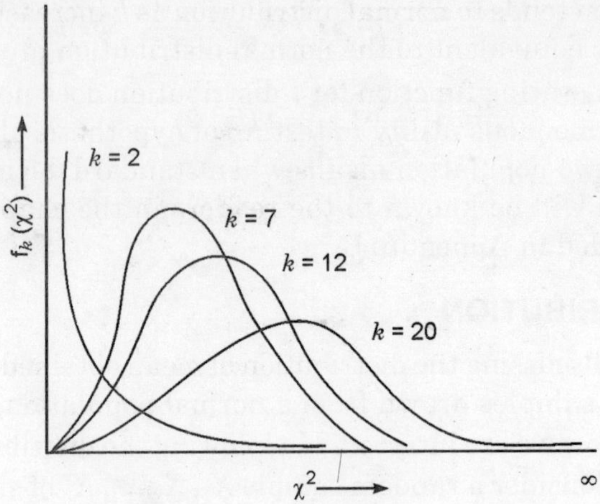

Figure 8.2 Chi-square Distribution Curves

3. Chi-square distribution curve is highly positive skewed.
4. It is an unimodal curve and its mode is at the point, $\chi^2 = (k-1)$.
5. The shape of the curve varies immensely especially when k is small. For $k = 1$ and 2, it is just like a hyperbola.
6. Chi-square distribution is completely defined by one parameter 'k', which is known as the *degrees of freedom* for chi-square distribution.
7. The constants for chi-square distributions are as follows:

$$\text{(Mean) } \mu = k$$

$$\text{(Variance) } \sigma^2 = 2k$$

$$\text{(Skewness) } \alpha_1 = 2\left(\frac{2}{k}\right)^{\frac{1}{2}}$$

8. The moment generating function for chi-square distribution is,

$$\phi_{\chi^2}(t) = (1-2t)^{-k/2}$$

9. r th raw moment of chi-square distribution is,

$$\mu'_r = \frac{2\Gamma\left(\frac{k}{2}+r\right)}{\Gamma k/2}$$

Putting $r = 1$,

$$\mu'_1 = \frac{2\Gamma\left(\frac{k}{2}+1\right)}{\Gamma k/2} = k$$

$$r = 2, \qquad \mu_2' = \frac{2^2\Gamma\left(\frac{k}{2}+2\right)}{\Gamma k/2}$$

$$= 4\left(\frac{k}{2}+1\right)\frac{k}{2} = k(k+2)$$

Again,

$$\mu_2 = \mu_2' - (\mu_1')^2$$

$$= k(k+2) - k^2 = 2k$$

and so on.

10. It can be shown that for large degrees of freedom say, $k \geq 100$, the variable $(\sqrt{2\chi^2} - \sqrt{2k-1})$ is distributed normally with mean 0 and variance 1.
11. If χ_1^2 and χ_2^2 are two independent chi-squares with degrees of freedom k_1 and k_2 respectively, their sum $(\chi_1^2 + \chi_2^2)$ will be distributed as chi-square with $(k_1 + k_2)$ d.f. This additive property of independent chi-squares, holds good for any number of chi-squares, i.e. if there are m independent chi-squares with $k_1, k_2, ...k_m$ d.f. respectively, the sum $\Sigma_i \chi_i^2 (i = 1, 2,..., m)$ will be distributed as chi-square with $\Sigma_i k_i$ d.f.

FISHER'S *z*-DISTRIBUTION

Sir Ronald A. Fisher defined a statistic z which is based upon the ratio of two-sample variances. Suppose s_1^2 and s_2^2 are two variances of random samples of sizes n_1 and n_2 respectively, drawn from two normal populations.

The statistic z is defined as,

$$z = \frac{1}{2}\log_e\left(\frac{s_1^2}{s_2^2}\right) \qquad ...(8.7)$$

or

$$z = \log_e s_1 - \log_e s_2 \qquad ...(8.7.1)$$

or

$$e^{2z} = \frac{s_1^2}{s_2^2} \qquad ...(8.7.2)$$

Putting

$$\frac{s_1^2}{s_2^2} = F,$$

we get

$$e^{2z} = F \qquad ...(8.7.3)$$

The letter F is the first letter of Fisher's name as a mark of respect. z-distribution is of the form,

$$y = \frac{ce^{k_1 z}}{(k_2 + k_1 e^{2z})^{(k_1+k_2)/2}} \qquad ...(8.8)$$

where c is a constant, $k_1 = (n_1 - 1)$ and $k_2 = (n_2 - 1)$.

Properties of z-Distribution

1. z-distribution is symmetrical about the point $z = 0$.
2. z-distribution is a family of distributions in which each one exists for a pair of degrees of freedom k_1 and k_2.

Here the readers are acquainted with Fisher's z-distribution as it is closely associated with F-distribution given below.

F-DISTRIBUTION

From (8.7.3) it is evident that the ratio of two independent sample variances is denoted as F. Now we will consider the distribution of the ratio of two-sample variances in another manner and based on this new approach, the distribution of F is given. The distribution of F was worked out by G.W. Snedecor.

Consider two normal populations $N(\mu_1, \sigma_1^2)$ and $N(\mu_2, \sigma_2^2)$. An independent sample of size n_1 is drawn from a population $N(\mu_1, \sigma_1^2)$, and of size n_2 from a population $N(\mu_2, \sigma_2^2)$. Let the sample variances be $s_1{}^2$ and $s_2{}^2$ respectively. From the chi-square distribution theory we know $k_1 s_1^2 / \sigma_1^2$ is distributed as chi-square with k_1 d.f., i.e.

$$\frac{k_1 s_1^2}{\sigma_1^2} \sim \chi_1^2 \qquad ...(8.9)$$

where χ_1^2 has d.f. $k_1 = (n_1 - 1)$.

Similarly,

$$\frac{k_2 s_2^2}{\sigma_2^2} \sim \chi_2^2 \qquad ...(8.10)$$

where χ_2^2 has d.f. $k_2 = (n_2 - 1)$.

From (8.9), and (8.10) we can write that,

$$\frac{s_1^2 / \sigma_1^2}{s_2^2 / \sigma_2^2} = \frac{\chi_1^2 / k_1}{\chi_2^2 / k_2} \qquad ...(8.11)$$

$$= F_{k_1, k_2} \qquad ...(8.11.1)$$

In (8.11.1), k_1 and k_2 are called the degrees of freedom of F. Dividing s_u^2 $(u = 1, 2)$ by its corresponding population variance standardizes the sample variance, in the sense that on the average both the numerator and denominator approach 1. Now we may be interested in testing the hypothesis that both the normal populations have the same variance, i.e. $\sigma_1^2 = \sigma_2^2$. Under thio hypothesis,

$$\frac{s_1^2}{s_2^2} = F_{k_1,\ k_2} \qquad ...(8.12)$$

As a norm, the greater sample variance is taken as the numerator.

From (8.11) it is apparent that the ratio of two independent chi-squares is distributed as F and (8.12) reveals that under the hypothesis $\sigma_1^2 = \sigma_2^2$, the ratio of two independent sample variances is distributed as F. The probability density function of F-distribution is,

$$f_{k_1,k_2}(F) = \frac{(k_1/k_2)^{k_1/2}}{B\left(\frac{k_1}{2},\frac{k_2}{2}\right)} \frac{F^{k_1/2-1}}{\left(1+\frac{k_1}{k_2}F\right)^{(k_1+k_2)/2}} \quad ...(8.13)$$

$$0 \le F < \infty$$

Obviously, F is always a positive number and the F-distribution curve wholly lies in the first quadrant. There are two parameters of F-distribution namely, k_1 and k_2. Hence the shape of F-distribution curve depends on k_1 and k_2. For two pairs of degrees of freedom (k_1, k_2), the shapes of the F-distribution are shown in Fig. 8.3.

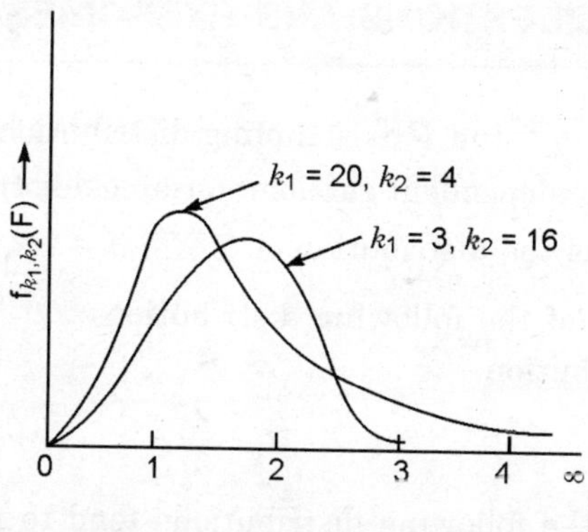

Figure 8.3 *F*-distribution Curves

Properties of *F*-Distribution

1. F-distribution curve extends on abscissa from 0 to ∞.
2. It is an unimodal curve and its mode lies on the point

$$F = \frac{k_2(k_1-2)}{k_1(k_2+2)}$$

which is always less than unity.

3. F-distribution curve is a positive skew curve. Generally the F-distribution curve is highly positive skewed when k_2 is small.
4. The constants of F-distribution are,

(mean) $\quad \mu = \dfrac{k_2}{k_2-2}$ for $k_2 \ge 3$.

(variance) $\quad \sigma^2 = \dfrac{2k_2^2(k_1+k_2-2)}{k_1(k_2-2)^2(k_2-4)}$ for $k_2 \ge 5$.

5. There exists a very useful relation for interchange of degrees of freedom k_1 and k_2, i.e.

$$F_{1-\alpha;(k_1,k_2)} = \frac{1}{F_{\alpha(k_2,k_1)}}$$

6. The moment generation function of F-distribution does not exist.

F-distribution is a very popular and useful distribution because of its utility in testing of hypothesis about the equality of several population means, two population variances and several regression coefficients in multiple regression etc. As a matter of fact, F-test is the backbone of analysis of variance.

Wide use and application of the sampling distributions has been made in different chapters ahead while testing different null hypotheses about a variety of population parameters. The relationships between t, χ^2 and F are given in Chapter 11.

QUESTIONS AND EXERCISES

1. Explain why we call t, χ^2 and F as sampling distributions?
2. If $X_1, X_2, ..., X_k$ are k independent random variables distributed normally with mean 0 and variance 1, what is the distribution of $\Sigma_i X_i^2$ $(i = 1,2, . . ., k)$?
3. Write the parameters of the following distributions:
   (*a*) Chi-square distribution.
   (*b*) t-distribution.
   (*c*) F-distribution.
4. In what situation do the following distributions tend to normal distribution?
   (*a*) t-distribution.
   (*b*) χ^2-distribution.
5. Does moment generating function exist for the following distributions?
   (*a*) t-distribution.
   (*b*) F-distribution.
   (*c*) χ^2-distribution.
6. Given $\alpha = 0.05$, $k_1 = 5$, $k_2 = 10$, find,
   (*i*) $F_{\alpha(k_2,k_1)}$.
   (*ii*) $F_{1-\alpha(k_1,k_2)}$.
7. In what respects does t-distribution differ from a normal distribution?
8. For the same value of t-variate and a normal variate x, write whether the area to the left of t will be larger or smaller than area to the left of x.
9. Determine the values of the following:
   (*a*) $t_{.01,18}$
   (*b*) $t_{.05,12}$
   (*c*) $t_{.10,15}$
   (*d*) Find the ninetieth percentile of the t-distribution with 10 d.f.

(e) Find $F(u \geq 2.086)$ where u has t-distribution with 20 d.f.

(f) Find $P(-2.583 \leq u \leq 2.583)$ where u has t-distribution with 16 d.f.

[*Hint.* Use t-table given in the appendix].

10. Obtain the values of the following:
(a) $\chi^2_{0.05,\ 12}$
(b) $\chi^2_{0.25,\ 20}$
(c) $\chi^2_{0.01,\ 16}$
(d) Find the ninety-fifth percentile of chi-square distribution with 12 d.f.
(e) Find the ninth decile of chi-square distribution with 15 d.f.

11. Give the relation between Fisher's z-distribution and F-distribution.

12. Give the probability density function for the following distributions and their moment generating functions if they exist.
(a) Chi-square distribution.
(b) F-distribution.
(c) t-distribution.

13. Compute the values of the following:
(a) $F_{0.01,\ (5,\ 8)}$
(b) $F_{0.05,\ (6,\ 12)}$
(c) $F_{0.10,\ (4,\ 15)}$
(d) Ninety-ninth percentile of the F-distribution with $k_1 = 8$ and $k_2 = 16$.
(e) Last decile of F-distribution with $k_1 = 6$, $k_2 = 10$.
(f) $P(F \leq 3.66)$ for $k_1 = 7$ and $k_2 = 21$.

14. Give the mean and the variance of the following distributions, along with the condition, if any, in which they exist.
(a) Chi-square distribution with n d.f.
(b) t-distribution based on a random sample of size n.
(c) F-distribution with n_1 and n_2 d.f. where n_1 is the d.f. for the sample variance in the numerator and n_2 is the d.f. for the sample variance in the denominator.

SUGGESTED READING

Bernard, Rosner (2005). *Biostatistics*, Thomson Brooks/Cole.

Burr, I.W. (1974). *Applied Statistical Methods,* Academic Press, New York.

Douglas, A. Downing and Jeff Clark (1997). *Statistics in Easy Way*, Barron's Educational Series.

Goon, A.M., M.K. Gupta and B. Dasgupta (1977). *An Outline of Statistical Theory,* The World Press, Vol. 1, Kolkata.

Lancaster, H.O. (1969). *The Chi-squared Distribution,* John Wiley, New York.

Larry J., Stephens (2004). *Advanced Statistics Demystified*, Mc-Graw Hill Professional.

Mood, A.M., F.A. Graybill and D.C. Boes (1974). *Introduction to the Theory of Statistics.,* International Student Edition, Mc-Graw Hill, Kogakusha, Tokyo.

Rao, C.R. (1973). *Linear Statistical Inference and its Applications,* Wiley Eastern, 2nd ed., New Delhi.

Shao J. (2003). *Mathematical Statistics,* Springer.

9

Chapter

Research Processes

Research is an ineluctable part of overall growth. It is a quest to gain knowledge about certain phenomenon. Any study carried out in a scientific manner for solving specific problem(s) is termed as research. For this, a survey or an experiment is conducted to collect certain information required in accordance to our objectives. This information is obtained for elaboration, verification of assertions, estimation of certain parameter(s) and/or testing of hypothesis[1]. As a matter of fact a hypothesis is used as a basis for investigation and reasoning. Broadly research can be classified into two types:

PURE/THEORETICAL RESEARCH

It adds new knowledge to the already existing knowledge.

Applied research

The research which is applied to practical situations and is useful in solving real life problems is categorised as applied research.

Statistics is the backbone of any research. Various techniques and tools are applied to manage the collection of information (data) and to analyse data for meaningful and correct inferences to the possible extent, may be regarded as research methodology.

Collection of facts, presentation, analysis of data and interpretation of results are the parts of research methodology. If one finds mean (average) of a sample, it is an estimation process and divulges some unknown facts. Undoubtedly the requirements of different researches engaged in various spheres of activity are different. A person in the area of social and marketing research will need to know about sampling designs, methods of investigation and enquiry, scaling techniques and suitable analysis techniques whereas a scientist in biological sciences will require more to know about experimental designs and analysis. Persons working for investigating about some complicated phenomena like human behaviour and psychology, meteorological studies, natural processes, economic changes etc., usually require multivariate analysis of data like principal component analysis, factor analysis, cluster analysis, discriminant analysis, conjoint analysis, etc.

---

1. A hypothesis is a small statement about certain theoretical concepts based on one's own experience or some knowledge gathered directly or indirectly.

One chapter presented here on research methodology in any way cannot cover the whole of research process. This chapter is meant to enable one to understand what research methodology is, what are its main constituents, what do they cover, what are their functions and intricacies, what purpose do they serve and from where their details can be held. For a detailed study, inquisitive minds can go through different volumes on research methodology pertaining to their areas of interest available in the market and moreover one can consult the literature as suggested at the end of this chapter.

STEPS INVOLVED IN A RESEARCH PROCESS

To organise and conduct a research systematically, one has to proceed step by step. Various steps that are usually involved in any research process are delineated below and each of them is explicated one after the other.

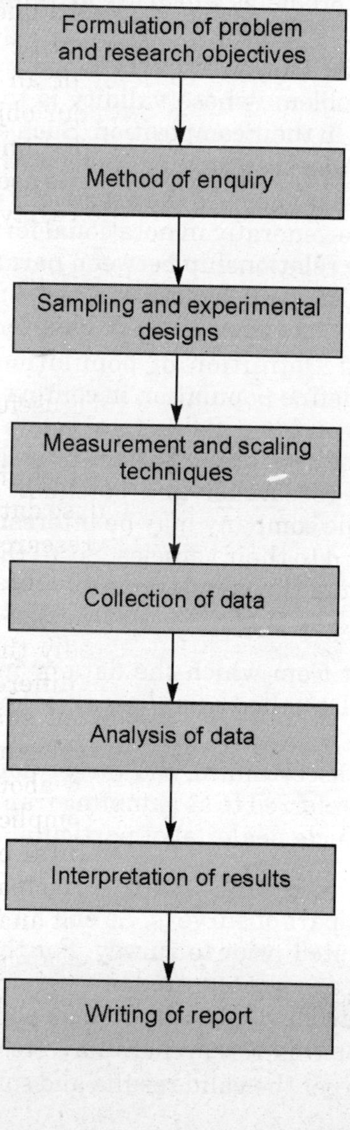

FORMULATION OF PROBLEM

All the succeeding steps involved in a research process depend on the problem formulated for investigation. So one should be wary about the objectives of the research project. First a researcher should clearly spell out the purpose and nature of research. Then he should jottle down the objectives of the research which he wants to fulfil. This will finalize the scope of the problem. Further, a **title** of the problem has to be given which would indicate the intention and aims of the research work. For instance, (*i*) a pharmaceutical company may be interested in knowing the efficacy of a drug, (*ii*) a marketing executive is usually interested to know the opinion and interest of customers in a product of his company. Then he will work out the ways and means to make it more popular to increase its sales, (*iii*) psychologist may be interested in knowing the impact of television and computers on the level of knowledge of adolescents, (*iv*) an agricultural scientist may be curious to know the effect of certain fertilizers or micronutrients on the yield of wheat or maize. On day-to-day basis, there are enumerable problems which are to be investigated for rational decision making.

(*a*) **Research Hypothesis:** They are the statements usually mentioned at the time of formulation of a problem, whose validity is to be ascertained. They are not very specific and exact in their composition. Such statements are termed as *weak hypothesis*. They are subject to modifications at the time of hypothesis testing.

(*b*) **Statistical Hypothesis:** They are the assertions about population parameter(s) either in words or more generally in notational form specifying parameter(s) and many times giving the relationship between parameters. There are two types of statistical hypothesis, (*i*) Null hypothesis and (*ii*) Alternative hypothesis. The description of the same has been given in chapter 10.

Target Population: Definition of population has already been given in chapter 7. Here we redefine population in context to market and allied research. A target population is an identifiable total group or an aggregate of subjects or objects e.g., people, products, organisations or institutions, physical entities that are of interest to the researcher and pertinent to the research problem. For instance, an automobile company may be interested in knowing about customer satisfaction with regard to their vehicles. So all those who purchased a vehicle of their company constitute the population.

Element

An individual or an object from which the data or information is to be collected is known as an element. This is also called *sampling unit.* For example vehicle owner is the element.

Sampling Frame. After ascertaining the target population, a list of all sampling units is prepared. Such a list is referred to as sampling frame. In earlier example sampling frame can be obtained from vehicle dealer(s) of particular region.

Methods of Enquiry

An enquiry is an essential part of surveys. So one has to concentrate on the methods of enquiry which has to be adopted prior to survey. For this he has to focus on construct development. It may be viewed as an integrated process in which an investigator puts his effort to decide what specific data should be collected for solving the problem and attaining the objectives of the study. For this researchers have to view the subjective properties which should be investigated to get the valid results and solution for the research problem.

Multidimensional Constructs

Summated scale measurements tend to be the most suitable scales. In these type of scales, each dimension represents some aspect of the construct. Thus, the construct is measured by the entire scale, not just by one component. Then one needs to measure the cohesiveness between scales that have multiple dimensions. That is known as *internal consistency*. It refers to the various dimension of a multidimensional construct that correlate with the scale. In other words, the set of attribute items that constitute the scale must be internally consistent and should not collide. There are two popular methods to assess internal consistency.

Method 1. Split Half Test

The items in the scale are divided into two halves (odd versus even) and the resulting halves summated scores are paired against one another and correlation is found out. A high correlation coefficient between halves is a sign of good internal consistency.

Method 2. Coefficient Alpha Method

In this method, the average is taken of all possible split half coefficients that are obtained by splitting the scale items in different ways. The value of coefficient alpha (α) lies between 0 and 1. A value of α equal to 0.6 or more indicates towards a satisfactory internal consistency and vice-versa. In general, research is meant to collect vital data, which are of following types.

Data – Types

There are two classes of data namely, (*i*) Primary data, (*ii*) Secondary data. Both of these are succinctly discussed in Chapter-1. As mentioned, secondary data are obtained through internal records, past reports, research journals, magazines, websites, computerised data stored in hard disc, CD's, floppies, etc. So the collection of secondary data is not a tedious problem. Problem lies only in making them available. A researcher should identify its relevance to his problem, authenticity, validity and correctness. But the collection of primary data has many facets which are discussed here.

Collection of primary data: Primary data are the information which are collected looking into the problem and objectives from the sampling elements. Only two methods of collection of data in surveys are in vogue namely, (*i*) through personal enquiry, i.e., through schedule, (*ii*) through mailed questionnaire. But with the tremendous expansion of telecommunication devices, internet facilities, e-mail etc., collection of information, particularly opinion, has become very quick and easier. But such surveys, hardly follow any rules of surveys like, choice of the type of population, knowledge of population or sampling frame, selection of random sample, etc. Still they are frequently used to get the opinion of masses quickly, may be in hours or days.

Direct and Indirect Observations

In case of direct observation, the information is sought by way of investigators' own observation without telling or asking the respondent. For instance, what does a man like to eat, whether a respondent smokes, consumes liquor or not, what conveyance does he use, etc. In indirect method, an investigator gathers information about a respondent through his neighbour or some other person intimately knowing the respondent. Investigator may guess the consumption of liquor by counting the empty liquor bottles found in garbage outside his house.

Observation method is good in cases where the respondents are not able to answer your queries or are expected not to reveal them. The reliability of such an information entirely depends on the integrity, sincerity and dexterity of the investigator. Undoubtedly this method is not free from investigator's bias.

Personal Enquiry Method

This is also known as *interview method*. This is a most commonly used method in social sciences, marketing research, psychology, education, opinion surveys, etc. Before starting a survey, a *schedule* is prepared which consists of a number of questions related to the research problem and its objectives. This should be as comprehensive as possible. Alternative answers are also given just below the question and often with a space for some unanticipated answers. Sometimes the answers are scaled like, strongly agree, agree, no opinion, disagree, strongly disagree. Method of preparing a schedule will be discussed under a heading separately. Prior to starting a survey, the schedule is tested on a small number of respondents randomly. This is known as *pilot survey* or *pretesting*. All the deficiencies realized in pretesting are removed and thus a schedule is finalized for complete survey. In personal enquiry method, the interviewer contacts the respondent personally and asks questions strictly in order given in the schedule. The replies of the respondent are either ticked ☑ out of alternative answers if it is there or noted in space separately if it is not there. Such a procedure of interviewing.is termed as *structured interview*. On the contrary, *unstructured interviews* are somewhat flexible in the sense that an interviewer can ask some additional question from the respondent besides those included in the schedule or omit some of them. There are some other kinds of interviews termed as *focused interview*, *clinical interview* and *non-directive* interview. In these types of interviews, more attention is given to the experience of the respondent to explore his feelings, motives, intention. Such interviews are called unstructured type interviews because in focussed interview, the interviewer has freedom to alter the sequence or the way in which the question to be asked. In clinical interview, it is at the interviewer's discretion to ask questions to elicit the required information whereas in case of non-directive interviews, the interviewer has no binding on himself and he tries to extract maximum information about the topic from the respondent putting minimum number of direct questions.

Structured interviews and unstructured interviews have their own merits and demerits as follows:

Structured Interviews: Merits

1. These facilitate the collection of information in a systematic and orderly manner.
2. An uniformity of information is maintained in spite of variability among interviews.
3. It makes the editing of data easier and smoother.
4. Pilot survey is feasible and meaningful only in case of structured interviews.
5. It is generally dovoid of the bias of the interviewer.

Demerits

1. It suffers from the limitation that some problem arises when the respondent is asked some personal and sensitive questions to get answers at the key motivational factor(s) face to face.

Unstructured Interview: Merits

1. This method works better when motivational factors are involved as the interviewer can ask some questions in an informal manner.
2. In case of unstructured interviews, the role of interviewer is far more important as compared to structured interviews. So unstructured interviews need much more competent, experienced and knowledgeable interviewers.

Demerits

The investigator faces more problem in editing and tabulation of information.

MAILED QUESTIONNAIRE METHOD

When a survey is widespread, i.e., a survey is to be conducted in the whole state, all over the country or even in some foreign countries, mailed questionnaire method is the only choice at hand. Of course such surveys are confined to educated persons or rather a section of society who are elite. In this method, a questionnaire is sent to the respondent through mail. The respondent finds some leisure time to fill up the questionnaire and return to the investigator. The respondent has more freedom to answer questions as compared to personal interview. But the preparation of a mailed questionnaire needs more skill, knowledge and caution than a schedule. Following are the positive and negative sides of this method:

Uppers

1. A survey can be planned covering a large area like country, continent or some highly scattered population.
2. The factors related to interviewer's biases and errors are totally eliminated.
3. A respondent has no pressure to reply a question immediately. He can take his own time to think and reply questions regarding policies, criminology, taxation, opinion, etc.
4. There remains no restriction on sample size. A large number of respondents can be included which is not possible in case of personal interviews.
5. A large survey can be conducted in a short time as all respondents may requested to return the questionnaire in one week, two weeks or a month.
6. The cost of survey is also much less as the cost of salary, travelling, boarding and lodging of the interviewers are completely saved.
7. Better supervision is possible over entire operations of the survey.
8. Answers of certain questions which are of very personal or confidential nature can be answered without any inhibitions because a respondent often hesitates to answer them before an interviewer.
9. The problem of non-availability of the respondent does not arise in case of mailed questionnaire method.

Downers

1. The foremost disadvantage of a mailed questionnaire method is very low response. This method seldom fails in case of very poor return of duly completed questionnaires.
2. This method is inappropriate if the questions are of sensitive and personal nature like, sexual behaviour, political affinities, attitude towards religions, etc. In such situations people refrain to commit anything in writing.
3. It cannot be used if the respondents knowledge is below certain level or they are illiterate.
4. The responses given in the questionnaire may be false, ambiguous or many questions may be left unanswered.
5. There is no control after mailing the questionnaire.
6. There is no check whether the questionnaire is filled by the respondent himself or someone else.
7. There is no way to confirm about the correctness of information supplied in the questionnaire.

DESIGNING OF A SCHEDULE OR A QUESTIONNAIRE

A schedule or a questionnaire is a document containing logically ordered questions to be answered by the respondents. There are many points which should be kept in mind at the time of preparing a schedule.

1. A researcher intending to collect primary data should very carefully decide what information has to be collected.
2. What is the structure, level and characteristics of the people from whom the information is to be collected?
3. How many questions are to be framed?
4. Sequence of questions be decided very carefully so that a respondent feels comfortable and confident in answering the questions. Rambling questions should totally be avoided.
5. The questions should be in simple and common words so that a respondent can understand and reply them easily. There should be no ambiguity in the questions, i.e., each respondent should carry the same meaning and sense so as to supply the same information as required for research. For example, if the question is about profit in the current financial year, it does not convey anything. There must be clarity regarding gross profit, net profit, profit before tax, etc.
6. The number of questions should not be large. If there are too many questions which need long time to fill it, the respondents may either refuse or start giving hurried answers which do not lead to factual information.
7. A schedule usually contains some introductory questions pertaining to the identification of respondent like, name, sex, age, qualification(s), marital status, number of children (if married), address, etc. In some cases it becomes necessary to maintain the anonymity of the respondent. So introductory questions are left out. Thereafter, it contains questions related to the problem under study. These

may be dichotomous, multiple choice or open ended questions. Dichotomous questions can be answered only in yes or no, agree or disagree, etc. For example, do you smoke, yes or no; are you married, yes or no. Multiple choice questions have more than two alternative answers; whereas open ended questions give full liberty to the respondents to answer a question in any form and length. Such questions are least preferred but are unavoidable in cases where one wants to know what does an interviewee actually thinks about an issue.

8. One should also keep in mind the variables included in the schedule or questionnaire and work out the feasibility of data.

DIFFERENCE BETWEEN A SCHEDULE AND A QUESTIONNAIRE

Basically a schedule and a questionnaire are same, yet due to their different usage, they slightly differ. A comprehensive list of questions used for interview method is called a *schedule* whereas when it is used for mailed enquiry, it is named as *questionnaire*. From the angle of research, both should be highly relevant to the problem, accurate, precise, clear, lexically sound. The trifling differences are as follows:

QUESTIONNAIRE VERSUS SCHEDULE

1. The meaning and sense of a question should convey exactly what we want to know from a respondent. But in a schedule, wording does not affect as much as in questionnaire since the questions are asked by the interviewer.
2. Sequence of questions should be well organised so that a respondent feels comfortable in answering them whereas it is not so momentous in case of a schedule.
3. If the answers are to be given in numerical terms, their units should also be specified there itself. For example, in case of income, it must be mentioned per month or per year, for age, it is to be given in years or years and months, etc. Whereas in personal enquiry method an interviewer can ask the question in that way.
4. High sounding and highly technical words should be avoided as far as possible as a respondent may be ignorant about them. While this is not necessary in a schedule as the interviewer can explain them.
5. Question should be such that answer can be given precisely, i.e., in a few words only whereas this is not so important in a schedule.
6. Certain questions of personal nature or on sensitive issues can be asked in a questionnaire whereas such question may cause problem to the interviewer in a personal interview. The respondents generally hesitate to answer such questions because of shyness and disclosure of identity.
7. Drafting of questions should be straight forward without any emphasis which may lead one to answer in affirmative or negative. Such a problem does not arise in case of a schedule.
8. More attention be paid to the time required in filling a questionnaire than a schedule. Because an interviewer can pursue a respondent to give more time for interview.

9. Wherever necessary, short explanation should be provided alongwith the question so that a respondent can understand the question in the same perspective as intended by the researcher. Whereas in case of schedule, this part is played by the interviewer.

OTHER SURVEY METHODS

From the foregoing discussion it is apparent that a structured interview is conducted by the interviewer at the house or office of a respondent. If the interview is conducted with business executive in his/her office, it is termed as *executive interview*. In marketing research, companies are interested to know the marketability of their product in terms of quality, liking, demand, prices, among customers. The way in which such surveys are carried out, they are named accordingly. Three instances are given below:

Mall Intercept Interview

A personal interview held face to face in a mall is termed as *mall intercept interview*. Mall shoppers are stayed and requested to provide required information about one or the other product(s) in a common area of mall.

Purchase Intercept Interview

In this type of survey, an interview of a buyer takes place immediately after the purchase of a product or service. It is different from mall-intercept interview in the sense that the intercept takes place when the buyer has already shown a prespecified behaviour with regard to the purchase of a particular product.

Telephone Interviews

In last one decade the number of telephone subscribers have tremendously increased. Telephone facility has reached upto village level. Mobile phones have also become the part of life of a common man. Thus, the continual advances in telecommunication, personal computer technologies have given rise to an innumerable methods of surveys. Telephone interviews are most commonly used in marketing research as they are cheaper and faster than other techniques. They are classified as *person administered, self-administered* or *telephone administered* survey. Recent emerging computer technology plays a significant role in modern surveys and they are called *Computer Assisted Techniques* (CAT) or simply *on line surveys*. The greatest advantage of these techniques is that they facilitate the interviewer to call the respondent any number of times and seek interview with him at his convenience.

Self Administered Survey

In this survey a person himself picks the questionnaire and fills it with his opinion on various aspects. This is most common in case of hotels and restaurants.

METHODS OF SAMPLING

Sampling methods may be divided into two categories: (*i*) probability sampling methods and (*ii*) non-probability sampling methods.

Probability Sampling Methods

The methods given in Chapter 7 are all probability sampling. To name, simple random sampling, stratified sampling, systematic sampling, cluster sampling, etc. Sequential sampling is described in Chapter 21. So the readers are advised to study thoroughly the same. Here some popularly used non-probability sampling methods are discussed with brevity.

Non-probability Sampling Methods

Non-probability sampling gives rise to those methods where the subjects, persons or objects are selected deliberately. No probability is attached or cannot be computed to an item being selected. All the methods given under non-probability sampling lead to almost same approach.

1. Convenience Sampling: In this type of sampling method, an investigator or an interviewer selects the sample at his own convenience, often as the study is being conducted. This method is based on the assumption that the target population is homogeneous and the individuals selected and interviewed yields similar information with regard to the characteristics under study. As persons selected from petrol pumps (stations) to collect information about the quality of petrol, service, correctness of measurements, etc., are supposed to represent the population of gasoline buyers. Such a sampling is known as convenience sampling.

2. Judgement Sampling: In this method respondents or sampling units are selected on the judgement of the person doing the study with the hope that they will meet the requirement of the study. The underlying assumption is that the person or unit selected truly represent the entire target population. For example, to find out the potential of drip irrigation technology, a researcher may go to the teachers of agricultural university.

3. Quota Sampling: In case of stratified sampling[2] if the cost of selecting random samples in each stratum is very high, then the interviewers are assigned a quota (fixed number of persons or subjects) in each stratum and the actual selection of persons is left at the discretion of the interviewer. It is to emphasize that quota samples are not random samples.

4. Snowball Sampling: This sampling technique involves the practice of identifying a set of respondents who can, in turn, help the interviewer to identify some other person who can be included in the study. After interviewing this person, he will contact the other person and interview him. Through him the interviewer would solicit that person for help to identify another person holding the same characteristics. In this way, a chain process continues till the required number of persons are interviewed. This type of sampling is most suitable in qualitative research. Reduced sample size and cost are the main advantages. Though snowball sampling is very likely to introduce bias in the research study, this is a frequently used method in marketing research.

CRITERIA FOR SELECTING AN APPROPRIATE SAMPLING DESIGN

A large number of sampling designs have been given in Chapter 7 and preceding section. Now the question arises which one to be chosen for research problem. No hard and fast rule can be given. Still there are certain criteria which can enable one to decide about a sampling plan as given below:

1. **Objectives of the Research:** One must consider what is the purpose and type of the research. Whether it is a qualitative research or quantitative research.

---

2. For stratified sampling, see Chapter 7.

2. **Target Population:** How much advanced knowledge about the target population is at hand? Is the sampling frame available? If not, how easy or difficult is to generate it?
3. **Time Frame:** What is the reference period for the project to be completed?
4. **Availability of Resources:** To what extent, the resources are available in terms of money and man power for the project.
5. **Degree of Accuracy:** How precisely the results are required? What degree of accuracy we want to attain in making prediction or in inductive research? As a general norm, greater the accuracy required, larger the sample is to be taken.
6. **Scope of the Research:** One has to keep in mind whether the research is conducted to apply its findings at international, national or regional level.
7. **Statistical Analysis Requirements:** Each method of estimation and testing of hypothesis or any other analysis have their own data requirement and conditions for their applicability. Only probability sampling techniques allow the researcher to apply estimation and testing methods. Anyhow non-probability methods of sampling are useful for qualitative and marketing research. But conclusions can be generalized for a larger population. Deliberate sampling is often used to develop hypothesis. So a researcher should choose a sampling design intelligibly.

MEASUREMENT AND SCALING

Measurement of persons or physical objects like height, length, weight, volume, hardness, etc., is the part of our daily life. Besides quantitative measurements based on some yardstick, one has to measure certain abstract concepts or phenomena. Such measure call for qualitative measurements in terms of attitudes and scales. There is a competition in all walks of life. People have a tendency to have as much amenities and latest articles as possible. Due to competition, every big company wants to know about the attitude and interest of public to promote their products and services. This needs marketing research. A study of attitude is a part of behavioural sciences like psychology and sociology. So we will first discuss about attitude and then scales.

Attitude

It can be expounded as a predisposition of a person to react in a consistent manner positively or negatively towards same physical object, phenomenon, idea or information. Attitude is purely a personal matter and it can vary from person to person. Thurstone defined attitudes as, the sum total of man's inclinations and feelings, prejudice or bias, preconceived notions, ideas, fears, threats and convictions about any specific topic. The term opinion is slightly different from attitude. Actually the verbal expression of attitude is opinion, not necessarily based on facts or knowledge. From theoretical point of view, a person's overall attitude consists of the interaction between three main components, the person's (*i*) beliefs (cognitive), (*ii*) feelings (affective component), (*iii*) outcome behaviour (conative).

Cognitive Component

This is a part of attitude which represents a person's beliefs, perception and knowledge about a particular subject, object or phenomenon.

Affective Component

The part of attitude that typifies a person's emotional feelings held towards an object, an individual or a plan.

Conative Component

The part of an attitude that reflects a person's intended or actual behavioural response to a given individual or object. This is an observable outcome of a person resulting from the interaction between the cognitive component and affective component as they emerge towards a given object.

SCALING

There is no problem when we require quantitative measurements. We have procedures and tools for it. The problem arises when a researcher is to measure some abstract and/or complex concept and there are no standardized tools and techniques. In the present context, we can say that there is a problem while measuring opinion and attitude particularly in the want of valid measure(s). In such situations scaling techniques come to our rescue. Scaling provides the procedures of assigning numerals to various degrees of opinion and attitudes and other concepts. For this two approaches can be adopted (*i*) firstly make a judgement about the degree of a response of an individual and place it directly on a predetermined scale about the characteristic in question and (*ii*) construct the questionnaire or schedule where the answers to the questions are given in terms of relative degree of preference or agreement. A variety of problems occur in researches and these problems need different scales. In view of the same, many researchers expounded various scales. Some of them are explicated here. Scales are classified into two categories, (*a*) measurement scales, (*b*) arbitrary scales.

(*a*) Measurement Scales

Measurement scales are classified into four categories in respect of their mathematical properties namely, (*i*) nominal scale, (*ii*) ordinal scale, (*iii*) interval scale and (*iv*) ratio scale.

Nominal scale: Nominal scale is most simple and widely used scale among the four measurement scales. It is a scale of measurement for a variable in which a number, descriptor or symbol is assigned to identify an attitude of an individual. Nominal data may be numeric or non-numeric. Nominal scales simply allow a researcher to divide the raw responses into distinct groups or categories on the basis of applicability, non-applicability; True, False; Yes, No, etc.

For example, an interviewer asks about the marital status of respondents and categorise them as,

Married ☐, Unmarried ☐, Divorcee ☐, Widow ☐, Widower ☐
Sex of the respondent as,
Male ☐, Female ☐

Number can also be used to serve as levels for nominal scales. In this we split a set of numbers into mutually exclusive and exhaustive subjects so that the characteristics under study are clearly identified. Following example is self-explanatory.

Impact of vaccination	*Preventive measure*		*Total*
	Vaccinated	*Not vaccinated*	
Suffered	12	38	100
Not suffered	166	34	200
Total	178	122	300

Similarly if two teams are given the number 1 and 2 or *A* and *B*. It just differentiates them and does not have any superiority or inferiority. This scale involves only the counting in each category and no ranking or ordering. Statistically, mode and percentage can be calculated.

Ordinal scale: This is a scale in which a variable or characteristic has the properties of nominal scale and the data or answers are ranked or ordered. Ordinal data can also be numeric or non-numeric. This type of scale enables an interviewer to record answers to a question in terms of relative magnitudes. Ordinal scale is extensively used in behavioural sciences and marketing research. Following illustration will make the concept clear.

Question: How are the working conditions in your company in respect of emoluments and environment? [Very good ☐, Good ☐, Average ☐, Bad ☐, Very bad ☐.] Here 'Very good' definitely denotes better opinion about working condition than good. Similarly 'Average' is a better opinion than bad. However, the difference between two successive opinions cannot be determined.

Ordinal scales depict only the ranks of companies, i.e., merely relative magnitudes and no comparison. Ordinal scale is also called ranking scale.

Interval scale: This is a scale of measurement in which distances among individuals or objects in respect of the characteristics are being measured. Intervals between numbers are taken to be equal or in other words interval between observations is expressed in terms of a fixed unit of measure. Interval data are always numeric. For example, scale showing the water level above sea level is an interval scale. Where the difference between –3 and 0 and 0 and 3 can be determined and it is same. However the problem with the scale is that this zero is an arbitrary zero and not an absolute zero. This inhibits the researcher to perform ratio and other calculations.

Ratio scale: Ratio scale is most valuable in physical sciences as this provides most precise description. All statistical tools and techniques are applicable in case of ratio scale data. All mathematical operations are also feasible with it. Hence ratio scale is of prime importance. Ratio scale has an absolute or true zero. A scale that allows a researcher not only to know the absolute differences between each scale but also allows to make comparisons is called ratio scale. All physical measures like weight, height, length, speed, price, number of children in a family, number of visit to doctor per family, etc., are examples of ratio scale.

(*b*) Arbitrary Scales: Construction Methods

We have read under the heading 'Measurement scales' that scaling is a procedure of assigning numbers to various degrees of opinion or attitude and other concepts. Measurement scales are basic in nature whereas following scales are itemized (arbitrary) rating scale measurements that are developed through researcher's own judgement after understanding the construct to be measured. These scale can be highly specific and problem oriented. Such scales are widely used. The main lacuna of such scales is that no justification can possibly be given that they measure the concept for which they are meant. Reliability of this type of scales depends on the insight and experience of the researcher.

DIFFERENTIAL OR THURSTONE SCALES

These scales were originally developed by Thurstone and Chave and are also known as *equal-appearing interval scales.* Thurstone scales can be adopted to measure attitudes or opinion towards any problem using the following procedure:

(*i*) A researcher collects a large number of statements related to the subject of enquiry usually in behavioural sciences and marketing research. The researcher should ensure that all statements belong to the attitude variable that is under consideration.

(*ii*) A large number of judges, possibly experts in that area, classify them in eleven groups from most favourable to extremely unfavourable. The median value of each group is calculated.

(*iii*) Twenty to twenty-five statements are finally selected which get maximum support from the expert judges as indicated by the scale values (median or mean) and interquartile range which measures the scatter of the judgements.

(*iv*) The retained statements are administered to the respondents in random order who are asked to conform all those statements with which they agree.

(*v*) Respondents' scale values are computed simply by finding out the mean or median of the median values of all statements which have been conformed. Thurstone and Chave used median of the distribution as the average.

Thurstone method is widely used for developing differential scales for measuring opinion for issues like war, religion, etc. They are most appropriate and reliable when utilized for measuring single attitude. At the same time, it suffers from the criticism that the attitude of judges will bias the selection of those statements which are finally used.

The method of construction of equal appearing intervals theoretically seems somewhat cumbersome. Hence it is elucidated through an example.

***Example* 9.1.** The data given in this example is fictitious. For the sake of brevity, the procedure is explained by taking only three statements, each having eleven categories. Cumulative frequencies (c.f.) are also shown just below frequencies.

Statement – 1,

$$Q_1 = 4.5 + \frac{\frac{150}{4} - 30}{18} \times 1 = 4.5 + 0.42 = 4.92$$

Sorting categories

Statement		1 0.5–1.5	2 1.5–2.5	3 2.5–3.5	4 3.5–4.5	5 4.5–5.5	6 5.5–6.5	7 6.5–7.5	8 7.5–8.5	9 8.5–9.5	10 9.5–10.5	11 10.5–11.5	*Scale value*	*I.R.*
1	f	3	6	6	15	18	27	30	24	12	0	9	6.50	2.89
	c.f.	3	9	15	30	48	75	105	129	141	141	150		
2	f	0	9	6	18	12	15	45	18	6	9	12	6.83	3.04
	c.f.	0	9	15	33	45	60	105	123	129	138	150		
3	f	6	3	12	18	30	24	36	9	12	0	0	5.75	2.62
	c.f.	6	9	21	39	69	93	129	138	150	150	150		

Scale values displayed in the above table are median values calculated by the formula (3.15),

$$\text{Scale value} = l_0 + \frac{N/2 - c}{f} \times I$$

$$\text{Statement 1, Scale value} = 5.5 + \frac{75-48}{27} \times 1 = 5.5 + 1 = 6.50$$

$$\text{Statement 2, Scale value} = 6.5 + \frac{75-60}{45} \times 1 = 6.5 + 0.33 = 6.83$$

$$\text{Statement 3, Scale value} = 5.5 + \frac{75-69}{24} \times 1 = 5.5 + 0.25 = 5.75$$

Now to obtain the interquartile range (I.R.) for each statement, calculate Q_1 and Q_3 by the formula (3.18) and I.R. by the formula (4.3)

$$Q_i = l_{io} + \frac{\frac{iN}{4} - c_i}{f_i} \times 1$$

and $$\text{I.R.} = Q_3 - Q_1$$

$$Q_3 = 7.5 + \frac{\frac{3\times150}{4} - 105}{24} \times 1 = 7.5 + .31 = 7.81$$

I. R. = 7.81 – 4.92 = 2.89

Statement – 2,

$$Q_1 = 4.5 + \frac{37.5 - 33}{12} \times 1 = 4.5 + 0.38 = 4.88$$

$$Q_3 = 7.5 + \frac{112.5 - 105}{18} \times 1 = 7.5 + 0.42 = 7.92$$

I. R. = 7.92 – 4.88 = 3.04

Statement – 3,

$$Q_1 = 3.5 + \frac{37.5 - 21}{18} \times 1 = 3.5 + 0.92 = 4.42$$

$$Q_3 = 6.5 + \frac{112.5 - 93}{36} \times 1 = 6.5 + 0.54 = 7.04$$

I. R. = 7.04 – 4.42 = 2.62

To construct the attitude scale by the method of equally appearing interval, one should select 20 to 30 statements (Taken 3 in the present example) for which the scale values are relatively equally spaced and I. R. values are relatively small. If two statements have the same scale values and only one out of them is to be retained, one may select the statement having lesser I. R. value. Once 20 – 30 statements are selected, they are embodied in the questionnaire in a random order to avoid any hierarchy. The questionnaire is administered to the respondents.

Each respondent is requested to endorse all those statements with which he agrees. The average (median) of the score values of all the statements which he endorses becomes his scale score. If this score is more than 6 in 11-point scale, then it is considered that the respondent has favourable attitude towards the object and vice-versa. In the given example, if we suppose that the repondents endorsed the statements 1 and 2 only, then the average score is (6.50 + 6.83)/2 = 6.6, which is greater than 6. Thus, if may be concluded that the respondent is favourable to the object. Besides many goods points, the scale suffers with many lacunae which are not discussed here.

LIKERT'S SCALE OR SUMMATED RATINGS SCALE

Likert's scale is an ordinal scale constructed to indicate the extent of respondents attitude towards an object related to the problem of survey to which they agree or disagree with a series of mental belief or feeling. It is named after its developer, Rensis Likert[3]. This scale consists of a set of five point scale: Strongly agree, agree, undecided, disagree, strongly disagree. Stepwise procedure of constructing Likert scale is as follows:

1. A large number of statements related to the subject of survey are collected by the researcher.

---

3. Likert Rensis (1932). A technique for the measurement of attitude, *Archives of Psychology*, No. 140, 44-53.

2. These statements are administered to some people of the target population whose attitudes are to be studied. They are requested to respond to each statement by indicating on any one of the scale point, strongly agree ☐, agree ☐, uncertain ☐, disagree ☐, fully disagree ☐.

   Usually in Likert's scale five point ratings are taken. But in many situations they may vary from 3 to 7. For example, in three point scale ratings, they are, agree ☐, undecided ☐, disagree ☐. In the sequel, we will pursue only with five point ratings.
3. Five ratings are numerically scored by giving numbers 5, 4, 3, 2 and 1 respectively in order of preference from strongly agree to strongly disagree as a tradition.
4. Work out the individual scores by totalling the itemwise scores of each statement.
5. For analysis purpose, the researcher uses only those statements which are capable to distinguish between high and low total scores. Suppose the instrument consists of 20 statements. Then the following criterion will help to decide about the statements. Maximum score for most favourable response = $20 \times 5 = 100$, Maximum number of neutral attitude = $20 \times 3 = 60$, Maximum number of most unfavourable attitude = $20 \times 1 = 20$.

So, the range of individual scores is 20 to 100. If the score is more than 60, it indicates favourable attitude and less than 60, unfavourable attitude. Of course, a total score 100 will show greater favourable opinion and 20, almost totally unfavourable opinion or attitude.

6. Now to select those statements which have highly discriminatory power, the researcher should prefer to select 25 per cent of statements with top scores and 25 per cent with bottom scores. These two groups are interpreted as criterion groups by which to evaluate individual statements.
7. Now itemwise analysis is carried out. To select the most discriminating items for each item, the correlation is calculated between item score and the total of all item scores. Those with highest correlation are finally retained in survey questionnaire. Number of items preferred is 20–25.

Strengths

1. Likert's scales are very popular as they are simple to construct as compared to Thurstone scales.
2. Likert's scales provide more information about the extent of agreement as against restricting the respondents to simple agree/disagree approbation in Thurstone scales.

Weaknesses

1. Likert's scales are not interval scales just like Thurstone scales.
2. In Likert's scale, often the same total of an individual respondent can be arrived by a variety of patterns. This causes problem.

For a detailed comparison of Thurstone and Likert's scales, readers are advised to read the research paper of Edwards and Kenny (1946).

SEMANTIC DIFFERENTIAL SCALE

An unique bipolar scale format that captures a subject's attitude or opinion about a given item is called semantic differential scale. This scale was expounded by Charles Osgood, George Suci and Percy Tannenbaun. This is given as good/bad, like/dislike; helpful/unhelpful, agree/disagree, true/false, etc.

GUTTMAN SCALE OR SCALOGRAM ANALYSIS

The method of developing attitude scales for items was propounded by Louis Guttman. Like other scales, the procedure consists of a series of statements to which a respondent expresses his feeling towards agreement or disagreement. Guttman held that attitude items can be arranged in order, higher to lower, in such a way that a respondent who consents to a particular item of a statement implies his consent for all succeeding statements. Hence, Guttman's technique gives rise to *cumulative scale*. This technique is also known as *scalogram analysis*. Suppose there are five problems of arithmetic say, *A, B, C, D* and *E* ordered from toughest to easiest. Here it is taken for granted that a respondent, who can solve the problem *A*, he will also be able to solve the next four problems *B, C, D* and *E*. If a person can solve the problem *B*, he will also be able to solve the problems *C, D, E* and so on.

If a problem is solved, weight 1 is given to it and items after it. Assign a weight 0 to the problems preceding it. Scalogram table can be prepared as follows:

Table 9.1 Scalogram analysis table

Respondents	*Ranks of problems*					*Scores of respondents*
	A	*B*	*C*	*D*	*E*	
	1	*2*	*3*	*4*	*5*	
R_1	1	1	1	1	1	5
R_2	0	1	1	1	1	4
R_3	0	0	1	1	1	3
R_4	0	0	0	1	1	2
R_5	0	0	0	0	1	1
R_6	0	0	0	0	0	0

From the Table 9.1, it can easily be deduced that a score of 5 shows that the respondent agrees with all the statement. A score of 4 shows that the respondent does not agree with the strongest statement *A*, but agrees with rest four statements and so on. This affirms that these items fall along a *unidimensional* continuum or there is no doubt to the rank order of the arithmetic problem from toughest to easiest.

Scalogram Analysis Procedure

In general we are not sure in advance that a given set of attitude items (statements, exactly fall in an unidimensional continuum from most to least favourable or vice versa). The purpose of scalogram analysis is to ascertain that the statements are in conformity with the hypothesis that the statements are in unidimensional scale.

Step 1: The universe of content, i.e., the issue we are to deal with, should specifically be defined. One should not talk in general terms such as attitude towards India's development. It should be in definite terms like agricultural development, population growth, market development, etc. Once the universe of content is exactly clarified, it becomes easy to obtain scalable set of statements.

Step 2: Now a researcher is to develop a number of statements related to the universe of content (issue/problem). All those statements which are ambiguous, irrelevant or impractical should be eliminated on the basis of intuition and experience.

Step 3: This step is concerned with pretesting whether the issue is scalable as suggested by Guttman. According to him one should start with 12 or more items and select 4 to 6 items for final survey. The number of respondents in the pretest survey may be small, say, 20–25.

In pretesting, the respondents are administered all selected items to have their opinion using a Likert type 5 point scale, i.e., strongest agree to, ..., totally disagree. If the strongest favourable statement is given the score 5 and weakest, the score 1, then for twelve items, a respondent's scores can range from 60 to 12.

The respondents' responses are arranged in order of total scores for the purpose of analysis. If they fall in cumulative scale, they are selected and if they do not show unidimensional continuum, they are either rejected or merged with other categories. After pretest, usually 4–6 items are chosen for final survey. For final survey, the number of respondents is relatively large, may it be 100 or more.

Step 4: Suppose out of twelve items, 5 items serialed as 3, 6, 7, 10 and 11 are selected for final scale and they are administered to 20 respondents. Their response to various items are tabulated alongwith cases which show nonunidimensionality, marked as errors. To test whether these items (a set of statements) may be regarded as unidimensional continuum (a perfect cumulative scale). Guttman gave a measure which he called the **coefficient of reproducibility**. Following formula was given for its measure:

$$\text{Coeff. of reproducibility} = 1 - \frac{e}{nN} \quad ...(9.1)$$

where, n — Number of items

N — Number of respondents

e — Number of errors

Guttman set the limit of coefficient of reproducibility as 0.9. A value of 0.9 or more confirms cumulative scale or unidimensionality and vice-versa. More explicitly, Guttman's coefficient is supposed to indicate the accuracy with which the responses to various items can be reproduced from the total scores. Following example will further elucidate the concept of reproducibility.

***Example* 9.2.** The example is given with five statements (items) and for only 20 respondents (in real survey it is 100 or more) whose responses to various items are tabulated alongwith errors, with rows corresponding to respondents and columns to statements.

Respondent	Statements (items)					Scores	Errors
	3	6	7	10	11		
1	1	1	1	1	1	5	0
2	1	1	1	1	1	5	0
3	0	1	1	1	1	4	0
4	0	1	0	1	1	3	1
5	0	0	1	1	1	3	0
6	0	0	0	1	1	2	0
7	0	0	1	0	0	1	2
8	0	1	1	1	1	4	0
9	0	0	0	0	1	1	0
10	0	0	0	0	0	0	0
11	0	1	1	0	1	3	1
12	0	0	0	0	0	0	0
13	1	1	1	1	1	5	0
14	0	0	1	0	0	1	2
15	0	0	1	1	1	3	0
16	1	1	1	1	1	5	0
17	0	1	1	0	1	3	1
18	1	1	1	1	1	5	0
19	0	0	0	1	1	2	0
20	0	0	1	1	1	3	0
$N = 20$	$n = 5$						$e = 7$

Substituting the values of N, n and e in the formula (9.1),

$$\text{Coeff. of reproducibility} = 1 - \frac{7}{5 \times 20} = 1 - 0.07 = 0.93$$

Since the computed value of coefficient of reproducibility is more than 0.9, it meets the requirement of the test of unidimensionality. The statements can be regarded in cumulative scale.

Merits

1. It ensures that only unidimensional attitude scale is being measured.
2. Researcher's subjective selection does not creep in the development of scale since it is based on the responses of the subjects.
3. It includes only a small number of statements. That makes it easy to administer to the respondents.
4. Guttman's scale is appropriate in personal, mailed and telephone surveys.

Demerits

1. The main difficulty is that it is rather impossible to develop a perfectly unidimensional continuum scale.
2. The scale developing technique is complex as compared to other scales.
3. Conceptually it is difficult to understand and analyse.

COLLECTION OF DATA

As a matter of fact this aspect has already been covered in the preceding sections. Once the survey has been conducted by any method discussed earlier, the information is at hand. The information is obtained either in the form of quantitative measures like height, weight, income, amount spent on purchases or services, etc. or in the form of opinion on various items as discussed under scaling techniques. If the information is in the form of statements, it is being coded and scores of each subject (respondent) work as data.

ERRORS IN SURVEYS

As discussed in Chapter 7, two types of errors in surveys are likely to creep in. One is *sampling error* which is associated with the process of selecting a sample. This can be taken care of by choosing a proper sampling design. Another is the *non-sampling error* which can happen in census and in sample surveys as well. Non-sampling error can occur in probability sampling as well as nonprobability sampling. Therefore, a researcher should be wary of the nonsampling error which can happen due to the following causes. They should be eliminated or reduced as far as possible.

(*i*) **Coverage errors:** This type of errors are caused due to fault in the sampling frame like inaccuracy, incompleteness, duplication, inappropriateness, obsolescence or incomplete coverage in field by the interviewer. These errors can be minimized by increasing the efficiency and care.

(*ii*) **Response error:** This error may occur because of inadequacy of schedule or questionnaire, the interviewer's carelessness, the respondents deliberate ill-intentions.

Interview Bias

Many times an interviewer ask some questions in such a manner that it prompts the respondent to give a derived answer. This introduces interview bias. This can be reduced by imparting proper training to the interviewers about, "how to conduct an interview."

Scaling Measurement Error

Such error occurs when various scale measures designed to collect primary data are inaccurate. Inaccuracy means incongruous questions, false scale attributes or inappropriate scale points used to respondent's answers.

Respondent Errors

Respondents are also likely to provide incorrect information due to lack of memory, tendency to exaggerate, underplay or to hide events. They may like to give common opinion rather than their own view.

Non-response Errors

Many times an interviewer fails to reach and contact a respondent as he is either not available or left the house or dwelling. In case of mailed questionnaire, many respondents selected in the sample have either left the place or do not return the duly completed questionnaire. This leads to *complete non-response* error. If this number is large, our results are very likely to be biased as the characteristics of the respondents may differ from those of non-respondents.

Even if respondents are available, there are certain questions which people do not understand. Further some questions are so personal which they do not want to reveal like income, extra-marital relations, diseases, etc. This leads to *incomplete non-response* error.

This error also causes bias. This can be reduced by properly designing and testing a questionnaire.

Processing Errors

These errors often creep at the time of preparing data files, i.e., when the data are coded, edited or imputed. Proper care can minimize such errors.

Estimation Error

If an inappropriate estimation method is adopted, then the results will be biased, regardless of the fact that how correctly the survey has been conducted and accurately the data have been collected.

Analysis Error

These errors occur due to application of improper analytical methods. Errors due to misinterpretation or faulty publication of results deliberately or inadvertently are also considered as analysis error. To avoid this type of errors, a researcher should not introduce any preconceived ideas and utmost care be taken while publishing the results.

ANALYSIS OF DATA

The raw material of any research process is primary data. To collect any relevant, reliable, unbiased and accurate information, it has to be analysed properly. The first step of analysis is to tabulate information in a proper format which paves the way for further analysis. Any calculations made to find out certain population constants or their estimates like mean, variance, finding out association between attributes or correlation between variables, testing of hypotheses; regression studies; analysis of variance or multivariate analysis; decision making; forecasting, etc. constitute the part of analysis of data. All these topics are well covered in various chapter of this book. They need no further elaboration. Of course some points will be pinned over here which will bring forth some concepts.

In the beginning of this chapter, it is made amply clear that there are two types of research processes, (*i*) survey method, (*ii*) experiments. Survey are conducted for behavioural research studies like opinion of people about a policy, a product, liking, market position, etc. Surveys are mostly conducted on animates. Of course geological and geographical survey are also conducted that are actually explorations in a sense. Experiments are controlled, systematic and well designed trials which are conducted to know the effect of certain treatments or to verify some theory or assertions. Experimental research designs have been covered in Chapter 12.

Analysis of data for survey designs usually involve estimation of proportions, percentages, association studies, comparison between different population or products. Multivariate analysis is also carried out when two or more than two dependent variables are involved and when a number of observations are taken for each subject or object.

Experimental univariate data analysis usually involves the method of *analysis of variance* (ANOVA) and multivariate analysis of variance (MANOVA) is conducted when one evaluates mean differences of two or more dependent criterion variables simultaneously. It is carried out in two steps:

Step 1. First an omnibus test is performed, i.e., to test the overall hypothesis of no difference in the means of different groups.

Step 2. A follow up test is conducted to explain the group differences.

MANOVA is a widely used technique in behavioral and social sciences. Besides MANOVA, there are many other multivariate analysis techniques. To name a few are: principal components analysis, factor analysis, discriminant analysis, cluster analysis, etc.

Analysis of variance is covered in Chapter 12. At the same time multivariate analysis techniques are kept out of the scope of this book except those which are already covered under multiple and partial correlation, multiple regression. For references to multivariate analysis, please go through suggested reading given at the end of this chapter.

INTERPRETATION OF RESULTS

Interpretation is the essence of any research. A survey or experiment might have been conducted absolutely-thoroughly and a most appropriate analysis of data been carried out. But if the results available after analysis are not interpreted skilfully and with dexterity, the purpose of research is completely vitiated. Prior to interpretation of results, one should ensure that –

(*a*) The data are free from sampling and non-sampling errors, biases and mistakes that may arise due to subjective and objective factors.

(*b*) The data are adequate, appropriate and trustworthy for drawing inferences.

(*c*) The data reflect good homogeneity as it leads to reliability.

(*d*) Pertinent analysis has been carried out unmistakably.

As a matter of fact, the process of interpretation is intertwined with analysis of data. A researcher should be clear in mind, what analysis has been carried out, what calculations are involved, what statistical values are worked out, for what do these figures stand and how far can they reveal. No one will be able to give exact interpretation of results unless he/she is not well versed with analysis process. For example, correlation coefficient value may be very high, but if the variable are such that they cannot be correlated, then such a value is to be outrightly rejected. For instance, a high correlation value between the demand of steel and medicines in India reveals nothing except nonsense relationship. In the want of statistical knowledge, it is always beneficial to consult an expert and experienced statistician. Further if any extraneous information is collected on auxiliary or concomitant variables, it must be considered and utilized at the time of interpreting the results.

While interpreting the results, a researcher should always consider what type of study has been conducted. If the study is of exploratory nature, it does not have a hypothesis to start with, but if provides basis to establish hypotheses. As such interpretation is involved in transition from exploratory to experimental research. Exploratory research elaborates knowledge and concepts. It is not conclusive. On the other side, the researches based on statistical theory, i.e., surveys employing probability sampling designs and random experiments lead to hypothesis testing and enable to draw inferences with some level of confidence. If the level of significance is 5 per cent, i.e., the level of confidence is 95 per cent, then it is expected that on repeating a survey or experiment under the same conditions, one would get the same result 95 times out of 100 repetitions as one gets at first time.

WRITING OF REPORT

Once the results are interpreted, it completes the research process. Still whole of research study remains unfinished until a report is written and presented to the sponsoring authorities and published to be known to others concerned and scientific world. Hence, report writing is considered as the last part of a research project. Report writing is not an easy task. It needs good skill and command on language. To maintain uniformity certain norms are set and a format is provided in which a scientific report has to be presented. Outline of a research report which should normally be adopted is as follows:

1. Preliminaries

(*a*) **Title or Cover Page:** It is a hard front page of a report which on the top expresses in words briefly and clearly about the topic which has been reported inside, so called 'title'. Title must not contain a verb as far as possible. Some people prefer to give a chart or diagram also on the cover page related to the study. In the middle it contains author's name(s). Below it, the year in which the report is finalised.

At the bottom, the name of the institution to which it belongs is given.

(*b*) **Preface:** A brief introductory statement authored by the researcher regarding the problem studies especially one that explains the aims and objectives of the study. Preface also contains the acknowledgements to all those who have meaningfully helped in the study. Some authors prefer to record acknowledgements under a separate heading.

(*c*) **Foreword:** It is a short introduction of the work done by the researcher alongwith its utility usually written by an eminent person other than the author but related to the study directly or indirectly.

(*d*) **Table of Contents:** It is a junctural list of chapters and their contents subsumed in the report alongwith the page numbers. This also provides the list of tables and illustrations with their page numbers.

2. Introduction

Introduction of a research report covers the following aspects:

(*a*) Statement of the problem.
(*b*) Purpose and objectives of the study.
(*c*) Hypothesis and definitions of the objects.
(*d*) Time, place and material that have been utilized in the duration of study.
(*e*) Scope, assumptions and limitations of study be delineated clearly.
(*f*) Organizations of research work may be outlined.

3. Review of Literature

In this chapter, the studies and researches conducted prior to the proposed study on similar or like topics are briefly cited chronologically as far as possible. The contents simply provide the reference material.

4. Abstract

It is a summary of the complete report. It is the most readable part of the report. It is a time saver. Even if one is going to read the complete report, he prefers to read it first as he gets an idea in advance what is to come out of it. It should be short in 2–3 pages. It should be self-contained, i.e., it should cover all aspects and recommendations available in the report in non-technical language as far as possible so that it can be perceived by all concerned.

5. Methodology and Research Design

This part of report should cover the following aspects:

(*a*) **Type of research:** It should first be clarified whether it is a survey/experimental/historical data research.

If it is a survey research, what is sampling design, sample size, method of survey, i.e., whether type of enquiry is observational, through interview or mailed questionnaire method, should elaborately be given. In case of observational method, instructions given to the observer should be specified. If the study is carried through interviews, details of schedule, coverage, type of scale used with justification, type of interviewers engaged with minimum qualification requirement, travelling plan, area of survey, time schedule and instructions given to the interviewer be delineated.

If the research is based on historical data, its sources and method of collection be discussed adequately.

In case of experimental research, the design of experiment with its layout be given. Details of experiment pertaining to the number of treatments, experimental units, number of replications, etc., be mentioned.

(*b*) **Analysis of data:** The method of analysis of data which is being used as objectives and requirements of the project should be explicated. All formulae involved should be given and decoded. What hypotheses are being tested and what statistical tests are being applied should be given in details alongwith test statistic.

In case of experimental design, analysis procedure is almost fixed as per design. So, skeleton ANOVA table and tests for pairwise comparisons should be presented.

If any instruments are used for measurements, their validity, accuracy, precision, etc., should also be given.

If any computer package is used for analysis, its details should be given.

6. Discussion of Results

Once the analysis is over, the results may be depicted in the form of tables, graphs, charts with appropriate illustrations. The rejection or acceptance of hypothesis should be construed specifying the test and level of significance (probability of type I error).

Inferences drawn from the results of analysed data are termed as interpretation of results. Enough guideline has been given with regard to interpretation in the previous section. That should be adhered to.

7. Footnotes

In case of quotations, quoted values, cross references, citation authorities and sources, explanation of a point, etc., are placed on the bottom of the pages (under a line) in which they occur marked with asterisk (*) or numerals 1, 2, 3, ... It is a supporting information.

8. Summary

It is customary to conclude a report with a very succinct summary. In business report it is called as executive summary. This covers the research report in capsule form.

9. Referencing and Bibliography

References are ineluctable part of a thesis, report or standard book. In thesis and reports, references are given in introduction, review of literature, material and method, analysis, discussion of results, etc. In short, references occur from beginning to end in the text in concise form, usually name and year of publication. Whereas bibliography is an alphabetical list providing complete details of the publications referred in the text. This helps the researchers and readers to go through the detailed contents of the same. Now we give below Harvard system of referencing.

Referencing in the Text

Documents cited in the text are given with author's name and year of publication for the purpose of identification. The norms are as follows:

Works of different authors cited in the text on similar or related topics be given in alphabetical order.

(*i*) In case of single authors (Cox, 1958; Evans, 1986; Stewart, 1981).

(*ii*) When referring to two authors of the same article (Enis and Keith, 1975; Moses and Kalton, 1979).

(*iii*) When joint authorship goes to more than two persons) (Nie *et al.*, 1991; Selltiz *et al.*, 1976).

(*iv*) A company's report with corporate author(s) (Bharat Sanchar Nigam Ltd., 2004).

(*v*) For official publications with no obvious author(s) (Census, 2001, Employment News, 2003).

(*vi*) In case of more than one publication by the same author(s) in the same year Bancroft, 1972 a, b).

(*vii*) When referring to more than one publication of the same author (Edards, 1957, 1967).

(*viii*) When an author is referred to another author without going through the original publication (Thurstone, 1928, cited by Beri 2003).

Referencing in Bibliography

Bibliography is the last part of a report which displays an alphabetical list of all those authors, scientists and workers who have been cited in the text. A reference contains complete information with regard to the name of author(s), year, title, name of publication, volume number, issue number, page numbers. In case of books, edition, chapter number and page number are also specified in a reference. We give below a few references without explanation which cover different situations. After going through them thoroughly, a researcher will be able to prepare the bibliography without difficulty.

It seems germane to point out that there are two types of publications, the books and journals. In case of books, title of book appears in italics and rest of the details in conventional print. Whereas in case of journal, the name of the journal is printed in italics either in full or in abbreviated form as per international convention.

1. Aaker, D.A. (1971), *Multivariate Analysis in Marketing*, Wadsworth Publishing Co.

2. Agarwal, B.L. (1990), Testing a Main Effect in a Three Factor Mixed Model, *Communications in Statistics, Theory and Methods*, 19, 2, 723–738.
3. Morris, C. (1973), *Quantitative Approaches to Business Studies*, Pitman Publishing, London.
4. Nachmias, Chava and David Nachmias (1982), *Research Methods in the Soil Sciences*, Edward Arnold (Publishers) Ltd., London.
5. Velleman, P.F. and Wilkinson L. (1993), Nominal ordinal, Interval and Ratio Typologies Are Misleading, *American statistician*, 47, 1, 65–72.

10. Appendix

This part of report contains relevant supporting material utilized in research process. To name, the schedule or questionnaire, sample information, data and result tables, like ANOVA table, maps, power of test(s), generated numbers, mathematical derivations, computer programs, etc.

QUESTIONS AND EXERCISES

1. What characteristics that makes the secondary data distinct from primary data? What are the main sources of secondary data?
2. Why is it necessary to review critically the secondary data before use?
3. Differentiate between a schedule and a questionnaire.
4. What are the limitations of a mailed questionnaire?
5. Distinguish between the following:
   (*a*) Direct and indirect observations.
   (*b*) Population and target population.
   (*c*) Structured and unstructured interviews.
   (*d*) Summated and Guttman scales.
6. What are the characteristics of a good questionnaire?
7. What do you understand by (*i*) open ended question, (*ii*) dichotomous questions and (*iii*) multiple choice questions?
8. What are the merits and demerits of three types of survey methods: personal interview, through mailed questionnaire and telephonic survey?
9. What is multidimensional construct and how can you measure cohesiveness between scales that have multiple dimensions?
10. Discuss judgement sampling and snowball sampling.
11. What are the criteria which enable a researcher to select an appropriate sampling design?
12. Give various components of a report with their important features.
13. In the absence of a reliable sampling frame, what sample design/designs would you prefer and why?
14. Why do many researchers these days emphasize on target population rather than a total population?
15. Compare the merits and demerits of probability and non-probability sampling.
16. What do you understand by mall intercept interviews?

17. Out of four measurement scales, which one provides the researcher with the most data and information?
18. Explain nominal, interval and ratio scales with examples.
19. What is an attitude? What are the factors that constitute attitude of a person?
20. Compare Thurstone and Likert scales.
21. What is meant by scalogram analysis and how is it carried out?
22. Discuss different causes of non-sampling errors and how to minimize them.
23. Write a note on semantic differential scale.
24. What are the factors responsible for bad questions in a mailed questionnaire?
25. What purpose is served by pretesting a questionnaire?
26. What are the various components of a research problem? Describe in brief their role.
27. In what respect an exploratory research differ from experimental research?
28. What has to be ensured prior to interpretation of results for reliable inferences?
29. Throw light on the advantages and shortcomings of observational method of survey.
30. Experimental method of research is not suitable in management field, "Discuss what are the problems in the introduction of this research design in business organisation"?
    (M.B.A.(Pt.I), Raj. Univ., 1985)
31. Distinguish between experiment and survey. Explain fully the survey method of research.
    (M.Phil (EAFM), Raj Univ., 1987)
32. When should a researcher use multivariate analysis?
33. Describe in brief editing, coding, classification and tabulation as components of data processing.
34. Compute Guttman's coefficient of reproducibility from the following information and draw conclusion.
    Number of subjects = 40
    Number of items = 5
    Number of errors = 8
35. Discuss widely used method of developing differential scale. Also discuss its merits.
36. (*a*) How is a research problem formulated? Describe in brief, the role of statistical hypothesis in examining the nature and significance of research problem.
    (*b*) Discuss various scaling techniques? Compare their merits and demerits.
    (M.B.A., Part-II, MLSU., 2001)
37. A consumer product manufacturer is planning to enter cooking medium market with a new brand of groundnut oil. The company wants to conduct a detailed study to identify users of the product and to collect information about usership and buying pattern in the capacity research executive in this company:
    (*a*) What type of research would you propose?
    (*b*) Explain the following aspects of the study:
    (*i*) Sampling design.
    (*ii*) Method of data collection.
    (*iii*) Format of the questionnaire.
    (*c*) How will you organize the field work and ensure reliability of data?
    (*d*) What analysis technique(s) will you suggest and why?
    (M.B.A. Part–II, MLSU, 2002)

38. What is a scientific enquiry? Why is it called scientific? Discuss a problem of research in social sciences.

(*M.B.A., Part–II, MLSU, 2000*)

39. (*a*) Describe the different types of research, clearly pointing out the differences between an experiment and a survey.

(*b*) Which different scaling techniques are you aware of? Suggest some rating and attitude measurement scales and also explain the situation in which rating scales are suitable.

(*M.B.A., Part–II, MLSU, 2002*)

40. There can be no research without statistics for reliable fact finding. Justify your answer with concrete reasoning whether you agree or disagree.

SUGGESTED READING

Agresti, A. (1990). *Categorical Data Analysis*, Wiley, New York.

Anderson, Ronald L., Tatham and William C. Black (1998). *Multivariate Data Analysis*, (5th ed.), Prentice Hall, (Upper Saddle River, NJ).

Anderson, T.W. (1958). *An Introduction to Multivariate Analysis*, John Wiley & Sons, New York.

Beri, G.C. (2000). *Marketing Research*, Tata McGraw Hill Publishing, 3rd ed., New Delhi.

David McNabb (2002). *Research Methods in Public Administration and Non-profit Management*, M.E. Sharpe.

Dennis, Child (1973). *The Essentials of Factor Analysis*, Holt, Rinethart and Winston.

Edwards, A.L. (1969). *Techniques of Attitude Scale Construction*, Vakils, Feffer and Simons.

Edwards A.L. and Kenny, Katherine C. (1946). A Comparison of Thurstone and Likert Techniques of Attitude Scale Construction, *Journal of Applied Psychology*, 30, pp. 374—84.

Garg, Rajendar K. (1996). The Influence of Positive and Negative Wording and Issues Involvement on Response to Likert Scales in Marketing Research, *Journal of Marketing Research Society*, 38, 3, pp. 235–46.

Ghosh, B.N. (1992). *Scientific Methods and Social Research*, Sterling Publishers.

Goodman, Leo A. (1961). Snowball sampling, *Annals of Mathematical Statistics*, 32, pp. 148–170.

Green, Paul E. and Carmone, F.J. (1970). *Multidimensional Scaling in Marketing Analysis*, Allyn & Bacon, Boston.

Green, Paul E. (1978). *Analysing Multivariate Data*, Hindsdale, III, Dryden Press.

Hair, J.F., Bush, R.P. and Ortinau, D.J. (2003). *Marketing Research*, Tata McGraw-Hill Publishing Company Ltd., 2nd ed., Delhi.

Jeremy J. Foster, Ema Barbus and Christian Yavorsky (2006). *Understanding and Using Advanced Statistics*, Sage Publication.

Jobson, J.D. (1991). *Applied Multivariate Data Analysis, Regression and Experimental Design*, Vol. I, Springer Verlag, New York.

Jobson, J.D. (1992). *Applied Multivariate Data Analysis, Categorical and Multivariate Methods*, Springer Verlag, Vol. II, New York.

Joseph, F. Healey (2004). *Statistics*, Thomson Wadsworth.

Karson, Marvin J. (1982). *Multivariate Statistical Methods*, The Iowa State University Press, Ames, Iowa.

Kerlinger, Fred N. (1983). *Foundation of Behavioural Research*, Surjeet Publications.

Kerlinger, Fred N. and Pedhazur, Elazar J. (1973). *Multivariate Regression in Behavioural Research*, Holt, Rinehart and Winston, New York.

Kothari, C.R. (1990). *Research Methodology, Methods & Techniques*, New Age International Private Ltd., 2nd ed., Delhi.

Lavrakas, Paul J. (1987). *Telephone Survey Methods: Sampling, Selection and Supervision*, Sage, Beverley Hills.

Peter M. Chisnall (1981). *Marketing Research, Analysis and Measurement*, McGraw Hill Book Co. Ltd., 2nd ed., U.K.

Riesman, C.K. (1994). *Quantitative Studies in Social Work*, Thousand Oaks (CA), Sage.

Ronald, Caulcutt (1991). *Statistics in Research and Development*, CRC Press.

Segal, M.N. (1984). Alternate Form Cojoint Reliability, *Journal of Advertising Research*, 4, pp. 31–38.

Shajahan, S. (2004). *Research Methods for Management*, Jaico Publishing House, 2nd ed., Mumbai.

Singer, E. and Presser, S.(Eds) (1989). *Research Methods: A Reader*, University of Chicago Press, Chicago.

Takeuchi, K, H. Yanai and B.N. Mukherjee (1982). *Foundations of Multivariate Analysis*, New Age International Private Ltd., New Delhi.

Taylor, Mark (1977). Ordinal and Interval Scaling, *Journal of Marketing Research Society*, 25, 4, pp. 297–303.

Thurtstone, Louis (1928). Attitude can be measured, *American Journal of Sociology*, Vol. 3.

Thurstone, L. and Chave, E. G. (1929). *The Measurement of Attitude,* University Chicago Press, Chicago.

Wilkinson, T.S. and P.L. Bhandarkar (1979). *Methodology and Techniques of Social Research*, Himalaya Publishing House, Mumbai.

10
Chapter

Test of Significance

A research worker or an experimenter has always some fixed ideas about certain population(s) vis-a-vis population parameter(s) based on prior experiments, surveys or experience. Sometimes these ideas might have been fixed in the mind vicariously. There is a need to ascertain whether these ideas or claims are correct or not, by collecting information in the form of data. In this way, we come across two types of problems, first is to draw inferences about the population on the basis of sample data and the other is to decide whether our sample observations have come from a postulated population or not. The first type of problem has almost been covered in Chapter 7. In this chapter, we would be dealing with the second type of problem.

Generally, a hypothesis is established beforehand. By hypothesis we mean to give postulated or stipulated value(s) of a parameter. Also, instead of giving values, some relationship between parameters is postulated in the case of two or more populations. On the basis of observational data, a test is performed to decide whether the postulated hypothesis should be accepted or not. This involves certain amount of risk. This amount of risk is termed as a level of significance. When the hypothesis is accepted, we consider it a non-significant result and if the reverse situation occurs, it is called a significant result. The tests, which are dealt within this chapter pertain to parametric tests. A test is defined as, "*A statistical test is a procedure governed by certain rules, which leads to take a decision about the hypothesis for its acceptance or rejection on the basis of sample values.*"

Statistical tests of hypothesis play an important role in industry, biological sciences, behavioral sciences and economics, etc. The use of tests has been made clear through a number of practical problems.

1. A feed manufacturer announces that his feed contains forty per cent protein. Now to make sure whether his claim is correct or not, one has to take a random sample of the product and by chemical analysis, find the protein percentages in the samples. From these observed values, he would decide about the manufacturer's claim for his product. This is done by performing a test of significance.
2. There is a process A which produces certain items. It is considered that a new process B is better than process A. Both the processes are put under operation and then the items produced by them are sampled and observations are taken on

them. A statistical test is performed based on these observations which enables us to decide whether process B is better than A or not.

3. Often we are interested to know what is the best dose of a chemical treatment? Two or more doses of the chemical are applied or administered on a number of subjects and response is observed. Now it is tested statistically whether the doses differ significantly or not.
4. Psychologists are often interested in knowing whether the level of IQ of a group of school boys is up to a certain standard or not. In this case, some boys are selected and an intelligence test is conducted. The scores obtained by them pass through a statistical test and a decision is made whether their IQ is up to the standard or not.

There is no end to such types of practical problems where statistical tests can be applied. These are only a few examples. Here, a very important point is to be noted. Whatever conclusions are drawn about the population(s), they are always subjected to some error. Hence there is always some risk involved in these decisions. Thus, a level of significance is always associated with these decisions. Now we will discuss various terms involved in testing of hypothesis in an exact way before describing the statistical tests.

TYPES OF HYPOTHESIS

"A hypothesis is an assertion or conjecture about the parameter(s) of population distribution(s)."

In case we are considering more than one population, it may be about the relationship between the similar parameters of the distributions. For example, the mean μ of a distribution is fifty, i.e., $H: \mu = 50$. The variance σ^2 of a distribution is 36, i.e., $H: \sigma^2 = 36$. For two populations, the hypothesis may be that the means μ_1 and μ_2 or variances σ_1^2 and σ_2^2 are equal, i.e., $H: \mu_1 = \mu_2$ or $H: \sigma_1^2 = \sigma_2^2$. Many times, the statement in the notational form can be given in the following manner as well.

$$H: \mu > 0,\ H: \mu < 0,\ H: \mu = 0,\ H: \mu = c,$$

$$H: \mu_1 > \mu_2,\ H: \mu_1 \leq \mu_2, \text{ etc.}$$

where c is a known constant value. Similarly for variance(s), the hypothesis may be given as,

$$H: \sigma^2 = \sigma_0^2,\ H: \sigma^2 > \sigma_0^2,\ H: \sigma_1^2 = \sigma_2^2,\ H: \sigma_1^2 < \sigma_2^2, \text{ etc.}$$

where σ_0^2 is a known fixed value. A hypothesis is further classified according to its nature and usage.

Null Hypothesis

A hypothesis which is to be actually tested for acceptance or rejection is termed as null hypothesis. It is denoted by H_0.

Alternative Hypothesis

It is a statement about the population parameter or parameters, which gives an alternative to the null hypothesis (H_0), within the range of pertinent values of the parameter, i.e., if H_0 is accepted, what hypothesis is to be rejected and vice versa. An alternative hypothesis is denoted by H_1 or H_A. The idea of alternative hypothesis was originated by Neyman. For instance,

if $H_0 : \mu = 0$, the alternatives are, $H_1 : \mu \neq 0$, $H_1 : \mu > 0$ or $H_1 : \mu < 0$,

if $H_0 : \mu_1 = \mu_2$, the alternatives are, $H_1 : \mu_1 \neq \mu_2$, $H_1 : \mu_1 > \mu_2$ or $H_1 : \mu_1 < \mu_2$.

if $H_0 : \sigma^2 = \sigma_0^2$, the alternatives are, $H_1 : \sigma^2 \neq \sigma_0^2$, $H_1 : \sigma^2 < \sigma_0^2$ or $H_1 : \sigma^2 > \sigma_0^2$

if $H_1 : \sigma_1^2 = \sigma_2^2$, the alternatives are, $H_1 : \sigma_1^2 \neq \sigma_2^2$, $H_1 : \sigma_1^2 > \sigma_2^2$ or $H_1 : \sigma_1^2 < \sigma_2^2$.

Simple and Composite Hypothesis

If the statistical hypothesis completely specifies the distribution, it is called a *simple hypothesis,* otherwise it is called a *composite hypothesis.* For instance, we consider a normal population $N(\mu, \sigma^2)$, where σ^2 is known and we want to test the hypothesis, $H_0 : \mu = 25$ against $H_1 : \mu = 30$. From these hypotheses we know that μ can take either of the two values, 25 or 30, In this case, H_0 and H_1 are both simple. But generally H_1 is composite, i.e. of the form, $H_1 : \mu \neq 25$, $H_1 : \mu < 25$ or $H_1 : \mu > 25$. Likewise, simple and composite hypothesis for any other parameter(s) can be stated.

TWO TYPES OF ERRORS

After applying a test, a decision is taken about the acceptance or rejection of null hypothesis vis-a-vis the alternative hypothesis. There is always some possibility of committing an error in taking a decision about the hypothesis. These errors can be of two types:

Type I error : Reject null hypothesis (H_0) when it is true.

Type II error : Accept null hypothesis (H_0) when it is false.

These two types of errors can be better understood with an example where a patient is given a medicine to cure some disease and his condition is scrutinised for some time. It is just possible that the medicine has a positive effect but it is considered that it has no effect or adverse effect. Thus, it is the *first kind of error* or *type I error.* On the contrary, if the medicine has an adverse effect but is considered to have a positive effect, it is called the *second kind of error* or *type II error.* Now let us consider the implications of these two types of error. If type I error is committed, the patient will be given another medicine, which may or may not be effective. But if type II error is committed, i.e., the medicine is continued in spite of an adverse effect, the patient is likely to develop some other complications or may even die. This means that the type II error is much more severe than the type I error. Hence in drawing inference about the null hypothesis, practice is followed that type II error can be minimized even at certain risk of type I error.

Level of Significance

It is the quantity of risk of the type I error which we are ready to tolerate in making a decision about H_0. In other words, it is the probability of type I error which is tolerable. The level of significance is denoted by α and is conventionally chosen as 0.05 or 0.01. Level $\alpha = 0.01$ is used for high precision and $\alpha = 0.05$ for moderate precision.

P-value Concept

Another approach is to find out the P-value at which H_0 is significant, i.e., to find the smallest level α at which H_0 is rejected. In this situation, it is not inferred whether H_0 is accepted or rejected at level 0.05 or 0.01 or any other level. But the statistician only gives the smallest level α at which H_0 is rejected. This facilitates an individual to decide for himself as to how much significant the data are. This approach avoids the imposition of a fixed level of significance. About the acceptance or rejection of H_0, the experimenter can himself decide the level α by comparing it with the P-value. The criterion for this is that if the P-value is less than or equal to α, reject H_0 otherwise accept H_0.

CRITICAL REGION (C.R.)

A statistic is used to test the hypothesis H_0. The test statistic follows some known distribution. In a test, the area under the probability density curve is divided into two regions, viz., the *region of acceptance* and the *region of rejection*. The region of rejection is the region in which H_0 is rejected. It means that if the value of test statistics lies in this region, H_0 will be rejected. The region of rejection is called a *critical region*. Moreover, the area of the critical region is equal to the level of significance α. The critical region is always on the tail of the distribution curve. It may be on both the tails or on one tail, depending upon the alternative hypothesis.

One- and Two-tailed Tests

If the alternative hypothesis, H_1 is of the type $\mu > \mu_0$; $\mu_1 <$ or $> \mu_2$; $\sigma^2 > \sigma_0^2$ or $\sigma_1^2 < \sigma_2^2$; etc., the critical region lies on only one tail of the probability density curve. In this situation the test is called *one-tailed test.* If H_1 is of the type $\mu > \mu_0$; $\mu_1 < \mu_2$; $\sigma^2 > \sigma_0^2$; $\sigma_1^2 > \sigma_2^2$; etc., the critical region is towards the right tail as shown in Figure 10.1.

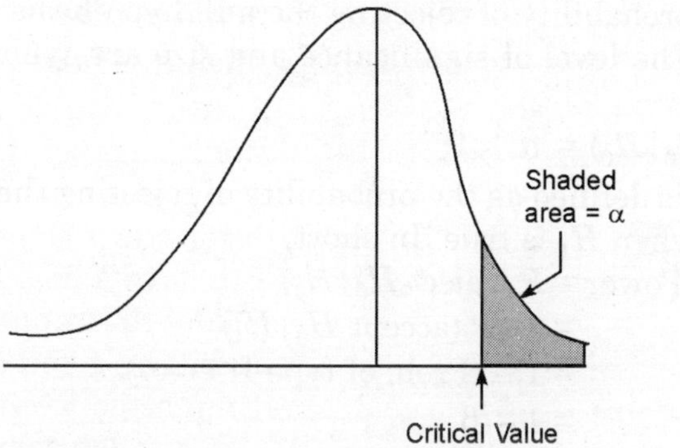

Figure 10.1 One-sided Right Tailed Critical Region

On the contrary, if H_1 is of the type $\mu < \mu_0$; $\sigma^2 < \sigma_0^2$, $\mu_1 > \mu_2$; $\sigma_1^2 > \sigma_2^2$ etc., the critical region lies on the left tail as depicted in Figure 10.2.

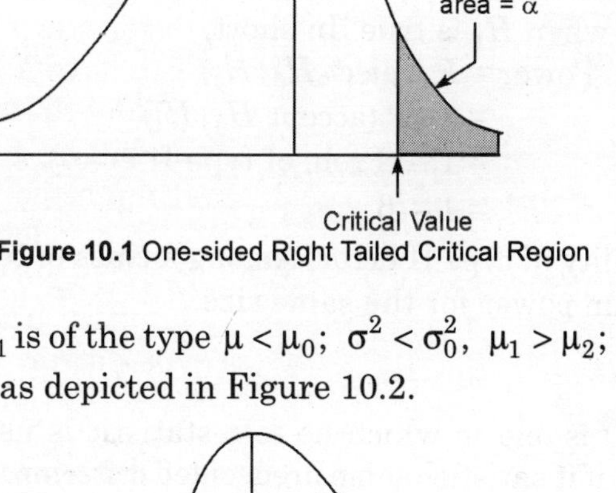

Figure 10.2 One-sided Left Tailed Critical Region

However, if H_1 is of the type $\mu \neq 0; \mu_1 \neq \mu_2; \sigma^2 \neq \sigma_0^2$, or $\sigma_1^2 \neq \sigma_2^2$ etc., the critical region lies on both the tails. In this situation a test is called a *two-tailed test.* In a two-tailed test, an area equal to $\alpha/2$ lies on both the tails, for a test of significance level α. The critical regions are shown in Figure 10.3.

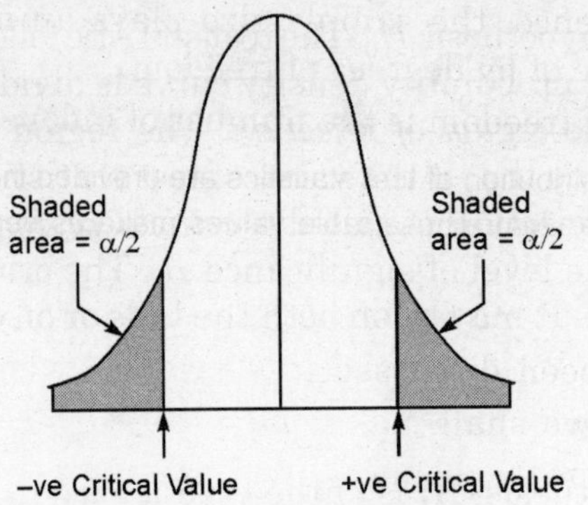

Figure 10.3 Two-tailed Critical Regions

SIZE AND POWER OF A TEST

The size of a test is the probability of rejecting the null hypothesis when it is true, and is usually denoted by α. The level of significance and size are synonymous in a practical sense. Therefore,

$$P(\text{reject } H_0 \mid H_0) = \alpha \qquad ...(10.1)$$

The power of a test is defined as the probability of rejecting the null hypothesis when it is actually false, i.e., when H_1 is true. In short,

$$\begin{aligned} \text{Power} &= P(\text{reject } H_0 \mid H_1) \\ &= 1 - P(\text{accept } H_0 \mid H_1) \\ &= 1 - (\text{Prob. of type II error}) \\ &= 1 - \beta \qquad ...(10.2) \end{aligned}$$

where β is the probability of type II error. Among a class of tests, the best test is the one which has the maximum power for the same size.

RANDOMIZED TEST

A randomized test (T°) is one in which no test statistic is used. The decision about the rejection of H_0 is taken, if it satisfies some predecided criterion. For instance, if it is decided that H_0 will be rejected if on tossing a coin it falls with the head on the upper side and will be accepted if it falls with the tail on the upper side. Since randomized test is rarely used, it is not explained further.

NON-RANDOMIZED TEST

A test T of a hypothesis H is said to be non-randomized if the hypothesis H is rejected on the basis that a test statistic belongs to the critical region c_T, i.e., $\Psi_T(X_1, X_2, ..., X_n) \in c_T$. Some of the commonly used non-randomized tests are given in this chapter as well as in the next chapter.

DEGREES OF FREEDOM (d.f.)

It is apparent from the discussion made so far that in a test of hypothesis, a sample is drawn from the population of which the parameter is under test. The size of the sample varies since its depends either on the experimenter or on the resources available. Moreover, the test statistic involves the estimated value of the parameter which depends on the number of observations. Hence, the sample size plays an important role in testing of hypothesis and is taken care of by degrees of freedom.

Definition: Degrees of freedom is the number of independent observations in a set.

Note: The table values for the distribution of test statistics are provided in the Appendix B for various levels of significance and degrees of freedom. These table values make us decide about the rejection of H_0.

STUDENT'S *t*-TEST

t-distribution has already been discussed in Chapter 8 where sampling distribution of $\bar{x}/s_{\bar{x}}$ was discussed. Here we shall make use of *t*-distribution in testing of hypothesis about the population mean or two population means.

Suppose, a small random sample $(X_1, X_2, ..., X_n)$ of size n has been drawn from a normal population having mean μ and variance σ^2 which are unknown. We want to test the hypothesis.

$$H_0 : \mu = \mu_0 \text{ against } H_1 : \mu \neq \mu_0$$

where μ_0 is some assumed value considered fit for μ. Let the observed values on random sample $(X_1, X_2, ..., X_n)$ be $(x_1, x_2, ..., x_n)$. Statistic t is given as,

$$t_{n-1} = \frac{\bar{x} - \mu_0}{s_{\bar{x}}} \qquad ...(10.3)$$

For the sample values, expression for t is,

$$t_{n-1} = \frac{\sqrt{n}(\bar{x} - \mu_0)}{s} \qquad ...(10.3.1)$$

where $\bar{x}$ is the sample mean, s is the standard deviation of the sample, $(n - 1)$ in suffix indicates the d.f. of t.

On substituting formula (7.3) for s, (10.3.1) can be written as,

$$t_{n-1} = (\bar{x} - \mu_0)\sqrt{\frac{n(n-1)}{\Sigma_i (x_i - \bar{x})^2}} \qquad ...(10.3.2)$$

where $i = 1, 2, ..., n$.

Definition: Student-*t* is the deviation of estimated mean from its population mean expressed in terms of standard deviation.

To decide about the acceptance or rejection of H_0 vis-a-vis H_1, the calculated value of t is compared with the table value of t for $(n - 1)$ d.f. and level of significance α. *t*-distribution table is provided in Appendix B (Table V) for different d.f. and various levels of significance. The tabulated *t*-value gives the critical value of *t*. More clearly, if $t_{cal} \geq t_{\alpha/2}$ for $(n - 1)$ d.f., reject H_0, otherwise accept it.

Notes : 1. In the above situation, a two-tailed test has to be applied since H_1 is $\mu \neq \mu_0$.

2. In case of one tailed test, i.e., for the alternative hypothesis, $H_1 : \mu > \mu_0$ reject H_0, if $t_{cal} \geq t_\alpha$ for $(n-1)$ d.f. The C.R. lies on the right tail. If the alternative hypothesis is, $H_1 : \mu < \mu_0$ reject H_0 if $t_{cal} \leq -t_\alpha$ for $(n-1)$ d.f. The C.R. lies on left tail.
3. If *t*-table is provided for a two-tailed critical region, it should be consulted as such. If a one tailed *t*-table has been provided, we should consult the table for level $\alpha/2$, where α is a prefixed level of significance.
4. If H_0 is rejected at $\alpha = 0.01$, calculated *t*-value is called a highly significant value.

Assumptions about *t*-Test

t-test is based on the following five assumptions:

1. The random variable X follows normal distribution. In other words the random sample has been drawn from a normal population.
2. All observations in the sample are independent.
3. The sample size is not large. There is no hard-and-fast rule which can be given to call a sample large. But, as a practice, a sample of size 30 or more is considered a large sample. At the same time one should note that at least five observations are desirable for applying a *t*-test.
4. The assumed value μ_0 of the population mean is the correct value.
5. The sample values are correctly taken and recorded.

In case the above assumptions do not hold good, the reliability of the test decreases. Further, some tests are very sensitive and some are not. The test which gives quite a satisfactory result in spite of some departure from the basic assumptions is called a *robust test.* It is interesting to point out that the student's *t*-test is a robust test.

***Example* 10.1.** A breeder claims that his variety of cotton contains, at the most, 40 per cent lint in seed cotton. Eighteen samples of 100 grams each were taken, and after ginning the following quantity of lint was found in each sample.

Sample No. :	1	2	3	4	5	6	7	8	9
Quantity of Lint in	36.3	37.0	36.6	37.5	37.5	37.9	37.8	36.9	36.7
100 g sample:	10	11	12	13	14	15	16	17	18
	38.5	37.9	38.8	37.5	37.1	37.0	36.3	36.7	35.7

To check the breeder's claim, a *t*-test is performed as under. Here we have to test,

$$H_0 : \mu = 40 \text{ against } H_1 : \mu < 40$$

To test H_0, the test statistic is

$$t_{n-1} = \frac{\sqrt{n}(\bar{x} - \mu_0)}{s}$$

Given $\mu_0 = 40$

Now we compute $\bar{x}$ and s.

$$\bar{x} = \frac{669.7}{18} = 37.206$$

$$s^2 = \frac{1}{n-1}\{\Sigma_i x_i^2 - (\Sigma_i x_i)^2 / n\}$$

$$= \frac{1}{17}\left\{24927.33 - \frac{(669.7)^2}{18}\right\}$$

$$= \frac{10.77}{17} = 0.633$$

$$s = 0.796$$

$$t = \frac{\sqrt{n}(\bar{x} - \mu_0)}{s}$$

$$= \frac{\sqrt{18}(37.206 - 40)}{0.796} = \frac{-11.854}{0.796} = -14.89$$

The table value of t at the prefixed $\alpha = 0.01$ and 17 d.f. is 2.567. Here, $t_{cal} < -2.567$. Hence H_0 is rejected. It means that the average percentage of lint in this cotton variety is less than 40 per cent.

***Example* 10.2.** The life expectancy of people in the year 1970 in Brazil is expected to be 50 years. A survey was conducted in eleven regions of Brazil and the data obtained are given below. Do the data confirm the expected view?

Life expectancy:	54.2,	50.4,	44.2,	49.7,	55.4,	57.0,
(years)	58.2,	56.6,	61.9,	57.5,	53.4,	

Here we have to test,

$$H_0 = \mu = 50 \text{ against } H_1 : \mu \neq 50$$

To test H_0, the statistic t is

$$t_{n-1} = \frac{\sqrt{n}(\bar{x} - \mu_0)}{s}$$

Now, we first compute $\bar{x}$ and s.

$$\bar{x} = \frac{598.5}{11} = 54.41$$

$$s^2 = \frac{1}{10}\{32799.91 - (598.5)^2/11\}$$

$$= \frac{1}{10}(236.07) = 23.607$$

$$s = 4.859$$

$$t = \frac{\sqrt{11}(54.41 - 50)}{4.859}$$

$$t = \frac{14.626}{4.859} = 3.01$$

The table value of t at $\alpha = 0.05$ and 10 d.f. is 2.228. Since $t_{cal} > 2.228$, reject H_0. It means that the life expectancy is more than 50 years. The chance of this result holding good for the whole population is 95 per cent.

Note: For t-test with the help of SPSS computer software, see Appendix.

TEST OF EQUALITY OF TWO POPULATION MEANS

Often, we have samples from two normal populations and want to test the hypothesis.

$$H_0 : \mu_1 = \mu_2 \text{ against } H_1 : \mu_1 \neq \mu_2$$

i.e.,
$$H_0 : \mu_1 = \mu_2 = 0 \text{ against } H_1 : \mu_1 - \mu_2 \neq 0$$

To test H_0 we come across either of the two situations, (*i*) $\sigma_1^2 = \sigma_2^2$, i.e., both the populations are distributed with the same variance, (*ii*) $\sigma_1^2 \neq \sigma_2^2$, i.e., two populations have unequal variances and are unknown for both the populations.

To test H_0 against H_1 in situation (*i*), the test statistic under H_0 based on two independent samples $X_{11}, X_{12}, \ldots, X_{1n_1}$ and $X_{21}, X_{22}, \ldots, X_{2n_2}$ of sizes n_1 and n_2, respectively from the two population is,

$$t = \frac{(\overline{X}_1 - \overline{X}_2) - (\mu_1 - \mu_2)}{S_p\sqrt{\dfrac{1}{n_1} + \dfrac{1}{n_2}}} \qquad \ldots(10.4)$$

Let the sample values be denoted by

$$(x_{11}, x_{12}, \ldots, x_{1n_1}) \text{ and } (x_{21}, x_{22}, \ldots, x_{2n_2}).$$

Then for sample observations, the expression for t is,

$$t = \frac{\bar{x}_1 - \bar{x}_2}{S_p\sqrt{\dfrac{1}{n_1} + \dfrac{1}{n_2}}} \qquad \ldots(10.4.1)$$

Since under H_0, $\mu_1 = \mu_2$.

Statistic t has $(n_1 + n_2 - 2)$ d.f.,

where $\bar{x}_1$ and $\bar{x}_2$ are the means of the samples I and II respectively, s_p is the pooled standard deviation which is equal to $\sqrt{s_p^2}$, whereas,

$$s_p^2 = \frac{\sum_{i=1}^{n_1}(x_{1i} - \bar{x}_1)^2 + \sum_{j=1}^{n_2}(x_{2j} - \bar{x}_2)^2}{(n_1 + n_2 - 2)} \qquad \ldots(10.5)$$

s_p^2 can also be calculated without taking the deviations from the mean by the formula

$$s_p^2 = \frac{\left\{\sum_{i=1}^{n_1} x_{1i}^2 - (\sum_{i=1}^{n_1} x_{1i})^2 / n_1\right\} + \left\{\sum_{j=1}^{n_2} x_{2j}^2 - (\sum_{j=1}^{n_2} x_{2j})^2 / n_2\right\}}{(n_1 + n_2 - 2)} \qquad \ldots(10.5.1)$$

In case the sample variances s_1^2 and s_2^2 are known or calculated earlier, then s_p^2 may be obtained by the formula,

$$s_p^2 = \frac{(n_1 - 1)s_1^2 + (n_2 - 1)s_2^2}{(n_1 + n_2 - 2)} \qquad \ldots(10.5.2)$$

Formulae (10.5.1) and (10.5.2) can easily be obtained from (10.5) using the formulae for the sample variance as given below.

$$s^2 = \frac{1}{n-1}\sum_{i=1}^{n}(x_i - \bar{x})^2$$

$$= \frac{1}{n-1}\left\{\sum_{i-1}^{n} x_i^2 - (\sum_{i=1}^{n} x_i)^2 / n\right\}$$

It should be noted that the pooled variance has been calculated because the two populations possess the same variability. The pooled variance s_p^2 will be a good estimate of the pooled variance of $(\bar{x}_1 - \bar{x}_2)$ and the expression $s_p\sqrt{\frac{1}{n_1}+\frac{1}{n_2}}$ is the standard deviation of $(\bar{x}_1 - \bar{x}_2)$. This is also called the standard error[1] of $(\bar{x}_1 - \bar{x}_2)$. Decision about the acceptance or rejection is taken according to the following rule.

(*i*) Given $H_1 : \mu_1 \neq \mu_2$ and α level of significance, reject H_0.

If $t_{cal} \geq t_{\alpha/2,\ (n_1+n_2-2)}$

or $t_{cal} \leq -t_{\alpha/2,\ (n_1+n_2-2)}$

otherwise H_0 is not rejected.

(*ii*) Given $H_1 : \mu_1 > \mu_2$, and α level of significance, reject H_0

if $t_{cal} \geq t_{\alpha,\ (n_1+n_2-2)}$

otherwise, H_0 is not rejected.

(*iii*) Given $H_1 : \mu_1 < \mu_2$, and α level of significance, reject H_0

if $t_{cal} \leq t_{\alpha,\ (n_1+n_2-2)}$

otherwise, H_0 is not rejected.

***Example* 10.3.** The following table gives the monthly average of total solar radiation on a horizontal and an inclined surface at a particular place.

Month	*Mean daily total radiation on horizontal surface (cal/cm²/day)*	*Mean daily total radiation on inclined surface (cal/cm²/day)*
Jan.	363	536
Feb.	404	474
Mar.	518	556
Apr.	521	549
May.	613	479
Jun.	587	422
Jul.	365	315
Aug.	412	414
Sept.	469	505
Oct.	468	552
Nov.	371	492
Dec.	330	507

1. By definition, standard deviation of an estimator is called its standard error.

To test whether the average daily total radiations in a year on a horizontal and an inclined surface are equal, amounts to testing H_0: $\mu_1 = \mu_2$ against H_1: $\mu_1 \neq \mu_2$. To test H_0 under the assumption that the population variances of average monthly total radiation on horizontal and inclined surfaces are equal, i.e., $\sigma_1^2 = \sigma_2^2$, the test statistic is

$$t = \frac{\bar{x}_1 - \bar{x}_2}{s_p\sqrt{\frac{1}{n_1} + \frac{1}{n_2}}}$$

Now make the following computations:

$$\sum_{i=1}^{12} x_{1i} = 5421;\ \bar{x}_1 = \frac{5421}{12} = 451.75;\ \sum_{i=1}^{12} x_{1i}^2 = 2543583$$

$$\sum_{j=1}^{12} x_{2j} = 5801;\ \bar{x}_2 = \frac{5801}{12} = 483.42;\ \sum_{j=1}^{12} x_{2j}^2 = 2859497$$

$$s_p^2 = \frac{\left\{\sum_{i=1}^{n_1} x_{1i}^2 - (\Sigma_i x_{1i})^2/n_1\right\} + \left\{\sum_{j=1}^{n_2} x_{2j}^2 - (\Sigma_j x_{2j})^2/n_2\right\}}{(n_1 + n_2 - 2)}$$

$$= \frac{\{2543583 - (5421)^2/12\} + \{2859497 - (5801)^2/12\}}{22}$$

$$= \frac{94646.3 + 55196.9}{22} = 6811.06$$

$$s_p = 82.53$$

The statistic

$$t = \frac{451.75 - 483.42}{82.53\sqrt{\frac{1}{12} + \frac{1}{12}}}$$

$$= \frac{-31.67}{33.69} = -0.94$$

The table value of t at $\alpha = 0.05$ and 22 d.f. is 2.074, since $t_{cal} > -2.074$; H_0 is not rejected. It means that on the whole, the average daily total radiations on the horizontal surface and the inclined surface are equal.

Situation (*ii*) when $\sigma_1^2 \neq \sigma_2^2$. In this situation the problem that arises is that the variances cannot be pooled and hence the degrees of freedom for t cannot be obtained. The test of difference between two means in this case is known as *Berhans-Fisher* problem.

Berhans and Fisher showed that the test statistic is

$$t = \frac{\bar{x}_1 - \bar{x}_2}{\sqrt{\frac{s_1^2}{n_1} + \frac{s_2^2}{n_2}}} \quad \text{...(10.6)}$$

where s_1^2 and s_2^2 are estimates of σ_1^2 and σ_2^2 respectively, obtained from two independent random samples of sizes n_1 and n_2, selected randomly from two populations. The statistic (10.6) does not follow the student's t-distribution under H_0. The theoretical considerations of Berhans-Fisher problem are omitted in this book. Here, we give the Cochran's approximation in which case an ordinary t-table can be used and this is sufficiently accurate for testing H_0.

For taking a decision about H_0, the calculated value of t is compared with t^* which is obtained by the formula,

$$t^* = \frac{t_1 s_1^2 / n_1 + t_2 s_2^2 / n_2}{s_1^2 / n_1 + s_2^2 / n_2} \quad \text{...(10.7)}$$

where t_1 and t_2 are the table values of t at a prefixed α level of significance with $(n_1 - 1)$ and $(n_2 - 1)$ d.f. respectively.

In case when $n_1 = n_2 = n$ (say), we obtain

$$t^* = t_\alpha \text{ with } (n-1) \text{ d.f.}$$

If $|t_{cal}| > t^*$, reject H_0, otherwise H_0 is not rejected.

Note: The test of significance by a t-test of the hypothesis about correlation coefficient, regression coefficient, etc., have been given in the respective chapters.

***Example* 10.4:** The following data give the gain in body weight (kilograms) per heifer of two different breeds under a grazing treatment:

Gain in body weight (kg)							
Breed 1:	57.3,	26.9,	53.2,	16.8,	44.8,	54.2,	71.4
Breed 2:	64.2,	52.2,	48.6,	26.6,	44.5,	71.8	

To test the equality of mean gain in the body weight of the two breeds, amounts to the testing of hypothesis,

$$H_0: \mu_1 = \mu_2 \text{ against } H_1: \mu_1 \neq \mu_2.$$

Here we assume that the population variances of gain in weight in the two breeds are different, i.e., $\sigma_1^2 \neq \sigma_2^2$.

H_0 can be tested by the statistic,

$$t = \frac{\bar{x}_1 - \bar{x}_2}{\sqrt{\frac{s_1^2}{n_1} + \frac{s_2^2}{n_2}}}$$

Now we calculate different constants in the formula:

Given $n_1 = 7$, $n_2 = 6$.

$$\sum_{i-1}^{7} x_{1i} = 324.6,\ \bar{x}_1 = 46.37,\ \sum_{i=1}^{7} x_{1i}^2 = 17162.02$$

$$\sum_{j=1}^{6} x_{2j} = 307.9,\ \bar{x}_2 = 51.32,\ \sum_{j=1}^{6} x_{2j}^2 = 17051.49$$

$$s_1^2 = \frac{1}{6}\{17162.02-(324.6)^2/7\} = 351.64$$

$$s_2^2 = \frac{1}{5}\{17051.49-(307.9)^2/6\} = 250.22$$

Substituting the values in the formula for t, we get

$$t = \frac{46.37-51.32}{\sqrt{\dfrac{351.64}{7}+\dfrac{250.22}{6}}}$$

$$= \frac{-4.95}{\sqrt{50.23+41.70}}$$

$$= \frac{-4.95}{9.59} = -0.516$$

To take the decision about H_0, at 5 per cent level of significance, we calculate t^*. From Table V in appendix B, we find

$$t_{0.025,6} = 2.447 \text{ and } t_{0.025,5} = 2.571$$

By formula (10.7),

$$t^* = \frac{2.447\times 50.23+2.571\times 41.70}{50.23+41.70}$$

$$= \frac{230.12}{91.93} = 2.50$$

The calculated value of $t > -2.50$. Hence, hypothesis H_0 is not rejected. It means that the average gain in weight of the two breeds is equal.

PAIRED *t*-TEST

This test is applicable only when two samples are not independent and the observations are taken in pairs. In this case, for each observation in one sample there is a corresponding observation in the other sample pertaining to the same character. It means that the paired observations are on the same unit or matching units. For example, a manufacturer wants to test the circularity of ball-bearing. For this one selects some ball-bearings randomly and measures the diameter along two mutually perpendicular diameters. Another example may be, say, there are sixteen students divided into eight pairs such that in each pair, both the students have the same IQ. Two groups are formed so that one student of each pair is taken in a group. The two groups are exposed to two teaching methods and a test is performed after one month. The experimenter is interested to test whether there is any difference in the effectiveness of teaching methods on the basis of test scores. From the discussion, it is amply clear that the paired *t*-test is applicable when the paired observations are taken on the same matching units or items.

Let the mean difference among the paired observations in the population be denoted by $\overline{D}$. The null hypothesis

$H_0 : \overline{D} = 0$ against $H_1 : \overline{D} \neq 0$ or $\overline{D} > 0$ or $\overline{D} < 0$ is tested as follows.

Suppose n observations in pairs and their differences, $(X - X') = d$, in the sample are as given below:

The test statistic for testing H_0 is

$$t_{n-1} = \frac{\bar{d}}{s_{\bar{d}}} \qquad \text{...(10.8)}$$

Pair no.	Sample values (X)	Sample values (X')	Difference (X–X') = d
1	x_1	x'_1	d_1
2	x_2	x'_2	d_2
3	x_3	x'_3	d_3
⋮	⋮	⋮	⋮
i	x_i	x'_i	d_i
⋮	⋮	⋮	⋮
n	x_n	x'_n	d_n

since $\overline{D} = 0$.

$$t_{n-1} = \frac{\sqrt{n}\ \bar{d}}{s_d} \qquad \text{...(10.8.1)}$$

Suffix $(n - 1)$ denotes the d.f. of t.

where $$\bar{d} = \sum_{i=1}^{n} d_i / n$$

and $$s_d^2 = \frac{1}{n-1} \sum_{i=1}^{n} (d_i - \bar{d})^2 \qquad \text{...(10.9)}$$

$$= \frac{1}{n-1} \left\{ \sum_{i=1}^{n} d_i^2 - (\Sigma_i d_i)^2 / n \right\} \qquad \text{...(10.9.1)}$$

while calculating $\bar{d}$ or $s_{\bar{d}}$ etc., the sign of the differences is taken into consideration.

The criterion for decision about H_0 is

Given $H_1 : \overline{D} \neq 0$, reject H_0 $\left[\begin{array}{l}\text{if } t_{cal} \geq t_{\alpha/2,\, n-1} \\ \text{if } t_{cal} \leq -t_{\alpha/2,\, n-1}\end{array}\right.$

otherwise H_0 is not rejected

Given $H_1 : \overline{D} > 0$, reject H_0 if $t_{cal} \geq t_{\alpha,\, n-1}$

otherwise H_0 is not rejected

Given $H_1 : \overline{D} < 0$, reject H_0 if $t_{cal} \leq -t_{\alpha,\, n-1}$

otherwise H_0 is not rejected.

Rejecting H_0 means that the difference is meaningful and cannot be ignored by considering it as a casual difference or the difference due to random error.

Note: We can take $(X - X')$ or $(X' - X)$ as difference d. But whatever we take once, it should be maintained uniformly.

***Example* 10.5.** The following table gives the pulsality index (PI) of 11 patients.

Patient no.	*PI value*		*Difference*
	During seizure (X)	*After seizure (X')*	$\lvert X'-X \rvert = d$
1	0.45	0.60	0.15
2	0.54	0.65	0.11
3	0.48	0.63	0.15
4	0.62	0.78	0.16
5	0.48	0.63	0.15
6	0.60	0.80	0.20
7	0.45	0.69	0.24
8	0.46	0.62	0.16
9	0.35	0.68	0.33
10	0.40	0.50	0.10
11	0.44	0.57	0.13

[*Source of data* : Gastroenterology, Vol. 84, 1983]

We want to test whether there is a significant increase on the average in PI values, after seizure as compared to during seizure. This amounts to testing the hypothesis,

$$H_0 : \overline{D} = 0 \text{ against } H_1 : \overline{D} > 0.$$

H_0 will be tested by the statistic,

$$t = \frac{\sqrt{n}\,\bar{d}}{s_d}$$

Now we calculate $\bar{d}$ and $s_{\bar{d}}$. The differences, d's, are entered in the last column along with the data.

$$\sum_{i=1}^{11} d_i = 1.88, \quad \bar{d} = \frac{1.88}{11} = 0.171, \sum_{i=1}^{11} d_i^2 = 0.3642$$

By formula (10.9.1).

$$s_d^2 = \frac{1}{10}\left\{0.3642 - \frac{(1.88)^2}{11}\right\} = 0.004289$$

$$s_d = 0.065$$

Thus, $$t = \frac{\sqrt{11} \times 0.171}{0.065} = 8.72$$

The table value of t at $\alpha = 0.05$ and 10 d.f. is 1.812. Since $t_{cal} > 1.812$, H_0 is rejected. It means that the PI value after seizure increases significantly as compared to during seizure.

***Example* 10.6.** The data below show the infiltration rate (cm/h) at an upstream and a downstream of the experimental plots.

Plot no.	*Infiltration rate*		*Difference*
	Upstream (X)	*Downstream (X')*	*(X–X') = d*
1	15.66	13.56	2.10
2	15.54	13.62	1.92
3	13.00	12.30	0.70
4	13.62	13.20	0.42
5	20.46	18.78	1.68
6	19.80	11.94	7.86
7	13.02	14.76	–1.74
8	22.08	15.18	6.90
9	17.40	10.86	6.54
10	13.80	11.52	2.28
11	18.18	15.30	2.88
12	11.16	12.00	–0.84
13	16.80	6.30	10.50
14	20.10	9.12	10.98
15	13.20	9.84	3.36
16	11.16	10.74	0.42

[*Source of data: Annals of Arid Zone,* Vol. 22, 1983]

To know whether the average difference in infiltration rate upstream and downstream is significant or not, amounts to testing the hypothesis,

$$H_0 : \bar{D} = 0 \text{ against } H_1 : \bar{D} \neq 0$$

H_0 can be tested by the statistic

$$t = \frac{\sqrt{n}\,\bar{d}}{s_d}$$

The difference d has been entered in the last column of the above table. Now compute $\bar{d}$ and $s_{\bar{d}}$.

$$\sum_{i=1}^{16} d_i = 55.96, \ \bar{d} = 3.50, \ \sum_{i=1}^{16} d_i^2 = 423.25$$

By formula (10.9.1),

$$s_d^2 = \frac{1}{15}\left\{423.25 - \frac{(55.96)^2}{16}\right\}$$

$$= \frac{227.53}{15} = 15.17$$

$$s_d = 3.89$$

Thus

$$t = \frac{\sqrt{16} \times 3.50}{3.89} = 3.60$$

The table value of t at $\alpha = 0.01$ and 15 d.f. is 2.602. Since $t_{cal} > 2.602$, H_0 is rejected. It shows that there is a highly significant difference between the infiltration rate along upstream and downstream.

Note: For paired *t*-test with the help of SPSS package, see Appendix.

INTERVAL ESTIMATION

The theory of interval estimation was developed by Jerzy Neyman. It was a breakthrough in the field of statistics. In point estimation, only one value is found through sample observations, as this represents the parameter. This value may or may not be a good representative of the parameter. But in an interval estimation, two limits (lower and upper) are found out through sample values within which any point may be taken as an acceptable value of the parameter, with certain confidence probability. The two limits are called the *confidence limits* (C.L.) and the difference between the upper and the lower confidence limits is called the *confidence interval*.

In case, different samples are drawn from the same population, then each sample will generally provide different estimates and these estimates themselves behave as a random variable. The standard deviation obtained by these estimated values is called the standard error and helps in finding the confidence interval.

Suppose, we are interested in finding out $(1 - \alpha)$ per cent confidence interval where α is the tolerable probability of the event that an estimated value may lie outside. Consider a parameter θ of a distribution. Let x' be the value of the deviate for the distribution, $f(x, \theta)$ corresponding to the confidence probability $(1 - \alpha)$. Let the sample estimate of θ be $\hat{\theta}$ and σ_θ the standard error of $\hat{\theta}$. The confidence interval is given by $\hat{\theta} \pm x'\sigma_\theta$. Generally σ_θ is not known and hence it is replaced by $s_{\hat{\theta}}$, the estimated value of $\sigma_{\hat{\theta}}$. Thus, the confidence limits are given by $(\hat{\theta} \pm x's_{\hat{\theta}})$. The lower limit is $(\hat{\theta} - x's_{\hat{\theta}})$. and upper limit is $(\hat{\theta} + x's_{\hat{\theta}})$. The confidence interval is $\{(\hat{\theta} + x's_{\hat{\theta}}) - (\hat{\theta} - x's_{\hat{\theta}})\}$, i.e. $2x'\ s_{\hat{\theta}}$.

The above general ideas will be implemented to the specific problems which will further elucidate the concepts about interval estimation. Let us draw a small sample of size n $(n < 30)$ from a normal population $N(\mu, \sigma^2)$. To find out the confidence limits for the mean μ when σ is unknown, we have to consider the statistic t. A value of sample mean is an acceptable value of population mean if and only if the statistic t lies between $-t_\alpha$ and t_α, i.e.,

$$-t_\alpha \le \frac{\bar{x} - \mu}{s/\sqrt{n}} \le t_\alpha \qquad \text{...(10.10)}$$

where t_α is the table value of t at α level of significance and $(n - 1)$ d.f.

Taking the left side of inequality (10.10), we get

$$-t_\alpha \frac{s}{\sqrt{n}} \le (\bar{x} - \mu)$$

or

$$\mu \le \bar{x} + t_\alpha . \frac{s}{\sqrt{n}} \qquad \text{...(10.11)}$$

Similarly, taking the right side of inequality (10.10) we get

$$\frac{\bar{x} - \mu}{s/\sqrt{n}} \le t_\alpha$$

or $$\bar{x} - t_{\alpha}.\frac{s}{\sqrt{n}} \leq \mu \qquad ...(10.12)$$

Combining (10.11) and (10.12) we obtain, $\bar{x} - t_{\alpha}.\frac{s}{\sqrt{n}} \leq \mu \leq \bar{x} + t_{\alpha}.\frac{s}{\sqrt{n}}$ ...(10.13)

Thus, $\left(\bar{x} - t_{\alpha}.\frac{s}{\sqrt{n}}\right)$ is the lower limit for μ and $\left(\bar{x} + t_{\alpha}.\frac{s}{\sqrt{n}}\right)$ is the upper limit for μ. $(1-\alpha)$ per cent confidence interval is $2t_{\alpha}.\frac{s}{\sqrt{n}}$. Similarly $(1-\alpha)$ per cent confidence limits for the difference between two normal population means, i.e. $(\mu_1 - \mu_2)$ are as follows: Let small samples $(x_{11}, x_{12}, \ldots x_{1n_1})$ and $(x_{21}, x_{22}, \ldots x_{2n_2})$ of size n_1 and n_2 be independently drawn from populations $N(\mu_1, \sigma_1^2)$ and $N(\mu_2, \sigma_2^2)$ respectively.

Consider the situation $\sigma_1^2 = \sigma_2^2$. In this situation the confidence limits for $(\mu_1 - \mu_2)$ are

$$(\bar{x}_1 - \bar{x}_2) \pm t_{\alpha}.s_p\sqrt{\frac{1}{n_1} + \frac{1}{n_2}} \qquad ...(10.14)$$

where $\bar{x}_1$ and $\bar{x}_2$ are sample means, t_{α} is the table value of t at α probability and $(n_1 + n_2 - 2)$ d.f. s_p is given by the formula (10.5) through (10.5.2). In a similar manner, the confidence limits for $(\mu_1 - \mu_2)$ in the situation $\sigma_1^2 \neq \sigma_2^2$ are,

$$(\bar{x}_1 - \bar{x}_2) \pm t^* \sqrt{\frac{s_1^2}{n_1} + \frac{s_2^2}{n_2}} \qquad ...(10.15)$$

where s_1^2 and s_2^2 are two sample variances and t^* is as given by (10.7). Similarly $(1-\alpha)$ per cent confidence limits for $\bar{D}$ are,

$$\bar{d} \pm t_{\alpha}.\frac{S_d}{\sqrt{n}} \qquad ...(10.16)$$

All the notations in (10.16) are as given with paired t-test.

***Example* 10.7.** For the data given in example 10.2, we find the 95 per cent confidence limits for μ.

All the calculations, made there, are used here directly. Thus, the confidence limits for μ by the formula (10.13) are,

$$\text{C.L.} = 54.41 \pm 2.228 \times \frac{4.859}{\sqrt{11}}$$

$$= 54.41 \pm 3.26$$

Upper limit = 57.67 and lower limit = 51.15.

***Example* 10.8.** Confidence interval for $(\mu_1 - \mu_2)$ for the data given in example (10.3) is computed here. All the calculations made in the solution of example (10.3) are used here directly.

Thus the 95 per cent confidence limits for $(\mu_1 - \mu_2)$ by the formula (10.14) are,

$$\text{C.L.} = (451.75 - 483.42) \pm 82.53 \sqrt{\frac{1}{12} + \frac{1}{12}} \times 2.074$$

$$= -31.67 \pm 33.69 \times 2.074$$
$$= -31.67 \pm 69.87$$

Upper limit = 38.20 and lower limit = – 101.54

The confidence interval = 38.20 – (–101.54)

= 139.74

LARGE SAMPLE TESTS

The test of hypothesis about a population mean or two population means, by the *t*-test, is applicable under the circumstances that population variance(s) is/are not known and the sample(s) is/are of small size. In cases where the population variance(s) is/are known, we use Z-test (normal test). Moreover, when the sample size is large, sample variance approaches population variance and is deemed to be almost equal to population variance. In this way, the population variance is known even if we have sample data and hence the normal test is applicable. The distribution of Z is always normal with a mean zero and a variance 1. The value of Z can be read from the table for the area under the normal curve, e.g., given $\alpha = 0.05$, $Z = 1.96$ and given $\alpha = 0.01$, $Z = 2.58$, when we are applying two-tailed test. Any other value of Z, for any given value of α, can be read from Table IV. For testing H_0: $\mu = \mu_0$ against $H_1 : \mu \neq \mu_0$, the test statistic is

$$Z = \frac{\bar{x} - \mu_0}{\sigma/\sqrt{n}} \qquad ...(10.17)$$

whereas in (10.17), $\bar{x}$ is the sample mean and σ is the standard deviation based on large sample of size n.

Also for testing $H_0 : \mu_1 = \mu_2 + \Delta$ vs. $H_1 : \mu_1 \neq \mu_2 + \Delta$, the expression is,

$$Z = \frac{(\bar{x}_1 - \bar{x}_2) - \Delta}{\sqrt{\dfrac{\sigma_1^2}{n_1} + \dfrac{\sigma_2^2}{n_2}}} \qquad ...(10.18)$$

where Δ is a known quantity.

In (10.18), σ_1^2 and σ_2^2 are the two population variances and all other notations are as in (10.6). Here it should be remembered that variances calculated from large samples are treated as population variances.

Note: In case of one-tailed test, the value of Z should be obtained from the table for the area under the normal curve, corresponding to the prescribed value of α. For traditional value of $\alpha = 0.05$, Z for one-tailed test is 1.645 and for $\alpha = 0.01$, Z is 2.33.

The test criterion for the three commonly encountered alternative hypothesis at α level of significance is,

Given $H_1 : \mu \neq \mu_0$ or $\mu_1 \neq \mu_2 + \Delta$,

reject H_0 if $Z \geq Z_{\alpha/2}$

or if $Z \leq -Z_{\alpha/2}$

Given $H_1 : \mu > \mu_0$, reject H_0 if $Z \geq Z_\alpha$.

Given $H_1 : \mu < \mu_0$, reject H_0 if $Z \leq Z_\alpha$.

***Example* 10.9.** The table below gives the total income in thousand rupees per year of 36 randomly selected persons from a particular class of people.

Income (thousand Rs.)					
6.5	10.5	12.7	13.8	13.2	11.4
5.5	8.0	9.6	9.1	9.0	8.5
4.8	7.3	8.4	8.7	7.3	7.4
5.6	6.8	6.9	6.8	6.1	6.5
4.0	6.4	6.4	8.0	6.6	6.2
4.7	7.4	8.0	8.3	7.6	6.7

On the basis of the sample data, can it be concluded that the mean income of a person in this class of people is Rs. 10,000 per year?

We have to test the hypothesis,

$$H_0 : \mu = 10 \text{ against } H_1 : \mu \neq 10$$

Since the sample size is 36, we will use a normal test for which the statistic is

$$Z = \frac{\bar{x} - \mu_0}{\sigma / \sqrt{n}}$$

Now we compute $\bar{x}$ and σ.

$$\sum_{i=1}^{36} x_i = 280.7, \bar{x} = 7.80, \sum_{i=1}^{36} x_i^2 = 2368.75$$

$$\sigma^2 = \frac{1}{35}\left\{2368.75 - \frac{(280.7)^2}{36}\right\}$$

$$= \frac{180.07}{35} = 5.14$$

$$\sigma = 2.27$$

Thus,

$$Z = \frac{\sqrt{36}(7.80 - 10)}{2.27}$$

$$= \frac{-13.2}{2.27} = -5.81$$

The table value of Z from Table IV at $\alpha = 0.05$ for a two-tailed test is 1.96. Since $Z < -1.96$, reject H_0. It means that the average annual income is less than rupees ten thousand.

Note: To know computer aided calculation for Z test, see Appendix.

***Example* 10.10.** Two samples were drawn from two normal populations $N(\mu_1, \sigma_1^2)$ and $N(\mu_2, \sigma_2^2)$. The following information was available on these samples regarding the expenditure in rupees per month per family.

Sample 1: $n_1 = 42$, $\bar{x}_1 = 744.85$, $\hat{\sigma}_1^2 = 158165.43$
Sample 2: $n_2 = 32$, $\bar{x}_2 = 516.78$, $\hat{\sigma}_2^2 = 26413.61$

On the basis of the available information it is required to test whether the average expenditure per month per family is equal. For the said problem we have to test the hypothesis,

$H_0 : \mu_1 = \mu_2$ against $H_1 : \mu_1 \neq \mu_2$

Since the sample sizes are large, H_0 is tested by the statistic,

$$Z = \frac{\bar{x}_1 - \bar{x}_2}{\sqrt{\frac{\sigma_1^2}{n_1} + \frac{\sigma_2^2}{n_2}}}$$

Substituting the values of various terms in the formula, we get

$$Z = \frac{744.85 - 516.78}{\sqrt{\frac{158165.43}{42} + \frac{26413.61}{32}}}$$

$$= \frac{228.07}{67.76} = 3.36$$

The table value of Z at $\alpha = 0.05$ is 1.96. Since $Z > 1.96$, reject H_0. It means that the average expenditure per month per family in the two populations is not equal.

Test of Hypothesis for Proportions

If the observations on various items or objects are categorised into two classes c_1 and c_2 (binomial population), we often want to test the hypothesis, whether the proportion of items in a particular class, say c_1, is p_0 or not. For example, the management of a manufacturing concern plans to introduce the new bonus scheme. Prior to implementation, the management wants to test whether 60 per cent employees shall favour the new bonus scheme. Thus for binomial population, the hypothesis

$$H_0 : P = p_0 \text{ against } H_1 : P \neq p_0 \text{ or } H_1 : P > p_0 \text{ or } H_1 : P < p_0$$

can be tested by Z-test where P is the actual proportion of items in the population belonging to class c_1. Proportions are mostly based on large samples and hence Z-test is given here. The test for a small sample case which involves a hypergeometric distribution is omitted. Let a large sample of n items be selected randomly. Out of n items, n_1 belong to class c_1 and n_2 belong to c_2 where $n_2 = (n - n_1)$. Also let the estimated proportion in class c_1 be denoted by $\hat{p}$. In this way we have the following configuration.

Classes	c_1	c_2	Total
No. of items:	n_1	n_2	n
Proportion:	$\hat{p}$	$\hat{q}$	1

where $\hat{p} = \frac{n_1}{n}, \hat{q} = \frac{n_2}{n}, \hat{p} = 1 - \hat{q}$

H_0 can be tested by the statistic,

$$Z = \frac{\hat{p} - p_0}{\sqrt{p_0 q_0 / n}} \quad \text{...(10.19)}$$

where $q_0 = 1 - p_0$

Decision about H_0 can be taken according to the following criterion.

Given $H_1 : P \neq p_0$, reject H_0 if $Z \geq Z_{\alpha/2}$ or $Z \leq Z_{\alpha/2}$

Given $H_1 : P > p_0$, reject H_0 if $Z \geq Z_\alpha$

Given $H_1 : P < p_0$, reject H_0 if $Z \leq Z_\alpha$

For prefixed $\alpha = 0.05$, $Z_{\alpha/2} = 1.96$ and $Z_\alpha = 1.645$ and for $\alpha = 0.01$, $Z_{\alpha/2} = 2.58$ and $Z_\alpha = 2.33$.

For any other level of significance α, the readers should obtain the value of Z_α or $Z_{\alpha/2}$ from Table IV for area under the normal curve given in the appendix.

***Example* 10.11.** To test the conjecture of the management that 60 per cent employees favour a new bonus scheme, a sample of 150 employees was drawn and their opinion was taken whether they favoured it or not. Only 55 employees out of 150 favoured the new bonus scheme.

Thus, we test the hypothesis,

$$H_0 : P = 0.60 \text{ against } H_1 : P \neq 0.60$$

The test for H_0 through (10.19) is,

$$Z = \frac{0.367 - 0.60}{\sqrt{\dfrac{0.60 \times .40}{150}}} \qquad \text{Since } \hat{p} = \frac{55}{150} = 0.367$$

$$= -5.825$$

At $\alpha = 0.01$, $Z < -2.58$. Hence H_0 is rejected. It means that 60 per cent employees do not favour the new bonus scheme.

Test of Equality of Proportions

If we have two populations and each item of a population belonged to either of the two classes c_1 and c_2. A person is often interested to know whether the proportion of items in class c_1 in both the populations is the same or not i.e., we want to test the hypothesis,

$$H_0: P_1 = P_2 \text{ against } H_1: P_1 \neq P_2 \text{ or } H_1: P_1 > P_2 \text{ or } H_1: P_1 < P_2$$

where P_1 and P_2 are the proportions of items in the two populations belonging to class c_1.

Two independent random samples of large sizes n_1 and n_2 are drawn from populations A and B respectively. Let the number of items belonging to classes c_1 and c_2 be as follows:

	Classes		
	c_1	c_2	*Total*
Sample from A	O_1	O_2	n_1
Sample from B	O'_1	O'_2	n_2
Total	$O_1 + O'_1$	$O_2 + O'_2$	$n_1 + n_2$

The estimated proportion in c_1 for the population A is $p_1 = \dfrac{O_1}{n_1}, q_1 = \dfrac{O_2}{n_1}$ and for population B is $p_2 = \dfrac{O'_1}{n_1}, q_2 = \dfrac{O'_2}{n_1}$.

H_0 against H_1 can be tested by the statistic,

$$Z = \frac{|p_1 - p_2|}{\sqrt{\hat{p}\hat{q}\left(\frac{1}{n_1} + \frac{1}{n_2}\right)}} \qquad ...(10.20)$$

under H_0, i.e. $P_1 = P_2$,

where
$$\hat{p} = \frac{n_1 p_1 + n_2 p_2}{n_1 + n_2} \text{ and } \hat{q} = 1 - \hat{p} \qquad ...(10.21)$$

$$= \frac{O_1 + O'_1}{n_1 + n_2} \qquad ...(10.21.1)$$

and $\sqrt{\hat{p}\hat{q}\left(\frac{1}{n_1} + \frac{1}{n_2}\right)}$ is the standard error of $(p_1 - p_2)$ under the assumption $P_1 = P_2 = p$. In case H_0 is suspected to be true, standard error of $(p_1 - p_2)$ should be restandardised using,

$$\sigma_{p_1 - p_2} = \sqrt{\frac{p_1 q_1}{n_1} + \frac{p_2 q_2}{n_2}}$$

The decision about H_0 against any of the three commonly encountered alternative hypotheses can be taken according to the rules discussed with one sample case.

***Example* 10.12.** A sample of 400 families in an old city is selected randomly, and a sample of 500 families is randomly selected from several new colonies of the same city. A survey is conducted for the number of houses possessing television (TV) sets. The number of TV holders in the old city is 48 out of 400 selected families and 120 in new colonies out of 500 families. Then the hypothesis whether the proportion of TV holders in old city and in the new colonies is the same, i.e.

H_0: $P_1 = P_2$ vs. H_1: $P_1 \neq P_2$

can be tested as under :

	Television		
	Holders	*Non-holders*	*Total*
Old city	48	352	400
New colonies	120	380	500

From the data,

$$p_1 = \frac{48}{400} = \frac{3}{25}, p_2 = \frac{120}{500} = \frac{6}{25}$$

From (10.21.1).

$$\hat{p} = \frac{168}{900} = \frac{14}{75}$$

$$\hat{q} = 1 - \frac{14}{75} = \frac{61}{75}$$

Thus, Z is computed by formula (10.20) as given below,

$$Z = \frac{|3/25 - 6/25|}{\sqrt{\frac{14}{75} \times \frac{61}{75}\left(\frac{1}{400} + \frac{1}{500}\right)}}$$

$$= \frac{3 \times 75}{25\sqrt{14 \times 61 \times 0.0045}} = 4.59$$

The table value of Z at $\alpha = 0.05$ for two-tailed test is 1.96. Since $Z > 1.96$, H_0 is rejected, which means that the proportion of TV holders in old city area and in new colonies is not the same at 5 per cent level of significance.

This chapter has covered the general theory of testing of hypothesis, t and Z tests. Besides these tests, there are a great number of test procedures suitable for test of significance in a variety of cases. It is impossible to cover all of them in one or two chapters. Hence, only two more tests namely, χ^2 and F test, which are widely applied and used, are discussed in the next chapter.

QUESTIONS AND EXERCISES

1. Throw light on the need of the testing of hypothesis.
2. Discuss a hypothesis. What types of hypotheses do you know? Discuss each of them.
3. Discuss two types of errors in the testing of hypothesis. What is their role in testing?
4. What is a critical region and on what basis, are we able to know about the position of critical region(s)?
5. Why are the degrees of freedom so important in taking a decision about the rejection or acceptance of a hypothesis?
6. Define the following terms:
   (*a*) Type II error.
   (*b*) Power of a test.
   (*c*) Degrees of freedom.
   (*d*) Level of significance.
   (*e*) Composite hypothesis.
7. What is the role of an alternative hypothesis in hypothesis testing?
8. Write short notes on:
   (*a*) Randomized test.
   (*b*) One-tailed test.
   (*c*) Critical region.
   (*d*) Statistic.
   (*e*) *P*-value concept.
9. Write the assumptions about t-test.
10. What do you understand by a large sample test?

11. Define the student's t-test. What kind of hypothesis can be tested by the t-test?
12. What is Cochran's approximation as an alternative to the Berhans-Fisher problem?
13. In what respect is a paired t-test different from a test of equality of two population means?
14. Explain the basic principle of interval estimation as invented by J. Neyman.
15. Write the appropriate statistics for testing the following hypothesis and give their corresponding theoretical degrees of freedom, if any:
    (*a*) H_0: $\mu_1 = \mu_2$, consider small samples case.
    (*b*) H_0: $\mu = 0$, when the sample is of small size.
    (*c*) H_0: $\mu = \mu_0$, when the population variance is known.
    (*d*) H_0: $\bar{D} = \Delta$, where Δ is a known constant.
    (*e*) H_0: $P = 0.5$.
    All the notations used above carry their usual meaning.
16. Select the correct answer:
    Student's t-test is applicable when (*a*) a sample size is large, (*b*) a sample size is less than five, (*c*) a sample size is less than thirty but greater than five.
17. Write 'Yes' if the statements given below are correct, otherwise write 'No'
    (*a*) Degrees of freedom take care of the sample size in a decision problem about a hypothesis.
    (*b*) Randomized test also involves some statistic.
    (*c*) Each statistic has some distribution.
    (*d*) Critical region is always on one tail only.
    (*e*) Standard deviation of an estimate and standard error are the same.
    (*f*) We can always pool variances in a two sample t-test.
    (*g*) Interval estimate is better than point estimate.
    (*h*) In a paired t-test, observations in two groups are correlated.
18. Write whether the following statements are correct:
    (*a*) t-value lies between $-\infty$ and ∞.
    (*b*) Z-value lies between 0 and ∞.
    (*c*) Variance of a sample can be any value between $-\infty$ and ∞.
    (*d*) When $\alpha = 0$, we have to accept H_0.
    (*e*) When $\alpha = 1$, we have to reject H_0.
19. Find the values for the following with the help of tables given in appendix:
    (*a*) $t_{0\cdot05,23}$
    (*b*) $t_{0\cdot01.28}$
    (*c*) $Z_{0\cdot025}$
    (*d*) $z_{0\cdot05}$
    (*e*) $t_{0\cdot1,15}$
20. In a nodulation study on *R.trifolii*, a sample of eleven plants gave the following shoot lengths. An earlier study reported that the mean shoot length is 15 cm.

Shoot length (cm):	10.1, 21.5, 11.7, 12.9, 14.8, 11.0, 19.2, 11.4, 22.6, 10.8, 10.2,

Test whether the experimental data confirm the old view at 5 per cent level of significance.

21. Following figures give the forage yield of ten randomly selected plots. On the basis of the following data test that the average yield of forage is 30 q/ha.

Forage yield (q/ha): 21.8, 24.8. 27.3, 29.3, 30.8, 31.8, 32.4, 32.5, 32.1, 31.3

22. A manufacturer of transistors claims that the defective pieces cannot be more than 10 per cent in any lot. From a consignment of 300 transistors, a sample of 60 transistors was drawn randomly. On testing it was found that 7 transistors were out of order. Test whether the manufacturer's claim is correct at $\alpha = 0.01$.
23. A sample of 3000 persons was selected randomly from a city. In the sample, there were 1632 males. Does this information support the view that the number of males and females in the city are equal?
24. The yield of two strains of a crop was found to be as given below:

	Yield (q/ha)
Strain 1:	15.4, 20.5, 15.9, 38.3, 8.7, 37.0, 39.2, 26.4
Strain 2:	33.3, 10.7, 6.5, 24.0, 42.5, 22.9

Test whether the mean yields of the two strains in general are equal. Perform the test at $\alpha = 0.05$.

25. A company wants to compare the mileage of two gasoline brands *X* and *Y*. Fourteen pairs of scooters, of different makes, having same BHP, were made to run the same distance at the same speed. The scooters gave the following mileage.

Pair no.	*Miles/litre*	
	Gasoline X	*Gasoline Y*
1.	32.95	32.00
2.	37.15	36.80
3.	32.35	32.50
4.	35.95	35.60
5.	30.55	28.45
6.	27.70	23.80
7.	40.45	39.55
8.	33.50	30.70
9.	34.30	34.10
10.	33.86	31.30
11.	42.00	40.90
12.	37.60	36.55
13.	39.00	36.10
14.	32.80	32.00

Test whether there is a significant mean difference between the average mileage of two gasoline brands.

26. Given that,

$$n = 28, \ \bar{x} = 1615 \text{ and } s = 235,$$

find the approximate *P*-value in test of the hypothesis H_0: $\mu = 1500$, that H_0 will be rejected.

27. Following data, based on samples of 1000 married women, give the distribution of marital fertility in two half centuries.

Half century	*No. of women*	
	Fertile	*Non-fertile*
1750-1799	423	577
1800-1850	413	587

Do the data give sufficient evidence, that the fertility rate per woman, in two half centuries is equal?

28. Test scores in mathematics, in two samples of students of the same class from two schools, were as given below.

School *A*:	65, 45, 63, 47, 84, 37, 48, 52, 95, 26, 68, 31
School *B*:	57, 39, 44, 76, 49, 83, 91, 68, 74

Can it be concluded that, on the average, the performance of students in the two schools is at par. Also state the assumptions made about the test of hypothesis.

29. In a life testing problem, the mean life of 15 cells of a company, *A,* was found to be 25 hours with variance 90. The mean life of 20 cells of company, B, was found to be 30 hours with variance 110. On the basis of this information, can it be inferred that company B's product is significantly better than company A's product?

30. Before an increase in excise duty on tea, 400 people, out of a sample of 500 persons, were found to be tea drinkers. After an increase in duty, 400 people were tea drinkers in a sample of 600 people. Using standard error of proportions, state whether there is a significant decrease in the consumption of tea. *(C.A., May, 1977)*

31. In a factory, 2 per cent fans were found defective in a lot of 2000 fans, and in another factory, $2\frac{1}{2}$ per cent fans were found defective in a lot of 3000 fans. Do you find that the fans in the second factory are significantly inferior compared to the fans in the first factory? *(M.Com., Meerut, 1978)*

32. In a study of ten business houses, it was found that their mean income is Rs. 6200 per month and standard deviation is Rs. 690. Test statistically the belief that the business houses have an average income of Rs. 5500.
[t = 2.26 at 9 d.f. and 5% level of significance].
(Translated from Hindi) *(M.Com., (Prev.), Meerut, 1977)*

33. The following change was observed in the blood pressure of 9 patients after administering a special medicine:

7, 3, –1, 4, 3, –3, –4, 6, –5

Do these data indicate that the injection will generally be accompanied by an increase in blood pressure (B.P.)? *(M.Com. (Prev.), Meerut, 1982)*

34. A group of 5 patients treated with medicine 'A' weigh 42, 39, 48, 60 and 41 kg; a second group of 7 patients from the same hospital treated with medicine *B* weigh 38, 42, 56, 64, 68, 69 and 62 kg. Do you agree with the claim that medicine *B* increases the weight significantly? [The value of t at 5% level of significance for 10 d.f. is 2.2281]
(I.C.W.A. (Final), June 1979)

35. (a) A random sample of 1000 workers, from South India, shows that their mean wages are Rs. 47 per week with a standard deviation of Rs. 28. A random sample of 1500 workers from North India gives a mean wage of Rs. 49 per week with a standard deviation of Rs. 40. Is there any significant difference between their mean level of wages.

(b) A random sample of 100 articles, selected from a batch of 2000 articles, shows that the average diameter of the articles = 0.354 mm with a standard deviation = 0.048 mm.

Find 95% confidence interval for the average diameter of this batch of 2000 articles. *(I.C.W.A. (Final), Dec. 1979)*

36. State the various applications of *t*-test. In a rat feeding experiment, the following results were obtained.

Diet	*Gain in weight (g)*
High Protein :	13, 14, 10, 11, 12, 16, 10, 8, 11, 12, 9, 12
Low Protein :	7, 11, 10, 8, 10, 13, 9

Do these data justify that both diets are just one and the same with respect to gain in weight? *(B.A./B.Sc., Jodhpur, 1982)*

37. (a) How do you test the significance of the difference between the means of two samples?

(b) Two samples of 6 and 5 items respectively gave the following data:

Mean of the first sample	40
Standard deviation of the first sample	08
Mean of the second sample	50
Standard deviation of the second sample	10

Is the difference of the means significant? The value of t for 9 degrees of freedom at 5% level is 2.26. *(C.A., May, 1981)*

38. A fertilizer-mixing machine is set to give 12 kg of nitrate for every quintal bag of fertilizer. Ten 100-kg bags were examined. The percentages of nitrate were as follows:

11, 14, 13, 12, 13, 12, 13, 14, 11, 12

Is there reason to believe that the machine was defective? Value of t for 9 degrees of freedom is 2.262. *(C.A., Nov. 1982)*

39. The mean breaking strength of the cables supplied by a manufacturer is 1800 with standard deviation 100. By a new technique in the manufacturing process it is claimed that the breaking strength of the cables have increased. In order to test this claim a sample of 200 cables is tested. It is found that the mean breaking strength is 1850. Can we support the claim at 0.01 level of significance?

$P(t > 2.236) = .01$ *(M.Com., Kolkata, 1986)*

40. An operator in a rice mill was told to fill bags with an average 100 kgs of rice bag. A random sample of six bags shows the following:

Bag No.	1	2	3	4	5	6
Weights (Kg.)	100.5	99.8	100.2	100.1	99.3	100.4

Test the hypothesis whether he was doing the job correctly. Also estimate 95% confidence interval for average of the rice bag.

[$t_{.005,5}$ = 4,023, $t_{.025,5}$ = 2.57]

[$t_{.005,6}$ = 3.707, $t_{.025,6}$ = 2.44] *(M.Com, Kolkata, 1985)*

41. Is it likely that a sample of size 300 whose mean is 12, is a random sample from a large population with mean 12.5 and S.D. 5.2. *[I.C.W.A. (Inter); Dec. 1992]*

42. It has been stated that potential respondents are more likely to reply to questionnaire on light coloured paper than on dark coloured paper. Questionnaires were sent out on a random basis yielding following results.

Colour	*Response received*	*No response*	*Total*
Light	120	80	200
Dark	100	100	200
Total	220	180	400

Use an appropriate test at 5% level of significance to find out whether or not light colour paper yields better response. *(M.B.A., Part II, MLSU, 2002)*

43. A sample of 100 units is found to have mean 74. Can it be reasonably regarded as a sample from a large population with mean 72 and standard deviation 8 ? (Take 5% level of significance) *(C.A.P.E.-I, Nov. 2004)*

44. Ten bulbs from each of the two brands A and B are selected at random and tested for the amount of electricity consumption per hour. The data are:

Brand *A*:	7 8 7 3 8 6 9 4 7 8
Brand *B*:	9 8 8 4 7 7 9 6 6 6

Test at 5% level, whether the average consumption between two brands statistically differ. *(M.B.A, Part II, MLSU, 2000)*

45. A soap manufacturing company was distributing a particular brand of soap through a large number of retailers. Before a heavy advertisement campaign, the mean sales per week was 160 dozens. After the campaign, a sample of 50 shops was taken and the mean sales was found to be 167 dozens with standard deviation 22.4. What conclusion do you draw on the impact of advertisement on sales? Use 5% significance level? *(C.A., P.E.–I, May, 2003)*

46. A sample of 900 members has a mean 3.4 cm and s.d. 2.61 cm. Can the sample be regarded as drawn from a population with mean 3.25 cm? Find the 95% confidence limits for the population mean. *(I.C.W.A. Inter, Dec., 2004)*

47. A sample of size 10 drawn from a normal population has a mean 31 and a variance 2.25. Is it reasonable to assume that the mean of the population is 30 ? (use 1% level of significance, given that $P(|t| > 3.25) = 0.01$ for 9 d.f.) *(C.A., Foundation, May, 2002)*

48. A random sample of 65 ball bearings produced by a machine has a mean diameter 0.24″ with standard deviation of 0.02″. Another batch of 65 ball bearings produced by the same machine next day, has a mean of 0.25″ with a standard deviation of 0.04″. Is the difference in the two mean values significant at 5% level of significance? *(M.B.A., Part II, MLSU, 2001)*

49. Explain two kinds of errors in testing of hypotheses. Also throw light on their applied aspect. *(RS-II, 1998)*

50. Given the following data from two independent samples.

Sample 1	*Sample 2*
A.M. $(\bar{x}_1) = 25.8$	A.M. $(\bar{x}_2) = 28.4$
S.D. $(s_1) = 12.6$	S.D. $(s_2) = 28.2$
No. of values $(n_1) = 15$	No. of values $(n_2) = 12$

Test the significance of difference between two means. *(B.Sc. (Ag.) Hons., Part I, RAU, 2001)*

SUGGESTED READING

David Ray Anderson, Dennis J, Sweeney and Thomas Arthur Williams (2004). *Statistics for Business and Economics*, Thomson South-Western.

Glen Cowan (1998). *Statistical Data Analysis*, Oxford University Press.

Goon, A.M., M.K. Gupta, and B. Dasgupta (1980). *An Outline of Statistical Theory, Vol. II,* The World Press, Kolkata.

Harshberger, D.V. and P. Billingsley (1977). *Elements of Statistical Inference,* Allyn and Bacon, London.

Jack D. Wchwager (1995). *Fundamental Analysis*, John Wiley.

Lehman, E.L. (1976). *Testing Statistical Hypothesis,* Wiley Eastern, New Delhi.

Lindgren, B.W. (1976). *Statistical Theory,* Collier Macmillan Publishers, London, 3rd ed.

Markos V. Koutras, C.A. Charalambides and N. Balakrishnan (2001). *Probability and Statistical Models with Application*, CRC Press.

Murray R. Spiegel (1998). *Schaum's Outline of Statistics.*

N. Balakrishnan (2001). *Probability and Statistical Models with Applications*, CRC Press.

Rao, C.R. (1973). *Linear Statistical Inference and its Applications,* Wiley Eastern, 2nd ed., New Delhi.

Sprott, D.A. (2000). *Statistical Inference in Science*, Springer-Verlag, New York.

Thomas Arthur Williams (2004). *Statistics for Business and Economics*, Thomson South-Western.

APPENDIX

SPSS WINDOW GUIDE FOR *t*-TESTS & *z*-TEST

Procedure for obtaining *t*-test

1. Click on **Analyze** in menu bar followed by **Compare Means & One-sample T-test** as given below to get next screen. Here select the variable, press arrow button and click on OK button to receive the *t*-test results given at the end.
   Example 10.2

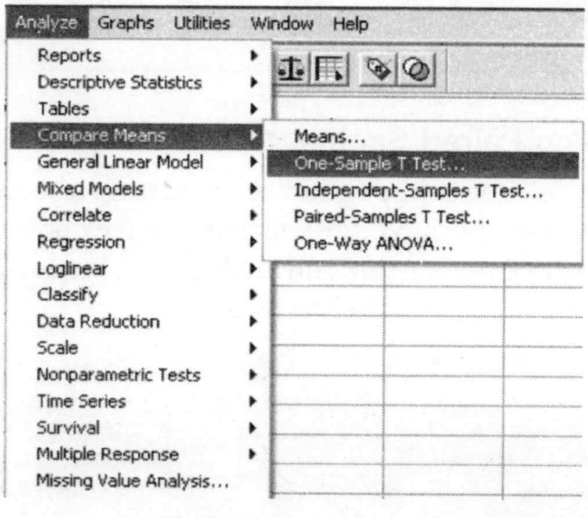

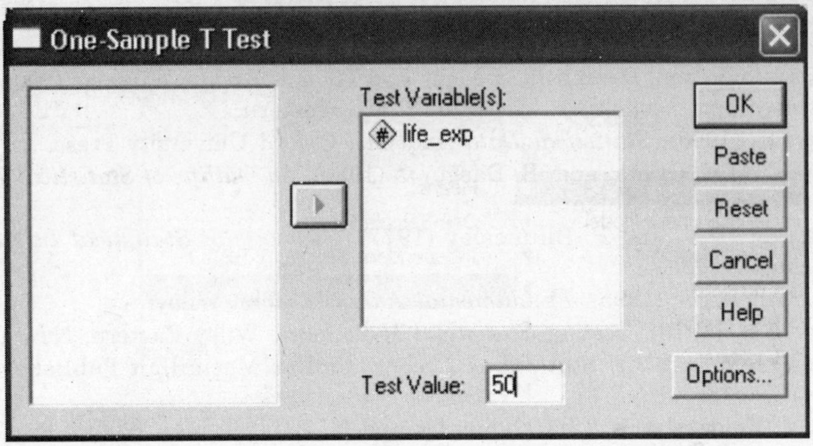

t-TEST

One-Sample Statistics

	N	Mean	Std. Deviation	Std. Error Mean
LIFE_EXP	11	54.4091	4.85869	1.46495

One-Sample Test

	Test Value = 50					
	t	df	Sig. (2-tailed)	Mean Difference	95% Confidence Interval of the Difference	
					Lower	Upper
LIFE_EXP	3.010	10	.013	4.4091	1.1450	7.6732

Procedure for Obtaining Paired Sample *t*-test

Click on **Analyze** in menu bar followed by **Compare means & paired sample *t*-test** as given below to get the next screen. Here select both the variables by pressing shift key in parallel, press arrow button and click on OK button to receive the *t*-test results given in the end.

Examples 10.5 and 10.6.

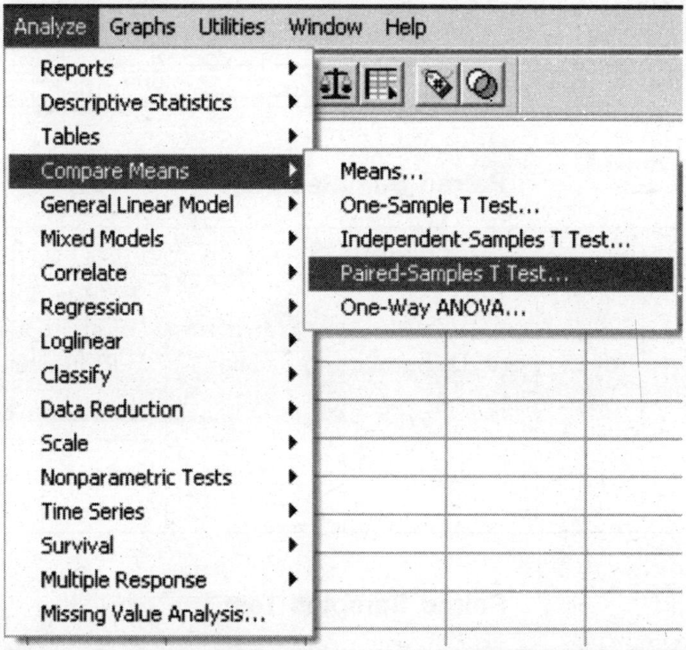

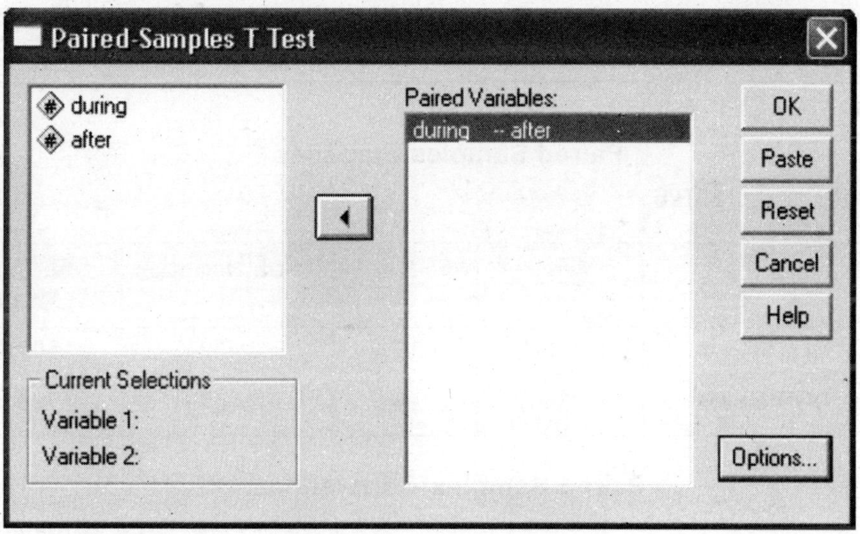

Paired Sample Statistics

Output of Example 10.5

		Mean	N	Std. Deviation	Std. Error Mean
Pair 1	DURING	.4791	11	.08043	.02425
	AFTER	.6500	11	.08660	.02611

Paired Samples Correlations

	N	Correlation	Sig.
Pair 1 DURING & AFTER	11	.695	.018

Paired Samples Test

	Paired Differences					
	Mean	Std. Deviation	Std. Error Mean	95% Confidence Interval of the Difference		*t*
				Lower	Upper	
Pair 1 DURING-AFTER	–.1709	.06549	.01975	–.2149	–.1269	–8.655

Paired Samples Test

	df	Sig. (2-tailed)
Pair 1 DURING-AFTER	10	.000

Paired Samples Statistics

Result of Example 10.6

		Mean	N	Std. Deviation	Std. Error Mean
Pair 1	UPSTR	15.9363	16	3.45252	.86313
	DOWNSTR	12.4388	16	2.90594	.72649

Paired Samples Correlations

	N	Correlation	Sig.
Pair 1 UPSTR & DOWNSTR	16	.259	.333

Paired Samples Test

		Paired Differences					
		Mean	Std. Deviation	Std. Error Mean	95% Confidence Interval of the Difference		*t*
					Lower	Upper	
Pair 1	UPSTR - DOWNSTR	3.4975	3.89469	.97367	1.4222	5.5728	3.592

Paired Samples Test

		df	Sig. (2-tailed)
Pair 1	UPSTR - DOWNSTR	15	.003

Z-TEST

In SPSS, *Z*-test also works like *t*-test. Follow the same steps as provided for *t*-test earlier. When you perform one sample *t*-test you will get following windows:

Example 10.9

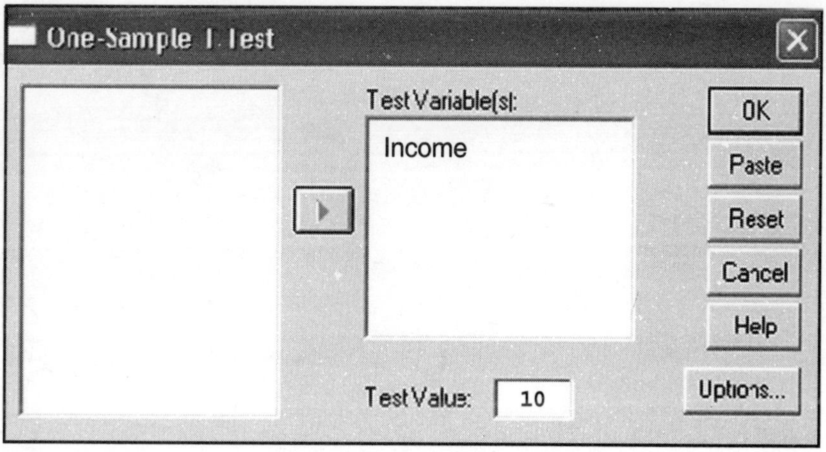

One-Sample Statistics

	N	Mean	Std. Deviation	Std. Error Mean
INCOME	36	7.797	2.2682	.3780

One-Sample Test

	Test Value = 10					
	t	df	Sig. (2-tailed)	Mean Difference	95% Confidence Interval of the Difference	
					Lower	Upper
INCOME	–5.827	35	.000	–2.203	–2.970	–1.435

11

Chapter

Chi-Square and F-Test

Chi-square test is one of the most commonly used tests of significance. All basic ideas concerning the test of significance remain the same as discussed in Chapter 10. The chi-square distribution as discussed in Chapter 8 has its importance in getting the critical values of χ^2 -variate. For convenience, the table for critical values of χ^2 at various levels of significance and for different degrees of freedom, is provided in Appendix B.

The chi-square test is applicable to test the hypotheses of the variance of a normal population, goodness of fit of the theoretical distribution to observed frequency distribution, in a one way classification having k-categories. It is also applied for the test of independence of attributes, when the frequencies are presented in a two-way classification called the contingency table. The chi-square test dates back to 1900, when Karl Pearson used it for frequency data classified into k-mutually exclusive categories. It is also a frequently used test in genetics, where one tests whether the observed frequencies in different crosses agree with the expected frequencies or not. Now chi-square tests of various hypotheses in sufficient details are given one by one.

TEST OF HYPOTHESIS FOR POPULATION VARIANCE

Suppose, on the basis of previous knowledge, we have a preconceived value, σ_0^2, of variance of a normal population. Draw a random sample of size n ($n < 30$) from this population. On the basis of n sample observations ($x_1, x_2, ..., x_n$), the postulated value σ_0^2 of the population variance σ^2 is to be either substantiated or refuted with the help of a statistical test. For this the hypothesis

$$H_0 : \sigma^2 = \sigma_0^2 \text{ vs } H_1 : \sigma^2 \neq \sigma_0^2$$

is tested by the statistic

$$\chi^2 = \frac{\Sigma_i (x_i - \overline{x})^2}{\sigma_0^2} \qquad ...(11.1)$$

$i = 1, 2, ..., n$

$$= \frac{(n-1)s^2}{\sigma_0^2} \qquad ...(11.1.1)$$

where s^2 is the variance of the sample, χ^2-statistic has $(n-1)$ d.f. Reject H_0 at pre-decided level of significance α, if $\chi^2_{cal} \geq \chi^2_{\alpha/2,n-1}$ or if $\chi^2_{cal} \leq \chi^2_{(1-\alpha/2),n-1}$.

In case of one-tailed test, i.e., testing H_0 against $H_1 : \sigma^2 > \sigma_0^2$, the test criterion is that reject H_0 if $\chi^2_{cal} \geq \chi^2_{\alpha,n-1}$.

Again for testing H_0 against $H_1 : \sigma^2 < \sigma_0^2$, the test criterion is that reject H_0 if $\chi^2_{cal} \leq \chi^2_{(1-\alpha),n-1}$

Example **11.1.** An owner of a big firm agrees to purchase the product of a factory, if the produced items do not have variance of more than 0.5 mm^2 in their length. To make sure of the specifications, the buyer selects a sample of 18 items from his lot. The length of each item was measured to be as follows:

Length (mm)					
18.57,	18.10,	18.61,	18.32,	18.33,	18.46,
18.12,	18.34,	18.57,	18.22,	18.63,	18.43,
18.37,	18.64,	18.58,	18.34,	18.43,	18.63

On the basis of the sample data, the hypothesis

$$H_0 : \sigma^2 = 0.5 \text{ vs } H_1 : \sigma^2 > 0.5$$

can be tested by the statistic

$$\chi^2 = \frac{\Sigma_i (x_i - \bar{x})^2}{\sigma_0^2}$$

$i = 1, 2, ..., 18$

We calculate, $\Sigma_i (x_i - \bar{x})^2 = \Sigma_i x_i^2 - \dfrac{(\Sigma_i x_i)^2}{n}$

For the given data,

$$\Sigma_i x_i^2 = 6112.64; \; \Sigma_i x_i = 331.69$$

$$\therefore \quad \Sigma_i (x_i - \bar{x})^2 = 6112.64 - \frac{(331.69)^2}{18}$$

$$= 6112.640 - 6112.125$$

$$= 0.515.$$

Thus, $\chi^2 = \dfrac{0.515}{0.5} = 1.03$

For $\alpha = 0.05$, $\chi^2_{0.05,17} = 27.587$. Since the calculated value of χ^2 is 1.03 which is not greater than 27.587, we accept the null hypothesis, $\sigma^2 = 0.5$ at $\alpha = .05$. It means that the buyer should purchase the lot.

TEST OF GOODNESS OF FIT

Generally the population under study has been taken to follow a known distribution such as normal, binomial or Poisson distribution. There is neither enough evidence nor enough logic, in the number of cases, to assume a particular distribution for the data. In such a situation one has every right to question the validity of such an assumption. To test the assertion of how closely the actual distribution approximates to a particular theoretical distribution, chi-square test is appropriate. To assume that the population is distributed normally is a common practice and hence we explain the test of goodness of fit of normal population first.

Let there be k class intervals and the corresponding frequencies be $f_1, f_2, ..., f_k$. The area of normal curve within each interval is found from the table of area under the normal curve, Appendix Table IV. On multiplying this area by the total of frequencies, we get the expected (theoretical) frequencies. In this way, the expected frequency for each interval is obtained. Since the tables are provided for standard normal curve, we first change each limit of class interval into a standard normal deviate by using the formula,

$$Z = \frac{x - \bar{x}}{s}$$

where $\bar{x}$ is the sample mean and s is the sample standard deviation.

Let the expected frequencies, as worked out in k classes, be $f_1', f_2', ..., f_k'$ respectively.

Chi-square statistic is

$$\chi^2 = \Sigma_i \frac{(f_i - f_i')^2}{f_i'} \quad ...(11.2)$$

$i = 1, 2, ..., k.$

Degrees of freedom for χ^2 in (11.2) are $(k - p - 1)$ where k is the number of class intervals and p is the number of parameters of the distribution estimated. One d.f. is reduced since $\Sigma_i f_i$ is a constant. For normal distribution two parameters μ and σ are estimated by $\bar{x}$ and s. Hence, in this case, chi-square has $(k - 3)$ degrees of freedom.

If the calculated value of χ^2 is greater than the table value of χ^2 for $(k - p - 1)$ d.f. and level of significance α, reject H_0. Rejection of H_0 means, that the postulated theoretical distribution is not fit to the observed data, or in other words the data do not support the assertion about the theoretical distribution.

***Example* 11.2.** The data regarding supplemental security income (SSI) programme, to escape from poverty, the poor people over 65 years as enrolled up to 1975 in an area are as follows:

Annual benefit ($)	*Mid-values (x)*	*No. of individuals in own home (f)*	*Expected frequency*
0 – 100	50	7	7.62
100 – 250	175	9	6.32
250 – 500	375	19	15.26
500 – 750	625	12	16.17
750 – 1000	875	8	11.52
1000 – 1250	1125	5 ⌉	5.24 ⌉
1250 – 1500	1375	4 ⌋	1.88 ⌋

Whether the given frequency distribution follows the normal distribution or not, can be tested by chi-square test.

The expected frequencies are worked out in the following manner:

To obtain the standard normal deviates, we calculate the mean $\overline{x}$ and standard deviation s.

The calculations are,

$$\Sigma_i f_i = 64,\ \Sigma_i f_i x_i = 34675, \text{ and } \Sigma_i f_i x_i^2 = 27668125$$

$$\overline{x} = \frac{34675}{64} = 541.8$$

$$s^2 = \frac{1}{63}\{27668125 - (541.8)^2 \times 64\}$$

$$= \frac{1}{63} \times 8881102 = 140969.87$$

$$\therefore \quad s = 375.46$$

The values of the standard normal deviates $(X - \overline{x})/s$ are,

$$Z_1 = \frac{0 - 541.8}{375.46} = -1.44$$

$$Z_2 = \frac{100 - 541.8}{375.46} = -1.18$$

Similarly,

$$Z_3 = -0.78,\ Z_4 = -0.11,\ Z_5 = 0.55$$
$$Z_6 = 1.22,\ Z_7 = 1.89,\ Z_8 = 2.55$$

From Table IV, the area between Z_1 and Z_2
$= 0.42507 - 0.38100 = 0.04407$

To calculate the expected frequency in the lowest class 0–100, the area to the left of 0 ($-\infty$ to 0), i.e., an area = 0.5 – 0.42507 = 0.07493 will also be included.

Hence, the area, to calculate the expected frequency for the lowest class = 0.07493 + 0.04407 = 0.11900

Area between Z_2 and Z_3 = 0.38100 – 0.28230 = 0.09870
Area between Z_3 and Z_4 = 0.28230 – 0.04383 = 0.23847
Area between Z_4 and Z_5 = 0.04383 + 0.20884 = 0.25267
Area between Z_5 and Z_6 = 0.38877 – 0.20884 = 0.17993
Area between Z_6 and Z_7 = 0.47062 – 0.38877 = 0.08185
Area between Z_7 and Z_8 = 0.49461 – 0.47062 = 0.02399

To calculate the expected frequency in the uppermost class (1250 – 1500), the area to the right of 1500 (1500 to ∞),

i.e., an area = 0.5 – 0.49461 = 0.00539

will also be included.

Hence, the area, to calculate the expected frequency for the upper most class = 0.02399 + 0.00539 = 0.02938

The expected frequencies are calculated as,

$$f'_1 = 0.11900 \times 64 = 7.62,\ f'_2 = 0.09870 \times 64 = 6.32$$
$$f'_3 = 0.23850 \times 64 = 15.26,\ f'_4 = 0.25267 \times 64 = 16.17$$
$$f'_5 = 0.17993 \times 64 = 11.52,\ f'_6 = 0.08185 \times 64 = 5.24$$
$$f'_7 = 0.02938 \times 64 = 1.88.$$

These frequencies are depicted in the last column of the frequency distribution table.

Note: As a check, it can easily be verified that the sum of the areas is 1.00 and the sum of the expected frequencies is 64.

Since the expected frequency of the uppermost class is less than five, this class is collapsed with the preceding class. In this way, the number of classes is reduced to six. This makes the chi-square test statistic a good indicator of the validity of the hypothesis under test.

The value of chi-square statistic by formula (11.2) is

$$\chi^2 = \frac{(7-7.62)^2}{7.62} + \frac{(9-6.32)^2}{6.32} + \frac{(19-15.26)^2}{15.26}$$
$$+ \frac{(12-16.17)^2}{16.17} + \frac{(8-11.52)^2}{11.52} + \frac{(9-7.12)^2}{7.12}$$
$$= 0.0504 + 1.1364 + 0.9166 + 1.0753 + 1.0756 + 0.4964$$
$$= 4.751$$

The table value of chi-square at α = 0.05 and (6 – 2 – 1) = 3 d.f. is 7.81.

The calculated value of chi-square is less than the table value, it means that χ^2_{cal} lies in the acceptance region. Hence, the null hypothesis that the given distribution follows a normal distribution is correct.

Goodness of Fit of a Poisson Distribution

When there are remote possibilities of occurrence of an event in a trial, very often we consider the variable to follow Poisson distribution. But the validity of Poisson's assumption is always questionable, until and unless it is supported by some proof. For example, a typist has typed few pages and the number of errors per page is counted. In this case, the distribution of the number of errors per page (per 300 words) is considered to be a Poisson variate. But we can test its validity by the chi-square test. For this, the expected frequencies of occurrence of errors can be calculated with the help of Poisson distribution, i.e., under the null hypothesis. Hence, obtain the probability of occurrence of the number of errors. The probability multiplied by the total frequency gives the corresponding expected frequency. The value of statistic χ^2 is calculated by formula (11.2). The decision about H_0 is taken as per rule.

***Example* 11.3.** A book containing 500 pages was thoroughly checked. The distribution of number of errors per page was as given below:

No. of errors (*X*)	*No. of pages* (*f*)
0	275
1	138
2	75
3	7
4	4
5	1

The null hypothesis H_0, that the distribution of errors follows Poisson's law, can be tested by the chi-square test.

By formula (6.57), we know that the probability of x successes of a Poisson variate is given by,

$$P(X = x) = \frac{e^{-\mu}\mu^x}{x!}$$

The estimated value of μ, say $\bar{x}$, is given as,

$$\bar{x} = \frac{\Sigma_i f_i x_i}{\Sigma_i f_i}$$

$i, = 1, 2, ..., 6$

$$\Sigma_i f_i x_i = 275 \times 0 + 138 \times 1 + 75 \times 2 + 7 \times 3 + 4 \times 4 + 5 \times 1$$
$$= 330$$
$$\Sigma_i f_i = 500$$

Thus,
$$\bar{x} = \frac{330}{500} = 0.66$$

From Table III,

$$e^{-0.66} = 0.517$$

Using the recurrence formula,

$$P(x+1) = \frac{\mu}{x+1} P(x)$$

we obtain the probabilities for $x = 0, 1, 2, ..., 5$.

$$p(0) = e^{-\bar{x}} = e^{-0.66} = 0.517$$
$$p(1) = \bar{x}p(0) = 0.66 \times 0.517 = 0.3412$$
$$p(2) = \frac{\bar{x}}{2}p(1) = \frac{0.66}{2} \times 0.3412 = 0.1126$$
$$p(3) = \frac{\bar{x}}{3}p(2) = \frac{0.66}{3} \times 0.1126 = 0.0248$$

$$p(4) = \frac{\overline{x}}{4}p(3) = \frac{0.66}{4} \times 0.0248 = 0.0041$$

$$p(5) = \frac{\overline{x}}{5}p(4) = \frac{0.66}{5} \times 0.0041 = 0.0005$$

The expected frequency for each class is obtained by multiplying the probability of occurrence by the total frequency, i.e., 500.

$$f_0' = 0.517 \times 500 = 258.5 = 258$$

$$f_0' = 0.3412 \times 500 = 170.6 = 171$$

Similarly,

$$f_2' = 56.3 = 56; \; f_3' = 12.4; \; f_4' = 2.05; \; f_5' = 0.25$$

Note that the last two classes have expected frequencies less than 5. Hence, to maintain the continuity of χ^2-distribution, these two classes are merged with fourth class. This makes the expected frequency of the fourth class 14.7, which is rounded to 15. In this way, the number of classes reduces to four. Also note that $\Sigma_i f_i = \Sigma_i f_i'$. The value of chi-square by formula (11.2) is

$$\chi^2 = \frac{(275-258)^2}{258} + \frac{(138-171)^2}{171} + \frac{(75-56)^2}{56} + \frac{(12-15)^2}{15}$$
$$= 1.120 + 6.368 + 6.446 + 0.60$$
$$= 14.534.$$

In this problem, we have $k = 4, p = 1$.

Hence, the d.f. for χ^2 are $4 - 1 - 1 = 2$.

The table value of χ^2 for 2 d.f. at $\alpha = 0.05$ from Table VI is 5.99. Since $\chi^2_{cal} > 5.991$ we reject H_0. It means that the given frequency distribution of errors does not follow Poisson distribution.

TEST IN ONE-WAY CLASSIFICATION

The test applies to the data when the occurrences are given in k mutually exclusive categories or class. Here we test the null hypothesis, that the probability of an item falling in ith category or class, is P_i or simply that the frequencies in k categories occur in the ratio $r_1 : r_2 : .... : r_k$. Suppose a random sample of n units falls in k categories as follows:

Categories :	C_1	C_2	C_3	---	C_i	---	C_k
Observed frequencies:	O_1	O_2	O_3	---	O_i	---	O_k

The hypothesis,

$H_0 : r_1 : r_2 : r_3 : ... r_i : ... : r_k$

against $H_1 : H_0$ is not true,

is tested by chi-square test in the manner given below.

Calculate first the expected frequencies.

we know, $O_1 + O_2 + ... + O_k = n$

and let, $r_1 + r_2 + ... + r_k = r$

The expected frequency E_i in the ith category is,

$$E_i = \frac{n}{r} \times r_i \text{ for } i = 1, 2, ..., k$$

i.e. $$E_1 = \frac{n}{r}\times r_1,\ E_2 = \frac{n}{r}\times r_2, ...,\ E_k = \frac{n}{r}\times r_k$$

The test statistic chi-square is,

$$\chi^2_{k-1} = \Sigma_i \frac{(O_i - E_i)^2}{E_i} \quad ...(11.3)$$

where the suffix $(k - 1)$ of χ^2 indicates the d.f. for chi-square. Reject H_0 at α level of significance if $\chi^2_{cal} \geq \chi^2_{\alpha,k-1.}$ Rejection of H_0 means that the observed data are not in agreement with the expected ratio.

Note: As a matter of fact formulae (11.2) and (11.3) are same. Only a difference of notations has been done according to the situation.

***Example* 11.4.** Mendel conducted a classic experiment on peas to know the genetic effect of colour and shape in the first generation, after taking four crosses namely, Round and Yellow (RY), Round and Green (RG), Wrinkled and Yellow (WY), and Wrinkled and Green (WG). According to his theory, the frequencies in these four classes should have been in the ratio 9 : 3 : 3 : 1. He found the frequencies in these four classes as follows:

Classes	RY	RG	WY	WG	Total
Obs. frequency :	315	108	101	32	556
Exp. frequency :	313	104	104	35	556

The expected frequencies are worked out in the manner given with the methodology. Given that, $n = 556$, $r_1 = 9$, $r_2 = 3$, $r_3 = 3$, $r_4 = 1$

and $r = 9 + 3 + 3 + 1 = 16$

Therefore $$E_1 = \frac{556}{16}\times 9 = 313$$

$$E_2 = \frac{556}{16}\times 3 = 104 \text{ and } E_3 = 104$$

$$E_4 = \frac{556}{16} = 35$$

The expected frequencies are rounded in such a way that the sum of expected frequencies is equal to the sum of observed frequencies, i.e., $\Sigma_i O_i = \Sigma_i E_i$ and written in the above table.

The hypothesis,

$$H_0 : 9:3:3:1$$

against $\quad H_1 : H_0$ is not true,

is tested by the statistic,

$$\chi_3^2 = \sum_{i=1}^{4} \frac{(O_i - E_i)^2}{E_i}$$

$$= \frac{(315-313)^2}{313} + \frac{(108-104)^2}{104} + \frac{(101-104)^2}{104} + \frac{(32-35)^2}{35}$$

$$\chi_3^2 = \frac{4}{313} + \frac{16}{104} + \frac{9}{104} + \frac{9}{35}$$

$$= 0.0128 + 0.1538 + 0.0865 + 0.2571$$

$$= 0.5102$$

At $\alpha = 0.05$, the table value of $\chi^2_{0.05,3} = 7.815$ which is greater than the calculated value of χ^2. Hence, the Mendel's theoretical ratio is not rejected.

***Example* 11.5.** Frequency of occurrence of modal verbs in a variety of discourses, of equal length, was as follows:

Discourses	Sports	Cultural articles	Letters to the editors	Regions	Novels	Total
Obs. frequency	137	162	167	189	197	852

If it is felt that a writer uses modal verbs at equal frequency in any type of discourse, i.e., we have to test the hypothesis.

$$H_0 : 1:1:1:1:1$$

against $H_1 : H_0$ is not true.

Given that $\quad n = 852, r_1 = r_2 = r_3 = r_4 = r_5 = 1$ and $r = 5$

Hence each $\quad E_i = \frac{852}{5} \times 1 = 170.4$ for $i = 1, 2, 3, 4, 5$,

H_0 can be tested by the statistic,

$$\chi_4^2 = \sum_{i=1}^{5} \frac{(O_i - E_i)^2}{E_i}$$

$$\chi_4^2 = \frac{(137-170.4)^2}{170.4} + \frac{(162-170.4)^2}{170.4} + \frac{(167-170.4)^2}{170.4} + \frac{(189-170.4)^2}{170.4} + \frac{(197-170.4)^4}{170.4}$$

$$= \frac{1}{170.4} \{(-33.4)^2 + (-8.4)^2 + (-3.4)^2 + (18.6)^2 + (26.6)^2\}$$

$$= \frac{2251.2}{170.4} = 13.21$$

At $\alpha = 0.05$, the table value of $\chi^2_{0.05,4} = 9.488$. Calculated value of χ^2 is greater than the table value, i.e., the value of χ^2_{cal} lies in the critical region. Hence, the null hypothesis is rejected which leads to the conclusion that the modal verbs are not used equal number of times in various types of discourses by a writer.

Special Case when $k = 2$

In many situations, there are only two classes c_1 and c_2 and the theory or experience calls for these frequencies to occur in these classes, in the ratio of $r_1 : r_2$. Let the observed frequencies in these classes be a and b. In such cases the value of chi-square, to test the null hypothesis.

$$H_0 = r_1 : r_2$$

against $H_1 : H_0$ is not true,

can directly be calculated by the formula

$$\chi_1^2 = \frac{(a - rb)^2}{r(a+b)} \qquad \text{...(11.4)}$$

where $r = \dfrac{r_1}{r_2}$

Obviously χ^2 has 1 d.f., since $k = 2$. Comparing the calculated value of χ^2 with the table value of χ^2 for 1 d.f., and $\alpha = 0.05$, i.e., 3.841, decision about H_0 is taken in the usual way.

Example **11.6.** Gene frequency of phenotypes of RR' and SS' groups was expected to be in the ratio of 1 : 2. The observed frequencies in these two classes were found to be 10 and 26. Whether the observed frequencies support the hypothetical ratio, can be confirmed by the chi-square test. Statistic χ^2 is given by (11.4).

Given that $r = \dfrac{1}{2}$, $a = 10$, $b = 26$.

Therefore,
$$\chi_1^2 = \frac{\left(10 - \frac{1}{2} \times 26\right)^2}{\frac{1}{2} \times 36} = \frac{9}{18} = 0.5$$

$\chi^2_{cal} < 3.841$, the table value of $\chi^2_{0.05,1}$. Hence the hypothetical ratio 1 : 2 of RR' to SS' is not rejected.

CONTINGENCY TABLE

The data are often based on counting of objects or units. These numbers fall in various categories of attributes in a two-way classification and are very well displayed systematically in a table known as contingency table. We can express a contingency table as a rectangular array of order ($m \times p$), having mp cells, where m denotes the number of rows which are equal to the number of categories of an attribute or criterion A, and p denotes the number of columns equal to the number of categories of attributes or criterion B. The matrix notation for contingency table is as follows:

Table 11.1: Contingency table

Attribute	*Attribute B*				*Total*
	B_1	B_2...	B_j...	B_p	
A_1	O_{11}	O_{12} ...	O_{1j} ...	O_{1p}	R_1
A_2	O_{21}	O_{22} ...	O_{2j} ...	O_{2p}	R_2
⋮	⋮		⋮		⋮
A_i	O_{i1}	O_{i2} ...	O_{ij} ...	O_{ip}	R_i
⋮	⋮				⋮
A_m	O_{m1}	O_{m2} ...	O_{mj} ...	O_{mp}	R_m
Total	C_1	C_2...	C_j...	C_p	n

In Table 11.1 cell frequency O_{ij} in (i, j)th cell represents the number of objects, units or individuals possessing the characteristics of A_i and B_j. Any of the row total R_i and column total C_j is called the *marginal total*, where $i = 1, 2, ..., m; j = 1, 2, ..., p$ and n is the grand total. Such a table eases out the process of calculations of corresponding expected frequencies and subsequently the value of chi-square statistics.

***Example* 11.7.** In a large manufacturing concern, an opinion survey was conducted regarding three types of bonus schemes. Total employees were divided into four categories, namely–labourers, clerical, technical and executives. The results obtained by way of opinion survey are presented in the form of contingency table as given below :

Employees category	*Bonus schemes*			*Total*
	Type I	*Type II*	*Type III*	
Labourer	190	243	197	630
Clerical	82	44	44	170
Technical	23	78	34	135
Executive	5	12	8	25
Total	300	377	283	960

The table indicates that out of 960 employees, 190 belonging to labour class, preferred type I scheme, and 243 preferred type II scheme. Similarly, any other cell frequency may be interpreted. 630, 170, 135 and 25 are the row marginal totals and 300, 377 and 283 are the column marginal totals.

TEST OF INDEPENDENCE OF FACTORS

It is apparent now, that a contingency table is a rectangular array having rows and columns associated with different factors. The hypothesis, that one factor is independent of the other or not, i.e.,

H_0 : Two factors are independent of each other

against H_1 : Two factors are dependent,
can be tested by chi-square test, where statistics,

$$\chi^2 = \sum_{i=1}^{m} \sum_{j=1}^{p} \frac{(O_{ij} - E_{ij})^2}{E_{ij}} \quad ...(11.5)$$

Statistic χ^2 has $(m-1)(p-1)$ d.f., whereas the data are presented in the form of the contingency table (11.1). In formula (11.5). E_{ij} is the expected frequency corresponding to (i, j)th cell observed frequency O_{ij}. Under the null hypothesis H_0, the expected frequency,

$$E_{ij} = \frac{i\text{th row total} \times j\text{th column total}}{\text{Sample size}} \quad ...(11.6)$$

$$E_{ij} = \frac{R_i \times C_j}{n} \quad ...(11.6.1)$$

Once the expected frequencies are calculated, the value of chi-square is obtained with the help of formula (11.5). To make a decision about H_0, calculated value of chi-square is compared with the table value of chi-square for $(m-1)(p-1)$ d.f. and α level of significance. If $\chi^2_{cal} \geq \chi^2_{\alpha,(m-1)(p-1)}$ reject H_0, which means that two factors are not independent.

***Example* 11.8.** For the data presented in example 11.7, we test the hypothesis H_0: Opinion about bonus schemes is independent of the types of employees against H_1: H_0 is not true, as follows:

The expected values are calculated with the help of (11.6.1) and presented in parentheses, adjacent to the observed frequency and the value of chi-square is calculated by (11.5).

Expected frequencies are calculated as,

$$E_{11} = \frac{630 \times 300}{960} = 196.88 = 197$$

$$E_{12} = \frac{630 \times 377}{960} = 247.41 = 247$$

$$\vdots$$

$$E_{43} = \frac{25 \times 283}{960} = 7.37 = 7$$

Employees category	*Bonus schemes*			*Total*
	Type I	*Type II*	*Type III*	
Labourer	190 (197)	243 (247)	197 (186)	630
Clerical	82 (53)	44 (67)	44 (50)	170
Technical	23 (42)	78 (53)	34 (40)	135
Executive	5 (8)	12 (10)	8 (7)	25
Total	300	377	283	960

$$\chi^2 = \frac{(190-197)^2}{197} + \frac{(243-247)^2}{247} + \frac{(197-186)^2}{186}$$

$$+ \frac{(82-53)^3}{53} + \frac{(44-67)^2}{67} + \frac{(44-50)^2}{50}$$

$$+ \frac{(23-42)^2}{42} + \frac{(78-53)^2}{53} + \frac{(34-40)^2}{40}$$

$$+ \frac{(5-8)^2}{8} + \frac{(12-10)^2}{10} + \frac{(8-7)^2}{7}$$

$$= 0.2487 + 0.0648 + 0.6505 + 15.8679 + 7.8955 + 0.7200 + 8.5952 + 11.7924 + 0.9000 + 1.1250 + 0.4000 + 0.1428$$

$$= 48.4028$$

The table value of chi-square for 6 d.f. and $\alpha = 0.05$ is 12.59. Since χ^2_{cal} is greater than 12.59, we reject H_0. It means that the opinion about bonus scheme is influenced by the category of employees.

***Example* 11.9.** Following table provides the number of teachers according to the time devoted to public activities by rank.

Time devoted	*Rank*			*Total*
	Professors	*Lecturers*	*Tutors*	
A good deal	25 (15.5)	13 (15.7)	9 (15.8)	47
Some	62 (54.1)	53 (54.7)	49 (55.2)	164
None	12 (29.4)	34 (29.6)	43 (30)	89
Total	99	100	101	300

The hypothesis,

H_0: Time devoted to public activities is independent of rank,

against H_1: H_0 is not true.

can be tested by chi-square test.

The expected frequencies are calculated by the formula (11.6.1) and are entered in the above table in parentheses.

$$E_{11} = \frac{47 \times 99}{300} = 15.5;$$

$$E_{12} = \frac{47 \times 100}{300} = 15.7;$$

$$E_{13} = \frac{47 \times 101}{300} = 15.8;$$

$$E_{21} = \frac{164 \times 99}{300} = 54.1;$$

$$E_{22} = \frac{164 \times 100}{300} = 54.7;$$

$$E_{23} = \frac{164 \times 101}{300} = 55.2;$$

$$E_{31} = \frac{89 \times 99}{300} = 29.4;$$

$$E_{32} = \frac{89 \times 100}{300} = 29.7;$$

$$E_{33} = \frac{89 \times 101}{300} = 30.0;$$

The statistic,

$$\chi^2 = \frac{(25-15.5)^2}{15.5} + \frac{(13-15.7)^2}{15.7} + \frac{(9-15.8)^2}{15.8} + \frac{(62-54.1)^2}{54.1} + \frac{(53-54.7)^2}{54.7} + \frac{(49-55.2)^2}{55.2} + \frac{(12-29.4)^2}{29.4} + \frac{(34-29.6)^2}{29.6} + \frac{(43-30)^2}{30}$$

$$\chi^2 = 5.822 + 0.464 + 2.926 + 1.153 + 0.0528 + 0.696 + 10.297 + 0.654 + 5.633 = 27.70$$

The table value of χ^2 for 4 d.f. and $\alpha = 0.05$ is 9.49, since χ^2_{cal} (27.70) is greater than 9.49, the null hypothesis H_0 is rejected. This leads to the conclusion that the time devoted to public activities depends on the rank of teachers.

2 × 2 Contingency Table

When a contingency table is of order (2 × 2), test of independence of factors can be performed in the same manner as for ($m \times p$) contingency table. But in this situation, the value of chi-square can also be calculated directly from the observed frequencies. It is nothing but a short-cut method of obtaining the calculated value of chi-square. Suppose the contingency table of order (2 × 2) for two factors A and B is as presented below:

Table 11.2: 2 × 2 Contingency table

Factor B	*Factor A*		*Total*
	A_1	A_2	
B_1	a	b	$(a + b)$
B_2	c	d	$(c + d)$
Total	$(a + c)$	$(b + d)$	$a + b + c + d = n$

The formula for calculating chi-square from observed frequencies a, b, c and d is,

$$\chi_1^2 = \frac{n(ad - bc)^2}{(a+c)(b+d)(a+b)(c+d)} \quad ...(11.7)$$

Obviously, χ^2 in this case has (2 – 1) (2 – 1) = 1 d.f. The decision about independence of factors A and B can be taken by comparing calculated value of the chi-square with table value of χ^2 for 1 d.f. and α = 0.05, i.e., 3.841.

***Example* 11.10.** Opinion about promotions, to be dependent on published work by persons interested in teaching or research was taken and displayed as below:

Interest	*Promotion dependent on published work*		*Total*
	Agree	*Disagree*	
Teaching	90	10	100
Research	70	30	100
Total	160	40	200

Here, H_0 : Interest and Promotion dependent on published work are independent. The value of statistic χ^2 by formula (11.7) is

$$\chi^2 = \frac{200(90\times30 - 70\times10)^2}{160\times40\times100\times100}$$

$$= \frac{200\times2000\times2000}{160\times40\times100\times100} = 12.50$$

Calculated value of χ^2 is greater than 3.841, the table value of χ^2 at 5 per cent level of significance and 1 d.f. Hence, H_0 is rejected. Here, it is concluded that the opinion about promotion scheme, too depends on published work, is influenced by the field of interest of persons.

YATES' CORRECTION

We know that the chi-square distribution is a continuous distribution. It has been proved that if any of the cell frequency in contingency table of order (2 × 2) is less than 5, the continuity of χ^2 - distribution curve is not maintained. So to remove this discrepancy, Yates suggested a correction which is extensively used. The correction is named after him. He suggested that add 0.5 in the frequency which is less than 5, and subtract and add 0.5 to the remaining cell frequencies in such a way that the marginal totals remain the same. Then calculate the value of χ^2 by formula (11.7) using the adjusted contingency table.

Instead of adjusting the contingency table of order (2 × 2), the formula (11.7) has been amended and this takes care of the correction. The value of chi-square under correction can directly be calculated by the formula,

$$\chi_1^2 = \frac{n\left(|ad - bc| - \frac{n}{2}\right)^2}{(a+c)(b+d)(a+b)(c+d)} \quad \text{...(11.8)}$$

Here, $|ad - bc|$ means that we consider only the absolute value of the difference. For instance $|23 - 75|$ will be taken as 52 instead of (– 52).

Moreover, if one does not use the formula given specifically for the (2 × 2) contingency table but follows the general procedure, under Yate's correction, the formula for the chi-square is,

$$\chi_1^2 = \sum_{i=1}^{2} \sum_{j=1}^{2} \frac{\left(|O_{ij} - E_{ij}| - \frac{1}{2}\right)^2}{E_{ij}} \quad \text{...(11.9)}$$

It is worthwhile to point out that all the three approaches yield the same value of the chi-square because they are fundamentally the same.

***Example* 11.11.** The number of licensor companies classified by the proportion of foreign profits derived from licence agreements were as follows:

Proportion of profit	*Licensor type*		*Total*
	Dominant product	*Diversified*	
Less than 5 per cent	1	6	7
5 per cent or more	7	6	13
Total	8	12	20

[*Source*: *Oxford Bulletin of Economic and Statistics*, **45** (3), Aug. 1983]

The hypothesis,

H_0 : Proportion of profit and licensor types are independent

vs. $H_1 : H_0$ is not true

can be tested by chi-square test.

Since one cell frequency is 1, the formula (10.8) is to be used.

$$\chi^2 = \frac{20 \times \left(|6\times1 - 7\times6| - \frac{20}{2}\right)^2}{8\times12\times7\times13}$$

$$= \frac{20\times(36-10)^2}{8\times12\times7\times13} = \frac{13520}{8736} = 1.55$$

Since the calculated value of χ^2 is less than 3.841, the table value of $\chi^2_{0.05,1}$, H_0 is not rejected. It means that the proportion of profit and licensor types are independent.

Note: For SPSS window guide to test independence of attribute in contingency table, see Appendix.

Coefficient of Contingency

If the hypothesis of independence of two factors is rejected, the extent of dependency can be measured by coefficient of contingency which is calculated by the formula,

$$C = \sqrt{\frac{\chi^2}{\chi^2 + n}} \qquad \ldots(11.10)$$

where χ^2 is the calculated value of statistic chi-square and n is the total frequency. The minimum value of C is zero and the maximum value never reaches 1 howsoever close to unity it may be. More is the degree of dependence between two factors as the value of C approaches unity. For a contingency table of order (5 × 5), the maximum value of C is 0.894, it is meaningless to calculate the value of C if the hypothesis of independence is not rejected.

F-TEST

A large number of surveys or experiments are conducted to draw conclusions about the effect of certain factors or treatments. Observations are taken pertaining to the character under study. *F*-test is used either for testing the hypothesis about the equality of two population variances or the equality of two or more population means. The equality of the two population means has been dealt with *t*-test. Besides a *t*-test, we can also apply a *F*-test for testing equality of two population means. *F*-distribution has already been discussed in Chapter 8. The expression (8.12) clearly indicates that the ratio of two sample variances is distributed as *F*. The same has been used in this chapter. The *F*-test is given below in adequate details for testing various hypothesis.

TEST OF EQUALITY OF TWO POPULATION VARIANCES

Let there be two normal populations $N(\mu_1, \sigma_1^2)$ and $N(\mu_2, \sigma_2^2)$. The hypothesis,

$$H_0 : \sigma_1^2 = \sigma_2^2 \text{ vs. } H_1 : \sigma_1^2 \neq \sigma_2^2$$

can be tested by *F*-test.

Let an independent sample of size n_1 be selected from population $N(\mu_1, \sigma_1^2)$ and of size n_2 from population $N(\mu_2, \sigma_2^2)$. Let the observations for these two samples be x_{11}, x_{12}, ..., x_{1n_1} and x_{21}, x_{22}, ..., x_{2n_2}. Then the sample variances are,

$$s_1^2 = \sum_{i=1}^{n_1}(x_{1i} - \bar{x}_1)^2/(n_1 - 1) \text{ and } s_2^2 = \sum_{j=1}^{n_2}(x_{2j} - \bar{x}_2)^2/(n_2 - 1)$$

s_1^2 and s_2^2 are the unbiased estimates of σ_1^2 and σ_2^2 respectively.

The statistic to test H_0 is,

$$F_{k_1,k_2} = \frac{s_1^2}{s_2^2} \qquad \ldots(11.11)$$

where $\qquad k_1 = (n_1 - 1)$ and $k_2 = (n_2 - 1)$

As a norm, larger variance is taken in the numerator of (11.11) and the d.f. corresponding to it is denoted as k_1. If the calculated value of F is greater than the table value of F for (k_1, k_2) d.f. and α level of significance, reject H_0, i.e., if $F_{cal} > F_{\alpha/2,(k_1,k_2)}$, reject H_0 or if $F_{cal} < F_{1-\alpha/2,(k_1,k_2)}$, reject H_0.

For $H_1 : \sigma_1^2 > \sigma_2^2$, reject H_0 if $F_{cal} > F_{\alpha, (k_1, k_2)}$.

For $H_1 : \sigma_1^2 < \sigma_2^2$, reject H_0 if $F_{cal} < F_{1-\alpha, (k_1, k_2)}$.

and in the reverse situation H_0 is not rejected.

Alternative Method

H_0 can also be tested by normal deviate test. We know from (8.7) that

$$z = \frac{1}{2}\log_e(s_1^2 / s_2^2) \qquad \ldots(11.12)$$

and conspicuously
$$\sigma_z^2 = \frac{1}{2}\left(\frac{1}{k_1} + \frac{1}{k_2}\right) \qquad \ldots(11.13)$$

The statistic (z/σ_z) is approximately a standard normal deviate for large or moderately large d.f. k_1 and k_2.

If the value of (z/σ_z) is greater or equal to the normal deviate value for α level of significance, reject H_0. For $\alpha = 0.05$, the normal deviate value is 1.96.

In case the experimenter knows whether $\sigma_1^2 < \sigma_2^2$ or $\sigma_1^2 > \sigma_2^2$, he should use one-tailed test. Table value of F or Z be obtained accordingly and decision about H_0 be taken in the usual manner.

***Example* 11.12.** Life expectancy in 9 regions of Brazil in 1900 and in 11 regions of Brazil in 1970 was as given in the table below:

Regions	*Life expectancy (years)*	
	1900	1970
1	42.7	54.2
2	43.7	50.4
3	34.0	44.2
4	39.2	49.7
5	46.1	55.4
6	48.7	57.0
7	49.4	58.2
8	45.9	56.6
9	55.3	61.9
10		57.5
11		53.4

[*Source : The Review of Income and Wealth*, Series 29, No. 2, June 1983]

It is desired to confirm, whether the variation in life expectancy in various regions in 1900 and in 1970 is same or not.

Let the population in 1900 and 1970 be considered as $N(\mu_1, \sigma_1^2)$ and $N(\mu_2, \sigma_2^2)$, respectively.

The hypothesis,

$$H_0 : \sigma_1^2 = \sigma_2^2 \text{ vs. } H_1 : \sigma_1^2 \neq \sigma_2^2$$

can be tested by F-test.

First we calculate s_1^2 and s_2^2,

$$s_1^2 = \frac{1}{8}\left\{\sum_{i=1}^{9} x_{1i}^2 - \frac{(\Sigma_i x_{1i})^2}{9}\right\}$$

$$\Sigma_i x_{1i} = 405, \ \Sigma_i x_{1i}^2 = 18527.78$$

$$s_1^2 = \frac{1}{8}\left\{18527.78 - \frac{(405)^2}{9}\right\}$$

$$= \frac{302.78}{8} = 37.848$$

$$s_2^2 = \frac{1}{10}\left\{\sum_{j=1}^{11} x_{2j}^2 - \frac{(\Sigma_j x_{2j})^2}{11}\right\}$$

$$\Sigma_j x_{2j} = 598.5, \ \Sigma_j x_{2j}^2 = 32799.91$$

$$s_2^2 = \frac{1}{10}\left\{32799.91 - \frac{(598.5)^2}{11}\right\}$$

$$= \frac{236.07}{10} = 23.607$$

The test statistic,

$$F = \frac{s_1^2}{s_2^2}$$

$$= \frac{37.848}{23.607} = 1.603$$

The table values of F at $\alpha = 0.05$ and (8, 10) d.f. for two-tailed test are $F_{0.025,(8,10)} =$ 3.85 and $F_{0.975,(8,10)} = 0.233$. Calculated value of F is less than 3.85 and greater than 0.233. Hence, H_0 is not rejected. This confirms the equality of variances in 1900 and 1970 in regions of Brazil.

TEST OF EQUALITY OF SEVERAL POPULATION MEANS

Frequently we come across situations where we have to test the validity of the hypothesis of equality of k normal population means *i.e.*, we want to test,

$$H_0 : \mu_1 = \mu_2 = \mu_3 = \ldots = \mu_k$$

vs. H_1 : at least two of the means (μ's) are not equal,
where $k > 2$.

Suppose the observations in k random samples of size $n_1, n_2, ..., n_k$ from k normal populations $N(\mu_i, \sigma_i^2)$ for $i = 1, 2, ..., k$ are as given below.

Table 11.3: Samples

	1	2	3	...	k
	x_{11}	x_{21}	x_{31}	...	x_{k1}
	x_{12}	x_{22}	x_{32}	...	x_{k2}
	⋮	⋮	⋮	⋮	⋮
	x_{1n_1}	x_{2n_2}	x_{3n_3}	...	x_{kn_k}
Total	$x_{1\cdot}$	$x_{2\cdot}$	$x_{3\cdot}$	...	$x_{k\cdot}$ $x_{\cdot\cdot} = G$

where x_{ij} denotes the jth observation in the ith sample for $i = 1, 2, ..., k$ and $j = 1, 2, ..., n_i$. If we assume that the population variances $\sigma_1^2, \sigma_2^2, ..., \sigma_k^2$ are homogeneous, F statistic is,

$$F = \frac{\sum_{i=1}^{k} n_i(\bar{x}_i - \bar{x})^2 / (k-1)}{\sum_{i=1}^{k}\sum_{j=1}^{n_j} (x_{ij} - \bar{x}_i)^2 / \sum_{i=1}^{k}(n_i - 1)} \qquad ...(11.14)$$

where mean of ith sample $\bar{x}_i = \sum_{j=1}^{n_i} x_{ij} / n_i$

Over mean, $\bar{x} = \sum_{i=1}^{k}\sum_{j=1}^{n_j} x_{ij} / n = \frac{G}{n}$

where, $n_1 + n_2 + ... + n_k = n$

Statistic F has $\{(k-1), (n-k)\}$ d.f.

The expression in the numerator of (11.14) denotes the sample variance between samples and the expression in the denominator denotes the variance within samples. The test criterion is that reject H_0 if $F_{cal} > F_{\alpha, k-1, n-k}$ where $F_{\alpha, k-1, n-k}$ is the table value of F at α level of significance and $(k-1, n-k)$ d.f.

Calculations involved in F-test can conveniently be carried out through a table known as *analysis of variance table.* Analysis of variance is extensively used in analysis of data pertaining to agricultural and biological experiments, the details of which are given in chapter 12. Here we give details of analysis of variance as applicable to survey designs, simple experiments and regression analysis, etc., in this chapter and the chapters ahead.

ANALYSIS OF VARIANCE (ANOVA)

When a number of populations are under study and from each population a random sample or a group of units is selected, analysis of variance is a powerful tool to analyse the data. The purpose of analysis of variance is two-fold.

(*i*) The total variance with respect to a variable (factor) is splitted into number of independent component variances, which are responsible for the total variance. Still, the sum of variances due to component factors never equals the total variance. Such a difference is attributed to error variance. This is the variance that occurs due to certain extraneous factors which cannot be held responsible for any known component.

(*ii*) The next step is to test the null hypothesis about each of the component factors individually. This hypothesis is tested by finding out the ratio of variance of a component factor to the error variance. In ANOVA table, estimated variances are termed as *mean sum of square* (M.S.). The skeleton of analysis of variance table is given below.

Table 11.4: ANOVA

Source of variation	*Degrees of freedom*	*Sum of squares*	*Mean sum of square*	*F-value*
Due to	*d.f.*	*S.S.*	*M.S.*	*F-value*
A B Error				
Total				

Table (11.4) in practice is given with abbreviated notations. Degrees of freedom for various components are written in the usual way. Error degrees of freedom are obtained by subtracting the components d.f. from total d.f. Similarly the error S.S. is obtained by subtracting the components S.S. from total S.S., whereas the total sum of square is calculated by taking the total of the square of each individual value and subtracting from it a factor which is known as *correction for mean* or *correction factor* (C.F.). Hence, the sum of squares for testing equality of k-population means, using the same notations as given in the preceding section are,

$$\text{(Correction for mean) C.F.} = \left(\sum_{i=1}^{k}\sum_{j=1}^{n_i} x_{ij}\right)^2 / n$$

$$= G^2/n$$

$$\text{Total S.S.} = \sum_{i=1}^{k}\sum_{j=1}^{n_i} x_{ij}^2 - \frac{G^2}{n} = T_{xx}$$

$$\text{Between samples S.S.} = \sum_{i=1}^{k} \frac{x_{i.}^2}{n_i} - \frac{G^2}{n} = S_{xx}$$

$$\text{Error S.S.} = \sum_{i=1}^{k}\sum_{j=1}^{n_i} x_{ij}^2 - \sum_{i=1}^{k} \frac{x_{i.}^2}{n_i} = T_{xx} - S_{xx}$$

$$= E_{xx}$$

Mean sum of squares are obtained by dividing the sum of squares by its corresponding d.f. F-value for a component is obtained by taking the ratio of a component M.S. to error M.S. Analysis of variance table with full details is as presented below:

Table 11.5: ANOVA

Due to	*d.f.*	*S.S.*	*M.S.*	*F-value*
Bet. samples	$(k-1)$	$\sum_{i=1}^{k} \frac{x_{i.}^2}{n_i} - \frac{G^2}{N} = S_{xx}$	$\frac{S_{xx}}{k-1} = S_x$	$S_x / E_x = F$
Within sample (Error)	$(n-k)$	$\sum_{i=1}^{k} \sum_{j=1}^{n_i} x_{ij}^2 - \sum_{i=1}^{k} \frac{x_{i.}^2}{n_i} = E_{xx}$	$\frac{E_{xx}}{n-k} = E_x$	
Total	$n-1$	$\sum_{i=1}^{k} \sum_{j=1}^{n_i} x_{ij}^2 - \frac{G^2}{n} = T_{xx}$		

The calculated value of F is compared with the table value of F for α level of significance and $(k-1, n-k)$ d.f. Traditionally α is chosen to be 0.05, and for more precision, α is chosen to be 0.01, though there is no hard-and-fast rule about it. We may choose any other value of α if it sounds more logical.

The above ANOVA is meant for one way classification. The ANOVA table may be extended for two or more way classification. In that situation, the component factors will increase in the ANOVA table accordingly. The methodology of analysis of variance is further explicated through a numerical example.

***Example* 11.13.** The following table gives the gain in body weight (kg) per heifer during four grazing treatments.

Heifer no.	*Treatments* T_1	T_2	T_3	T_4	*Total*
	Gain in body weight (kg) x_{ij}				
1	67.3	74.2	63.1	48.7	
2	36.9	42.2	32.9	49.0	
3	63.2	58.6	59.2	62.0	
4	26.8	36.6	42.4	38.8	
5	54.8	54.6	34.0	48.2	
6	64.2	81.8	65.6		
7	81.4				
Total	394.6	348.0	297.2	246.7	1286.5

The hypothesis that the mean gain in weight of heifers under four treatments is equal or not, can be tested by F-test, i.e., the hypothesis,

$$H_0 : \mu_1 = \mu_2 = \mu_3 = \mu_4$$

against H_1 : at least two means are different,
can be tested through analysis of variance technique.

For the given data, $n_1 = 7$, $n_2 = 6$, $n_3 = 6$, $n_4 = 5$ and $n = 24$,

$$G = 1286.5,\ x_{1\cdot} = 394.6,\ x_{2\cdot} = 348.0,\ x_{3\cdot} = 297.2,\ x_{4\cdot} = 246.7$$

$$\sum_{i=1}^{4}\sum_{j=1}^{n_i} x_{ij}^2 = (67.3^2 + 36.9^2 + ... + 38.8^2 + 48.2^2)$$

$$= 74357.57$$

$$\frac{G^2}{n} = \frac{(1286.5)^2}{24} = 68961.76$$

Total S.S.
$$= 74357.57 - 68961.76$$
$$= 5395.81$$

$$\sum_{i=1}^{4}\frac{x_{i.}^2}{n_i} = \frac{(394.6)^2}{7} + \frac{(348.0)^2}{6} + \frac{(297.2)^2}{6} + \frac{(246.7)^2}{5}$$

$$= 22244.16 + 20184.00 + 14721.31 + 12172.18$$
$$= 69321.65$$

Between treatment S.S.,

$$\sum_{i=1}^{4}\frac{x_{i.}^2}{n_i} - \frac{G^2}{n} = 69321.65 - 68961.76$$
$$= 359.89$$

Error S.S.
$$= 5395.81 - 359.89$$
$$= 5035.92$$

Due to	*d.f.*	*S.S.*	*M.S.*	*F-value*
Treatments	3	359.89	119.96	$\frac{199.96}{251.80} = 0.794$
Error	20	5035.92	251.80	
Total	23	5395.81		

From Table VII (*ii*), value of $F_{0.05,\ (3,\ 20)} = 3.10$.

Since the calculated value of F is less than the table value, H_0 is not rejected. It leads to the result that the mean increase in weight of heifers, under four grazing treatments, is not significantly different at 5 per cent level of significance.

RELATION BETWEEN t, χ^2, F AND z

It is worth pointing out that for some hypothesis, more than one test can be used. For instance, the equality of two population means can be tested by t-test as well as F-test. The reascn is that some relationship exists between t, χ^2 and F-distribution in particular situations and hence these tests become equivalent, permitting the use of either of these. Thus, the relationship for $k_1 = 1$, $k_2 = n$ is,

$$t_n^2 = F_{1,n} \qquad ...(11.15)$$

$$t_n = e^z = \sqrt{F_{1,n}} \qquad ...(11.15.1)$$

where z is given by (11.12).

If $k_1 = n$, $k_2 = \infty$, z is related to chi-square and the relation is

$$z = \frac{1}{2}\log_e\left(\frac{\chi^2}{n}\right) \quad ...(11.16)$$

$$e^{2z} = \chi^2/n \quad ...(11.16.1)$$

or

$$F = \chi^2/n \quad ...(11.16.2)$$

Since we know, $F = e^{2z}$

If $k_1 = 1$, $k_2 = \infty$, then

$$F_{1,\infty} = \chi_1^2 \quad ...(11.17)$$

where suffix 1 denotes the d.f. for χ^2.

Also from (11.15),

$$t_\infty^2 = \chi_1^2 \quad ...(11.18)$$

If F-table is available only for the upper percentage points, the following identity enables us to obtain the F-values on the left-tail distribution. Let α be the level of the test and F be distributed with (k_1, k_2) d.f., the identity is,

$$1/F_{\alpha,(k_1,k_2)} = F_{1-\alpha,(k_2,k_1)} \quad ...(11.19)$$

The identity (11.19) is very useful and easy to prove.

If the degrees of freedom for a chi-square are large, *i.e.*, more than 100, then the chi-square can be approximated to a standard normal variate using the relation,

$$Z = \sqrt{2\chi^2} - \sqrt{2k-1} \quad ...(11.20)$$

where k is the d.f. for a chi-square and $Z \sim N(0, 1)$. In this situation, the significance of null hypothesis can be tested by using the normal table for one tail.

These tests will be used in subsequent chapters also as and when the need arises to test various hypotheses.

QUESTIONS AND EXERCISES

1. What are the kinds of hypotheses that can be tested by the chi-square test?
2. What are the types of observational data suitable for the chi-square test, in a contingency table?
3. What do you understand by the test of goodness of fit?
4. Discuss a contingency table.
5. What is Yates' correction and its need?
6. Answer the following in not more than three lines
   (*a*) Expected frequencies are obtained under which hypothesis?
   (*b*) Why can the chi-square not be negative?
   (*c*) Why can the value of F-statistic not be negative?

(d) Write the use of coefficient of contingency.

(e) Give the relations between t, χ^2 and F.

7. Write short notes on:
   (a) Analysis of variance.
   (b) F-statistic.
   (c) Chi-square test in a (2 × 2) contingency table.
   (d) Test of hypothesis about a population variance.
   (e) Normal deviate test for the equality of two population variances.

8. Obtain the values of the following F and χ^2 distribution points from the tables given in appendix.
   (i) $F_{0.05,\ (9,\ 15)}$ (ii) $F_{0.90,\ (8,\ 18)}$ (iii) $F_{0.01,\ (12,\ 20)}$
   (iv) $F_{0.99,\ (20,\ 12)}$ (v) $F_{0.1,\ (7,\ 15)}$ (vi) $\chi^2_{0.05,6}$
   (vii) $\chi^2_{0.05,1}$

9. The household net income from property and entrepreneurship in France and Germany, in two samples of households, as percentage of total inflationary gap was as follows:

Germany :	15.0, 8.0, 3.8, 6.4, 27.4, 19.0, 35.3, 13.6
France:	18.8, 23.1, 10.3, 8.0, 18.0, 10.2, 15.2, 19.0, 20.2

Test the equality of variances of household net income in France and Germany.

10. A wire of metal will be considered suitable for use, if the variance of the tensile strength is not more than 5 units. A sample of 12 pieces of wire of equal lengths yielded the sample variance as 7.8 units. Perform the statistical test and suggest whether the wire should be accepted for use.

11. Following data give the distribution of women ever married by age.

Age group	*No. of women*
15–19	3
19–23	43
23–27	62
27–31	38
31–35	24
35–39	14
39–43	11
43–47	5
47–51	2

Test whether the data have come from a normal population.

12. The following table gives the distribution of a number of breaks, in 100 metre length of wire, in a sample of 50 coils of 100 metre length.

No. of breaks	*No. of coils*
0	12
1	15
2	9
3	10
4	4

Do the given frequency distribution follows Poisson distribution?

13. A cross was performed between two breeds of cows namely, Brownswiss (R) and Sahiwal (S). The frequencies in three phenotypes RR, RS and SS were expected to occur in the ratio 1 : 6 : 9. A breeding experiment yielded the frequencies as RR — 2, RS — 16 and SS — 18. Do the observed frequencies support the hypothetical ratio.
14. Following table gives the data regarding the field of study in the University and their field of specialization in Secondary School.

Specialization in Secondary School	*Field of study in the University*		
	Biology	*Medicine*	*Agriculture*
Biology	26	52	23
Physics and Maths	3	44	8
Agriculture	4	1	15
Humanities	6	11	10

[*Source* : *Higher Education* (International Journal) 9 (4), July, 1980]
Test wheathr the field of study in the University is influenced by the specialization in High School.
15. It is expected that the ratio of the number of men and women married in the age group 24–30 years is 3 : 2. A pilot survey was conducted in a region and found that 52 men and 47 women were married in the age group 24—30 years. Do the survey data support the expected ratio?
16. Following table gives the number of births according to their sex and condition at the time of birth.

	Condition	
Sex	*Normal*	*Abnormal*
Male	19	5
Female	30	6

Test at $\alpha = 0.05$, whether the condition at birth depends on the sex of the child.
17. In a departmental examination, the candidates of both the sexes yielded results as presented here in the (2 × 2) table.

Sex	*Pass*	*Fail*
Male	42	2
Female	14	6

Can it be inferred that the result of the test is related to the sex of the candidates. Perform a suitable statistical test to arrive at the correct decision, using a 5 per cent level.
18. A coaching school claims that 60% of the students, coached in the school, will be selected in a competition, 55 candidates sought admission in the school and only 24 candidates got selected. Do the results of the candidates justify the claim of the school authorities at 1 per cent level of significance?

19. Total green forage yield (tonnes/ha) during three years 1973–76 based on experimental plots situated at different locations is as follows:

1973-74	*1974-75*	*1975-76*
11.1	18.3	17.3
15.2	21.8	22.5
17.8	24.8	26.7
19.9	27.3	29.5
21.3	29.3	31.1
21.8	30.8	31.3
21.5	32.4	30.3
20.5	32.5	24.4
18.6	31.8	
15.9		
12.5		

Test at 0.01 level, whether the average yield during three years is the same or not.

20. Given the following information about two samples from two normal populations,

$n_1 = 9$, $s_1 = 1.97$, $n_2 = 7$ and $s_2 = 3.21$.

Can it be concluded that both the samples have come from populations having the same variability.

21. Describe the use of the χ^2-test in testing of independence of attributes in a (2×2) contingency table. *(B.A., Mumbai, 1970)*

22. Two random samples taken from two normal populations are as follows. Estimate the variances of populations and test that the two populations have equal variances.

Sample I:	20,	16,	26,	27,	23,	22,	18,	24,	25,	19		
Sample II:	17,	23,	32,	25,	22,	24,	28,	18,	31,	33,	20,	27

(Translated from Hindi) *(M.Com. (Final), Meerut, 1980)*

23. The following table reveals the condition of the house and the condition of the children.

	Condition of house		
Condition of children	*Clean*	*Not clean*	*Total*
Very clean	76	43	119
Clean	38	17	55
Dirty	25	47	72
Total	139	107	246

Using the chi-square test, find out whether the condition of house affects the condition of children. *(M.A.(Final) Econ., Agra, 1982)*

24. Given below are the number of accidents of aeroplanes that occurred on different days of a week. Find out whether the aeroplane accidents are uniformly distributed over the seven days of the week.

Days :	Sun	Mon	Tues	Wed	Thurs	Fri	Sat	Total
No. of Accidents :	16	18	10	14	13	11	16	98

(Translated from Hindi) *(M.A. (Final), Econ., Agra, 1979)*

25. The following mistakes per page were observed in a book.

No. of mistakes per page	*No. of times the mistake occurred*
0	59
1	27
2	9
3	1

Fit a Poisson distribution to the above data. (*M.Com., Meerut, 1982*)

26. The following table contains the yield in quintals of five plots for each of the three strains of wheat. Decide whether there is any significant difference in the yields of strains of wheat? Variation between plots be considered immaterial.

Strains	*Plots*				
	I	*II*	*III*	*IV*	*V*
A	20	21	23	16	20
B	18	20	17	15	25
C	25	28	22	28	32

[For (2, 12) d.f. $F_{0.05}$ = 3.88] (*M.A. (Final), Econ., Agra, 1981*)

27. Following table gives the number of those plants which have some special qualities. Test the hypothesis that the colour of flowers is independent to the flatness of leaves.

	Flat leaves	*Curved leaves*	*Total*
White flowers	99	36	135
Red flowers	20	5	25
Total	119	41	160

(*Translated from Hindi*) (*M.Com. (Prev.), Meerut, 1978*)

28. A survey of 320 families with five children each reveal the following distribution.

No. of boys	5	4	3	2	1	0
No. of girls	0	1	2	3	4	5
No. of families	14	56	110	88	40	12

Is this result consistent with the hypothesis that the male and female births are equally probable. You may use chi-square test. (*M.Com., Delhi, 1975*)

[*Hint*: Find the expected number of families from 320 $\left(\frac{1}{2}+\frac{1}{2}\right)^n$]

29. The following data relate to a random sample of government employees in two states of the Indian Union.

	State I	*State II*
Sample size	16	25
Mean monthly income (Rs.) of the sampled employees	440	460
Sample variance	40	42

First carry out a test of hypothesis that the variance of the two populations are equal. In the light of the result of the above test, carry out a test of the hypothesis that the means of the two populations are equal. *(M.A. Econ., Delhi, 1971)*

30. Among 64 offsprings of a certain cross between guinea pigs, 34 were red, 10 were black and 20 were white. According to the genetic model, these numbers should be in the ratio 9 : 3 : 4, Are the data consistent with the model at the five per cent level? (You are given that the value of χ^2 is 5.99 for $v = 2$ and 3.84 for $v = 1$). *(I.A.S., 1965)*

31. Two samples are drawn from two normal populations. From the following data, test whether the two samples have the same variance at 5% level:

Sample 1 :	60	65	71	74	76	82	85	87		
Sample 2 :	61	66	67	85	78	63	85	86	88	91

(C.A., May, 1983)

32. (*a*) Discuss the importance of χ^2 test. How is it used to test the association between attributes?

    (*b*) In a survey of 200 boys, of which 75 were intelligent, 40 had skilled fathers; while 85 of the unintelligent boys had unskilled fathers. Do these figures support the hypothesis that skilled fathers have intelligent boys. Use χ^2 test. Value of χ^2 for 1 degree of freedom at 5% level is 3.84. *(C.A., Nov., 1982)*

33. In a textile factory, 100 pieces of cloth were inspected and the number of defects in each piece were recorded. In this way, the following distribution was obtained. Fit a Poisson distribution to the following data:

Number of defects:	0	1	2	3	4 or more
Frequency:	79	18	2	1	0

$[e^{-1.25} = .0821, e^{-.25} = .788, e^{-1} = .3679, e^{-2} = .1353, e^{-3} = .0498]$

(M.Com. Kolkata, 1985)

34. The variance of a random sample of 10 observations is found to be 81.3. Test the hypothesis that the true value of the population variance is 125.

$[\chi^2_{.025,9} = 19.013,\ \ \chi^2_{0.025,10} = 21.483,\ \ \chi^2_{.975,9} = 2.70,\ \ \chi^2_{.975,10} = 3.247]$

(M.Com. Kolkata, 1985)

35. The following table gives the joint distribution of 120 fathers and sons with respect to hair colour.

Son's hair colour	*Father's hair colour*			
	Black	*Grey*	*Brown*	*Total*
Black	8	12	10	30
Grey	7	18	20	45
Brown	10	10	25	45
Total	25	40	55	120

On the hypothesis of chance, find out if there is significant association between fathers and sons with respect to hair colour. Use contingency coefficient C.

(Mumbai, M.Ed., 1986)

36. Three samples, each of size 5, were drawn from three uncorrelated normal populations with equal variances. Test the hypothesis that the population means are equal at 5% level.

Sample	*1*	*2*	*3*
	10	9	14
	12	7	11
	9	12	15
	16	11	14
	13	11	16

(*I.C.W.A., Dec., 1988*)

37. A die is thrown 120 times with the following results:

Face:	1	2	3	4	5	6
Frequency:	16	30	22	18	14	20

Test the hypothesis that the die is unbiased. (Given $\chi^2_{0.05;5} = 11.07, \chi^2_{0.05;6} = 12.59$)

(*I.C.W.A., Inter, June, 2000*)

38. In a recent diet survey the following results were obtained in a city:

	Community A	*Community B*
No. of families taking tea	1236	164
No. of families not taking tea	564	36

Test whether there is any significant difference between the two communities in the matter of taking tea? (*C.A. P.E. – I, May, 2004*)
($\chi^2_{1 d.f.} = 3.84$)

39. An experiment with an immunization of cattle from tuberculosis gave the following results:

	Died/Affected	*Unaffected*
Innoculated	12	26
Not innoculated	16	6

Examine the effect of vaccine in controlling susceptibility to tuberculosis. $\chi^2_{(1)}$ at 5% level of significance = 3.84. (*I.C.W.A., Inter, June, 2002*)

40. A certain drug was administered to 456 males out of a total 720 in a certain locality to test its efficacy against typhoid. The incidence of typhoid is shown below. Find out the effectiveness of the drug against the disease.

	Infection	*No infection*	*Total*
Administered the drug	144	312	456
Without administering the drug	192	72	264
Total	336	384	720

(*M.B.A., Delhi Univ., 1982*)

41. Following results were obtained from two samples each drawn from two different populations A and B.

Population	:	A	B
Sample	:	I	II
Sample size	:	$n_1 = 16$	$n_2 = 9$
Sample S.D.	:	$s_1 = 3$	$s_2 = 2$

Test the hypothesis that variance of Brand A is more than that of Brand B.

(C.A., P.E.-I, Nov. 2003)

42. Fit a Poisson distribution to the following data and calculate the theoretical frequencies.

x	:	0	1	2	3	4
Frequency	:	122	60	15	2	1

Given that : $e^{-0.5} = 0.61$ *(I.C.W.A., Inter, Dec. 2003)*

43. In a locality 200 persons were randomly selected and asked about their educational achievements. The results are presented in the following table:

	Education		
Sex	*Middle*	*High School*	*College*
Male	20	30	50
Female	50	20	30

Does education depends on sex. *(C.A. Foundation, Nov. 2002)*

44. A manufacturer of TV sets was trying to find out what variables influenced the purchase of a TV set. Level of income was suggested as possible variable influencing the purchase of TV sets. A sample of 500 households was selected and the information obtained is classified as shown below:

	Have TV set	*Do not have TV set*
Low Income Group	0	250
Middle Income Group	50	100
High Income Group	80	20

Is there evidence from the above data of relation between ownership of TV sets and level of income? *(M.B.A., Delhi Univ., 1988)*

45. A sample of 100 gave a mean of 7.4 kg and a standard deviation of 1.2 kg. Find 95% confidence limits for the population mean. *(C.A., Foundation, Nov. 2001)*

SUGGESTED READING

David Ray Anderson, Dennis J, Sweeney and Thomas Arthur Williams (2004). *Statistics for Business and Economics*, Thomson South-Western.

Glen Cowan (1998). *Statistical Data Analysis*, Oxford University Press.

Goon, A.M., M.K. Gupta, and B. Dasgupta (1980). *An Outline of Statistical Theory, Vol. II,* The World Press, Kolkata.

Harshberger, D.V. and P. Billingsley (1977). *Elements of Statistical Inference,* Allyn and Bacon, London.

Jack D. Wchwager (1995). *Fundamental Analysis*, John Wiley.

Lehman, E.L. (1976). *Testing Statistical Hypothesis,* Wiley Eastern, New Delhi.

Lindgren, B.W. (1976). *Statistical Theory,* Collier Macmillan Publishers, London, 3rd ed.

Markos V. Koutras, C.A. Charalambides and N. Balakrishnan (2001). *Probability and Statistical Models with Application*, CRC Press.

Murray R. Spiegel (1998). *Schaum's Outline of Statistics.*

N. Balakrishnan (2001). *Probability and Statistical Models with Applications*, CRC Press.

Rao, C.R. (1973). *Linear Statistical Inference and its Applications,* Wiley Eastern, 2nd ed., New Delhi.

Sprott, D.A. (2000). *Statistical Inference in Science*, Springer-Verlag, New York.

Thomas Arthur Williams (2004). *Statistics for Business and Economics*, Thomson South-Western.

APPENDIX

SPSS WINDOW GUIDE FOR CHI-SQUARE TEST OF INDEPENDENCE IN CONTINGENCY TABLE

Procedure for Performing Chi-Square Test

1. Click on Analyze menu. Select **Descriptive Frequencies** option followed by **Cross tabs** to get following window:

   Example 11.11

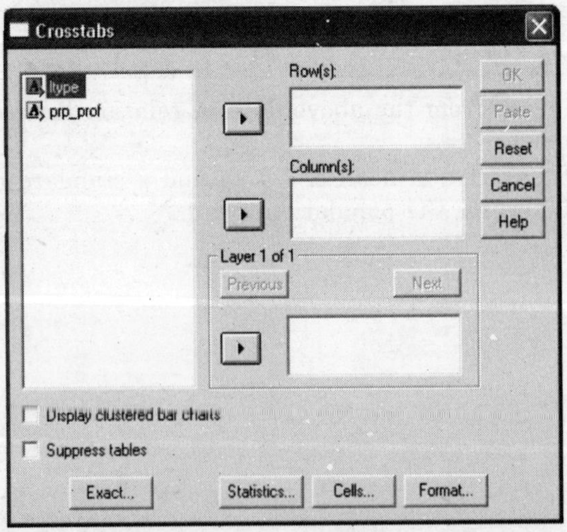

2. Select the variable prp_prof and press the arrow button to send it to the Row(s) pane. Similarly select the variable type & press another arrow button so that it appears on the column(s) pane. Now click on **statistics** button in the bottom and tick on chi-square check box at the top as given below.

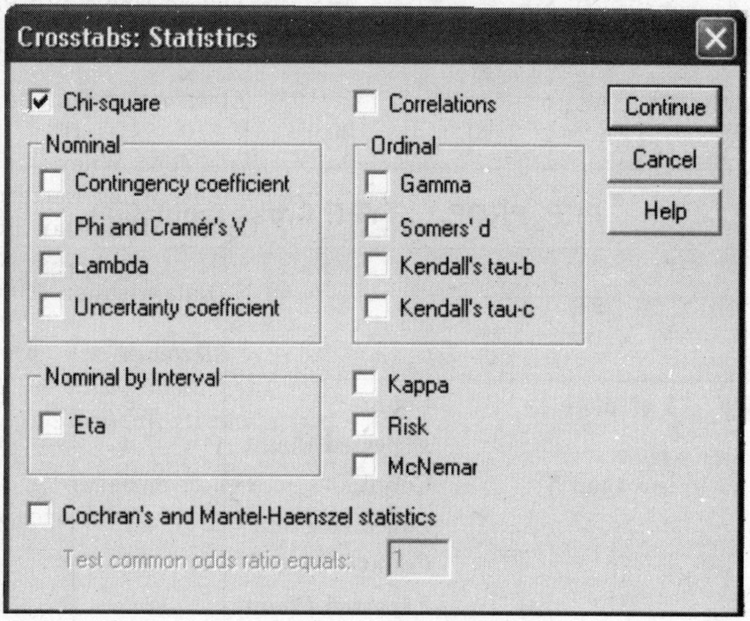

3. In order to return to the main window, press **Continue** button. Now click on **Cells** button in the bottom and select on check box before **expected** as given below. Again press continue button to return to main window.

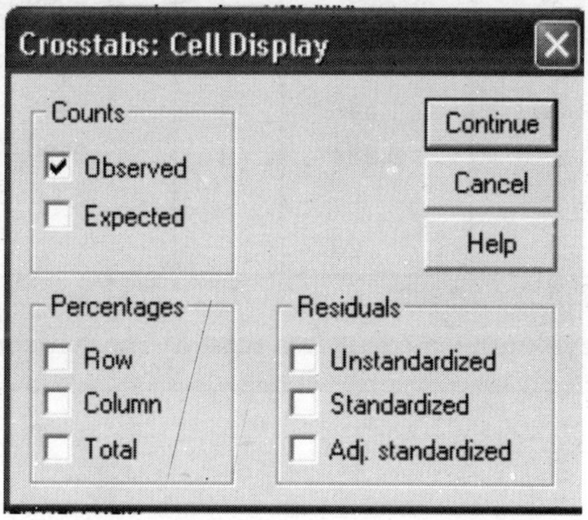

4. When you press OK button, you get following output:

Cross tabs

Example 11.11. Case Processing Summary

	Cases					
	Valid		Missing		Total	
	N	Per cent	N	Per cent	N	Per cent
PRP_PROF * LTYPE	20	100.0%	0	.0%	20	100.0%

PRP_PROF * LTYPE Cross tabulation

			LTYPE		
			Diversified	Dominant product	Total
PRP_PROF	5 or more	Count	6	7	13
		Expected Count	7.8	5.2	13.0
	less than 5	Count	6	1	7
		Expected Count	4.2	2.8	7.0
Total		Count	12	8	20
		Expected Count	12.0	8.0	20.0

Chi-Square Tests

	Value	df	Asymp. Sig. (2-sided)	Exact Sig. (2-sided)	Exact Sig. (1-sided)
Pearson Chi-Square	2.967(b)	1	.085		
Continuity Correction(a)	1.548	1	.213		
Likelihood Ratio	3.234	1	.072		
Fisher's Exact Test				.158	.106
No. of Valid Cases	20				

(a) Computed only for a 2 × 2 table

(b) 2 cells (50.0%) have expected count less than 5. The minimum expected count is 2.80.

12

Chapter

Experimental Research Designs

Research is an inseparable part of academic, scientific, social, medical, economic, industrial and management studies. The purpose of a research is to explore, to describe, to establish the validity of a statement, to establish the relationship between parameters, to find out the cause and effect relationship, etc. A variety of strategies have been developed to fulfil these purposes. These strategies include sample surveys, pre-experimental designs, true experimental designs, quasi experiments. Sample surveys entail probability and non-probability sampling designs which have been discussed adequately in Chapters 7 and 9. So, sampling designs do not form the part of this chapter. Only remaining three aspects of research designs will be covered in this chapter to the extent they are usually required as a part of curriculum of the courses for which this book is meant. Before discussing experimental designs, it seems germane to explain and define the terms that are commonly associated with experimental designs.

RESEARCH DESIGNS

It is most important to clearly and conceptually understand what is meant by a research design. It can be spelled out as, "A research design is a plan to collect data from individuals or units which are subjected to certain conditions or treatments in such a way that the individuals or units are free from the influences or effects of all extraneous factors (nuisance variables) and have full freedom to show the effect of conditions or treatments to which the individuals or units are exposed to." "Research designs also include analysis of data and interpretation of results."

DATA

Numerical values of a variable collected on individuals or units are known as data.

VARIABLE

Definitions and explanations of continuous and discrete variables, dependent and independent variables have already been dealt in Chapters 2, 6 and 9. Still dependent and independent variables will be discussed in context to experimental designs.

Independent Variable

The variable (conditions or substances) that is manipulated by a researcher to see its effect(s) on experimental units is called independent variable. The terms treatment and independent variable are used in the same sense and hence are interchangeable. For instance, subjects are exposed to different advertising themes, students are imparted instructions under various teaching methods, patients are administered various composition of medicines, different doses of fertilizers be applied to plots, different feeds be given to cows, etc. Advertising themes and teaching methods lead to the term *conditions* whereas medicines, fertilizer doses, feed types are usually called *treatments*.

Dependent Variable

Measurements are taken in respect of a variable on each and every experimental unit so as to estimate the effect of certain treatments and to test the equality of their effects. Such a variable is known as dependent variable. Milk yield of cows in feeding experiments, yield of crops in fertilizer experiment, blood pressure of patients in drug experiment, impact of advertising themes on sales of a product, increase in knowledge in teaching methods experiment, are examples of dependent variables. Such variables are also termed as *criterion variables*.

Nuisance Variables

Extraneous variables which influence the dependent variable and cause undesired variation are called nuisance variable. For example, the inherent knowledge of a person in teaching method experiment, initial weight of cows in feeding experiment, temperament of patients in drug experiment, percentage germination in fertilizer experiment. Some of the nuisance variables may be controlled by choosing a proper design and some cannot be. Nuisance variables confound with the dependent variable in some way that weakens and sometimes invalidates the results of the experiment. Hence they should be controlled in so far as possible.

EXPERIMENTAL UNIT

An individual or a group of individuals to which a single condition or treatment is applied independently of other individual or group is called an experimental unit. Experimental unit is one whose response to the treatment is being examined and this observation is taken on each unit as a separate identity. In experiment on teaching method, a person; in drug experiment, a patient; in feeding experiment, a cow; in field experiment, a plot; in marketing research, a family; are a few examples of experimental units.

Experimental Error

The error caused by extraneous factors in an experiment which are beyond the control or not controlled by the researcher is called experimental error. More simply, we can say that experimental error is the characteristic of two or more experimental units behave differently even if they are treated all alike. These differences whether large or small contribute to experimental error. For example, if on two or more field plots, the seed is sown on the same day and are treated similarly in all respects, their yields are not same. This difference is attributed to experimental error.

Control in Experiments

One important aspect of planning a good research design is to minimize influence of extraneous variable(s) in so far as possible. So the techniques used in designing of experiments for minimizing the influence of extraneous independent variable(s) are called control in experiments. In experimental researches, the term control is used to restrict undesired variability.

Nota Bene

The terms, level of significance, Type I and Type II errors, degrees of freedom, types of hypotheses, analysis of variance have already been discussed in Chapters 9 and 10. So they are not repeated here.

VALIDITY IN EXPERIMENTATION

An experiment is conducted with two aims : (*i*) to draw valid inferences about the effects of treatments (independent variable) on the subjects under investigation and, (*ii*) to generalize our results to a larger population of interest. The first aim concerns ***internal validity*** whereas the second to ***external validity***. Now both the validities will be discussed in brief.

Internal Validity

It is mainly concerned with drawing the correct conclusion that whatever variation is observed in the dependent variable is really due to the effect of the treatment(s). Thus, internal validity checks whether the observed effect on the subjects or test group could have occurred due to some extraneous factors. If the observed effects are confounded with the extraneous variable(s), then it would not be reasonable to draw conclusions about causal relationship between the treatment effect and response. Hence, internal validity is a must for correct and valid inferences. To ensure internal validity, extraneous factors should be controlled.

There are many threats to internal validity. We discuss here some of them.

1. **History :** In many experimental designs, measurement (O_1) about the criterion variable is taken on the test units prior to the manipulation X. When the manipulation is over, an after measurement (O_2) on the same criterion variable is taken. The difference ($O_2 - O_1$) measures the effect of X. But there is a possibility that in the mean time between O_1 and O_2, many events might have occurred which could have influence O_2 besides X. Such events are known as ***history.*** For instance, the management of a company wants to convince his workers about a new bonus scheme. Managers give a test to all its employees to know their existing opinion (O_1) about the bonus scheme. Again at the end of a campaign, a test is conducted to known their present opinion (O_2) about the bonus scheme. Diagramatically the experiment can be depicted as follows:

Pre-test	Treatment	Post-test
O_1	X	O_2

   Such experiments are called *one-group Pre-test – Post-test design experiment.* But between O_1 and O_2, many events could have occurred like some union leaders might have conveyed their views, some articles would have appeared in newspapers. Such intervening events are called *history* and have an influence on O_2. So the difference $(O_2 - O_1)$ cannot be taken exclusively due to campaign because the campaign effect might have been confounded with history. For valid conclusion history must be controlled, lesser the gap between O_2 and O_1 better is the check on history.

2. **Maturation :** It concerns to the changes occurring within subjects or test units themselves with the passage of time. These changes are not due to the effect of the treatment at all. For instance, a subject may get bored, tired, uninterested, knowledgeable, etc. Maturation is more vulnerable when the study continues for a long time, such as tracking and market studies span over months. Maturation effect can also happen in cases other than persons. For example, malls may also change in respect of decoration, prices, counters etc. Possibility of maturation can be minimized by conducting interviews at the convenience of the respondents and completing the studies in short periods.
3. **Testing Effects :** The effects which are caused due to taking a measure on the dependent variable before and after the application of the treatment on the test units are called testing effects. These are further classified into two types of effects, (*i*) main testing effect (MT), (*ii*) interactive testing effect (IT).

   The effect that occurs when a prior observation (O_1) affects a latter observation (O_2) is known as *main testing effect.*

   An effect in which a prior measurement (O_1) has an influence on the independent variable and hence affecting the test unit response is called *interactive testing* effect.
4. **Instrumentation (I) :** Any changes made in the calibration of measuring instrument during interviews cause threats to internal validity.
5. **Selection Bias (SB) :** The differential selection of subjects to experimental and control groups is a major threat to the internal validity. Selection bias is almost eliminated if the subjects are assigned to control and experimental groups randomly or matching the members of both the groups on key factors.
6. **Statistical Regression (SR) :** This refers to the threat where the measurements of the dependent variable have a tendency that the extreme scores regress towards mean scores. To elucidate further, if we select 25% workers (w_1) of a factory which have minimum output (scores) and 25% workers (w_2) with maximum output (scores) and then they are exposed to certain treatment. It is observed that the scores of w_1 tend to increase and that of w_2 tend to decline towards the average output (scores). Such a tendency is termed as *statistical regression* and is inversely related to the validity of the test.
7. **Experimental Mortality :** This term does not refer to only death of the experimental unit(s) but also pertains to the changes in composition of the study group(s) during experimentation. Such changes often occur due to death of subjects or some subjects refuse to continue in the experiment. This alters the distribution of the subjects and one cannot ensure that the units lost would have responded to the treatments in the same manner as the remaining ones. Suppose

various compensation schemes have been tried on workers and some workers withdraw from the test group as they do not like the changes in their compensation. So the comparison of the test group with the control group would be distorted. As a remedy, random assignment of group may reduce the treat to internal validity to a great extent.

8. **Imitation of Treatment:** In many studies, the independent variable entails varied information as treatment levels that is passed on selectively to the subjects. In case, the subjects under various information levels communicate with each other, then the differences in responses under various treatment levels get compromised. To overcome this problem, the researcher should not allow the subjects to meet and discuss with one another about the topics under study.
9. **Resentful Demoralization :** If the subjects come to know that the treatment level assigned to them are inferior in terms of benefits, goods or services, they may feel demoralized and hence show their resentment. They are very likely to perform very low. This will create larger difference than the real one between desirable and undesirable treatment levels. Confidentiality of treatment levels be maintained to reduce this type of threat.

External Validity

External validity is concerned with the generalization of research findings to and across the population from which we select the subjects or settings. In other words, external validity means to ensure whether the cause and effect relationship established in the experiment can be generalized to other similar population beyond the subjects involved in the experiment. In applying the results of an experiment to population in general, there are many threats to external validity. Some of the important ones are enucleated below:

1. **Interaction of testing and treatment (X) :** It refers to sensitizing the subjects to a topic via a pretest as it may focus attention on the topic. So this may very likely either enhance the effectiveness of *X* or reduce the effectivity of *X*. Hence, pretesting be done on the subjects of the population other than the selected subjects.
2. **Interaction of selection and *X*:** The process by which the test subjects are selected for an experiment may not be a representative of the population to which the researcher wishes to generalize the research findings. For instance, the opinion of a buyer about a product in the mall cannot be generalized to the public.
3. **Reactive factors:**
   (*i*) If the subjects know, that they are being observed, they will act and respond differently than those who are not being observed. So, the results cannot be generalized.
   (*ii*) There are situations in which the experimental settings are such that they may have biasing effect. For example, a group of workers receiving incentive pay are kept away from the control group to avoid any likely menace. The new environment will create a strong reactive condition and the results cannot be generalized.

External validity can be secured by selecting the subjects from a population to which the research findings are to be generalized and also controlling reactive factors as far as possible.

Conclusion Validity

It refers to the threats to draw valid inferences that can be made from random error and adopting inadequate statistical procedures. Well known threats for conclusion validity are as follows:

1. **Low statistical power :** If the power of a test is low, then a research will very likely fail to reject a false null hypothesis. This may happen due to inadequate sample size, non-control of nuisance variables or due to use of an inappropriate test.
2. **Violation of assumptions :** All tests are based on certain assumptions. If such assumptions are violated, then there is every likelihood that incorrect inferences shall be drawn.
3. **Reliability of measures :** If the reliability of measure on dependent variable is low, it results into increase of error variance, a false null hypothesis will not be rejected. In this way one would be drawing wrong conclusion.
4. **Random irrelevancies :** If the conditions, in which the treatment levels are administered, change during experimentation, then error variance may inflate. This may result into non-rejection of false null hypothesis. This is obviously a threat to conclusion validity.
5. **Respondents random heterogeneity :** Idiosyncratic variation of the respondents may inflate the error variance which may lead to acceptance of a false null hypothesis. So idiosyncrasy is a threat to conclusion validity.

Above mentioned threats to conclusion validity can be minimized by strictly observing the rules and requirements of a good design.

CLASSIFICATION OF EXPERIMENTAL DESIGNS

Experimental designs may be divided into classes according to their settings namely, (*i*) Pre-experimental designs, (*ii*) True experimental designs and (*iii*) Quasi-experimental designs.

Pre-experimental Designs

These designs do not employ randomization in assigning the experimental units to treatment or condition. So, they are weak in their measurement power, i.e., the chances of threats to internal validity are more. Three types of experiments fall in this category as discussed here.

On shot case study : In this design a single group of subjects is exposed to a treatment or condition X and at some prefixed time, measurements in respect of dependent variable are taken on the subjects of the study group. Diagramatically,

Treatment	**Measurement**
X	O

In such an experiment, there is no control on extraneous factors and thereby there is a great threat to internal validity. An example of this type of study is, telephonic interviews conducted with a fixed number of television (TV) viewers about a TV programme held previous night with regard to seeing a commercial about a product's qualities. This experiment will only reveal how much people remember about the product's quality after seeing the advertisement. It fails to disclose what was the status of viewers' knowledge about the product prior to experimentation.

One-group pre-test—post-test design : This design has already been discussed under the heading history while explaining threats to internal validity. So it will be redundant to repeat.

Static group design : This is a two nonrandomized equal group design in which one group is a controlled group and other is experimental group (EG). The experimental group is exposed to an intervention (treatment) having no random assignment. Measurements on both the groups are taken at the same time only after exposure of the treatment to the experimental group. It can be represented by a simple diagram as follows:

Groups	Treatment	Measurement
CG	–	O_1
EG	*X*	O_2

Estimated treatment effect would be $(O_2 - O_1)$. This difference may be as a result of two factors namely, (i) selection differences as the respondents in groups are not selected randomly, (ii) due to treatment effect. Further, there is no evidence which affirms that the groups are equivalent due to absence of pretest. For example, two groups of television viewers are selected on the basis of convenience, in which one group is taken as experimental group and other is not. Now, the attitude of both the groups towards the product is measured separately. This post-test difference $(O_2 - O_1)$ is not devoid of flaws. Hence, the reliability of this design is in jeopardy.

True Experimental Designs

True experimental designs differ from pre-experimental designs mainly in respect of randomization and also have better control over extraneous factors. In true experimental designs, test units are assigned randomly to experimental groups and treatments are allotted to experimental groups randomly. These experiments ensure greater internal and external validity. Also statistical tests for testing the significance of the difference can be applied. Now we shall discuss three true designs which are usually exploited for market and social research.

Pre-test–post-test control group design: This design involves two groups and two measurements of dependent variable in both the groups. In this design, firstly the test units are assigned randomly to the experimental and control group and a pre-treatment measure of the dependent variable is taken on both the groups. Now only the experimental group is exposed to treatment. Again post-test measurements for the same dependent variable are taken on both the groups. Diagramatically this can be depicted as below.

Group	Symbol of randomization	Pre-measurement	Treatment	Post-measurement
CG	R	O_1	–	O_2
EG	R	O_3	X	O_4

Treatment effect = $(O_4 - O_3) - (O_2 - O_1)$ This design controls almost all nuisances except that of interactive testing effect. Largely it maintains high level internal and external validity. The example given with static group design can be moulded for this design.

Post-test only control group design: This design differs from the preceding design only in one sense that the pretest measurements in both the groups are omitted. Following the same symbols as in the preceding design, it can be represented as:

$$\begin{array}{ccc} R & - & O_1 \\ R & X & O_2 \end{array}$$

Treatment effect = $O_2 - O_1$

This design is simpler than the previous one and controls threats to internal validity like history, maturation, selection and statistical regression. This is also devoid of interactive testing effect as only post-measurements are taken. Problem of mortality in two groups remains there.

Solomon four group design : This design overcomes the limitations of the last two designs. Besides controlling various extraneous variable effects, Solomon design also controls interactive testing effect. But due to complexity, practical constraints like heavy cost and greater time requirement, etc. This design is practically not viable. Hence, the details of this design are omitted.

STATISTICAL DESIGNS

In the category of true experimental designs, there are a large number of statistical designs that allow the control of extraneous variables to a great extent. All these designs are randomized designs and have their origin in field experiments especially meant for agricultural research. But soon their utility was realised in chemical, industrial, medical, sociological researches, etc. They are largely used because of their merits. Some common advantages are:

1. The effects of more than one treatment or condition can be estimated and compared from one experiment.
2. Interaction effects can also be measured and tested.
3. Many extraneous factors (variables) can be statistically controlled.
4. The designs are generally economical and convenient.
5. Each design has a fixed analysis procedure and hence the chances of researcher's bias are negligible.
6. Threats to internal and external validity are very less as compared to other types of experiments.

REQUIREMENTS FOR A GOOD EXPERIMENTAL DESIGN

A design is considered good if it meets certain conditions. A design should have no researcher's bias and statistical tests must be applicable while analyzing the data. This requirement is met by randomly assigning the experimental units to treatments or vice versa. Secondly the error variance should be as small as possible. This is maintained by replicating the treatments. Thirdly, all extraneous factors be controlled in so far as possible. This control is incorporated through local control. So, the three requirements, randomization, replication and local control are discussed here adequately. As a matter of fact all the three approaches serve for controlling the nuisance variables. These approaches appear under one head, *experimental control*. Some authors call them as the *basic principles of experimental designs.*

Besides the above, there is another approach known as *statistical control.* In this approach observations on an auxiliary (concomitant) variable are taken side by side of the dependent variable. The variability in dependent variable is controlled by regression method which is referred to as *analysis of covariance.*

Randomization

The process in which each and every experimental unit has the same chance of being allocated to treatments is known as *randomization*. This is best performed with the help of random number tables. Randomization eliminates researcher's bias. In this way, a researcher will have no choice to assign a treatment which he wants to prove better, to a better responding unit and others to inferior units. Further randomization makes sure that no treatment will continually be favored or handicapped by extraneous source(s) of variation which are out of control of the experimenter.

From experiments, valid statistical inferences are based on the assumption that errors are independently and normally distributed. Randomization ensures the validity of this assumption.

Replication

Repetition of each treatment on several experimental units is called *replication*. In spite of randomization, a treatment may be favoured by some unit and handicapped by other unit. So, replications neutralize the advantage and thus the response tends towards real value. It provides an estimate of experimental error variance which is the basic requirement to test the significance of the treatment differences and finding the estimate of the standard error of mean, i.e., $s_e/\sqrt{r}$ where s_e^2 is the mean square error variance and r-the number of replication of the treatment.

Number of replications depend upon various factors like heterogeneity among experimental units, precision required, experimental materials available, nature of the experiment etc. The details are omitted. As a general norm, the number of replications be such that it provides at least 12 degrees of freedom (d. f.) for error variance. More the error d.f., better it is.

Nota Bene

Repeated measurements on an experimental unit receiving a treatment are not replications.

Local Control

It is a technique of controlling a known extraneous variable. In field experiments, we know that adjacent plots are more alike in respect of fertility as compared to those which lie apart. In human population, persons with almost same income will have similar attitudes and opinions, cows of the same breed will lactate almost equally. So the patch of land with same fertility, persons with same income or cows of same breed are kept in one block. Such a phenomenon is known as *blocking* and *balancing*. A complete block has as many experimental units or plots as the number of treatments. Blocking is a device of local control.

The purpose of local control is to make the design more efficient, i.e., it makes the test of significance more sensitive and powerful. Local control results into reduction of error variance. Local control can be accomplished in many ways other than blocking, depending on the type of variability present in the experimental units.

ANALYSIS OF VARIANCE (ANOVA)

Purpose of analysis of variance and ANOVA table have been given in Chapter 11. This would have developed some insight about ANOVA. Here some additional points are delineated.

ANOVA is used in the situations where we want to test simultaneously the equality of more than two population means e.g., through ANOVA, one may compare the average yield of several varieties of seed of a crop, gasoline average mileage of five brands of cars of same HP, testing the efficacy of four drugs which are prescribed for the patients of the same disease, etc.

Analysis of variance cannot be used in all situations and for all types of variables. It is based on certain assumptions and if the data of an experiment do not fulfil these assumptions, the validity of the tests and thereby of the results is always in jeopardy. The assumptions underlying the application of ANOVA are:

1. The observations follow normal distribution.
2. Experimental units are assigned to treatments randomly and vice-versa.
3. Appropriate statistical model is adopted for the experimental design.
4. All the components involved in the model are additive and independent.
5. Experimental errors are independently and identically distributed normally with mean 0 and variance σ_e^2.
6. The tests involved in ANOVA are quite robust. So one should ensure that the experimental data meet the requirements.

STATISTICAL MODEL

It is a linear relationship of an observation with the overall mean, treatment effects, manipulating factors (blocking) and residual effect (error), i.e.,

Observation = Overall mean + Treatment effects + Residual ...(12.1)

Overall mean is estimated by grand mean (GM). If we denote the observation by y, treatment effect by TE, fitted value by FV, treatment mean by TM, residual by RE, then by (12.1), Observed value = Overall mean + Treatment effect + Residual

Fitted value = Overall mean + Treatment effect

Observed value = Fitted value + Residual

or Residual = Observed value – Fitted value

Also, Treatment effect = Treatment mean – Grand mean

Symbolically,

$$TE = TM - GM \quad ...(12.2)$$

$$FV = GM + TE = GM + (TM - GM) = TM \quad ...(12.3)$$

$$y = FV + RE$$

or

$$RE = y - FV = y - TM \quad ...(12.4)$$

Model (12.1)

$$y = GM + (TM - GM) + (y - TM)$$

or

$$y - GM = (TM - GM) + (y - TM) \quad ...(12.5)$$

Equation (12.5) suggests that ANOVA can be carried by taking the deviations of observed values from grand mean and same results would be obtained.

It is trivial to prove that the relation (12.5) not only holds for observed values but is also true for sum of squares of these deviations, i.e.,

$$\Sigma (y - GM)^2 = \Sigma (TM - GM)^2 + \Sigma (y - TM)^2 \quad ...(12.6)$$

This is known as the *method* of *sweeping*. But with the popularization of electronic calculators and computers, short-cut methods have lost their identity. So any short-cut method will be out of context in this chapter. Methods of analysis of variance based on the respective models will be explicated alongwith the respective designs in the sequel.

WHAT NEXT AFTER ANOVA?

In ANOVA an experimenter tests the null hypothesis of equality of k treatment mean effects i.e., H_0: $\mu_1 = \mu_2 = \text{----} = \mu_k$ against H_1: at least two of them are not equal i.e.,

$\mu_i \neq \mu_m$ for some $i \neq m$; $i, m = 1, 2, \text{----}, k$.

The test employed for testing H_0 is F-test. If calculated F is non-significant, then it is inferred that all treatments are equally effective and no further test is required. But if calculated F for treatment is significant, then H_0 is rejected. This signifies that all the treatment mean effects are not equal. Some of them may be equally effective and some will not. So there is a need to perform a test for testing the significance of all pairs of treatment means. But ANOVA fails to provide any such test. Many times a researcher also carries out test for individual contrasts (comparisons) which were planned prior to data collection. An introduction to contrasts is as follows:

CONTRASTS

A contrast is a linear combination of treatments such that the sum of the coefficients of treatments is zero. For example, the contrasts 'Z' for three treatments T_1, T_2 and T_3 can be of the form,

$$Z_1 = T_1 - 2T_2 + T_3$$
$$Z_2 = T_1 - T_3$$

For four treatments; T_1, T_2, T_3 and T_4 the contrast can be of the form,

$$Z_3 = -3T_1 - T_2 + T_3 + 3T_4$$
$$Z_4 = T_1 - T_2 - T_3 + T_4$$
$$Z_5 = -T_1 + 3T_2 - 3T_3 + T_4$$

In general, for k treatments, each having the same number of replications r, the linear combination,

$$Z_c = l_1T_1 + l_2T_2 + \ldots, + l_kT_k$$

will be a contrast, if the sum of coefficients

$l_1, l_2, \ldots\ldots, l_k$ is zero, i.e., $\sum_i l_i = 0$

Two contrasts are said to be orthogonal if the sum of the products of the corresponding coefficients, involving the same set of treatments, is zero. It is trifling to verify that contrasts z_1 and z_2 are orthogonal. Also contrasts z_3, z_4 and z_5 are orthogonal among themselves.

Sum of square due to a contrast Z_c among k treatments where each treatment is replicated r times is, $Z_c^2 / r\sum_i l_i^2$. Each contrast has 1 d.f.

Estimated standard error of a contrast Z_c is,

$$\text{S.E. } (Z_c) = \frac{s_e}{\sqrt{r}}\sqrt{l_1^2 + l_2^2 + \ldots.. + l_k^2} \quad \ldots(12.7)$$

where s_e^2 is the mean sum of square for error. If the *ith* treatment has r_i replications for $i = 1, 2, ..., k$, then a linear combination of k treatment total,

$$Z_u = l_{u_1} T_1 + l_{u_2} T_2 + ... + l_{u_k} T_k$$

is said to be contrast if,

$$r_1 l_{u_1} + r_2 l_{u_2} + ... + r_k l_{u_k} = 0$$

i.e. $\sum_i r_i l_{u_i} = 0$

Sum of square due to the contrast Z_u is,

$$Z_u^2 / \sum_i r_i l_{u_i}^2 \qquad ...(12.8)$$

Estimate of the standard error Z_u is,

$$= s_e \sqrt{\frac{l_{u_1}^2}{r_1} + \frac{l_{u_2}^2}{r_2} + ... + \frac{l_{u_k}^2}{r_k}} \qquad ...(12.9)$$

Any other contrast among the same treatment total,

$$Z'_u = l'_{u_1} T_1 + l'_{u_2} T_2 + ... + l'_{u_k} T_k$$

is orthogonal to Z_u iff,

$$r_1 l_{u_1} l'_{u_1} + r_2 l_{u_2} l'_{u_2} + ... + r_k l_{u_k} l'_{u_k} = 0$$

MULTIPLE COMPARISON TESTS

To test the significance of all pairs of treatment means or a contrast, a large number of tests are available in the literature. But only two most popular tests are discussed here.

Least Significant Difference Test (lsd. Test)

R.A. Fisher propounded a multiple comparison procedure in 1935 for testing the significance of pairwise treatment means at preselected level of significance α.

$$lsd = \text{SE(d)} \times t_{v;\alpha} \qquad ...(12.10)$$

where, n – total no. of observations

$t_{v;\alpha}$ – tabulated value of t for two-tailed test at α level of significance and v, error d.f.

$$\text{SE(d)} = \sqrt{\frac{2s_e^2}{r}} \qquad ...(12.11)$$

s_e^2 – error mean sum of square

r – No. of replications for each treatment. If treatment T_i is replicated r_i times, $i = 1, 2, ..., k$.

Then,

$$\text{SE(d)} = \sqrt{s_e^2\left(\frac{1}{r_i} + \frac{1}{r_j}\right)} \quad \text{for } i \neq j \qquad ...(12.12)$$

If the difference between a pair of means is larger than or equal to lsd, then it is significant, otherwise not. But later it was proved that if the number of treatments is more than three, then the chance of type I error is greater than α and this error increases briskly as k increases. To overcome this deficiency, alternative procedures were evolved by a number of statisticians. Only one procedure is given here as this can be applied in general.

DUNN'S MULTIPLE COMPARISON TEST

Dunn developed a procedure for testing the significance of pairwise treatment contrast or any other contrast among treatment means using student t-statistic and sampling distribution. The test statistic under Dunn's procedure is denoted by tD, which is obtained by the formula,

$$tD = \frac{l_1\overline{T}_1 + l_2\overline{T}_2 + ... + l_k\overline{T}_k}{\sqrt{s_e^2\left(\frac{l_1^2}{r_1} + \frac{l_2^2}{r_2} + ... + \frac{l_k^2}{r_k}\right)}} \qquad ...(12.13)$$

where,

$\Sigma r_i l_i = 0$, T_i has r_i replications,

$\overline{T}_i$ is the *ith* treatment mean for $i = 1, 2, ..., k$.

For pairwise contrast where each treatment is replicated r times, the statistic reduces to,

$$tD = \frac{l_1\overline{T}_i + l_2\overline{T}_j}{\sqrt{\frac{2s_e^2}{r}}} \qquad ...(12.14)$$

For $i \neq j$ and $l_1 + l_2 = 0$

A two sided null hypothesis is rejected if the absolute value of tD i.e., $|tD|$ is greater than or equal to the critical value of $tD_{\alpha/2}$, C, ν, where α is the preselected level of significance, C is the total number of contrasts to be tested and ν is the error d.f. Critical values of tD tabulated by O.J. Dunn can be obtained from a modern book on experimental designs or can be seen in the journal of American Statistical Association, 1961, vol. 56, pp. 52 – 64. This test is more powerful than Fisher's **lsd** procedure and is also better than many other tests as far as the power of the test is concerned. Some people call it *Bonferroni procedure* as it is based on Bonferroni's inequality.

BASIC EXPERIMENTAL DESIGNS

Experimental design is a vast subject and hundreds of experimental designs have been constructed. No design is perfect in itself. One design may be very suitable for some problem under investigation and may not be appropriate for the other. For this reason, the quest for new designs never ends. But keeping in view the requirement of the courses for which this book is written, only three basic designs namely, Completely randomized design (CRD), Randomized block design (RBD) and Latin square design (LSD) are elucidated. Lastly an introduction to factorial experiments is given:

Completely Randomized Design

This design is frequently used when all the experimental units are homogeneous. It means, the experimenter knows that the units have no inherent variability which could influence the treatment effect. In such a case, CRD is the most suitable design.

Suppose in a CRD there are k treatments and ith treatment has r_i replications. Total number of experimental units is n i.e., $\Sigma_i r_i = n$ for $i = 1, 2, ..., k$. There is no restriction on the number of replications of the treatments. No. of replications depend upon the availability of material and experimental units. Treatments are allocated to experimental units randomly or vice-versa. It is a non-restrictional design in the sense that there is no blocking. Also any treatment can be replicated any number of times. The observations on the experimental units are taken as soon as the required period after application of treatment is over. In field experiments yield is recorded when crop is ripe, in drug experiments observations are taken on patients when the course of the drug is over, to see the impact of different types of packings, the sale at selected stores is recorded at the end of prefixed time period, etc. We shall confine our discussion to one observation per unit.

Linear statistical model as given in (12.1) for CRD in notational form is,

$$y_{ij} = \mu + \tau_i + \varepsilon_{ij} \qquad ...(12.15)$$

for $i = 1, 2, ..., k$ and $j = 1, 2, ..., r_i$

where, y_{ij} measurement on jth unit receiving the treatment i.

μ – true mean effect

τ_i ~ true effect of treatment i

ε_{ij} – true effect of the jth unit subjected to ith treatment.

Customarily it is assumed that μ is a constant and errors Σ_{ij} are identically and independently distributed $N(0, \sigma_\varepsilon^2)$. y_{ij} are also independent and identically normally distributed. If the researcher's interest lies in the treatments that are present in the experiment, then $\Sigma\ \tau_i = 0$. Model (12.15) is known as *fixed effect model* or Model-I. If the researcher considers the treatments as a sample from a population of treatments, then τ_i are $N(0, \sigma_\tau^2)$. In this case, model (12.15) is known as *random effect model* or Model-II. Choice of Model-I and Model-II depends on the nature of treatments.

Table 12.1: Data table

Treatments	1	2	----	*i*	----	*k*	*Overall*
	y_{11}	y_{21}	----	y_{i1}	----	y_{k1}	
	y_{12}	y_{22}	----	y_{i2}	----	y_{k2}	
	⋮	⋮		⋮		⋮	
	y_{1r_1}	y_{2r_2}	----	y_{ir_i}	----	y_{kr_k}	
Calculation							
Treat. Total	y_1	$y_{2.}$	----	$y_{i.}$	----	$y_{k.}$	$y_{..} = G$
No. of reps.	r_1	r_2	----	r_i	----	r_k	$\Sigma_i r_i = n$
Treat. mean	$\bar{y}_1$	$\bar{y}_2$	----	$\bar{y}_i$	----	$\bar{y}_k$	$\bar{y} = y_{..}/n$

under Model-I,

$$H_0 : \tau_1 = \tau_2 = ... = \tau_k = 0$$

$$\text{vs. } H_1 : \tau_i \neq \tau_m \text{ for some } i \neq m \text{. where } i, m = 1, 2, ..., k$$

under Model-II,

$$H_0 : \sigma_\tau^2 = 0 \text{ vs. } H_1 : \sigma_\tau^2 \neq 0$$

Correction factor, $\text{C.F.} = \dfrac{G^2}{n}$

$$\text{Total S.S.} = \sum_i \sum_i y_{ij}^2 - \frac{G^2}{n} = SSY$$

$$\text{Treat. S.S.} = \frac{1}{r_i} \sum_i y_i^2 - \frac{G^2}{n} = SST$$

$$\text{Error S.S.} = SSY - SST = SSE$$

Table 12.2: ANOVA for CRD

Source of variation	*d.f.*	*S.S.*	*M.S.*	*F-value*
Treats	$k - 1$	SST	$SST/(k-1) = MST$	$\dfrac{MST}{MSE} = F$
Error	$n - k$	SSE	$SSE/(n-k) = MSE$	
Total	$n - 1$	SSY		

F is distributed with $[(k-1), (n-k)]$ d.f. If the calculated value of F is greater than or equal to the tabulated value of F for predecided level of significance α and $[(k-1), (n-k)]$ d.f., then reject H_0, otherwise accept H_0. F-value can be obtained from table VII given in the appendix.

Merits of CRD

1. It is a non-restrictional design and hence total material can be used.
2. Layout is very simple.
3. Maximum error d.f. are available in this design as compared to any other design.
4. Analysis of data is easy and interpretation of results is straight forward.
5. If there is any missing value, it is left as if it was not there. The analysis of data is carried from the remaining values. So missing value in this design causes no problem.

Demerits

1. Usually experimental units are not as homogeneous as they are taken to be.
2. As the number of replications differ from one treatment to the other, the treatments, having larger number of replications, will be estimated and tested more precisely than those who are repeated only a few times.

***Example* 12.1.** In a factory producing edible oil and marketing its product in 15 kg tins, uses five filling machines. Random samples of the packed tins were taken for each machine and weighed the quantity of oil in each tin. The weights found in each tin under five machines A, B, C, D and E were presented as below:

Machines				
A	*B*	*C*	*D*	*E*
14.85	14.28	14.16	15.25	14.60
15.00	14.42	14.15	15.30	14.84
15.25		14.19	15.10	14.82
15.10		14.50	15.35	14.74
14.80			15.00	

Analysis of data to test the equality of efficiency of machines is as follows:

In this problem we consider fixed effect model and test,

$$H_0 : W_1 = W_2 = W_3 = W_4 = W_5$$

vs. $$H_1 : W_i \neq W_j \text{ for } i \neq j = 1, 2, 3, 4, 5.$$

where W_i is the mean weight of tins for the machine i.

Treat totals,

$$A = 75.00,\ B = 28.70,\ C = 57.00,\ D = 76.00,\ E = 59.00$$

$$\overline{A} = 15.00,\ \overline{B} = 14.35,\ \overline{C} = 14.25,\ \overline{D} = 15.20,\ \overline{E} = 14.75$$

$$r_1 = 5,\ r_2 = 2,\ r_3 = 4,\ r_4 = 5,\ r_5 = 4,\ n = 20.$$

$$G = 295.70,\ \text{C.F.} = \frac{(295.70)^2}{20} = 4371.92$$

$$\text{Total S.S.} = (14.85^2 + 15.00^2 + ... + 14.82^2 + 14.74^2) - \text{C.F.}$$
$$= 4374.89 - 4371.92 = 2.97$$

$$\text{Treat. S.S.} = \frac{75.00^2}{5} + \frac{28.70^2}{2} + \frac{57.00^2}{4} + \frac{76.00^2}{5} + \frac{59.00^2}{4} - \text{C.F.}$$
$$= 4374.54 - 4371.92 = 2.62$$

$$\text{Error S.S.} = 2.97 - 2.62 = 0.35$$

ANOVA

Source of variation	*d.f.*	*S.S.*	*M.S.*	*F–value*
Machines	4	2.62	0.655	$\frac{.655}{.023} = 28.48$
Error	15	0.35	0.023	
Total	19	2.97		

Tabulated value of F from table VII$_{ii}$ for $\alpha = 0.05$ and (4, 15) d.f. = 3.06.

Calculated value of F is greater than the tabulated F-value. Hence, we reject the null hypothesis concluding that all the machines are not equally efficient. Now it remains still to find out which machines are equivalent and which differ significantly. There are 10 paired comparisons. Since number of pairs is large, we will prefer to use Dunn's test and calculate 10 values of $|tD|$ by the formulae (12.13) and (12.14).

Differences between paired means, no. of respective replications and calculated values of tD are tabulated below.

$$\overline{A}-\overline{B} = 15.00 - 14.35 = 0.65,\ r_1 = 5,\ r_2 = 2,\ tD_1 = \frac{0.65}{\sqrt{0.023\left(\frac{1}{5}+\frac{1}{2}\right)}} = 5.12$$

$$\overline{A}-\overline{C} = 15.00 - 14.25 = 0.75,\ r_1 = 5,\ r_3 = 4,\ tD_2 = \frac{0.75}{\sqrt{0.023\left(\frac{1}{5}+\frac{1}{4}\right)}} = 7.35$$

$$\overline{A}-\overline{D} = 15.00 - 15.20 = -0.20,\ r_1 = 5,\ r_4 = 5,\ tD_3 = \frac{-0.20}{\sqrt{0.023\left(\frac{1}{5}+\frac{1}{5}\right)}} = -2.08$$

$$\overline{A}-\overline{E} = 15.00 - 14.75 = 0.25,\ r_1 = 5,\ r_5 = 4,\ tD_4 = \frac{0.25}{\sqrt{0.023\left(\frac{1}{5}+\frac{1}{4}\right)}} = 2.45$$

$$\overline{B}-\overline{C} = 14.35 - 14.25 = 0.10,\ r_2 = 2,\ r_3 = 4,\ tD_5 = \frac{0.10}{\sqrt{0.023\left(\frac{1}{2}+\frac{1}{4}\right)}} = 0.76$$

Similarly,

For $\overline{B}-\overline{D},\ tD_6 = -6.69$; $\overline{B}-\overline{E},\ tD_7 = -3.05$;

$\overline{C}-\overline{D},\ tD_8 = -9.31$; $\overline{C}-\overline{E},\ tD_9 = -4.67$; $\overline{D}-\overline{E},\ tD_{10} = 4.41$

Critical value of Dunn's statistic from the table for $\alpha = 0.05$, No. of pairs = 10 and $v = 15$ is 3.29. Now on comparing the calculated values of $|tD|$ with 3.29, we infer that machine A differs significantly from B and C, machine B is significantly inferior than D, machine C differs from D and E significantly. Also there is a significant difference between the machines D and E.

Note: For analysing data of CRD with the help of SPSS software, see Appendix.

Randomized Block Design (RBD)

Completely randomized design is suitable only when all experimental units are homogeneous. But such an ideal condition rarely exists. If there is only one nuisance variable which is likely to influence the treatment effect, then similar units or subjects are grouped together which are known as *blocks*. Each block is homogeneous itself and has as many experimental units as the number of treatments. So the blocks are said to be complete blocks. Each and every treatment occurs once in a block and the design is known as *randomized complete block design* (RCBD). But in common parlance it is called RBD. For instance, to see the impact of different levels of pricing, blocks of subjects are formed on the basis of high, medium and low income; in feeding experiments on cows, blocks are formed by keeping the cows of same breed in a block, in field experiments block are constituted on the basis of fertility gradient, etc. In this way there is intrablock homogeneity and interblock heterogeneity due to blocking factor.

Once the blocks are formed, the treatments are assigned randomly to experimental units in each block independently. The layout of a RBD with 6 treatments and 4 blocks is of the type as shown below.

Block 1	*Block 2*	*Block 3*	*Block 4*
T_3	T_3	T_4	T_3
T_2	T_6	T_2	T_5
T_1	T_1	T_3	T_1
T_5	T_2	T_6	T_2
T_6	T_5	T_5	T_4
T_4	T_4	T_1	T_6

STATISTICAL MODEL FOR RBD

Linear model with one observation per unit can be presented as

$$y_{ij} = \mu + \tau_i + \beta_j + \varepsilon_{ij} \qquad ...(12.16)$$

for $i = 1, 2, ..., k$ and $j = 1, 2, ..., b$

In this design there are two independent variables namely, treatments and blocks.

There is one blocking factor. Hence, it is known as *one restrictional design* or *two way classification*.

In the above model,

y_{ij} – observation for the ith treatment in jth block.

β_j – jth block effect

μ, τ_i and ε_{ij} represent the same factors as in model (12.15)

In addition, $\Sigma_j \beta_j = 0$ and $\varepsilon_{ij} \sim NID(0, \sigma_e^2)$. Hypothesis for treatment remain the same as in case of CRD depending on whether we choose Model-I or Model-II. For blocks, $H_0: \beta_1 = \beta_2 = ... = \beta_b$ *vs.* $H_1 : \beta_j \neq \beta'_j$ for $j \neq j'$. Data of a RBD can be tabulated as depicted in table (12.3).

Table 12.3: Data of a RBD

Treatments	Blocks 1	2	---	j	---	b	*Total*
1	y_{11}	y_{12}	---	y_{1j}	---	y_{1b}	$y_{1.}$
2	y_{21}	y_{22}	---	y_{2j}	---	y_{2b}	$y_{2.}$
.	.	.		.			.
.	.	.		.			.
i	y_{i1}	y_{i2}		y_{ij}	---	y_{ib}	$y_{i.}$
.	.	.		.			.
.	.	.		.			.
.	.	.		.			.
k	y_{k1}	y_{k2}	---	y_{kj}	---	y_{kb}	$y_{k.}$
Total	$y_{\cdot 1}$	$y_{\cdot 2}$	---	$y_{\cdot j}$	---	$y_{\cdot b}$	$y_{..} = G$

Calculations:

$$i\text{th treatment mean} = \frac{y_{i.}}{b} = \bar{y}_i$$

$$j\text{th block mean} = \frac{y_{.j}}{k} = \bar{y}_j$$

$$\text{C.F.} = \frac{G^2}{bk}$$

$$\text{Total S.S.} = y_{11}^2 + y_{12}^2 + \ldots + y_{kb}^2 - \text{C.F.} = SSY$$

$$\text{Treatment S.S.} = \frac{1}{b}(y_{1.}^2 + y_{2.}^2 + \ldots + y_{k.}^2) - \text{C.F.} = SST$$

$$\text{Block S.S.} = \frac{1}{k}(y_{.1}^2 + y_{.2}^2 + \ldots + y_{.b}^2) - \text{C.F.} = SSB$$

$$\text{Error S.S.} = SSY - SST - SSB = SSE$$

Table 12.4: ANOVA for RBD

Source of variation	*d.f.*	*S.S.*	*M.S.*	*F-value*
Blocks	$b-1$	SSB	$SSB/(b-1) = MSB$	$\frac{MSB}{MSE} = F_B$
Treatments	$k-1$	SST	$SST/(k-1) = MST$	$\frac{MST}{MSE} = F_T$
Error	$(b-1)(k-1)$	SSE	$\frac{SSE}{(b-1)(k-1)} = MSE$	
Total	$bk-1$	SSY		

F for blocks has d.f. $[(b-1), (b-1)(k-1)]$ and F for treatments has d.f. $[(k-1, (b-1)(k-1)]$. If calculated value of F for treatment is greater than or equal to the tabulated value for α level of significant and ν d.f., then reject H_0, otherwise accept it. Similarly if $F_B \geq F_{(b-1),\nu;\alpha}$, reject H_0 for blocks, otherwise accept it. Similarly if H_0 is rejected for treatments, the researcher has to perform the test for pairwise treatment comparisons by a suitable procedure.

Merits of RBD

1. One nuisance variable is isolated in this design. This reduces the experimental error and thereby power of the test is increased.
2. Any number of blocks and treatments can be used.
3. Number of replications per treatment is same as the number of blocks.
4. Analysis of data is straight forward.
5. RBD is most used design in various areas of research.

Demerits

1. If the number of treatments is large enough, then it becomes difficult to maintain the homogeneity of blocks.
2. If there is a missing value, it cannot be ignored. It has to be estimated and analysis should be carried out using the estimated value. Certain adjustments are to be made in the analysis procedure. This make the analysis somewhat complex.

***Example* 12.2.** A factory manager wanted to compare the efficiency of four factory workers with respect to cotton spinning. He had four machines. Four workers A, B, C and D were allotted a machine randomly on each day for 6 days. Hereafter we consider days as blocks and machines as experimental units. Cotton thread yield (in kg) for each worker was recorded as shown in the layout displayed below. All machines were of the same make.

Blocks	*Machines*				*Block Totals*
	1	2	3	4	
I	C 22	A 14	B 12	D 23	71
II	A 16	B 18	C 20	D 25	79
III	A 15	C 23	D 28	B 14	80
IV	A 17	D 21	C 19	B 11	68
V	B 18	C 20	A 13	D 24	75
VI	D 18	C 21	A 10	B 17	66

Analysis of data to test whether there is any significant difference in the efficiency of workers is as follows:

Here we test,

H_0 : All workers are equally efficient

vs. H_1 : At least two of them differ significantly.

Calculation:

$$G = 439,\ \text{C. F.} = \frac{(439)^2}{24} = 8030.04$$

$$\begin{aligned}\text{Total S.S.} &= 22^2 + 14^2 + \dots + 10^2 + 17^2 - \text{C.F.}\\ &= 8527.00 - 8030.04\\ &= 496.96\end{aligned}$$

$$\begin{aligned}\text{Block S.S.} &= \frac{1}{4}(71^2 + 79^2 + 80^2 + 68^2 + 75^2 + 66^2) - \text{C.F.}\\ &= 8041.75 - 8030.04\\ &= 41.71\end{aligned}$$

Treatment totals : $A = 85$, $B = 90$, $C = 125$, $D = 139$

Treatment means : $\overline{A}$ – 14.17, $\overline{B} = 15.00$, $\overline{C} = 20.83$, $\overline{D} = 23.17$

$$\text{Treatment S.S.} = \frac{1}{6}(85^2 + 90^2 + 125^2 + 139^2) - \text{C.F.}$$
$$= 8378.50 - 8030.04$$
$$= 348.46$$
$$\text{Error S.S.} = 496.96 - 41.71 - 348.46$$
$$= 106.79$$

ANOVA

Source of variation	*d.f.*	*S.S.*	*M.S.*	*F-value*
Blocks	5	41.71	8.34	$\frac{8.34}{7.12} = 1.17$
Workers	3	348.46	116.15	$\frac{116.15}{7.12} = 16.31$
Error	15	106.79	7.12 (s_e^2)	
Total	23	496.96		

From Appendix table VII$_{ii}$ for $\alpha = 0.05$, $F_{5,\,15} = 2.90$ and $F_{3,\,15} = 3.29$.

On comparing the *F*-value for blocks, we find $F_{cal} < F_{tab}$. So there is no significant difference between days. It means total production per day is same.

Calculated value of *F* for treatments is 16.31 which is greater than 3.29. Hence, we conclude that there is a marked difference between the efficiency of workers. Now to explore further which worker is significantly better than the other or equivalent, we will use lsd. By the formula (12.10),

$$\text{lsd} = \sqrt{\frac{2s_e^2}{r}} \times t_{0.05,15}$$

From appendix table V, $t_{0.05,\,15} = 2.131$

$$\text{lsd} = \sqrt{\frac{2 \times 7.12}{6}} \times 2.131$$
$$= 3.28$$

The difference between means are,

$$\overline{A} - \overline{B} = 14.17 - 15.00 = -0.83,\ \overline{A} - \overline{C} = 14.17 - 20.83 = -6.66$$

Similarly, $\overline{A} - \overline{D} = -9.00$, $\overline{B} - \overline{C} = -5.83$, $\overline{B} - \overline{D} = -8.17$, $\overline{C} - \overline{D} = -2.34$

On comparing the absolute differences of paired mean as above with the value of lsd = 3.28, we find that *A* and *B* are significantly less efficient than *C* and *D* whereas *A* is at par with *B*. Also *C* and *D* are at par.

Note: For data analysis of RBD with the help of SPSS software, see Appendix Chapter-12.

LATIN SQUARE DESIGN (LSD)

Randomized block design isolates the variation due to one nuisance variable. But in many situations it is known that there are two nuisance variables which are likely to influence the effect of treatments. For example, in field experiment fertility gradient may be varying in two directions, milk yield of cows depends on breed and lactation number, interest in purchasing a product may be influenced by the education level and income of persons, etc. LSD controls two way variability and hence it is regarded as an improvement over RBD.

A Latin square design has the following properties.

1. It was named as latin square design because it was originally constructed using latin letters.
2. The term square is used because the number of rows and number of columns in this design are always equal.
3. Number of rows, columns and treatments are always equal.
4. In each row and each column, a treatment occurs only once.
5. Each row and each column is a complete block in itself.
6. This is a two restrictional design.
7. In LSD there are three sources of variation namely, rows, columns and treatments. Hence, it is known as a three way classification design.
8. A LSD having r treatments is called a design of order $(r \times r)$ and has r^2 units in all.
9. A latin square design with $r < 3$ is practically irrelevant as it provides zero d.f. for error.
10. Latin square designs are frequently used in agriculture and industry. Their use in management and marketing research is increasing gradually.

Plans of LSD for r = 3, 4 and 5 are displayed below to further elucidate the above points.

Latin square designs

3 × 3

A	B	C
B	C	A
C	A	B

4 × 4

D	A	B	C
C	D	A	B
A	B	C	D
B	C	D	A

5 × 5

B	C	E	A	D
D	E	A	B	C
C	A	B	D	E
E	B	D	C	A
A	D	C	E	B

STATISTICAL MODEL FOR LSD

Linear model for LSD of order $(r \times r)$ in notational form with one observation per unit is,

$$y_{jk(i)} = \mu + \tau_i + \rho_j + \gamma_k + \varepsilon_{jk(i)} \quad \ldots(12.17)$$

$$i, j, k = 1, 2, \ldots, r$$

$$\sum_i \tau_i = \sum_j \rho_j = \sum_k \gamma_k = 0$$

Suffix (i) shown in parentheses indicates that it refer to the unit belonging to jth row, kth column to which the treatment i is allocated.

ρ_j is the true effect of jth row and γ_k is the true effect of kth column.

ANALYSIS

The observations on each unit are taken and recorded in the layout itself. Sum of squares for all component factors are calculated in the same manner as in case of RBD. Here one more factor is added in ANOVA i.e., either row or column. Also $b = k = r$ and $n = r^2$.

Configuration of analysis of variance table for LSD will be as follows:

Table 12.5: ANOVA for LSD of order $(r \times r)$

Source of variation	*d.f.*	*S.S.*	*M.S.*	*F-value*
Treatments	$r-1$	SST	$\frac{SST}{(r-1)} = MST$	$\frac{MST}{MSE} = F_T$
Rows	$r-1$	SSR	$\frac{SSR}{(r-1)} = MSR$	$\frac{MSR}{MSE} = F_R$
Columns	$r-1$	SSC	$\frac{SSC}{(r-1)} = MSC$	$\frac{MSC}{MSE} = F_C$
Error	$(r-1)(r-2)$	SSE	$\frac{SSE}{(r-1)(r-2)} = MSE$	
Total	r^2-1	SSY		

Each F in ANOVA is distributed with $[(r-1), (r-1)(r-2)]$ d.f. Decision about the rejection or acceptance of the hypotheses are taken in the usual manner by comparing calculated value of F with the critical value F_α for $[(r-1), (r-1)(r-2)]$ d.f. Solved numerical example will remove the apprehension if any.

Merits of LSD

1. Two way variation is isolated in this design. Hence, there is a greater reduction in error variance.
2. The tests in this design have greater power than CRD and RBD.
3. Analysis of variance is simple and straight forward.

Demerits

1. For large number of treatments, Latin square designs are not used for various reasons.
2. Error degrees of freedom is less than CRD and RBD for the same number of treatments and replications.
3. If there is a missing value, it has to be estimated and analysis be carried out with necessary amendments. This makes the analysis complex.
4. A latin square of order less than (5 × 5) does not yield required d.f. for error. Hence, lower order LSD is inadequate.

***Example* 12.3.** Five levels of a fertilizer were tried in a 5 × 5 latin square to see its effect on the yield of wheat. The yield of wheat is given below in kg. per plot alongwith the layout.

5 × 5 Latin square
Grain yield in kg. per (1/100 hectare/plot)

						Row Total
	B 37.0	C 35.9	E 30.9	A 28.2	D 35.8	167.8
	D 37.3	E 38.3	A 26.9	B 36.6	C 37.6	176.7
	C 34.8	A 27.4	B 34.2	D 37.4	E 34.4	168.2
	E 31.3	B 38.4	D 38.0	C 39.4	A 30.3	177.4
	A 24.2	D 38.0	C 36.8	E 30.8	B 34.5	164.3
Column Total	164.6	178.0	166.8	172.4	172.6	854.4

Nitrogen fertilizer levels,
A – no fertilizer, B – 20 kg/ha, C – 40 kg/ha, D – 60 kg/ha, E – 80 kg/ha.
Row and column totals are also given with the layout to save space.
Data analysis for comparing the effect of five levels of fertilizer is as given below.
Analysis

H_0 : Mean effect of all fertilizer levels is same.
vs. H_1 : At least two fertilizer levels differ significantly from each other.

Treatment totals,
$A = 137.0, \quad B = 180.7, \quad C = 184.5, \quad D = 186.5, \quad E = 165.7$
Treatment means,
$\overline{A} = 27.40, \quad \overline{B} = 36.14, \quad \overline{C} = 36.90, \quad \overline{D} = 37.30, \quad \overline{E} = 33.14$

$$G = 854.4, \quad \text{C.F.} = \frac{(854.4)^2}{25} = 29199.97$$

$$\text{Total S.S.} = 37.0^2 + 35.9^2 + \ldots + 34.5^2 - \text{C.F.}$$
$$= 29629.64 - 29199.97 = 429.67$$

$$\text{Row S.S.} = \frac{1}{5}(167.8^2 + 176.7^2 + 168.2^2 + 177.4^2 + 164.3^2) - \text{C.F.}$$
$$= 29227.24 - 29199.97 = 27.27$$

$$\text{Col. S.S.} = \frac{1}{5}(164.6^2 + 178.0^2 + 166.8^2 + 172.4^2 + 172.6^2) - \text{C.F.}$$
$$= 29222.38 - 29199.97 = 22.41$$

$$\text{Treat. S.S.} = \frac{1}{5}(137.0^2 + 180.7^2 + 184.5^2 + 186.5^2 + 165.7^2) - \text{C.F.}$$
$$= 29540.10 - 29199.97$$
$$= 340.13$$

ANOVA

Source of variation	*d.f.*	*S.S.*	*M.S.*	*F-value*
Treatments	4	340.13	85.03	$\frac{85.03}{3.32} = 25.61$
Rows	4	27.27	6.82	$\frac{6.82}{3.32} = 2.05$
Columns	4	22.41	5.60	$\frac{5.60}{3.32} = 1.69$
Error	12	39.86	3.32	
Total	24	429.67		

Tabulated value of F at $\alpha = 0.05$ and for (4, 12) d.f. from Appendix table VII_{ii} is 3.26. On comparing the calculated values of F from the critical value 3.26, it is inferred that there is no significant difference between rows and also between columns. Of course the fertilizer levels differ significantly. To investigate further which of the fertilizer levels differ significantly and which do not, we apply Dunn's test statistic as given by the formula (12.14).

For comparison, calculated values of tD for all pairwise contrast are as follows:

$\sqrt{\frac{2s_e^2}{r}}$ is same for all pair in (12.14) i.e., $\sqrt{\frac{2\times3.32}{5}} = 1.15$

So by dividing each value of paired contrast of treatment means by 1.15, we obtain the values of tD.

$$\overline{A} - \overline{B} = 27.40 - 36.14 = -8.74,\ tD_1 = \frac{-8.74}{1.15} = -7.60$$

$$\overline{A} - \overline{C} = 27.40 - 36.90 = -9.5,\ tD_2 = \frac{-9.5}{1.15} = -8.26$$

$$\overline{A} - \overline{D} = 27.40 - 37.30 = -9.9,\ tD_3 = \frac{-9.9}{1.15} = -8.61$$

Similarly

$$\overline{A} - \overline{E} = -5.74,\ tD_4 = -4.99$$

$$\overline{B} - \overline{C} = -0.76,\ tD_5 = -0.66$$

$$\overline{B} - \overline{D} = -1.16,\ tD_6 = -1.00$$

$$\overline{B} - \overline{E} = 3.00,\ tD_7 = 2.61$$

$$\overline{C} - \overline{D} = -0.4,\ tD_8 = -0.34$$

$$\overline{C} - \overline{E} = 3.76,\ tD_9 = 3.27$$

$$\overline{D} - \overline{E} = 4.16,\ tD_{10} = 3.62$$

For $\alpha = 0.05$, $C = 10$, $\nu = 12$, tabulated value of Dunn's statistic is 3.43. Comparing this value with absolute calculated values of tD for all 10 pairs one by one, we conclude that all doses of fertilizer are significantly superior than control i.e., A. Further out of other four doses of fertilizer, B is at par with C, D and E, C is at par with D and E. But there is a significant difference between D and E.

Note: For analysis data of LSD using SPSS software, see Appendix.

INTRODUCTION TO FACTORIAL EXPERIMENTS

An experiment involving two or more treatments each at two or more levels and all possible combinations of treatment levels occur together in the design is known as factorial experiment. These combinations are considered as treatments and are assigned in any of the CRD, RBD and LSD. If there are p levels of a factor A and q levels of other factor B, then there shall be $p \times q$ combinations. Each of the $p \times q$ combinations may be allocated randomly to experimental units of any basic design.

Analysis of variance of data for all combinations will be carried out as usual for treatment effects. But the treatment effect will consist of three components: (*i*) main effect of A, (*ii*) main effect of B, and (*iii*) interaction $A \times B$. Truly speaking, interaction effect is an additional information that is obtained due to combined influence of two or more factors. Main effect and interaction may be defined as follows. We will confine our discussion to two factors only.

Main Effect

It is a measure of change in the response of a dependent variable subject to changes in the level of a factor (usually lower to higher level) averaged over all levels of other factor (s) applied in combination of the factor of which the main effect is under consideration.

Interaction Effect

It is the difference in response of one factor at varying levels of the other factor applied simultaneously. In other words, interaction is the failure of a factor to give the same response in presence of various levels of the other factor.

We will explain main and interaction effects by considering only two factors each at two levels and also assume that each combination is replicated equal number of times.

Let there be a factor A with two levels 0 and 1 denoted as a_0 and a_1. Also there is another factor B with levels 0 and 1 denoted by b_0 and b_1. Thus, there will be four combinations as a_0b_0, a_0b_1, a_1b_0 and a_1b_1.

As per definition,

Effect of A at 0 level of $B = a_1b_0 - a_0b_0$ ...(*i*)

Effect of A at 1 level of $B = a_1b_1 - a_0b_1$ ...(*ii*)

Main effect of A is the average of (*i*) and (*ii*) i.e.,

$$A = \frac{1}{2}\left[(a_1b_0 - a_0b_0) + (a_1b_1 - a_0b_1)\right]$$

$$= \frac{1}{2}\left[(b_1 + b_0)\, a_1 - (b_1 + b_0)\, a_0\right]$$

$$= \frac{1}{2}(a_1 - a_0)(b_1 + b_0) \qquad \text{...}(iii)$$

Similarly, main effect of B,

$$B = \frac{1}{2} [(a_1 + a_0)\, b_1 - (a_1 + a_0)\, b_0]$$

$$= \frac{1}{2} (a_1 + a_0)(b_1 - b_0) \quad ...(iv)$$

Interaction between A and B: By definition,

$$AB = \frac{1}{2} [(a_1b_1 - a_0b_1) - (a_1b_0 - a_0b_0)]$$

$$= \frac{1}{2} (a_1 - a_0)(b_1 - b_0) \quad ...(v)$$

Two factors interaction is known as *first order interaction*, three factor interactions say, ABC is known as *second order interaction* and so on.

***Example* 12.4.** To illustrate the calculation of main effects and interaction, consider the following two way table having given the yield due to four combinations in the respective cells.

A/B	b_1	b_0	*Total*
a_1	83	57	140
a_0	61	43	104
Total	144	100	244

$$A = \frac{1}{2}(140 - 104) = 18$$

$$B = \frac{1}{2}(144 - 100) = 22$$

$$\text{AB} = \frac{1}{2}(83 - 57 - 61 + 43) = 4$$

Now we will illustrate the method of analysis of variance of a RBd in case of 2 × 2 factorial treatments.

***Example* 12.5.** An experiment in RBD with two instructors (I_1 and I_0) and two methods of teaching (M_1 and M_0) was conducted at four schools. The scores out of 10 were as given in the following layout.

Schools

I	II	III	IV
$I_0\, M_1$ 6	$I_1\, M_1$ 7	$I_0\, M_0$ 6	$I_0\, M_0$ 4
$I_1\, M_0$ 3	$I_0\, M_1$ 5	$I_0\, M_1$ 7	$I_1\, M_0$ 7
$I_0\, M_0$ 2	$I_1\, M_0$ 3	$I_1\, M_1$ 9	$I_0\, M_1$ 6
$I_1\, M_1$ 8	$I_0\, M_0$ 4	$I_1\, M_0$ 5	$I_1\, M_1$ 8

Fictitious example

Analysis of data can be carried out as per the following procedure.

Four treatments are $I_1 M_1$, $I_1 M_0$, I_0M_1, I_0M_0.

Schools are blocks. Therefore, No. of blocks = 4

Computation

Treatment Totals: $I_1M_1 = 32$, $I_1M_0 = 18$, $I_0M_1 = 24$, $I_0M_0 = 16$.

$$G = 90,\ C.F. = \frac{(90)^2}{16} = 506.25$$

School Totals : $S_I = 19$, $S_{II} = 19$, $S_{III} = 27$, $S_{IV} = 25$

$$\text{Total S.S.} = 6^2 + 3^2 + ... + 6^2 + 8^2 - C.F.$$
$$= 568.00 - 506.25 = 61.75$$

$$\text{Treat. } S.S. = \frac{1}{4}\ (32^2 + 18^2 + 24^2 + 16^2) - C.F.$$
$$= 545.00 - 506.25 = 38.75$$

$$\text{School } S.S. = \frac{1}{4}\ (19^2 + 19^2 + 27^2 + 25^2) - C.F.$$
$$= 519.00 - 506.25 = 12.75$$

Treat *S.S.* consists of three effects' *S.S.* i.e., the sum of square due to main effect *I*, main effect *M* and interaction $I \times M$.

Now to calculate S.S. due to *I*, *M* and $I \times M$, we prepare a two way table.

Effects	M_1	M_0	*Total*
I_1	32	18	50
I_0	24	16	40
Total	56	34	90

Nota bene: A divisor in the calculation of sum of squares is always equal to the number of experimental units on which a figure is based.

$$\text{S.S. due to } I = \frac{1}{8}\ (50^2 + 40^2) - \text{C.F.}$$
$$= 512.50 - 506.25 = 6.25$$

$$\text{S.S. due to } M = \frac{1}{8}\ (56^2 + 34^2) - \text{C.F.}$$
$$= 536.50 - 506.25 = 30.25$$

$$S.S. \text{ due to } I \times M = \text{Table } S.S - S.S.\ (I) - S.S.\ (M) - C.F.$$
$$= \frac{1}{4}(32^2 + 18^2 + 24^2 + 16^2) - 6.25 - 30.25\ - C.F.$$
$$= 545.00 - 6.25 - 30.25 - 506.25$$
$$= 2.25$$

Check

1. The sum of square due to treatments is always equal to the aggregate of sum of squares due to main effects and interaction effects.
2. Degrees of freedom for the interaction is the product of the d.f. of the factors involved in the interaction.

ANOVA

Source of variation	*d.f.*	*S.S.*	*M.S.*	*F-value*
Schools	3	12.75	4.25	$\frac{4.25}{1.14} = 3.72$
Treatments	3	38.75		
I	1	6.25	6.25	$\frac{6.25}{1.14} = 5.48$
M	1	30.25	30.25	$\frac{30.25}{1.14} = 24.56$
I × M	1	2.25	2.25	$\frac{2.25}{1.14} = 1.97$
Error	9	10.25	1.14	
Total	15	61.75		

From the table VII_{ii}, value of F at $\alpha = 0.05$ and (3, 9) d.f. is 3.86 and for (1, 9) d.f. is 5.12. Calculated value of $F = 3.72$ for schools is less than 3.86. This leads to the conclusion that the standard of school is same. Further calculated values of F for I and M are larger than 5.12. It means there is a significant difference between the instructors, as well as teaching methods. F-value for $I \times M$ in ANOVA is less than 5.12, hence it leads to the conclusion that there is no interaction between instructors and methods teaching.

QUASI-EXPERIMENTS

A quasi-experimental design is similar to full experiments except that they lack random assignment of treatments to subjects or units. Such experiments are unavoidable in situations when the researcher has no control on experimental units such as the availability of persons suffering from a particular disease, the study of buyers who have been supplied imitative packs of a product, sexually abused women, etc. Also it is not possible to randomize the population of those who suffer from water treatments like adding chloride or iodide or fluoride in water supply of the city, etc.

CONCLUDING REMARK

The coverage in this chapter is not an iota of theory and practice of designs. Topic of experimental design is so vast that even the great volumes have not been able to cover it in full. Anyhow a thorough study of this chapter will enable the students to do well in examinations. Also it will be of help for those who are engaged in research in various areas. For a detailed study one should read an exclusive book on the topic. Some books are referred in suggested reading at the end of this chapter. Please go through them in need.

QUESTIONS AND EXERCISES

1. What do you understand by internal validity? List any seven extraneous variables that can be a threat to internal validity.
2. When does a causal relationship exists between two variables?
3. Distinguish between pre-experimental designs and true designs.
4. Describe a pre-test – post-test control group design through an example.
5. What is meant by imitation of treatments? Show by an illustration how it affects an experiment?
6. Delineate external validity and list the threats to it with a brief description.
7. When should one group pre-test–post-test design be used? How is it performed?
8. Elucidate static group design.
9. How a pre-test–post-test control group design differs from a pre-test–post-test design?
10. In what respects statistical designs are superior to pre-experimental designs?
11. What are the three basic requirements of a good experimental design? Explain their role also.
12. What is a statistical model of a design and what are the assumptions on which it is based?
13. Define a contrast and give its utilities.
14. Explicate Fisher's LSD method for comparing pairwise treatment means.
15. Why LSD test is not good? Give an alternative test to LSD test which is more powerful.
16. What are the merits and demerits of a completely randomised design?
17. Which design is known as one restrictional design? Explain this design adequately.
18. What are the advantages and limitations of a latin square design?
19. Which design yields maximum degrees of freedom out of CRD, RBD and LSD?
20. Define the terms, main effect and interaction with reference to field experiment.
21. What is the main advantage of factorial experiments?
22. Describe the practical situations for which each of the following design is appropriate.
    (*a*) One group pre-test–post-test design.
    (*b*) One shot case design.
    (*c*) Pre-test–Post-test control group design.
    (*d*) Completely randomized design.
    (*e*) Latin square design.
    (*f*) Randomized block design.
23. What problems generally arise in conducting experiments with people?
24. What characteristics distinguish a true experiment with other experimental research designs?
25. Discuss the term experimental mortality.
26. An experiment was conducted in RBD to test the effect of three temperatures 20°C, 60°C and 100°C (T_0, T_1 and T_2) and two levels of humidity 10% and 50% (H_0 and H_1). The resistance values of resistors were recorded under six combinations of temperatures and humidities on three consecutive weeks.

Combinations	Weeks		
	I	II	III
$T_0 H_0$	33	35	26
$T_1 H_0$	28	26	24
$T_2 H_0$	34	26	23
$T_0 H_1$	36	30	25
$T_1 H_1$	38	28	24
$T_2 H_1$	40	34	31

* *Coded values*

Analyse the data and interpret results.

27. Following table presents the field plan and yield of five varieties of barley tried in CRD.

Yield/plot (kg.)

V_1 3.2	V_4 3.4	V_5 4.0	V_4 3.6	V_3 3.5
V_2 3.7	V_2 4.5	V_3 4.2	V_1 4.2	V_5 3.6
V_3 4.0	V_1 3.5	V_5 3.3	V_1 3.1	V_4 3.6
V_4 3.7	V_5 3.4	V_2 3.8	V_5 3.0	V_3 2.8
V_2 3.8	V_3 2.8	V_4 2.7	V_2 3.1	V_1 4.0

Analyse the data and state conclusions.

28. Four cultivars A, B, C, and D of dwarf beans were arranged in a latin square design. The layout of the design and leaf area (cm^2) of leaves were as shown below, five days after germination.

B 10	C 17	D 7	A 15
C 15	D 8	A 19	B 13
D 6	A 18	B 12	C 16
A 16	B 9	C 12	D 9

Test whether there is a significant difference in the cultivars with respect to leaf area.

29. A farmer applies three types of fertilizers on 4 separate plots. The figures on yield per acre are tabulated below.

	Yields				
Fertilizers | Plots	A	B	C	D	Total
Nitrogen	6	4	8	6	24
Potash	7	6	6	9	28
Phosphate	8	5	10	9	32

Find out if the plot are materially different in fertility, as also, if the three fertilizers make any material difference in yields. *(C.A. Foundation, May 1998)*

30. Four operators are tested for their efficiency in terms of no. of units produced per hour on 5 different types of machines A, B, C, D and E. Test at 5 per cent level of significance whether the operators differ in terms of their efficiency? Data are as follows:

	Machine Types				
Operators	A	B	C	D	E
I	8	10	7	12	6
II	12	13	8	9	12
III	7	8	6	8	8
IV	5	5	3	5	14

(M.B.A. Part II, MLSU, 2000)

31. Following are the weekly sale records (in Rs.) of three salesmen A, B and C of a company during 13 sale calls:

A :	300	400	300	500	
B :	600	300	300	400	
C :	700	300	400	600	500

Test whether the sales of three salesmen are different.

$F_{2\ 11,\ 0.05} = 3.98$ and $F_{2,\ 13,\ 0.05} = 3.81$ *(C.A. Foundation, Nov. 2001)*

32. Following is the layout and yield data of a latin square design to compare 5 treatments.

A 6	E 14	B 10	D 9	C 6
B 10	D 11	A 5	C 4	E 16
D 11	B 12	C 7	E 18	A 5
E 20	C 8	D 14	A 8	B 8
C 5	A 3	E 12	B 13	D 15

Give the complete ANOVA table and compare treatment means.

(B.Sc (Ag.) Hons. Part I, RAU, 2001)

33. In order to determine whether there is significant difference in the durability of three makes of computer, samples of size $n = 5$ are selected from each make and the frequency of repair during the first year of purchase is observed.
The results are as follows:

Computer make	*Sample observations*				
A	5	6	8	9	7
B	8	10	11	12	4
C	7	3	5	4	1

Analyse the data and draw your conclusions, given that $F_{2,\ 12}$ at 5% level of significance is 3.89. *(C.A. Foundation, Nov. 2002)*

34. A reputed marketing agency in India has three different training programmes for salespersons. Three programmes are known as Method – A, Method – B, Method – C. To assess the success of the programme, 4 salesmen from each of the programmes were sent to the field. Their performance in terms of sales is given in the following table.

Salesmen	*Methods*		
	A	B	C
1	4	6	2
2	6	10	6
3	5	7	4
4	7	5	4

Test whether there is a significant difference between methods and between salesmen.
(M.B.A. Part II, MLSU, 2001)

35. Discuss in detail the basic principles of experimental design alongwith their roles.
(B.Sc. (Ag.) Hons. Part I, RAV. 2001)

SUGGESTED READING

Cochran, W. G., and G. M. Cox (1957). *Experimental Designs,* John Wiley, New York.

Cook, T. D., and D. T. Campbell (1979). *Quasi-experimentation, Design and analysis issues for field settings,* Rand McNally, Chicago.

Dean, A. and Daniel Voss (1999). *Design and Analysis of Experiments,* Springer, New York.

Dunn, O. J. (1961). Multiple Comparisons Among Means. *Journal of the American Statistical Association,* Vol. 56, pp. 52 – 64.

Elazar, J. Pedhazur (1991). *Measurement Design and Analysis,* Lawrence Eribaum Associates.

Fabio, Sani and John Todman (2006). *Experimental Design and Statistics for Psychology,* Blackwell Publishing.

Kish, R. E. (1995). *Experimental Design: Procedures for the Behavioural Sciences,* Brooks/Cole Publishing Company, 3rd ed., U.S.A.

Leslie, Kish (2004). *Statistical Design for Research,* John Wiley.

Neter, John (1990). *Applied Statistical Models– Regression Analysis of Variance and Experimental Design,* Irwin, Homewood.

APPENDIX

SPSS WINDOW GUIDE FOR ANALYSIS OF VARIANCE

Procedure for performing ANOVA for one way classification

1. Enter the data as given in example 12.1. While feeding the data, prepare two variables, *mach* for types of treatment and *tinwt* for values of dependent variable. Ensure that the mach variable is taken as a numerical value & later feed 1, 2, ..., 5 in place of A, B, ..., E.
2. Select the **Analyze** menu followed by **Compare Means** and **One-Way ANOVA** as shown in following window:

Example 12.1

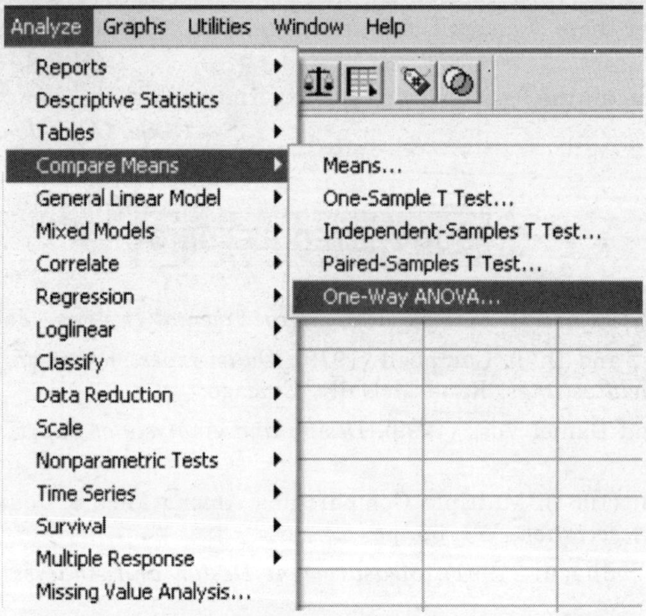

3. When you obtain following window, select each variable and press the corresponding arrow button to shift them to respective panes as shown below.

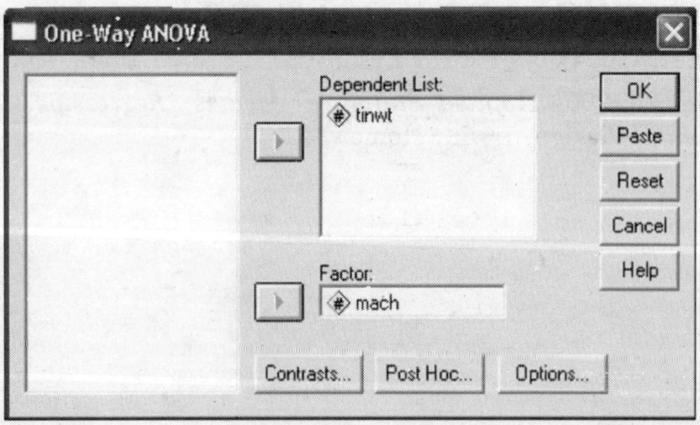

4. Now click on **Post Hoc...** button and in the new window, click on any test you want to apply for comparing the paired treatment means as shown below:

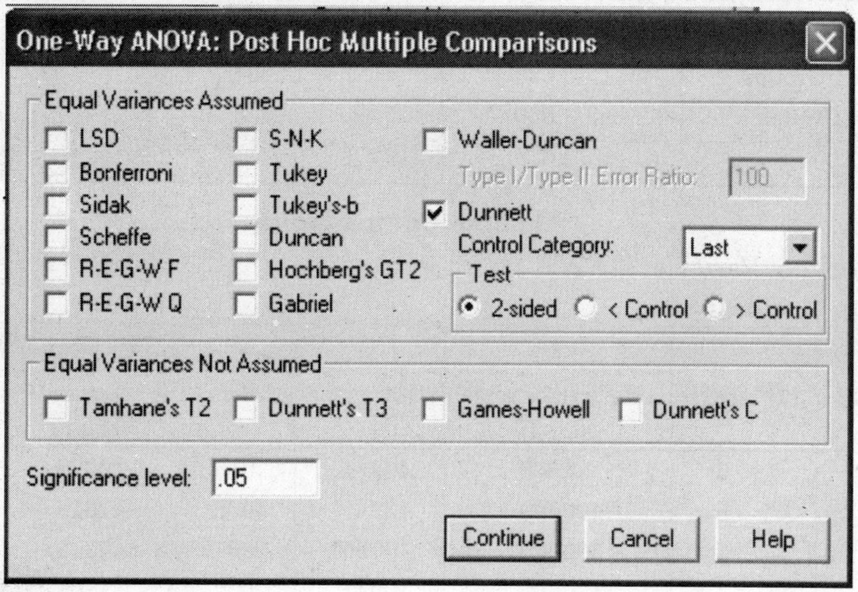

5. Click on Continue button to move to the original window. You can click on Options button and select the Descriptives checkbox to get mean, standard deviations and other relevant statistics.
6. Finally, click on OK button to get the following output:

One way

Descriptives

TINWT

	N	Mean	Std. Deviation	Std. Error	95% Confidence Interval for Mean		Minimum	Maximum
					Lower Bound	Upper Bound		
1	5	15.0000	.18371	.08216	14.7719	15.2281	14.80	15.25
2	2	14.3500	.09899	.07000	13.4606	15.2394	14.28	14.42
3	4	14.2500	.16753	.08377	13.9834	14.5166	14.15	14.50
4	5	15.2000	.14577	.06519	15.0190	15.3810	15.00	15.35
5	4	14.7500	.10893	.05447	14.5767	14.9233	14.60	14.84
Total	20	14.7850	.39537	.08841	14.6000	14.9700	14.15	15.35

ANOVA

TINWT

	Sum of squares	df	Mean square	F	Sig.
Between Groups	2.620	4	.655	28.109	.000
Within Groups	.350	15	.023		
Total	2.970	19			

Multiple Comparisons

Dependent Variable: TINWT
Dunnett *t* (2-sided)

(I) MACH	(J) MACH	Mean difference (I – J)	Std. error	Sig.	95% Confidence interval	
					Lower bound	Upper bound
1	5	.2500	.10241	.086	–.0298	.5298
2	5	–.4000(*)	.13221	.028	–.7612	–.0388
3	5	–.5000(*)	.10795	.001	–.7949	–.2051
4	5	.4500(*)	.10241	.002	.1702	.7298

* The mean difference is significant at the .05 level.

a Dunnett *t*-tests treat one group as a control, and compare all other groups against it.

Procedure for analyzing data of RBD (explained using example 12.2)

1. Arrange the data as per the format given in Window 1.

Example 12.2

Window 1: RBD Data Sheet

	treat	block	cospn	var
1	a	1	14.00	
2	a	2	16.00	
3	a	3	15.00	
4	a	4	17.00	
5	a	5	13.00	
6	a	6	10.00	
7	b	1	12.00	
8	b	2	18.00	
9	b	3	14.00	
10	b	4	11.00	
11	b	5	18.00	
12	b	6	17.00	
13	c	1	22.00	
14	c	2	20.00	
15	c	3	23.00	
16	c	4	19.00	
17	c	5	20.00	
18	c	6	21.00	
19	d	1	23.00	
20	d	2	25.00	
21	d	3	28.00	
22	d	4	21.00	
23	d	5	24.00	
24	d	6	18.00	

2. Click on **Analyze** menu followed by **General Linear Model** and **Univariate** options subsequently as shown in Window 2. You will receive Window 3.

Window 2 :

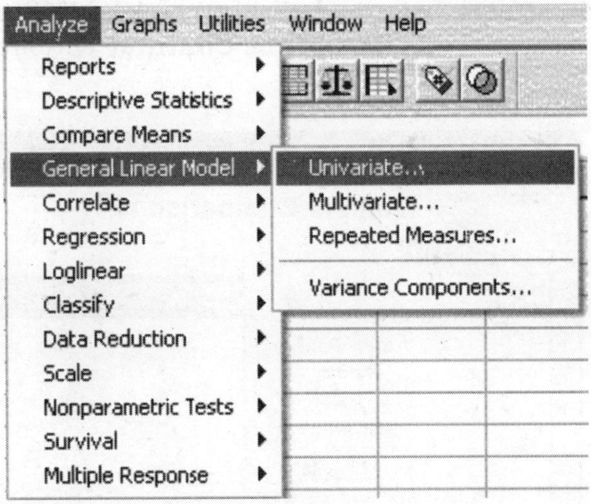

3. Now select the variable cospn and click on arrow button corresponding to Dependent Variable. Similarly, choose other two variables and click on the arrow button of Fixed Factor(s) so as to get Window3.

Window 3: Univariate

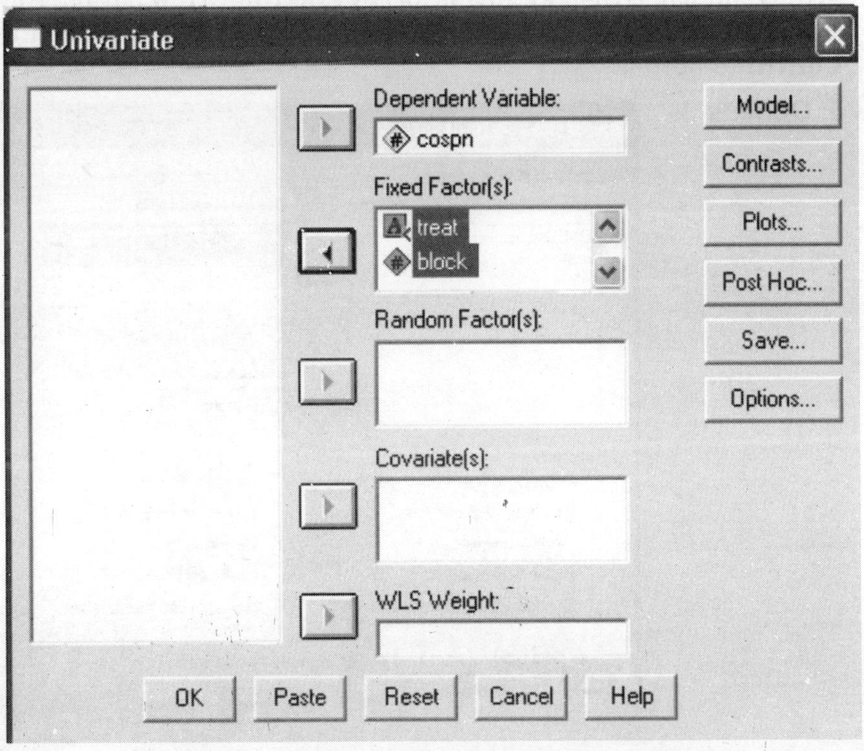

4. Now click on **Model** button to get the following window. In this window, click on Custom and then send both the variables in the right pane by selecting & clicking the arrow button. You also need to click on the check box below the arrow and select **Main effects**. In the end, click on check box of **Sum of squares** shown in bottom and choose **Type III**. Click on **Continue** button to return to main menu.

Window 4: Model

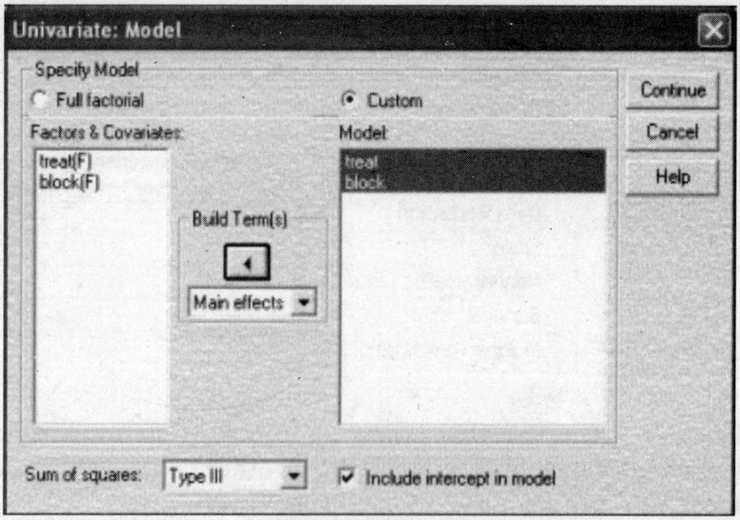

5. Now click on **Options** button to get the following window. Send both the variables to the right pane (Display Means for) by selecting arrow button. Now click on the check box before comparing main effects. Return to main menu by clicking on **Continue** button.

Window 5: Options

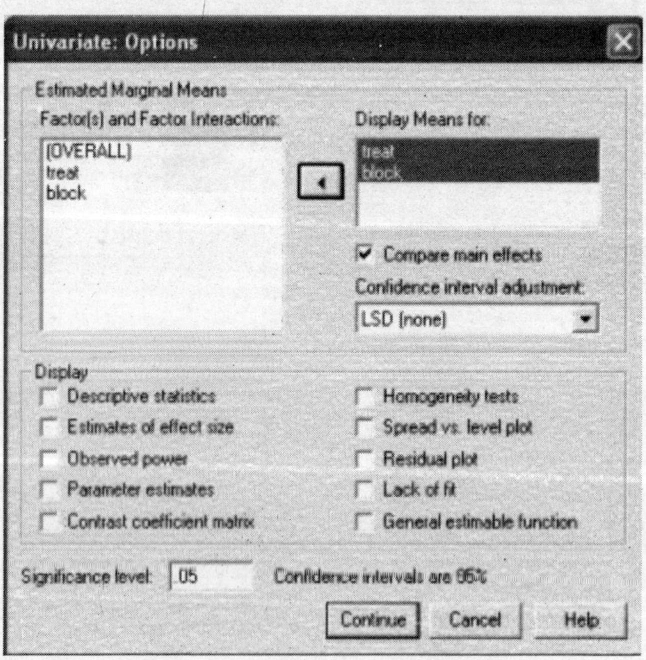

6. Click on **OK** button to get the following output.

Window 6:

Univariate Analysis of Variance

Between-Subjects Factors

		N
TREAT	a	6
	b	6
	c	6
	d	6
BLOCK	1	4
	2	4
	3	4
	4	4
	5	4
	6	4

Tests of Between-Subjects Effects

Dependent Variable: COSPN

Source	Type III sum of squares	df	Mean square	F	Sig.
Corrected Model	390.167(a)	8	48.771	6.850	.001
Intercept	8030.042	1	8030.042	1127.903	.000
BLOCK	41.708	5	8.342	1.172	.368
TREAT	348.458	3	116.153	16.315	.000
Error	106.792	15	7.119		
Total	8527.000	24			
Corrected Total	496.958	23			

a R Squared = .785 (Adjusted R Squared = .671)

ESTIMATED MARGINAL MEANS

1. TREAT

Estimates

Dependent Variable: COSPN

TREAT	Mean	Std. error	95% Confidence interval	
			Lower bound	Upper bound
a	14.167	1.089	11.845	16.488
b	15.000	1.089	12.678	17.322
c	20.833	1.089	18.512	23.155
d	23.167	1.089	20.845	25.488

Procedure for analyzing data of LSD (explained using example 12.3)

1. Arrange the data as per the format given in Window 1.

Example 12.3

Window 1: LSD Data Sheet

	row	col	fertlev	yield
1	1	1	b	37.00
2	2	1	d	37.30
3	3	1	c	34.80
4	4	1	e	31.30
5	5	1	a	24.20
6	1	2	c	35.90
7	2	2	e	38.30
8	3	2	a	27.40
9	4	2	b	38.40
10	5	2	d	38.00
11	1	3	e	30.90
12	2	3	a	26.90
13	3	3	b	34.20
14	4	3	d	38.00
15	5	3	c	36.80
16	1	4	a	28.20
17	2	4	b	36.60
18	3	4	d	37.40
19	4	4	c	39.40
20	5	4	e	30.80
21	1	5	d	35.80
22	2	5	c	37.60
23	3	5	e	34.40
24	4	5	a	30.30
25	5	5	b	34.50

2. Click on **Analyze** menu followed by **General Linear Model** and **Univariate** options subsequently as shown in Window 2. You will receive Window 2.

Window 2:

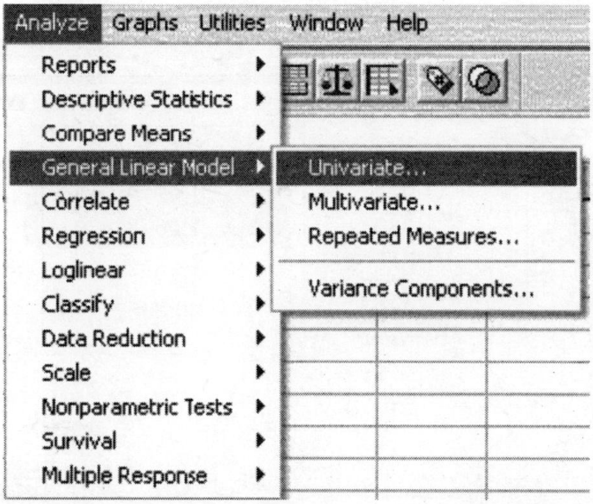

3. Now select the variable yield and click on arrow button corresponding to Dependent Variable. Similarly, choose other three variables and click on the arrow button of Fixed Factor(s) so as to get Window 3.

Window 3: Univariate

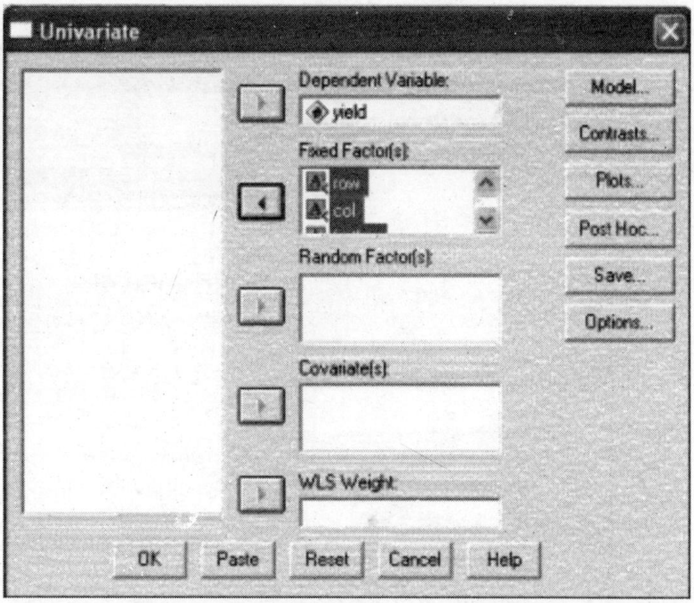

4. Now click on **Model** button to get following window. In this window, click on **Custom** and then send all the variables in the right pane by selecting & clicking

the arrow button. You also need to click on the check box below the arrow and select **Main effects**. In the end, click on check box of **Sum of squares** shown in bottom and choose **Type III**. Click on Continue button to return to main menu.

Window 4: Model

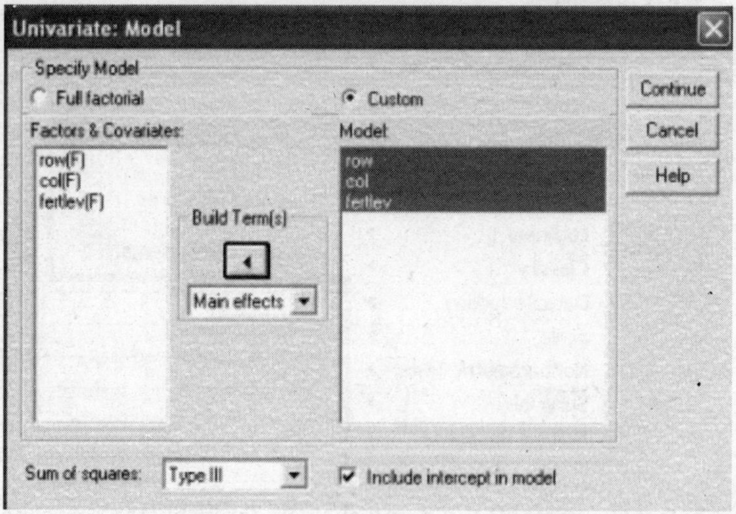

5. Now click on **Options** button to get the following window. Send all the variables to the right pane (*Display Means for*) by selecting arrow button. Now click on the check box before **Compare main effects**. Return to main menu by clicking on Continue button.

Window 5: Options

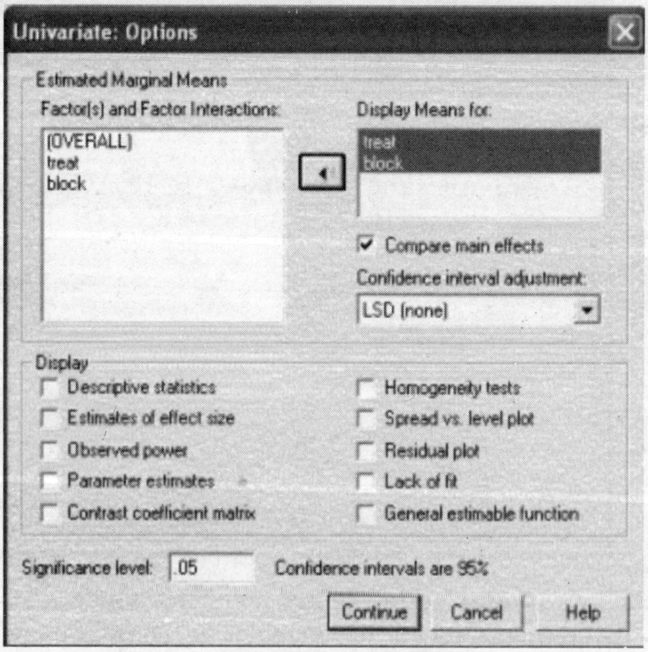

6. Click on **OK** button to get the following output.

Window 6:

Univariate Analysis of Variance

Between-Subjects Factors

ROW	1	5
	2	5
	3	5
	4	5
	5	5
COL	1	5
	2	5
	3	5
	4	5
	5	5
FERTLEV	a	5
	b	5
	c	5
	d	5
	e	5

Tests of Between-Subjects Effects

Dependent Variable: YIELD

Source	Type III sum of squares	df	Mean square	F	Sig.
Corrected Model	389.801(a)	12	32.483	9.778	.000
Intercept	29199.974	1	29199.974	8789.702	.000
ROW	27.270	4	6.817	2.052	.151
COL	22.410	4	5.602	1.686	.217
FERTLEV	340.122	4	85.030	25.596	.000
Error	39.865	12	3.322		
Total	29629.640	25			
Corrected Total	429.666	24			

a R Squared = .907 (Adjusted R Squared = .814)

ESTIMATED MARGINAL MEANS

3. FERTLEV

Estimates

Dependent Variable: YIELD

FERTLEV	Mean	Std. error	95% Confidence interval	
			Lower bound	Upper bound
a	27.400	.815	25.624	29.176
b	36.140	.815	34.364	37.916
c	36.900	.815	35.124	38.676
d	37.300	.815	35.524	39.076
e	33.140	.815	31.364	34.916

13

Chapter

Nonparametric Tests

Chapters 10 and 11 cover a number of tests of hypothesis. All these tests are based on the assumption that the variable follows normal distribution or that the sample has been drawn from a normal population. The importance of the normal distribution theory is justified under the umbrella of the central limit theorem. However it is often doubtful whether the basic distribution is such that the central limit theorem is applicable and hence the estimates and tests based on the assumption of normal distribution are not accurate to the desired degree. In the last two chapters, the hypotheses about the parameter(s) of the distribution(s) were tested and the decision about the hypothesis taken with the help of the critical region which is determined by the distribution that is not known, one needs statistical methods which do not require the form of the parent distribution. Such methods are called *nonparametric* or *distribution-free methods*.

The two terms, nonparametric and distribution-free are not synonymous though they are used in the same sense and cover the same statistical techniques. The term 'nonparametric' is used in the sense that no hypothesis is established about the indexing parameters of the density function, whereas the term 'distribution-free' is used in the sense that no assumption is made about the form of the population density and thereby the decision about a hypothesis is not based on the density of the parent population.

Some problems are categorised as parametric and others as nonparametric. The distinction, however, is not very clear. Interestingly, the chi-square test is taken as a parametric as well as a nonparametric test.

Whichever technique be adopted for testing a hypothesis, the definitions and implications of terms like hypothesis, two types of error, critical region, level of significance and degrees of freedom remain the same, as in Chapter 10 on Tests of Significance. The desired significance level α in nonparametric tests is called the *nominal* α. It cannot, usually, be determined exactly because of the discreteness of the sampling distribution. It should be noted that nonparametric statistics are applicable to the set of observations which are either ranked or ordered. Let a random sample of n observations $X_1, X_2, ..., X_n$ be drawn from a population. These observations can always be arranged in ascending or descending order. However, the observations in this chapter will usually be arranged in ascending order, *i.e.*, from the lowest to the highest value in increasing order of magnitude. Suppose the observations arranged in increasing order of magnitude are $x_{(1)}, x_{(2)}, ..., x_{(n)}$, where $x_{(1)}$ is the lowest value of X and $x_{(n)}$ the largest value of X. Numerically $x_{(1)} \leq x_{(2)} \leq ... \leq x_{(n)}$.

In performing any nonparametric test, it is required to know whether the random variable follows continuous or discrete distribution. It is well known that the area of the density curve between any two ordered observations is free from the form of the density function. Also, it is always possible to divide the total area under the density curve into $(n + 1)$ equal parts such that the area of each part is equal to $1/(n + 1)$. Therefore, techniques like quartiles, deciles, percentiles, rank correlation, etc. come under the category of nonparametric techniques although they are concerned with estimation. This chapter contains only some popular nonparametric tests.

TREATMENT OF TIES IN RANK TESTS

It has been mentioned in the above discussion that nonparametric tests are based on the ranks of the ordered observations of a sample. Even though the population has been assumed continuous, all observations are not distinct owing to rounding of values. Hence, the sample values arranged in order of magnitude produce a set of p groups of sample observations. Let the number of tied observations in a group be r_i with $r_i \geq 2$. In such a situation, the ranks are no longer well defined. Suppose $\sum_{i=1}^{p} r_i = m$. For any set having p groups of tied observations, there are $\prod_{i=1}^{p} r_i!$ possible arrangements of ranks of the ordered sample observations. Each arrangement will lead to its own value of rank test statistics. Consequently, the decision about the hypothesis will not be uniformly made. To overcome this problem there should either be a unique procedure to assign the ranks to the tied observations or a method of combining the values of all rank-test statistics so as to reach a single-decision. Of the two, the former procedure is more commonly used than the later.

The unique procedure of assigning ranks to the tied sample values is called *midranks method*. In this method, the simple average of the ranks of tied values, which they would have if distinguishable, is assigned as the rank of each tied value, *i.e.*, the tied values receive tied ranks. However, under this method, null distribution (the distribution under null hypothesis) is affected as the mean rank remains the same but variance is reduced. To improve, a correction for ties is introduced in the rank test statistics depending upon the availability of correction.

As suggested, another way is to calculate the values of the rank test statistics for all possible $\prod_{i=1}^{p} r_i!$ arrangements and use the simple average of all the test statistics as a single value to take a decision about the null hypothesis. In this method too, the test statistic would have the same mean but a smaller variance.

Sometimes, an easy method of dealing with the problem of ties is to discard all tied observations and reduce sample size by the same number. This method is least recommended as there is a loss of information contained in the sample. But in cases where the sample size is large enough as compared to the number of tied values, this method may be used as the loss of information will be negligible.

Assumptions

1. For nonparametric tests, the only assumption is about the continuity of the distribution function. This is postulated to determine the sampling distributions.
2. Median is as good as index of central tendency as mean. We know, for symmetrical distributions, mean and median coincide. Hence, in nonparametric statistics median is taken as a measure of location parameter instead of mean.

ONE-SAMPLE NONPARAMETRIC TESTS

A random sample of size n is drawn from a population and the sample values are arranged in order of magnitude and ranked accordingly, if need be. Different tests evolved in one sample case for the test of hypothesis are discussed here. These tests lead us to decide whether the sample has come from a particular population. Also, we test whether the median of the population is equal to a known value or not. Such tests are classified as tests for goodness of fit like chi-square test.

Kolmogorov-Smirnov (K-S) One-Sample Test

A random sample $X_1, X_2, ..., X_n$ of size n is drawn from an unknown population having the cumulative distribution function (c.d.f.) $F(x)$. Let the ordered valued be $x_{(1)}, x_{(2)}, ..., x_{(n)}$. The K-S test is based on the Glivenko-Cantelli theorem which states that the step function $S_n(x)$, with jumps occurring at the values of the ordered statistics $x_{(1)}, x_{(2)}, ..., x_{(n)}$ for the sample, approaches the true distribution for all x. Making use of this theorem, the comparison of the empirical distribution function[1] $S_n(x)$ of the sample for any value x is made with the population c.d.f. under H_0, $F_0(x)$. This comparison is made by defining the distance between the two cumulative distribution functions which is taken as the supremum[2] of the absolute deviations *i.e.*, Sup $|S_n(x) - F_0(x)|$ over all x. The hypothesis for the test of goodness of fit is,

$$H_0 : F(x) = F_0(x) \text{ vs. } H_1: F(x) \neq F_0(x).$$

where F_0 is a completely specified continuous distribution.

To test H_0, the actual numerical difference $|S_n(x) - F_0(x)|$ is used in K-S test. Since this difference depends on x, the K-S statistics is taken to be the supremum of such differences, *i.e.*,

$$D_n = \text{Sup } |S_n(x) - F_0(x)| \qquad \text{...(13.1)}$$

---

1. The empirical (sample) distribution function of an ordered random sample $x_{(1)}, x_{(2)}, ..., x_{(n)}$ of size n, denoted by $S_n(x)$ for all real x, is the proportion of sample values which do not exceed x. $S_n(x)$ is a set function which increases by $1/n$ at the jump points which are the values of the ordered sample. $S_n(x)$ is also known as the statistical image of the population distribution function.

   Symbolically, $S_n(x)$ is defined as,

$$S_n(x) = \begin{cases} 0 & \text{if} \quad x \le x_{(1)} \\ k/n & \text{if} \quad x_{(k)} \le x \le x_{k+1} \quad \text{for } k = 1, 2, ..., n-1 \\ 1 & \text{if} \quad x \ge x_{(n)} \end{cases}$$

2. Supremum (sup) means least upper bound. Similarly, infimum (inf) means greatest lower bound.

where D_n is known as the K-S statistic. Under H_0, the statistic D_n has a distribution which is independent of the c.d.f. $F(x)$ that defines H_0. The statistic D_n is distribution-free. To decide about H_0, the test criterion is, reject H_0 if D_n (max $|S_n(x) - F_0(x)|$), exceeds the tabulated value for given n and prefixed significance level α. Otherwise, H_0 is not rejected. The critical values of D_n for prefixed α are given in Appendix B, Table IX.

***Example* 13.1.** On tossing five coins 192 times, the frequencies of 0 to 5 heads are:

No. of heads:	0	1	2	3	4	5
Frequency:	6	26	73	66	14	7

The fairness of the coin by the K-S test can be ascertained. The null hypothesis under test is,

$$H_0: F(x) = F_0(x) \text{ vs. } H_1: F(x) \neq F_0(x)$$

The hypothetical frequencies are calculated with the help of the binomial function, $\binom{n}{r} p^r q^{n-r}$. Here, $n = 5$, $p = 0.5$.

Thus, the frequencies for $r = 0, 1, 2, 3, 4, 5$ are

$$f_0 = \binom{5}{0}\left(\frac{1}{2}\right)^0\left(\frac{1}{2}\right)^5 \times 192 = 6,\ f_1 = \binom{5}{1}\left(\frac{1}{2}\right)^1\left(\frac{1}{2}\right)^{5-1} \times 192 = 30,$$

and similarly, $f_2 = 60$, $f_3 = 60$, $f_4 = 30$, $f_5 = 6$. Actual and theoretical frequencies, the sample or empirical c.d.f., theoretical c.d.f. and the differences are tabulated below.

No. of heads	*0*	*1*	*2*	*3*	*4*	*5*
Actual frequencies	6	26	73	66	14	7
Empirical c.d.f.	$\frac{6}{192}$	$\frac{32}{192}$	$\frac{105}{192}$	$\frac{171}{192}$	$\frac{185}{192}$	$\frac{192}{192}$
Theoretical frequencies	6	30	60	60	30	6
Theoretical c.d.f.	$\frac{6}{192}$	$\frac{36}{192}$	$\frac{96}{192}$	$\frac{156}{192}$	$\frac{186}{192}$	$\frac{192}{192}$
Difference: D_n	0	$\frac{4}{192}$	$\frac{9}{192}$	$\frac{15}{192}$	$\frac{1}{192}$	0

$$\text{Max. } D_n = \frac{15}{192} = 0.078$$

Suppose the prefixed significance level $\alpha = 0.1$. The critical value of D_n from Table IX is $\frac{1.22}{\sqrt{192}} = 0.088$. Since the value of statistic D_n does not exceed the critical value 0.088, H_0 is not rejected. This means that the sample c.d.f. is similar to the hypothetical distribution function.

Ordinary Sign Test

Let a random sample $X_{(1)}, X_{(2)}, ..., X_{(n)}$ of size n be drawn from a population $F(x)$ where $F(x)$ is assumed to be continuous in the close vicinity of the median. Suppose the median of $F(x)$ is M. In this situation, $P(X = M) = 0$.

The hypothesis which has to be tested by sign test is,

$$H_0 : M = M_0 \quad \text{vs.} \quad H_1 : M \neq M_0$$

where M_0 is a given value of the population median. We know,

$$P(X > M_0) = P(X < M_0) = 0.5$$

Hence, the null hypothesis H_0 under test is equivalent to

$$H_0 : P(X > M_0) = P(X < M_0) \text{ vs. } H_1 : P(X > M_0) \neq P(X < M_0)$$

If the randomly selected sample comes from a population having the median value equal to M_0 on the average, half of the observations will be below M_0 and half above M_0. To perform the sign test, we take the differences $(X_{(i)} - M_0)$ for $i = 1, 2, ..., n$ and consider their signs. Let the number of positive signs be r and negative signs $(n - r)$. For the test statistic, we consider only the positive signs. In this way the data have been dichotomised which consist of the number of positive and negative signs. The distribution of r for given n is a binomial distribution with $p = P(X > M_0)$. Thus, the null hypothesis H_0 changes to,

$$H_0 : p = 0.5 \text{ vs. } H_1 : p \neq 0.5$$

It is not necessary to use the two-sided alternative. In case there is pre-information that the sample will have an excess number of positive signs, we may use the one-sided alternative, *i.e.*, $H_1 : p > 0.5$. The only difference between one-sided and two-sided tests is that of critical values for a prefixed α. Similarly, the alternative hypothesis $H_1 : p < 0.5$ will be chosen when it is expected that the sample will have few positive signs.

The decision criterion for a two-sided test is, reject H_0 if $r \geq r'_{\alpha/2}$ where $r'_{\alpha/2}$ is the critical value at significance level α. $r_{\alpha/2}$ is the smallest integer which satisfies the condition,

$$\sum_{r=r_{\alpha/2}}^{n} \binom{n}{r} \left(\frac{1}{2}\right)^r \left(\frac{1}{2}\right)^{n-r} \leq \alpha/2 \qquad ...(13.2)$$

or $r \leq r'_{\alpha/2}$ where $r'_{\alpha/2}$ is the largest integer such that,

$$\sum_{r=0}^{r'_{\alpha/2}} \binom{n}{r} \left(\frac{1}{2}\right)^r \left(\frac{1}{2}\right)^{n-r} \leq \alpha/2 \qquad ...(13.3)$$

For the one-sided alternative $H_1 : p > 1/2$, reject H_0 if $r \geq r_\alpha$ where r_α is the smallest integer such that,

$$\sum_{r=r_\alpha}^{n} \binom{n}{r} \left(\frac{1}{2}\right)^r \left(\frac{1}{2}\right)^{n-r} \leq \alpha \qquad ...(13.4)$$

and for $H_1 : p < 1/2$, reject H_0 if $r \leq r'_\alpha$ where r'_α is the largest integer such that,

$$\sum_{r=0}^{r'_\alpha} \binom{n}{r} \left(\frac{1}{2}\right)^r \left(\frac{1}{2}\right)^{n-r} \leq \alpha \qquad ...(13.5)$$

In any problem, the probability of the event $X \leq r$ is computed by the binomial probability provided $n < 25$. For ease, the probabilities are tabulated and given in Appendix *B*, Table *X* for different values of n and r. If the calculated value of $P(X \leq r)$ is less than the predecided significance level α, H_0 is rejected.

For a two-sided test, the calculated probability is doubled and then compared with level α. The decision about H_0 is taken as per the criterion given above.

If $n \geq 25$, the value of Z is computed and the normal test is applied to decide about H_0. Z is given by the statistic,

$$Z = \frac{(r+0.5) - np_0}{\sqrt{np_0(1-p_0)}} \quad \text{when } r < np_0 \qquad \text{...(13.6)}$$

or

$$Z = \frac{(r-0.5) - np_0}{\sqrt{np_0(1-p_0)}} \quad \text{when } r > np_0 \qquad \text{...(13.7)}$$

Remember that $p_0 = 0.5$.

If $Z \leq Z_{\alpha/2}$ or $Z \geq Z_{1-\alpha/2}$, H_0 is rejected. For the one-sided test, adjustment is made, as discussed, with parametric tests.

Theoretically, none of the differences $(X_{(i)} - M_0)$ should be zero since $F(x)$ has been assumed continuous. But, in practice, there are zero differences in some problems. In such a situation, the zero differences are omitted and the sample size is reduced by the number of zero differences. For instance, there are 18 observations in the ordered sample. On taking the deviation from M_0, two zero deviations occur. Then the sample size is taken as 16 ignoring two zeros.

***Example* 13.2.** Following are the data arranged in order of magnitude of a random sample drawn from a continuous population with median $M = 13$.

9.62, 10.19, 10.27, 11.13, 12.26, 13.55, 14.16
14.46, 15.02, 15.92, 16.26

The test of the null hypothesis,

$$H_0 : M = 13$$

against $\quad H_1 : M > 13$

at significance level $\alpha = 0.10$ can be performed by the ordinary sign test in the following manner. The signs of difference $(X_{(i)} - 13)$ are,

$$- - - - - + + + + + +$$

In this case, $n = 11$ and number of positive signs, $r = 6$.

With the help of Table X in Appendix B, the probability, $P(X \leq r)$ is 0.7256. The given alternative hypothesis leads to one sided test. Since the calculated value of $P(X \leq r)$ is greater than the prefixed level $\alpha = 0.10$, the null hypothesis, $M = 13$ is not rejected.

Wilcoxon Signed-Rank Test

The ordinary sign test was based on only the sign of the deviations of the ordered sample values from the hypothesised median M_0. No heed was paid to the magnitude of the differences. The Wilcoxon signed rank test utilizes the signs as well as the magnitudes of the differences. This test is more sensitive and powerful than the ordinary sign test.

If we are prepared to assume that the population is continuous and symmetric, the Wilcoxon signed-rank test is a much improved test in comparison to the ordinary sign test for testing the same null hypothesis against an alternative hypothesis discussed with the sign test. In this case also we have a random sample $X_1, X_2, \ldots, X_n$ from a continuous and symmetric population with median M. The null hypothesis is,

$$H_0 : M = M_0$$

where M_0 is the hypothesised value of M. Let the difference $X_i - M_0$ be denoted by d_i, *i.e.*, $d_i = X_i - M_0$ for $i = 1, 2, ..., n$. The difference d_i will be distributed symmetrically about the median zero so that positive and negative differences of equal absolute magnitude have equal probabilities of occurrences. First arrange the differences in ascending order ignoring their signs and rank them from 1 to n. Now assign the same sign to the ranks which their original differences possessed. In this way, the data consist of a set of n integers and a corresponding set of plus and minus signs. Let the sum of the ranks of positive d_i' s be denoted by T^+ and that of ranks of negative d_i's by T^-. For a symmetrical distribution it is expected that T^+ will be approximately equal to T^-. Obviously $T^+ + T^-$ is equal to the sum of n integers, *i.e.*,

$$T^+ + T^- = \sum_{i=1}^{n} i = n(n+1)/2.$$

Since the sum of all the ranks is a constant, the tests based on T^+, T^- and $T^+ - T^-$ will be equivalent. In practice, the smaller of T^+ and T^- is used for conducting the test. However, the test is discussed further taking T^+.

Let the rank of the absolute differences $|d_i|$ be denoted by $r(|d_i|)$ and a variable Z_i be defined as,

$$Z_i = \begin{cases} 1 & \text{if } d_i > 0 \\ 0 & \text{if } d_i < 0 \end{cases}$$

T^+ may be written as,

$$T^+ = \sum_{i=1}^{n} Z_i r(|d_i|) \qquad ...(13.8)$$

If we take the subscripts on the original sample such that all $|d_i|$, $i = 1, 2, ..., n$ are ordered statistics, replace $r(|d_i|)$ by i and Z_i by $Z_{(i)}$ where

$$Z_{(i)} = \begin{cases} 1 & \text{if } d_i \text{ with rank } i \text{ is positive} \\ 0 & \text{if } d_i \text{ with rank } i \text{ is negative} \end{cases}$$

Now T^+ may be given as,

$$T^+ = \sum_{i=1}^{n} i Z_{(i)} \qquad ...(13.9)$$

$Z_{(i)}$ *s* are independent Bernoulli random variables but are not identically distributed, $Z_{(i)}$ has mean p_i and variance $p_i q_i$ for $q_i = 1 - p_i$ and cov $(Z_{(i)}, Z_{(j)}) = 0$ for $i \neq j$.

Thus, the variable T^+ is distributed with mean $\sum_{i=1}^{n} ip_i$ and variance $\sum_{i=1}^{n} i^2 p_i(1-p_i)$.

Under H_0, $p_i = 1/2$ and hence,

$$E(T^+) = \sum_{i=1}^{n} ip_i = \frac{1}{2}\sum_{i=1}^{n} 1 = \frac{1}{2}.\frac{n(n+1)}{2}$$

$$= \frac{n(n+1)}{4} \qquad ...(13.10)$$

$$V(T^+) = \frac{1}{4}\sum_{i=1}^{n} i^2 = \frac{n(n+1)(2n+1)}{24} \qquad ...(13.11)$$

Similar expressions may be developed for T^-. It has already been stated that it is convenient to perform the test with smaller values of T^+ and T^-. Let $T = \min(T^+, T^-)$. If t_α is a number such that $P(T \le t_\alpha) = \alpha$, the nominal, the regions of rejection of size α for the test of H_0: $M = M_0$ are given as,

$$T^+ \le t_\alpha \text{ for } H_1 : M < M_0$$
$$T^- \le t_\alpha \text{ for } H_1 : \text{M} > \text{M}_0$$
$$T^+ \le t_{\alpha/2} \text{ or } T^- \le t_{\alpha/2} \text{ for } H_1 : M \ne M_0$$

The sample space contains 2^n points which are equally likely under H_0.

Thus,

$$P[T^+ = t \mid H_0 \mid] = k_t/2^n \qquad ...(13.12)$$

where k_t is the number of ways of assigning the plus and minus signs to the ranks 1, 2, ..., n such that $T^+ = t$. The critical values of T may either be calculated or obtained directly from Table XIII prepared by Wilcoxon. For large n say $n \ge 25$, the sum T^+ follows normal distribution. Under H_0, the statistic

$$Z = \frac{T^+ - n(n+1)/4}{\sqrt{n(n+1)(2n+1)/24}} \qquad ...(13.13)$$

where Z ~ N(0, 1)as $n \to \infty$

The decision about H_0 is taken in the same manner as discussed with the large-sample test in Chapter 10.

Run Test

In statistical theory, it has normally been assumed that a sample drawn from a population is random. Whether the assumption of randomness is true or not needs verification. The run test is one device to test randomness. Before discussing the test, it is essential to discuss the runs.

Definition

A *run* is a sequence of like symbols which are followed and preceded by other kinds of symbols or no symbol at either side. For clarity, a vertical line is drawn in between two consecutive sequences of symbols to mark the runs. A sequence of symbols exhibiting a pattern of symbols is usually indicative of lack of randomness. For instance, looking at a queue of persons waiting for the bus the following sequence of males (*M*) and females (*F*) is observed.

$$M|F|M|F|M|F|M|F|M|F|M|F|M|F$$

This sequence shows a definite pattern, i.e., the males and females are standing alternately. This sequence clearly shows a lack of randomness. Again a sequence of type,

MMMMMMM | *FFFFFFF*

shows clustering of males and females which is again indicative of lack of randomness. From this, it may be deduced that an excessive number of runs or too few runs for a given set of symbols provide the basis for nonrandomness.

It is not always that we have sequences of symbols. Any data at hand can be converted into runs. Take the deviation of each observation of the set from the median (any other constant) and denote the positive and zero difference by a and negative difference by b. In this way we get a sequence of symbols a and b. For example, the marks of 15 students are 55, 52, 43, 49, 36, 61, 44, 47, 67, 78, 63, 57, 41, 28, 50. On taking the deviations from 50, the following sequence is obtained.

$$aa \mid bbb \mid a \mid bb \mid aaaa \mid bb \mid a$$

The above sequence has seven runs. Positive and negative signs may also be taken in place of a and b taking zero as positive quantity, to mark the runs.

Test for Randomness

The null hypothesis, H_0: the symbols a and b occur in random order in the sequence against the alternative, H_1: symbols a and b do not occur in random order, can be tested by the run test. Let the sample of size n contains n_1 symbols of one type, say a, and n_2 symbols of the other type, say b. Thus, $n = n_1 + n_2$. Also suppose the number of runs of symbol a is r_1 and that of symbol b is r_2. Suppose $r_1 + r_2 = r$. In order to perform a test of hypothesis based on the random variable R, we need to know the probability distribution of R under H_0. The probability distribution function of R is given as,

$$f_R(r) = 2\begin{pmatrix} n_1 - 1 \\ r/2 - 1 \end{pmatrix}\begin{pmatrix} n_2 - 1 \\ r/2 - 1 \end{pmatrix} \Big/ \begin{pmatrix} n_1 + n_2 \\ n_1 \end{pmatrix}$$

when r is even.

For r even, the number of runs of both types must be the same, *i.e.*, $r_1 = r_2 = r/2$. Again,

$$f_R(r) = \left\{\begin{pmatrix} n_1 - 1 \\ \frac{r-1}{2} \end{pmatrix}\begin{pmatrix} n_2 - 1 \\ \frac{r-3}{2} \end{pmatrix} + \begin{pmatrix} n_1 - 1 \\ \frac{r-3}{2} \end{pmatrix}\begin{pmatrix} n_2 - 1 \\ \frac{r-1}{2} \end{pmatrix}\right\} \Big/ \begin{pmatrix} n_1 + n_2 \\ n_1 \end{pmatrix} \quad \text{...(13.14)}$$

when r is odd.

For r odd, $r_1 = r_2 \pm 1$. In this situation, the sum is taken over two pairs of values, $r_1 = (r - 1)/2$ and $r_2 = (r + 1)/2$ and vice versa.

To decide about H_0 the critical number of runs are obtained from Tables XI-F_i and XI-F_{ii} given in Appendix B. Table XI-F_i and XI-F_{ii} provide the lower and upper critical values of the number of runs at level 0.05 respectively. If the number of runs in the sample lies between these critical values, the hypothesis H_0 is not rejected, otherwise rejected. Rejecting H_0 means that the data are not in random order.

***Example* 13.3.** Given the following sequence as given in the above text.

$$aa \mid bbb \mid a \mid bb \mid aaaa \mid bb \mid a$$

The null hypothesis H_0: the observations occur in random order, against H_1 : the observations do not occur in random order, can be tested by runs test as follows:

$$n_1 = 8,\ n_2 = 7,\ n = 15$$
$$r_1 = 4,\ r_2 = 3,\ r = 7$$

For $\alpha = 0.05$, $n_1 = 8$, $n_2 = 7$, the lower critical value = 4 (see Table XI-F_i)

For $\alpha = 0.05$, $n_1 = 8$, $n_2 = 7$, the upper critical value = 13 (see Table XI-F_{ii}). The number of runs in the sample is 7 which lies between 4 and 13. It means that the observations occur in random order with five per cent significance level.

TWO-SAMPLE NONPARAMETRIC TESTS

Kolmogorov-Smirnov Two-Sample Test

It is an extension of the one sample K-S test as applied to a two-sample problem. In the one-sample test, the empirical distribution is compared with the population c.d.f. But in the two-sample K-S test, the two empirical distributions of two samples are compared and a decision is taken on the basis of the distance between these empirical distributions.

Let two random samples of sizes n_1 and n_2 be drawn from two continuous populations F_1 and F_2, respectively. Also, it is assumed that the two samples are independent. The observations are taken at least on ordinal scale. If these assumptions hold good, two-sample K-S test can be performed in the following manner. Let the empirical distribution functions be given by $S_{n_1}(x)$ and $S_{n_2}(x)$.

The hypothesis,

$$H_0 : F_1(x) = F_2(x) \text{ for all } x$$
$$\text{vs. } H_1 : F_1(x) \neq F_2(x) \text{ for some } x$$

can be tested by the K-S statistic

$$D_{n_1,n_2} = \max_x | S_{n1}(x) - S_{n2}(x) | \qquad \text{...(13.15)}$$

In a real problem, obtain the cumulative step functions of two samples and find the maximum difference. Compare this value with the critical value of D_{n_1,n_2} given in Table XII of Appendix *B*. Table XII gives the acceptance limits of D_{n_1,n_2} for n_1, $n_2 \leq 15$ at two significance levels $\alpha = 0.05$ and $\alpha = 0.01$. Reject H_0, if calculated D_{n_1,n_2} exceeds the tabulated value, otherwise not.

For large values of n_1, $n_2 > 15$, acceptance limits of D_{n_1,n_2} are calculated by the approximate formulae given below the table for various level of significance α. The decision about H_0 is taken in the same way as for small samples.

If there is any prior information whether $F_1(x) > F_2(x)$ or $F_1(x) < F_2(x)$, the one-tailed K-S test will be applied. Now we calculate either $D^+_{n_1,n_2} = \max | S_{n_1}(x) - S_{n_2}(x) |$ or $D^-_{n_1,n_2} = \max_x | S_{n_2}(x) - S_{n_1}(x) |$ as the case may be and perform the test in the usual way. Table XII can be used by doubling the level of significance.

Example **13.4.** A sample of 26 male patients and another of 25 female patients suffering from respiratory tuberculosis (TB) are randomly selected. The frequency distributions according to the age of males and females are given below. The c.d.f. and the differences $| S_{n_1}(x) - S_{n_2}(x) |$ are shown simultaneously.

	Age group							
	0–5	5–15	15–25	25–35	35–45	45–55	55–65	above 65
Males suffering from TB	1	1	3	2	2	4	6	7
c.d.f. $\{S_{n_1}(x)\}$	$\frac{1}{26}$	$\frac{2}{26}$	$\frac{5}{26}$	$\frac{7}{26}$	$\frac{9}{26}$	$\frac{13}{26}$	$\frac{19}{26}$	$\frac{26}{26}$
Females suffering from TB	1	2	4	3	6	4	2	3
c.d.f. $\{S_{n_2}(x)\}$	$\frac{1}{25}$	$\frac{3}{25}$	$\frac{7}{25}$	$\frac{10}{25}$	$\frac{16}{25}$	$\frac{20}{25}$	$\frac{22}{25}$	$\frac{25}{25}$
Difference $\mid S_{n_1}(x) - S_{n_2}(x) \mid$	$\frac{1}{25\times 26}$	$\frac{28}{25\times 26}$	$\frac{57}{25\times 26}$	$\frac{85}{25\times 26}$	$\frac{191}{25\times 26}$	$\frac{195}{25\times 26}$	$\frac{97}{25\times 26}$	0

The hypothesis, that the age distribution of males and females in respect of susceptibility to respiratory tuberculosis is same, can be tested by the K-S statistic given by (13.15).

From the above table,

$$D_{n_1,n_2} = \max_x \mid S_{n_1}(x) - S_{n_2}(x) \mid = \frac{195}{25\times 26} = 0.300$$

The acceptance limit for $n_1 = 26$, $n_2 = 25$ at the level $\alpha = 0.05$ with the help of the formula given in Table XII is

$$= 1.36\sqrt{\frac{n_1+n_2}{n_1 n_2}} = 1.36\sqrt{\frac{26+25}{26\times 25}} = 0.381$$

Since the calculated difference D_{n_1,n_2} does not exceed the acceptance limit, H_0 is not rejected. It means that the male and female populations have the same proportion of respiratory TB in different age groups.

Sign Test for Paired Samples

The procedure for the ordinary sign test is extended to paired-samples problems. In paired-samples problems we have random samples of n pairs, say (X_1, Y_1), (X_2, Y_2), ..., (X_n, Y_n). Just like the t-test in a parametric case, take the differences of the paired observations. Here establish the hypothesis about the median of the differences. The n differences are given as,

$$D_i = X_i - Y_i \quad \text{for} \quad i = 1, 2, ..., n$$

If the population of D_i is assumed continuous at its median say, M_D, then $P(D = M_D) = 0$ The hypothesis which is to be tested in this case is,

$$H_0 : P(D > M_D^0) = P(D < M_D^0) \text{ vs. } H_1 : H_0 \text{ is not true.}$$

where M_D^0 is a hypothesised value of the median of differences.

In a nutshell, it can be said that the ordinary sign test procedure is applicable for paired samples, taking D_i as X_i. Therefore, further details are omitted. One should bear in mind that the test applied for the median difference is not the same as for the difference of two medians, $(M_X - M_Y)$.

Wilcoxon Paired-Sample Signed-Rank Test

Wilcoxon's test for one sample can be applied in a way to paired-samples problems as well. Consider a paired sample of size n as, $(X_1, Y_1), (X_2, Y_2), ..., (X_n, Y_n)$. As in the case of the sign test for paired samples, the differences $(X_1 - Y_1), (X_2 - Y_2), ..., (X_n - Y_n)$, which are denoted by D_i and $i = 1, 2, ..., n$, are assumed to have come from a continuous and symmetric population of differences.

In this case, the hypothesis,

$$H_0 : M_D = M_D^0 \text{ vs. } H_1 : M_D \neq M_D^0$$

where M_D is the median of the population of differences D and M_D^0 is a hypothesised value of M_D.

In case there is any prior information about the differences that an excess number of difference will be less than M_D or few differences will be less than M_D, then one-sided test should be used. To apply the test, find the differences

$$D_i = X_i - Y_i \quad \text{for} \quad i = 1, 2, ..., n.$$

Now, from a practical point of view, the differences D_i are as good as X_i in one-sample case. Apply Wilcoxon's signed-rank test on D_i's similar to one-sample case, *i.e.*, find T^+ or T^- and test the hypothesis in a like manner as in one-sample problems. Table XIII given in Appendix B provides the critical values of T which can directly be used to take a decision about H_0.

Median Test

This test is attributed to Westenberg (1948) and Mood (1950). The sign test for two-sample problems has been applicable only when the observations are paired. But such a situation is not always possible. Often we have samples of different sizes from two populations. In such a situation, the median test is quite-efficient. Suppose two random samples $X_1, X_2, ..., X_{n_1}$ and $Y_1, Y_2, ..., Y_{n_2}$ of sizes n_1 and n_2 are drawn from two populations F_X and F_Y respectively. Suppose, $n_1 + n_2 = n$. The median test is a test of equality of location parameters of the two populations under consideration. Here, we test the hypothesis

$$F_X(x) = F_Y(x) \text{ for all } x$$

against the shift alternative.

$$F_X(x) = F_Y(x - \delta) \text{ for all } x \text{ and } \delta \neq 0.$$

where δ is the shift in the location parameter which is the median in this test.

Without indulging into the theoretical aspects of the test, the methodology of using the test has been given directly.

Combine the samples and arrange them in order. Find the median of the combined order statistics. The median may be one of the X's or Y's. Let it be denoted by θ. Again, count the number of X's and Y's to the left of the median. Let the number of X's to the left of θ be u and that of Y's be v. Obviously, the number of X's on the right side of θ is $(n_1 - u)$

and that of Y's is $(n_2 - v)$. These results are summarized in the table below :

	On the left of the median θ	*Not on the left of the median θ*	*Total*
Sample X	u	$n_1 - u$	n_1
Sample Y	v	$n_2 - v$	n_2
	$(u + v)$	$(n_1 + n_2) - (u + v)$	n

If p is the probability that any observation is less than θ, the probability of $u + v = t$ (say) is,

$$f(t) = \binom{n_1 + n_2}{t} p^t (1-p)^{n_1+n_2-t} \qquad \text{...(13.16)}$$

for $t = 0, 1, 2, ..., n_1 + n_2$.

The conditional distribution of u, given t, is

$$f(u \mid t) = \frac{\binom{n_1}{u}\binom{n_2}{t-u}}{\binom{n_1+n_2}{t}} \qquad \text{...(13.17)}$$

for $u = 0, 1, 2, ..., n_1$.

The distribution given by (13.17) is the hypergeometric probability distribution.

It is worth pointing out that $n = n_1 + n_2$ may be odd or even. To eliminate inconsistencies in the application of this procedure, θ can be defined as the $\left(\frac{n+1}{2}\right)$th ordered statistic if n is odd and any number between the $\left(\frac{n}{2}\right)$th and $\left(\frac{n+2}{2}\right)$th ordered statistics if n is even. In this way, a unique value of u is obtained for any set of n observations. That is why θ is taken to be the median of the combined sample. Expression (13.17) gives the conditional probability of u where $t = n/2$ for n even and $t = \frac{n-1}{2}$ for n odd. The test based on u, the number of observations belonging to the X-sample which are less than the median of the combined sample is called the *median test.*

If two samples are drawn from identical populations with respect to the location parameter, *i.e.*, median in this case, the probability distribution $U = u$ for given t is,

$$f_U(u) = \frac{\binom{n_1}{u}\binom{n_2}{t-u}}{\binom{n_1+n_2}{t}} \qquad \text{...(13.18)}$$

for $\quad u = 0, 1, 2, ..., n_1$

and $\quad t = n/2.$

The rejection regions for significance level α are obtained by the following inequalities:
Reject H_0, if $u \leq C$ or $u \geq C'$ for $H_1 : \delta \neq 0$
Reject H_0, if $u \geq C'_\alpha$ for $H_1 : \delta > 0$
Reject H_0, if $u \leq C_\alpha$ for $H_1 : \delta < 0$
where C and C' are any two integers such that

$$P(U \leq C) + P(U \geq C') \leq \alpha.$$

Also C_α and C'_α are, respectively, the largest and smallest integers such that $P(U \leq C_\alpha) \leq \alpha$ and $P(U \geq C'_\alpha) \leq \alpha$.

The critical values C, C', C_α, C'_α can be obtained from (13.18) or from the tables of the hypergeometric distribution given by Lieberman and Owen in 1961. As an alternative, calculate the probability by (13.18) and compare it with a prefixed level of significance α. For a one-tailed test, if calculated probability is less than or equal to α, H_0 is rejected, otherwise not. Also, for a two-tailed test, if calculated probability is less than or equal to $\alpha/2$, reject H_0; otherwise H_0 is not rejected.

For large $n \geq 40$, the normal deviate test can be used. The distribution of U tends to normal. The mean and variance of U given t, are

$$\text{mean} = \frac{n_1 t}{n} \text{ and variance} = \frac{n_1 n_2 t(n-t)}{n^2(n-1)}$$

Thus, the distribution of

$$Z = \frac{U - n_1 t/n}{\sqrt{\dfrac{n_1 n_2 t(n-t)}{n^2(n-1)}}} \qquad \text{...(13.19)}$$

is approximately standard normal, *i.e.*, $Z \sim N(0, 1)$. Putting $t = u + v$ in (13.19) and doing certain algebraic manipulations, the above test statistic can be rewritten as,

$$Z = \frac{\dfrac{u}{n_1} - \dfrac{v}{n_2}}{\sqrt{\hat{p}\hat{q}\left(\dfrac{1}{n_1} + \dfrac{1}{n_2}\right)}} \qquad \text{...(13.19.1)}$$

where $\hat{p} = \dfrac{u+v}{n_1+n_2}$ and $\hat{q} = 1 - \hat{p}$. 0.5 is added to u or v, whichever is less, and 0.5 is subtracted from u or v, whichever is greater. This correction leads to the more reliable results. The decision about H_0 is taken in the usual way.

***Example* 13.5.** The data of 10 plots each, under two treatments are as given below.

(Treat. 1) X:	46,	45,	32,	42,	39,	48,	49,	30,	51,	34
(Treat. 2) Y:	44,	40,	59,	47,	55,	50,	47,	71,	43,	55

The hypothesis of equality of median response under two treatments can be tested by the median test. Here we test,

$$H_0 : F_1(x) = F_2(x) \text{ vs. } H_1 : F_1(x) = F_2(x - \delta) \text{ for } \delta \neq 0.$$

Arranging the data in ascending order, we have

30	32	34	39	40	42	43	44	45	46
47	47	48	49	50	51	55	55	59	71

In the above ordered statistics, the observations belonging to treatment 2 are underlined just to differentiate them from observations under treatment 1. The median of the combined data is 46.5. Here we have 10 observations on the left of the median, and 10 observations on the right of the median, *i.e.*, $t = 10$. Also

$$n = 20, \quad u = 7, \quad v = 3$$

By formula (13.18),

$$P(u \mid t) = \frac{\binom{10}{7}\binom{10}{3}}{\binom{20}{10}}$$

$$= \frac{120 \times 120}{19 \times 17 \times 4 \times 13 \times 11} = 0.078$$

Take the prefixed significance level $\alpha = 0.05$. Since $P(u \mid t)$ is greater than 0.05, H_0 is not rejected. This means that the treatments are equally effective with regard to their median effects.

Wald-Walfowitz Runs Test

This test is used for testing the identity of two populations. To avoid any confusion between one-sample runs test and this test procedure, we will consider two random samples of sizes m and n respectively, instead of sizes n_1 and n_2. Let the two independent samples $X_1, X_2, ..., X_m$ and $Y_1, Y_2, ..., Y_n$ combine into a single sequence of ordered statistics. Assuming that the samples have come from continuous probability distributions, a unique sequence of ordered statistics is always possible as, theoretically, no ties should occur. In the combined sequence some identification mark must be put with observations of one type so as to identify whether an observation belongs to X-sample or Y-sample. The definition of runs remains the same as in the one-sample case. Let the combined sequence of order statistics with $m = 5$ and $n = 4$ be,

$$XX \mid Y \mid X \mid YY \mid XX \mid Y$$

In this case, there are three runs of X's and 3 runs of Y's. In all we have six runs. From this it may be concluded that the two populations are identical as the total number of runs r is quite large. If the populations are different, we expect that r will be small as the two samples are not well mixed. Here we test,

$$H_0 : F_X(x) = F_Y(x) \text{ for all } x.$$

vs. $H_1 : F_X(x) \neq F_Y(x)$ for some x.

We define a random variable R, the total number of runs in pooled ordered arrangement of m X's and n Y's. As already mentioned, too few runs tend to reject H_0 in favour of H_1 as this indicates that either most of the X's are greater than or less than the Y's. The Wald-Wolfowitz runs test of nominal α has a critical region given by

$$R \leq r_\alpha$$

where r_α is chosen to be the largest integer such that $P(R \leq r_\alpha) \leq \alpha$ under H_0.

Since X and Y constitute a completely random sequence under H_0 as the letters a and b do in case of single random sample, the probability distribution of R is exactly the same as given by (13.14). In this case, $m = n_1$ and $n = n_2$. The only difference in the Wald-Wolfowitz runs test from the one-sample runs test is that only the one-sided test is being used here. Tables of critical values of r at significance level α are prepared by Swed and Eisenhart. Table XI-$F_{(i)}$ can be used for this test also at the 0.05 level.

For large $m, n > 10$, a normal approximation may be made assuming that $m/(m + n)$ and $n/(m + n)$ remain constant as $m + n \to \infty$.

The mean and variance of R are given as,

$$\text{mean }(R) = \frac{2mm}{m+n} + 1 \qquad \text{...(13.20)}$$

and

$$\text{var }(R) = \frac{2mn(2mn - n - m)}{(m+n)^2(m+n-1)}$$

Thus, the normal deviate is,

$$Z = \frac{R - \text{mean }(R)}{\sqrt{\text{var}(R)}} \qquad \text{...(13.21)}$$

where $Z \sim N(0, 1)$.

The decision about H_0 is taken in the usual way.

In working, ties sometimes occur though theoretically it should not. This happens due to the rounding of figures. If the ties occur within same sample, there is no problem, but if they occur across samples, we face a problem as the number of runs would not be uniquely obtained. In that situation, we break the ties in all possible ways and compute r for each way of breaking ties. Then, the largest r value will be used, since that is the one value least likely to lead to the rejection of H_0.

***Example* 13.6.** The following are the rates of flow of a certain gas through two soil samples collected from two different places.

Sample X:	23,	27,	19,	24,	22,	30		
Sample Y:	21,	29,	34,	32,	26,	28,	36,	26

The hypothesis that the populations of soil types are the same with respect to the rates of flow through the soils, *i.e.*, symbolically,

$$H_0 : F_X(x) = F_Y(x) \text{ for all } x$$

vs. $\quad H_1 : F_X(x) \neq F_Y(x)$ for some x

can be tested by the Wald-Wolfowitz test.

The sequence of combined samples with the clearly marked runs is,

19 | 21 | 22, 23, 24 | 26, 26 | 27 | 28, 29 | 30 | 32, 34, 36 |

In this case $m = 6$, $n = 8$ and the number of runs $r = 8$. The probability for $r = 8$ (even) from (13.14) is,

$$f(r) = \frac{2\binom{5}{3}\binom{7}{3}}{\binom{14}{6}} = 0.233$$

Supposing the predecided level of significance $\alpha = 0.1$. Since the probability $f(r)$ is greater than 0.1, we accept H_0 which means that the two soils have identical distributions in respect of rates of flow of a certain gas.

Mann-Whitney U-test

Just like the Wald-Wolfowitz runs test, the Mann-Whitney U-test is based on the idea that the pattern of X's and Y's exhibited by combined ordered statistics provides information about the relationship between their parent populations. Unlike previous runs test, the Mann-Whitney test is based on the criterion of magnitudes of Y's in relation to X's, or vice versa. If most Y's are greater or less than X's, the null hypothesis of equality of two populations is most likely to be refuted.

Let the two independent random samples of sizes n_1 and n_2 be $X_1, X_2, \ldots, X_{n_1}$ and $Y_1, Y_2, \ldots Y_{n_2}$ and be drawn from two populations having the distribution functions F_X and F_Y respectively. It has been assumed that F_X and F_Y are continuous. This assumption avoids, theoretically, the chances of tied observations.

The hypothesis

$H_0 : F_X(x) = F_Y(x)$ for all x

vs. $H_1 : F_X(x) \neq F_Y(x)$ for some x

or $H_1 : F_X(x) \leq F_Y(x)$

or $H_1 : F_X(x) \geq F_Y(x)$

can be tested in the following manner. Write the combined sequence of n_1 X's and n_2 Y's in order of increasing magnitude. Let the combined sequence for $n_1 = 5$ and $n_2 = 3$ be

$$Y_1\, X_5\, X_1\, Y_3\, X_2\, X_3\, X_4\, Y_2$$

The Mann-Whitney U-statistic is defined as the number of times the Y's precedes the X's in the combined sequence of $(n_1 + n_2)$ variables. The Mann-Whitney U-statistic can be defined with the help of an indicator variable D_{ij} where,

$$D_{ij} = \begin{bmatrix} 1 & \text{if} & Y_j < X_i & \text{for} & i & = & 1,2,\ldots,n_1 \\ 0 & \text{if} & Y_j > X_i & & j & = & 1,2,\ldots,n_2 \end{bmatrix}$$

and

$$U = \sum_{i=1}^{n_1} \sum_{j=1}^{n_2} D_{ij} \qquad \ldots(13.22)$$

The random variables D_{ij} are Bernoulli variables with

$$P(D_{ij} = 1) = P(Y < X) = \pi \text{ (say)}.$$

If H_0 is true for all x, $P(Y < X) = P(X < Y) = \frac{1}{2} = \pi$ and H_1 can be given any one of the alternatives $\pi \neq \frac{1}{2}$ or $\pi < \frac{1}{2}$ or $\pi > \frac{1}{2}$ for some x as the situation demands. Also,

$$\text{mean } (D_{ij}) = \pi \text{ and var } (D_{ij}) = \pi(1 - \pi)$$

The critical values of U for nominal α are obtained by making use of the null probability distribution of U. Instead of deriving the null probability distribution of U, we would advise readers to make use of the tables given in Appendix-B for small values of n_1 and n_2. An alternative approach to determine the value of U is also given here. Readers may find it simpler than the procedure of D_{ij}.

In the ordered sequences of combined samples, the ranks of either X's or Y's are found out. In case, the ranks of Y's are taken into consideration (the case when Y precedes X) and their sum is S_2, the Mann-Whitney U-statistic is given as,

$$U = n_1 n_2 + \frac{n_2(n_2+1)}{2} - S_2 \qquad ...(13.23)$$

Similarly, if the ranks of X's are counted, *i.e.*, the case when X precedes Y and their sum is S_1, the statistic U is given as,

$$U' = n_1 n_2 + \frac{n_1(n_1+1)}{2} - S_1 \qquad ...(13.24)$$

It is interesting to point out that both the approaches yield the same value of U. For instance, consider the ordered sequence given earlier for $n_1 = 5$ and $n_2 = 3$.

Sequence:	Y_1	X_5	X_1	Y_3	X_2	X_3	X_4	Y_2
Ranks :	1	2	3	4	5	6	7	8

First we consider $D_{ij} = 1$ when $Y_j < X_i$, otherwise zero. In the given sequence,

Y_1 is less than X_5, X_1, X_2, X_3, X_4, hence, $D_{i1 = 5}$

Y_3 is less than X_2, X_3, X_4 and hence, $D_{i3} = 3$

Y_2 is less than none and hence, $D_{i2} = 0$

$$U = \sum_{j=1}^{3} \sum_{i=1}^{5} D_{ij} = 5 + 3 + 0 = 8$$

Now, from (13.23), statistic U can be calculated as follows:

$$n_1 = 5,\ n_2 = 3,\ S_2 = 1 + 4 + 8 = 13.$$

$$U = 5 \times 3 + \frac{3 \times 4}{2} - 13 = 8$$

Similarly, if we consider $D_{ij} = 1$ for $X_i < Y_j$, otherwise zero, we get,

$$D_{5j} = 1 + 1 = 2, \quad D_{1j} = 1 + 1 = 2, \quad D_{2j} = 1,\ D_{3j} = 1, \quad D_{4j} = 1$$

and
$$U = \sum_{i=1}^{5} \sum_{j=1}^{3} D_{ij} = 2 + 2 + 1 + 1 + 1 = 7.$$

From (13.24),

$$U' = 5 \times 3 + \frac{5 \times 6}{2} - 23$$

$$= 7$$

Since,
$$S_1 = 2 + 3 + 5 + 6 + 7 = 23.$$

From the above discussion, it is evident that the value of the statistic U remains the same, no matter which of the two approaches is adopted.

For small values of n_2, say, 8 or less, Table XIV-*a* given in Appendix-B provides the probability associated with the calculated value of U and n_1. One should make it a point to note that n_2 in the table is the size of the Y sample for which the sum of ranks have been used. If the probability obtained from the table is less than or equal to the significance level α, we reject H_0, otherwise H_0 is not rejected.

If the probability for the given value of U is not provided in the table, the value of U' for the other group can be calculated by the relation,

$$U' = n_1 n_2 - U \qquad ...(13.25)$$

Also, $P(U' \geq U) = P(U \leq n_1 n_2 - U')$

Now the test is applied to U'.

For n_2 lying between 9 and 20 and $n_1 \leq 20$, the critical value of U can be seen in Table XIV-b for the desired nominal α. The table is provided for $\alpha = 0.05$ only for a two-tailed test. If the calculated U is less than or equal to the tabulated value of U, H_0 is rejected at level α, otherwise not.

When n_1 and n_2 are so large that the critical values cannot be determined by Table XIV-a and XIV-b, a normal approximation may be made under H_0. Under the null hypothesis,

$$\text{mean } (U) = \frac{n_1 n_2}{2} \text{ and } \text{var}(U) = \frac{n_1 n_2 (n_1 + n_2 + 1)}{12}$$

The large sample test statistic is,

$$Z = \frac{U - n_1 n_2/2}{\sqrt{n_1 n_2 (n_1 + n_2 + 1)/12}} \qquad ...(13.26)$$

where $Z \sim N(0, 1)$.

The approximation has been found accurate enough for equal sample sizes as small as 6. The decision about H_0 can be taken in the same way as we have been doing previously, in case of normal deviate test.

***Example* 13.7.** The following are the scores of certain randomly selected students at mid term (MT) and final examinations.

MT scores X:	55,	57,	72,	90,	57,	74	
Final scores Y:	80,	76,	63,	58,	56,	37,	75

The hypothesis H_0 that the distribution of scores at two occasions is same against H_1, *i.e.*,

$$H_0 : F_Y(x) = F_X(x) \text{ vs. } H_1 : F_Y(x) \neq F_X(x)$$

can be tested by the Mann-Whitney U-test.

The combined scores in a sequence in increasing order of magnitude are,

	37,	55,	56,	57,	57,	58,	63,	72,	74,	75,	76,	80,	90
	Y	X	Y	X	X	Y	Y	X	X	Y	Y	Y	X
Ranks of Y:	1		3			6	7			10	11	12	

Considering the ranks of Y's, the Mann-Whitney statistic for $n_1 = 6$, $n_2 = 7$ is,

$$U = 7 \times 6 + \frac{7 \times 8}{2} - 50$$
$$= 20$$

From Table XIV-a, for $n_2 = 7$, $n_1 = 6$ and $U = 20$, the probability is 0.473. Suppose that the test has been performed at significance level $\alpha = 0.05$. The tabulated probability is greater than 0.05, hence we infer that the distribution of scores at two occasions is same.

K-SAMPLE PROBLEM ($K \geq 3$)

The tests given so far are confined to one or two sample cases. But in real life one comes across many problems involving more than two independent samples. The analysis of variance is most commonly used.

But analysis of variance is based on the assumptions that the samples are drawn from normal populations and their variances are same. When these assumptions are not likely to hold good, the F-test cannot be applied. In such a situation nonparametric tests come to our rescue. The nonparametric tests for K-sample problems require no assumption except that the populations are continuous. Three nonparametric tests for three or more sample problems are given here.

Median Test for Three or More Samples

This is an extension of the median test for two sample problems. The test is applied in the same way with little modification. Let k samples of sizes $n_1, n_2, ..., n_k$ be selected independently from k populations $F_1(x), F_2(x), ..., F_k(x)$, respectively. The hypothesis that the k samples have come from identical populations, *i.e.*,

$$H_0 : F_1(x) = F_2(x) = ... = F_k(x)$$

vs. H_1 : at least two of them are not identical.

can be tested by the median test.

All the samples are pooled and the overall median of the combined ordered statistics is found out. Track should be kept as to which observation belongs to which sample in the pooled sequence of observations. Let the median be designated by θ. Suppose $\sum_{i=1}^{k} n_i = N$. Obviously, θ will be the $\left(\frac{N+1}{2}\right)$th observation if N is odd, and an average of the $\frac{N}{2}$th and $\frac{N+2}{2}$th observations when n is even. Again, the observations are dichotomized according as they are less than θ or more than θ. Consider a random variable U_i defined as the number of observations which are less than θ in the i-th sample for $i = 1, 2, ..., k$. Supposing

$$r = \sum_{i=1}^{k} U_i = \begin{bmatrix} N/2 & \text{if } N \text{ is even} \\ \dfrac{N-1}{2} & \text{if } N \text{ is odd.} \end{bmatrix}$$

Under null hypothesis, all the $\binom{N}{r}$ possible sets of observations are equally likely which are in the less than θ category. Therefore, the null probability function of U's is a multivariate hypergeometric distribution given as,

$$f(U_1, U_2, ..., U_k \mid r) = \frac{\binom{n_1}{U_1}\binom{n_2}{U_2}...\binom{n_k}{U_k}}{\binom{N}{r}} \qquad ...(13.27)$$

If one or more U_i differ largely from their expected value, H_0 should be rejected. For an exact test, the best way is to calculate the probabilities for observed and extreme values of $U_1, U_2, ..., U_k$ and cumulate these probabilities. In practice, if the sum of probabilities so obtained is less than the desired significance level α, reject H_0; otherwise H_0 is not rejected.

The calculation of probabilities is a tedious process. Hence an alternative test criterion is used which is sufficiently accurate for N as small as 25 and no individual sample is of size less than 5. Each element in the combined sequence is classified according to two criteria, the sample number to which it belongs and whether it is less than θ. Hence, the test statistic is approximately chi-square. Thus, we find out the observed and expected frequencies as in the k-classification case. Let an observed frequency be denoted by f_{ij} and the expected frequency be e_{ij} for $i = 1, 2, ... k$ and $j = 1, 2$.

$f_{i1} = U_i$, the no. of observations in sample i which are less than θ.

$f_{i2} = n_i - U_i$, the no. of observation in sample i which are not less than θ.

Similarly, the expected frequencies,

$$e_{i1} = \frac{r}{N} n_i$$

and
$$e_{i2} = \frac{N-r}{N} n_i$$

The test statistic for $2k$ categories is,

$$q = \sum_{i=1}^{k} \sum_{j=1}^{2} \frac{(f_{ij} - e_{ij})^2}{e_{ij}} \qquad ...(13.28)$$

Substituting the values of f_{ij} and e_{ij} in terms of U_i, N and r, we obtain

$$q = \frac{N^2}{r(N-r)} \sum_{i=1}^{k} \frac{\left(U_i - \frac{r}{N} n_i\right)^2}{n_i} \qquad ...(13.28.1)$$

q has an approximately chi-square distribution with $(k - 1)$ d.f.

The approximation is improved if q is multiplied by the fraction $(N - 1)/N$.

The test criterion is, reject H_0 if the value of $(N - 1)\, q/N$ is greater than or equal to the tabulated value of χ^2 for $(k - 1)$ d.f. and desired level α. Otherwise, H_0 is not rejected.

In actual problems, if two middle values in the combined sequence are equal to θ, a conservative approach is adopted, *i.e.,* the ties are broken in a way which leads to the maximum value of q.

Kruskal-Wallis Test

This is a nonparametric test for one-way classification just like one-way analysis of variance. The Kruskal-Wallis test is an improvement on the median test. In the median test, the magnitude of the observations was compared with one value only, *i.e.,* the median. But in this method the magnitude of observations is compared with every other observation by considering the ranks.

Again the pooled sequence of k samples of size n_i, $i = 1, 2, ..., k$, in order of increasing magnitudes, will have ranks from 1 to N. The sum of the ranks is equal to $N(N + 1)/2$. Under H_0, the sum of the ranks would be divided in proportion to sample size among k samples. For the *ith* sample of size n_i, the expected sum of ranks is,

$$\frac{n_i}{N}\cdot\frac{N(N+1)}{2} = \frac{n_i(N+1)}{2}$$

Suppose R_i is the actual sum of ranks of the elements in sample i. A reasonable test based on a function of the deviations between the observed and expected rank sums has been given by Kruskal and Wallis. The Kruskal-Wallis test statistic is

$$H = \frac{12}{N(N+1)}\sum_{i=1}^{k}\frac{R_i^2}{n_i} - 3(N+1) \qquad ...(13.29)$$

The statistic H is distributed as chi-square with $(k - 1)$ d.f. Reject H_0 at significance level α if,

$$H \geq \chi^2_{\alpha,k-1}$$

Otherwise H_0 is not rejected.

***Example* 13.8.** The green yield (kg) under four treatments is as tabulated below:

No. of plots	*Treatments*			
	1	2	3	4
1	3.17	3.44	3.15	2.48
2	3.40	2.88	2.69	2.37
3	3.50	2.97	3.10	2.58
4	2.87	3.27	2.80	2.84
5	3.88	3.94	3.45	3.00
6	4.00	3.87		2.48
7	3.60	3.25		

The hypothesis that there is no difference among four treatments can be tested by the median test.

Here $k = 4$, $n_1 = 7$, $n_2 = 7$, $n_3 = 5$, $n_4 = 6$ and $N = 25$. The ordered statistics of the pooled samples is,

(2.37), (2.48), (2.48), (2.58), 2.69, 2.80, (2.84), 2.87, $\overline{2.88}$, $\overline{2.97}$
(3.00), 3.10, 3.15, 3.17, $\overline{3.25}$, $\overline{3.27}$, 3.40, $\overline{3.44}$, 3.45, 3.50, 3.60,
$\overline{3.87}$, 3.88, $\overline{3.94}$, 4.00

$$M_d = 3.15$$

For treatment 1; $U_1 = 1$
For treatment 2; $U_2 = 2$
For treatment 3; $U_3 = 3$
For treatment 4; $U_4 = 6$

$$r = \sum_{i=1}^{4} U_i = 1 + 2 + 3 + 6 = 12$$

To show the method of calculations, the test will be performed at 5 per cent significance level by using (*i*) hypergeometric distribution and (*ii*) chi-square statistic.

(*i*) The probability,

$$f(U_1, U_2, U_3, U_4|r) = \frac{\binom{7}{1}\binom{7}{2}\binom{5}{3}\binom{6}{6}}{\binom{25}{12}}$$

$$= \frac{21}{74290}$$

$$= 0.00028$$

The calculated probability is less than 0.05. Hence, we reject H_0 which means that the treatments differ significantly.

(*ii*) Observed frequencies in the two categories are,

Treatment	*Category 1 (Less than θ)*		*Category II (More than θ)*	
	Observed freq.	*Expected freq.*	*Observed freq.*	*Expected frequency*
1	1	$\frac{12}{25} \times 7 = 3.4$	6	$\frac{13}{25} \times 7 = 3.6$
2	2	$\frac{12}{25} \times 7 = 3.4$	5	$\frac{13}{25} \times 7 = 3.6$
3	3	$\frac{12}{25} \times 5 = 2.4$	1	$\frac{13}{25} \times 5 = 2.6$
4	6	$\frac{12}{25} \times 6 = 2.8$	0	$\frac{13}{25} \times 6 = 3.2$

By formula (13.28)

$$\chi^2 = 11.86$$

By formula (13.28.1)

$$\chi^2 = \frac{25 \times 25}{12 \times 13}\ (0.796 + 0.264 + 0.072 + 1.622)$$

$$= 11.03$$

Tabulated value of $\chi^2_{0.05,3} = 7.815$

Again, the conclusion is the same as in procedure (*i*)

***Example* 13.9.** For the experimental data given in example (13.8), test of H_0 by Kruskal-Wallis test can be carried out as follows.

The sequence of the combined sample in increasing order of magnitude is,

(2.37),	(2.48),	(2.48),	(2.58),	*2.69,*	*2.80,*	(2.84),
1	2.5	2.5	4	5	6	7
2.87,	2.88,	2.97,	(3.00),	*3.10,*	*3.15,*	3.17,
8	9	10	11	12	13	14
3.25,	3.27,	3.40,	3.44,	*3.45,*	3.50,	3.60,
15	16	17	18	19	20	21
3.87,	3.88,	3.94,	4.00			
22	23	24	25			

The sum of ranks for each individual treatment is,

Treat. — 1 ; $R_1 = 8 + 14 + 17 + 20 + 21 + 23 + 25 = 128$

Treat. — 2 ; $R_2 = 9 + 10 + 15 + 16 + 18 + 22 + 24 = 114$

Treat. — 3 ; $R_3 = 5 + 6 + 12 + 13 + 19 = 55$

Treat. — 4 ; $R_4 = 1 + 2.5 + 2.5 + 4 + 7 + 11 = 28$

The Kruskal-Wallis test statistic by formula (13.29) is,

$$H = \frac{12}{25\times 26}\left(\frac{128^2}{7}+\frac{114^2}{7}+\frac{55^2}{5}+\frac{28^2}{6}\right)-3\times 26$$

$$= \frac{12}{25\times 26}\times 4932.81-3\times 26$$

$$= 91.067 - 78$$

$$= 13.067$$

The table value of $\chi^2_{0.05,3} = 7.815$.

The hypothesis of equality of treatments' effect is rejected.

Friedman's Test

This is a nonparametric test for k-related samples of equal size, say n, parallel to two-way analysis of variance. Here we have k-related samples of size n arranged in n blocks and k columns in a two-way table as given below:

Blocks	*Samples (Treatments)*			*Block totals*
	1	2............................	k	
1	R_{11}	R_{12}............................	R_{1k}	$k(k + 1)/2$
2	R_{21}	R_{22}............................	R_{2k}	$k(k + 1)/2$
3	R_{31}	R_{32}............................	R_{3k}	$k(k + 1)/2$
⋮	⋮			⋮
n	R_{n1}	R_{n2}............................	R_{nk}	$k(k + 1)/2$
Col. Total	R_1	R_2............................	R_k	$\frac{nk(k+1)}{2}$

where R_{ij} is the rank of the observation belonging to sample j in block i for $j = 1, 2, ..., k$ and $i = 1, 2, ..., n$. This is the same situation in which there are k treatments and each treatment is replicated n times. Here it should be carefully noted that the observations in a block receive ranks from 1 to k. The smallest observation receives rank 1 at its place and the largest observation receives rank k at its place. Intermediary observations receive ranks accordingly. Hence, the block totals are constant and equal to $\frac{k(k+1)}{2}$, the sum of k integers.

The null hypothesis H_0 to be tested is that all the k samples have come from identical population. In case of experimental design, the null hypothesis H_0 is that there is no difference between k treatments. The alternative hypothesis H_1 is that at least two samples (treatments) differ from each other.

Under H_0, the test statistic is,

$$F = \frac{12}{nk(k+1)}\sum_{j=1}^{k} R_j^2 - 3n(k+1) \qquad ...(13.30)$$

The statistic F is distributed as chi-square with $(k - 1)$ d.f. At level α, reject H_0 if $F \geq \chi^2_{\alpha,k-1}$, otherwise H_0 is not rejected.

***Example* 13.10.** The iron determinations (ppm) in five pea-leaf samples, each under three treatments, were as tabulated below.

Samples no. (Blocks)	*Treatments*			*Block total*
	1	2	3	
1	591 (1)	682 (2)	727 (3)	6
2	818 (2)	591 (1)	863 (3)	6
3	682 (2)	636 (1)	773 (3)	6
4	499 (1)	625 (2)	909 (3)	6
5	648 (1)	863 (3)	818 (2)	6
Col. total	7	9	14	30

The null hypothesis H_0, that the iron content in leaves under three treatments is same against H_1, that at least two of them have different effect, can be tested by Friedman's test. The ranks of observations in each block are shown below each value in parentheses. Friedman's test statistic by formula (13.30) is,

$$F = \frac{12}{5 \times 3 \times 4}(7^2 + 9^2 + 14^2) - 3 \times 5 \times 4$$
$$= 65.2 - 60$$
$$= 5.2.$$

For $\alpha = 0.05$, the table value of $\chi^2_{0.05,2} = 5.99$. Since the calculated F-value is less than 5.99, H_0 is not rejected. This means that there is no difference in the iron content of pea leaves due to the treatments.

Many other tests have appeared in the literature. But they are not commonly used and are beyond the scope of the prescribed curriculum. Hence, they are not included in this chapter.

QUESTIONS AND EXERCISES

1. What is ordered statistics? Describe the role of ordered statistics in nonparametric tests.
2. Write a short essay on the uses of nonparametric tests.
3. Throw light on the implication of ties in the samples. Also describe the ways in which ties can be tackled.
4. Describe three nonparametric tests for two-sample problems. Also discuss their salient features.
5. How is the Wilcoxon-signed rank test superior to ordinary sign-test?

6. Justify the statement that Runs test is good for testing the randomness of a sample.
7. Differentiate between critical region and critical value.
8. Which nonparametric tests are substitutes for the analysis of variance? Describe their methodology.
9. A die was rolled 132 times and the following results were obtained.

No. of spots	1	2	3	4	5	6
Frequency	12	24	38	32	16	10

Use Kolmogorov-Smirnov statistic to test the hypothesis that the die is perfect.

10. Two quality control laboratories independently collected samples of 25 articles from a number of sales depots and tested them. The number of defectives per sales depot were as follows.

Lab A :	9	3	1	3	0	7	2	11
Lab B :	12	6	6	4	8	5	4	

Test the hypothesis that the two laboratories have samples from the same lot by, (*i*) Median test, (*ii*), Mann-Whitney U-test, (*iii*) Wald-Wolfowitz runs test.

11. The following 30 numbers are taken from a two-digited numbers table:

51,	68,	30,	81,	90,	46,	99,	98,	11,	06
19,	43,	95,	82,	65,	85,	65,	81,	00,	50
53,	69,	51,	97,	79,	69,	60,	15,	05,	35

Test the randomness of the numbers by the Runs test on the basis of runs up and runs down.

12. Given the following ten-paired sample observations.

X-sample:	42.7	50.4	44.2	49.7	49.4	55.3	46.1	49.8	48.7	45.9
Y-sample:	54.2	43.7	34.0	46.1	55.4	58.2	53.4	43.6	57.0	61.9

Test the hypotheses that the two samples have come from identical populations by (a) Ordinary sigin test and (b) Wilcoxon signed rank test.

13. On tossing a coin 15 times, the following sequence of heads (H) and tails (T) was obtained.

$$T\,T\,H\,H\,H\,T\,H\,T\,H\,H\,H\,T\,T\,H\,H$$

Test whether the coin is unbiased by the Runs test.

14. School children taking coaching in three english schools secured the following scores out of 100.

No. of children	*Schools*		
	1	2	3
1	33	32	55
2	38	15	68
3	39	87	27
4	48	32	88
5	58	22	46
6	70	63	52
7	61	56	76
8	41	57	
9	45	44	
10	49		

Test the hypothesis that the students studying in the three coaching schools have identical distribution of marks by applying the (*i*) Median test and (*ii*) Kruskal-Wallis test, at significance level $\alpha = 0.1$.

15. The quantity of serum albumin (gms) per 100 ml in lepers under three different drugs and a control group was as follows:

Group No.	*Control*	*Drug I*	*Drug II*	*Drug III*
1	4.30	3.65	3.05	3.90
2	4.00	3.60	4.10	3.10
3	4.10	2.70	4.20	3.20
4	3.80	3.15	3.70	4.20
5	3.30	3.75	3.60	3.00
6	4.50	2.95	4.80	3.40

Apply Friedman's test to confirm whether the content of serum albumin in different groups of persons is same.

SUGGESTED READING

Adrian, Pagan and Aman Ullah (1999). *Nonparametric Econometrics*, Cambridge University Press.

Antony, Stewart (2002). *Basic Statistics and Epidemiology*, Radcliffe Publishing.

Braverman, J.D. (1978). *Fundamentals of Business Statistics,* Academic Press, New York.

Byrkit, D.R. (1979). *Elementary Business Statistics*, D. Van Nostrand Company, New York.

Gibbons, J.D. (1971). *Nonparametric Statistical Inference*, McGraw-Hill Book Company, Kogakusha, Tokyo.

John, Townend (2002). *Practical Statistics for Environmental and Biological Scientists*, John Wiley.

Lieberman, G.J. and Owen, D.B. (1961). *Tables of Hypergeometric Probability Distribution,* Stanford University Press, Stanford, Calif.

Lindgren, B.W. (1976). *Statistical Theory*, Collier Macmillan Publishers, London.

Mills, R.L. (1977). *Statistics for Applied Economics and Business*, McGraw-Hill Book Company, New York.

Siegel, S. (1956). *Nonparametric Statistics for the Behavioral Sciences*, McGraw-Hill Book Company, New York.

Sprent, P. (1993). *Applied Nonparametric Statistical Methods*, 2nd ed., Chapman & Hall, London.

Swed, F. and Eisenhart, C. (1943). *"Tables for Testing Randomness of Grouping in a Sequence of Alternatives"*, *Ann. Math. Stat.* 14, pp. 66–87.

Wilcoxon, F. (1945). *"Probability Tables for Individual Comparisons by Ranking Methods"*, *Biometrics*, 1, pp. 80–83.

Yakov, Nikitin (1995). *Asymptotic Efficiency for Nonparametric Test*, Cambridge University Press.

14
Chapter

Association of Attributes

In any study, the observations on units or individuals are of two types. Firstly, the observation may be about the measurement of certain characters of the units, e.g., height, weight, yield, income, expenditure, volume etc. Secondly, the observations may be for some characters or attributes of the units or respondents which they possess, e.g., the level of education, blindness, liking, environment etc. Moreover, it has been experienced that there are many such factors which are influenced by some other factor(s) or character(s). Often the need to know the relationship or the extent of association between two or more qualitative or quantitative characters arises. In cases where both the factors are such that the measurements are numerical values, statistical methods like correlation, regression etc. are applied to find out the association between the factors. This is further elaborated in Chapter 15.

The method of obtaining association between two qualitative characters, has already been dealt with earlier, while explaining chi-square test. In this chapter we shall consider another statistical tool for measuring the degree of association between two or more attributes. Here, the data pertain to the presence or absence of certain attributes in the units under study. Methods of tabulation for a two-way classification (dichotomy) or manifold classification, have been given in Chapter 2 and are not repeated here. Before going into the details, it is necessary to know the notations used in the discussions to follow.

NOTATIONS

Introductory discussion clearly reveals that the data (information) are classified according to the attributes. Hence the *order of a class* is defined as the number of attributes involved in the classification. If there is only one attribute under consideration, it is called the class of first order, e.g., *A*, *a* or *B*, *b*, etc., and in the case of two attributes, it is called the class of second order, e.g., *Ab*, *AB*, etc., and the classes with three attributes are known as the classes of the third order, e.g., *ABC*, *AbC*, *Abc*, *abc*, etc. In general, if k attributes are involved in the constitution of the classes, they are called the classes of k-th order.

The presence of an attribute, say *A*, in a unit under observation is denoted by the capital letter *A* and is termed *positive attribute*. At the same time the absence of an attribute *A* is denoted by the small letter *a* and is termed as *negative attribute*. The same pattern is followed for other attributes, say, *B*, *C*, etc. The presence of the two attributes i.e. *A* and *B*, is denoted by AB and their absence by ab. In case of the presence of A and absence of B, it is denoted by Ab and the absence of A and presence of B is denoted by aB. The classes which possess qualities of some attributes and do not have qualities of other attribute(s) are called *contrary classes*. In the case of the three attributes A, B and C, the combinations for the presence and absence of one, two and three attributes can be given in a similar manner. The number of units possessing or not possessing attributes are called the *frequency* of an attribute or of the combination of attributes. These frequencies are symbolically denoted by writing the attribute or the combination of attributes in parentheses. For example, the number of units possessing the attribute A is denoted by (A) and similarly the frequency (Ab) denotes the number of units which possess the attribute A but not B. This denotation system can be extended to any number of attributes.

The total number of units N under study which is always equal to the sum of all the class frequencies is called the *frequency of the zero order*. The reason is that no attribute is attached to this frequency. These ideas can be summarized in a tabular form, in the manner given below. Here we present three tables taking two and three attributes respectively and the total number of objects or units equal to N.

Table 14.1: For two attributes *A* and *B*

	A	a	*Total*
B	(AB)	(aB)	(B)
b	(Ab)	(ab)	(b)
Total	(A)	(a)	N

The above table is similar to a contingency table and hence certain relations are obvious.

$$\left.\begin{aligned} &(A)=(AB)+(Ab);(B)=(AB)+(aB)\\ &(a)=(aB)+(ab);(b)=(Ab)+(ab)\\ &(AB)+(aB)+(Ab)+(ab)=N\\ &(A)+(a)=(B)+(b)=N \end{aligned}\right] \qquad ...(14.1)$$

All above relations are helpful in finding out any one of the missing class (cell) frequency.

Table 14.2: For three attributes *A*, *B* and *C*

	A		a		
	B	b	B	b	*Total*
C	(ABC)	(AbC)	(aBC)	(abC)	(C)
c	(ABc)	(Abc)	(aBc)	(abc)	(c)
Total	(AB)	(Ab)	(aB)	(ab)	N

The totals and subtotals of all frequencies given in Table 14.2 are depicted through Table 14.3.

Table 14.3: Expanded table showing totals and sub-totals

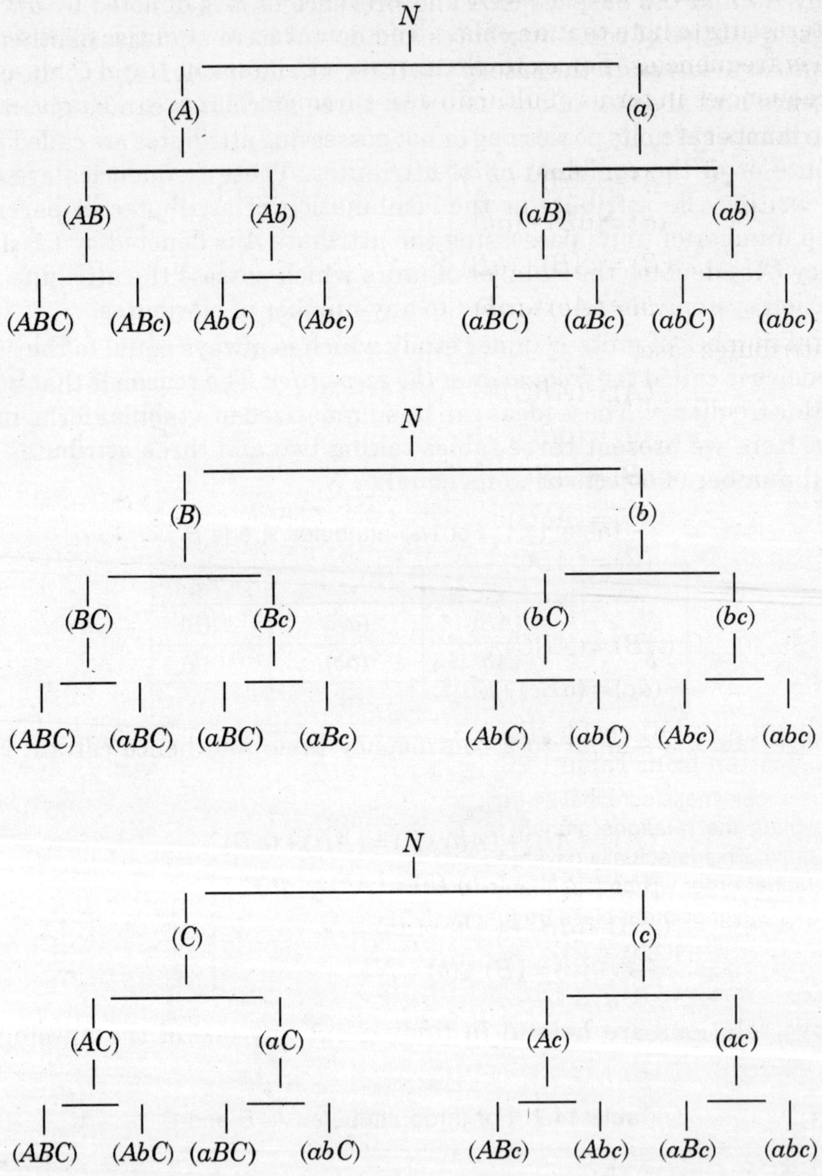

CLASS FREQUENCIES

The number of subjects attached to any class is termed its class frequency. For example, (*A*), (*B*), (*a*), (*b*), (*AB*), (*Ab*), (*aB*), (*ab*), (*ABC*), (*Abc*), (*abc*), etc.

Ultimate Class Frequency

In the classification of units of a population, according to certain attributes, the classes of the highest order are called the *ultimate classes*. The frequency of any ultimate class is called its *ultimate class frequency*. For example, the ultimate class frequencies of order two are (AB), (aB), (Ab), (ab) and the ultimate frequencies of order three are (ABC), (aBC), (aBc), (ABc), (abC), (Abc), (AbC), (abc).

It is interesting to note that any class frequency can always be expressed in terms of ultimate class frequencies. For example, in case of classes of the second and the third order, the frequencies in terms of ultimate class frequencies can be expressed as follows:

Two attributes case,

$$\left.\begin{aligned}(A) &= (AB) + (Ab)\\(a) &= (aB) + (ab)\\(B) &= (AB) + (aB)\\(b) &= (Ab) + (ab)\end{aligned}\right] \qquad \ldots(14.2)$$

Three attributes case:

$$\left.\begin{aligned}(A) &= (ABC) + (AbC) + (ABc) + (Abc)\\(a) &= (aBC) + (abC) + (aBc) + (abc)\\(B) &= (ABC) + (ABc) + (aBC) + (aBc)\\(b) &= (AbC) + (Abc) + (abC) + (abc)\\(C) &= (ABC) + (AbC) + (aBC) + (abC)\\(c) &= (ABc) + (Abc) + (aBc) + (abc)\\(AB) &= (ABC) + (ABc)\\(ac) &= (aBc) + (abc)\end{aligned}\right] \qquad \ldots(14.3)$$

Similarly other relations for class frequencies, in terms of ultimate class frequencies can easily be written from Table 14.3.

Note: One should make sure that no frequency is negative. If it occurs, it is sure that an error has been committed in writing the relations among cell frequencies. Such a mistake can easily be rectified by examining the table. This is actually covered under *consistency of data*. It should be noted that any class frequency of a higher order will be less than or equal to the class frequency of lower order involving some of the attributes of a higher order class frequency. For example,

$$\begin{aligned}&(AB) \le (A);\ (AB) \le (B)\\&(ABC) \le (AB);\ (ABC) \le (AC);\ (ABC) \le (BC)\\&(AB) + (AC) - (BC) \le A\\&(AB) + (BC) - (AC) \le B\\&(AC) + (BC) - (AB) \le C\end{aligned} \qquad \ldots(14.4)$$

INCONSISTENCY OF DATA

When the data pertaining to two attributes are collected, the data will be *inconsistent* if any of the following inequality holds.

$$\left.\begin{aligned}&(i)\ (AB) < 0 \Rightarrow (AB) \text{ will be} - \text{ve.}\\&(ii)\ (AB) > (A) \Rightarrow (Ab) \text{ will be} - \text{ve.}\\&(iii)\ (AB) > (B) \Rightarrow (aB) \text{ will be} - \text{ve.}\\&(iv)\ (AB) > (A) + (B) - N \Rightarrow (ab) \text{ will be} - \text{ve.}\end{aligned}\right] \qquad \ldots(14.5)$$

When three attributes are under consideration, the data will be *inconsistent* if any of the following inequalities hold good.

$$\left.\begin{array}{l}(i)\ (ABC) < 0 \Rightarrow (ABC) \text{ will be} - \text{ve.}\\(ii)\ (ABC) < (AB) + (AC) - (A) \Rightarrow (Abc) \text{ will be} - \text{ve.}\\(iii)\ (ABC) < (AB) + (BC) - (B) \Rightarrow (aBc) \text{ will be} - \text{ve.}\\(iv)\ (ABC) < (AC) + (BC) - (C) \Rightarrow (abC) \text{ will be} - \text{ve.}\\(v)\ (ABC) > (AB) \Rightarrow (ABc) \text{ will be} - \text{ve.}\\(vi)\ (ABC) > (AC) \Rightarrow (AbC) \text{ will be} - \text{ve.}\\(vii)\ (ABC) > (BC) \Rightarrow (aBC) \text{ will be} - \text{ve.}\\(viii)\ (ABC) > (AB) + (AC) + (BC) - (A) - (B) - (C)\\\qquad + N \Rightarrow abc \text{ will be} - \text{ve.}\end{array}\right] \quad \ldots(14.6)$$

Inconsistency of data always leads to the conclusion that the information given for studying the phenomenal relationship is incorrect, and the data are unsuitable for further treatment. Hence it should either be corrected, if possible, or rejected.

CONSISTENCY OF DATA

The data are said to be consistent if any of the ultimate frequency, associated with the same population, is not negative. It means that the frequencies are in conformity with each other and do not conflict in any way. For the test of consistency of data, the sign of the inequalities given under inconsistency of data should be reversed, and word negative be changed to positive. For instance if $(A) = 40$, $(AB) = 42$, (A) and (AB) are inconsistent, since there cannot be more than 40 units which possess the attributes of A as well as of B. On the basis of these considerations it can be stated that "*The necessary and sufficient condition for consistency of a set of independent class frequencies is that no class frequency must be negative.*"

Example **14.1.** Consider the following data for two attributes A and B and test its consistency.

$$(A) = 80,\ (b) = 280,\ (AB) = 50,\ N = 400$$

To test the consistency, prepare the following table using the relations between class frequencies and ultimate class frequencies.

	A	a	*Total*
B	(AB) 50	(aB) 70	(B) 120
b	(Ab) 30	(ab) 250	(b) 280
Total	(A) 80	(a) 320	N 400

The relations are:

$$(B) = N - (b) = 400 - 280 = 120$$
$$(aB) = (B) - (AB) = 120 - 50 = 70$$
$$(a) = N - (A) = 400 - 80 = 320$$
$$(ab) = a - (aB) = 320 - 70 = 250$$
$$(Ab) = (A) - (AB) = 80 - 50 = 30$$

Since all the ultimate class frequencies are positive, the data are consistent.

***Example* 14.2.** Consider the following data for two attributes A and B and test its consistency.

$$N = 400, (A) = 80, (B) = 120, (AB) = 130, (ab) = 330$$

As in example (14.1), we prepare the following table.

	A	*a*	*Total*
B	(*AB*) 130	(*aB*) – 10	(*B*) 120
b	(*Ab*) – 50	(*ab*) 330	(*b*) 280
Total	(*A*) 80	(*a*) 320	*N* 400

In the above table, we note that the ultimate frequencies (Ab) and (aB) are negative. Hence the given data are inconsistent.

***Example* 14.3.** The following information was supplied by an investigator about three attributes A, B and C.

$$N = 1{,}000;\ (A) = 300;\ (B) = 180,\ (C) = 100$$
$$(AB) = 180;\ (AC) = 240;\ (BC) = 120 \text{ and } (ABC) = 400$$

The consistency of data, supplied by the investigator, can be tested by the relation

$$(ABC) > (AB) + (AC) + (BC) - (A) - (B) - (C) + N$$

Substituting the frequencies we obtain,

$$(ABC) > 180 + 240 + 120 - 300 - 180 - 100 + 1000 > 960$$

Since it is given that $(ABC) = 400$ which is less than 960, the inequality does not hold. This leads to the conclusion that the data are inconsistent.

KINDS OF ASSOCIATION OF ATTRIBUTES

Two attributes A and B may be (*i*) positively associated, (*ii*) negatively associated or (*iii*) independent.

(*i*) Two attributes A and B are said to the *positively associated* if the presence of one attribute 'A' is accompanied by the presence of the other attribute 'B'. For instance, health and food quality are positively associated attributes.

(*ii*) When the presence of an attribute A ensures the absence of the other attribute B or vice versa, the attributes A and B are said to be *negatively associated.*

(*iii*) Two attributes A and B are called *independent* in case the presence or absence of one attribute has no relationship with the presence or absence of the other attribute. If A and B are independent it is expected that proportion of B's in A's is the same as that of a's in B and vice versa. Mathematically it can be expressed as,

$$\frac{(AB)}{(A)} = \frac{(aB)}{(a)}$$

$$1 - \frac{(AB)}{(A)} = 1 - \frac{(aB)}{(a)}$$

$$\frac{(A)-(AB)}{(A)} = \frac{(a)-(aB)}{(a)}$$

With the help of Table 14.1, we get

$$\frac{(Ab)}{A} = \frac{(ab)}{a} \qquad \text{...(14.7)}$$

Similarly for proportion of A's in B's under the assumption of independence, the following relations hold.

$$\frac{(aB)}{(B)} = \frac{(ab)}{(b)} \qquad \text{...(14.8)}$$

and

$$\frac{(AB)}{(B)} = \frac{(Ab)}{(b)} \qquad \text{...(14.9)}$$

$$\frac{(AB)}{(aB)} = \frac{(Ab)}{(ab)} \qquad \text{...(14.9.1)}$$

or

$$\frac{(AB)}{(B)} = \frac{(AB)+(Ab)}{(B)+(b)} = \frac{(A)}{N}$$

or

$$(AB) = \frac{(A)(B)}{N} \qquad \text{...(14.10)}$$

$$\frac{(AB)}{N} = \frac{(A)}{N}\frac{(B)}{N} \qquad \text{...(14.10.1)}$$

Relation (14.10) leads to the rule that if two attributes A and B are independent, the frequency of AB in the population under consideration is equal to the product of frequencies of A and B divided by the total of frequencies.

In other words, relation (14.10.1) leads to the rule that the proportion of AB's in the population is equal to the product of proportions of A's and B's in the population under consideration. This is a sort of relationship parallel to the formula for expected frequency of a cell in a (2 × 2) contingency table given for chi-square test under the assumption of independence.

COEFFICIENT OF ASSOCIATION

The extent of association between two or more attributes may be measured mathematically. The measure is known as *coefficient of association.* The sign of the coefficient depends on whether the attributes are positively or negatively associated. The positive value shows positive association and negative value shows negative association. Some commonly used coefficients of association are given here.

Yule's Coefficient of Association

This coefficient was invented by G.V. Yule and is named after him. For two attributes A and B using table (14.1), the coefficient of association is given as,

$$Q = \frac{(AB)(ab)-(Ab)(aB)}{(AB)(ab)+(Ab)(aB)} \qquad ...(14.11)$$

Value of Q lies between −1 and +1.

(i) If $Q = 1$, A and B possess a perfect positive association. It is trivial to verify that under complete positive association, the following relationships hold good.

$$(AB) = (A) \Rightarrow (Ab) = 0$$
$$(AB) = (B) \Rightarrow (aB) = 0$$

(ii) If $Q = -1$, A and B possess perfect negative association.

(iii) If $Q = 0$, A and B are independent.

(iv) Any other value in between −1 and +1 tells the extent of association between two attributes. If $Q > 0.5$, the association between two attributes is considered to be of high order and a value of Q less than 0.5 shows a low degree of association between the attributes.

Coefficient of Colligation

It is another type of measure of association given by Professor Yule and is denoted by Y where Y is determined by the formula,

$$Y = \frac{1-\sqrt{\dfrac{(Ab)(aB)}{(AB)(ab)}}}{1+\sqrt{\dfrac{(Ab)(aB)}{(AB)(ab)}}} \qquad ...(14.12)$$

Coefficient of colligation Y has the same properties as Q i.e. Y also lies between −1 and 1. To show this, we will first establish the relationship between Q and Y.

Suppose $\dfrac{(Ab)(aB)}{(AB)(ab)} = \theta$

From (14.12), we obtain

$$Y = \frac{1-\sqrt{\theta}}{1+\sqrt{\theta}}$$

$$Y^2 = \frac{1+\theta-2\sqrt{\theta}}{1+\theta+2\sqrt{\theta}}$$

$$1+Y^2 = \frac{2(1+\theta)}{(1+\sqrt{\theta})^2}$$

$$\frac{Y}{1+Y^2} = \frac{1-\sqrt{\theta}}{1+\sqrt{\theta}} \times \frac{(1+\sqrt{\theta})^2}{2(1+\theta)}$$

$$\frac{2Y}{1+Y^2} = \frac{1-\theta}{1+\theta}$$

Substituting the expression for θ, we get

$$\frac{2Y}{1+Y^2} = \frac{1-\dfrac{(Ab)(aB)}{(AB)(ab)}}{1+\dfrac{(Ab)(aB)}{(AB)(ab)}}$$

$$= \frac{(AB)(ab)-(Ab)(aB)}{(AB)(ab)+(Ab)(aB)}$$

$$= Q \qquad \text{...(14.13)}$$

Now we find the range of Y.

If $Q = 1, \dfrac{2Y}{1+Y^2} = 1$

$$Y^2 - 2Y + 1 = 0$$
$$(Y-1)^2 = 0$$
$$Y = 1$$

If $Q = -1, \dfrac{2Y}{1+Y^2} = -1$

$$Y^2 + 2Y + 1 = 0$$
$$(Y+1)^2 = 0$$
$$Y = -1$$

If $Q = 0, \dfrac{2Y}{1+Y^2} = 0$

$$2Y = 0$$

Since $2 \neq 0, Y = 0$

From the relationship (14.13) between Q and Y it can easily be inferred that we get the same value of Y as is obtained for Q. Thus, the two coefficients hold the same properties. Since it is comparatively easier to work out Q than Y, Q is commonly worked out.

Example **14.4.** The following table gives the effect of measles immunizing vaccination on 12 month care and cohort infants.

Immunization effect

	Suffered from measles A	*Did not suffer from measles* a	
Vaccinated B	(AB) 6	(aB) 56	(B) 62
Not-vaccinated b	(Ab) 84	(ab) 18	(b) 102
Total	(A) 90	(a) 74	N 164

The coefficient of association between vaccination and immunization can be computed by the formula,

$$Q = \frac{(AB)(ab)-(Ab)(aB)}{(AB)(ab)+(Ab)(aB)}$$

$$= \frac{6\times18-84\times56}{6\times18+84\times56}$$

$$= -\frac{4596}{4812}$$

$$= -0.96$$

There is a high degree of negative association between immunization and suffering from measles. It means, the vaccination has an immunization effect.

***Example* 14.5.** A survey study of 366 students about the performance of matured and fresh certificate holder students admitted in first year of the Arts faculty yielded the following information.

Let A denotes the maturedness and B the good performance, and a denotes the fresh students and b the poor performance.

On the basis of the given information, the extent of association between maturedness and performance is obtained by (*i*) Yule's coefficient and (*ii*) Coefficient of colligation.

The information in hand is,

$$N = 366,\ (A) = 192,\ (B) = 172 \text{ and } (ab) = 100$$

The other cell frequencies of a (2 × 2) table of attributes can be obtained by the relations (14.1),

$(A) + (a) = N;$ $\quad$ $(B) + (b) = N$

$192 + (a) = 366;$ $\quad$ $172 + (b) = 366$

$(a) = 174$ $\quad$ $(b) = 194$

$(a) = (aB) + (ab)$ $\quad$ $(b) = (Ab) + (ab)$

$174 = (aB) + 100$ $\quad$ $194 = (Ab) + 100$

$(aB) = 74$ $\quad$ $(Ab) = 94$

and $\quad (A) = (AB) + (Ab)$

$192 = (AB) + 94$

$(AB) = 98$

Thus, a two-way table of attributes is

Performance

	Good A	*Poor* a	*Total*
Matured students *B*	(*AB*) 98	(*aB*) 74	(*B*) 172
Fresh students *b*	(*Ab*) 94	(*ab*) 100	(*b*) 194
Total	(*A*) 192	(*a*) 174	*N* 366

(*i*) Yule's coefficient of association,

$$Q = \frac{(AB)(ab)-(Ab)(aB)}{(AB)(ab)+(Ab)(aB)}$$

$$= \frac{98\times100-94\times74}{98\times100+94\times74}$$

$$= \frac{2844}{16756}$$

$$= 0.17$$

There is a positive association between maturedness and performance but of a very low degree. It means that maturedness has little to do with the performance.

(*ii*) Coefficient of colligation can be calculated by the formula,

$$Y = \frac{1-\sqrt{(Ab)(aB)/(AB)(ab)}}{1+\sqrt{(Ab)(aB)/(AB)(ab)}}$$

Substituting the value of cell frequencies we get,

$$Y = \frac{1-\sqrt{94\times74/98\times100}}{1+\sqrt{94\times74/98\times100}}$$

$$= \frac{1-\sqrt{0.7098}}{1+\sqrt{0.7098}}$$

$$= \frac{1-0.84}{1+0.84}$$

$$= \frac{0.16}{1.84}$$

$$= 0.087$$

The value of Y can be checked by the relation (14.13),

$$\frac{2Y}{1+Y^2} = \frac{2\times0.087}{1+(0.087)^2}$$

$$= \frac{0.174}{1.008}$$

$$= 0.17 = Q$$

The interpretation for association with Y remains the same as given with Q value.

Example **14.6**. The data, in a survey on the preference to study medicine and agriculture in the university by the students of biology and agriculture at the school level was found to be as given below:

We denote the attributes as follows:

(*A*) — Biology students at school level
(*a*) — Agriculture students at school level
(*B*) — Preference to medicine
(*b*) — Preference to agriculture

Thus, the two-way table based on the survey data is,

	B	*b*	*Total*
A	(*AB*) 52	(*Ab*) 23	(*A*) 75
a	(*aB*) 1	(*ab*) 15	(*a*) 16
Total	(*B*) 53	(*b*) 38	*N* 91

The association between the field of study at school level and preference to study medicine and agriculture in the university can be computed as,

$$Q = \frac{(AB)(ab) - (Ab)(aB)}{(AB)(ab) + (Ab)(aB)}$$

$$= \frac{52 \times 15 - 23 \times 1}{52 \times 15 + 23 \times 1}$$

$$= \frac{757}{803}$$

$$= 0.94$$

The value of Q is 0.94 which is near to 1. Hence it can be concluded that there is a strong positive association between the field of study at the school level and choice of a particular subject of study at the university level.

PARTIAL ASSOCIATION

Generally we consider association between two attributes, say, A and B. If it exists, it is inferred that there is a cause and effect relationship between A and B. But it may not always be true. The reason is that in many situations, the relationship between A and B may be existing due to a third attribute C. Hence, it becomes logical to find out the association between A and B in view of C. Attributes A and B would be associated if and only if they are associated in the sub-populations C and c.

Definition

The association between two attributes A and B in the sub-populations C and c is called the *partial association* between A and B and is denoted as $Q_{AB \cdot C}$ or $Q_{AB \cdot c}$.

Similarly we can define the partial associations $Q_{AC \cdot B}$ or $Q_{AC.b}$ and $Q_{BC .A}$ or $Q_{BC . a}$.

The need for considering partial association can easily be justified through these instances. If we consider two factors viz. educational level of fathers and intelligence of sons, it is expected that sons of educated fathers will generally be more intelligent than the sons of uneducated fathers. It means that the educational level of fathers and intelligence of their sons are associated. But this association cannot be taken for granted, because the intelligence of sons may be due to the extra coaching and facilities provided by the fathers. Hence, the association between fathers' educational level and intelligence of sons can be worked out in two groups of persons viz., where guidance and extra facilities are provided and where guidance and extra facilities are not provided. In this way the effect of the third factor, guidance and extra facilities, can be neutralised.

As a second example, consider the effect of vaccination to prevent tuberculosis (T.B.). If a survey is conducted in a posh colony and concluded that vaccination prevents T.B., it is not convincing, because the people living in posh colonies have highly hygienic conditions and take good diet, whereas people living in slums or congested area have no hygienic conditions and take poor diet. Thus, these people (in slums) have more chances of T.B. infection. Therefore, to know the real association between vaccination and prevention of T.B., the association should be determined separately for both types of localities. The results so obtained will give the true picture of the association between vaccination and prevention of T.B. In such situations the role of a third factor cannot be ignored and hence partial association is a more realistic approach.

Formulae for partial association between two attributes A and B in the subpopulations with attributes C and c are,

$$Q_{AB.C} = \frac{(ABC)(abC)-(AbC)(aBC)}{(ABC)(abC)+(AbC)(aBC)} \quad ...(14.14)$$

and

$$Q_{AB.c} = \frac{(ABc)(abc)-(Abc)(aBc)}{(ABc)(abc)+(Abc)(aBc)} \quad ...(14.15)$$

Formulae for $Q_{AC.B}$, $Q_{AC.b}$ and $Q_{BC.a}$ can easily be written by interchanging the letters in (14.14) and (14.15).

The idea about the sign of coefficient of association Q can be had, with the help of the following inequalities.

Two attributes A and B in the sub-population C will be positively associated if,

$$(ABC) > \frac{(AC)(BC)}{(C)} \quad ...(14.16)$$

and will be negatively associated, if the inequality (14.16) is reversed.

Similarly in the sub-population c, two attributes A and B will be positively associated if,

$$(ABc) > \frac{(Ac)(Bc)}{(c)} \quad ...(14.17)$$

and will be negatively associated if the inequality (14.17) is reversed.

***Example* 14.7.** A survey study was conducted in an urban area and in a suburban area to know the liking of 50 males and 50 females, in the technical programmes and humorous programmes on television (TV). The number of persons belonging to different combinations of attributes are presented in the following table. Suppose the attributes are denoted as:

Males — A;
Females — a;
Technical programme — B;
Humorous programme — b;
Urban population — C;
Suburban population — c.

Urban population — C				Suburban population — c			
	Tech. program B	Hum. program b			Tech. program B	Hum. program b	
Males A	(AB) 30	(Ab) 20	(A) 50	Males A	(AB) 25	(Ab) 25	(A) 50
Females a	(aB) 5	(ab) 45	(a) 50	Females a	(aB) 15	(ab) 35	(a) 50
	(B) 35	(b) 65	N 100		(B) 40	(b) 60	N 100

It is thought that the place of residence affects the likes and dislikes of a person. Hence the association between sex and the liking of two types of performances has been computed in the two populations separately. The coefficient of association between sex and the liking in urban population C is computed by formula (14.14).

$$Q = \frac{(ABC)(abC)-(AbC)(aBC)}{(ABC)(abC)+(AbC)(aBC)}$$

$$= \frac{30\times45-20\times5}{30\times45+20\times5}$$

$$= \frac{1250}{1450}$$

$$= 0.86$$

Similarly the coefficient of association between A and B in the suburban population c is obtained by formula (14.15) i.e.,

$$Q = \frac{(ABc)(abc)-(Abc)(aBc)}{(ABc)(abc)+(Abc)(aBc)}$$

$$= \frac{25\times35-25\times15}{25\times35+25\times15}$$

$$= \frac{500}{1250}$$

$$= 0.40$$

In urban population there is a high positive value of coefficient of association, hence it is inferred that sex and liking to the two types of programmes are strongly associated in urban areas. But the coefficient of association in suburban area is of low degree. Hence the place of residence affects the opinion and thus there is an association between sex and liking for the type of programmes.

ILLUSORY ASSOCIATION

It has been pointed out under the discussion of partial association, that in many situations, the association existing between two attributes is due to the influence of the third attribute (factor), rather than the real association. Hence the association between two attributes ignoring the influence of a third factor, if it is there, is known as *illusory association*. Besides this, illusory association can occur due to many other factors or causes as well.

Some commonly known causes are enucleated here.

1. When we calculate the association between two attributes ignoring the third factor which is very likely to influence it, we get illusory association.
2. Illusory association arises due to the biased attitude of the investigator. Sometimes the investigator is more liberal in recording the presence of an attribute rather than its absence.
3. When the attributes are not distinct, the investigator will be confused and will mis-classify the individuals in a specified class. Thus, the results based on such data will lead to illusory association.
4. In case, the study is based on sampling, illusory association will occur if a proper sample is not selected from the population.

Association of attributes is used by some economists and social scientists. But it is loosing ground day by day as the chi-square statistic gives better measure of dependence between qualitative factors (attributes). The chi-square test is very robust in nature and hence the use of coefficient of association has been very limited. Moreover, in sampling studies, no test statistic has been provided to test the significance of Yule's coefficient of association. Hence, the association found in the sample cannot be ascertained to have occurred in the population even with a certain amount of risk. At the end, the readers are advised to understand it as a part of statistical theory and use it wherever it appears appropriate.

QUESTIONS AND EXERCISES

1. State the purpose of the association of attributes. Also express the suitability of this type of study.
2. Explain what do you understand by the inconsistency of data? Illustrate with examples.
3. Discuss the following terms:
   (*a*) Ultimate class frequency.
   (*b*) Independence of attributes.
   (*c*) Yule's coefficient of association.
   (*d*) Order of a class.
   (*e*) Partial association.
4. Write whether the following statements are true or false and why?
   (*a*) The value of Yule's coefficient of association Q lies between 0 and 1.
   (*b*) The value of coefficient of colligation Y and coefficient of association Q are equal.
   (*c*) Ultimate class frequency is not greater than the lower order class frequency.
   (*d*) Any lower order class frequency can be obtained from the ultimate class frequencies.
   (*e*) If the attributes are independent, the value of Q is zero.
5. The following table gives the number of people according to their ranks who have given time to public activities.

Time	*Rank*	
	Highup	*Lower cadre*
A good deal	25	9
None	12	13

Find the coefficient of association between the time given and rank.

6. A study of 1000 units was classified according to three attributes A, B and C. The letters a, b and c denote the absence of A, B and C, respectively. Given the following ultimate class frequencies,

$$(ABC) = 280,\ (ABc) = 220,\ (AbC) = 30,\ (Abc) = 70,$$
$$(aBC) = 140,\ (aBc) = 60,\ (abC) = 110 \text{ and } (abc) = 90$$

Test the consistency of data.

7. Given,
$N = 820$, $(A) = 250$, $(aB) = 50$ and $(AB) = 35$.
Test the consistency of data.

8. Given the following cell frequencies,
$(ABC) = 60$, $(AB) = 80$, $(BC) = 32$, $(B) = 38$.
Comment whether the data are consistent.

9. According to a survey, the following results were obtained:

	Boys	*Girls*
Number of candidates who appeared at an examination	800	200
Married	150	50
Married and successful	70	20
Unmarried and successful	550	110

Find the association between marital status and the success in the examination both for boys and girls. *(M.A. Econ., Jabalpur, 1975)*

10. The following information relates to literacy and unemployment in 500 persons. Find out Yule's coefficient of association and its implications:

Illiterate unemployed	220
Literate employed	20
Illiterate employed	180

(M. Com., Vikram, 1972)

11. 1660 candidates appeared for a competitive examination, 442 were successful, 256 had attended a coaching class and of these 150 came out successful. Estimate the utility of the coaching class. *(M. Com., Meerut, 1973, M.A., Jiwaji, 1971)*

12. Find out the association between darkness of eye-colour in father and son from the following data:
Fathers with dark eyes and sons with dark eyes = 50
Fathers with no dark eyes and sons with dark eyes = 89
Fathers with dark eyes and sons with no dark eyes = 79
Fathers with no dark eyes and sons with no dark eyes = 782
What would have been the frequency of fathers with dark eyes and sons with dark eyes, for the same total number, has there been complete independence.
(M.A., Punjab, 1973)

13. In two towns A and B, the following information was supplied by an investigator. Total population (thousands)–Town A (240), Town B (234), Literates (thousands)–Town A (40), Town B (34), Illiterate criminals (thousands)–Town A (40) and Town B (20) and literate criminals (thousands)–Town A (5) and Town B (2). Compare the degree of association between literacy and crime in each of the two towns.
(B.A., Hons., Delhi, 1973)

14. The total population of a city was 12,000. The total males were 5000, out of which 4000 were unmarried. The number of married females was 8000. Do you find any inconsistency in the figures. *(M.Com, Agra, 1973)*
15. A universe consists of three attributes, each of which is divisible into two parts. What are the different class frequencies obtainable?

    A market investigator returns the following—Of 1000 people consulted, 811 liked chocolates, 752 liked toffee and 418 liked boiled sweets, 570 liked chocolates and toffee, 356 liked chocolates and boiled sweets and 348 liked toffee and boiled sweets and 297 liked all three. Show that this information as it stands must be incorrect.

    (M.A., Delhi, 1960, M.Sc., Agra, 1956)
16.
    (*a*) What do you understand by association of attributes and coefficient of association?

    (*b*) 300 people of German and French nationalities were interviewed for finding their preference for music of their own language. The following facts were gathered: Out of 100 German nationals, 60 liked music of their own language, whereas 70 French nationals out of 200 liked German music. Out of 100 French nationals, 55 liked music of their own language and 35 German nationals out of 200 Germans liked French music. Using coefficient of association, state whether Germans prefer their own music in comparison with Frenchmen. *(C.A., May, 1982)*
17. In a sample of 500 children, 200 came from higher income group and the rest from lower income group. The number of delinquent children in these groups respectively was 25 and 100.

    Calculate the coefficient of association between delinquency and income group.

    (C.A., May, 1981)

SUGGESTED READING

Goodman, L.A., and W.H. Kruskal (1979). *Measures of Association for Cross Classification*, Springer-Verlag, Berlin.

Hand, D.J. (EDT) (1993). *Artificial Intelligence Frontiers in Statistics*, CRC Press.

Herbert, Avon David (2001). *Annotated Readings in the History of Statistics*, Springer.

Parker, R.E. (1991). *Introductory Statistics for Biology*, Cambridge University Press.

Peter, Spirtes, Clark N.G. Lymour and Richard Scheines (2000). *Causation, Prediction and Search*, MIT Press.

15
Chapter

Regression and Correlation

In the previous chapter, we have considered the association between attributes. It has been a measure of dependence between two or more variates of qualitative nature or those which indicate categories. In this chapter, we shall deal with the dependence of factors or variables which take only numerical values. Very often, the interest lies in establishing the actual relationship between two or more variables. This problem is dealt with regression. On the other hand, we are often not interested to know the actual relationship but are only interested in knowing the degree of relationship between two or more variables. This problem is dealt with correlation analysis. For both the studies, the number of variables may be two or more. But keeping in view the course for which the book is meant, we shall discuss in detail only the bivariate data. First regression shall be discussed and then correlation in this chapter.

The concept of regression was first given by Sir Francis Galton (1822–1911) in the study of inheritance of stature in human being. To prove this biometrical fact, Karl Pearson found thc regression of son's height on father's height. But soon the use of regression technique became too common for a variety of problems. The relationship between variables, if it exists, may be linear or curvilinear. In this chapter a detailed discussion of linear regression and a brief discussion of curvilinear regression have been given.

Linear relationship between two variables is represented by a straight line which is known as a *regression line. The line of average relationship* is another name for a regression line. In the study of linear relationship between two variables Y and X, suppose the variable Y is such that it depends on X, then we call it the regression line of Y on X. If X depends on Y, it is called the regression of X on Y. To find out the regression line, the observations (x_i, y_i) on the variables X and Y are necessarily taken in pairs, on the units which may be people, animals, plots, spare parts, plants or any other thing. For example, if the height of Johar is measured, only the weight of Johar has to be taken to form a pair for establishing the relationship between height and weight. It should not be such that we form a pair of Johar's height and Madan's weight. If a pair is formed of a father's height and eldest son's height at a particular age, in all cases this has to be maintained and not a combination of different sons with the father should form a pair of observations. Generally the studies are based on samples of size n, and hence n pairs of sample observations can be written as (x_1, y_1), (x_2, y_2), ..., (x_n, y_n). Before entering into the method of estimation or fitting of regression line, it will be appropriate to explain first the scatter diagram.

SCATTER DIAGRAM

When a regression equation is to be specified, n paired observations are plotted on the graph paper, setting the vertical scale for the dependent variable Y and horizontal scale for the independent variable X. From the plotted points, it can easily be visualized, whether or not the plotted points lie in a straight line or appear to lie on a curve of a known type. As a matter of fact, scatter diagram may be considered as a basis of deciding the type of regression equation, suited for the relationship, between the two variables, Y and X. In case, the plotted points are scattered in a haphazard manner, *i.e.*, no pattern is observed, then it can be inferred that the variables are not related. Now we discuss the scatter diagram with special reference to the regression line. In practice, when we plot various paired observations, one would hardly come across a situation in which all the points are lying exactly in a line. But if a line is drawn suitably, some points will be lying on the line and others will be lying in the close vicinity of this line as depicted in Fig. 15.1.

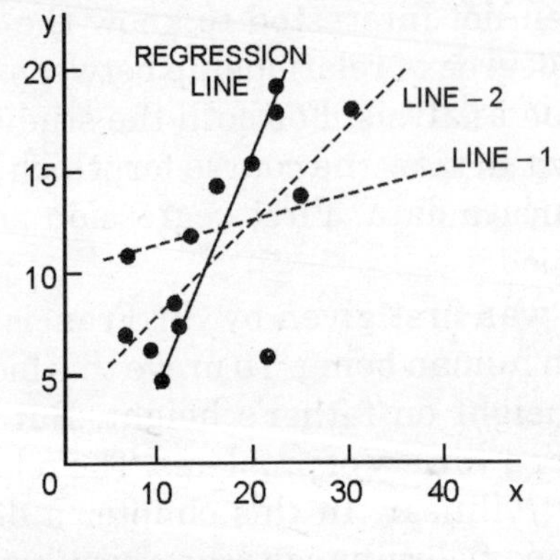

Figure 15.1: Fitting of a Regression Line

It is observed that a few points are lying away from all the fitted lines. These extreme points may sometimes be considered outliers. As evident from the figure, a number of lines may be drawn and considered suitable. But the best line will be one for which the algebraic sum of the perpendicular distances of all the points from the line is zero. Hence, dotted lines in the figure are not such a good fit as the smooth straight line. In short, the scatter diagram can be thought of as a device to know how closely the two variables are related and in what form *i.e.*, linear or curvilinear. If no path is discernable, it means that the two variables are independent. Independence of two variables means that the change in one variable does not cause any change in the other variable, according to any rule. Scatter diagram pertaining to independent variables is shown in Fig. 15.2.

From the above figure, it is easily verifiable that if any line is drawn through the plotted points, not more than two points will be lying on the line and most of the other points will be at a considerable distance from this line.

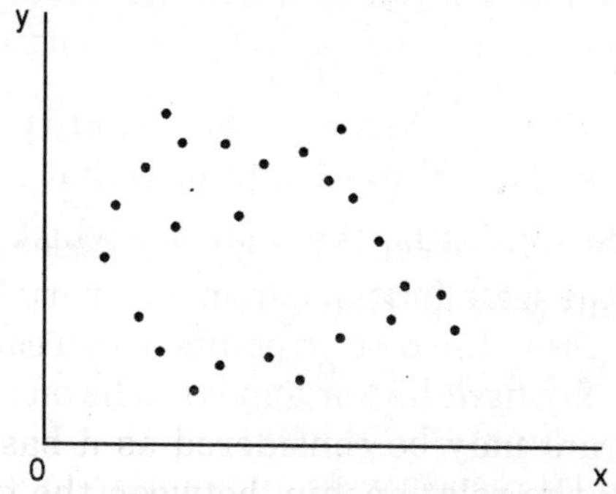

Figure 15.2: Scatter Diagram

Once it is decided on the basis of prior information or scatter diagram that the two variables are linearly related, the problem arises on deciding which of the many possible lines is the best fitted line. To cope with this problem, mathematical basis leads to the most logical and accurate solution. The least square method is the most widely accepted method of fitting a straight line and is discussed here adequately.

LEAST SQUARE METHOD OF FITTING A REGRESSION LINE

The equation for a regression line of Y on X for the population is given as

$$Y = \alpha + \beta X + e \qquad \text{...(15.1)}$$

Equation (15.1) is also known as the *statistical model* for linear regression. The main difference between the cartesian equation of a line and a regression line is that the regression line is a probabilistic model which enables one to develop procedures for making inferences about the parameters α and β of the model. In this model, the expected value of Y is a linear function of X, but for fixed X, the variable Y differs from its expected value by a random amount. As a special case, the form $y = \alpha + \beta x$ is called the *deterministic model.* In this model, the actual observed value of y is a linear function of x. In equation (15.1) α is the intercept which the line cuts on the axis of Y and β is the slope of the line. β is also called the *regression coefficient* and is defined as, "*β is the measure of change in the dependent variable* (Y) *corresponding to a unit change in the independent variable* (X)." β is often written as β_{YX} to indicate that it is the regression coefficient of Y on X. In case no suffix is attached to β, it is considered by itself. β can take any real value within the range $-\infty$ to ∞.

Suppose the regression line given by (15.1) is to be fitted on the basis of n pairs of sample observations, $(x_1, y_1), (x_2, y_2), ..., (x_n, y_n)$. Each pair (x_i, y_i) for $i = 1, 2, ..., n$ will satisfy the regression line (15.1).

Thus, $$y_i = \alpha + \beta x_i + e_i \qquad \text{...(15.1.1)}$$

or $$e_i = (y_i - \alpha - \beta x_i) \qquad \text{...(15.1.2)}$$

e_i may be positive or negative in case y_i is greater than or less than $(\alpha + \beta x_i)$ respectively. Whether the error is positive or negative, it does not matter as an error is after all an error. So to avoid the sign of error and confining to its magnitude only, square both sides of (15.1.2) and take the sum over n pairs of observations.

This gives,

$$\Sigma_i e_i^2 = \Sigma_i (y_i - \alpha - \beta x_i)^2 \qquad ...(15.1.3)$$

In Legendre's principle of least squares, the quantity which is minimized is the *residuals* or *error sum of squares*. Here the assumption is that each e_i is normally distributed with mean zero and variance σ_e^2. Thus, the quantity which is to be minimized here is $\Sigma_i e_i^2$. Let us denote this quantity by Q. Hence,

$$Q = \Sigma_i (y_i - \alpha - \beta x_i)^2 \qquad ...(15.1.4)$$

To get the least square estimates of α and β, so that Q is minimum, differentiate Q partially with respect to α and β respectively and equate to zero. Also replace α and β by their estimated values, say a and b respectively. Thus, we get two equations as given below. These equations are called normal equations.

$$\frac{\partial Q}{\partial \alpha} = -2\,\Sigma_i (y_i - a - bx_i) = 0 \qquad ...(15.2)$$

$$\frac{\partial Q}{\partial \beta} = -2\,\Sigma_i (y_i - a - bx_i)x_i = 0 \qquad ...(15.3)$$

On rearranging we get,

$$na + b\Sigma_i x_i = \Sigma_i y_i \qquad ...(15.4)$$

$$a\Sigma_i x_i + b\Sigma_i x_i^2 = \Sigma_i y_i x_i \qquad ...(15.5)$$

From (15.4)

$$a + b\frac{1}{n}\Sigma_i x_i = \frac{1}{n}\Sigma_i y_i \qquad ...(15.6)$$

$$a + b\bar{x} = \bar{y}$$

or $$a = (\bar{y} - b\bar{x}) \qquad ...(15.7)$$

Substituting the value of a from (15.6) in (15.5), we get,

$$\left(\frac{1}{n}\Sigma_i y_i - b\frac{1}{n}\Sigma_i x_i\right)\Sigma_i x_i + b\Sigma_i x_i^2 = \Sigma_i y_i x_i$$

or $$b\left\{\Sigma_i x_i^2 - \frac{1}{n}(\Sigma_i x_i)^2\right\} = \Sigma_i x_i y_i - \frac{1}{n}(\Sigma_i x_i)(\Sigma_i y_i)$$

or $$b = \frac{\Sigma_i x_i y_i - \frac{1}{n}(\Sigma_i x_i)(\Sigma_i y_i)}{\Sigma_i x_i^2 - \frac{1}{n}(\Sigma_i x_i)^2} \qquad ...(15.8)$$

Expression (15.8) can easily be written as,

$$b = \frac{\Sigma_i (x_i - \bar{x})(y_i - \bar{y})}{\Sigma_i (x_i - \bar{x})^2} \qquad ...(15.8.1)$$

Suppose $x_i - \bar{x} = u_i$ and $y_i - \bar{y} = v_i$, under this transformation,

$$b = \frac{\Sigma_i u_i v_i}{\Sigma_i u_i^2} \qquad ...(15.8.2)$$

If we divide the numerator and denominator by n in (15.8.1), we get

$$b = \frac{\text{cov}(X,Y)}{\text{var}(X)} \qquad ...(15.8.3)$$

or
$$b = \frac{s_{XY}}{s_X^2} \qquad ...(15.8.4)$$

b is the estimated regression coefficient of Y on X and is also symbolised as b_{YX}.

With the help of the formula (15.36.1) given ahead we can write,

$$S_{XY} = rS_X S_Y$$

Substituting the value of s_{XY} in terms of r, s_X and s_Y in (15.8.4) we obtain,

$$b_{YX} = r\frac{s_Y}{s_X} \qquad ...(15.8.5)$$

where r is the sample correlation coefficient between X and Y.

Properties of Regression Coefficient

1. It can take any value between $-\infty$ and ∞.
2. Its sign is same as that of s_{XY} *i.e.*, cov(X, Y).

Further, if the whole population has been studied, i will vary from 1 to N for all the N units of the population. In this situation obtain population regression coefficient β_{YX} directly, for which the formula is

$$\beta_{YX} = \frac{\sigma_{XY}}{\sigma_x^2} \qquad ...(15.9)$$

In case of population regression coefficient β of Y on X, which can elaborately be specified as β_{YX} we can express it as,

$$\beta_{YX} = \rho\frac{\sigma_Y}{\sigma_X} \qquad ...(15.9.1)$$

where ρ is the population correlation coefficient between X and Y.

As a and b are the estimated values of α and β respectively, the equation of the estimated regression line is

$$\hat{Y} = a + bX \qquad ...(15.10)$$

where, the hat ($\wedge$) over Y indicates that Y is an estimated value. Substituting the value of a from (15.7), the line of best fit is,

$$\hat{Y} = (\bar{y} - b\bar{x}) + bX \qquad ...(15.10.1)$$

or
$$(\hat{Y} - \bar{y}) = b(X - \bar{x}) \qquad ...(15.10.2)$$

Prediction Equation

The regression line is also known as *prediction equation*. Once the constants a and b are calculated, there remains two unknown variables in the regression equation viz., Y and X. Moreover, we know Y depends on X in the case of regression equation of Y on X. Under the presumption that the trend of change in Y corresponding to X remains the same, the value of Y can be estimated for any value of X. But such a presumption rarely holds good for a very wide range of X values. Hence, the fitted regression line gives a better estimate of Y for a given value of X, which is within the range of X values, taken into consideration at the time of calculation of a and b or not much beyond the values of X involved in the calculations. For example, we know that the crop yield increases with the increases in the quantity of fertilizers applied in the field. But beyond certain fertilizer-dose, the increase in yield is negligible. Hence the estimation of the yield of a crop for a fertilizer dose should be restricted only for doses within certain limits. In industry, the production of a product depends on the consumption of electricity. But it does not mean that if we go on increasing the consumption of electricity, the production of a product will keep on increasing in the same proportion. It holds true only up to a certain limit because many other factors besides consumption of electricity affect the production. The fitting of a regression line through actual data is given below.

***Example* 15.1.** The table below, gives the data regarding industrial consumption index of electricity and industrial production index (taking 1960 = 100) from 1951 to 1970.

Year	*Index of industrial consumption of electricity (X)*	*Index of industrial production (Y)*
1951	36.6	54.8
1952	39.5	57.2
1953	43.4	58.1
1954	47.6	63.4
1955	53.4	72.5
1956	58.5	78.4
1957	66.1	82.7
1958	74.9	84.4
1959	87.1	90.3
1960	100.0	100.0
1961	115.1	109.2
1962	131.7	119.8
1963	150.0	129.7
1964	162.6	140.8
1965	176.3	153.8
1966	190.4	153.2
1967	209.4	152.6
1968	233.6	163.0
1969	255.7	175.3
1970	271.4	184.3

It is known that the production (Y) depends on the consumption of electricity (X) and the relation between the two variables is linear. Hence, a regression line can be fitted to the bivariate data by calculating the values of a and b. First make the following calculations.

$$\Sigma_i x_i = (36.6 + 39.5 + ... + 271.4) = 2503.3$$

$$\Sigma_i y_i = (54.8 + 57.2 + ... + 184.3) = 2223.5$$

$$\Sigma_i x_i^2 = (36.6^2 + 39.5^2 + ... + 271.4^2) = 425211.85$$

$$\therefore \quad \bar{x} = \frac{2503.3}{20} = 125.17$$

$$\bar{y} = \frac{2223.5}{20} = 111.18$$

Also $n = 20$

$$\Sigma_i x_i y_i = (36.6 \times 54.8 + 39.5 \times 57.2 + \ldots + 271.4 \times 184.3)$$
$$= 339769.87$$

Using the formula (15.8) we get

$$b = \frac{339769.87 - \frac{1}{20}(2503.3)(2223.5)}{425211.85 - \frac{1}{20}(2503.3)^2}$$
$$= \frac{61465.49}{111886.31}$$
$$= 0.55$$

and from (15.7) $a = 111.18 - 0.55 \times 125.17$
$$= 42.34$$

Hence, the estimated equation of the regression line is,

$$\hat{Y} = 42.34 + 0.55\ X$$

Given the value of $X = 150$, we can estimate the value of Y from the estimated equation, that is

$$\hat{Y} = 42.34 + 0.55 \times 150 = 124.84$$

If we see the data, we find that the actual value of Y for $X = 150$ is 129.7. The difference between the actual and estimated value is not much. Hence, the line seems to be a good fit. Again, if we want the projection for the increased consumption of electricity, *i.e.*, $X = 350$, the estimated value of Y is,

$$\hat{Y} = 42.34 + 0.55 \times 350$$
$$= 234.84$$

From this we infer, that, if the industrial consumption index of electricity rises to the level of 350, production will rise to the level of 234.84.

Note: To fit the regression line with the help of SPSS software, see Appendix.

***Example* 15.2.** A departmental store gives in-service training to salesmen followed by a test. It is experienced that the performance regarding sales of any salesman is linearly related to the scores secured by him. The following data give test scores and sales made by nine salesmen during fixed period.

Test scores (X):	16	22	28	24	29	25	16	23	24
Sales ('00 Rs) (Y):	35	42	57	40	54	51	34	47	45

The sales Y of any salesman are considered to depend on his ability as judged by his test scores X. The regression line of Y on X can be fitted to the data in the following manner.

$$\Sigma_i x_i = 207 \text{ and } \Sigma_i y_i = 405 \text{ for } i = 1, 2, \ldots, 9.$$

$$\bar{x} = \frac{207}{9} = 23 \text{ and } \bar{y} = \frac{405}{9} = 45$$

Since the means of x and y observations are whole numbers, it is preferable to use the formula (15.8.1). To show the calculations clearly, it is better to prepare the following table.

Observation number	x	y	$x-\bar{x}$	$y-\bar{y}$	$(x-\bar{x})^2$	$(x-\bar{x})(y-\bar{y})$
1	16	35	– 7	– 10	49	70
2	22	42	– 1	– 3	1	3
3	28	57	5	12	25	60
4	24	40	1	– 5	1	– 5
5	29	54	6	9	36	54
6	25	51	2	6	4	12
7	16	34	– 7	– 11	49	77
8	23	47	0	2	00	00
9	24	45	1	0	1	00
Total	207	405	00	00	166	271

$$b = \frac{271}{166}$$
$$= 1.63$$

Hence, the estimated regression line as given by (15.10.2) is,

$$(\hat{Y} - 45) = 1.63\ (X - 23)$$

$$\hat{Y} = 7.51 + 1.63\ X$$

The predicted sales due to a salesman having the scores 30 is,

$$\hat{Y} = 7.51 + 1.63 \times 30$$
$$= 56.41$$

Thus, the estimated sale is Rs. 56.41.

Regression Line of X on Y

Often we come across situations in which two variables (Y and X) are such that not only Y depends on X but X also depends on Y. For example, the heights and weights of people are two variables where heights of people depend on weights and weights depend on heights. In such a case we can find not only the regression line of Y on X but also of X on Y. Suppose the regression line of X on Y is,

$$X = \alpha_1 + \beta_1 Y + e_1 \qquad \text{...(15.11)}$$

The parameters α_1 and β_1 can be estimated in the same way as α and β in (15.1). Instead of repeating the derivation, it will be worthwhile to write directly the estimated values of α_1 and β_1, say, a_1 and b_1 (by interchanging the variable Y by X and X by Y in the formulae for a and b respectively). Thus, the estimates are,

$$a = (\bar{x} - b_1\bar{y}) \qquad \text{...(15.12)}$$

$$b_1 = \frac{\Sigma_i (x_i - \bar{x})(y_i - \bar{y})}{\Sigma_i (y_i - \bar{y})^2} \qquad \text{...(15.13)}$$

$$= \frac{\Sigma_i x_i y_i - (\Sigma_i x_i)(\Sigma_i y_i)/n}{\Sigma_i y_i^2 - (\Sigma_i y_i)^2/n} \quad ...(15.13.1)$$

$$= \frac{s_{XY}}{s_Y^2} \quad ...(15.13.2)$$

We can express b_1, which is the estimated regression coefficient of X on Y and symbolically denoted as b_{XY}. In terms of r, s_X, s_Y, as in case of (15.8.5), we can write,

$$b_{XY} = r\frac{s_X}{s_Y} \quad ...(15.13.3)$$

where r is the sample correlation coefficient between X and Y.

The equation of the estimated regression line of X on Y is,

$$(\hat{X} - \bar{x}) = b_1(Y - \bar{y}) \quad ...(15.14)$$

Also, the population regression coefficient of X on Y may be given as follows,

$$\beta_1 = \frac{\sigma_{XY}}{\sigma_Y^2} \quad ...(15.15)$$

The population regression coefficient β_1 of X on Y, which is often symbolised as β_{XY}, can be expressed as,

$$\beta_{XY} = \rho\frac{\sigma_X}{\sigma_Y} \quad ...(15.15.1)$$

where ρ is the population correlation coefficient between X and Y.

It is trivial to prove that the two regression lines given by (15.10.2) and (15.14) intersect each other at a point having coordinates $(\bar{x}, \bar{y})$, *i.e.*, at the mean of two variables.

***Example* 15.3.** Using the data and partial calculations of example (15.1), we fit in the regression line.

$$(\hat{X} - \bar{x}) = b_1(Y - \bar{y})$$

First, we calculate, $\Sigma_i y_i^2 = (54.8^2 + 57.2^2 + ... + 184.3^2)$

$= 281790.03$

Now from (15.13.1), $b_1 = \dfrac{61465.49}{281790.03 - \frac{1}{20}(2223.5)^2}$

$= \dfrac{61465.49}{34592.42}$

$= 1.78$

Hence, the required equation of regression line is,

$$(\hat{X} - 125.17) = 1.78(Y - 111.18)$$

or

$$\hat{X} = 1.78\,Y - 72.73$$

The value of X can be estimated for any given value of Y, in the manner followed in example (15.1).

Regression Coefficient from Coded Data

Coding of data has already been discussed in Chapter 4. We have to calculate the variance and covariance for calculating β or b and the methodology given in Chapter 4 is applicable. Coding is useful to reduce the labour of calculations. This not only saves time but also reduces the chances of errors in calculations. Since ages, coding has been a very popular device as a short cut method of calculations, but now it is losing its importance with the increasing use of modern electronic calculators. Still in many examinations calculators are not provided and hence it is worthwhile to discuss it here.

Let a constant c_1 be subtracted from X observations and c_2 from Y observations. Then the reduced values of X and Y are divided by d_1 and d_2, respectively. Thus, the coded variate values are

$$dx_i = \frac{x_i - c_1}{d_1} \text{ and } dy_i = \frac{y_i - c_2}{d_2}$$

for $i = 1, 2, ..., n$.

For calculating the regression coefficient from coded data, prepare the Table 15.1 given on next page.

Under the transformation,

$$\overline{dx} = \frac{1}{n}\Sigma_i dx_i = \frac{1}{n}\Sigma_i \frac{(x_i - c_1)}{d_1}$$

$$= \frac{1}{d_1}\left\{\frac{1}{n}\Sigma_i x_i - \frac{1}{n}\Sigma_i c_1\right\}$$

$$\overline{dx} = \frac{\bar{x} - c_1}{d_1} \qquad ...(15.16)$$

or $$\bar{x} = d_1\overline{dx} + c_1 \qquad ...(15.16.1)$$

Similarly, $$\overline{dy} = \frac{\bar{y} - c_2}{d_2} \qquad ...(15.17)$$

or $$\bar{y} = d_2\overline{dy} + c_2 \qquad ...(15.17.1)$$

Now the regression coefficient from coded observations is,

$$b_c = \frac{\Sigma_i(dx_i - \overline{dx})(dy_i - \overline{dy})}{\Sigma_i(dx_i - \overline{dx})^2} \qquad ...(15.18)$$

$$= \frac{\Sigma_i dx_i dy_i - (\Sigma_i dx_i)(\Sigma_i dy_i)/n}{\Sigma_i dx_i^2 - (\Sigma_i dx_i)^2/n} \qquad ...(15.18.1)$$

Substituting the transforms for dx_i and dy_i etc., we get,

$$b_c = \frac{\Sigma_i\left(\frac{x_i - c_1}{d_1} - \frac{\bar{x} - c_1}{d_1}\right)\left(\frac{y_i - c_2}{d_2} - \frac{\bar{y} - c_2}{d_2}\right)}{\Sigma_i\left(\frac{x_i - c_1}{d_1} - \frac{\bar{x} - c_1}{d_1}\right)^2}.$$

$$= \frac{\frac{1}{d_1 d_2}\Sigma_i(x_i - \bar{x})(y_i - \bar{y})}{\frac{1}{d_1^2}\Sigma_i(x_i - \bar{x})^2} \qquad ...(15.18.2)$$

$$= \frac{d_1}{d_2} b_{YX} \qquad ...(15.18.3)$$

Table 15.1

x	y	$x - c_1$	$y - c_2$	$dx = \frac{x - c_1}{d_1}$	$dy = \frac{y - c_2}{d_2}$	$dx.dy$	d^2x	d^2y
x_1	y_1	$x_1 - c_1$	$y_1 - c_2$	$dx_1 = \frac{x_1 - c_1}{d_1}$	$dy_1 = \frac{y_1 - c_2}{d_2}$	$dx_1 dy_1$	d^2x_1	d^2y_1
x_2	y_2	$x_2 - c_1$	$y_2 - c_2$	$dx_2 = \frac{x_2 - c_1}{d_1}$	$dy_2 = \frac{y_2 - c_2}{d_2}$	$dx_2 dy_2$	d^2x_2	d^2y_2
⋮	⋮	⋮	⋮	⋮	⋮	⋮	⋮	⋮
x_i	y_i	$x_i - c_1$	$y_i - c_2$	$dx_i = \frac{x_i - c_1}{d_1}$	$dy_i = \frac{y_i - c_2}{d_2}$	$dx_i dy_i$	d^2x_i	d^2y_i
⋮	⋮	⋮	⋮	⋮	⋮	⋮	⋮	⋮
x_n	y_n	$x_n - c_1$	$y_n - c_2$	$dx_n = \frac{x_n - c_1}{d_1}$	$dy_n = \frac{y_n - c_2}{d_2}$	$dx_n dy_n$	d^2x_n	d^2y_n
Total $\Sigma_i x_i$	$\Sigma_i y_i$	$\Sigma_i x_i - nc_1$	$\Sigma_i y_i - nc_2$	$\Sigma_i dx_i$	$\Sigma_i dy_i$	$\Sigma_i dx_i dy_i$	$\Sigma_i d^2x_i$	$\Sigma_i d^2y_i$

where i varies from 1to n.

or
$$b_{YX} = \frac{d_2}{d_1} b_c \qquad ...(15.18.4)$$

From (15.18.4) it is clear that the regression coefficient is independent of the change of origin but is affected by the change of scale. To obtain the value of regression coefficient for original observations, from regression coefficient based on coded data, it should be multiplied by d_2/d_1.

Notes: (*i*) c_1, c_2, d_1 and d_2 need not necessarily be different. Any of them may be equal if found appropriate. d_1 and d_2 should never be taken as zero because the coded value will become infinity and d_2/d_1 will become an indeterminate quantity.

(*ii*) Often we like to do only one operation, *i.e.*, we subtract a constant and no divisor is taken. In this situation $d_1 = d_2 = 1$. Hence the value of b_{YX} will directly be equal to the value obtained from coded data. When the divisors are taken but no constants are subtracted from the observed values, then $c_1 = c_2 = 0$.

***Example* 15.4.** The table below gives the total grain production and production of cereals in Lakh tonnes (rounded figures) for nine years.

Year:	1	2	3	4	5	6	7	8	9
Total grain production (*y*):	400	440	480	550	620	650	660	740	760
Cereal production (*x*):	50	60	70	85	95	100	105	115	120

We know that total production is directly proportional to the cereal production. Hence a regression line of total production (*y*) on cereal production (*x*) can be fitted. Since the figures are large enough, we will use coding of data. Therefore, subtract 620 from each value of *y*. Also divide each subtracted figure by 10. Also subtract 95 from each value of *x* and divide the reduced figure by 5. In other words, $c_2 = 620$, $c_1 = 95$, $d_2 = 10$ and $d_1 = 5$. The calculations for fitting of regression line, using the coding technique, are presented in the following table.

Year	*Total production* y	*Cereal production* x	$\frac{y-620}{10} = dy$	$\frac{x-95}{5} = dx$	$dxdy$	dx^2
1.	400	50	– 22	– 9	198	81
2.	440	60	– 18	– 7	126	49
3.	480	70	– 14	– 5	70	25
4.	550	85	– 7	– 2	14	4
5.	620	95	0	0	00	00
6.	650	100	3	1	3	1
7.	660	105	4	2	8	4
8.	740	115	12	4	48	16
9.	760	120	14	5	70	25
Total			– 28 $\equiv \Sigma_i dy_i$	– 11 $\equiv \Sigma_i dx_i$	537 $\equiv \Sigma_i dx_i dy_i$	205 $\equiv \Sigma_i d^2 x_i$

From (3.6),

$$\bar{x} = 95 - \frac{11}{9} \times 5$$
$$= 95 - 6.1$$
$$= 88.9$$
$$\bar{y} = 620 - \frac{28}{9} \times 10$$
$$= 620 - 31.1$$
$$= 588.9$$

Now the regression coefficient from (15.18.1) is,

$$b_c = \frac{537 - \frac{(-28)(-11)}{9}}{205 - \frac{(-11)^2}{9}}$$

$$= \frac{537 - 34.22}{205 - 13.44}$$

$$= \frac{502.78}{191.56}$$

$$= 2.6247$$

From (15.18.4), $b_{YX} = \frac{10}{5} \times 2.6247$

$$= 5.2494$$

$$= 5.25$$

Equation of the estimated regression line is,

$$(\hat{Y} - 588.9) = 5.25(X - 88.9)$$

$$\hat{Y} = 588.9 + 5.25\,X - 466.72$$

$$= 122.18 + 5.25X$$

From the fitted regression line, we can estimate the total production for the cereal production of 90 Lakh tonnes.

Thus, $\hat{Y} = 122.18 + 5.25 \times 90$

$$= 122.18 + 472.50$$

$$= 594.68$$

$$= 595 \text{ Lakh tonnes.}$$

Test of Significance of Regression Parameters

The estimators of α and β have already been given by (15.7) and (15.8) respectively based on n paired observations. The experimenter is interested to test whether the parameters α and β, involved in the regression line, are of practical relevance or not. To do so, we have to test the hypotheses $\beta = 0$ and $\alpha = 0$. These hypotheses can be tested provided we know the distribution of b and a. The estimators a and b are random variables such that,

$$b \sim N(\beta, \sigma_b^2) \quad ...(15.19)$$

and $$a \sim N(\alpha, \sigma_a^2) \quad ...(15.20)$$

where $$\sigma_b^2 = \sigma_e^2 / \Sigma_i (x_i - \bar{x})^2 \quad ...(15.21)$$

and $$\sigma_a^2 = \sigma_e^2 \left\{ \frac{1}{n} + \frac{\bar{x}^2}{\Sigma_i (x_i - \bar{x})^2} \right\} \quad ...(15.22)$$

The variances σ_b^2 and σ_a^2 are not known and are thus estimated from sample observations. In (15.21) and (15.22) if σ_e^2 is estimated, say, by s_e^2, then the estimators s_b^2 and s_a^2 of σ_b^2 and σ_a^2 respectively, are obtained. There are only n paired observations (x_i, y_i) where $i = 1, 2, ..., n$ and s_e^2 is to be estimated from $\Sigma_i e_i^2$. The expression (15.1.3) for

$\Sigma_i e_i^2$ involves two parameters α and β which are estimated by a and b. The estimate of $\Sigma_i e_i^2$ is,

$$\Sigma_i e_i^2 = \Sigma_i (y_i - a - bx_i)^2$$

The appropriate divisor to obtain s_e^2 from $\Sigma_i e_i^2$ is $(n-2)$. Thus,

$$s_e^2 = \frac{1}{(n-2)} \Sigma_i (y_i - a - bx_i)^2 \quad \text{...(15.23)}$$

The divisor $(n-2)$ is used because the two parameters α and β are estimated resulting into a loss of two d.f. Moreover, s_e^2 so obtained is an unbiased estimate of σ_e^2, s_e^2 is also called the mean square error (MSE).

With the help of simple algebra, it is easy to show that

$$s_e^2 = \frac{1}{(n-2)} \{\Sigma_i (y_i - \bar{y})^2 - b\Sigma_i (x_i - \bar{x})(y_i - \bar{y})\} \quad \text{...(15.23.1)}$$

Putting $x_i - \bar{x} = u_i$ and $y_i - \bar{y} = v_i$, we get

$$s_e^2 = \frac{1}{(n-2)} \{\Sigma_i v_i^2 - b\Sigma_i u_i v_i\} \quad \text{...(15.23.2)}$$

In (15.23.2), the quantity $b\Sigma_i u_i v_i$ is called the sum of squares due to regression and the quantity within the braces is called the residual sum of squares.

Substituting the value of b as $\Sigma_i u_i v_i / \Sigma_i u_i^2$, we obtain,

$$s_e^2 = \frac{1}{(n-2)} \left\{ \Sigma_i v_i^2 - \frac{(\Sigma_i u_i v_i)^2}{\Sigma_i u_i^2} \right\} \quad \text{...(15.23.3)}$$

Now using the estimate s_e^2 for σ_e^2, we get the estimates s_b^2 and s_a^2 for σ_b^2 and σ_a^2 respectively, viz.,

$$s_b^2 = \frac{s_e^2}{\Sigma_i (x_i - \bar{x})^2} \quad \text{...(15.24)}$$

$$= \frac{s_e^2}{\Sigma_i u_i^2} \quad \text{...(15.24.1)}$$

and

$$s_a^2 = s_e^2 \left\{ \frac{1}{n} + \frac{\bar{x}^2}{\Sigma_i (x_i - \bar{x})^2} \right\} \quad \text{...(15.25)}$$

$$= s_e^2 \left\{ \frac{1}{n} + \frac{\bar{x}^2}{\Sigma_i u_i^2} \right\} \quad \text{...(15.25.1)}$$

The test for testing the hypothesis

$$H_0 : \beta_{YX} = 0 \text{ vs. } H_1 ; \beta_{YX} \neq 0$$

will be as follows:

H_0 against H_1 can be tested by t-statistic which is given as:

$$t_{n-2} = \frac{b}{s_b} \qquad ...(15.26)$$

where the suffix $(n-2)$ indicates the degrees of freedom for t and s_b is the standard error of b which is the square root of s_b^2 given by (15.24). If $t_{n-2} \geq t_\alpha$, reject H_0 where t_α is the table value of t for $(n-2)$ d.f. at prefixed level of significance α. If $t_{n-2} < t_\alpha$, accept H_0. Accepting H_0 means that the regression coefficient of Y on X has no practical significance *i.e.*, the change in Y corresponding to a unit change in X is practically meaningless.

Similarly we can perform the test for testing the hypothesis,

$$H_0 : \alpha = 0 \text{ vs. } H_1 : \alpha \neq 0$$

by using the statistic,

$$t_{n-2} = \frac{a}{s_a} \qquad ...(15.27)$$

where s_a is the standard deviation of a, which is the square root of s_a^2 given by (15.25). If the value of $\alpha = 0$ is tenable, then it would be desirable to use the regression equation $Y = \beta X + e$, *i.e.*, the line is passing through the origin.

Alternative Test. The hypothesis

$$H_0 : \beta_{YX} = 0 \text{ vs. } H_1 : \beta_{YX} \neq 0$$

can also be tested by the F-test using the analysis of variance technique. For this the ANOVA table is as given below:

Table 15.2: ANOVA table

Source	*d.f.*	*S.S.*	*M.S.*	*F-value*
Due to regression	1	$b\Sigma_i u_i v_i$	$\frac{b\Sigma_i u_i v_i}{1}$	$\frac{b\Sigma_i u_i v_i}{s_e^2} = F$
Deviation from regression	$(n-2)$	$(\Sigma_i v_i^2 - b\Sigma u_i v_i)$	$\frac{(\Sigma_i v_i^2 - b\Sigma u_i v_i)}{(n-2)} = s_e^2$	
Total	$(n-1)$	$\Sigma_i v_i^2$		

If $F > F_{\alpha,(1, n-2)}$, reject H_0 otherwise accept H_0. The physical interpretation for rejection or acceptance of H_0 remains the same as given with t-test of H_0.

Confidence Limits for Regression Parameters

Following the same principle as given in Chapter 10, an expression analogous to (10.13) is given for $(1-\alpha)$ per cent confidence limits.

Confidence limits for β_{YX} are,

$$b \pm s_b\, t_{\alpha,\,(n-2)} \qquad ...(15.28)$$

where $t_{\alpha,(n-2)}$ is the table value for two-tailed t-test at α level of significance and for $(n-2)$ degree of freedom. b and s_b are as given earlier.

Again (1 – α) per cent confidence limits for the intercept are,

$$a \pm s_a\, t_{\alpha,\,(n-2)} \qquad ...(15.29)$$

where a and s_a are as given earlier. $t_{\alpha,(n-2)}$ has been explained just before.

***Example* 15.5.** In this example the tests of significance is given for the data given in example (15.1).

Test of significance of regression coefficient amounts to testing of hypothesis,

$$H_0 : \beta_{YX} = 0 \text{ vs. } H_1 : \beta_{YX} \neq 0$$

To test H_0, we make use of the test statistic,

$$t_{n-2} = \frac{b}{s_b}$$

We will make use of all the calculations made in example (15.1).

To perform the test, we need b and s_b. We have b = 0.55 and now calculate s_b.

From (15.23.2),

$$s_e^2 = \frac{1}{18}\left[\left\{281790.03 - \frac{(2223.5)^2}{20}\right\} - 0.55 \times 61465.49\right]$$

Since $\qquad \Sigma_i y_i^2 = 54.8^2 + 57.2^2 \,...\, + 184.3^2 = 281790.03$

$$s_e^2 = \frac{1}{18}\,[34592.42 - 33806.02]$$

$$= \frac{786.40}{18}$$

$$= 43.69$$

From (13.24), $\quad s_b^2 = \dfrac{43.69}{111886.31}$

$$= 0.00039$$

or $\qquad s_b = 0.0197$

The statistic, $\quad t_{18} = \dfrac{0.55}{0.0197}$

$$= 27.92$$

The table value of t for 18 d.f. and 5 per cent level of significance is 2.101. Since the table value of t is less than the calculated t-value, we reject H_0 which means that the regression coefficient plays a significant role in determining Y through X.

95 per cent confidence interval for β_{YX} from (15.28) is

$$0.55 \pm 0.0197 \times 2.101$$

i.e., $\qquad 0.55 \pm 0.0414$

Upper limit for β_{YX} is 0.5914 and lower limit is 0.5086.

Again the hypothesis, whether or not the line passes through the origin, is equivalent to testing,

$$H_0 : \alpha = 0 \text{ vs. } H_1 : \alpha \neq 0$$

H_0 can be tested by the statistic,

$$t_{n-2} = \frac{a}{s_a}$$

we know, $a = 42.34$

Now we calculate s_a by (15.25)

$$s_a^2 = 43.69\left\{\frac{1}{20}+\frac{125.17^2}{111886.31}\right\}$$

$$= 43.69\ (0.05 + 0.14)$$

$$= 8.30$$

or $s_a = 2.88$

Now, $$t_{18} = \frac{42.34}{2.88}$$

$$= 14.70$$

The calculated value of t is greater than the table value of $t_{0.05,\ 18} = 2.101$. Hence, we reject H_0. This means that the regression line does not pass through the origin.

95 per cent confidence limits for α from (15.29) are,

$$42.34 \pm 2.88 \times 2.101$$

i.e., $$42.34 \pm 6.05$$

The upper limit for α is 48.39 and lower limit is 36.29.

CURVILINEAR REGRESSION

It has already been stated in the beginning of this chapter that the relationship between the dependent variable Y and the independent variable X can be curvilinear in many cases. The shape of the curve depends on the rate of change in Y corresponding to the change in the value of X. Some of the commonly used curves are given here along with their mathematical equations. These curves may be fitted to the data and used.

Second Degree Curve

Mathematical equation of the curve is,

$$Y = \alpha + \beta X + \gamma X^2 \qquad \text{...(15.30)}$$

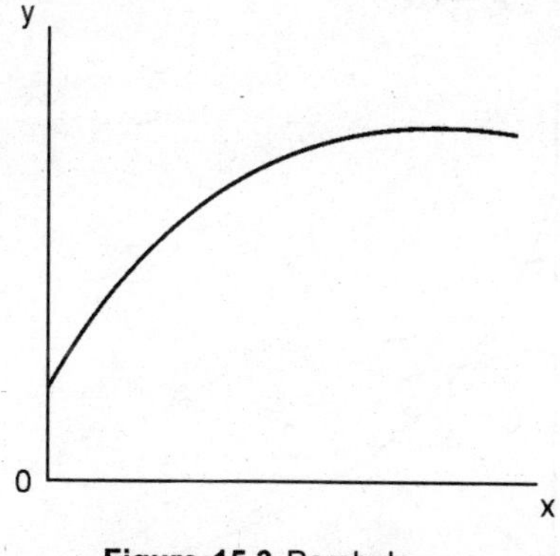

Figure 15.3 Parabola

The shape of the curve is the upper half of the *parabola*. It is generally used for a relationship between the production of a crop and the quantity of fertilizer applied per unit area.

Exponential Growth Curve

Mathematical equation of the curve is,

$$Y = \alpha\beta^X \quad ...(15.31)$$

If we put $\beta = 1 + i$, where i is the rate of interest and X the number of years, then, Y gives the amount to which the initial amount α will rise. By taking the logarithm of both sides, the model becomes linear in log terms.

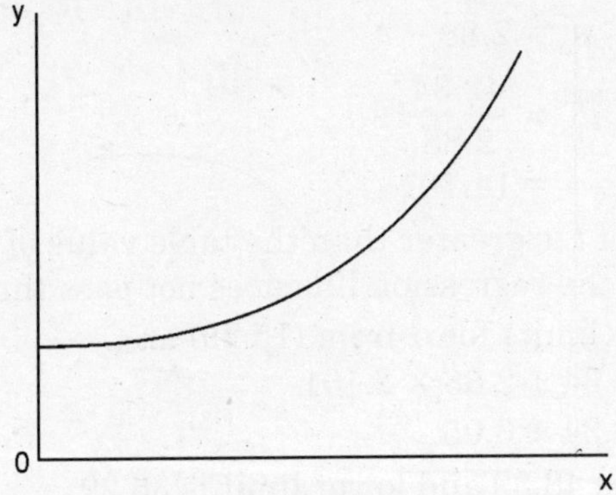

Figure 15.4 Growth Curve

Mathematical equation of exponential growth curve is also given as

$$Y = \alpha e^{\delta X} \quad ...(15.32)$$

Exponential Decay Curve

Mathematical model is,

$$Y = \alpha\beta^{-X} \quad ...(15.33)$$

If $\beta < 1$, then it represents the decay curve. The decay of the emission of particles of a radioactive element follows this law.

Another mathematical form of the above curve is,

$$Y = \alpha e^{-\delta X} \quad ...(15.34)$$

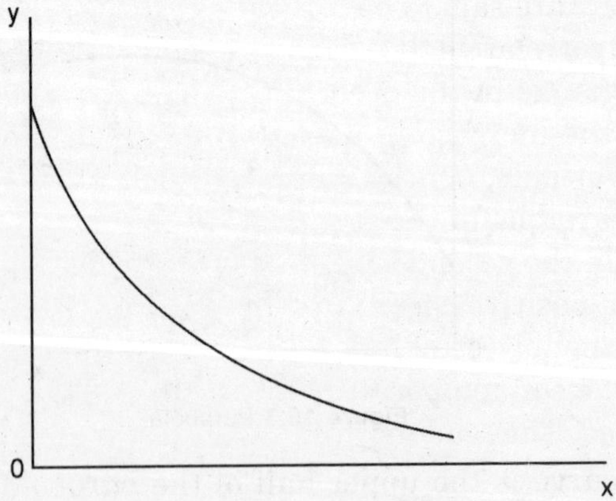

Figure 15.5 Decay Curve

Logistic Growth Curve

The mathematical model is,

$$\frac{1}{Y} = \alpha\beta^{X} + \gamma \qquad ...(15.35)$$

This curve is often suitable to the growth of human populations of some countries.

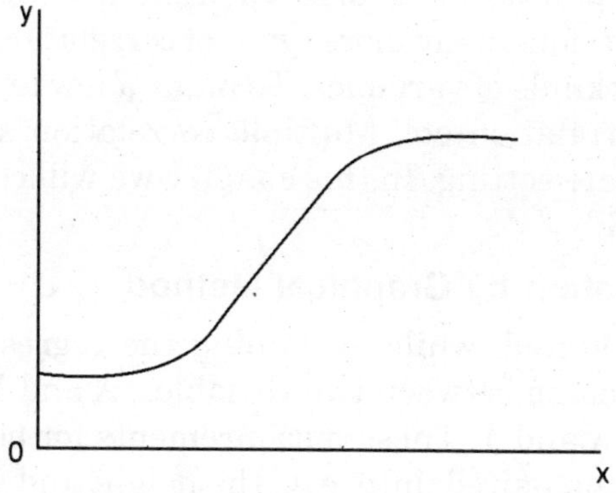

Figure 15.6 Logistic Growth Curve

It is worth pointing out, that it is not possible to enumerate all situations in which a particular linear or curvilinear regression model is suitable. Moreover, neither one can enunciate all possible equations. It is through experience and certain norms that an analyst has to arrive at the conclusion as to which equation is most suited for the data at hand.

CORRELATION METHODS

Regression technique provides the actual relationship between two or more variables. But the scientists are not always interested in this linear or curvilinear relationship. Often the interest lies only in knowing the extent of interdependence between two or more variables. In this situation, correlation methods serve our purpose. If the two variables, say X and Y, are linearly related, they are said to be correlated. The correlation between two variables is also known as simple correlation. It means that the change in one variable is accompanied by the proportionate change in the other variable. The change is likely to occur in both directions namely, (*i*) the increase in one variable is accompanied by the proportionate increase in the other variable, (*ii*) the increase in one variable causes the proportionate decrease in the other variable. In the first case, the two variables are said to be positively interrelated, whereas in the second case, they are said to be negatively interrelated. For example, there exists a positive correlation between the age of a husband and age of his wife, the income and expenditure of families. On the other hand, the price of a commodity and its consumption, the soil temperature and germination period are the variables that are negatively correlated. The readers will come across many more correlation problems in numerical examples.

The mathematical measure of correlation was given by the statistician Karl Pearson in 1896 in the form of correlation coefficient. This was extensively used by Sir Francis Galton to explain many phenomena in biology and genetics. Its use in economics was emphasized by Professor Neiswanger as he wrote, "correlation analysis contributes to the understanding of economic behaviour, aids in locating the critically important variable on which others depend, may reveal to the economist the connections by which disturbances spread and suggest to him the paths through which stabilising forces may become effective." Since its innovation the application of correlation methods has always been increasing. Besides Pearsonian correlation, many more types of correlations are being invented which are suitable for particular kinds of variables. To name a few are: rank correlation, biserial correlation, intraclass correlation etc. Multiple correlation and partial correlation are associated with multivariate setting. In this chapter we will confine to simple correlation and rank correlation.

Determination of Correlation by Graphical Method

It has already been stated, while explaining the regression, that *scatter diagram* gives a fair idea of relationship between two variables, *X* and *Y*. Here too, we have paired observations of variables *X* and *Y*. These measurements for both the variables are taken either on the same unit or on paired units *e.g.*, the height and weight of a person form one pair, the age of husband and his wife form one pair, the income and expenditure of a family form one pair, the cost price and selling price of an article form one pair. When the paired observations are plotted on the graph paper for all the objects or units under consideration, their pattern of location gives a fair idea of correlation between two variables, Six figures of scatter diagrams are given here to show the extent of relationship between two variables. The population correlation coefficient is denoted by ρ (rho).

(*i*) This scatter diagram shows the perfect positive correlation, as all the points lie on a straight line. As the variate value of *X* increases, *Y* also increases and vice-versa.

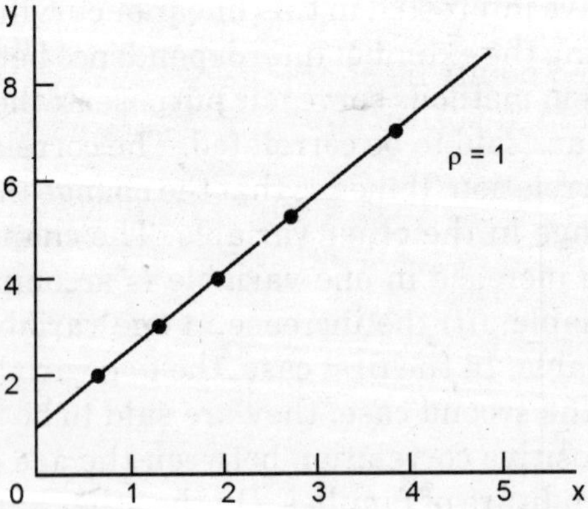

Figure 15.7 Perfect Positive Correlation

(*ii*) This scatter diagram depicts a perfect negative correlation. All points lie on the straight line. The slope of the line is such that as *X* increases, *Y* decreases proportionately.

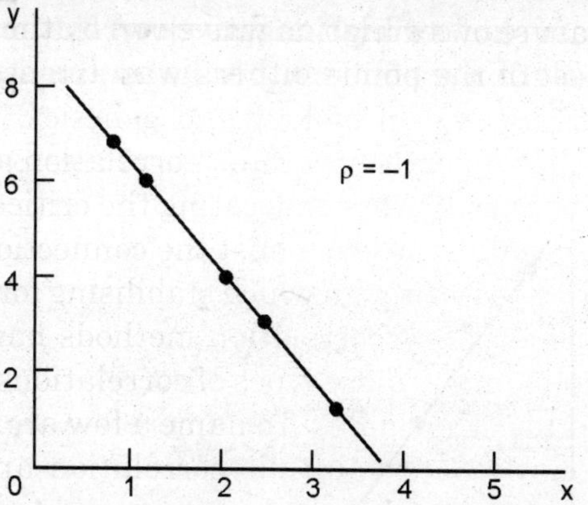

Figure 15.8 Perfect Negative Correlation

(*iii*) No line can be drawn passing through most of the plotted points. The points are totally scattered. Hence, it shows no correlation between the variables *X* and *Y*.

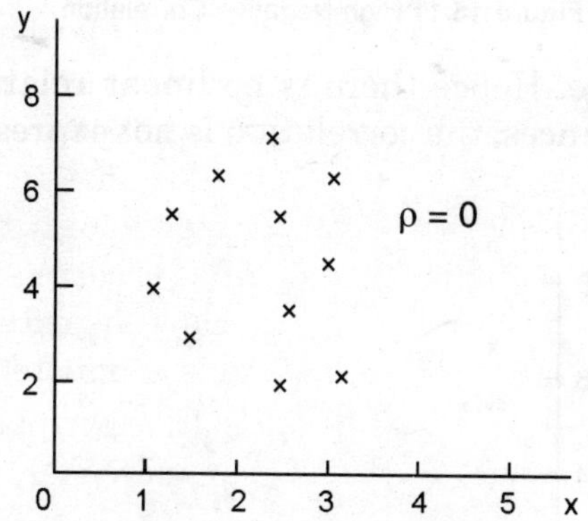

Figure 15.9 Scatter Diagram

(*iv*) Most of the plotted points lie on the line. Others are near to this line. Hence, the diagram shows a high positive correlation.

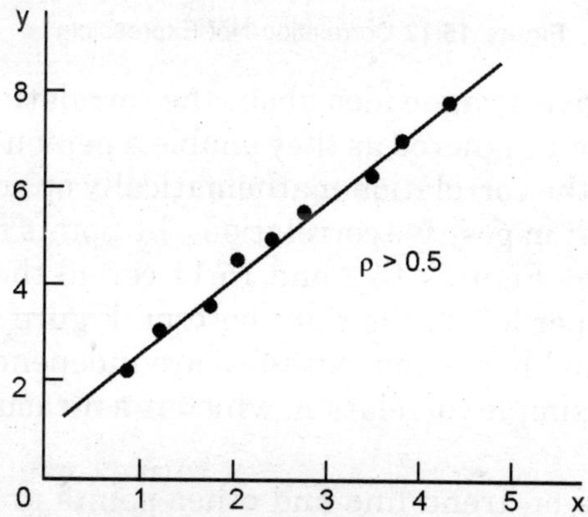

Figure 15.10 High Positive Correlation

(*v*) This scatter diagram shows a high negative correlation as the slope of the line is more than 90°. Most of the points either lie on the straight line or are in close vicinity.

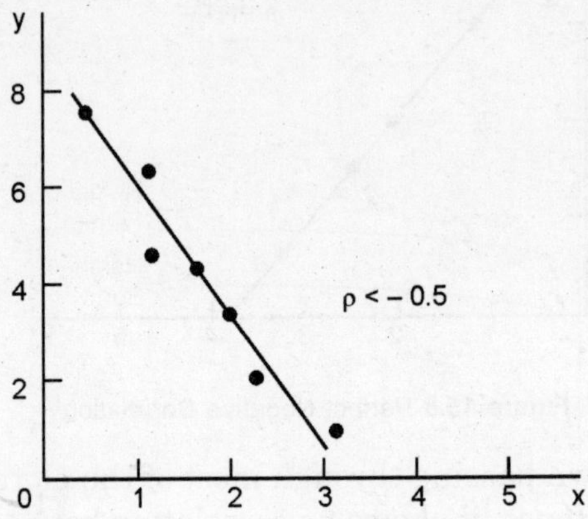

Figure 15.11 High Negative Correlation

(*vi*) Points lie on a curve. Hence there is no linear relationship between X and Y. Under the circumstances, the correlation is not expressible.

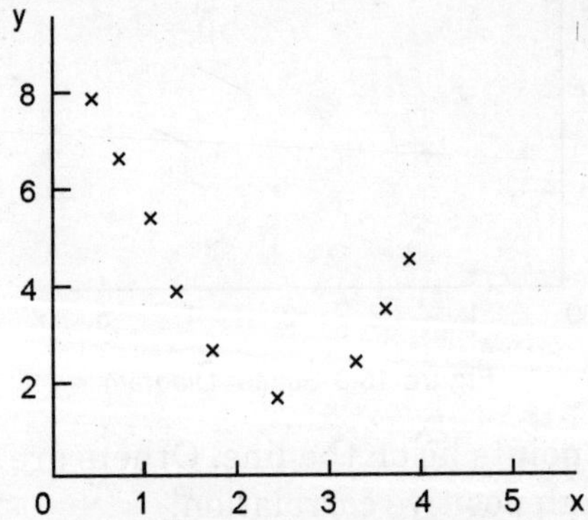

Figure 15.12 Correlation Not Expressible

The above six figures give a vague idea about the correlation between two variables. Still their importance cannot be ignored as they enable a person to know whether the data are suitable for finding out the correlation mathematically or not. From the Figures (15.7 and 15.10, it is apparent that in positive correlation, the points flow from lower left corner to the right top. Whereas the Figures 15.8 and 15.11 reveal that in negative correlation, the points flow from the upper left to the right bottom. Figure 15.9 shows that points do not follow any set pattern and hence the variables are independent. Figure 15.12 depicts a curvilinear trend and the simple correlation, which is a measure of linear association, is not expressible.

If only a few points lie on trend line and other points are away from this line, we consider that there is a low degree of linear relationship between the two variables.

Another way of judging the correlation between two variates is, to plot both the variate values on the same axis corresponding to each paired number and see the trend of both the graphs. If both these trend lines or curves are parallel to each other, they are positively correlated.

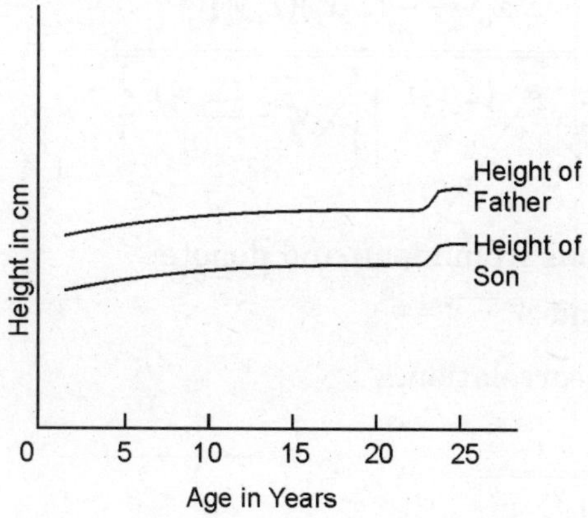

Figure 15.13 High Positive Correlation

Fig. 15.13 shows that there is a high degree of positive correlation between the height of a father and his son.

CORRELATION COEFFICIENT

The correlation between two variables is termed as simple correlation and its general measure is *Karl Pearson coefficient of correlation*. The estimated value of population correlation coefficient ρ between two variables X and Y is denoted by r. Here we shall give all the formulae for r. If in some study all the units of the population are measured, we should use the formulae given for r over all the observations of the population and, instead of r, use the symbol ρ. But in rare cases we study the whole population. Therefore, we have given the formulae for sample observations. Sometimes the suffix XY is added to r, *i.e.*, r_{XY}, to connote that it is the correlation coefficient between the variables X and Y. Theoretically, the sample correlation coefficient is given as,

$$r_{XY} = \frac{\operatorname{cov}(X,Y)}{\sqrt{v(X)v(Y)}} \quad \text{...(15.36)}$$

$$= \frac{s_{XY}}{s_X s_Y} \quad \text{...(15.36.1)}$$

where s_X and s_Y are the sample standard deviations of variables X and Y respectively, and s_{XY} is the estimated covariance between X and Y. If we have n pairs of sample observations, (x_1, y_1), (x_2, y_2), (x_3, y_3), ...(x_n, y_n), then the correlation coefficient,

$$r = \frac{\frac{1}{n-1}\Sigma_i(x_i - \bar{x})(y_i - \bar{y})}{\sqrt{\left\{\frac{1}{n-1}\Sigma_i(x_i - \bar{x})^2\right\}\left\{\frac{1}{n-1}\Sigma_i(y_i - \bar{y})^2\right\}}} \quad \text{...(15.37)}$$

for $i = 1, 2, ..., n$

$$= \frac{\Sigma_i (x_i - \bar{x})(y_i - \bar{y})}{\sqrt{\Sigma_i (x_i - \bar{x})^2 \Sigma_i (y_i - \bar{y})^2}} \qquad ...(15.37.1)$$

$$= \frac{\Sigma_i x_i y_i - \frac{1}{n}(\Sigma_i x_i)(\Sigma_i y_i)}{\sqrt{\left\{\Sigma_i x_i^2 - \frac{(\Sigma_i x_i)^2}{n}\right\}\left\{\Sigma_i y_i^2 - \frac{(\Sigma_i y_i)^2}{n}\right\}}} \qquad ...(15.37.2)$$

for $i = 1, 2, ..., n$.

If we take the deviations from mean and denote

$$x_i - \bar{x} = u_i \text{ and } y_i - \bar{y} = v_i,$$

then the coefficient of correlation,

$$r = \frac{\Sigma_i u_i v_i}{\sqrt{\Sigma_i u_i^2 \Sigma_i v_i^2}} \qquad ...(15.37.3)$$

The correlation coefficient r is a pure number *i.e.*, r is independent of the units in which X and Y are measured.

Note: All said about r holds true for ρ except that *r* is an estimated value of the population parameter ρ.

Assumptions about Correlation Coefficient

There are three assumptions made in giving the correlation coefficient by the above formulae. They are:

1. The random variables X and Y are distributed normally.
2. The variables X and Y are linearly related.
3. There is a cause and effect relationship between factors affecting the values of X and Y in the series of data.

Limits of Correlation Coefficient

Formula (15.37.3) gives,

$$r^2 = \frac{(\Sigma_i u_i v_i)^2}{\Sigma_i u_i^2 \Sigma_i v_i^2} \qquad ...(15.38)$$

We know from the Schwartz inequality that if u_i and v_i are real quantities for all $i = 1, 2, ..., n$, then

$$(\Sigma_i u_i v_i)^2 \le (\Sigma_i u_i^2)(\Sigma_i v_i^2) \qquad ...(15.39)$$

The sign of equality holds if and only if

$$\frac{u_1}{v_1} = \frac{u_2}{v_2} = \cdots = \frac{u_n}{v_n} \qquad ...(15.40)$$

Thus using (15.39), we can write that

$$r^2 \le 1 \qquad ...(15.41)$$

which implies that $-1 \le r \le 1$. ...(15.42)

Hence it is clear that the correlation coefficient can never be greater than 1 and less than – 1. When ρ (or r) = 1, it means that there exists a perfect positive correlation between two variables and when ρ (or r) = – 1, it is called the perfect negative correlation. When two variables are independent, the correlation between them is zero. But its converse is not true *i.e.*, if the correlation between two variables is zero, they are not necessarily independent. Zero correlation coefficient shows the absence of linear relationship between the two variables. The values between 1 and – 1 are interpreted accordingly.

***Example* 15.6.** The age in years of fourteen young couples is given below:

Husband (X):	21	25	26	24	22	30	19	24	28	32	31	29	21	18
Wife (Y):	19	20	24	21	21	24	18	22	19	30	27	26	19	18

To know the extent of relationship between the age of husbands and wives, we calculate the coefficient of correlation r from the given data. For the given variate values,

$$n = 14,$$

$$\Sigma_i x_i = 350,$$

$$\bar{x} = 25$$

$$\Sigma_i y_i = 308,$$

$$\bar{y} = 22$$

Since means are whole numbers, it is convenient to make use of the formula (15.37.1). To do the calculations systematically, prepare the following table.

	x	y	$x-\bar{x}$	$y-\bar{y}$	$(x-\bar{x})^2$	$(y-\bar{y})^2$	$(x-\bar{x})(y-\bar{y})$
	21	19	– 4	– 3	16	9	12
	25	20	0	– 2	00	4	00
	26	24	1	2	1	4	2
	24	21	– 1	– 1	1	1	1
	22	21	– 3	– 1	9	1	3
	30	24	5	2	25	4	10
	19	18	– 6	– 4	36	16	24
	24	22	– 1	0	1	00	00
	28	19	3	– 3	9	9	– 9
	32	30	7	8	49	64	56
	31	27	6	5	36	25	30
	29	26	4	4	16	16	16
	21	19	– 4	– 3	16	9	12
	18	18	– 7	– 4	49	16	28
Total	350	308	0	0	264	178	185

From the above table we have,

$$\Sigma(x_i-\bar{x})^2 = 264, \Sigma_i \; (y_i-\bar{y})^2 = 178, \Sigma_i \; (x_i-\bar{x})(y_i-\bar{y}) = 185$$

Putting these values in the formula (15.37.1) we get,

$$r = \frac{185}{\sqrt{264 \times 178}} = \frac{185}{216.78} = 0.85$$

The coefficient of correlation between the age of husband and that of the wife is 0.85 which is close to 1. Hence it can be said that there is a high degree of positive relationship between the age of husbands and wives.

***Example* 15.7.** The birth rate and death rate per thousand persons in Switzerland from 1968 to 1980 were as follows:

Birth rate (*X*):	17.1	16.5	15.8	15.2	14.3	13.6	12.9	12.3	11.7	11.5	11.3	11.3	11.6
Death rate (*Y*):	9.3	9.3	9.1	8.2	8.9	8.9	8.5	9.7	9.0	8.7	9.1	9.0	9.2

The correlation between the birth rate and the death rate can be calculated in the following manner.

First, we make the following table and compute various values involved in the formula.

Obs. no.	x	y	x^2	y^2	xy
1	17.1	9.3	292.41	86.49	159.03
2	16.5	9.3	272.25	86.49	153.45
3	15.8	9.1	249.64	82.81	143.78
4	15.2	8.2	231.04	67.24	124.64
5	14.3	8.9	204.49	79.21	127.27
6	13.6	8.9	184.96	79.21	121.04
7	12.9	8.5	166.41	72.25	109.65
8	12.3	9.7	151.29	94.09	119.31
9	11.7	9.0	136.89	81.00	105.30
10	11.5	8.7	132.25	75.69	100.05
11	11.3	9.1	127.69	82.81	102.83
12	11.3	9.0	127.69	81.00	101.70
13	11.6	9.2	134.56	84.64	106.72
Total	175.1 $= \Sigma_i x_i$	116.9 $= \Sigma_i y_i$	2411.57 $= \Sigma_i x_i^2$	1052.93 $= \Sigma_i y_i^2$	1574.77 $= \Sigma_i x_i y_i$

There are 13 pairs of observations, hence $n = 13$. Now we make use of formula (15.37.2) because the means of x and y values are not exact.

$$r = \frac{1574.77 - (175.1)(116.9)/13}{\sqrt{\left(2411.57 - \frac{175.1^2}{13}\right)\left(1052.93 - \frac{116.9^2}{13}\right)}}$$

$$= \frac{0.22}{\sqrt{53.11 \times 1.73}} = \frac{0.22}{9.58} = 0.02$$

The coefficient of correlation between the birth rate and the death rate is 0.02, which is very close to zero, hence it can be inferred that they are not linearly related to each other.

Note: To calculate correlation coefficient with the help of SPSS software, see Appendix.

Correlation Coefficient from Coded Data

Using the same coding as in case of regression coefficient, *i.e.*, $dx_i = (x_i - c_1)/d_1$ and $dy_i = (y_i - c_2)/d_2$ and also making use of table (15.1) as such and relations from (15.16) to (15.17.1), the correlation coefficient from coded data as per formula (15.37.1) is,

$$r_c = \frac{\Sigma_i (dx_i - \overline{dx})(dy_i - \overline{dy})}{\sqrt{\Sigma_i (dx_i - \overline{dx})^2 \Sigma_i (dy_i - \overline{dy})^2}} \quad ...(15.43)$$

$$= \frac{\Sigma_i \left(\frac{x_i - c_1}{d_1} - \frac{\overline{x} - c_1}{d_1}\right)\left(\frac{y_i - c_2}{d_2} - \frac{\overline{y} - c_2}{d_2}\right)}{\sqrt{\Sigma_i \left(\frac{x_i - c_1}{d_1} - \frac{\overline{x} - c_1}{d_1}\right)^2 \Sigma_i \left(\frac{y_i - c_2}{d_2} - \frac{\overline{y} - c_2}{d_2}\right)^2}}$$

$$= \frac{\Sigma_i \left(\frac{x_i - \overline{x}}{d_1}\right)\left(\frac{y_i - \overline{y}}{d_2}\right)}{\sqrt{\Sigma_i \left(\frac{x_i - \overline{x}}{d_1}\right)^2 \Sigma_i \left(\frac{y_i - \overline{y}}{d_2}\right)^2}} \quad ...(15.43.1)$$

$$= \frac{\Sigma_i (x_i - \overline{x})(y_i - \overline{y})}{\sqrt{\Sigma_i (x_i - \overline{x})^2 \Sigma_i (y - \overline{y})^2}} \quad ...(15.43.2)$$

$$= r_{YX} \quad ...(15.44)$$

Relation (15.44) reveals that the correlation from coded data is independent of the constants involved in coding of the data. This result helps in reducing the labour of calculation of r to a great extent by choosing the suitable constants c_1, c_2, d_1 and d_2. Some or none or all of them may be equal. Moreover, c_1 and /or c_2 should be taken as zero if the origin is not shifted. Also d_1 and d_2 should be taken as unity if the scale of measurement is not to be changed.

***Example* 15.8.** First an example is given for the assumed set of paired observations showing that the correlation coefficient calculated with and without coding remains the same.

X:	8	6	12	14	16	10
Y:	15	10	20	25	30	20

We have done the coding by taking $c_1 = 10$, $d_1 = 2$, $c_2 = 20$ and $d_2 = 5$. The calculations are shown in the following table:

First we will calculate r with the help of formula (15.37.2) using the columns from (*i*) to (*v*).

$$r = \frac{1450 - \frac{66 \times 120}{6}}{\sqrt{\left(796 - \frac{66^2}{6}\right)\left(2650 - \frac{120^2}{6}\right)}}$$

	(i)	(ii)	(iii)	(iv)	(v)	(vi)	(vii)	(viii)	(ix)	(x)
	x	y	x^2	y^2	xy	$(x-10)/2 = dx$	$(y-20)/5 = dy$	d^2x	d^2y	$dxdy$
	8	15	64	225	120	– 1	– 1	1	1	1
	6	10	36	100	60	– 2	– 2	4	4	4
	12	20	144	400	240	1	0	1	0	0
	14	25	196	625	350	2	1	4	1	2
	16	30	256	900	480	3	2	9	4	6
	10	20	100	400	200	0	0	0	0	0
Total	66 $\equiv \Sigma_i x_i$	120 $\equiv \Sigma_i y_i$	796 $\equiv \Sigma_i x_i^2$	2650 $\equiv \Sigma_i y_i^2$	1450 $\equiv \Sigma_i x_i y_i$	3 $\equiv \Sigma_i dx_i$	0 $\equiv \Sigma_i dy_i$	19 $\equiv \Sigma_i d^2x_i$	10 $\equiv \Sigma_i d^2y_i$	13 $\equiv \Sigma_i dx_i dy_i$

$$= \frac{130}{\sqrt{70 \times 250}}$$

$$= \frac{13}{13.23}$$

$$= 0.98$$

Now we calculate r with the help of coded data from columns (*vi*) to (*x*) of the above table. The formula for r is,

$$r = \frac{\Sigma_i dx_i dy_i - \dfrac{(\Sigma_i dx_i)(\Sigma_i dy_i)}{n}}{\sqrt{\left\{\Sigma_i d^2 x_i - \dfrac{(\Sigma_i dx_i)^2}{n}\right\}\left\{\Sigma_i d^2 y_i - \dfrac{(\Sigma_i dy_i)^2}{n}\right\}}}$$

$$= \frac{13 - \dfrac{3 \times 0}{6}}{\sqrt{\left(19 - \dfrac{3^2}{6}\right)\left(10 - \dfrac{0}{6}\right)}}$$

$$= \frac{13}{\sqrt{17.5 \times 10}}$$

$$= 0.98$$

We get the same value of r in both ways. Hence, it justifies numerically that $r_c = r_{XY}$.

***Example* 15.9.** Correlation coefficient between the variables, total grain production and cereal production for the data given in example (15.4) is worked out.

Make use of coded values, since the data are too heavy. The partial calculations made in the example (15.4) have been used as such. Formula for r from coded values is used in the form as given in the example (15.8).

$$r=\frac{537-\frac{(-28)\times(-11)}{9}}{\sqrt{\left(205-\frac{(-11)^2}{9}\right)\left(1418-\frac{(28)^2}{9}\right)}}$$

Since, $\Sigma_i d^2 y_i = (-22)^2 + (-18)^2 + (-14)^2 + (-7)^2 + 0^2 + 3^2 + 4^2 + 12^2 + 14^2 = 1418$

$$r=\frac{502.78}{\sqrt{191.56\times 1330.89}}$$

$$=\frac{502.78}{504.92}$$

$$= 0.9958$$

The correlation between total grain production and cereal production is of high order.

Test of Significance of Correlation Coefficient

As already stated in Chapter 10, the random sample(s) is/are drawn from the population or universe under consideration. Whatever conclusions are derived or deduced from the sample values, are meant to draw inferences about the parent population. The estimates are not unique and hence a sort of confirmation is sought by way of test of significance, for the validity of inferences drawn from the sample about the population. Of course, these results are subjected to certain probability of wrong decision which is covered by level of significance.

The test of significance of correlation coefficient means to test the hypothesis, whether or not the correlation coefficient is zero in the population *i.e.*, we test,

$$H_0 : \rho = 0 \text{ vs. } H_1 : \rho \neq 0$$

The test statistic for testing H_0 is,

$$t_{n-2}=\frac{r}{s_r} \quad \text{...(15.45)}$$

where r is the estimated value of ρ based on n paired observations and s_r is the standard error of r. Suffix $(n-2)$ denotes the degrees of freedom of t. Also,

$$s_r=\sqrt{\frac{1-r^2}{n-2}}$$

Thus,
$$t_{n-2}=\frac{r\sqrt{n-2}}{\sqrt{1-r^2}} \quad \text{...(15.45.1)}$$

If the calculated value of t is greater than the table value of t for α level of significance and $(n-2)$ d.f., reject H_0, otherwise accept H_0. Rejection of H_0 leads to the conclusion that the two variables are not independent. This means that the correlation between them is worth considering. If H_0 is accepted, it means that the value of r is due to sampling whereas in reality two variables are uncorrelated in the population.

***Example* 15.10.** In the example (15.9),

$$r = 0.9958 \text{ and } n = 9.$$

To test the significance of the population correlation coefficient, we test

$$H_0 : \rho = 0 \text{ vs. } H_1 : \rho \neq 0$$

by the statistic (15.45.1). Hence,

$$t = \frac{0.9958\sqrt{9-2}}{\sqrt{1-(0.9958)^2}}$$

$$= \frac{0.9958 \times \sqrt{7}}{\sqrt{.0084}}$$

$$= \frac{2.63}{0.092}$$

$$= 28.59$$

The table value of t at $\alpha = 0.05$ and 7 d.f. is 2.365. Since the calculated value of t is greater than the table value of t, we reject H_0. It means that there is a significant correlation between total grain production and cereal production.

***Example* 15.11.** From example (15.6) we have,

$$r = 0.85 \text{ and } n = 14.$$

We test the hypothesis,

$$H_0 : \rho = 0 \text{ vs. } H_1 : \rho \neq 0$$

by the statistic (15.45.1), That is,

$$t = \frac{0.85\sqrt{14-2}}{\sqrt{1-(0.85)^2}}$$

$$= \frac{2.944}{0.527}$$

$$= 5.587$$

The table value of t at $\alpha = 0.01$ and 12 d.f. is 3.499 which is less than the calculated value of t. Hence, we reject H_0. This leads to the conclusion that the heights of husbands and their wives are highly correlated.

Tests under Fisher's Z-Transformation

When the hypothesis, $\rho = 0$, is rejected, then it will be worthwhile to test H_0 for some other postulated value of ρ. Even though the hypothesis $\rho = 0$ is not tested. Often on the basis of some prior information, we expect a value of correlation coefficient, say ρ_0 to exist between two variables X and Y. Moreover, from the sample, we want to ascertain whether the value ρ_0 is to be accepted or not. To achieve this objective, Sir Ronald A. Fisher suggested the Z-test for the test of hypothesis,

$$H_0 : \rho = \rho_0 \text{ vs. } H_1 : \rho \neq \rho_0.$$

In this situation H_0 cannot be tested directly. Hence he suggested a transformation which is known as Fisher's Z-transformation which is as follows:

$$Z_r = \frac{1}{2}\log_e\left(\frac{1+r}{1-r}\right) \qquad ...(15.46)$$

Generally, we are provided with log tables to the base 10. So we use logarithmic relationship for the change of base, *i.e.*, $\log_e a = \log_{10} a \log_e 10$. We also know that $\log_e 10 = 2.3026$. Thus,

$$Z_r = 1.1513 \log_{10}\left(\frac{1+r}{1-r}\right) \qquad \text{...(15.46.1)}$$

Corresponding to any value of r, the value of Z_r can be calculated. To save time and labour, the Table VIII is provided from which the value of Z_r corresponding to any value of r between 0 and 0.99 can directly be read and made use of.

The variable Z_r is distributed approximately normally with mean μ_z and standard deviation σ_z, where,

$$\mu_z = 1.1513 \log_{10}\left(\frac{1+\rho_0}{1-\rho_0}\right) \text{ and } \sigma_z = \frac{1}{\sqrt{n-3}}$$

Thus, the rationale for the transformation (15.46) has been to obtain a function of r which has variance independent of ρ. This transformation should be used only when n is not very small. Because if n is small, approximation to normal distribution will not be valid.

Test of H_0 is performed using the normal deviate test. The test statistic is,

$$Z = \frac{Z_r - \mu_z}{\sigma_z} \qquad \text{...(15.47)}$$

If the calculated value of Z obtained from (15.47) is greater than Z_α, the table value of normal deviate at α level, then reject H_0, otherwise accept H_0. Rejection of H_0 leads us to conclude that the postulated value ρ_0 of population correlation coefficient is not supported by the data. If H_0 is accepted, it means that there is no evidence against the value of ρ as ρ_0 and hence it is acceptable, of course, with risk α.

For a two-tailed test, the table value of Z at 5 per cent level of significance is 1.96 and at 1 per cent level of significance, it is 2.58. These table values can be used at the time of taking a decision about H_0 provided the prefixed level of significance is either of the two.

***Example* 15.12.** Making use of the data and the results of the example (15.6), test of hypothesis that the correlation coefficient between the age of husbands and wives is 0.9 amounts to test,

$$H_0 : \rho = 0.9 \text{ vs. } H_1 : \rho \neq 0.9$$

In the example (15.6) we have got $r = 0.85$ and $n = 14$. To test H_0 we apply Fisher's Z-transformation. The value of Z_r corresponding to $r = 0.85$ from Table VIII is 1.256 and for $\rho_0 = 0.9$, $\mu_z = 1.472$.

Also $$\sigma_z = \frac{1}{\sqrt{14-3}} = \frac{1}{\sqrt{11}}$$

Hence, the test statistic,

$$Z = \frac{1.256 - 1.472}{1/\sqrt{11}}$$
$$= -0.216 \times 3.32$$
$$= -0.72$$

The calculated value of Z is less than 1.96, the normal deviate value at 5 per cent level of significance. So, we accept H_0, which means that the expectation of the scientist is correct.

***Example* 15.13.** Now the test is performed based on the data given in example (15.7) where the experience tells that the coefficient of correlation between the birth rate and the death rate is 0.5. To confirm our assertion, we test the hypothesis,

$$H_0 : \rho = 0.5 \text{ vs. } H_1 : \rho \neq 0.5$$

In the referred example we have,

$$r = 0.02 \text{ and } n = 13.$$

Using the Table VIII for Fisher's Z-transformation, we get,

$$Z_r = 0.02 \text{ and } Z_{\rho_0} = Z_{0.5} = 0.549$$

or $$\mu_z = 0.549$$

Now the test statistic is,

$$Z = \frac{0.02 - 0.549}{1/\sqrt{10}}$$

$$= -0.529 \times \sqrt{10}$$

$$= -0.529 \times 3.16$$

$$= -1.67$$

The calculated value of absolute Z is greater than 1.64, the table value of normal deviate at 10 per cent level of significance. Hence, we reject H_0. It is worth noting that the calculated value of r is very low. The test reveals that the correlation coefficient in the population, of the order 0.5, is not acceptable for $\alpha = 0.10$.

Test of Equality of Two Population Correlation Coefficients

Let there are two bivariate normal populations and the correlation coefficients between two variables X and Y in each population are ρ_1 and ρ_2 respectively.

Here the hypothesis,

$$H_0 : \rho_1 = \rho_2 \text{ vs. } H_1 : \rho_1 \neq \rho_2$$

is to be tested.

Suppose two random samples of sizes n_1 and n_2 are drawn independently from two bivariate normal populations and the sample correlation coefficients between the variables X and Y are r_1 and r_2 respectively.

To test H_0, we will have to make Fisher's Z-transformation.

$$Z_1 = \frac{1}{2}\log_e\left(\frac{1+r_1}{1-r_1}\right) \quad ...(15.48)$$

and $$Z_2 = \frac{1}{2}\log_e\left(\frac{1+r_2}{1-r_2}\right) \quad ...(15.49)$$

The value of Z_1 and Z_2 can directly be read from table-VIII for the values r_1 and r_2 respectively.

The distribution of $(Z_1 - Z_2)$ is normal with mean,

$$\left\{\frac{\rho}{2(n_1-1)} - \frac{\rho}{2(n_2-1)}\right\}$$

(where ρ is the common correlation coefficient) and variance,

$$\left\{\frac{1}{n_1-3} + \frac{1}{n_2-3}\right\}$$

Z-statistics to test H_0 is, $Z = \dfrac{Z_1 - Z_2}{\sqrt{\dfrac{1}{n_1-3} + \dfrac{1}{n_2-3}}}$ ...(15.50)

Statistic Z is distributed normally with mean 0 and variance 1. To decide about H_0, compare the value of Z with tabulated value of Z with α level of significance. For $\alpha = 0.05$, $Z_{1-\alpha/2} = 1.96$. Hence, if $Z_{cal} \geq 1.96$, reject H_0. It means ρ_1 cannot be taken equal to ρ_2. Again, if $Z_{cal} < 1.96$, accept H_0, it means $\rho_1 = \rho_2$. In this situation, two correlation coefficients can be pooled. For any other value of α, the value of $Z_{1-\alpha/2}$ can be obtained from table IV and a decision about H_0 can be taken in the like manner.

***Example* 15.14.** In a research study, the correlation coefficients between dietary intake of vitamin A and serum levels of vitamin A in rural males and urban males based on samples of sizes 30 and 28 respectively were as follows:

Rural males	Urban males
$r_1 = 0.90$	$r_2 = 0.99$

The test of hypothesis that the correlation coefficients between intake of vitamin A and serum level of vitamin A in rural population (ρ_1) and in urban population (ρ_2) are equal *i.e.*, the test of

$$H_0 : \rho_1 = \rho_2 \text{ versus } H_1 ; \rho_1 \neq \rho_2$$

can be performed in the manner described just before,

The values of Z_1 and Z_2 from table VIII corresponding to $r_1 = 0.90$ and $r_2 = 0.99$ are,

$$Z_1 = 1.4722 \text{ and } Z_2 = 2.6467.$$

Also given that $n_1 = 30$ and $n_2 = 28$.

Hence, the test statistic Z from the formula (15.50) is,

$$Z = \frac{1.4722 - 2.6467}{\sqrt{\dfrac{1}{30-3} + \dfrac{1}{28-3}}}$$

$$Z = \frac{-1.1745}{\sqrt{0.0370 + 0.04}}$$

$$= \frac{-1.1745}{0.2776}$$

$$= -4.23$$

The tabulated value of Z for $\alpha = 0.05$ is 1.96, which is less than the absolute calculated value of Z. Hence H_0 is rejected. This leads to infer that the correlation between vitamin A intake and serum level of vitamin A in rural and urban male populations is not the same at 5 per cent level of significance.

Pooling of Several Correlation Coefficients

Suppose we have K samples ($K > 2$) of sizes n_i ($i = 1, 2, ..., K$) are selected randomly from K populations or at K occasions. Paired observations (x, y) are taken for all the samples and correlation coefficient calculated for each sample. Now the question arises whether we can pool these correlations to get a single estimate of the population correlation coefficients or not. Pooling of correlation coefficients is possible only if the population correlation coefficients are homogeneous. It amounts to testing,

$$H_0 : \rho_1 = \rho_2 = \rho_3 = ... = \rho_k$$

versus H_1 :at least two of them are not equal.

Let the simple correlation coefficient between the variables X and Y from K samples are $r_1, r_2, ..., r_K$ respectively, if the bias is so small that it can be neglected, then the test of homogeneity of correlation coefficients is equivalent to testing the homogeneity of Z-values. Hence, we make use of Fishers Z-transformation. Null hypothesis H_0 can be tested by χ^2 - test. The value of statistic χ^2 can be calculated with the help of the following table (15.3).

Table 15.3

(i)	(ii)	(iii)	(iv)	(v)	(vi)	(vii)
Sample No.	Sample size	Correlation coefficient	$Z = \text{Tanh}_r^{-1} = \frac{1}{2}\log_e \frac{1+r}{1-r}$	Reciprocal of variance of $r = (n - 3)$	$(n - 3)Z$	$(n - 3)Z^2$
1	n_1	r_1	Z_1	$(n_1 - 3)$	$(n_1 - 3)Z_1$	$(n_1 - 3) Z_1^2$
2	n_2	r_2	Z_2	$(n_2 - 3)$	$(n_2 - 3)Z_2$	$(n_2 - 3) Z_2^2$
3	n_3	r_3	Z_3	$(n_3 - 3)$	$(n_3 - 3)Z_3$	$(n_3 - z) Z_3^2$
⋮	⋮	⋮	⋮	⋮	⋮	⋮
⋮	⋮	⋮	⋮	⋮	⋮	⋮
K	n_K	r_K	Z_K	$(n_K - 3)$	$(n_K - 3)Z_K$	$(n_K - 3) Z_K^2$
Total				$\sum_i (n_i - 3)$	$\sum_i (n_i - 3)Z_i$	$\sum_i (n_i - 3)Z_i^2$

The value of statistic χ^2 in terms of the quantities calculated in the table (15.3) is,

$$\chi^2 = \sum_{i=1}^{K} (n_i - 3)Z_i^2 - \frac{\left\{\sum_{i=1}^{K} (n_i - 3)Z_i\right\}^2}{\sum_{i=1}^{K} (n_i - 3)} \quad ...(15.51)$$

Statistic χ^2 has $(K-1)$ d.f.

To test H_0 vs. H_1, compare calculated value of χ^2 with the tabulated value of χ^2 for $(K-1)$ d.f. and α level of significance. The values for χ^2 are tabulated in table (VI).

If $\chi^2_{cal} \geq \chi^2_{(K-1).\alpha}$, reject H_0 which means that the correlation coefficients are not homogeneous and hence they cannot be pooled. If $\chi^2_{cal} < \chi^2_{(K-1).\alpha}$, accept H_0 which leads to the conclusion that correlation coefficients are not heterogeneous and can be pooled.

***Example* 15.15.** In a survey on children below 5 years age, the simple correlation in weights in kg (X) and height in cms (Y) of children in four age groups were as follows:

Age group (years)	*Number of children*	*Correlation coefficients*
0 – 1	$n_1 = 25$	$r_1 = 0.88$
1 – 2	$n_2 = 27$	$r_2 = 0.78$
2 – 3	$n_3 = 25$	$r_3 = 0.52$
3 – 4	$n_4 = 10$	$r_4 = 0.70$

The hypothesis, $H_0 = \rho_1 = \rho_2 = \rho_3 = \rho_4$
against H_1 = at least two of them are not equal.
can be tested by χ^2 – test.

To get the value of statistic χ^2, prepare the following table. The value of Z corresponding to r are obtained from table (VIII).

Age groups	*Sample size n*	*Corr. coeff. r*	$\frac{1}{2}\log_e\left(\frac{1+r}{1-r}\right)$ Z	$(n-3)$	$(n-3)$ Z	$(n-3)Z^2$
0 – 1	25	0.88	1.3758	22	30.2676	41.6422
1 – 2	27	0.78	1.0454	24	25.0896	26.2287
2 – 3	25	0.52	0.5763	22	12.6786	7.3066
3 – 4	10	0.70	0.8673	7	6.0711	5.2655
Total				75	74.1069	80.4430

The value of χ^2 from the formula (15.51),

$$\chi^2 = 80.4430 - \frac{(74.1069)^2}{75}$$
$$= 80.4430 - 73.2244$$
$$= 7.2186$$

Tabulated value of χ^2 for 3 d.f. and $\alpha = 0.05$, level of significance is 7.815. Calculated value of χ^2 is less than the tabulated value of χ^2. Hence, we conclude that the correlation coefficients in different age groups are homogeneous. Hence, a common correlation coefficient obtained by pooling the data of all age groups is valid.

Correlation in Grouped Bivariate Data

Many studies are based on a very large number of people or units. For example we consider correlation between the number of days, lost by the workers of a production unit, and their age. In such a case it is not advisable to deal with every worker's age and days lost individually. So the data are grouped and the correlation is calculated. Here the basic formula and interpretation remains the same. But a change in approach is made in doing the calculation by using the following bivariate table which is similar to the contingency table.

Suppose, the bivariate frequency table in general obtained after grouping is as follows:

Table 15.4

Groupings of variable X	*Groupings of variable Y*						
	$Y_1 - Y_2$	$Y_2 - Y_3$	....	$Y_j - Y_{j+1}$	....	$Y_q - Y_{q+1}$	*Total*
$X_1 - X_2$	f_{11}	f_{12}	....	f_{1j}	....	f_{1q}	R_1
$X_2 - X_3$	f_{21}	f_{22}	....	f_{2j}	....	f_{2q}	R_2
⋮	⋮	⋮		⋮		⋮	⋮
$X_i - X_{i+1}$	f_{i1}	f_{i2}	....	f_{ij}	....	f_{iq}	R_i
⋮	⋮	⋮		⋮		⋮	⋮
$X_p - X_{p+1}$	f_{p1}	f_{p2}	....	f_{pj}	....	f_{pq}	R_p
Total	C_1	C_2	....	C_j	....	C_q	n

In the above table certain points are to be noted:

(*i*) It is not necessary that the number of groupings of one variable is equal to the number of groupings of the other variable, *i.e.*, p may or may not be equal to q.

(*ii*) The frequency f_{ij} of any cell may be zero.

(*iii*) R_i $(i = 1, 2, ..., p)$ represents the total frequency for the ith group of variable X, and similarly C_j $(j = 1, 2, ..., q)$ represents the total frequency of the jth group of variable Y.

(*iv*) n represents the total number of people or units in the sample.

The correlation coefficient, for the data presented in the table (15.5), can be calculated by the procedure given below:

First, find out the mid-values of each group for both the variables. The mid-value of each class works as variate value, under the assumption that the frequencies are centered at the mid-point of each class. Also let us suppose, the coding of data has been done and thus denote the coded value of variable X by dx and of Y by dy. The formula for calculating the correlation coefficient in terms of dx and dy is,

$$r = \frac{\Sigma_i \Sigma_j f_{ij}\, dx_i dy_j - \dfrac{(\Sigma_i R_i\, dx_i)(\Sigma_j C_j\, dy_j)}{n}}{\sqrt{\left\{\Sigma_i R_i\, d^2 x_i - \dfrac{(\Sigma_i R_i dx_i)^2}{n}\right\}\left\{\Sigma_i C_j\, d^2 y_j - \dfrac{(\Sigma_j C_j\, dy_j)^2}{n}\right\}}} \quad ...(15.52)$$

where $\Sigma_i \Sigma_j f_{ij} = n$.

Table 15.5

Variable X						Variable Y					
Groups	*Mid-values x*	*Freq. R*	$\frac{x-c_1}{d_1}$ $= dx$	Rdx	Rd^2x	*Groups*	*Mid-values y*	*Freq. C*	$\frac{y-c_2}{d_2}$ $= dy$	Cdy	Cd^2y
$X_1 - X_2$	x_1	R_1	dx_1	R_1dx_1	$R_1d^2x_1$	$Y_1 - Y_2$	y_1	C_1	dy_1	C_1dy_1	$C_1d^2y_1$
$X_2 - X_3$	x_2	R_2	dx_2	R_2dx_2	$R_2d^2x_2$	$Y_2 - Y_3$	y_2	C_2	dy_2	C_2dy_2	$C_2d^2y_2$
$\vdots$	$\vdots$	$\vdots$	$\vdots$	$\vdots$	$\vdots$	$\vdots$	$\vdots$	$\vdots$	$\vdots$	$\vdots$	$\vdots$
$X_i - X_{i+1}$	x_i	R_i	dx_i	R_idx_i	$R_id^2x_i$	$Y_j - Y_{j+1}$	y_j	C_j	dy_j	$C_j\,dy_j$	$C_jd^2y_j$
$\vdots$	$\vdots$	$\vdots$	$\vdots$	$\vdots$	$\vdots$	$\vdots$	$\vdots$	$\vdots$	$\vdots$	$\vdots$	$\vdots$
$X_p - X_{p+1}$	x_p	R_p	dx_p	R_pdx_p	$R_pd^2x_p$	$Y_q - Y_{q+1}$	y_q	C_q	dy_q	C_qdy_q	$C_qd^2y_q$
Total				$\Sigma_iR_idx_i$	$\Sigma_iR_id^2x_i$					$\Sigma_iC_j\,dy_j$	$\Sigma_jC_j\,d^2y_j$

The quantities required in the formula (15.52) can be calculated by preparing the following tables.

Table 15.6

dy / dx	dy_1	dy_2	...	dy_j	...	dy_q	*Total*
dx_1	dx_1dy_1 f_{11} $f_{11}dx_1dy_1$	dx_1dy_2 f_{12} $f_{12}dx_1dy_2$	...	dx_1dy_j f_{1j} $f_{1j}\ dx_1dy_j$	...	—	$\Sigma_i f_{1j}\ dx_1dy_j$
						$dx_2\ dy_q$ f_{2q} $f_{2q}\ dx_2\ dy_q$	$\Sigma_j\ f_{2j}\ dx_2\ dy_j$
. d_{x_i}	— . .	dx_idx_2 f_{i2} $f_{i2}dx_idy_2$	...	—	...	—	$\Sigma_j\ f_{ij}\ dx_i\ dy_j$
. . dx_p	dx_pd_{y1} f_{p1} $f_{p1}dx_pdy_1$	—	...	—	...	dx_pdy_q f_{pq} $f_{pq}dx_pdy_q$	$\Sigma_jf_{pj}dx_pdy_j$
Total	$\Sigma_i\ f_{i1}\ dx_i\ dy_1$	$\Sigma_i\ f_{i2}\ dx_i\ dy_2$	...	$\Sigma_i\ f_{ij}\ dx_i\ dy_j$	...	$\Sigma_i\ f_{iq}\ dx_i\ dy_q$	$\Sigma_{ij}\ f_{ij}\ dx_i\ dy_j$

Now, we are to calculate $\Sigma_{ij}\ f_{ij}\ dx_i\ dy_1$ to make use of the formula (15.52). For this, prepare another Table 15.6 as given above. In this table, some cell frequencies f_{ij} are shown and the rest are taken to be zero. Even if all frequencies are present, similar procedure can be followed for all the cell frequencies.

In each cell of the Table 15.6, three figures appear. The upper part contains the product of the coded values of X and Y corresponding to that cell, *i.e.*, *dxdy*; in the middle there is cell frequency; the lower part is the product of the upper two quantities of the cell *i.e.*, *fdxdy*. Thus the (i, j)th cell contents as given in the table are as shown in the rectangle. The last column of the table gives the marginal totals, *fdxdy* over all y. Similarly the last row of the table shows the marginal totals, *fdxdy* over all x. The sum of all the marginal totals along the rows or along the columns gives the quantity $\Sigma f_{ij}\ dx_i\ dy_j$. It is to be noted that the sum of marginal totals along rows is always equal to the sum of marginal totals along columns. It works as a check to the calculations.

dx_idy_i f_{ij} $f_{ij}\ dx_i\ dy_j$

Substituting the values of all the terms in the formula (15.52) and solving the expression, we get the value of correlation coefficient.

Remarks: 1. Coding of data, is not a must. If no coding has been done, $c_1 = c_2 = 0$ and $d_1 = d_2 = 1$.

2. If needed coding of one variable alone can be done.
3. The test of significance remains the same irrespective of the way, the value of correlation coefficient has been calculated.

***Example* 15.16.** In a survey of factories, the number of days with double duty, per month, by workers of different age groups, were as follows:

Age groups	*Number of days with double duty per month*						*Total*
	1 – 3	3 – 5	5 – 7	7 – 9	9 – 11	11 – 13	
20 – 30	2	8	14	—	1	—	25
30 – 40	5	9	6	3	—	—	23
40 – 50	6	7	5	—	—	1	19
50 – 60	2	6	3	1	—	—	12
60 – 70	1	—	—	—	—	—	1
Total	16	30	28	4	1	1	80

The correlation coefficient between the age and the number of days with double duty per month can be calculated easily by preparing the tables on the lines of Tables 15.5 and 15.6 and using the formula 15.52. Here we give the calculations without any explanation, as we follow exactly the same procedure as already described. (see table on page 424).

Now prepare the second table to calculate the cross product terms.

dy / *dx*	– 2	– 1	0	1	2	3	*Total*
– 2	4 2 8	2 8 16	0 14 0	– 2 0 0	– 4 1 – 4	– 6 0 0	+ 20
– 1	2 5 10	1 9 9	0 6 0	– 1 3 – 3	– 2 0 0	– 3 0 0	+ 16
0	0 6 0	0 7 0	0 5 0	0 0 0	0 0 0	0 1 0	00
1	– 2 2 – 4	– 1 6 – 6	0 3 0	1 1 1	2 0 0	3 0 0	– 9
2	– 4 1 – 4	– 2 0 0	0 0 0	2 0 0	4 0 0	6 0 0	– 4
Total	10	19	0	– 2	– 4	0	23

From these two tables, we get values for all the required terms in the formula (15.52). Thus on substituting we obtain,

$$r = \frac{23 - \dfrac{(-59)(-53)}{80}}{\sqrt{\left\{139 - \dfrac{(-59)^2}{80}\right\}\left\{111 - \dfrac{(-53)^2}{80}\right\}}}$$

Variable X						Variable Y					
Classes	Mid-values	Freq. R	$\frac{x-45}{10} = dx$	Rdx	Rd^2x	Classes	Mid-values	Freq. C	$\frac{y-6}{2} = dy$	Cdy	Cd^2y
20 – 30	25	25	– 2	– 50	100	1 – 3	2	16	– 2	– 32	64
30 – 40	35	23	– 1	– 23	23	3 – 5	4	30	– 1	– 30	30
40 – 50	45	19	0	00	00	5 – 7	6	28	0	00	00
50 – 60	55	12	1	12	12	7 – 9	8	4	1	4	4
60 – 70	65	1	2	2	4	9 – 11	10	1	2	2	4
						11 – 13	12	1	3	3	9
Total		80		– 59	139			80		– 53	111

$$= \frac{23 - 39.09}{\sqrt{(139 - 43.51)(111 - 35.11)}}$$

$$= \frac{-16.09}{85.12}$$

$$= -0.19$$

The correlation between the age of workers and the number of double duty days is negative. It means that as the age increases, the workers avoid double duty. Of course, the correlation is of a low degree.

RELATIONSHIP BETWEEN CORRELATION COEFFICIENT AND REGRESSION COEFFICIENTS

It has been said that simple correlation is expressed only when there exists a linear relation between two variables. Hence, it should be possible to establish the mathematical relationship between the correlation coefficient and the two regression coefficients namely, b_{YX} and b_{XY}. We know,

$$r = \frac{\Sigma_i (x_i - \bar{x})(y_i - \bar{y})}{\sqrt{\Sigma_i (x_i - \bar{x})^2 \Sigma_i (y_i - \bar{y})^2}}$$

for $i = 1, 2. ..., n$

or $$r^2 = \frac{\{\Sigma_i (x_i - \bar{x})(y_i - \bar{y})\}^2}{\Sigma_i (x_i - \bar{x})^2 \Sigma_i (y_i - \bar{y})^2}$$

Also $$b_{YX} = \frac{\Sigma_i (x_i - \bar{x})(y_i - \bar{y})}{\Sigma_i (x_i - \bar{x})^2}$$

and $$b_{XY} = \frac{\Sigma_i (x_i - \bar{x})(y_i - \bar{y})}{\Sigma_i (y_i - \bar{y})^2}$$

$\therefore$ $$b_{YX} b_{XY} = \frac{(\Sigma_i (x_i - \bar{x})(y_i - \bar{y})\}^2}{\Sigma_i (x_i - \bar{x})^2 \Sigma_i (y_i - \bar{y})^2}$$

$$= r^2$$

or $$r = \sqrt{b_{YX} . b_{XY}} \qquad ...(15.53)$$

Relation (15.53) shows that the correlation coefficient is the geometric mean of the two regression coefficients. The sign of r will be the same as that of either b_{YX} or $b_{XY.}$

Again, $$b_{YX} = \frac{s_{XY}}{s_X^2}$$

and $$r = \frac{s_{XY}}{s_X s_Y}$$

$$s_{XY} = r s_X s_Y$$

Substituting for s_{XY} we get,

$$b_{YX} = r\frac{s_Y}{s_X} \quad ...(15.54)$$

Similarly, $$b_{XY} = r\frac{s_X}{s_Y} \quad ...(15.55)$$

RANK CORRELATION

It is not always possible to take measurements on units or objects. Many characters are expressed in comparative terms such as beauty, smartness, temperament, etc. In such cases the subjects are ranked pertaining to that particular character instead of taking measurements on them. Sometimes, the units are also ranked according to their quantitative measure. In these types of studies, two situations arise, (*i*) the same set of units is ranked according to two characters A and B, (*ii*) Two judges give ranks to the same set of units independently, pertaining to one character only. In both these situations, we get paired ranks for a set of units. For examples, (*i*) two judges rank the girls independently in a beauty competition, (*ii*) The students are ranked according to their marks in Mathematics and Statistics. In all these situations, the usual Pearsonian correlation coefficient cannot be obtained. Hence, the psychologist, Charles Edward Spearman (1906) developed a formula for correlation coefficient, which is known as *rank correlation* or *Spearman's correlation*. It is denoted by r_s. Suffix S to r is a connotation for Spearman, the name of the inventor.

The formula for r_s is derived as the ratio of covariance to the product of standard deviation of two series of ranks. Here the derivation is omitted and thus the formula for rank correlation is,

$$r_s = 1 - \frac{6\Sigma_i d_i^2}{n(n^2-1)} \quad ...(15.56)$$

where $i = 1, 2, ..., n$,

d_i is the difference between the ranks of the i-th units and n is the total number of units.

The value of r_s also lies between – 1 and 1.

***Example* 15.17.** Two judges gave the following ranks (from the highest to the lowest) to eleven girls who contested in a beauty competition. Whether or not, there is an agreement between the independent rankings of the two judges, can be ascertained only by finding out the rank correlation between the ranks awarded by two judges.

Girl no.	1	2	3	4	5	6	7	8	9	10	11
	Ranks										
Judge A	3	4	1	2	5	10	11	7	9	8	6
Judge B	2	4	3	1	7	9	6	11	10	5	8

Following the usual procedure, the rank correlation is calculated.

d	1	0	– 2	1	– 2	1	5	– 4	– 1	3	– 2	Total
d^2	1	0	4	1	4	1	25	16	1	9	4	66

Here $\Sigma_i d_i^2 = 66$ and $n = 11$

From (15.56),

$$r_s = 1 - \frac{6 \times 66}{11 \times 120} = 1 - 0.30 = 0.70$$

The value of rank correlation $r_s = 0.70$, which is quite high. Hence it can be concluded that there is an agreement between judges with regard to the beauty of the girls.

Example **15.18.** The ranks of 12 students according to their marks in Mathematics and Statistics were as follows:

Student no.	1	2	3	4	5	6	7	8	9	10	11	12
Mathematics	5	2	1	6	8	11	12	4	3	9	7	10
Statistics	4	3	2	7	6	9	10	5	1	11	8	12

The curiosity lies to know whether or not students who are good in Mathematics also excel in Statistics and vice versa. This objective can be met by finding out the rank correlation coefficient. For this the calculations are,

													Total
d	1	– 1	– 1	– 1	2	2	2	– 1	2	– 2	– 1	– 2	0
d^2	1	1	1	1	4	4	4	1	4	4	1	4	30

Here $\Sigma_i d_i^2 = 30$ and $n = 12$

From (15.56)

$$r_s = 1 - \frac{6 \times 30}{12 \times 143}$$
$$= 1 - 0.105$$
$$= 0.895$$

The correlation between the ranks of marks in the two subjects is very high. From this, it is inferred that the students who are good in Mathematics are also good in Statistics.

Problem of Tied Observations

Formula (15.56) is based on the assumption that n units received n sets of paired ranks from 1 to n independently assigned in each set. As a matter of fact no ties should occur in case of samples from continuous population. But ties seldom occur due to rounding of measurements. Hence, the problem of ties comes in while calculating Spearman's rank correlation.

If ties occur between measurements across sets x and y, it creates no problem. But if ties occur within a set of sample values, the problem of ties cannot be ignored. In this situation, of course, the ranks are assigned by mid-rank method. Under this process, the sum of ranks remain the same as $n(n + 1)/2$, but there is a decrease in the sum of squares of ranks. Hence, adjustment has to be made in the formula of Spearman's rank correlation. It is given here without proof.

Suppose m_h is the number of tied measurements in the ith group of tied values ($h = 1, 2, ..., K$) for the set x. It means there are K groups of tied values in the set x. Then the correction factor u_x for ties for the set x is given as,

$$u_x = \sum_{h=1}^{K} m_h(m_h^2 - 1)$$

A similar expression v_y *i.e.*, the correction factor for groups of tied measurements within the set y can be given as,

$$v_y = \sum_{j=1}^{l} g_j(g_j^2 - 1)$$

where g_j is the number of tied measurements in the jth group of tied values for $j = 1, 2, ..., l$. In case of ties in both the sets, the amended formula for Spearman's rank correlation is,

$$r = \frac{n(n^2-1) - 6\sum_{i=1}^{n} d_i^2 - (u_x + v_y)/2}{\sqrt{(n^2(n^2-1)^2 + (u_x + v_y)(n^3 - n) + u_x v_y}} \quad ...(15.56.1)$$

$$= \frac{(n^3 - n) - 6\sum_{i=1}^{n} d_i^2 - (u_x + v_y)/2}{\sqrt{(n^3 - n)^2 - (n^3 - n)(u_x + v_y) + u_x v_y}} \quad ...(15.56.2)$$

In the above formula, if no ties occur in the set x, $u_x = 0$ and if no ties occur in the set y, $v_y = 0$. If no ties occur in both the sets, $u_x = 0$, $v_y = 0$ and thus formula (15.56.2) reduces to formula (15.56).

***Example* 15.19.** The percentage marks secured by eleven students in I.C.W.A. and C.A. examinations are as follows:

Student:	1	2	3	4	5	6	7	8	9	10	11
I.C.W.A. Marks (x)%	40	55	40	60	62	78	58	96	85	60	60
C.A. Marks (y) %	65	45	68	65	70	75	69	88	75	72	82

Spearman's rank correlation between percentage of marks in I.C.W.A. and C.A. examinations by eleven students is calculated in the manner explained in theory.

From percentage of marks it is apparent that the ties occur in both the sets. Further there are two groups of tied percentages in each set.

Using mid-rank method, the ranks of percentages for I.C.W.A. (x) and C.A. (y) and their differences $d_i (i = 1, 2, ..., 11)$ are displayed in the following table.

Students	1	2	3	4	5	6	7	8	9	10	11
Ranks for x	1.5	3	1.5	6	8	9	4	11	10	6	6
Ranks for y	2.5	1	4	2.5	6	7.5	5	11	7.5	9	10
Difference d_i	– 1	2	– 2.5	3.5	2	1.5	– 1	0	2.5	– 3	– 4

Calculation of correction factors —

For the set x, $m_1 = 2, m_2 = 3$ and $h = 1, 2$.

Hence, $u_x = (2^3 - 2) + (3^3 - 3)$

$= 6 + 24 = 30$

Similarly for the set y,

$g_1 = 2, g_2 = 2$ and $l = 1, 2$

$v_y = (2^3 - 2) + (2^3 - 2)$

$= 6 + 6 = 12$

$$\Sigma d_i^2 = (-1)^2 + 2^2 + (-2.5)^2 + 3.5^2 + 2^2 + 1.5^2 + (-1)^2 + 0^2 + 2.5^2 + (-3)^2 + (-4)^2$$

$$= 1 + 4 + 6.25 + 12.25 + 4 + 2.25 + 1 + 0 + 6.25 + 9 + 16$$

$$= 62.00$$

Also, $n^3 - n = (11^3 - 11) = 1320$

Thus, from the formula (15.56.2), Spearman's correlation is,

$$r_s = \frac{1320 - 6 \times 62 - (30 + 12)/2}{\sqrt{(1320)^2 - 1320(30 + 12) + 30 \times 12}}$$

$$= \frac{1320 - 372 - 21}{\sqrt{1687320}}$$

$$= \frac{927}{1298.97}$$

$$= 0.714$$

Since, the value of r_s is high, it shows that a high positive correlation exists between percentage of marks in I.C.W.A. and C.A. earned by the eleven students.

COEFFICIENT OF DETERMINATION

The coefficient of determination, which is given as r^2, explains to what extent the variation of dependent variable Y is being expressed by the independent variable X.

$$r^2 = \frac{\text{variance explained}}{\text{total variance}} \qquad ...(15.57)$$

More the value of r^2, better it is. A high value clearly shows that a good linear relation exists between the two variables. Obviously, if $r = 1$, then $r^2 = 1$, which is an indicator of perfect relationship between the two variables. Also the quantity $(1 - r^2)$ is called the *coefficient of non-determination* or *coefficient of alienation.* $(1 - r^2)$ is thus a measure of deviation from perfect linear relationship. For example, if $r = 0.8$, it means high degree of correlation. But $r^2 = 0.64$, which means that only 64% of variations in the dependent variable are due to the independent variable, remaining 36% variations are due to other independent variables yet to be located.

SPURIOUS CORRELATION

If we have paired observations on two variables and the assumptions hold good, it is always possible to calculate the correlation coefficient between the two variables. But correlation coefficient is not always meaningful unless the two variables are properly chosen. For example, if we find out the correlation between the total imports and the number of shoes produced per year, it would not lead to any conclusion. Because there is no cause and effect relationship between the total imports and number of shoes produced per year. Such a correlation is known as *spurious* or *non-sense* correlation between two variables. Another example of spurious correlation is the correlation between the number of tourists who visited Taj Mahal and the number of TV sets produced. From this discussion, we come to the conclusion that it is not enough to find out the correlation coefficient only, but it is more important to see the nature of the variables. If they have a cause and effect relationship, and if one variable can be explained with the help of the other, then the correlation has sense, otherwise it is spurious.

The description of correlation coefficient, in this chapter, does not cover all types of correlation coefficients. Those not covered in this chapter are correlation ratio, intraclass correlation, biserial correlation etc. Whatever has been embodied in this chapter is in accordance to the requirement of the syllabi.

QUESTIONS AND EXERCISES

1. What do you understand by a regression model? What are its uses?
2. What is a scatter diagram and what role does it play in regression theory?
3. Explain the method of estimating parameters of a regression equation.
4. Can a regression equation be used for projections? If so, what are the assumptions underlying it? Also give some examples.
5. Explain the regression of Y on X and X on Y. At what point do the two regression lines intersect? Also derive the relation of two regression coefficients with correlation coefficient.
6. Answer the following questions with reasoning in a line or two.
   (*a*) Can regression coefficient be negative?
   (*b*) Can correlation coefficient be negative?
   (*c*) If the regression coefficient is negative, then correlation coefficient will also be negative.
   (*d*) If the regression coefficient of Y on X is negative, does it mean that regression coefficient of X on Y will also be negative?
   (*e*) What inference would you draw by a negative value of regression coefficient?
   (*f*) If the two coefficients of regression are negative, does it mean that the correlation would be positive?

7. Write whether the following statements are true or false.
   (*a*) Regression coefficient lies between 0 and ∞.
   (*b*) Correlation coefficient lies between 0 and 1.
   (*c*) Shift of origin has no effect on the value of r_{XY}.
   (*d*) Shift of origin effects the value of regression coefficient.
   (*e*) Regression coefficient can be zero.
8. What is the importance of the test of significance of a regression coefficient?
9. What is Fisher's *Z*-transformation, and when do you use it?
10. How will you test the significance of population correlation coefficient?
11. Sketch the scatter diagrams for the following value of correlation coefficient *r*,
   (*i*) $r = 0.11$, (*ii*) $r = 0.98$, (*iii*) $r = -1$, (*iv*) $r = 1$ and (*v*) $r = 0.50$
12. Give the formulae for standard error of b_{YX} and *a*. Also write the situations in which these standard errors are used. (Notations b_{YX} and *a* carry their usual meaning).
13. What is rank correlation? How is it different from Pearsonian correlation?
14. Write which of the following statements are correct or wrong and why?
   (*a*) $r_{XY} = r_{YX}$
   (*b*) $b_{YX} = b_{XY}$
   (*c*) If $r = 1$, then $b_{YX} = 1$
   (*d*) If $r = 0$, then $b_{XY} = 0$
   (*e*) $r^2 = b_{YX}\, b_{XY}$
   (*f*) $r_{XY} = 0.9$, $b_{XY} = 2.04$, $b_{YX} = -3.2$
   (*g*) $r_{XY} = 0.9$ and $b_{YX} = -1$
   All the above notations carry their usual meaning.
15. (*a*) What formula do you use to calculate the correlation coefficient from a bivariate frequency table?
   (*b*) Can you calculate regression coefficient from a bivariate frequency table? If so, explain how will you do it?
16. What is coefficient of determination? Explain its uses.
17. Is it useful to calculate the correlation coefficient between any two variables? Justify your answer.
18. (*a*) If each value of a variable is increased by 5, then how much will be the increase in the value of regression coefficient?
   (*b*) If each value of a variable *Y* is divided by 10 and of a variable *X* by 5, how will the value of (*i*) regression coefficient be affected and (*ii*) correlation coefficient be affected.
19. How can you fit in the following curve, by the method of least squares?
   (*a*) $Y = \alpha e^{\beta X}$
   (*b*) $Y = \alpha X^{\beta}$
   [*Hint*: Take logarithm, you will get linear equations of the line. Follow the usual procedure.]
20. The household net income from property and entrepreneurship in France and Germany for the years 1971 to 1978 as a percentage of total inflationary gap were as follows:

Year:	1971	1972	1973	1974	1975	1976	1977	1978
France:	18.8	23.1	10.3	8.0	18.0	10.2	15.2	19.0
Germany:	15.0	8.0	3.8	6.4	27.4	19.0	35.3	13.6

   Find the correlation coefficient between net incomes of France and Germany. Also test its significance.

21. Mean morphometic values of workers of Apis Cerana measured in mm were as follows at thirteen locations.

Labrum length:	0.42	0.43	0.40	0.33	0.36	0.40	0.32	0.40	0.38	0.36	0.40	0.33	0.35
Labrum breadth:	1.10	1.02	1.00	1.00	1.02	0.99	1.00	1.00	1.00	1.00	1.01	1.00	0.99

(*a*) Find the regression of labrum breadth on labrum length.
(*b*) Estimate labrum breadth for labrum length = 0.5.
(*c*) Test the significance of the regression coefficient.

22. Aggregate figures for merchandise exports and imports in India for eight years in millions of rupees are as follows:

Export:	1960	2170	2420	3020	3850	4690	5360	5210
Import:	2330	2110	2580	3540	4070	4000	4550	5920

Calculate correlation coefficient between the import and the export using the method of coding of data.

23. Following are the data pertaining to the production and export of sugar in lakh tonnes in India from 1971 to 1982.

Production (X):	37.4	31.1	38.7	39.5	47.9	42.6	48.4	64.6	58.4	38.6	51.4	84.0
Export (Y):	3.90	1.33	1.10	4.39	9.41	9.67	3.41	2.51	8.62	9.90	6.64	6.50

(*a*) Find the regression of Y on X.
(*b*) Test the significance of the regression coefficient.
(*c*) Test whether the regression line in the population passes through the origin.
(*d*) What export of sugar can be expected when the production is 50 lakh tonnes?

24. The age groups and monthly income of 80 workers of a manufacturing unit were as given in the following bivariate frequency table.

Monthly pay Rs.	*Age groups*				
	20 – 30	30 – 40	40 – 50	50 – 60	60 – 70
300 – 350	5	2	1	—	—
350 – 400	4	4	2	3	—
400 – 450	2	6	4	1	—
450 – 500	2	3	5	2	—
500 – 550	1	4	7	5	—
550 – 600	—	2	3	2	—
600 – 650	—	—	1	—	1
650 – 700	1	1	2	2	—
700 – 750	—	—	1	1	—

Calculate the coefficient of correlation between age and monthly income.

25. Fourteen singers in a music competition were ranked by two judges as follows:

Singers:	*A*	*B*	*C*	*D*	*E*	*F*	*G*	*H*	*I*	*J*	*K*	*L*	*M*	*N*
Judge I:	13	4	5	11	2	6	8	9	12	1	3	7	10	14
Judge II:	10	9	7	8	1	3	6	14	11	2	4	5	12	13

Using the method of rank correlation, find whether the ranks given by the two judges have concordance.

26. The I.Q.'s of a group of 6 persons were measured, and then they were made to appear in a certain examination. Their I.Q's and examination marks were as follows:

Person:	*A*	*B*	*C*	*D*	*E*	*F*
I.Q.:	110	100	140	120	80	90
Exam. marks:	70	90	80	60	10	20

Compute the coefficient of correlation and rank correlation. Why are the correlation figures obtained different? *(B.Sc., Chennai, 1975)*

27. The following calculations have been made for closing prices of twelve stocks (X), on the Mumbai Stock Exchange on a certain day, along with the volume of sales in thousands of Shares (Y). From these calculations, find the regression equation:

$\Sigma X =$ Rs 580, $\Sigma Y =$ Rs 370, $\Sigma XY =$ Rs 11494, $\Sigma X^2 =$ Rs 41658 and $\Sigma Y^2 =$ Rs. 17206

(B.A. Hon. Econ., Delhi, 1971)

28. From the two regression equations, find the value of r, $\overline{X}$ and $\overline{Y}$:

$4Y = 9X + 15$ and $25X = 6Y + 7$ *(M.A., Agra, 1974)*

29. A departmental store gives in-service training to its salesmen followed by a test to consider whether it should terminate the services of any of the salesman whc does not qualify in the test. The following data give the test scores and sales made by nine salesmen during a certain period.

Test score:	14	19	24	21	28	22	15	20	19
Sales ('00 Rs.):	31	36	48	37	50	45	33	41	39

Calculate the coefficient of correlation between the test scores and the sales. Does it indicate that the termination of services of the low test scorer is justified? If the firm wants a minimum sales volume of Rs. 3000, what is the minimum test score that will ensure continuation of the service? *(C.A., Nov. 1974)*

30. (*a*) Given,

	X series	*Y series*
Mean	24	140
S.D.	16	48
	$r = 0.6$	

(*i*) Find out the most probable value of Y if X is 50 and the most probable value of X if Y is 180.

(*ii*) What would be the coefficient of correlation if the two regression coefficients are 0.6 and 0.4?

(*b*) The following data are given for marks in English and Mathematics in a certain examination.

	English	*Mathematics*
Mean marks	39.5	47.5
S.D. of marks	10.8	16.8

Coefficient of correlation between marks in English and Mathematics = 0.42. Find the two regression equations. (*M.Com., Delhi, 1974*)

31. Calculate the coefficient of correlation from the following data:

X:	1	2	3	4	5	6	7	8	9
Y:	9	8	10	12	11	13	14	16	15

Also obtain the equations of two lines of regression. (*C.A. Final, 1978*)

32. What are regression lines? Why is it necessary to consider two lines of regression? If the two lines are identical, prove that the correlation coefficient is either + 1 or – 1. The correlation between two variables X and Y is $r = 0.60$. If the variance of $X = 2.25$, the variance of $Y = 4.00$, mean of $X = 10$ and mean of $Y = 20$, find the equations of regression lines of (*i*) Y on X and (*ii*) X on Y. (*C.A. Final, 1979*)

33. In the estimation of regression equations of two variables X and Y, the following results were obtained:

$$\overline{X} = 90, \quad \overline{Y} = 70, \quad N = 10$$

$$\Sigma x^2 = 6300, \ \Sigma y^2 = 2860, \ \Sigma xy = 3900.$$

Find the two regression equations. (*C.A., May, 1983*)

34. The ranks according to two attributes in a sample are given below:

R_1:	1	2	3	4	5
R_2:	5	4	3	2	1

The rank correlation between them is:
0, + 1, – 1, none of these. (*C.A., Nov., 1982*)

35. The following table gives the age of cars of a certain make and annual maintenance costs. Obtain the regression equation for costs related to age.

Age of cars in years:	2	4	6	8
Maintenance cost in hundreds of Rs:	10	20	25	30

(*C.A., May, 1981*)

36. Find the rank correlation coefficient for the following data.

X :	30	48	54	62	48	60	50	55
Y:	40	35	48	54	36	50	30	54

(*B. Com., 1 Yr., Andhra, 1989*)

37. Calculate Karl Pearson's coefficient of correlation for the data given below, taking 66 and 63 as assumed means of x and y respectively.

Heights of Husbands (in inches)	x : 60	62	64	66	68	70	72
Heights of wives: (in inches)	y : 61	63	63	63	64	65	67

(B. Com., 1 Yr. Andhra, 1988)

38. The lines of regression of y on x and x on y are respectively $y = x + 5$ and $16x = 9y - 94$. Find the variance of x if the variance of y is 16. Also find the covariance of x and y. *(I.C.W.A. Dec., 1986)*

39. In a study of sales, a company obtained the following least squares trend equation:

$$y = 16 + 2x$$

(origin: 1975, x units = 1 year, y – total number of units sold per year)

The company has physical facilities to produce only 30 units a year and it believes that at least for the next decade the trend will continue as before.

(*i*) What is the average annual increase in the number of units sold?

(*ii*) By what year the company's expected sales have equalled its present capacity.

(*iii*) Estimate the annual sales for the year 1988. *(I.C.W.A. June, 1988)*

40. A building contractor is interested in knowing whether relationship does exist between the number of building permits issued and the volume of sales of such buildings in some past years. He collects data about sales (y–in thousands of rupees) and the number of building permits issued (x–in hundreds) in past ten years. The results worked out are as under:

$\Sigma X = 117$, $\Sigma Y = 78$, $\Sigma XY = 981$, $\Sigma X^2 = 1491$, $\Sigma Y^2 = 662$.

(*i*) What level of sales can you expect next if it is hoped that 2000 building permits would be issued.

(*ii*) What change in sales is likely to take place with an increase of 100 building permits. *(C.A. (Inter); May, 1993)*

41. For n pairs of values of x and y, the following results were found:

$r_{xy} = 0.5$, $\sigma_y = 8$, $\Sigma u^2 = 90$, $\Sigma uv = 120$, where

$u = x - \bar{x}$ and $v = y - \bar{y}$.

Find n, σ_x and the two regression coefficients. *(I.C.W.A. (Inter), June, 1992)*

42. Fit the curve $y = ax^b$ to the following data:

x:	1	2	3	4	5	6
y:	1200	900	600	200	110	50

(I.C.W.A. (Inter), Dec., 1991)

43. From the following data calculate the rank correlation coefficient after making adjustment for tied ranks.

x :	48	33	40	9	16	16	65	24	16	57
y :	13	13	24	6	15	4	20	9	6	19

(I.C.W.A. (Inter), June., 2003)

44. How can you perform the test of hypothesis for a specified value ρ_0 of the population correlation coefficient? Also establish the formula for $(1 - \alpha)$ 100 per cent confidence limits for the population coefficient of correlation ρ. *(Rs-II, 1998)*

45. For a certain bivariate data, following results are obtained.
$n = 25, \Sigma x = 125, \Sigma y = 100, \Sigma x^2 = 650, \Sigma y^2 = 436, \Sigma xy = 520.$
Determine the regression coefficients and the correlation coefficient.
(I.C.W.A. Inter, Dec., 2004)

46. The following are the marks obtained by 8 students in English and History papers. Compute rank coefficient of correlation.

Marks in English :	15	20	28	12	40	60	20	80
Marks in History :	40	30	50	30	20	10	30	60

(M.B.A., I-yr., MLSU, Udaipur, 2002)

47. Regression equations of two variables x and y are as follows:
$8x - 10y = 64$ and $40x - 18y = 320$
Find *(i)* The means, *(ii)* The regression coefficients and *(iii)* The coefficient of correlation between x and y. *(C.A., P.E.-I, Nov., 2004)*

48. Following data have been collected on experience of operators (in years) and their performance rating.

Operators:	A	B	C	D	E	F	G	H
Experience:	16	12	18	4	3	10	5	12
Rating:	87	88	89	68	78	80	75	83

Find the correlation between the two, and the regression equation of rating on experience. *(M.B.A., Part-II, MLSU, Udaipur, 2000)*

49. (*a*) Why there are two lines of regression and where do they intersect? What will be the correlation if they intersect at 90° and 180°? Also state properties of regression coefficient.
(*b*) Find correlation coefficient (r_{xy}) if variance of $x = 2.25$, standard deviation of $y = 4$ and regression equation of x on y is $x = 0.3\,y + 1.8$.
(Dairy Technology, III Yr, RAU, 2001)

50. Calculate the correlation coefficient from the following data:

X:	12	9	8	10	11	13	7
Y:	14	8	6	9	11	12	3

Let now each value of X is multiplied by 2 and then 6 is added to it. Similarly, each value of Y is multiplied by 3 and 2 is subtracted from it. What will be the correlation coefficient between X and Y? *(C.A., Foundation, May, 1997)*

51. Obtain the second degree parabola which best fits the following data.

x :	1	2	3	4	5	6	7	8	9
y:	2	6	7	8	10	11	11	10	9

(I.C.W.A., Inter, June, 2003)

SUGGESTED READING

Achen, Christopher (1982). *Interpreting and Using Regression, Sage*, Beverley Hills.

Chang, Few Lee, John C. Lee and Alice Lee (1998). *Statistics for Business and Financial Economics*, World Scientific.

Dobson, A. (1990). *An Introduction to Generalized Linear Models*, 2nd ed. Chapman and Hall, London.

Draper, N.R. and H. Smith (1998). *Applied Regression Analysis*, John Wiley, 3rd ed., New York.

Goodman, L.A. and W.H. Kruskal (1979). *Measures of Association for Cross Classification.* Springer-Verlag, Berlin.

Grey, Attwood (2000). *Statistics*, Ca-print Harcourt Heineman.

Hoel, P.G. and Jessen, R.J. (1971). *Basic Statistics for Business and Economics,* John Wiley, New York.

J.Keithord, Maurice Kendall and Steven Arnold (1999). *Advanced Theory of Statistics*, Oxford University Press.

John, A. Rafter, Martha L. Abell and James P. Braselton (2002). *Statistics with Maple*, Elsevier.

Joseph, F. Healey (2004). *Statistics*, Thomson Wadsworth.

Meter, J., W. Wasserman and G.A. Whitmore (1982). *Applied Statistics*, Allyn and Bacon, London.

Muller, Keith E. and Bethel A. Fetterman (2003). *Regression and ANOVA*, John Wiley, SAS Publishing, New York.

Neter, J. *et al.* (1996). *Applied Linear Regression Models*, Richard D. Irwin, 3rd ed., Chicago, IL.

Ronald M. Weiers (2004). *Introduction to Business Statistics*, Thomson South-Western.

Seber, G.A.F. (1977). *Linear Regression Analysis,* John Wiley, New York.

Seber, G.A.F. and Wild, C.J. (1989). *Nonlinear Regression*, John Wiley, New York.

APPENDIX

SPSS WINDOW GUIDE FOR REGRESSION & CORRELATION

Procedure for obtaining linear regression and correlation

1. Click on Analyze in the menu bar followed by regression in sub-menu as given in window 1.
2. Choose appropriate option for regression (Linear, Curve estimation etc.)

Example 15.1

Window 1:

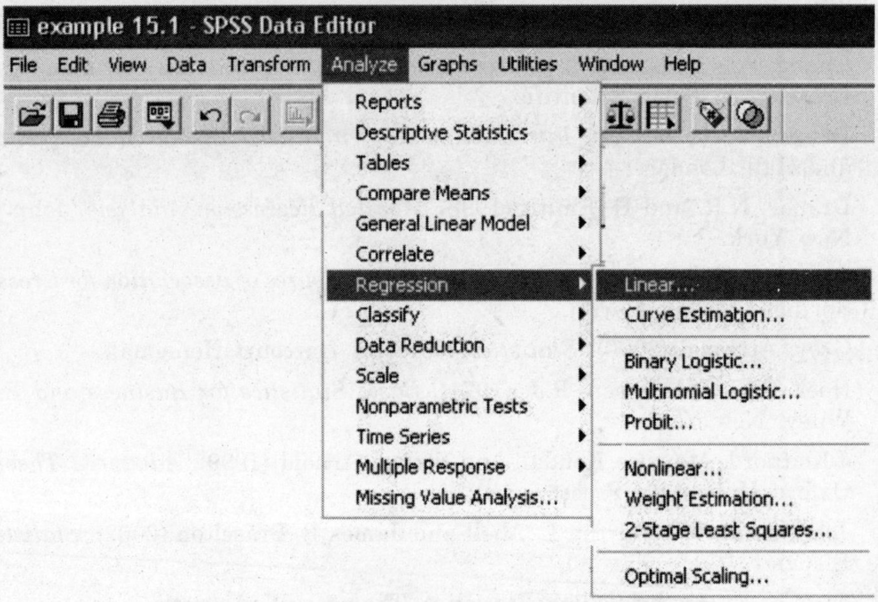

3. On clicking linear option, you will receive window 2. Select dependent and independent variables by clicking on particular variable and pressing corresponding arrow button. In the same window, required statistics (R, R2, test of significance) can also be specified as given in window 3. When we click on OK button, we receive regression results as given in window 4.

Window 2:

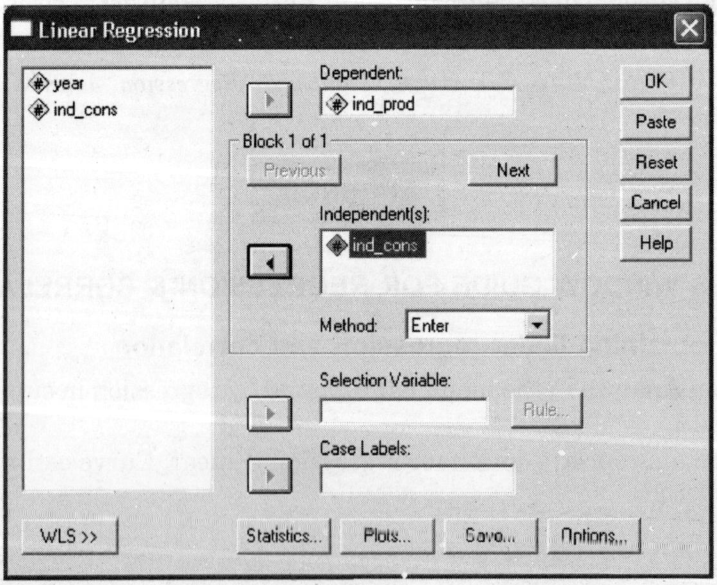

Window 3:

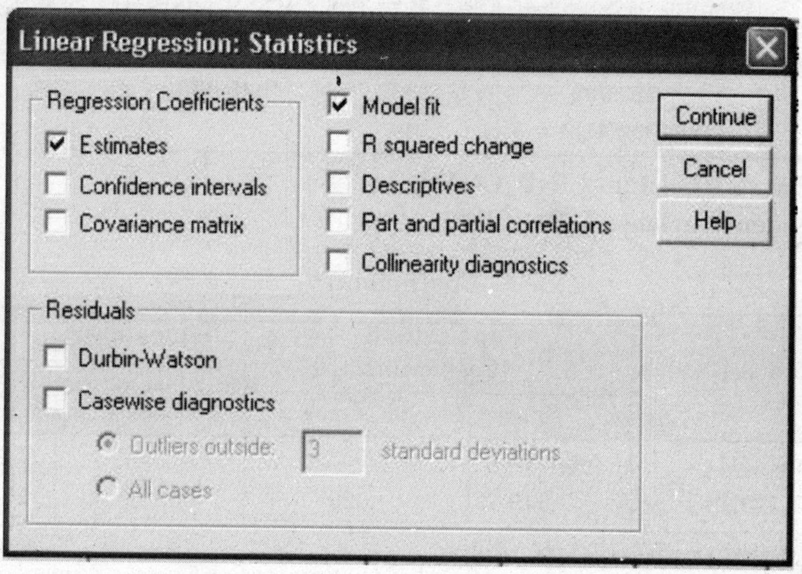

Window 4:

Variables Entered/Removed[b]

Model	Variables Entered	Variables Removed	Method
1	IND_CONS[a]		Enter

a. All requested variables entered.

b. Dependent Variable: IND_PROD

Model Summary

Model	R	R Square	Adjusted R Square	Std. Error of the Estimate
1	.988[a]	.976	.975	6.77387

Model Summary

Model	Change Statistics				
	R Square	F change	df1	df2	Sig. F change
1	.976	735.888	1	18	.000

a. Predictors: (Constant), IND_CONS

ANOVA[b]

Model	Sum of Squares	df	Mean Square	F	Sig.
1 Regression	33766.481	1	33766.481	735.888	.000[a]
Residual	825.937	18	45.885		
Total	34592.418	19			

a. Predictors: (Constant), IND_CONS
b. Dependent Variable: IND_PROD

Coefficients[a]

Model		Unstandardized Coefficients		Standardized Coefficients	T	Sig.
		B	Std. Error	Beta		
1	(Constant)	42.415	2.953		14.364	.000
	IND_CONS	.549	.020	.988	27.127	.000

a. Dependent Variable: IND_PROD

Procedure for calculating correlation using SPSS

1. Click on analyze in the menu bar followed by correlate in sub-menu as given in window 1.
2. Choose appropriate option for correlation.

Example 15.6

Window 1:

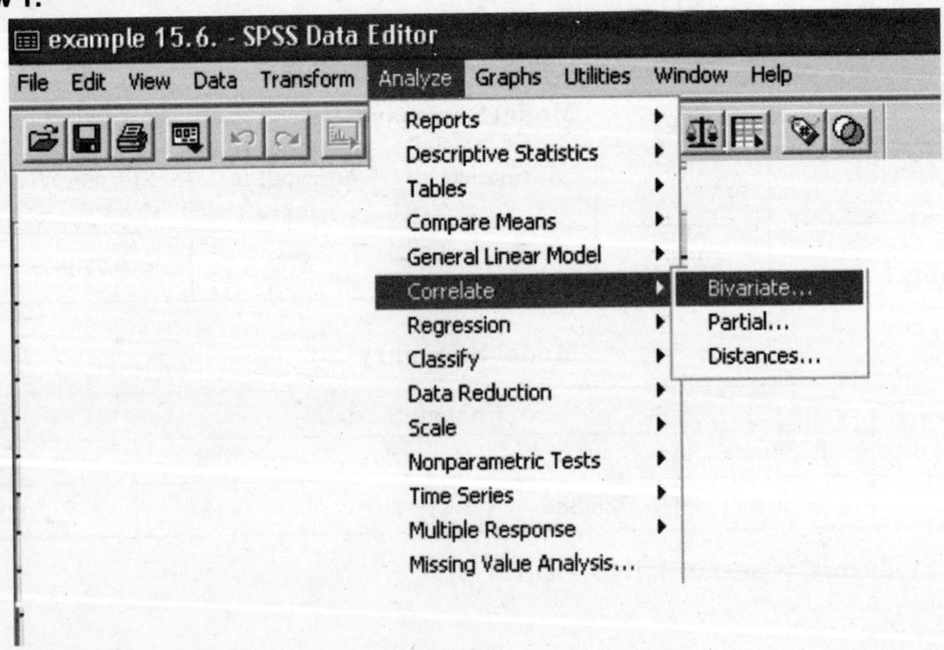

3. On clicking bivariate option, you will receive window 2. Select appropriate variables for establishing correlation. In the same window, correlation coefficients, test of significance and other options can be specified. When we click on OK button, we receive correlation results as given in window 3.

Window 2:

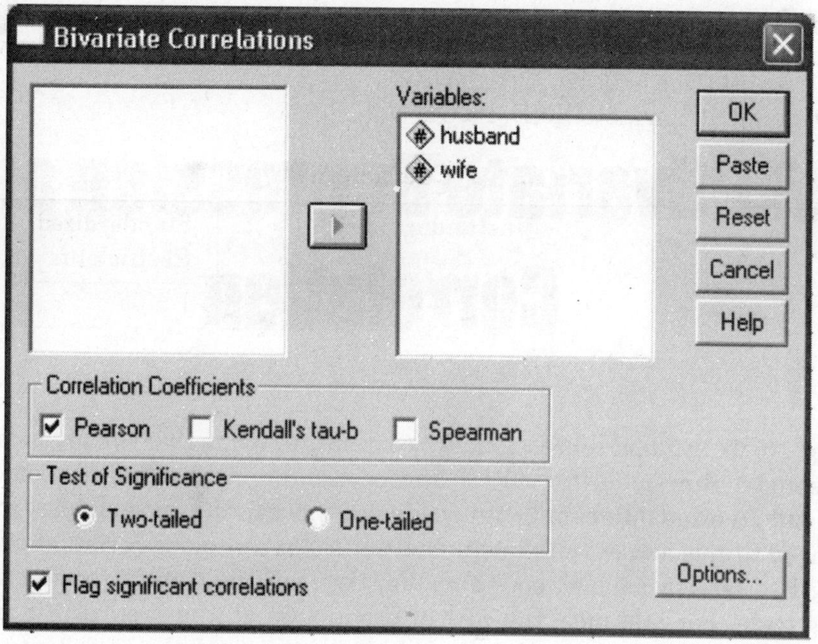

Window 3:

Correlations

		HUSBAND	WIFE
HUSBAND	Pearson Correlation	1	.853(**)
	Sig. (2-tailed)		.000
	N	14	14
WIFE	Pearson Correlation	.853(**)	1
	Sig. (2-tailed)	.000	
	N	14	14

** Correlation is significant at the 0.01 level (2-tailed).

16

Chapter

Multivariate Regression and Correlation

In Chapter 15, we studied regression and correlation when two variables are under study simultaneously. But scientific, social and economic phenomena do not confine to two variables only. A large number of studies involve more than two variables. In these studies, we often need to give actual relationship between three or more variables and/or to explain the strength of association between them. For this, multivariate regression and correlation are strong tools. For instance, the cost of production of a manufactured product mainly depends on the cost of raw material, the labour charges and the cost of energy. The cost of a crop mainly depends upon the cost of seeds, fertilizer, irrigation, pesticides and many farm operations. In both the examples, the cost of the produced product is a dependent factor, while others are independent factors. If we want to establish the relationship between the dependent variable and the independent variable, a mathematical equation can be given to do this. This type of mathematical equation is known as a mathematical model. The equation pertaining to such a relationship may be of any type. But we will only deal with a linear relationship which represents a plane or hyper-plane according to the number of variables involved.

Multivariate Regression Equations

First, we will discuss the mathematical model before giving its fitting. Fitting of a regression equation means, the estimation of parameters involved in the model. A mathematical model with dependent variable Y and k independent variables $X_1, X_2..., X_k$ is,

$$Y = \beta_0 + \beta_1 X_1 + \beta_2 X_2 + ... + \beta_k X_k + e \qquad ...(16.1)$$

This type of regression is also known as multiple regression equation or the prediction equation, with Y as predictant and X_1, X_2, ...X_k as predictors. e is the error which is distributed normally with mean 0 and variance σ^2, i.e. $e \sim N(0, \sigma^2)$. To fit the equation (16.1), we have to estimate the parameters β_0, β_1, β_2, ..., β_k on the basis of n sample observations in which each observation is $(k + 1)$-tuple, n composite sample observations can be presented in the following format.

Table 16.1: Presentation of Sample Observations

Composite observation no.	*Variables*			
	Y	X_1	X_2 .... X_j	X_k
1	y_1	x_{11}	$x_{21}...x_{j1}....$	x_{k1}
2	y_2	x_{12}	$x_{22}...x_{j2}....$	x_{k2}
.	.	.	. .	.
.	.	.	. .	.
.	.	.	. .	.
i	y_i	x_{1i}	$x_{2i}...x_{ji}....$	x_{ki}
.	.	.	. .	.
.	.	.	. .	.
.	.	.	. .	.
n	y_n	x_{1n}	$x_{2n}...x_{jn}....$	x_{kn}
Total	$\Sigma_i y_i$	$\Sigma_i x_{1i}$	$\Sigma_i x_{2i}...\Sigma_i x_{ji}...$	$\Sigma_i x_{ki}$

where $i = 1, 2, ..., n$ and $j = 1, 2, ..., k$.

Making use of the data given in table (16.1) we want to fit the regression equation (16.1). It means that we want to estimate the parameters $\beta_0, \beta_1, \beta_2, ..., \beta_k$. Let the estimated values of the parameters be $b_0, b_1, b_2, ..., b_k$ respectively. These estimates should be such that the error e is minimum, preferably zero. Hence to achieve this objective, we adopt the *method of least squares* for estimation of partial regression coefficients $\beta_1, \beta_2, ..., \beta_k$ and the intercept β_0. The advantage of least square method is, that these estimates are unbiased. Before giving the estimates, we define partial regression coefficient β_j which is the coefficient of X_j ($j = 1, 2, ..., k$) in equation (16.1).

PARTIAL REGRESSION COEFFICIENT

β_j is the measure of change in the dependent variable Y corresponding to a unit change in the independent variable X_j, whereas the other independent variables are kept fixed.

Estimation of β's by Least Square Method

For the ith-tuple, the regression model is

$$y_i = \beta_0 + \beta_1 x_{1i} + \beta_2 x_{2i} + ... + \beta_k x_{ki} + e_i \quad ...(16.2)$$

where each $e_i \sim N(0, \sigma^2)$, $i = 1, 2, ..., n$

Again, $e_i^2 = (y_i - \beta_0 - \beta_1 x_{1i} - \beta_2 x_{2i} - ... - \beta_k x_{ki})^2$

Taking the sum over all n-tuples, we obtain

$$\Sigma_i e_i^2 = \Sigma_i (y_i - \beta_0 - \beta_1 x_{1i} - \beta_2 x_{2i} - ... - \beta_k x_{ki})^2$$

For minimization, we have considered the square of errors summed over all observation. Squaring has the advantage of being able to remove the problem of the direction of errors. Let the quantity $\Sigma_i e_i^2$ be denoted by Q. To minimize Q, the overall squared error, differentiate Q partially with respect to $\beta_0, \beta_1, \beta_2, ..., \beta_k$ respectively and equate them to zero. Also replace β's by b's. In this way, we get $(k + 1)$ normal equations in $(k + 1)$ unknowns. Solving these equations, we get the expressions for $b_0, b_1, b_2, ..., b_k$ in terms of observed values. Substituting these estimates, we obtain the estimated regression equation.

The normal equations are,

$$\begin{aligned}
\Sigma_i y_i &= \Sigma_i b_0 + b_i \Sigma_i x_{1i} + b_2 \Sigma_i x_{2i} + \ldots + b_k \Sigma_i x_{ki} \\
\Sigma_i x_{1i} y_i &= b_0 \Sigma_i x_{1i} + b_1 \Sigma_i x_{1i}^2 + b_2 \Sigma_i x_{1i} x_{2i} + \ldots + b_k \Sigma_i x_{1i} x_{ki} \\
\Sigma_i x_{2i} y_i &= b_0 \Sigma_i x_{2i} + b_1 \Sigma_i x_{1i} x_{2i} + b_2 \Sigma_i x_{2i}^2 + \ldots + b_k \Sigma_i x_{2i} x_{ki} \qquad \ldots(16.3) \\
&\vdots \\
\Sigma_i x_{ki} y_i &= b_0 \Sigma_i x_{ki} + b_1 \Sigma_i x_{1i} x_{ki} + b_2 \Sigma_i x_{2i} x_{ki} + \ldots + b_k \Sigma_i x_{ki}^2
\end{aligned}$$

where $i = 1, 2, ..., n$.

If we place the observed data in the form of vectors and matrices, the set of normal equations given by (16.3) can be given as follows. Following the standard notations as,

$$Y_{n\times 1} = \begin{bmatrix} y_1 \\ y_2 \\ \cdot \\ \cdot \\ \cdot \\ y_n \end{bmatrix}; \beta_{(k+1)\times 1} = \begin{bmatrix} \beta_0 \\ \beta_1 \\ \cdot \\ \cdot \\ \cdot \\ \beta_k \end{bmatrix}; B_{(k+1)\times 1} = \begin{bmatrix} b_0 \\ b_1 \\ \cdot \\ \cdot \\ \cdot \\ b_k \end{bmatrix}$$

and $$X_{n\times(k+1)} = \begin{bmatrix} 1 & x_{11} & x_{21} & x_{k1} \\ 1 & x_{12} & x_{22} & x_{k2} \\ \cdot & \cdot & \cdot & \cdot \\ \cdot & \cdot & \cdot & \cdot \\ \cdot & \cdot & \cdot & \cdot \\ 1 & x_{1n} & x_{2n} & x_{kn} \end{bmatrix}$$

and $e' = (e_1, e_2, \ldots e_n)$

The regression equations (16.2) for $i = 1, 2, ..., n$ in matrix notation are,

$$Y = X\beta + e \qquad \ldots(16.2.1)$$

and its estimated equation is

$$Y = XB$$

whereas the set of normal equations (16.3) in matrix notation is

$$X'Y = X'XB \qquad \ldots(16.3.1)$$

or $$B = (X'X)^{-1} X'Y \qquad \ldots(16.3.2)$$

provided $(X'X)$ is a non-singular matrix.

In (16.3.2), $X'Y$ is the left hand side of (16.3) and

$$\underset{(k+1)\times(k+1)}{X'X} = \begin{bmatrix} n & \Sigma x_{1i} & \Sigma x_{2i} \ldots\ldots \Sigma x_{ki} \\ \Sigma x_{1i} & \Sigma x_{1i}^2 & \Sigma x_{1i}x_{2i} \ldots\ldots \Sigma x_{1i}x_{ki} \\ \Sigma x_{2i} & \Sigma x_{1i}x_{2i} & \Sigma x_{2i}^2 \ldots\ldots \Sigma x_{2i}x_{ki} \\ . & . & . \\ . & . & . \\ . & . & . \\ \Sigma x_{ki} & \Sigma x_{1i}x_{ki} & \Sigma x_{2i}\, x_{ki} \ldots\ldots \Sigma x_{ki}^2 \end{bmatrix}$$

Notes: 1. The method of inversion of non-singular matrix is given in the appendix.

2. The matrix $X'X$ can easily be obtained by writing the first row elements and then multiplying the first row elements by $x_{1i}, x_{2i}, \ldots, x_{ki}$ in succession, we obtain the subsequent rows of the matrix $X'X$. The same approach is true for generating the other k-normal equations from the first normal equation.

From the first equation of set (16.3) we obtain,

$$\Sigma_i b_0 = \Sigma_i y_i - b_1\Sigma_i x_{1i} - b_2\Sigma_i x_{2i} - \ldots - b_k\Sigma_i x_{ki}$$

Since $\quad \Sigma_i x_{ji} = n\bar{x}_j$ for $j = 1, 2, \ldots, k$.

and $\quad \Sigma_i y_i = n\bar{y}$,

$$nb_0 = n(\bar{y} - b_1\bar{x}_1 - b_2\bar{x}_2 - \ldots - b_k\bar{x}_k)$$

or

$$b_0 = \bar{y} - b_1\bar{x}_1 - b_2\bar{x}_2 - \ldots - b_k\bar{x}_k \qquad \ldots(16.4)$$

Substituting the value of $\Sigma_i b_0$ in the second equation of the set of normal equations, we get

$$\Sigma_i\, x_{1i}\, y_i = n\bar{x}_1(\bar{y} - b_1\bar{x}_1 - b_2\bar{x}_2 - \ldots - b_k\bar{x}_k) + b_1\Sigma_i x_{1i}^2 + b_2\Sigma_i x_{1i}x_{2i} + \ldots + b_k\Sigma_i x_{1i}x_{ki}$$

$$\Sigma_i x_{1i}y_i - n\bar{x}_1\bar{y} = -nb_1\bar{x}_1^2 - nb_2\bar{x}_1\bar{x}_2 - \ldots - nb_k\bar{x}_1\bar{x}_k + b_1\Sigma_i x_{1i}^2 + b_2\Sigma_i x_{1i}x_{2i} + \ldots + b_k\Sigma_i x_{1i}x_{ki}$$

$$\Sigma_i(x_{1i} - \bar{x}_1)(y_i - \bar{y}) = b_1\Sigma_i(x_{1i} - \bar{x}_1)^2 + b_2\Sigma_i(x_{1i} - \bar{x}_1)(x_{2i} - \bar{x}_2) + \ldots + b_k\Sigma_i(x_{1i} - \bar{x}_1)(x_{ki} - \bar{x}_k)$$

Suppose, $\quad x_{ji} - \bar{x}_j = u_{ji}, y_i - \bar{y} = v_i$

for $i = 1, 2, \ldots, n$ and $j = 1, 2, \ldots, k$.

The above equation is,

$$\Sigma_i u_{1i}v_i = b_1\Sigma_i u_{1i}^2 + b_2\Sigma u_{1i}u_{2i} + \ldots + b_k\Sigma_i u_{1i}u_{ki}$$

Similarly the other equations of the set are,

$$\Sigma_i u_{2i}v_i = b_1\Sigma_i u_{1i}u_{2i} + b_2\Sigma_i u_{2i}^2 + \ldots + b_k\Sigma_i u_{2i}u_{ki} \qquad \ldots(16.5)$$

$$\vdots$$

$$\Sigma_i u_{ki}v_i = b_1\Sigma_i u_{1i}\, u_{ki} + b_2\Sigma_i\, u_{2i}\, u_{ki} + \ldots + b_k\, \Sigma_i u_{ki}^2$$

In the matrix notation, the set of normal equation (16.5) can be represented as,

$$\begin{bmatrix} \Sigma_i u_{1i} v_i \\ \Sigma_i u_{2i} v_i \\ \cdot \\ \cdot \\ \cdot \\ \Sigma_i u_{ki} v_i \end{bmatrix} = \begin{bmatrix} \Sigma_i u_{1i}^2 & \Sigma_i u_{1i} u_{2i} \ldots & \Sigma_i u_{1i} u_{ki} \\ \Sigma_i u_{1i} u_{2i} & \Sigma_i u_{2i}^2 \quad \ldots & \Sigma_i u_{2i} u_{ki} \\ \cdot & \cdot & \cdot \\ \cdot & \cdot & \cdot \\ \cdot & \cdot & \cdot \\ \Sigma_i u_{1i} u_{ki} & \Sigma_i u_{2i} u_{ki} \quad \ldots & \Sigma_i u_{ki}^2 \end{bmatrix} \begin{bmatrix} b_1 \\ b_2 \\ \cdot \\ \cdot \\ \cdot \\ b_k \end{bmatrix} \qquad \ldots(16.6)$$

$$Y_{k \times 1} \qquad\qquad A_{k \times k} \qquad\qquad B_{k \times 1}$$

Thus, the set of equations (16.6) may be written as,

$$Y = AB \qquad \ldots(16.6.1)$$

In the above equations,

$$\Sigma_i u_{ji}^2 = \Sigma_i x_{ji}^2 - (\Sigma_i x_{ji})^2 / n$$

$$\Sigma_i u_{ji} u_{j'i} = \Sigma_i x_{ji} x_{j'i} - (\Sigma_i x_{ji}) (\Sigma_i x_{j'i})/n$$

for $j \neq j'$

$$\Sigma_i u_{ji} v_i = \Sigma_i x_{ji} y_i - (\Sigma_i x_{ji}) (\Sigma_i y_i)/n$$

Matrix A is known as the *coefficient matrix*. From (16.6.1), the solution of equation (16.6.1) is,

$$B = A^{-1} Y \qquad \ldots(16.7)$$

where A^{-1} is the inverse of A. The inverse of A is possible only if A is a non-singular matrix. For the method of finding out the inverse of A, see appendix. Let the inverse matrix be $[c_{jj'}]$ where $j, j' = 1, 2, \ldots, k$.

In the expanded form, the matrix

$$A^{-1} = \begin{bmatrix} c_{11} & c_{12} & \ldots & c_{1k} \\ c_{21} & c_{22} & \ldots & c_{2k} \\ \cdot & & & \cdot \\ \cdot & & & \cdot \\ \cdot & & & \cdot \\ c_{k1} & c_{k2} & \ldots & c_{kk} \end{bmatrix}$$

Matrix A^{-1} is symmetric and hence $c_{jj'} = c_{j'j}$.

Hence (16.7) in expanded form is,

$$\begin{bmatrix} b_1 \\ b_2 \\ \cdot \\ \cdot \\ \cdot \\ b_j \\ \cdot \\ \cdot \\ \cdot \\ b_k \end{bmatrix} = \begin{bmatrix} c_{11} & c_{12} & \ldots & c_{1j} & \ldots & c_{1k} \\ c_{21} & c_{22} & \ldots & c_{2j} & \ldots & c_{2k} \\ \cdot & & & & & \\ \cdot & & & & & \\ \cdot & & & & & \\ c_{j1} & c_{j2} & \ldots & c_{jj} & \ldots & c_{jk} \\ \cdot & & & & & \\ \cdot & & & & & \\ \cdot & & & & & \\ c_{k1} & c_{k2} & \ldots & c_{kj} & \ldots & c_{kk} \end{bmatrix} \begin{bmatrix} \Sigma_i u_{1i} v_i \\ \Sigma_i u_{2i} v_i \\ \cdot \\ \cdot \\ \cdot \\ \Sigma_i u_{ji} v_i \\ \cdot \\ \cdot \\ \cdot \\ \Sigma_i u_{ki} v_i \end{bmatrix} \qquad \ldots(16.7.1)$$

From (16.7.1), the estimates of the partial regression coefficients are,

$$b_1 = c_{11}\,\Sigma_i\, u_{1i}\, v_i + c_{12}\,\Sigma_i\, u_{2i}\, v_i + \ldots + c_{1k}\,\Sigma_i\, u_{ki}\, v_i$$

$$b_2 = c_{21}\,\Sigma_i\, u_{1i}\, v_i + c_{22}\,\Sigma_i\, u_{2i}\, v_i + \ldots + c_{2k}\,\Sigma_i\, u_{ki}\, v_i$$

$$\vdots$$

$$b_j = c_{j1}\,\Sigma_i\, u_{1i}\, v_i + c_{j2}\,\Sigma_i\, u_{2i}\, v_i + \ldots + c_{jk}\,\Sigma_i\, u_{ki}\, v_i \qquad \ldots(16.8)$$

$$\vdots$$

$$b_k = c_{k1}\,\Sigma_i\, u_{1i}\, v_i + c_{k2}\,\Sigma_i\, u_{2i}\, v_i + \ldots + c_{kk}\,\Sigma_i\, u_{ki}\, v_i$$

In (16.8), b_j is the general term for $j = 1, 2, \ldots, k$.

Had we not taken the deviations from means of the respective variables, the partial regression coefficients could have been found in the usual way. But the advantage of taking the deviations is that the order of the coefficient matrix is reduced, which makes the calculations easier and also a considerable time is saved in finding out A^{-1}.

Once we have obtained $b_1, b_2 \ldots, b_k$, estimated linear regression equation can easily be written as,

$$(\hat{Y} - \bar{y}) = b_1(X_1 - \bar{x}_1) + b_2(X_2 - \bar{x}_2) + \ldots + b_k(X_k - \bar{x}_k) \qquad \ldots(16.9)$$

The estimated value of Y will be obtained by substituting the given values $X_1, X_2, \ldots, X_k$ in the prediction equation (16.9).

TEST OF SIGNIFICANCE

Generally, the problem before us is which of the X's should be included in the estimation of Y through X's and which should be excluded. In other words, we want to decide whether all or some of the k-independent variables be retained in the prediction equation. This decision can be taken by testing the significance of each of the partial regression coefficient i.e., test

$$H_0 : \beta_j = 0 \text{ against } H_1 : \beta_j \neq 0$$

for $j = 1, 2, \ldots, k$.

If H_0 is not rejected, it means that the corresponding X_j should be omitted from the equation, otherwise it can be retained. The test statistic under H_0 is,

$$t_{n-k-1} = \frac{b_j}{s_{b_j}} \qquad \ldots(16.10)$$

Suffix $(n - k - 1)$ indicates the degrees of freedom of statistic t. b_j is the estimated value of β_j and s_{b_j} is the standard error of b_j.

Where, $$S_{b_j}^2 = S_E^2\, c_{jj} \qquad \ldots(16.11)$$

where c_{jj} is the (j, j)th cell element of A^{-1}

and $$S_E^2 = \frac{\Sigma_i (Y_i - \hat{Y})^2}{(n-k-1)}$$

$$= \frac{1}{(n-k-1)}\{\Sigma_i v_i^2 - R^2 \Sigma_i v_i^2\} \qquad \ldots(16.12)$$

$$= \frac{1}{(n-k-1)}(1-R^2)\Sigma_i v_i^2 \qquad ...(16.12.1)$$

where, $R^2\Sigma_i v_i^2 = b_1\Sigma_i u_{1i}v_i + b_2\Sigma_i u_{2i}v_i + ... + b_k\Sigma_i u_{ki}v_i$ ...(16.13)

Again, $s_{b_j} = \sqrt{s_{b_j}^2}$

Putting the values of b_j and s_{bj} in (16.10), we calculate the value of t. This value of t is compared with the table value of t for $(n - k - 1)$ d.f. and α level of significance. If $t_{cal} \geq t_{\alpha/2, (n-k-1)}$ or $t_{cal} \leq -t_{\alpha/2, (n-k-1)}$, reject H_0, otherwise H_0 is not rejected. If H_1 is accepted, it means that the variable X_j makes considerable contribution in the prediction of Y. Non-significance of any β_j infers that its inclusion in the regression equation is superfluous.

In many problems, we may like to know which of the X's are more important than the other. The priority may be fixed in order of their importance by considering the quantities $b_j \sqrt{\Sigma_i u_{ji}^2 / \Sigma_i v_i^2}$, known as the standard partial regression coefficients. The greater the value of this quantity, the more important the variable X_j is. Thus, X's can be ranked in order of magnitude of these quantities, ignoring the sign. This determines the preference for X's.

Interval Estimate for β_j

In case, we are interested to find out $(1 - \alpha)$ per cent confidence interval estimate of a partial regression coefficient, say, β_j for $j = 1, 2, ..., k$, it is given by

$$b_j \pm s_{b_j} t_{\alpha/2,(n-k-1)} \qquad ...(16.14)$$

where $t_{\alpha/2, (n-k-1)}$ is the table value of t at α level and $(n - k - 1)$ d.f., b_j and s_{b_j} are as explained earlier.

ANALYSIS OF VARIANCE FOR REGRESSION

Analysis of variance helps to test,

$H_0 : \beta_1 = \beta_2 = ... = \beta_k = 0$

against H_1 : at least one of the β's is not zero.

H_0 can be tested easily by the following ANOVA table.

Table 16.2 ANOVA for Multiple Regression

Due to	*d.f.*	*S.S.*	*M.S.*	*F-value*
Regression	k	$R^2\Sigma_i v_i^2$	$R^2\Sigma_i v_i^2/k$	$\frac{(n-k-1)R^2}{k(1-R^2)}$
Residual	$(n - k - 1)$	$(1-R^2)\Sigma_i v_i^2$	$\frac{(1-R^2)\Sigma_i v_i^2}{n-k-1}$	
Total	$n - 1$	$\Sigma_i v_i^2$		

Statistic F in the above ANOVA table has $(k, n - k - 1)$ d.f. If the calculated value of $F > F_{\alpha, (k, n-k-1)}$, reject H_0 at α level of significance. It leads to the conclusion that at least one of the partial regression coefficient is not zero.

In the above ANOVA, the quantity $R^2\Sigma_i v_i^2$ is known as regression sum of squares and $(1 - R^2)\ \Sigma_i v_i^2$ is the measure of the quantity $\Sigma_i\ (Y_i - \hat{Y}_i)^2$, which is the sum of the square of deviations of the actual values of Y from its estimated values.

In case, H_0 is not rejected by the F-test, there is no need to test the individual β's. Therefore, one must use the F-test first and if it gives a significant value, only then the significance of individual β's be tested by t-test.

A statistician's aim is to select a model which can best explain the relationship for a body of data. As a safeguard for this, we choose too many parameters for it. But this unnecessarily makes the analysis of data more complicated. So we should have parsimony in choosing parameters. By parsimony in parameters, we mean that the parameters be introduced in the model sparingly in such a way that a significant contribution is made by each and every parameter opted in the model. For this, the test of significance of parameters is a viable device.

MULTIPLE CORRELATION

While fitting a regression equation, the interest lies to know how far this equation serves our purpose. That is we want to confirm whether the equation is a good fit or not. In other words to what extent do the predictors explain the predictant Y? One way of describing the relative goodness of fit is the coefficient of determination R^2. R^2 tells what part of the total variation $\Sigma_i (y_i - \bar{y})^2$ in Y is explained by X-variables. Formula for R^2 is,

$$R^2 = \frac{R^2\Sigma_i v_i^2}{\Sigma_i v_i^2} \qquad \ldots(16.15)$$

where $i = 1, 2, \ldots, n$

$$\Sigma_i v_i^2 = \Sigma_i (y_i - \bar{y})^2 = \Sigma_i y_i^2 - (\Sigma_i y_i)^2/n$$

$R^2\Sigma_i v_i^2$ is given by (16.13). Moreover, $R^2\Sigma_i v_i^2$ can never exceed $\Sigma_i v_i^2$. Hence, R^2 lies between 0 and 1. The positive square root of R^2 i.e., R is known as the *multiple correlation coefficient.* In full form, it is denoted as $R_{y.12\ldots,k}$. Instead in general, the connotation for the multiple correlation coefficient of a variable X_j, with the remaining variables $X_1, X_2, \ldots, X_{J-1}, X_{j+1}, \ldots, X_k$ is $R_{j.12\ldots(j-1).(j+1),\ldots,k}$. But for convenience, the suffixes are omitted and are understood by himself.

Definitions

(*i*) Multiple correlation coefficient is a measure of linear association of a variable Y (say) with X-variables.

(*ii*) Multiple correlation coefficient is the simple correlation between

$$Y \text{ and } \hat{Y} \text{ where } \hat{Y} = \bar{Y} + b_1X_1 + b_2X_2 + \ldots + b_kX_k.$$

The range of R is also from 0 to 1.

It is advisable to find the value of R. If the value of R is near 1, the regression equation is a good fit. Otherwise, there is every justification to doubt the postulated regression model and hence a search for better model be made.

Multiple Correlation in Terms of Simple Correlation

If we consider only k variables $X_1, X_2, ..., X_k$, the simple correlation coefficients between all possible pairs of k-variables can easily be arranged in a correlation matrix P as given below.

$$P = \begin{bmatrix} 1 & r_{12} & r_{13} & \cdots & r_{1k} \\ r_{21} & 1 & r_{23} & \cdots & r_{2k} \\ r_{31} & r_{32} & 1 & \cdots & r_{3k} \\ \cdot & & & & \\ \cdot & & & & \\ \cdot & & & & \\ r_{k1} & r_{k2} & r_{k3} & \cdots & 1 \end{bmatrix}$$

Recall $r_{ij} = r_{ji}$ and $r_{ii} = r_{jj} = 1$ for $i, j = 1, 2, 3, ..., k$. Therefore, P is always a symmetric square matrix.

Multiple correlation coefficient of a variable x_j with the rest of the variables is given as,

$$R_{j.12...(j-1)(j+1)...k} = \left(1 - \frac{|P|}{P_{jj}}\right)^{\frac{1}{2}} \quad ...(16.15.1)$$

where $|P|$ is the determinant of the correlation matrix P and P_{jj} is the cofactor of r_{jj}.

Please note that the sign of $|P|$ and P_{jj} is always the same. Otherwise the value of R (suffix omitted) will become greater than one which is impossible. Also $|P| \leq P_{jj}$.

If $R = 0$, it means that X_j has no linear relationship with the other variables. Again if $R = 1$, it means that X_j has a perfect linear relationship with the other variables.

In case of three variables X_1, X_2 and X_3, multiple correlation coefficient of X_1, X_2 and X_3 in terms of simple correlation coefficients can be expressed as,

$$R_{1.23} = \sqrt{\frac{r_{12}^2 + r_{13}^2 - 2r_{12}r_{13}r_{23}}{1 - r_{23}^2}} \quad ...(16.15.2)$$

Similarly, $$R_{2.13} = \sqrt{\frac{r_{21}^2 + r_{23}^2 - 2r_{21}r_{23}r_{13}}{1 - r_{13}^2}} \quad ...(16.15.2)$$

A parallel expression can be given for $R_{3.12}$.

In case of three variables X_1, X_2 and X_3 the regression planes of X_1 on X_2 and X_3; X_2 on X_1 and X_3 & X_3 on X_1 and X_2 will be coincident if

$$r_{12}^2 + r_{13}^2 + r_{23}^2 - 2r_{12}r_{13}r_{23} = 1.$$

This condition is necessary and sufficient for the three regression planes to be coincident. Further, if $1 - r_{12}^2 - r_{13}^2 - r_{23}^2 + 2r_{12}r_{13}r_{23} > 0$, Then r_{12}, r_{13}, r_{23} are said to be consistent and if < 0, then inconsistent.

Partial Correlation Coefficient

Another measure of importance in a multivariate problem is the partial correlation.

Definition. Partial correlation coefficient is a measure of the degree of linear association between any two variables out of a set of variables, when the influence of the remaining variables is eliminated from both of them.

Suppose, there are k-variables $X_1, X_2, ..., X_k$. We want to know the degree of relationship between X_1 and X_2, which is free from the influence of $X_3, X_4, ..., X_k$. It is measured by partial correlation coefficient and is denoted by $\rho_{12.34...k}$. Similarly, if we find out the partial correlation between X_2 and X_4, eliminating the influence of the variables $X_1, X_3, X_5, ..., X_k$, it will be denoted by $\rho_{24.135..k}$. The range of partial correlation coefficient is from – 1 to + 1. Here, we give the formulae for partial correlation coefficient only in cases when $k = 3$ and $k = 4$.

Suppose, there are three variables X_1, X_2 and X_3. The partial correlation coefficient between X_1 and X_2 eliminating the influence of X_3 is given as

$$\rho_{12.3} = \frac{\rho_{12} - \rho_{13}\rho_{23}}{\sqrt{1-\rho_{13}^2}\sqrt{1-\rho_{23}^2}} \quad ...(16.16)$$

Let the estimate of $\rho_{12.3}$ be given by $r_{12.3}$. To find $r_{12.3}$, we replace all simple population correlation coefficients by their estimated values. Thus,

$$r_{12.3} = \frac{r_{12} - r_{13}r_{23}}{\sqrt{1-r_{13}^2}\sqrt{1-r_{23}^2}} \quad ...(16.17)$$

$r_{12.3}$ is also known as the *first order partial correlation coefficient.*

For calculating $r_{12.3}$ we have to consider the triplets. The data and partial calculations are shown in the following Table 16.3.

Table 16.3: Sample Observations and Calculations

	X_1	X_2	X_3	X_1X_2	X_1X_3	X_2X_3	X_1^2	X_2^2	X_3^2
	x_{11}	x_{21}	x_{31}	$x_{11}x_{21}$	$x_{11}x_{31}$	$x_{21}x_{31}$	x_{11}^2	x_{21}^2	x_{31}^2
	x_{12}	x_{22}	x_{32}	$x_{12}\ x_{22}$	$x_{12}x_{32}$	$x_{22}\ x_{32}$	x_{12}^2	x_{22}^2	x_{32}^2
	⋮	⋮	⋮	⋮	⋮	⋮	⋮	⋮	⋮
	x_{1n}	x_{2n}	x_{3n}	$x_{1n}x_{2n}$	$x_{1n}\ x_{3n}$	$x_{2n}\ x_{3n}$	x_{1n}^2	x_{2n}^2	x_{3n}^2
Total	$\Sigma_i x_{1i}$	$\Sigma_i x_{2i}$	$\Sigma_i x_{3i}$	$\Sigma_i x_{1i}\ x_{2i}$	$\Sigma_i x_{1i}\ x_{3i}$	$\Sigma_i x_{2i}\ x_{3i}$	$\Sigma_i x_{1i}^2$	$\Sigma_i x_{2i}^2$	$\Sigma_i x_{3i}^2$

In the margin, all summations are taken over i where $i = 1, 2, 3, ..., n$.

We know that simple correlation coefficient,

$$r_{jm} = \frac{\Sigma_i x_{ji}x_{mi} - (\Sigma_i x_{ji})(\Sigma_i x_{mi})/n}{\sqrt{\{\Sigma_i\, x_{ji}^2 - (\Sigma_i x_{ji})^2/n\}\{\Sigma_i x_{mi}^2 - (\Sigma_i x_{mi})^2/n\}}} \quad ...(16.18)$$

for $\qquad j \neq m = 1, 2, 3, ..., k$

Also $\qquad r_{jm} = r_{mj}$

Substituting the value of simple correlation coefficients calculated in 16.17 from 16.18, we obtain the value of $r_{12.3}$. The other partial correlation coefficients can be obtained in the same way using the formulae.

$$r_{13.2} = \frac{r_{13} - r_{12}r_{23}}{\sqrt{1-r_{12}^2}\sqrt{1-r_{23}^2}} \qquad \text{...(16.19)}$$

and $$r_{23.1} = \frac{r_{23} - r_{12}\,r_{31}}{\sqrt{1-r_{12}^2}\sqrt{1-r_{31}^2}} \qquad \text{...(16.20)}$$

If there are four variables X_1, X_2, X_3 and X_4 under consideration for the joint study, and we want to calculate the partial correlation coefficient between X_1 and X_2 independent of the effect of X_3 and X_4, the formula for $r_{12.34}$, the estimated value of $\rho_{12.34}$ is

$$r_{12.34} = \frac{r_{12.4} - r_{13.4}r_{23.4}}{\sqrt{(1-r_{13.4}^2)(1-r_{23.4}^2)}} \qquad \text{...(16.21)}$$

or alternatively,

$$r_{12.34} = \frac{r_{12.3} - r_{14.3}r_{24.3}}{\sqrt{(1-r_{14.3}^2)(1-r_{24.3}^2)}} \qquad \text{...(16.22)}$$

It is worth pointing out that the formulae (16.21) and (16.22) are identical and hence the same value of $r_{12.34}$ is obtained from both the formulae. Formula for other partial correlation coefficient like $r_{13.24}$ or $r_{14.23}$ can be written by interchanging the suffixes in either of the formula (16.21) or (16.22). $r_{12.34}$ is known as the *second order partial correlation coefficient*. Partial correlation coefficient is often calculated between Y and independent variable X_i, whereas the effect of other independent variables is eliminated. In this situation, we may denote the partial correlation coefficient by

$$r_{Yi.12\,...\,(i-1)\,(i+1)\,...\,k}$$

In the similar manner as (16.20) to (16.22), the formulae can be given as,

$$r_{Y1.2} = \frac{r_{Y1} - r_{Y2}r_{12}}{\sqrt{(1-r_{Y2}^2)(1-r_{12}^2)}} \qquad \text{...(16.23)}$$

and $$r_{Y1.23} = \frac{r_{Y1.3} - r_{Y2.3}\,r_{12.3}}{\sqrt{(1-r_{Y2.3}^2)(1-r_{12.3}^2)}} \qquad \text{...(16.24)}$$

or alternately $$r_{Y1.23} = \frac{r_{Y1.2} - r_{Y3.2}\,r_{13.2}}{\sqrt{(1-r_{Y3.2}^2)(1-r_{13.2}^2)}} \qquad \text{...(16.25)}$$

Further Explanation: Often the correlation between two variables X_1 and X_2, may be partly due to the influence of a third variable X_3 which is correlated to X_1 and X_2 both. We are interested in working out the pure correlation between X_1 and X_2 after eliminating the linear effect of X_3 from X_1 and X_2. In this situation, we define the two residual variables $X_{1.3}$ and $X_{2.3}$ where $X_{1.3} = X_1 - b_{13}X_3$ and $X_{2.3} = X_2 - b_{23}X_3$. Here b_{13} and b_{23} are the simple linear regression coefficients of X_1 on X_3 and X_2 on X_3 respectively. The simple correlation between $X_{1.3}$ and $X_{2.3}$ is equivalent to partial correlation coefficient between X_1 and X_2, eliminating the influence of X_3 on X_1 and X_2, i.e.

$$r_{12.3} = \frac{\text{cov}(X_{1.3}, X_{2.3})}{\sqrt{\text{var}(X_{1.3})\text{var}(X_{2.3})}} \quad ...(16.26)$$

Formula (16.26) ultimately reduces to (16.17).

If the number of variables is more than four then the formula for partial correlation coefficient becomes complicated. In such a situation, it is easy to work out the partial correlation coefficient $r_{ij.12...k}$(for $i \neq j$ and 12...*k* in suffix do not include *i* and *j*) in case of *k*-variables $X_1, X_2,..., X_k$ with the help of correlation matrix *P*. Formula for $r_{ij.12...k}$ is,

$$r_{ij.12....k} = \frac{P_{ij}}{(P_{ii}P_{jj})^{1/2}}$$

where P_{ij}, P_{ii} and P_{jj} are the cofactors of r_{ij}, r_{ii} and r_{jj} respectively in the determinant of the correlation matrix.

***Example* 16.1.** The data regarding total expenditure and its four main components as percentage of gross domestic product for eleven years are presented in the table below:

Year	*Total expenditure* (y)	*Interest payments* (x_1)	*Subsidies* (x_2)	*Security expenditure* (x_3)	*Grants* (x_4)
1.	10.5	1.7	0.6	3.0	4.3
2.	11.6	1.7	1.2	2.9	4.7
3.	12.2	1.7	1.3	2.7	4.8
4.	13.5	1.9	1.3	2.7	5.3
5.	13.3	2.1	1.4	2.9	4.8
6.	13.0	2.1	1.2	2.8	4.6
7.	13.4	2.2	1.2	2.8	4.5
8.	14.5	2.4	1.4	3.0	5.0
9.	12.8	2.5	1.4	2.9	5.0
10.	14.8	2.8	1.8	3.0	5.4
11.	15.4	3.0	2.0	3.1	6.3
Total	$145.0 \equiv \Sigma_i y_i$	$24.1 \equiv \Sigma_i x_{1i}$	$14.8 \equiv \Sigma_i x_{2i}$	$31.8 \equiv \Sigma_i x_{3i}$	$54.7 \equiv \Sigma_i x_{4i}$

where $i = 1, 2, ..., 11$.

Using the given data we will,

(*a*) Fit in the linear regression equation of *Y* on X_1, X_2, X_3 and X_4.

(*b*) Estimate the total expenditure for the given independent variate values, $X_1 = 2.5$, $X_2 = 1.5$, $X_3 = 3.0$ and $X_4 = 5.0$.

(*c*) Find the multiple correlation coefficient *R* and interpret it.

(*d*) Test the significance of regression coefficients through analysis of variance.

(*e*) Test the significance of the individual regression coefficient β_2.

(*a*) For the given data,

$$n = 11,\ k = 4,\ \bar{y} = \frac{145.0}{11} = 13.182,$$

$$\bar{x}_1 = \frac{24.1}{11} = 2.1909,\ \bar{x}_2 = \frac{14.8}{11} = 1.3454,$$

$$\bar{x}_3 = \frac{31.8}{11} = 2.8909,\ \bar{x}_4 = \frac{54.7}{11} = 4.9727$$

To fit in the linear regression equation,

$$\hat{Y} = \bar{y} + b_1(X_1 - \bar{x}_1) + b_2(X_2 - \bar{x}_2) + b_3(X_3 - \bar{x}_3) + b_4(X_4 - \bar{x}_4),$$

we calculate the sum of squares and sum of cross products as given below.

$$\Sigma_i y_i^2 = (10.5)^2 + (11.6)^2 + \ldots +(15.4)^2$$
$$= 110.25 + 134.56 + \ldots + 237.16$$
$$= 1931.64$$

$$\Sigma_i x_{1i}^2 = (1.7)^2 + (1.7)^2 + \ldots + (3.0)^2$$
$$= 2.89 + 2.89 + \ldots + 9.00$$
$$= 54.79$$

Similarly,

$$\Sigma_i x_{2i}^2 = 21.8,\ \Sigma_i x_{3i}^2 = 92.10,\ \Sigma_i X_{4i}^2 = 275.01.$$

$$\Sigma_i x_{1i} x_{2i} = 1.7 \times 0.6 + 1.7 \times 1.2 + \ldots + 3.0 \times 2.0$$
$$= 1.02 + 2.04 + \ldots + 6.00$$
$$= 33.74$$

Similarly,

$$\Sigma_i x_{1i} x_{3i} = 70.03,\ \Sigma_i x_{1i} x_{4i} = 121.69$$
$$\Sigma_i x_{2i} x_{3i} = 42.94,\ \Sigma_i x_{2i} x_{4i} = 75.31$$

and $\Sigma_i x_{3i} x_{4i} = 158.43$

$$\Sigma_i x_{1i} y_i = 1.7 \times 10.5 + 1.7 \times 11.6 + \ldots + 3.0 \times 15.4$$
$$= 17.85 + 19.72 + \ldots + 46.20$$
$$= 323.11$$

Similarly,

$$\Sigma_i x_{2i} y_i = 199.59$$
$$\Sigma_i x_{3i} y_i = 419.78, \text{ and } \Sigma_i x_{4i} y_i = 727.16$$

Now we calculate again the above quantities taking into consideration the deviations from respective means. Thus, we have

$$\Sigma_i v_i^2 = \Sigma_i y_i^2 - \frac{(\Sigma_i y_i)^2}{n}$$
$$= 1931.64 - \frac{(145.0)^2}{11}$$
$$= 20.2760$$

$$\Sigma_i u_{1i}^2 = \Sigma_i x_{1i}^2 - \frac{(\Sigma_i x_{1i})^2}{n}$$

$$= 54.79 - \frac{(24.1)^2}{11}$$

$$= 1.9891$$

Similarly,

$$\Sigma_i u_{2i}^2 = 1.2673,\ \Sigma_i u_{3i}^2 = 0.1691,\ \Sigma_i u_{4i}^2 = 3.0018$$

$$\Sigma_i u_{1i} u_{2i} = \Sigma_i x_{1i} x_{2i} - \frac{(\Sigma_i x_{1i})(\Sigma_i x_{2i})}{n}$$

$$= 33.74 - \frac{24.1 \times 14.8}{11}$$

$$= 1.3145$$

Similarly,

$$\Sigma_i u_{1i} u_{3i} = 0.3591,\ \Sigma_i u_{1i} u_{4i} = 1.8473$$

$$\Sigma_i u_{2i} u_{3i} = 0.1545,\ \Sigma_i u_{2i} u_{4i} = 1.7136$$

and $\Sigma_i u_{3i} u_{4i} = 0.2973$

$$\Sigma_i u_{1i} v_i = \Sigma_i x_{1i} y_i - \frac{(\Sigma_i x_{1i})(\Sigma_i y_i)}{n}$$

$$= 323.11 - \frac{24.1 \times 145.0}{11}$$

$$= 5.4282$$

Similarly,

$$\Sigma_i u_{2i} v_i = 4.4991,\ \Sigma_i u_{3i} v_i = 0.5982,$$

and $\Sigma_i u_{4i} v_i = 6.1145$

The coefficient matrix (16.6) for the values obtained after taking the deviations from means is,

$$A_{4\times4} = \begin{bmatrix} 1.9891 & 1.3145 & 0.3591 & 1.8473 \\ 1.3145 & 1.2673 & 0.1545 & 1.7136 \\ 0.3591 & 0.1545 & 0.1691 & 0.2973 \\ 1.8473 & 1.7136 & 0.2973 & 3.0018 \end{bmatrix}$$

The inverse of the matrix A is calculated by pivotal condensation method given in appendix-A on pages 739–742.

From the relation (16.7.1), we obtain the values of b_1, b_2, b_3, and b_4. The inverse has been taken only up to eight decimal places.

$$\begin{bmatrix} b_1 \\ b_2 \\ b_3 \\ b_4 \end{bmatrix} = \begin{bmatrix} 2.78548404 & -2.70529343 & -3.80798645 & 0.20730246 \\ -2.70529343 & 6.10663094 & 4.07743252 & -2.22501662 \\ -3.80798645 & 4.07743252 & 12.40762356 & -1.21306599 \\ 0.20730246 & -2.22501662 & -1.21306599 & 1.59587020 \end{bmatrix} \begin{bmatrix} 5.4282 \\ 4.4991 \\ 0.5982 \\ 6.1145 \end{bmatrix}$$

$$\begin{aligned} b_1 &= 2.78548404 \times 5.4282 - 2.70529343 \times 4.4991 \\ &\quad - 3.80798645 \times 0.5982 + 0.20730246 \times 6.1145 \\ &= 15.1202 - 12.1714 - 2.2779 + 1.2676 \\ &= 1.9385 \end{aligned}$$

Similarly,

$$\begin{aligned} b_2 &= 2.70529343 \times 5.4282 + \ldots - 2.22501662 \times 6.1145 \\ &= -14.6849 + 27.4743 + 2.4391 - 13.6049 \\ &= 1.6236 \end{aligned}$$

and $b_3 = -2.3208,\ b_4 = 0.1470$

(*a*) Thus, the linear regression of $\hat{Y}$ on X_1, X_2, X_3 and X_4 is,

$$\begin{aligned} \hat{Y} &= 13.182 + 1.9385\,(X_1 - 2.1909) + 1.6236\,(X_2 - 1.3454) \\ &\quad - 2.3208\,(X_3 - 2.8909) + 0.1470\,(X_4 - 4.9727) \end{aligned}$$

$$\hat{Y} = 12.7288 + 1.9385\,X_1 + 1.6236\,X_2 - 2.3208\,X_3 + 0.1470\,X_4$$

where

$$\begin{aligned} b_0 &= 13.182 - 1.9385 \times 2.1909 - 1.6236 \times 1.3454 \\ &\quad + 2.3208 \times 2.8909 - 0.1470 \times 4.9727 \\ &= 13.182 - 4.2470 - 2.1844 + 6.7092 - 0.7310 \\ &= 12.7288 \end{aligned}$$

(*b*) We can estimate the total expenditure for given values of X's i.e., $X_1 = 2.5$, $X_2 = 1.5$, $X_3 = 3.0$ and $X_4 = 5.0$. By substituting the values of X_1, X_2, X_3 and X_4 in the estimated regression equation, we get

$$\begin{aligned} \hat{Y} &= 12.7288 + 1.9385 \times 2.5 + 1.6236 \times 1.5 \\ &\quad - 2.3208 \times 3.0 + 0.1470 \times 5.0 \\ &= 12.7288 + 4.8462 + 2.4354 - 6.9624 + 0.7350 \\ &= 13.7830 \end{aligned}$$

(*c*) Now calculate the value of $R^2\ \Sigma_i v_i^2$ by the relation (16.13).

$$\begin{aligned} R^2\Sigma_i v_i^2 &= 1.9385 \times 5.4282 + 1.6236 \times 4.4991 \\ &\quad - 2.3208 \times 0.5982 + 0.1470 \times 6.1145 \\ &= 10.5226 + 7.3047 - 1.3883 + 0.8988 \\ &= 17.3378 \end{aligned}$$

we know, $\Sigma_i v_i^2 = 20.2760$

The multiple correlation coefficient,

$$\begin{aligned} R^2 &= \frac{R^2\Sigma_i v_i^2}{\Sigma_i v_i^2} \\ &= \frac{17.3378}{20.2760} = 0.8551 \\ R &= 0.9247 \end{aligned}$$

The value of multiple correlation coefficient R is more than 0.9. This indicates that there exists a high degree of linear association between Y and independent variables X_1, X_2, X_3, and X_4.

	1.9891	1.3145	0.3591	1.8473	1	0	0	0
	1.3145	1.2673	0.1545	1.7136	0	1	0	0
	0.3591	0.1545	0.1691	0.2973	0	0	1	0
	1.8473	1.7136	0.2973	3.0018	0	0	0	1
I Pivotal row	1	0.660851641	0.180533909	0.928711477	0.502739932	0	0	0
	0	0.398610517	–0.082811824	0.492808763	–0.660851641	1	0	0
	0	–0.082811824	0.104270273	–0.036200290	–0.180533909	0	1	0
	0	0.492808763	–0.036200290	1.286191289	–0.928711476	0	0	1
II Pivotal row		1	–0.207751227	1.236316509	–1.657888121	2.508714541	0	0
		0	0.087066014	0.066183350	–0.317826648	0.207751227	1	0
		0	0.066181335	0.676923679	–0.11168968	–1.236316510	0	1
III Pivotal row			1	0.760128228	–3.650409998	2.386134583	11.48553786	0
			0	0.626617378	0.129899327	–1.394234082	–0.760128228	1
IV Pivotal row				1	0.207302464	–2.225016623	–1.213065987	1.595870199

Now rewrite the Pivotal rows, change the left hand matrix into I, so that the right hand matrix is changed to A^{-1}.

1	0.660851641	0.180533909	0.928711477	0.502739932	0	0	0
0	1	–0.207751227	1.236316509	–1.657888121	2.508714541	0	0
0	0	1	0.760128228	–3.650409998	2.386134583	11.48553786	0
0	0	0	1	0.207302464	–2.225016623	–1.213065987	1.595870199
1	0	0.317826648	0.111689683	1.598358017	–1.657888121	0	0
0	1	0	1.394234081	–2.416265277	3.004436928	2.386134583	0
0	0	1	0	–3.807986453	4.077432526	12.40762356	–1.213065987
0	0	0	1	0.207302464	–2.225016623	–1.213065987	1.595870199
1	0	0	0.111689683	2.808637587	–2.953804833	–3.943473406	0.385544696
0	1	0	0	–2.705293437	6.106630935	4.077432525	–2.22501662
0	0	1	0	–3.807986453	4.077432526	12.40762356	–1.213065987
0	0	0	1	0.207302464	–2.225016623	–1.213065987	1.595870199
1	0	0	0	2.78548404	–2.70529343	–3.80798645	0.20730246
0	1	0	0	–2.70529343	6.10663094	4.07743252	–2.22501662
0	0	1	0	–3.80798645	4.07743252	12.40762356	–1.21306599
0	0	0	1	0.20730246	–2.22501662	–1.21306599	1.59587020

1. Pivotal condensation method : See appendix A.

(*d*) All the calculations required for ANOVA to test the hypothesis.

$$H_0 : \beta_1 = \beta_2 = \beta_3 = \beta_4$$

vs. H_1 : at least one of the $\beta's$ is not zero.

have already been done.

Thus, ANOVA table is as given below.

Due to	*d.f.*	*S.S.*	*M.S.*	*F—value*
Regression	4	17.3378	4.3344	8.8511*
Residual	6	2.9382	0.4897	–
Total	10	20.2760		

*Significant at 5% level of significance

Table value of *F* for (4, 6) d.f. and α = 0.05 is 4.53. Since the calculated value of *F* is greater than tabulated value of *F*. H_0 is rejected. It means that one or more β'*s* are significant.

(*e*) Now we test the significance of individual partial regression coefficient β_2 by formula (16.10).

First we calculate S_E^2 by formula (16.12).

$$S_E^2 = \frac{1}{11-4-1}(20.2760 - 17.3378)$$

$$= \frac{2.9382}{6}$$

$$= 0.\ 4897$$

By formula (16.11),

$$S_{b_2}^2 = 0.4897 \times 6.10663094$$

$$= 2.9904$$

$$\therefore \quad S_{b_2} = 1.7293$$

Hence,

$$t = \frac{1.6236}{1.7293} = 0.94$$

Tabulated value of *t* for 6 d. f. and α = 0.05 is 2.447, which is greater than the calculated value of *t* = 0.94. Hence, we conclude that β_2 is non-significant.

MULTIPLE LINEAR REGRESSION WITH TWO INDEPENDENT VARIABLES

In the earlier discussion, the regression model has been treated in general and its solution is explicated through the matrices. The reason for this being the ease with which the solution of the normal equations is found. But if the number of normal equations is two or three, they can easily be solved by the method of elimination for the values of b_1 and b_2.

Let the linear regression model with two independent variables X_1 and X_2 be

$$Y = \beta_0 + \beta_1 X_1 + \beta_2 X_2 + e \qquad ...(16.27)$$

Following the same procedure as before, and taking the deviations from the mean of the respective variable, two normal equations are,

$$b_1 \Sigma_i u_{1i}^2 + b_2 \Sigma_i u_{1i} u_{2i} = \Sigma_i u_{1i} v_i \qquad ...(16.28)$$

$$b_1 \Sigma_i u_{1i} u_{2i} + b_2 \Sigma_i u_{2i}^2 = \Sigma_i u_{2i} v_i$$

Solving the equations given in (16.28) we obtain,

$$b_1 = \frac{(\Sigma_i u_{1i} v_i)(\Sigma_i u_{2i}^2) - (\Sigma_i u_{1i} u_{2i})(\Sigma_i u_{2i} v_i)}{(\Sigma_i u_{1i}^2)(\Sigma_i u_{2i}^2) - (\Sigma_i u_{1i} u_{2i})^2} \qquad ...(16.29)$$

$$b_2 = \frac{(\Sigma_i u_{2i} v_i)(\Sigma_i u_{1i}^2) - (\Sigma_i u_{1i} u_{2i})(\Sigma_i u_{1i} v_i)}{(\Sigma_i u_{1i}^2)(\Sigma_i u_{2i}^2) - (\Sigma_i u_{1i} u_{2i})^2} \qquad ...(16.30)$$

The estimated regression equation with two independent variables is,

$$\hat{Y} = \bar{y} + b_1(X_1 - \bar{x}_1) + b_2(X_2 - \bar{x}_2) \qquad ...(16.31)$$

All other formulae concerning regression analysis can be obtained by putting $k = 2$ in the general case. Anyhow, we give direct method of computing c_{11}, c_{12} and c_{22}, the elements of the inverse matrix of the coefficient matrix. We know, $AA^{-1} = I$.

In the expanded form,

$$\begin{bmatrix} \Sigma_i u_{1i}^2 & \Sigma_i u_{1i} u_{2i} \\ \Sigma_i u_{1i} u_{2i} & \Sigma_i u_{2i}^2 \end{bmatrix} \begin{bmatrix} c_{11} & c_{12} \\ c_{21} & c_{22} \end{bmatrix} = \begin{bmatrix} 1 & 0 \\ 0 & 1 \end{bmatrix}$$

On multiplication we get the following four equations,

$$c_{11} \Sigma_i u_{1i}^2 + c_{21} \Sigma_i u_{1i} u_{2i} = 1 \qquad ...(16.32)$$

$$c_{12} \Sigma_i u_{1i}^2 + c_{22} \Sigma_i u_{1i} u_{2i} = 0 \qquad ...(16.33)$$

and

$$c_{11} \Sigma_i u_{1i} u_{2i} + c_{21} \Sigma_i u_{2i}^2 = 0 \qquad ...(16.34)$$

$$c_{12} \Sigma_i u_{1i} u_{2i} + c_{22} \Sigma_i u_{2i}^2 = 1 \qquad ...(16.35)$$

Since A^{-1} is symmetric, $c_{12} = c_{21}$.

Solving (16.32) and (16.34) we obtain,

$$c_{11} = \frac{\Sigma_i u_{2i}^2}{D} \qquad ...(16.36)$$

where

$$D = |\Sigma_i u_{1i}^2 \Sigma_i u_{2i}^2 - (\Sigma_i u_{1i} u_{2i})^2|$$

and

$$c_{12} = -\frac{\Sigma_i u_{1i} u_{2i}}{D} \qquad ...(16.37)$$

From equations (16.33) and (16.35) we obtain,

$$c_{22} = \frac{\Sigma_i u_{1i}^2}{D} \qquad ...(16.38)$$

All the quantities required to calculate c_{11}, c_{12} and c_{22} in (16.36) to (16.38) have already been calculated. So we easily get c_{11}, c_{12} and c_{22}. The elements of the inverse matrix help in calculating S_{b1} and S_{b2}. All these formulae will be used in the example below.

Some Useful Relations

(*i*) In a trivariate distribution with variables X_1, X_2 and X_3 having known the means $\bar{x}_1, \bar{x}_2, \bar{x}_3$ and standard deviations s_1, s_2, s_3 of the three variables respectively and the simple correlation coefficients r_{12}, r_{13} and r_{23}. The multiple linear regression equation of X_1 on X_2 and X_3 can be obtained by the following determinant equation,

$$\begin{bmatrix} \dfrac{X_1-\bar{x}_1}{s_1} & \dfrac{X_2-\bar{x}_2}{s_2} & \dfrac{X_3-\bar{x}_3}{s_3} \\ r_{21} & 1 & r_{23} \\ r_{31} & r_{32} & 1 \end{bmatrix} = 0 \qquad ...(16.39)$$

$$\frac{(X_1-\bar{x}_1)}{s_1}(1-r_{23}^2)-\frac{(X_2-\bar{x}_2)}{s_2}(r_{21}-r_{31}r_{23})$$

$$+\frac{(X_3-\bar{x}_3)}{s_3}(r_{21}r_{32}-r_{31}) = 0 \qquad ...(16.39.1)$$

(*ii*) The partial regression coefficients $b_{12.3}$ and $b_{21.3}$ can be obtained by the following formulae:

$$b_{12.3} = \frac{r_{12}-r_{23}r_{13}}{1-r_{23}^2}\cdot\frac{s_1}{s_2} \qquad ...(16.40)$$

$$b_{21.3} = \frac{r_{21}-r_{23}r_{13}}{1-r_{13}^2}\cdot\frac{s_2}{s_1} \qquad ...(16.41)$$

(*iii*) The relation between two partial regression coefficients and partial correlation coefficient is,

$$b_{12.3} \times b_{21.3} = r_{12.3}^2 \qquad ...(16.42)$$

***Example* 16.2.** In a trivariate population of random variables X_1, X_2, X_3, following results about means, S.D. and correlation coefficients were found in a sample of size 20.

$$\bar{x}_1 = 40,\ \bar{x}_2 = 50,\ \bar{x}_3 = 60;$$

$$s_1 = 3,\ s_2 = 4,\ s_3 = 5;$$

$$r_{12} = 0.6,\ r_{13} = 0.5,\ r_{23} = 0.4.$$

Making use of the given information, we would, (*i*) find regression equation of X_1 on X_2 and X_3, (*ii*) estimate X_1 when $X_2 = 70$ and $X_3 = 75$, (*iii*) calculate $b_{12.3}$, (*iv*)work out $r_{12.3}$.

(*i*) Regression equation of X_1 on X_2 and X_3 by the equation (16.39.1) is,

$$\frac{X_1-40}{3}(1-.4^2)-\frac{(X_2-50)}{4}(.6-.5\times.4)+\frac{X_3-60}{5}(.6\times.4-.5)=0$$

$$\frac{X_1-40}{3}\times 0.84-\frac{X_2-50}{4}\times 0.4+\frac{X_3-60}{5}\times(-0.26)=0$$

$$0.28\ (X_1 - 40) - 0.10\ (X_2 - 50) - 0.052\ (X_3 - 60) = 0$$

$$0.28\ X_1 - 0.10\ X_2 - 0.052\ X_3 = 3.08 \quad ...(1)$$

(*ii*) Putting $X_2 = 70$ and $X_3 = 75$ in (1), we get the estimated value of X_1 as follows:

$$0.28\ \hat{X}_1 = 0.10 \times 70 + 0.052 \times 75 + 3.08 = 13.98$$

$$\therefore \quad \hat{X}_1 = 49.93 \quad ...(2)$$

(*iii*)
$$b_{12.3} = \frac{.6-.4\times.5}{1-.4^2}\times\frac{3}{4} = \frac{.40}{.84}\times\frac{3}{4} = 0.357$$

(*iv*)
$$b_{21.3} = \frac{.6-.4\times.5}{1-.5^2}\times\frac{4}{3} = \frac{.40}{.75}\times\frac{4}{3} = 0.711$$

$$r^2_{12.3} = \frac{.40}{.84}\times\frac{3}{4}\times\frac{.40}{.75}\times\frac{4}{3} = 0.254$$

$$\therefore \quad r_{12.3} = \sqrt{0.254} = 0.504$$

***Example* 16.3.** A modulation study on *R. Trifoli* yields the following data.

	Dry weight of plants (mg) Y	*Root length (cm)* X_1	*Shoot length (cm)* X_2
	412	28.7	21.5
	226	13.4	11.7
	292	14.6	12.9
	323	18.0	14.8
	233	12.1	11.0
	368	23.4	19.2
	239	12.6	11.4
	382	30.2	22.6
	218	11.6	10.8
	222	12.0	10.2
	214	12.4	10.1
Total	3129	189.0	156.2

[*Source: Indian J. Exp. Biol.* **21** (9). Sept. 83]

Considering that the dry weight of plants depend on root length and shoot length, we would (*i*) fit in the linear regression equation of Y on X_1 and X_2, (*ii*) estimate Y for given $X_1 = 12$ and $X_2 = 10$, (*iii*) find the value of R and interpret it, (*iv*) test the significance of each partial regression coefficient, (v) find 95 per cent confidence limits for β_1 and (vi) calculate partial correlation coefficient $r_{y1.2}$.

(i) First the following calculations are made which will be required in almost all formulae.

$$\Sigma_i y_i^2 = 412^2 + 226^2 + ... + 214^2$$
$$= 169744 + 51076 + ...+ 45796$$
$$= 945775$$
$$\Sigma_i x_{1i}^2 = 28.7^2 + 13.4^2 + ... + 12.4^2$$
$$= 823.69 + 179.56 + ... + 153.76$$
$$= 3737.50$$

Similarly,

$$\Sigma_i x_{2i}^2 = 2437.64$$
$$\Sigma_i x_{1i} x_{2i} = 28.7 \times 21.5 + 13.4 \times 11.7 + ... + 12.4 \times 10.1$$
$$= 617.05 + 156.78 + ... + 125.24$$
$$= 3010.03$$
$$\Sigma_i x_{1i} y_i = 28.7 \times 412 + 13.4 \times 226 + ... + 12.4 \times 214$$
$$= 11824.4 + 3028.4 + ... + 2653.6$$
$$= 58754.7$$

Similarly,

$$\Sigma_i x_{2i} y_i = 47816.0$$

Also
$$n = 11, \bar{y} = \frac{3129}{11} = 284.45,$$
$$\bar{x}_1 = \frac{189.0}{11} = 17.182, \bar{x}_2 = \frac{156.2}{11} = 14.20$$

The sum of squares and the sum of the cross products taking deviations from the means are calculated in the same manner as in example 16.1.

$$\Sigma_i v_i^2 = 945775 - (3129)^2/11 = 55716.73$$
$$\Sigma_i u_{1i}^2 = 3737.5 - (189)^2/11 = 490.136$$
$$\Sigma_i u_{2i}^2 = 2437.64 - (156.2)^2/11 = 219.6$$
$$\Sigma_i u_{1i} u_{2i} = 3010.03 - (189)(156.2)/11 = 326.23$$
$$\Sigma_i u_{1i} v_i = 58754.7 - (189)(3129)/11 = 4992.79$$
$$\Sigma_i u_{2i} v_i = 47816.0 - (156.2)(3129)/11 = 3384.2$$

From the formulae (16.29) and (16.30) we obtain,

$$b_1 = \frac{219.6 \times 4992.79 - 326.23 \times 3384.2}{490.136 \times 219.6 - (326.23)^2}$$

$$= -\frac{7610.9}{1207.85}$$

$$= -6.30$$

and $$b_2 = \frac{490.136 \times 3384.2 - 326.23 \times 4992.79}{490.136 \times 219.6 - (326.23)^2}$$

$$= \frac{29920.4}{1207.85}$$

$$= 24.77$$

The regression equation from (16.31) is

$$\hat{Y} = 284.45 - 6.30\ (X_1 - 17.182) + 24.77\ (X_2 - 14.2)$$
$$= 40.96 - 6.30\ X_1 + 24.77\ X_2$$

(*ii*) The estimated value of the dry weight of plant for given values, $X_1 = 12$ and $X_2 = 10$, is calculated by putting the values of X_1 and X_2 in the above prediction equation.

$$\hat{Y} = 40.96 - 6.30 \times 12 + 24.77 \times 10$$
$$= 213.06 \text{ mg.}$$

(*iii*) From formula (16.13), the regression sum of square,

$$R^2\Sigma_i v_i^2 = -6.30 \times 4992.79 + 24.77 \times 3384.2$$
$$= 52372.06$$

The multiple correlation coefficient from (16.15) is obtained as,

$$R^2 = \frac{52372.06}{55716.73}$$
$$= 0.94$$
$$R = \sqrt{0.94} = 0.97$$

The value of R is nearly equal to 1. This shows that the linear regression equation is a good fit.

(*iv*) The hypothesis

$$H_0 : \beta_1 = 0 \text{ vs } H_1 : \beta_1 \neq 0$$

is tested by the statistic (16.10).

The quantity.

$$\Sigma_i v_i^2 - R^2\Sigma_i v_i^2 = 55716.73 - 52372.06$$
$$= 3344.67$$

$$\therefore \qquad S_E^2 = \frac{1}{(11-2-1)} \times 3344.67$$
$$= 418.08.$$

Using formulae (16.36) to (16.38), we obtain the elements of the inverse matrix as,

$$c_{11} = \frac{219.6}{1207.85} = 0.1818$$

$$c_{12} = -\frac{326.23}{1207.85} = -0.2701$$

$$c_{22} = \frac{490.136}{1207.85} = 0.4058$$

The variance of b_1 from (16.11) is

$$S_{b_1}^2 = 418.08 \times 0.1818$$
$$= 76.007$$

$\therefore$ $$S_{b_1} = 8.718$$

The test statistic

$$t = \frac{-6.30}{8.718}$$
$$= -0.722$$

The table value of t at $\alpha = 0.05$ and 8 d.f. is 2.306. The calculated value of t is greater than – 2.306. Hence, we accept H_0 i.e., β_1 is nonsignificant. It means that the unit increase in the root length does not make a significant change in the dry weight of the plant.

Similarly the test for the hypothesis,

$$H_0 : \beta_2 = 0 \text{ vs. } \beta_2 \neq 0$$

can be performed.

In this case,

$$S_{b_2}^2 = 418.08 \times 0.4058$$
$$= 169.6568$$
$$S_{b_2} = 13.02$$

The statistic,

$$t = \frac{24.77}{13.02}$$
$$= 1.902$$

Again, the regression coefficient β_2 is nonsignificant since $t_{cal} < 2.306$. Its physical interpretation remains the same as for β_1.

(*v*) 95 per cent confidence interval for β_1 by formula (16.14) is,

$$\text{C.I.} = -6.30 \pm 8.718 \times 2.306$$
$$= -6.30 \pm 20.10$$

Hence, the confidence limits are,

Lower limit = – 6.30 – 20.10 = – 26.40

Upper limit = – 6.30 + 20.10 = 13.80.

(*vi*) The partial correlation coefficient $r_{Y1.2}$ will be calculated by the formula (16.23). First, we calculate the simple correlation coefficients, required in the formulae (16.23), by the formula (16.18). Using the sum of squares and the sum of the cross products found out by taking the deviations from the means,

$$r_{Y1} = \frac{4992.79}{\sqrt{55716.73 \times 490.136}} = \frac{4992.79}{5225.78} = 0.9554$$

$$r_{Y2} = \frac{3384.2}{\sqrt{55716.73 \times 219.6}} = \frac{3384.2}{3497.91} = 0.9675$$

and

$$r_{12} = \frac{326.23}{\sqrt{490.136 \times 219.6}} = \frac{326.23}{328.08} = 0.9944$$

The partial correlation coefficient from (16.23) is,

$$r_{Y1.2} = \frac{0.9554 - 0.9675 \times 0.9944}{\sqrt{(1 - 0.9675^2)(1 - 0.9944^2)}} = -\frac{0.0067}{0.0268} = -0.257$$

This shows that a very low degree of negative correlation exists between Y and X_1 eliminating the effect of X_2.

Note: For fitting of multiple regression equation, see Appendix Chapter-16.

To conclude we would like to say that multiple regression equations are widely used in economics, industry and biological sciences. Its use as a prediction model has been increasing day by day.

QUESTIONS AND EXERCISES

1. What do you understand by multiple linear regression model? Explain a few situations in which it can be used.
2. Give the method of fitting of a multiple linear regression equation by the least square method using matrix notations.

3. What does the significance of a partial regression coefficient indicate?
4. Define the following terms and give their range:
   (*a*) Partial regression coefficient.
   (*b*) Partial correlation coefficient.
   (*c*) Multiple correlation coefficient.
5. Explain the term coefficient of determination. Also give its use in fitting of a multiple linear regression equation.
6. Write whether the following statements are true or false:
   (*a*) Multiple correlation coefficient lies between — 1 and 1.
   (*b*) Partial correlation coefficient lies between 0 and 1.
   (*c*) Partial regression coefficient lies between 0 and ∞.
   (*d*) Regression sum of square is always less than total sum of squares.
   (*e*) We test the significance of individual partial regression coefficient by analysis of variance.
7. How will you decide about the relative importance of various independent variables?
8. What inference would you draw, when a partial regression coefficient in multiple regression, with two independent variables, comes out to be non-significant?
9. The following table gives the data with regard to the cost of produce of wheat per hectare and the cost of inputs in rupees at different farmer's fields.

S.no.	*Output* (Y)	*Seed* (X_1)	*Labour* (X_2)	*Fertilizer* (X_3)
1	2905	185	475	578
2	2850	198	336	356
3	2910	197	242	680
4	3050	160	245	584
5	2845	195	255	695
6	2960	212	235	650
7	3012	155	275	710
8	3108	165	280	595
9	3197	185	215	440
10	2278	216	376	655
11	3118	212	235	745
12	2956	204	256	465
13	2926	198	260	730
14	3085	242	466	715

   (*i*) Fit in the linear regression equation of Y on X_1, X_2 and X_3.
   (*ii*) Test the significance of partial regression coefficient by F-test.
   (*iii*) Test the significance of partial regression coefficient of X_3.
   (*iv*) Estimate the cost of product if the inputs in rupees are X_1 = 160, X_2 = 250 and X_2 = 560.

(*v*) Find the coefficient of determination and interpret it.

(*vi*) Find the multiple correlation coefficient.

10. The data with regard to the output of gram and the cost of seed and labour per hectare at ten farmers' fields, are as given below.

S.no.	*Cost of produce (Y) (Rs/ha)*	*Cost of seed (X_1) (Rs/ha)*	*Labour cost (X_2) (Rs/ha)*
1	1127	235	128
2	840	236	82
3	735	238	205
4	570	241	71
5	462	238	110
6	614	233	130
7	916	235	200
8	460	190	170
9	1540	235	180
10	1065	243	165

(*i*) Fit the regression equation $\hat{Y} = b_0 + b_1X_1 + b_2X_2$

(*ii*) Estimate the cost of produce per hectare given that $X_1 = 230$ and $X_2 = 125$.

(*iii*) Test the significance of partial regression coefficients.

(*iv*) Find the partial correlation coefficient $r_{YX_2.X_1}$

11. The following zero-order correlation coefficients are given:

$$r_{12} = 0.98, r_{13} = 0.44, r_{23} = 0.54$$

Calculate the partial correlation coefficient between first and third variable keeping the effect of second variable constant.

(*M. Com., Delhi, 1975*).

12. Suppose that the correlation coefficients r_{12}, r_{13} and r_{23} between variables x_1 and x_2, x_1 and x_3, x_2 and x_3 are each r. Find the values of multiple correlation coefficient $R_{1.23}$ and partial correlation coefficient $r_{12.3}$.

(*M.Sc. Descriptive and Industrial Statistics, Andhra, 1986*)

13. If $r_{12} = \frac{1}{2}$, $r_{23} = \frac{3}{4}$, $r_{31} = \frac{2}{3}$, find the values of $r_{1.23}$ and $r_{13.2}$ (use usual notations).

(*I.C.W.A. Inter, June, 1992*)

14. In a certain trivariate distribution $s_1 = 2$, $s_2 = 4$, $s_3 = 2$, $\bar{x}_1 = 50$, $\bar{x}_2 = 60$, $\bar{x}_3 = 40$, $r_{12} = .7$, $r_{23} = r_{31} = .5$ where $\bar{x}_i$, s_i are mean and s.d. of variable x_i, $i = 1, 2, 3$ and r_{ij} = correlation coefficient between x_i and x_j, $i \neq j$; $i, j = 1, 2, 3$.
Find the multiple regression line of x_1 on x_2 and x_3 and estimate x_1 for $x_2 = 62$, $x_3 = 45$.

(*I.C.W.A., Inter, Dec., 2004*)

15. In a certain trivariate distribution, $s_1 = 3$, $s_2 = s_3 = 5$, $r_{12} = 0.7$, $r_{23} = r_{31} = 0.6$. Find (*i*) the partial correlation coefficient $r_{12.3}$ and (*ii*) regression coefficient, $b_{12.3}$. Hence (not otherwise) find the value of $b_{21.3}$.

(*I.C.W.A., June, 2002*)

16. (*a*) For a trivariate distribution, the following correlation coefficients were obtained. $r_{12} = 0.77$, $r_{13} = 0.72$ and $r_{23} = 0.52$. Find the partial correlation coefficient $r_{12.3}$ and multiple correlation coefficient $R_{1.23}$.

(b) If $r_{12} = 0.80$, $r_{13} = 0.60$, $r_{23} = -0.20$, then show that these are inconsistent.

(*I.C.W.A., Inter, June, 2003*)

SUGGESTED READING

Anderson, T.W. (1958). *An Introduction to Multivariate Analysis,* John Wiley, New York.

Gudmund R. Iversen and Mary M. Gergen (1997). *Statistics,* Springer.

Jaccard, J., Turrisi, R. and C.K. Wan (1990). *Interactive Effects in Multiple Regression,* Sage, Newbury Park.

James Stevens (2001). *Applied Multivariate Statistics for the Social Sciences,* Lawrence Eribaum Associates.

Joseph F. Healey (2004). *Statistics,* Thomson Wadsworth.

Kshirsagar, A.M. (1972). *Multivariate Analysis,* Marcel Dekker, New York.

Manly, Bryan F.J. (1986). *Multivariate Statistical Models: A Primer.,* Chapman & Hall, New York.

Perry R. Hinton (1995). *Statistics Explained,* Routledge.

Peter J. A. Shaw (2003). *Multivariate Statistics for the Environmental Sciences,* Oxford University Press.

Rao, C.R. (1952). *Advanced Statistical Methods in Biometric Research,* John Wiley, New York.

Rao, C.R. (1973). *Linear Statistical Inference and its Applications,* Wiley Eastern, 2nd ed., New Delhi.

APPENDIX

SPSS WINDOW GUIDE TO MULTIPLE REGRESSION

Procedure for obtaining Multiple Regressions

1. Select **Analyze** in the menu bar followed by **Regression** and **Linear** in the menu and sub-menu you get thereof the following window.
2. After selecting dependent variable, click on the corresponding arrow button. Perform similar activity with the independent variables. Click on OK button to get the output as given below.

Example 16.3

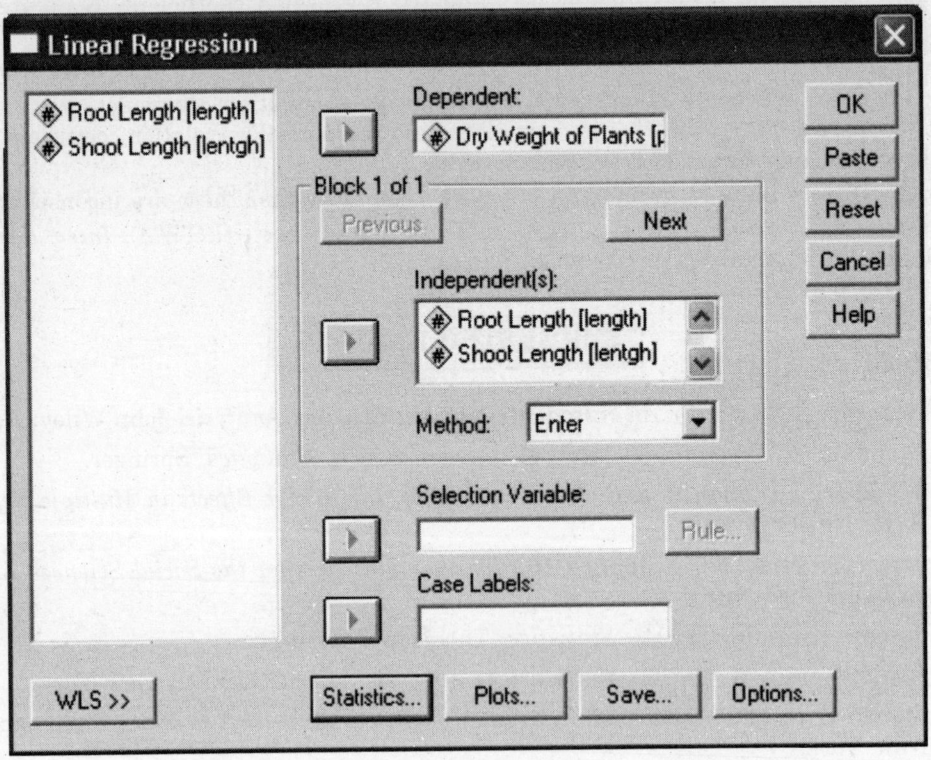

ANOVA[b]

Model		Sum of squares	df	Mean square	F	Sig.
1	Regression	52371.409	2	26185.704	62.621	.000[a]
	Residual	3345.318	8	418.165		
	Total	55716.727	10			

a. Predictors: (Constant), Shoot Length, Root Length
b. Dependent Variable: Dry Weight of Plants

Coefficients[a]

Model		Unstandardized coefficients		Standardized coefficients	t	Sig.
		B	Std. error	Beta		
1	(Constant)	40.966	39.826		1.029	.334
	Root Length	– 6.301	8.719	– .591	– .723	.490
	Shoot Length	24.771	13.026	1.555	1.902	.094

a. Dependent Variable: Dry Weight of Plants

Residuals Statistics[a]

	Minimum	Maximum	Mean	Std. deviation	N
Predicted Value	213.02	410.51	284.45	72.368	11
Residual	– 28.51	28.84	.00	18.290	11
Std. Predicted Value	– .987	1.742	.000	1.000	11
Std. Residual	– 1.394	1.410	.000	.894	11

a. Dependent Variable: Dry Weight of Plants

CHARTS

REGRESSION

Descriptive Statistics

	Mean	Std. deviation	N
Dry Weight of Plants	284.45	74.644	11
Root Length	17.1818	7.00097	11
Shoot Length	14.2000	4.68615	11

Correlations

		Dry weight of plants	Root length	Shoot length
Pearson Correlation	Dry Weight of Plants	1.000	.955	.967
	Root Length	.955	1.000	.994
	Shoot Length	.967	.994	1.000
Sig. (1-tailed)	Dry Weight of Plants	.	.000	.000
	Root Length	.000	.	.000
	Shoot Length	.000	.000	.
N	Dry Weight of Plants	11	11	11
	Root Length	11	11	11
	Shoot Length	11	11	11

Variables Entered/Removed(b)

Model	Variables entered	Variables removed	Method
1	Shoot Length, Root Length[a]		Enter

a. All requested variables entered.
b. Dependent Variable: Dry Weight of Plants

Model Summary[b]

Model	R	R square	Adjusted R square	Std. error of the estimate
1	.970[a]	.940	.925	20.449

Model Summary[b]

	Change statistics				
Model	R Square Change	F Change	df1	df2	Sig. F Change
1	.940	62.621	2	8	.000

a. Predictors: (Constant), Shoot Length, Root Length

b. Dependent Variable: Dry Weight of Plants

CORRELATIONS

Correlations

		Dry weight of plants	Root length
Dry Weight of Plants	Pearson Correlation	1	.922**
	Sig. (2-tailed)	.	.000
	N	11	11
Root Length	Pearson Correlation	.922**	1
	Sig. (2-tailed)	.000	.
	N	11	11

17

Chapter

Time Series Analysis

There are many factors which change with the passage of time, *i.e.*, as time passes, their values also change. For example, the population of a country, geomorphology, demand of items, prices, etc. The set of data with one or more variables, which is attuned to periodical changes, are generally suitable for a time series analysis. In social sciences, specially economics, and earth sciences and its branches like seismology, metereology and oceanography, time series analysis is very useful. *Time series may be considered as a sequence of measurements of some variable or composite of variables, taken periodically through time.*

Sometimes, sets of observations which do not vary with the passage of time, but are the measurements made at equidistant points, may be regarded as time series data. In this situation spacing is the variable in place of time. Such data at equal spacing are often suitable for time series analysis. For example, measurements regarding the coal face at consecutive 100 metre depths, measurements of marine animal population at consecutive 50 metre depths, etc., are the cases where spacing is the independent variable.

The purpose of time series study is to measure chronological variations. W.Z. Hirsch had correctly said, "*The main objective in analysing time series is to understand, interpret and evaluate change in economic phenomena in the hope of more correctly anticipating the course of future events.*" In the study of time series, a comparison of the past and the present data is also made. It also compares two or more series at a time e.g., the production of steel over the last ten years may be compared with the production of machines and steel appliances over the same sequence of years. Another example for this may be the comparison of agricultural production with population growth in the same sequence of years. Some other uses of time series analysis are:

(*i*) Time series analysis provides knowledge about the fluctuations in economic and business phenomena. The causes of changes can also be found out. Though some fluctuations may take place under the same circumstances.

(*ii*) Time series analysis also helps to evaluate the achievements.

(*iii*) Time series analysis is suitable for forecasting as well. The past trends can be projected into future trends, to predict the changes which are likely to occur in the economic activity of trade cycle.

It can be said that time series analysis is a big tool in the hands of the executives, to plan their sales, prices, policies, production, etc.

As stated in the preceding paragraph, one or more variables, which vary with time, may be measured and included in the time series data. But keeping in view the scope of the book, we shall consider only one variable, say Y changing with time, for time series analysis. Let the observation at time t be denoted by y_t for $t = 1, 2, ..., n$. It will not be wrong to assume that observations taken at equal intervals of time, forming a sample of observations, is a continuous observable phenomenon. Throughout this chapter, we will denote the observed value at time t by y without subscript and the independent coded variable by X for the time period t.

An economy is a dynamic phenomenon which is akin to time factor. The periodical movements are being studied through graphical methods and mathematical methods. Firstly, we discuss the type of variations which are likely to occur in time series and then find mathematical methods for their measurement. Basically in a graphical approach we have to plot the data on a graph paper and see the crests and troughs (ups and downs) present in it. Then we use a composite force so that the troughs are pushed up and crests are pulled down until a straight line is attained.

MATHEMATICAL MODEL

In a mathematical approach, the objective is to build a model from past observations and use this model for future occurrences. For building the model, we first measure various influences and then combine them to build the model. Variations present in a time series data can be attached to four components which are as follows:

(1) Trend T, (2) Seasonal variation S, (3) Cyclical variation C, (4) Irregular variation I.

Let the original observations in a time series data be represented by O. The following multiplicative relation between the original observations and four components exists. This is known as a *multiplicative model.*

$$O = T \times S \times C \times I \qquad ...(17.1)$$

Time series analysis is a device through which an effort is made to isolate these component effects in the series of data and measure them if possible.

ADDITIVE MODEL

Sometimes the relation between the observed values and four components of time series are additive. In this case the additive model is,

$$O = T + S + C + I \qquad ...(17.2)$$

Any of the component or components in it can be estimated by transposition in formula (17.2).

In most of the situations, the multiplicative model is appropriate for use. But it will be advisable to use additive model, provided, some features as given here are not noticed.

(*a*) Four components of time series are not influencing each other.

(*b*) The seasonal variations remain fixed in spite of the growth or decline in the trend. Since, there are hardly any ways to detect such situations in which the additive model can be used, we will confine ourselves to the discussion of multiplicative model only.

EDITING OF DATA

Before we use data for analysis, it needs critical examination. One has to see the purpose for which the data are going to be used. Since the time series data are always given over specified periods and one value is generally compared with the other, to ensure comparability among observed values, one must make certain adjustment(s) in the data. Mainly one or more out of four types of adjustments are needed: (*i*) Calendar variations, (*ii*) Price variations, (*iii*) Population changes, (*iv*) Miscellaneous changes.

Calendar Variations

In many cases, monthly consumption of an item is compared within a year. Since the number of days are different in different months, the data should be adjusted to thirty days in a month and then these values be compared. A similar statement can be given for production values. if we do not do so, it will be wrong to compare the production of the month January with February as the month January has thirtyone days whereas February has only 28 days. One should take care that wages are not to be adjusted as the salary in India is paid on monthly basis. Number of other examples can be thought of where adjustment is required or not required.

Price Variations

The sales of a business organisation, if expressed only in monetary terms, will mislead the management. Similarly, if we assess the production merely in terms of returns, it will be highly misleading. Because with the rising prices, the returns may be more inspite of less production. Hence, a logical way of comparison of sales or production over different periods is to compare the quantity which is given by the formula,

$$q = v/p \qquad ...(17.3)$$

where q = the quantity of sales or production in a specified period,

v = the sales value in terms of money, and

p = the price per unit which should be obtained from the price index of that period.

Population Changes

The consumption of cloth, sugar and food grains, etc. totally depends on the number of consumers. The more the population, the greater will be the consumption. As the population of India has doubled within the last thirty years, the consumption has also doubled. Hence, it is necessary that the consumption be calculated on the basis of per capita or per thousand people. This will form the correct basis of comparison for two different decades rather than comparing the consumption figures as such.

Miscellaneous Changes

Many changes occur with the lapse of time. Some years ago, the synthetic fibre was not available in our country. Nowadays, it is produced in bulk. Hence, to compare its production now to some years back would be wrong.

Units of measurements have also changed. Earlier it was seers, yards and miles, now it is kilogram, metre and kilometre. Therefore, to compare the old figures with the new figures, the data should be changed into the same units of measurements. For example, miles into kilometres, seers into kilograms etc.

The above discussion clearly reveals that editing of data avoids many false conclusions which would have been drawn otherwise.

TREND

The term trend is more often termed *secular trend,* which means long term movements. The production, sales, exports and imports, population, employment etc., have an increasing or decreasing tendency over periods of time. These changes are as a consequence of consistent movement of factors over a long period. These periods are generally taken as yearly, quinquennial or decadal. Since the short term fluctuations are irregular, they hardly deserve any meaningful attention. So one should attempt to estimate long term movements only. The growth or decline, with the passage of time has to reveal a number of things at a time. For example, population growth means more demand of consumer goods like food, cloth and shelter. The increasing demand may force the producers to develop new technology for mass production. New synthetic fibres and plastic goods may be produced to replace naturally produced items like cotton and rubber. If the natural resources are going to be exhausted soon, efforts are to be made to find out alternative *e.g.,* coal by electricity and other sources of energy. In short, the trend exposes a lot regarding the business phenomenon and also helps the government of a country to chalk out plans and policies which maintain a balanced economy, and a balance in supply and demand position, etc.

METHODS OF MEASURING SECULAR TREND

The precondition for the measurement of the secular trend is that the data must be available for a long period, otherwise it will not be possible to isolate and estimate the growth or decline in the trend. In case, the data show a constant rate of growth or decline, the trend is apparent and the graph would be a straight line. Such an ideal situation, in practice, does not exist and the graph is a zig-zag one. Hence an operation that removes erratic and short term changes is called *smoothening operation,* because it makes the time series graph smooth. This smoothened graph is known as a *trend line.* The idea of measuring the trend is to estimate the average growth or decline. Moreover, the two series can easily be compared by comparing the angles, which the lines make with abscissa, so called the slopes of the lines. The projection for future through a trend line is known as *forecasting.* Various methods for measuring trends are as follows:

Free Hand Method

This is one of the most preliminary and easy way of fitting a trend line. Firstly, we plot the data on a graph paper, taking the variable time on X-axis, and the corresponding values of the other factor, on Y-axis. After that we join these plotted points, in order, by straight lines. In this way, we get a zig-zag graph. Now fit a trend line with the help of a transparent ruler or a smooth line by hand, in such a way that the fluctuations in one direction are equal to the fluctuations in the opposite direction. Such a line shows the long term trend. The line will be good, if vertical distance of the plotted points above the trend line, is equal to the vertical distance of those points which are below the trend line. In a way, it will be a commendable line if the sum of the vertical distances of all the plotted points, from the trend line, is zero. But such an optimacy is hardly attainable in practice, as one would not like to draw all possible lines, and see whether the sum of vertical distances in opposite directions equals each other. Hence, it is preferable to draw a trend which passes through the middle of each cycle. But it is not possible in many cases, unless we divide the line or curve into long term segments. There is no rule for this except the experience of the statistician, which works in drawing a trend line, merely by inspection.

It is one of the simplest and most flexible methods and sometimes yield good results. Still, it cannot be recommended for use as it is too subjective. In this method, the trend line varies from person to person, as it depends on individual's judgement. Hence it cannot be used as a basis of prediction. But for a rough estimation and to have an idea of the change, one is advised to use it.

Example **17.1.** The data below gives the rate of gross capital formation from 1965–66 to 1981–82 in Rs. crores at 1970–71 prices.

Years :	1965—66	—67	—68	—69	—70	—71	—72	—73	—74
Gross capital : formation (Rs.crores)	19.3	20.9	17.8	16.1	17.6	17.8	18.3	17.3	21.4
Years :	1974—75	—76	—77	—78	—79	—80	—81		
Gross capital : formation (Rs.crores)	19.3	18.1	19.5	19.2	22.2	20.9	21.5		

The trend line by a free-hand method is drawn with the help of a transparent ruler as shown in Fig. 17.1. Years are taken on X-axis and gross capital formation on Y-axis.

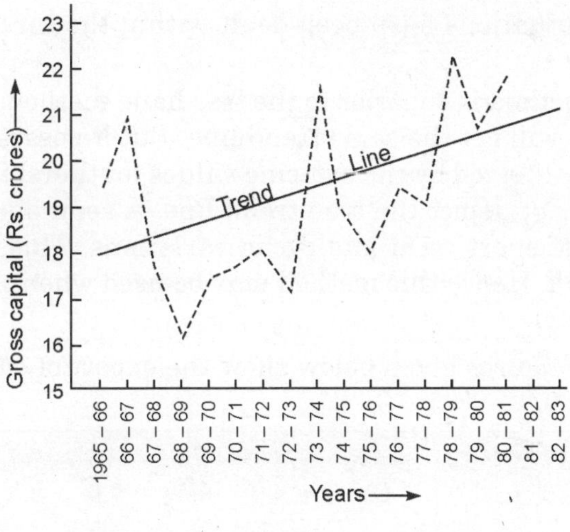

Figure 17.1 Trend line by Free-hand Method

Semi-average Method

In this method, the series is divided into two parts. The first part consists of the first half years (periods) and the second part of the remaining years (periods). In case the series consists of an even number of years say, $2k$ where k is an integer, the series is divisible into two halves each consisting of k years. Find the average of k years of the two parts of series and place these values in the mid-year of each of the half-series. It is easy to locate the mild-year if k is odd. In this case $(k + 1)/2$th year will be the mid-year for the first half series and $(3k + 1)/2$th year for the second half series. For example, if $2k = 10$, then

$k = 5$. In this case the third year will be the mid-year for the first half series and the eighth year for the second half series. But in the case where k is even, none of the year in the half series will be a mid-year. Here the middle point of the two mid-years will be the mid-period where the average of half series has to be located. For example, the data pertain to 12 years, *i.e.* from 1971 to 1982. The half series will consist of 1971 to 1976 and 1977 to 1982. The mid-period for the first half will be the middle of 1973–74, *i.e.*, 1st July, 1973, and similarly the mid-period of the second half series will be the mid-point of 1979–80, *i.e.*, 1st July, 1979, Enter the average values against these mid-points in the table. Plot the data on graph paper and these two average values at the mid-points. The original data should be joined by dotted lines and the two average values by a smooth straight line. This straight line shows the trend.

Now we consider the case, when the number of years (periods) in the series is odd, say $(2k + 1)$, where k is an integer. In this case, it is not possible to divide the series into two equal halves. Here, the first k years form the first half series and the last k years form the last half series. The value for $(k + 1)$th year is either included in both the half series or it is excluded completely. The later part is generally implemented. Keeping in view the convenience, it is advisable to include this value in both the half series if k is even and omit it if k is odd. For instance, if there are 11 years in the series, $2k + 1 = 11$ and thus, $k = 5$. Here the 6th value in the series will have to be either included or excluded. Once the series is divided into halves, the rest of the procedure remains the same as given in the last paragraph. All the situations have been dealt within the three numerical examples given below.

The semi-average method is superior to the free hand method, as it is not subjective. In this method, everyone will get the same trend line. But it possesses all the demerits of an average, *i.e.*, it will be affected by the extreme values (outliers) if present in the series. In this situation, it does not depict the true trend line. A semi-average method does not ensure the elimination of short term and cyclic variations. This danger is more if the period for average is small. Hence this method may be used when the data are given for a longer period.

***Example* 17.2.** The figures given below show the export of sugar from India for the years 1970–71 to 1979–80.

Years	: 1970—71	—72	—73	—74	—75	—76	—77	—78	—79	—80
Export (Lakh Tons)	: 3.9	1.3	1.1	4.4	9.4	9.6	3.4	2.5	8.6	2.9

The trend of the export of sugar from India can be found by the semi-average method in the manner given in theory.

Here, $2k = 10$ or $k = 5$, an odd integer. So, divide the series into halves consisting of the first five years and the last five years.

$$\text{The average of the first five years} = \frac{1}{5}(3.9 + 1.3 + 1.1 + 4.4 + 9.4) = 4.02$$

$$\text{The average of the last five years} = \frac{1}{5}(9.6 + 3.4 + 2.5 + 8.6 + 2.9) = 5.4$$

Plot the data on a graph paper and join them by dotted lines.

Plot the average value of the first half series against the year 1972-73 and the average of the last half series against 1977-78 on the same graph. On joining these two points, we get the trend line as shown in Fig. 17.2.

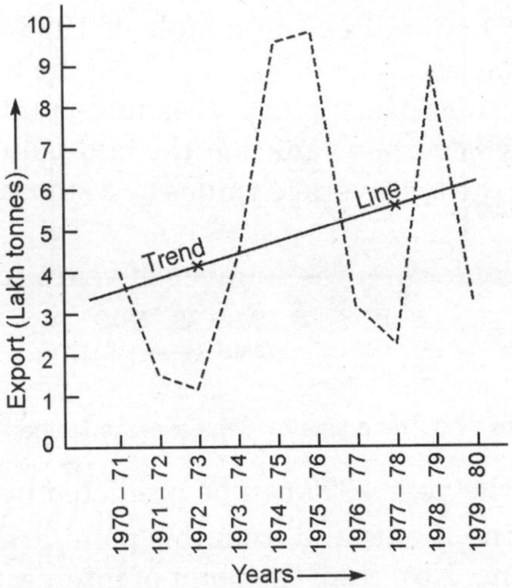

Figure 17.2 Trend line by Semi-average Method

***Example* 17.3.** The following table gives the export data of a country from 1968 to 1976. The trend of export can be shown by a trend line in the manner given below.

Year :	1968	1969	1970	1971	1972	1973	1974	1975	1976
Export (Rs.Crores) :	720	681	723	666	679	951	1093	1031	1144

The given series contains data for the nine years, hence, $2k + 1 = 9$ or $k = 4$.

We take the first four years' figures in half series and the last four years' data to form the last half of the series. The year 1972 is not included in either of the half series. Since the number of years in the half series is four, so include 1972's data in both the half series. Now the half series consist of five years' data each.

Find the average of each half series separately.

$$\text{The average of the first half series} = \frac{1}{5}(720 + 681 + 723 + 666 + 679)$$
$$= 693.8$$

$$\text{The average of the last half series} = \frac{1}{5}(679 + 951 + 1093 + 1031 + 1144)$$
$$= 979.6$$

Plot the data on a graph paper and join the plotted points by dotted lines.

Plot the average values against the years 1970 and 1974 respectively.

Join these average values by a straight line which gives the trend of export as shown in Fig. 17.3.

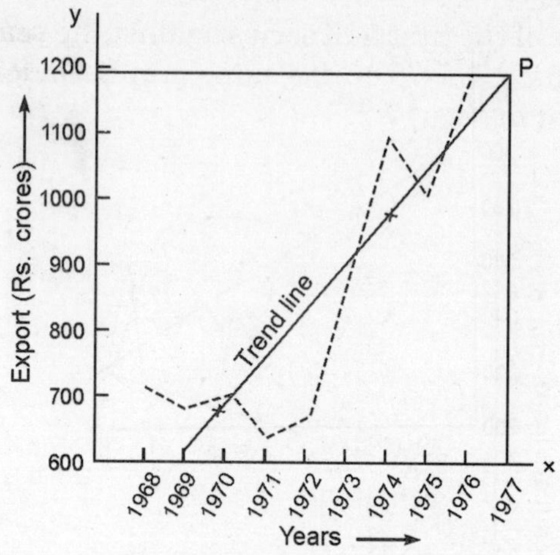

Figure 17.3 Trend Line by Semi-average Method

The extent of exports in the year 1977 can be predicted by the trend line.

Locate the year 1977 on the *X*-axis and from this point draw a line parallel to the *Y*-axis so that it cuts the trend line. Now from the point of intersection *P* draw a line parallel to the *X*-axis so that it touches the *Y*-axis. The reading at this point on the vertical scale, which is the ordinate of point *P*, gives the predicted value of exports for the year 1977. The estimated value of exports comes out to be Rs.1190 crores.

***Example* 17.4.** The following table gives the number of black and white films produced in India from the year 1970 to 1977. The trend of films production can be depicted by a trend line as delineated below.

Years	:	1970	1971	1972	1973	1974	1975	1976	1977
No. of films	:	311	289	236	278	225	243	267	217

The number of years in the given series is eight. Therefore, the first half series consists of the first four years' data and second half series consists of the last four years' data.

$$\text{The average of the first half series} = \frac{1}{4}(311 + 289 + 236 + 278)$$

$$= 278.5$$

$$\text{The average of the last half series} = \frac{1}{4}(225 + 243 + 267 + 217)$$

$$= 238.0$$

The average of the first half series has to be plotted against the mid-point of 1971-72 and the last half series average has to be plotted against the mid-point of 1975-76. Plot the data and join the points, in order, by dotted lines to show the variability of the series.

By plotting the average values as stated above and joining these two points by a straight line, we get the trend of production of black and white films as shown in Fig. 17.4.

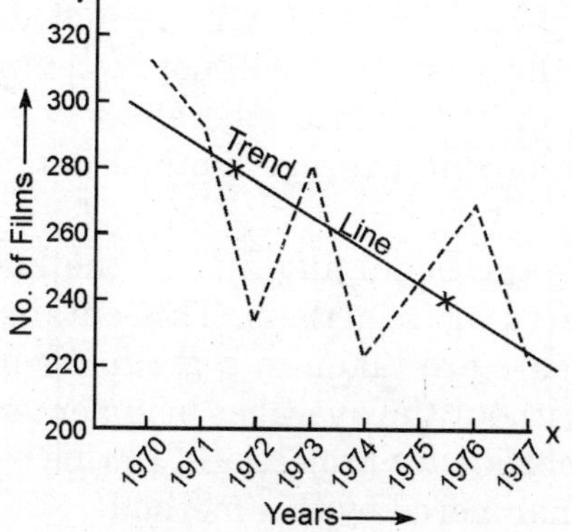

Figure 17.4 Trend of Production of Black and White Films by Semi-average Method

Moving Average Method

The semi-average method is definitely an improvement over the free hand method. But by this method, short term fluctuations except seasonal variations which are of little or no interest cannot be eliminated from the time series. The moving average method removes short term variations also. Thus, the moving average method is an improvement over the semi-average method, which isolates the trend in the time series, in an effective manner because it eliminates the short term fluctuations. It is better to know the meaning of the term *moving average* first.

"*Moving average is a series of arithmetic means of variate values of a sequence of fixed number of years (periods).*"

To obtain the moving average, take a few years' data of the series, in a group, and find its average. Then, delete the first year (any period according to which the time series is given) from this group of years and add a succeeding year to this group. In this way, the number of observed values for averaging remains the same. Enter the average value of each group against the mid-year of that group. The mid-year is located in the same way, as described, with semi-average method. Continue this process till the data of all the years, beginning from the first to the last, are exhausted.

Now the question that arises is to determine the years to be taken to form the first group, so that the trend is reflected as a straight line. There is no hard and fast rule for it. As a principle, the minimum number of years be taken together in a group, which result in a straight line for the trend. As a thumb rule, the minimum number of years in a group, should be equal to the number of years (periods) which form a business cycle. An idea of cycles can be got by studying the short term fluctuations as adjudged by plotting the time-series data. Once the number of years to be included in the first group is finalised, the method follows mechanically.

Plot the moving average values on a graph paper, choosing a suitable scale on the ordinate, against the years (periods) taken along abscissa. The plotted points are joined in sequence of time periods. the resulting graph gives the trend. In case, these points do not fall in a straight line, we should think of a suitable curvilinear trend. The moving average method gives a clear and a correct picture of the trend provided the trend is almost linear. For this, cyclical variations should be regular in periodicity and amplitude in the time series under consideration, otherwise, they will not be completely removed. The greatest advantage of this method is that it reduces the effect of extreme values for respective years to a great extent. The moving average method is not devoid of demerits as well. They are as follows:

1. Few of the years in the beginning and at the end are such that the average values are not entered against them. This entails the loss of information. For example, if three years are taken in a group for moving average, the first and last years are left without the averages being entered against them. Hence, this method is not appropriate for projections. In this way, one of the main objectives of the trend line is hampered by this method.
2. The experience shows that there is hardly any series which has regular cyclic variations (periodicity). In practice, the cycles are not fixed as they are taken to be. Their periodicity varies within a series.
   One way to remove this lacuna is to find the period of different cycles and average them. This average number of years (periods) is considered as effective length of cycles. Generally, it will not be a whole number, therefore, it must be rounded to the nearest integer. Even this approach is not easily feasible, as it is a big problem to isolate cycles in a series.
3. Moving average deflates or depresses the magnitude of oscillations in a time series. The more the number of years taken in a group for moving averages, the greater will be the deflation. Thus, the greater the degree of deflation, the less realistic will be the resulting trend. Moreover, the moving averages not only deflate but also anticipate faster changes before they actually occur.
4. This method is not suitable for the comparison of the two series as it is not fully mathematical.
5. In case the cycle consists of an even number of years then, as a rule, the average value is entered in the centre of two mid-years of that group. This central position is not an existing period in the given series of data. To remove this anomaly, the moving average of the moving averages, taken in pairs, is calculated and entered against their mid-period, which is the $(k + 1)$th year of that group. For trend, the last sequence of averages is plotted on the graph.
6. The moving average method takes care of cyclic and short term fluctuations very well. But there is subjectivity in deciding the number of years (periods) in a group for the moving average. This can lead to any number of trend lines for the same time series data.

In spite of the above demerits, moving average is considered to be a nice method for finding secular trend provided (*a*) the trend is linear, (*b*) the cyclical variations are regular both in period and amplitude.

***Example* 17.5:** For the moving average we consider the data given in example 17.1. We take the gross capital formation at the end of the financial year and prepare the following table directly for the moving averages.

In this case consider a cycle consisting of five years.

The average of the first five years is entered against the third year from the beginning. While deleting one year from the beginning and adding one succeeding year in every subsequent cycles, the moving averages are calculated and entered against the mid-position of each cycle. A table with moving averages is given below:

Year	*Gross capital formation (Rs. crores)*	*Moving average*
1966	19.3	
1967	20.9	
1968	17.8	18.34
1969	16.1	18.04
1970	17.6	17.52
1971	17.8	17.42
1972	18.3	18.48
1973	17.3	18.82
1974	21.4	18.88
1975	19.3	19.12
1976	18.1	19.50
1977	19.5	19.66
1978	19.2	19.98
1979	22.2	20.66
1980	20.9	21.40
1981	21.5	
1982	21.9	

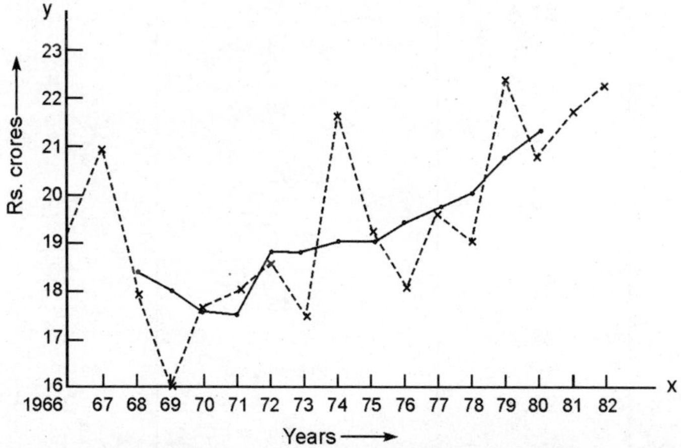

Figure 17.5 Trend by Moving Average Method

The trend is almost linear as the average points do not have much of variation.

***Example* 17.6.** Again we find the trend for the data given in example 17.1, taking four years in each cycle.

The moving averages of four years are entered in the mid-period of the two middle years, as shown in column (*iii*) of the table given below.

The moving average of the moving averages taken in pairs are entered in the mid-position of the two averages under consideration. Thus, the final moving average has its first entry against the year 1968 and advances year to year up to 1980 as given in column (*iv*).

The actual data and the final moving averages are plotted on the graph paper separately. A zig-zag graph in continuous lines of the final moving averages depicts the trend as shown in Fig. 17.6.

Year (i)	*Gross capital formation (ii)*	*Four yearly moving average (iii)*	*Centered moving average (iv)*
1966	19.3		
1967	20.9		
		18.52	
1968	17.8		18.31
		18.10	
1969	16.1		17.71
		17.32	
1970	17.6		17.38
		17.45	
1971	17.8		17.60
		17.75	
1972	18.3		18.22
		18.70	
1973	17.3		18.89
		19.08	
1974	21.4		19.05
		19.02	
1975	19.3		19.30
		19.58	
1976	18.1		19.30
		19.02	
1977	19.5		19.38
		19.75	
1978	19.2		20.10
		20.45	
1979	22.2		20.70
		20.95	
1980	20.9		21.28
		21.62	
1981	21.5		
1982	21.9		

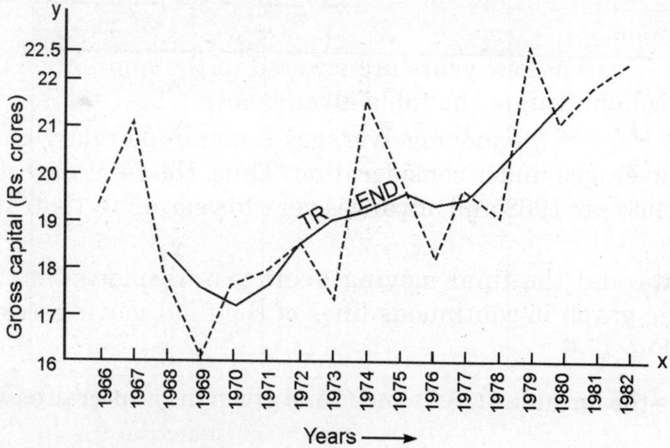

Figure 17.6 Trend by Four Years moving Average

Note: Comparing graphs 17 .5 and 17.6, it is easy to arrive at the conclusion that five years moving average gives a better trend line than the trend obtained by taking four years moving averages.

Least Square Method

This is a completely mathematical method and hence, there is no subjectivity in this method. It is considered very appropriate because it possesses all the merits, discussed in chapter 15 with fitting of regression equations. Here we assume a mathematical model which is suitable for the trend and fit this equation to the time series data. It may be recalied that fitting of a model means the estimation of parameters, involved in it, based on the principle that the sum of squares of deviations of actual values from the corresponding estimated values, from the fitted trend, is minimum. First we consider the linear model.

$$Y = \alpha + \beta X + e \qquad ...(17.4)$$

where α and β are two parameters and e is the error distributed as $N(0, \sigma_e^2)$. Let a and b be the estimates of α and β, respectively. The fitted equation is,

$$Y_c = a + bX \qquad ...(17.5)$$

where a is the intercept which the estimated line cuts from the axis of Y or, in other words, a is the trend value at $X = 0$, and b is the slope of the trend line which gives the rate of growth or depression. Also Y_c is the estimated value of Y. Y_c has actually estimated T of model 17.1.

Under the least square method, the quantity $\Sigma (Y - Y_c)^2$ is minimized. The line so obtained is a *dynamic average* of the movement through time, as given in the original data, and thus is an average path. Also this method possesses another characteristic that $\Sigma (Y - Y_c) = 0$. The trend as average path is also known as the *line of best fit.*

If we denote the coded time-variable by X with the starting year (period) as 0 and subsequent years by 1, 2, 3, ... and the sample values of the dependent variable in sequence of time be $y_0, y_1, ..., y_n$, the time series data will be of the form:

Year	*X*	*Y*
1970	$x_1 = 0$	y_0
1971	$x_2 = 1$	y_1
1972	$x_3 = 2$	y_2
1973	$x_4 = 3$	y_3
1974	$x_5 = 4$	y_4
1975	$x_6 = 5$	y_5
⋮	⋮	⋮

We repeat here the formulae (15.7) and (15.8) given in chapter fifteen for the estimates a and b.

$$a = \bar{y} - b\bar{x} \quad ...(17.6)$$

$$b = \frac{\Sigma_i x_i y_i - (\Sigma_i x_i)(\Sigma_i y_i)/n}{\Sigma_i x_i^2 - (\Sigma_i x_i)^2/n} \quad ...(17.7)$$

The values of a and b can be calculated in the same way as in the fitting of a regression line.

Alternatively, the labour of calculations can considerably be reduced by coding the values of X in a different way. Instead of coding the first year as 0, take the mid-year of the series as zero and give the values –1, –2, –3, ... to the preceding years (periods) and 1, 2, 3, ... to the succeeding years. Following is the coding plan for a seven years time series [See Plan (*a*)].

Plan (a)

Year	*X*	*Y*
1970	$x_1 = -3$	y_1
1971	$x_2 = -2$	y_2
1972	$x_3 = -1$	y_3
1973	$x_4 = -0$	y_4
1974	$x_5 = -1$	y_5
1975	$x_6 = -2$	y_6
1976	$x_7 = -3$	y_7

Again, if the number of years in the time series are even say $2k$, there will be no single year as mid-year. Two years, namely, kth year and $(k + 1)$th year, will be the mid-years. Code the kth year as –1 and the preceding years as –3, –5, –7, ... Code the $(k + 1)$th year as 1 and the succeeding years as 3, 5, 7, ... As a matter of fact, in this case, the middle period of two mid-years, i.e. 1st July is taken as zero and every half year period on either side is counted as one unit distance. Since no mid-point of two mid-years exists in the yearly time series data, zero code value does not appear as coded value. We give the codings for eight years of a time series [See Plan (*b*)].

Plan (b)

Year	*X*	*Y*
1975	– 7	y_1
1976	– 5	y_2
1977	– 3	y_3
1978	– 1	y_4
1979	1	y_5
1980	3	y_6
1981	5	y_7
1982	7	y_8

The main advantage of such coding system is that the $\Sigma_i x_i$ is always equal to zero. Thus, by putting $\Sigma_i x_i = 0$, the formulae for a and b reduce to the form as under:

$$a = \bar{y} \qquad ...(17.8)$$

$$b = \Sigma_i x_i y_i / \Sigma_i x_i^2 \qquad ...(17.9)$$

On substituting the values of a and b (calculated by any appropriate formula) in equation (17.5), we get the trend line.

The fitted line is good for interpolation as well as for extrapolation. For example, we know that the population census is done after every decade. Once we have fitted a trend line to the census data, we can estimate population for any intermediary year. Also we can find projections for any future year. For example, we may like to interpolate a value for the year 1973 or extrapolate a value for the year 1998.

It is worthwhile to point out that the results obtained for interpolation are better than those obtained for extrapolation. The reason for this is, that the variations occurring within the periods of time series are taken care of under interpolation, but one cannot predict changes which may occur in the future while extrapolating a value. Anyway, extrapolation also provides good projections (estimates) if the circumstances (growth or depletion) continue to remain the same in the coming periods.

The method of least square is mathematically sound and has no ambiguity and subjectivity. The estimates are unbiased and have minimum variance. Still this method is not optimum from practical considerations. The trend is meant to find out the long term movements in sequence of time. In fitting a trend line, it has been assumed that the variable Y depends on a time period. Such an assumption is often not true as the changes occurring in Y could be due to other explanatory variables. For instance, it is well known that the population of India is increasing at a very fast rate. Hence, the increasing trend of demand of all commodities is due to the increase of population and not due to the passage of time. Although per capita consumption may decrease, even then the demand may increase consistently. This leads to infer that the least square method gives the line of best fit but fails to throw light on the reasons of the upward or the downward trend of the same series. Particularly extrapolation from this method seldom leads to ridiculous projections. If population control becomes effective, all the projections made on the basis of existing data will become meaningless. Therefore, it is advisable that before using any of the methods described so far, the method should be justified on logical grounds.

Example **17.7.** The production of pig iron and ferro-alloys in thousand Metric Tons in India is as given below.

Years (X)	:	1974	1975	1976	1977	1978	1979	1980	1981	1982
Production ('000 M Tons)	:	620	713	833	835	810	745	726	806	861

The trend line can be fitted to the given data by the method of least squares. Coding the years as 0, 1, 2, 3, ..., 8, the sums, sum of squares, sum of cross products are calculated as per the table given below.

Hence, $\bar{y} = \dfrac{6949}{9} = 772.11 \text{ and } \bar{x} = \dfrac{36}{9} = 4$

Substituting the values of various terms in the formulae (17.7) and (17.6), we obtain the values of b and a as given below.

$$b = \frac{28735 - (36)(6949)/9}{204 - (36)^2/9} = \frac{28735 - 27796}{204 - 144}$$

Year (X)	*Production ('000, M. Tons) (y)*	*Coded x-values*	*xy*	x^2	y^2
1974	620	0	00	00	384400
1975	713	1	713	1	508369
1976	833	2	1666	4	693889
1977	835	3	2505	9	697225
1978	810	4	3240	16	656100
1979	745	5	3725	25	555025
1980	726	6	4356	36	527076
1981	806	7	5642	49	649636
1982	861	8	6888	64	741321
Total	$6949 = \Sigma_i y_i$	$36 = \Sigma_i x_i$	$28735 = \Sigma_i x_i y_i$	$204 = \Sigma_i x_i^2$	$5413041 = \Sigma_i y_i^2$
Average	772.11	4.0			

$$b = \frac{939}{60} = 15.65$$

$$a = 772.11 - 15.65 \times 4 = 772.11 - 62.60 = 709.51.$$

Thus, the estimated equation of the trend line is,

$$\hat{Y} = 709.51 + 15.65\, X$$

Example **17.8.** Consider the time series data given in example 17.7. The calculations given in the last example are quite lengthy. Hence, to reduce the labour of calculations, we do the coding of data as per details given in chapter 15 on regression and correlation. Hcro, take deviations for y-values from 810 and for x-values from 4. Prepare the table to evaluate the various terms as follows:

Under the operation of coding, the value of b is given by the formula,

$$b = \frac{\Sigma_i dx_i dy_i - (\Sigma_i dx_i)(\Sigma_i dy_i)/n}{\Sigma_i dx_i^2 - (\Sigma_i dx_i)^2/n}$$

Year (X)	*Production (y)*	*y–810 = dy*	*x*	*x –4 = dx*	*dx.dy*	*dx²*
1974	620	–190	0	–4	760	16
1975	713	–97	1	–3	291	9
1976	833	23	2	–2	–46	4
1977	835	25	3	–1	–25	1
1978	810	00	4	0	00	0
1979	745	–65	5	1	–65	1
1980	726	–84	6	2	–168	4
1981	806	–4	7	3	–12	9
1982	861	51	8	4	204	16
Total	$6949 = \Sigma_i y_i$	$-341 = \Sigma_i dy_i$	$36 = \Sigma_i x_i$	$00 = \Sigma_i dx_i$	$939 = \Sigma_i dx_i\, dy_i$	$60 = \Sigma_i d^2 x_i$

Here $\Sigma_i dx_i = 0$, hence the above formula reduces to

$$b = \frac{\Sigma_i dx_i dy_i}{\Sigma_i dx_i^2}$$

Substituting the values in the numerator and denominator, we get

$$b = \frac{939}{60} = 15.65$$

From coded data, the mean

$$\bar{y} = 810 - \frac{341}{9} = 810 - 37.89 = 772.11$$

Thus, the estimated regression line is,

$$\hat{Y} = 772.11 + 15.65\ X$$

Note: It should be kept in mind that X will be given the coded value while estimating Y for a given year.

The readers may recall that the subtraction of a constant from each value does not affect the regression coefficient. This fact is verified in this example as well.

***Example* 17.9.** Considering example 17.8, we can notice that taking the deviations from the mid-year value '4', amounts to the coding system given for the odd number of years in time series data. We may not code the values of the dependent variable Y. Making use of the formula (17.9), we obtain the same equation of the trend line as found in example (17.7) and (17.8). The readers can easily verify this fact themselves.

CONVERTING THE PERIOD OF TREND VALUES

Sometimes, there is a need for converting the annual trend line to per month or half-yearly values. The problem is a part of the coding of data. In general, we fit a straight line $Y = a + bX$ as trend. In case b is calculated for annual data, b is the annual increase (or decrease) in Y for the entire year. If we divide b by 12, we obtain a monthly increment (or decrement) in the yearly totals. Since we still have yearly totals, we must divide by 12 to reduce the figure to per month basis and here the value of a in monthly terms would be one-twelfth of a. In short, to convert an annual trend equation to a per-month value divide a by 12 and b by 144. Similarly, to convert the annual trend to a half-yearly trend, divide a by 2 and b by 4.

***Example* 17.10.** The trend line obtained for annual data in example 17.8 is,

$$\hat{Y} = 772.11 + 15.65X$$

(*i*) To convert the trend values from annual values, to half-yearly trend values, we divide a by 2 and b by 4.

Hence, for the half-yearly trend line, the constants are,

$$a = \frac{772.11}{2} = 386.06$$

$$b = \frac{15.65}{4} = 3.91$$

The half-yearly trend line is,

$$\hat{Y} = 386.06 + 3.91X$$

(*ii*) To convert the annual trend to a monthly trend, we divide a by 12 and b by 144. For the monthly trend line, the constants are,

$$a = \frac{772.11}{12} = 64.34$$

$$b = \frac{15.65}{144} = 0.1087$$

Thus, the monthly trend equation is,

$$\hat{Y} = 64.34 + 0.1087X$$

CURVILINEAR TREND

So far, the discussion about trend is confined mostly to the linear trend. But the linear trend does not always exist. The linear trend means a constant rate of growth or decay, which in many situations is refuted. Thus, one has to switch over to some other kind of trend which would naturally be a curvilinear trend. Such a situation generally arises when the x-values for years (periods) are in arithmetic progression and corresponding y-values are either in geometric progression, or follow some other law except arithmetic progression. For instance, if some money is invested at compound interest, the money rises more rapidly in the succeeding years as compared to the early years of investment and is in a geometric progression. The same phenomenon may be observed in population growth. In the beginning of a period, the population growth will be slow but will start to multiply at a faster rate in the later period. The consumption of nylon cloth went on rising gradually for a number of years but declined sharply in the recent years due to the manufacturing of terecotton cloth and some other synthetic fibre clothes. For such types of time series data, a non-linear trend would depict a better trend than the linear one. Here we give some well known methods of determining non-linear trends.

Free-Hand Method

It has already been said in the discussion of linear trend that the statistician will choose a curve if he feels that it will give a better picture of the trend. This method is not encouraged by most of the scientists because of its subjectivity.

Moving Average Method

In the discussion of linear trend by the moving average method, it has already been mentioned that the moving averages are plotted on the graph paper and joined in sequence of time. These moving averages generally do not fall in a straight line. They are mostly zig-zag. On joining these points we often get a curve to show the trend of time series data. The zig-zag graph, obtained by joining the moving averages, may be smoothened by a freehand. This curve will enable us to give projections. All other merits and demerits stand true for moving average method as given with the linear trend.

Least Square Method

The theory of least square method has been discussed in Chapter 15 and its application for time series linear trend in the preceding section. If the trend is changing direction frequently, a curve will give a picture of the trend. Which curve is best suited to the data may be guessed by plotting the time series data on the graph. When the shape of the curve is known, the mathematical equation for it may be given. Once the equation is decided, it can be fitted to the available time series data. Some of the commonly used curves are discussed below.

PARABOLA

The most popular and the simplest non-linear trend is a parabolic curve which is mathematically represented by a second degree polynomial,

$$Y = \alpha_0 + \alpha_1 X + \alpha_2 X^2 + e \qquad ...(17.10)$$

The second degree curve is also known as a *response curve.* Its geometrical shape is as given in Fig. 17.7.

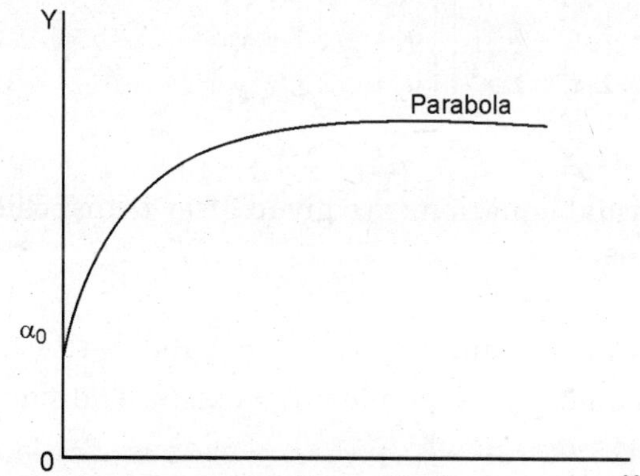

Figure 17.7 Response Curve

Suppose the estimated values of α_0, α_1 and α_2 are a_0, a_1 and a_2, respectively. The estimated equation of parabola is

$$Y_c = a_0 + a_1 X + a_2 X^2 \quad ...(17.11)$$

Now we have to determine the values of a_0, a_1, and a_2 in terms of the observed values of the variates X and Y.

Under the method of least squares, we have to minimize the sum of squares of the errors, *i.e.*, $\Sigma_i e_i^2$ for all the n paired observations (x_i, y_i) of a time series data. From equation (17.10) we get, say,

$$Q = \Sigma_i e_i^2 = \Sigma_i (y_i - \alpha_0 - \alpha_1 x_i - \alpha_2 x_i^2)^2 \quad ...(17.12)$$

where $i = 1, 2, ... n$.

Partially differentiate Q with respect to α_0, α_1 and α_2 respectively and equate them to zero. Also replace α_0, α_1 and α_2 by their estimates. In this way we get a set of normal equations which are as follows:

$$\begin{aligned} \Sigma_i y_i &= \Sigma_i a_0 + a_1 \Sigma_i x_i + a_2 \Sigma_i x_i^2 \\ \Sigma_i x_i y_i &= a_0 \Sigma_i x_i + a_1 \Sigma_i x_i^2 + a_2 \Sigma_i x_i^3 \\ \Sigma_i x_i^2 y_i &= a_0 \Sigma_i x_i^2 + a_1 \Sigma_i x_i^3 + a_2 \Sigma_i x_i^4 \end{aligned} \quad ...(17.13)$$

It is worth pointing out, that any paired observation (x_i, y_i) will satisfy the model. The first normal equation is a sum over all observations in the equation (17.11). The second equation is obtained from (17.11) by multiplying it first by x_i and then taking the summation over all observations. Whereas, the third equation is obtained on multiplying (17.11) by x_i^2 and then taking the summation over all observations. Solving the three normal equations, we get the expressions for a_0, a_1 and a_2 in terms of observed values of X and Y.

The normal equations given by (17.13) can be represented through matrices. The notations and the approach is the same as given in chapter 16 for multivariate regression equation. In model (17.10), X^2 is equivalent to X_2. Thus, the normal equations in matrix notations are,

$$\underset{A}{\begin{bmatrix} n & \Sigma_i x_i & \Sigma_i x_i^2 \\ \Sigma_i x_i & \Sigma_i x_i^2 & \Sigma_i x_1^3 \\ \Sigma_i x_i^2 & \Sigma_i x_i^3 & \Sigma_i x_i^4 \end{bmatrix}} \underset{a'}{\begin{bmatrix} a_0 \\ a_1 \\ a_2 \end{bmatrix}} = \underset{Y'}{\begin{bmatrix} \Sigma_i y_i \\ \Sigma_i x_i y_i \\ \Sigma_i x_i^2 y_i \end{bmatrix}} \quad ...(17.14)$$

In (17.14), the normal equations are given after transposition in (17.13). In short, they can be represented as,

$$Aa' = Y' \quad ...(17.15)$$

where A is the coefficient matrix and $a = (a_0, a_1, a_2)$ and $Y = (\Sigma_i y_i, \Sigma_i x_i y_i, \Sigma_i x_i^2 y_i)$.

The solution of the equations is simple if A^{-1} exists. The solution is,

$$a' = A^{-1}\ Y' \quad ...(17.16)$$

The expressions for a_0, a_1 and a_2 are omitted here, as the readers can write them themselves by making equivalence with multivariate normal equations. Here it would be easy to solve the normal equations by the elimination process, particularly after coding the variate X in such a way that the mid-period is coded as zero, the preceding and succeeding years by gradually decreasing and increasing integers respectively. In this way, all sums over odd powers of x_i's will reduce to zero i.e., $\Sigma_i x_i = 0, \Sigma_i x_i^3 = 0$. Hence, the normal equations are,

$$\begin{aligned} na_0 + a_2\Sigma_i x_i^2 &= \Sigma_i y_i \\ a_1\Sigma_i x_i^2 &= \Sigma_i x_i y_i \\ a_0\Sigma_i x_i^2 + a_2\Sigma_i x_i^4 &= \Sigma_i x_i^2 y_i \end{aligned} \qquad \text{...(17.17)}$$

The solution of these equations is quite simple. Substituting the calculated value of a_0, a_1 and a_2 in equation (17.11), we get the estimated equation of the curve, which is a parabola.

In case, a third degree polynomial is considered suitable for curvilinear trend, the mathematical model is,

$$Y = \alpha_0 + \alpha_1 X + \alpha_2 X^2 + \alpha_3 X^3 + e \qquad \text{...(17.18)}$$

Let the estimated values of $\alpha_0, \alpha_1, \alpha_2$ and α_3 be a_0, a_1, a_2 and a_3, respectively. Using the estimates, the fitted equation of the curve is

$$Y_c = a_0 + a_1 X + a_2 X^2 + a_3 X^3 \qquad \text{...(17.19)}$$

The estimated values of a_0, a_1, a_2 and a_3 can be obtained by solving the following set of normal equations for a time series data over n periods.

$$\left.\begin{aligned} \Sigma_i y_i &= na_0 + a_i\Sigma_i x_i + a_2\Sigma_i x_i^2 + a_3\Sigma_i x_i^3 \\ \Sigma_i x_i y_i &= a_0\Sigma_i x_i + a_1\Sigma_i x_i^2 + a_2\Sigma_i x_i^3 + a_3\Sigma_i x_i^4 \\ \Sigma_i x_i^2 y_i &= a_0\Sigma_i x_i^2 + a_1\Sigma_i x_i^3 + a_2\Sigma_i x_i^4 + a_3\Sigma_i x_i^5 \\ \Sigma_i x_i^3 y_i &= a_0\Sigma_i x_i^3 + a_1\Sigma_i x_i^4 + a_2\Sigma_i x_i^5 + a_3\Sigma_i x_i^6 \end{aligned}\right\} \qquad \text{...(17.20)}$$

The solution of these equations for a_0, a_1, a_2 and a_3 can be obtained either by the elimination method or with the help of matrices. Substituting the values of the constants in (17.19), we get the fitted equation of the curve.

There is no limit of the degree of a polynomial which can be chosen. But the experience tells that there is hardly any situation where we need to go beyond the third degree polynomial. Any way, if the need arises, the equation of polynomial may be extended to any degree and following the given procedure, it can be estimated.

There is no strict rule by which the degree of the polynomial for the curvilinear trend can be decided. As a thumb rule, it can be suggested that (*i*) if the first differences of y-values (see Chapter 19) are constant (approx), use a first degree polynomial for trend, i.e. a straight line, (*ii*) if the second differences of y-values are constant (approx.), use a second degree polynomial, i.e. a parabola, (*iii*) if the third differences of y-values are constant (approx.), use a third degree polynomial and so on.

Any polynomial can be fitted in the same manner as a multiple linear regression equation in Chapter 16. In this case X should be taken equivalent to X_1, X^2 equivalent to X_2, X^3 equivalent to X_3 and so on. The fitting of the polynomial becomes evident.

Some special methods of fitting a polynomial also exist. But they are kept out of scope of this book.

SEMI-LOGARITHMIC TREND LINE

This trend is generally observed by the data in which the X-variate is in arithmetic progression and Y-variate is in geometric progression. The net amount with compound interest for a number of years shows a semi-logarithmic trend. Some people call it a *geometric trend line* also. If we plot the time series data as such, it would be a curve, but if we take the logarithm of equation (17.21) it reduces to a straight line. In this case, the curve is referred to as exponential curve and its mathematical equation is of the form,

$$Y = \alpha\beta^X \qquad ...(17.21)$$

The shape of the exponential curve is as shown in Fig. 17.8.

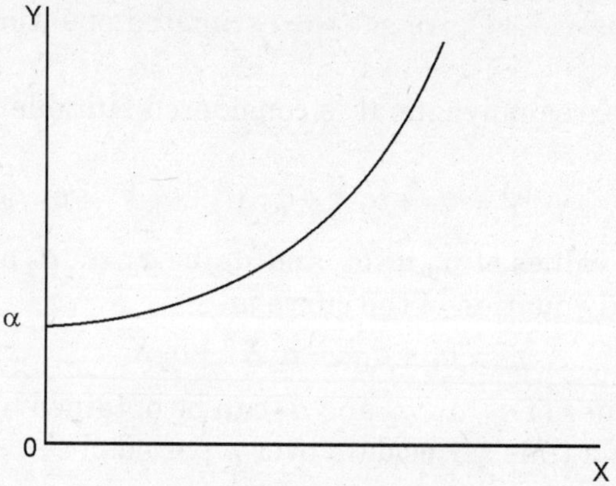

Figure 17.8 Exponential curve

Taking logarithm (log) of equation (17.21), the equation of the exponential curve transforms to a straight line of which the equation is,

$$\log Y = \log \alpha + X \log \beta \qquad ...(17.22)$$

From (17.22), it is apparent that the equation involves logarithm of Y-values and X occurs as such. If we put $\log Y = Z$, $\log \alpha = a$ and $\log \beta = b$, (17.22) changes to the form,

$$Z = a + bX \qquad ...(17.22.1)$$

which is the equation of a straight line. Its fitting can be done by the method described earlier in this chapter. Here we give directly the expressions for a and b in a particular case when the mid-period of the time series is coded as zero.

$$a = \frac{1}{n}\Sigma_i \log y_i \qquad ...(17.23)$$

where $i = 1, 2, ..., n$ and

$$b = (\Sigma_i x_i \log y_i)/(\Sigma_i x_i^2) \qquad ...(17.24)$$

where the pair (x_i, y_i) stands for i-th time period and the corresponding i-th Y-value. The original form of the curve can be regained by taking anti-logarithm.

PEARL REED CURVE

It is useful to bring forward the pattern of a matured industry. The growth of the steel industry in India is one example which the *Pearl Reed curve* depicts very well. The shape of this curve is like that of an elongated S as shown in Fig. 17.9. The mathematical equation for Pearl Reed curve is,

$$Y = \frac{1}{a + bc^X} \qquad ...(17.25)$$

The curve depicts three things:

(*i*) Slow growth in the early stage.

(*ii*) Intermediate period of rapid growth.

(*iii*) An approach to maturity.

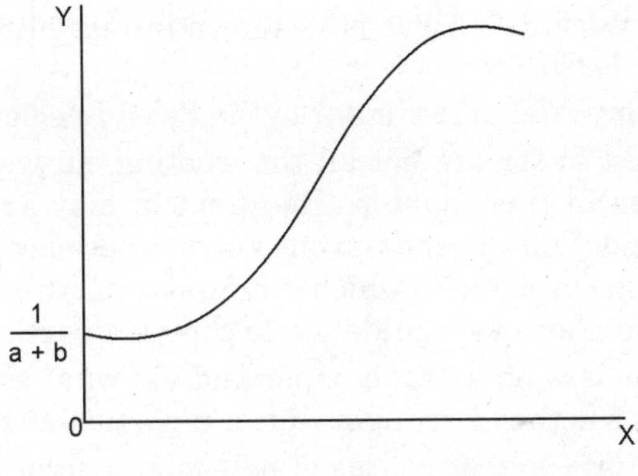

Figure 17.9 Pearl Reed Curve

MODIFIED EXPONENTIAL CURVE

The trend pattern of an economic time series, which tends to level off and approaches the horizontal axis, may be described by a modified exponential curve. The shape of this curve is like that of an inverted exponential curve, as shown in Fig. 17.10. The mathematical equation for modified exponential curve is,

$$Y = a - bc^X \qquad ...(17.26)$$

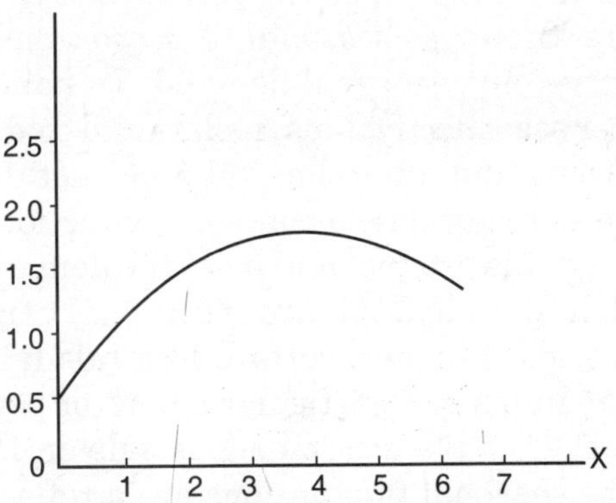

Figure 17.10 Modified Exponential Curve

The curve shows growth in the beginning and then it becomes stationary for some period before it begins to decline.

COMPERTZ CURVE

When the beginning and the latest stages of growth of an organisation are to be represented by a trend pattern, either Pearl Reed curve or *simple compertz curve* is appropriate. The mathematical equation of simple compertz curve is

$$Y = \alpha\beta^{c^X} \qquad ...(17.27)$$

Taking logarithm of equation (17.27), we get

$$\log Y = \log \alpha + c^X \log \beta \qquad ...(17.27.1)$$

Suppose $\log \alpha = a$, $\log \beta = b$. Then equation (17.27.1) reduces to the form

$$\log Y = a + bc^X \qquad ...(17.27.2)$$

The shape of the curve is almost similar to the Pearl Reed curve.

The curves described so far are not all the existing curves. Only a few, which are popularly used, are given in this chapter. The problem may arise as to the choice of a curve suitable for the trend. This depends on one's own experience, the deep understanding of the data at hand, and the problem to which it refers to. All this cannot be attained soon. Hence, some tips are given here as a guideline to choose a particular kind of curve.

(*i*) Firstly, plot the data on a graph paper and see what shape it takes? This gives some idea as to whether a straight line or a particular type of curve is to fitted.

(*ii*) Use the second or a higher degree of polynomial according as second or higher order of Newton's differences[1] tend to be constant.

(*iii*) If Newton's first differences of log values tend to be constant, use the second degree polynomial to the log-values.

(*iv*) If Newton's first differences decrease almost by a constant percentage, use a modified exponential curve.

MEASUREMENT OF SEASONAL VARIATION

Under the heading 'Trend', we studied long term fluctuations which occur yearly or in a still longer time series of data. But the short term fluctuations in a quarterly, monthly, fortnightly or weekly series of data are of no less importance in business and management. *Short term fluctuations* are known as *seasonal.* A *season* means the periods within the year. A number of items have only seasonal demand. To name a few, wool and woollens have a market during winter season only; fans, coolers and cold drinks are in great demand in summer; whereas rain coats and umbrellas get a market during rainy season mainly. Hence, a manufacturer or a stockiest has to manage production, finances and personnel in such a way that he can market his product and meet the demand properly and in time. For this, a businessman should have a clear picture of seasonal variations occurring from year to year during the same period. Further, certain festivals falling in a particular month also create demand for some items in a particular month or period. Such a demand is also seasonal. *For example,* crackers have a tremendous sale on Deepawali festival. Thus, it can be said that most of the seasonal fluctuations are a reflection of underlying climatic conditions and/or customs. This makes us realise the importance of the study of seasonal variation. Under the study of the isolation of the seasonal variation, we are doing two

1. For Newton's differences, read Chapter 19 on Interpolation and Extrapolation.

things, (*i*) determination of increase or decrease in the size of variable under study in a time series data and (*ii*) elimination of the seasonal effect that is to determine the size of the variable, which would have been, had there been no seasonal effect. The first part of the study enables an executive to know the extent of variation and plan accordingly. The second part provides the safeguard against many risks. Further, the study of a number of seasons as a whole helps in forecasting of the future trends.

In our study, we have two types of seasonals. When we refer to a season in a particular year, it will be termed as *specific seasonal* whereas the average of specific seasonality for a number of years is known as *typical seasonal*. It is worth pointing out, that when we consider the season comprising of many months in a year, the months which constitute the season should not be arithmetical quarters but should be the months in which season actually occurs. For instance, if November, December and January constitute the winter season, neither October, November and December nor January, February and March constitute the winter season. Also it should be decided whether the seasonality has to be studied weekly, fortnightly, monthly, quarterly or half-yearly. All this depends on the nature and objective of the study of seasonality.

COMPUTATION OF SHORT TERM FLUCTUATIONS

Model (17.1) reveals that an observation in a time series data is under the influence of four components viz., T, S, C, I. To isolate S, we must eliminate T, C and I. Thus, the computation of seasonal variation is based on this idea. Various methods of measuring seasonal variation are given below:

Simple Average Method

Under this method, the yearwise time series data are arranged according to the periods of seasonals, which may be weekly, monthly, quarterly or any other span of time within a year. Generally, monthly or quarterly data are taken for seasonality. The steps for measuring seasonal variations are:

1. Take the simple average for each period during all the years under study. These averages give typical seasonals.
2. Compute periodic indices by the formula,

$$\frac{\text{Average of a period}}{\text{Average of the periodic average}} \times 100 \qquad \ldots(17.28)$$

   The periodic indices obtained by (17.28) give the periodic fluctuations, which are taken to give seasonal variation. But the periodic indices, obtained in this manner are not free from long term fluctuations, i.e. the trend influence. This method yields good results provided time series is free from the trend. But such an ideal situation rarely exists in actual life. Hence the seasonal indices are adjusted for the trend, so that one gets the pure seasonal indices. For this, we have to make further calculations which are as follows:

3. Find the trend equation which is usually taken as a straight line, for which the equation is, $Y = a + bX$. In this equation, b is connotative of the trend. The trend line is fitted for Y, the yearly average value over all the periods X, the coded values of years. Here b gives the trend value for the whole year. Periodic trend is

obtained by dividing the value of b by the number of periods in the year. For example, if monthly data is taken, the divisor will be twelve. In case of quarterly data, the divisor will be four and likewise any other divisor can be chosen as the need arises. The average of the periodic average is the trend at the middle point of the series. This average value is adjusted for trend by adding or subtracting the proportionate trend values. The values yield the secular trend.

4. The seasonal indices are obtained by finding out the percentage of periodic average to the secular trend value calculated under preceding operations.
5. The seasonal indices obtained in this manner may not have an average seasonal index equal to hundred. But it is always preferable to standardize them, so that their average is equal to 100. For this, each seasonal index is multiplied by the factor,

$$\frac{\text{Number of periods}}{\text{Total of seasonal indices}} \times 100 \qquad ...(17.29)$$

In this way, we obtain the final seasonal indices.

Although the average method is simple, it is not very appropriate for the simple reason that it does not remove the cyclical and irregular variations. Hence, we resort to some other methods.

Ratio to Trend Method

This is another method of measuring seasonal variation free from the trend. Under this method, first the estimated value for each period from the estimated trend equation must be found. Enter the estimated values against each corresponding period for all the years under study. Calculate the percentage ratio of periodic value to the corresponding estimated value. In this process the effect of trend is removed. Further, the cyclic and irregular variations are eliminated by using a central measure. Find the average for each period separately considering percentage ratio over all the years. These periodic averages are free from cyclical and irregular influence.

In case, time series data show some extreme values, during a period in various years, the median can be found out instead of the average, as the median is not affected by extreme values. Usually these extreme values are associated with irregular variations. These values represent seasonal indices. But often, their average is not equal to 100. So to standardize it, multiply each central value by the quantity, 1200/(sum of the mean or median for all the seasons). The values so obtained indicate seasonal indices.

***Example* 17.11.** The table (*i*) gives the data of production of nonfat milk in U.S.A. (human food).

From formulae (17.8) and (17.9), we obtain

$$a = 95.07 \text{ and } b = \frac{-96.77}{10} = -9.68$$

The equation of the trend line is,

$$\hat{Y} = 95.07 - 9.68\,X$$

The trend values obtained from the estimated trend line are entered in the last column of the table – (*i*). They are obtained by putting $X = -2, -1, 0, 1$ and 2, respectively.

Table: (i)

	Production (million lbs)																	
	Months																	
Year	Jan.	Feb.	Mar.	Apr.	May	June	July	Aug.	Sept.	Oct.	Nov.	Dec.	Total	Av.per month (y)	Coded (x)	xy	x^2	Monthly trend values $\hat{y}$
1971	115.8	111.8	131.1	149.2	174.6	177.8	137.3	117.6	92.2	93.5	77.4	95.4	1473.7	122.81	–2	–245.62	4	114.43
1972	98.5	100.0	118.0	128.9	153.0	160.0	127.4	99.4	77.0	69.6	61.6	75.8	1269.2	105.77	–1	–105.77	1	104.75
1973	85.2	79.9	86.4	87.2	118.9	115.8	86.2	65.0	49.5	54.4	44.2	58.2	930.9	77.58	0	00	00	95.07
1974	58.4	56.0	75.3	95.0	121.2	129.0	117.1	97.4	64.7	58.3	52.8	80.1	1005.3	83.78	1	83.78	1	85.39
1975	83.5	81.6	95.8	111.5	131.4	126.5	98.7	76.2	53.2	50.3	49.3	67.1	1025.1	85.42	2	170.4	4	75.71
Total	441.4	429.3	506.6	571.8	699.1	709.1	566.7	455.6	336.6	326.1	285.3	376.6	5704.2	475.35	00	–96.77	10	
Average	88.28	85.86	101.32	114.36	139.82	141.82	113.34	91.12	67.32	65.22	57.06	75.32	1140.84	95.07	00			

Table: (*ii*)

Monthly trend values													
Months													
Year	*Jan.*	*Feb.*	*Mar.*	*Apr.*	*May*	*June*	*July*	*Aug.*	*Sept.*	*Oct.*	*Nov.*	*Dec.*	*Total*
1971	118.87	118.06	117.25	116.45	115.64	114.83	114.03	113.22	112.41	111.61	110.80	109.99	1373.16
1972	109.19	108.38	107.58	106.77	105.96	105.16	104.35	103.54	102.74	101.93	101.12	100.32	1257.04
1973	99.51	98.70	97.89	97.08	96.28	95.47	94.67	93.86	93.05	92.25	91.44	90.63	1140.83
1974	89.83	89.02	88.21	87.41	86.60	85.79	84.99	84.18	83.37	82.57	81.76	80.95	1024.68
1975	80.15	79.34	78.53	77.73	76.92	76.11	75.31	74.50	73.69	72.89	72.08	71.27	908.52

Monthly increment = $\frac{-9.68}{12}$ = – 0.8067 = c (say).

The trend value for the middle of the year (1971), *i.e.* on 1st July = 114.43.

We may consider the trend values centered in the mid of every month.

The trend values for the month of June will be

$$= 114.43 - \left(\frac{c}{2}\right)$$

$$= 114.43 + \frac{0.8067}{2} = 114.83$$

The trend value for May = 114.43 – $\left(\frac{3c}{2}\right)$ = 115.64

The trend value for July = 114.43 + $\left(\frac{c}{2}\right)$ = 114.03

The trend value for August = 114.43 + $\left(\frac{3c}{2}\right)$ = 113.22

The trend value for Feb. = 114.43 – $\left(\frac{9c}{2}\right)$ = 118.06

The trend value for Jan. = 114.43 – $\left(\frac{11c}{2}\right)$ = 118.87

In a similar manner, we can find the monthly trend values for each month, in all the five years, by gradual increment or decrement in the trend value. These values are displayed in the table (*ii*).

Now we calculate the percentage ratio of each periodic value to the corresponding trend value, e.g.

For January 1971, the percentage ratio = $\frac{115.8}{118.87} \times 100 = 97.42$

For February 1971, the percentage ratio = $\frac{111.8}{118.06} \times 100 = 94.70$ and so on.

All the calculated percentage ratios are displayed in the table (*iii*).

The seasonal indices for each month are obtained by expressing each month's average percentage as the percentage of their own average *i.e.* by formula (17.29). This has been done to bring forth the average seasonal index equal to 100, e.g. The

January seasonal index = $\frac{88.49}{1198.00} \times 1200 = 88.64$

February seasonal index = $\frac{86.74}{1198.00} \times 1200 = 86.88$

and so on.

Table: (*iii*)

Given values as percentage of trend values

Year	*Jan.*	*Feb.*	*Mar.*	*Apr.*	*May*	*Jun.*	*Jul.*	*Aug.*	*Sept.*	*Oct.*	*Nov.*	*Dec.*	*Total*
1971	97.42	94.70	111.81	128.12	150.98	154.48	120.41	103.87	82.02	83.77	69.86	86.74	
1972	90.21	92.27	109.68	120.73	144.39	152.15	122.09	96.00	74.95	68.28	60.92	75.56	
1973	85.62	80.95	88.26	89.82	123.49	121.29	91.05	69.25	53.20	58.97	48.34	64.22	
1974	65.01	62.91	85.36	108.68	139.95	150.37	137.78	115.70	77.60	70.61	64.58	98.95	
1975	104.18	102.85	121.99	143.44	170.83	166.21	131.06	102.28	72.19	69.01	68.40	94.15	
Total	442.44	433.68	517.10	590.79	729.64	744.50	602.39	487.10	359.96	350.64	312.10	419.62	
Ave.	88.49	86.74	103.42	118.16	145.93	148.90	120.48	97.42	71.99	70.13	62.42	83.92	1198.00
Sea. Index	88.64	86.88	103.60	118.36	146.17	149.15	120.68	97.58	72.11	70.24	62.52	84.07	1200
Med.	90.21	92.27	109.68	120.73	144.39	152.15	122.09	102.28	74.95	69.01	64.58	86.74	1229.08
Final Sea. Index	88.08	90.09	107.08	117.87	140.97	148.55	119.20	99.86	73.18	67.38	63.05	84.69	1200.00

Alternative

The production in various months of 1971 is comparatively higher than the other succeeding four years. These figures may be considered as extreme values. Hence, to avoid the influence of extreme values, use median instead of the average of each month as an indicative of seasonal index. The median values are given in the last but one row of the previous table. The last row gives the seasonal indices obtained by multiplying each median index by $\frac{1200}{1229.08}$. These seasonal indices average to 100.

Ratio to Moving Average Method

This is one of the most commonly used method, as it is better than others in many respects, as discussed at the end of this method. The methodology is explained here for monthly time series data. The same may be applied for any other periodic data like quarterly, fortnightly, weekly etc. Various operations under this method are:

1. Write the monthly data for each year chronologically.
2. Find the twelve month average for the first year and enter it against the middle position, between June and July.
3. Delete the January value of the first year and add the January value of subsequent year. Again, calculate the average and enter it between mid-positions of July and August of the first year. Continue the process of deleting and adding the one month value and entering the average value in mid position, till all the monthly data are exhausted.
4. Again find the moving average of the two average values starting from the first two. Enter the first moving average against July and subsequently against August, September, etc.
5. Calculate the percentage ratio of each monthly value from its corresponding moving average, and enter it against the same month.
6. Now, prepare another two-way table containing these monthwise percentage ratios for all the years.
7. Find the median for each month and calculate the average of these medians. Divide the median of each month by the average value and multiply it by 100. This amounts to performing the same operation as multiplying the indices by the factor given by (17.29).

Here it may be noted that the method has been explained by taking a twelve month average though this is not necessary. One has to choose the number of periods for moving average, which constitutes a cycle. In case a cycle is completed in a six month period, one should calculate a six monthly moving average. The method has been explained for the case which is usually in practice. Also, it has been said that the median for the percentage ratios for each month be found out, though this too is not a compulsion. One may prefer the average, but the use of median is better as it is devoid of the effect of extreme values.

In this method, the trend and cyclical variations are removed by taking the twelve months' averages. In other words, it removes linear and curvilinear trends. Obtaining the median (may be mean) of percentage ratios, eliminates the influences of irregular variations. In this way the seasonal indices so obtained are free from all the three component variations namely, T, C and I.

Ratio to moving average method entails too much of labour but is still the most adopted method because of its accuracy.

Example **17.12.** We consider the five years data given in example (17.11) and calculate seasonal indices by the moving average method. Proceeding step by step, as discussed in the methodology, prepare the following table.

In the table,

First moving average entered between June and July $= \dfrac{1473.7}{12} = 122.81$

Second moving average entered between July and August,

$$= \frac{1473.7 - 115.8 + 98.5}{12}$$

$$= \frac{1456.4}{12} = 121.37$$

Third moving average entered between August and September,

$$= \frac{1456.4 - 111.8 + 100}{12}$$

$$= \frac{1444.6}{12} = 120.38$$

First moving average of the first two average value

$$= \frac{122.81 + 121.37}{2} = 122.09$$

Table: (*iv*)

Year/Month		*Production (Lbs.)*	*12 months moving average*	*2–months moving average from col. 3*	*Percentage ratio of monthly value to the final moving average (col. 2 + col. 4) × 100*
(1)		(2)	(3)	(4)	(5)
1971	Jan.	115.8			
	Feb.	111.8			
	Mar.	113.1			
	Apr.	149.2			
	May	174.6			
	Jun.	177.8			
			122.81		
	Jul.	137.3		122.09	112.46
			121.37		
	Aug.	117.6		120.88	97.29
			120.38		
	Sept.	92.2		119.84	76.94
			119.29		
	Oct.	93.5		118.44	78.91
			117.60		

(1)		(2)	(3)	(4)	(5)
	Nov.	77.4		116.70	66.32
			115.80		
	Dec.	95.4		115.06	82.91
			114.32		
1972	Jan.	98.5		113.90	86.48
			113.49		
	Feb.	100.0		112.73	88.71
			111.98		
	Mar.	118.0		111.34	105.99
			110.71		
	Apr.	128.9		109.71	117.49
			108.72		
	May	153.0		108.05	141.60
			107.40		
	Jun.	160.0		106.57	150.14
			105.77		
	Jul.	127.4		105.20	121.10
			104.66		
	Aug.	99.4		103.82	95.74
			102.98		
	Sept.	77.0		101.66	75.74
			100.35		
	Oct.	69.6		98.60	70.59
			96.88		
	Nov.	61.6		95.45	64.54
			94.03		
	Dec.	75.8		92.18	82.23
			90.35		
1973	Jan.	85.2		88.62	96.14
			86.92		
	Feb.	79.9		85.48	93.47
			84.05		
	Mar.	86.4		82.90	104.22
			81.76		
	Apr.	87.2		81.12	107.50
			80.49		
	May	118.9		79.76	149.07
			79.04		

(1)		(2)	(3)	(4)	(5)
	Jun.	115.8		77.92	148.61
			76.81		
	Jul.	86.2		75.80	113.72
			74.82		
	Aug.	65.0		74.34	87.44
			73.89		
	Sept.	49.5		74.20	66.71
			74.54		
	Oct.	54.4		74.62	72.90
			74.73		
	Nov.	44.2		75.27	58.72
			75.83		
	Dec.	58.2		77.11	75.48
			78.41		
1974	Jan.	58.4		79.75	73.23
			81.11		
	Feb.	56.0		81.73	68.52
			82.38		
	Mar.	75.3		82.52	91.25
			82.70		
	Apr.	95.0		83.04	114.40
			83.42		
	May	121.2		84.32	143.74
			85.24		
	Jan.	129.0		86.28	149.51
			87.33		
	Jul.	117.1		88.38	132.50
			89.47		
	Aug.	97.4		90.30	107.86
			91.18		
	Sept.	64.7		91.85	70.44
			92.55		
	Oct.	58.3		92.14	63.27
			93.40		
	Nov.	52.8		91.62	57.63
			93.19		
	Dec.	80.1		90.76	83.25
			91.66		
1975	Jan.	83.5		89.10	93.71
			89.89		
	Feb.	81.6		87.74	93.00
			87.26		

(1)		(2)	(3)	(4)	(5)
	Mar.	95.8		86.93	110.20
			86.60		
	Apr.	111.5		86.45	128.98
			86.30		
	May	131.4		85.76	153.22
			85.22		
	Jun.	126.5		85.32	148.26
			85.42		
	July	98.7			
	Aug.	76.2			
	Sept.	53.2			
	Oct.	50.3			
	Nov.	49.3			
	Dec.	67.1			

Second moving average of the second and third average values

$$= \frac{121.37 + 120.38}{2} = 120.88$$

Now prepare another two way table giving monthwise percentage ratio for each of the five years as given in Table (*v*).

The seasonal index given in the last row of this table is obtained by multiplying each monthly median value by 1200/1200.41. This has been done to bring the average of the monthly seasonal indices to 100.

From the seasonal indices, it is easily deduceable that thc production has been almost one and a half times more than the average in the month of May and June, whereas in the month of November it has been 61.61 per cent of the average.

Link Relative Method

Some people call it Pearson's method as a mark of respect to its inventor, Karl Pearson. Various steps involved in this method are:

1. *Calculation for link relatives*

   Express each periodic or seasonal (quarterly, monthly or weekly) value, of a time series data, as the percentage of the preceding seasonal value. The percentages so obtained are called *link relatives.* The process of calculating every seasonal percentage of the preceding periodic value, eliminates the influence of the trend. Hence, it reduces the labour of calculating the trend separately. Besides this, the cyclic effects are also nullified to a great extent.

2. *Calculation of median*

   Calculate median of the percentage values of each period separately. This eliminates the irregular effects from the time series. This is done by making use of basic definitions. Two points are worth noting here.

   (*a*) Under this process, median is preferred to the mean of every periodic percentage value.

Table: (v)

Year	Jan.	Feb.	Mar.	Apr.	May.	Jun.	Jul.	Aug.	Sept.	Oct.	Nov.	Dec.	Total
1971							112.46	97.29	76.94	78.94	66.32	82.91	
1972	86.46	88.71	105.98	117.49	141.60	150.14	121.10	95.74	75.74	70.59	64.54	82.23	
1973	96.14	94.37	104.22	107.50	149.07	148.61	113.72	87.44	66.71	72.90	58.72	75.48	
1974	73.23	68.52	91.25	114.40	143.74	149.51	132.50	107.86	70.44	63.27	57.63	88.25	
1975	93.71	93.00	110.20	128.98	153.22	148.26							
Mec.	90.10	90.85	105.10	115.94	146.40	149.06	117.41	96.52	73.09	71.74	61.63	82.57	1200.41
Sea Index	90.07	90.82	105.06	115.90	146.35	149.01	117.37	96.49	73.06	71.72	61.61	82.54	1200

(*b*) These medians do not represent seasonal indices. They are simply the medians for link relatives. These medians are the basis for calculating the seasonal indices. The medians obtained for each period are tabulated columnwise.

3. *Calculation of chain relative medians*

Now assume the median for the first season (period) i.e., the first quarter or first month etc. as 100 and calculate the *chain relative medians* by the formula,

$$\frac{\text{median for the season} \times \text{previous seasonal chain relative median}}{100} \quad \text{...(17.30)}$$

4. *Calculation of chain relative for the first season*

The chain relative of the first season is calculated on the basis of the last season i.e., I season (I-quarter or I-month etc.) chain relative is,

$$= \frac{\text{median for I season} \times \text{chain relative median for the last season}}{100} \quad \text{...(17.31)}$$

The chain relative calculated by (17.31) for the first season under step (4) will have some difference, between the chain relative obtained by (17.30). The difference is obvious due to long variations. Therefore, a correction is necessary in the chain relatives which is as follows:

5. *Calculation of correction factor*

The chain relative medians represent the crude seasonal variation. Hence, they need some adjustment, so that the adjusted value of chain relative median for the first season equals to hundred. For this, the adjustment factor c is obtained by the formula,

$$c = \frac{100 - \text{chain relative for first season}}{\text{number of seasons}} \quad \text{...(17.32)}$$

In the case where there is quarterly data, the number of seasons = 4 and for the monthly data, the number of seasons = 12. Hence, the corrections for seasonal indices from the first season to the last season are $0 \times c$, $1 \times c$, $2 \times c$, ... respectively. These correction factors are added in the respective seasons's chain median values resulting into adjusted chain medians.

6. *Calculation of seasonal indices*

Find the mean of the adjusted medians. Divide adjusted median of each season by the mean of adjusted medians. The resulting values are the required seasonal indices. The advantage of dividing by mean is that the seasonal indices obtained in this manner average to 100.

Note: Some people give seasonal indices in whole numbers by rounding of the figures. It is tolerable because it does not effect the physical interpretations.

It has its own *merits and demerits* as given below:

(*i*) The link relative method is good because link relatives eliminate cyclic and trend effects.

(*ii*) In this method, link relatives are calculated for each and every season, so that no information is left unused.

(*iii*) The use of the correction factor further eliminates the trend effect.

(*iv*) The link relative method is more laborious than others. Still it is a popular method because of its merits.

Comments: Besides the methods described so far, for measuring seasonal influences, there are many more methods. The Bauman moving average difference method, the Carmichael first difference method and the Falkner method are a few rarely used methods and hence the description of these methods has been abandoned.

The practical utility of seasonal index in business may be understood with this example, a bookseller has a yearly sale of Rs.2,40,000, which means he has an average sale of Rs.60,000 per quarter. But the quarterly seasonal index shows that the indices for the four quarters are 100, 50, 180 and 70 respectively. Hence the bookseller will expect his sales of Rs.60,000 in the first quarter (Jan. to Mar.) Rs.30,000 in the second quarter (Apr. to June), Rs.1,08,000 in the third quarter (July to Sept.) and a sales of Rs. 42,000 in the fourth quarter (Oct. to Dec.). This enables the bookseller to manage his stocks and finances accordingly.

***Example* 17.13.** The data given here pertain to the quarterly export of wheat from United States for the years 1969 to 1975.

Following the procedure described theoretically, step by step, prepare the table of link relatives and calculate seasonal indices.

Quarterly export (million bushels)

Year	*I*	*II*	*III*	*IV*
1969	66.4	139.5	114.6	127.1
1970	147.7	146.1	154.1	191.8
1971	167.0	160.8	145.0	116.4
1972	131.9	173.8	196.9	273.4
1973	292.9	363.7	395.9	332.1
1974	219.8	167.6	260.4	271.9
1975	244.9	219.5	336.4	337.7

For the above table, calculations are done as follows:

Step 1: The link relative for II quarter of 1969 = $\frac{139.5}{66.4} \times 100 = 210.09$

The link relative for III quarter of 1969 = $\frac{114.6}{139.5} \times 100 = 82.15$

The link relative for IV quarter of 1969 = $\frac{127.1}{114.6} \times 100 = 110.91$

The link relative for I quarter of 1970 = $\frac{147.7}{127.1} \times 100 = 116.21$

The link relative for II quarter of 1970 = $\frac{146.1}{147.7} \times 100 = 98.92$

and so on.

Step 2: The median for I quarter = $\frac{90.07+107.13}{2}$ = 98.60

The median for II quarter = 98.92

and so on.

Step 3: The chain relative medians by formula (17.30) are calculated,

I quarter chain relative median = 100

II quarter chain relative median = $\frac{100 \times 98.92}{100}$ = 98.92

III quarter chain relative median = $\frac{108.85 \times 98.92}{100}$ = 107.67

IV quarter chain relative median = $\frac{104.42 \times 107.67}{100}$ = 112.43

Step 4: The chain relative for the I quarter of 1969 by the formula (17.31) is

$$= \frac{98.60 \times 112.43}{100} = 110.85$$

This value is given in the above table enclosed in the box □

Step 5: Now the adjustment factor from formula (17.32) is

$$c = \frac{100 - 110.85}{4} = -2.71$$

Quarterly link relatives and seasonal indices

Year	*I*	*II*	*III*	*IV*
1969	110.85	210.09	82.15	110.91
1970	116.21	98.92	105.48	124.46
1971	87.07	96.29	90.17	80.28
1972	113.32	131.77	113.29	138.85
1973	107.13	124.17	108.85	83.88
1974	66.18	76.25	155.37	104.42
1975	90.07	89.63	153.26	100.39
Median	98.60	98.92	108.85	104.42
Chain relative median	100.00	98.92	107.67	112.43
Adjusted chain relative median	100.00	96.21	102.25	104.30
Seasonal indices	99.31	95.55	101.55	103.58

The quantities to be adjusted are:

The adjustment factor for I quarter = 0 × (–2.71) = 0

The adjustment factor for II quarter = 1 × (–2.71) = – 2.71

The adjustment factor for III quarter = 2 × (–2.71) = – 5.42

The adjustment factor for IV quarter = 3 × (–2.71) = – 8.13

The adjusted chain relative medians are, 100, (98.92 – 2.71), (107.67 – 5.42) and (112.43 – 8.13) respectively.

Step 6: The mean of the adjusted medians

$$= \frac{100 + 96.21 + 102.25 + 104.30}{4} = 100.69$$

$$\text{I quarter seasonal index} = \frac{100}{100.69} \times 100 = 99.31$$

$$\text{II quarter seasonal index} = \frac{96.21}{100.69} \times 100 = 95.55$$

$$\text{III quarter seasonal index} = \frac{102.25}{100.69} \times 100 = 101.55$$

$$\text{IV quarter seasonal index} = \frac{104.30}{100.69} \times 100 = 103.58$$

The sum of seasonal indices is 399.99, which is almost equal to 400. The existing slight differences have occurred due to the rounding of figures.

MEASUREMENT OF CYCLIC VARIATIONS

Firstly, one must be clear about the meaning of cycle. In the time series, a cycle means a business cycle which should normally exceed a year in length. This is obvious, because the changes that occur in a particular period, within a year, are considered as seasonal changes. The yearly changes are studied under trend, therefore, the changes that occur for periods more than one year come under the category of cyclic changes. These cycles are never regular in periodicity and amplitude, and therefore, it should be kept in mind that there is hardly any time series which possesses strict cycles. All that can be expected is that, there is a fair degree of approximation of one or more cycles present in the time series. That is why, more realistically, analyst use the term *undulation* or *oscillation* rather than a cycle. In the strict sense, cycles imply a more regular pattern, whereas oscillations or undulations are less regular in occurrences.

Fluctuation in business is an inevitable phenomenon. The cyclical pattern for any time series tells about the prosperity and recession, ups and downs, booms and slumps, of a business. In most of the business there is an upward trend for some time and then the down fall, touching its low level. Again, a rise starts which touches its peak. This process of prosperity and recession continues and may be considered a natural phenomenon. Thus, the cycles reflect on the behaviour of the particular time series under investigation. Moreover, a cycle generally consists of a number of years. This shows that for measurement and/or depiction of cycles, we need data for a large number of years. Otherwise, the data would be insufficient for the purpose.

Various reasons may be attached to cyclic variations present in a time series. Some are (*i*) People always want change and after some years, certain current items are discarded and new ones are patronized. After a few years, people may adopt the old ones. (*ii*) Some items are banned by the government while others are given the incentive to flood the market. (*iii*) The changes in social customs affect the consumption of items. (*iv*) New scientific and technological inventions also affect the production and consumption of items *e.g.* the market of terry cloth has seen a massive decline due to the invention of terrycotton and polyester cloth. Many theories have been propounded by the economists and statisticians to reveal the causes of cycles and the ensuing effects, but hardly any one has succeeded in defining, precisely, the cycles and giving their quantification, regarding their periodicity and amplitude.

MEASUREMENT AND ISOLATION OF CYCLES

The booms and slumps in business are of great interest to businessmen and economists. A businessman has to reduce his production and stocks according to the receding demands. He should also increase his production and supply according to the promoted demands. The study of cycles enables him to know the approximate period for which the recession or upward trend will continue. The simplest way of roughly judging and depicting cycles is to plot the yearly data on the graph paper and see the troughs and crests present in the graph. An adjacent trough and crest forms one *cycle.* One should not confuse cycles with fortuitous or random fluctuations, which do recur in a series as there is always some periodicity and regularity in cycles.

One method of isolation of cycles, is to eliminate the trend and seasonal effect from the time series data. The series will be left only with the cyclic and irregular variations. If irregular influences are also removed from the data, we will be able to isolate the cycles. In case this yearly data are given in the time series, this will be devoid of seasonality. Hence, in this case we have to eliminate only the trend and, if possible, the irregular influence. Symbolically,

$$C \times I = \frac{T \times S \times C \times I}{T \times S} \qquad ...(17.33)$$

For this, we have to divide the observed data by the trend value and multiply it by 100, resulting a series, free from the trend. If the seasonality is there, divide the values obtained by seasonal indices and obtain the percentages. The series now contains only the cyclic and irregular influences. Now the data free from the trend and seasonality are plotted on the graph, which clearly depicts the cycles through troughs and crests. This method is known as the *residual method* and is widely used. The irregular fluctuations can easily be identified by observing the periods of the series and corresponding observations. If any irregular effects are observed, they may be removed by logic itself or applying the moving average method to $C \times I$ values obtained in the manner stated above.

The residual method is based on the assumption that the trend values and seasonal indices completely indicate only trend and seasonal effects. But such an ideal situation is rarely found in practice. In case the distortion from the trend ordinates and seasonal indices is not much, residual method may be used. Otherwise, we must delve for other appropriate method. A few are given below.

First Difference Method

This method is applicable only when the yearly data in the time series is given. It has already been given, that the yearly data is devoid of seasonality. Hence, by this method we remove only secular trend. To do so, take difference of a year from its preceding year and note the differences with its sign, positive or negative. Naturally under this method, the difference for first year will not appear. Plot the yearwise differences on the graph paper taking the years on the abscissa and the differences on the ordinate. Joining the plotted points we get the cycles present in the time series. Even without the graph, the idea can be had but the graph depicts a better picture through the troughs and crests.

Percentage Ratio Method

In this method, divide each year's observed value by its preceding year's observed value, and multiply it by hundred to get the percentages. Plot these percentage values on the graph paper. The concave and convex portions of the plotted graph give a clear picture of cyclic variations. This method is equivalent to the first difference method, in the sense that here we have considered relative change instead of actual differences. As a matter of fact both methods yield similar results.

IRREGULAR VARIATIONS

The components of the time series, which we have studied so far, were to a great extent regular and had some direction and amplitude. But, as the name implies, irregular variations are irregular, in the sense that, neither they are predictable nor can the extent of their impact be thought of. Hence, such influences in the time series data have to be isolated and removed. The irregular influences can be divided into two categories.

(*i*) The first category consists of thousands of minute environmental factors, which affect a time series either in uplifting it or depressing it at any time. But none of them holds enough importance to be singled out and given individual treatment.

(*ii*) The second category, consists of those influences which affect the time series at a time significantly, and change the pattern of the time series. Such forces should explicitly be singled out and given a proper treatment. For example, the effect of an earthquake, widespread floods, a war or an internal revolution etc. Now the task before us is to find a way to measure these effects.

MEASUREMENT OF IRREGULAR INFLUENCES

One fundamental method of isolating and measuring irregular influences, is to remove the trend, seasonality (if it is there) and cyclical variation from the series.

The variations present in the series will merely be due to irregular effects. Symbolically,

$$I = \frac{T \times S \times C \times I}{T \times S \times C} \qquad \text{...(17.34)}$$

Since, nothing can be predicted about the occurrence of irregular influences and the magnitude of such effects, no standard method has been evolved. The only method available is of identifying and isolating them. The adjustments may be made in the time series on the basis of historical background.

It is worth mentioning that the time series analysis is an important tool for businessmen and economic policy makers. The methods given in this chapter are not exhaustive and description given is also not comprehensive. But the matter covered is sufficient and up-to-date for students and some people involved in Economics and Commerce.

QUESTIONS AND EXERCISES

1. Discuss a time series and its importance.
2. What are the components of a time series? Are they all distinct and completely determinable?
3. Name different methods of estimating the trend. Which of them you consider the best and why?
4. Explain each of the following method and for which component(s) of a time series is it used to estimate.
   (*a*) Least square method.
   (*b*) Moving average method.
   (*c*) Semi-average method.
   (*d*) Link relative method.
   (*e*) First difference method.
5. Given below are the equations of different curves, name the curves and give their shape.
   (*a*) $Y = a + bX + cX^2$
   (*b*) $Y = 1/(a + bc^X)$
   (*c*) $Y = a + b^{cX}$
   (*d*) $Y = \alpha\beta^{c^X}$
   (*e*) $Y = \alpha\beta^X$
6. Write short notes on:
   (*a*) Periodicity
   (*b*) Irregular fluctuations
   (*c*) Business cycles
   (*d*) Editing of data
   (*e*) Additive model of times series.
7. Compare the moving average method with the link relative method on the basis of their merits and demerits.
8. Explain the importance and the role of graphical method in determining and isolating various components of a time series.
9. Think and describe three situations of your own, where a time series analysis is required.
10. Define the following terms:
    (*a*) Specific and typical seasonal
    (*b*) Moving average
    (*c*) Dynamic average
    (*d*) Forecasting
    (*e*) Season.
11. To which type of data, a simple compertz curve is suitable for fitting?
12. Discuss the various steps involved in a link relative method, while estimating the seasonal indices.
13. What are the adjustments needed in a time series, before using it for time series analysis? Discuss them adequately.

14. Why is the least square method for the trend considered better than other methods?
15. What is the criterion for selecting a second or a higher degree polynomial?
16. Production of petroleum products from 1970–71 to 1979–80 was as follows:

Years:	1970–71	—72	—73	—74	—75	—76	—77	—78	—79	—80
Production (Lakh Tonnes):	171.1	186.4	178.3	195.0	196.0	208.3	214.3	232.2	231.9	258.3

Find the trend line and plot it on the graph.

17. The data below give the index of industrial production from 1961 to 1970.

Years:	1961	1962	1963	1964	1965	1966	1967	1968	1969	1970
Index of Production:	109.2	119.8	129.7	140.8	153.8	153.2	152.6	163.0	175.3	184.3

Fit in the trend line and predict the index of production for the year 1972 by (*i*) a semi-average method, (*ii*) the least square method, (*iii*) a 3 years moving average method.

18. The household net income from property and enterpreneurship in France, for the years 1971 to 1978, as a percentage of total inflationary gap, was as follows:

Years :	1971	1972	1973	1974	1975	1976	1977	1978
Income :	18.8	23.1	10.3	8.0	18.0	10.2	15.2	19.0

Find the trend line by (*i*) a graphical method, (*ii*) the least square method.

19. Aggregate figures for merchandise export (f.o.b.) in India, for eight years, in Rs. Crores, are as follows:

Years :	1971	1972	1973	1974	1975	1976	1977	1978
Export (Rs. Crores):	196.2	217.4	241.9	302.4	385.2	468.8	535.5	521.2

Find the trend line of merchandise export and predict the amount of export for the year 1980.

20. Depict the following figures of the net national product (NNP) of India, at 1970–71 prices, in the form of graph and superimpose the trend by computing the five years moving average.

Year	*NNP (Rs 00, crores)*	*Years*	*NNP (Rs. 00, crores)*	*Year*	*NNP (Rs. 00, crores)*
1961	259	1969	335	1977	444
1962	269	1970	356	1978	482
1963	275	1971	378	1979	513
1964	292	1972	386	1980	487
1965	315	1973	382	1981	521
1966	301	1974	397	1982	550
1967	299	1975	400		
1968	324	1976	440		

21. Assuming that the trend is absent, determine if there is any seasonality in the data given below:

Year	*Quarters*			
	I	*II*	*III*	*IV*
1996	3.7	4.1	3.3	3.5
1997	3.7	3.9	3.6	3.6
1998	4.0	4.1	3.3	3.1
1999	3.3	4.4	4.0	4.0

What are the seasonal indices for various quarters by ratio to moving average method taking three quarters moving averages?

22. The following are the number of books borrowed from a public library, on six working days, for a period of six weeks. Compute the seasonal daily index for the series.

Week	*Number of books borrowed (hundreds)*					
	Mon.	*Tue.*	*Wed.*	*Thu.*	*Fri.*	*Sat.*
1	2.5	4.3	4.4	4.6	5.1	6.2
2	1.8	3.4	5.2	4.9	5.3	6.8
3	1.2	2.5	4.8	5.1	6.2	7.0
4	1.9	2.2	4.9	6.1	7.1	6.9
5	2.1	3.2	4.3	5.3	6.1	7.2
6	1.2	3.1	2.7	4.8	5.3	6.2

(*B.Com. Bombay, 1968*)

23. What is a time series? Distinguish between the secular trend, the seasonal variations and the cyclical fluctuations. How would you measure secular trend in any given data? (*M.A. (Prev.), Econ., Meerut, 1980*)

24. Given the following data, pertaining to the expenditure on imports by the Government of India, find out the average seasonal variation.

Year	*Quarterly*			
	Apr.-Jun. (Rs crores)	*July-Sept. (Rs. crores)*	*Oct.-Dec. (Rs crores)*	*Jan.-Mar. (Rs. crores)*
1979-80	36	43	44	102
1980-81	39	44	57	98
1981-82	47	53	58	104
1982-83	47	56	60	130

(*M.Com. (Final), Agra, 1983*)

25. Given the following time series data, find out the trend by the least square method.

Year :	1974	1975	1976	1977	1978	1979
Production (Lakh tonnes):	5	7	9	10	12	17

(*M.Com. (Final), Agra, 1980*)

26. Apply the method of least squares to determine the sales figures for the year 1976 from the following data.

Years :	1968	1969	1970	1971	1972	1973	1974
Sales of Refrigerators:	100	110	130	125	170	168	191

(*M.B.A., Delhi, 1975*)

27. The following table shows urban population as the percentage of the total population from 1921 to 1961:

Census year :	1921	1931	1941	1951	1961
Per cent of total population	11.4	12.1	13.9	17.3	18.0

Compute the second degree trend line, for the data given above, and from the equation determine the trend value of the census year 1971. (*M.Com., Raj., 1969*)

[*Hint:* Write the normal equations and solve them for the unknown constants by the elimination method.]

28. Calculate the seasonal indices, by ratio to trend method, from the following data:

Year	I Quarter	II Quarter	III Quarter	IV Quarter
1986	36	34	38	32
1987	38	48	52	42
1988	42	56	50	52
1989	56	74	68	62
1990	82	90	88	80

(*M.Com. Madras, 1975*)

29. The sales of a company, in thousands of rupees, for the years 1965 to 1971 are given below:

Year :	1965	1966	1967	1968	1969	1970	1971
Sales	32	47	65	92	132	190	275

Estimate sales for the year 1972 by using an equation of the form $y = ab^x$ where x = years and y = sales. (*M.Com., Delhi, 1974*)

[*Hint:* Take logarithm of the equation $y = ab^x$. We get, $\log y = \log a + x \log b$. Fit this equation like a trend line $Z = a_1 + b_1 x$ where $Z = \log y$, $a_1 = \log a$ and $b_1 = \log b$]

30. Calculate trend value by 3 yearly moving average from the following data:

Year:	1960	1961	1962	1963	1964	1965	1966	1967
Sales (Thousand units):	5	7	9	12	11	10	8	12
Year:	1968	1969	1970	1971	1972	1973	1974	
Sales (Thousand units):	13	17	19	14	13	12	15	

(*B.A. Hon., Kurukshetra, 1975*)

31.(*a*) What do you understand by Seasonal Variations? What are the methods used to determine them?

(*b*) Enumerate the steps you take in computing seasonal indices by the link relative method. (*C.A. May, 1981*)

32.(*a*) What do you understand by Seasonal Indices? What methods are used to determine them?

(*b*) Use the method of monthly average to determine the monthly indices for the following data of *production of a commodity for the years* 1979, 1980, 1981:

Month	*1979*	*1980*	*1981*
	Production (Lacs tons)		
January	12	15	16
February	11	14	15
March	10	13	14
April	14	16	16
May	15	16	15
June	15	15	17
July	16	17	16
August	13	12	13
September	11	13	10
October	10	12	10
November	12	13	11
December	15	14	15

(*C.A., May, 1982*)

33.(*a*) Give the addition and multiplication models of the time series equation and explain briefly the components of a time series.

(*b*) Explain the meaning of deseasonalising data. What purpose does it serve?

(*c*) Deseasonalise the following data with the help of the seasonal index given against:

Month	*Cash balance ('000 Rs)*	*Seasonal index*
January	360	120
February	400	80
March	550	110
April	360	90
May	350	70
June	550	100

(*C.A., May, 1983*)

34. Fit a linear trend by the method of least squares to the following data:

Year :	1981	1982	1983	1984	1985	1986	1987
Profit (Rs., 000):	57	65	63	72	69	78	82

(*B.Com. 1 Yr., Andhra, 1989*)

35. What are the advantages and limitations of the moving average method of trend fitting?

(*B.Com.I Yr., Andhra, 1989*)

36. Find the trend values by the method of least squares and estimate the production for the year 1988.

Year :	1981	1982	1983	1984	1985	1986	1987
Production (Lakh tons):	9	12	14	16	20	26	35

(*B.Com. I Yr., Andhra, 1988*)

37. You are given the population figures of India as follows:

Census year (x):	1911	1921	1931	1941	1951	1961	1971
Population (y): (crores)	25.0	25.1	27.9	31.9	36.1	43.9	54.7

Fit in exponential trend $y = ab^x$ to the above data by the method of least squares and find the trend value. Estimate the population in 1981.
[Hints: Take logarithm and then fit] (*Diploma in Appld. Stat., Andhra, 1987*)

38.(*a*) Explain the method of curve fitting by the principle of least squares to a set of given data.

(*b*) What are the components of time series and explain the method of moving averages for measuring secular trend? (*P.G.Certificate, Andhra, 1987*)

39. Deseasonalise the following data using a multiplicative model:

Quarter:	1	2	3	4
Sales (Rs '000):	65.4	25.2	23.7	21.4
Seasonal Index:	148	124	78	59

(*I.C.W.A. Dec., 1988*)

40. Fit a straight line trend by least square method to the following data and estimate the production for the year 1993.

Year:	1985	1986	1987	1988	1989	1990
Production ('000 tons):	75	83	109	129	134	148

(*I.C.W.A. (Inter); June, 1993*)

41. Following information is collected for the number of units produced of a particular product between 1992 and 1999.

Year :	1992	1993	1994	1995	1996	1997	1998
Units Produced: (in million)	98	105	116	135	156	177	208

(*i*) Find the equation that describes the secular trend of projection. Also project the units produced in 2000 with the help of trend equation.

(*ii*) Plot the original data and the trend values on a graph paper.

(*M.B.A., Part-II, MLSU, Udaipur, 2001*)

42. Calculate the seasonal indices from the following ratio to moving average values expressed in percentage.

Year/Season	*Summer*	*Rainy*	*Winter*
1999	–	101.75	107.14
2000	96.18	92.30	114.00
2001	92.45	95.20	118.18

(*C.A. Foundation, May, 2002*)

43.(a) Using the method of least squares, fit a straight line to the following data and find the trend values and short term fluctuations.

Year :	1990	1991	1992	1993	1994	1995	1996	1997	1998
Values :	232	226	220	180	190	168	162	152	144

(b) For the following seris of observations, verify that the 2–year centered moving average is equivalent to a 3–year weighted moving average with weights 1, 2, 1 respectively.

Year:	1994	1995	1996	1997	1998	1999	2000
Values:	2	4	5	7	8	10	13

(*I.C.W.A., Inter, June, 2002*)

44. The figures of quarterly income of a municipal corporation (in Rs. Lakhs) for 2 years are given below.

Year :	Q_1	Q_2	Q_3	Q_4
1995 :	74	56	48	69
1996 :	83	52	49	81

Using a four quarterly average estimate the trend values. (*I.C.W.A., Inter, Dec. 1998*)

45. Below are given the figures of production (in thousand tons) of a sugar factory.

Year :	1989	1990	1991	1992	1993	1994	1995
Production ('000 *tons*) :	77	88	94	85	91	98	90

(*i*) Fit a straight line by the method least squares and find the trend values.
(*ii*) Find the monthly increase in production. (*M.B.A., I-Yr, MLSU, Udaipur, 2003*)

SUGGESTED READING

Anderson, T.W. (1958). *The Statistical Analysis of Time Series,* John Wiley, New York.

Berenson, M.L. and D.M. Levine (1979). *Business Statistics,* Prentice Hall, Englewood Cliffs.

Byrkit, D.R. (1979). *Elementary Business Statistics,* D. Van Nostrand Company, New York.

Chris Chatfield (2003). *The Analysis of Time Series*, CRC Press.

David Ray Anderson, Dennis J. Swelney and Thomas Arthur Williams (2004). *Statistics for Business and Economics*, Thomson South-Western.

Enns, P.G. (1985). *Business Statistics,* Richard D. Irwin, Illinois.

Fuller, W.A. (1976). *Introduction to Statistical Time Series,* John Wiley, New York.

Hannan, E.J. (1970). *Multiple Time Series,* John Wiley, New York.

Judy L. Klein (1977). *Statistical Vision in Time*, Cambridge University Press.

Maurice B. Priestley, T. Subba Rao and S. Subba Rao (1993). *Developments in Time Series Analysis*, CRC Press.

Mohsen Pourahmadi (2001). *Foundations of Time Series Analysis and Prediction Theory*, Wiley - IEEE.

Robert H. Shumway and David S. Stofer (2005). *Time Series Analysis and its Applications*, Springer.

18
Chapter

Index Numbers

The index numbers are intended to show the average percentage changes, in the value of certain product(s), at a specific time, place or situation as compared to any other time, place or situation. Such a study is of great importance in the industry, management and business, and largely to the governments for chalking out the wage policy or fixing of prices, import-export policy etc. For example, when the workers demand more wages and the employers try to remain static, a conflict occurs. The only feasible solution to this problem is to adopt a uniform wage policy, depending on the cost of living. Sometimes, we need to compare the cost of living at Bombay with the cost of living at Delhi, Lucknow or Kolkata etc. As a matter of fact, the index number is an economic barometer as it always measures the economic pressure on the consumers directly or indirectly. Besides this, index numbers also reveal the state of inflation or deflation. Although a good number of statisticians and economists have defined index number in their own way. All these definitions are the same in a broader sense. Some definitions are given below.

DEFINITIONS

Irving Fisher:

"The purpose of index number is that it shall fairly represent so far as one single figure can, the general trend of the many diverging ratios from which it is calculated."

John I. Griffin:

"An index number is a quantity which by reference to a base period, shows by its variations, the changes in the magnitude over a period of time. In general, index numbers are used to measure changes overtime, in magnitudes which are not capable of direct measurement."

Wessel, Willet and Simone:

"An index number is a special type of an average that provides a measurement of relative changes from time to time or place to place."

Clark and Schkade:

"An index number is a percentage relative that compares economic measure, in a given period, with those same measures at a fixed time period in the past."

From these definitions and the initial discussion, it is apparent that the index number is the ratio of two quantities of the same products or variables, with reference to two timings, places or situations. These ratios are usually expressed as percentages which are most suited for comparability. In the twentieth century, index numbers are quite popular for production and consumption besides price indices, which are most prevalent.

Index numbers are mostly given for a time period, in comparison to any earlier time period, which is known as *reference period or base period.* Hence, for calculations of index numbers, the data are collected for prices and quantities consumed or produced at two different timings, one-named as *current period* and the other as *base period.* Data at two timings are collected for the same or similar items. The ratio of the sum of the products of the prices and the quantities at the current period to the base period, multiplied by hundred gives the index number in per cent. The method expressed here is the basic idea, where as the methods and the formulae are given in the body of this chapter. In general, the formulae are based on the value ratio V which is the product of the measure of the total price influence P in V and of a measure of the total quantity influence Q in V. That is,

$$V = P \times Q \qquad ...(18.1)$$

Before we discuss various aspects and methods of construction of index number, it will be useful to explain the notations used in this chapter.

I_{01} = Index number at the current period 1 as compared to the base period '0'.

P_{01} = Price index for the current period '1' as compared to the base period '0'.

Q_{01} = Quantity index for the current period '1' as compared to the base period '0'.

N_0 = Number of items and/or commodities included in the base period '0'.

N_1 = Number of items and/or commodities included in the current period '1'.

N_{01} = Number of items and/or commodities which are common in the base period and the current period. Such items and/or commodities are called *binary items* and/or *commodities.*

From the above notations, it is easy to deduce that the number of items uncommon to the current period and the base period are

$$= (N_1 - N_{01}) + (N_0 - N_{01})$$
$$= N_1 + N_0 - 2N_{01}$$

Further, it may be worthwhile to point out that, all the notations, given earlier for sample values will be given by p_{01}, n_0, n_1 and n_{01} respectively.

Suppose, there are n_1 items included in the sample in the current period and n_0 items in the base period. Let the prices and quantities in the current period be denoted as p_{11}, $p_{12}, ..., p_{1n_1}$ and $q_{11}, q_{12}, ..., q_{1n_1}$, respectively. The prices and quantities in the base period are denoted as $p_{01}, p_{02}, ... p_{0n_0}$ and $q_{01}, q_{02}, ..., q_{0n_0}$ respectively. Then the total price value for the current period is $\sum_{i=1}^{n_1} p_{1i}\, q_{1i}$ and for the base period is $\sum_{i=1}^{n_0} p_{0i}\, q_{0i}$. Similar expression can be given for total quantity values. Also the total price value of binary items at the kth period is $\sum_{i=1}^{n_{0k}} p_{ki} q_{ki}$ where k refers to any period in the given series of data as 1st, 2nd, 3rd period, and so on.

For the construction of index numbers, we have to decide on a reference period or a base period in comparison to which the indices are to be worked out at a particular time. The base year should be a normal year. Its choice mostly depends upon the purpose of the study. The items which are to be included for the calculation of index numbers also depends on the objective of these indices *i.e.*, what we want to express through these index numbers. In case of consumer price index number, we should take retail prices and the quantities sold through retailers. If we take the wholesale prices and the quantities from the manufacturers, the index numbers will give distorted figures which will lead to unrealistic conclusions.

METHODS OF CONSTRUCTION OF INDEX NUMBERS

Index numbers are a special type of average, *i.e.*, the weighted averages. The difficulty lies in the choice of the type of average, *i.e.*, the arithmetic mean, geometric mean, harmonic mean, median or mode etc. As a matter of fact, the harmonic mean, median and mode are not used at all. Thus, from the remaining two, the geometric mean is preferred to the arithmetic mean because in the construction of index numbers, we mostly deal with the ratios and the relative changes. The geometric mean is not affected much by the extreme values often occurring in the observed data. Often, we have to reverse the whole process of the index number, *i.e.*, from one base period to the other base period. From this angle too, geometric mean is the most convenient. Inspite of these theoretical points in favour of geometric mean, the use of arithmetic mean has not been totally ruled out. Mostly, it is used for the convenience of calculations. With the development of computers, calculations are no longer a problem and hence geometric mean can easily be used.

In the previous paragraph, it has been noted that index numbers are mostly weighted averages. Now an important point to be discussed is the choice of weights. As you have noted in the chapter on measures of central tendency the weights refer to the relative importance of a variate value. In the construction of index numbers a number of items are included and all these items are not equally important. For example, if the price of butter is reduced and the price of milk is increased proportionately and equal weight is given to both, the index number will remain unchanged; whereas the rise in price of milk will affect most of the people while the price of butter will affect a few. Hence, the equal weights will not reveal the real situation. In case the quantities of consumptions of butter and milk are used as their respective weights, the index number will go up definitely and will measure the actual impact of the price rise of milk and butter on the masses. This clearly shows that weighting of prices by proper weights will definitely improve the results. When some items are unweighted, it means their weights are unity. Generally, in calculation of a price index, the weights are the quantities consumed, produced or distributed through various agencies which are denoted in the formulae by q.

Another point of importance is the uniformity of units. If certain rates are expressed as rupees per kilogram, it should be uniformly maintained, but this is not possible for all the items. For example, in a consumer price index, the consumption of cereals is expressed in terms of rupees and kilograms, whereas the consumption of cloth will have to be expressed in terms of rupees and metres. Since these two units are not compatible it would be logical to consider the value ratio, $p \times q$, which gives the value of an item in terms of rupees only. Hence, mostly the value ratio is used.

Three types of indices are commonly found out, namely, the price index number, the quantity index number and the consumers price index number. A *numerical value that summarizes price levels is called a price index.* The price index numbers are of prime importance in explaining the purchasing power (inflation or deflation) from one period to another, whereas the quantity index number is the measure of changing production or consumption. The consumer price index is a price index with special reference to a class or category of people for whom it is meant. In this type of index number, items to be included for calculating index numbers vary from one group to another under consideration. Different statisticians and economists have given different formulae for index numbers, giving their own logic befitting to a situation. Some commonly used methods are discussed here.

Two types of measures of variation in price or quantity are as follows:

(1) The actual change in prices, $p_{01} = p_1 - p_0$ and in quantity, $q_{01} = q_1 - q_0$

(2) The relative change in price = p_1/p_0 and in quantity, = q_1/q_0

The actual change approach is totally discarded as its magnitude is influenced by the units in which the price (quantity) is quoted. For example, if the price of petrol is quoted in Rs. per ton, its magnitude will look much higher than the change, if the price of petrol is quoted in Rs. per litre. The relative change approach is appropriate when this is not affected by the unit of measurement, in which the price or quantity is quoted. Of course p_1 and p_0 or q_1 and q_0 should be expressed in the same units. Hence, the relative change approach is universally accepted. The relative price change, $(p_{1i}/p_{0i}) \times 100$ per cent, have limited usefulness, as it does not reflect a general movement in price. So, a composite index covering a large number of commodities of common use will be a better measure of change.

Unweighted Aggregate Price Index

Suppose there are n items which are in common use, the formula of unweighted aggregate price index is given as,

$$I_{01} = \frac{\sum_i p_{1i}}{\sum_i p_{0i}} \times 100 \qquad \text{...(18.2)}$$

where $i = 1, 2, ..., n$.

This type of index is not good because it is affected by the units upon which the prices are based. In most of the cases, the units of prices of various items will not be compatible. Thus, the use of this formulae is ruled out.

Choice of Weights

The price or quantity relatives should always be weighted. The difficulty lies in the choice of weights. The accepted practice is to use value figures pq as weights. The dilemma lies in the choices whether our weights should be p_0q_0, the value of a commodity in the base year or p_1q_1, the value of the same commodity in the current year. Besides this, the workers also used some other value figure $p'q'$ which is a value figure for some period other than the base year or current year. But such a value figure is outrightly rejected because this figure neither belongs to the base year nor to the current year. Since this in no way purports the changes under measurement, it is condemned. We consider the value figure p_0q_0 which is the amount of expenditure on an item for purchasing the quantity q_0 at the price p_0 in the base year. When the price relative (p_1/p_0) is multiplied by p_0q_0, that is $(p_1/p_0)\, p_0q_0$, we have to pay the sum p_1q_0 for the quantity q_0 in the current year. If the number of items included in the list is n, the total sum of money is $\sum_i p_{1i}q_{0i}$ where $i = 1, 2, ..., n$. The value $\sum_i p_{1i}q_{0i}$ is the hypothetical sum of the money to be spent on purchasing the same quantity of articles as in the base year, at the current price. The value $\Sigma_i\, p_{0i}\, q_{0i}$ is the sum of money spent for quantities q_{0i} in the base year. The ratio of the two value figures gives the price index number for the current year, relative to the base period. In general,

$$LL_{01} = \frac{\Sigma_i \left(\frac{p_{1i}}{p_{0i}} \times 100 \right) \omega_i}{\Sigma_i\, \omega_i} \qquad ...(18.3)$$

where $i = 1, 2,, ..., n$.

When $\omega_i = p_{0i}\, q_{0i}$, we obtain Laspeyre's price index formula as follows:

$$L_{01} = \frac{\Sigma_i \left(\frac{p_{1i}}{p_{0i}} \times 100 \right) p_{0i} q_{0i}}{\Sigma_i\, p_{0i} q_{0i}} \qquad ...(18.3.1)$$

$$= \frac{\Sigma_i\, p_{1i}\, q_{0i}}{\Sigma_i\, p_{0i}\, q_{0i}} \times 100 \qquad ...(18.3.2)$$

The ratio of the two aggregate values given by (18.3.2) is the measure of price change for the same quantities of items, from the base period to the current period. The ratio is multiplied by 100 to get the index in per cent. The idea of using base year quantities as weights was mooted out first by **Laspeyre.** That is why the price index is denoted by L_{01}. But, to use the quantities of base period as weights is not binding. As a norm, it can be neither for the base year or for the given year. In view of this, **Paasche** suggested another measure which consist of taking the current year quantities as weights. Thus Paasche's formula for index number is given as,

$$P_{01} = \frac{\Sigma_i\, p_{1i}\, q_{1i}}{\Sigma_i\, p_{0i}\, q_{1i}} \times 100 \qquad ...(18.4)$$

where $i = 1, 2, ..., n$.

The connotation P_{01} is used as a mark of respect to its inventor **Paasche**. The L and P formulae for quantity index numbers can be obtained by interchanging p by q and q by p in formulae (18.3.2) and (18.4). Elaborately,

$$\text{for quantities,} \quad L_{01} = \frac{\Sigma_i\, q_{1i}\, p_{0i}}{\Sigma_i\, q_{0i}\, p_{0i}} \times 100 \qquad ...(18.5)$$

$$\text{for quantities,} \quad P_{01} = \frac{\Sigma_i\, q_{1i}\, p_{1i}}{\Sigma_i\, q_{0i}\, p_{1i}} \times 100 \qquad ...(18.6)$$

where $i = 1, 2, ..., n$.

Of course, their meaning and interpretation should be thought of for quantity influence. Now a pertinent question arises which one of the two formulae is to be preferred over the other as both the formulae are logically sound. To resolve this problem, some norms may be formed.

1. If the values of L_{01} and P_{01} are close to each other, one can choose either of the two formulae. Alternatively, it would be wise to use the average of L_{01} and P_{01} as the price index number, which is the measure of price influence in the value ratio V_{01}, where V_{01} is the ratio of $P \times Q$ for period 1 to period 0.

2. In case L_{01} and P_{01} are far apart, none of the two should be accepted and some other criteria have to be set. For brevity, we will write L for Laspeyre's formula and P for Paasche's formula. To decide whether L and P are compatible, we use the following test.

D-Test for Consistency in L and P

The number D is a measure of the lack of agreement between L and P. It is given as,

$$D = L - P \qquad ...(18.7)$$

If $D \leq 2$, L and P are consistent and if $D > 2$, none of them will be considered satisfactory.

Comparison of L and P

Paasche's index is based on the logic of the changing tastes of consumers. Newer items in this index will tend to supplant other items, in importance. Thus, Paasche's index may be more realistic than Laspeyre's index, in the sense that, the former index reflects the tastes and earnings of consumers more realistically.

Paasche's index is more difficult to work out as compared to Laspeyre's index because it is very expensive to collect data to find out new quantity weight for the current year. To overcome the difficulties of shifting consumers emphasis of various items, the base period may be revised from time to time, every ten years or so, to make an index up-to-date.

Fixed Weight Aggregate Price Index

Some workers suggested that instead of taking weights for any period, fixed weights, which may be the average of quantities consumed or produced in a number of years, should be used. The Laspeyre's price index is

$$L_{01} = \frac{\sum_i p_{1i}\, q_{ai}}{\sum_i p_{0i}\, q_{ai}} \times 100 \qquad ...(18.8)$$

where $i = 1, 2, ..., n$.

The main advantage of this more general index is that it is free from the year to year changes. But this approach is mostly discarded on the ground that the weights belong to none of the periods involved in the calculation of index number.

***Example* 18.1.** The table given below contains the prices per kilogram of few selected items.

Year	*Prices per kg*			
	Rice	*Wheat*	*Pure ghee*	*Edible oil*
1978	2.54	1.36	24.00	46.50
1979	2.44	1.44	25.00	54.40
1980	2.41	1.41	25.10	55.50

The price relative change for each commodity to the base 1978 can be calculated by the formula,

$$I = \frac{p_1}{p_0} \times 100$$

Percentage price relative change:

Item	Year	
	1979	1980
Rice	$\frac{2.44}{2.54}\times 100 = 96$	$\frac{2.41}{2.54}\times 100 = 95$
Wheat	$\frac{1.44}{1.36}\times 100 = 106$	$\frac{1.41}{1.36}\times 100 = 104$
Pure ghee	$\frac{25.00}{24.00}\times 100 = 104$	$\frac{25.10}{24.00}\times 100 = 105$
Edible oil	$\frac{54.40}{46.50}\times 100 = 117$	$\frac{55.50}{46.50}\times 100 = 119$

The above price changes in each single commodity do not reflect the general movement of the prices.

Unweighted aggregate price index for the given four commodities for 1979 to the base 1978, can be calculated by the formula (18.2) *i.e.*,

$$I_{01} = \frac{\Sigma_i\, p_{1i}}{\Sigma_i\, p_{0i}}\times 100$$

for $i = 1, 2, 3, 4$

The price aggregate for the year 1979, is

$$\sum_{i=1}^{4} p_{1i} = 2.44 + 1.44 + 25.00 + 54.40 = 83.28$$

The price aggregate for the year 1978, is

$$\sum_{i=1}^{4} p_{0i} = 2.54 + 1.36 + 24.00 + 46.50 = 74.40$$

The percentage relative price index, $I_{01} = \frac{83.28}{74.40}\times 100 = 112$.

The index shows that the aggregate price of the four commodities has increased by 12 per cent in a period of one year.

Note : In all the problems, the indexes are given in round figures.

***Example* 18.2.** The following table gives the data with regard to the prices and consumption of a few selected items for the year 1972 and 1981 of a centre:

Items	Prices		Quantity assumed	
	1972	1981	1972	1981
Vegetable oil (Rs/q)	512	1590	239 (q)	796 (q)
Sugar (Rs/q)	309	437	1325 (q)	2577 (q)
Milk (Rs/100 litres)	160	306	2291 ('00 litres)	6217 ('00 litres)
Egg (each)	0.30	0.55	2600	2900
Kerosene (Rs/litre)	0.66	1.86	1033 (litres)	3428 (litres)

The percentage price relative indices for each item for 1981 to the base 1972, are calculated by the formula,

$$I = \frac{p_1}{p_0} \times 100$$

Items	*Price relative Index Base = 1972*
Vegetable oil	$\frac{1590}{512} \times 100 = 311$
Sugar	$\frac{437}{309} \times 100 = 141$
Milk	$\frac{306}{160} \times 100 = 191$
Egg	$\frac{0.55}{0.30} \times 100 = 183$
Kerosene	$\frac{1.86}{0.66} \times 100 = 282$

Laspeyre's index 1981 to the base 1972 is calculated by formula (18.3.2), that is

$$L_{01} = \frac{\Sigma_i \, p_{1i} \, q_{0i}}{\Sigma_i \, p_{0i} \, q_{0i}} \times 100$$

For the given data,

$$\begin{aligned} \sum_{i=1}^{5} p_{1i} \, q_{0i} &= 1590 \times 239 + 437 \times 1325 + 306 \times 2291 + 0.55 \times 2600 + 1.86 \times 1033 \\ &= 380010 + 579025 + 701046 + 1430 + 1921.38 \\ &= 1663432.38 \end{aligned}$$

$$\begin{aligned} \sum_{i=1}^{5} p_{0i} \, q_{0i} &= 512 \times 239 + 309 \times 1325 + 160 \times 2291 + 0.30 \times 2600 + 0.66 \times 1033 \\ &= 122368 + 409425 + 366560 + 780 + 681.78 \\ &= 899814.78 \end{aligned}$$

$$L_{01} = \frac{1663432.38}{899814.78} \times 100 = 185$$

Paasche's index for 1981 to the base 1972 is calculated by formula (18.4), that is

$$P_{01} = \frac{\Sigma_i \, p_{1i} \, q_{1i}}{\Sigma_i \, p_{0i} \, q_{1i}} \times 100$$

For the given data,

$$\begin{aligned} \sum_{i=1}^{5} p_{1i} \, q_{1i} &= 1590 \times 796 + 437 \times 2577 + 306 \times 6217 + 0.55 \times 2900 + 1.86 \times 3428 \\ &= 1265640 + 1126149 + 1902402 + 1595 + 6376.08 \\ &= 4302162.08 \end{aligned}$$

$$\sum_{i=1}^{5} p_{0i}\, q_{1i} = 512 \times 796 + 309 \times 2577 + 160 \times 6217 + 0.30 \times 2900 + 0.66 \times 3428$$

$$= 407552 + 796293 + 994720 + 870 + 2262.48$$

$$= 2201697.48$$

$$P_{01} = \frac{4302162.08}{2201697} \times 100 = 195$$

The difference between Paasche's index and Laspeyre's index is 10 which is quite high.

Weighting Diagram

In formula (18.3), it is given that the weights are assigned to various items in proportion to the market value of the commodities transacted or consumed in the area or group of people for whom the indices are being prepared, and are multiplied by the average price per unit during the base year, *i.e.*, calculate the quantity $p_{0i}q_{0i}$ for the ith commodity.

In practice, price quotations of the specified commodities are collected on every Friday by fixed reporting agencies from fixed markets and centres. The average of the prices of a commodity gives the required average price of that commodity. The consumption data have been taken through the survey conducted during the base year or any other period as required. To prepare the weighting diagram we write the weights for each commodity or item groupwise and then reduce them to 100 or 1000 or any other number. The method of preparing the weighting diagram has been shown in the table given below:

Group	*Commodity*	*Weights*	*Weights reduced to 1000*
I	*Food articles*		
	Rice	29	32
	Wheat	268	295
	Gram	81	89
	Pulses (excluding gram)	60	66
	Milk	190	209
	Pure ghee	178	196
	Sugar	37	41
	Spices	66	72
	Total	909	1000
II	*Industrial raw material*		
	Raw wool	35	427
	Raw cotton	29	354
	Hides	11	134
	Mica	7	85
	Total	82	1000

III	*Fuel, light and power*		
	Coal	18	254
	Kerosene7	99	
	Petrol	16	225
	Diesel oil17	239	
	Electricity	13	183
	Total	71	1000
IV	*Manufactured items*		
	Cloth	117	504
	Iron and steel	26	112
	Handloom	34	147
	Steel utensils	7	30
	Fertilizers	5	22
	Soaps	7	30
	Shoes	28	121
	Building materials	8	34
	Total	232	1000

The figures given in the last column against each item show their corresponding weights.

The group weights are calculated by writing the weights of each group and then reducing them into 1000 or 100 etc. Group weights for the above four groups are calculated as given below.

Group	*Weights*	*Group weights reduced to 1000*
Food articles	909	702
Industrial raw materials	82	63
Fuel, light and power	71	55
Manufactured items	232	180
Total	1294	1000

Formulae for Group Indices

The price index for the jth group can be calculated by the formula,

$$I_j^p = \frac{\Sigma_i (p_{1ij} / p_{0ij}) \times \omega_{ij}}{\Sigma_i \omega_{ij}} \times 100 \qquad ...(18.9)$$

and formula for quantity index of jth group is,

$$I_j^q = \frac{\Sigma_i (q_{1ij} / q_{0ij}) \times \omega_{ij}}{\Sigma_i \omega_{ij}} \times 100 \qquad ...(18.10)$$

For the combined groups, the price index is,

$$I_G = \frac{\Sigma_j I_j \omega_j}{\Sigma_j \omega_j} \qquad ...(18.11)$$

***Example* 18.3.** The table below gives the data for the construction of the index of the industrial production for the month of May 1972 to the fixed based 1970 in a region.

Group	*Industry group/Items*	*Weights*	*Production during*	
(i)	*(ii)*	*(iii)*	*May, 70 (M.T.) (iv)*	*May, 72 (M.T.) (v)*
I	*Textiles*	52.2716		
	(1) Cotton cloth	8.8600	689	717
	(2) Cotton yarn	24.8539	2787	2975
	(3) Nylon yarn	14.4902	276	309
	(4) Tyre fabrics	4.0674	217	254
II	*Basic industrial chemical*	21.2007		
	(1) P.V.C. compound	5.0482	807	281
	(2) P.V.C. Resins	1.7204	580	1080
	(3) Caustic soda	1.3493	1407	1556
	(4) Fertilizers	13.0828	16856	22295
III	*Cement*	10.6448		
	(1) Cement	10.6448	128931	134347
IV	*Electrical machinery*	8.0027		
	(1) Electric motors	2.6683 (No.)	44525	39948
	(2) A.C. conductors	3.5234	345.4	285.95
	(3) Paper insulated cables	1.8110 (K.M.)	18.25	29.19
V	*Scientific instruments*	7.8800		
	(1) Dynamic meter	3.6947 (No.)	57	80
	(2) Pneumatic instruments	1.6229 (No.)	74	16
	(3) Controllers	1.2369 (No.)	141	13
	(4) Water meters	1.3254 (No.)	1137	1038

For the given data, we would first work out the group indices, and then the index of industrial production for all the items will be worked out. Group index,

$$I_j^q = \frac{\Sigma_i (q_{1ij} / q_{0ij} \times 100)\omega_{ij}}{\Sigma_i \omega_{ij}}$$

where $j = 1, 2, 3, 4, 5$.

For group I,

$$I_1 = \frac{1}{52.2716}\left\{\frac{717}{689}\times 8.86 + \frac{2975}{2787}\times 24.8539 + \frac{309}{276}\times 14.4903 + \frac{254}{217}\times 4.0674\right\}\times 100$$

$$= \frac{1}{52.2716}\{922.0058 + 2653.0444 + 1622.2835 + 476.0919\}$$

$$= \frac{5673.4256}{52.2716} = 108.537$$

For group II,

$$I_2 = \frac{1}{21.2007}\left\{\frac{281}{807}\times 5.0482 + \frac{1080}{580}\times 1.7204 + \frac{1556}{1407}\times 1.3493 + \frac{22295}{16865}\times 13.0828\right\}\times 100$$

$$= \frac{1}{21.2007}\{175.7799 + 320.3503 + 149.2190 + 1730.4284\}$$

$$= \frac{2375.7776}{21.2007} = 112.061$$

For group III,

$$I_3 = \frac{1}{10.6448}\left\{\frac{134347}{128931}\times 10.6448\right\}\times 100$$

$$= 104.201$$

For group IV,

$$I_4 = \frac{1}{8.0027}\left\{\frac{39948}{44525}\times 2.6683 + \frac{285.95}{345.40}\times 3.5234 + \frac{29.19}{18.25}\times 1.8110\right\}\times 100$$

$$= \frac{1}{8.0027}\{239.4009 + 291.695 + 289.6607\}$$

$$= \frac{820.7566}{8.0027} = 102.560$$

For group V,

$$I_5 = \frac{1}{7.88}\left\{\frac{80}{57}\times 3.6947 + \frac{16}{74}\times 1.6229 + \frac{13}{141}\times 1.2369 + \frac{1038}{1137}\times 1.3254\right\}\times 100$$

$$= \frac{1}{7.88}\{518.5543 + 35.0897 + 11.4040 + 120.9996\}$$

$$= \frac{686.0476}{7.88} = 87.062$$

The general index of industrial production is calculated with the help of formula (18.11), that is

$$I_G = \frac{\Sigma_j I_j \omega_j}{\Sigma_j \omega_j}$$

$$= \frac{1}{100}\{108.537\times 52.2716 + 112.061\times 21.2007 + 104.201\times 10.6448 + 102.560\times 8.0027 + 87.062\times 7.88\}$$

$$= 106.654 = 107$$

Other Formulae

Besides L and P, many more formulae in terms of L and P are available in the literature. Some of these are given here. Since L and P stand on equal footing, the compromise formulae are the arithmetic cross (mean) and the geometric cross (mean) of L and P. The arithmetic cross, for price index is,

$$\frac{1}{2}(L+P) = \frac{1}{2}\left(\frac{\Sigma_i\, p_{1i}\, q_{0i}}{\Sigma_i\, p_{0i}\, q_{0i}} + \frac{\Sigma_i\, p_{1i}\, q_{1i}}{\Sigma_i\, p_{0i}\, q_{1i}}\right) \times 100 \qquad \text{...(18.12)}$$

The arithmetic cross is due to Drobisch and Bowley in 1901.

The geometric cross for price index is,

$$\sqrt{LP} = \sqrt{\frac{\Sigma_i\, p_{1i}\, p_{0i}}{\Sigma_i\, p_{0i}\, q_{0i}} \times \frac{\Sigma_i\, p_{1i}\, q_{1i}}{\Sigma_i\, p_{0i}\, q_{1i}}} \times 100 \qquad \text{...(18.13)}$$

The formulae for the quantity index can be obtained by interchanging p by q and q by p.

Professor Bowley recommended arithmetic cross on the ground that the overestimate through L is compensated by the underestimate through P. But the geometric cross suggested by **Walsh** in 1901 has been a much accepted formula, due to its many virtues. In 1920, **Fisher** called it an ideal formula for index number. Some people call the geometric cross and *Fisher's ideal formula*. In addition to these, the other two crossed weight formulae are as follows:

Arithmetically Crossed-Weight Formula

Here the weights used are the sum of the quantities for the current period and the base period. Symbolically the formula is,

$$P_{01} = \frac{\Sigma_i\, p_{1i}\,(q_{1i} + q_{0i})}{\Sigma_i\, p_{0i}\,(q_{1i} + q_{0i})} \times 100 \qquad \text{...(18.14)}$$

The arithmetically crossed weight formula is due to **Marshal and Edgeworth. Irving Fisher** advocated that this formula yields a good index number.

Geometrically Crossed-Weight Formula

In this formula, the weights used are the geometric mean of the quantities transacted during the given period and the base period. Symbolically the formula is,

$$P_{01} = \frac{\Sigma_i\, p_{1i}\sqrt{q_{1i}\, q_{0i}}}{\Sigma_i\, p_{0i}\sqrt{q_{1i}\, q_{0i}}} \times 100 \qquad \text{...(18.15)}$$

As already stated, Walsh formula (18.13) is the choicest formula in theory. The reason for this is that it fulfils most of the conditions and satisfies various tests innovated for testing the validity and appropriateness of various formulae. They are adequately discussed here.

FORMULA ERROR

Different formulae yield different values of an index number. Moreover, all formulae stand on equal footing as they are correct on one or the other logical ground. Now the problem is how to judge which of the formula is better than the other. For this, **Irving Fisher** and others suggested some tests. If any formula satisfies these conditions, it is considered to be a good formula and the formula which can stand all the tests is considered to be the best. But unfortunately no such optimum formula is available.

Time Reversal Test

Fisher contributed a lot towards the measurement of formula error. He stated that a formula will be accurate if it maintains the time consistency, *i.e.*, if it satisfies the following criterion.

$$P_{01} \times P_{10} = 1 \qquad \text{...(18.16)}$$

In case the condition (18.16) is not satisfied, **Fisher** called it a joint error, because neither P_{01} nor P_{10} can be held responsible for this formula error. Thus, the measure of joint error is,

$$E_1 = (P_{01} \times P_{10} - 1) \qquad \text{...(18.17)}$$

It can be verified that the geometric cross of L and P satisfies the condition (18.16) and thus $E_1 = 0$. Suppose,

$$P_{01} = \sqrt{L.P.}$$

$$= \sqrt{\frac{\Sigma_i\, p_{1i}\, q_{0i}}{\Sigma_i\, p_{0i}\, q_{0i}} \times \frac{\Sigma_i\, p_{1i}\, q_{1i}}{\Sigma_i\, p_{0i}\, q_{1i}}}$$

Similarly, $$P_{10} = \sqrt{\frac{\Sigma_i\, p_{0i}\, q_{1i}}{\Sigma_i\, p_{1i}\, q_{1i}} \times \frac{\Sigma_i\, p_{0i}\, q_{0i}}{\Sigma_i\, p_{1i}\, q_{0i}}}$$

$$P_{01} \times P_{10} = \sqrt{\frac{\Sigma_i\, p_{1i}\, q_{0i}}{\Sigma_i\, p_{0i}\, q_{0i}} \times \frac{\Sigma_i\, p_{1i}\, q_{1i}}{\Sigma_i\, p_{0i}\, q_{1i}} \times \frac{\Sigma_i\, p_{0i}\, q_{1i}}{\Sigma_i\, p_{1i}\, q_{1i}} \times \frac{\Sigma_i\, p_{0i}\, q_{0i}}{\Sigma_i\, p_{1i}\, q_{0i}}} = 1$$

This implies $E_1 = 0$. Hence, geometric cross of L and P satisfies the time reversal test.

Factor Reversal Test

Fisher originated this test with the idea that a formula which correctly gives price change should also give correctly the change in quantity. Hence,

$$P_{01}\; Q_{01} = V_{01} \qquad \text{...(18.18)}$$

where V_{01} represents the ratio of the value of fixed articles in the given year to the base year, *i.e.*,

$$V_{01} = \frac{\Sigma_i\, p_{1i}\, q_{1i}}{\Sigma_i\, p_{0i}\, q_{0i}}$$

Formula (18.18) can be written as,

$$\frac{P_{01}\, Q_{01}}{V_{01}} = 1 \qquad \text{...(18.18.1)}$$

If any formula does not satisfy (18.18.1), it will be considered a joint formula error. The word 'joint' has been used because it is not possible to attach error to either P_{01} or Q_{01}. The joint error expressed in percentage is,

$$E_2 = \frac{P_{01}\,Q_{01}}{V_{01}} = 1 \qquad \text{...(18.19)}$$

E_2 may be positive or negative.

Now we prove that geometric cross satisfies this test. We know,

$$P_{01} = \sqrt{\frac{\Sigma_i\, p_{1i}\, q_{0i}}{\Sigma_i\, p_{0i}\, q_{0i}} \times \frac{\Sigma_i\, p_{1i}\, q_{1i}}{\Sigma_i\, p_{0i}\, q_{1i}}}$$

$$Q_{01} = \sqrt{\frac{\Sigma_i\, q_{1i}\, p_{0i}}{\Sigma_i\, q_{0i}\, p_{0i}} \times \frac{\Sigma_i\, q_{1i}\, p_{1i}}{\Sigma_i\, q_{0i}\, p_{1i}}}$$

$$P_{01} \cdot Q_{01} = \sqrt{\frac{\Sigma_i\, p_{1i}\, q_{0i}}{\Sigma_i\, p_{0i}\, q_{0i}} \times \frac{\Sigma_i\, p_{1i}\, q_{1i}}{\Sigma_i\, p_{0i}\, q_{1i}} \times \frac{\Sigma_i\, q_{1i}\, p_{0i}}{\Sigma_i\, q_{0i}\, p_{0i}} \times \frac{\Sigma_i\, q_{1i}\, p_{1i}}{\Sigma_i\, q_{0i}\, p_{1i}}}$$

$$= \sqrt{\left(\frac{\Sigma_i\, p_{1i}\, q_{1i}}{\Sigma_i\, p_{0i}\, q_{0i}}\right)^2} = \frac{\Sigma_i\, p_{1i}\, q_{1i}}{\Sigma_i\, p_{0i}\, q_{0i}} = V_{01}$$

Therefore,

$$\frac{P_{01}\,Q_{01}}{V_{01}} = 1$$

This proves that Fisher's ideal formula satisfies the time reversal test.

Geometric cross of L and P as an ideal formula, was endorsed by **Pigou and Bowley, Fisher** called it superior not only on the grounds of formula error but due to the fact that it completely utilizes the information about prices and quantities collected for both, the current period and the base period. Fisher's ideal formula does not satisfy circular test as given below. Even then its superiority is not marred because of the fact that, hardly one or two uncommon formulae satisfy circular test.

Circular Test

In this test, time series data regarding prices and quantities are considered. The price index for each of the following year is calculated taking the preceding year as the base year. This process continues till we obtain the index for the first year (0 year), taking the last year (kth year) as the base year. Symbolically, we calculate P_{01}, P_{12}, P_{23}, ..., $P_{(k-1)k}$ and P_{k0}. If a formula stands the circular test, it must satisfy the condition

$$P_{01}\, P_{12}\, P_{23} \ldots P_{(k-1)k}\, P_{k0} = 1 \qquad \text{...(18.20)}$$

Formula (18.20) can also be written as,

$$P_{01}\, P_{12}\, P_{23} \ldots P_{(k-1)k} = P_{0k} \qquad \text{...(18.20.1)}$$

This formula will be proved under the chain base method for index numbers.

Example **18.4.** The data regarding prices and quantities consumed for a few items other than food articles for the years 1960 and 1983, are presented in the table below. Cross product terms are also shown in the last four columns. Values of L and P are calculated and the verification of tests is left to the readers.

	1960		1983					
Items (i)	Price (p_0) per piece (ii)	Quantity (q_0) no. (iii)	Price (p_1) per piece (iv)	Quantity (q_1) no. (v)	p_0q_0 (ii) × (iii) (vi)	p_1q_o (iii) × (iv) (vii)	p_0q_1 (ii) × (v) (viii)	p_1q_1 (iv) × (v) (ix)
Shirts	4.75	272	28.00	342	1292.00	7616.00	1624.50	9576.00
Shoes	15.55	137	86.35	354	2130.35	11829.95	5504.70	30567.90
Chappals	5.46	224	26.12	415	1223.04	5850.88	2265.90	10839.80
Books	1.50	108	3.20	387	162.00	345.60	580.50	1238.40
Toys	0.25	349	0.75	612	87.25	261.75	153.00	459.00
Soap	1.06	460	7.79	890	487.60	3583.40	943.40	6933.10
Watches	80.00	53	244.00	62	4240.00	12932.00	4960.00	15128.00
Total					9622.24	42419.58	16032.00	74742.20

From the table,

$$\Sigma_i p_{0i}\, q_{0i} = 9622.24, \qquad \Sigma_i p_{1i}\, q_{0i} = 42419.58$$

$$\Sigma_i p_{0i}\, q_{1i} = 16032.00 \qquad \Sigma_i p_{1i}\, q_{1i} = 74742.20$$

$$L = \frac{\Sigma_i p_{1i}\, q_{0i}}{\Sigma_i p_{0i}\, q_{0i}} = \frac{42419.58}{9622.24} \times 100 = 440.85$$

$$P = \frac{\Sigma_i p_{1i}\, q_{1i}}{\Sigma_i p_{0i}\, q_{1i}} = \frac{74742.20}{16032.00} \times 100 = 466.21$$

Readers can easily verify that the geometric cross satisfies the time reversal test and the factor reversal test in case of the given data.

SAMPLING ERROR

The concept of sampling error originates from the fact that while calculating the index number, we are actually not including the total list of items (commodities) present in the two periods but only select a few of them, e.g., the total number of items is N and out of these N we include only n for the purpose of the calculation of index number. If the price index based on n items is p_{01}^{n} and for all N items is $p_{01}^{N}.(P_{01}^{n} - P_{01}^{N})$ called the sampling error of price index number. Similar expression can be given for the quantity index by using Q in place of P. In principle, this error may be reduced by selecting a random sample of n items out of N. In practice, we are generally including the items which are of vital importance rather than those which are of rare use. Hence, a purposive sample of individual items is often used. Instead, the standard sample of data for index number calculations is a stratified random sample from finite populations. Anyway, in practice, we should try to include as many items as possible for the collection of sample data. The complicated aspects of sampling errors are omitted.

HOMOGENEITY ERROR

The formula for calculating index numbers, clearly reveals that the index numbers are based only on binary articles or commodities. If the number of such commodities in the periods 1 and 0 is almost the same, index number will be a good index of change from period 0 to 1. But on the contrary, if the number of common articles between two periods is less, it will not give the correct picture. This situation mostly arises when there is a long gap between the current period and the base period. In this developing world, the articles which are in use are quickly replaced by new articles. For example, cotton clothes have been replaced by synthetic clothes, brass utensils and crockery mostly replaced by stainless steel and coal by cooking gas. In such a situation, the comparability of two periods becomes more difficult. *Hence, the error caused by considering only the binary articles omitting the unique articles, is termed as homogeneity error.* To know the extent of homogeneity, we give here a test known as R-test for homogeneity.

R-Test for Homogeneity

A real number R is defined as the ratio of the number of unique articles to the total number of articles in both the periods 0 and 1. If N_0 and N_1 are the numbers of articles in the base period and the current period respectively, and N_{01} is the number of articles common to both the periods, the value,

$$R = \frac{N_0 + N_1 - 2N_{01}}{N_0 + N_1} \qquad \text{...(18.21)}$$

If all articles are present in both the periods, $N_0 + N_1 = 2\,N_{01}$ and thus $R = 0$. If there is no article common to both the periods, $N_{01} = 0$ and hence, $R = 1$. As the value of R approaches 0, there is less and less homogeneity error and as the value of R approaches 1, we conclude that there is a high degree of homogeneity error. Homogeneity error can be reduced by choosing the base year, not too far, from the given period.

Besides the three errors discussed so far, there are chances of some other error also. For instance, the prices and quantities are not obtained from the fixed sources. The data do not exactly pertain to the period of reference, but such errors can be minimized by utilizing the service of trained and skilled personnel.

***Example* 18.5**. Given data,

$$N_0 = 15,\ N_1 = 19 \text{ and } N_{01} = 12$$

The value of homogeneity error,

$$R = \frac{15+19-2\times 12}{15+19} = \frac{10}{34} = 0.29$$

The value of R is small, hence there is tolerable homogeneity error.

FIXED BASE METHOD

When we have a series of data for a number of years, with regard to prices and quantities consumed, produced or transacted, we often calculate index number for each year with respect to a fixed year. Such indices are termed as *fixed base indices.* Suppose we have a series of data for $(k + 1)$ years, say, 0, 1, 2, ..., k years. Taking 0 year as base year, we can calculate price index number P_{0j} by Laspeyre's formula, where $j = 1, 2, ..., k$. Elaborately,

$$P_{01} = \frac{\Sigma_i\, p_{1i}\, q_{0i}}{\Sigma_i\, p_{0i}\, q_{0i}} \times 100$$

$$P_{02} = \frac{\Sigma i\, p_{2i}\, q_{0i}}{\Sigma i\, p_{0i}\, q_{0i}} \times 100 \qquad ...(18.22)$$

$$\vdots$$

$$P_{0k} = \frac{\Sigma_i\, p_{ki}\, q_{0i}}{\Sigma_i\, p_{0i}\, q_{0i}} \times 100$$

for $i = 1, 2, 3, ..., n$ where n represents the number of commodities.

By this method, we are able to know the gradual price change in each subsequent year for the same base. The above indices are correct, provided it is possible to conform that these indices require constant weights. Such a situation is not called for particularly when k is large.

AVERAGE BASE METHOD

According to **Croxton** and **Cowden**, it is possible, that no one year is sufficiently normal to be a good base for comparison. Prices are always advancing or receding with the business cycle. Thus, in case of the unavailability of one suitable year as the base, the averages of prices of items taken over a number of years, are taken as a basis of comparison. Commonly four or five years average is considered suitable for the base. Some workers used this technique when the market rates varied at a fast rate.

CHAIN BASE METHOD

When calculating indices chain base method for a series of data, as considered in the preceding section, is necessary to obtain each link of the chain. Thus, we have to calculate indices, such as P_{01}, P_{12}, P_{23}, ..., $P_{(k-1)k}$, taking the preceding year to any year as base year. Thus, the individual links in the chain can be given by the formula,

$$P_{(j-1)j} = \frac{\Sigma_i P_{ji}\, q_{(j-1)i}}{\Sigma_i P_{(j-1)i} q_{(j-1)i}} \quad \text{...(18.23)}$$

$j = 1, 2, ..., k$
$i = 1, 2, ..., n$

Giving different values to j from 1 to k, we get the link relatives as follows:

$$\text{For} \quad j = 1, \quad P_{01} = \frac{\Sigma_i P_{1i}\, q_{0i}}{\Sigma_i P_{0i}\, q_{0i}}$$

$$j = 2, \quad P_{12} = \frac{\Sigma_i P_{2i}\, q_{1i}}{\Sigma_i P_{1i}\, q_{1i}} \quad \text{...(18.24)}$$

$$j = 3, \quad P_{23} = \frac{\Sigma_i P_{3i}\, q_{2i}}{\Sigma_i P_{2i}\, q_{2i}}$$

$$j = k, P_{(k-1)k} = \frac{\Sigma_i P_{ki}\, q_{(k-1)i}}{\Sigma_i P_{(k-1)i}\, q_{(k-1)i}}$$

The various terms of the series by chain base method can be obtained by the following relations:

$$\begin{aligned} P_{01} &= P_{01} \text{ as a first link} \\ P_{02} &= P_{01}\, P_{12} \\ P_{03} &= P_{01}\, P_{12}\, P_{23} = P_{02}\, P_{23} \\ P_{04} &= P_{01}\, P_{12}\, P_{23}\, P_{34} = P_{03}\, P_{34} \\ &\vdots \\ P_{0k} &= P_{01}\, P_{12}\, P_{23} \ldots P_{(k-1)k} = P_{0(k-1)}\, P_{(k-1)k} \end{aligned} \quad \text{...(18.25)}$$

To obtain the index numbers in percentages, each index should be multiplied by 100.

If we used fixed weights q_a, *i.e.*, the average quantities consumed, produced or supplied from base year to the last year of the series, the two types of indices namely, fixed based indices and chain base indices become equivalent. This phenomenon is shown here only for a three year series. If the readers want, they can extend it for a series consisting of any number of years. We write it here using Laspeyre's formula.

	Fixed base	*Chain base*
P_{01}	$\frac{\Sigma_i p_{1i}\, q_{ai}}{\Sigma_i p_{0i}\, q_{ai}}$	$\frac{\Sigma_i p_{1i}\, q_{ai}}{\Sigma_i p_{0i}\, q_{ai}}$
P_{02}	$\frac{\Sigma_i p_{2i}\, q_{ai}}{\Sigma_i p_{0i}\, q_{ai}}$	$\frac{\Sigma_i p_{1i}\, q_{ai}}{\Sigma_i p_{0i}\, q_{ai}} \times \frac{\Sigma_i p_{2i}\, q_{ai}}{\Sigma_i p_{1i}\, q_{ai}} = \frac{\Sigma_i p_{2i}\, q_{ai}}{\Sigma_i p_{0i}\, q_{ai}}$
P_{03}	$\frac{\Sigma_i p_{3i}\, q_{ai}}{\Sigma_i p_{0i}\, q_{ai}}$	$\frac{\Sigma_i p_{1i}\, q_{ai}}{\Sigma_i p_{0i}\, q_{ai}} \times \frac{\Sigma_i p_{2i}\, q_{ai}}{\Sigma_i p_{1i}\, q_{ai}} \times \frac{\Sigma_i p_{3i}\, q_{ai}}{\Sigma_i p_{2i}\, q_{ai}} = \frac{\Sigma_i p_{3i}\, q_{ai}}{\Sigma_i p_{0i}\, q_{ai}}$

The formula, given above having fixed weights, satisfy the circular test. For this reason, many workers who believed in circular test accepted a fixed weight approach. But **Fisher** said that a circular test is theoretically wrong. He condemned it totally on the grounds that such weights belong to none of the periods under consideration. But some researchers working on the index numbers accept the theory of fixed weight aggregative formula. Such a controversy is not yet over. In some situation, one may prove more correct than the other.

From (18.20), it is interesting to note that if we find out the fixed base indices for the years (periods) of the series, the index of individual links can easily be obtained by the chain base formulae.

$$P_{12} = \frac{P_{02}}{P_{01}} \times 100$$

$$P_{23} = \frac{P_{03}}{P_{02}} \times 100$$

and so on.

***Example* 18.6.** All India sale price index number for the manufactured products from 1976 to 1980 to the base year 1970 – 71 = 100, are given below.

Year:	1976	1977	1978	1979	1980
Index number:	171.7	179.4	177.9	203.5	248.6
P_{0j}:	P_{01}	P_{02}	P_{03}	P_{04}	P_{05}

The link relatives can be calculated as,

$$P_{12} = \frac{P_{02}}{P_{01}} \times 100 = \frac{179.4}{171.7} \times 100 = 104.48$$

$$P_{23} = \frac{P_{03}}{P_{02}} \times 100 = \frac{177.9}{179.4} \times 100 = 99.16$$

$$P_{34} = \frac{P_{04}}{P_{03}} \times 100 = \frac{203.5}{177.9} \times 100 = 114.39$$

$$P_{45} = \frac{P_{05}}{P_{04}} \times 100 = \frac{248.6}{203.5} \times 100 = 122.16$$

Comments

The advantage of the chain base index is that we are able to know the gradual changes of prices or quantity from period to period. Moreover, the number of binary commodities in consecutive periods is also large. The chain base index is superior to the fixed base index, due to the fact that the chain base formula includes prices and quantities for all the periods from 0 to k, except for the last period. On the other hand, the fixed base method includes data for the base year and the given year, neglecting the changes occurring in the intervening periods between 0 and k. **Walsh** had been a strong exponent of the chain base system.

Besides the good points given above, for the chain base system, it has many drawbacks too. Only the main drawbacks or lacunae are discussed here. The chain base index is tedious and laborious, in the sense that, it needs data for prices and quantities for all the periods, from the base period to the given period, except for quantities in the last period. To collect data for all the periods is a difficult and a costly affair. It involves the calculation of all link relatives, which is quite cumbersome job.

Chain base gradually drifts away from the fixed base and is thus subjected to a cumulative error. But this statement is valid only if we believe that the fixed base system is correct. The fixed base indices are easy to conceive as compared to the chain base indices. **Fisher** considered the chain base system of very little use or no use. Perhaps the controversy still persists. It is the individual's thinking and interpretation, on the basis of which one propounds it or discards it.

CONSUMER PRICE INDEX NUMBER (CPI)

Meaning

Until a few years back it was known as the *cost of living index.* The general price index does not reflect exactly the impact of price changes on the cost of living of different sections of the society. This is due to the fact that all people do not consume similar commodities and utilize similar services. For example, people belonging to the low and middle income groups do not buy unseasonal fruits and vegetables, butter and cheese etc. They do not use refrigerator, TV, cooler etc. Also neither they consult costly doctors for medical care. In short, while constructing CPI for a section of population, one should include only those items which are generally used and utilised. From this discussion it is amply clear that the price rise or fall of certain items will affect certain sections of society, whereas it will have no impact on the others. For instance, minuscule percentage of people are affected by the price rise of cars, paintings, etc. Therefore, to know how a particular population group is affected with the rise or fall in prices of certain items, it is necessary to construct consumer price index for different population groups separately.

The consumer price index is intended to measure the average percentage change in prices paid by the consumer, at different time periods, belonging to a group of population for which it is referred to. The group may be the average income class of people of a city or region, labourers of a factory or income tax payers in a city etc. The percentage change is measured on monthly basis with respect to a fixed base. The basic principle of calculating index remains the same as discussed earlier. Still some special considerations are to be made in the construction of CPI. The prominent step of all CPI is the determination of a list of articles and services which are commonly consumed and utilized by the referred group of persons. Such a list is known as the *basket of goods and services,* in short *basket.* The measurement of the prices of the basket of goods and services enables us to know the increased or the decreased burden on the consumer, through CPI, at a point of time, as compared to a fixed base period. If one has to spend Rs. 100 for a basket in 1960 and Rs 230 in 1970, it means that the cost has gone up by 130 per cent.

Here we would like to pinpoint the difference between the cost of living index and the consumer price index. The cost of living is affected by the standard of living *i.e.*, taste, changes in the quality of the commodities, the consumption, the services utilized, the prices etc. Whereas consumer price index measures only one aspect of the cost of living index, *i.e.*, the effect of price changes which has the maximum impact on the cost of living. Thus, for the clarity of their meaning, the government decided to change the name from *cost of living index* to *consumer price index.*

Uses

The consumer price index numbers are meant for various purposes. To name a few are (*i*) the regulation of the dearness allowance of employees to compensate for the rise in prices, (*ii*) to measure the purchasing power of the rupee (currency), (*iii*) the real income of a population group for which consumer price index is constructed, (*iv*) at government level these indices are used in determining economic policies, particularly regarding wages (pay scales), prices, taxation, house rent allowance etc., (*v*) it enables us to make long term comparison of the cost of living, at a particular time or place, in respect to any other time or place, for the same or similar class of society.

Defining the Purpose

The purpose of the indices should clearly be defined, since the consumer price index measures the effect of price changes over a time for the same set of commodities at the unchanged level of consumption. In this regard, it is necessary to clearly define the population group to which the index is to relate the base and the current periods. At present the government of India has been using 2002–03 as the base year.

Selection of Items

The consumption level and the pattern of the population group should be determined at a fixed period of time, which is taken as the base period for the calculation of index number. From this, the basket of goods and services is decided for inclusion in the index. The basket of goods and services broadly consists of the following items:

(*a*) *Food items*: Wheat, rice, pulses, milk, meat, edible oils, condiments and spices, sugar, tea, etc.

(*b*) *Tobacco, pan, supari and other intoxicants*: Cigarettes, chewing tobacco, katha, liquors, etc.

(*c*) *Fuel and light*: Electricity, kerosene, coke, firewood, coal, etc.

(*d*) *Services*: Medical, entertainment, transport, banker's charges, etc.

(*e*) *Miscellaneous*: Soap, hair oil, face cream, face power, utensils, crockery, etc.

The number of commodities and services included in the basket is about one hundred and ten. While including the commodities in the list, it will be necessary to specify the quality for each commodity by its brand, local name, grade as superior, medium or low, cloth by its fibre name or companies name, texture, etc. For example, rice of many varieties is available in the market and their rates vary largely. *Basmati* and *Hansraj* are costlier than *saila*. Once the quality or brand is described, the prices are accounted for those quality or brands of items only. As a general principle those items which are most popularly consumed by the population group are included in the basket and the prices for those specific items only are collected from the market.

Collection of Price Data

The important task is to organize the regular collection of price data for various commodities and services, included in the basket. The prices are collected from the base period to the current period of the index. Prices should be collected only from selected retailers, which are mostly patronised by the consumers of the population group. The prices are to be noted in the uniform units, e.g., commodities in rupees per kilogram, cloth in rupees per metre, services in rupees per month, match box per piece, etc. The prices are collected on fixed days of a month to represent the price trend for the whole month. The prices are to be collected for specified qualities as mentioned in the basket. Of course, for some items more than one quality or brand is included in the list of price collection. The whole process of collecting data is based on sampling and thus, in all these matters, selection is made on the basis of judgement after a close study of buying pattern and the consumption potential of the population group under consideration. In short, to measure pure price changes, it is necessary to keep the quality, shops, price collection days and time as fixed as possible.

Adjustment for Quality Changes

The aim is to keep the prices strictly comparable from one pricing period to another and the index should reflect pure price changes only. An important part is to guard the prices against the quality changes. For example, broken rice is much cheaper than whole rice of the same quality. Such an accuracy may be maintained by keeping the actual physical sample of various commodities, but so far this practice is not in vogue in India. Moreover, with the passage of time certain qualities or brands of items disappear from the market and new one replace them. In this situation, the practice is to collect prices for another variety or brand in the same quality range and that meets the same specifications. This procedure is known as a *substitution* and is mainly followed in case of textile because new synthetic fibres enter the market at short intervals. For some items, a listed variety totally disappears from the market. In such a situation, the price collector furnishes a price for a variety most popularly consumed at the time, which is adjusted properly to conform to the prescribed quality before it is used for calculation of index number. There are some accepted technical methods for such an adjustment but their details are not dealt with here.

Fixing of Weights for CPI

The use and importance of weights has already been discussed. Here, we shall discuss weights in reference to consumer price index. Weights are meant to account for the relative importance associated with the percentage of change in prices, paid by the consumer for the items of the basket. For example, the rise in the prices of wheat will affect the consumer more than the rise in the prices of cosmetics. The relative importance of price changes recorded for an item is termed as *weight.*

"The weight is nothing but the percentage of expenditure on each item of goods and services of the basket, in relation to the total expenditure." In the calculation of the index number, weights are assigned to each individual item of a group first and later to groups like food, clothing, housing, services etc. The whole structure of weights is known as *weighting diagram.*

The question that arises is how does one determine these weights for the CPI? They are obtained by making a *family budget enquiry.* A survey is conducted among a sample of families, selected from the population group under study. The data on the consumption pattern for a short period say, per month or per week, are collected from each selected family, by conducting a family budget enquiry. The whole enquiry is spread over one full year, in an appropriate manner, to account for the seasonal variations. Such an enquiry yields data on characteristics like size of the family and its composition, family income, expenditure incurred by the family members. The data so collected are arranged to yield the average budget of expenditure for all the items. This provides the necessary information for required weights, in terms of percentage expenditure, for items in each group and for the groups as well.

Selection of Base Period

Generally the base period for CPI is the year declared by the government. The weighting diagram is based on the family budget enquiry conducted in the declared base year. Sometimes, a base period of CPI is chosen, which is not far apart from the period of family budget enquiry, so that the weights obtained can be taken as the weights for the proposed base period. In practice, the weighting diagram, determined once, remains fixed for ten to fifteen years, depending on the life of a series, Here, it is assumed that the spending pattern of the families on various items remains the same for about 10 -15 years.

Imputation of Expenditure

In the basket, a limited number of items are included. But experience tells one that families do spend money on many items which are not included in the basket. Now the problem that arises is how does one adjust such expenditure in the calculation of CPI. The approach is simple. The weights of such expenditure are distributed (added) to the weights of items included in the basket, so that the total family budget is taken into account. For instance, the weights of curd and cheese are added to that of milk, weights of maize, jowar, bajra are added to that of cereal etc. This process of adjusting the weights is known as the *imputation of weights.*

Computation of CPI

The computation of CPI is based on Laspeyre's formula. There are two methods of computation as discussed below:

Weighted Aggregative Method. This method has already been dealt with while describing the calculation of the general price index by Laspeyre's method. We know that the formula for it is,

$$\text{(CPI) } P_{01} = \frac{\Sigma_i\, p_{1i}\, q_{0i}}{\Sigma_i\, p_{0i}\, q_{0i}} \times 100 \qquad \text{...(18.26)}$$

This method can be used when it is possible to give the weight in terms of quantities, for all items of the basket. But, we know that the quantity of weights cannot be determined for services, hence, the second method is in use. If the basket includes only consumable articles, this formula can be used which gives similar results as obtained by the second method.

Family Budget Method

By this method, the consumer price index is calculated in two steps. At the first step, all items are divided into broad groups like food, fuel, light, house rent, health care, medical fee, etc. For each item of a group, an average price is calculated in the base period as well as for the current period separately. The monthly average price is mostly based on a weekly price data. The ratio of the current price of an item to the average price of the same item during the base period expressed in percentage is calculated. This is called the price relative of an item. Symbolically, we calculate $p_{1i}/p_{0i} \times 100$. After price relative of each item is multiplied by its respective weight ω_i which is usually in terms of the percentage of expenditure, *i.e.*, we calculate the quantity $\left(\frac{p_{1i}}{p_{0i}} \times 100\right)\omega_i$. The sum of the products for all the items of a group, divided by the sum of the weights, $\Sigma_i \omega_i$, gives the consumer price index where i varies from 1 to n, the number of items in the group. The formula for the jth group index is,

$$G_{01}^{j} = \frac{\Sigma_i (p_{1ij} / p_{0ij} \times 100)\omega_{ij}}{\Sigma_i \omega_{ij}} \tag{18.27}$$

Note: If the prices for more than one variety of an item are collected, calculate the price relative for each variety exclusively. A simple average of these price relatives is taken as the price relative for that commodity.

As a second step, the group index numbers are multiplied by the respective group weights. The sum of these products divided by the sum of group weights, provides the consumer-price index number. Generally, the consumer price index is obtained on a monthly basis and is known as *general index* for the mid of that month. The formula for general CPI is,

$$P_{01} = \frac{\Sigma_j G_{01}^{j} \times \omega_j}{\Sigma_j \omega_j} \tag{18.28}$$

where j varies over all the groups.

Summary Remarks on CPI

As discussed earlier, the population group is constituted by a set of families. These families vary in size, income, likes and dislikes (for various items included in the basket), standard of living, consumption pattern etc. Hence, an index number should not be taken as to reflect on ones' own family budget alone but should be taken as the price change effects experienced, on an average, by each family of the population group. More elaborately, if the effect of price changes experienced by all the families of the population group are pooled and averaged. The average experience would be reflected by the consumer price index.

***Example* 18.7.** The price data for various items included in a basket for industrial workers, for September 1983 and 1960 as base year, alongwith the weights for each item, are presented in the table given below,

Items	*Weights*	*Unit*	*1960 Base prices*	*Sept. 1983 current prices*
(i)	*(ii)*	*(iii)*	*(iv)*	*(v)*
1. *Cereals & Products*				
(i) Rice	4.11	Per kg	0.93	4.71
(ii) Wheat	51.27	"	0.47	2.23
(iii) Atta	1.16	"	0.53	2.37
(iv) Bajra	3.63	"	0.43	1.70
(v) Barley	30.76	"	0.35	1.74
(vi) Gram	5.82	"	0.39	2.91
(vii) Grinding charges	3.25	"	0.03	0.15
Total	100.00			

2. *Pulses and Products*				
(*i*) Arhar dal	6.85	Per kg.	0.80	7.00
(*ii*) Gram dal	38.69	"	0.44	3.50
(*iii*) Moong dal	28.27	"	0.74	5.00
(*iv*) Masur dal	11.90	"	0.63	4.28
(*v*) Urad dal	14.29	"	0.69	5.97
Total	100.00			
3. *Oils and Fats*				
(*i*) Mustard oil	9.21	Per kg.	2.26	16.22
(*ii*) Gingelly oil	57.53	"	2.21	16.17
(*iii*) Vanaspati ghee	33.26	"	2.74	15.83
Total	100.00			
4. *Meat, Fish and Eggs*				
(*i*) Goat's meat	96.43	Per kg.	1.65	16.00
(*ii*) Fish	2.04	"	2.18	22.50
(*iii*) Eggs	1.53	"	0.17	0.58
Total	100.00	Each		
5. *Milk and Products*				
(*i*) Milk	51.44	Per litre	0.70	5.03
(*ii*) Curd	4.51	Per kg.	1.01	6.62
(*iii*) Desi ghee	44.05	"	6.19	39.61
Total	100.00			
6. *Other Foods*				
(*i*) Sugar	40.94	Per kg.	1.26	4.20
(*ii*) Gur	15.21	"	0.59	3.75
(*iii*) Tea (leaves)	10.23	"	7.20	35.54
(*iv*) Refreshment taken outside	8.33	Per head	1.61	14.42
(*v*) Jalebi	7.16	Per kg.	1.62	10.75
(*vi*) Tea (readymade)	18.13	Per cup	0.08	0.68
Total	100.00			
7. *Fuel and Light*				
(*i*) Firewood	57.70	Per 40 kg.	3.14	26.10
(*ii*) Coke	4.52	Per kg.	0.50	2.75
(*iii*) Kerosene oil	8.13	Per litre	0.37	1.99
(*iv*) Electricity charges	5.26	Per unit	0.37	0.46
(*v*) Cowdung cake	6.32	Per 100	0.63	5.25
(*vi*) Coal	12.78	Per 40 kg.	9.30	70.00
(*vii*) Match box	5.29	Each	0.05	0.25
Total	100.00			

8.	*Miscellaneous*				
	(*i*) Doctor's fee	1.03	Per visit	5.00	14.50
	(*ii*) Medicine	80.53	Per phial of 4 doses	1.12	2.00
	(*iii*) E.S.I. premium	18.44	Per head	0.50	0.50
	Total	100.00			
9.	*Transport and Communication*				
	(*i*) Railway fare	16.08	Per adult	1.09	3.70
	(*ii*) Bus fare	23.53	"	0.14	0.70
	(*iii*) Bicycle tyre	54.12	Each	6.28	19.41
	(*iv*) Postage	6.27	Per card	0.05	0.15
	Total	100.00			

CPI from the given data can be calculated in the following manner.

First the index for each group is calculated by formula (18.27).

1. For cereals and products group,

$$G_{01}^{1} = \frac{1}{100}\left\{\frac{4.71}{0.93}\times 4.11+\frac{2.23}{0.47}\times 51.27+\frac{2.37}{0.53}\times 1.16+\frac{1.70}{0.43}\times 3.63\right.$$

$$\left.+\frac{1.74}{0.35}\times 30.76+\frac{2.91}{0.39}\times 5.82+\frac{0.15}{0.03}\times 3.25\right\}\times 100$$

[since $\Sigma_i \omega_{ij} = 100$]

$$G_{01}^{1} = 20.82 + 243.26 + 5.19 + 14.35 + 152.92 + 43.43 + 16.25$$

$$= 496.22$$

2. For pulses and products group,

$$G_{01}^{2} = \frac{1}{100}\left\{\frac{7.00}{0.80}\times 6.85+\frac{3.50}{0.44}\times 38.69+\frac{5.00}{0.74}\times 28.27\right.$$

$$\left.+\frac{4.28}{0.63}\times 11.90+\frac{5.97}{0.69}\times 14.29\right\}\times 100$$

$$= 59.94 + 307.76 + 191.01 + 80.84 + 123.64$$

$$= 763.19$$

3. For oils and fats group,

$$G_{01}^{3} = \frac{1}{100}\left\{\frac{16.22}{2.26}\times 9.21+\frac{16.17}{2.21}\times 57.53+\frac{15.83}{2.74}\times 33.26\right\}\times 100$$

$$= 66.10 + 420.93 + 192.16$$

$$= 679.19$$

4. For meat, fish and eggs group,

$$G_{01}^{4} = \frac{1}{100}\left\{\frac{16.00}{1.65}\times 96.43+\frac{22.50}{2.18}\times 2.04+\frac{0.58}{0.17}\times 1.53\right\}\times 100$$

$$= 935.08 + 21.06 + 5.22 = 961.36$$

5. For milk and its products group,

$$G_{01}^5 = \frac{1}{100}\left\{\frac{5.03}{0.70}\times 51.44 + \frac{6.62}{1.01}\times 4.51 + \frac{39.61}{6.19}\times 44.05\right\}\times 100$$

$$= 369.63 + 29.56 + 281.88 = 681.07$$

6. For other foods group,

$$G_{01}^6 = \frac{1}{100}\left\{\frac{4.20}{1.26}\times 40.94 + \frac{3.75}{0.59}\times 15.21 + \frac{35.54}{7.20}\times 10.23 + \frac{14.42}{1.61}\times 8.33 + \frac{10.75}{1.62}\times 7.16 + \frac{0.68}{0.08}\times 18.13\right\}\times 100$$

$$= 136.47 + 96.67 + 50.50 + 74.61 + 47.51 + 154.10$$

$$= 559.86$$

7. For fuel and light group,

$$G_{01}^7 = \frac{1}{100}\left\{\frac{26.10}{3.14}\times 57.70 + \frac{2.75}{0.50}\times 4.52 + \frac{1.99}{0.37}\times 8.13 + \frac{0.46}{0.37}\times 5.26 + \frac{5.25}{0.63}\times 6.32 + \frac{70.00}{9.30}\times 12.78 + \frac{0.25}{0.05}\times 5.29\right\}\times 100$$

$$= 479.61 + 24.86 + 43.73 + 6.54 + 52.67 + 96.19 + 26.45$$

$$= 730.05$$

8. For miscellaneous groups,

$$G_{01}^8 = \frac{1}{100}\left\{\frac{14.50}{5.00}\times 1.03 + \frac{2.00}{1.12}\times 80.53 + \frac{0.50}{0.50}\times 18.44\right\}\times 100$$

$$= 2.99 + 143.80 + 18.44 = 165.23$$

9. For transportation and communication group,

$$G_{01}^9 = \frac{1}{100}\left\{\frac{3.70}{1.09}\times 16.08 + \frac{0.70}{0.14}\times 23.53 + \frac{19.41}{6.28}\times 54.12 + \frac{0.15}{0.05}\times 6.27\right\}\times 100$$

$$= 54.58 + 117.65 + 167.27 + 18.81 = 358.31$$

The general consumers price index is calculated by formula (18.28). In the given example, each $\omega_j = 100$ for $j = 1, 2, ..., 9$.

Hence, $P_{01} = \frac{1}{9}\sum_{j=1}^{9} G_{01}^j$

$$= \frac{1}{9}\{496.22 + 763.19 + 679.19 + 961.36 + 681.07 + 559.86 + 730.05 + 165.23 + 358.31\}$$

$$= \frac{5394.48}{9} = 599 \text{ (rounded)}$$

PROBLEMS AND PRECAUTIONS IN THE CONSTRUCTION OF INDEX NUMBERS

Defining the Object

Before one starts working on the construction of index numbers, it is most important to clearly define the objective of index numbers. Otherwise, the whole labour of constructing indices may go waste, since no index number is an all purpose index. The primary requirement is to decide what we are going to measure and for what it is meant. All the successive steps involved in the construction of index numbers depend on the objective. For example, the population, base period, basket of goods, choice of formula etc.

Selection of Items

The items in the basket depend on the purpose of the index number and the class of population, *i.e.*, for whom it is meant. Hence, they should be selected accordingly.

Generally CPI does not take into account the quality improvement of the goods. But, in some countries an attempt is made to factor out the quality changes that can be detected in items considered for the calculation of CPI. For example, the cotton cloth is replaced by synthetic fibre clothes. Though the synthetic fibre clothes are costlier than the cotton clothes, they are liked because of their durability. Hence, the quality factor must be considered. It is extremely difficult to measure the worth of increased quality and make adjustments accordingly.

Selection of Base Period

Every index number calculation needs a base period which plays a very important role. Generally one should choose a base period with normal or average economic activity. It means that the base period should be devoid of abnormal conditions like war, drought, flood and earthquake etc. The idea of a normal year (period) was perhaps originated by Mitchell but such a condition is neither feasible nor required for the reasons given here. A formula that satisfies the time reversal test, uses each period 0 and 1 as a base period. This result does not require the normality condition in any way for either period 1 or 0.

Sometimes, the government declares the base year for CPI or gross national product (GNP). In this case, there is no option but to accept the declared year as the base year. The average base and the chain base methods do not stick to a particular base year. Thus, we conclude that the normality of a base period is only a desirable condition and not a necessary one.

Collection of Data

The rate of different articles should strictly be collected from fixed markets and centres. The data regarding the quantities or expenditure should be collected through the survey under strict surveillance.

Selection of Formula

The selection of formula and system depends on the purpose of the index number and the data at hand. The selection of formula should be made on the merits and demerits of the formulae which have already been discussed.

Selection of Weights

The importance of weights has already been discussed. On providing quantities consumed as weights to the prices, the index numbers are inflated or deflated. Generally, the price relatives are weighted by the respective values and thus this system of weighting is known as *value weighting.*

Explicit and Implicit Weights

Explicit weights are those which can be expressed with definiteness e.g., the quantities consumed or produced. In most of the studies, explicit weights are used. On the other hand when some items are to be given more weight as compared to the other, a number of varieties of a particular item according to its importance are included. Such a weighting system is known as implicit weighting system. For instance, if wheat is to be given three fold more importance than ghee, three varieties of wheat will have to be included in the list, in comparison to one brand of ghee. Nevertheless, such a weighting system is rarely used.

WHOLESALE PRICE INDEX (W.P.I.)

Wholesale price index gives an indication of price movements in all markets other than the retail markets. For a country, as a whole, or for a very large area, generally the wholesale price index is worked out. In this type of price index, the prices are collected from the wholesale dealers only. The method of construction of index number remains the same.

The wholesale price index and consumer price index are generally different. The reasons for this are, (*i*) a lag between the movement of the wholesale prices and the retail prices. The retail prices increase much faster than the wholesale prices. (*ii*) wholesale price index is based on different weighting system and has a different coverage than CPI. Of course both these indices do not reflect the same magnitude of price change, but they do reflect a similar pattern of price change.

TIME SERIES OF INDEX NUMBERS

When the indices in a time series are given, we often come across two types of problems.

1. How the base period of indices may be shifted to another base. This is known as the problem of *base shifting*.
2. How two series of indices covering different periods of time may be combined into a single series. This operation of linking the series is known as *splicing*.

Base Shifting

Often a series of indices is based on an old base year but is left to be meaningless now for a comparison. In this situation, it becomes necessary to shift the old base year to a more meaningful recent year. For this, a new series of indices has to be formed by shifting the old base year to the new base year. The operation of the base shifting can be carried out by two approaches as described below.

Recomputation Method

In this method, firstly the price relatives for all the current years are calculated a fresh, by taking the new base year values as 100. Then the average of these price relatives is calculated and this enables us to know the indices based on the new base. This method is hardly in use because it involves too much of labour.

Short-cut Method

This method is applicable only if the indices are obtained with the help of geometric mean. In this method, the indices on the original base are expressed as the percentage of the indices of the period to be adopted as the shift base (new base). The formula for calculating the index numbers to the shifted base is,

$$\text{New base index no.} = \frac{\text{Old index no. of current year}}{\text{Index no. of new base year}} \times 100 \qquad ...(18.29)$$

Example **18.8.** Given below are the all India wholesale general price index numbers from 1971 to 1980 to the fixed base 1970 – 71.

Year:	1971	1972	1973	1974	1975	1976	1977	1978	1979	1980
Index No:	105.0	113.0	131.6	169.2	175.8	172.4	185.4	185.0	206.2	246.8

From the given indices, the index numbers to the new base 1975 are calculated by formula (18.29) as shown in the following table.

Year	*Index no.*	*Index number with base 1975*
1971	105.0	$\frac{105.0}{175.8} \times 100 = 59.73$
1972	113.0	$\frac{113.0}{175.8} \times 100 = 64.28$
1973	131.6	$\frac{131.6}{175.8} \times 100 = 74.86$
1974	169.2	$\frac{169.2}{175.8} \times 100 = 96.24$
1975	175.8	$\frac{175.8}{175.8} \times 100 = 100.00$
1976	172.4	$\frac{172.4}{175.8} \times 100 = 98.06$
1977	185.4	$\frac{185.4}{175.8} \times 100 = 105.46$
1978	185.0	$\frac{185.0}{175.8} \times 100 = 105.23$
1979	206.2	$\frac{206.2}{175.8} \times 100 = 117.29$
1980	246.8	$\frac{246.8}{175.8} \times 100 = 140.39$

The figures in the last column show index numbers to the new base 1975.

Splicing

The problem of linking two series of indices arises, when a new series is based on a new base period and the old series is stopped. This new series of price indices is released when there is a major change in quantity weights. The new base period is always the last year of the old series. But, the indices are still required with the base of the old series. If this is not done, the two series are not comparable. Hence to make them comparable, splicing is done. Combining of the two series of indices can be carried through the following formula.

$$\text{Spliced index no.} = \frac{\dfrac{\text{Index no. of the given year} \times \text{Old index no. of new base year}}{100}}{} \qquad ...(18.30)$$

By the above formula, the indices based on the new base year are shifted to the old base year. Splicing is also a sort of base shifting. The major difference between the base shifting and splicing is that, in base shifting all the given indices are based to the same base year. While in splicing, there are two series of indices on two different base years and the indices are converted to one base year as required.

***Example* 18.9.** The following table contains two series of index numbers for labourers. The first series of index numbers is from 1966 to 1971 with base 1960. Second series of indices is from 1971 to 1980 with base 1971.

Series-II index numbers with base 1971 are spliced to series-I index numbers with the base 1960. Spliced index numbers are calculated from formula (18.30) and are shown in the last column of the following table along with their calculations.

Year (i)	*Index nos. with base 1960 series-I (ii)*	*Index nos. with base 1971 series-II (iii)*	*Index nos. spliced to the base 1960 (iv)*
1966	155		
1967	180		
1968	175		
1969	181		
1970	188		
1971	188	100	$\frac{188 \times 100}{100} = 188$
1972		113	$\frac{188 \times 113}{100} = 212$
1973		124	$\frac{188 \times 124}{100} = 233$
1974		126	$\frac{188 \times 126}{100} = 237$
1975		159	$\frac{188 \times 159}{100} = 299$
1976		168	$\frac{188 \times 168}{100} = 316$
1977		175	$\frac{188 \times 175}{100} = 329$
1978		196	$\frac{188 \times 196}{100} = 368$
1979		253	$\frac{188 \times 253}{100} = 476$
1980		276	$\frac{188 \times 276}{100} = 519$

The index numbers of the first series are well comparable with the spliced index numbers for the second series given in the last column of the above table.

DEFLATION OF INDEX NUMBERS

The money value of our earnings, changes according to the rise or fall in prices of commodities and services. Hence, one would like to know his real earning at any point of time. This can be achieved by making use of the following formulae.

$$\text{Real wage} = \frac{\text{Money wage (Income of the current year)}}{\text{Price index number of the current year}} \times 100 \qquad (18.31)$$

$$\text{Money income index no.} = \frac{\text{Real wage}}{\text{Income of base year}} \times 100 \qquad (18.32)$$

$$\text{Real income index no.} = \frac{\text{Money income index no.}}{\text{CPI number}} \times 100 \qquad (18.33)$$

The application of these three formulae for deflating index numbers has been shown through the following example.

***Example* 18.10.** The annual income of an executive from 1975 to 1980 and consumer price index to the base 1975 were as follows:

Year	:	1975	1976	1977	1978	1979	1980
Income (Rs.)	:	12025	12260	15520	15910	17556	17866
CPI No.	:	100	98	105	105	117	140

The index numbers and the changes in real income of the executive by formulae (18.31) through (18.33) are presented in the table below.

Year (*i*)	*Income (Rs.)* (*ii*)	*Index no.* (*iii*)	*Real wage* (*iv*)	*Money income index no.* (*v*)	*Real income index no.* (*vi*)
1975	12025	100	$\frac{12025}{100}\times100=12025$	$\frac{12025}{12025}\times100=100.0$	$\frac{100.0}{100}\times100=100$
1976	12260	98	$\frac{12260}{98}\times100=12510$	$\frac{12510}{12025}\times100=104.0$	$\frac{104.0}{98}\times100=106$
1977	15520	105	$\frac{15520}{105}\times100=14781$	$\frac{14781}{12025}\times100=122.9$	$\frac{122.9}{105}\times100=117$
1978	15910	105	$\frac{15910}{105}\times100=15152$	$\frac{15152}{12025}\times100=126.0$	$\frac{126.0}{105}\times100=120$
1979	17556	117	$\frac{17556}{117}\times100=15005$	$\frac{15005}{12025}\times100=124.8$	$\frac{124.8}{117}\times100=107$
1980	17866	140	$\frac{17866}{140}\times100=12761$	$\frac{12761}{12025}\times100=106.1$	$\frac{106.1}{140}\times100=76$

The real income index numbers in column (*vi*) reveal that the real income has been increasing from 1975 to 1978 but has considerably reduced in 1979 and it further declined sharply, in 1980, in spite of the fact that the annual income consistently registered an increase from 1975 to 1980.

GROSS NATIONAL PRODUCT (GNP)

The gross national product at the factor cost is the value at factor cost of the product attributable to the factors of production, supplied by the normal residents of the country, prior to the deduction of the consumption of capital. It is equal to the gross domestic product at the factor cost plus the net factor income from abroad.

The gross national product is the basic measure of economic growth. This enables one to determine how much the physical goods and services have grown over time, where the increase in value of goods and services, due to rise in prices, should be eliminated. If this is not done, there will be a fall in quantity of goods and services and the inflation will cause the GNP to rise merely due to the rise in prices. Hence, to determine the real economic growth we may use the price index to deflate the GNP values.

To isolate changes in real GNP, the effect of rising prices may be eliminated, by transforming the actual value in terms of rupees (in terms of currency of a country) into their equivalent for the current year. This is achieved by dividing the original GNP for the year by an adjustment factor, known as deflator index number. The details are omitted.

NET NATIONAL PRODUCT (NNP)

It is the value of the product, at the factor cost, attributable to the factors of production supplied by the normal residents of the country, after the deduction of the consumption of fixed capital.

INDEX FOR INDUSTRIAL PRODUCTION (IIP)

It measures changes in the manufacturing output and is a weighted average of quantity relative indices. For this, we have to collect data about production in the base year and the current year for various industrial items, alongwith information about suitable weights (generally the prices). The data include the production of private as well as public sectors.

The formula for calculating index number for industrial production for the current year 1, to the year 0 is,

$$IIP_{01} = \frac{\Sigma_i \left(\dfrac{q_{1i}}{q_{0i}}\right)\omega_i}{\Sigma_i \omega_i} \times 100 \qquad \text{...(18.34)}$$

where i varies over all items of industrial production.

Formula (18.34) is similar to (18.10).

The index of industrial production throws lights on the development of a country and also the availability of industrial goods for use.

DEVELOPMENTS ABOUT CPI

As per the recommendations of the International Labour Organisation (ILO), the family income and expenditure survey should be conducted at fixed intervals, generally, of not more than ten years in order to revise the base and weighting diagrams of CPI. The 25th session of the Indian Labour Conference held in 1968, also made the same recommendations. The Index Review Committee known as the Rath Committee, had also recommended that fresh family income and expenditure survey should be conducted in 1981–82. A survey was conducted in 1971 and a new series of CPI was to be released, but due to certain reasons it is was abandoned.

Keeping in view the ILO recommendation vis-a-vis Rath Committee, a survey had been planned to derive new weighting diagrams, for the compilation of a new series of CPI numbers for individual centres as well as an average all India Index and the basis of new consumption system. On recommendations of the Rath Committee, it is to cover the following seven employments, namely, (*i*) Factories, (*ii*) Mines, (*iii*) Plantations, (*iv*) Railways, (*v*) Motor transport undertakings, (*vi*) Electricity undertakings (*vii*) Ports and Decks, during the proposed survey. In the survey conducted during 1958–59 and 1971 only the first three employments were covered. In 1981–82 survey, 45300 working class families were proposed to be interviewed at 70 centres all over the country. In addition, another 3000 families were covered at the additional 6 centres. Care had been taken that sample size is not reduced at any centre. A number of centres had been allocated to different states on prorata basis, according to the number of industrial workers belonging to 7 employments in each state. The survey at additional six centres had been integrated with the all India survey at 70 centres.

The survey was conducted during 1981–82. The National Sample Survey Organization (NSSO) had been responsible for conducting the field work of the survey, on behalf of the Labour Bureau. The survey relating to the collection of retail prices, had however been the responsibility of the Labour Bureau. The schedules for the price collection had been prepared in consultation with the representatives of the employers, employees and the government. The schedule for the family budget survey had been the same as for earlier surveys in 1958–59 and 1971.

At present the calendar year 2002–03 is taken, as the base year for the compilation of a new series of CPI which would eventually replace the existing Labour Bureau series of CPI, relating to industrial workers. This pattern of construction of CPI is followed in many countries.

CONCLUDING REMARKS

Index numbers are the best indicators of economic status of an individual, a group or section of people, agricultural production and industrial production of a country and the world as a whole. Because of its importance, weekly, monthly, quarterly and yearly index numbers are published regularly by various agencies and organizations in the form of bulletins and reports. Main organizations which publish index numbers are:

1. Ministry of Food and Agriculture.
2. Reserve Bank of India.
3. Food and Agricultural Organization.
4. Central Statistical Organization.
5. Department of Commercial Intelligence and Statistics.
6. Labour Bureau.

QUESTIONS AND EXERCISES

1. Define and discuss index numbers and give their uses.
2. Discuss the merits and demerits of Laspeyre's and Paasche's formulae.
3. Why is weighting so important in the construction of index numbers?
4. Why is the geometric cross L and P considered an ideal formula?

5. Write short notes on:
   (a) Time reversal test.
   (b) Factor reversal test.
   (c) Homogeneity error.
   (d) R-test of homogeneity.
   (e) Deflating of index numbers.
6. Establish the relationship between the fixed base and the chain base index numbers.
7. Why is the consumer price index so important in the economy of a country?
8. Give the chain base method of constructing a price index number.
9. What information is gathered through quantity index numbers?
10. Give various steps involved in the construction of consumer price index.
11. Differentiate between the following:
    (a) Cost of living index and consumer price index.
    (b) Base shifting and splicing.
    (c) Wholesale index number and consumers price index number.
    (d) Gross national product and net national product.
    (e) Chain base and fixed base methods.
12. Write whether the following statements are correct or not. Also justify your answer in a line or two.
    (a) Index numbers can be negative.
    (b) Index number cannot be less than 100.
    (c) L and P yield the same index numbers.
    (d) The chain base method is more difficult than the fixed base method.
    (e) The circular test is a good test.
13. Discuss the problem of (a) the choice of the base period, (b) the selection of weights, (c) the selection of items.
14. The following are the group index numbers and the group weights of monthly index of industrial production.

Groups	*Weight*	*Index no.*
Mill products	16	148
Sugar	16	40
Food	21	129
Metal products	26	111
Electricity	18	200
Scientific equipment	3	194

Construct the general index of industrial production.

15. Construct an index of prices for 1982 to the base of 1975 from the following data.

Commodity	*1975*		*1982*
	Price	*Quantity*	*Price*
Wheat	1.57 (per kg)	58 (kg)	1.94 (per kg)
Urad dal	3.17 (per kg)	5 (kg)	4.45 (per kg)
Milk	1.80 (per litre)	30 (litres)	3.00 (per litre)
Onion	0.50 (per kg)	15 (kg)	0.75 (per kg)
Sugar	4.00 (per kg)	6 (kg)	4.70 (per kg)
Tea leaf	17.00 (per kg)	0.5 (kg)	22.00 (per kg)
Kerosene oil	1.12 (per litre)	20 (litres)	1.85 (per litre)

16. From the following fixed base index numbers for fuel and light group from 1965 to 1976, for the month of April of each year, calculate the index numbers to the base of 1970.

Years	:	1965	1966	1967	1968	1969	1970
Index Nos.	:	125	131	139	161	177	187
Years	:	1971	1972	1973	1974	1975	1976
Index Nos.	:	184	193	199	275	293	321

17. The following table gives the data, pertaining to the prices of different commodities, groupwise, along with the weights of each commodity for March 72 and March 82.

	Group	*Weights*	*Unit*	*Price March 72 Rs.*	*Price March 82 Rs.*
(*a*)	*Cereals*				
	Wheat	55.5	Per kg	1.28	1.95
	Bajra	4.8	"	0.75	2.00
	Gram	7.2	"	1.10	3.00
	Barley	32.5	"	0.70	1.45
(*b*)	*Pulses*				
	Arhar dal	6.8	Per kg	1.98	5.00
	Moong dal	28.3	"	2.00	4.60
	Masur dal	11.9	"	2.12	4.10
	Gram dal	38.7	"	1.30	3.50
	Urad dal	14.3	"	2.40	4.45
(*c*)	*Oils and Fats*				
	Mustard oil	25.6	Per kg	5.40	14.25
	Vanaspati ghee	74.4	"	5.45	15.40
(*d*)	*Fuel and Light*				
	Coke	10.5	Per kg	0.25	1.60
	Kerosene	18.6	Per litre	0.66	1.85
	Electricity charges	14.5	Per unit	0.43	0.46
	Firewood	56.4	Per quintal	25.40	65.50
(*e*)	*Education and Recreation*				
	School fee	47.1	Each kid	1.50	5.50
	Books	14.7	"	2.75	3.20
	Copies	8.4	"	0.45	0.75
	Newspaper	1.2	"	0.25	0.50
	Cinema	28.6	Per head	1.10	3.20

Construct consumer price index for each group and the general consumer price index for 1982 to the base 1972.

18. Given the fixed base index numbers of the cost of building construction, prepare the chain base index numbers.

Years :	1991	1992	1993	1994	1995	1996	1997
Index Nos. :	100	109.8	117.8	128.2	143.0	150.5	159.6

19. The following table gives two series of index numbers.

Years	*Index no. base = 1967*	*Index no.base = 1971*
1968	101.5	
1969	104.5	
1970	86.4	
1971	95.5	100
1972		113
1973		150
1974		188
1975		180
1976		149
1977		167

Make the two series comparable by changing the index numbers to the same base.

20. The following table gives annual wages of agricultural labourers from 1961 to 1968.

Years :	1961	1962	1963	1964	1965	1966	1967	1968
Annual Income (Rs.) :	1440	1560	1600	1880	2000	2050	2100	2150
Index Nos. :	100	101	103	132	140	167	173	182

Compute the index numbers of real wages and give your comments.

21. Calculate the Laspeyre's and Paasche's index numbers from the following data.

	Base year		*Current year*	
	Quantity (lbs)	*Price (Rs/lbs)*	*Quantity (lbs)*	*Price (Rs/lbs)*
Bread	6	40 Paise	7	30 Paise
Meat	4	45 Paise	5	50 Paise
Tea	0.5	90 Paise	1.5	40 Paise

(*B.Com., Delhi, 1969*)

22.(*a*) Explain the fixed base index numbers and the chain base index numbers with examples.

(*b*) From the fixed base index numbers given below, prepare chain base index numbers.

Years :	1955	1956	1957	1958	1959	1960
Index numbers :	188	196	204	190	196	200

(*B.Com., Agra, 1969*)

23. For the following data, calculate index number by Fisher's formula.

Commodity	*Base year quantity*	*Base year price*	*Current year quantity*	*Current year price*
A	12	10	15	12
B	15	07	20	05
C	24	05	20	09
D	05	16	05	14

(*M.A. (Econ.), Agra 1983*)

24. In the working class consumer price index number in a particular town, the weight corresponding to the different groups of items are as follows:
Food 55, Fuel 15, Clothing 10, Rent 8 and Miscellaneous 12.
In October 1972, the dearness allowance was fixed by a mill of that town at 182% of the worker's wage which fully compensated for the rise in the prices of food and rent, but did not for anything else. Another mill of the same town paid dearness allowance of 46.5%, which compensated rise in fuel and miscellaneous group. It is known that rise in food is double that of fuel and miscellaneous double that of rent. Find the rise in food, fuel, rent and miscellaneous groups. *(M.Com., Delhi, 1973)*

25. Calculate the cost of living index from the following data.

Item	*Quantity consumed per year in the given year*	*Price per unit in rupees*	
		Base year	*Given year*
Rice	$2\frac{1}{2}$ qntl. × 12	12	25
Pulses	3 kg × 12	4	6
Oil	2 kg × 12	1.5	2.2
Clothing	6 meters × 12	0.75	1.0
Housing	—	20 per month	30 per month
Miscellaneous	—	10 per month	15 per month

(I.C.W.A., 1972)

26. Construct cost of living index number for the following data:

Items	*Weights*	*Price relatives*
A	55	140
B	30	120
C	12	130
D	3	110

(B.Com. I Yr., Andhra, 1989)

27. Calculate Fisher's Ideal Index from the following data:

Commodity	*Base year 1982*		*Current year 1987*	
	Price (Rs.)	*Quantity (Qtls.)*	*Price (Rs.)*	*Quantity (Qtls.)*
A	10	13	14	15
B	15	18	22	24
C	12	15	15	18
D	8	11	10	15
E	6	19	9	19

(B.Com. I yr. Andhra, 1988)

28. Describe the method of construction of Index Numbers for wholesale prices and cost of living Index Numbers in India.(*M.Sc. Descriptive & Industrial Statistics, Andhra, 1985*)

29. If the ratio between Laspeyre's index number and Paasche's index number is 28 : 27, find the missing figure in the following table:

Commodity	*Base year*		*Current year*	
	Price	*Quantity*	*Price*	*Quantity*
x	1	10	2	5
y	1	5	—	2

30 Prepare price index number for 1980 with 1971 as base year from the following data by using (*i*) Laspeyre's, (*ii*) Paasche's and (*iii*) Fisher's method (correct upto-4 places of decimal).

Year	*Article*							
	I		*II*		*III*		*IV*	
	P	*Q*	*P*	*Q*	*P*	*Q*	*P*	*Q*
1971	12.50	9	9.63	4	7.75	6	5.00	5
1980	12.75	9	7.75	6	8.80	10	6.50	7

(P: Price; Q: Quantity)

With the help of above data prove that the Time Reversal test is satisfied by Fisher's formula, but not necessarily by the Laspeyre's and Paasche's index number.

(*I.C.W.A. June, 1989*)

31. During a certain period the cost of living index goes up from 110 to 200 and the salary of a worker is also raised from Rs 330 to 500. Does he really gain, and if so, by how much in real terms? (*I.C.W.A. (Inter), Dec., 1992*)

32. Compute Fisher's ideal index and verify that it satisfies the Factor Reversal test with the help of the following data:

	Item					
	A		B		C	
	P	*Q*	*P*	*Q*	*P*	*Q*
1970	40	50	30	10	40	5
1980	100	40	80	8	40	4

(P: Price in Rs per kg; Q: Quantity in kg) (*I.C.W.A. (Inter), June, 1992*)

33. The following data show the prices and the quantities of four commodities in the base and current years:

Commodity	*Base year*		*Current year*	
	Price	*Quantity*	*Price*	*Quantity*
A	10	40	12	50
B	12	25	15	20
C	15	10	20	12
D	20	5	30	2

Using the above data, check whether Fisher's Ideal Index satisfies the Time Reversal and Factor Reversal Tests. *(C.A. (Inter) Nov. 1993)*

34. From the table given below, construct Fisher's ideal index and show that it satisfies time reversal and factor reversal tests.

	Articles			
	I	*II*	*III*	*IV*
Price in 1991	12.5	9.63	7.75	5.00
Qty. in 1991	9	4	6	5
Price in 1992	12.75	7.75	8.80	6.5
Qty. in 1992	9	6	10	7

(M.B.A, Part-I, MLSU, Udaipur, 2001)

35. Calculate the index number of prices for 1995 on the basis of 1990 from the data given below:

Commodity	*Weight*	*Price/unit (Rs.)*	
		1990	*1995*
A	40	16	20
B	25	40	50
C	20	12	15
D	15	2	3

If the weights of commodities A, B, C, D are increased in the ratio 1 : 2 : 3 : 4, then what will be the increase/decrease in the index number?

[I.C.W.A., Inter (Revised), June, 2004]

36. Compute Fisher's ideal index from the following data :

Commodities	*Base year*		*Current year*	
	Price	*Quantity*	*Price*	*Quantity*
A	5	2	8	1
B	6	3	8	3
C	8	1	11	1
D	3	2	3	4

Show, how it satisfies the time and factor reversal tests. *(C.A., P.E.-I, Nov. 2003)*

37. The following table gives the index numbers for different groups with their respective weights for the year 2000 (Base year 1995).

Group	*Group index number*	*Weights*
Food	130	60
Clothing	280	5
Lighting and fuel	190	7
Rent	300	9
Miscellaneous	200	19

(*i*) Find out the overall cost of living index number for the year 2000.

(*ii*) Suppose a person was earning Rs 1500 per month in 1995. What should be his salary in 2000, if his standard of living in that year to be the same as in 1995?

(*I.C.W.A., Inter, Dec., 2003*)

38. From the data given below, construct Laspeyre's and Paasche's index numbers:

	Base year		*Current year*	
Commodities	*Price*	*Expenditure*	*Price*	*Expenditure*
A	2	40	5	75
B	4	16	8	40
C	1	10	2	24
D	5	25	10	60

(*C.A., P.E.-I, May, 2004*)

SUGGESTED READING

Batra, J. and Arthur Vogt (2001). *The Making of Tests for Index Numbers*, Springer.

Berenson, M.L. and Levine, D.M. (1979). *Basic Business Statistics,* Prentice Hall, Englewood Cliffs.

Cheng Few Lee, John C. Lee and Alice C. Lee (1998). *Statistics for Business and Financial Economics*, World Scientific.

Chow, Ya Lun (1975). *Statistical Analysis with Business and Economic Applications,* Holt, Rinehart and Winston, New York.

Enns, P.G. (1985). *Business Statistics,* Richard D. Irwin, Illinois.

Jessica M. Utts (2004). *Seeing Through Statistics*, Thomson Brooks/Cole.

Louise J. Clark (1995). *Essentials of Business Statistics II, Research and Education Associates.*

Moya McCloskey (2002). *Business Statistics*, Oxford University Press.

Richards, L.E. and Lacava, J.J. (1978). *Business Statistics,* McGraw-Hill Book Company, New York.

Ronald L. Moy (2000). *Study Guide for Statistics for Business and Financial Economics,* World Scientific.

19 Chapter

Interpolation and Extrapolation

We often come across a series of data consisting of values of a variable, Y, corresponding to some other variable, X. In general, we may say that Y is a function of X. For any pair (x, y), $y = f(x)$.The variable y is said to be a function of x because, for any value of x, we can always find a definite value of y, e.g., $y = f(x) = x^2$; $y = f(x) = a + bx + cx^2$ or $y = f(x) = ae^x$, etc. The series of data in Y will generally emerge for different values of X which occur at certain intervals within some assigned range or period. But we often need to know the value of Y corresponding to a value of X which is not existing in the given series. This type of problem has already been dealt with under the regression technique. Analysis of time series data, is also helpful in determining an intermediate value of a given time series. But in this chapter, we shall be discussing another technique, which is known as *Interpolation* and *Extrapolation*. This technique is a part of numerical analysis and has been extremely useful for estimating a value of the dependent variable Y, corresponding to a given value of the independent variable X. The values of the independent variable are usually called *arguments*.

If the value of y is estimated for a given value of x which lies within its given range of values, it is known as *interpolation*, and if y is estimated for a given value of x which lies outside the existing range of given values of x, it is known as *extrapolation*. The estimated value of y for a given value of x is generally denoted by y_x. Consider a well-known example of population census. Population census in India takes place at ten years interval. The years of census are 1911, 1921, 1931, 1941, 1951, 1961 1971, 1981, 1991 and 2001. If the population is to be estimated for any year between the two census years, e.g., the population is to be estimated for the year 1975, it is an interpolation problem. But in case, the population is to be estimated for a year before 1911 and after 2001, e.g., let the population be estimated for the year 1908 or for 2008, it is an extrapolation problem. In a statistical table for some distribution, quantities (per cent points) are given corresponding to various degrees of freedom. But often, we need to know the value of the percentage point corresponding to some specific degrees of freedom, lying between two given values of degrees of freedom. The value of the percentage point for the required degrees of freedom can be estimated with the help of interpolation. In a logarithm table, sometimes a logarithmic value is not available for a certain number. But it can be estimated with the help of interpolation. It has already been given in Chapter 3, how the value of median and mode are obtained by the method of interpolation in case of a grouped data. Besides these, there are many other situations as well where interpolation and extrapolation are required.

ASSUMPTIONS AND ACCURACY

All the methods of interpolation and extrapolation are based on certain assumptions, which are, (i) no violent fluctuations occur within the series of data. It means that the values of Y, corresponding to the values of X, increase or decrease regularly. Thus, a continuity is maintained without any sudden change, (*ii*) the change in one variable corresponding to the other is governed by certain rules. Often two variables are assumed to be connected by a polynomial relationship. Most of the interpolation formulae are based on the assumption that Y is a polynomial function of X with a fair degree of accuracy.

The methods given in the body of this chapter are based on the above assumptions. But, it is always doubtful whether these assumptions are absolutely true. The departure from these assumptions will lead to faulty and inaccurate estimates. Hence, it would be a folly to expect an absolute accuracy. Moreover, the estimates are never the actual values. Instead, they are always subjected to a certain amount of error. The less the error, the better it is. The accuracy of the estimates can be adjudged by inspecting the fluctuations occurring in the series of data. The events connected with the referred period of the series also throw light on the accuracy of the results. As, in the example of the census data from 1911 to 2001, the comparison of the population of the pre-independence period and the post-independence period is meaningless. Because, the dimension of the post-independent India is not the same as that of India before independence. The population pattern has also changed. Hence, for the population of present India, 1951 census is the first census. However, all the census years are to be considered, and adjustments should be made in the pre-independence population of India.

Interpolation is more frequently used as compared to extrapolation. Therefore, most of the methods applicable for interpolation and extrapolation are discussed for interpolation only. But the same method, if applicable, can be used for extrapolation too. Wherever necessary, extrapolation is also discussed. This has been done for brevity.

METHODS OF INTERPOLATION

The methods are classified into two types:

(1) Graphic method.

(2) Algebraic methods.

Graphic Method

In this method, the given paired values (x, y) are plotted on the graph paper. It has already been discussed in chapter 2 that the independent variable must be taken on the X-axis (abscissa) and the dependent variable on the Y-axis (ordinate). The plotted points are joined by straight line(s), then the graph is smoothened. Now, to estimate a value of Y for a given value of X, locate the given point on the X-axis and draw a line parallel to the axis of Y so that it cuts the smoothened graph. From the point of intersection, draw a line parallel to the axis of X towards the left so that it touches the Y-axis. The reading of this point on the vertical scale gives the estimated value of Y corresponding to a given value of X.

For extrapolation, the plotted straight line or curve may be extended and the value of Y for the given value of X may be estimated.

The Graphic method gives a rough estimate as the smoothening of the plotted graph can be done in a way desired by the person and is not exact. The estimate becomes quite accurate if the plotted points lie in a straight line.

***Example* 19.1.** The following table gives the value of output of the natural fibres other than cotton, jute and mesta for the years 1974-75 to 1980-81. But the figure for 1977-78 has been missing in the table. The missing value by the graphical method can be estimated in the following manner.

Years:	1974-75	1975-76	1976-77	1977-78	1978-79	1979-80	1980-81
Value of output (Rs. lacs):	128	168	177	?	252	423	453

From the graph, it is clear that the point P has its Y-coordinate as 215. Hence, the estimated value of output is Rs 215 lac.

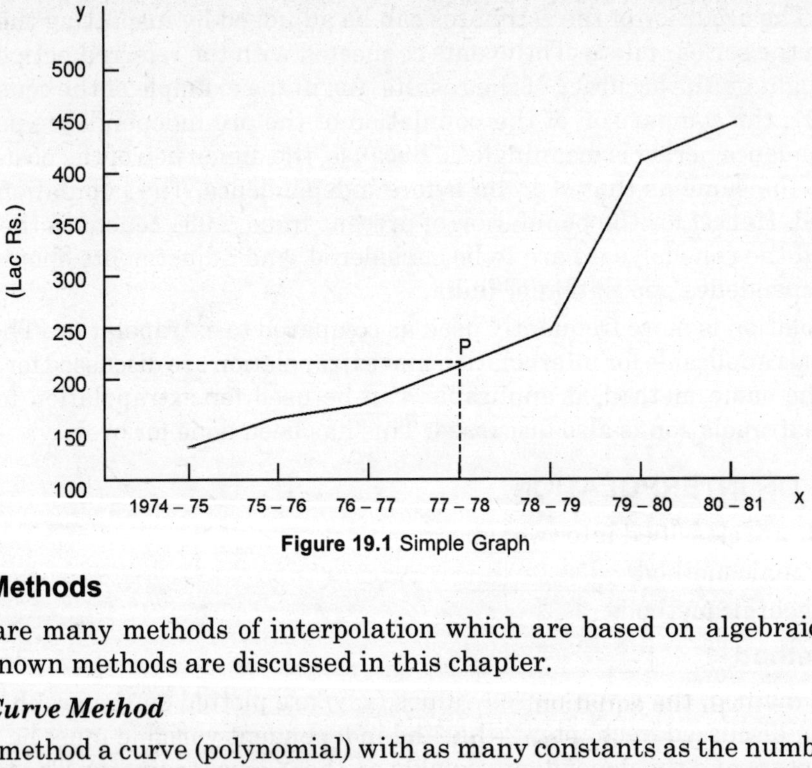

Figure 19.1 Simple Graph

Algebraic Methods

There are many methods of interpolation which are based on algebraic principles. Some well known methods are discussed in this chapter.

Parabolic Curve Method

In this method a curve (polynomial) with as many constants as the number of known paired values, is taken. If n paired values are known, the curve with n constant coefficients, which is a polynomial of degree $(n - 1)$ of the variable X is chosen. The equation of the polynomial is,

$$Y = a_1 + a_2X + a_3X^2 + \ldots + a_nX^{n-1} \qquad \ldots(19.1)$$

where Y is the dependent variable and X is the independent variable. Now to fit the parabolic curve of degree $(n - 1)$, the paired values of (X, Y) are substituted in (19.1), one by one. On each substitution, we get one equation in the unknown constants $a_1, a_2, \ldots, a_n$. In all, we get n simultaneous equations. Solving these equations for $a_1, a_2, \ldots, a_n$, we get the values of these unknowns. Now, putting the value of these coefficients in (19.1), we get the estimated equation of the parabola. Thus, from the fitted parabolic equation of the curve, Y can be estimated for any value of X.

This is a general method and can be applied in any case. Both interpolation and extrapolation can be worked out in the same manner. The curve is expected to be a good fit, as it passes through all the given points. But this method suffers from the defect that it is very lengthy to follow. If there are ten pairs of values, one would be required to solve ten simultaneous equations, and that is why it is not in common use. When $n = 4$ or less, this method is easily applicable, Because of the use of simultaneous equations, it is also known as the *method of simultaneous equations.*

Example **19.2.** The following table gives the expectation of life in years at different ages in years.

Age (X)	10	15	20	30
Expectation of life (l_x):	35.4	32.3	29.2	23.2

The expectation of life at the age of 16 years can be estimated by parabolic curve method.

Since there are 4 pairs of values known to us, we have to fit in a third degree equation of the curve, i.e.

$$y = a_1 + \alpha_2 x + a_3 x^2 + a_4 x^3$$

where $y = l_x$.

Now we make a transformation,

$$v = \frac{x-10}{5}$$

Using the above transformation, we prepare the following table.

x	$l_x = y$	$v = \dfrac{x-10}{5}$	v^2	v^3
10	35.4	0	0	0
15	32.3	1	1	1
20	29.2	2	4	8
30	23.2	4	16	64

Now we fit in the equation.

$$y = a_1 + a_2 v + a_3 v^2 + a_4 v^3$$

where $v = 0$, ...(*i*)

$$a_1 = 35.4$$

when $v = 1$,

$$32.3 = a_1 + a_2 + a_3 + a_4 \quad ...(ii)$$

when $v = 2$,

$$29.2 = a_1 + 2a_2 + 4a_3 + 8a_4 \quad ...(iii)$$

when $v = 4$,

$$23.2 = a_1 + 4a_2 + 16a_3 + 64a_4 \quad ...(iv)$$

From (*i*) and (*ii*), we get

$$a_2 + a_3 + a_4 = -3.1 \quad ...(v)$$

Subtracting (*iii*) from (*iv*), we obtain

$$2a_2 + 12a_3 + 56a_4 = -6.0 \quad ...(vi)$$

Subtracting (*ii*) from (*iii*), we get

$$a_2 + 3a_3 + 7a_4 = -3.1 \quad ...(vii)$$

Equations (*v*) and (*vii*) give,

$$2a_3 + 6a_4 = 0 \quad ...(viii)$$

Multiplying (*vii*) by 2 and subtracting it from (*vi*), we obtain

$$6a_3 + 42a_4 = 0.2 \quad ...(ix)$$

Multiplying (*viii*) by 3 and subtracting it from (*ix*) we get,

$$24a_4 = 0.2 \text{ or } a_4 = \frac{0.2}{24} = 0.0083$$

Substituting the value of a_4 in (*ix*), we obtain

$$a_3 = -0.0248$$

Putting the values of a_3 and a_4 in equation (*v*), we get

$$a_2 = -3.1 + 0.0248 - 0.0083 = -3.0835$$

Thus, the fitted parabolic equation in v is,

$$y = 35.4 - 3.0835\, v - 0.0248\, v^2 + 0.0083\, v^3$$

Now decoding v in x, the equation becomes,

$$y = 35.4 - 3.0835\left(\frac{x-10}{5}\right) - 0.0248\left(\frac{x-10}{5}\right)^2 + 0.0083\left(\frac{x-10}{5}\right)^3$$

$$= 41.4008 - 0.5768\, x - 0.003\, x^2 + 0.00007\, x^3$$

when $x = 16$,

$$y = 41.4008 - 0.5768 \times 16 - 0.003 \times 16^2 + 0.00007 \times 16^3$$

$$= 41.4008 - 9.2288 - 0.768 + 0.2867 = 31.69.$$

The expectation of life at the age of 16 years is 31.69 years.

***Example* 19.3.** Rental income by private organised sectors in India during the three financial years was as follows :

Years (X)	:	1977	1979	1981
Rental income (Y) (Rs. crores)	:	164	256	279

Rental income for the year 1980 can be estimated by parabolic curve method.

Since three years data are available we choose a second degree parabola,

$$y = a_1 + a_2x + a_3x^2$$

For the sake of convenience, we take 1979 as the origin. Hence, the values of x will be –2, 0, 2. For three pairs of values, three simultaneous equations are,

$$a_1 - 2a_2 + 4a_3 = 164 \quad ...(i)$$

$$a_1 = 256 \quad ...(ii)$$

$$a_1 + 2a_2 + 4a_3 = 279 \quad ...(iii)$$

Adding (*i*) and (*iii*) we get,

$$2a_1 + 8a_3 = 443 \quad ...(iv)$$

or

$$8a_3 = 443 - 2 \times 256$$

$$a_3 = -8.625$$

From equations (*iii*),

$$2a_2 = 279 - 4 \times (-8.625) - 256 \quad ...(v)$$

$$a_2 = 28.75$$

Putting the values of a_1, a_2 and a_3 in the second degree equation, we get the estimated equation as,

$$y = 256 + 28.75\,x - 8.625\,x^2 \quad ...(vi)$$

To estimate the rental income for the year 1980, we put $x = 1$ in (*vi*) which gives,

$$y = 276.125$$

Thus, the estimated rental income for the year 1980 is 276.125 Rs crores.

METHODS OF INTERPOLATION FOR EQUAL INTERVALS

Newton's methods, Gauss methods and some other interpolation formulae are based on *finite differences*. Hence, it seems very logical to clear the idea about finite differences first. The problem is simplified, if we consider the value of Y for equidistant values of X. Moreover, it is convenient to arrange the series of data with x-values in ascending order. Hence, in this chapter, it will generally be followed. If we denote x_0 as the origin in the series of data for x-values, any other entry of x-values may be given as $(x_0 + ih)$ where i is an integer (positive or negative) and h stands for the uniform difference between x-values. The variable y is expressed as a function of x say, $f(x)$. The differences are tabulated for the functional values y, *i.e.*, $f(x)$. Subscripts are used for indexing variable to make it easy to refer to a particular entry. Let an entry be chosen as the origin and x is subscripted by zero, *i.e.*, the entry is denoted as x_0. The entries following this value are denoted as x_1, x_2, x_3, etc., and entries preceding it are denoted as x_{-1}, x_{-2}, x_{-3}, etc. y-values or $f(x)$ receive the same subscripts as x-values i.e. they are denoted as y_1, y_2, y_3, etc. and y_{-1}, y_{-2}, y_{-3}, etc., or for functional values as f_1, f_2, f_3, etc., and f_{-1}, f_{-2}, f_{-3}, etc. The subscripting simplifies the job of preparing the finite difference table to a great extent. We shall tabulate finite differences, taking y-values, and maintain it throughout the chapter. If one wants, f can be used in place of y.

Let the ordered series of $(n + 1)$ paired (x, y) observations be as follows.

x:	x_0	x_1	x_2..........x_i..........x_{n-1}	x_n
y:	y_0	y_1	y_2..........y_i..........y_{n-1}	y_n

We define the first differences as

$$\Delta y_0 = y_1 - y_0;\ \Delta y_1 = y_2 - y_1;\ ...\Delta y_i = y_{i+1} - y_i\ , ...$$

and

$$\Delta y_{n-1} = y_n - y_{n-1} \quad ...(19.2)$$

The second and the higher order differences are obtained by taking the difference of the previous differences. For example,

$$\Delta^2 y_0 = \Delta y_1 - \Delta y_0 \quad ...(19.3)$$

$$= (y_2 - y_1) - (y_1 - y_0) \quad ...(19.3.1)$$

$$= y_2 - 2y_1 + y_0 \quad ...(19.3.2)$$

In general,

$$\Delta^2 y_i = y_{i+2} - 2y_{i+1} + y_i \qquad ...(19.3.3)$$

Similarly,

$$\Delta^3 y_0 = y_3 - 3y_2 + 3y_1 - y_0 \qquad ...(19.4)$$

In general,

$$\Delta^3 y_i = y_{i+3} - 3y_{i+2} + 3y_{i+1} - y_i \qquad ...(19.4.1)$$

Using the recurrence re'ations, we can write,

$$\Delta^n y_i = y_{i+n} - \binom{n}{1} y_{i+n-1} + \binom{n}{2} y_{i+n-2} - \binom{n}{3} y_{i+n-3} + ... \qquad ...(19.5)$$

where $\binom{n}{r} = \frac{n(n-1)(n-2)...(n-r+1)}{r(r-1)(r-2)...3.2.1}$

The first and higher order differences given above show that the first difference represents the first degree polynomial, i.e. a linear relationship, the second order differences represent a second degree polynomial and the third order differences a cubic and so on. The moment, all the ith order differences become equal, it indicates that a y-value is a polynomial function of the ith degree in x. If there are $(n + 1)$ paired value (x, y), at the most there can be nth order differences. Hence, y can at the most be a nth degree polynomial function of x. Thus, we state the following proposition without proof.

For equally spaced independent variable, nth differences of a polynomial of degree n are constant. Conversely, if the nth differences of a function of x (y-values) at equally spaced intervals are constant, the function is a nth degree polynomial.

Differences are usually tabulated in the form of diagonal difference table as shown in table (19.1). Here we give a table taking seven entries only.

In many situations, we have to choose an origin other than the first entry. x-entries are subscripted according to the position of the origin x_0, as already discussed. A difference table is customarily prepared as given in table 19.2 and is known as *central difference table.*

The central difference table focuses attention upon the differences around the horizontal line, through the value taken as origin. Here, it is observed that only the even order differences entries come into existence.

Check : There are chances of arithmetic error in a difference table inspite of great care. Hence, it is advisable to check the correctness of the differences. The best way of checking the mistake (s) is to add the sum of differences, in each column, to the top entry of its left hand column. This sum should be equal to the last entry of its left hand column. If this holds true, there is no mistake in the table and if not, the differences should be checked again.

Divided Differences

If a difference in the y-values is divided by the interval length of the independent variable x, it is called a divided difference. For example, the first difference for any two pairs of observations (x_i, y_i) and (x_j, y_j) where $i < j = 1, 2, ..., n$ is,

$$\Delta y_i = \frac{y_j - y_i}{x_j - x_i}$$

Table 19.1: Diagonal Difference Table

x	y	*First difference* Δy	*Second difference* $\Delta^2 y$	*Third difference* $\Delta^3 y$	*Fourth difference* $\Delta^4 y$	*Fifth difference* $\Delta^5 y$	*Sixth difference* $\Delta^6 y$
x_0	y_0						
		$y_1 - y_0 = \Delta y_0$					
x_1	y_1		$\Delta y_1 - \Delta y_0 = \Delta^2 y_0$				
		$y_2 - y_1 = \Delta y_1$		$\Delta^2 y_1 - \Delta^2 y_0 = \Delta^3 y_0$			
x_2	y_2		$\Delta y_2 - \Delta y_1 = \Delta^2 y_1$		$\Delta^3 y_1 - \Delta^3 y_0 = \Delta^4 y_0$		
		$y_3 - y_2 = \Delta y_2$		$\Delta^2 y_2 - \Delta^2 y_1 = \Delta^3 y_1$		$\Delta^4 y_1 - \Delta^4 y_0 = \Delta^5 y_0$	
x_3	y_3		$\Delta y_3 - \Delta y_2 = \Delta^2 y_2$		$\Delta^3 y_2 - \Delta^3 y_1 = \Delta^4 y_1$		$\Delta^5 y_1 - \Delta^5 y_0 = \Delta^6 y_0$
		$y_4 - y_3 = \Delta y_3$		$\Delta^2 y_3 - \Delta^2 y_2 = \Delta^3 y_2$		$\Delta^4 y_2 - \Delta^4 y_1 = \Delta^5 y_1$	
x_4	y_4		$\Delta y_4 - \Delta y_3 = \Delta^2 y_3$		$\Delta^3 y_3 - \Delta^3 y_2 = \Delta^4 y_2$		
		$y_5 - y_4 = \Delta y_4$		$\Delta^2 y_4 - \Delta^2 y_3 = \Delta^3 y_3$			
x_5	y_5		$\Delta y_5 - \Delta y_4 = \Delta^2 y_4$				
		$y_6 - y_5 = \Delta y_5$					
x_6	y_6						

Table 19.2: Central Difference Table

x	y	Δy	$\Delta^2 y$	$\Delta^3 y$	$\Delta^4 y$	$\Delta^5 y$
x_{-2}	y_{-2}					
		$y_{-1} - y_{-2} = \Delta y_{-2}$				
x_{-1}	y_{-1}		$\Delta y_{-1} - \Delta y_{-2} = \Delta^2 y_{-2}$			
		$y_0 - y_{-1} = \Delta_{y_{-1}}$		$\Delta^2 y_{-1} - \Delta^2 y_{-2} = \Delta^3 y_{-2}$		
x_0	y_0		$\Delta y_0 - \Delta y_{-1} = \Delta^2 y_{-1}$		$\Delta^3 y_{-1} - \Delta^3 y_{-2} = \Delta^4 y_{-2}$	
		$y_1 - y_0 = \Delta y_0$		$\Delta^2 y_0 - \Delta^2 y_{-1} = \Delta^3 y_{-1}$		$\Delta^4 y_{-1} - \Delta^4 y_{-2} = \Delta^5 y_{-2}$
x_1	y_1		$\Delta y_1 - \Delta y_0 = \Delta^2 y_0$		$\Delta^3 y_0 - \Delta^3 y_{-1} = \Delta^4 y_{-1}$	
		$y_2 - y_1 = \Delta y_1$		$\Delta^2 y_1 - \Delta^2 y_0 = \Delta^3 y_0$		
x_2	y_2		$\Delta y_2 - \Delta y_1 = \Delta^2 y_1$			
		$y_3 - y_2 = \Delta y_2$				
x_3	y_3					

The higher order divided differences are obtained, by taking the differences of the preceding order differences and dividing them by the difference of the corresponding x-values. Divided differences are extremely useful for interpolation in case of data having unequally spaced x-values.

INTERPOLATION FORMULAE BASED ON POLYNOMIALS

There are many interpolation formulae based on finite differences, which have emerged out of polynomials. The classical polynomial formulae are meant to interpolate values of function $y = f(x)$ other than those which have already been tabulated, provided a sufficient number of differences are available to attain a desirable degree of accuracy. There are special situations in which a particular polynomial formula is appropriate. The individual formula has been displayed and discussed ahead. Here, some general ideas about the polynomial approach have been given.

Let us consider a function $y = f(x)$ which takes on values $y_0, y_1, y_2, \ldots y_n$ corresponding to the equidistant values $x_0, x_1, x_2, \ldots, x_n$ of the independent variable X. Let $P(x)$ be a polynomial of nth degree and is written in the form,

$$P(x) = a_0 + a_1 (x - x_0) + a_2 (x - x_0)(x - x_1) + a_3 (x - x_0)(x - x_1)(x - x_2) + \ldots + a_n (x - x_0)(x - x_1) \ldots (x - x_{n-1}) \quad (19.6)$$

To fit this polynomial, we have to determine the coefficients $a_0, a_1, a_2, \ldots, a_n$ such that,

$$P(x_0) = y_0,\ P(x_1) = y_1,\ P(x_2) = y_2,\ \ldots,\ P(x_n) = y_n$$

Since the values x_i ($i = 0, 1, 2, \ldots, n$) are chosen at equal distance, we have

$$x_i = x_0 + ih \quad \ldots(19.7)$$

where h is the interval.

Now putting different values of x as $x_0, x_1, \ldots, x_n$ in (19.6), we get

$$\begin{aligned}
P(x_0) &= y_0 = a_0 \\
P(x_1) &= y_1 = a_0 + a_1 (x_1 - x_0) = a_0 + a_1(h) \\
P(x_2) &= y_2 = a_0 + a_1 (x_2 - x_0) + a_2 (x_2 - x_0)(x_2 - x_1) \\
&= a_0 + a_1 \{(x_2 - x_1) + (x_1 - x_0)\} + a_2 \{(x_2 - x_1) + (x_1 - x_0)\} (x_2 - x_1) \\
&= a_0 + a_1 (2h) + a_2 (2h)(h) \quad \ldots(19.8) \\
&\vdots \\
P(x_i) &= y_i = a_0 + a_1(ih) + a_2(ih) \{(i - 1)\} h + \ldots + a_i (i!) h^i \\
&\vdots \\
P(x_n) &= a_0 + a_1 (nh) + a_2 (nh)(n - 1) h + \ldots + a_n (n!) h^n \\
P(x_n) &= y_n = a_0 + a_1 (nh) + a_2 (nh)(n - 1)h + \ldots + a_n (n!) h^n
\end{aligned}$$

The set of equations (19.8) can be solved for the coefficients $a_0, a_1, a_2, \ldots, a_n$ by the method of substitution. Recalling the definition of finite differences, we have

$$\begin{aligned}
a_0 &= y_0 \\
a_1 &= \frac{y_1 - y_0}{h} = \frac{\Delta y_0}{h} \\
a_2 &= \frac{1}{2h^2}(y_2 - 2y_1 + y_0) = \frac{\Delta^2 y_0}{2h^2} \quad \ldots(19.9)
\end{aligned}$$

$$\vdots$$

$$a_i = \frac{\Delta^i y_0}{i!h^i}$$

$$\vdots$$

$$a_n = \frac{\Delta^n y_0}{n!h^n}$$

On substituting the value of the coefficients, the polynomial (19.6) may be written as

$$P(x) = y_0 + \frac{\Delta y_0}{h}(x - x_0) + \frac{\Delta^2 y_0}{2h^2}(x - x_0)(x - x_1) + \ldots$$

$$\ldots + \frac{\Delta^n y_0}{n!h^n}(x - x_0)(x - x_1)\ldots(x - x_{n-1}) \qquad \ldots(19.10)$$

Now make a transformation on the variable x by letting

$$u = \frac{x - x_0}{h} \qquad \ldots(19.11)$$

We know, $x_i = x_0 + ih$

or $x_0 = x_i - ih$

for $i = 1, 2, \ldots, n$.

Again, $$\frac{x - x_i}{h} = \frac{x - x_0 - ih}{h} = \left(\frac{x - x_0}{h} - i\right) = (u - i) \qquad \ldots(19.12)$$

Putting $i = 1, 2, 3, \ldots n$, we obtain

$$\frac{x - x_1}{h} = (u - 1),$$

$$\frac{x - x_2}{h} = (u - 2),$$

$$\vdots$$

$$\frac{x - x_n}{h} = (u - n)$$

Using these relations, equation (19.10) reduces to the form

$$P(x) = y_0 + u\Delta y_0 + \frac{u(u-1)}{2!}\Delta^2 y_0 + \ldots + \frac{u(u-1)(u-2)\ldots(u-n+1)}{n!}\Delta^n y_0$$

$$= y_0 + \binom{u}{1}\Delta y_0 + \binom{u}{2}\Delta^2 y_0 + \ldots + \binom{u}{n}\Delta^n y_0 \qquad \ldots(19.13)$$

where $\binom{u}{i}$ is the binomial coefficient.

Formula (19.13) is known as *Newton's Forward Interpolation formula.* The other details of this formula are discussed ahead. Other interpolation formulae based on finite differences have also been discussed which can be derived on the basis of the polynomial of nth degree. But, the other polynomial formulae are not derived in this chapter. The readers may try themselves, if they desire so.

Newton-Gregory (N-G) Forward Formula

This formula is also known as *Newton's formula of advancing differences.* The method is applicable only when the independent variable X advances with equal increment, i.e. X takes on values $x + h$, $x + 2h$, $x + 3h$, and so on. This formula gives good estimate of the dependent variable Y, if the interpolating item lies in the beginning of the series of data. The reason for this is that in this method, we use only leading differences and these occur in the beginning only. A diagonal difference table is prepared. To be more specific, if there are n entries in the series, the maximum possible number of difference columns will be $(n - 1)$. A difference table (19.3) taking five entries is displayed. The sign of the differences should be retained and considered for further calculations. The first difference $\Delta^i y_0$ ($i = 1, 2, ..., n - 1$) in each column is known as the *leading difference* and is used in Newton's advancing formula. Suppose the value of y corresponding to a given value x, say y_x, is to be estimated. Now transform the given value x to a value, say u which is obtained by the formula.

$$u = \frac{\text{Given } x\text{– value for interpolation – First } x\text{ – value of the series}}{\text{Difference between two consecutive } x \text{ values}} \quad ...(19.14)$$

$$= \frac{x - x_0}{x_1 - x_0} \quad ...(19.14.1)$$

u can take non-integral values as well, y_x may be obtained by the following polynomial formula,

$$y_x = y_0 + \binom{u}{1}\Delta y_0 + \binom{u}{2}\Delta^2 y_0 + \binom{u}{3}\Delta^3 y_0 + \binom{u}{4}\Delta^4 y_0 + ... \quad ...(19.15)$$

$$= y_0 + u\Delta y_0 + \frac{u(u-1)}{2.1}\Delta^2 y_0 + \frac{u(u-1)(u-2)}{3.2.1}\Delta^3 y_0$$

$$+ \frac{u(u-1)(u-2)(u-3)}{4.3.2.1}\Delta^4 y_0 + ... \quad ...(19.15.1)$$

The calculations for estimating y_x are simplified if we establish the following relationship between binomial coefficients.

Suppose $\binom{u}{1} = n_{11}$

Again, $\binom{u}{2} = \frac{1}{2}(u-1)n_{11} = n_{12}$

$\binom{u}{3} = \frac{1}{3}(u-2)n_{12} = n_{13}$

Table 19.3: Diagonal differences table for a fourth degree polynomial

x	y	Δy	$\Delta^2 y$	$\Delta^3 y$	$\Delta^4 y$
x_0	y_0				
		$y_1 - y_0 = \Delta y_0$			
x_1	y_1		$\Delta y_1 - \Delta y_0 = \Delta^2 y_0$		
		$y_2 - y_1 = \Delta y_1$		$\Delta^2 y_1 - \Delta^2 y_0 = \Delta^3 y_0$	
x_2	y_2		$\Delta y_2 - \Delta y_1 = \Delta^2 y_1$		$\Delta^3 y_1 - \Delta^3 y_0 = \Delta^4 y_0$
		$y_3 - y_2 = \Delta y_2$		$\Delta^2 y_2 - \Delta^2 y_1 = \Delta^3 y_1$	
x_3	y_3		$\Delta y_3 - \Delta y_2 = \Delta^2 y_2$		
		$y_4 - y_3 = \Delta y_3$			
x_4	y_4				

$$\binom{u}{4} = \frac{1}{4}(u-3)n_{13} = n_{14}$$

$$\binom{u}{r} = \frac{1}{r}(u-r+1)n_{1(r-1)} = n_{1r}$$

Thus, the polynomial (19.15.1) can again be written as,

$$y_x = y_0 + n_{11}\Delta y_0 + \tfrac{1}{2}(u-1)n_{11}\Delta^2 y_0 + \tfrac{1}{3}(u-2)n_{12}\Delta^3 y_0 + \tfrac{1}{4}(u-3)n_{13}\Delta^4 y_0 + \ldots \qquad \ldots(19.15.2)$$

$$= y_0 + n_{11}\Delta y_0 + n_{12}\Delta^2 y_0 + n_{13}\Delta^3 y_0 + n_{14}\Delta^4 y_0 + \ldots \qquad \ldots(19.15.3)$$

Formula (19.15) may be extended for a series with any finite number of entries by adding the terms further. Newton-Gregory's polynomial utilizes y_0 and the higher order differences on a diagonally downward path to the right side.

Note : The series should always be arranged in ascending order of x - values.

***Example* 19.4.** The following table gives the net domestic saving at the closing of the financial years from 1956 to 1981 at the interval of five years.

Years :	1956	1961	1966	1971	1976	1981
Net domestic saving: (00, Rs. crores)	9.8	13.3	25.6	45.7	108.0	200.2

Net domestic saving for the year 1963 can be estimated by Newton's method of advancing differences.

First prepare the table of finite differences as given under methodology.

The value of u by formula (19.14) is,

$$u = \frac{1963-1956}{5}$$

$$= 1.4$$

The estimated value of y for the year 1963 from (19.15.3) can easily be calculated.

Here,

$$n_{11} = \binom{1.4}{1} = 1.4$$

$$n_{12} = \frac{1}{2}(1.4-1)\times 1.4 = 0.28$$

$$n_{13} = \frac{1}{3}(1.4-2)\times 0.28 = -0.056$$

$$n_{14} = \frac{1}{4}(1.4-3)\times(-0.056) = 0.0224$$

$$n_{15} = \frac{1}{5}(1.4-4)(0.0224) = -0.0116$$

Putting the value of n's in (19.15.3) we get

$$y_x = 9.8 + 1.4 \times 3.5 + 0.28 \times 8.8 + (-0.056)(-1.0) + 0.0224 \times 35.4 + (-0.0116) \times (-82.1)$$

x	y	Δy	$\Delta^2 y$	$\Delta^3 y$	$\Delta^4 y$	$\Delta^5 y$
1956 $= x_0$	9.8 $= y_0$					
		$3.5 = \Delta y_0$				
1961 $= x_1$	13.3 $= y_1$		$8.8 = \Delta^2 y_0$			
		$12.3 = \Delta y_1$		$-1.0 = \Delta^3 y_0$		
1966 $= x_2$	25.6 $= y_2$		$7.8 = \Delta^2 y_1$		$35.4 = \Delta^4 y_0$	
		$20.1 = \Delta y_2$		$34.4 = \Delta^3 y_1$		$-82.1 = \Delta^5 y_0$
1971 $= x_3$	45.7 $= y_3$		$42.2 = \Delta^2 y_2$		$-46.7 = \Delta^4 y_1$	
		$62.3 = \Delta y_3$		$-12.3 = \Delta^3 y_2$		
1976 $= x_4$	108.0 $= y_4$		$29.9 = \Delta^2 y_3$			
		$92.2 = \Delta y_4$				
1981 $= x_5$	200.2 $= y_5$					

$= 9.8 + 4.90 + 2.464 + 0.056 + 0.7930 + 0.9524$
$= 18.965$

Thus, the estimated net domestic saving at the close of the financial year 1963 is 18.965 hundred crore rupees.

***Example* 19.5**. From the following data, estimate the number of persons in the income group of Rs. 200 to 250 per month.

Income below (Rs./month):	100	200	300	400	500
No. of persons :	20	45	115	210	325

To estimate the number of persons having an income of Rs. 200 to 250 per month, we first estimate the number of people having an income upto Rs. 250 by Newton's forward formula. Prepare the diagonal finite difference table as given on next page.

From (19.14),

$$u = \frac{250-100}{100} = 1.5$$

To make use of formula (19.15.3), we find out

x	y	Δy	$\Delta^2 y$	$\Delta^3 y$	$\Delta^4 y$
$100 = x_0$	$20 = y_0$	$25 = \Delta y_0$			
$200 = x_1$	$45 = y_1$		$45 = \Delta^2 y_0$		
		$70 = \Delta y_1$		$-20 = \Delta^3 y_0$	
$300 = x_2$	$115 = y_2$		$25 = \Delta^2 y_1$		$15 = \Delta^4 y_0$
		$95 = \Delta y_2$		$-5 = \Delta^3 y_1$	
$400 = x_3$	$210 = y_3$		$20 = \Delta^2 y_2$		
		$115 = \Delta y_3$			
$500 = x_4$	$325 = y_4$				

$$n_{11} = 1.5;\ n_{12} = \frac{1}{2}(1.5-1)\times 1.5 = 0.375$$

$$n_{13} = \frac{1}{3}(1.5-2)\times 0.375 = -0.0625;$$

$$n_{14} = \frac{1}{4}(1.5-3)\times(-0.0625) = 0.0234$$

Thus, the estimated value,

$$y_x = 20 + 1.5 \times 25 + 0.375 \times 45 + (-0.0625)(-20) + 0.0234 \times 15$$
$$= 20 + 37.5 + 16.875 + 1.25 + 0.351$$
$$= 75.976 = 76$$

The number of people earning upto Rs. 200 per month is 45. Hence, the number of people having an earning between Rs. 200 and 250 is,

$76 - 45 = 31.$

Interpolation in a Frequency Table

If in a frequency table, the x-variate values are in a continuous series with equal class intervals, it is necessary that a cumulative frequency table be prepared. The upper limit of each class in a grouped data be taken as the values of the variate X, and the cumulative frequencies as the variate values of Y. The rest of the procedure is exactly the same as given with Newton's method of advancing differences, or other methods based on finite differences coming ahead. In case of discrete data, the methods will directly be applicable without any change in the series.

***Example* 19.6.** The following table gives the frequency distribution of food expenditure per family per month among the working class families of a locality. Find the number of families whose monthly expenditure on food is not more than Rs. 110.

Range of expenditure	*No. of families*
60 – 80	40
80 – 100	260
100 – 120	400
120 – 140	210
140 – 160	70
160 – 180	20

To interpolate the value of y for $x \leq 110$, we prepare the finite difference table by converting first the frequently distribution into less than type cumulative frequency distribution. (See table given on page 440).

From formula (19.14)

$$u = \frac{110-80}{20} = 1.5 .$$

Determine the coefficients of leading differences and substitute them in (19.15.3) to get the estimate of y_{110}.

$$n_{11} = 1.5, n_{12} = \frac{1}{2}(1.5-1)\times 1.5 = 0.375,$$

$$n_{13} = \frac{1}{3}(1.5-2)\times 0.375 = -0.0625,$$

$$n_{14} = \frac{1}{4}(1.5-3)\times(-0.0625) = 0.0234,$$

$$n_{15} = \frac{1}{5}(1.5-4)\times 0.0234 = -0.0117.$$

The estimated value,

$$\begin{aligned} y_{110} &= 40 + 1.5 \times 260 + 0.375 \times 140 + (-0.0625) \times (-330) + (0.0234) \\ &\quad \times 380 + (-0.0117) \times (-340) \\ &= 40 + 390 + 52.5 + 20.625 + 8.892 + 3.978 \\ &= 515.995 = 516 \end{aligned}$$

Number of families which have expenditure on food less than Rs. 110 is 516.

Newton-Gregory Backward Formula

It is another interpolating polynomial and should preferably be used when it is desired to estimate values of the variate y, near the end of the series. The condition of equidistance in x-values is necessary in this case as well. We make use of the difference table (19.3)

Monthly expenditure (Rs.)	*No. of families*	Δy	$\Delta^2 y$	$\Delta^3 y$	$\Delta^4 y$	$\Delta^5 y$
Less than 80	40 $= y_0$					
		$260 = \Delta y_0$				
Less than 100	300 $= y_1$		$140 = \Delta^2 y_0$			
		$400 = \Delta y_1$		$-330 = \Delta^3 y_0$		
Less than 120	700 $= y_2$		$-190 = \Delta^2 y_1$		$380 = \Delta^4 y_0$	
		$210 = \Delta y_2$		$50 = \Delta^3 y_1$		$-340 = \Delta^5 y_0$
Less than 140	910 $= y_3$		$-140 = \Delta^2 y_2$		$40 = \Delta^4 y_1$	
		$70 = \Delta y_3$		$90 = \Delta^3 y_2$		
Less than 160	980 $= y_4$		$-50 = \Delta^2 y_3$			
		$20 = \Delta y_4$				
Less than 180	1000 $= y_5$					

again. The interpolating backward polynomial formula is,

$$y_n = y_n + \binom{u}{1}\Delta y_{n-1} + \binom{u+1}{2}\Delta^2 y_{n-2} + \binom{u+2}{3}\Delta^3 y_{n-3} + \binom{u+3}{4}\Delta^4 y_{n-4} + \ldots \quad \ldots(19.16)$$

An inter-relationship between binomial coefficients can be established which simplifies the calculations.

If we take,

$$\binom{u}{1} = u = n_{21}$$

$$\binom{u+1}{2} = \frac{1}{2}(u+1)u = \tfrac{1}{2}(u+1)n_{21} = n_{22}$$

$$\binom{u+2}{3} = \frac{1}{3}(u+2)n_{22} = n_{23}$$

$$\binom{u+3}{4} = \frac{1}{4}(u+3)n_{23} = n_{24}$$

$$\binom{u+r}{r+1} = \frac{1}{r+1}(u+r)n_{2r} = n_{2(r+1)}$$

using the above relations, formula (19.16) can be written as,

$$y_x = y_n + n_{21}\Delta y_{n-1} + n_{22}\Delta^2 y_{n-2} + n_{23}\Delta^3 y_{n-3} + \ldots \quad \ldots(19.16.1)$$

This formula utilizes the differences lying on the upward diagonal of table (19.3) from Δy_{n-1} and to the right.

The value of u is determined by the formula,

$$u = \frac{\text{Given value of } x \text{ for interpolation} - \text{Last } x\text{-value of the series}}{\text{Difference between two consecutive } x\text{-values}} \quad \ldots(19.17)$$

$$= \frac{x - x_n}{h} \quad \ldots(19.17.1)$$

when h is the constant interval between x-values. The value of u will be negative and usually a fraction.

Note : It can be seen that Newton-Gregory forward and backward polynomials are analogous. The analogy can be shown by choosing the subscripts suitably. There is much ado in many books about the use of Newton's forward formula, when the value to be interpolated lies at the beginning of the series, and backward polynomial, when it lies at the end of the series. But the fact is that, we may use either formula for a value anywhere in the table by suitably subscribing the x's. Tho two formulae yield exactly identical results by an interpolating polynomial that ends on the same difference entry.

Example **19.7.** To verify the above fact we solve the problem of example 19.4 by Newton's backward formula.

The value of u from (19.17.1) is,

$$u = \frac{1963-1981}{5} = -\frac{18}{5}$$
$$= -3.6$$

The value of y for given $x = 1963$ from the formula (19.16.1) is obtained as follows:

$$n_{21} = \begin{pmatrix} -3.6 \\ 1 \end{pmatrix} = -3.6$$

$$n_{22} = \frac{1}{2}(-3.6+1)(-3.6) = 4.68$$

$$n_{23} = \frac{1}{3}(-3.6+2)(4.68) = -2.496$$

$$n_{24} = \frac{1}{4}(-3.6+3)(-2.496) = 0.3744$$

$$n_{25} = \frac{1}{5}(-3.6+4)\times 0.3744 = 0.0299$$

using the difference table given with example 19.4 we obtain,

$$y = 200.2 - 3.6 \times 92.2 + 4.68 \times 29.9 + (-2.496) \times (-12.3)$$
$$+ 0.3744 \times (-46.7) + 0.0299 \times (-82.1)$$
$$= 200.2 - 331.92 + 139.932 + 30.7008 - 17.484 - 2.454$$
$$= 18.97$$

It can be noted that the same interpolated value was obtained by Newton's forward formulae in example 19.4.

Example **19.8.** Using the data and the difference table given in example 19.4, we again interpolate the value of net domestic savings for the year 1978.

The value of u from formula (19.17.1) is,

$$u = \frac{1978-1981}{5} = -0.6$$

The estimated value of y for given $x = 1978$ from formula (19.16.1) is obtained as follows.

$$n_{21} = \begin{pmatrix} -0.6 \\ 1 \end{pmatrix} = -0.6$$

$$n_{22} = \begin{pmatrix} u+1 \\ 2 \end{pmatrix} = \frac{1}{2}(-0.6+1)(-0.6) = -0.12$$

$$n_{23} = \begin{pmatrix} u+2 \\ 3 \end{pmatrix} = \frac{1}{3}(-0.6+2)(-0.12) = -0.056$$

$$n_{24} = \begin{pmatrix} u+3 \\ 4 \end{pmatrix} = \frac{1}{4}(-0.6+3)(-0.056) = -0.0336$$

$$n_{25} = \binom{u+4}{5} = \frac{1}{5}(-0.6+4)(-0.0336) = -0.0228$$

Thus,

$$\begin{aligned} y &= 200.2 + (-0.6)(92.2) + (-0.12)(29.9) + (-0.056)(-12.3) \\ &\quad + (-0.0336)(-46.7) + (-0.0228)(-82.1) \\ &= 200.2 - 55.32 - 3.59 + 0.69 + 1.57 + 1.87 \\ &= 145.42 \end{aligned}$$

Thus, the estimated net domestic saving at the closing of financial year 1978 is Rs. 145.42 crores.

Gauss Forward Polynomial Formula

The two polynomial formulae given earlier, used only the difference Δy occurring either at the beginning or at the end of each column. But, there are many more formulae which utilize intermediate differences also. Gauss formula is applicable when (*i*) the independent variable X advances with equal increment, (*ii*) the value which is to be interpolated lies in the mid of the given series of data. Gauss forward method is not much different from Newton's advancing difference method. Hence, the development of Gauss forward polynomial is evident itself. In this method, the nearest lower value to the given value of x for interpolation is taken as x_0 (initial value) and corresponding value of y as y_0. Hence, y_0, the initial value of the function can arbitrarily be chosen according to the value of x, given for interpolation. In this situation, a central difference table like table (19.2) can be adopted. In this table, the given value of x for interpolation lies at the position three from the top. However, in such cases it is better, to utilize values of $\Delta^i{}_y$ on both sides of the horizontal line through y_0. For Gauss forward formula, we focus attention on the horizontal line between values y_0 and y_1 which we may call $y_{1/2}$ line. The line of attention can be depicted as below.

y_0		$\binom{u}{1}$		$\Delta^2 y_{-1}$		$\binom{u+1}{3}$		$\Delta^4 y_{-2}$	$\binom{u+2}{5}$
	Δy_0		$\binom{u}{2}$		$\Delta^3 y_{-1}$		$\binom{u+1}{4}$		$\Delta^5 y_{-2}$
y_1		$\binom{u-1}{1}$		$\Delta^2 y_0$		$\binom{u}{3}$		$\Delta^4 y_{-1}$	$\binom{u+1}{5}$

Diagram 19.1

Gauss forward formula involves y_0 and finite differences, starting from Δy_0, and alternately one in horizontal line through y_0 and one below it. The coefficient of y_0 is always unity. The path is a zig-zag one. The binomial coefficients in the formula have been obtained from diagram (19.1), starting from $\binom{u}{1}$, for Δy_0 and taking other coefficients as one in the middle line and one coefficient in the horizontal line, through y_0, alternately. The derivation of the formula has been omitted. Gauss forward formula for interpolating y for a given value of x is,

$$y_x = y_0 + \binom{u}{1}\Delta y_0 + \binom{u}{2}\Delta^2 y_{-1} + \binom{u+1}{3}\Delta^3 y_{-1} + \binom{u+1}{4}\Delta^4 y_{-2}$$

$$+ \binom{u+2}{5}\Delta^5 y_{-2} + \ldots \qquad \ldots(19.18)$$

where the value of u is determined by the formula,

$$u = \frac{\text{Given value of } x - \text{Initial value of } x}{\text{Difference between two consecutive } x\text{-values}} \qquad \ldots(19.19)$$

$$= \frac{x - x_0}{h} \qquad \ldots(19.19.1)$$

where h is the constant interval between x-values.

Example **19.9.** For the data given in the example 19.6, we estimate the number of families having monthly expenditure on food of Rs. 130 or less per family.

Prepare the central difference table given on page 586.

$$u = \frac{130 - 120}{20} = \frac{10}{20} = 0.5$$

The estimated number of families y for given $x \leq 130$ is obtained by Gauss forward formula (19.18).

$$y_x = 700 + \binom{0.5}{1}\times 210 + \binom{0.5}{2}\times(-190) + \binom{0.5+1}{3}\times 50$$

$$+ \binom{0.5+1}{4}\times 380 + \binom{0.5+2}{5}\times(-340)$$

$$= 700 + 105 + 23.75 - 3.125 + 8.906 - 3.984$$

$$= 830.547$$

$$= 830 \text{ families.}$$

Gauss Backward Polynomial Formula

The application of this formula is appropriate when the value to be interpolated lies towards the end of the series. The basic approach of finding the finite differences remains the same as in Gauss forward formula. The condition for the application of this method is that, the increment in the values of x in the series must be equal. Here we make use of the central difference table (19.2). But in this method, the origin x_0 is the x-value just succeeding the given value of x. Other subscripts follow as per rule. Gauss backward formula can be understood in the light of the following diagram, which arises with the help of the table (19.2).

Monthly expenditure (Rs.)	No. of families	Δy	$\Delta^2 y$	$\Delta^3 y$	$\Delta^4 y$	$\Delta^5 y$
Less than $80 = x_{-2}$	$40 = y_{-2}$					
		$260 = \Delta y_{-2}$				
Less than $100 = x_{-1}$	$300 = y_{-1}$		$140 = \Delta^2 y_{-2}$			
		$400 = \Delta y_{-1}$		$-330 = \Delta^3 y_{-2}$		
Less than $120 = x_0$	$700 = y_0$		$-190 = \Delta^2 y_{-1}$		$380 = \Delta^4 y_{-2}$	
		$210 = \Delta y_0$		$50 = \Delta^3 y_{-1}$		$-340 = \Delta^5 y_{-2}$
Less than $140 = x_1$	$910 = y_1$		$-140 = \Delta^2 y_0$		$40 = \Delta^4 y_{-1}$	
		$70 = \Delta y_1$		$90 = \Delta^3 y_0$		
Less than $160 = x_2$	$980 = y_2$		$-50 = \Delta^2 y_1$			
		$20 = \Delta y_2$				
Less than $180 = x_3$	$1000 = y_3$					

y_{-1}	Δy_{-1}	$\binom{u+1}{2}$	$\Delta^3 y_{-2}$	$\binom{u+2}{4}$
y_0	$\binom{u}{1}$	$\Delta^2 y_{-1}$	$\binom{u+1}{3}$	$\Delta^4 y_{-2}$
y_1	Δy_0	$\binom{u}{2}$	$\Delta^3 y_{-1}$	$\binom{u+1}{4}$

Diagram 19.2

Gauss backward formula involves, term y_0 and the differences on the entry, diagonally upward and on the horizontal line through y_0 alternately. The coefficients are taken for the upper line differences given below it and the middle line differences given above it. The coefficient of y_0 is unity. The formula should include as many terms as available in the central difference table. The terms are considered for the inclusion according to the plan of diagram (19.2). Gauss backward interpolating polynomial is,

$$y_x = y_0 - \binom{u}{1}\Delta y_{-1} + \binom{u+1}{2}\Delta^2 y_{-1} - \binom{u+1}{3}\Delta^3 y_{-2} + \binom{u+2}{4}\Delta^4 y_{-2} \ldots \quad \ldots(19.20)$$

In the above formula, the odd order differences are taken with a negative sign.

The value of u is determined by the formula,

$$u = \frac{\text{The value of } x \text{ succeeding} - \text{Given value of } x \text{ for the given } x\text{-valuc interpolation}}{\text{Difference between two consecutive } x\text{-values}} \quad \ldots(19.21)$$

$$= \frac{x_0 - x}{h} \quad \ldots(19.21.1)$$

where h has its usual meaning.

***Example* 19.10.** The following table gives critical values of the chi-square distribution, at 5 per cent probability for various degrees of freedom.

Degrees of freedom (X) :	5	10	15	20	25	30
Critical values (Y):	1.145	3.940	7.260	10.850	14.610	18.491

Critical values of chi-square distribution for 17 degrees of freedom can be interpolated by Gauss backward formula.

Prepare the central difference table given on page 588.

From the formula (19.21.1)

$$u = \frac{20-17}{5} = 0.6$$

x	y	Δy	$\Delta^2 y$	$\Delta^3 y$	$\Delta^4 y$
$5 = x_{-3}$	$1.145 = y_{-3}$				
		$2.795 = \Delta y_{-3}$			
$10 = x_{-2}$	$3.940 = y_{-2}$		$0.525 = \Delta^2 y_{-3}$		
		$3.320 = \Delta y_{-2}$		$-0.255 = \Delta^3 y_{-3}$	
$15 = x_{-1}$	$7.260 = y_{-1}$		$0.270 = \Delta^2 y_{-2}$		$0.155 = \Delta^4 y_{-3}$
		$3.590 = \Delta y_{-1}$		$-0.100 = \Delta^3 y_{-2}$	
$20 = x_0$	$10.850 = y_0$		$0.170 = \Delta^2 y_{-1}$		$0.051 = \Delta^4 y_{-2}$
		$3.760 = \Delta y_0$		$-0.049 = \Delta^3 y_{-1}$	
$25 = x_1$	$14.610 = y_1$		$0.121 = \Delta^2 y_0$		
		$3.881 = \Delta y_1$			
$30 = x_2$	$18.491 = y_2$				

The interpolated value of y for given $x = 17$ from the formula (19.20) is,

$$y = 10.850 - \binom{0.6}{1} \times 3.590 + \binom{0.6+1}{2} \times 0.170 - \binom{0.6+1}{3} \times (-0.100) + \binom{0.6+2}{4} \times 0.051$$

$$= 10.850 - 2.1540 + 0.0816 - 0.0064 - 0.0021$$

$$= 8.77.$$

[It is interesting to reveal that the actual critical value of chi-square distribution at $\alpha = 0.05$ and 17 d.f. is 8.682, which is very near to the interpolated value.]

Stirling's Formula

In Gauss forward formula, the terms included were initiated by y_0 and the diagonally downward ones were multiplied by the entries above it, and those in the horizontal line through y_0 were multiplied by the entries below it. In Gauss backward formula, the terms included were initiated by y_0 and those diagonally upward were multiplied by the entry below it, and the finite differences in the horizontal line, through y_0, were multiplied by the entries above it. The coefficient of y_0 is always unity. But Stirling's formula includes the entries lying in the horizontal line through y_0, multiplied by the average of the entries above and below it. It can be better understood and written with the help of the following diagram.

	Δy_{-1}		$\binom{u+1}{2}$		$\Delta^3 y_{-2}$		$\binom{u+2}{4}$
y_0		$\binom{u}{1}$		$\Delta^2 y_{-1}$		$\binom{u+1}{3}$		$\Delta^4 y_{-2}$
	Δy_0		$\binom{u}{2}$		$\Delta^3 y_{-1}$		$\binom{u+1}{4}$

Diagram 19.3

The interpolated value of y for the given value of x, by Stirling's formula is given by,

$$y_x = y_0 + \binom{u}{1}\frac{\Delta y_0 + \Delta y_{-1}}{2} + \frac{\binom{u+1}{2} + \binom{u}{2}}{2}\Delta^2 y_{-1} + \binom{u+1}{3}\frac{\Delta^3 y_{-1} + \Delta^3 y_{-2}}{2} + \frac{\binom{u+1}{4} + \binom{u+2}{4}}{2}\Delta^4 y_{-2} + \ldots \quad \ldots(19.22)$$

Further terms in the formula can be added by symmetry.

BINOMIAL EXPANSION METHOD OF INTERPOLATION

The binomial expansion method is applicable if the value of X increases with equal magnitude and the given value of X, for which the interpolation is to be done, is also a term in the series. This method is not considered appropriate for extrapolation, as it gives misleading results. Method of Binomial expansion is based on the assumption that in a series of $(n + 1)$ entries, the $(n + 1)$th finite leading difference becomes zero. For example, if there are five entries in the series, the fifth leading difference will be zero. Newton's leading difference arises as a result of binomial expansion. Here we expand $(y - 1)^n$ and equate it to zero, i.e.

$$\Delta^n y_0 = (y - 1)^n = 0$$

In the expanded equation if we put $y^i = y_i$ where $i = 0, 1, 2, \ldots, n$ and y_i denotes the ith term in a series arranged in the ascending order of x-values.

Let the given set of data is

X	x_0 x_1 x_2.....x_i.......x_n
Y	y_0 y_1 y_2......y_i......y_n

The equation $\Delta^n y_0 = 0$ in the expanded form is,

$$\Delta^n y_0 = (y - 1)^n$$

$$y_n - \binom{n}{1} y_{n-1} + \binom{n}{2} y_{n-2} - \binom{n}{3} y_{n-3} + \ldots + (-1)^n y_0 = 0 \quad \ldots(19.23)$$

Again when,

$$n = 3, \Delta^3 y_0 = y_3 - 3y_2 + 3y_1 - y_0 = 0$$
$$n = 4, \Delta^4 y_0 = y_4 - 4y_3 + 6y_2 - 4y_1 + y_0 = 0$$
$$n = 5, \Delta^5 y_0 = y_5 - 5y_4 + 10y_3 - 10y_2 + 5y_1 - y_0 = 0$$
$$n = 6, \Delta^6 y_0 = y_6 - 6y_5 + 15y_4 - 20y_3 + 15y_2 - 6y_1 + y_0 = 0$$

and so on.

Now we explain this phenomenon through an operator E.

Suppose $\quad \Delta = (E - 1) \quad \ldots(19.24)$

$$\Delta^n y_i = (E - 1)^n y_i \quad \ldots(19.25)$$

$$E^r y_i = y_{r+i} \quad \ldots(19.26)$$

where r and i are integers.

Again we define,

$$\Delta^n y_0 = (\mathrm{E} - 1)^n y_0 = 0$$

i.e.

$$\Delta^n y_0 = \left\{ E^n - \binom{n}{1} E^{n-1} + \binom{n}{2} E^{n-2} - \binom{n}{3} E^{n-3} + \ldots + (-1)^n \right\} y_0 = 0$$

$$\Delta^n y_0 = E^n y_0 - \binom{n}{1} E^{n-1} y_0 + \binom{n}{2} E^{n-2} y_0 - \binom{n}{3} E^{n-3} y_0 + \ldots + (-1)^n y_0 = 0$$

$$= y_n - \binom{n}{1} y_{n-1} + \binom{n}{2} y_{n-2} - \binom{n}{3} y_{n-3} + \ldots + (-1)^n y_0 = 0 \quad \ldots(19.27)$$

Similarly,

$$\Delta^n y_1 = (E-1)^n y_1$$

$$= y_{n+1} - \binom{n}{1} y_n + \binom{n}{2} y_{n-1} - \binom{n}{3} y_{n-2} + ... + (-1)^n y_1 = 0 \quad ...(19.28)$$

In a similar manner, we can write as many equations as we want by taking $\Delta^n y_2 = 0$; $\Delta^n y_3 = 0$, etc.

When there is one missing value y, only one equation (19.23), which is the same as (19.27), is sufficient.

When there are two or more than two missing values of Y, in a series of data, we have to form as many equations as the number of unknowns, by taking $\Delta^n y_0 = 0$; $\Delta^n y_1 = 0$; $\Delta^n y_2 = 0$, etc. On solving the simultaneous equations, we get the estimated values of unknown y-values. The method is simple as it involves simple algebra.

***Example* 19.11.** From the following data, find out the missing value.

X	:	0	3	6	9
Y	:	30	?	80	120

The missing value of y can be interpolated by the binomial expansion method. In the given series we have three known terms. Hence, the third order leading difference will be zero, i.e.

$$\Delta^3 y_0 = (E-1)^3 y_0 = 0$$

or

$$\left\{E^3 - \binom{3}{1}E^2 + \binom{3}{2}E - 1\right\} y_0 = 0$$

$$y_3 - 3y_2 + 3y_1 - y_0 = 0$$

Putting the y-values in the above equation, we have

$$120 - 3 \times 80 + 3 \times y_1 - 30 = 0$$

$$3y_1 = 150$$

or

$$y_1 = 50.0$$

***Example* 19.12.** The following table gives the expectation of life at different ages, having two missing values.

Age x (years) :	10	15	20	25	30	35
Expectation of life y (years):	35.4	?	29.2	?	23.2	20.4

The missing values can be estimated by the binomial expansion method. Since, there are four known y-values, we have to take $\Delta^4 y_0 = 0$ and $\Delta^4 y_1 = 0$, Thus the equations are,

$$(E-1)^4 y_0 = y_4 - 4y_3 + 6y_2 - 4y_1 + y_0 = 0$$

$$23.2 - 4y_3 + 6 \times 29.2 - 4y_1 + 35.4 = 0$$

$$4y_3 + 4y_1 = 233.8 \quad ...(i)$$

$$(E-1)^4 y_1 = y_5 - 4y_4 + 6y_3 - 4y_2 + y_1 = 0$$

$$20.4 - 4 \times 23.2 + 6y_3 - 4 \times 29.2 + y_1 = 0$$

$$6y_3 + y_1 = 189.2 \quad ...(ii)$$

Multiplying equation (*ii*) by 4 and subtracting equation (*i*) from it, we get

$$20y_3 = 523$$

or

$$y_3 = 26.15 \quad ...(iii)$$

Substituting the value of y_3 in (*ii*) we obtain,

$$y_1 = 189.2 - 156.9$$
$$= 32.3 \quad ...(iv)$$

Thus, for $x = 15$, $y = 32.3$ yrs and for $x = 25$, $y = 26.15$ yrs.

NEWTON'S METHOD OF DIVIDED DIFFERENCES

So far Newton and Gauss methods were applicable, provided the values of independent variable x has been advancing with equal increment. But such a situation does not always exist. Newton's method of divided differences is applicable when x-values are not equally spaced. In this case too, the given set of paired observations is to be arranged in ascending order of the values of x.

The present method is similar to Newton's method of advancing differences.

In this method, the difference between two consecutive values of Y is divided by the difference of the corresponding values of X's. This reduces each difference to the unit interval of x-values. Suppose, there are $(n + 1)$ pairs of observations say, (x_i, y_i) for $i = 0, 1, 2, ..., n$. A value of y for a given value x, is interpolated by the formula,

$$y_x = y_0 + (x - x_0)\,\Delta\, y_0 + (x - x_0)(x - x_1)\,\Delta^2 y_0 + (x - x_0)(x - x_1)(x - x_2)\,\Delta^3\, y_0 + ... \quad ...(19.29)$$

Formula (19.29) is known as *Newton's formula of divided differences.* Δy_0, $\Delta^2 y_0$, $\Delta^3 y_0$, etc. denote the leading divided differences which are determined in the manner given in the Table (19.4). The divided difference table is prepared by taking only five pairs of observations and given on page 593.

Substituting the values of different terms in the formula (19.29), we obtain the value of y_x.

***Example* 19.13.** The data given below provided the amount of expenditure of the Government of India, due to the payment of pension, on the closing date of various financial years.

Year (X)	:	1971	1975	1977	1980	1981
Amount of Pension (Y) (Rs. crores)	:	105	191	309	487	643

The amount of expenditure on account of pension at the end of 1979 financial year, can be estimated with the help of Newton's divided difference polynomial formula (19.29).

The divided difference table is given on page 594.

Given that $x = 1979$.

The interpolated value of y for the year 1979 is,

$$y_x = 105 + (1979 - 1971) \times 21.5 + (1979 - 1971)(1979 - 1975) \times 6.25$$
$$+ (1979 - 1971)(1979 - 1975)(1979 - 1977)(-0.687)$$
$$+ (1979 - 1971)(1979 - 1975)(1979 - 1977) \times (1979 - 1980) \times 0.4704$$
$$= 105 + 172 + 200 - 43.968 - 30.08$$
$$= 402.95$$

Here, it would be interesting to disclose, that the actual expenditure on payment of pension in the year 1979, had been Rs. 407 crores. The estimated figure above is quite close to the actual value.

Table 19.4: Divided Difference Table

x	y	Δy	$\Delta^2 y$	$\Delta^3 y$	$\Delta^4 y$
x_0	y_0				
		$\frac{y_1 - y_0}{x_1 - x_o} = \Delta y_0$			
x_1	y_1		$\frac{\Delta y_1 - \Delta y_0}{x_2 - x_0} = \Delta^2 y_0$		
		$\frac{y_2 - y_1}{x_2 - x_1} = \Delta y_1$		$\frac{\Delta^2 y_1 - \Delta^2 y_0}{x_3 - x_0} = \Delta^3 y_0$	
x_2	y_2		$\frac{\Delta y_2 - \Delta y_1}{x_3 - x_1} = \Delta^2 y_1$		$\frac{\Delta^3 y_1 - \Delta^3 y_0}{x_4 - x_0} = \Delta^4 y_0$
		$\frac{y_3 - y_2}{x_3 - x_2} = \Delta y_2$		$\frac{\Delta^2 y_2 - \Delta^2 y_1}{x_4 - x_1} = \Delta^3 y_1$	
x_3	y_3		$\frac{\Delta y_3 - \Delta y_2}{x_4 - x_2} = \Delta^2 y_2$		
		$\frac{y_4 - y_3}{x_4 - x_3} = \Delta y_3$			
x_4	y_4				

x	y	Δy	$\Delta^2 y$	$\Delta^3 y$	$\Delta^4 y$
$1971 = x_0$	$105 = y_0$	$\frac{86}{4} = 21.5 = \Delta\, y_0$			
			$\frac{37.5}{6} = 6.25 = \Delta^2 y_0$		
$1975 = x_1$	$191 = y_1$	$\frac{118}{2} = 59 = \Delta\, y_1$		$-\frac{6.184}{9} = -0.687 = \Delta^2 y_0$	
			$\frac{0.33}{5} = 0.066 = \Delta^2 y_1$		$\frac{4.704}{10} = 0.4704 = \Delta^4 y_0$
$1977 = x_2$	$309 = y_2$	$\frac{178}{3} = 59.33 = \Delta\, y_2$		$\frac{24.104}{6} = 4.017 = \Delta^3 y_1$	
			$\frac{96.67}{4} = 24.17 = \Delta^2 y_2$		
$1980 = x_3$	$487 = y_3$	$\frac{156}{1} = 156 = \Delta y_3$			
$1981 = x_4$	$643 = y_4$				

Lagrange's Interpolation Polynomial

When the x-values are not equally spaced, most of the earlier methods of interpolation fail. The only alternative has been the divided difference method. The other simple and an appropriate approach is the Lagrangian interpolating polynomial. This method can also be used for extrapolation. Let there be (n + 1) given values of y, a function of x, *i.e.*, $f(x)$, corresponding to (n + 1) values of x. Thus, we have (n + 1) paired values as,

x	:	x_0,	x_1,	$x_2, ..., x_i, ..., x_n$
y	:	y_0,	y_1,	$y_2, ..., y_i, ..., y_n$

nth degree polynomial due to Lagrange's is,

$$P(x) = \frac{(x-x_1)(x-x_2)...(x-x_n)}{(x_0-x_1)(x_0-x_2)...(x_0-x_n)}y_0$$
$$+\frac{(x-x_0)(x-x_2)...(x-x_n)}{(x_1-x_0)(x_1-x_2)...(x_1-x_n)}y_1$$
$$... ... ...$$
$$... ... ...$$
$$+\frac{(x-x_0)(x-x_1)...(x-x_{i-1})(x-x_{i+1})...(x-x_n)}{(x_i-x_0)(x_i-x_1)...(x_i-x_{i-1})(x_i-x_{i+1})...(x_i-x_n)}y_i \quad ...(19.30)$$
$$... ... ...$$
$$... ... ...$$
$$+\frac{(x-x_0)(x-x_1)...(x-x_{n-1})}{(x_n-x_0)(x_n-x_1)...(x_n-x_{n-1})}y_n$$

In the notational form, the above polynomial can be written as

$$\sum_{i=0}^{n} y_i \prod_{j=0}^{n} \frac{(x-x_j)}{(x_i-x_j)} \quad \text{for} \quad j \neq i \qquad ...(19.30.1)$$

The value of y for any given x can be interpolated from (19.30), in which case $P(x)$ is equivalent to y_x, the interpolated value of y for a given value of x.

Example **19.14.** The normal weight of an animal during the first six years was as given below:

Age in year (X):	0	2	3	5	6
Weight in kg (Y):	5	7	8	10	12

The weight of the animal at the age of four years can be estimated by Lagrange's formula as the variable X is not equally spaced.

Given that $x = 4$ and

x_0	x_1	x_2	x_3	x_4
0	2	3	5	6
y_0	y_1	y_2	y_3	y_4
5	7	8	10	12

From formula (19.30)

$$y_x = \frac{(4-2)(4-3)(4-5)(4-6)}{(0-2)(0-3)(0-5)(0-6)}\times 5 + \frac{(4-0)(4-3)(4-5)(4-6)}{(2-0)(2-3)(2-5)(2-6)}\times 7 + \frac{(4-0)(4-2)(4-5)(4-6)}{(3-0)(3-2)(3-5)(3-6)}\times 8 + \frac{(4-0)(4-2)(4-3)(4-6)}{(5-0)(5-2)(5-3)(5-6)}\times 10 + \frac{(4-0)(4-2)(4-3)(4-5)}{(6-0)(6-2)(6-3)(6-5)}\times 12$$

$$= \frac{4}{180}\times 5 - \frac{8}{24}\times 7 + \frac{16}{18}\times 8 + \frac{16}{30}\times 10 - \frac{8}{72}\times 12$$

$$= 0.111 - 2.333 + 7.111 + 5.333 - 1.333$$

$$= 8.889.$$

The weight of the animal at the age of 4 years is 8.889 kg.

***Example* 19.15.** Given the following logarithmic values,

$\log_{10} 200 = 2.3010$, $\log_{10} 210 = 2.3222$,

$\log_{10} 225 = 2.3522$, $\log_{10} 230 = 2.3617$.

The value of $\log_{10} 220$ can be estimated by Lagrange's polynomial formula.

The arguments and the values of the function $\log_{10} x$ are as tabulated below.

x_0		x_1		x_2		x_3
... ...	... ...	... ...	... ...	... ...	... ...	... ...
200		210		225		230
y_0		y_1		y_2		y_3
... ...	... ...	... ...	... ...	... ...	... ...	... ...
2.3010		2.3222		2.3522		2.3617

Given $x = 220$

From Lagrange's formula (19.30),

$$\log_{10} 220 = \frac{(220-210)(220-225)(220-230)}{(200-210)(200-225)(200-230)}\times 2.3010 + \frac{(220-200)(220-225)(220-230)}{(210-200)(210-225)(210-230)}\times 2.3222 + \frac{(220-200)(220-210)(220-230)}{(225-200)(225-210)(225-230)}\times 2.3522 + \frac{(220-200)(220-210)(220-225)}{(230-200)(230-210)(230-225)}\times 2.3617$$

$$= -\frac{500}{7500}\times 2.3010+\frac{1000}{3000}\times 2.3222+\frac{2000}{1875}\times 2.3522-\frac{1000}{3000}\times 2.3617$$
$$= -0.1534 + 0.7741 + 2.5090 - 0.7872$$
$$= 2.3425$$

The interpolated value of $\log_{10} 220$ is 2.3425 which is almost equal to the exact value.

INVERSE INTERPOLATION

In an inverse interpolation, it is required to interpolate x, the argument for a given value of $f(x)$, i.e. y which lies between any two tabulated values of y. The necessity of this type of interpolation often arises in trigonometry, where one needs to find an angle from its trigonometric function.

A simple way is to consider Y as independent variable and X as a dependent variable and follow any of the methods described earlier. But this approach is not suitable in most of the cases; because the variable X is considered as a function of Y say $g(y)$ which cannot be approximated by the same polynomial as $f(x)$. For example, if $y = x^2$, then $x \neq y^2$. The techniques for inverse interpolation which are simple and readily accomplishable are (*i*) method of iteration, (*ii*) method of successive approximations. These methods involve less tedious calculations as compared to some other methods and provide good estimates. Hence, these methods are discussed here.

Iterative Method

Let us consider Newton's forward polynomial formula (19.15). This polynomial can be written as,

$$y = y_0 + u\Delta y_0 + \sum_{i=2}^{n} \binom{u}{i} \Delta^i y_0 \qquad \text{...(19.31)}$$

Solving for u we get,

$$u = \frac{y - y_0}{\Delta y_0} - \frac{1}{\Delta y_0}\sum_{i=2}^{n} \binom{u}{i} \Delta^i y_0 \qquad \text{...(19.31.1)}$$

Formula (19.31.1) is an iteration formula, which expresses u as a function of u alone. The reader should recall that u is a term which involves x, the origin x_0 and a constant divisor. So if we know u, immediately x is known.

We obtain first approximation by taking

$$u_1 = \frac{y - y_0}{\Delta y_0} \qquad \text{...(19.32)}$$

Suppose, $$I(u) = \frac{1}{\Delta y_0}\sum_{i=2}^{n} \binom{u}{i} \Delta^i y_0 \qquad \text{...(19.33)}$$

Using the first approximate value u_1, we can obtain the second approximation,

$$u_2 = u_1 - I(u_1) \qquad \text{...(19.34)}$$

A third approximation is obtained by putting $u = u_2$ in $I(u)$ and thus,

$$u_3 = u_1 - I(u_2) \qquad \text{...(19.35)}$$

The iteration process is continued until a constant value of u is obtained.

It appears important to point out that it is not a compulsion to use Newton's forward polynomial alone. It is chosen here to explain the methodology. As a matter of fact, one has to choose polynomial which is appropriate in a particular situation. Prepare the difference table accordingly. Proceed as per the dictum described above to obtain the value of the argument for the given value of the function. The iteration technique is further elucidated through the following example.

***Example* 19.16.** Having known the angles x in degrees and the corresponding values of $\sin x$ as given below:

x:	30	40	50	60
$\sin x$:	0.5000	0.6428	0.7660	0.8660

One needs to find the value of angle x for a given value of $\sin x = 0.6200$.

In the given example we have to interpolate the argument for a given value of the function. So we use the inverse interpolation. In the given example $\sin x = y$. To apply the iteration technique, prepare the diagonal difference table.

x	y	Δy	$\Delta^2 y$	$\Delta^3 y$
$30 = x_0$	$0.5000 = y_0$			
		$0.1428 = \Delta y_0$		
$40 = x_1$	$0.6428 = y_1$		$-0.0196 = \Delta^2 y_0$	
		$0.1232 = \Delta y_1$		$-0.0036 = \Delta^3 y_0$
$50 = x_2$	$0.7660 = y_2$		$-0.0232 = \Delta^2 y_1$	
		$0.1000 = \Delta y_2$		
$60 = x_3$	$0.8660 = y_3$			

Given value of $y = 0.6200$

From (19.32),

$$u_1 = \frac{0.6200 - 0.5000}{0.1428} = 0.8403$$

From (19.34),

$$u_2 = 0.8403 - \frac{1}{0.1428}\left\{\binom{0.8403}{2}\times(-0.0196) + \binom{0.8403}{3}\times(-0.0036)\right\}$$

$$= 0.8403 - \frac{1}{0.1428}\{0.0013 - 0.0001\}$$

$$= 0.8403 - 0.0084$$

$$= 0.8319$$

Putting $u = 0.8319$ in $I(u)$ and repeating the process, we obtain,

$$u_3 = 0.8403 - \frac{1}{0.1428}\left\{\binom{0.8319}{2}\times(-0.0196) + \binom{0.8319}{3}\times(-0.0036)\right\}$$

$$= 0.8403 - \frac{1}{0.1428}\{0.0014 - 0.0001\}$$

$$= 0.8403 - 0.0091$$
$$= 0.8312$$

Taking $u = 0.8312$ in $I(u)$ and repeating the process, we get,

$$u_4 = 0.8403 - \frac{1}{0.1428}\left\{\binom{0.8312}{2}\times(-0.0196) + \binom{0.8312}{3}\times(-0.0036)\right\}$$
$$= 0.8403 - \frac{1}{0.1428}\{0.00138 - 0.0001\}$$
$$= 0.8403 - 0.0090$$
$$= 0.8313.$$

Since u_3 and u_4 are almost equal, we accept

$$u = 0.8313$$

we know,

$$u = \frac{x - x_0}{h}$$

or $$0.8313 = \frac{x - 30}{10}$$

or $$x = 38.313$$
$$= 38° \ 18.98''$$

From the trigonometrical table, it is easily verifiable that the inverse interpolation by iterative method has yielded the exact value of the angle.

Inverse Interpolation by Successive Approximation

This method also involves the writing of the polynomial, deemed suitable for interpolation according to the situation. Consider again Newton's forward polynomial for interpolation.

The formula is,

$$y = y_0 + \binom{u}{1}\Delta y_0 + \binom{u}{2}\Delta^2 y_0 + \binom{u}{3}\Delta^3 y_0 + \ldots\ldots + \binom{u}{n}\Delta^n y_0 \quad \ldots(19.36)$$

Rearrange the polynomial as,

$$u = \frac{y - y_0}{\Delta y_0} - \frac{1}{\Delta y_0}\left\{\binom{u}{2}\Delta^2 y_0 + \binom{u}{3}\Delta^3 y_0 + \ldots\ldots + \binom{u}{n}\Delta^n y_0\right\} \quad \ldots(19.36.1)$$

In this method, find u by neglecting all the terms involving u on the right side of (19.36.1). This provides the first estimate of u by successive approximation method, i.e.

$$u_1 = \frac{y - y_0}{\Delta y_0} \quad \ldots(19.37)$$

The second approximation is made by taking $u = u_1$ and including one more term of (19.36.1) in u_1. We obtain,

$$u_2 = \frac{y - y_0}{\Delta y_0} - \frac{1}{\Delta y_0}\binom{u_1}{2}\Delta^2 y_0 \quad \ldots(19.38)$$

For the third approximation, put $u = u_2$ and add one more term of (19.36.1) in u_2. Thus,

$$u_3 = \frac{y - y_0}{\Delta y_0} - \frac{1}{\Delta y_0}\left\{\binom{u_2}{2}\Delta^2 y_0 + \binom{u_2}{3}\Delta^3 y_0\right\} \qquad \text{...(19..39)}$$

Continue this process till the last term of the interpolating polynomial is exhausted. If the polynomial involves too many terms, one may stop after making a few approximations, provided a sufficiently stable value of u is obtained.

***Example* 19.17.** The previous example is tried again by successive approximation method using the same data. From the finite difference table and the calculation of example (19.16), we have,

$$u_1 = 0.8403$$

From (19.38)

$$u_2 = 0.8403 - \frac{1}{0.1428}\binom{0.8403}{2} \times (-0.0196)$$

$$= 0.8403 - 0.0092$$

$$= 0.8311$$

Taking $u = 0.8311$ and using (19.39) we obtain,

$$u_3 = 0.8403 - \frac{1}{0.1428}\left\{\binom{0.8311}{2} \times (-0.0196) + \binom{0.8311}{3}(-0.0036)\right\}$$

$$= 0.8403 - \frac{1}{0.1428}(0.0014 - 0.0001)$$

$$= 0.8403 - 0.0091$$

$$= 0.8312$$

Since, there is no more leading finite difference, we stop our process of successive approximation at this stage. Now taking $u = 0.8312$, we obtain the value of x. This gives,

$$0.8312 = \frac{x - 30}{10}$$

or $$x = 38.312$$

$$= 38^\circ\ 18.9''$$

The interpolated value is exact.

This chapter does not cover all the interpolation and extrapolation formulae. Moreover, the formulae given inside can be presented in many different forms. Therefore, the reader should not get confused if he finds the same formula in a different form, in other books and texts. Many topics, pertaining to interpolation, have been omitted as they do not form part of the prescribed course work. A variety of examples illustrated in the text might have made the subject matter more comprehensible.

QUESTIONS AND EXERCISES

1. What is the importance of interpolation for Businessmen and Scientists?
2. Can we always apply interpolation and extrapolation techniques? Justify your answer on the basis of certain factual example.
3. Which of the following techniques are appropriate for extrapolation?
   (*a*) Newton's forward formula.
   (*b*) Lagrange's method.
   (*c*) Binomial expansion method.
   (*d*) Parabolic curve method.
   (*e*) Gauss backward formula.
4. What are the main assumptions made for interpolation by Newton's method and Gauss' method?
5. What are the merits and demerits of graphical method for interpolation and extrapolation?
6. What is inverse interpolation? In what situations it can be used?
7. Describe one method of inverse interpolation which you consider the best.
8. What are the restrictions which prevent us from applying binomial expansion method in general?
9. Which of the following methods of interpolation are applicable when the arguments are not equally spaced?
   (*a*) Graphical method
   (*b*) Gauss backward formula
   (*c*) Lagrange's method
   (*d*) Binomial expansion method
   (*e*) Newton's method of divided differences.
10. Do we obtain an exact value of interpolation? Justify your answer on logical grounds.
11. Interpolation generally gives better estimates than extrapolations, explain why it is so?
12. Explain the following:
    (*a*) Interpolation
    (*b*) Extrapolation
    (*c*) Central difference table
    (*d*) Lagrange's method of extrapolation
    (*e*) Stirling's formula.
13. Explain how a leading difference represents a polynomial.
14. What degree of polynomial is required to fit exactly to all six pairs of observation? In what situation do we have to stop at a lower degree polynomial and why?
15. Complete the following difference table given one entry in each column.

x	y	Δy	$\Delta^2 y$	$\Delta^3 y$	$\Delta^4 y$	$\Delta^5 y$
0	—	—				
2	—	32	26	—		
4	—	—	—	—	—	–8
6	—	—	—	54	2	
8	—	—	—			
10	754					

16. The rate of gross capital formation in India at five years interval was as follows:

Years:	1960	1965	1970	1975	1980
Rate:	14.5	16.8	17.6	19.3	20.9

Interpolate the value of the rate of gross capital formation for the year 1972, by a suitable formula.

17. From the following table, find the number and percentage of students who obtained less than 45 marks.

Marks:	30–40	40–50	50–60	60–70	70–80
No. of students:	31	42	51	35	31

18. Given the following data, find out the number of workers earning Rs. 24 or more but less than Rs. 25 by interpolation technique.

Earning less than:	20	25	30	35	40
No. of workers:	296	599	804	918	966

19. The population of women of reproductive age in a city in different age groups is as shown below:

Age group of mother	*No. of mothers (lakhs)*
15—20	2.0
20—25	2.5
25—30	4.0
30—35	2.8
35—40	1.5
40—45	1.0

Estimate the number of women in the city between age group 20—23.

20. If l_x represents the numbers living at age x in a life table, interpolate the values l_x for the values (*i*) $x = 45$ (*ii*) $x = 25$ (*iii*) $x = 35$, $l_{20} = 572$, $l_{30} = 439$, $l_{40} = 346$, $l_{50} = 243$.

21. Given the following logarithms,
$\log_{10} 100 = 2.000$, $\log_{10} 120 = 2.0792$, $\log_{10} 140 = 2.1461$, $\log_{10} 150 = 2.1761$. Estimate the value of $\log_{10} 130$ by a suitable interpolation formula.

22. A person loaned Rs. 100 on interest to five persons for different number of years. He calculated the amount which he will receive at the end of the period of the loan. But a figure got rubbed off. Estimate the missing figure by binomial expansion method.

No. of years	:	5	10	15	20	25
Amount with interest (Rs.)	:	128	163	?	265	339

23.(*a*) Discuss merits and demerits of graphical method of interpolation and extrapolation.

(*b*) The age of mothers and the average number of children, born per mother, are given in the table below. Interpolate the average number of children, born per mother in the age group 30—34 by (*i*) graphical method, (*ii*) binomial expansion method.

Age of mothers:	15—19	20—24	25—29	30—34	35—39	40—44
Av. no. of children:	0.7	2.1	3.5	?	5.7	5.8

24. Table below gives the values of x and $f(x)$. Estimate the missing values of $f(x)$.

x :	1.2	1.4	1.6	1.8	2.0	2.2	2.4
$f(x)$:	1.24	?	1.96	2.44	?	3.64	4.36

25. Estimate the value of the cubic function for $x = 1.5$ given the four points (1.0), (– 2, 15), (– 1, 0), (2, 9) by (*i*) Lagrangian form of the polynomial, (*ii*) Binomial expansion method.

26. Given that $\Gamma 0.5 = \sqrt{\pi}$; $\Gamma 1 = 1$; $\Gamma 1.5 = \frac{1}{2}\sqrt{\pi}$; $\Gamma 2.0 = 1.0$; $\Gamma 3 = 2.0$; find $\Gamma 1.7$ by Lagrangian interpolation formula.

27. Given the values of Γx for different values of x, estimate the value of $\Gamma 3.0$ by Gauss formula.

x:	1.5	2.5	3.5	4.5
Γx:	$\frac{1}{2}\sqrt{\pi}$	$\frac{3}{4}\sqrt{\pi}$	$\frac{15}{8}\sqrt{\pi}$	$\frac{105}{16}\sqrt{\pi}$

28. Given below are the angles in degrees and the values of cos θ, find the angle for the value of cos θ = 0.9730.

θ:	10°00′	15°00′	20°00′	25°00′
cos θ:	0.9848	0.9659	0.9397	0.9063

29. Following are the annual premiums charged by the Life Insurance Corporation of India, for a policy of 1000. Calculate the premium payable at the age of (*i*) 38 years, (*ii*) 24 years.

Age in years:	20	25	30	35	40
Premium Rs:	23	26	30	35	42

30. In a certain test 468 candidates secured marks as given below:

Marks less than :	40	45	50	55	60	65
No. of candidates :	190	215	292	352	385	468

Find the number of candidates who obtained marks from 48 to 50.

31. Estimate the data for the years 1972 and 1975 by binomial expansion method.

Years :	1970	1971	1972	1973	1974	1975	1976
Export (*crore Rs*) :	16	20	?	28	31	?	42

(*M.Com., Agra, 1980*)

32. Obtain estimates of the missing figure in the following table:

x:	2.0	2.1	2.2	2.3	2.4	2.5	2.6
y:	0.135	—	0.111	0.100	—	0.082	0.074

(*I.C.W.A., Dec., 1982*)

33. Estimate by Newton's method of interpolation, the expectation of life at age 22 from the following data:

Age	:	10	15	20	25	30	35
Expectation of life (in yrs)	:	35.4	32.2	29.1	26.0	23.1	20.4

(*M.A. (Prev.) Meerut, 1979*)

34. The following table gives the normal weight of babies, during the first twelve months after birth:

Age in months	:	0	2	5	8	10	12
Weight (lbs.)	:	$7\frac{1}{2}$	$10\frac{1}{4}$	15	16	18	21

Find the weight of a 7 month old baby. (*M.A. Econ., Delhi, 1964*)

35. Interpolate the value of premium to be paid, by using the Newton's method, when the age at next birthday is 17, from the following table:

Age at next birthday (in years)	:	15	25	35	45	55
Premium in Rs.	:	11.1	12.6	14.3	16.1	18.3

(*B. Com., Mysore, 1969*)

36. Apply Newton's divided difference method to find out the number of persons getting Rs. 6.

Income per day (Rs.)	:	3	5	7	8	10
No. of persons	:	180	154	123	110	90

(*Dip. in Apply. Stat., Andhra, 1987*)

37. Construct a difference table and hence find $f(x)$ from the following:
$f(0) = 1, f(1) = 3, f(2) = 7, f(3) = 13$. Also calculate $f(4)$. (*I.C.W.A. June, 1987*)

38. Given

x	:	1	2	3	4	5
$y = f(x)$	:	1	8	27	64	125

(*i*) Estimate $f(2.5)$ using Newton's Forward Interpolation formula.
(*ii*) Estimate $f(2.5)$ by least square method assuming $y = a + bx + cx^2$.
(*iii*) Compare the two estimates. (*I.C.W.A. (Inter); Dec., 1992*)

SUGGESTED READING

Andrew B. Gelman and Deborah Ann Nolan (2002). *Teaching Statistics*, Oxford University Press.

Gerald, C.F. (1970). *Applied Numerical Analysis,* Addison-Wesley Publishing Company, Philippines.

Hilderbrand, F.B. (1974). *Introduction to Numerical Analysis,* Tata McGraw-Hill Publishing Company, New Delhi.

Johnson, L.W. and Riefs, R.D. (1977). *Numerical Analysis,* Addison-Wesley Publishing Company, Philippines.

Maron, M.J. (1982). *Numerical Analysis,* Macmillan Publishing Company, New York.

Stan Gibilisco (2004). *Statistics Demystified*, McGraw-Hill Professional.

20

Chapter

Elementary Decision Theory

Decision making is a routine of life. A person has to take decisions every day which may be of vital importance or of little importance and may be involving more or little risk. Whatever, may be the situation, one has to take a decision, whenever it is required. For example, a person has to take decision whether he should carry an umbrella or not on a particular day and such a decision involves little risk. Sometimes, a person has to decide whether he should undergo an operation for a disease or not. It is a vital as well as a difficult decision. Another decision problem could be whether a contractor should take a contract or not on the given terms and conditions and what option should the contractor take, out of the many options given to him. One decides many things merely on the basis of experience or intuition. But this is not always fair. Hence, the mathematicians, particularly probabilists, developed a *decision theory* which contains elements of statistics, economics and psychology. The decision theory is also termed as *decision analysis*. The contents in this chapter are like a drop in the ocean about the decision theory, as only some elementary ideas specially with regard to business and management have been given.

A decision is taken under three situations, namely, (*a*) certainty, (*b*) uncertainty and (*c*) conflict. It is trivial to take a decision under *certainty* because a decision maker knows what will be the result when a particular decision is taken. For example, a person has to decide which tie should he put on with a particular suit. It may take a little time to take a decision about this and moreover it involves almost no risk. But, a decision which involves many random factors makes the decision making more complex. Such a decision is referred to as a decision under uncertainty. A decision under uncertainty means the choice of an action out of many courses of action at hand, when the outcome of any action is unknown. Thus, the decision making always involves a chance factor. For example, there are two types of investment schemes announced by a person or an organisation. Types of investment schemes are termed as *portfolio* in financial analysis. A person who wants to invest five lakh rupees has to decide which scheme would be more profitable and safe. Alternatively, he may prefer to invest in both so that the risk is minimized or the gain is maximized. All such decisions need a basis. The basis of taking decision under uncertainty is governed by certain norms of decision analysis. As mentioned, the outcomes are not known but the probabilities of outcomes are always found out either objectively or through a series of results or subjectively.

Another type of decision making is to take a decision under a conflict. In decision making under conflict, the decisions are based not only on one person, but depend on what the other person, so called the counterpart, decides about his move. Such situations often occur in business and specially in the theory of games, where opposite players adopt varying moves, and each move of a player makes the opponent decide his next move accordingly. The decision problems under certainty and under conflict are kept out of scope of this text. Thus, the matter discussed in this chapter pertains only to the decisions under risk.

A decision problem arises when there are more than one outcome out of any single decision. Further, a decision structure always involves three elements which are as follows:

(*i*) **Acts** A decision maker has to first determine the alternative courses of action so called, 'Acts or Strategies' from which he has to choose one considered to be the best.

(*ii*) **States of nature** The circumstances, which affect the outcome of a decision problem but are beyond the control of the decision maker, are known as **states of nature** or events.

(*iii*) **Payoff** For each combination of act and event, there exists an outcome, which is dearer to the decision maker, is known as **Payoff.** Usually, the payoffs are expressed in terms of profits or present values. A payoff table may be presented as follows:

Table 20.1: Payoffs

States of nature (or events)	*Acts (strategies)*			
	A_1	A_2	A_j	A_k
E_1	a_{11}	a_{12}	a_{1j}	a_{1k}
E_2	a_{21}	a_{22}	a_{2j}	a_{2k}
$\vdots$	$\vdots$	$\vdots$	$\vdots$	$\vdots$
$\vdots$	$\vdots$	$\vdots$	$\vdots$	$\vdots$
$\vdots$	$\vdots$	$\vdots$	$\vdots$	$\vdots$
E_i	a_{i1}	a_{i2}	a_{ij}	a_{ik}
$\vdots$	$\vdots$	$\vdots$	$\vdots$	$\vdots$
$\vdots$	$\vdots$	$\vdots$	$\vdots$	$\vdots$
$\vdots$	$\vdots$	$\vdots$	$\vdots$	$\vdots$
E_n	a_{n1}	a_{n2}	a_{nj}	a_{nk}

Above table consists of n events and k strategies. a_{ij} is the payoff in terms of project or cost corresponding to ith state of nature and jth strategy.

Decision Making in Case of Unknown Probability of Events

In many situations, only payoffs are known and nothing is known about the likelihood of occurrence of various events (states of nature). To make a decision in these conditions, several persons have propounded different criteria. Some of the popular ones are given here.

1. **Maximin criterion** This criterion is based on the pessimistic approach that the worst is going to happen. Hence, a decision maker considers each strategy and select the minimum payoff for each of them. Then out of these minimum payoffs, he selects that strategy for which the payoff is maximum.
2. **Minimax criterion** It is a little optimistic approach. Under this approach a decision maker first locates the maximum payoff for each alternative act. Then out of these maximum payoffs, he selects the alternative which has minimum payoff.
3. **Maximax criterion** This is based on extreme optimism. In this criterion, first select maximum payoff for each alternative strategy and then select that strategy which corresponds to maximum of the maximum payoffs.
4. **Minimin criterion** This criterion is as a consequence of extreme pessimism. Here we first select the minimum payoff for each act and then out of these minimum, select the act corresponding to minimum payoff.
5. **Laplace criterion** Laplace thought to utilize full information *i.e.*, the payoffs for all act-event combinations. He considered that each payoff is equally likely and hence assigned equal probability $\left(\frac{1}{n}\right)$ to each payoff of a strategy having n payoffs. Work out the expected payoff for each strategy by the formula $\sum_i p_i a_{ij}$. As a matter of fact, expected payoff is simply the average payoff for each course of action. Select the strategy having the maximum payoff as best strategy. Laplace criterion is also known as the **criterion of rationality**.
6. **Savage method** This method is also known as **minimax regret criterion**. Leonard Savage proposed to workout first the opportunity loss (regret) associated with each state of nature when a particular course of action is taken. The formula for finding out the regret is as follows:

   Regret = Max. payoff for jth course of action – Payoff for each (i, j)th cell.

   Once the regret table is ready, follow the two steps for decision making as:

   (*a*) identify the maximum regret for each alternative course of action.

   (*b*) select the act corresponding to minimum regret out of the maximum regrets.
7. **Hurwicz criterion** The method proposed by Hurwicz is also known as the **criterion of realism**. Because this method has a compromising approach between extreme pessimistic and optimistic decision criterion. This concept allows to choose an appropriate degree of optimism depending on the view of decision maker. Suppose α is the degree of optimism and thus $1-\alpha$ is the degree of pessimism, where $0 \le \alpha \le 1$. Greater the value of α, more is the optimistic view of the decision maker about the course of events. Hurwicz decision procedure can be carried out in the following steps:

   (*i*) Determine a suitable degree of optimism 'α' of the decision maker.

   (*ii*) Identify the maximum and minimum payoff for each strategy (course of action).

(*iii*) Calculate the quantity 'H' for each strategy where,
$H = \alpha \times \text{max. payoff} + (1-\alpha) \times \text{min. payoff}$

(*iv*) The strategy which corresponds to the maximum value of H is selected as the best strategy.

***Example* 20.1** A businessman has five options to stock a product from suppliers and four categories of demand under consideration. The payoffs for each act - event combination are presented in the following table.

Category of demand	*Supplies level (strategy)*				
	S_1	S_2	S_3	S_4	S_5
Very high demand	17	22	32	35	43
High demand	20	24	22	32	30
Medium demand	29	28	34	33	35
Low demand	25	36	30	29	41
Max. Payoff	29	36	34	35	43
Min. Payoff	17	22	22	29	30

Note: Maximum and minimum payoffs are identified and shown in the last two rows for the sake of brevity.

The selection of the best course of action will be made on the basis of, (*i*) Maximin criterion, (*ii*) Minimax criterion, (*iii*) Maximax criterion, (*iv*) Minimin criterion, (*v*) Laplace criterion, (*vi*) Savage method, (*vii*) Hurwicz criterion, when businessman degree of optimism $\alpha = 0.7$.

Solution:

(*i*) From the last row of the table, maximum of the minimum payoff is 30. Hence, adopt S_5.

(*ii*) Minimum of maximum payoff is 29. Hence, under minimax criterion, select S_1.

(*iii*) Maximum of the max. payoff is 43. Therefore, the businessman should opt the action S_5.

(*iv*) According to minimin criterion, businessman should take the course of action S_1. Since minimum of min. payoff is 17.

(*v*) Under Laplace criterion, we will first work-out the expected payoffs for each course of action.

$$E(S_1) = \frac{1}{4}(17 + 20 + 29 + 25) = \frac{91}{4} = 22.75$$

$$E(S_2) = \frac{1}{4}(22 + 24 + 28 + 36) = \frac{110}{4} = 27.50$$

Similarly,

$$E(S_3) = \frac{118}{4} = 29.50,\ E(S_4) = \frac{129}{4} = 32.25,\ E(S_5) = \frac{149}{4} = 37.25$$

Maximum expected payoff is 37.25. Hence, businessman has to choose action S_5.

(*vi*) To apply the Savage method of decision making, we will first prepare regret table as per the procedure explicated in methodology.

Regret Table

Demand	*Actions*				
	S_1	S_2	S_3	S_4	S_5
Very high	12	14	2	0	0
High	9	12	12	3	13
Medium	0	8	0	2	8
Low	4	0	4	6	2
Max. regret	12	14	12	6	13

Out of maximum regrets, 6 is the minimum regret. Therefore, businessman should select the alternative S_4.

(*vii*) To apply Hurwicz criterion, for $\alpha = 0.7$ we calculate H for each strategy.

$H_1 = 0.7 \times 29 + 0.3 \times 17 = 25.4$

$H_2 = 0.7 \times 36 + 0.3 \times 22 = 31.8$

$H_3 = 0.7 \times 34 + 0.3 \times 22 = 30.4$

$H_4 = 0.7 \times 35 + 0.3 \times 29 = 33.2$

$H_5 = 0.7 \times 43 + 0.3 \times 30 = 39.1$

Maximum value of H is 39.1 for strategy S_5. So action S_5 is to be adopted by the businessman.

DECISION TABLE

A decision table is one which summarizes a decision problem. Each column of the table corresponds to an *act* and each row of the table corresponds to an *event*. The *outcomes* as a sequence of a combination of an act and an event are displayed as entries in each cell of the table. Let us consider a simple problem. A person wants to decide whether he should undergo an operation or not. Various outcomes of undergoing an operation are given in the following table.

Table 20.2: Decision table for undergoing an operation

	Act	
Event	*Operated*	*Not operated*
Cured	Stay free from ailment	Cured without trouble
Not cured	Bear trouble unnecessarily	Bear consequences of ailment

If we do not consider other complications of undergoing an operation, or the effects of an ailment, the acts as well as the events are mutually exclusive and exhaustive. Each cell entry is a result of a combination of an act and an event.

DECISION TREE

A decision table can accommodate a limited number of acts and events. It becomes difficult to portray a decision problem through a table, where a large number of choices are to be made at various stages. To overcome this difficulty, a diagram so called *decision tree* is appropriate for the portrayal of any problem having a number of choices and subsequent results. Each decision tree has three main items, namely, acts, events and outcomes. The acts and events are displayed through forks, having as many branches as the number of acts, and each act has as many forks as the number of events attached to it. In a decision tree, there may sometimes be a sequence of acts-events-acts-event-outcome. The outcome is depicted at the end position of the fork. The problem of distinguishing between forks, representing the acts and events is solved by taking a *square* for act-forks node and *circle* for the events-forks node. The basic rule for constructing a decision tree is that the flow should be chronological from left to right. The problem of undergoing an operation is represented by a decision tree as shown below:

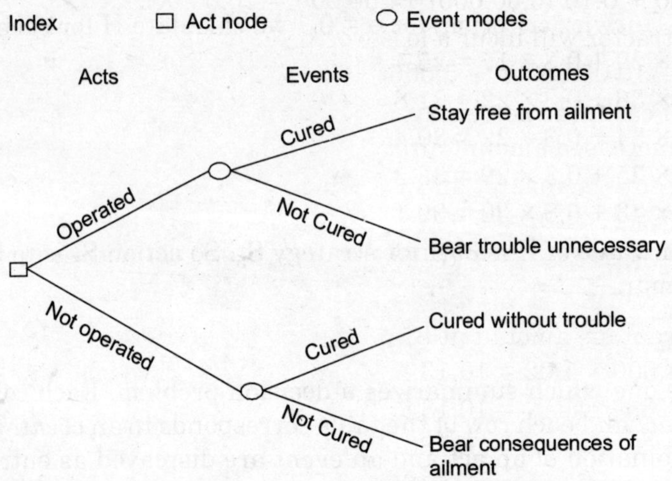

Figure 20.1 Decision Tree for Operation Problem

A decision tree is appropriate, when there is a sequence of acts-events-acts-events-outcome. The above diagram has been displayed with two acts and two events only to create better understanding without complications.

DECISIONS UNDER UNCERTAINTY

We consider a simple practical problem, and explains how and why a particular choice is made out of a set of alternatives.

***Example* 20.2**. Consider the problem of a building contractor who has been given two options and has to decide one out of the two. One option is that he takes the contract on a fixed price and the other is that he takes the contract on the basis of total cost plus a certain percentage. The implications of the two options are as follows. Prices are rising and hence a fixed price contract may not be profitable. Whereas the second option has an assured profit but of a limited amount. Hence, the contractor is in a dilemma about taking a decision under an uncertainty of an expected price rise. Now, we consider the various eventualities attached to the various events. Suppose the contract is for Rs.10 lakhs. Out of 10 lakh rupees, Rs. 5.5 lakhs are towards the cost of the material and Rs. 4 lakhs are towards the wages. If the material cost increases by 5 per cent, the amount spent by the contractor will be,

$$5,50,000 + 0.05\ (5,50,000) + 4,00,000 = 9,77,500$$

The contractor's profit = 10,000,00 – 9,77,500 = 22500

If the material cost increases by 8 per cent, the contractor will have to spend the amount,

$$5,50,000 + 0.08\ (5,50,000) + 4,00,000 = 9,94,000$$

The contractor's profit = 10,00,000 – 9,94,000 = 6,000

If the material cost increases by 10 per cent, the contractor will have to spend the amount

$$5,50,000 + 0.10\ (5,50,000) + 4,00,000 = 10,05,000$$

Thus, the contractor will incur a loss worth,

$$10,00,000 - 10,05,000 = -5,000$$

If the terms of cost plus percentage are that he will receive 102 per cent of the total cost including the increased amount after 5, 8 or 10 per cent increase in the material cost.

Cost plus percentage amount at 5% increase is,

$$977500 \times 1.02 = 9,97,050$$

Profit after 5% increase = 9,97,050 – 9,77,500
= 19,550

Cost plus percentage amount at 8% increase is,

$$9,94,000 \times 1.02 = 10,13,880$$

Profit after 8% increase = 10,13,880 – 9,94,000
= 19,880

Cost plus percentage amount at 10% increase is,

$$10,05,000 \times 1.02 = 10,25,100$$

Profit after 10% increase = 10,25,100 – 10,05,000
= 20,100

A comparison of profits under three different percentages of price rise, reveals that a fixed price contract is better if the price rise is up to 5 per cent. On the other hand, in case of an increase in price by 8 per cent or more, the cost plus percentage contract is better. The above payoffs can easily be summarised in the form of a table. The table depicting the elements of a decision problem is termed as a *payoff table. Payoffs* are usually represented by profits, revenues or any other measures which is dearer to the decision maker like time, fuel, etc. Since the payoffs depend on the choice of a particular act and are conditional and subject to the happening of an event, are often termed as *conditional values* and the payoff table is termed the *conditional value table.*

INADMISSIBLE ACT

An act is said to be inadmissible, if it is dominated by any other act. In a payoff table, if the payoffs for an act are less than any other act, the act is called an *inadmissible* act and is eliminated from the payoff table. The elimination process reduces the labour of further calculations and simplifies the process of decision making.

***Example* 20.3:** Consider the following payoff table with five acts and four events.

Table 20.3

Events	*Acts*				
	A_1	A_2	A_3	A_4	A_5
E_1	5	7	4	3	6
E_2	6	4	7	9	8
E_3	12	9	11	8	14
E_4	18	12	14	10	17

In the above table, the payoffs for act A_3 are less than the payoffs for act A_5 (for each event). Hence A_3 is inadmissible and should be deleted from the payoff table for further considerations.

***Example* 20.4:** Now the payoff table is given for the contractor's problem of example 20.2.

Table 20.4 clearly reveals that the fixed price contract is better than cost plus percentage contract, only in case of 5% price increase.

Table 20.4: Payoff table showing profits

Events	*Act*	
	Fixed price contract	*Cost plus two per cent contract*
5% rise	22,500	19,550
8% rise	6,000	19,880
10% rise	– 5,000	20,100

Now the question arises, what should be the criterion for the decision making. This will be done by attaching probabilities to the various events. In this way, a fourth factor of 'probabilities' has been introduced to the decision problem, besides act, event and outcome. These probabilities are utilized in calculating the *Expected Monetary Value* (EMV) for a decision problem. Expected monetary value is also termed as *expected payoff.* As a rule, we will choose an act having the maximum EMV. The criterion of selecting the maximum EMV of an act is often referred to as *Bayes decision rule,* named after Thomas Bayes. The Bayesian approach makes use of prior information available about the events. Let us assume that the uncertainties can be considered to be unknown numerical quantities and are represented by θ, possibly a vector of uncertainties. Bayes decision rule involves a *risk function,* $R(\theta, a)$, *i.e.*, the risk involved in taking a decision about θ, when the action a has been taken . $R(\theta, a)$ is nothing but the expected loss incurred in taking action a about θ . Thus,

$$R(\theta, a) = E\{L(\theta, a)\} \quad ...(20.1)$$

Loss is usually taken to mean the opportunity loss (OL) of money or any other measure, which reflects something not to be lost by the decision maker, e.g., time, material or quality etc.

The concept of the loss function is a pessimistic view taken by the statisticians. Contrary to this, economists take an optimistic view and talk of an *utility function.* Statistician talks about minimising the risk, vis-a-vis, the expected loss, whereas, an economist talks about maximising the utility function.

Avoiding theoretical complications, we will explain the working rules through practical problems. One thing to be remembered is that Bayes principle always involves some apriori probabilities. For this, we return to the contractor's problem and rediscuss the matter through the particular problem.

***Example* 20.5.** The probabilities to different percentages of price rise are attached on the basis of the assessment of the contractor. The probability of 5% price rise in a specified period of contract is 0.4, and that of 8% rise is 0.5, and of 10% rise is 0.1. It should be noted that, the sum of probabilities is always equal to 1. To arrive at a decision about the type of contract to be taken, we will calculate EMV for both. Suppose X_i denotes the ith event in an act, and P_i is the probability when X_i takes place. The expected monetary value of an act is given as,

$$\text{EMV} = \sum_i X_i P_i \qquad \text{...(20.2)}$$

where $i = 1, \quad 2, \quad 3, \ ...$

EMV for fixed price contract is

$$= 22500 \times 0.4 + 6000 \times 0.5 - 5000 \times 0.1$$
$$= 9000 + 3000 - 500 = 11{,}500$$

EMV for cost plus percentage contract is

$$\text{EMV}^* = 19550 \times 0.4 + 19880 \times 0.5 + 20100 \times 0.1$$
$$= 7820 + 9940 + 2010 = 19770$$

Taking EMV as the decision criterion, the contractor would choose the cost plus percentage contract, as the expected gain in this case is Rs.19,770 in comparison to Rs.11,500 in case of fixed price contract. In the former type of contract, the gain is Rs. 8270 more than the later type.

Expected monetary value as a decision criterion appears to be quite logical, as it gives the average payoff value in the long run, provided there is a certainty of the long run. But, a decision problem is not repeated a number of times in most of the cases. This leads to the conclusion that EMV is a good criterion but unpalatable. Hence, the use of EMV is considered logical when the payoffs are relatively small, as compared to the total outfit. Such a practice does not jeopardise the organisation.

EXPECTED VALUE OF PERFECT INFORMATION (EVPI)

The expected value of perfect information indicates the worth of the best possible decision in the process of decision making. The perfect information will incur some expenditure, may be the charges made by the clairvoyant person or the cost of an experiment or survey to obtain the perfect information. Suppose the contractor is making use of a perfect forecast, say, the probability of 5% price rise as 0.4 and that of 8% rise as 0.5 and of 10% rise as 0.1. These are the probabilities used by the contractor. First, we calculate the *expected value under certainty* (EVUC) as the sum over all rows of the maximum payoff value in a row of payoff table, multiplied by the probability of the corresponding row event. The calculation of EVUC, in case of the contractor's problem, is demonstrated in the table 20.5. The payoffs have been taken from table 20.4.

From table 20.5, the expected value of the payoff under certainty is Rs. 20,950. This is also known as *expected profit under certainty* (EPC). To calculate EVPI, choose an act having the highest EMV. Let the highest EMV is denoted as EMV*. Thus EVPI is the difference of EVUC and EMV*, *i.e.*,

$$\text{EVPI} = \text{EVUC} - \text{EMV}^* \qquad ...(20.3)$$

Table 20.5: Calculation of EVUC for contractor's problem

Event	*Probability*	*Payoffs*		*Row maximum (Rs.)*	*Row max.× probability (Rs.)*
		Fixed price contract (Rs.)	*Cost plus per-cent contract (Rs.)*		
5% rise	0.4	22,500	19,550	22,500	9,000
8% rise	0.5	6,000	19,880	19,880	9,940
10% rise	0.1	– 5,000	20,100	20,100	2,010
Total					20,950

In the above example,

$$\text{EVPI} = 20{,}950 - 19{,}770$$
$$= \text{Rs. } 1180$$

EXPECTED OPPORTUNITY LOSS (EOL)

As the name implies, the loss incurred by a decision maker, due to missing of better opportunity, is termed as expected opportunity loss. EOL is an alternative to best EMV and EVPI for decision making. The advantage of EOL is that it makes a combined use of best EMV and EVPI. Thus, *the expected opportunity loss for an outcome is the difference between the best payoff for an event and the payoff for the outcome of that event under an act*. In other words, it is the gain missed for not selecting the best act for an event. We first explain the expected opportunity loss through a very simple example and then come back to the contractor's problem.

***Example* 20.6.** Consider, that a shopkeeper purchases a particular item of fireworks for Rs. 10 each and sells it for Rs. 16.00 each on the occasion of Diwali. Now the problem that lies before the shopkeeper is that of determining the number of items that should be stocked because any item left unsold will be spoiled and would be a net loss. For example, the merchant expects the sale of 5 items with probability of 0.5 and 10 items with probability of 0.3 and 15 items with probability of 0.2. In this case, the opportunity loss table will be constructed as given in table 20.6.

Table 20.6: Opportunity loss table for items of fireworks

Events	*Probability*	*Acts*		
		Stock 5	*Stock 10*	*Stock 15*
		Rs.	Rs.	Rs.
Demand 5 items	0.5	0	50	100
Demand 10 items	0.3	30	0	50
Demand 15 items	0.2	60	30	0

The entries in table 20.6 are easily obtained. When the shopkeeper stocks 5 items and the demand is also for five items, there is no loss or opportunity of gain. Hence, the entry is zero. When the shopkeeper stocks 10 items against the demand of 5 items, his cost for 5 items *i.e.*, Rs. 50 has been wasted. So there is an opportunity loss of Rs. 50 due to a wrong decision. Similarly, we obtain OL in the last column of the first row. Now, consider the act, stock 5 items where the demand is for 10 items. In this situation there was an opportunity to earn the profit on the sale of another 5 items *i.e.*, a possible gain of Rs. 30, but it has been lost due to the wrong decision of stocking only 5 items. Similarly, other entries have been obtained in the table 20.6. It should be noted that table 20.6 does not contain the expected opportunity loss, but only contains the opportunity losses. The expected opportunity loss for an act would be obtained by taking the sum of the product of its entries with its corresponding probabilities. Thus,

$$\text{EOL (Act–stock 5)} = 0 \times 0.5 + 30 \times 0.3 + 60 \times 0.2 = 21$$

$$\text{EOL (Act–stock 10)} = 50 \times 0.5 + 0 \times 0.3 + 30 \times 0.2 = 31$$

$$\text{EOL (Act–stock 15)} = 100 \times 0.5 + 50 \times 0.3 + 0 \times 0.2 = 65$$

Since the minimun expected opportunity loss is Rs.21.00 for the act, stock 5 items, the shopkeeper should stock 5 items of fireworks.

***Example* 20.7.** Consider again the contractor's problem and prepare the opportunity loss table.

The entries in the table 20.7 are obtained from the payoff table 20.4 using the working rule as,

$$\text{OL} = \text{row maximum} - \text{payoff in the row}$$

Table 20.7: Opportunity loss table for contractor's problem

Events	*Probability*	*Act*	
		Fixed price contract	*Cost plus per cent contact*
5% rise	0.4	0	2950
8% rise	0.5	13,880	0
10% rise	0.1	25,100	0

The entry for OL in the cell (1, 1) = 22,500 – 22,500 = 0
The entry for OL in the cell (1, 2) = 22,500 – 19,550 = 2950
The entry for OL in the cell (2, 1) = 19,880 – 6,000 = 13,880
The entry for OL in the cell (2, 2) = 19,880 – 19,880 = 0
The entry for OL in the cell (3, 1) = 20,100 – (–5,000) = 25,100
The entry for OL in the cell (3, 2) = 20,100 – 20,100 = 0
The expected opportunity loss for two acts is,

$$\text{EOL (Fixed price)} = 0 \times 0.4 + 13{,}880 \times 0.5 + 25{,}100 \times 0.1 = \text{Rs. } 9450$$

$$\text{EOL (cost plus)} = 2950 \times 0.4 + 0 \times 0.5 + 0 \times 0.1 = \text{Rs. } 1180$$

The expected opportunity loss for the act cost plus percentage, is less than the fixed price contract. Hence, the contractor should choose the cost plus percentage contract. This is the same decision as has been taken on the criterion of EMV.

Now we display the contractor's problem through a decision tree.

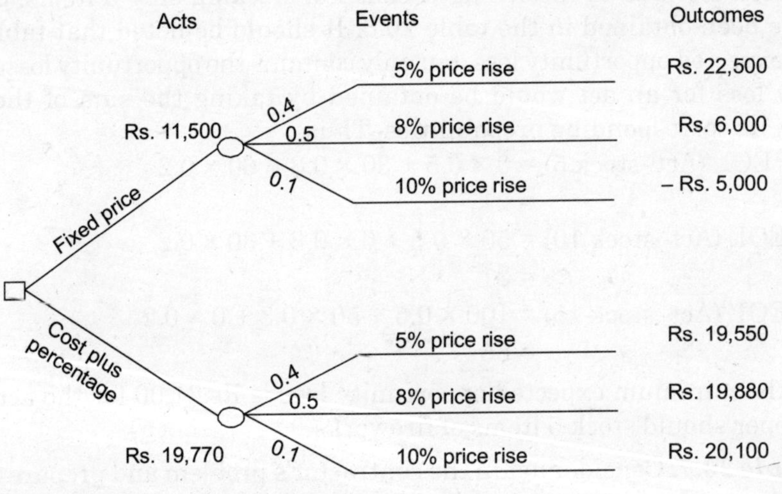

Figure 20.2 Decision tree for contractor's problem.

In the above decision tree, the figures at the terminals of the forks, originated from the square, indicate expected monetary values for the two acts. The figures at the terminals of the forks, originated from the circles, indicate the payoff values. The percentage of price rise has been shown on the forks from the circle. The probabilities of occurrence of the three events are indicated on the forks near the event nodes.

DECISION MAKING WITH IMPERFECT INFORMATION

If the cost of obtaining the perfect information, which may be the payment to the clairvoyant person or some other agency, is more than or equal to the gain due to perfect information, thus the purpose of receiving the perfect information is defeated. In the contractor's problem,

EMVI is Rs. 1180. If the charges for perfect information exceed Rs. 1180, no purpose is served in getting it. Therefore, it is desirable to base our decision on imperfect information. In this situation, the information is based on forecasts or the experiments consisting of selecting a random sample from a population, whose characteristics affect the ultimate payoffs. Thus, a decision maker's choice of an act depends on the forecast or the sample results. It is always beneficial to bear in mind that the study of sample units may be pertaining to the quantitative or the qualitative characters. In business and management, we are mostly concerned with the quantitative characters, specially the payoffs. Rather than discussing a variety of examples and lengthening our discussion, we confine ourselves to the calculation of posterior probabilities, on the basis of the forecast. This amounts to the revision of prior probabilities, on the basis of added imperfect information. Now we explain the way, the forecast or the sampling information can be integrated into the basic structure of decision making. Such an approach is based on Bayes' conditional probability rules. The whole process of decision making is re-examined by making use of posterior probabilities in contractor's problem.

***Example* 20.8.** A professional economist, approaches the contractor to make use of his forecast. The consultant actually does not tell the exact probabilities of a fixed percentage of a price rise, but only tells about the trend *i.e.*, whether there will be a fast rise in prices or whether the prices will rise at the slow rate during the period of contract. For brevity, we write the forecasts as 'Fast' and 'Slow'. On the basis of this information, the economist also gives the reliability statement for various price rise as, the probability of 5% price rise in view of forecast 'Fast' is 0.2 *i.e.*,

$$P\,(\text{Fast} \mid 5\%) = 0.2$$

and for forecast 'slow' is 0.8 *i.e.*, $P\,(\text{Slow} \mid 5\%) = 0.8$

For 8% price rise, the probability under forecast 'Fast' is 0.7 *i.e.*, $P\,(\text{Fast} \mid 8\%) = 0.7$ and 0.3 for forecast 'Slow', $P\,(\text{Slow} \mid 8\%) = 0.3$. For 10% price rise, the probability under the forecast 'fast' is 0.9, *i.e.*, $P\,(\text{Fast} \mid 10\%) = 0.9$ and 0.1 for forecast 'Slow', *i.e.*, $P\,(\text{Slow} \mid 10\%) = 0.1$. We know that the prior probabilities assessed by the contractor in EVPI are:

$$P\,(5\%) \equiv P\,(5\%\text{ price rise}) = 0.4$$
$$P\,(8\%) \equiv P\,(8\%\text{ price rise}) = 0.5$$
$$P\,(10\%) \equiv P\,(10\%\text{ price rise}) = 0.1$$

The posterior probabilities are given by,

$$P\,(\text{Event} \mid \text{Forecast result}) \qquad \text{...(20.4)}$$

$$= \frac{P(\text{Event} \cap \text{Forecast result})}{P(\text{Forecast result})} \qquad \text{...(20.4.1)}$$

By Bayes' formula (5.11) we obtain,

$$P\,(\text{Event} \cap \text{Forecast}) = P\,(\text{Forecast} \mid \text{Event}) \times P\,(\text{Event}) \qquad \text{...(20.5)}$$

We first calculate P (Event $\cap$ Forecast result) for the forecast 'Fast' and 'Slow' separately by formula (20.5), making use of the probabilities given with the reliability statements and the prior probabilities.

$$P\,(5\% \cap \text{Fast}) = P\,(\text{Fast} \mid 5\%)\,P\,(5\%) = 0.2 \times 0.4 = 0.08$$
$$P\,(5\% \cap \text{Slow}) = P\,(\text{Slow} \mid 5\%)\,P\,(5\%) = 0.8 \times 0.4 = 0.32$$
$$P\,(8\% \cap \text{Fast}) = P\,(\text{Fast} \mid 8\%)\,P\,(8\%) = 0.7 \times 0.5 = 0.35$$

$$P(8\% \cap \text{Slow}) = P(\text{Slow} \mid 8\%)\, P(8\%) = 0.3 \times 0.5 = 0.15$$

$$P(10\% \cap \text{Fast}) = P(\text{Fast} \mid 10\%)\, P(10\%) = 0.9 \times 0.1 = 0.09$$

$$P(10\% \cap \text{Slow}) = P(\text{Slow} \mid 10\%)\, P(10\%) = 0.1 \times 0.1 = 0.01$$

The probability of price rise 'Fast' = 0.08 + 0.35 + 0.09 = 0.52

The probability of price rise 'Slow' = 0.32 + 0.15 + 0.01 = 0.48

The posterior probabilities by the formula (20.4.1) are,

$$P(5\% \mid \text{Fast}) = \frac{P(5\% \cap \text{Fast})}{P(\text{Fast})} = \frac{0.08}{0.52} = 0.1538$$

$$P(5\% \mid \text{Slow}) = \frac{P(5\% \cap \text{Slow})}{P(\text{Slow})} = \frac{0.32}{0.48} = 0.6667$$

$$P(8\% \mid \text{Fast}) = \frac{P(8\% \cap \text{Fast})}{P(\text{Fast})} = \frac{0.35}{0.52} = 0.6731$$

$$P(8\% \mid \text{Slow}) = \frac{P(8\% \cap \text{Slow})}{P(\text{Slow})} = \frac{0.15}{0.48} = 0.3125$$

$$P(10\% \mid \text{Fast}) = \frac{P(10\% \cap \text{Fast})}{P(\text{Fast})} = \frac{0.09}{0.52} = 0.1731$$

$$P(10\% \mid \text{Slow}) = \frac{P(10\% \cap \text{Slow})}{P(\text{Slow})} = \frac{0.01}{0.48} = 0.0208$$

It can be verified that the sum of the probabilities,

$$\sum_{3\text{ events}} P(\text{Event} \mid \text{Fast}) = 0.1538 + 0.6731 + 0.1731 = 1.0$$

$$\sum_{3\text{ events}} P(\text{Event} \mid \text{Slow}) = 0.6667 + 0.3125 + 0.0208 = 1.0$$

Once we have got the posterior probabilities, there is no sense in confining ourselves to the use of prior probabilities. Hence, we calculate the expected monetary values under the forecast 'Fast' and 'Slow' separately, for a fixed price and cost plus percentage contract.

For the forecast 'Fast',

$$\begin{aligned} \text{EMV (Fixed price)} &= 22500 \times 0.1538 + 6000 \times 0.6731 - 5000 \times 0.1731 \\ &= 3460.50 + 4038.60 - 865.50 \\ &= 6633.60 \end{aligned}$$

$$\begin{aligned} \text{EMV (Cost plus)} &= 19550 \times 0.1538 + 19880 \times 0.6731 + 20100 \times 0.1731 \\ &= 3006.79 + 13381.23 + 3479.31 \\ &= 19867.33 \end{aligned}$$

EMV for cost plus percentage contract is greater than EMV for fixed price contract, in spite of the use of posterior probabilities under the new forecast 'Fast'.

For the forecast 'Slow',

$$\begin{aligned} \text{EMV (Fixed price)} &= 22500 \times 0.6667 + 6000 \times 0.3125 - 5000 \times 0.0208 \\ &= 15000.75 + 1875.00 - 104 \\ &= 16771.75 \end{aligned}$$

$$\begin{aligned}\text{EMV (Cost plus)} &= 19550 \times 0.6667 + 19880 \times 0.3125 + 20100 \times 0.0208 \\ &= 13033.98 + 6212.50 + 418.08 \\ &= 19664.56\end{aligned}$$

Again, for the price rise forecast 'Slow', cost plus percentage contract is better than fixed price contract. We can also calculate the expected value, for selecting cost plus percentage contract in both kind of forecasts. For contractor's problem, the expected value is,

$$19867.33 \times 0.52 + 19664.56 \times 0.48 = 19770.00$$

To avoid confusion, it is worthwhile to point out, that a situation may arise in which a decision maker may select one course of action with the forecast 'Fast' and the other course of action with the forecast 'Slow'.

If the contractor has to pay fee to the consultant say, Rs. 500, this amount has to be deducted from the expected value. In the present example, there is no gain after paying any fee, and the contractor would not like to buy the forecast.

The contractor's problem with apriori probabilities and posteriori probabilities has been displayed in the decision tree 20.3.

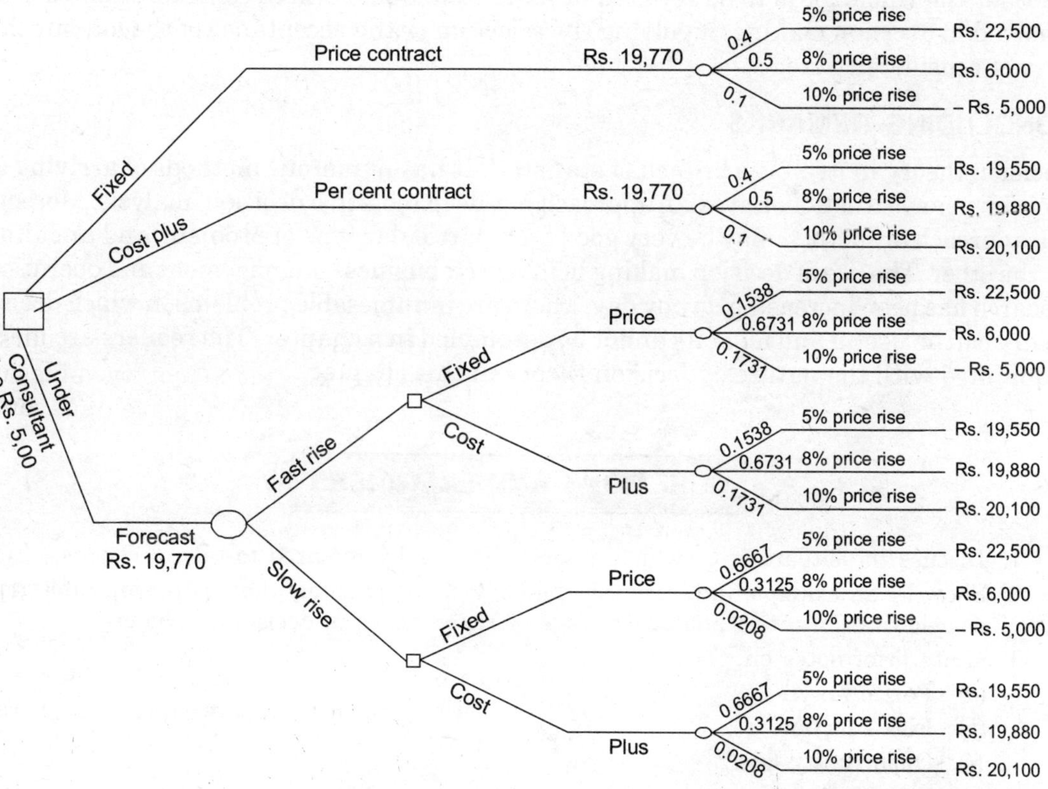

Figure 20.3 Decision tree for contractor's problem with forecast

In the above problem, it is by chance that the expected value with forecast, and EMV without forecast, in the act of cost plus percentage are the same. Hence, paying for the forecast is not profitable. As a general rule, the net gain under the consultant's forecast is the difference between the expected value after deducting the consultation fee, if any, and the maximum EMV for an act without forecast.

USE OF SAMPLE INFORMATION IN DECISION MAKING

Such type of studies often occur in factories. Suppose, a manufacturer expects that his system will not produce more than two per cent defective items and to make sure of his belief, the manufacturer asks the quality control section to test the lot. At the best, the quality control section can select a random sample of adequate size, as it is not possible to test each and every item of the lot. Tests are performed on the selected items to know what percentage of items are defective in the sample which gives an estimate for the whole lot. In this way, an additional information is obtained. Such an information is known as *information result* or *sample result* and is as good as the forecast. Therefore, the procedure for decision making adopted with forecast, can be applied with sample information also. On the basis of additional information, he has to revise his probability of percentage of defectives in the lot. Having this much of information, a decision has to be taken as to whether the whole lot is to be rejected or marketed. Some others considerations are also involved in decision making, involving the rejection or the acceptance of the lot, but these are not considered here.

CONCLUDING REMARKS

Decision theory in itself is a branch of statistics. It has numerous methods of arriving at a decision in any situation. Bayesian approach has deep roots in a decision analysis. Moreover, one approach or method may be very good for a particular type of problem, and unsuitable for the other. The use of decision making in industry, business, management and operational research has been increasing day by day. There are innumerable problems in which decision theory can be useful and all of it cannot be assembled in a chapter. The readers are merely acquainted with the nature of decision theory in this chapter.

QUESTIONS AND EXERCISES

1. Discuss the situations in which a person is usually required to take decisions.
2. Show by an example (not given in the body of the chapter) that a decision table and a decision tree are two analogous ways of representing a decision problem.
3. Write brief notes on;
   (*a*) Portfolio
   (*b*) Risk function
   (*c*) Opportunity loss
   (*d*) Payoffs
   (*e*) Posterior probabilities.

4. Write three situations where the decision making with imperfect information is necessitated.
5. Define expected monetary value and expected monetary value of perfect information. How are they used as decision criterion?
6. A person is allowed to travel by an aeroplane, by train in Ist class and by car from Delhi to Mumbai. Travel by aeroplane costs him Rs. 400 more than train and Rs. 300 more by car than train. Travelling by plane saves 14 hours and by car he save 8 hours. Travelling by car gives him the enjoyment worth 10 units and by train worth 4 units and by plane worth 1 unit. Prepare a payoff table in terms of the three types of payoff measures.
7. Write whether the following statements are true or false.
   (*a*) The entries in a payoff table can be negative.
   (*b*) The entries in an opportunity loss table can be negative.
   (*c*) The value of an expected monetary value may be zero or negative.
   (*d*) The sum of the revised probabilities, after the sample information, may exceed one.
   (*e*) Expected opportunity loss can lead to a wrong decision.
8. A dealer stocks three types of machines namely, hand operated (HO), semiautomatic (SA) and fully automatic (FA). The cost price of a HO machine is Rs. 5300 and involves installation charges per machine as Rs. 500. A HO machine is sold for Rs. 6200. The cost price of SA machine is Rs. 7000 and its installation involves an expenditure of Rs. 600 per machine. A SA machine is sold for Rs. 8100. The cost price of a FA machine is Rs. 12,000 and its installation involves an expenditure of Rs. 370 per machine. A FA machine is sold for Rs. 12,900. The overhead costs on the three types of machines (HO, SA and FA) per year are Rs. 5,500, Rs. 7,750 and Rs. 11,250. The demand of machines is categorised as follows:
   Light demand — 30 machines per year.
   Moderate demand — 80 machines per year.
   Heavy demand — 120 machines per year.
   The dealer assessed the probabilities as light demand (L) = 0.2; moderate demand (M) = 0.3 and heavy demand (H) = 0.5.
   (*a*) Calculate the expected monetary values for the three acts, *i.e.*, the sale of three types of machines. Also suggest what type of machine should the dealer stock to sale?
   (*b*) Depict the dealers problem through a decision tree.
   (*c*) Find the expected value of perfect information.
9. For the dealer's problem given in question No. 8, an agency forecasts the conditional probabilities of light (X_1), moderate (X_2) and heavy (X_3) demand as given in the table below. Using the additional information, find the expected monetary value and take a decision as to which type of a machine should the dealer stock to sale.

State of nature θ	*Conditional probabilities* $P(X \mid \theta)$			*Prior probabilities*
	demand HO X_1	*demand SA* X_2	*demand FA* X_3	
L	.25	.60	.15	.2
M	.20	.30	.50	.3
H	.20	.10	.70	.5

10. Identify whether there is any inadmissible act in the following payoff table.

Event	Act A_1	A_2	A_3	A_4	Probability
E_1	20	–12	–10	–30	0.4
E_2	40	40	44	30	0.5
E_3	65	72	75	70	0.1

Calculate the maximum expected payoff and state to which act does it correspond?

11. Given the following opportunity loss table, find which act leads to the maximum expected opportunity loss.

Events	Acts A_1	A_2	A_3	A_4	Probability
E_1	4	0	8	16	0.2
E_2	0	8	16	24	0.1
E_3	12	8	4	0	0.3
E_4	8	4	0	8	0.4

12. A vegetable grower wants to make a contract with a canning factory, about one vegetable which he will grow in his entire field of 50 acres and supply to the factory. The factory has given him the option to grow any one of the three vegetables, Tomatoes, Peas and Cauliflowers. The farmer knows that the yield of vegetables greatly depend on the rains. The farmer collects the following information. The given table also contains the rates of vegetables offered by the factory.

Rainfall	Yield (quintal/acre) Tomato	Pea	Cauliflower	Probability
Little	40	24	60	0.4
Good	50	32	100	0.6
Rate/quintal	Rs. 50	Rs. 100	Rs. 80	

(*a*) Prepare the payoff table, for returns to the farmer in terms of total cash receipts.

(*b*) Which act has the maximum expected monetary value?

(*c*) Which vegetable should the farmer grow to have the maximum receipt?

(*d*) The meteorologist gives one word forecast as 'poor' or 'good'. The reliability statement with forecast 'poor' is, that the probability of little rainfall is 0.7 and of good rainfall is 0.2. The reliability statement with forecast 'better' is, that the probability of little rainfall is 0.3 and of good rainfall is 0.8. Suggest which vegetable should the farmer grow after the forecast?

13. A person has the choice of running a hot snack stall or an ice-cream and cold drink shop at a certain holiday resort during the coming summer season. If the weather during the season is cool and rainy he can expect to make a profit of Rs. 15,000 and if it is warm he can expect to make a profit of only Rs. 3,000 by running a hot snack stall. On the other hand, if his choice is to run an ice-cream and cold drinks shop, he can expect to make a profit of Rs. 18,000 if the weather is warm and only Rs. 3,000 if the weather is cool and rainy. The meteorological authorities predict that there is 40% chance of the weather being warm during the coming season. You are to advise him as to the

choice between the two types of stalls. Base clearly your argument on the expectation of the results of the two courses of action and show the result in a tabular form.

(*C.A. May, 1983*)

14. A group of volunteers of a service organisation raises money each year by selling gift articles outside the stadium after a football match between Teams X and Y. They can buy any of the three different types of gift articles from a dealer. Their sales are mostly dependent on which team wins the match. A conditional pay-off table is as under:

	Type of gift articles		
	I	II	III
Team X wins	Rs.1,000	900	600
Team Y wins	Rs. 400	500	800

(*i*) Construct the Opportunity Loss Table and

(*ii*) Which type of gift article should the volunteers buy if the probability of Team X's winning is 0.8? (*C.A. Inter; Nov., 1993*)

15. Calculate EMV and thus select the best act for the following payoff table.

State of nature	*(Prob.)*	*Pay-off (Rs.) by the player*		
		A	*B*	*C*
X	(0.3)	–2	–5	20
Y	(0.4)	20	–10	–5
Z	(0.3)	40	60	30

(*I.C.W.A., Inter, June, 2003*)

16. (*a*) You are given the following payoffs of three acts A_1, A_2 and A_3 and states of nature S_1, S_2, S_3.

	Acts		
States of nature	A_1	A_2	A_3
S_1	25	–10	–125
S_2	400	440	400
S_3	650	740	750

The probability of the three states of nature are respectively 0.1, 0.7 and 0.2. Calculate and tabulate E.M.V. and conclude which of the acts can be chosen as the best.

(*b*) Marketing department of a company calculated the payoffs in terms of yearly net profits for each of the strategies of expected sale price in the following table:

	States of nature of sale		
Strategies ↓	n_1	n_2	n_3
P_1	7000	3000	1500
P_2	5000	4500	0
P_3	3000	3000	3000

Which strategy should the marketing executive choose on the basis of (*i*) maximin criterion, (*ii*) minimax criterion, and (*iii*) Laplace criterion.

(*I.C.W.A., Inter, June, 2004*)

17. Which criteria are based on extreme optimism and pessimism in decision process?
18. What do you understand by minimax regret table and where is it used?
19. Given is the following payoff matrix.

State of nature	*Probability*	*Acts*		
		Do not expand	*Expand 100 units*	*Expand 200 units*
High demand	0.2	3,500	4,500	6,000
Medium demand	0.3	3,500	4,500	3,500
Low demand	0.5	3,500	3,500	2,000

Using EMV criterion decide the best act. *(C.A., Foundation, May, 2002)*

20. Consider the following payoff (profit) matrix.

		States			
		S_1	S_2	S_3	S_4
	a_1	5	10	18	25
	a_2	8	7	8	23
Action	a_3	21	18	12	21
	a_4	30	22	19	15

No probabilities are known for the occurrence of the nature states. Compare the solutions obtained by each of the following criteria:

(*i*) Laplace (*ii*) Maximin (*iii*) Minimax (*iv*) Hurwicz (assume that $\alpha = 0.5$)

(I.C.W.A., Inter, June, 2002)

21. What is the theme behind Hurwicz criterion of selecting the best act?
22. The table below gives the payoffs of the acts A_1, A_2 and A_3 and the states of nature E_1, E_2 and E_3 with their respective probabilities. Find the optimum value of expected opportunity loss and the optimum action.

Acts		*States of nature*		
		E_1	E_2	E_3
	Probability	0.2	0.4	0.4
A_1		90	60	–15
A_2		80	65	–10
A_3		60	50	0

(C.A., Foundation, May, 2001)

23. Based on the following payoff matrix:

States of nature	*Payoff matrix*			
	Acts			
	A	*B*	*C*	*D*
P	5	10	18	25
Q	8	7	8	23
R	21	18	12	21
S	30	22	19	15

Determine the alternative to be chosen under (*i*) Maximax, (*ii*) Maximin and (*iii*) Minimax regret criterion. (*C.A., Foundation, Nov., 1999*)

24. Which criterion is known as the criterion of rationality? Describe it.
25. What is the structure of decision theory? Explain adequately.

SUGGESTED READING

Berger, J.O. (1980). *Statistical Decision Theory,* Springer-Verlag, Berlin.

Braverman, J.D. (1978). *Fundamentals of Business Statistics,* Academic Press, New York.

Byrkit, D.R. (1979). *Elementary Business Statistics,* D. Van Nostrand Company, New York.

Charles, A. (1979). *Decision-making under Uncertainty: Models and Choices,* Prentice-Hall, Englewood Cliffs.

David Ray Anderson, Dennis J-Sweeney and Thomas Arthur Williams (2004). *Statistics for Business and Economics*, Thomson South-Western.

Felix Klein (2004). *Elementary Mathematics from an Advanced Standpoint*, Courier Dover Publications.

Hoel, P.G. and R.J. Jessen (1982). *Basic Statistics for Business and Economics,* John Wiley, New York.

Lapin, L.L. (1981). *Quantitative Methods for Business Decisions,* Harcourt Brace Jovanovich, 2nd ed. New York.

Levin, R.L., C.A. Kirkpatrick and D.S. Rubin (1982). *Quantitative Approach to Management,* McGraw-Hill Book Company, New York.

Panchapakesan, S. and N. Balakrishnan (1977). *Advances in Statistical Decision Theory and Applications*, Birhauser.

Raiffa, H. (1970). *Decision Analysis: Introductory Lectures on Choices under Uncertainty,* Addison-Wilsey Publishing Company, California.

Wermuth, N., Mark J. Schervish and K. Krickebery (1995). *Theory of Statistics,* Springer.

21 Chapter

Statistical Quality Control

General Discussion

The quality of a product is the most important property that one desires while purchasing it. A product is of good quality, if it meets the required specifications, otherwise not. In this competitive world, the success of a manufacturer mostly depends on quality of his product. Also, the quality of the product should be maintained so that the reputation of the company does not suffer. The quality of every product or article can be defined, but statistical quality control deals with the quality of the articles produced in an industry. It is commonly felt that all the articles produced by a machine will be exactly similar, but this is not true as variation is inherent and unavoidable. On taking measurements pertaining to certain characteristics of articles, it is found that they do differ from one another. If this difference is negligible from the desired measurements, the article is acceptable and if it differs much from the specifications, it is to be rejected.

A manufacturer cannot afford the rejection of his finished product so often. Therefore, it is necessary to keep constant vigil on the quality of the finished product. For instance, the ball bearing is exactly circular and of a specified diameter, the size of the bolt is 5 cm exactly, each match box contains 50 sticks, a battery cell gives current at 2 volts etc. These objectives can be fulfilled by the statistical technique named statistical quality control (S.Q.C.). With the aid of statistical methods we can find out whether the variation in the articles is of random nature, or whether some reason can be assigned for this variation. Thus, statistical quality control methods are applied to two phases of the manufacturing process.

(*i*) A control is to be maintained during the process of manufacturing of the articles. This facilitates the manufacturer to keep a constant vigil during the process. At this stage, it is statistically tested whether the variation occurring in various pieces is by chance or due to some defect in the manufacturing process like some fault in the machine. S.Q.C. is applicable to any repetitive manufacturing process and is known as a *process control*. It is to be kept in mind, that the population in a repetitive process consists of an infinite number of items. The process control, which is carried through the inspection of samples collected at regular intervals, guards the producer against the production of poor quality product, and assists to determine whether the manufacturing process is running under control or not.

(*ii*) The second phase is the checking of the quality of the manufactured product in respect of its acceptability. This is achieved through an acceptance inspection or a sampling inspection plan. The purpose of this is to test whether the product, which is in existence, is acceptable to the consumer or not. Such a sampling inspection is often termed as *product control* or *lot control.* Product control is carried through the inspection of a sample of items, selected randomly from the lot under consideration. If this sampling inspection conforms to the quality of the product as desired, the lot is accepted, otherwise it is rejected. The variation, in quality characteristics of product, can be divided into two categories.

Chance Variation

A product shows some deviation from the desired specification of the product in spite of all care. As a matter of fact, such a variation is unavoidable. By *chance variation,* we mean the variation occurring in the pieces due to minor causes or the variation to which no reason can be assigned, and is of random nature. This type of variation is tolerable and does not affect the quality and the utility of the articles or product. If there exists only chance variation, the process is said to be under *statistical control.*

Assignable Variation

Sometimes, the articles show marked deviation from the given specifications of a product. This affects the utility of the product and causes worry to the manufacturer. Such a major variation from the standard measurements may be due to various reasons, such as the change in the quality of raw material, a defect in the machine, non-expertise of the mechanic etc. If the variation from standard in the product occurs due to assignable causes, the process is said to be out of control. The causes can be traced out from the type of defect observed in the product and the process is rectified.

As already said, the statistical quality control is mainly confined to the finished product, manufactured by a factory. Statistically, it is ascertained whether the variation occurring in the manufactured units, is a chance variation or is due to certain lacunae, which can be removed to improve the quality of the articles or items. This is done through certain charts such as $\overline{X}$, R, p, c charts etc. *The control chart is a statistical device mainly used for the study and control of a repetitive process.* Statistical techniques for controlling the quality of the finished industrial product, were developed by Dr. Walter A. Shewhart, a physicist of Bell Telephone laboratory in 1924 and subsequent years. The methodology, developed by Shewhart, could not get full recognition until world war II. The pressing needs of production, with precision and accuracy, made the people realize the importance and utility of statistical methods. The advantages of statistical quality control are summarised below.

1. Statistical quality control makes it possible to discriminate whether the deviation from the standard occurring in the product, during manufacturing process, is due to chance factors or due to assignable causes.
2. The items, which meet the specifications under statistical control, get a good market for sale and the demand increases day by day.
3. Quality control indicates the defects, if any in the machinery or the inefficiency of the operator.

4. Statistical quality control is extremely helpful, particularly in the case, where the units are destroyed under inspection e.g., the life of an electric bulb, bullets or bombs, life of a battery cell etc.
5. The greatest advantage is the low cost of inspection and the assurance for the product to be of standard quality.
6. It minimizes the risk of the consumer as well as the producer.
7. A quality control scheme alerts the personnel about any ensuing defects. Moreover, one can think of certain improvement.
8. Quality control techniques provide protection to the manufacturer against losses, due to the rejection of manufactured products, likely to be made at a late stage.
9. Further, a factory can also check the quality of the raw material before its consumption, through quality control scheme. This protects the producer from further losses.

As already mentioned, the statistical quality control is carried through the control charts. These charts may be divided into two categories namely, (1) control charts for quality measurements (continuous variable), (2) control charts for attributes. The main idea behind Shewhart's control charts lies in the division of observations into groups or so called *rational sub-groups.* When the subgroups of a production process are formed in such a way that the variation within a sub-group may be attributed to chance factors only, whereas systematic variation, if at all present, can occur only between the sub-groups. In other words, the units belonging to a sub-group are as homogeneous as possible, where as, one sub-group differs from another, indicating the presence of a systematic variation, if it exists. Such sub-groups are termed as rational sub-groups.

Whichever type of control charts may have been used, manufactured units have to be inspected. In the use of control charts, all the manufactured units are not inspected, but a sample of units is inspected. In process control, a sample of unit is selected at regular intervals. For product control, a sample is drawn from a lot which is known as *acceptance sampling.* The sampling scheme may consists of a single stage or a multistage. Many times a sequential sampling plan is also used. The sampling plans are discussed ahead. On the basis of inspection of sample units which take into consideration certain measurements or attributes, a whole lot (population of units) is to be accepted or rejected according to some criterion. *By a lot, we mean a finite number of units produced during a definite period of time.* Once the units are inspected, control charts help us to decide whether the process is under control or not i.e., whether there occurs a chance variation or an assignable variation. On the other hand, the acceptance sampling plans help us to decide whether the lot is to be accepted or not. Sampling inspection is generally an accepted procedure, though in some situations, inspection of the whole lot is called for. Such situations arise when,

(*i*) a defective unit may cause danger to the life e.g., the insulation defect in a high voltage unit.

(*ii*) a defective part may spoil the whole machinery e.g., the failure of certain resistance may fuse the radio bulbs.

(*iii*) total number of units manufactured, is small.

(*iv*) there is a lack of confidence on the consistent performance of a manufacturing process.

CONTROL CHARTS FOR PROCESS CONTROL

Shewhart's Charts for Variables

The quality of a large number of products is adjudged on the basis of measurements of characteristics, such as length, diameter, weight, tensile strength, life of bulbs, chemical composition etc. These variables are of a continuous type. For continuous variable, Shewhart developed control charts known as $\overline{X}$, σ and R charts, to keep a control on the quality of the product. These charts involve the location parameter 'the mean', the scale parameters, 'the range and the standard deviation'.

$\overline{X}$-Chart

Some variations do occur from unit to unit, as no two units are alike in respect of certain characteristics. To keep a control on the measurable characteristic of articles, we use $\overline{X}$-chart, which involves the mean $\overline{X}$ and the standard deviation σ. $\overline{X}$- chart is a graphic device, which depicts the measurements revealing the state of their scatteredness from the standard value. The control charts have three horizontal lines – the lower line, the middle line and the upper line. The middle line or the central line (C.L.) shows the standard value of the quality characteristic (variable) of the manufactured units. The lower line is the lower control limit (L.C.L.) of the variate values and the upper line is the upper control limit (U.C.L.) of the variate values, as shown in Fig. 21.1.

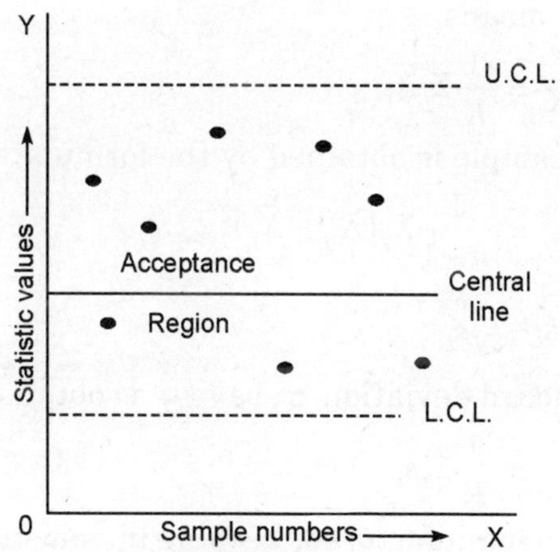

Figure 21.1 A Control Chart, in General

As a tradition, the lines indicating the upper and the lower control limits are shown by dotted lines, while the central line is kept smooth. A small sample of units (around 5 units) is drawn at regular intervals and the decision about the process, whether, it is under control or not is taken on the basis of the plotted points, which in this case are mean values of the samples plotted against sample numbers. The decision criterion is, if all the plotted points lie on or in between upper and lower control limits, the process is under control. On the contrary, if any one or more points lie outside the control limits, it is concluded that the process is not under control, which indicates the presence of some assignable causes. Such a variation arises because of increased dispersion beyond the tolerance limits.

Setting of Control Limits

Let μ be the mean and σ be the standard deviation of variate values for all the units of the process. We know that 99.73% units fall within $\mu \pm 3\sigma$ limits in case of normal population. Hence, the process is considered under control if the mean values of the samples fall within plus and minus, three times the standard deviation of the statistic from the true mean. The standard error of a sample mean $\bar{x}$, based on a sample of size n, is $\sigma/\sqrt{n}$. Often the mean value and standard deviation for all the units of the process are not known. Hence, the estimated values of population mean μ and the standard deviation σ are used to set the control limits. The mean of the sample means is taken as the standard value, *i.e.*, estimated value of the population mean and the mean of standard deviations of K samples, say, $\overline{S}$ is taken as the estimate of the standard deviation σ.

Let K samples, of equal size n, be taken at regular intervals of the process. Suppose, the variate values on ith random sample are $X_{i1}, X_{i2}, ..., X_{in}$. The ith sample mean,

$$\overline{X}_i = \frac{1}{n}\Sigma_j X_{ij} \qquad ...(21.1)$$

$i = 1, 2, ..., K$ and $j = 1, 2, ..., n$.

From formula (21.1), we can calculate the means $\overline{X}_1, \overline{X}_2, \overline{X}_3, ..., \overline{X}_K$.

The mean of the sample means,

$$\overline{\overline{X}} = \frac{1}{K}\Sigma_i \overline{X}_i \qquad ...(21.2)$$

The variance of the ith sample is obtained by the formula

$$s_i^2 = \frac{1}{n-1}\Sigma_j (X_{ij} - \overline{X}_i)^2 \qquad ...(21.3)$$

and

$$s_i = \sqrt{s_i^2} \qquad ...(21.3.1)$$

The estimate of the standard deviation σ, say, $\overline{S}$ is obtained as

$$\overline{S} = \frac{1}{K}\Sigma_i s_i \qquad ...(21.4)$$

The units or products are manufactured, keeping in view the purpose for which it is to be used. If the units produced are spare parts, they will have to be set in a particular type and size of machine. If the product is a chemical compound, it will be used for some specific purpose. In all these cases, the average size and variance are predecided, *i.e.*, the standard values are prefixed. Suppose μ' and σ' are the known values of mean μ and S.D. σ respectively. The control limits are given by

$$\mu' \pm 3\frac{\sigma'}{\sqrt{n}}$$

$$\text{Thus} \quad \left.\begin{aligned} \text{U.C.L.} &= \mu' + A\sigma' \\ \text{C.L.} &= \mu' \\ \text{L.C.L.} &= \mu' - A\sigma' \end{aligned}\right\} \qquad ...(21.5)$$

where $A = 3/\sqrt{n}.$

Often, the standard deviation is not used as a measure of dispersion. Instead, the range is used. In this case, we find the range R_i for each sample by the formula,

$$R_i = max\, X_{ij} - min\, X_{ij}$$

$$i = 1, 2, ..., K$$

$$j = 1, 3, ..., n$$

and overall the mean range is obtained by the formula,

$$\overline{R} = \frac{1}{K}\Sigma_i R_i$$

$$i = 1, 2, ..., K.$$

The mean range is used in the formulae given ahead.

In a large number of cases, the statistics personnel are not told the standard values of the mean and the variance. Hence, in such cases the estimated values of μ and σ are used. Let the estimated values of μ and σ be $\hat{\mu}$ and $\hat{\sigma}$ which can be obtained by the following relations.

$$\hat{\mu} = \overline{X} \text{ and } \hat{\sigma} = \frac{\overline{S}}{c_2}$$

The control limits are

$$\overline{X} \pm 3\frac{\overline{S}}{c_2\sqrt{n}} \qquad ...(21.6)$$

where c_2 is a constant factor obtained from the distribution of sample standard deviation such that $E(\overline{S}/c_2) = \sigma$. The constant,

$$c_2 = \sqrt{\frac{2}{n}}\frac{\Gamma\frac{n}{2}}{\Gamma\frac{n-1}{2}} \qquad ...(21.7)$$

$$= \sqrt{\frac{2}{n}}\frac{\left(\frac{n-2}{2}\right)!}{\left(\frac{n-3}{2}\right)!} \qquad ...(21.7.1)$$

Since $\Gamma_n = (n-1)\,!$

Thus, the limits given in (21.6) can be rewritten as,

$$\left.\begin{aligned} \text{U.C.L.}_{\overline{X}} &= \overline{X} + A_1\overline{S} \\ \text{C.L.} &= \overline{X} \\ \text{L.C.L.}_{\overline{x}} &= \overline{X} - A_1\overline{S} \end{aligned}\right\} \quad ...(21.8)$$

where $$A_1 = \frac{3}{c_2\sqrt{n}} = \frac{A}{c_2} \quad ...(21.9)$$

The values of A_1 for different values of n are being tabulated. The same can be obtained from table XV.

σ-Chart

Instead of considering the mean as a quality characteristic, standard deviation σ may also be considered. Let s be the sample standard deviation. By definition, the variance of s is given as,

$$V(s) = E\,(s^2) - \{E\,(s)\}^2$$

Also we know,

$$E\,(s^2) = \frac{(n-1)}{n}\sigma^2$$

and $$E\,(s) = c_2\,\sigma$$

where n is the sample size and c_2 is given by (21.7). Hence,

$$\begin{aligned} V\,(s) &= \frac{n-1}{n}\sigma^2 - c_2^2\sigma^2 \\ &= \left(\frac{n-1}{n} - c_2^2\right)\sigma^2 \\ &= c_3^2\sigma^2 \end{aligned} \quad ...(21.10)$$

Also, $$\text{S.D.}(s) = c_3\,\sigma \quad ...(21.10.1)$$

where, $$c_3^2 = \left(\frac{n-1}{n} - c_2^2\right) \quad ...(21.11)$$

The control limits for σ-chart are,

$$\left.\begin{aligned} \text{U.C.L.}_s &= E(s) + 3\,\text{S.E.}_{(s)} = (c_2 + 3c_3)\sigma \\ \text{C.L.} &= c_2\sigma \\ \text{L.C.L.}_s &= E(s) - 3\,\text{S.E.}_{(s)} = (c_2 - 3c_3)\sigma \end{aligned}\right\} \quad ...(21.12)$$

The σ-limits given by (21.12) can be rewritten as,

$$\left.\begin{aligned} \text{U.C.L.}_s &= B_2\sigma \\ \text{C.L.} &= c_2\sigma \\ \text{L.C.L.}_s &= B_1\sigma \end{aligned}\right\} \quad ...(21.12.1)$$

where, $B_1 = (c_2 - 3c_3)$ and $B_2 = (c_2 + 3c_3)$.

The values of B_1 and B_2 are tabulated in table XV for different values of n. Often, the value of σ is neither specified nor known. In this situation, we use the estimated value of σ *i.e.*, $\bar{S}$ where $\bar{S}$ is defined in (21.4). Obviously

$$\bar{S} = c_2\sigma \text{ or } \sigma = \frac{\bar{S}}{c_2}$$

Hence, the σ-control limits when σ is not known are obtained by replacing σ by $\bar{S}/c_2$. Thus, we get

$$\left.\begin{aligned} \text{U.C.L.}_s &= (c_2 + 3c_3)\frac{\bar{S}}{c_2} = \left(1 + \frac{3c_3}{c_2}\right)\bar{S} = B_4\bar{S} \\ \text{C.L.} &= \bar{S} \\ \text{L.C.L.}_s &= (c_2 - 3c_3)\frac{\bar{S}}{c_2} = \left(1 - \frac{3c_3}{c_2}\right)\bar{S} = B_3\bar{S} \end{aligned}\right\} \quad ...(21.13)$$

where, $B_4 = \left(1 + \frac{3c_3}{c_2}\right) = \frac{B_2}{c_2}$ and $B_3 = \left(1 - \frac{3c_3}{c_2}\right) = \frac{B_1}{c_2}$

B_3 and B_4 have been tabulated for different values of n, and are given in table XV.

Note: In case the lower control limit comes out to be negative. It is taken to be zero, since the standard deviation can never be negative.

R-Chart

Experience reveals that, in case of small samples, the standard deviation s and the range R fluctuate simultaneously. Elaborately, if s is small, R is also small and vice-versa. But this relation does not hold good for large samples. In statistical quality control, generally, small samples are drawn and hence the range can be used in place of a standard deviation. The charts constructed on using the range are termed 'R-charts'. As we know, it is simpler to find a range compared to a standard deviation. Hence, the use of a range as a substitute to a standard deviation is not bad, even with a little loss of efficiency. The relation between R and σ from the sampling distribution of the range are obtained as,

$$\left.\begin{aligned} E(R) &= d_2\sigma \\ \text{S.D.}(R) &= d_3\sigma \end{aligned}\right\} \quad ...(21.14)$$

We also know that $E(R_i) = \bar{R}$, where R_i is the ith sample range. Hence,

$$\bar{R} = d_2\,\sigma \text{ or } \sigma = \bar{R}/d_2$$

The control limits for various charts using R in place of σ are as follows:

Case (*i*) When the range R' and the standard deviation $\sigma_{R'}$ are the known values of range R and S.D σ_R. The control limits are given as,

$$\begin{aligned} \text{U.C.L}_{R'} &= E(R') + 3\sigma_{R'} \\ &= d_2\,\sigma_{R'} + 3d_3\sigma_{R'} \\ &= (d_2 + 3d_3)\,\sigma_{R'} \end{aligned}$$

Similarly,

$$\left.\begin{aligned} &= D_2\sigma_{R'} \\ \text{C.L.} &= d_2\sigma_{R'} \\ \text{L.C.L.}_{R'} &= (d_2 - 3d_3)\sigma_{R'} \\ &= D_1\sigma_{R'} \end{aligned}\right\} \quad ...(21.15)$$

where, $D_2 = (d_2 + 3d_3)$ and $D_1 = (d_2 - 3d_3)$

Case (ii) When the value of population range R is not known. In this case we make use of an estimated range $\overline{R}$.

For $\overline{X}$ - chart:

$$\text{U.C.L.}_{\overline{X}} = \overline{X} + 3\sigma_{\bar{x}}$$

$$= \overline{X} + \frac{3}{d_2\sqrt{n}}\overline{R}$$

Similarly

$$\left.\begin{aligned} &= \overline{X} + A_2\overline{R} \\ \text{C.L.} &= \overline{X} \\ \text{L.C.L}_{\bar{x}} &= \overline{X} - A_2\overline{R} \end{aligned}\right\} \quad \text{...(21.16)}$$

where $A_2 = \dfrac{3}{d_2\sqrt{n}}$

For R- chart,

$$\text{U.C.L.}_R = E(\overline{R}) + 3\,\text{S.D.}(\overline{R})$$

$$= d_2\sigma + 3d_3\sigma$$

$$= d_2\frac{\overline{R}}{d_2} + 3d_3\frac{\overline{R}}{d_2}$$

$$= \left(1 + 3\frac{d_3}{d_2}\right)\overline{R}$$

Similarly,

$$\left.\begin{aligned} &= D_4\overline{R} \\ \text{C.L.} &= \overline{R} \\ \text{L.C.L.}_R &= \left(1 - \frac{3d_3}{d_2}\right)\overline{R} = D_3\overline{R} \end{aligned}\right\} \quad \text{...(21.17)}$$

where, $D_4 = \left(1 + \dfrac{3d_3}{d_2}\right)$ and $D_3 = \left(1 - \dfrac{3d_3}{d_2}\right)$.

The values of d_2, d_3, A_2, D_3, D_4, etc. are being tabulated by Dodge and Roming. The use of the same can be made.

Remarks on $\overline{X}$, R and σ charts

(*i*) R- charts and σ-charts give an almost similar picture of the variability of plotted points.

(*ii*) In case of small samples, the use of R-charts is easy and economical, without the loss of efficiency.

(*iii*) Experience tells us that R-chart is generally under control. Hence, to prepare a R-chart after a $\overline{X}$-chart will be a sheer waste of time and money.

(*iv*) If the sample size is large, the use of R-chart should be avoided as, σ-chart will provide more reliable results than R-chart.

(v) $\overline{X}$-chart should not be constructed unless a R-chart shows that the process is under control.

(vi) A $\overline{X}$-chart discovers the variability between rational sub-groups, whereas a R-chart discovers the assignable causes within sub-groups.

(vii) When $\overline{X}$-chart and R-chart both are constructed, they reveal the assignable causes between samples and within samples. It is expected, that there is a rare chance for the assignable causes not to be detected. Hence, to judge whether the process is really under control, both the charts should be constructed.

Interpretation of $\overline{X}$, R and σ charts

While plotting the points on the control charts, the values of $\overline{X}$, R or σ are always taken on Y-axis and the sample numbers on the X-axis. If any point falls outside the control band, it indicates that the process is out of control and the assignable causes are to be thrashed out. Also, any trend depicted by the plotted sample points indicates presence of assignable causes. If the values of $\overline{X}$ or R are continuously increasing or decreasing, it means that the process is not functioning normally and a resetting is required either in the machines or in the operation. Sometimes, the plotted sample points show a cyclic pattern. This is also an indicator of assignable causes. Such a variation may occur due to the quality difference of the raw material or due to the malfunctioning of the machine. Once the statistical quality control unit reports the presence of assignable causes, the job of finding out the causes is left to the production engineer.

***Example* 21.1.** A factory was producing screws. It was desired to test whether the process was under control or not. For this purpose, twenty samples of 4 screws were drawn at an interval of one hour and the diameter of each sampled screw was measured. The measurements were as given on page 636.

(i) The manufacturer wanted the screws of the diameter 0.35 mm which can vary with a standard deviation of 0.12 mm.

Control limits for $\overline{X}$-chart, when the standards are known, can be obtained as follows:

Given that $\mu' = 0.35$ mm. and $\sigma' = 0.12$ mm.

The control limits for $\overline{X}$-chart from (21.5) are,

$$\text{U.C.L.}_{\overline{X}} = 0.35 + \frac{3}{\sqrt{20}} \times 0.12$$

$$= 0.35 + 0.08 = 0.43$$

$$\text{C.L.} = 0.35$$

$$\text{L.C.L.}_{\overline{X}} = 0.35 - 0.08 = 0.27$$

To test, whether the process is under control or not, draw the control lines on the graph and plot the points $\overline{X}_i$, against sample numbers as shown in Fig. 21.2.

No point lies outside the control limits and hence, it indicates that the process is under control.

(ii) The control limits for σ-chart, when σ is known, are obtained from (21.12.1).

Sample no.	Diameter of screws (mm). (X)				Total	Mean	Standard deviation	Range
	1	2	3	4		$\overline{X}_i$	S_i	R_i
(i)	(ii)				(iii)	(iv)	(v)	(vi)
1	.33	.36	.42	.40	1.51	.38	.040	.09
2	.38	.42	.32	.43	1.55	.39	.050	.11
3	.35	.40	.33	.34	1.42	.36	.031	.07
4	.34	.37	.40	.32	1.43	.36	.035	.08
5	.37	.31	.34	.34	1.36	.34	.024	.06
6	.41	.39	.36	.37	1.53	.38	.022	.05
7	.30	.30	.31	.31	1.22	.30	.006	.01
8	.40	.32	.34	.36	1.42	.36	.034	.08
9	.36	.42	.38	.35	1.51	.38	.031	.07
10	.28	.30	.31	.39	1.28	.32	.048	.11
11	.39	.34	.33	.36	1.42	.36	.026	.06
12	.34	.35	.34	.34	1.37	.34	.005	.01
13	.36	.30	.34	.33	1.33	.33	.025	.06
14	.37	.40	.35	.32	1.44	.36	.034	.08
15	.32	.34	.36	.34	1.36	.34	.016	.04
16	.37	.40	.33	.30	1.40	.35	.044	.10
17	.41	.32	.34	.35	1.42	.36	.039	.09
18	.36	.34	.30	.33	1.33	.33	.025	.06
19	.34	.36	.42	.37	1.49	.37	.034	.08
20	.35	.37	.34	.33	1.39	.35	.017	.04
Total					28.18	7.06	0.586	1.35

From the table XV, for $n = 4$,

$$B_1 = 0,\ B_2 = 1.808 \text{ and } c_2 = 0.798$$

$$\text{U.C.L.}_s = 1.808 \times 0.12 = 0.217$$

$$\text{C.L.} = 0.798 \times 0.12 = 0.096$$

$$\text{L.C.L.}_s = 0 \times 0.12 = 0$$

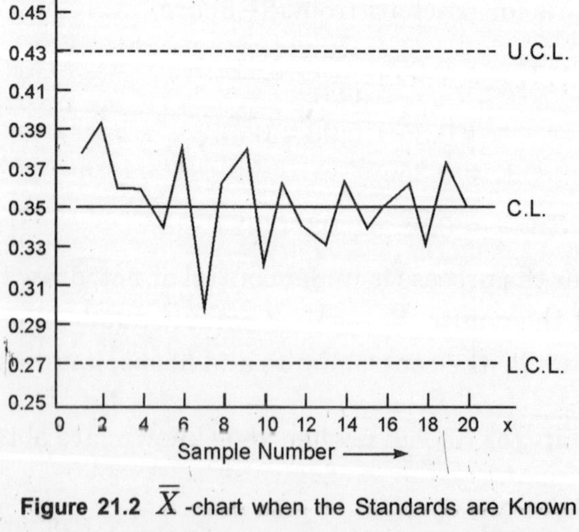

Figure 21.2 $\overline{X}$ -chart when the Standards are Known

There is no value of standard deviation which is greater than 0.217. Hence it is considered that the process is under control. The plotting of the chart for limits from (21.12) is left to the reader.

***Example* 21.2.** For the data given in example 21.1, we test whether the process is under control or not, when the standard values of mean diameter and standard deviation are not known.

In this situation, we estimate constants required to set up the statistical control limits.

Estimated value of μ by (21.2) is,

$$\overline{X} = \frac{7.06}{20} = 0.353$$

s_i-values given in column (v) along with the data in example 21.1 are calculated with the help of formula (21.3.1). The estimated value of σ from (21.4) is,

$$\overline{S} = \frac{0.586}{20} = 0.029$$

The control limits for $\overline{X}$-chart, when the standard values of parameters are not known, can be obtained from (21.8).

From table XV, the value of A_1 for $n = 4$ is 1.880

$$\text{U.C.L.}_{\overline{X}} = 0.353 + 1.880 \times 0.029$$

$$= 0.4075$$

$$\text{C.L.} = 0.353$$

$$\text{L.C.L.}_{\overline{X}} = 0.353 - 1.880 \times 0.029$$

$$= 0.297$$

To test whether the process is under control or not, we draw the control limits on the graph paper and plot $\overline{X}_i$-values against sample numbers.

Fig. (21.3) depicts $\overline{X}$-chart when μ and σ are unknown. All the point lie within the control limits and hence it is concluded that the control chart does not indicate the presence of any assignable cause.

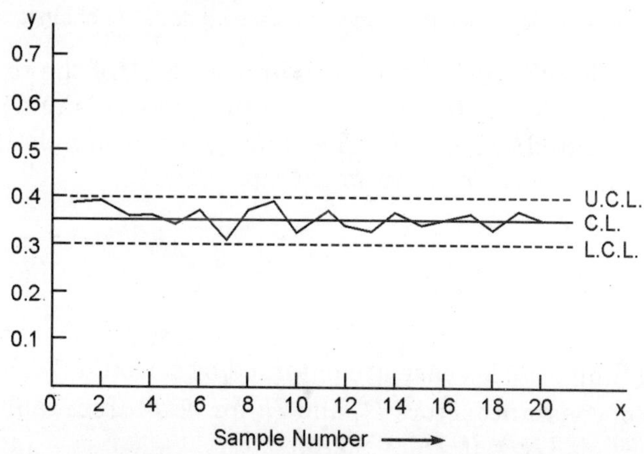

Figure 21.3 $\overline{X}$ - chart when μ and σ are unknown

***Example* 21.3.** We test the process of manufacturing screws for the data given in example 21.1 by R-chart in both the cases (*i*) When the given value of the range of the diameters is 0.04 mm. and S.D. of the range of the diameters of the screws is given as 0.03 mm., (*ii*) When the range and S.D. of the range of the diameters are not known.

(*i*) We find out the control limits, given that $R' = 0.04$ and $\sigma_{R'} = 0.03$ from the formulae given in (21.15).

For $n = 4$, the values of d_2, D_1 and D_2 from table XV are,

$$d_2 = 2.059,\ D_1 = 0,\ D_2 = 4.698.$$

Thus,
$$\text{U.C.L.}_{R'} = 4.698 \times 0.03 = 0.1409$$
$$\text{C.L.} = 2.059 \times 0.03 = 0.0618$$
$$\text{L.C.L.}_{R'} = 0 \times 0.03 = 0$$

Draw the control limits and plot the points R_i against the sample numbers on the graph paper as displayed below.

All the points lie within the control limits. Hence, the process is under control.

(*ii*)

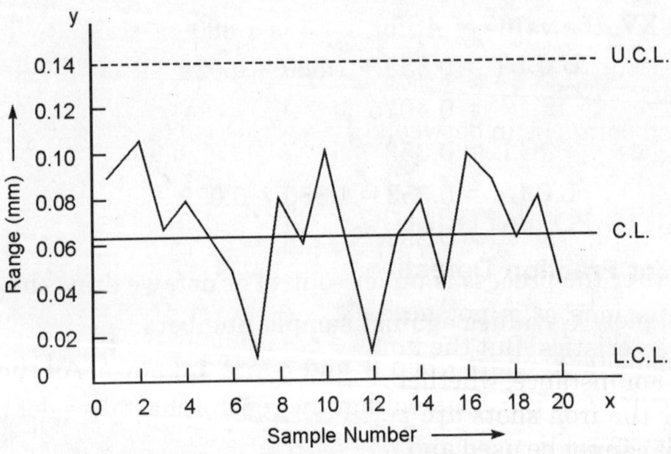

Figure 21.4 Control chart when the range and standard deviation of range are known

When the specified value of the range and the S.D. of the range are not known, the R-chart can be used to test whether the process is under control or not, by using the estimated value of R. The range of each sample has been entered in column (*vi*) along with the data in example (21.1)

The mean range,

$$\overline{R} = \frac{1.35}{20} = 0.0675$$

The control limits in this case are obtained by formula (21.17).

The values of constant factors D_3 and D_4 for $n = 4$ from table XV are,

$$D_3 = 0,\ D_4 = 2.282$$

Thus, $U.C.L._R = 2.282 \times 0.0675 = 0.154$

$C.L. = 0.067$

$L.C.L._R = 0 \times 0.0675 = 0$

The control lines and points R plotted against the sample numbers are shown in the Figure (21.5) given below.

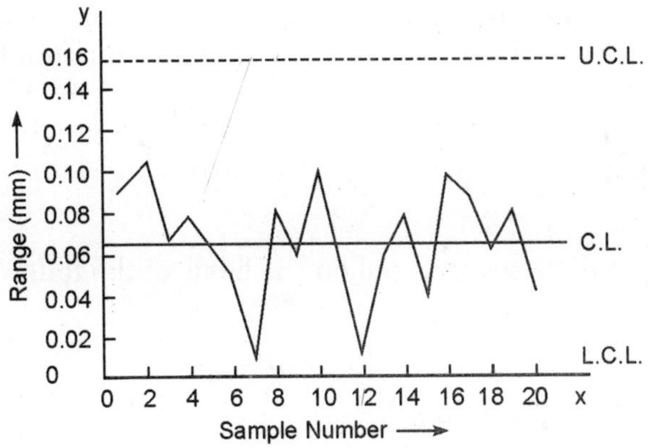

Figure 21.5 The R-chart when Standard Values are not known

All the plotted points lie in between the control lines. Hence, the production process is under control.

CONTROL CHARTS FOR ATTRIBUTES

Control Charts for Fraction Defectives (p-Chart)

In many situations, it is not necessary to find the variation pertaining to certain measurable characteristics. But the units are checked to see whether they possess certain attributes or not. For instance, whether the ball-bearings produced by a factory are perfectly circular, whether the iron shots are perfectly spherical. If not, they are defective. If the unit is defective it cannot be used and if non-defective, it is acceptable. Moreover, if the lot contains a proportion of defectives more than a certain percentage, it is not to be marketed. In case, more defective items come in the market for sale, the reputation of the company will go down and the product may lose the market. Hence, the process is tested to see whether it is under control with regard to fraction defectives.

Suppose P is the population fraction defective, in a process during a fixed period, *i.e.*, in the lot of items produced during that fixed period, the judgement about the process is based on the fraction defective, p, in a sample of size n. Let the sample contains d defectives.

Hence, $p = \dfrac{d}{n}$

Also,

$$E(p) = E\left(\frac{d}{n}\right) = P \quad \text{or} \quad E(d) = nP$$

and $$\text{S.D.}\ (p) = \text{S.D.}\left(\frac{d}{n}\right) = \sqrt{\frac{P.Q}{n}}$$

where $Q = 1 - P$

To test whether the process is under control or not, we construct a *p*-chart. For this, the samples of items are taken at regular intervals or from sub-groups and inspected. The proportion of defectives in each sample is calculated. In this chart, *p*-values are taken on the *Y*-axis and the sample numbers on the *X*-axis. Since, an unit can either be defective or non-defective, the variable is dichotomous and will follow binomial distribution. Let p' be the specified value of *P*. Then,

$$\text{S.D.}\ (p') = \sqrt{\frac{p'q'}{n}}$$

where $q' = 1 - p'$

The control chart will be constructed on the basis of the following limits.

$$\left.\begin{aligned} \text{U.C.L.}_{p'} &= p' + 3\sigma_{p'} = p' + 3\frac{p'q'}{n} \\ \text{C.L.} &= p' \\ \text{L.C.L.}_{p'} &= p' - 3\sigma_{p'} = p' - 3\frac{p'q'}{n} \end{aligned}\right\} \quad ...(21.18)$$

If the values of *p*, plotted against sample numbers, lie within the control limits, it indicates that there is no evidence that the process is out of control. In case, any point goes out of the control band, the process is not under control and some assignable causes should be searched out.

When the standard value of *P* is not known, it is estimated on the basis of sample. Let a sample of size n_i ($i = 1, 2, ..., \kappa$) be drawn from the process at regular intervals in a fixed period, *i.e.*, from sub-groups and inspected. Suppose d_i is the number of defectives out of n_i units of the *i*th sample.

The fraction defective,

$$p_i = \frac{d_i}{n_i} \quad ...(21.19)$$

The estimated value of *P*,

$$\bar{p} = \frac{\Sigma_i d_i}{\Sigma_i n_i} \quad ...(21.20)$$

$i = 1, 2, ..., \kappa$

In general, it is preferred that the samples of equal size be selected. Supposing $n_1 = n_2 = ... = n_\kappa = n$, we have,

$$\bar{p} = \frac{1}{n\kappa}\Sigma_i d_i = \frac{1}{\kappa}\Sigma_i p_i \quad ....(21.21)$$

It is trivial to verify that $\bar{p}$ is an unbiased estimate of *P*.

When P is not known, the control limits are,

$$\left.\begin{aligned} \text{U.C.L.}_p &= \bar{p}+3\frac{\bar{p}\bar{q}}{n} \\ \bar{q} &= 1-\bar{p} \\ \text{where} \qquad \text{C.L.} &= \bar{p} \\ \text{L.C.L.}_p &= \bar{p}-3\frac{\bar{p}\bar{q}}{n} \end{aligned}\right\} \qquad \ldots(21.22)$$

Sample p-values are plotted on the graph against sample numbers. If any point lies outside the control limits, it is concluded that the process is out of control, otherwise not. The points which lie outside the upper control line are called *high spots.* These points indicate a deterioration in the production process. Such a situation should immediately be reported to the production incharge. Again, the points which fall below the lower control line, they are called *low spots.* These points show an improvement in the production process or give greater assurance of the good quality of the product. But, it should be confirmed that there is no slackness on the part of the checker.

Control Chart for Number of Defectives

It is not necessary to calculate the proportion of defectives to set up the control limits. Instead, we can construct the control chart for the actual number of defectives. It is known that for a sample of size n having d defectives,

$$d = np$$

The control limits in two situations are given below.

Situation (*i*): *Control Limits When the Specified Value p' of P is Known:* Number of defectives (d') in a sample of size n for given p' is,

$$d' = np'$$

and $\qquad \sigma_d' = \sqrt{np'q'}$

where $q' = 1 - p'$

The control limits are,

$$\left.\begin{aligned} \text{U.C.L.}_{d'} &= d'+3\sigma_{d'} = np'+3\sqrt{np'q'} \\ \text{C.L.} &= d' = np' \\ \text{L.C.L.}_{d'} &= d'-3\sigma_{d'} = np'-3\sqrt{np'q'} \end{aligned}\right\} \qquad \ldots(21.23)$$

Situation (*ii*): *Control Limits When the Specified Value of Proportion P is not Known:* In this situation, we estimate the value of P by $\bar{p}$ as given by (21.21).

Also, the control limits similar to (21.22) are,

$$\left.\begin{aligned} \text{U.C.L}_d &= d+3\sigma_d = n\bar{p}+3\sqrt{n\bar{p}(1-\bar{p})} \\ \text{C.L}_d &= n\bar{p} \\ \text{L.C.L}_d &= d-3\sigma_d = n\bar{p}-3\sqrt{n\bar{p}(1-\bar{p})} \end{aligned}\right\} \qquad \ldots(21.24)$$

Control lines are drawn on graph paper. Sample d-values are plotted on the graph against sample numbers. The decision about the state of the process is taken in the same manner as for proportion defectives.

***Example* 21.4.** Twenty five boxes, each containing 20 electric switches were randomly selected and inspected for the number of defectives in each box. The number of defectives found in each box were as follows:

Box number	:	1	2	3	4	5	6	7	8	9
No. of defectives	:	3	2	1	0	4	2	1	2	3
Fraction defectives	:	.15	.10	.05	0	.20	.10	.05	.10	.15
		10	11	12	13	14	15	16	17	
		0	2	1	2	0	3	5	4	
		0	.10	.05	.10	0	.15	.25	.20	
		18	19	20	21	22	23	24	25	
		2	1	3	0	3	1	2	1	
		.10	.05	.15	0	.15	.05	.10	.05	

Standard value of fraction defective P is not known.

Hence, to test whether the process is under control, we will find the estimated value $\overline{p}$ of fraction defectives and set up the control limits given by (21.22). For the given data,

$$\Sigma_i d_i = 48$$

$$\overline{p} = \frac{1}{25 \times 20} \times 48 = 0.096$$

$$\therefore \quad \overline{q} = 1 - 0.096 = 0.904$$

Also given that $n = 20$

The control limits are,

$$\text{U.C.L.}_p = 0.096 + 3\sqrt{\frac{0.096 \times 0.904}{20}}$$

$$= 0.096 + 0.198 = 0.294$$

$$\text{C.L.} = 0.096$$

$$\text{L.C.L.}_p = 0.096 - 0.198 = -0.102$$

Since L.C.L._p is negative, it is taken as zero. To test whether the process of the production of switches is under control or not, we draw the control limits on the graph and plot the points p_i against sample numbers as depicted below.

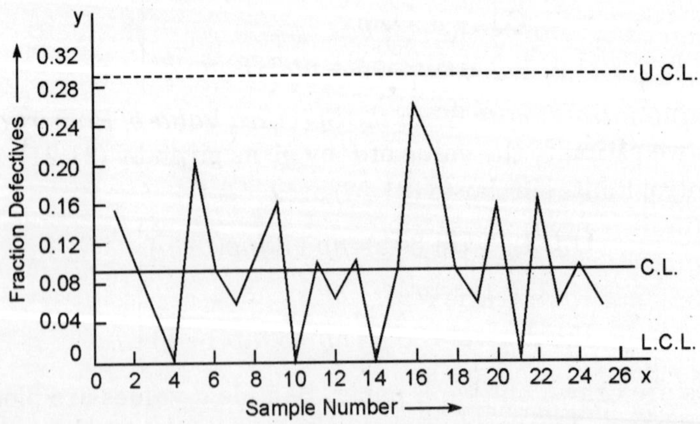

Figure 21.6 *p*-chart when the Proportion of Defectives in the process is unknown

The above graph leads to the conclusion, that the process is under statistical control as no point lies outside the control limits.

***Example* 21.5.** For the data given in example 21.4, we set up the control limits for a number of defectives with the help of the formula (21.24).

We known that $n = 20, \bar{p} = 0.096.$

Thus, $d' = n\bar{p} = 20 \times 0.096 = 1.92.$

The control limits for number of defectives are

$$\text{U.C.L.}_d = 1.92 + 3\sqrt{20 \times 0.096 \times 0.904}$$
$$= 1.92 + 3 \times 1.317$$
$$= 1.92 + 3.95 = 5.87$$
$$\text{C.L.} = 1.92$$

Similarly, $\text{L.C.L.}_d = 1.92 - 3.95 = -2.03$

Since the number of defectives can never be negative, the lower control limit is taken as zero. The control chart is prepared in the usual manner and displayed below.

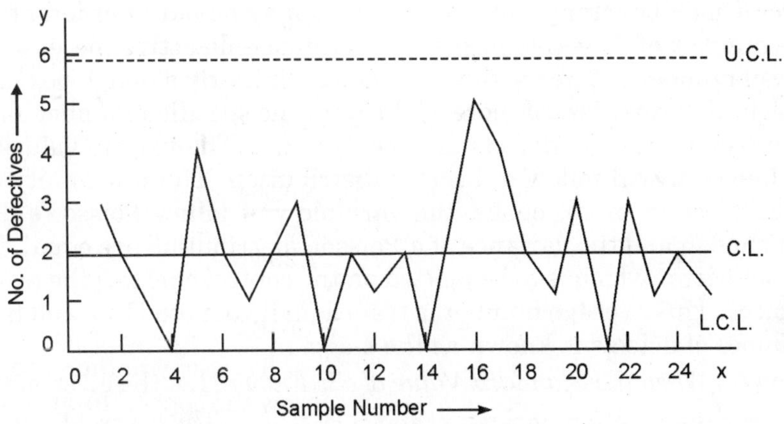

Figure 21.7 *np*-chart for Number of Defectives

No plotted point lies outside the control limits, hence it is inferred that there is no reason to believe that there is any assignable cause which can be attached to the variation in the production units. Therefore, the process is under statistical control.

Samples of Unequal Size

Sometimes samples of unequal size are selected from each sub-group. In this situation, one set of control limits cannot be used for all samples under inspection. If the number of units in the samples vary, control limits in *p*-chart for each sample has to be set up separately. Of course the central line remains the same as $\bar{p} = \Sigma_i d_i / \Sigma_i n_i$, $i = 1, 2, ..., K$. In case a *d*-chart is drawn, the central line also changes for each sample as $d_i = n_i \bar{p}$. The control limits in such a situation are known as *variable limits.*

If the sample size does not vary appreciably, a single set of central limits can be used, taking the average value of sample size as the constant sample size, *i.e.*, $\bar{n} = \Sigma_i n_i / K$ for

$i = 1, 2, ..., K$. As a common norm, the difference between the largest and smallest sample size should not be more than 20% of the smallest sample size.

To reduce the labour of finding out the limits for each sample separately, an alternative method may be used. First, find the limits for the sample of the smallest size and then for the sample of the largest size. Plot these two sets of limits on the same graph paper. Plot all the sample points for p or d-values on this graph paper. Three situations may arise, (*i*) if all the points lie within the inner set of limits, the process is taken under statistical control, (*ii*) if any point lies outside the outer set of limits, it is considered that the process is out of control. In this situation, the assignable causes should be found out and rectified, (*iii*) if the points lie above the inner set of limits and below the outer set of limits, separate limits for various samples are to be set up and the points are plotted for performing the tests. The decision about the process control is taken in the usual manner.

Control Charts for Number of Defects

In the preceding section, we considered only one criterion, *i.e.*, an item is either perfect or defective. But in many situations it will be advantageous to know the number of defects in a piece. For instance, a radio set may have many defects, namely, its bulbs may be out of order, circuit may be wrong, some resistances may be out of order, etc. But, from the angle of the number of defective pieces, it is only one defective piece, whereas from the point of view of number of defects, they are many. Similarly a match box may have broken sticks, may contain either less or more sticks than the specified number, or have improper labelling, etc. The number of defects may be 0, 1, 2, ... The variate values are discrete in nature and hence, it will follow a discrete distribution. The probability of a defect in a manufactured piece is small, hence, the variable will follow Poisson's distribution. We know that the mean and the variance of a Poisson distribution are equal. In this case, the quality characteristic, which is to be plotted on the control chart, is the average number of defects per piece. This average number is traditionally denoted by c and hence the control chart for number of defects is known as the *c-chart*.

Situation (i): When the Standard Value of c is Known: Let the given standard value of c be c'. For Poisson distribution, mean $= c'$ and S.D. $= \sqrt{c'}$. The control limits for c-chart are,

$$\left.\begin{aligned} \text{U.C.L.}_c &= \text{mean} + 3\,\text{S.D.}(c) = c' + 3\sqrt{c'} \\ \text{C.L.} &= \text{mean} = c' \\ \text{L.C.L.}_c &= \text{mean} - 3\,\text{S.D.}(c) = c' - 3\sqrt{c'} \end{aligned}\right\} \quad ...(21.25)$$

Situation (ii): When the Standard Value of c is Not Known: Most often, the value of c is not specified. Hence, it has to be estimated from the sample values. Let c_i be the number of defects for the sample taken from the ith sub-group. The estimated value of c is,

$$\bar{c} = \frac{1}{K}\Sigma_i c_i \quad ...(21.26)$$

where $i = 1, 2, ... K$

Thus, the control limits are

$$\left.\begin{aligned} \text{U.C.L.}_c &= \bar{c} + 3\sqrt{\bar{c}} \\ \text{C.L.} &= \bar{c} \\ \text{L.C.L.}_c &= \bar{c} - 3\sqrt{\bar{c}} \end{aligned}\right\} \quad ...(21.27)$$

c-values for the samples are plotted against the sample numbers on the graph paper. If the plotted points lie within the control band, the process is considered to be under control and vice-versa. c-chart should be used when the number of samples is from 20 to 25 and the value of c is around 5.

***Example* 21.6.** Twenty two samples, of bundles of a dozen of match boxes, were selected at regular intervals. The match boxes in each sample were inspected and the number of defects were noted down, with regard to the number of broken sticks, box shape, the labelling, and the paste on the sticks etc. The number of defects were as follows:

Sample no. :	1	2	3	4	5	6	7	8	9	10	11	12	13	14	15
No. of defects:	5	7	8	4	2	5	7	3	0	2	4	9	6	7	3
:	16	17	18	19	20	21	22								
:	5	1	4	5	6	3	12								

The control chart for the number of defects can be prepared in the following manner. From (21.26).

$$\Sigma_i c_i = 108, \kappa = 22$$

$$\bar{c} = \frac{1}{22} \times 108 = 4.91$$

The control limits from (21.27) are,

$$\text{U.C.L.}_c = 4.91 + 3\sqrt{4.91}$$
$$= 4.91 + 6.65$$
$$= 11.56$$
$$\text{C.L.} = 4.91$$

Similarly,

$$\text{L.C.L.}_c = 4.91 - 6.65$$
$$= -1.74$$

Lower control limit is taken as zero, as the number of defects cannot be negative.

The control limits are drawn and c_i-values are plotted against sample numbers as shown below.

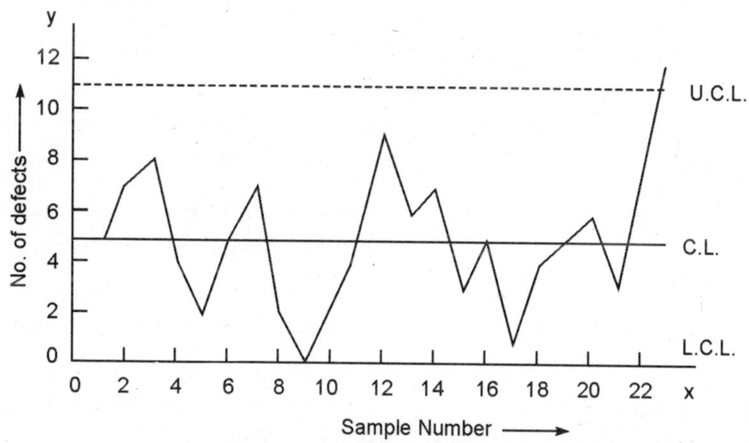

Figure 21.8 c-chart for Number of Defects in the Bundles of Match Boxes

The chart has one point lying above the upper control limit. This indicates that the process is out of control. Thus, the process engineer should be informed to trace out the assignable causes and rectify them.

Uses of the c-Chart: It is apparent that the *c*-chart is applicable only when the probability of occurrence of defects, at any stage, is small; *c*-charts are used for the data on counts. Some of the examples are:

(*a*) *c* is the number of defects per roll of 20 metres cloth.

(*b*) *c* is the number of missing rivets in an aircraft.

(*c*) *c* is the number of breaks in 100 metres of insulated wire coils.

(*d*) It is also used for sampling acceptance procedures based on a number of defects per unit. e.g., for radio sets, television sets, military equipments, etc.

(*e*) *c*-charts can also be used for non-manufacturing units, e.g., for accidents at a particular place in a fixed duration, in chemical laboratories, in case of incidence of deaths due to an epidemic in a particular region in a fixed span of time, etc.

Note: The fraction defectives, number of defects or the number of defectives can never be less than zero. Hence, in case, lower control limit for attributes comes out to be negative, it should be taken as zero.

Comparison of Control Charts of Variables vs. Attributes

Control charts for variables	*Control charts for attributes*
1. A separate chart is needed for each quality characteristic under consideration.	A single chart is enough to decide for a number of quality characteristics under consideration.
2. Small samples serve the purpose very well.	Large samples are needed for correct conclusions.
3. The cost of inspection of units is large.	Cost of inspection of units is small as compared to measurement data.
4. It involves more computational labour.	The computations are simple.
5. The control charts are sensitive to assignable causes.	The control charts are less sensitive to assignable causes.
6. Control charts provide better quality control.	These charts are not very effective in keeping the quality control.
7. A control chart for variable can hardly be used for attributes.	Control charts for attributes can be used in lieu of charts for variables.
8. Samples from sub-groups should preferably be of equal size.	The need for equal size of samples is not as much as in the case of control charts for variables.

ADVANTAGES OF STATISTICAL QUALITY CONTROL

There are two options before a manufacturer. He should either get each and every item checked and decide about the quality or he should use the statistical quality control methods. S.Q.C. involves the inspection of a small number of items and decides about the quality of the whole lot of the product. S.Q.C. has many advantages over 100 per cent inspection which are recorded below.

1. S.Q.C. involves inspection of only a fraction of items produced in a fixed period. Hence, it is very economical.
2. The inspection of each and every item has hardly been feasible, as the rate of production in many cases will be faster than the time required for the inspection of items. Hence, 100 per cent inspection would cost too much. Also, in cases where the units are destroyed during inspection (testing), 100 per cent inspection is impossible.
3. The inspection of each and every unit will reduce the efficiency of the quality inspectors because of boredom. S.Q.C. keeps the quality control personnel alert.
4. S.Q.C. can be carried by persons who do not possess a high degree in engineering or statistics. As a matter of fact, great skill and intelligence is required to develop the statistical method for quality control in a particular case rather than applying the methods set for the purpose.
5. S.Q.C. keeps consistent vigilance on the quality of the product. The moment it is found that the process is out of control, the production engineer is informed about it. In this way, there is an incalculable reduction in losses.
6. Variation is inherent and unavoidable. So merely measuring the variation from the standard values does not serve the purpose. We have to decide whether the variation is within the tolerance limits or not. Such a variation is termed as chance variation. If the variation is beyond tolerance limits, it is said to be due to assignable causes. Thus, with the help of S.Q.C., the process is kept under control so that the product meets the specifications within tolerance limits.
7. Process control provides the basis to the producer, for deciding about the specifications. It makes no sense to fix up the specifications, which cannot be maintained economically.
8. S.Q.C. enables the manufacturers to know whether the changes brought in the production by installing new machines or by changing the system of the process or by employing more skilled persons has improved the quality of the product or not.
9. S.Q.C. is a basis for compromise between the machine operators and engineers. The engineers may expect a total adherence to specifications whereas the operators may emphasize their performance up to the mark, in spite of large variability in the units. Hence, S.Q.C. is a good device to keep both the sections satisfied.
10. S.Q.C. provides protection against losses to the producer as well as to the consumer.

Limitations of S.Q.C.

A number of advantages of S.Q.C. have been given above. The readers should not be misguided into believing that S.Q.C. is a panacea against any evil of production. Many more considerations are to be made in the production of units besides S.Q.C. The main consideration is the requirement of the consumer and the demand in the market. Many more factors are involved and overall responsibility of maintaining the quality and running of the process lies with the production manager. S.Q.C. is a part of the production process rather than the production being a part of S.Q.C.

ACCEPTANCE SAMPLING PLAN

Control charts can also be used in acceptance inspection, to give the general picture of the quality history to which it has been applied. In quality control analysis, the data from a number of lots is combined in a way, that gives a more revealing description of the quality of the product in the long run, rather than the data from each lot alone. Control charts are chiefly meant for process control. Sampling inspection is carried out to inspect the raw material, and the spares of a machine and his own product in the finished form. In short, sampling inspection is meant for product control. As a matter of fact, it is not practically possible to inspect each and every unit produced in a large factory. Hence, one has to resort to *sampling inspection.* It means that a small fraction of items, selected randomly from a lot, are inspected to decide, as to whether the lot should be accepted or rejected on the basis of the information supplied by the sample inspection. Some people call it *acceptance sampling.* Thus, under sampling inspection plan, a decision is taken about the acceptance or rejection of a lot. Sampling inspection serves the following purposes.

(*i*) It provides the basis to know whether the manufacturing process is yielding the product up to the mark or not.

(*ii*) It tells about the quality of the product at hand.

(*iii*) It minimizes the risk of the purchaser and protects the producer from future losses.

Sampling inspection is of two types:

(*a*) Sampling inspection by attributes.

(*b*) Sampling inspection by variables.

Two types of sampling inspection leads to the same conclusion. Due to simplicity we will be discussing the sampling inspection by attributes. The quality of items will be adjudged only as defective or non-defective. The acceptance or rejection of a lot is decided on the basis of fraction defectives in the sample. As a matter of fact, the sampling plan can lead to two types of decisions (*i*) acceptance-rejection type, (*ii*) acceptance-rectification type. In the first type, the lot is either accepted or rejected. If the lot is accepted, the items found defective in the sample are replaced by non-defectives and the whole lot is released for marketing. If the lot is rejected, all the items produced are wasted. Such a plan is very costly for the producer. Hence, the second course *i.e.*, acceptance-rectification plan is better. In this type of sampling plan, if the sampling inspection does not lead to the acceptance of the lot, each and every unit of the lot is inspected. The defectives found in the lot are replaced by non-defective items and the lot is released for sale. This is a practical approach. But from the theoretical point of view, we shall consider the two approaches as equivalent. Rejection and replacement will be considered as interchangeable terms. Before we discuss various sampling plans, it is worthwhile to explain certain terms which are to be used in different sampling plans.

Producer's Risk

A producer is a person who produces goods for use or consumption of others. It may happen in practice, that a sampling inspection plan leads to the rejection of a lot of satisfactory quality. Such a possibility is termed as *producer's risk.* Suppose the producer's process is set for a level of fraction defectives $\overline{p}$. *The average fraction defective $\overline{p}$ is known as producer's process average.* The probability of rejecting a lot, which has actually the producer's process average equal to p, is called the producer's risk and is denoted by P_p. The value of P_p decreases as $\overline{p}$ increases. Hence, P_p can be made as small as the producer pleases by taking larger and larger $\overline{p}$. Symbolically,

$$P_p = \text{Prob. [Reject a lot having } \overline{p} \text{ defectives]} \quad \text{...(21.28)}$$
$$= \alpha \text{ (The probability of type I error).}$$

Consumer's Risk

A consumer is a person who buys goods for his own need, and not for resale or for use in the production of other goods for sale. The consumer has always the risk of getting a lot which is not up to the mark. He finds, on testing through sampling inspection, that the number of items in the lot do not meet the requirements. Let p_t be the maximum fraction defective of the lot which the consumer is ready to tolerate. Then the probability of accepting a lot with fraction defectives p_t under the sampling inspection plan, is known as consumer's risk and is denoted by p_c. Thus,

$$P_c = \text{Prob. [Accept a lot having } p_t \text{ defective]} \quad \text{...(21.29)}$$
$$= \beta \text{ (The probability of type II error)}$$

Acceptance Quality Level (A.Q.L.)

A producer always tries to maintain the quality of his product, maintaining a specified level, which is acceptable to the consumers. Let the fraction defective be p_1 in a lot, which is quite a small fraction to call a lot as standard quality lot, and is acceptable to the consumer. In this situation, the producer will not like to reject the lot. p_1 is known as *acceptance quality level.*

Lot Tolerance Percentage Defective (L.T.P.D.)

A consumer is ready to accept a lot, if the lot does not contain more than a specified proportion of defectives. Let this limit of defectives be p_t. Obviously, the consumer will reject a lot having fraction defectives more than the quantity p_t. The quantity 100 p_t is referred to as *lot tolerance percentage defective.* As a tradition, this value is usually taken as 10 per cent.

Average Outgoing Quality Limit (A.O.Q.L.)

A producer always guarantees certain quality level after inspection, irrespective of the fact what quality is really being maintained by the producer. Suppose, the actual fraction defectives in the lot is p. p is termed as an *incoming quality.* The expected proportion of defectives remaining in the lot after sampling inspection, is called *average outgoing quality.* Let it be denoted by **p. p** is evidently a function of p. The maximum limit of average outgoing quality p is known as *average outgoing quality limit* in respect of p. Suppose, the number of items in the lot is N. Let n be the sample size and P_a the probability of accepting a lot of acceptance quality level p. Then the average outgoing quality limit,

$$\text{A.O.Q.L.} = \mathbf{p} = \frac{p(N-n)P_a}{N} \qquad \text{...(21.30)}$$

If the sampling fraction n/N is negligible, the probability,

$$\mathbf{p} = p\,P_a \qquad \text{...(21.30.1)}$$

Average Sample Number (ASN)

The expected sample size, required to arrive at a decision about the acceptance or rejection of the lot under sampling inspection, is known as *average sample number*. This is obviously a function of p, the actual proportion of defectives in the lot. If a graph is drawn in ASN against p-values, it is a curve known as *ASN curve*. A sampling plan having the lowest ASN curve, is considered better than any other sampling plan, provided all other factors are kept fixed.

Operating Characteristic (O.C.)

Operating characteristic is a mathematical function $L(p)$ which is equal to the probability of accepting a lot, with p as the proportion of defectives in the lot. The curve obtained on plotting $L(p)$ against p is known as OC curve. Naturally, more steep the OC curve, the better it is, as this provides the greater protection to the consumer.

SAMPLING PLANS

Here we shall discuss some of the commonly used plans, in brief, merely to acquaint the readers with the use and application of sampling schemes.

Single Sampling Plan

When the decision about the acceptance or rejection of a lot is based on a single sample, it is known as a *single sampling plan*. This plan involves three numbers namely, N–the number of units in the lot, n–the sample size, c–the maximum number of allowable defective units in the sample. N is generally known. The quantities n and c can be determined either by a *lot quality protection* approach or by an *average quality protection* approach. Let D units in the lot, out of N units, be defective. Also let a sample of size n from this lot contain d defective units as revealed by sampling inspection. Suppose c is the maximum allowable number of defectives in the sample. The single sampling procedure to arrive at a decision about the lot is as follows:

(*i*) Draw a random sample or n units from the lot.

(*ii*) Inspect each and every unit of the sample and classify it as defective or non-defective. Let the number of defectives in the sample be d.

(*iii*) If $d \leq c$, accept the lot and replace all defective units found in the sample by non-defectives and release the lot for marketing.

(*iv*) If $d > c$, inspect the whole lot and replace all the defectives in the lot by non-defectives. Release the lot for sale.

In this case, the variable d follows hypergeometric distribution. Various probabilities under single sampling plan can be worked out by the following expressions.

(1) Probability of getting d defectives in a sample of size n is,

$$P_d = \frac{\binom{Np}{d}\binom{N-Np}{n-d}}{\binom{N}{n}} \qquad \ldots(21.31)$$

where $D = Np$

(2) Probability of accepting the lot is,

$$P_a = \sum_{d=0}^{c} P_d = \sum_{d=0}^{c} \frac{\binom{Np}{d}\binom{N-Np}{n-d}}{\binom{N}{n}} \qquad \ldots(21.32)$$

(3) Consumer's risk when $p = p_t$ is,

P_c = Prob. (Accepting a lot having p_t defectives)

$$= \sum_{d=0}^{c} \frac{\binom{Np_t}{d}\binom{N-Np_t}{n-d}}{\binom{N}{n}} \qquad \ldots(21.33)$$

(4) Producer's risk when $p = \overline{p}$ is,

P_p = Prob. (Rejecting a lot having $\overline{p}$ defectives)

$$= \sum_{d=c+1}^{n} \frac{\binom{N\overline{p}}{d}\binom{N-N\overline{p}}{n-d}}{\binom{N}{n}} \qquad \ldots(21.34)$$

$$= 1 - \sum_{d=0}^{c} \frac{\binom{N\overline{p}}{d}\binom{N-N\overline{p}}{n-d}}{\binom{N}{n}} \qquad \ldots(21.34.1)$$

Notes: (*i*) All notations used in the above expressions have already been defined, hence, their clarification is not repeated.

(*ii*) From (21.33), it is apparent that the consumer's risk does not depend on $\overline{p}$, the process average fraction defectives whereas (21.34) reveals that the producer's risk depends on $\overline{p}$.

(*iii*) In general *p* is not known and hence it is taken to be equal to $\overline{p}$.

(*iv*) The number of defectives *d*, may follow Binomial or Poisson distribution, depending on the values of *N*, *n* and *p*. In that situation, the probabilities are to be calculated with the help of the respective distributions.

Double Sampling Plan

If a single sampling plan does not lead to the satisfaction about the acceptance or rejection of the lot, one has to resort to some other sampling plan. Such a situation arises when only one point may be just above the upper control limit or just below the lower control limit. A person may not be willing to reject the lot, on the basis of a single point, lying little outside the control limits. In other words, a single sample is not bad enough to reject a lot straightway or good enough to accept the lot. In this situation, a second sample is drawn and a decision is taken on the basis of the results of the first and second samples combined. Selecting a second sample to arrive at a more reliable decision is known as double sampling plan. A second sample throws another chance to confirm our results and it is more convincing to the producer as well as to the consumer. Double sampling scheme was originated by Dodge and Roming. In this scheme a second sample is drawn from the same lot and the decision is taken according to the procedure given below.

The notations used in the procedure are:

N = Number of units in the lot.

n_1 = Size of the first sample.

c_1 = Acceptance number of the first sample.

d_1 = Number of defectives in the first sample.

n_2 = Size of the second sample.

c_2 = Acceptance number for both the samples combined.

d_2 = Number of defectives in the second sample.

Different steps of the procedure:

(*i*) Draw a random sample of size n_1 from the lot.

(*ii*) If $d_1 \leq c_1$, accept the lot and release it for sale after replacing the defectives in the sample by non-defectives.

(*iii*) If $d_1 > c_2$, reject the lot. Inspect each and every unit of the lot, and replace all the defectives by non-defectives, before the lot is released for sale.

(*iv*) If d_1 lies between $(c_1 + 1)$ and c_2 *i.e.*, $c_1 + 1 \leq d_1 \leq c_2$, draw a second sample randomly from the lot and inspect it.

(*v*) If $d_1 + d_2 \leq c_2$, accept the lot and release the lot for sale, after replacing the defectives in the two samples by non-defectives.

(*vi*) If $d_1 + d_2 > c_2$, reject the lot. Each and every unit of the lot should be inspected. All the defectives should be replaced by non-defectives, before the lot is released for sale.

Multiple Sampling Plan

The process of second sampling can be extended to the third, and the fourth sampling stage etc. Such a sampling plan is known as multiple sampling plan. The details are omitted.

Sequential Sampling Plan

Sequential sampling may be thought of as a special type of multiple sampling plan, which consists of a sequence of samples of size one. In this type of sampling, the statistician has the option to terminate the sampling after each observation and makes the final decision. The theory of sequential analysis was developed by A. Wald in 1947. In the sequential analysis theory, the sample size n is a random variable instead of a fixed number. In a decision problem under sequential sampling plan, the total space is divided into three regions namely, (*i*) the acceptance region, (*ii*) the region of rejection and (*iii*) the region of continuance. Hence, in taking a decision about the acceptance or rejection of the lot, one by one item is randomly selected from the lot and inspected. If the lot is accepted or rejected at any stage, the sampling is terminated. The decision procedure is explained below.

Suppose p is the unknown proportion of defectives in the lot. It is not difficult to find two values of p *i.e.*, p_0 and $p_1 (p_0 < p_1)$ such that the producer will not like to reject the lot if $p \leq p_0$ and a consumer will not like to accept the lot if $p \geq p_1$. At the same time, both would be reluctant to take a final decision if $p_0 < p < p_1$. Also it would be possible to fix two values α and β such that the producer wants the probability of rejecting the lot to be less than or equal to α when $p \leq p_0$ and the consumer wants the probability of accepting the lot less than or equal to β when $p \geq p_1$. In terms of operating characteristic it is desired that,

$$L(p) \geq 1-\alpha \qquad \text{when } p \leq p_0 \qquad \text{...(21.35)}$$

$$L(p) \leq \beta \qquad \text{when } p \geq p_1 \qquad \text{...(21.36)}$$

Sequential sampling plan is implemented to the acceptance-rejection problem in the following manner. We perform a test known as Wald's *sequential probability ratio test* (S.P.R.T.). Here we test,

$$H_0 : p = p_0 \text{ vs. } H_1 : p = p_1$$

Let $X_1, X_2, ..., X_m$ be the random sample selected up to the mth stage and X_i' s be independently and identically distributed with joint probability density or mass function $f(x, \theta)$. When we are considering whether the units in the lot are defective or non-defective, $f(x, \theta)$ can be given by Bernoulli's distribution, *i.e.*, $\prod_{i=1}^{m} p_1^{x_i}(1-p_1)^{1-x_i}$. Under H_1, the probability mass function for the sample $x_1, x_2, ..., x_m$ is

$$p_{1m} = \prod_{i=1}^{m} p_1^{x_i}(1-p_1)^{1-x_i} \qquad \text{...(21.37)}$$

and under H_0, probability mass function is

$$p_{0m} = \prod_{i=1}^{m} p_0^{x_i}(1-p_0)^{1-x_i} \qquad \text{...(21.38)}$$

To test H_0 against H_1, SPRT is defined in terms of the ratio p_{1m}/p_{0m}. Thus,

$$\frac{p_{1m}}{p_{0m}} = \frac{\prod_{i-1}^{m} p_1^{x_i}(1-p_1)^{1-x_i}}{\prod_{i=1}^{m} p_0^{x_i}(1-p_0)^{1-x_i}} \qquad \text{...(21.39)}$$

Suppose $x_i = 1$, if the ith unit is found defective and $x_i = 0$, if the ith unit is found non-defective. Let d_m = number of defectives found up to the mth stage.

The readers should note that one has to proceed up to the mth stage provided no decision is taken up to $(m - 1)$th stage.

Under sequential sampling inspection plan, the expression (21.39) reduces to,

$$\frac{p_{1m}}{p_{0m}} = \frac{p_1^{d_m}(1-p_1)^{m-d_m}}{p_0^{d_m}(1-p_0)^{m-d_m}} \qquad \text{...(21.40)}$$

The decision about the acceptance or rejection is taken according to the rules given below.

Accept the lot if

$$\frac{p_{1m}}{p_{0m}} \le \frac{\beta}{1-\alpha} \qquad \text{...(21.41)}$$

Reject the lot if

$$\frac{p_{1m}}{p_{0m}} \ge \frac{1-\beta}{\alpha} \qquad \text{...(21.42)}$$

and continue sampling till

$$\frac{\beta}{1-\alpha} < \frac{p_{1m}}{p_{0m}} < \frac{1-\beta}{\alpha} \qquad \text{...(21.43)}$$

Rewrite the inequality (21.41) in full form and solve for d_m.

$$\frac{p_1^{d_m}(1-p_1)^{m-d_m}}{p_0^{d_m}(1-p_0)^{m-d_m}} \le \frac{\beta}{1-\alpha}$$

Taking logarithm on both sides we get,

$$d_m \log\frac{p_1}{p_0} + (m-d_m)\log\frac{1-p_1}{1-p_0} \le \log\frac{\beta}{1-\alpha}$$

$$d_m\left\{\log\frac{p_1}{p_0} - \log\frac{1-p_1}{1-p_0}\right\} \le \log\frac{\beta}{1-\alpha} \div m\log\frac{1-p_0}{1-p_1}$$

or

$$d_m \le \frac{\log\frac{\beta}{1-\alpha}}{\log\frac{p_1}{p_0}-\log\frac{1-p_1}{1-p_0}} + m\frac{\log\frac{1-p_0}{1-p_1}}{\log\frac{p_1}{p_0}-\log\frac{1-p_1}{1-p_0}} \qquad \text{...(21.44)}$$

Suppose,

$$a_m = \frac{\log\frac{\beta}{1-\alpha}}{\log\frac{p_1}{p_0}-\log\frac{1-p_1}{1-p_0}} + m\frac{\log\frac{1-p_0}{1-p_1}}{\log\frac{p_1}{p_0}-\log\frac{1-p_1}{1-p_0}}$$

Therefore, accept the lot if

$$d_m \le a_m$$

Similarly, reject the lot if

$$d_m \ge r_m \qquad \text{...(21.45)}$$

where,

$$r_m = \frac{\log\frac{1-\beta}{\alpha}}{\log\frac{p_1}{p_0}-\log\frac{1-p_1}{1-p_0}} + m\frac{\log\frac{1-p_0}{1-p_1}}{\log\frac{p_1}{p_0}-\log\frac{1-p_1}{1-p_0}}$$

and continue sampling if

$$a_m < d_m < r_m$$

The sequential test procedure can be carried out graphically in the following manner. Draw two lines namely, a_m, the line of acceptance and r_m, the line of rejection respectively.

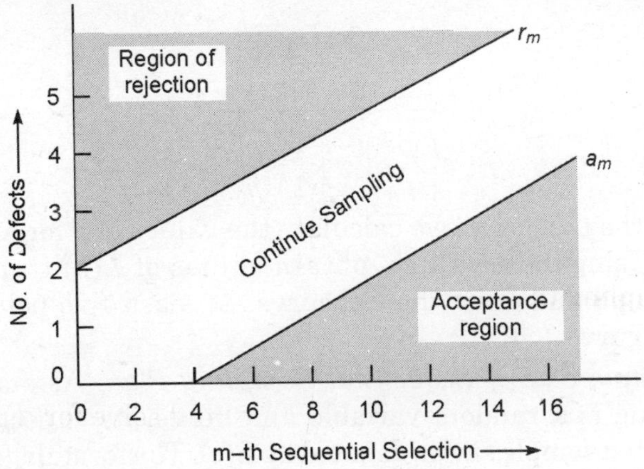

Figure 21.9 Sequential test procedure for acceptance-rejection of a lot

Plot the point (m, d_m). If the plotted point lies on or below the line a_m, accept the lot. If the point (m, d_m) lies on or above the line r_m, reject the lot. If the point lies in between the lines a_m and r_m, no decision is taken about the acceptance or rejection of the lot. Repeat the process, *i.e.*, select another unit randomly and plot the point (m, d_m). See where this point lies and take the decision as per rule.

Sequential sampling plan is easy to implement as it involves only four quantities p_0, p_1, α and β. At each stage, the quantities a_m and r_m can be calculated and a decision about acceptance, rejection or continuance can be taken according to the rule.

Sequential sampling plan gives an impression that we might have to continue the process infinitely, to arrive at a decision. But it has been proved mathematically, that the process always terminates after a finite number of stages, *i.e.*, the sequential process terminates with probability 1. Also, it is found that the average sample number is about half of the sample size required for single sampling inspection plan that provides the same control on probabilities of type I and type II errors.

O.C. Function of Sequential Sampling Plan. The O.C. function of a SPRT for testing $H_0: p = p_0$ against $H_1: p = p_1$ is given by

$$L(p) = \frac{\left(\frac{1-\beta}{\alpha}\right)^h - 1}{\left(\frac{1-\beta}{\alpha}\right)^h - \left(\frac{\beta}{1-\alpha}\right)^h} \qquad \text{...(21.46)}$$

where $h = h(p)$.

The value of h is obtained by the equation,

$$p\left(\frac{p_1}{p_0}\right)^h + (1-p)\left(\frac{1-p_1}{1-p_0}\right)^h = 1 \qquad \text{...(21.47)}$$

To solve the equation (21.47) for h is a tedious job. Therefore, we solve this equation for p in terms of h. So we get,

$$p = \frac{1 - \left(\frac{1-p_1}{1-p_0}\right)^h}{\left(\frac{p_1}{p_0}\right)^h - \left(\frac{1-p_1}{1-p_0}\right)^h} \qquad \text{...(21.48)}$$

Now to draw the OC curve, we calculate the values of p for arbitrarily chosen values of h from (21.48). Using these values, obtain values of $L(p)$ from (21.46). Plot the point $\{p, L(p)\}$ on the graph and draw the OC curve. At least, five points should be plotted to determine the OC curve.

Expected Sample Size of Sequential Sampling Plan. As stated earlier, the size in sequential sampling is a random variable and hence, its expected value can be found. Suppose, the expected sample size is denoted by $E(n)$. The formula for $E(n)$ under sequential sampling plan with A.Q.L., p_0 and least tolerance fraction defective p_1 *i.e.*, for testing $H_0 : p = p_0$ against $H_0 : p = p_1$ through SPRT is given as

$$E(n) = \frac{L(p)\log\frac{\beta}{1-\alpha} + \{1 - L(p)\}\log\frac{1-\beta}{\alpha}}{E(z)} \qquad \text{...(21.49)}$$

where $$E(z) = p\log\frac{p_1}{p_0} + (1-p)\log\frac{1-p_1}{1-p_0}$$

Thus, $$E(n) = \frac{L(p)\log\frac{\beta}{1-\alpha} + \{1 - L(p)\}\log\frac{1-\beta}{\alpha}}{p\log\frac{p_1}{p_0} + (1-p)\log\frac{1-p_1}{1-p_0}} \qquad \text{...(21.49.1)}$$

Comparison of Three Sampling Plans

Single and double sampling are equally good in respect of operating characteristic and average sample number. But generally, double sampling requires 25–33 per cent less inspection of units on the average and sequential sampling needs 33–50 per cent less inspection of units on the average as compared to single stage sampling.

SAMPLING INSPECTION PLAN FOR VARIABLES

The charts for continuous variables have already been discussed. The sampling inspection plans have been discussed here in adequate detail for fraction defectives. The theory developed for fraction defectives can be applied for quantity characteristics, which are measured for continuous variables e.g., diameter, weight, length, tensile strength, percentage of a chemical etc. In this type of quality control, the whole process of quality control has to be carried out for each of the variable separately. This makes the process of quality control quite cumbersome. While in fraction defective approach, a unit not meeting the specifications is categorised as defective, otherwise they are non-defective. Hence, the inspection cost is reduced to a great extent in the latter case. Suppose, there are 20 variables under consideration, 20 charts are to be prepared and on the basis of each chart a decision is taken about the acceptance or rejection of the lot. The results may be contradictory and confusing. Hence, to avoid this difficulty, one or two variables of prime importance are considered and a decision is taken on the basis of these variables only.

Statistical quality control is one of the keys to success, for the producers. In this competitive world, one cannot market sub-standard goods. Particularly, the spares used in the machinery are useless if they do not meet the specifications and sometimes, they may prove dangerous as well. Hence, quality control methods are strong tools in the hands of the producers to maintain the quality of the product vis-a-vis their reputation.

QUESTIONS AND EXERCISES

1. Throw light on the use and applications of statistical quality control.
2. Do the control charts indicate the fault in the process? Clarify your answer with examples.
3. What are the broad categories of control charts and the basis for them?
4. Discuss the basic principle underlying the preparation of control charts.
5. Distinguish between the following.
   (*a*) $\overline{X}$ and R charts.
   (*b*) Single sampling and sequential sampling plans.
   (*c*) Charts for attributes and variables.
   (*d*) Number of defectives and number of defects.
   (*e*) p and d charts.
6. Write an essay on the advantages of statistical quality control.
7. Explain the following terms:
   (*a*) Acceptance quality level.
   (*b*) Lot tolerance percentage defective.
   (*c*) Average outgoing quality limit.
   (*d*) Operating characteristic.
   (*e*) Average sample number.
8. Define the following terms:
   (*a*) Consumer's risk
   (*b*) Producer's risk
   (*c*) Sequential probability ratio test.
9. Explain the procedure of statistical quality control under sequential sampling plan.
10. Set up the control limits for the following, when the process values are not known.
    (*a*) $\overline{X}$-chart
    (*b*) R-chart
    (*c*) c-chart
    (*d*) p-chart
    (*e*) σ-chart.
11. In what respects, is sequential sampling plan better than single stage sampling?
12. Describe briefly the need and utility of statistical quality control in industry.

    (*M.B.A., Delhi, 1969*)

13. Distinguish between process control and product control. Define producer's risk. If the average fraction defectives of a large sample of a product is 0.1537, calculate the control limits. (Given that sub-group size is 2000). What modifications do you need if the sub-group size is not constant. *(I.C.W.A., Final Exam., Dec., 1979)*
14. The following figures were obtained on inspecting the five rational sub-groups.

Groups	*No. of units inspected*	*No. of units found defective*
1	300	20
2	350	35
3	275	24
4	270	16
5	325	8

Prepare a suitable control chart and comment whether the process is in a state of statistical quality control.

15. Fifteen groups of 6 tape-recorder cum transistor sets were randomly selected for inspection in a factory on consecutive days. The number of defects found in each group were as follows.

Group	*No. of defects per group*	*Group*	*No. of defects per group*
1.	34	9.	11
2.	23	10.	28
3.	13	11.	35
4.	32	12.	22
5.	48	13.	18
6.	16	14.	14
7.	9	15.	7
8.	12		

Plot the control chart for the number of defects and comment whether the process is under control.

16. 12 samples of 4 bulbs were selected at regular intervals from a light bulb manufacturing company. If bulbs have the mean life equal to 1000 hours, it is considered satisfactory. The standard deviation of life of bulbs is expected to be 522 hours. On testing the samples, the failure times (in hours) were recorded as given below.

Sample number	*Life of bulbs (hours)*			
1.	1081	363	1092	1385
2.	528	330	1053	945
3.	984	1384	1194	456
4.	728	972	647	792
5.	804	845	1132	1024
6.	1002	804	760	1035
7.	994	1023	1136	842
8.	616	832	497	692
9.	982	1342	1132	945
10.	1132	998	554	777
11.	1134	1140	756	994
12.	749	948	1050	857

(i) Prepare the $\overline{X}$ - chart when the mean life and the standard deviation of the life of bulbs are known.

(ii) Prepare $\overline{X}$ and R charts as if the mean and the standard deviation of the life of bulbs are not known.

On the basis of each of these charts, comment whether the process is under control or not.

17. Explain the terms: Control charts for variables and control charts for attributes. The following table shows the number of missing rivets observed at the time of the inspection of 12 aircrafts. Find the control limits for the number of defects chart and comment on the state of control.

Aircraft number	1	2	3	4	5	6	7	8	9	10	11	12
No. of missing rivets	7	15	13	18	10	14	13	10	20	11	22	15

(*I.C.W.A., Final Exam., Dec., 1978*)

18. Explain the following terms.

(i) (a) Rational sub-groups.

(b) Operating characteristic curve.

(ii) A machine is set to deliver packets of a given weight. 10 samples of size 5 were recorded. Below are given the relevant data:

Sample No.:	1	2	3	4	5	6	7	8	9	10
Mean ($\overline{X}$):	15	17	15	18	17	14	18	15	17	16
Range (R):	7	7	4	9	8	7	12	4	11	5

Calculate the values for the central line and the control limits for the mean chart and range chart. Also comment on the state of control.

[Conversion factors for $n = 5$ are $A_2 = 0.58$, $D_3 = 0$, $D_4 = 2.11$]

(*I.C.W.A., Final Exam., Dec., 1980*)

19. The following data show the values of sample mean $\overline{X}$ and range (R) for 10 samples of size 6 each. Calculate the values for the central line and the control limits for the Mean-chart and the Range-chart. Draw the control charts and comment on the state of control.

Sample No.	1	2	3	4	5	6	7	8	9	10
Mean ($\overline{X}$):	43	49	37	44	45	37	51	46	43	47
Range (R):	3	6	5	7	7	4	8	6	4	6

[Conversion factors for $n = 6$ are $A_2 = 0.483$, $D_3 = 0$, $D_4 = 2.004$]

(*I.C.W.A., Final Exam., June, 1979*)

20. Write a brief note on the method of constructing control charts for $\overline{X}$ and R, giving the formulae for the upper and the lower control limits, in both the cases.

(*M.Com., Meerut, 1970*)

21. Quality control is maintained in a factory with the help of the mean ($\overline{X}$) and the standard deviation (σ) charts. Ten items are chosen in every sample. 18 samples were chosen whose ΣX was 595.8 and $\Sigma\sigma$ was 8.28. Determine 3σ limits for $\overline{X}$ and σ - charts. You may use the following factors for finding the 3σ limits.

n	A_1	B_3	B_4
10	1.03	0.28	1.72

(M. Com., Delhi, 1970)

22. (*a*) What do you understand by Acceptance Sampling?

(*b*) In order to determine whether or not a process producing bronze castings is in control, 20 sub-groups of size 6 are taken. The quality characteristic of interest is the weight of the castings and it is found that X is 3.126 gm and $R = 0.009$ gm.

(*i*) Estimate the standard deviation of the weight of castings.

(*ii*) Assuming that the process is in control, find the upper and lower control limits for the sub-group means.

(*iii*) Assuming that the process is in control, find the upper and lower control limits for the sub-group ranges.

(*iv*) Using (*i*) above, within what limits would you expect 99.73 per cent of all individual measurements to fall.

You may use the following control chart constants.

n	d_2	A_2	D_3	D_4	B_3	B_4
4	2.059	0.729	0	2.282	0	2.266
5	2.326	0.577	0	2.115	0	2.089
6	2.534	0.483	0	2.004	0	1.970

(M.Com., Delhi, 1972)

23. Explain the meanings of *LTPD, AQL, L(p)*, producer's risk, consumer's risk and *AOQL* and explain their relevance in determining an appropriate sampling inspection scheme for acceptance of lots. *(M.Sc. Descriptive & Industrial Statistics, Andhra, 1986)*

SUGGESTED READING

Cowden, D.J. (1960). *Statistical Methods in Quality Control,* Asia Publishing House, Bombay.

Dan Trietsch (1999). *Statistical Quality Control*, World Scientific.

Ekambram, S.K. (1963). *The Statistical Basis of Acceptance Sampling,* Asia Publishing House, Bombay.

Irwing W. Burr (1979). *Elementary Statistical Quality Control*, Marcell Dekker.

Kenneth Walter Kemp (2001). *The Efficient Use of Quality Control Data*, Oxford University Press.

M.J. Ćhandra (2001). *Statistical Quality Control*, CRC Press.

Metron R. Hubbard (2001). *Statistical Quality Control for the Food Industry*, Springer.

22 Chapter

Statistical Organisation in India

General Discussion

Statistical information about a place, region, state or nation is necessary for running the administration efficiently. Its origin dates back to the period of Ramayana when statistics, regarding employment and taxes, were collected during the rule of Raja Bharat. Arthashastra written by Kautilya also throws light on the collection machinery of statistical information regarding land, area, agricultural production, population, taxes etc. During the Moghul period, statistics were collected and used for administrative purposes. The main documents related to statistical information were Tuzke-Babri and Ain-i-Akbari. Ain-i-Akbari was considered to be one of the very informative and standard documents of Emperor Akbar's period. From the details given in Ain-i-Akbari, it is evident that there has been an organised machinery for collecting statistical information.

After the Moghul period, the British period started in India. Ryotwari system was introduced in some parts of India during the 18th century and the land revenue officers were appointed by East India Company to collect land revenue. The revenue rate was based on agricultural production and fertility of soils. The procedure continued till the existence of Zamindari system in India.

The need for statistical information was felt more and more in the nineteenth century due to the recurrence of famine. The famine of 1860 is a historical famine in India. Till that time, government had no knowledge about the population and its food requirements. A partial census in India took place in 1872. The first census covering the whole of India was conducted in 1881. Since then, decennial census is a regular feature. The famine commission of 1880 recommended the creation of the department of agriculture and some posts of statistical officers. The statistics of foreign trade, prices and industries, on the other hand, were collected and published by the Department of Finance and Commerce. This led to the publication of "Agricultural Statistics of British India" in 1886.

In order to collate and compile enormous data at the state level, a *statistical Bureau* was established at the centre in 1895. Besides agricultural statistics it was entrusted to collect statistics with regard to the trade and industries. In 1905, the Directorate of Commercial Intelligence and statistics was established and the Statistical Bureau was merged with it. Till the commencement of World War I, the Department of Commercial intelligence published the following journals.

(i) *Review of Trade of India.*
(ii) *Statement of Foreign Sea-borne Trade and Navigation of British India.*
(iii) *Statistical Abstract of British India.*
(iv) *Estimates of Area and yield of Principal Crops in India.*
(v) *Agricultural Statistics of British India.*
(vi) *The Indian Trade Journal (Quarterly).*

In addition to these, a number of other Journals were also published.

An enquiry committee named as 'Economic Enquiry Committee' was constituted in 1925, under the chairmanship of Sir M. Visvesraya. The objective of the committee was to look into the adequacy of the data available at hand, and the possibility of supplementing it. The committee made the following recommendations for the improvement of statistical information. It said that (*a*) a census of large scale industries be instituted, (*b*) data be collected about the quantity and value of the products raised and the raw material consumed by the factories, (*c*) statistics of all departments (provincial and state) should come under the supervision of a central authority. It further recommended the publication of a year book on the lines of the Dominion Year Book.

Immediately after the report of the Economic Enquiry Committee, the report of the *Royal Commission on Agriculture* was out in 1928. The Royal Commission recommended the constitution of an *Imperial Council of Agricultural Research,* to coordinate agricultural research and to collect data about agriculture and animal husbandry. An important event that occurred in 1933 was the establishment of *Statistical Research Bureau.* Another committee was set up in 1934 known as *Bowley-Robertson Committee.* The committee recommended and gave details of the census of the production and the measurement of the National Income. It also recommended the appointment of a Directorate of Statistics to collect data. In 1939, there was an outbreak of World War II. The need for statistical information was felt more and more. The *Department of Industries and Civil Supplies* meant for controlling the civil supplies was entrusted with the job of collection of the statistical information, relating to essential commodities. To ensure completeness of data on industries, an act known as *Industrial Statistics Act* was passed in 1942. This act compelled the industries to furnish the required information for statistical purposes. More and more developments took place from time to time, regarding the collection of statistical information, making the data more complete and reliable. Also, an effort was made to collect statistical data, in varied fields, related to economy and manpower. Since statistical information has been the backbone of government activities and planning, it has been paid great attention after the independence of India in 1947.

Post-Independence Period

Indian Government has a federal set up as far as the administration of the country is concerned. Hence, there is a combined responsibility of the states as well as the centre for internal matters. In view of this, all the jobs are taken either by state government or by the central government or by both. Different categories of works are covered by different ministries of the states or the centre. For a systematic organisation and the collection of statistical information, Government of India established different departments at the centre and state levels. The Cabinet Secretariat has a Department of Statistics. One wing of this department is *National Sample Survey Organisation* (NSSO) set up in January, 1950. Another wing is the *Central Statistical Organisation* (CSO) set up in May, 1951. These two are important statistical wings of the Government of India and hence it becomes necessary to know about them in details.

CENTRAL STATISTICAL ORGANISATION OF INDIA

Central government established Central Statistical Organisation (CSO), under cabinet secretariat with the objective of creating coordination of large variety of statistical information, collected at the centre and state level. It performs many more functions as listed below:

1. Coordination of statistical activities at the centre and the state.
2. Advisory work concerning the statistical matter, particularly standardization of concepts and definitions to maintain uniformity, throughout the country.
3. Collection of statistical data related to planning.
4. Training of statistical personnel.
5. Compilation of national income estimates.
6. To provide statistical data of the nation to the United Nations statistical offices and other international institutions.
7. To plan and coordinate the conduct of the annual survey of industries and publish the results.
8. To attend to the work of International Statistical Institutes (conferences) held in India and abroad.
9. The display of charts and graphs pertaining to the national data which are of administrative interest.
10. Circulation of regular publications.

This organisation does many other things concerning statistical matter, needed from time to time. Each of the above mentioned functions is looked after by a separate division with its headquarters in Delhi, except the Industrial Statistics Wing at Kolkata. We will give here the brief account of the above mentioned functions.

The CSO examines various schemes running at the state level and makes specific suggestions for their improvement. Now CSO has a network all over the country. CSO coordinates statistics collected by different ministries. It also coordinates with National Sample Survey Organisation.

The Central Statistical Organisation, supplies statistical information about India to United Nations Statistical Office and International Agencies. It provides data for publication in (*i*) The U.N. Monthly Bulletin of Statistics; (*ii*) U.N. Quarterly Bulletin on Commodity Trade Statistics; (*iii*) U.N. Demographic Year Book and (*iv*) The Economic Council for Asia and Far East (ECAFE), Quarterly Bulletin and Annual Surveys. Besides these, CSO supplies compiled data to many other international agencies for publication. It also supplies information regarding the methodology adopted in the collection of data, the coverage and the scope.

The Directorate of Industrial Statistics was set up in 1944 at Kolkata. But later in 1957, it was merged with Central Statistical Organisation. Its main function has been the annual census of manufacturing industries, which is known as the *Annual Survey of Industries* (ASI). This unit of CSO has various functions such as (*i*) to coordinate the conduct of annual survey of industries in all states, and process the data for publication, (*ii*) to give monthly account of the production of selected industries through a monthly Bulletin, (*iii*) to compute and publish the monthly index of industrial production, obtained for selected industries and (*iv*) to function in many other ways. The CSO renders advice to various ministries, in the central government. It examines the bulletins of the state level. It lays down the definitions and concepts, in conformity, with international standards e.g., International Standard Industrial Classification (ISIC); International Standard Classification of Occupation (ISCO) and Standard Occupational Classification (SOC) for India. The adoption of standard definitions and classifications, makes the information comparable within the country and at the international level.

A planning cell was set up in CSO in 1955, to maintain liason between the Indian Statistical Institute and the planning division. All statistical matters related to planning are dealt within this wing.

The CSO conducts regular training courses at its offices, to train the personnel in statistical services throughout the country.

The CSO makes national income estimates for the centre as well as for the states in collaboration with various statistical agencies at the state level. A National Income Unit (NIU) was created in 1955. The unit exclusively collects the data concerning the national income. A white paper on national income is published by an industrial intelligence unit with regards to industries in India. This unit assists the private and public sectors in many ways, particularly, giving information about imports, exports, demand etc.

The pertinent information of administrative and public interest is displayed through charts, graphs and diagrams. Such diagrams are displayed in an exhibition hall maintained by the CSO.

As a matter of fact, statistical information is collected and compiled in a vast field of economic activity-like motor vehicles, civil aviation, foreign trade, inland trade, taxation and revenue, agriculture, forest, fishery, livestock, etc. All this compiled information is published in one or another form in the journals and bulletins. A few publications of CSO are enlisted below :

1. *Monthly Abstract of Statistics.* It represents data about diferent facets of Indian economy such as (*i*) Labour and Employment; (*ii*) Fuel and Power; (*iii*) Minerals; (*iv*) Industrial production; (*v*) Transport; (*vi*) Foreign trade; (*vii*) Banking and Currency; (*viii*) Consumption and Stocks; (*ix*) Postal traffic ;(*x*) Prices etc.
2. *Monthly Statistics of the Production of Selected Industries.* It gives the monthly production statistics. Two months statistics are published in a combined issue, covering a large number of items. It also contains the index of industrial production and mill stock position. Separate production figures for different states are presented in it.
3. *Annual Survey of Industries.* The National Sample Survey Organisation, carries out annually a survey of industries known as *Annual Survey of Industries* (ASI). Industrywise estimates of employment, output, input and capital are displayed

separately for the census and sample sectors. Because of the time lag in the availability of results of ASI, the net value added estimates for more recent years are prepared from *Summary Result of Factory Sector,* containing combined results of census and sample sectors. The report is brought out within a year of the completion of the survey. Data with regard to defence are kept out of the purview of this survey, as they are not covered under ASI. This is an annual publication. Till 1958, it was published under the name 'Census of Indian Manufacturers'.

4. *Statistical Abstract of India.* This publication is of general nature. It gives an account of area, population, climate, agriculture, mining, banks, motor vehicles, balance of payments etc. Large number of tables are presented relating to social, economic and natural factors.
5. *National Accounts Statistics* (NAS). This annual publication is also known as *white paper.* It incorporates the estimates of capital formation, saving, private consumption, expenditure, factor incomes and the disaggregated tables. The white paper published in January, 1978 introduced for the first time, a more recent base 1970-71 for the series at constant prices replacing the earlier base 1960-61. The issue of NAS published in April, 1980 contains data up to 1977-78. Since 1956, the publication of NAS is brought out annually. The base year of new series of NAS is 1999–2000.

There are many other publications of CSO, which are referred ahead in this chapter.

NATIONAL SAMPLE SURVEY ORGANISATION (NSSO)

Census studies have been very expensive and time consuming. In many situations, we cannot afford to wait for long, to get the overall picture of various aspects of socio-economic study. Hence, the emphasis was laid down to sampling studies which led to the creation of National Sample Survey Organisation. As given earlier, it was established in January, 1950 in the Department of Economic Affairs, Ministry of Finance, to conduct countrywide multipurpose sample surveys, covering all aspects of national economy required by *National Income Committee* (NIC), Planning Commission and other ministries of Government of India. The Directorate of National Sample Survey, used to work under the Statistics Department of the cabinet secretariat. Its main functions were:

(*i*) Collection of socio-economic data relating to demographic conditions for the whole country on regular basis.

(*ii*) To provide statistical data for national income and planning.

(*iii*) To conduct annual surveys in the organised industrial sector.

(*iv*) Training of personnel and providing guidance to the states in the conduct of surveys.

The work of NSSO was being done under dual control for two decades. The field work was carried out by the Directorate of NSS, whereas designing of surveys, processing of data and preparation of reports was entrusted to the Indian Statistical Institute. In March 1970, the Government of India accepted the recommendation that all aspects of the NSS be brought under an unified control, with a Governing Council to govern its activities. The council was given the requisite independence and autonomy in decision making. In the real sense, it materialised in 1972. Now NSSO is under the Department of Statistics, Ministry of Planning, Government of India. The objective of the NSSO, as laid down in the background of the aims of government statistical work, as an autonomous organisation, are:

(*i*) To provide statistical and other information needed for the efficient conduct of government business.

(*ii*) To evolve statistical technique to bear on the analysis of information, the solution of administrative problems and the estimation of future trends.

(*iii*) To collect and publish information which will be of use to those engaged in economic activities in the country.

(*iv*) To provide and analyse information which are useful to the research workers.

(*v*) To assist in keeping the public informed of the new developments in the economic and the social fields.

In short, NSSO has unified control of the governing council with regard to survey designs, field operations, data processing, economic analysis and publication of NSS data. The present structure of NSSO consists of four functional divisions, with a Chief Executive Officer at the apex. The four divisions are:

(*a*) Survey Design and Research.

(*b*) Field Operations.

(*c*) Data Processing.

(*d*) Economic Analysis.

The Executive Officer, as the member secretary of the Governing Council, obtains the approval of the council to the programme of work and directs the appropriate Division to implement it. The National Sample Survey Organisation works in close coordination with CSO in respect of certain projects and programmes. The tabulation and analysis of data are attended by the CSO and, partly, by the Labour Bureau and National Building Organisation (NBO). As far as the agriculture is concerned, the Field Operations Division (FOD) is responsible for all activities.

With the increasing intake of new personnel, NSSO felt the need for reorientation of its staff. For this purpose, it conducts training programmes. Accordingly, 41 regions of FOD have been grouped into five zones, with headquarters at Bangalore, Nagpur, Jaipur, Allahabad and Kolkata. Each zone has been placed under the charge of a Deputy Director, who is responsible for organising training courses for his zonal staff.

In case of the socio-economic surveys, decisions on subject coverage are taken from round to round, keeping in view the request for data from the central and the state governments. The council considers the requirements of the planners, research workers and other users in the country. It conducts surveys on demography, health and family planning, debt and investment, capital formation, land holdings, Livestock enterprises (quinquennially), employment, rural labour, consumer expenditure and self employment in non-agricultural sector. NSSO also conducts survey on special demands.

It makes no sense to give the account of all the rounds completed by NSSO, so we give brief account of the three rounds. The thirty-seventh round field operation was initiated in January 1982 and was over by December, 82. The enquiries on land holdings and livestock, debt and investment formed the core of the 37th round programme. The First survey on land holdings was taken up in 8th round as a part of Food and Agricultural Organisation (FAO) programme of the World Agricultural Census.

It was repeated in the 16th and the 17th rounds. The next NSSO survey was in 26th round when it was integrated with a survey on debt and investment at the instance of the Reserve Bank of India. According to the ten years programme of the NSSO, the enquiry on the above topics has to be the carried out once in ten years and accordingly 37th round is essentially a repetition of the 26th round survey. However, some items covered in the 26th round survey had been excluded from the scope of the present survey. It covered the whole country excepting Ladakh, and Kargil districts of Jammu and Kashmir, and the rural areas of Nagaland.

By the end of December 1983, NSSO had completed the thirty-eighth round. The period of the 38th round was from January to December, 1983. This round was the third quinquennial survey on the household consumer expenditure, employment and unemployment. The two previous surveys of this series were carried out in the 27th round (Oct. 1972 to Sept. 1973) and the 32nd round (July 1977 to June 1978). The 32nd round was different from the 27th round in some ways. But the 38th round was similar to the 32nd round and thus, the two rounds were very well comparable. The survey covered the whole of the country, excepting Ladakh and Kargil Districts of Jammu and Kashmir and the rural areas of Nagaland.

The field work of the thirty-ninth round had started in January, 1984. The survey period of this round was from Jan. to June, 1984. An enquiry of the population, the births and the deaths, was conducted in the 39th round of NSS. Two schedules were canvassed—one for the enumeration of population as on the date of survey and the enumeration of births and deaths occurring during the preceding two years; the other schedule for re-enumeration of population, enumeration of births and deaths occurring to household members found existing during a previous visit one year earlier, and to elicit certain information on the fertility.

The price enquiry was also being conducted in this round in 419 fixed villages, selected for the collection of data, on rural retail prices, through a schedule. The geographical coverage in this round had been the same as in the 38th round. National Sample Survey Organisation, publishes a report on each round, for the use of various departments and research workers.

To update and acquaint the readers with the latest rounds of surveys conducted by the National sample survey organisation; it looks germane to give a brief account of 46th to 49th rounds.

NSSO conducted 46th round from July, 1990 to June, 1991. This survey was on *wholesale and retail trade transacted by non-directory trading establishments* (NDTE's) and own account trade enterprises (OATE's). The area of survey was whole of India except some regions namely, Ladakh and Kargil, interior villages of Nagaland and some villages in Andaman & Nicobar islands. The survey design was stratified two stage sampling. Villages and urban blocks were taken as first stage units, NDTE's and OATE's were taken as second stage units. A consolidated report had been published by NSSO.

47th round of NSSO consisted of the survey on *disability, literacy* and *culture*. The duration of the survey was July to December, 1991. Geographical coverage and sampling design was same as in 46th round. In this survey, urban blocks and villages were taken as first stage units and households as second stage units. The report of the survey has been out for use.

A *consumer expenditure survey* was also organised side by side clubbed with 47th round on a thin sample basis. In this survey two households per village or per urban block were surveyed. Survey report had been published by NSSO in 54th issue.

In 48th round, NSSO conducted a survey on land holding, livestock holding, debt and investment. Duration of this survey was Jan.–Dec., 1992. Geographical area of coverage remained the same as in 46th round. Sampling design was again stratified into two stage sampling. Urban blocks or villages were taken as first stage units and households as second stage units. This survey was different from other surveys in respect of collecting information from households. Two visits were made to every household. First visit in the first six months i.e., in between January and June, 1992 and second visit in the last half of the year i.e., at any time from July to December, 1992. The report of the survey has been out for information.

49th round of NSSO is on housing conditions, construction and migration. The period of survey is from January to July, 1992. The coverage of area being the same as in previous rounds.

Conducting surveys is a regular function of NSSO. Sixty-first round of survey started in June, 2004. This round pertains to employment and unemployment. Its term ended on June, 2005. The 65th round of socioeconomic survey was commensed from Ist July 2008 to 30th June, 2009. This round covered Domestic Tourism, Housing condition and Urban Slums.

POPULATION STATISTICS

Population statistics is the oldest in the history of statistics, collected and compiled by any Kingdom or country. Population statistics at that time used to mean only the counting of heads which was necessary to know the manpower of a Kingdom, to protect oneself from other Kingdoms or to win the other Kingdoms. Nowadays, population statistics is a part of demography. Demography is a science which covers genealogy, human eugenics, population census, vital statistics, biometrics and statistical pathology. Here we shall briefly discuss the collection of data pertaining to the population census and the vital statistics only.

Population Census

Enumeration of individuals under state direction at regular intervals is called population census.

Vital Statistics

It is a branch of statistics, which deals with the registration of facts concerning birth, marriage, divorce, sickness and death under the state direction.

Methods of Conducting Population Census

Population census in India, started in 1881 for the first time. Before independence of India, census was not conducted under a permanent legislation. But after independence, Government of India passed on an act known as the *Indian Census Act,* 1948 which empowers the central government to take a census, appoint necessary census staff, delegate authority and the status of public servants as census officers, assume the power to call upon persons to give assistance and any person is legally bound to answer any questions asked of him by a census officer for the census information. It also authorises the census enumerators to enter a house and interrogate people. Any defiance to this rule shall be punishable. After independence, there has been five censuses, the last was conducted in 2001. In fact, two methods of census are there.

1. *De facto* method or Date system.
2. *De jure* method or period system.

Both these methods are further sub-divided into canvasser's method and household method.

De facto Method. In this method, persons are counted, wherever they are, on the date of census. In this way, counting takes place on the date and that is the reason it is called the *date system* as well. This gives good information about the number of people in a country but suffers from many lacunae. Firstly, it excludes people where enumerators cannot reach. Moreover, it involves a very huge number of enumerators and hence this method is uneconomical.

De jure Method. In this method, people are counted on the basis of their normal (habitual) residence. Any person found temporarily at a place is excluded from enumeration and counted by an enumerator at his place of residence, even if he is absent. In this method, census is not conducted on a fixed date but is conducted in a particular period. That is why, it is known as a *period system.* The *De jure canvasser method* provides geographical and regional distribution of population more exactly than *de facto method.* The period of census under the de jure method since 1941 has been extended to three weeks.

Slip System. Instead of filling the schedules, the slip system of census was introduced for the first time in India during the census of 1941. In this system, one slip was assigned to each individual on which the entire information about the person concerned was noted. The slip system is very convenient for the compilation and the analysis of data. Answers to various questions were recorded in the form of symbol codes on the slip. This saves a lot of labour and time of the enumerator and eases the process of compilation of information, with the help of mechanical tabulation.

Census 1951. The first census of free India, was conducted in 1951. The Census Act of India 1948, was passed for the conduct of the census. The office of the census commissioner was created on a permanent basis. Otherwise, this office used to be bound up when the census operations were over. The full designation of the posts were that of a Census Commissioner and a Registrar General of India. The officer worked as a Census Commissioner during the period of census and carried on the duties of Registrar General during inter-censal period.

It was for the first time in 1951, that a distinction between House and Household was made. House was defined as a dwelling place with a separate main entrance. Household was defined on the basis of chulha i.e., group of persons living together and dining from a common kitchen were regarded as the member of the same household. This helped in estimating the family size. Enumeration of population was conducted on the basis of household in 1951 census.

A national register of citizens had been prepared for the first time, which served as an inventory for various official and non-official investigations. This register had been prepared for every village and every town. The Registrar General keeps this register uptodate, by recording births and deaths. The Registrar General is required to keep a copy of the relevant portion at the village block and district headquarters. This register is also used in preparing the electoral lists.

To acquire more information about the economic characteristics of the population, the changes were made in the existing slip of 1941 for the census in 1951.

Census 1961 – De jure census method was adopted at this time and hence, each individual was contacted at his place of residence. Some improvements were made in 1961 census over the census 1951. The changes are mentioned in brief. Each house was identified by a location code. In census 1961, three categories were defined instead of two, namely (*i*) Building; (*ii*) Housing and (*iii*) Household. The word building referred to an entire structure raised on the ground whereas, a census house may be a whole or a part of a building. Hence, a building can have one or more census houses.

The questionnaire for 1961 census was prepared in consultation with the planning commission. The questionnaire consisted of two parts namely (*i*) household schedule and (*ii*) the individual census slip. Besides these, a special form was prepared to collect information from technical diploma or degree holders.

A new occupational classification was used in this census. The whole population was divided into two categories namely, working and non-working.

1961 census covered Jammu and Kashmir and other snow bound areas for the first time. The first publication of the census – 1961 results for the whole country appeared on March 25, 1961 i.e., just after three weeks of the enumeration work.

Census 1971 – The preparation for census 1971 started as early as 1967. A seminar was held in New Delhi from the 3rd to 6th May, 1967, for evolving a procedure and preparing schedules and questionnaire to remove the deficiencies of the census of 1961 and to obtain any other required information. After the seminar, a questionnaire was prepared and tested in the field. The experiences of pre-testing were discussed again in the conference of superintendents of the census operations of the states at Delhi in January, 1968. The enumeration work of census was carried out from the 10th March to the 31st March, 1971. The enumerators revisited their area from 1st to 3rd April, to make the information more complete with regard to the birth and deaths that occurred before the sunrise of 1st April, 1971 and also, on the night of 31st March, 1971. Each enumerator counted the number of homeless persons in their areas of survey.

The special features of 1971 census were, (*i*) the data were collected on current fertility, (*ii*) a separate card known as, 'Degree holders and technical personnel card' was filled in the 1971 census, (*iii*) for the first time, detailed information was collected on migration, (*iv*) for the first time, census data were computerised.

Economic Census

The Central Statistical Organisation had taken a major step during 1977, in collaboration with the state statistical bureaus to remove data gaps in the unorganised sectors of non-agricultural economy, covering unregistered manufacturing, trade, transport and services, by launching a central plan scheme on economic census and surveys. This economic survey of non-agricultural establishments, employing at least one hired person was complete in the last quarter of 1977. The information regarding the type of activity, number of working persons and type of ownership etc., were collected and used in the sample survey of selected establishments in different sectors, conducted during 1978-79 and 1979-80. These surveys collected information relating to the quantity of inputs, outputs, investment, emoluments, employment etc. The manufacturing sector was covered in the 33rd round of NSS during 1978-79 and the sectors of the trade, transport, hotel and restaurants, storage and warehousing were covered in the 34th round of NSS, conducted in 1979-80. The small establishment were also covered in the 33rd and the 34th rounds.

The census covered large number of small establishments, which were subject to high morbidity and mortality and the variation in their input and output. Hence, the need was felt for conducting the economic census at regular intervals. Five year interval for such a census was considered. As such, the second census was due in 1982. But the preparations were going on in 1980 for census 1981, particularly with regard to the preparation of house lists. Hence, it was considered beneficial that the second economic census be synchronised with the house listing operation meant for the 1981 population census. Economic census of 1980 may be considered as a by-product of the 1981 population census.

The synchronisation increased the scope of economic survey. The small villages which were not covered in 1977 census could be covered in 1980 economic census. In this census, own account enterprises were covered for the first time on a census basis. In addition to non-agricultural establishments, some agricultural enterprises (excluding crop production and plantation) were also covered for the first time in 1980 economic census. This survey collected information about the location, the type of activity, the type of ownership, the power and fuel used, the number of persons engaged in the enterprise.

The schedules to be canvassed were finalised by the technical experts of the centre and the states, some non-government researchers and users. They, of course, made use of the experience of 1977 economic census.

The survey work was the responsibility of the Registrar General of India. The technical guidance and supervision rested with CSO at the centre and with the Directorate of Economics and statistics at the state level. The entire district administration coordinated with the District Statistical Officer and his staff. At Tehsil level, Tehsildar was designated as Charge Officer, whereas in municipal areas, Executive Officers were designated as Municipal Census Officer. About 62000 enumerators were engaged in economic census vis-a-vis house listing operation.

The results of the economic census 1980 pertaining to the number of enterprises (rural and urban), the number of persons (rural and urban) engaged on their own account and hired persons, percentage distribution of enterprises with principal characteristics etc. were published in the form of an economic census report.

Census 1981. It is well known to all that census is a phenomenon of national importance and is the base of all the future planning and development programmes. The house listing operation was conducted from the 15th of September to the 11th of October

1980. The enumeration work was carried out from 9th to 28th February 1981. The number of homeless persons was counted by the enumerator on the night of the 28th of February, 1981 in the areas assigned to him. The enumerators revisited their allocated areas, to note down new births and deaths, any member added in the household after the date of their previous visit and before the sunrise of March 1, 1981 and any new family residing in the block after the day of enumeration. A new baby borned in his new place of residence was counted as a member. In all such cases, previous records had to be corrected. The records were deposited by the enumerators on the 6th of March, 1981.

Two schedules were canvassed this time also as in the case of 1971 census, one related to household and the other one to the individual slip. The enumerators were required to fill in the location code on each household schedule and individual slips. The information about the household with regard to the number and distribution of family members, religion of the head of the family, whether schedule caste/tribe, mother tongue, ownership of house, availability of water and electricity, number of rooms in the house, land holding etc., were recorded. Information on individual slips was collected from each individual of India. The individual slip contained information about demographic data like relationship to the head of the household, sex, age, birth place, marital status, sociological information like nationality, religion, education, mother tongue and economic data like occupation, business establishment, employment etc.

Individual slips from sampled blocks were also filled by the enumerators for specific information. Separate cards were filled by persons holding a recognised degree or diploma in science, engineering, technology or medicine etc. This card contained information about his biodata and employment.

Census 1991 – It was the fifth census of independent India and thirteenth since the inception of census of India in 1872. The enumeration period of census 1991 was from 9–28 February, 1991 and the reference point of time being the sunrise of March 1, 1991. To update the information regarding new births and deaths and/or any new family residing before the sunrise of March 1, 1991, a revisional round was conducted during 1–5 March, 1991. The homeless people were enumerated on the night of February 28 and in some cases on February 27, 1991 due to Holi festival.

The census operation was carried out throughout the country at a time except for those areas or regions where the census was not feasible due to heavy snowfall, bad weather or some other valid reasons. For instance, in mountain areas of Uttar Pradesh like Uttarkashi, Chamoli and Pithoragarh; Himachal Pradesh and certain parts of Andaman Nicobar islands, enumeration was done in September 1990. Here the reference date was kept at October 1, 1990.

In census 1991, around 1.7 million enumerators and supervisors were involved. An enumerator had to canvas the schedules for about 600–750 people. A supervisor was appointed for every five enumerators. The questionnaires were presented at the first data users conference which was held during 18–20 April, 1988. The data users conference was attended by the representatives of the important ministries of the Government of India, the planning commission, the state governments, universities, demographic and population institutes, expert bodies, research institutions and individuals. The questionnaires were amended in the conference and later placed before the Advisory Committee on Technical Issues connected with the holding of 1991 census which was appointed by Government of India on August 31, 1988. The Advisory Committee vetted the census questionnaires which were tested in selected areas during Nov.–Dec., 1988 and finalised as a result of first pretest.

The whole of the villages and wards of the country were divided into enumeration blocks in such a way that in rural area an enumeration block consisted of around 750 people and in urban area 600 people. After preliminary preparations, houselisting operations were carried out from Apr.–Sept., 1990 in all states and union territories except for Uttar Pradesh where it was completed between 10–25 Sept., 1990.

Alongwith house listing operation which constituted the first phase of census 1991, the Central Statistical Organisation of India concurrently canvassed an enterprise list as a part of the *Third Economic* Census. Each financial undertaking had to fill up an enterprise list furnishing information with regard to the nature of activity, classification, type of ownership, number of workers employed, type of energy used by the enterprise etc. A quick report of economic census had been very helpful in finalising the eighth five year plan commencing from 1st April, 1992 to 31st March, 1997.

In census 1991, the information was collected through the family schedule having 34 columns. Columns 1–7 contained the information like family serial number, name of person, relation with regard to the head of family, sex, age, mother language and marital status. Rest of the columns contained almost the same information which was collected in individual slip with some more details regarding the profession.

The individual slip canvassed pertains to the information about an individual. Questions 1–13 were of general nature i.e., with regard to his name, relation with head of the family, sex, age, marital status, mother tongue and any other two languages known to him, religion, whether a member of schedule caste or schedule tribe, caste, literate or illiterate, educational standard, whether attending a school/college or not. Children of the age group 0–6 were classified as illiterate immaterial of the fact whether they have learnt some reading or writing or not. In census – 1991, this age group was 0–4. Three questions 14–16 were regarding the detailed enquiry about economic activity. Question 17 was specially included for retired military personnel to know whether they are getting pension or not. Question 18–20 were in respect of place of birth, migration and reason(s) for migration. Question 21st was with regard to the length of stay at the place of enquiry at the time of enumeration. Question 22nd was asked from only those women who were not married, divorced or widow. The enquiry was made with regard to the age at the time of marriage, number of children present and their sex ratio. The last question No. 23 was asked from married women whether they gave live birth during last one year or not.

A special form called "Post Graduate Degree Holders and Technical Personnel Schedule" (PGDHTP) was distributed to all the post graduates and technical degree holders on behalf of the Council for Scientific and Industrial Research to meet their needs for planning for technical and professional manpower. The form was designed in the shape of the postage prepaid inland letter to be filled by the respondent concerned. The enumerator was asked to collect it back, failing which the respondent was requested to mail it. The processing of this schedule and dissemination of the data was the responsibility of the Council for Scientific and Industrial Research.

Census 2001 In the first phase of census, Houselisting Operation was conducted between April-September, 2000 as a prelude to the exercise of undertaking the decennial population census 2001. During this houselisting operation, information on house conditions, amenities and assets available to the households were also collected.

The second phase of census i.e., Population Enumeration was undertaken between 9-28 February, 2001 with a revisional round from 1st to 5th March, 2001. The census moment was 00 hours of March 1, 2001 and the referral time at which the snapshot of the population of the country was taken. In certain snow bound and inaccessible areas of the country, the census operations were either extended or postponed to different time periods. Population data were obtained for Location Particulars, Individual Particulars, Cultivation /Plantation, Migration, etc. The final census data were released in parts. Their publication started from December, 2001 and was almost completed by 2006.

Census 2011 Population census in India is a regular decennial national feature to collect information about the people of India at a fixed point of time. As usual, Census of India was conducted in two phases:

Phase I–It consisted of listing and counting the number of houses. In this round, the enumerators were assigned the job of recognizing census houses and families which would have been included in final survey. They will also capture the biometric details (face, iris, and ten finger prints) of every citizen over the age of 15 so that a 12-digit unique identification number can be assigned to all Indians by the Unique Identification authority of India (UDAI). Biometric information will be maintained in the National Population Register (NPR). These census houses were counted and systematically listed in the duration of April to September, 2010. Some additional information consisted of 35 items was also collected regarding identification of house, family head, caste status, ownership of the house, its size, availability of drinking water, lighting, drinking water, latrine, bathroom and kitchen within premises, fuel used, availability of radio, television, computer, telephone, scooter, motor bicycle, car and banking services. This is only one instance of a caste count in post-independent India. In pre-independent India, information on caste was collected only once as a part of Census of India - 1931.

Phase II–Population enumeration was conducted from 9th to 28th February, 2011. The schedule for population enumeration contained 29 items with regard to person's relationship to head of the family, sex , age, marital status, languages known, education level, working, birth place, place of last residence, reason for migration, schedule caste/ tribe, disability, mother tongue, category of activity, occupation, number of children ever born and during last year.

Once the population enumeration work was completed, the data were compiled and tabulated. Some provisional data were released by the census office on March 31, 2011.

Distinct Features:

1. Information for National Population Register was collected for the first time in first phase of census 2011. On the basis of this information ID card shall be issued to every individual. This ID card is expected to help in preventing infiltration and unlawful activities.

2. In post-independent India, this is the first instance that information was collected on caste of all individuals as a part of census-2011.

3. Once the information would be collected and degitalized, finger prints and photos shall be collected. Later a unique 12-digit identification number to all individuals will be issued sometime in 2011.

To have a comparative picture of population of India that emerged after Census 2001 and 2011, data are tabulated below.

India's Comparative Census Data 2001 and 2011 at a Glance

Heads	Census 2001	Provisional data Released on March 31, 2011 Census 2011
Population		
Persons	102,87,37,436	121,01,93,422
Males	53,22,23,090	63,37,24,248
Females	49,65,14,346	58,64,69,174
	(1991 to 2001)	(2001 to 2011)
Persons Added	18,30,84,386	18,14,55,986
State with highest population–Uttar Pradesh	16,61,97,921	19,95,81,477
State with lowest population–Sikkim	5,40,851	6,07,688
UT with highest population–Delhi	1,35,80,507	1,67,53,235
UT with lowest population–Lakshadweep	60,650	64,429
Decadal Growth Rate-GR		
Decadal GR – India	21.34%	17.64%
State with highest GR	64.41% (Nagaland)	27.80% (Meghalaya)
State with lowest GR	9.42% (Kerala)	– 0.50% (Nagaland)
UT with highest GR		
Dadara & Nagar Haveli	59.20%	55.50%
UT with lowest GR- Lakshadweep	17.19%	6.20%
Population Density – PD	**[per sq. km]**	**[per sq. km]**
India	324	382
State with highest PD	903 (West Bengal)	1102 (Bihar)
State with lowest PD –		
Arunachal Pradesh	13	17
UT with highest PD-Delhi	9294	9340
UT with lowest PD –		
Andaman & Nicobar Islands	43	46
Sex ratio – SR	**[Females/1000 M]**	**[Females/1000 M]**
India	933	940
State with highest SR – Kerala	1058	1084
State with lowest SR – Haryana	861	877
UT with highest SR – Puducherry	1001	1038
UT with lowest SR – Daman & Diu	710	618

Contd...

Literacy rate – LR			
India		64.84%	74.04%
	Males	75.96%	82.14%
	Females	54.28%	65.46%
State with highest LR – Kerala		90.92%	90.90%
	Males	94.20%	94.20%
	Females	87.86%	87.70%
States with lowest LR – Bihar		47.53%	63.82%
	Males	59.68%	73.39%
	Females	33.12%	53.33%
UT with highest LR – Lakshadweep		87.52%	92.28%
	Males	93.15%	96.11%
	Females	81.56%	88.25%
UT with lowest LR – Dadara & Nagar Haveli		60.03%	77.65%
	Males	73.32%	86.46%
	Females	42.99%	65.93%

Compiled census data have been published for India as a whole and in parts for each state and union territory, district and tehsils in the form of reports. Various aspects covered during the census have been tabulated and published systematically. Final data of census – 2011 are expected to be released by the Office of the Registrar General and Census of India sometime in the year 2012.

AGRICULTURAL STATISTICS

India is an agricultural country and its economy largely depends on agriculture. In ancient days, agriculture had been the main source of income of all the rulers. They collected money in the form of *Land Revenue.* Therefore, most of the rulers maintained records of agricultural land and their categories on the basis of fertility and production. Records were also maintained for orchards. The main objective of keeping these records was the collection of revenue.

After independence, a lot of emphasis has been given to agriculture. Indian economy is based mostly on agriculture even today, hence a comprehensive and reliable statistics are necessary for good planning and development of agriculture and that for the country. As a matter of fact, all statistics which have an impact on agricultural economy may be regarded as *agricultural statistics.* Here, we shall use the term agricultural statistics in a narrower sense. The statistics pertaining to land utilization, production of crops, livestock and agricultural prices, poultry, forestry, etc., will come under the category of agricultural statistics.

Agricultural statistics is mostly collected by the Directorate of Economics and Statistics (DES) at the centre, as well as at the state level. Each state has a Directorate of Economics and Statistics. The statistics regarding area, crop production, poultry and forests are collected.

Total area statistics are obtained from two sources, (*i*) the Surveyor General of India (*ii*) the village records maintained by the Revenue Department. The area is further classified as forest, land put to non-agricultural uses, barren and unculturable land, permanent pastures and other grazing lands, culturable waste, current fallows, other fallow land, new area sown (irrigated and unirrigated). The irrigated area is found out from the availability of irrigation by canals, tanks and wells.

The area under crops is obtained by two sources (*i*) official series based on village records and (*ii*) NSS series based on sample surveys, NSS collects data during the regular rounds of survey on area under different crops. The area figures provided by these two sources are far apart, because of the difference in method of the coverage of crops, difference in the field work, the classification of area under feed and the fodder crops, the allocation of area under mixed crops and due to sampling error in NSS estimates. The land utilisation statistics are published in *Indian Agricultural Statistics.* The individual states publish these statistics in *Season and Crop Reports.* Land utilisation statistics are also published in (*i*) Agricultural situation in India (monthly); (*ii*) Abstract of Agricultural Statistics (DES Annual) and (*iii*) Statistical Abstract of the Indian Union (CSO, Annual).

Agricultural Production Statistics

Agricultural production includes the production of food and non-food crops but forests, livestock and fisheries are excluded at this place. We will give a brief account of these separately. Crop output statistics cannot be collected at the time of harvesting, as millions of farmers harvest their crops at the same time. Mostly they are uneducated and maintain no record. Hence, the output is estimated by multiplying the area under a crop by the average expected yield per hectare, in the season. The yield statistics are collected by official machinery and NSSO. As official machinery, the work of the survey is undertaken by the Directorate of Economics and Statistics. Two methods are adopted to collect yield statistics of various crops.

(*a*) the traditional method, (*b*) the random sampling method.

Traditional Method : This method of estimation is known as *Annawari system.* In this system, the condition of the crop is judged by Patwari or any other official in relation to the normal crop. This is known as the *condition factor* or the *Annawari estimate.* The yield estimate is obtained by the Annawari system, by the formula,

$$\text{Crop yield} = \frac{\text{Annas judged}}{\text{Total Annas}} \times \text{normal yield} \times \text{Area} \qquad ...(22.1)$$

This system suffers from two main lacunae. One is that the condition factor depends totally on the judgement of Lekhapals or Patwaris, which is very subjective. Secondly, the total annas representing the normal condition of a crop is not uniform in all the states. For instance, some states take fifteen annas as normal condition while Madhya Pradesh takes 13.3 annas to represent normal condition of a crop.

Random Sampling Method : This method was recommended by the Board of Agriculture as early as 1919 but was abandoned due to the huge financial burden on the states. The Indian Council of Agriculture introduced the random sampling method again in 1942, for cotton crops. This method was later extended for other crops in all states, except West Bengal and Orissa, where the job was entrusted to Indian Statistical Institute, Kolkata. In random sampling method, villages were randomly selected in tehsils of a state and within each village few fields were selected randomly. To be more specific, stratified multi-stage random sampling design is adopted for the crop cutting experiments. Crop cutting experiments have been conducted since 1943. Now the experiments are conducted by the Directorate of Economics and Statistics and statistical section of the Board of Revenue, through its field staff and separately by National Sample Survey Organisation. The NSSO conducts crop cutting experiments on major cereal crops, during the course of their regular survey rounds. The yields data collected by two agencies differ in their estimates quite widely due to the difference in the shape and the size of the cuts, the difference in the driage factors, the difficulties of harvesting at a proper time by NSSO investigators, the difference in the methods of estimation and overall difference in the field work.

The results of the survey are published mainly in (*i*) the Agricultural situation in India (monthly), (*ii*) the weekly Bulletin of Agricultural prices, (*iii*) the Agricultural Statistics. A long list of other publications providing statistics related to agriculture can be seen on the back side of the Journal, 'Agricultural Situation in India'.

World Agricultural Census, 1980

First a detailed Agricultural Census in India was conducted in the year 1970–71 from July 1, 1970 to 30th June, 1971. In this survey, information was collected about land holding, land use under different crops (irrigated and unirrigated), water sourcewise irrigated area etc. The second Agricultural Census was conducted during the agricultural year 1976–77 i.e. from July 1, 1976 to June 30, 1977. This covered one kharif and one rabi season completely. In this census, additional information was collected from the land holders of 2 per cent villages about the use and consumption of fertilizers, insecticides, livestock, farm implements, saline and alkaline lands, in addition to the information which was collected in 1970–71 Agricultural Census.

Agricultural Census 1980–81 is the third of its kind in India, sponsored by United Nations Food and Agricultural Organisation (FAO). In India, it is being conducted under the patronage of the Ministry of Agriculture in the Centre and Department of Revenue, in the States. In this Census, Department of Agriculture, District Statistical Officer and other government officials actively participated to get the enumeration work done properly. This census was conducted in two phases, as was done in 1976–77 census. In the first phase, enumeration work had been completed and in the second phase, the information was collected from land holders as per revenue records. The work of the second phase was carried out by the Revenue Department. The results of the survey had been published.

Another agricultural survey named, the *Input Survey,* was conducted during the agricultural year 1981–82 i.e. from 1st July 1981 to 30th June, 1982. The input survey was conducted in about 7 per cent of inhabited villages. Institutional holdings were kept out of the sampling frame. City people were also not included in the input survey. For the selection of land holdings from a selected village, the land holders were divided into five groups i.e., farmers with the holding less than 1 hectare, 1–2, 2–4, 4–10 and more than 10 hectares. From each group of farm holding, 4 families were selected randomly. If any group contained 4 or less than four farmers, all were included in the sample. The enumerators collected the information in a single visit for both the seasons i.e., kharif and rabi. Information was collected about the individual and the joint holdings.

The enumerators collected information about (1) the number of plots; (2) the multiple cropping pattern in irrigated and unirrigated areas; (3) the saline, alkaline and water logged areas; (4) the application of chemical fertilizers, manures and insecticides in main crops (separately for irrigated and unirrigated sown areas); (5) livestock ;(6) agricultural implements and (7) agricultural credits.

The results of the survey were published in the form of a report, by the Directorate of Economics and Statistics.

Output from Agriculture

For the purpose of evaluation of output, 68 agricultural crops, including by-products are considered. These are divided into four broad categories viz. (*i*) 35 items of principal crops[1] (*ii*) 10 items of minor crops[2]. (*iii*) 11 items of miscellaneous and unspecified crops groups[3] (*iv*) 12 other products and by-products[4].

Estimates of area and the outturn for principal crops are based on the estimates of crop surveys, conducted annually by the state government agencies. The results are published annually by the Directorate of Economics and Statistics in *Estimates of Area and Production of Principal Crops in India* with a time lag of one year. Data on area under unspecified crops are available annually in *Indian Agricultural Statistics,* published by DES with a time lag of two to three years. Some other publications (regular and adhoc) giving Agricultural Statistics are as given below:

1. *Bulletin of Food Statistics* (DES, Annual)
2. *Oilseeds in India* (DES, 1955, 1961)
3. *Bulletin on Commercial Crop Statistics* (DES).
4. *Farm Management/Cost of Cultivation Studies* (DES, adhoc).
5. *NSS Reports* Nos.–32 (Part I to III), 140.

LIVESTOCK AND POULTRY STATISTICS

On the initiative of the Government, the first cattle census, on all India basis, was conducted from December, 1919 to April, 1920. Since then the livestock census is held quinquennially by the Directorate of Economics and Statistics. Statistics regarding livestock and poultry are published in *Indian Livestock Census* (quinquennial). This publication contains information related to cattle and poultry.

For the purpose of the estimation of the gross value of output from livestock and poultry, eight broad groups are taken into consideration, namely, (*i*) milk and milk products; (*ii*) meat and meat products; (*iii*) hides and skins; (*iv*) eggs and poultry meat; (*v*) wool and hair; (*vi*) dung; (*vii*) increment in livestock and (*viii*) other products. The information about these are available in a number of publications of the NSSO and the Indian

---

1. Rice, wheat, jowar, bajra, maize, ragi, small millets, gram, tur, urad, moong, masoor, other pulses, linseed, sesamum, groundnut, rapeseed and mustard, castor, coconut, sugarcane, cotton (unginned i.e. kapas), jute, mesta, sannhemp, tobacco, dry chillies, dry ginger, black pepper, turmeric, arecanut, cardamom, potato, banana and tapioca.
2. Indigo, opium, sweet potato, cashewnut, tea, coffee, rubber, citrus fruits, grapes and mangoes.
3. Other cereals, other oilseeds, other sugars, other fibres, other dyes and tanning materials, other drugs and narcotics, other condiments and spices, other fruits and vegetables, fodder, miscellaneous food crops and miscellaneous non-food crops.
4. Gur, bagasse, cotton sticks, sesamum sticks, jute sticks, arhar sticks, rice bran, rice husk, cane trash, grass, stalks and straws and farmyard wood.

Agricultural Statistics Research Institute (IASRI), the Directorate of Economics and Statistics of the States, the Directorate of Marketing and Inspection (DMI), the Animal Husbandry Departments of the states. Some of the popular publications are:

1. *Indian Livestock Census* (Quinquennial)
2. *Indian Livestock Statistics* (Annual)
3. Marketing reports issued from time to time (DMI)
4. *Agricultural Statistics of India* (Vol. I and II).
5. *Reports of NSS* Nos., 97, 281.
6. *Statistical Abstract of India* (CSO).

FOREST STATISTICS

Forest statistics includes the information relating to the volume of timber, the round wood, the match and pulp wood, the bamboo, the sandal wood, the charcoal and the lac etc. Data relating to area, the volume of standing timber, the annual outturn, the value of timber (fire wood and forest products) are released annually in the *Indian Forest Statistics* by DES. For major products statewise, data on quantities and the royalty value are reported annually in the *Forestry in India,* in a mimeograph form, with a time lag of three to four years. Other publications which contain forest statistics are:

(*i*) *Abstract of Agricultural Statistics* (DES)
(*ii*) *Forestry in India* (DES, Annual)
(*iii*) *Statistical Abstract of India* (CSO, Annual)
(*iv*) Annual Administrative Reports of Forest Department of Different States in India.

FISHERIES STATISTICS

Fishing in India is an age old trade, but the data relating to the quantity of fish catching and the consumption were inadequate and non-comprehensive prior to 1950. The fishery statistics is available only in the published reports of the Department of Fisheries, Madras and Bengal. Data about commerical fishing is based on two sectors: (*i*) ocean, coastal and offshore water fishing, (*ii*) inland waters e.g., rivers, canals, tanks etc. Besides commercial fishing. Millions of people are engaged in fishing for their consumption and earning their livelihood. No statistics for such fish catch is available. Estimates of fish catch are made from figures supplied by, (*i*) Fish curing (salting and sun-drying) yards, (*ii*) Fish boats in use, (*iii*) import and export of preserved fish and fish products, (*iv*) movement by rails, (*v*) arrival of fish at the market centres, (*vi*) sample surveys conducted by research institutes etc.

The estimates of the value of the output of fish are worked out separately for marine and inland fish at the state level. The data on landing of marine fish are collected by the Central Marine Fisheries Research Institute (CMFRI), Cochin. For Maharashtra, Kerala, Gujarat, Pondicherry, Goa, Daman and Diu, the estimates of marine fish are collected by the State Fisheries Departments (SFD). Data regarding inland fishing are also obtained by the SFDs. The sources of Fishery Statistics are:

1. *Report on the Marketing of Fish in the Indian Union* (DMI).
2. Reports published by CMFRI.

3. Data available with Fisheries Development Adviser and in state's Statistical Bureaus.
4. Data regarding consumption are collected by the Directorate of NSSO and are available in the reports of the rounds.

There is a lot of scope and need for improvement in the process of collecting fishery statistics.

MINING AND QUARRYING STATISTICS

Economic activities, covered in this sector, comprise the extraction of minerals which occur in nature as solid, liquid and gases in underground and surface mines, quarries and oil wells. Mines and mineral statistics are not very popular and adequate in India, except the coal statistics. Coal statistics are regularly published in the Annual Report of the Chief Inspector of Mines, Dhanbad. Another annual publication which provides statistics is made by the Geological Survey of India. It concerns the value of minerals production, number of people employed in the mining industry, exports and imports of minerals in India. Some other worth mentioning publications are:

1. *Quinquennial Review of Mineral Production in India:* This review provides comparative figures of production and foreign trade of minerals.
2. *Monthly Coal Bulletin* (Director General of Mines Safety, DGMS).
3. *Mineral Statistics of India* (Indian Bureau of Mines, IBM, biannual). Monthly data of mineral output are published in it with a lag of about six months.
4. *Bulletin of Mineral Statistics and Information* (IBM, bimonthly). It gives data about quantity and value of output of minerals.
5. *Indian Petroleum and Chemical Statistics* (Ministry of Petroleum and Chemicals, Annual).
6. *Indian Coal Statistics*: It is published by the Department of Commercial Intelligence and Statistics, Kolkata. It provides statistical information relating to production, price, freight, employment, export and import, etc.
7. *Statistical Abstracts of India* (CSO, Annual). It contains figures of quantity and value of output of each mineral for the preceding years.
8. *Indian Trade Journal*: It gives data about the manufacturing and the import of salt in India.
9. *Monthly Survey of Business Conditions in India*: It is published by the Chief Inspector of Mines, Dhanbad. It gives figures of production of coal, petroleum and kerosene in India.
10. Statewise and mineralwise values of the output are published by the Indian Bureau of Mines, Nagpur.

Besides the above, there are some other publications, which report data pertaining to Mines and Minerals.

INDUSTRIAL STATISTICS

This is an industrial age. India is making her best efforts in the direction of industrialisation. As such India has come under the category of industrially advanced countries. There is a need to collect and publish industrial statistics. For the purpose of domestic product estimation, the entire manufacturing industry is sub-divided into two broad sectors viz., manufacturing registered and manufacturing unregistered. The registered manufacturing sector covers all organised manufacturing and processing establishments (classified as factories) which are registered under *Indian Factories Act* (IFA), 1948. Unregistered manufacturing sector covers all manufacturing units which are not registered under the IFA, 1948. It covers all manufacturing units employing less than 10 workers if using power, or less than 20 workers if not using power.

The history of industrial statistics begins from the year 1942, when the *Industrial Statistical Act,* 1942 was passed. This act empowered the state governments to collect data from factories with regards to any statistical information. *A Directorate of Industrial Statistics* was set up at the centre to enforce this Act. The first census of manufacturing industries was conducted in 1946 and the results were published in a bound volume. From 1959, the census of the manufacturing industries and sample survey of industries was discontinued and the Annual Survey of Industries (ASI) was started. The NSSO carries out the annual survey of industries regularly. This survey provides industry-wise estimates of employment, output, input and capital employed separately for the census and sample sectors[1]. Data in respect of Defence production are collected independently as they are not covered under ASI. The result of annual survey of the census sector are published in bound volumes by CSO and the results of the sample sector are published by NSSO in their regular reports.

As regards statistics of unregistered manufacturing units, NSSO conducts surveys on small scale manufacturers and self employed households in non-agricultural enterprises. NSSO conducted surveys in the 23rd and the 29th rounds respectively. The 23rd round included the small scale manufacturing in rural and urban areas in 1968–69. The results of the survey were presented in NSS Report no. 205. The 29th round was the survey of self-employed household in non-agricultural enterprises in 1974–75. Tables with notes are published in NSS Report no. 280/6.

The NSS surveys only cover effectively the household establishments and do not provide information on the value added per worker for the non-household enterprises. However, data are available from the survey results conducted under the centrally sponsored scheme on the *Survey of Small Scale Industries* by the Ministry of Industrial Development with 1970–71 as the reference period. All India Report on the small scale industrial units, covering mainly urban areas, was published in 1977 by Development Commissioner Small Scale Industries (DCSSI).

Different publications for Industrial Statistics are:

1. *Monthly Statistics of the Production of Selected Industries*: It is a publication of the Industrial Statistics Wing of the CSO.
2. *Monthly Abstract of Statistics* (CSO): It contains data pertaining to industrial production, index number of industrial production, consumption and stocks, etc.
3. *Statistical Abstract of the Indian Union* (CSO, Annual): It covers data on various aspects of industry and power. Statewise figures are provided for the latest year.

---

1. Factories employing 50 or more workers with power or 100 or more workers without power constitute the census sector.
The remaining factories constitute the sample sector.

4. *Monthly Jute Bulletin*: It is a publication of the Indian Central Jute Committee, Kolkata. It contains statistics of production, stocks, consumption and export of jute goods etc.
5. *Monthly Statistical Bulletin, Indian Cotton Textile Industry.*
6. *Indian Sugar*: It is published by the Sugar Manufacturers Association.

Besides the above publications, the number of other Reports, Bulletins and Journals are regularly published by various departments, Statistical Bureaus, Directorates, Associations, etc.

TRADE STATISTICS

Trade statistics is compiled and published regularly by the Directorate of Commercial Intelligence and Statistics (DCIS), Kolkata. The data for trade statistics emerge as a byproduct of official administrative data of the nation. These statistics are given with regard to, (*i*) inland wholesale and retail trade, (*ii*) foreign trade of India, (*iii*) index number of inland and foreign trade. The Directorate of Commercial Intelligence and Statistics started the publication of *Indian Trade Journal* in 1906. Different publications which give data on trade are:

1. *Accounts Relating to the Inland* (*Rail and River borne*) *Trade of India* (DCIS, Quarterly). The journal contains data as provided by railways and steamer authorities to whom the traders have to submit their invoices.
2. Statistics relating to the coasting trade of India are published in the Bulletins:
   (*a*) *Statistics of Foreign and Coastal Cargo Movements of India* (DCIS, Monthly).
   (*b*) *Statistics of Coasting Trade of India* (DCIS, Annual)
   (*c*) *Statistics of Maritime Navigation of India* (DCIS): It contains data available with the DGCIS. Coasting trade is registered separately by the traders in custom houses.
3. *Indian Trade Journal*: (DCIS, weekly). It contains some data about retail trade of India.

   Some publications which supply compiled information about foreign trade are:

(*i*) (*a*) *Monthly Statistics of Foreign Trade of India,* Vol. I & II (DCIS): Volume I contains information related to the exports and re-exports. Volume II contains data about the imports. This publication uses the trade classification based on standard International Trade classification.

(*b*) *Supplement to the Monthly Statistics by the Foreign Trade of India,* Vol. I & II (DCIS, Quarterly): This publication contains mostly the information which has already been published in a monthly series.

(*ii*) *Annual Statistics of Foreign Trade of India by Countries:*

This issue contains total of the monthly statistics, with certain revision and corrections. These revisions and corrections arise due to short and shut-out shipment in exports and finalisation of note pass transactions in imports.

Besides the above mentioned publication, there are many more which contain statistics of merchandise imports and exports, internal trade statistics, etc.

LABOUR STATISTICS

The term labour refers to the workers whose work is characterised largely by physical exertion. Generally, they are the persons engaged wholly or partly in the production of goods and services. These persons may be engaged in agriculture and allied activities, forestry and logging, fishing, mining and quarrying, manufacturing, construction, transport, storage, communication, trade, hotel and management, banking and insurance, education and research, health and medicines, etc. But the term labour is mainly in connotation to the workers in industry, agriculture and construction. Out of the three, main emphasis is laid on industrial labour. International Labour Organisation (ILO) is playing a significant role in the collection and publication of labour statistics. The main function of ILO is to maintain uniformity of labour statistics in all the countries. This makes comparison feasible on an international level.

The labour statistics is collected and compiled relating to average daily employments in Factories, Mines, Plantation, Railways, Post and Telegraph, Commercial Establishments and Central Government Establishments, wages and hours of work, levels of living, family living, statistics of accidents and occupational diseases, statistics of trade unions and disputes, social security, migration, etc.

There are three main sources of employment statistics in India namely, *(i)* Decennial Population Census, *(ii)* National Sample Survey, *(iii)* Employment Exchange. The statistics of wages are the indicator of the economic condition of the fixed salaried people. Level of living is adjudged in terms of the wages paid to the workers and the consumer price index, at a time. The Minimum Wage Act, 1948 provides protection to the labourers against price rise of essential commodities and services.

Statistics of accidents and occupational diseases are collected under the workmen's compensation Act of 1923. The figures for the number of injuries and accidents, for which the compensation is paid, are collected. The Accidents include data relating to deaths, permanent disablement and temporary disablement. Social security is provided to the employees getting less than Rs. 500 per month, under the Employees State Insurance Act of 1948, in all the registered factories. Benefits under this scheme accrue to the employees with regard to sickness, maternity, disablement and dependents.

There are three organisations which are mainly responsible for the collection and publication of labour statistics. They are given below with a brief description of their functioning.

Labour Bureau

It comes under the Ministry of Labour, Employment and Rehabilitation, Government of India. Labour Bureau is the main source of labour statistics, as it publishes a number of journals, books and ad hoc reports. Its main publications are:

(i) *Indian Labour Journal* (Monthly)
(ii) *Indian Labour Year Book* (Annual)
(iii) *Indian Labour Statistics* (Annual)
(iv) *Trade Union in India* (Biennial)
(v) *Statistics of Factories* (Annual)
(vi) *Pocket Book of Labour Statistics* (Annual)

These publications contain information about the items given earlier.

Directorate of Employment and Training (DET)

This Directorate is located in New Delhi. The Director General collects and analyses the data on the occupational pattern of the employees. The employment exchanges are the main source of data. The data are published in the form of journals and reports.

(i) *Quarterly Employment Review*: The journal contains data about the employment in public and private sector, industrywise, statewise and zonewise. It also gives information relating to women employees.

(ii) *Area Employment Market Report* (Quarterly and Annual)

(iii) *State Employment Report* (Quarterly)

(iv) Reports on Occupational Pattern of Employees (Biennial)

(v) Report on Biennial Survey of Establishments employing workers in Private sector (Biennial).

Director General of Mines Safety

The Directorate of Mines Safety, collects data relating to labour employed in collieries, their wages and hours of work, productivity, general health, accidents, etc. The information about all aspects is published in the *Monthly Coal Bulletin*.

Statistics of Agricultural Labour

The statistical information regarding agricultural labour has been collected through *Labour Enquiry Committees,* appointed from time to time. The first enquiry was conducted in 1950–51, under the supervision of *Directorate of Economics and Statistics.* The second enquiry was conducted in 1956–57, under the ministry of labour in collaboration with CSO, NSSO and ASI. In both these surveys only landless agricultural households were selected for investigation. The Directorate of Economics and Statistics collects information about Agricultural Labour (skilled and unskilled) regularly. Collected statistics are published in the following two journals:

(i) *Agricultural Wages in India*

(ii) *Agricultural Situation in India.*

NATIONAL INCOME STATISTICS

National income estimates are of great importance to get a broad view of the entire economy of a country. They also provide the information about the changes occurring in economy from year to year. The economic policies and planning are mostly framed keeping in view, the national income of a nation. The National Income Committee (NIC) set up by the Government of India in 1949 produced for the first time, national income estimates for the entire Indian union. The estimates along with the methodology were published in the first and final report of the National Income Committee (Ministry of Finance) in 1951 and 1954. Efforts were made to improve the empirical data and overcome the gaps. The first results of these efforts were presented by the CSO in the National Income Statistics. The result of the earlier studies along with the revised series of national income were published in *Brochure on the Revised Series of National Product* for 1961–62 to 1964–65 by CSO in 1967. Two more Brochures were published by the CSO.

(i) *National Income Statistics*: Estimates of Capital Formation in India from 1960–61 to 1965–66 were presented in 1969.

(ii) *National Income Statistics*: Estimates of Savings in India from 1960–61 to 1965–66 were released in 1969.

Here, it would be worthwhile to give some idea about the national income of a nation. Different economists defined national income in various ways. Without entangling with these controversies, we give the definition :—

"*Sum of the employees compensation and the net income from property and enterpreneurship, that is the distributed factors income, represents the national income of the country.*"

The national income becomes gross, when added with the consumption of fixed capital. By definition, it is equivalent to the national product at factor cost, gross and net.

In simple words, national income may be defined as, 'The value of commodities and services produced during a particular period counted without duplication.'

Net Factor Income from Abroad

Income attributable to factor services rendered by the normal residents of the country, to the rest of the world, less factor services rendered to them by the rest of the world. It also includes retained earnings of foreign controlled rupee companies, and branches of foreign companies in the domestic territory. Residents include both individuals and institutions. Tourists or commercial travellers of a given country travelling abroad are also treated as residents. The factor income generated by diplomats and consulars' representatives and members of armed forces stationed abroad are the domestic product of the resident country. Factor incomes of locally recruited staff of the foreign diplomatic military establishments are included in the factor income from abroad.

Uses of National Income

1. The first and foremost use of national income estimate is that, it gives us a correct picture of the structure of the economy of the nation, as well as the distribution of income according to regions, industrial origin and income from functional services and persons during a specified period of time.
2. National income estimates give us an idea of the purchasing power of the people in the country. Inflationary and deflationary gaps of purchasing power are revealed by income and product figures. This is of great value in working out the details and timing of anti-inflationary and deflationary programmes.
3. National income statistics provide a useful guideline in the formulation of the budget of a country.
4. National income figures help forecast the level of business activity for months and years ahead, since it enables us to compare and analyze changes in the output, income and expenditure of the various sectors, as well as the entire economy over a period of time. These figures are absolutely fundamental to the analysis of the overall economic and business situation, particularly with regard to its cyclical aspects.
5. National income figures have been found useful for studies of the problems of the economically underdeveloped countries.
6. National income statistics help in making the interregional and interstate comparisons of national income distribution. It is also useful in comparing the economic conditions of a country over a period of time.

7. National income statistics give us an idea about the standard of living of the nationals of a country. If we consider the national income only on current prices, the per capita income may increase, but it may not lead to the income in standard of living since the increase in prices causes the fall in the real income of the consumers. To estimate the real national increase, at present the base year is 2004–2005.
8. National income estimates provide a basis for the future planning of a country. In the absence of such statistics, no comprehensive economic plan can be chalked out. It also helps in evaluating the success of an economic plan.

Methods of National Income Estimation

The methods used to estimate the national income of a country necessarily depend upon the availability of statistics. Commonly, the following three methods are used for the calculation of national income:

1. Output or production method.
2. Income method.
3. Expenditure method.

Output Method. Output or production method is also called *inventory method.* It consists of finding out the market value of all goods and services produced by the individuals and business enterprises during a specified period of time. The national income or net domestic product can be calculated by the following equation.

National Income = (value of goods and services + self consumption + increase in stock – depreciation of capital – income from abroad) ... (22.2)

The above sum of income contributes the national income at the factor cost.

Income Method. The income method consists of adding together all incomes by the way of wages, interests, rents and profits. Wages include the value of services (mental and physical), in terms of money rendered by the nationals. Interest is the amount of money, received by the entrepreneurs, by way of capital investment. Similarly, rent may be defined as the factor income generated by the letting and the use of land for agricultural and other purposes, buildings (residential and non-residential), machinery, equipment and other fixed assets. It is treated as rental income from property. Also any amount of money saved by the individuals or institutions, after deducting the expenditure on production, may be termed as profit.

Expenditure Method. The national income is equal to the sum of consumption and saving. Symbolically, we can write.

$$Y = C + S \qquad ...(22.3)$$

where, Y – National income
C – Consumption
S – Saving

The method is rarely used because of the non-availability of data required for its calculation. Because of the predominance of unorganised sectors in underdeveloped and developing countries, there is a lack of proper maintenance of records of consumption, expenditure, savings, etc.

As a matter of fact, all the three methods lead to the same value of national income estimates. These are three angles from which we can look at the national income.

Problems in the Estimation of National Income

Every country, advanced or underdeveloped, faces some difficulty in computing national income. However, underdeveloped countries are faced with some special difficulties arising out of the peculiar nature of such economies. The important problems that are faced while estimating national income are:

1. There is substantial non-monetised sector which makes the calculation of national income difficult. A great deal of what is produced in the subsistence sector is either exchanged for other goods or is kept for personal consumption. This tends to understate the national income.
2. In underdeveloped countries due to the lack of occupational specialisation, calculation of national income by industrial origin becomes rather difficult. For instance, besides the crops, farmers often produce a variety of products like — eggs, milk, articles of clothing, etc., that are not included in the calculation of national income estimates due to the lack of availability of such data.
3. In developing countries, people are mostly illiterate and do not keep any accounts and even if they do, they are reluctant to disclose their income correctly. In such a situation only rough estimates are possible.
4. The computation of national income in terms of money, underestimates the real income, because it does not include the real cost of the produced articles. The income earned by two people may be the same, but if one works for longer hours than the other, there is some justification in saying that the real income of the former is lower than the later.
5. National income estimates fail to measure adequately, the changes in output due to the changes in the price level. Index numbers, used to measure changes in the price level are simply rough estimates. Therefore, the national figures under such circumstances are often misleading.
6. National income estimates include only those goods and services, which are commercially used. People living in rural areas usually manufacture articles of consumption, from traditional goods/raw materials, are able to avoid many expenses. For example, they build their own huts, garments and other items of necessity. The value of such goods are not included in the national income estimates.
7. The international comparison of national income is inaccurate and misleading due to the exchange rate conversion of different countries into a common currency i.e., U.S. dollars. The rates of exchanges are primarily based on the prices of internationally traded goods. Unlike developed countries, in underdeveloped countries there are many goods and services that are never traded internationally and are also priced low. This makes international comparisons of national incomes misleading and superfluous.
8. While computing national income of a country, the problem of double counting may crop up. Double counting refers to the possibility of a commodity or raw material or labour being included in national income calculation more than once. An example will elucidate this point. Suppose we calculate the total money value of a book published in a particular year and include it as part of the national

income of the country for that year and suppose at the same time, we calculated the money value of paper used in the printing of books and add it up to the national income of the year. The value of paper has entered the national income calculation twice-once directly and second time indirectly through the value of the books. This is a problem of double counting. The best way to avoid this duplication error is to calculate only the value of those goods and services that enter into the final consumption stage.

FINANCIAL STATISTICS

Financial statistics are the best source of understanding the state of economy of a country. These statistics contain compiled data relating to Banking, Currency, Exchanges and Bullion, Public Finances, Statistics of Insurance Companies. Financial Institutions are also the part of financial statistics.

The Reserve Bank of India (RBI) has a full fledged department of research and statistics. This department compiles data and publishes information on banking, exchange, currency, finances, etc. These data are used by the Government of India, Foreign Governments and International Monetary Fund (IMF) and private sectors. Some important publications are:

1. *Reserve Bank of India Bulletin* (Monthly): Besides other things, it contains data on banking, money and credit.
2. *Statistical Tables Relating to Banks in India* (RBI, Annual): These tables furnish data on scheduled and non-scheduled Banks, whether registered in India or abroad.
3. *Report on Currency and Finance* (RBI, Annual): This report has two parts. Part- I covers information about investment, finance and advances for agriculture, external assistance, international monetary situation, etc. Part-II gives details in respect of price trends, rural credit, capital market trade, tariffs and exchange control, world trade, currency, coinage, etc.
4. *Report on the Trend and Progress of Banking in India* (RBI, Annual): This publication gives data relating to liabilities and assets of the RBI, consolidated position of other scheduled banks, position of investment of banks, interest, money rate, etc.
5. *Statistical Statements Relating to Cooperative Movement in India* vol. I & II (RBI, Annual): This publication contains data relating to provincial and central cooperative banks, credit societies, land mortgage banks and other types of cooperative societies.
6. *Banking Statistics—Basic Statistical Returns* (RBI, Annual).
7. *Reserve Bank of India* (Annual Report).
8. *Analysis of the Accounts of the Joint Stock Companies* (RBI Bulletin).
9. *Balance of Payment Statistics* (RBI Bulletin).
10. *Results of Sample Studies on Analysis of Finance of Medium and Large Public Companies,* (RBI, Bulletin).
11. *Survey of Finances of Local Authorities,* (RBI, Bulletin).

12. *Study of Company Finance,* (RBI, Bulletin).
13. *Annual Report and Accounts* (L.I.C. of India).
14. *Abstract and Statements in Respect of Valuation of Assets and Liabilities* (L.I.C. of India).
15. *Finance Accounts of the Central and State Governments* (Ministry of Finance, Annual).

Besides the above publications there are many more as Annual Reports, Regular Journals, Brochures, Bulletins, etc., which furnish financial statistics. All are not listed here. Financial statistics also take into account a number of sectors which are not covered in the discussion here.

The statistical organisation in India is very widespread. It covers hundreds of sectors which are functionally important and contribute a lot to the private and public sector. In this chapter, a brief description of some important organisations have been given. Some of the uncovered sectors are Trade, Hotel and Restaurants, Transport, storage and communication. Anyhow, the information given in this chapter is enough to obtain any allied information as well. The names of other publications will become available in the publications named in this chapter.

QUESTIONS AND EXERCISES

1. What purpose is served by the collection, compilation and publication of data?
2. Give the historical background of the collection of data.
3. Is the collection of statistical data, a statutory provision? Support your answer.
4. Write notes on the following:
   (*a*) Central statistical organisation.
   (*b*) National sample survey organisation.
   (*c*) Census commissioner.
5. What are the various methods of census in India? Describe each method adequately.
6. Is the census of livestocks equally important as that of human beings? Support your answer by arguments.
7. "*Financial statistics is the backbone of economic planning.*" Do you agree with this statement? Give reasons to your answer.
8. What purpose is served with the creation of National Sample Survey Organisation?
9. Describe in brief the functions of the Central Statistical Organisation and name at least five of its publications.
10. Under what regulation, is labour statistics collected? What aspects are covered under labour statistics?
11. What are the sectors covered in Annual Survey of Industries? Define unregistered and registered manufacturing sectors.
12. What do you understand by crop cutting experiments and for what are they conducted?
13. Name ten statistical organisations of India.
14. Is fisheries statistics adequate? Justify your answer.

15. What do you understand by national income? Give various methods of estimation of the national income. Which body mainly collects and publishes it?
16. Explain the meaning of mining and quarrying. What are the different sources of statistics with regard to mining and quarrying?
17. Do the forests add to our national income? If so in what form?
18. Write the full form of the following abbreviations.
(*i*) CSO, (*ii*) NSSO (*iii*) ASI (*iv*) NAS (*v*) FOD (*vi*) ILO (*vii*) FAO (*viii*) DMI (*ix*) SFD (*x*) IBM (*xi*) DCSSI (*xii*) DCIS.
19. What do you understand by Economic Census? Discuss the economic census, 1980.
20. Throw light on the salient features of the World Agricultural Census 1980–81 and the input survey 1981–82.
21. What are the various products taken into enumeration of the Forest statistics? Name some publications in which Forest statistics appear.
22. Write a note on the evaluation of the present statistical organisation of India and point out its main short comings. (*M.Com., Gorakhpur, 1968*)
23. Explain in brief, the functions performed by the following units in India.
(*a*) Directorate of Economics and Statistics.
(*b*) Department of Commercial Intelligence and Statistics.
(*c*) Department of Research and Statistics (Reserve Bank of India).
(*B.Com., Punjab, 1966*)
24. Explain how yield statistics in our country is collected through random sampling technique. How is this method better than the traditional method?
(*M.Com., Agra, 1970*)
25. Write a note on the Annual Survey of Industries–scope and coverage.
(*M.Com., Delhi, 1961*)
26. Write a critical note on the Foreign Trade Statistics of India.
(*M.A. Econ., Punjab, 1963*)
27. State the difference between the *de-jure* and *de-facto* methods of conducting a census of population.
Appraise the special features of the census of population recently held in India.
(*M.Com., Delhi, 1971*)
28. Discuss briefly the design and organisation of the National Sample Survey and indicate some of its broad results. (*M.A. Econ., Lucknow, 1964*)
29. How are the Agricultural Statistics of area and yield collected in India? What are their weaknesses? Suggest remedies. (*M.Com., Raj., 1983*)
30. '*Planning without statistics is simply unthinkable*', In the light of this statement, comment upon the growth of statistical organisation in India since the introduction of planning. (*M.Com., Raj., 1983*)
31. "*Planning without statistics is a ship without rudder and compass.*" Discuss.
(*M.A. Econ., Meerut, 1976*)
32. Discuss the importance of statistics in the present socio-economic life.
[*Translated from Hindi.*] (*M.A. Econ., Meerut, 1982*)
33. Define national income. Describe briefly the methods used for calculating it.
[*Translated from Hindi.*] (*M.A. Econ., Agra, 1979*)

34. Describe two common defects of Indian Agricultural Statistics and suggest methods for improvement.
[*Translated from Hindi*] (*M.A. Econ., Agra, 1981*)
35. Write a critical note on Indian Industrial Statistics.
[*Translated from Hindi.*] (*M.A. Econ., Agra, 1982*)
36. What are the functions of Central Statistical Organisation? What are your suggestions to make it more effective and useful.
[*Translated from Hindi*] (*M.Com., Agra, 1983*)
37. How is the census conducted in India? Give a critical review of the information collected in the census 1981.
[*Translated from Hindi.*] (*M.Com., Agra, 1983*)
38. Define national income. Discuss briefly the various methods followed for its calculation in India. (*B.Com., Nagpur,* 1968)
39. Write a short note on the Labour Statistics in India—its Nature and Sources.
(*M.Com., Delhi, 1967*)
40. Examine the nature, scope and limitations of the Trade Statistics of India.
(*B.Com., Kerala, 1969*)
41. What is the base year for estimating the real national income of India at present? Explain the methods estimating National Income in our country.
(*M.A.* (*Prev.*) *Econ., Rajasthan, 1983*)
42. (*a*) What are the organisational set up and functions of the central statistical organisation and the State Statistical Bureaux?
(*b*) In what way does the National sample survey help Government of India in evaluating the economic status of the country from time to time.
(*M.Sc., Descriptive & Industrial Statistics, Andhra 1985*)
43. (*a*) Briefly outline the procedures followed in the estimation of acreage and yield of any major crop in India.
(*b*) How is national income estimated? How accurate do you think the estimates are?
(*M.Sc., Descriptive & Industrial Statistics, Andhra, 1985*)

SUGGESTED READING

Asthana, B.N. and S.S. Srivastava (1969). *Applied Statistics of India,* Chaitanya Publishing House, Allahabad.

Bansil, P.C. (1970). *Agricultural Statistics in India,* Dhanpat Rai and Sons, Delhi.

Gupta, C.B. (1978). *An Introduction to Statistical Methods,* 8th ed., Vikas Publishing House, New Delhi.

Gupta, S.P. (1981). *Statistical Methods,* 15th ed., Sultan Chand and Sons, New Delhi.

23 Chapter

Business Forecasting

Business is an inseparable part of human life. One may be a producer, a stockist, a seller or a consumer, but one is connected with business in one way or the other. The former three comes under the category of businessman, but the consumer, somehow, is not considered to be a businessman. There is one common objective for every businessman, *i.e.*, to maximize the profit and to safeguard against any likely loss. Of course, the past has passed, the present is under dealing and the future is to be planned. The success of the businessman depends mainly on future planning based on past and present experiences. Therefore, it is the future which worries him most. No one can predict the future exactly, but the experiences of past and present situations can always lead him to make certain predictions about the future of his business. The experiences may be based on quantitative and/or qualitative factors. The combination of these two types of information helps in business forecasting.

Projections and predictions have already been dealt with in the previous chapters on correlation and regression, time series analysis, index numbers, interpolation and extrapolation. In all these chapters, predictions are based merely on quantitative data. Quantitative data cannot contribute more than a certain fraction of the information required for business forecasting. The statistical methods used for forecasting in previous chapters ignored multitudinous and varied forces which are not easily reduced to a numerical basis or cannot be quantified, but have a lot of bearing upon businesses like fashion, life styles, taste, politics, etc.

From the foregoing description, it is evident that a businessman, on the basis of his forecasts, has to plan a number of factors which directly or indirectly affect his trade. These factors include the increase in production, increase in the number of inventories, acquiring land, constructing new buildings, expansion of production plants, arrangement of additional funds, curtailment of loans, raising prices, creating new markets and many other factors. If the forecast is not reliable, all his efforts will go waste and the business may flop.

The importance of statistics lies in the extent to which it serves as the basis for making reliable forecasts, against arbitrary forecasts with no statistical background. The interpretation of statistical analysis, in the light of judgement, experience and knowledge of the particular trade or industry, makes the forecasts more sound and reliable.

Different persons have defined business forecasting according to their view points. Some of the well known definitions are given below.

1. *"Business forecasting is not so much the estimation of certain figures of sales, production, profits, etc., as the analysis of known data, internal and external, in a manner which will enable policy to be determined to meet probable future conditions to the best advantage."* H.J. Wheldon
2. *"Business forecasting refers to the statistical analysis of the past and current movements in a given time series, so as to obtain clues about the future pattern of the movements."*
Neter and Wasserman
3. *"Forecasting is using the knowledge we have at one time to estimate what will happen at some future moment of time."*
T.S. Lewis and R.A. Fox
4. *"All business proceed on beliefs or judgements of probabilities and not on certainties."*
Charles W. Elliot
5. *"The aim of forecasting is to establish, as accurately as possible, the probable behaviour of economic activity based on all data available and to set policies in terms of these probabilities."*
Leo Barness

From the above discussion, it is clear that the aim of forecasting is to forewarn a businessman about the future state of business activity on the basis of statistical analysis of the quantitative data of the past and the present, plus qualitative factors. Forecasting is a scientific process which aims at reducing the uncertainty of the future state of business and trade. With the help of forecasting, a businessman is not dependent merely on guess work, but has a sound footing for his decision on the future course of action.

Prediction, Projection and Forecasting

To be more specific, the three terms prediction, projection and forecasting are not same in usage and meaning. The difference among them is explained here for a clear understanding of these terms. *Prediction* is an estimate based on the analysis of a past series of data for a point outside the series. *Projection* is a prediction based on certain assumptions. For instance, the population projection for 2019 is based on the assumption that the present growth rate will continue in ensuing years. A *forecast* is an estimate for some future point of time, partly based on past and present data and partly on subjective estimates arising out of the experience and judgement of the forecaster. In short, prediction is a mechanical extrapolation, and projection is a prediction with certain assumptions(s), whereas forecast is a prediction based on quantitative as well as qualitative factors.

METHODS OF FORECASTING

The science of business forecasting has developed only in some developed countries. These countries have certain private agencies which have taken up forecasting as a profession. The statisticians and economists working in these institutions developed their own methodology which appeared germane to them on mathematical and logical grounds. Whatever may be the method, it involves two types of analysis. The first may be categorised as *historical analysis of past events,* and the second as *cross section analysis of present conditions.* Many methods have been developed which use a combination of both types of analysis. One method may be more suitable in one situation than another. The techniques developed by a number of agencies can be classified under three basic methods, namely,

(*a*) Naive method.
(*b*) Barometric methods.
(*c*) Analytical methods.

Each of these methods covers a number of techniques and theories as mentioned and discussed below:

Naive Method

(*i*) The economic rhythm theory.

The Barometric Methods

(*i*) Specific historical analogy
(*ii*) Lead-lag relationship
(*iii*) Diffusion index
(*iv*) Action-reaction theory

The Analytical Methods

(*i*) The factor listing methods
(*ii*) Cross-cut analysis theory
(*iii*) Opinion polling
(*iv*) Exponential smoothing
(*v*) Econometric methods.

Economic Rhythm Method

This method implies the forecasting of a time series by itself. This is often used by a manufacturer to forecast his production, sales, dividends, etc. In this method, the manufacturer analyses the time series for the components, trend, seasonal variation and cycles of his firm. The forecasts are made simply on projections obtained from time series data of his own firm. The forecast may be made for each component of time series independently, or by synthesising the three components, i.e. a single factor may be given by combining the three projected values by a process of multiplication. It has been mentioned in the chapter of time-series analysis that a time series is a multiplicative model of the four components — trend, seasonal, cycles and irregular variations. Such an analysis of time series helps to determine whether the increase or decrease in demand is a continued process or cyclical. A forecast of increasing trend in demand serves for long-term planning to expand the plant for more production and greater investment. Seasonal and cyclical variations forewarn the businessman for production scheduling, arranging finances, transport of finished product, etc. It is difficult to forecast the turning point and amplitude of a cycle by the series itself. Hence, a promising method for overcoming this difficulty is to predict the cycle of one series by the cycle of another series that leads. The forecasts under the naive method are valid only for the individual firm and are not very reliable as no subjective considerations are made.

Specific Historical Analogy

This technique is based on the theory that history repeats itself. This method implies that there exist certain uniformities in a series under consideration and a past series which had occurred under a similar situation. The inferences drawn from past series are applicable straightway to the present state of economy. The method of historical analogy can be applied to a specific series or a series in general.

There is hardly any situation in the past which is exactly similar to the present situation. Thus, a total analogous situation is impossible. Hence, a situation of maximum resemblance is sought out and an allowance is made for the differences occurring in the two situations. If similar situations at two occasions are not traceable or one fails to make an allowance for dissimilarities in two situations, this method will lead us astray.

Lead-Lag Relationship

Lead-Lag theory is also known as *sequence theory.* This theory is based on the principle that the changes in business are not simultaneous but successive, i.e., the changes occur with a time lag. For example, in the state of inflation, the exchange rate is adversely affected. The decrease in exchange rate leads to increase in wholesale prices which subsequently causes the increase in retail prices and thereby, the increase in wages takes place. Hence, the impact of inflation on various aspects of business is not simultaneous, but takes place in stages. Similarly, the impact of deflation will be in the opposite direction to that of inflation. The preceding example shows that most of the variables attached to business activity have lead and lag relationship. Under this theory, an attempt is made to determine the approximate lapse of time between the movement of one or more series and general business cycles. This theory received greater attention due to the fact that for any series whose turning point leads by a certain period (generally 2 to 10 months) with enough regularity, the turning points of general business in the past help forecast what is going to happen to general business activity.

The lead-lag technique of forecasting is geared to some hypothetical or observed relationship among variables. Lead-lag relationships are usually developed by the inspection of graphs of different series and by correlation studies between the series. The famous *Harvard Index of General Business Conditions* was comprised of three prediction curves: (*a*) Speculation, the leading series, (*b*) Business, the coincident series, and (*c*) Money, the lagging series. The rise and fall of the speculation curve was used to forecast the movement of the business curve. It is worth pointing out that the speculation curve and money curve have movements in opposite directions. Obviously, the upturn of the speculation curve is accompanied by the downturn of the money curve. Such a situation marks a boom in business within a few months, while the downturn of the speculation curve and upturn of the money curve forewarns a recession in business within a couple of months.

It is apparent from the above discussion that three types of indicators are involved in the lead-lag approach. First, the *lead indicators* like price indices of equity shares, bank reserves, exchange rates of currency, borrowings from banks and financing bodies, creation of new companies, new orders, etc. Second *coincident indicators* like employment, industrial production index, gross national product at current prices, business profits, total freight traffic, etc. Third, *lag indicators* like personal income payments, total sales from retail storos, business loans (quarterly), interest rates, inventories of finished products, etc.

The lead-lag tecbnique has many difficulties. First, it is not always easy to interpret the movement of indicators correctly because of the variability of timing and presence of irregular movements in the series. Choice of indicators itself is a problem. Some indicators fail to signal at all. It is also difficult to forecast the amplitude of the cycle. Keeping in view the difficulties arising from this technique, the lead-lag method can be taken as a supplement to forecasting techniques, not beyond it.

Diffusion Index

Different factors, affecting the business, do not reach their peaks and troughs simultaneously. There is always a time lag between them. The diffusion index is based only on this proposition. This method has the convenience, of not having to identify which series has a lead and which a lag. The diffusion index depicts the movement of broad groups of series as a whole without bothering about individual series. The diffusion index shows the percentage of a given set of series as expanding (contracting) from month to month, or any other interval of time chosen suitably. The diffusion index, evidently, is the index of general business activity. However, it is to be carefully noted that the peaks and troughs of the diffusion index are not the peaks and troughs of business cycle. It is easy to note that all series do not expand or contract at the same time. Some series expand and other contract at a given time, *i.e.*, some are attaining their peaks while others are attaining their troughs. In such a situation, if more than 50 per cent of the series are expanding, the business is in the process of booming. On the contrary, if less than 50 per cent series are expanding, the business in general is in a state of contraction. A graphic method is used to work out the diffusion index. The per cent of series expanding out of a large number of series (may be hundreds), are plotted for each year, or half yearly, as the case may be. Then, from the graph, we note the period in which the diffusion index has crossed the 50 per cent line, from above, that the peak of business cycle has reached. For comparison, the per cent of trend of the series are also plotted against years, and the index of business activity is noted. In practice, the lead-lag relationship between the diffusion index and the index of business activity is often observed. It is worth noting that the diffusion index can be constructed for a group of business variables like prices, working hours, investment, profits, etc., of all the related industries.

Action Reaction Theory

Newton's celebrated third law of motion, in the realm of Physics, which states that for every action there is an equal and opposite reaction, has been applied to the theory of economics. Enough reliance has been placed in this action-and-reaction law as it has been observed that in business activity there is always a recession after prosperity and prosperity after a recession. Babson found that the area covered by a time series or index of activity curve above the line of normal business activity is approximately equal to the area below the normal line. The span of the recession after a long period of prosperity may not be the same, but it does occur. It clearly shows that one phase of the trade cycle comes after the other and this sequence of recession and prosperity continues eternally.

In this method also, there are some difficulties. The first one is of ascertaining the line of normal business activity. In practice, the trend line is taken as the line of normal business activity. The second problem is of determining the phase of the business cycle through which an industry or business is passing at the time of the forecast. The business statistics organisation mainly uses the action-reaction theory for business forecasting.

Factor Listing Method

In this method, various factors which influence business activity are sorted out and assembled by the analyst. Each factor is analysed separately with the objective of assessing whether the probable impact of the factor upon aggregate business activity is favourable or not. No mathematical tool is applied for the analysis of each factor. Inferences are drawn regarding the effect of each factor on the business and then aggregated, merely by a mental process, to forecast the condition of the business in the near future.

This approach has some merits as well as demerits. It has the advantage that it is not based on any theory. There is no restriction on the type and number of variables to be included in the analysis. Hence, new variables may be included and old variables deleted at any stage. The method is capable of giving due weightage to each factor according to its importance for explaining the business condition. A judgement of likely turning points through dominating variables has been easy and handy. Such a facility is not available with other methods.

The main defect of this method is that it is based totally on the judgement of the analyst. Hence, conclusions will vary from person to person. This method is entirely subjective. A factor may be taken as favourable for a swing in business by one analyst, and unfavourable by another. The forecasts given, by this method, by an analyst depend upon his knowledge of economic theories, understanding of the present situation and economic policies of the government. Most likely, this method may prove more effective if it is used in combination with other methods.

Cross-cut Analysis Theory

This theory is opposite to the historical analogy theory. Here, the convention is that historical cycles cannot be thrusted upon future cycles, i.e. conditions which occurred in the past cannot be a guide for forecasting. Under this theory each of the variables, like technological advancement, government policies, demand, availability of inputs, styles, fads, etc., concerned with the present economic activity, is thoroughly analysed and an effort is made to estimate the composite effect of all the variables. This method takes into account the views of the managerial staff, economists, consumers, etc., prior to forecasting. As a consequence of the cumulative effect of all the factors, the forecast is made on the state of business in near future.

This method suffers with the lacuna that people do not express their views sincerely, honestly and clearly. Also, it is very difficult to analyse each variable separately and to pool their effects for a forecast.

Opinion Polling

This device of forecasting makes use of the reports and opinion obtained from surveys. The theme behind this method is that the present attitudes towards business can be the real guide for evaluating the expected changes in business conditions in near future. Opinions are invited from business experts, persons in strategic positions, the sales force and consumers. The opinions are analysed to make a forecast. In this process it is common to come across divergent or totally opposite views, but a consensus is reached on the median value. This value is taken as a guide for prediction. The firms usually apply this method for forecasting their sales by collecting anticipatory data covering consumer's spending plans. Delphin's method implements this technique.

The forecasts made by the opinion polling method are simple and the least expensive. Often, these surveys are best suited for short-term forecasts but are unlikely to give long-term forecasts of the aggregate business condition.

Exponential Smoothing

This is a mathematical device for improving trend by the moving average method. Finding out a trend by the moving average method has already been discussed in the chapter on Time Series Analysis, where equal weights have been given to all items. Under exponential smoothing, the weights are assigned in geometric progression. Greater weights are assigned to recent observations and smaller weights to distant observations. Suppose the weights in geometric series are as given below.

$$1, (1-\omega), (1-\omega)^2, .., (1-\omega)^{n-1}$$

where $0 < \omega < 1$

and n = number of observations.

Thus, the weighted average till the current period t is given by the expression,

$$\overline{X}_t = \frac{1.X_t + (1-\omega)X_{t-1} + (1-\omega)^2 X_{t-2} + \ldots + (1-\omega)^{n-1} X_{t-(n-1)}}{1 + (1-\omega) + (1-\omega)^2 + \ldots + (1-\omega)^{n-1}} \quad ..(23.1)$$

Similarly,

$$\overline{X}_{t+1} = \frac{1.X_{t+1} + (1-\omega)X_t + \ldots + (1-\omega)^{n-1} X_{t-n+2}}{1 + (1-\omega) + \ldots + (1-\omega)^{n-1}} \quad ...(23.2)$$

Taking n large and neglecting higher powers of ω and $(1-\omega)$ and doing certain algebraic manipulations, the following relationship between $\overline{X}_{t+1}$, the forecast value for the next period and $\overline{X}_t$, the forecast for the current period can be established as given below.

$$\overline{X}_{t+1} = \omega X_{t+1} + (1-\omega)\overline{X}_t \quad ...(23.3)$$

i.e., New forecast = ω × observed value + $(1-\omega)$ × old forecast ...(23.3.1)

In relation (23.3), $\overline{X}_{t+1}$, the smoothed value at the next period of time is ω times the observed value plus $(1-\omega)$ times the preceding smoothed value which is itself an average smoothed value. Now, to make a forecast for each successive period, these smoothed values are used to find out a change in each period. ω is called the *smoothing coefficient* and $(1-\omega)/\omega$, the *trend factor*. For example, if smoothing coefficient $\omega = 1/3$, the trend factor $(1-\omega)/\omega = 2$.

Since only one smoothing constant ω is used in this procedure, it is referred to as *single parameter exponential smoothing*. The forecast for the first period is usually taken from some old forecast, if available, or is often assumed.

Trend Adjusted Exponential Smoothing

A situation often arises in which the trend is going upward but the forecast is low or, conversely, the trend is going downwards but the forecast is high. Somehow, to minimize this effect, a factor is added and the calculations under trend-adjusted exponential smoothing are made as per the following procedure. This procedure adjusts the forecast according to the trend. It has been observed that the trend-adjusted forecasted value comes pretty close to the actual value.

Relationship (23.3) may be rewritten as,

$$\overline{X}_{t+1} = \omega(X_{t+1} - \overline{X}_t) + \overline{X}_t \qquad ...(23.4)$$

By induction,

$$\overline{X}_t = \omega X_t + (1-\omega)\overline{X}_{t-1} \qquad ...(23.4.1)$$

or

$$\overline{X}_t = \omega(X_t - \overline{X}_{t-1}) + \overline{X}_{t-1} \qquad ...(23.4.2)$$

The quantity $(X_t - \overline{X}_{t-1})$ is called the error.

Thus, the forecast for the period t is the preceding average $\overline{X}_{t-1}$ plus ω times the error.

The trend coefficient which is required for preparing the forecast is calculated by the formula,

Trend coefficient, $\theta_t = \omega \times$ change in smoothed value + $(1-\omega) \times$ preceding trend coefficient ...(23.5)

The forecast F_t is obtained by the relation,

F_t = Smoothed value + Trend factor × Trend coefficient ..(23.6)

Also, error in forecast,

$$E_t = X_t - F_t \qquad ...(23.7)$$

Choice of Weight ω. The value of ω is chosen arbitrarily. There is no rule which governs to the choice of ω. Anyhow, as a general norm, some tips may be given. If the fluctuation in production, sales, demand, etc., appears to be random, a smaller value of ω is preferred. Also, in case the actual value turns down but the forecast does not turn down, a larger value of ω will be more suitable, and vice-versa.

The calculation of the forecast for any period and error in forecast has been illustrated through the numerical problem given below.

***Example* 23.1.** Monthly pattern of off-take of sugar in India in '000 tonnes, during the year 1983–84, by the public distribution system is as follows:

Apr.	May	Jun.	Jul.	Aug.	Sep.	Oct.	Nov.	Dec.	Jan.	Feb.	Mar.
444	464	524	554	574	614	693	643	613	638	638	668

The smoothed values and trend adjusted forecasts for the above time series have been calculated, taking the value of ω to be equal to 0.6, and displayed in the table given ahead. The step by step calculations are explained just below and displayed in the table on page 701.

Also, the trend factor, $\dfrac{(1-\omega)}{\omega} = \dfrac{2}{3}$

Calculations: Smoothed forecast for the months are obtained from relation (23.4.1).

Suppose, predetermined $\overline{X}_1 = 428.0$

For May; $\overline{X}_2 = 0.6 \times 464 + (1 - 0.6) \times 428 = 449.6$

For Jun; $\overline{X}_3 = 0.6 \times 524 + (1 - 0.6) \times 449.6 = 494.2$

$\vdots$

For Mar.; $\overline{X}_{12} = 0.6 \times 668 + (1 - 0.6) \times 636.1 = 655.2$

S.no.	*Month*	*Observed value* X_t	*Smoothing coefficient* ω	*Smoothed forecast* $\overline{X}_t$	*Change in smoothed values* $\overline{X}_{t+1} - \overline{X}_t$	*Trend coefficient* $\theta_t = \omega \times col.5 + (1-\omega)\,\theta_{t-1}$	*Forecast* F_t = *col. 4* $+\left(\frac{1-\omega}{\omega}\right)\theta_t$	*Error* $E_t = X_t - F_t$
	(1)	(2)	(3)	(4)	(5)	(6)	(7)	(8)
1	Apr.	444	0.6	(Predetermined) 428.0	—	—	—	—
2	May	464	0.6	449.6	21.6	12.96	458.24	5.76
3	Jun.	524	0.6	494.2	44.6	31.94	515.49	8.51
4	Jul.	554	0.6	530.1	35.9	34.32	552.98	1.02
5	Aug.	574	0.6	556.4	26.3	29.50	576.07	–2.07
6	Sep.	614	0.6	591.0	34.6	32.56	612.71	1.29
7	Oct.	693	0.6	652.2	61.2	49.74	685.36	7.64
8	Nov.	643	0.6	646.7	–5.5	16.60	657.77	–14.77
9	Dec.	613	0.6	626.2	–20.5	–5.66	622.43	–9.43
10	Jan.	638	0.6	633.3	7.1	2.00	634.63	3.37
11	Feb.	638	0.6	636.1	2.8	2.48	637.75	0.25
12	Mar.	668	0.6	655.2	19.1	14.45	664.83	3.17

In column (5), change in smoothed values is calculated from smoothed values only.

May; change = 449.6 – 428.0 = 21.6

Jun.; change = 494.2 – 449.6 = 44.6

⋮ ⋮

Mar.; change = 655.2 – 636.1 = 19.1

In column (6), the trend coefficients are calculated by formula (23.5)

May; $\theta_2 = 0.6 \times 21.6 + (1 - 0.6) \times 0 = 12.96$

Jun.; $\theta_3 = 0.6 \times 44.6 + (1 - 0.6) \times 12.96 = 31.94$

⋮ ⋮

Mar.; $\theta_{12} = 0.6 \times 19.1 + (1 - 0.6) \times 2.48 = 12.45$

Trend adjusted forecasts in col. 7 are calculated in the following manner by formula (23.6).

May; $F_2 = 449.6 + \dfrac{1-0.6}{0.6} \times 12.96 = 458.24$

Jun.; $F_3 = 494.2 + \dfrac{2}{3}\ 31.94 = 515.49$

⋮ ⋮

Mar.; $F_{12} = 655.2 + \dfrac{2}{3} \times 12.45 = 663.50$

Errors in forecast in col. 8 are obtained by taking the difference between col. 2 and col. 7.

May ; $E_2 = 464.0 - 458.24 = 5.76$

Jun.; $E_3 = 524.0 - 515.49 = 8.51$

⋮ ⋮

Mar.; $E_{12} = 668.0 - 664.83 = 3.17$

Comparing the values in col. 4 and col. 7, it is apparent that the trend-adjusted forecast is much closer to the actual value as compared to simple-smoothed values.

Two Parameter Exponential Smoothing

It has been observed that whenever there is a pronounced upward trend in the actual value of a time series, the forecast resulting from the single-parameter exponential smoothing procedure is consistently low. To overcome this deficiency of the single-parameter exponential smoothing method, a second smoothing constant is chosen for the trend itself. Let the two parameters be ω and δ. This smoothing process involves three equations only.

$$V_t = \omega X_t + (1-\omega)(V_{t-1} + b_{t-1}) \qquad ...(23.8)$$

$$b_t = \delta(V_t - V_{t-1}) + (1-\delta) b_{t-1} \qquad ...(23.9)$$

$$F_t = V_{t-1} + b_{t-1} \qquad ...(23.10)$$

For $0 < \omega < 1$ and $0 < \delta < 1$

where, V_t – Smoothed value at period t.

b_t = Smoothed trend at period t.

F_t = Forecast at period t.

Also, b_2 is the difference between the actual value for period 2 and actual initial value. Subsequent values of b's are calculated by relation (23.9). The final forecast for the period t is available from equation (23.10).

The exponential smoothing procedure is popular because of two major advantages. First, the calculations are simple. Second, it has a self-adjusting device for forecasts, i.e., the procedure regulates forecast values by increasing or decreasing them in the opposite direction of the error, like a thermostat.

***Example* 23.2.** The following are employment figures in quasi-government institutions at the end of March. The figures are rounded to the nearest thousand.

Year :										
1973	1974	1975	1976	1977	1978	1979	1980	1981	1982	1983
Employment (Lakhs):										
25.8	29.1	31.9	33.9	36.8	39.3	41.7	43.4	45.8	48.1	50.4

The time series data has a clear cut upward trend. Hence, the two-parameter exponential smoothing method will be used taking $\omega = 0.2$ and $\delta = 0.3$. Also, the 1973 figure for actual employment has been used as the smoothed value for 1974. With the help of relations (23.8) to (23.10), the following table is prepared presenting the values of V_t, b_t and F_t,

Calculations: Smoothed values,

$$V_3 = 0.2 \times 31.9 + 0.8\,(25.80 + 3.30) = 29.66$$
$$V_4 = 0.2 \times 33.9 + 0.8\,(29.66 + 3.47) = 33.28$$
$$\vdots$$
$$V_{11} = 0.2 \times 50.4 + 0.8\,(50.74 + 2.77) = 52.86$$

Smoothed trend values,

$$b_2 = 29.1 - 25.8 = 3.30$$
$$b_3 = 0.3\,(29.66 - 25.80) + 0.7 \times 3.30 = 3.47$$
$$\vdots$$
$$b_{11} = 0.3\,(52.89 - 50.74) + 0.7 \times 2.77 = 2.58$$

The forecast under two smoothing coefficients,

$$F_3 = 25.80 + 3.30 = 29.10$$
$$F_4 = 29.66 + 3.47 = 33.13$$
$$\vdots$$
$$F_{11} = 50.74 + 2.77 = 53.51$$

The error,

$$E_3 = 31.9 - 29.10 = 2.80$$
$$E_4 = 33.9 - 33.13 = 0.77$$
$$\vdots$$
$$E_{11} = 50.4 - 53.51 = -\,3.11$$

The table clearly reveals that the forecasts from this procedure are quite close to the actual values of employment.

S.no.	Year	Actual employment X_t	ω	Smoothed value V_t	δ	Smoothed trend b_t	Forecast F_t	Error $E_t = X_t - F_t$
1	1973	25.8	0.2	—	0.3	—	—	—
2	1974	29.1	0.2	25.80	0.3	3.30	—	—
3	1975	31.9	0.2	29.66	0.3	3.47	29.10	2.80
4	1976	33.9	0.2	33.28	0.3	3.52	33.13	0.77
5	1977	36.8	0.2	36.80	0.3	3.52	36.80	0.00
6	1978	39.3	0.2	40.12	0.3	3.46	40.32	– 1.02
7	1979	41.7	0.2	43.20	0.3	3.35	43.58	– 1.88
8	1980	43.4	0.2	45.92	0.3	3.17	46.55	– 3.15
9	1981	45.8	0.2	48.43	0.3	2.97	49.09	– 3.29
10	1982	48.1	0.2	50.74	0.3	2.77	51.40	– 3.30
11	1983	50.4	0.2	52.89	0.3	2.58	53.51	– 3.11

ECONOMETRIC METHODS

Econometrics is a science which expresses economic theories in mathematical terms. It is a branch of statistics because mathematical relations, which explain the impact of one or more variables on some dependent variable, are verified statistically. The behaviour of an economic system is analysed through econometric methods which have proved very useful in economic theory. A number of variables influence an economic system whose inter-relationship is expressed by a set of equations. These equations involve two types of variables, namely, *endogenous variables* and *exogenous variables*. The variables which belong to the economic system itself are called endogenous variables, like production, stocks, interest, rent, prices, money reserves, employment, wages, etc. On the other hand, exogenous variables are those which do effect the economic system but do not belong to it, e.g. politics, customs, life styles, nature, environment, etc. Econometric methods try to discover and measure the quantitative aspects of an economic phenomenon which enable one to forecast the magnitude of the economic change with certain probability level. Some such methods are discussed here.

Econometric methods start basically with model building. Econometric models take the form of a set of simultaneous equations. The values of constants involved in an econometric model are estimated by using some part of time series data. Often, a large number of equations are needed to estimate precisely the parameters involved in the model. The invention of electronic computers has eased the process of solving the simultaneous equations. Due to computer facility, the econometric methods of forecasting are becoming more and more popular.

To clarify, we discuss the model for Gross National Product (GNP) for a given period t. The model is,

$$y_t = C_t + I_t + G_t \qquad ..(23.11)$$

where, Y_t = GNP for period t.

C_t = Consumption for period t.

I_t = Gross investment in period t

G_t = Government expenditure in period t.

Now, each variable on the right side of model (23.11) will be expressed as a function of other variables.

We know that the consumption in any period depends on the GNP of the preceding period. Also, it is observed that the increments in GNP, irrespective of the initial value of GNP, are equal to the increments in consumption. This incremental value is known as the *marginal propensity* to consume and is denoted by β. Further, even if the GNP is zero. There will be some minimum consumption. Let this be denoted by α. Thus, the mathematical equation for consumption is,

$$C_t = \alpha + \beta y_{t-1} \qquad ...(23.12)$$

The gross investment I_t is the sum of induced private investment and autonomous investment. The induced private investment in any given period is proportional to the difference in consumption between the given period and the preceding one. The constant proportionality is called the *relation* and is denoted by i. Thus, the size of the induced investment may be given by $i\,(C_t - C_{t-1})$. Autonomous investment refers to capital formation for replacement and adoption of new inventions. Let this amount be denoted by k and is assumed to be independent of consumption level. Thus,

$$I_t = k + i\,(C_t - C_{t-1}) \qquad \text{...(23.13)}$$

Government expenditure is an exogenous variable. It may be considered a constant amount say, G_0. Hence,

$$G_t = G_0 \qquad \text{...(23.14)}$$

Substituting the functional values of C_t, I_t and G_t from (23.12) to (23.14) in (23.11), the model for GNP takes the form,

$$y_t = \alpha + \beta \;\; y_{t-1} + k + i(C_t - C_{t-1}) + G_0 \qquad \text{...(23.15)}$$

with the help of (23.12), equation (23.15) can be rewritten as,

$$\begin{aligned} y_t &= \alpha + \beta y_{t-1} + k + i(\alpha + \beta y_{t-1} - \alpha - \beta y_{t-2}) + G_0 \\ &= \alpha + \beta(1+i)\, y_{t-1} - i\beta y_{t-2} + k + G_0 \end{aligned} \qquad \text{...(23.15.1)}$$

The parameters α, β, i and k in (23.15.1) can be estimated on the basis of the past time series data. A suitable method, which has already been discussed with the fitting of a regression equation or time series model can be used to estimate the parameters and finally obtain the workable forecasting model. We may take GNP and consumption figures for a good length of time, say ten or more years and estimate α and β. Similarly, associating the investment, expenditure and changes in consumption figures, estimates of k and i are obtained. Substituting the estimated values of these parameters in (23.15.1), the workable model is obtained. Let the estimated values of α, β, i and k be a, b, i' and k' respectively. The estimated economic equation is,

$$\hat{y}_t = a + b\,(1 + i')\, y_{t-1} - i'\, b y_{t-2} + k' + G_0 \qquad \text{...(23.16)}$$

On substituting the predetermined values of y_{t-1}, y_{t-2} and G_0 in (23.16), the estimated value of y_t is readily available for the forecast period.

The model for any other forecast can also be built up in the like manner, for instance the production model, input-output models, demand function, etc.

The forecasts made through econometric models are mathematically sound and without subjectivity. Moreover, the econometric model has quantified forecasting techniques which are verifiable at any time. But they too are not always exact and reliable because the estimates of parameters are subject to sampling errors. The validity of the model itself is questionable as it may be suitable at a certain past or present moment of time, but not for a future period when new forces may enter and play a dominant role, Therefore, new forces should be incorporated in the model to get a reliable forecast rather than doing it mechanically. The success of the econometric method of forecasting depends mainly on the selection of the model, collection of reliable past data, scientific knowledge of statistical methods and economic theories.

Econometric models can be built for individual firms and industries for forecasting of production, prices, demand and other factors, as required. Forecasting models can also be built up at the national or international level.

FORECASTING AGENCIES AND THEIR PUBLICATIONS

Forecasting agencies exist mainly in economically and industrially developed countries like U.S.A., England and Canada. In India it is still a luxury. Of course, there has been some development in India over the last decades, but of a negligible magnitude. Forecasting is done by individual firms in different countries for their own use, and also by private agencies in U.S.A.

India

1. Associated Cement Company (ACC) established a Corporate Planning (CP) cell in 1975 to feed necessary information to the management to help in planning for their sales, production, expansion, diversification, etc.
2. Larsen and Toubro (L & T) has developed a separate corporate planning cell within its planning and development unit.
3. Other companies, namely Imperial Chemical Industries (ICI) India, Dunlop India, Indian Textile Corporation (ITC), Hindustan Levers, Metal Box, Texmaco and Coal India Ltd., are also engaged in corporate planning and forecasting. In India, forecasting has received hardly any importance. Either most of the businessmen believe in their own guess work or they don't feel the necessity of forecasting. But in advanced countries, forecasting agencies play a prominent role in the planning and expansion of industries.

Abroad

The Econometric Institute and the Index Number Institute, New York, U.S.A. The econometric institute is organised to help the management and executives solve their various problems by forecasting business condition for short terms of three months to a year i.e., intermediate terms of two to four years to regulate their production, sales, transportation, finances, etc., and long term of five to twenty years with regard to the expansion of plants, change of location, etc.

The institute analyzes data and measures the trend, i.e. rate of growth, cycles about these trends, their leads and lags about each other or phase differences, the systematic patterns fo residuals and econometric relationships.

The institute publishes a forecasting bulletin, *Economic Measures.*

Bussiness Statistics Organisation, Washington. It is one of the oldest and best known forecasting service organisation. Formerly, it was known as *Babson's Statistical Organisation* after its founder Roger W. Babson. The forecasts of this organisation are based on the law of action and equal and opposite reaction theory as applied to economics. It has an affiliated organisation in Canada named Babson's Canadian Reports Ltd., Toronto, Ontario. The publications of this institute are:

(*i*) *Investment and Barometer Letter* (Weekly).

(*ii*) *Confidential Barometer Letter* (Weekly).

(*iii*) *Business Inventory–Commodity Price Forecasts* (Monthly).

(*iv*) *Babson's Washington Forecasts.*

Standard and Poor's Trade and Securities Service, New York. This institute does not follow any single theory for the purpose of forecasting. Of course, it believes little in the economic rhythm theory. The institute analyses data for forecasts according to the existing situations with a fresh outlook.

This organisation publishes the following weekly and monthly bulletins:

(i) *Industry Surveys–Trends and Projections.*

(ii) *The Outlook*

(iii) *The Stock Guide*

(iv) *Basic Statistics*–a set of statistical bulletins

(v) *Basic Surveys* – irregular reports.

The *Brookmire Economic Service, New York.* This service emphasises the theory of cross-section analysis. They consider business cycles a permanent and unavoidable phenomenon. Their belief is that there are many indirectly effective forces and all of them cannot be discovered by any one method. These forces vary in intensity, and wane and die out. Thus, dominating forces of one cycle may have little or no effect on the next cycle. The forecasts of this service are based on this principle. The Brookmire Economic Service has the following publications:

(i) *Brookmire bulletin*

(ii) *Brookmire Special Report* (Weekly)

Moody's Investors Service, New York. This is one of the leading services which analyses business situations. This service does not rigidly follow any single forecasting device or mathematical model, but chooses the method which is considered suitable for a particular set of conditions. This institute usually makes studies of individual industrial and business units. It publishes two regular bulletins.

(i) *Moody's Stock Survey.*

(ii) *Moody's Bond Survey.*

The International Statistical Bureau, New York. The bureau is not confined to any one rigid method of forecasting. It makes use of a methodology which appears most suitable at a particular instance. It has one publication.

(i) *Business and Investment* (Weekly).

The Real Estate Analyst Service, St. Louis. This service covers a number of factors that affect business activity. It measures, analyses and forecasts the likely changes in real estate and construction activity. This agency publishes one monthly and many supplementary bulletins. Some are named below.

(i) *Real Estate Analyst* (Monthly).

(ii) *National Events* (Monthly).

(iii) *Construction* (Quarterly).

(iv) *Mortgage Conditions* (Quarterly).

(v) *Agriculture* (Triannually).

(vi) *General Business Conditions* (Biannually).

(vii) *Real Estate Taxes* (biannually).

National Bureau of Economic Research, Massachusetts. This bureau has carried out most careful and comprehensive work on lead-and-lag relationships, as initiated by the Harward Committee on Economic Research in the early twenties. It publishes a weekly report.

There are also a great number of organisations run by the governments, public and private sectors which are engaged in the job of forecasting. Almost all organisations publish their findings and forecasts in bulletins, reports, journals or magazines. It is not possible to list all of them. A few are named just to acquaint readers with the type of institutional services devoted to the work of economic analysis and forecasting.

From the matter discussed in this chapter it is easy to conclude that business forecasting does not depend on the determination of a figure that can determine the future situation. Forecasting is based on the measurement of a number of composite and complex forces which influence the future. The methods usually adopted for analysis of the composite forces may be of qualitative and/or quantitative nature. They provide guidelines for drawing certain conclusions to make the forecasts. The reliability of a forecast depends upon the experience, knowledge of economic theory, mathematical background and statistical insight of the forecaster. Of importance above all is the ready availability of data at the proper time with the maximum accuracy. Thus, a combination of knowledgeable persons, collection of timely and correct informations, choice of proper tools and techniques can result in good forecasts. It is to be remembered, however, that any forecasts has some probability of occurrence but is never certain.

QUESTIONS AND EXERCISES

1. Explain what is meant by forecasting. How does it differ from prediction and projection?
2. What are the general assumptions on which a forecast is based?
3. In what respects are econometric methods for forecasting better than non-econometric methods?
4. Name five organisations which exclusively deal with business forecasting. Also discuss their approach in brief.
5. Write a short note on business forecasting. *(C.A. Intermediate, Nov. 1977)*
6. What is business forecasting? What are the assumptions on which business forecasts are made? Describe the techniques of forecasting that are commonly employed by big business houses. *(M.Com., Delhi, 1977)*
7. Examine critically the time-lag and the action-and-reaction theory of business forecasting. Which of these, in your opinion, is better, and why? *(M. Com., Allahabad, 1975)*
8. How does an econometric model differs from a mathematical model?
9. In your opinion, will it ever be possible to develop an infallible system of forecasting? Give supporting reasons for your answer.
10. Describe the services and approach of the Business Statistics Organisation.
11. Name seven publications which bringforth business forecasts or general business conditions. Also give names of the organisations with which they are linked.
12. Describe the method of exponential smoothing. What does the value of the smoothing coefficient indicate? What are its limiting values and what do they indicate?

    An old forecast of 39 is given initially and the smoothing coefficient is 0.1. Smooth exponentially the following observations:

    41, 41, 34, 39, 36, 35, 40, 36, 41, 33

    (C.A. Intermediate, Nov. 1974)

13. Differentiate between long-term and short-term forecasting. Examine the place of time series analysis in forecasting.
14. The domestic production of crude oil in million tonnes from 1975–76 to 1984–85 is as given below.

1975—76	77	78	79	80	81	82	83	84	85
8.4	8.9	10.8	11.6	11.8	10.5	16.2	21.1	26.0	29.0

Taking the initial forecast of 7.4 Mn. tonnes and following the two-parameter exponential smoothing procedure with $\omega = 0.3$ and $\delta = 0.4$, find the forecast values.
15. The consumption of foodgrains supplied through public distribution systems during fourteen years is as follows:

Year :	1971	1972	1973	1974	1975	1976	1977	1978
Food grains : (Mn tonnes)	7.82	10.49	11.41	10.79	11.25	9.17	11.73	10.18
	1979	1980	1981	1982	1983	1984		
	11.66	14.99	13.01	14.77	16.21	13.42		

Find the forecast values by the exponential smoothing method taking the value of smoothing coefficient $\omega = 0.6$.

SUGGESTED READING

Anderson, O.D. (1976). "Forecasting", *Proceedings of the Institute of Statisticians Annual Conference,* Cambridge, North Holland Publishing Company, Amsterdam, New York.

Douglas A. Downing and Jeffery Clark (2003). *Business Statistics*, Barron's Educational Series.

Firth, M. (1977). *Forecasting Methods in Business and Management,* Edward Arnold, London.

G. Peter Zhang (2003). *Neural Networks in Business Forecasting*, Idea Group Incs.

Jae K. Shim (2002). *Strategic Business Forecasting*, CRC Press.

Lapin, L.L. (1981). *Quantitative Methods for Business Decisions,* Harcourt Brace Jovanovich, New York.

Levin, R.I., A. Kirkpatrick and D.S. Rubin (1982). *Quantitative Approach to Management,* McGraw-Hill International Book Company, New York. 5th ed.

Michael K. Evans (2002). *Practical Business Forecasting*, Black Well Publishing.

Nelson, C.R. (1973). *Applied Time Series Analysis for Managerial Forecasting,* Holden Day, San Francisco.

Richard, L.E. and J.J. Lacava (1978). *Business Statistics,* McGraw-Hill Book Company, New York.

Robert Dransfield (2003). *Understanding Business Statistics Made Easy*, Nelson Thornes.

Ronard M. Weiers (2004). *Introduction to Business Statistics*, Thomson South-Western.

Wheel, W., and S. Makridakis (1978). *Forecasting: Methods and Applications,* John Wiley, London.

24

Chapter

Vital Statistics

People of a country and the world, as a whole, are more important than all other living beings. The human population plays a very important role in the development of a country. Hence, its study is very important. **Demography** is the science which pertains to the study of population. Demography covers a large number of aspects concerning the human population like births, age, sex, caste, literacy and educational level, workers and non-workers, income patterns, marital status, natality and fecundity, immigration and emigration, diseases, deaths, etc. Such studies reveal a number of facts and figures which help in the planning so as to achieve the desired socio-economic standards. For centuries, many theories have been propounded regarding population growth. The Malthusian theory is one of the most famous theories. This theory is based on the meticulous proposition that population, when unchecked, increases in a geometrical ratio while subsistence increases only in an arithmetical ratio. If population grows in a geometrical ratio, it is inevitable that the population would ultimately outstrip the available resources. Food grains, particularly, will become scarce and population growth would not be limited by any means other than starvation. Hence, the study of population is a must.

Demography has many facets, and vital statistics is one of them. Vital statistics deal exclusively with marriages, births, morbidity and deaths of the human population. These factors are mainly responsible for population growth. In other words, we limit our discussion to population growth. For a marked region, immigration and emigration affect population growth and thus these two factors also come within the purview of vital statistics. Births depend on the age at marriage, fertility and fecundity— still births, infant mortality and birth intervals are some other factors responsible for the growth rate.

Deaths due to epidemics like the plague, cholera, small pox, malaria, dengue, etc., and fatal diseases like cancer, tuberculosis and heart diseases cannot be ruled out. In the last few decades, a check has been made on the spread of epidemics like the plague, cholera and small pox. But many other diseases are still prevalent among the masses. Tuberculosis and cancer are taking a great toll. Natural calamities like cyclones, earthquakes, floods and famines are no less disastrous. In the modern age, wars cause innumerable deaths within no time. However, discussion of these factors is out of the scope of this chapter. Of course, deaths due to various diseases are recorded to maintain vital statistics.

Nowadays, family planning is one of the most important programmes of the governments of various countries. In India, it has attracted the special attention of the government due to the population explosion. The study of vital statistics enables the government to assess the impact of family planning on population growth.

Though a general idea of vital statistics has been given in the preceding paragraphs, a few definitions of vital statistics are quoted below:

Definitions

Arthur Newsholme gave two definitions of vital statistics:

1. The branch of biometry which deals with data and the laws of human mortality, morbidity and demography.
2. Vital statistics may be interpreted in two ways—in a broader sense it refers to all types of population statistics collected by whatever mode, while in a narrower sense it refers only to the statistics derived from the registration of births, deaths and marriages.

According to Benjamin:

"Vital statistics are conventional numerical records of marriages, births, sickness and deaths by which the health and growth of a community may be studied."

From the above description, it is amply clear that vital statistics are useful to individuals, various agencies, medical sciences, business communities, planners, policy makers and researchers.

A judicious discussion of the factors which fall within the framework of vital statistics have been covered in this chapter.

Collection of Vital Statistics

There are five methods usually adopted for collecting data for vital statistics:

1. Registration method.
2. Census enumeration method.
3. Survey method.
4. Sample registration system.
5. Analytical method.

Registration Method

This method is a perpetual process which entails the registration of vital events such as births, marriages, deaths, etc. A large number of countries have adopted this system which is a legal binding on each individual. Registration is done with the proper authorities as appointed by the government of a country. In India, registration of births and deaths is compulsory by legislation, through an act known as 'The Registration of Births and Deaths Act, 1969'. It came into force throughout the country through a gazette notification in 1970. In case of birth, the information with regard to the date of birth, place, name of father, sex of the newborn, nationality, religion and profession of the parents has to be reported to the appropriate authority in the area. In case of death of a person, information in respect of date of death, name of the deceased, his/her father's/husband's name, place at which the death occurred, age, sex, marital status, religion, nationality, permanent address and cause of death has to be supplied to the registering authority. In the act, various terms are defined as follows:

Birth means live birth or still birth.

Live Birth means the complete expulsion or extraction from its mother of a product of conception, irrespective of the duration of pregnancy, which, after such expulsion or extraction, breathes or shows any other evidence of life. Each product of such birth is considered live born.

Still Birth means foetal death where a product of conceptions has attained at least the prescribed period of gestation.

Death means the permanent disappearance of all evidence of life at any time after live birth has taken place.

Foetal death means absence of all evidence of life prior to the complete expulsion or extraction from its mother of a product of conception, irrespective of the period of pregnancy.

The legal responsibility of giving the information in respect of births and deaths to the registering authority lies with the following persons:

(*a*) Head of the household, and in absence of any such person, the eldest male present therein during the said period.

(*b*) In case of births and deaths in a hospital, health centre, nursing home or other like institutions, the medical officer in charge or any person authorised by him on his behalf.

(*c*) In respect of births and deaths in a jail, the jailor incharge.

(*d*) In respect of births and deaths in a choultry, hostel, dharamsala, boarding house, lodging house, tavern, barrack, toddy shop or place of public resort, the person in charge thereof.

(*e*) In respect of a new-born child or dead body found deserted in a public place, the headman or other corresponding officer of the village, in case of a village, and the officer in charge of the local police station, elsewhere.

(*f*) In any other place, such person as may be prescribed.

The registration office issues a certificate on registration of a birth and/or death. This certificate is of great use. The birth certificate is a legal document and helps a person at the time of entering a school, taking a job, insurance policy and ration card. Similarly, a death certificate helps in getting insurance money and in disputes of land and property.

The registration method is easy in operation and very effective. Yet it suffers from the lacuna that a large number of births and deaths are not reported to the registration office as the law has not been enforced effectively.

Census Enumeration Method

A census presents a comprehensive profile of a country's population. Census operation are conducted in almost all countries at intervals of ten years. In a census, the enumeration of every individual of all habitational areas is carried out at a specific time. In India, the 1991 census record was updated by the enumeration from March 1 to March 5, 1991. So was the census 2001. Census enumeration usually covers data regarding age, sex, marital status, educational level, occupation, religion and other factors needed for vital statistics. But this information is available for the census year only. Hence, census data fail to produce vital statistics for intercensal years, whereas population growth rate is needed from time to time. Moreover, the data obtained in respect of births and deaths are not complete even for the census year. Hence, the census enumeration method fails to provide data suitable for vital statistics.

Survey Method

Ad hoc surveys are conducted in areas or regions where the system of recording births and deaths has not been functioning properly and efficiently. It becomes necessary, particularly in those areas where registration offices have not been established. The survey records make vital statistics available for that region.

Sampling Registration System (SRS)

Vital rates are needed from time to time for an idea of population growth, specially for the purpose of evaluation of family planning programmes in terms of their ultimate objective of reduction in fertility.

In organising the post enumeration check of a census, the continuing sample registration of births and deaths in a reasonably large sample covering all parts of the state or country has been taken as a useful source for recording information. Sample registration system is operated under the aegis of the Registrar General and Census Commissioner. In India, the sample registration system has been in operation since June 1967 in rural areas and since July 1968 in urban areas. Under this scheme, census blocks are selected by a random sampling method in rural and urban areas, separately, as sampling units. The sample covers less than one per cent of the rural and urban population. Regular information about births, marriages, deaths, etc., are collected by the recorders appointed for the purpose. Half-yearly enumeration is done for each family in the selected blocks, by a team of investigators. The anomalies found in the daily records and periodic enumeration are removed after revisiting the families under conflict by a totally new team of personnel. At present, several methods are built in SRS to aid full coverage. The scheme of permanent house marking has been introduced so that no households are missed at the time of half-yearly checking. All old sampling units have been gradually replaced by new ones based on the frame of the latest census. The following studies are undertaken by the sample registration unit:

At All National Level

(*a*) Infant mortality.
(*b*) Age-specific mortality rates in rural areas.
(*c*) Sampling variability of vital rates.

At State Level

(*a*) Differences in birth rates with education, religion and parity.
(*b*) Extent of institutional and domiciling event.
(*c*) Sex ratio of vital statistics.
(*d*) Seasonality in birth and death rates.

The types of events missed by the enumerator and supervisor are:

(*a*) Volume of migration in the sample area.
(*b*) Age and sex composition of the population in sample areas.
(*c*) Errors in matching.

The sample registration system is a continuous process for estimating the vital rates and is very effective besides certain lacunae. The SRS is designed to give estimates of urban and rural vital rates separately. The estimates of vital rates based on the records provided by SRS are a good barometer in the evaluation of family planning programmes.

Analytical Methods

It is generally not possible to conduct ad hoc surveys to assess the population at any period in between two censal years. The population estimates at a given time can be obtained without ad hoc surveys by mathematical methods. The estimates are based on the assumption that the population grows at a constant rate during the intercensal years. For example, given the birth and death rates, population growth may be estimated for an intercensal period. The number of births or deaths at a given time in a population sub-group can also be estimated. Analytical methods are algebraic methods which make use of available data without requiring any fresh survey. Some analytical methods are given below.

1. Estimation of population in a given intercensal year can be done by the formula,

$$\hat{P}_t = P_0 + \frac{n}{N}(P_1 - P_0) \qquad \text{...(24.1)}$$

where,

$\hat{P}_t$ – Estimated population at some intercensal year t.

P_0 – Population in the previous census.
P_1 – Population in the succeeding census.
N – Number of years between the censuses.
n – Number of years between the given year and the previous census year.
Formula (24.1) is a linear interpolation formula and yields good estimates provided population changes occur at a constant rate all over the intercensal years.

***Example* 24.1.** The population of Jaipur city, according to censuses 1991 and 2001, are 7,45,876 and 12,50,532 respectively.

1. The population estimate for the year 1995 is obtained by (24.1).

In this problem,

$$P_1 = 12{,}50{,}532,\ P_0 = 7{,}45{,}876,\ N = 10,\ n = 4.$$

Thus $$\hat{P}_t = 7{,}45{,}876 + \frac{4}{10}(12{,}50{,}532 - 7{,}45{,}876)$$

$$= 9{,}47{,}738.$$

2. Population for any intercensal year can be estimated provided accurate records regarding birth, deaths and migration are available. The formula is,

$$\hat{P}_t = P_0 + (B - D) + (I - E) \qquad \text{...(24.2)}$$

where,

$\hat{P}_t$ and P_0 are the same as in (24.1).

B – Total number of births during the period 0 to t.

D – Total number of deaths during the period 0 to t.
I – Total number of immigrants during the period 0 to t.
E – Total number of emigrants during the period 0 to t.

3. *Compound Interest Formula.* Population increase take place in a geometrical progression. In case, the population growth rate r is known, the population estimate at any time t can be obtained by the formula,

$$\hat{P}_t = P_0\,(1 + r)^n \quad \text{...(24.3)}$$

where, n is the number of years between 0 to t. $\hat{P}_t$ and P_0 have already been explained.

If r is not known, it can be estimated by using the formula given below.

Let P_n be the known population at any period subsequent to t. Then,

$$r = \sqrt[n]{\frac{P_n}{P_0}} - 1 \quad \text{...(24.3.1)}$$

where, n is the gap between period 0 and the end period.

***Example* 24.2.** The population of a town in two census years is as follows:

Year	*Population*
1981	54,892
2001	1,08,431

(*a*) The rate of increase in population per thousand per annum,

(*b*) The estimate of the population in 1995, and

(*c*) The estimate of the population in 2011;

(*a*) By formula (24.3.1),

$$r = \sqrt[30]{\frac{108431}{54892}} - 1$$

$$= \sqrt[30]{1.9754} - 1$$

$$\log (r + 1) = \frac{1}{30}\log(1.9754)$$

$$= \frac{0.2956}{30}$$

$$= 0.009853$$

Taking antilog,

$$r + 1 = 1.023$$

$$r = 0.023$$

The rate per thousand = 0.023 × 1000 = 23.

(*b*) The population estimate for 1995 from (24.3) is,

$$\hat{P}_{1995} = 54,892\ (1 + 0.023)^{24}$$

Taking log,

$$\log \hat{p} = \log 54,892 + 24 \log (1.023)$$
$$= 4.7395 + 0.2370$$
$$= 4.9765$$

Taking antilog,

$$\hat{P}_{1995} = 94,733$$

(*c*) Similarity as in part (*b*),

$$\hat{P}_{2011} = 54,892\ (1.023)^{36}$$
$$= 1,24,460$$

4. *Geometric Mean Formula.* The mid-year population between any two consecutive census years can be estimated by the geometric mean formula,

$$\hat{P}_{1-2} = \sqrt{P_1 \times P_2} \quad \text{...(24.4)}$$

where P_1 – Population at the first census.

P_2 – Population at the second census.

5. *Logistic Curve.* The logistic curve was originally developed by Verhulst and later studied by Pearl, R. and Read, L. The curve is also known as the *Pearl – Read curve.* The curve, in its simplest form, is given by

$$Y_c = \frac{K}{1+10^{a+bx}} \quad \text{...(24.5)}$$

where, Y_c – Estimated value of population.

$$K = \frac{2y_0y_1y_2 - y_1^2(y_0 + y_2)}{y_0y_2 - y_1^2}$$

$$a = \log \frac{K - y_0}{y_0}$$

$$b = \frac{1}{n} \log \frac{y_0(K - y_1)}{y_1 K - y_0}$$

where, x — the year for which the value has to be interpolated.

y_0 — Geometric mean of the first 3 years of the series.

y_1 — Geometric mean of the middle 3 years of the series.

y_2 — Geometric mean of the last 3 years of the series.

The theory propounded by Pearl and Read is not universally accepted. Moreover, this theory involves high level mathematics.

CALCULATION OF VITAL RATES

As a matter of fact, all the significant events related to life come under the category of vital statistics. Hence, the vital statistics rates are of prime importance and can be calculated by the formulae given ahead.

$$\text{Rate of vital event} = \frac{\text{No. of cases of the event under consideration}}{\text{Total population exposed to the risk of the event}} \quad ...(24.6)$$

The *rate of vital events* is mostly expressed on the basis of per thousand (‰) persons. Formula (24.6) may be considered a fundamental formula which leads to all the subsequent formulae.

MEASURES OF MORTALITY

The study of mortality can be made through the following death rates. Three types of death rate are calculated which enable us to know about the depletion of population. The rates are,

(1) Crude death rate.
(2) Specific death rate.
(3) Standardised death rate.

Crude Death Rate (C.D.R.)

This is the simplest type of death rate and is defined as the number of deaths in a specific community or region in a given period, preferably on a yearly basis, per thousand persons. The formula is,

$$\text{C.D.R.} = \frac{\text{No. of deaths in a specified area in the given period}}{\text{Total population of the area in that period}} \times 1000 \quad ...(24.7)$$

or $$\text{C.D.R.} = \frac{\text{No. of deaths in a year}}{\text{Annual mean population}} \times 1000 \quad ...(24.7.1)$$

$$= \frac{D_A}{T_A} \times 1000 \quad ...(24.7.2)$$

The formula for C.D.R. resembles to that for probability and thus C.D.R. gives the probability of death of a person belonging to the population under reference in the specified year. Here, the death rate is crude in the sense that no attention has been paid to the age and sex distribution of the population. The information revealed by C.D.R. is not complete. We know that the death rate is high in infants and old persons, but this has not been considered in C.D.R.

Specific Death Rate

Here the death rates are calculated for a section of the population exclusively. For instance, the death rates for males and females are calculated separately, the death rates for persons belonging to age groups, say 0 to 5 years, 5 to 15 years, 50 to 60 years, etc., are calculated.

The formula for specific death rate is,

$$\text{S.D.R.} = \frac{\text{No. of deaths in the specified section of the population in given period}}{\text{Mean population of the specified section in the given period.}} \times 1000 \quad ...(24.8)$$

$$= \frac{D_s}{P_s} \times 1000 \quad ...(24.8.1)$$

Specified death rate may be found for any section of the population. However, *Infant mortality rate* is usually calculated and may be formulated as given below.

$$\text{Infant mortality rate} = \frac{\begin{array}{c}\text{No. of deaths of children under one year of}\\ \text{age in a population in a given year}\end{array}}{\begin{array}{c}\text{No. of births in the same population}\\ \text{during the same year}\end{array}} \times 1000 \qquad ..(24.9)$$

Similarly, for the neonatal mortality rate, the number of deaths of children under one month are recorded in formula (24.9). Other things remain the same.

Specific death rates can be calculated for any age group, sex, religion, caste or community. There is no end to the type of specifications. Anyway, formula (24.8) can easily be applied with a slight modification in its numerator. S.D.R. reveals more glaring facts about various sections of a population than C.D.R. If the death rate is high in a particular age group, except very old age, measures can be taken to improve upon the situation. S.D.R's are very helpful in planning and research.

***Example* 24.3.** The number of live births and deaths of children under one year of age, in a city, in the year 1983 are reported as given below:

No. of births = 4721

No. of deaths = 101

The infant mortality rate by formula (24.9) is,

$$= \frac{101}{4721} \times 1000$$

$$= 21.39 \text{ per thousand.}$$

Standardized Death Rate (S_T.D.R.)

When it is required to compare the death rates of two regions or community, heterogeneity factors have to be removed. In the formulae for death rates, the overall population of the region plays a dominant role and, thus, causes heterogeneity. Hence, the population has to be standardized. For this, the population in various categories or groups of one region are taken as standard and death rates are calculated on the basis of this population classification alone.

For calculating the standardized death rate, the death rate of each group, obtained separately for each region, is multiplied by the respective population of the group of the standard region and summed up. This sum is divided by the total population of the standard region. The ratio so obtained is called the standardised death rate. The formula is,

$$S_T\text{.D.R} = \frac{\Sigma_x p_x^s D_x}{\Sigma_x P_x^s} \times 1000 \qquad ...(24.10)$$

where, P_x^s — Standard population for group x

D_x — Death rate for group x in the original, *i.e.*, S.D.R. for a region.

Σ_x — Summation overall groups.

The comparability of S_T.D.R. provides a logical solution of the problem and the conclusion whether the death rate of one region is lower or higher than the other is valid.

Sometimes one comes across a situation in which the S.D.R's of a population are not known but the distribution of population in various age groups is known. Hence, standard death rate cannot be calculated. In such a situation, an indirect approach is adopted which provides an approximate S_T.D.R. In this approach, known age-specific death rates, of a standard population are taken as standard values of age-specific death rates. First, a quantity known as the Index death rate (I.D.R.) of the population is calculated. The formula for index death rate is,

$$\text{I.D.R.} = \frac{\Sigma_x p_x^q D_x}{\Sigma_x P_x^q} \times 1000 \qquad \text{...(24.11)}$$

where, P_x^q – Population in the region under question for the group x.

D_x – Group specific death rate of the standard population.

Also calculated the crude death rate of the standard population. Calculate an adjustment factor A which is obtained by the formula,

$$A = \frac{\text{C.D.R. of Standard Population}}{\text{I.D.R.}} \qquad \text{...(24.12)}$$

The approximate standardised death rate of the population under consideration is calculated by the relation.

$$S_T\text{.D.R.} = \text{C.D.R.} \times \text{A} \qquad \text{...(24.13)}$$

***Example* 24.4.** The following are the data of two districts for the year 1981.

Age group (Years)	*District A*		*District B*		*Age S.D.R. Distt. A* D_x^a	*Age S.D.R. Distt. B* D_x^b
	Population	*No. of deaths*	*Population*	*No. of deaths*		
(1)	(2)	(3)	(4)	(5)	(6)	(7)
0 – 5	45,860	338	41,169	784	7.37	19.04
5 – 15	99,120	308	88,163	415	3.11	4.71
15 – 35	1,52,050	602	1,48,440	724	3.96	4.88
35 – 50	1,04,600	1,827	1,02,632	977	17.47	9.52
50 & above	2,14,770	2,885	1,98,887	1383	13.43	6.95
Total	6,16,400	5,960	5,79,291	4,283		

The computation of (*i*) the crude death rate, (*ii*) age specific death rates for both the districts and, (*iii*) the standard death rate, taking the population of district *A* as standard population, is shown below.

(*i*) The crude death rate for district *A* by formula (24.7) is,

$$\text{C.D.R.} = \frac{5{,}960}{6{,}16{,}400} \times 1000$$
$$= 9.67 ‰$$

The crude death rate for district B is,

$$\text{C.D.R.} = \frac{4{,}283}{5{,}79{,}291} \times 1000$$
$$= 7.39\ \text{‰}$$

(ii) Specific death rate for district A by formula (24.8) are,

Age group 0 – 5 $\quad \text{S.D.R.} = \dfrac{338}{45{,}860} \times 1000 = 7.37‰$

Age group 0 – 15, $\quad \text{S.D.R.} = \dfrac{308}{99{,}120} \times 1000 = 3.11\ ‰$

Age group 15 – 35, $\quad \text{S.D.R.} = \dfrac{602}{1{,}52{,}050} \times 1000 = 3.96\ ‰$

Age group 35 – 50, $\quad \text{S.D.R.} = \dfrac{1{,}827}{1{,}04{,}600} \times 1000 = 17.47\ ‰$

Age group 50 & above, $\quad \text{S.D.R.} = \dfrac{2{,}885}{2{,}14{,}770} \times 1000 = 13.43‰$

Similarly, the S.D.R's for district B are calculated and entered in column 7 alongwith the data.

(iii) Computation of standardised death rates has been explicated below:

Age group	*Standard Population*	*District A*		*District B*	
		S.D.R.		*S.D.R.*	
	P_x^s	D_x^a	$P_x^s \times D_x^a$	D_x^b	$P_x^s \times D_x^b$
(1)	(2)	(3)	(4)	(5)	(6)
0 – 5	45,860	7.37	3,37,988.2	19.04	8,73,174.4
5 – 15	99,120	3.11	3,08,263.2	4.71	4,66,855.2
15 – 35	1,52,050	3.96	6,02,118.0	4.88	7,42,004.0
35 – 50	1,04,600	17.47	18,27,362.0	9.52	9,95,792.0
50 & above	2,14,770	13.43	28,84,361.1	6.95	14,92,651.5
Total	6,16,400		59,60,092.5		45,70,477.1

The standard death rate for the district A, by formula (24.10), is,

$$S_T.\text{D.R.} = \frac{59{,}60{,}092.5}{6{,}16{,}400}$$
$$= 9.67\ ‰$$

Similarly, for district B,

$$S_T.\text{D.R.} = \frac{45{,}70{,}477.1}{6{,}16{,}400}$$
$$= 7.41\ ‰$$

The standardized death rate in district B is less than that in district A. Hence, it can be concluded that the health hazards in district B are less than that in district A.

MEASURES OF FERTILITY

Fertility rates are the barometer for the increase in population due to births in a specified period, usually a year.

The fertility rate may be defined as, "*The number of births to the women of child bearing or reproductive ages as against the total population.*"

The rates are expressed per thousand women capable of child bearing. In India's 1981 census, four questions relating to fertility were canvassed. The questions were about the age at marriage, number of surviving children, number of children ever born during the last one year. The last question was canvassed in case of newly married women. Different types of fertility rates are discussed adequately as given below.

(1) General fertility rate.
(2) Age specific fertility rate.
(3) General marital fertility rate.
(4) Age specific marital fertility rate.
(5) Total marital fertility rate.
(6) Total fertility rate.

General Fertility Rate (GFR)

This is defined as the number of children born alive per thousand women of child-bearing age (in India 15–49 years), in a year and region.

The formula is,

$$\text{GFR} = \frac{\text{No. of live births}}{\text{No. of women of child bearing age}} \times 1000 \qquad \ldots(24.14)$$

The fecundity of women in all age groups is not the same. Hence, for the control of population growth, the study of fertility rates of women in various age groups is of special interest. The marital status of women also has an impact on fertility rates. Hence, marital fertility rates and age specific fertility rates should have been studied in detail rather than being confined to the general fertility rate.

Age Specific Fertility Rate (ASFR)

In this, fertility rates are calculated separately for various age groups of females of child bearing age. The number of live births to women of a particular age group are taken into account, *e.g.*, 15–20, 20–25, and so on. Also, the population consists of the total number of females of that group alone. The age specific fertility rate may be defined as, "*The number of children born alive during a year, per thousand women of a particular age group.*"

The formula is,

$$\text{ASFR} = \frac{\begin{array}{c}\text{No. of live births to women in the age}\\ \text{group } x \text{ to } (x+c)\end{array}}{\begin{array}{c}\text{Average no. of women in the age}\\ \text{group } x \text{ to } (x+c)\end{array}} \times 1000 \qquad \ldots(24.15)$$

***Example* 24.5.** The female population and live births with age of mother, in 1979, of a country, are given below. General fertility rates and age specific fertility rates have been calculated.

Age group (years)	*Female population*	*Live births*
15 – 19	1,16,410	10,468
20 – 24	1,13,610	16,983
25 – 29	1,02,930	12,522
30 – 34	93,300	7,083
35 – 39	73,920	3,456
40 – 44	62,700	1,140
Total	5,62,870	51,652

The general fertility rate by formula (24.14) is,

$$\text{GFR} = \frac{51{,}652}{5{,}62{,}870} \times 1000$$
$$= 91.76 \text{ ‰}.$$

Age specific fertility rates are calculated by the formula (24.15).

Age group	*ASFR*
15 – 19	$\frac{10{,}468}{1{,}16{,}410} \times 1000 = 89.92$ ‰
20 – 24	$\frac{16{,}983}{1{,}13{,}610} \times 1000 = 149.48$ ‰
25 – 29	$\frac{12{,}522}{1{,}02{,}930} \times 1000 = 121.65$ ‰
30 – 34	$\frac{7.083}{93{,}300} \times 1000 = 75.92$ ‰
35 – 39	$\frac{3{,}456}{73{,}920} \times 1000 = 46.75$ ‰
39 – 44	$\frac{1{,}140}{62{,}700} \times 1000 = 18.18$ ‰

The above ASFR's show the maximum fertility rate in the age group 20–24 years.

General Marital Fertility Rate (GMFR)

This type of fertility rate is slightly different from the general fertility rate. In GMFR, the population of married women of child bearing age only is considered, whereas in GFR, all women of child bearing age are taken into consideration. The general marital fertility rate can be defined as, "*The number of children born alive during a year per thousand married women of child bearing age.*"

The formula is,

$$GMFR = \frac{\text{No. of live births to married women}}{\text{No. of married women of child bearing age}} \times 1000 \qquad ...(24.16)$$

As fertility varies in various age groups of married women, it is preferable to calculate the age specific marital fertility rate.

Age Specific Marital Fertility Rate

(ASMFR) Fertility rates are considered only for married women of a specific age group. It may be defined as, " *The number of children born alive during a given year, per thousand married women of a particular age group.*"

The formula is,

$$ASMFR = \frac{\text{No. of live births to married women in the age group } x \text{ to } (x+c)}{\text{Average no. of married women in the age group } x \text{ to } (x+c)} \times 100 \qquad ...(24.17)$$

***Example* 24.6.** If we consider the data given in example (24.5) as if the female population consists of married women, the GMFR and ASMFR are the same as the GFR and ASFR.

Total Marital Fertility Rate (TMFR)

This rate gives the total number of children that would have been born alive per thousand married women, had the current schedule of age specific marital fertility rates been applicable for the entire child bearing period. It is calculated as the sum of age specific marital fertility rates in the age groups x to $(x + c)$ multiplied by c where c is the interval.

The formula for this may be given as,

$$TMFR = \text{Sum of ASMFR} \times c \qquad ...(24.18)$$

Total Fertility Rate (TFR)

In this type of fertility rate all females of reproductive age are considered. It may be defined as, "*The total number of children that would have been born alive per thousand women, had the current schedule of age specific fertility rates been applicable for the entire child bearing period.*"

It is calculated as the sum of age specific fertility rates in the age group x to $(x + c)$ multiplied by c where, c is the interval. Thus,

$$TFR = \text{sum of ASFR} \times c \qquad ...(24.19)$$

***Example* 24.7.** The following are the fertility rates in Rajasthan (India) in various age groups of women of child bearing age for the census year 1981.

Age group	:	15–19	20–24	25–29	30–34	35–39	40–44	45–49
Fertility rate	:	73	270	290	237	166	93	40

The sum of the fertility rates

$= (73 + 270 + 290 + 237 + 166 + 93 + 40)$

$= 1169$

Class interval c $= 5.$

Total fertility rate by formula (24.19) is,

$$TFR = 1169 \times 5 = 5845 \text{ per thousand woman of child bearing age}$$
$$= 5.845 \text{ per woman of child bearing age.}$$

The total fertility rate per woman may be interpreted as the average number of children produced by a woman in her entire child-bearing span of life.

Fertility rates can be worked out for different religions and regions separately to make comparisons. Such comparisons reveal interesting facts, like TFR for Jains is much lower than for Hindus and Muslims. Particularly in India, fertility rates are not very accurate as many sensitive questions on births are not canvassed in case of single, divorced or widow-women. These might have given birth during the last one year but such births are not recorded in census operations. Women who died in the last year but gave birth are also omitted. All these limitations lead to under-estimation of fertility rates. Anyway, fertility rates presented after any census or obtained for intencensal periods are indicative of broad trends rather than actual levels. Such information is good enough for chalking out family planning operations, population projections, estimation of demand of various commodities, etc.

LIFE TABLE

Concept

A life table exhibits the numbers living and dying at each age, on the basis of the experience of a cohort. It also gives the probability of dying and living separately. The probability of dying manifests the mortality rate. The life table is mainly based on the assumption that the cohort experiences the age specific mortality in the population under consideration. More so, the deaths are evenly distributed over the whole year. The life table also reveals the expectation of life at any stage or age. A life table is essentially a more detailed expression of mortality rates.

Ulpian's life table, consisting of a series of values diminishing with increasing age, came into existence first. But the manner in which it was constructed and its purpose, was uncertain. Valid life tables were developed only at the end of the eighteenth century, for the purpose of life assurance. It was soon realised that the mortality rate is not the same in all age groups. Hence, age specific mortality rates were taken into consideration. Also, the mortality rates were found to differ widely for male and female populations. Hence, life tables are prepared separately for both sexes.

Uses of Life Table

(1) Life tables are of maximum utility to actuaries to work out the rate of premium for persons of different age groups.

(2) Population projections may be construed by age and sex with the help of life tables. The life table for any specific section of the society can be prepared and used to deduce many conclusions about population growth, specific death rate, etc., of that section of society.

(3) A life table clearly depicts the distribution of people according to age which is useful for planning in respect of education, employment, availability of persons for labour and military forces, etc.

(4) The life table helps to assess the accuracy of census figures, death and birth registrations.

(5) The computation of measure of intrinsic natural increase, such as net production rate and the true rate of natural increase, makes use of life tables.
(6) It helps to evaluate the impact of family planning on population growth.
(7) How far the new scientific inventions, sophisticated medical treatment and better living conditions have increased the span of life can be assessed through life tables.
(8) Estimates of migration can also be made from life tables.

Construction of a Life Table

As expressed earlier, life tables depict the mortality vis-a-vis survival rate of cohorts or groups of people. George Barclay has rightly defined it as, "*The life table is a life history, as it diminishes gradually by deaths. The record begins at the birth of each member and continues until all have died.*"

A life table usually begins with a population of one lakh people or any other convenient figure like 10,000, 1000, etc. This figure is known as the *radix* of the table. A life table consists of eight columns as expressed below.

(1) The age in years = x
(2) Persons living at age $x = l_x$
(3) Dying between age x and $x + 1 = d_x = l_x - l_{x+1}$
(4) Prob. of dying between age x and $x + 1 = q_x = \dfrac{d_x}{l_x}$
(5) Prob. of surviving between age x and $x + 1 = p_x = 1 - q_x = \dfrac{l_{x+1}}{l_x}$
(6) Living between age x and $x + 1 = L_x = \dfrac{l_x + l_{x+1}}{2} = l_x - \dfrac{1}{2}dx$
(7) Living above the age $x = T_x = L_x + L_{x+1} + ... = L_x + T_{x+1}$
(8) Expectation of life at age $x = e_x^0 = T_x / l_x$

Each symbol has been further explicated so that one makes their correct usage.

x — Exact age in years till last birthday.

l_x — the number of survivors at the exact age x out of the initial cohort which is usually taken 1,00,000.

d_x — the number of deaths in the interval x to $(x + 1)$ in the initial cohort. (The interval taken can be more than one year also if desired). It gives the number of those who could celebrate their xth birthday but not the $(x + 1)$th birthday.

q_x — It is the proportion of persons dying between the ages of x and $x + 1$ to the number of persons alive at the age of x, *i.e.*, at the beginning of the interval.

p_x — It gives the proportion of persons surviving upto the end of the interval, *i.e.*, at age $(x + 1)$ years to the number of persons alive at the beginning of the interval, *i.e.*, at age x.
Either a person will die or remain alive. Therefore, $p_x + q_x = 1$ or $p_x = 1 - q_x$.

L_x — The number of persons lived between the age x and $(x + 1)$ in the hypothetical life table stationary population.

T_x — The number of years lived by the cohort after x years of age. In other words, T_x denotes the total future years lived by l_x persons of the cohort who have attained age x.

e_x^0— The average remaining life time. It gives the average number of years a person of age x is likely to survive under the existing mortality rate.

Assumptions. Certain assumptions are made while constructing a life table.

They are:

(*i*) There is no effect of immigration and emigration on the cohort. It means that the reduction in number of the initial cohort is merely due to deaths.

(*ii*) The deaths occurring in between two consecutive birthdays are evenly distributed.

(*iii*) The deaths recorded for a cohort through any method are correct without any errors and omissions.

(*iv*) The cohort begins with a convenient figure of 1,00,000 ; 10,000 ; 1,000 ; etc. Now a life table is presented to understand its working for live data.

Single year age returns and number of deaths are obtained from census data. The age returns for each year are converted to the base 1,00,000 and, accordingly, the data for mortality are adjusted. Third to eighth columns of the life table are prepared as per the clarifications of the symbols. The table is self-explanatory.

Table 24.1 Life Table

x	l_x	d_x	q_x	p_x	L_x	T_x	e_x^0
(*i*)	(*ii*)	(*iii*)	(*iv*)	(*v*)	(*vi*)	(*vii*)	(*viii*)
0	1,00,000	9,872	.09872	.90128	95,064	57,68,318	57.68
1	90,128	3,939	.04370	.95630	88,158	56,73,254	62.95
2	86,189	2,654	.03079	.96921	84,862	55,85,096	64.80
3	83,535	2,476	.02964	.97036	82,297	55,00,234	65.84
4	81,059	1,772	.02186	.97814	80,173	54,17,937	66.84
5	79,287	1,234	.01556	.98444	78,670	53,37,764	67.32
6	78,053	987	.01264	.98736	77,560	52,59,094	67.38
7	77,066	765	.00993	.99007	76,684	51,81,534	67.24
8	76,301	477	.00625	.99375	76,062	51,04,850	66.90
9	75,824	462	.00609	.99391	75,593	50,28,788	66.32
10	75,362	418	.00555	.99445	75,153	49,53,195	65.72
.	.	.	.	.	.	.	.
.	.	.	.	.	.	.	.
.	.	.	.	.	.	.	.
96	371	158	.42588	.57412	292	788	2.12
97	267	104	.38951	.61049	215	496	1.86
98	210	57	.27143	.72857	182	281	1.34
99	181	29	.16022	.83978	166	99	0.55

***Example* 24.8.** A life table with two years age returns with certain missing values is presented below.

Age (years)	l_x	d_x	p_x	q_x	L_x	T_x	e_x^0
35	9,345	?	?	?	?	1,63,819	?
36	9,243	149	?	?	?	?	?

The life table has been completed using the relationship of unknown terms with other terms.

$$d_{35} = 9,345 - 9,243 = 102$$

$$q_{35} = \frac{102}{9,345} = 0.0109, \; p_{35} = 1 - 0.0109 = 0.9891$$

$$q_{36} = \frac{149}{9,243} = 0.0161, \; p_{36} = 1 - 0.0161 = 0.9839$$

$$L_{35} = 9,345 - \frac{1}{2} \times 102 = 9,294$$

$$L_{36} = 9,243 - \frac{1}{2} \times 149 = 9,168.5$$

$$T_{36} = T_{35} - L_{35} = 1,63,819 - 9,294 = 1,54,525$$

$$e_{35}^0 = \frac{1,63,819}{9,345} = 17.53$$

$$e_{36}^0 = \frac{1,54,525}{9,243} = 16.72$$

Substituting the values of unknown terms, the complcted life table is,

Age (years)	l_x	d_x	p_x	q_x	L_x	T_x	e_x^0
35	9,345	102	.9891	.0109	9,294	1,63,819	17,53
36	9,243	149	.9839	.0161	9,168.5	1,54,525	16.72

MEASURES OF POPULATION GROWTH

The growth of the population of a country or region can be measured by the following methods:

(1) Crude rate of natural increase
(2) Vital index
(3) Gross reproduction rate.
(4) Net reproduction rate.
(5) Replacement index.

Crude Rate of Natural Increase

This is the simplest kind of measure of population growth and can easily be obtained by subtracting the crude death rate (CDR) from the crude birth rate (CBR). This is also known as the *crude rate of natural survival.* Symbolically,

The crude rate of natural increase = CBR – CDR.

In case the total number of births and deaths of a country or region for a given year are known, then the annual crude rate of natural increase can be calculated by the formula,

$$\text{Annual crude rate of natural increase} = \frac{\text{Total birth} - \text{Total death}}{\text{Mid-year population}} \times 1000 \quad ...(24.20)$$

***Example* 24.9.** The following are the figures for the year 1982 obtained from the sample registration system under operation in Rajasthan.

Mid-year population = 3,52,72,000

Total births = 1,87,236

Total deaths = 72,299

The annual crude rate of natural increase by formula (24.20) is,

$$= \frac{187236 - 72299}{3,52,72,000} \times 1000$$

$$= \frac{114937}{3,52,72,000} \times 1000$$

= 3.26 per thousand persons

Vital Index

This is an index which takes into account the two most vital events, namely, births and deaths. For a specific period and region, the vital index is given by the formula,

$$\text{Vital index} = \frac{\text{Total births}}{\text{Total deaths}} \quad ...(24.21)$$

The vital index may be equal to 1 or less than 1 or greater than 1. The value 1 indicates stagnation in population growth. A value greater than 1 throws light on the expected increase in population whereas a value less than 1 is indicative of a decline in the population.

Gross Reproduction Rate (GRR)

Fertility rates include the birth of children of both the sexes. But the population growth depends mainly on the birth of female children who are the future mothers. Hence, population growth is mainly a function of the fertility rate, restricted to female children. The demographic year book published by United Nations, 1954, has defined GRR as, "*The gross reproduction rate indicates the average number of daughters who would be born to a group of girls beginning life together in a population where none died before the upper limit of child bearing age and where the given set of fertility rates was in operation.*"

If S_{ix} is the fertility rate at age x, restricted to the births of the female infants, the function $\sum_{x=0}^{n} S_{i_x}$ is called the GRR, where n is the upper child bearing age. GRR is based on the assumptions,

(*i*) There is no mortality of newly born female children till they attain the highest reproductive age. In India this is 49 years.

(*ii*) There are no gains or losses due to migration.

(*iii*) The current fertility rate is maintained till their highest child-bearing age.

In other words, the GRR is the sum of age specific birth rates of women of child-bearing age restricted to female births only. The working formula for GRR may be written as,

$$\text{GRR} = \frac{\begin{array}{c}\text{No. of daughters}\\ \text{expected to be borned to 1000 newly born}\\ \text{girls under the current ASFR without}\\ \text{mortality and with no migration}\end{array}}{1000} \quad ...(24.22)$$

All GRR may be calculated from the formula,

$$\text{GRR} = \text{TFR} \times \frac{\text{No. of female births}}{\text{Total births}} \quad ...(24.23)$$

$$= \text{TFR} \times \frac{B_g}{B} \quad ...(24.23.1)$$

GRR is usually given for female births. But male births have an equal role in the reproduction system. Hence, the GRR for males can also be calculated in a like manner.

***Example* 24.10.** The demographic year book published by the United Nations (1978–80) gives the following figures for female births and the total number of births in Sweden for the year 1979.

No. of female births = 46,842

Total births = 96,255

Taking the total fertility rate = 3.6, the gross reproduction rate by the formula (24.23) is,

$$\text{GRR} = 3.6 \times \frac{46842}{96255}$$

$$= 1.75$$

Net Reproduction Rate (NRR)

It is clear from the description of gross reproduction rate that it has its significance in relation to the replacement of one generation by the next one. This replacement may be towards increasing the population or decreasing it. But the GRR overestimates the next generation as the loss due to mortality was ignored and it was assumed that all the newborn female children attain their maximum reproductive age. This made the GRR quite artificial. Of course, other losses like migration, unmarried persons, etc., do affect the next generation. But these factors are not so important as mortality. Hence, by making use of the life table, it is possible to make some allowance for mortality losses and obtain the reproduction rate which is devoid of the losses due to mortality. The net reproduction rate, as defined in the Demographic year book, United Nations, 1954 is, "*The net reproduction rate may be interpreted as the average number of daughters that would be produced by women throughout their life-time if they were exposed at each age to the fertility and mortality rates on which the calculation is based.*"

From the above discussion, it is evident that NRR measures the extent to which the female infants, who continue to survive their maximum reproductive age, can reproduce infants of the same sex. The formula for net reproduction rate is,

$$\text{NRR} = \sum_{\substack{all\,age\\groups}} \left(\frac{B_g}{P_g} \times S \right) \times \text{class interval of the age group} \qquad ...(24.24)$$

where, B_g — No. of female infants born to women of specific reproductive age groups.

P_g — No. of women in each specific reproductive age group.

S — Survival rate p_x per woman, which is obtained from the life table.

In brief, vital statistics is mainly concerned with births and deaths. The accountability of births and deaths depends on the effectiveness of the registration system. Incompleteness of registration of births and deaths, in spite of the existing laws, has made it difficult to give a correct picture of fertility and mortality rates. In the absence of such correct and up-to-date information, all other statistical estimates also produce a distorted picture of the present population and population projections. The life table, which depends entirely on the number of deaths, also leads to faulty conclusions due to the lack of accurate data regarding the number of deaths. Anyway, more and more emphasis on the registration system is improving the vital statistics. Whatever vital statistics are available, they provide enough reliable information for planning.

Vital statistics have many aspects. The salient facets are covered in this chapter. For greater details, readers are advised to go through various books and reports on vital statistics.

QUESTIONS AND EXERCISES

1. What are the areas covered by vital statistics?
2. Why is vital statistics so important in national life?
3. Define vital statistics.
4. Write short notes on:
   (*a*) Analytical methods of estimation of population.
   (*b*) Sample registration system.
   (*c*) Standardised death rate.
   (*d*) General marital fertility rate.
   (*e*) Life table.
5. Differentiate between the following:
   (*a*) Crude death rate and specific death rate.
   (*b*) Gross and net reproduction rate.
   (*c*) General fertility rate and total fertility rate.
6. (*a*) Define crude and specific death rates. Explain why the mortality situations of two places cannot usually be compared. Describe, in this connection, the construction and usefulness of standardised death rates.
   (*b*) Distinguish between crude and specific birth and death rates. How are the two types of rates calculated? What are their uses?
   (B.A. (Econ. Hons.), Calcutta, 1975)

7. Explain the gross and net production rate. Discuss their suitability as measures of fertility. *(B.A. (Econ. Hons.), Delhi 1976)*

8. Explain the concepts of crude death rates and standardised death rates. Why is standardisation necessary for comparing mortality in different populations?
How does one select a standard population? What would you choose as the standard population for comparing the mortality levels of Madhya Pradesh and Uttar Pradesh? *(B. Com., Bombay, 1976)*

9. The population and deaths of two towns, according to age groups, are given below.

	Town X		*Town Y*	
Age group	*Population*	*No. of deaths*	*Population*	*No. of deaths*
Under 5	6,040	215	93,000	904
5–15	12,645	241	1,54,100	523
15–35	13,300	294	1,86,200	618
35–50	4,625	362	81,900	1237
over 50	6,710	463	64,800	1475

Calculate (*i*) the crude death rates, (*ii*) standardised death rates taking the population of Town *X* as standard population and compare their health conditions.

10. Given the following information about a city.

Mid-year population	*Total live births*	*Total deaths*
1,96,200	13,071	3,048

Calculate the crude rate of natural increase.

11. Complete the following incomplete life table.

Age (years)	l_x	d_x	q_x	p_x	L_x	T_x	e_x^0
72	4,412	×	×	×	×	×	×
73	3,724	×	×	×	×	×	×
74	3,201	642	×	×	×	26,567	×

12. From the following figures, calculate the gross and net reproduction rates.

Age group (years)	*No. of female children born to 1000 women*	*Per cent survival rate*
15–19	200	85
20–24	365	80
25–29	300	70
30–34	188	65
35–39	115	60
40–44	42	50
45–49	5	45

13. The following data pertain to the female population and number of live births in different age groups of reproductive age. Calculate the general and specific fertility rates.

Age group:	15-19	20-24	25-29	30-34	35-39	40-44	Total
Female population:	29,240	24,565	21,138	18,319	15,661	13,035	1,21,958
No. of live births:	2,046	6,313	5,792	4,048	2,380	1,094	21,673

14. Estimate the standard death rate for the following two countries.

Age group (years)	*Death rate per 1,000*		*Standardised population in lakhs*
	Country I	*Country II*	
0 – 4	10.1	5.0	100
5 – 14	1.0	2.0	200
15 – 24	1.4	1.0	190
25 – 34	2.0	1.0	180
35 – 44	3.3	2.0	120
45 – 54	7.0	5.0	100
55 – 64	15.0	12.0	70
65 – 74	40.0	35.0	30
75 and over	120.0	110.0	10

(*B.A.(Hons.), Delhi, 1973*)

15. From the data given below, calculate the gross reproduction rate, assuming that for the given population, the ratio of female babies to total birth is 48.8 %.

Age group (years)	16–20	21–25	26–30	31–35	36–40	41–45	46–50
Fertility rate per 1000 women:	19	173	253	201	157	67	9

(*M. Com., Delhi, 1962*)

16. Fill up the blanks in a portion of a life table given below:

Age	l_x	d_x	p_x	q_x	L_x	T_x	e
4	95,000	500	×	×	×	48,50,300	×
5	×	400	×	×	×	×	×

(*M. Com., Delhi, 1973*)

17. What do you understand by net reproduction rate? Calculate such rate from the following data—

Age group of child bearing females	*No. of female children born to 1000 women passing through each age group*	*No of survivors out of each 1000 female children*
15 – 20	50	850
20 – 25	180	800
25 – 30	450	750
30 – 35	500	700
35 – 40	300	650
40 – 45	100	600
45 – 50	40	500
15 – 50	1620	

(*T.D.C. (Final) Com., Raj., 1972*)

18. From the data given below, calculate the gross reproduction rate assuming that the ratio of female births to total birth is 49 %.

Age group:						
16–20	21–25	26–30	31–35	36–40	41–45	46–50
Fertility rate per 1000 women:						
20	170	242	200	167	69	9

(*M.Com., Delhi, 1980*)

19. Which of the two places, for which mortality data are given below, is in your opinion more healthy?

Age group	*Locality A*		*Locality B*	
	Standard population	*Population deaths*	*Local population*	*Population deaths*
Under 5	4,500	135	4,000	144
5–15	10,000	40	10,500	63
15–65	12,500	75	13,500	81
above 65	3,000	140	2,000	102
Total	30,000	390	30,000	390

(*B. Com., Madras, 1977*)

20. Compute the crude and standardised death rates of the two population *A* and *B* from the following data.

Age group (years)	*A*		*B*	
	Population	*Deaths*	*Population*	*Deaths*
Below 5	15,000	360	40,000	1,000
5–30	20,000	400	52,000	1,040
above 30	10,000	280	8,000	240
Total	45,000	1,040	1,00,000	2,280

(*B.Com., Andhra, 1977*)

SUGGESTED READING

Cassen, R.H. (1979). *India: Population, Economy and Society,* The Macmillan Company of India, Delhi.

Census of India, 1981-Publications.

Cox, P.R. (1979). *Demography*, Vikas Publishing House, Delhi.

Freeman, D. et al. (1988). *The Life History Calendar : A Technique for Collecting Retrospective Data in Sociological Methodology*, Vol. 18, pp. 37-68, Edited by C. Clogg., American Sociological Association, Washington D.C.

Kohli, K.L. (1977). *Mortality in India (Statewise study),* Sterling Publishers, Delhi.

Norman J. Ornstein, Thomas E. Mann and Michael J. Malbin (2002). *Vital Statistics on Congress 2001-2002*, American Enterprise Institutes.

Appendix A
Mathematics for Statistics

A-1 INTRODUCTION TO SET THEORY

Consider a collection of certain objects, items or numbers, so large that it includes all objects under reference. Each object of this collection is called an element or a point. The collection of all these elements or points is called a *space* or a universe set. For example, the collection of books in a shelf is the space, whereas each book in the shelf is an element of the space or a set. Suppose x is an element of a set A. Symbolically, it is denoted as $x \in A$ ($\in$ – belongs to). Similarly, if the element x is not an element in the set A, is denoted as $x \notin A$. ($\notin$ – does not belong to).

Subset If there are two sets A and B, such that every element of set B is also the element of A, B is said to be a subset of A. It is denoted as $B \subset A$ ($\subset$ – contained in) or $A \supset B$ ($\supset$ – contains).

If A and B are such that $A \subset B$ and $B \subset A$, the set A and B are said to be equal or equivalent.

Null Set If a set contains no element, it is known as *null set* or an *empty set* and is denoted by ϕ.

Complementary Set Suppose Ω is the space and A is any set in Ω. The complementary set of A is set of those points, which are in Ω but not in A. A complementary set is denoted by A', $\overline{A}$ or $A^c \equiv \Omega - A$.

Disjoint Sets Suppose A and B are two subsets of Ω. Then the sets A and B are said to be disjoint if there is no element in common to A and B, i.e. $A \cap B = \phi$ ($\cap$ – intersection).

Operations of Sets

Union of Sets Suppose A and B are two sets such that each is a subset of Ω, then the set of all those points, which contains the elements of A, B and common to both, is defined as the union of sets A and B. It is denoted as $A \cup B$ ($\cup$ – union). The concept of union can be extended to any number of sets in Ω.

Intersection of Two Sets Suppose A and B are two sets, both in Ω. Then the set of all those points which are in A are also in B and vice-versa, is known as intersection of two sets. It is denoted as $A \cap B$ or AB.

Difference Set Suppose A and B are two sets in Ω. The set of all those points of A, that are not in B, is known as a difference set and is denoted by $(A - B)$. In other words this a set of all those points of A which exclude the elements of A which are common with B.

Laws on Sets

Here we shall use A, B, C for sets that are subsets of Ω. All the notations given above shall be used without explanation in these laws.

Commutative Laws

(*i*) $A \cup B = B \cup A$

(*ii*) $A \cap B = B \cap A$

This law can be extended to any number of subsets of Ω.

Associative Laws

(*i*) $A \cap (B \cup C) = (A \cap B) \cup (A \cap C)$

(*ii*) $A \cup (B \cap C) = (A \cup B) \cap (A \cup C)$

Law of Identity

$A \cup \phi = A = \phi \cup A$

Idempotent Laws

(*i*) $A \cup A = A$

(*ii*) $A \cap A = A$

Complement Laws

(*i*) $A \cup A' = \Omega$

(*ii*) $A \cap A' = \phi$

DeMorgan's Laws

(*i*) $(A \cup B)' = A' \cap B'$

(*ii*) $(A \cap B)' = A' \cup B'$

Double Complementation

$(A')' = A$

A-2 MATRICES AND DETERMINANTS

Matrix

A matrix is a rectangular arrangement of pq elements in rows and columns. The element a_{ij} of a matrix A is the (i, j)-th positional entry in the rectangular array, i.e. it is an element belonging to the ith row and j th column. In full, matrix A will be denoted as given below.

$$A_{p\times q}=\begin{bmatrix} a_{11} & a_{12}\ldots a_{1j}\ldots a_{1q} \\ a_{21} & a_{22}\ldots a_{2j}\ldots a_{2q} \\ a_{31} & a_{32}\ldots a_{3j}\ldots a_{3q} \\ \vdots & \\ a_{i1} & a_{i2}\ldots a_{ij}\ldots a_{iq} \\ \vdots & \\ a_{p1} & a_{p2}\ldots a_{pj}\ldots a_{pq} \end{bmatrix} \quad \ldots\text{(A-2.1)}$$

$$= [a_{ij}]_{p\times q}$$

for $i = 1, 2, ..., p$
$j = 1, 2, ..., q$

The matrix A is said to be of the order $(p \times q)$. It means that the matrix A has p rows and q columns.

Properties of a Matrix

(*i*) If the number of rows of a matrix are equal to its number of columns, i.e. $p = q$, it is said to be a *square matrix.*

(*ii*) If (i, j) th entry in a matrix A is same as (j, i) th entry, i.e., $a_{ij} = a_{ji}$, it is said to be a *symmetric matrix.*

(*iii*) If in a matrix, A, $a_{ij} = -a_{ji}$, it is said to be a *skew symmetric* or *asymmetric matrix.*

(*iv*) A matrix of order $(p \times 1)$ is known as a *column vector* and is denoted as a'. A matrix of order $(1 \times q)$ is known as a row vector and is denoted as a. In full form, the column and row vectors can be written as given below.

$$a'=\begin{bmatrix} a_1 \\ a_2 \\ a_3 \\ \vdots \\ a_p \end{bmatrix};\ a=[a_1,a_2,\cdots,a_q]$$

(*v*) A square matrix, which has all entries zero, excepting diagonal entries, is called a *diagonal matrix.* For example,

$$A=\begin{bmatrix} d_1 & 0 & 0 \\ 0 & d_2 & 0 \\ 0 & 0 & d_3 \end{bmatrix} \quad \ldots\text{(A-2.2)}$$

(*vi*) A square matrix, which has all its diagonal elements unity and the off-diagonal elements zero, is said to be a *unit* or *identity matrix.* Unit matrix is denoted by I.

Thus a unit matrix of order (4 × 4) is,

$$I = \begin{bmatrix} 1 & 0 & 0 & 0 \\ 0 & 1 & 0 & 0 \\ 0 & 0 & 1 & 0 \\ 0 & 0 & 0 & 1 \end{bmatrix} \qquad \text{...(A-2.3)}$$

(*vii*) A matrix with all its elements zero is said to be a null matrix and is denoted by 0. Thus, a null matrix of order (3 × 3) is,

$$O = \begin{bmatrix} 0 & 0 & 0 \\ 0 & 0 & 0 \\ 0 & 0 & 0 \end{bmatrix} \qquad \text{...(A-2.4)}$$

(*viii*) A matrix A' obtained by interchanging the rows and columns of A, is called the transpose of A, In other words, if the rows of a matrix A are written as columns and columns as rows, the matrix so obtained is called the transpose of A. For example, if

$$A = \begin{bmatrix} a_{11} & a_{12} & a_{13} \\ a_{21} & a_{22} & a_{23} \\ a_{31} & a_{32} & a_{33} \end{bmatrix}; \; A' = \begin{bmatrix} a_{11} & a_{21} & a_{31} \\ a_{12} & a_{22} & a_{32} \\ a_{13} & a_{23} & a_{33} \end{bmatrix} \qquad \text{...(A-2.5)}$$

Operations on Matrices

Scalar Multiplication If a matrix A is multiplied by a scalar quantity c, each element of the matrix A is multiplied by c. In the expanded form,

$$cA_{p \times q} = \begin{bmatrix} ca_{11} & ca_{12} & ca_{1q} \\ ca_{21} & ca_{22} & ca_{2q} \\ \vdots & & \vdots \\ ca_{p1} & ca_{p2} & ca_{pq} \end{bmatrix} = [ca_{ij}] \qquad \text{...(A-2.6)}$$

Addition of Two Matrices Two matrices A and B can be added if they are of the same order. Suppose $A_{p \times q} = [a_{ij}]$ and $B_{p \times q} = [b_{ij}]$, then the elements of the matrix $(A + B)$ are $[a_{ij} + b_{ij}]$. If the matrices A and B are of the order $(p \times q)$, the order of the matrix $(A + B)$ shall also be $(p \times q)$. Also,

$$A + B = B + A \qquad \text{...(A-2.7)}$$

$$(A + B)' = A' + B' \qquad \text{...(A-2.8)}$$

Multiplication of Two Matrices The product AB of two matrices A and B is possible only when the number of columns, in the premultiplying matrix A, is equal to the number of rows in the post multiplying matrix B. The (i, j)th entry of the product matrix is the product element of i-th row with j-th column vector. If $A_{p \times n} = [a_{ij}]$ and $B_{n \times q} = [b_{ij}]$, the entries c_{ij} of the product matrix AB are given by the relation

$$c_{ij} = \sum_n a_{in} b_{nj} \qquad \text{...(A-2.9)}$$

The order of the product matrix is $(p \times q)$.

For example, if

$$A_{2\times3} = \begin{bmatrix} 3 & 2 & 6 \\ 5 & 4 & -1 \end{bmatrix}$$

and
$$B_{3\times4} = \begin{bmatrix} 7 & 3 & 2 & 10 \\ 11 & 6 & -5 & 4 \\ 8 & 4 & 9 & -3 \end{bmatrix}$$

$$AB_{2\times4} = \begin{bmatrix} (3\times7+2\times11+6\times8) & (3\times3+2\times6+6\times4) & (3\times2-2\times5+6\times9) & (3\times10+2\times4-6\times3) \\ (5\times7+4\times11-1\times8) & (5\times3+4\times6-1\times4) & (5\times2-4\times5-1\times9) & (5\times10+4\times4+1\times3) \end{bmatrix}$$

$$= \begin{bmatrix} 91 & 45 & 50 & 20 \\ 71 & 35 & -19 & 69 \end{bmatrix}$$

Also if A' is the transpose of A and B' is the transpose of B, the transpose of AB is given as

$$(AB)' = B'A'$$

Rank of a Matrix

A matrix consists of rows and columns written in an order. The number of independent rows, which is the same as the number of independent columns in a matrix, is known as the rank of a matrix.

DETERMINANT

Definition

A real valued function of the elements of a square matrix say, of order $(p \times p)$, is said to be a determinant of the order p. The determinant A of the order p is given as,

$$|A| = \begin{vmatrix} a_{11} & a_{12} & a_{1p} \\ a_{21} & a_{22} & a_{2p} \\ \vdots & \vdots & \vdots \\ a_{p1} & a_{p2} & a_{pp} \end{vmatrix} \qquad \text{...(A-2.10)}$$

For a determinant A of order 2,

$$|A| = \begin{vmatrix} a_{11} & a_{12} \\ a_{21} & a_{22} \end{vmatrix} = (a_{11}a_{22} - a_{12}a_{21}) \qquad \text{...(A-2.11)}$$

Properties of Determinants

(*i*) If any two rows or columns of a determinant are identical or one row (column) can be expressed as a constant multiple of any other row (column), the value of the determinant is zero. Again, if $|A| = 0$, it means that the rank of the square matrix is not full and vice-versa.

(*ii*) If all the elements of any row or column of a determinant A are zero, then $|A| = 0$.

(*iii*) The sign of the determinant changes if any two rows (columns) are interchanged with each other. Evidently, if the number of such changes is even, the sign of the determinant remains unchanged and if it is odd, the sign of the determinant changes.

(*iv*) If A is a diagonal matrix, $|A|$ is equal to the product of the diagonal elements.

(*v*) If A and B are any two square matrices such that $AB = C$, then $|A| \times |B| = |C|$ ...(A-2.12)

(*vi*) If in a determinant for an entry a_{ij}, the *i*-th row and *j*-th column are deleted, the determinant with the remaining elements is known as the *minor* of a_{ij}. For example, if

$$|A| = \begin{vmatrix} a_{11} & a_{12} & a_{13} \\ a_{21} & a_{22} & a_{23} \\ a_{31} & a_{32} & a_{33} \end{vmatrix}$$

The minor of a_{22} is $\begin{vmatrix} a_{11} & a_{13} \\ a_{31} & a_{33} \end{vmatrix}$

and the minor of a_{21} is $\begin{vmatrix} a_{12} & a_{13} \\ a_{32} & a_{33} \end{vmatrix}$ ...(A-2.13)

In the same way, the minor of any other element can be found.

(*vii*) If the minor of an element, a_{ij} is written with its proper sign, it is known as the cofactor of a_{ij}. The sign of the minor is determined by the quantity $(-1)^{i+j}$. The cofactor of a_{ij} is denoted by A_{ij}. For example, as in property (*vi*) the cofactor of a_{22} is

$$A_{22} = (-1)^{2+2}\begin{vmatrix} a_{11} & a_{13} \\ a_{31} & a_{33} \end{vmatrix} = \begin{vmatrix} a_{11} & a_{13} \\ a_{31} & a_{33} \end{vmatrix} \qquad \text{...(A-2.14)}$$

and cofactor of a_{21} is

$$A_{21} = (-1)^{2+1}\begin{vmatrix} a_{12} & a_{13} \\ a_{32} & a_{33} \end{vmatrix} = -\begin{vmatrix} a_{12} & a_{13} \\ a_{32} & a_{33} \end{vmatrix} \qquad \text{...(A-2.15)}$$

(*viii*) The value of a determinant A of order p can be calculated by the formula,

$$|A| = \sum_{j=1}^{p} a_{ij} \times (\text{cofactor of } a_{ij}) \quad ...(A\text{-}2.16)$$

$$i, j = 1, 2, ..., p$$

$$= \sum_{j=1}^{p} a_{ij} (\text{cofactor of } a_{ij}) \quad ...(A\text{-}2.17)$$

From the above formulae, it is apparent that the value of a determinant is obtained as a sum of the product of the elements of a row or a column, multiplied by the cofactors of the corresponding elements.

Back to Matrices

(1) A square matrix A is said to be *singular* if $|A| = 0$.

(2) If $|A|$ of a matrix is not zero, the matrix is said to be *non-singular*. The rank of a *nonsingular* matrix is full, i.e. it is equal to be order of the matrix.

(3) *Inverse of a matrix.* If any non-singular matrix A, of order $(p \times p)$, exists then one can find another non-singular matrix B of order $(p \times p)$ so that $AB = I$, the matrix B is said to be the inverse of matrix A. Notationally $B = A^{-1}I = A^{-1}$. Hence $AA^{-1} = I$.

Suppose, $A = [a_{ij}]$ is a non-singular matrix. The elements of the inverse matrix A^{-1} are denoted by c_{ij}. Hence $A^{-1} = [c_{ij}]$. The elements of A^{-1} can be obtained by the formula,

$$c_{ij} = \frac{\text{cofactor } a_{ji}}{|A|} = \frac{A_{ji}}{|A|} \quad ...(A\text{-}2.18)$$

The inverse of the matrix A can be obtained by a direct method without difficulty, if it is of the order (3×3) or less. But, for higher order matrices, the direct method for finding out the inverse becomes quite cumbersome. Hence, some other methods are applied which involve comparatively less labour. Here only one method named as *Pivotal Condensation Method* has been given. The same has been used in chapter 16.

Pivotal Condensation Method

Consider a non-singular matrix A, whose elements are a_{ij}. The inverse of A can be found out by the basic principle, that is put, $A = I$. Then, do some operations on A and I simultaneously such that the matrix A is reduced to I. The right hand matrix I automatically changes to A^{-1} since,

$$AA^{-1} = IA^{-1} \quad ...(A\text{-}2.19)$$

or

$$I = A^{-1} \quad ...(A\text{-}2.19.1)$$

For simplicity, we will consider a matrix of the order (4×4) and describe the method of inversion with adequate details. Step-by-step operations are explained.

Step 1 Divide the first row entries by a_{11}, so that the entry (1, 1) reduces to 1. If the first entry is zero, bring some other row as the first row by interchanging the rows. The entries after division are shown in row 5.

The entries of the fifth row are 1, $b_{12} = a_{12}/a_{11}$, $b_{13} = b_{13}/a_{11}$, $b_{14} = a_{14}/a_{11}$ and $d_{11} = 1/a_{11}$. The fifth row is known as *first pivotal row.*

	Row no.	A				I			
	1.	a_{11}	a_{12}	a_{13}	a_{14}	1	0	0	0
	2.	a_{21}	a_{22}	a_{23}	a_{24}	0	1	0	0
	3.	a_{31}	a_{32}	a_{33}	a_{34}	0	0	1	0
	4.	a_{41}	a_{42}	a_{43}	a_{44}	0	0	0	1
I Pivotal row	5.	1	b_{12}	b_{13}	b_{14}	d_{11}	0	0	0
	6.	0	$b_{12.1}$	$b_{13.1}$	$b_{14.1}$	$-a_{21}d_{11}$	1	0	0
	7.	0	$b_{12.2}$	$b_{13.2}$	$b_{14.2}$	$-a_{31}d_{11}$	0	1	0
	8.	0	$b_{12.3}$	$b_{13.3}$	$b_{14.3}$	$-a_{41}d_{11}$	0	0	1
II Pivotal row	9.		1	b_{23}	b_{24}	d_{21}	d_{22}	0	0
	10.		0	$b_{23.1}$	$b_{24.1}$	$b_{21.1}$	$-b_{12.2}d_{22}$	1	0
	11.		0	$b_{23.2}$	$b_{24.2}$	$d_{21.2}$	$-b_{12.3}d_{22}$	0	1
III Pivotal	12.			1	b_{34}	d_{31}	d_{32}	d_{33}	0
	13.			0	$b_{34.1}$	$d_{31.1}$	$d_{32.1}$	$-b_{23.2}d_{32}$	1

IV Pivotal row 14.				1	c_{41}	c_{42}	c_{43}	c_{44}
15.	1	b_{12}	b_{13}	b_{14}	d_{11}	0	0	0
16.	0	1	b_{23}	b_{24}	d_{21}	d_{22}	0	0
17.	0	0	1	b_{34}	d_{31}	d_{32}	d_{33}	0
18.	0	0	0	1	c_{41}	c_{42}	c_{43}	c_{44}
19.	1	0	$b_{42.1}$	$b_{44.1}$	$b_{41.1}$	$-b_{12}\,d_{22}$	0	0
20.	0	1	0	$b_{54.1}$	$d_{51.1}$	$d_{52.1}$	$-b_{23}\,d_{33}$	0
21.	0	0	1	0	c_{31}	c_{32}	c_{33}	c_{34}
22.	0	0	0	1	c_{41}	c_{42}	c_{43}	c_{44}
23.	1	0	0	$b_{44.1}$	$d_{61.1}$	$d_{62.1}$	$d_{63.1}$	$d_{64.1}$
24.	0	1	0	0	c_{21}	c_{22}	c_{23}	c_{24}
25.	0	0	1	0	c_{31}	c_{32}	c_{33}	c_{34}
26.	0	0	0	1	c_{41}	c_{42}	c_{43}	c_{44}
27.	1	0	0	0	c_{11}	c_{12}	c_{13}	c_{14}
28.	0	1	0	0	c_{21}	c_{22}	c_{23}	c_{24}
29.	0	0	1	0	c_{31}	c_{32}	c_{33}	c_{34}
30.	0	0	0	1	c_{41}	c_{42}	c_{43}	c_{44}
		I					A^{-1}	

Step 2 Now we make the other entries of the first column as zero. To make the entry of (2, 1)-th cell as zero, multiply the 5th row by a_{22} and subtract it from row 2. The other entries of row 6 are, $b_{12.1} = a_{22} - a_{21}\, b_{12}$; $b_{13.1} = a_{23} - a_{21}\, b_{13}$; $b_{14.1} = a_{24} - a_{21}\, b_{14}$. Similarly, we obtain the elements of row 7 by multiplying the row 5 by a_{31} and subtracting it from row 3. Row 8 is obtained by multiplying row 5 by a_{41} and subtracting it from row 4.

Step 3 Delete I pivotal row, i.e. row 5 and first column. This gives the matrix of order (3 × 3).

Step 4 Repeat the process on the reduced matrix to provide second pivotal row, *i.e.*, row 9. To obtain this divide row 6 by $b_{12.1}$. Then make the other first column entries zero of the reduced matrix in the same manner as in step 2. Here, $b_{23} = b_{13.1}/b_{12.1}$ $b_{24} = b_{14.1}/b_{12.1}$; $d_{21} = -a_{21}\, d_{11}/b_{12.1}$; $d_{22} = 1/b_{12.1}$. Also, $b_{23.1} = b_{13.2} - b_{12.2}\, b_{23}$; $b_{24.1} = b_{14.2} - b_{12.2}\, b_{24}$; $d_{21.1} = -a_{31}\, d_{11} - b_{12.2}\, d_{21}$ and so on.

Step 5 Again delete the second pivotal row and the first column of the reduced matrix. This gives another matrix of order (2 × 2). Repeat the first three steps which give the third pivotal row and a matrix of order (1 × 1); i.e. single entry. Divide row 13 by $b_{34.1}$, and obtain the fourth pivotal row. The right hand elements are written as c_{41}, c_{42}, c_{43}, c_{44} where $c_{41} = d_{31.1}/b_{34.1}$, $c_{42} = d_{31.1}/b_{34.1}$, $c_{43} = -b_{23.2}\, d_{33}/b_{34.1}$ and $c_{44} = 1/b_{34.1}$.

Step 6 Now rewrite the four pivotal rows. The left hand matrix has the lower triangle elements as zero, whereas the upper triangle elements are not zero. To change this left side matrix to *I*, we reduce the upper triangle elements to zero.

Step 7 First we make the entry (1, 2) zero by multiplying row 16 by b_{12} and subtracting it from row 15.

Step 8 Multiply row 17 by b_{23} and subtract it from row 16. This makes the entry (2, 3) zero.

Step 9 Multiply row 18 by b_{34} and subtract it from row 17. This makes the entry (3, 4) zero. Here $c_{31} = d_{31} - b_{34}c_{41}$, $c_{32} = d_{32} - b_{34}c_{42}$ and so on. In like manner, we make the elements, b_{13}, b_{14} and b_{24} zero. The elements on the right hand side are adjusted according to the operations and are denoted by new symbols. For instance, $d_{41.1} = d_{11} - b_{12}d_{21}$; $d_{31.1} = d_{41.1} - b_{43.1}\, c_{31}$ and $c_{11} = d_{61.1} - c_{41}\, b_{44.1}$ and so on.

In this way, the left hand matrix is reduced to *I* and the right hand matrix is changed to A^{-1}. The product matrix will be *I*. If not, the calculations must be checked again. The advantages and the various uses of pivotal condensation method have not been given because of the brevity.

A-3 SOME USEFUL FORMULAE

Logarithm

If $10^x = a,$

Then $\log_e 10 = x$ ...(A-3.1)

and if $e^x = a$

$\log_e a = x$ ...(A-3.2)

In (A-3.1), the logarithm is to the base 10 and in (A-3.2), the logarithm is to the base *e*. The logarithm to the base *e* is called a *natural logarithm*.

If *a* and *b* are two real numerical numbers and the logarithm is taken to the base *e*, the following relations hold

$$\log_e (ab) = \log_e a + \log_e b \qquad \text{...(A-3.3)}$$

$$\log_e \left(\frac{a}{b}\right) = \log_e a - \log_e b \qquad \text{...(A-3.4)}$$

$$\log_e (a)^n = n \log_e a \qquad \text{...(A-3.5)}$$

Generally, the formulae are developed to the base *e*. But the tables are provided to the base 10. So the values of logarithm to the base *e* can be evaluated by using the relation,

$$\log_e a = \log_{10} a \times \log_e 10 \qquad \text{...(A-3.6)}$$

Also,

$$\log_e 10 = 2.3026 \qquad \text{...(A-3.7)}$$

From (A-3.6), it is clear that the logarithmic value found out to the base 10, when multipled by 2.3026, is converted to the base *e*.

Formulae for Permutations and Combinations

The number of permutation of *r* objects or items selected or arranged in order out of *n* objects or items, are denoted by $(n)_r$. The formula is,

$$(n)_r = n\,(n-1)\,(n-2)\,...\,(n-r+1) \qquad \text{...(A-3.8)}$$

The number of combinations of *r* objects or items selected or arranged out of *n* objects or items, when the ordering does not matter, are denoted by $\begin{pmatrix} n \\ r \end{pmatrix}$. The formula is,

$$\begin{pmatrix} n \\ r \end{pmatrix} = \frac{n(n-1)(n-2)...(n-r+1)}{r(r-1)(r-2)...3.2.1} \qquad \text{...(A-3.9)}$$

$$= \frac{(n)_r}{r!} \qquad \text{...(A-3.9.1)}$$

$$= \frac{n!}{(n-r)\,!\,r!}$$

where

$$n! = n\,(n-1)\,(n-2)\,...\,3.2.1$$

Also

$$\begin{pmatrix} n \\ 0 \end{pmatrix} = 1, \begin{pmatrix} n \\ n \end{pmatrix} = 1,\ 0! = 1 \text{ and } 1! = 1$$

Binomial Expansion Formula

$$(a+b)^n = a^n + \begin{pmatrix} n \\ 1 \end{pmatrix} a^{n-1} b + \begin{pmatrix} n \\ 2 \end{pmatrix} a^{n-2} b^2 + ... + \begin{pmatrix} n \\ r \end{pmatrix} a^{n-r} b^r + ... + b^n \qquad \text{...(A-3.10)}$$

$$= a^n + na^{n-1}\,b + \frac{n(n-1)}{1.2} a^{n-2} b^2 + ...$$

$$... + \frac{n(n-1)(n-2)...(n-r+1)}{r(r-1)(r-2)...3.2.1} a^{n-r} b^r + ... + b^n \qquad \text{...(A-3.10.1)}$$

In the above expansion formula, $\binom{n}{r} a^{n-r} b^r$ is the $(r + 1)$ term. This is also known as the general term. All the $(n + 1)$ terms of the binomial expansion can be obtained one by one putting $r = 0, 1, 2 ..., n$ in the general term.

Exponential Series

$$e^x = 1 + x + \frac{x^2}{2!} + \frac{x^3}{3!} + ... \quad ...(A\text{-}3.11)$$

$$e^{-x} = 1 - x + \frac{x^2}{2!} - \frac{x^3}{3!} + ... \quad ...(A\text{-}3.12)$$

Exponential series are infinite series.

Logarithmic Series

$$\log_e (1 + x) = x - \frac{x^2}{2} + \frac{x^3}{3} - \frac{x^4}{4} + ... \quad ...(A\text{-}3.13)$$

$$\log_e (1 - x) = -x - \frac{x^2}{2} - \frac{x^3}{3} - \frac{x^4}{4} - ... \quad ...(A\text{-}3.14)$$

$$\log_e \left(\frac{1+x}{1-x}\right) = 2\left(x + \frac{x^3}{3} + ...\right) \quad ...(A\text{-}3.15)$$

Gamma Function For any two positive numbers α and n, such that $\alpha > 0$ and $n > 0$, the gamma function $G(\alpha, n)$ is given as,

$$G(\alpha, n) = \int_0^\infty x^{n-1} e^{-\alpha x} dx \quad ...(A\text{-}3.16)$$

$$= \frac{\Gamma n}{\alpha^n} \quad ...(A\text{-}3.16.1)$$

If $\alpha = 1$,

$$G(1, n) = \int_0^\infty x^{n-1} e^{-x} dx \quad ...(A\text{-}3.16.2)$$

$$= \Gamma n$$

where $\Gamma n = (n - 1)(n - 2)...3.2.1$ ...(A-3.16.3)

since, $\Gamma(n + 1) = n\Gamma n$

Beta Function For any two positive numbers, m and n, the beta function is given as,

$$B(m, n) = \int_0^1 x^{m-1}(1-x)^{n-1}\, dx \quad \text{...(A-3.17)}$$

$$= \int_0^\infty \frac{x^{m-1}}{(1+x)^{m+n}} dx \quad \text{...(A-3.17.1)}$$

$$= \frac{\Gamma m \Gamma n}{\Gamma(m+n)} \quad \text{...(A-3.17.2)}$$

Appendix B
Statistical Tables

Table I. Logarithms

	0	1	2	3	4	5	6	7	8	9	1	2	3	4	5	6	7	8	9
10	0000	0043	0086	0128	0170						5	9	13	17	21	26	30	34	38
						0212	0253	0294	0334	0374	4	8	12	16	20	24	28	32	36
11	0414	0453	0492	0531	0569						4	8	12	16	20	23	27	31	35
						0607	0645	0682	0719	0755	4	7	11	15	18	22	26	29	33
12	0792	0828	0864	0899	0934						3	7	11	14	18	21	25	28	32
						0969	1004	1038	1072	1106	3	7	10	14	17	20	24	27	31
13	1139	1173	1206	1239	1271						3	6	10	13	16	19	23	26	29
						1303	1335	1367	1399	1430	3	7	10	13	16	19	22	25	29
14	1461	1492	1523	1553	1584						3	6	9	12	15	19	22	25	28
						1614	1644	1673	1703	1732	3	6	9	12	14	17	20	23	26
15	1761	1790	1818	1847	1875						3	6	9	11	14	17	20	23	26
						1903	1931	1959	1987	2014	3	6	8	11	14	17	19	22	25
16	2041	2068	2095	2122	2148						3	6	8	11	14	16	19	22	24
						2175	2201	2227	2253	2279	3	5	8	10	13	16	18	21	23
17	2304	2330	2355	2380	2405						3	5	8	10	13	15	18	20	23
						2430	2455	2480	2504	2529	3	5	8	10	12	15	17	20	22
18	2553	2577	2601	2625	2648						2	5	7	9	12	14	17	19	21
						2672	2695	2718	2742	2765	2	4	7	9	11	14	16	18	21
19	2788	2810	2833	2856	2878						2	4	7	9	11	13	16	18	20
						2900	2923	2945	2967	2989	2	4	6	8	11	13	15	17	19
20	3010	3032	3054	3075	3096	3118	3139	3160	3181	3201	2	4	6	8	11	13	15	17	19
21	3222	3243	3263	3284	3304	3324	3345	3365	3385	3404	2	4	6	8	10	12	14	16	18

Table I *(Contd.)*

	0	1	2	3	4	5	6	7	8	9	1	2	3	4	5	6	7	8	9
22	3434	3444	3464	3483	3502	3522	3541	3560	3579	3598	2	4	6	8	10	12	14	15	17
23	3617	3636	3655	3674	3692	3711	3729	3747	3766	3784	2	4	6	7	9	11	13	15	17
24	3802	3820	3838	3856	3874	3892	3909	3927	3945	3962	2	4	5	7	9	11	12	14	16
25	3979	3997	4014	4031	4048	4065	4082	4099	4116	4133	2	3	5	7	9	10	12	14	15
26	4150	4166	4183	4200	4216	4232	4249	4265	4281	4298	2	3	5	7	8	10	11	13	15
27	4314	4330	4346	4362	4378	4393	4409	4425	4440	4456	2	3	5	6	8	9	11	13	14
28	4472	4487	4502	4518	4533	4548	4564	4579	4594	4609	2	3	5	6	8	9	11	12	14
29	4624	4639	4654	4669	4683	4698	4713	4728	4742	4757	1	3	4	6	7	9	10	12	13
30	4771	4786	4800	4814	4829	4843	4857	4871	4886	4900	1	3	4	6	7	9	10	11	13
31	4914	4928	4942	4955	4969	4983	4997	5011	5024	5038	1	3	4	6	7	8	10	11	12
32	5051	5065	5079	5092	5105	5119	5132	5145	5159	5172	1	3	4	5	7	8	9	11	12
33	5185	5198	5211	5224	5237	5250	5263	5276	5289	5302	1	3	4	5	6	8	9	10	12
34	5315	5328	5340	5353	5366	5378	5391	5403	5416	5428	1	3	4	5	6	8	9	10	11
35	5441	5453	5465	5478	5490	5502	5514	5527	5539	5551	1	2	4	5	6	7	9	10	11
36	5563	5575	5587	5599	5611	5623	5635	5647	5658	5670	1	2	4	5	6	7	8	10	11
37	5682	5694	5705	5717	5729	5740	5752	5763	5775	5786	1	2	3	5	6	7	8	9	10
38	5798	5809	5821	5832	5843	5855	5866	5877	5888	5899	1	2	3	5	6	7	8	9	10
39	5911	5922	5933	5944	5955	5966	5977	5988	5999	6010	1	2	3	4	5	7	8	9	10
40	6021	6031	6042	6053	6064	6075	6085	6096	6107	6117	1	2	3	4	5	6	8	9	10
41	6128	6138	6149	6160	6170	6180	6191	6201	6212	6222	1	2	3	4	5	6	7	8	9
42	6232	6243	6253	6263	6274	6284	6294	6304	6314	6325	1	2	3	4	5	6	7	8	9
43	6335	6345	6355	6365	6375	6385	6395	6405	6415	6425	1	2	3	4	5	6	7	8	9
44	6435	6444	6454	6464	6474	6484	6493	6503	6513	6522	1	2	3	4	5	6	7	8	9
45	6532	6542	6551	6561	6571	6580	6590	6599	6609	6618	1	2	3	4	5	6	7	8	9
46	6628	6637	6646	6656	6665	6675	6684	6693	6702	6712	1	2	3	4	5	5	7	7	8
47	6721	6730	6739	6749	6758	6767	6776	6785	6794	6803	1	2	3	4	5	5	6	7	8
48	6812	6821	6830	6839	6848	6857	6866	6875	6884	6893	1	2	3	4	4	5	6	7	8
49	6902	6911	6920	6928	6937	6946	6955	6964	6972	6981	1	2	3	4	4	5	6	7	8
50	6990	6998	7007	7016	7024	7033	7042	7050	7059	7067	1	2	3	4	4	5	6	7	8
51	7076	7084	7093	7101	7110	7118	7126	7135	7143	7152	1	2	3	3	4	5	6	7	8
52	7160	7168	7177	7185	7193	7202	7210	7218	7226	7235	1	2	2	3	4	5	6	7	7

Table I *(Contd.)*

	0	1	2	3	4	5	6	7	8	9	1	2	3	4	5	6	7	8	9
53	7243	7251	7259	7267	7275	7284	7292	7300	7308	7316	1	2	2	3	4	5	6	6	7
54	7324	7332	7340	7348	7356	7364	7372	7380	7388	7396	1	2	2	3	4	5	6	6	7
55	7404	7412	7419	7427	7435	7443	7451	7459	7466	7474	1	2	2	3	4	5	5	6	7
56	7482	7490	7497	7505	7513	7520	7528	7536	7543	7551	1	2	2	3	4	5	5	6	7
57	7559	7566	7574	7582	7589	7597	7604	7612	7619	7627	1	2	2	3	4	5	5	6	7
58	7634	7642	7649	7657	7664	7672	7679	7686	7694	7701	1	1	2	3	4	4	5	6	7
59	7709	7716	7723	7731	7738	7745	7752	7760	7767	7774	1	1	2	3	4	4	5	6	7
60	7782	7789	7796	7803	7810	7818	7825	7832	7839	7846	1	1	2	3	4	4	5	6	6
61	7853	7860	7868	7875	7882	7889	7896	7903	7910	7917	1	1	2	3	4	4	5	6	6
62	7924	7931	7938	7945	7952	7959	7966	7973	7980	7987	1	1	2	3	3	4	5	6	6
63	7993	8000	8007	8014	8021	8028	8035	8041	8048	8055	1	1	2	3	4	4	5	5	6
64	8062	8069	8075	8082	8089	8096	8102	8109	8116	8122	1	1	2	3	3	4	5	5	6
65	8129	8136	8142	8149	8156	8162	8169	8176	8182	8189	1	1	2	3	3	4	5	5	6
66	8195	8202	8209	8215	8222	8228	8235	8241	8248	8254	1	1	2	3	3	4	5	5	6
67	8261	8267	8274	8280	8287	8293	8299	8306	8312	8319	1	1	2	3	3	4	5	5	6
68	8325	8331	8338	8344	8351	8357	8363	8370	8376	8382	1	1	2	3	3	4	4	5	6
69	8388	8395	8401	8407	8414	8420	8426	8432	8439	8445	1	1	2	2	3	4	4	5	6
70	8451	8457	8463	8470	8476	8482	8488	8494	8500	8506	1	1	2	2	3	4	4	5	6
71	8513	8519	8525	8531	8537	8543	8549	8555	8561	8567	1	1	2	2	3	4	4	5	5
72	8573	8579	8585	8591	8597	8603	8609	8615	8621	8627	1	1	2	2	3	4	4	5	5
73	8633	8639	8645	8651	8657	8663	8669	8675	8681	8686	1	1	2	2	3	4	4	5	5
74	8692	8698	8704	8710	8716	8722	8727	8733	8739	8745	1	1	2	2	3	4	4	5	5
75	8751	8756	8762	8768	8774	8779	8785	8791	8797	8802	1	1	2	2	3	3	4	5	5
76	8808	8814	8820	8825	8831	8837	8842	8848	8854	8859	1	1	2	2	3	3	4	5	5
77	8865	8871	8876	8882	8887	8893	8899	8904	8910	8915	1	1	2	2	3	3	4	4	5
78	8921	8927	8932	8938	8943	8949	8954	8960	8965	8971	1	1	2	2	3	3	4	4	5
79	8976	8982	8987	8993	8998	9004	9009	9015	9020	9025	1	1	2	2	3	3	4	4	5
80	9031	9036	9042	9047	9053	9058	9063	9069	9074	9079	1	1	2	2	3	3	4	4	5
81	9085	9090	9096	9101	9106	9112	9117	9122	9128	9133	1	1	2	2	3	3	4	4	5
82	9138	9143	9149	9154	9159	9165	9170	9175	9180	9186	1	1	2	2	3	3	4	4	5
83	9191	9196	9201	9206	9212	9217	9222	9227	9232	9238	1	1	2	2	3	3	4	4	5
84	9243	9248	9253	9258	9263	9269	9274	9279	9284	9289	1	1	2	2	3	3	4	4	5

Table I *(Contd.)*

	0	1	2	3	4	5	6	7	8	9	1	2	3	4	5	6	7	8	9
85	9294	9299	9304	9309	9315	9320	9325	9330	9335	9340	1	1	2	2	3	3	4	4	5
86	9345	9350	9355	9360	9365	9370	9375	9380	9385	9390	1	1	2	2	3	3	4	4	5
87	9395	9400	9405	9410	9415	9420	9425	9430	9435	9440	0	1	1	2	2	3	3	4	4
88	9445	9450	9455	9460	9465	9469	9474	9479	9484	9489	0	1	1	2	2	3	3	4	4
89	9494	9499	9504	9509	9513	9518	9523	9528	9533	9538	0	1	1	2	2	3	3	4	4
90	9542	9547	9552	9557	9562	9566	9571	9576	9581	9586	0	1	1	2	2	3	3	4	4
91	9590	9595	9600	9605	9609	9614	9619	9624	9628	9633	0	1	1	2	2	3	3	4	4
92	9638	9643	9647	9652	9657	9661	9666	9671	9675	9680	0	1	1	2	2	3	3	4	4
93	9685	9689	9694	9699	9703	9708	9713	9717	9722	9727	0	1	1	2	2	3	3	4	4
94	9731	9736	9741	9745	9750	9754	9759	9763	9768	9773	0	1	1	2	2	3	3	4	4
95	9777	9782	9786	9791	9795	9800	9805	9809	9814	9818	0	1	1	2	2	3	3	4	4
96	9823	9827	9832	9836	9841	9845	9850	9854	9859	9863	0	1	1	2	2	3	3	4	4
97	9868	9872	9877	9881	9886	9890	9894	9899	9903	9908	0	1	1	2	2	3	3	4	4
98	9912	9917	9921	9926	9930	9934	9939	9943	9948	9952	0	1	1	2	2	3	3	4	4
99	9956	9961	9965	9969	9974	9978	9983	9987	9991	9996	0	1	1	2	2	3	3	3	4

Table II. antilogarithms

	0	1	2	3	4	5	6	7	8	9	1	2	3	4	5	6	7	8	9
.00	1000	1002	1005	1007	1009	1012	1014	1016	1019	1021	0	0	1	1	1	1	2	2	2
.01	1023	1026	1028	1030	1033	1035	1038	1040	1042	1045	0	0	1	1	1	1	2	2	2
.02	1047	1050	1052	1054	1057	1059	1062	1064	1067	1069	0	0	1	1	1	1	2	2	2
.03	1072	1074	1076	1079	1081	1084	1086	1089	1091	1094	0	0	1	1	1	1	2	2	2
.04	1096	1099	1102	1104	1107	1109	1112	1114	1117	1119	0	1	1	1	1	2	2	2	2
.05	1122	1125	1127	1130	1132	1135	1138	1140	1143	1146	0	1	1	1	1	2	2	2	2
.06	1148	1151	1153	1156	1159	1161	1164	1167	1169	1172	0	1	1	1	1	2	2	2	2
.07	1175	1178	1180	1183	1186	1189	1191	1194	1197	1199	0	1	1	1	1	2	2	2	2
.08	1202	1205	1208	1211	1213	1216	1219	1222	1225	1227	0	1	1	1	1	2	2	2	3
.09	1230	1233	1236	1239	1242	1245	1247	1250	1253	1256	0	1	1	1	1	2	2	2	3
.10	1259	1262	1265	1268	1271	1274	1276	1279	1282	1285	0	1	1	1	1	2	2	2	3
.11	1288	1291	1294	1297	1300	1303	1306	1309	1312	1315	0	1	1	1	2	2	2	2	3
.12	1318	1321	1324	1327	1330	1334	1337	1340	1343	1346	0	1	1	1	2	2	2	2	3
.13	1349	1352	1355	1358	1361	1365	1368	1371	1374	1377	0	1	1	1	2	2	2	3	3
.14	1380	1384	1387	1390	1393	1396	1400	1403	1406	1409	0	1	1	1	2	2	2	3	3
.15	1413	1416	1419	1422	1426	1429	1432	1435	1439	1442	0	1	1	1	2	2	2	3	3
.16	1445	1449	1452	1455	1459	1462	1466	1469	1472	1476	0	1	1	1	2	2	2	3	3
.17	1479	1483	1486	1489	1493	1496	1500	1503	1507	1510	0	1	1	1	2	2	2	3	3
.18	1514	1517	1521	1524	1528	1531	1535	1538	1542	1545	0	1	1	1	2	2	2	3	3
.19	1549	1552	1556	1560	1563	1567	1570	1574	1578	1581	0	1	1	1	2	2	3	3	3
.20	1585	1589	1592	1596	1600	1603	1607	1611	1614	1618	0	1	1	1	2	2	3	3	3
.21	1622	1626	1629	1633	1637	1641	1644	1648	1652	1656	0	1	1	2	2	2	3	3	3
.22	1660	1663	1667	1671	1675	1679	1683	1687	1690	1694	0	1	1	2	2	2	3	3	3
.23	1698	1702	1706	1710	1714	1718	1722	1726	1730	1734	0	1	1	2	2	2	3	3	4
.24	1738	1742	1746	1750	1754	1758	1762	1766	1770	1774	0	1	1	2	2	2	3	3	4
.25	1778	1782	1786	1791	1795	1799	1803	1807	1811	1816	0	1	1	2	2	2	3	3	4
.26	1820	1824	1828	1832	1837	1841	1845	1849	1854	1858	0	1	1	2	2	3	3	3	4
.27	1862	1866	1871	1875	1879	1884	1888	1892	1897	1901	0	1	1	2	2	3	3	3	4
.28	1905	1910	1914	1919	1923	1928	1932	1936	1941	1945	0	1	1	2	2	3	3	4	4
.29	1950	1954	1959	1963	1968	1972	1977	1982	1986	1991	0	1	1	2	2	3	3	4	4
.30	1995	2000	2004	2009	2014	2018	2023	2028	2032	2037	0	1	1	2	2	3	3	4	4
.31	2042	2046	2051	2056	2061	2065	2070	2075	2080	2084	0	1	1	2	2	3	3	4	4
.32	2089	2094	2099	2104	2109	2113	2118	2123	2128	2133	0	1	1	2	2	3	3	4	4
.33	2138	2143	2148	2153	2158	2163	2168	2173	2178	2183	0	1	1	2	2	3	3	4	4
.34	2188	2193	2198	2203	2208	2213	2218	2223	2228	2234	1	1	2	2	3	3	4	4	5
.35	2239	2244	2249	2254	2259	2265	2270	2275	2280	2286	1	1	2	2	3	3	4	4	5
.36	2291	2296	2301	2307	2312	2317	2323	2328	2333	2339	1	1	2	2	3	3	4	4	5
.37	2344	2350	2355	2360	2366	2371	2377	2382	2388	2393	1	1	2	2	3	3	4	4	5
.38	2399	2404	2410	2415	2421	2427	2432	2438	2443	2449	1	1	2	2	3	3	4	4	5
.39	2455	2460	2466	2472	2477	2483	2489	2495	2500	2506	1	1	2	2	3	3	4	5	5
.40	2512	2518	2523	2529	2535	2541	2547	2553	2559	2564	1	1	2	2	3	4	4	5	5
.41	2570	2576	2582	2588	2594	2600	2606	2612	2618	2624	1	1	2	2	3	4	4	5	5
.42	2630	2636	2642	2649	2655	2661	2667	2673	2679	2685	1	1	2	2	3	4	4	5	6
.43	2692	2698	2704	2710	2716	2723	2729	2735	2742	2748	1	1	2	3	3	4	4	5	6
.44	2754	2761	2767	2773	2780	2786	2793	2799	2805	2812	1	1	2	3	3	4	4	5	6

Table II (*Contd.*)

	0	1	2	3	4	5	6	7	8	9	1	2	3	4	5	6	7	8	9
.45	2818	2825	2831	2838	2844	2851	2858	2864	2871	2877	1	1	2	3	3	4	5	5	6
.46	2884	2891	2897	2904	2911	2917	2924	2931	2938	2944	1	1	2	3	3	4	5	5	6
.47	2951	2958	2965	2972	2979	2985	2992	2999	3006	3013	1	1	2	3	3	4	5	5	6
.48	3020	3027	3034	3041	3048	3055	3062	3069	3076	3083	1	1	2	3	4	4	5	6	6
.49	3090	3097	3105	3112	3119	3126	3133	3141	3148	3155	1	1	2	3	4	4	5	6	6
.50	3162	3170	3177	3184	3192	3199	3206	3214	3221	3228	1	1	2	3	4	4	5	6	7
.51	3236	3243	3251	3258	3266	3273	3281	3289	3296	3304	1	2	2	3	4	5	5	6	7
.52	3311	3319	3327	3334	3342	3350	3357	3365	3373	3381	1	2	2	3	4	5	5	6	7
.53	3388	3396	3404	3412	3420	3428	3436	3443	3451	3459	1	2	2	3	4	5	6	6	7
.54	3467	3475	3483	3491	3499	3508	3516	3524	3532	3540	1	2	2	3	4	5	6	6	7
.55	3548	3556	3565	3573	3581	3589	3597	3606	3614	3622	1	2	2	3	4	5	6	7	7
.56	3631	3639	3648	3656	3664	3673	3681	3690	3698	3707	1	2	3	3	4	5	6	7	8
.57	3715	3724	3733	3741	3750	3758	3767	3776	3784	3793	1	2	3	3	4	5	6	7	8
.58	3802	3811	3819	3828	3837	3846	3855	3864	3873	3882	1	2	3	4	4	5	6	7	8
.59	3890	3899	3908	3917	3926	3936	3945	3954	3963	3972	1	2	3	4	5	5	6	7	8
.60	3981	3990	3999	4009	4018	4027	4036	4046	4055	4064	1	2	3	4	5	6	6	7	8
.61	4074	4083	4093	4102	4111	4121	4130	4140	4150	4159	1	2	3	4	5	6	7	8	9
.62	4169	4178	4188	4198	4207	4217	4227	4236	4246	4256	1	2	3	4	5	6	7	8	9
.63	4266	4276	4285	4295	4305	4315	4325	4335	4345	4355	1	2	3	4	5	6	7	8	9
.64	4365	4375	4385	4395	4406	4416	4426	4436	4446	4457	1	2	3	4	5	6	7	8	9
.65	4467	4477	4487	4498	4508	4519	4529	4539	4550	4560	1	2	3	4	5	6	7	8	9
.66	4571	4581	4592	4603	4613	4624	4634	4645	4656	4667	1	2	3	4	5	6	7	9	10
.67	4677	4688	4699	4710	4721	4732	4742	4753	4764	4775	1	2	3	4	5	7	8	9	10
.68	4786	4797	4808	4819	4831	4842	4853	4864	4875	4887	1	2	3	4	5	7	8	9	10
.69	4898	4909	4920	4932	4943	4955	4966	4977	4989	5000	1	2	3	5	6	7	8	9	10
.70	5012	5023	5035	5047	5058	5070	5082	5093	5105	5117	1	2	4	5	6	7	8	9	11
.71	5129	5140	5152	5164	5176	5188	5200	5212	5224	5236	1	2	4	5	6	7	8	10	11
.72	5248	5260	5272	5284	5297	5309	5321	5333	5346	5358	1	2	4	5	6	7	9	10	11
.73	5370	5383	5395	5408	5420	5433	5445	5458	5470	5483	1	3	4	5	6	8	9	10	11
.74	5495	5508	5521	5534	5546	5559	5572	5585	5598	5610	1	3	4	5	6	8	9	10	12
.75	5623	5636	5649	5662	5675	5689	5702	5715	5728	5741	1	3	4	5	7	8	9	10	12
.76	5754	5768	5781	5794	5808	5821	5834	5848	5861	5875	1	3	4	5	7	8	9	11	12
.77	5888	5902	5916	5929	5943	5957	5970	5984	5998	6012	1	3	4	5	7	8	10	11	12
.78	6026	6039	6053	6067	6081	6095	6109	6124	6138	6152	1	3	4	6	7	8	10	11	13
.79	6166	6180	6194	6209	6223	6237	6252	6266	6281	6295	1	3	4	6	7	9	10	11	13
.80	6310	6324	6339	6353	6368	6383	6397	6412	6427	6442	1	3	4	6	7	9	10	12	13
.81	6457	6471	6486	6501	6516	6531	6546	6561	6577	6592	2	3	5	6	8	9	11	12	14
.82	6607	6622	6637	6653	6668	6683	6699	6714	6730	6745	2	3	5	6	8	9	11	12	14
.83	6761	6776	6792	6808	6823	6839	6853	6871	6887	6902	2	3	5	6	8	9	11	13	14
.84	6918	6934	6950	6966	6982	6998	7015	7031	7047	7063	2	3	5	6	8	10	11	13	15
.85	7079	7096	7112	7129	7145	7161	7178	7194	7211	7228	2	3	5	7	8	10	12	13	15
.86	7244	7261	7278	7295	7311	7328	7345	7362	7379	7396	2	3	5	7	8	10	12	13	15
.87	7413	7430	7447	7464	7482	7499	7516	7534	7551	7568	2	3	5	7	9	10	12	14	16
.88	7586	7603	7621	7638	7656	7674	7691	7709	7727	7745	2	4	5	7	9	11	12	14	16

Table II (*Contd.*)

	0	1	2	3	4	5	6	7	8	9	1	2	3	4	5	6	7	8	9
.89	7762	7780	7798	7816	7834	7852	7870	7889	7907	7925	2	4	5	7	9	11	13	14	16
.90	7943	7962	7980	7998	8017	8035	8054	8072	8091	8110	2	4	6	7	9	11	13	15	17
.91	8128	8147	8166	8185	8204	8222	8241	8260	8279	8299	2	4	6	8	9	11	13	15	17
.92	8318	8337	8356	8375	8395	8414	8433	8453	8472	8492	2	4	6	8	10	12	14	15	17
.93	8511	8531	8551	8570	8590	8610	8630	8650	8670	8690	2	4	6	8	10	12	14	16	18
.94	8710	8730	8750	8770	8790	8810	8831	8851	8872	8892	2	4	6	8	10	12	14	16	18
.95	8913	8933	8954	8974	8995	9016	9036	9057	9078	9099	2	4	6	8	10	12	15	17	19
.96	9120	9141	9162	9183	9204	9226	9247	9268	9290	9314	2	4	6	8	11	13	15	17	19
.97	9333	9354	9376	9397	9419	9441	9462	9484	9506	9528	2	4	7	9	11	13	15	17	20
.98	9550	9572	9594	9616	9638	9661	9683	9705	9727	9750	2	4	7	9	11	13	16	18	20
.99	9772	9795	9817	9840	9863	9886	9908	9931	9954	9977	2	5	7	9	11	14	16	18	20

Table III. Values of e^{-x}

x	.1	.2	.3	.4	.5	.6	.7	.8	.9	1.0
–0	0.9048	0.8187	0.7408	0.6703	0.6065	0.5488	0.4966	0.4493	0.4066	0.3679
–1	0.3329	0.3012	0.2725	0.2466	0.2231	0.2019	0.1827	0.1653	0.1496	0.1353
–2	0.1225	0.1108	0.1003	0.0907	0.0821	0.0743	0.0672	0.0608	0.0550	0.0498
–3	0.0450	0.0408	0.0369	0.0334	0.0302	0.0273	0.0247	0.0224	0.0202	0.0183
–4	0.0166	0.0150	0.0136	0.0123	0.0111	0.0101	0.0091	0.0082	0.0074	0.0067
–5	0.0061	0.0055	0.0050	0.0045	0.0041	0.0037	0.0033	0.0030	0.0027	0.0025
–6	0.0022	0.0020	0.0018	0.0017	0.0015	0.0014	0.0012	0.0011	0.0010	0.0009
–7	0.0008	0.0007	0.0007	0.0006	0.0006	0.0005	0.0005	0.0004	0.0004	0.0003
–8	0.0003	0.0003	0.0002	0.0002	0.0002	0.0002	0.0002	0.0002	0.0001	0.0001
–9	0.0001	0.0001	0.0001	0.0001	0.0001	0.0001	0.0001	0.0001	0.0001	0.0000

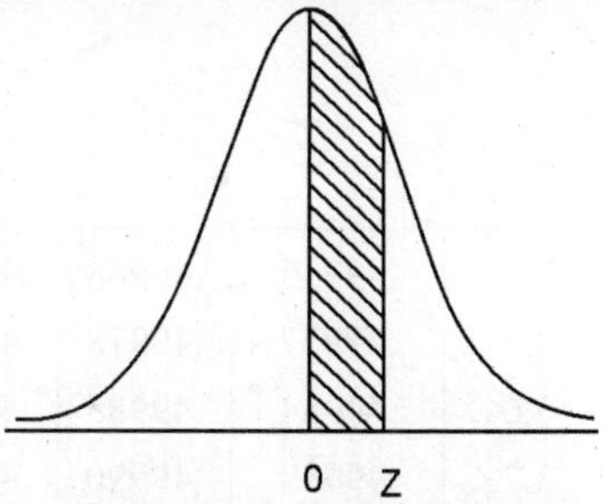

Table IV. Area Under the Standard Normal Curve

Z	.00	.01	.02	.03	.04	.05	.06	.07	.08	.09
0.0	.00000	.00399	.00798	.01197	.01595	.01994	.02392	.02790	.03188	.0.3586
0.1	.03983	.04383	.04776	.05172	.05567	.05962	.06356	.06749	.07142	.07535
0.2	.07926	.08317	.08706	.09095	.09483	.09871	.10257	.10642	.11026	.11409
0.3	.11791	.12172	.12552	.12930	.13307	.13683	.14058	.14431	.14803	.15173
0.4	.15542	.15910	.16276	.16640	.17003	.17364	.17724	.18082	.18439	.18793
0.5	.19146	.19497	.19847	.20194	.20540	.20884	.21226	.21566	.21904	.22240
0.6	.22575	.22907	.23237	.23565	.23891	.24215	.24537	.24857	.25175	.25490
0.7	.25804	.26115	.26424	.26730	.27035	.27337	.27637	.27935	.28230	.28524
0.8	.28814	.29103	.29389	.29673	.29955	.30234	.30511	.30785	.31057	.31372
0.9	.31594	.31859	.32121	.32381	.32639	.32894	.33147	.33398	.33646	.33891
1.0	.34134	.34375	.34614	.34849	.35083	.35314	.35543	.35769	.35993	.36214
1.1	.36433	.36650	.36864	.37076	.37286	.37493	.37698	.37900	.38100	.38298
1.2	.38493	.38686	.38877	.39065	.39251	.39435	.39617	.39796	.39973	.40147
1.3	.40320	.40490	.40658	.40824	.40988	.41198	.41309	.41466	.41621	.41774
1.4	.41924	.42073	.42220	.42364	.42507	.42647	.42785	.42922	.43056	.43189
1.5	.43319	.43448	.43574	.43699	.43822	.43943	.44062	.44179	.44295	.44408
1.6	.44520	.44630	.44738	.44845	.44950	.45053	.45154	.45254	.45352	.45449
1.7	.45543	.45637	.45728	.45818	.45907	.45994	.46080	.46164	.46246	.46327
1.8	.46407	.46485	.46562	.46638	.46712	.46784	.46856	.46926	.46995	.47062
1.9	.47128	.47193	.47257	.47320	.47381	.47441	.47500	.47558	.47615	.47670
2.0	.47725	.47784	.47831	.47882	.47932	.47982	.48030	.48077	.48124	.48169
2.1	.48214	.48257	.48300	.48341	.48382	.48422	.48461	.48500	.48537	.48574
2.2	.48610	.48645	.48679	.48713	.48745	.48778	.48809	.48840	.48870	.48899
2.3	.48928	.48956	.48983	.49010	.49036	.49061	.49086	.49111	.49134	.49158
2.4	.49180	.49202	.49224	.49245	.49266	.49286	.49305	.49324	.49343	.49361
2.5	.49379	.49396	.49413	.49430	.49446	.49461	.49477	.49492	.49506	.49520
2.6	.49534	.49547	.49560	.49573	.49585	.49598	.49609	.49621	.49632	.49643
2.7	.49653	.49664	.49674	.49683	.49693	.49702	.49711	.49720	.49728	.49736
2.8	.49744	.49752	.49760	.49767	.49774	.49781	.49788	.49795	.49801	.49807
2.9	.49813	.49819	.49825	.49831	.49836	.49841	.49846	.49851	.49856	.49861
3.0	.49865	.49869	.49874	.49878	.49882	.49886	.49889	.49893	.49896	.49900
3.1	.49903	.49906	.49910	.49913	.49916	.49918	.49921	.49924	.49926	.49929
3.2	.49931	.49934	.49936	.49938	.49940	.49942	.49944	.49946	.49948	.49950
3.3	.49952	.49953	.49955	.49957	.49958	.49960	.49961	.49962	.49964	.49965

Table IV (*Contd.*)

3.4	.49966	.49968	.49969	.49970	.49971	.49972	.49973	.49974	.49975	.49976
3.5	.49977	.49978	.49978	.49979	.49980	.49981	.49981	.49982	.49983	.49983
3.6	.49984	.49985	.49985	.49986	.49986	.49987	.49987	.49988	.49988	.49989
3.7	.49989	.49990	.49990	.49990	.49991	.49991	.49992	.49992	.49992	.49992
3.8	.49993	.49993	.49993	.49994	.49994	.49994	.49994	.49995	.49995	.49995
3.9	.49995	.49995	.49996	.49996	.49996	.49996	.49996	.49996	.49997	.49997
4.0	.49997	–	–	–	–	–	–	–	–	–
4.5	.499997	–	–	–	–	–	–	–	–	–
5.0	.4999997	–	–	–	–	–	–	–	–	–

Table is taken from Table 11_1 of Fisher and Yates, *Statistical Tables for Biological, Agricultural and Medical Research,* Longman Group Ltd., London, (previously published by Olivers and Boyd, Edinburgh), by the permission of the authors and publishers.

Table V. Percentage Points of the t-Distribution

υ	$\alpha = 0.4$ $2\alpha = 0.8$	0.25 0.5	0.1 0.2	0.05 0.1	0.025 0.05	0.01 0.02	0.005 0.01	0.0025 0.005	0.001 0.002	0.0005 0.001
1	0.325	1.000	3.078	6.314	12.706	31.821	63.657	127.320	318.31	636.620
2	.289	0.816	1.886	2.920	4.303	6.965	9.925	14.089	22.326	31.593
3	.277	.765	1.638	2.353	3.182	4.541	5.841	7.453	10.213	12.924
4	.271	.741	1.533	2.132	2.776	3.747	4.604	5.598	7.173	8.610
5	0.267	0.727	1.476	2.015	2.571	3.365	4.032	4.773	5.893	6.889
6	.265	.718	1.440	1.943	2.447	3.143	3.707	4.317	5.208	5.959
7	.263	.711	1.415	1.895	2.365	2.998	3.499	4.029	4.785	5.408
8	.262	.706	1.397	1.860	2.306	2.896	3.355	3.833	4.501	5.041
9	.261	.703	1.383	1.833	2.262	2.821	3.250	3.690	4.297	4.781
10	0.260	0.700	1.372	1.812	2.228	2.764	3.169	3.581	4.144	4.587
11	.260	.697	1.363	1.796	2.201	2.718	3.106	3.497	4.025	4.437
12	.259	.695	1.356	1.782	2.179	2.681	3.055	3.428	3.930	4.318
13	.259	.694	1.350	1.771	2.160	2.650	3.012	3.372	3.852	4.221
14	.258	.692	1.345	1.761	2.145	2.624	2.977	3.326	3.787	4.140
15	0.258	0.691	1.341	1.753	2.131	2.602	2.947	3.286	3.733	4.073
16	.258	.690	1.337	1.746	2.120	2.583	2.921	3.252	3.686	4.015
17	.257	.689	1.333	1.740	2.110	2.567	2.898	3.222	3.646	3.965
18	.257	.688	1.330	1.734	2.101	2.552	2.878	3.197	3.610	3.922
19	.257	.688	1.328	1.729	2.093	2.539	2.861	3.174	3.579	3.883
20	0.257	0.687	1.325	1.725	2.086	2.528	2.845	3.153	3.552	3.850
21	.257	.686	1.323	1.721	2.080	2.518	2.831	3.135	3.527	3.819
22	.256	.686	1.321	1.717	2.074	2.508	2.819	3.119	3.505	3.792
23	.256	.685	1.319	1.714	2.069	2.500	2.807	3.104	3.485	3.767
24	.256	.685	1.318	1.711	2.064	2.492	2.797	3.091	3.467	3.745
25	0.256	0.684	1.316	1.708	2.060	2.485	2.787	3.078	3.450	3.725
26	.256	.684	1.315	1.706	2.056	2.479	2.779	3.067	3.435	3.707
27	.256	.684	1.314	1.703	2.052	2.473	2.771	3.050	3.421	3.690
28	.256	.683	1.313	1.701	2.048	2.467	2.763	3.047	3.408	3.674
29	.256	.683	1.311	1.699	2.045	2.462	2.756	3.038	3.396	3.659
30	0.256	0.683	1.310	1.697	2.042	2.457	2.750	3.030	3.385	3.646
40	.255	.681	1.303	1.684	2.021	2.423	2.704	2.971	3.307	3.551
60	.254	.679	1.296	1.671	2.000	2.390	2.660	2.915	3.232	3.460
120	.254	.677	1.289	1.658	1.980	2.358	2.617	2.860	3.160	3.373
∞	.253	.674	1.282	1.645	1.960	2.326	2.576	2.807	3.090	3.291

$\alpha = 1 - P(t/\upsilon)$ is the upper-tail area of the distribution for υ degrees of freedom, appropriate for use in a single tail test. For a two-tail test, 2α must be used.

Source: The table is reproduced with the kind permission of the trustees of Biometrika from E.S. Pearson and H.O. Hartley (eds.), Biometrika Table for Statisticians. Vol. 1, 3rd edn., 1966.

Table VI. Percentage Points of the χ^2-Distribution

ν \ α	0.250	0.100	0.050	0.025	0.010	0.005	0.001
1	1.32330	2.70554	3.84146	5.02389	6.63490	7.87944	10.828
2	2.77259	4.60517	5.99147	7.37776	9.21034	10.5966	13.816
3	4.10835	6.25139	7.81473	9.34840	11.3449	12.8381	16.266
4	5.38527	7.77944	9.48773	11.1433	13.2767	14.8602	18.467
5	6.62568	9.23635	11.0705	12.8325	15.0863	16.7496	20.515
6	7.84080	10.6446	12.5916	14.4494	16.8119	18.5476	22.458
7	9.03715	12.0170	14.0671	16.0128	18.4753	20.2777	24.322
8	10.2188	13.3616	15.5073	17.5346	20.0902	21.9550	26.125
9	11.3887	14.6837	16.9190	19.0228	21.6660	23.5893	27.877
10	12.5489	15.9871	18.3070	20.4831	23.2093	25.1882	29.588
11	13.7007	17.2750	19.6751	21.9200	24.7250	26.7569	31.264
12	14.8454	18.5494	21.0261	23.3367	26.2170	28.2995	32.909
13	15.9839	19.8119	22.3621	24.7356	27.6883	29.8194	34.528
14	17.1170	21.0642	23.6848	26.1190	29.1413	31.3193	36.123
15	18.2451	22.3072	24.9958	27.4884	30.5779	32.8013	37.697
16	19.3688	23.5418	26.2962	28.8454	31.9999	34.2672	39.252
17	20.4887	24.7690	27.5871	30.1910	33.4087	35.7185	40.790
18	21.6049	25.9894	28.8693	31.5264	34.8053	37.1564	42.312
19	22.7178	27.2036	30.1435	32.8523	36.1908	38.5822	43.820
20	28.8277	28.4120	31.4104	34.1696	37.5662	39.9968	45.315
21	24.9348	29.6151	32.6705	35.4789	38.9321	41.4010	46.797
22	26.0393	30.8133	33.9244	36.7807	40.2894	42.7956	48.268
23	27.1413	32.0069	35.1725	38.0757	41.6384	44.1813	49.728
24	28.2412	33.1963	36.4151	39.3641	42.9798	45.5585	51.179
25	29.3389	34.3816	37.6525	40.6465	44.3141	46.9278	52.620
26	30.4345	35.5631	38.8852	41.9232	45.6417	40.2899	54.052
27	31.5284	36.7412	40.1133	43.1944	46.9630	49.6449	55.476
28	32.6205	37.9159	41.3372	44.4607	48.2782	50.9933	56.892
29	33.7109	39.0875	42.5569	45.7222	49.5879	52.3356	58.302
30	34.7998	40.2560	43.7729	46.9792	50.8922	53.6720	59.703
40	45.6160	51.8050	55.7585	59.3417	63.6907	66.7659	73.402
50	56.3336	63.1671	67.5048	71.4202	76.1539	79.4900	86.661
60	66.9814	74.3970	79.0819	83.2976	88.3794	91.9517	99.607
70	77.5766	85.5271	90.5312	95.0231	100.425	104.215	112.317
80	88.1303	96.5782	101.879	106.620	112.329	116.321	124.839
90	98.6499	107.565	113.145	118.136	124.116	128.299	137.208
100	109.141	118.498	124.342	129.561	135.807	140.169	149.449
X	+0.6745	+1.2816	+1.6449	+1.9600	+2.3263	+2.5758	+3.0902

For $\nu > 100$ take

$$\chi^2 = \nu\left\{1 - \frac{2}{9\nu} + X\sqrt{\frac{2}{9\nu}}\right\}^3 \quad \text{or} \quad \chi^2 = \frac{1}{2}\{X + \sqrt{(2\nu - 1)}\}^2$$

according to the degree of accuracy required. X is the standardized normal deviate corresponding to $P = 1 - \alpha$, and is shown in the bottom line of the table.

Source: The table is reproduced with the kind permission of the Trustees of Biometrika from E.S. Pearson and H.O. Hartley (eds.) Biometrika Tables for Statisticians, Vol. 1 , 3rd. edition, 1966.

Table VII$_i$. Percentage Points of the F-Distribution

Upper 1% points

υ_2 \ υ_1	1	2	3	4	5	6	7	8	9
1	4052	4999.5	5403	5625	5764	5859	5928	5982	6022
2	98.50	99.00	99.17	99.25	99.30	99.33	99.36	99.37	99.39
3	34.12	30.82	29.46	28.71	28.24	27.91	27.67	27.49	27.35
4	21.20	18.00	16.69	15.98	15.52	15.21	14.98	14.80	14.66
5	16.26	13.27	12.06	11.39	10.97	10.67	10.46	10.29	10.16
6	13.75	10.92	9.78	9.15	8.75	8.47	8.26	8.10	7.98
7	12.25	9.95	8.45	7.85	7.46	7.19	6.99	6.84	6.72
8	11.26	8.65	7.59	7.01	6.63	6.37	6.18	6.03	5.91
9	10.56	8.02	6.99	6.42	6.06	5.80	5.61	5.47	5.35
10	10.04	7.56	6.55	5.99	5.64	5.39	5.20	5.06	4.94
11	9.65	7.21	6.22	5.67	5.32	5.07	4.89	4.74	4.63
12	9.33	6.93	5.95	5.41	5.06	4.82	4.64	4.50	4.39
13	9.07	6.70	5.74	5.21	4.86	4.62	4.44	4.30	4.19
14	8.86	6.51	5.56	5.04	4.69	4.46	4.28	4.14	4.03
15	8.68	6.36	5.42	4.89	4.56	4.32	4.14	4.00	3.89
16	8.53	6.23	5.29	4.77	4.44	4.20	4.03	3.89	3.78
17	8.40	6.11	5.18	4.67	4.34	4.10	3.93	3.79	3.68
18	8.29	6.01	5.09	4.58	4.25	4.01	3.84	3.71	3.60
19	8.18	5.93	5.01	4.50	4.17	3.94	3.77	3.63	3.52
20	8.10	5.85	4.94	4.43	4.10	3.87	3.70	3.56	3.46
21	8.02	5.78	4.87	4.37	4.04	3.81	3.64	3.51	3.40
22	7.95	5.72	4.82	4.31	3.99	3.76	3.59	3.45	3.35
23	7.88	5.66	4.76	4.26	3.94	3.71	3.54	3.41	3.30
24	7.82	5.61	4.72	4.22	3.90	3.67	3.50	3.36	3.26
25	7.77	5.57	4.68	4.18	3.85	3.63	3.46	3.32	3.22
26	7.72	5.53	4.64	4.14	3.82	3.59	3.42	3.29	3.18
27	7.68	5.49	4.60	4.11	3.78	3.56	3.39	3.26	3.15
28	7.64	5.45	4.57	4.07	3.75	3.53	3.36	3.23	3.12
29	7.60	5.42	4.54	4.04	3.73	3.50	3.33	3.20	3.09
30	7.56	5.39	4.51	4.02	3.70	3.47	3.30	3.17	3.07
40	7.31	5.18	4.31	3.83	3.51	3.29	3.12	2.99	2.89
60	7.08	4.98	4.13	3.65	3.34	3.12	2.95	2.82	2.72
120	6.85	4.79	3.95	3.48	3.17	3.96	2.79	2.66	2.56
∞	6.63	4.61	3.78	3.32	3.02	2.80	2.64	2.51	2.41

Table VII$_i$ (*contd.*)

10	12	15	20	24	30	40	60	120	∞
6056	6106	6157	6209	6235	6261	6287	6313	6339	6366
99.40	99.42	99.43	99.45	99.46	99.47	99.77	99.48	99.49	99.50
27.23	27.05	26.87	26.69	26.60	26.50	26.41	26.32	26.22	26.13
14.55	14.37	14.20	14.02	13.93	13.84	13.75	13.65	13.56	13.46
10.05	9.89	9.72	9.55	9.47	9.38	9.29	9.20	9.11	9.02
7.87	7.72	7.56	7.40	7.31	7.23	7.14	7.06	6.97	6.88
6.63	6.47	6.31	6.16	6.07	5.99	5.91	5.82	5.74	5.65
5.81	5.67	5.52	5.36	5.28	5.20	5.12	5.03	4.95	4.86
5.26	5.11	4.96	4.81	4.73	4.65	4.57	4.48	4.40	4.31
4.85	4.71	4.56	4.41	4.33	4.25	4.17	4.08	4.00	3.91
4.54	4.40	4.25	4.10	4.02	3.94	3.86	3.78	3.69	3.60
4.30	4.16	4.01	3.86	3.78	3.70	3.62	3.54	3.45	3.36
4.10	3.96	3.82	3.66	3.59	3.51	3.43	3.34	3.25	3.17
3.94	3.80	3.66	3.51	3.43	3.35	3.27	3.18	3.09	3.00
3.80	3.67	3.52	3.37	3.29	3.21	3.13	3.05	2.96	2.87
3.69	3.55	3.41	3.26	3.18	3.10	3.02	2.93	2.84	2.75
3.59	3.46	3.31	3.16	3.08	3.00	2.92	2.83	2.75	2.65
3.51	3.37	3.23	3.08	3.00	2.92	2.84	2.75	2.66	2.57
3.43	3.30	3.15	3.00	2.92	2.84	2.76	2.67	2.58	2.49
3.37	3.23	3.09	2.94	2.86	2.78	2.69	2.61	2.52	2.42
3.31	3.17	3.03	2.88	2.80	2.72	2.64	2.55	2.46	2.36
3.26	3.12	2.98	2.83	2.75	2.67	2.58	2.50	2.40	2.31
3.21	3.07	2.93	2.78	2.70	2.62	2.54	2.45	2.35	2.26
3.17	3.03	2.89	2.74	2.66	2.58	2.49	2.40	2.31	2.21
3.13	2.99	2.85	2.70	2.62	2.54	2.45	2.36	2.27	2.17
3.09	2.96	2.81	2.66	2.58	2.50	2.42	2.33	2.23	2.13
3.06	2.93	2.78	2.63	2.55	2.47	2.38	2.29	2.20	2.10
3.03	2.90	2.75	2.60	2.52	2.44	2.35	2.26	2.17	2.06
3.00	2.87	2.73	2.57	2.49	2.41	2.33	2.23	2.14	2.03
2.98	2.84	2.70	2.55	2.47	2.39	2.30	2.21	2.11	2.01
2.80	2.66	2.52	2.37	2.29	2.20	2.11	2.02	1.92	1.80
2.63	2.50	2.35	2.20	2.12	2.03	1.94	1.84	1.73	1.60
2.47	2.34	2.19	2.03	1.95	1.86	1.76	1.66	1.53	1.38
2.32	2.18	2.04	1.88	1.79	1.70	1.59	1.47	1.32	1.00

$F = \dfrac{s_1^2}{s_2^2} = \dfrac{S_1}{v_1} / \dfrac{S_2}{v_2}$ where $s_1^2 = S_1 / v_1$ and $s_2^2 = S_2 / v_2$ are independent mean squares estimating a common variance σ^2 and based on v_1 and v_2 degrees of freedom, respectively.

Table VII$_{ii}$. Percentage Points of the F-Distribution

Upper 5% points

υ_2 \ υ_1	1	2	3	4	5	6	7	8	9
1	161.4	199.5	215.7	224.6	230.2	234.0	236.8	238.9	240.5
2	18.51	19.00	19.16	19.25	19.30	19.33	19.35	19.37	19.38
3	10.13	9.55	9.28	9.12	9.01	8.94	8.89	8.85	8.81
4	7.71	6.94	6.59	6.39	6.26	6.16	6.09	6.04	6.00
5	6.61	5.79	5.41	5.19	5.05	4.95	4.88	4.82	4.77
6	5.99	5.14	4.76	4.53	4.39	4.28	4.21	4.15	4.10
7	5.59	4.74	4.35	4.12	3.97	3.87	3.79	3.73	3.68
8	5.32	4.46	4.07	3.84	3.69	3.58	3.50	3.44	3.39
9	5.12	4.26	3.86	3.63	3.48	3.37	3.29	3.23	3.18
10	4.96	4.10	3.71	3.48	3.33	3.22	3.14	3.07	3.02
11	4.84	3.98	3.59	3.36	3.20	3.09	3.01	2.95	2.90
12	4.75	3.89	3.49	3.26	3.11	3.00	2.91	2.85	2.80
13	4.67	3.81	3.41	3.18	3.03	2.92	2.83	2.77	2.71
14	4.60	3.74	3.34	3.11	2.96	2.85	2.76	2.70	2.65
15	4.54	3.68	3.29	3.06	2.90	2.79	2.71	2.64	2.59
16	4.49	3.63	3.24	3.01	2.85	2.74	2.66	2.59	2.54
17	4.45	3.59	3.20	2.96	2.81	2.70	2.61	2.55	2.49
18	4.41	3.55	3.16	2.93	2.77	2.66	2.58	2.51	2.46
19	4.38	3.52	3.13	2.90	2.74	2.63	2.54	2.48	2.42
20	4.35	3.49	3.10	2.87	2.71	2.60	2.51	2.45	2.39
21	4.32	3.47	3.07	2.84	2.68	2.57	2.49	2.42	2.37
22	4.30	3.44	3.05	2.82	2.66	2.55	2.46	2.40	2.34
23	4.28	3.42	3.03	2.80	2.64	2.53	2.44	2.37	2.32
24	4.26	3.40	3.01	2.78	2.62	2.51	2.42	2.36	2.30
25	4.24	3.39	2.99	2.76	2.60	2.49	2.40	2.34	2.28
26	4.23	3.37	2.98	2.74	2.59	2.47	2.39	2.32	2.27
27	4.21	3.35	2.96	2.73	2.57	2.46	2.37	2.31	2.25
28	4.20	3.34	2.95	2.71	2.56	2.45	2.36	2.29	2.24
29	4.18	3.33	2.93	2.70	2.55	2.43	2.35	2.28	2.22
30	4.17	3.32	2.92	2.69	2.53	2.42	2.33	2.27	2.21
40	4.08	3.23	2.84	2.61	2.45	2.34	2.25	2.18	2.12
60	4.00	3.15	2.76	2.53	2.37	2.25	2.17	2.10	2.04
120	3.92	3.07	2.68	2.45	2.29	2.17	2.09	2.02	1.96
∞	3.84	3.00	2.60	2.37	2.21	2.10	2.01	1.94	1.88

Table VII$_{ii}$. (*Contd.*)

10	12	15	20	24	30	40	60	120	∞
241.9	243.9	245.9	248.0	249.1	250.1	251.1	252.2	253.3	254.3
19.40	19.41	19.43	19.45	19.45	19.46	19.47	19.48	19.49	19.50
8.79	8.74	8.70	8.66	8.64	8.62	8.59	8.57	8.55	8.53
5.96	5.91	5.86	5.80	5.77	5.75	5.72	5.69	5.66	5.63
4.74	4.68	4.62	4.56	4.53	4.50	4.46	4.43	4.40	4.36
4.06	4.00	3.94	3.87	3.84	3.81	3.77	3.74	3.70	3.67
3.64	3.57	3.51	3.44	3.41	3.38	3.34	3.30	3.27	3.23
3.35	3.28	3.22	3.15	3.12	3.08	3.04	3.01	2.97	2.93
3.14	3.07	3.01	2.94	2.90	2.86	2.83	2.79	2.75	2.71
2.98	2.91	2.85	2.77	2.74	2.70	2.66	2.62	2.58	2.54
2.85	2.79	2.72	2.65	2.61	2.57	2.53	2.49	2.45	2.40
2.75	2.69	2.62	2.54	2.51	2.47	2.43	2.38	2.34	2.30
2.67	2.60	2.53	2.46	2.42	2.38	2.34	2.30	2.05	2.21
2.60	2.53	2.46	2.39	2.35	2.31	2.27	2.22	2.18	2.13
2.54	2.48	2.40	2.33	2.29	2.25	2.20	2.16	2.11	2.07
2.49	2.42	2.35	2.28	2.24	2.19	2.15	2.11	2.06	2.01
2.45	2.38	2.31	2.23	2.19	2.15	2.10	2.06	2.01	1.96
2.41	2.34	2.27	2.19	2.15	2.11	2.06	2.02	1.97	1.92
2.38	2.31	2.23	2.16	2.11	2.07	2.03	1.98	1.93	1.88
2.35	2.28	2.20	2.12	2.08	2.04	1.99	1.95	1.90	1.84
2.32	2.25	2.18	2.10	2.05	2.01	1.96	1.92	1.87	1.81
2.30	2.23	2.15	2.07	2.03	1.98	1.94	1.89	1.84	1.78
2.27	2.20	2.13	2.05	2.01	1.96	1.91	1.86	1.81	1.76
2.25	2.18	2.11	2.03	1.98	1.94	1.89	1.84	1.79	1.73
2.24	2.16	2.09	2.01	1.96	1.92	1.87	1.82	1.77	1.71
2.22	2.15	2.07	1.99	1.95	1.90	1.85	1.80	1.75	1.69
2.20	2.13	2.06	1.97	1.93	1.88	1.84	1.79	1.73	1.67
2.19	2.12	2.04	1.96	1.91	1.87	1.82	1.77	1.71	1.65
2.18	2.10	2.03	1.94	1.90	1.85	1.81	1.75	1.70	1.64
2.16	2.09	2.01	1.93	1.89	1.84	1.79	1.74	1.68	1.62
2.08	2.00	1.92	1.84	1.79	1.74	1.69	1.64	1.58	1.51
1.99	1.92	1.84	1.75	1.70	1.65	1.59	1.53	1.47	1.39
1.91	1.83	1.75	1.66	1.61	1.55	1.50	1.43	1.35	1.25
1.83	1.75	1.67	1.57	1.52	1.46	1.39	1.32	1.22	1.00

$F = \dfrac{s_1^2}{s_2^2} = \dfrac{S_1}{\upsilon_1} / \dfrac{S_2}{\upsilon_2}$ where $s_1^2 = S_1/\upsilon_1$ and $s_2^2 = S_2/\upsilon_2$ are independent mean squares estimating a common variance σ^2 and based on υ_1 and υ_2 degrees of freedom, respectively.

Table VII$_{iii}$. Percentage Points of the F-Distribution

Upper 10% points

ν_2 \ ν_1	1	2	3	4	5	6	7	8	9
1	39.86	49.50	53.59	55.83	57.24	58.20	58.91	59.44	59.86
2	8.53	9.00	9.16	9.24	9.29	9.33	9.35	9.37	9.38
3	5.54	5.46	5.39	5.34	5.31	5.28	5.27	5.25	5.24
4	4.54	4.32	4.19	4.11	4.05	4.01	3.98	3.95	3.94
5	4.06	3.78	3.62	3.52	3.45	3.40	3.37	3.34	3.32
6	3.78	3.46	3.29	3.18	3.11	3.05	3.01	2.98	2.96
7	3.59	3.26	3.07	2.96	2.88	2.83	2.78	2.75	2.72
8	3.46	3.11	2.92	2.81	2.73	2.67	2.62	2.59	2.56
9	3.36	3.01	2.81	2.69	2.61	2.55	2.51	2.47	2.44
10	3.29	2.92	2.73	2.61	2.52	2.46	2.41	2.38	2.35
11	3.23	2.86	2.66	2.54	2.45	2.39	2.34	2.30	2.27
12	3.18	2.81	2.61	2.48	2.39	2.33	2.28	2.24	2.21
13	3.14	2.76	2.56	2.43	2.35	2.28	2.23	2.20	2.16
14	3.10	2.73	2.52	2.39	2.31	2.24	2.19	2.15	2.12
15	3.07	2.70	2.49	2.36	2.27	2.21	2.16	2.12	2.09
16	3.05	2.67	2.46	2.33	2.24	2.18	2.13	2.09	2.06
17	3.03	2.64	2.44	2.31	2.22	2.15	2.10	2.06	2.03
18	3.01	2.62	2.42	2.29	2.20	2.13	2.08	2.04	2.00
19	2.99	2.61	2.40	2.27	2.18	2.11	2.06	2.02	1.98
20	2.97	2.59	2.38	2.25	2.16	2.09	2.04	2.00	1.96
21	2.96	2.57	2.36	2.23	2.14	2.08	2.02	1.98	1.95
22	2.95	2.56	2.35	2.22	2.13	2.06	2.01	1.97	1.93
23	2.94	2.55	2.34	2.21	2.11	2.05	1.99	1.95	1.92
24	2.93	2.54	2.33	2.19	2.10	2.04	1.98	1.94	1.91
25	2.92	2.53	2.32	2.18	2.09	2.02	1.97	1.93	1.89
26	2.91	2.52	2.31	2.17	2.08	2.01	1.96	1.92	1.88
27	2.90	2.51	2.30	2.17	2.07	2.00	1.95	1.91	1.87
28	2.89	2.50	2.29	2.16	2.06	2.00	1.94	1.90	1.87
29	2.89	2.50	2.28	2.15	2.06	1.99	1.93	1.89	1.86
30	2.88	2.49	2.28	2.14	2.05	1.98	1.93	1.88	1.85
40	2.84	2.44	2.23	2.09	2.00	1.93	1.87	1.83	1.79
60	2.79	2.39	2.18	2.04	1.95	1.87	1.82	1.77	1.74
120	2.75	2.35	2.13	1.99	1.90	1.82	1.77	1.72	1.68
∞	2.71	2.30	2.08	1.94	1.85	1.77	1.72	1.67	1.63

Table VII$_{iii}$ (Contd.)

10	12	15	20	24	30	40	60	120	∞
60.19	60.71	61.22	61.74	62.00	62.26	62.53	62.79	63.06	63.33
9.39	9.41	9.42	9.44	9.45	9.46	9.47	9.47	9.48	9.49
5.23	5.22	5.20	5.18	5.18	5.17	5.16	5.15	5.14	5.13
3.92	3.90	3.87	3.84	3.83	3.82	3.80	3.79	3.78	3.76
3.30	3.27	3.24	3.21	3.19	3.17	3.16	3.14	3.12	3.10
2.94	2.90	2.87	2.84	2.82	2.80	2.78	2.76	2.74	2.72
2.70	2.67	2.63	2.59	2.58	2.56	2.54	2.51	2.49	2.47
2.54	2.50	2.46	2.42	2.40	2.38	2.36	2.34	2.32	2.29
2.42	2.38	2.34	2.30	2.28	2.25	2.23	2.21	2.18	2.16
2.32	2.28	2.24	2.20	2.18	2.16	2.13	2.11	2.08	2.06
2.25	2.21	2.17	2.12	2.10	2.08	2.05	2.03	2.00	1.97
2.19	2.15	2.10	2.06	2.04	2.01	1.99	1.96	1.93	1.90
2.14	2.10	2.00	2.01	1.98	1.96	1.93	1.90	1.88	1.85
2.10	2.05	2.08	1.96	1.94	1.91	1.89	1.86	1.83	1.80
2.06	2.02	1.97	1.92	1.90	1.87	1.85	1.82	1.79	1.76
2.03	1.99	1.94	1.89	1.87	1.84	1.81	1.78	1.75	1.72
2.00	1.96	1.91	1.86	1.84	1.81	1.78	1.75	1.72	1.69
1.98	1.93	1.89	1.84	1.81	1.78	1.75	1.72	1.69	1.66
1.96	1.91	1.86	1.81	1.79	1.76	1.73	1.70	1.67	1.63
1.94	1.89	1.84	1.79	1.77	1.74	1.71	1.68	1.64	1.61
1.92	1.87	1.83	1.78	1.75	1.72	1.69	1.66	1.62	1.59
1.90	1.86	1.81	1.76	1.73	1.70	1.67	1.64	1.60	1.57
1.89	1.84	1.80	1.74	1.72	1.69	1.66	1.62	1.59	1.55
1.88	1.83	1.78	1.73	1.70	1.67	1.64	1.61	1.57	1.53
1.87	1.82	1.77	1.72	1.69	1.66	1.63	1.59	1.56	1.52
1.86	1.81	1.76	1.71	1.68	1.65	1.61	1.58	1.54	1.50
1.85	1.80	1.75	1.70	1.67	1.64	1.60	1.57	1.53	1.49
1.84	1.79	1.74	1.69	1.66	1.63	1.59	1.56	1.52	1.48
1.83	1.78	1.73	1.68	1.65	1.62	1.58	1.55	1.51	1.47
1.82	1.77	1.72	1.67	1.64	1.61	1.57	1.54	1.50	1.46
1.76	1.71	1.66	1.61	1.57	1.54	1.51	1.47	1.42	1.38
1.71	1.66	1.60	1.54	1.51	1.48	1.44	1.40	1.35	1.29
1.65	1.60	1.55	1.48	1.45	1.41	1.37	1.32	1.26	1.19
1.60	1.55	1.49	1.42	1.38	1.34	1.30	1.24	1.17	1.00

$F = \dfrac{s_1^2}{s_2^2} = \dfrac{S_1}{\upsilon_1} / \dfrac{S_2}{\upsilon_2}$ where $s_1^2 = S_1/\upsilon_1$ and $s_2^2 = S_2/\upsilon_2$ are independent mean squares estimating a common variance σ^2 and based on υ_1 and υ_2 degrees of freedom, respectively.

Tables VII, (*i*), (*ii*) and (*iii*) are adopted from table V or Fisher and Yates, Statistical Tables for Biological, Agricultural and Medical Research, Longman Group Ltd., London, with the kind permission of the authors and the publisher.

Table VIII. Transformation from r to $Z = \frac{1}{2}\log_e\left(\frac{1+r}{1-r}\right)$

r	0.00	0.01	0.02	0.03	0.04	0.05	0.06	0.07	0.08	0.09
0	0.0000	0.0100	0.0200	0.0300	0.0400	0.0500	0.0601	0.0701	0.0802	0.0902
.1	0.1003	0.1104	0.1206	0.1307	0.1409	0.1511	0.1614	0.7117	0.1820	0.1923
.2	0.2027	0.2132	0.2237	0.2342	0.2448	0.2554	0.2661	0.2769	0.2877	0.2986
.3	0.3005	0.3205	0.3316	0.3428	0.3541	0.3654	0.3769	0.3884	0.4001	0.4118
.4	0.4236	0.4356	0.4477	0.4599	0.4722	0.4847	0.4973	0.5101	0.5230	0.5361
.5	0.5493	0.5627	0.5763	0.5901	0.6042	0.6184	0.6328	0.6475	0.6625	0.6777
.6	0.6931	0.7089	0.7250	0.7414	0.7582	0.7753	0.7928	0.8107	0.8291	0.8480
.7	0.8673	0.8872	0.9076	0.9287	0.9505	0.9730	0.9962	1.0203	1.0454	1.0714
.8	1.0996	1.1270	1.1568	1.1881	1.2212	1.2562	1.2933	1.3331	1.3758	1.4219
.9	1.4722	1.5275	1.5890	1.6584	1.7380	1.8318	1.9459	2.0923	2.2976	2.6467

Table IX. Acceptance Limits for the Kolmogoroy-Smirnov Test of Goodness of Fit

Sample size (n)	*Significance level*				
	.20	.15	.10	.05	.01
1	.900	.925	.950	.975	.995
2	.684	.726	.776	.842	.929
3	.565	.597	.642	.708	.829
4	.494	.525	.564	.624	.734
5	.446	.474	.510	.563	.669
6	.410	.436	.470	.521	.618
7	.381	.405	.438	.486	.577
8	.358	.381	.411	.457	.543
9	.339	.360	.388	.432	.514
10	.322	.342	.368	.409	.486
11	.307	.326	.352	.391	.468
12	.295	.313	.338	.375	.450
13	.284	.302	.325	.361	.433
14	.274	.292	.314	.349	.418
15	.266	.283	.304	.338	.404
16	.258	.274	.295	.328	.391
17	.250	.266	.286	.318	.380
18	.244	.259	.278	.309	.370
19	.237	.252	.272	.301	.361
20	.231	.246	.264	.294	.352
25	.21	.22	.24	.264	.32
30	.19	.20	.22	.242	.29
35	.18	.19	.21	.23	.27
40				.21	.25
50				.19	.23
60				.17	.21
70				.16	.19
80				.15	.18
90				.14	
100				.14	
Asymptotic Formula	$\frac{1.07}{\sqrt{n}}$	$\frac{1.14}{\sqrt{n}}$	$\frac{1.22}{\sqrt{n}}$	$\frac{1.36}{\sqrt{n}}$	$\frac{1.63}{\sqrt{n}}$

Reject the hypothetical distribution $F(x)$ if $D_a = \max | F_a(x) - F(x) |$ exceeds the tabulated value. (For $\alpha = .01$ and .05, asymptotic formulae give values which are too high – by 1.5 per cent for $n = 80$). This table is taken from F.J. Massey, Jr., "The Kolmogorov Smirnov Test for Goodness of Fit, "*J.Am. Stat. Assn.* 46, 68–78 (1951), except that certain corrections and additional entries are from Z.W. Birnbaum, "Numerical Tabulation of the Distribution of Kolmogorov's Statistic for Finite Sample Size, "*J.Am. Stat. Assn*, 47, 425–41 (1952), with the kind permission of the authors and the *J.Am. Stat. Assn.*

Table X. Cumulative Probabilities Associated with Values as small as $x = r$ in the Binomial test when $P = Q = \frac{1}{2}$ Under H_0.

n \ r	0	1	2	3	4	5	6	7	8	9
5	.0312	.1875	.5000	.8125	.9688	1.00				
6	.0156	.1094	.3437	.6562	.8906	.9843	1.00			
7	.0078	.0625	.2266	.5000	.7734	.9375	.9922	1.00		
8	.0039	.0352	.1445	.3633	.6367	.8555	.9648	.9961	1.00	
9	.0020	.0196	.0899	.2540	.5000	.7462	.9102	.9805	.9981	1.00
10	.0010	.0108	.0547	.1719	.3770	.6230	.8281	.9453	.9893	.9990
11	.0005	.0058	.0327	.1133	.2744	.5000	.7256	.8867	.9673	.9941
12	.0002	.0029	.0193	.0730	.1938	.3872	.6127	.8061	.9269	.9807
13	.0001	.0017	.0112	.0461	.1334	.2905	.5000	.7095	.8666	.9538
14	6×10^{-5}	.0009	.0065	.0287	.0898	.2120	.3953	.6048	.7880	.9102
15	3×10^{-5}	.0005	.0037	.0176	.0592	.1509	.3036	.5000	.6964	.8491
16	1.5×10^{-5}	2.6×10^{-4}	.0021	.0106	.0384	.1050	.2272	.4018	.5982	.7728
17	7.6×10^{-6}	1.4×10^{-4}	.0012	.0064	.0245	.0717	.1661	.3145	.5000	.6855
18	3.8×10^{-6}	7.2×10^{-5}	.0007	.0038	.0154	.0481	.1189	.2403	.4073	.5927
19	1.9×10^{-6}	3.8×10^{-5}	.0004	.0022	.0096	.0318	.0835	.1796	.3238	.5000
20	9.5×10^{-7}	2.0×10^{-5}	.0002	.0013	.0059	.0207	.0576	.1316	.2517	.4119
21	4.8×10^{-7}	$1.0\times10^{015-5}$	.0001	.0007	.0036	.0133	.0392	.0946	.1916	.3318
22	2.4×10^{-7}	5.5×10^{-6}	6.6×10^{-5}	.0004	.0022	.0084	.0262	.0668	.1431	.2617
23	1.2×10^{-7}	2.8×10^{-6}	3.3×10^{-5}	.0002	.0013	.0053	.0173	.0466	.1050	.2024
24	6.0×10^{-8}	1.5×10^{-6}	1.8×10^{-5}	.0001	.0008	.0033	.0113	.0320	.0758	.1538

Table X (*Contd.*)

n \ r	10	11	12	13	14	15	16	17	18	19	20
5											
6											
7											
8											
9											
10	1.00										
11	.9995	1.00									
12	.9968	.9997	1.00								
13	.9888	.9983	.9999	1.00							
14	.9713	.9936	.9991	.9999							
15	.9408	.9824	.9963	.9995							
16	.8949	.9616	.9894	.9979	.9997						
17	.8338	.9283	.9755	.9936	.9988	.9999					
18	.7596	.8810	.9519	.9846	.9962	.9993	.9999				
19	.6762	.8204	.9165	.9682	.9904	.9978	.9996	.9999			
20	.5881	.7483	.8684	.9423	.9793	.9941	.9987	.9998			
21	.5000	.6682	.8083	.9054	.9608	.9867	.9964	.9992	.9999		
22	.4158	.5840	.7382	.8568	.9330	.9737	.9915	.9978	.9995	.9999	
23	.3388	.5000	.6612	.7976	.8950	.9534	.9826	.9947	.9987	.9998	.9999
24	.2707	.4194	.5806	.7294	.8463	.9242	.9681	.9887	.9967	.9993	.9999

Given in the bodies of Table F_i and Table F_{ii} are various critical values of r for various values of n_1 and n_2. For the one sample runs test, any value of r which is equal to or smaller than that shown in Table XI. F_i or equal to or larger than that shown in Table XI F_{ii} is significant at the .05 level. For the Wald-Wolfwitz two-sample runs test, any value of r which is equal or smaller than that shown in Table XI F_{ii} is significant at the .05 level.

Table XI F_i

n_1/n_2	2	3	4	5	6	7	8	9	10	11	12	13	14	15	16	17	18	19	20
2											2	2	2	2	2	2	2	2	2
3					2	2	2	2	2	2	2	2	2	3	3	3	3	3	3
4				2	2	2	3	3	3	3	3	3	3	3	4	4	4	4	4
5			2	2	3	3	3	3	3	4	4	4	4	4	4	4	5	5	5
6		2	2	3	3	3	3	4	4	4	4	5	5	5	5	5	5	6	6
7		2	2	3	3	3	4	4	5	5	5	5	5	6	6	6	6	6	6
8		2	3	3	3	4	4	5	5	5	6	6	6	6	6	7	7	7	7
9		2	3	3	4	4	5	5	5	6	6	6	7	7	7	7	8	8	8
10		2	3	3	4	5	5	5	6	6	7	7	7	7	8	8	8	8	9
11		2	3	4	4	5	5	6	6	7	7	7	8	8	8	9	9	9	9
12	2	2	3	4	4	5	6	6	7	7	7	8	8	8	9	9	9	10	10
13	2	2	3	4	5	5	6	6	7	7	8	8	9	9	9	10	10	10	10
14	2	2	3	4	5	5	6	7	7	8	8	9	9	9	10	10	10	11	11
15	2	3	3	4	5	6	6	7	7	8	8	9	9	10	10	11	11	11	12
16	2	3	4	4	5	6	6	7	8	8	9	9	10	10	11	11	11	12	12
17	2	3	4	4	5	6	7	7	8	9	9	10	10	11	11	11	12	12	13
18	2	3	4	5	5	6	7	8	8	9	9	10	10	11	11	12	12	13	13
19	2	3	4	5	6	6	7	8	8	9	10	10	11	11	12	12	13	13	13
20	2	3	4	5	6	6	7	8	9	9	10	10	11	12	12	13	13	13	14

* Adapted from Swed. Frieda S., and Eisenhart, C., 1943. Table for testing randomness of grouping in a sequence of alternative, *Ann. Math. Statist.* 14, 83–86 with the kind permission of the author and the publisher.

Table XI F_{ii}

n_1/n_2	2	3	4	5	6	7	8	9	10	11	12	13	14	15	16	17	18	19	20
2																			
3																			
4				9	9														
5			9	10	10	11	11												
6			9	10	11	12	12	13	13	13	13								
7				11	12	13	13	14	14	14	14	15	15	15					
8				11	12	13	14	14	15	15	16	16	16	16	17	17	17	17	17
9					13	14	14	15	16	16	16	17	17	18	18	18	18	18	18
10					13	14	15	16	16	17	17	18	18	18	19	19	19	20	20
11					13	14	15	16	17	17	18	19	19	19	20	20	20	21	21
12					13	14	16	16	17	18	19	19	20	20	21	21	21	22	22
13						15	16	17	18	19	19	20	20	21	21	22	22	23	23
14						15	16	17	18	19	20	20	21	22	22	23	23	23	24
15						15	16	18	18	19	20	21	22	22	23	23	24	24	25
16							17	18	19	20	21	21	22	23	23	24	25	25	25
17							17	18	19	20	21	22	23	23	24	25	25	26	26
18							17	18	19	20	21	22	23	24	25	25	26	26	27
19							17	18	20	21	22	23	23	24	25	26	26	27	27
20							17	18	20	21	22	23	24	25	25	26	27	27	28

* Adapted from Swed, Frieda S., amd Eisenhart, C. 1943. Tables for testing randomness of grouping in a sequence of alternatives. *Ann. Math. Statist.* 14, 83–86 with the kind permission of the authors and the publisher.

Table XII. Acceptance-Limits for the Two-sample Kolmogorov-Smirnov Test

Sample size n_2	Sample size n_1: 1	2	3	4	5	6	7	8	9	10	12	15
1	* *	* *	* *	* *	* *	* *	* *	* *	* *	* *		
2		* *	* *	* *	* *	* *	* *	7/8 *	16/18 *	9/10 *		
3			* *	* *	12/15 *	5/6 *	18/21 *	18/24 *	7/9 8/9		9/12 11/12	
4				3/4 *	16/20 *	9/12 10/12	21/28 24/28	6/8 7/8	27/36 32/36	14/20 16/20	8/12 10/12	
5					4/5 4/5	20/30 25/30	25/35 30/35	27/40 32/40	31/45 36/45	7/10 8/10		10/15 11/15
6						4/6 5/6	29/42 35/42	16/24 18/24	12/18 14/18	19/30 22/30	7/12 9/12	
7							5/7 5/7	35/56 42/56	40/63 47/63	43/70 53/70		
8								5/8 6/8	45/72 54/72	23/40 28/40	14/24 16/24	
9									5/9 6/9	52/90 62/90	20/36 24/36	
10										6/10 7/10		15/30 19/30
12											6/12 7/12	30/60 35/60
15												7/15 8/15

Note 1: Reject H_0 if $D = \max \mid F_{n2}(x) - F_{n1}(x)$ exceeds the tabulated value. The upper value gives a level at most. 05 and the lower at most .01.

Note 2: Where * appears, do not reject H_0 at the given level.

Note 3: For large values of n_1 and n_2, the following approximately formulas may be used:

$$\alpha = .10 : 1.22\sqrt{\frac{n_1+n_2}{n_1n_2}};\alpha = .05 : 1.36\sqrt{\frac{n_1+n_2}{n_1n_2}};\alpha = .025 : 1.48\sqrt{\frac{n_1+n_2}{n_1n_2}}$$

$$\alpha = .005 : 1.73\sqrt{\frac{n_1+n_2}{n_1n_2}};\alpha = .01 : 1.63\sqrt{\frac{n_1+n_2}{n_1n_2}};\alpha = .001 : 1.95\sqrt{\frac{n_1+n_2}{n_1n_2}}$$

This table is derived from E.J. Massey, "Distribution Table for the Deviation between Two Sample Cumulatives," *Ann. Math. Stat.* 23, 425–41 (1952). Adapted with the kind permission of the author and the *Ann. Math. Stat.* Formulas for large-sample sizes were given by N. Smirnov , "Tables for Estimating the Goodness of Fit of Empirical distributions," *Ann. Math. Stat.*, 19, 280–81 (1948).

Table XIII. Critical Values of T in the Wilcoxon Matched-Pairs Signed-Ranks Test*

N	*Level of significance for one-tailed test.*		
	.025	.01	.005
	Level of significance for two-tailed test		
	.05	.02	.01
6	0	–	–
7	2	0	–
8	4	2	0
9	6	3	2
10	8	5	3
11	11	7	5
12	14	10	7
13	17	13	10
14	21	16	13
15	25	20	16
16	30	24	20
17	35	28	23
18	40	33	28
19	46	38	32
20	52	43	38
21	59	49	43
22	66	56	49
23	73	62	55
24	81	69	61
25	89	77	68

* Adapted from table 1 of Wilcoxon, F, 1949, Some rapid approximate Statistical procedures, New York American Cyanamid Company, p. 13, with the kind permission of the author and publisher and the American Cyanamid Company.

Table XIV-a. Probabilities associated with Values as small as observed values of U in the Mann-Whitney Test.

$n_2 = 3$

U/n_1	1	2	3
0	.250	.100	.050
1	.500	.200	.100
2	.750	.400	.200
3		.600	.350
4			.500
5			.650

$n_2 = 4$

U/n_1	1	2	3	4
0	.200	.067	.028	.014
1	.400	.133	.057	.029
2	.600	.267	.114	.057
3		.400	.200	.100
4		.600	.314	.171
5			.429	.243
6			.571	.343
7				.443
8				.557

Table XIV-a *(Contd.)*

$n_2 = 5$

U/n_1	1	2	3	4	5
0	.167	.047	.018	.008	.004
1	.333	.095	.036	.016	.008
2	.500	.190	.071	.032	.016
3	.667	.286	.125	.056	.028
4		.429	.196	.095	.048
5		.571	.286	.143	.075
6			.393	.206	.111
7			.500	.278	.155
8			.607	.365	.210
9				.452	.274
10				.548	.345
11					.421
12					.500
13					.579

$n_2 = 6$

U/n_1	1	2	3	4	5	6
0	.143	.036	.012	.005	.002	.001
1	.286	.071	.024	.010	.004	.002
2	.428	.143	.048	.019	.009	.004
3	.571	.214	.083	.033	.015	.008
4		.321	.131	.057	.026	.013
5		.429	.190	.086	.041	.021
6		.577	.214	.129	.063	.032
7			.357	.176	.089	.047
8			.452	.238	.123	.066
9			.548	.305	.165	.090
10				.381	.214	.120
11				.457	.268	.155
12				.545	.331	.197
13					.396	.242
14					.465	.294
15					.535	.350
16						.409
17						.469
18						.531

Table XIV-a (*Contd.*)

$n_2 = 7$

U/n_1	1	2	3	4	5	6	7
0	.125	.028	.008	.003	.001	.001	.000
1	.250	.056	.017	.006	.003	.001	.001
2	.375	.111	.033	.012	.005	.002	.001
3	.500	.167	.058	.021	.009	.004	.002
4.	.625	.250	.092	.036	.015	.007	.003
5		.333	.133	.055	.024	.011	.006
6		.444	.192	.082	.037	.017	.009
7		.556	.258	.115	.053	.026	.013
8			.333	.158	.074	.037	.019
9			.417	.206	.101	.051	.027
10			.500	.264	.134	.069	.036
11			.583	.324	.172	.090	.049
12				.394	.216	.117	.064
13				.464	.265	.147	.082
14				.538	.319	.183	.104
15					.371	.223	.130
16					.438	.267	.159
17					.500	.314	.191
18					.526	.365	.228
19						.418	.267
20						.473	.310
21						.527	.355
22							.402
23							.451
24							.500
25							.549

Table XIV-a (*Contd.*)

$n_2 = 8$

U/n_1	1	2	3	4	5	6	7	8	t	Normal
0	.111	.022	.006	.002	.001	.000	.000	.000	3.308	.001
1	.222	.044	.012	.004	.002	.001	.000	.000	3.203	.001
2	.333	.089	.024	.008	.003	.001	.001	.000	3.098	.001
3	.444	.133	.042	.014	.005	.002	.001	.001	2.993	.001
4	.556	.200	.067	.024	.009	.004	.002	.001	2.888	.002
5		.267	.097	.036	.015	.006	.003	.001	2.783	.003
6		.356	.139	.055	.023	.010	.005	.002	2.678	.004
7		.444	.188	.077	.033	.015	.007	.003	2.573	.005
8		.556	.248	.107	.047	.021	.010	.005	2.462	.007
9			.315	.141	.064	.030	.014	.007	2.363	.009
10			.387	.184	.085	.041	.020	.010	2.258	.012
11			.461	.230	.111	.054	.027	.014	2.153	.016
12			.539	.285	.142	.071	.036	.019	2.048	.020
13				.341	.177	.091	.047	.025	1.943	.026
14				.404	.217	.114	.060	.032	1.838	.033
15				.467	.262	.141	.076	.041	1.733	.041
16				.533	.311	.172	.095	.052	1.628	.052
17					.362	.207	.116	.065	1.523	.064
18					.416	.245	.140	.080	1.418	.078
19					.472	.286	.168	.097	1.313	.094
20					.528	.331	.198	.117	1.208	.113
21						.377	.232	.139	1.102	.135
22						.426	.268	.164	.998	.159
23						.475	.306	.191	.893	.185
24						.525	.347	.221	.788	.215
25							.389	.253	.683	.247
26							.433	.287	.578	.282
27							.478	.323	.473	.318
28							.522	.360	.363	.356
29								.399	.263	.396
30								.439	.158	.437
31								.480	.052	.481
32								.520		

*Reproduced from Mann H.B. and Whitney, D.R., 1947, on a test of whether one of two-random variables is stochastically larger than the other, *Ann. Math. Statist.*, 18,52-54 with the kind permission of the authors and the publisher.

Table XIV-b. Critical Values of *U* in the Mann-Whitney Test*

(Critical values of *U* for a one-tailed Test at *a* = .025 or for a two-tailed Test at *a* = .05)

n_1/n_2	9	10	11	12	13	14	15	16	17	18	19	20
1												
2	0	0	0	1	1	1	1	1	2	2	2	2
3	2	3	3	4	4	5	5	6	6	7	7	8
4	4	5	6	7	8	9	10	11	11	12	13	13
5	7	8	9	11	12	13	14	15	17	18	19	20
6	10	11	13	14	16	17	19	21	22	24	25	27
7	12	14	16	18	20	22	24	26	28	30	32	34
8	15	17	19	22	24	26	29	31	34	36	38	41
9	17	20	23	26	28	31	34	37	39	42	45	48
10	20	23	26	29	33	36	39	42	45	48	52	55
11	23	26	30	33	37	40	44	47	51	55	58	62
12	26	29	33	37	41	45	49	53	57	61	65	69
13	28	33	37	41	45	50	54	59	63	67	72	76
14	31	36	40	45	50	55	59	64	67	74	78	83
15	34	39	44	49	54	59	64	70	75	80	85	90
16	37	42	47	53	59	64	70	75	81	86	92	98
17	39	45	51	57	63	67	75	81	87	93	99	105
18	42	48	55	61	67	74	80	86	93	99	106	112
19	45	52	58	65	72	78	85	92	99	106	113	119
20	48	55	62	69	76	83	90	98	105	112	119	127

*Adopted and abriged from tables 1,3,5 and 7 of Auble, D., 1953. "Extended tables for the Mann-Whitney statistic." *Bulletin of the Institute of Educational Research at Indian University,* Vol. 1, No. 2 with the kind permission of the authors and the publisher.

Table XV. Factors Useful in the Construction of Control Charts*

Sample size	Mean chart			Standard deviation chart					Range chart				
	Factors for control limit			Factor for central line	Factor for control limits				Factor for central line	Factors for control limit			
n	A	A_1	A_2	c_2	B_1	B_2	B_3	B_4	d_2	D_1	D_2	D_3	D_4
2	2.121	3.760	1.880	0.5642	0	1.843	0	3.267	1.128	0	3.686	0	3.267
3	1.732	2.394	1.023	0.7236	0	1.858	0	2.568	1.693	0	4.358	0	2.575
4	1.500	1.880	0.729	0.7979	0	1.808	0	2.266	2.059	0	4.698	0	2.282
5	1.342	1.596	0.577	0.8407	0	1.756	0	2.089	2.326	0	4.918	0	2.115
6	1.225	1.410	0.483	0.8686	0.026	1.711	0.030	1.970	2.534	0	5.078	0	2.004
7	1.134	1.277	0.419	0.8882	0.105	1.672	0.118	1.882	2.704	0.205	5.203	0.076	1.924
8	1.061	1.175	0.373	0.9027	0.167	1.638	0.185	1.815	2.847	0.387	5.307	0.136	1.864
9	1.000	1.094	0.337	0.9139	0.219	1.609	0.289	1.761	2.970	0.546	5.394	0.184	1.816
10	0.949	1.028	0.308	0.9227	0.262	1.584	0.284	1.716	3.078	0.687	5.469	0.228	1.777
11	0.905	0.973	0.285	0.9300	0.299	1.561	0.321	1.679	3.173	0.812	5.538	0.256	1.744
12	0.866	0.925	0.266	0.9359	0.331	1.541	0.354	1.646	3.258	0.924	5.592	0.284	1.716
13	0.832	0.884	0.249	0.9410	0.359	1.523	0.382	1.618	3.336	1.026	5.646	0.308	1.692
14	0.802	0.848	0.235	0.9453	0.384	1.507	0.406	1.594	3.407	1.121	5.693	0.329	1.671
15	0.775	0.816	0.223	0.9490	0.406	1.492	0.428	1.572	3.472	1.207	5.737	0.348	1.652
16	0.750	0.788	0.212	0.9523	0.427	1.478	0.448	1.552	3.532	1.285	5.779	0.364	1.636
17	0.728	0.762	0.203	0.9551	0.445	1.465	0.466	1.534	3.583	1.359	5.817	0.379	1.621
18	0.707	0.738	0.194	0.9576	0.461	1.454	0.482	1.518	3.640	1.426	5.854	0.392	1.608
19	0.688	0.717	0.187	0.9599	0.477	1.443	0.497	1.503	3.689	1.490	5.888	0.404	1.596
20	0.671	0.697	0.180	0.9619	0.491	1.433	0.510	1.490	3.735	1.548	5.922	0.414	1.586
21	0.655	0.679	0.173	0.9638	0.504	1.424	0.523	1.477	3.778	1.606	5.950	0.425	1.575
22	0.640	0.662	0.167	0.9655	0.516	1.415	0.534	1.466	3.819	1.659	5.979	0.434	1.566
23	0.626	0.647	0.162	0.9670	0.527	1.407	0.545	1.455	3.858	1.710	6.006	0.443	1.557
24	0.612	0.632	0.157	0.9684	0.538	1.399	0.555	1.445	3.895	1.759	6.031	0.452	1.548
25	0.600	0.619	0.153	0.9696	0.548	1.392	0.565	1.435	3.931	1.804	6.058	0.459	1.541

*Reprinted with permission from the "American Society for Testing and Materials", 1916 Race Street, Philadelphia, PA 19103, STP 15C.

Appendix C
Common Distributions

We record here the most commonly used distributions in probability and statistics as well as some of their basic characteristics.

C-1 DISCRETE DISTRIBUTIONS

1. *Bernoulli* (θ), $\theta \in [0, 1]$ (same as Binomial (1, (θ)).
probability function: $p(x) = \theta^x (1-\theta)^{1-x}$ for $x = 0, 1$.
mean : θ.
variance: $\theta(1-\theta)$.
moment-generating function: $m(t) = (1 - \theta + \theta e^t)$ for $t \in R^1$.

2. *Binomial* (n, θ), $n > 0$ an integer, $\theta \in [0, 1]$.
probability function: $p(x) = \binom{n}{x}\theta^x (1-\theta)^{n-x}$ for $x = 0, 1, ..., n$.
mean : $n\theta$.
variance: $n\theta(1-\theta)$.
moment-generating function: $m(t) = (1 - \theta + \theta e^t)^n$ for $t \in R^1$.

3. *Geometric* (θ), $\theta \in [0, 1]$ (same as Negative-Binomial (1, (θ)).
probability function: $p(x) = (1-\theta)^x \theta$ for $x = 0, 1, 2, ...$
mean : $(1-\theta) / \theta$.
variance: $(1-\theta)/ \theta^2$.
moment-generating function: $m(t) = \theta\,(1 - (1-\theta)\, e^t)^{-1}$ for $t < -\ln(1-\theta)$.

4. *Hypergometric* (N, M, n), $M \le N$, $n \le N$ all positive integers.
probability function:

$$p(x) = \binom{M}{x}\binom{N-M}{n-x}\Big/\binom{N}{n} \text{ for } \max(0, n + M - N) \le x \le \min(n, M).$$

mean : $n\dfrac{M}{N}$

variance: $n\dfrac{M}{N}\left(1-\dfrac{M}{N}\right)\dfrac{N-n}{N-1}$

5. *Multinomial* $(n, \theta_1, ..., \theta_k)$, $n > 0$ an integer, each $\theta_i \in [0, 1]$, $\theta_1 + ... + \theta_k = 1$.
probability function:

$$p(x_1, ..., x_k) = \binom{n}{x_1..x_k}\theta_1^{x_1}...\theta_k^{x_k} \text{ where each } x_i \in \{0, 1, ..., n\}.$$

$$\text{and } x_1 + ... + x_k = n.$$

mean : $E(X_i) = n\theta_i$.
variance: $\text{Var}(X_i) = n\theta_i(1 - \theta_i)$.
covariance : $\text{Cov}(X_i, X_j) = -n\theta_i\theta_j$ when $i \neq j$.

6. *Negative-Binomial* (r, θ), $r > 0$ an integer, $\theta \in (0, 1]$.

probability function: $$p(x) = \binom{r-1+x}{x}\theta^r(1-\theta)^x \text{ for } x = 0, 1, 2, 3, ...$$

mean : $r(1 - \theta)/\theta$.
variance: $r(1 - \theta)/\theta^2$.
moment-generating function: $m(t) = \theta^r(1 - (1 - \theta)e^t)^{-r}$ for $t < -\ln(1 - \theta)$.

7. *Poisson* (λ), $\lambda > 0$.

probability function: $$p(x) = \frac{\lambda^x}{x!}e^{-\lambda} \text{ for } x = 0, 1, 2, 3, ...$$

mean : λ.
variance: λ.
moment-generating function: $m(t) = \exp\{\lambda(e^t - 1)\}$ for $t \in R^1$.

C-2 ABSOLUTELY CONTINUOUS DISTRIBUTIONS

1. *Beta* (a, b), $a > 0$, $b > 0$ (same as Dirichlet (a, b)).

density function: $$f(x) = \frac{\Gamma(a+b)}{\Gamma(a)\Gamma(b)}x^{a-1}(1-x)^{b-1} \text{ for } x \in (0, 1).$$

mean : $a/(a + b)$.
variance: $ab/(a + b + 1)(a + b)^2$.

2. *Bivariate Normal* $(\mu_1, \mu_2, \sigma_1^2, \sigma_2^2, \rho)$ for $\mu_1, \mu_2 \in R^1, \sigma_1^2, \sigma_2^2 > 0, \rho \in [-1,1]$.

density function:

$$f_{X_1,X_2}(x_1,x_2) = \frac{1}{2\pi\sigma_1\sigma_2\sqrt{1-\rho^2}}\exp\left\{-\frac{1}{2(1-\rho^2)}\left[\left(\frac{x_1-\mu_1}{\sigma_1}\right)^2 + \left(\frac{x_2-\mu_2}{\sigma_2}\right)^2 - 2\rho\left(\frac{x_1-\mu_1}{\sigma_1}\right)\left(\frac{x_2-\mu_2}{\sigma_2}\right)\right]\right\}.$$

$$\text{for } x_1 \in R^1,\ x_2 \in R^1.$$

mean : $E(X_i) = \mu_i$.

variance: Var $(X_i) = \sigma_i^2$.

covariance: Cov $(X_1, X_2) = \rho\sigma_1\sigma_2$.

3. *Chi-squared* (α), or $\chi 2$ (α), $\alpha > 0$ (same as Gamma ($\alpha/2$, 1/2)).
density function: $f(x) = 2^{-\alpha/2} (\Gamma(\alpha/2)^{-1} x^{(\alpha/2)-1} e^{-x/2}$ for $x > 0$.
mean : α.
variance: 2α.
moment-generating function: $m(t) = (1 - 2t)^{-\alpha/2}$ for $t < 1/2$.

4. *Dirichlet* (α_1, ..., α_{k+1}), $\alpha_i > 0$ for each i.
density function:

$$f_{X_1,...,X_k}(x_1,...,x_k) = \frac{\Gamma(\alpha_1 + ... + \alpha_{k+1})}{\Gamma(\alpha_1)...\Gamma(\alpha_{k+1})} x_1^{\alpha_1 - 1} ... x_k^{\alpha_k - 1}(1 - x_1 - ... - x_k)^{\alpha_{k+1}-1}$$

for $x_i \geq 0$, $i = 1, ..., k$ and $0 \leq x_1 + ... + x_k \leq 1$.

mean :

$$E(X_i) = \frac{\alpha_i}{\alpha_1 + ... + \alpha_{k+1}}.$$

variance:

$$\text{Var}(X_i) = \frac{\alpha_i(\alpha_1 + ... + \alpha_{k+1} - \alpha_i)}{(\alpha_1 + ... + \alpha_{k+1})^2(1 + \alpha_1 + ... + \alpha_{k+1})}.$$

covariance: when $i \neq j$

$$\text{Cov}(X_i, X_j) = \frac{-\alpha_i\alpha_j}{(\alpha_1 + ... + \alpha_{k+1})^2(1 + \alpha_1 + ... + \alpha_{k+1})}.$$

5. *Exponential* (λ), $\lambda > 0$ (same as Gamma (1, λ)).
density function: $f(x) = \lambda e^{-\lambda x}$ for $x > 0$.
mean : λ^{-1}.
variance: λ^{-2}.
moment-generating function: $m(t) = \lambda(\lambda - t)^{-1}$ for $t < \lambda$.
Note that some books and software packages instead replace λ by $1/\lambda$ in the definition of the Exponential (λ) distribution — always check this when using software to generate from this distribution.

6. $F(\alpha, \beta)$, $\alpha > 0$, $\beta > 0$.

density function: $$f(x) = \frac{\Gamma\left(\frac{\alpha+\beta}{2}\right)}{\Gamma\left(\frac{\alpha}{2}\right)\Gamma\left(\frac{\beta}{2}\right)}\left(\frac{\alpha}{\beta}x\right)^{\alpha/2-1}\left(1+\frac{\alpha}{\beta}x\right)^{-(\alpha+\beta)/2}\frac{\alpha}{\beta} \text{ for } x > 0.$$

mean : β / (β – 2) when β > 2.
variance: $2\beta^2 (\alpha + \beta - 2) / \alpha(\beta - 2)^2 (\beta - 4)$ when β > 4.

7. *Gamma* (α, λ), α > 0, λ > 0.

density function: $$f(x) = \frac{\lambda^\alpha x^{\alpha-1}}{\Gamma(\alpha)} e^{-\lambda x} \text{ for } x > 0.$$

mean : α/λ.
variance: α/λ^2.
moment-generating function: $m(t) = \lambda^\alpha(\lambda - t)^{-\alpha}$ for $t < \lambda$.
Note that some books and software packages instead replace λ by 1/λ in the definition of the Gamma (α, λ) distribution — always check this when using software to generate from this distribution.

8. Lognormal or log N(μ, σ²), $\mu \in R^1$, $\sigma^2 > 0$.
density function:

$$f(x) = (2\pi\sigma^2)^{-1/2} x^{-1} \exp\left(-\frac{1}{2\sigma^2}(\ln x - \mu)^2\right) \text{ for } x > 0.$$

mean : $\exp(\mu + \sigma^2/2)$.
variance: $\exp(2\mu + \sigma^2)(\exp(\sigma^2) - 1)$.

9. *N*(μ, σ²), $\mu \in R^1$, $\sigma^2 > 0$.
density function:

$$f(x) = (2\pi\sigma^2)^{-1/2} \exp\left(-\frac{1}{2\sigma^2}(x - \mu)^2\right) \text{ for } x \in R^1.$$

mean : μ.
variance: σ^2.
moment-generating function: $m(t) = \exp(\mu t - \sigma^2 t^2/2)$ for $t \in R^1$.

10. *Student* (α) or *t*(α), α > 0 (α = 1 gives the Cauchy distribution).

density function: $$f(x) = \frac{\Gamma\left(\frac{\alpha+1}{2}\right)}{\Gamma\left(\frac{1}{2}\right)\Gamma\left(\frac{\alpha}{2}\right)}\left(1+\frac{x^2}{\alpha}\right)^{-(\alpha+1)/2} \frac{1}{\sqrt{\alpha}} \text{ for } x \in R^1.$$

mean : 0 when α > 1.
variance: α/(α – 2) when *a* > 2.

11. *Uniform* [L, R], R > L.
density function: $f(x) = 1/(R - L)$ for $L < x < R$.
mean : $(L + R)/2$.
variance: $(R + L)^2 / 12$.
moment-generating function: $m(t) = (e^{Rt} - e^{Lt}) / t(R - L)$.

Appendix D
Some Important Terms

Terminology used frequently in the field of Probability and Statistics is compiled here from various sources.

***p*-Value:** The smallest significance level at which a null hypothesis can be rejected.

***t*-Distribution:** A continuous distribution with a specific type of bell-shaped curve with its mean equal to 0 and standard deviation equal to $\sqrt{df/(df-2)}$.

***y*-intercept:** The point at which the regression line intersects the vertical axis on which the dependent variable is marked. It is the value of y when x is zero.

***z*-Score Formula:** The difference between the observation and the mean, divided by the standard deviation. That is, $z = (x - \mu)/\sigma$

α (Alpha): The probability that the statistical test will incorrectly reject the null hypothesis.

β (Beta): The probability of making a *Type II error* when making a statistical hypothesis test. One minus this probability is power, the probability of correctly rejecting the null hypothesis.

μ_d: The mean of the paired differences for the population.

σ (Sigma): The significance level of a test of hypothesis that denotes the probability of rejecting a null hypothesis when it is actually true. (The probability of committing a Type I error.)

σ_d: The standard deviation of the paired differences for the population.

***d*:** The difference between two matched values in two samples collected from the same source. It is called the *paired difference*.

$\bar{d}$ **:** The mean of the paired differences for a sample.

Absolute Dispersion: The actual variation or dispersion is called the absolute dispersion.

Absolute Error: The difference, without sign, between the actual value and a statistically determined model value.

All those value that would not be rejected with $p = 0.05$.

Alternative Hypothesis: A claim about a population parameter that will be true if the null hypothesis is false.

Analysis of Variance (ANOVA): A statistical technique used to test whether the means of three or more populations are equal.

Array: An array is an arrangement of raw numerical data in ascending or descending order of magnitude.

Average: Another name for the mean. The sum of all the data values divided by the number of data values.

Bar Graph: A graph made of bars whose heights represent the frequencies of respective categories.

Bernoulli Trial: Consider a process that consists of a sequence of n independent trials, where the outcome of each trial is a success or a failure. These are called Bernoulli trials.

Biased Estimator: See *unbiased estimator*.

Bimodal Distribution: A distribution that has two modes.

Binomial Experiment: An experiment that contains n identical trials such that each of these n trials has only two possible outcomes, the probabilities of these two outcomes remain constant for each trial, and the trials are independent.

Binomial Parameters: The total trials n and the probability of success p for the binomial probability distribution.

Binomial Probability Distribution: The probability distribution that gives the probability of x successes in n trials when the probability of success is p for each trial of a binomial experiment.

Box Plot: The box represents the middle 50% of the data values; that is, the data values from the first to third quartiles. The line or dot in the middle of the box denotes the median. Whiskers – lines extending from the box – extend either to the limits of the data or to a maximum length equal to 1.5 times the length of the box. In the latter case, points beyond the lines indicate outliers.

Box-and-Whisker Plot: A plot that shows the centre, spread and skewness of a data set by drawing a box and two whiskers using the median, the first quartile, the third quartile, and the smallest and the largest values in the data set between the lower and the upper inner fences.

Categorical Variable: The values of a categorical variable are discrete categories. Usually the categories cannot be ordered from *highest* to *lowest* in any meaningful way. Rather, the categories just define different groups. Gender and religions are examples of categorical variables. Compare *continuous variable*. See also *variable*.

Census: A survey conducted by including every element of the population.

Central Limit Theorem: The theorem from which it is inferred that for a large sample size ($n \geq 30$), the shape of the sampling distribution of $\bar{x}$ is approximately normal. Also, by the same theorem, the shape of the sampling distribution of $\hat{p}$ is approximately normal for a sample for which $np > 5$ and $nq > 5$.

Chebyshev's Theorem: For any number k greater than 1, at least $(1 - 1/k^2)$ of the values for any distribution lie within k standard deviations of the mean.

chi-square Distribution: A distribution, with degrees of freedom as the only parameter, that is skewed to the right for small *df* and looks like a normal curve for large *df*.

chi-square Test: A statistical test for determining whether two categorical variables are related.

Class Boundary: The midpoint of the upper limit of one class and the lower limit of the next class.

Class Frequency: The number of values in a data set that belongs to a certain class.

Class Length: See *class size*

Class Midpoint or Mark: The class midpoint or mark is obtained by dividing the sum of the lower and upper limits (or boundaries) of a class by 2.

Class: An interval that includes all the values in a (quantitative) data set that fall within two numbers, the lower and the upper limits of the class.

Class Size: The size or width of a class interval is the difference between the lower and the upper class boundary. It is also referred to as the class width, class size, or class length.

Classical Probability Rule: The method of assigning probabilities to outcomes or events of an experiment with equally likely outcomes.

Cluster: A subgroup (usually geographical) of the population that is representative of the whole population.

Cluster Sampling: The sampling technique under which the population is divided into clusters and a sample is chosen from one or a few clusters.

Coefficient of Determination: A measure that gives the proportion (or percentage) of the total variation in a dependent variable that is explained by a given independent variable.

Coefficient of Variation: A measure of relative variability that expresses standard deviation as percentage of the mean.

Combinations: The number of ways x elements can be selected from n elements.

Complementary Events: Two events that are taken together include all the outcomes for an experiment but do not contain any common outcomes.

Compound Event: An event that contains more than one outcome of an experiment. It is also called a *composite event*.

Conditional Probability: The probability of an event subject to the condition that another event has already occurred.

Confidence Interval: All the values for a parameter that would not be rejected if they were used as the null hypothesis in a statistical test of that parameter. A 95% confidence interval includes the true mean of the population.

Confidence Level: Confidence level, denoted by $(1 - \alpha)$ 100%, states how much confidence we have that a confidence interval contains the true population parameter. This may be thought of as the probability that a given assertion is true. More precisely a statement is true at C confidence level if it is true for fraction C of all notional populations that give the same sampling result as the one actually observed.

Confidence Limit: Stated at *C* confidence level, the *C* confidence limits are the endpoints of the *C* confidence interval.

Consistent Estimator: A sample statistic with a standard deviation that decreases as the sample size increases.

Contingency Coefficient: Quantifies the degree of relationship between two categorical variables.

Continuity Correction Factor: Addition of 0.5 and/or subtraction of 0.5 from the value(s) of x when the normal distribution is used as an approximation to the binomial distribution, where x is the number of successes in n trials.

Continuous Data: Data, which can be described by a continuous variable, are called continuous data.

Continuous Random Variable: A random variable that can assume any value in one or more intervals. A random variable whose values are countable.

Continuous Variable: A variable, which can theoretically assume any value between two given values, is called a continuous variable, otherwise it is called a discrete variable.

Control Group: The group on which no condition is imposed.

Controllable Factor: A design variable that is considered to influence the response and is included in the experiment. The experimenters can control its level.

Convenient Sample: A sample in which the most accessible members of the population are selected.

Covariance: Assesses the degree to which two variables co-vary or vary together. If the two variables are independent, then the covariance will equal zero. It is computed as the mean of the products of the mean deviations for each variable.

Critical Value or Critical Point: One or two values that divide the whole region under the sampling distribution of *s* sample statistic into rejection and non-rejection regions.

Cross-Section Data: Data collected on different elements at the same point in time or for the same period of time.

Cumulative Frequency: The cumulative frequency of a class is the frequency of the class divided by the total frequency of all classes and is generally expressed as a percentage.

Cumulative Frequency Distribution: The total frequency of all values less than the upper class boundary of a given class interval is called the cumulative frequency. A table representing such cumulative frequencies is called a cumulative frequency distribution, or cumulative frequency table; or simply a cumulative distribution.

Cumulative Percentage: The cumulative relative frequency multiplied by 100.

Cumulative Probability: The sum of the probabilities from the minimum possible value up to a certain value.

Cumulative Probability Distribution: By cumulating probabilities we obtain cumulative probability distribution, which are analogous to cumulative relative frequency distributions. The function associated with this distribution is often called a distribution function.

Cumulative Relative Frequency: The cumulative frequency of a class divided by the total number of observations.

Curve Fitting: The general problem of finding equations of approximating curves, which gives best fit to the sets of data, is called curve fitting.

Data or Data Set: Collection of observations or measurements on a variable.

Degrees of Freedom (*df*): The number of observations that can be chosen freely. For the estimation of μ using the t-distribution, the degrees of freedom are $n - 1$.

Degrees of Freedom for a Simple Linear Regression Model: Sample size minus 2, that is, $n - 2$.

Dependent Events: Two events for which the occurrence of one changes the probability of the occurrence of the other.

Dependent Variable: The variable to be predicted or explained.

Descriptive Statistics: Collection of methods that are used for organising, displaying and describing data using tables, graphs and summary measures.

Designed Experiment: A study in which the experiment controls the assignment of elements to different treatment groups.

Deterministic Model: A model in which the independent variable determines the dependent variable exactly. Such a model gives an exact relationship between two variables.

Discrete Data: Data, which can be described by a discrete variable, are called discrete data.

Discrete Probability Distribution: Of a variation x can assume a discrete set of values with respective probabilities where we can say that a discrete probability distribution for x has been defined.

Discrete Random Variable: A random variable whose values are countable.

Discrete Variable: A variable that can have only certain discrete values. The same as a categorical variable.

Dispersion: The degree to which numerical data tend to spread apart an average value is called the variation or dispersion of the data. The different measure of valuation or dispersion available is the range, mean deviation, semi-interquartile range, and the standard deviation.

Distribution Function: A function giving, for every value of x, the probability that a random variable X is lower than or equal to x.

Dot Plot: A simple graph in which each observation is represented by a dot at its score.

Efficient Estimator: If the sampling distributors of the two statistics have the same mean (or expectation), the statistic with the smaller variance is called an efficient estimator of the mean while the other statistic is called an inefficient estimator.

Element or Member: A specific subject or object included in a sample or population.

Empirical Rule: For a specific bell-shaped distribution, about 68% of the observations fall in the interval $(\mu - \sigma)$ to $(\mu + \sigma)$, about 95% fall in the interval $(\mu - 2\sigma)$ to $(\mu + 2\sigma)$, and about 99.7% fall in the interval $(\mu - 3\sigma)$ to $(\mu + 3\sigma)$.

Equally Likely Outcomes: Two (or more) outcomes or events that have the same probability of occurrence.

Error: The amount of variation in the response caused by factors other than controllable factors included in the experiment.

Estimate: The value of a sample statistic that is used to find the corresponding population parameter.

Estimated or Predicted Value of *y*: The value of the dependent variable, denoted by $\hat{y}$, that is calculated for a given value of x using the estimated regression model.

Estimation: Estimation is the process of analysing a sample result in order to predict the corresponding value of the population parameter. The sample statistic that is used to estimate a population parameter.

Estimator: The sample statistic that is used to estimate a population parameter.

Event: A collection of one or more outcomes of an experiment.

Expected Frequencies: The frequencies for different categories of a multinomial experiment or for different cells of a contingency table that are expected to occur when a given null hypothesis is true.

Experiment: A process with well-defined outcomes that, when performed, results in one and only one of the outcomes per repetition.

***F*-Distribution:** A probability distribution for ratios of variances. Most commonly used in *analysis of variance* to compare if the ratio of the variance of the means from a number of groups were the same.

Factorial: Denoted by the symbol "!" or $\lfloor$

Factorial *n*: Factorial n, denoted by $n!$ is simply defined as $n! = n\ (n-1)\ (n-2)... 1$.

First Quartile: The value in a ranked data set such that about 25% of the measurements are smaller than this value and about 75% are larger. It is the median of the values that are smaller than the median of the whole data set.

Frequency Distribution: A tabular arrangement of data by classes put together with the corresponding class frequencies is called a frequency distribution or frequency table.

Frequency: The number of times a certain data value occurs in the set of observations.

Frequency Polygon: A frequency polygon is a line graph made by connecting the mid-points of the bars in a histogram by straight lines.

Gaussian Distribution: Another name for the *normal distribution*.

Goodness-of-Fit Test: A test of the null hypothesis that the observed frequencies for an experiment follow a certain pattern or theoretical distribution.

Grouped Data: Data organised and summarised in a frequency-distributed manner are called grouped data.

Histogram: A graph in which classes are marked on the horizontal axis and frequencies, relative frequencies, or percentages are marked on the vertical axis. Bars that are drawn adjacent to each other represent the froquencies, relative frequencies, or percentages or various classes.

Hypothesis: A hypothesis is an assertion made about a population.

Hypothesis Test: A test of whether or not the null hypothesis should be rejected based on the data.

Impossible Event: An event that cannot occur.

Independent Events: Two events for which the occurrence of one does not change the probability of occurrence of the other.

Independent or Explanatory Variable: The variable included in a model to explain the variation in the dependent variable.

Independent Samples: Two samples drawn from two populations such that the selection of one does not affect the selection of the other.

Independent Variable: In an experiment, the levels of independent variables are controlled by the experimenter. Independent variables serve as inputs. Compare *dependent variable*.

Inefficient Estimator: See *efficient estimator*.

Inferential Statistics: Collection of methods that help make decisions about a population based on sample results.

Interaction: Two factors are said to have interaction with each other if the influence of one on the response function is dependent on the value of the other.

Intercept: In the equation for a line such as a regression model, the parameter a is the intercept.

y-intercept: The point at which the regression line intersects the vertical axis on which the dependent variable is marked. It is the value of y when x is zero.

Interquartile Range (IQR): The difference between the third Quartile (Q_3) and the first quartile (Q_1). The IQR indicates the range of scores spanned n by the middle half of the data values. The box in a box plot represents the IQR.

Intersection of Events: Intersection of events is given by the outcomes that are common to two (or more) events.

Interval Estimate: An estimate of a population parameter given by two numbers between which the parameter may be considered to lie is called an interval estimate of the parameter.

Joint Probability: The probability that two (or more) events occur together.

Judgment Sample: A sample that includes the elements of the population selected based on the judgment and prior knowledge of an expert.

Kruskal-Wallis Test: A non-parametric statistical procedure for comparing medians across groups.

Kurtosis: Kurtosis is the degree of peakedness of a distribution relative to a normal distribution.

Large Sample: The samples of size greater than 30 are called large samples.

Law of Large Numbers: If an experiment is repeated again and again, the probability of an event obtained from the relative frequency approaches the actual or theoretical probability.

Least-Squares Estimates of *a* and *b*: The values of *a* and *b* that are calculated by using the sample data.

Least-Squares Method: The method used to fit a regression line through a scatter diagram such that the error sum of squares is a minimum.

Least-Squares Regression Line: A regression line obtained by using the least squares method.

Left-Tailed Test: A test in which the rejection region lies in the left tail of the distribution curve.

Level of Significance: The maximum probability in testing a hypothesis that was set for commiting a type I error is called the level of significance of the test.

Linear Correlation Coefficient: A measure of the strength of the linear relationship between two variables.

Linear Regression Model: A regression model that gives a straight-line relationship between two variables.

Lower Inner Fence: The value in a data set that is 1.5 × IQR below the first quartile.

Lower Outer Fence: The value in a data set that is 3.0 × IQR below the first quartile.

Lower Quartile: The lowest 25% of the scores are equal to or less than the lower quartile score. Often represented as Q_1; equal to the 25th *percentile*.

Marginal Probability: The probability of one event or characteristic without consideration of any other event.

Maximum Error of Estimate: The quantity that is subtracted from and added to the value of a sample statistic to obtain a confidence interval for the corresponding population parameter.

Maximum: The largest data value in a set of observations.

Mean of a Discrete Random Variable: The mean of a discrete random variable x is the value that is expected to occur per repetition, on average, if an experiment is performed a large number of times. The mean of a discrete random variable is also called its *expected value*.

Mean of $\hat{p}$: The mean of the sampling distribution of $\bar{x}$, denoted $\mu_{\bar{x}}$, is equal to the population mean μ.

Mean Square Between Samples or MSB: A measure of the variation among means of samples taken from different populations.

Mean Square Within Samples or MSW: A measure of the variation within data of all samples taken from different populations.

Mean: The average of the data values, that is, the sum of all the data values divided by the number of data values. The mean makes the *sum of squared errors* as small as possible.

Measure of Dispersion: Measures that give the spread of a distribution. The range, variance and standard deviation are three such measures.

Measures of Central Tendency: Measures that describe the centre of a distribution. The mean, median and mode are three of the measures of central tendency.

Measures of Position: Measures that determine the position of a single value in relation to other values in a data set. Quartiles, percentiles, and percentile rank are examples of measures of position.

Median Absolute Deviation (MAD): The median of all the absolute errors or deviations. The MAD describes the spread of the data values away from the model value.

Median: The middle data value in a set of observation. To find the median, reorder the data from smallest to largest and find the middle observation; that is the median. If there is an even number of observations, then there will be two middle values; in that case, the average of those two middle values is the median. The median is also the 50th *percentile*.

Minimum: The lowest data value in a set of observations.

Mode: A value (or values) that occurs with highest frequency in a data set.

Model: Specifies a predicted or representative value of each observation in a data set. Simple models are the mean or the median for a set of observations. More complex models are, for example, regression lines.

Multimodal Distribution: A distribution that has more than two modes.

Multinomial Experiment: An experiment with n trials for which (1) the trials are identical, (2) there are more than two possible outcomes per trial, (3) the trials are independent, and (4) the probabilities of various outcomes remain constant for each trial.

Multiple Regression Model: A regression model that contains two or more independent variables.

Mutually Exclusive Events: Two or more events that do not contain any common outcome and, hence, cannot occur together.

Negative Relationship between Two Variables: The value of the slope in the regression line and the correlation coefficient between two variables are both negative.

Nominal Variable: Same as *categorical variable*. Levels of these variables are *noms* or *names*. For example, the names for the levels of the gender variable are *male* and *female*.

Non-linear (simple) Regression Model: A regression model that does not give a straight-line relationship between two variables.

Non-parametric Statistics: Statistical methods that make no assumption that the data are from a *normal distribution*.

Non-random Sample: A sample in which some members of the population may have no chance of being selected.

Non-sampling Errors: The errors that occur during the collection, recording, and tabulation of data.

Non-sampling or Systematic Error: The errors that occur in the collection, recording and tabulation of data.

Normal Distribution: The probability distribution that describes or approximates the distribution of many variables. Most observations in a normal distribution occur near the mean.

Normal Probability Distribution: The probability distribution of a continuous random variable that, when plotted, gives a specific bell-shaped curve. The parameters of the normal distribution are the mean μ and the standard deviation σ.

Null Hypothesis: The hypothesis that nothing is happening in the data that would not be expected by chance. Some null hypotheses are (*a*) the means of two groups are equal, (*b*) the slope in a simple regression is zero, (*c*) the correlation between two variables is zero, and (*d*) the classification of the data according to one nominal variable is independent of the classification of that data according to a second nominal variable.

Number of Degrees of Freedom: The number of degrees of freedom (n) of a statistic generally is defined as the number N of the independent observatory in the sample (sample size) minus the number k of population parameters estimated from the sample observations.

Observation: A person, place, or thing for which a data value is available or is measured.

Observation or Measurement: The value of a variable for an element.

Observation Study: A study in which the assignment of elements to different treatment is voluntary and the researcher simply observes the results of the study.

Observed Frequencies: The frequencies actually obtained from the performance of an experiment.

Observed Value of *z* or *t*: The value z or t calculated for a sample statistic such as the sample mean or the sample proportion.

Ogive: A curve drawn for a cumulative frequency distribution.

One-Way ANOVA: The analysis of variance technique that analyses one variable only.

One-Tailed Test: A test in which there is only one rejection region, either in the left tail or in the right tail of the distribution curve.

Ordinal Variable: A variable whose values indicate only rank and not the distance between values. For example, in a race, an ordinal variable would indicate who was first, second, third, etc., but would not give the time or distance between the racers.

Outcome: An outcome is one particular result of an experiment.

Outlier: An extreme or a typical value that is very different from other data values in the set of observations.

Outliers or Extreme Values: Values that are very small or very large relative to the majority of the values in a data set.

Paired or Matched Samples: Two samples drawn in such a way that they include the same elements and two data values are obtained from each element, one for each sample. Also called *dependent samples*.

Parameter: An unknown value in a model that is estimated from the data. Examples: mean, median, intercept, and slope.

Percentage: The percentage for a class or category is obtained by multiplying the relative frequency of that class or category by 100.

Percentile Rank: The percentile rank of a value gives the percentage of values in the data set that are smaller than this value.

Percentile: The Pth percentile data value is the score that is equal to or greater than P% of all the data values. For example, the score equal to the 25th percentile is equal to or greater than one quarter of all the data values (and is also the first *quartile*). The 50th percentile necessarily is the median. 99 values that divide a rankod data set into 100 equal parts.

Permutations: A permutation of n different objects taken r at a time is an arrangement of r out of the n objects with no special attention given to the order of arrangement.

$${}^nP_r = \frac{n!}{(n-r)!}$$

Pie Chart: A circle divided into portions that represent the relative frequencies or percentages of different categories or classes.

Point Estimate: An estimate of a population parameter given by a single number is called a point estimate of the parameter.

Poisson Parameter: The average occurrences, denoted by λ, during an interval for a Poisson probability distribution.

Poisson Probability Distribution: The probability distribution that gives the probability of x occurrences in an interval when the average occurrences in that interval are λ.

Polygon: A graph formed by joining the mid-points of the tops of successive bars in a histogram by straight lines.

Population: A population consists of all the individuals or objects in a well-defined group about which information is desired to answer a question.

Population Distribution: The probability distribution of the population data.

Population or Target Population: The collection of all elements whose characteristics are being studied.

Population Parameters: The estimation of unknown population quantities (such as population mean, variance, etc.) often called population parameters from a knowledge of corresponding sample quantities (sample mean, variance, etc.), often called sample statistics.

Population Parameters for a Simple Regression Model: The values of A and B for the regression model $y = A + Bx + \in$ that are obtained by using population data.

Population Proportion p: The ratio of the number of elements in a population with a specific characteristic to the total number of elements in the population.

Positive Relationship Between Two Variables: The value of the slope in the regression line and the correlation coefficient between two variables are both positive.

Power: The probability that a statistical test will reject the *null hypothesis* given that some specific alternative model is true. Equivalently, the probability that a *Type II error* will be avoided.

Prediction Interval: The confidence interval for a particular value of y for a given value of x.

Probabilistic or Statistical Model: A model in which the independent variable does not determine the dependent variable exactly.

Probability: The probability of an event occurring in an experiment equals the proportion of times the event occurs if the experiment is repeated a very large (infinite) number of times.

Probability Distribution of a Discrete Random Variable: A list of all the possible values that a discrete random variable can assume and their corresponding probabilities.

Probability Distribution: A distribution that determines the probability that a random variable takes any given value or belongs to a given set of values.

Qualitative or Categorical Variable: A variable that cannot assume numerical values but is classified into two or more categories.

Quantitative Data: Data generated by a quantitative variable.

Quartiles: Summary measures that divide all the scores into four quarters. One-fourth of the data values are equal to or less than the first or *lower quartile* (Q_1), one half of the values are equal to or less than the second quartile (Q_2, also known as the *median*), and three fourths of all the data values are equal to or less than the third or *upper quartile* (Q_3).

Quota Sample: A sample selected in such a way that each group or subpopulation is represented in the sample in exactly the same proportion as in the target population.

Random Error Term (∈): The difference between the actual and predicted value of *y*.

Random Sample: A sample drawn in such a way that each element of the population has same chance of being included in the sample.

Random Sampling: Each member of a population, which has an equal chance of being included, is called random sampling.

Random Variable: A variable, denoted by *x*, whose value is determined by the outcome of a random experiment. Also called a *chance variable*.

Randomisation: The procedure under which elements are assigned to different (treatment and control) groups at random.

Range: The difference between the largest and smallest numbers is called the range of the data.

Ranks: Data values, which indicate only the order of the observations. See *ordinal variable*.

Raw Data: Data recorded in the sequence in which they are collected and before they are processed.

Relative Cumulative Frequency: The relative cumulative frequency or percentage cumulative frequency is the cumulative frequency divided by the total frequency.

Relative Dispersion: Relative dispersion is defined as the ratio of absolute dispersion and the average value.

Relative Frequency: The frequency of a class or category divided by the sum of all frequencies.

Representative Sample: A sample that contains the characteristics of the corresponding population.

Right-Tailed Test: A test in which the rejection region lies in the right tail of the distribution curve.

Sample: A selection of observations from a larger population of all possible observations. Ideally, the sample is selected randomly from the population.

Sample Point: An outcome of an experiment.

Sample Proportion $\hat{p}$: The ratio of the number of elements in a sample with a specific characteristic to the total number of *elements in that sample.*

Sample Space: A sample space is the set of all possible outcomes of an experiment. These outcomes are also called the *elements of the sample space.*

Sample Statistics: See *population parameters.*

Sample Survey: A survey that includes elements of a sample.

Sampling Distribution: The probability distribution of the statistic one would get by sampling over and over again.

Sampling Distribution of $\bar{x}$: The probability distribution of all the values of $\bar{x}$ calculated from all possible samples of the same size selected from a population.

Sampling Distribution of $\hat{p}$: The probability distribution of all the values of $\hat{p}$ calculated from all possible samples of the same size selected from a population.

Sampling Error: The difference between the values of a sample statistic calculated from a random sample and the value of the corresponding population parameter. This type of error occurs due to chance.

Sampling Frame: The list of elements of the target population that is used to select a sample.

Sampling or Chance Error: The difference between the results obtained from a sample survey and the result that would be obtained from the census.

Scatter Diagram or Scattergraph: A plot of the paired observations of x and y.

Scatter Plot or Scattergram: A two-variable plot in which each point represents the levels of an observation on each variable. Often the variable on the horizontal axis is to be used to predict the variable on the vertical axis. Scatter plots are useful for viewing *correlations* and for *simple regression.*

S_d: The standard deviation of the paired differences for a sample.

Second Quartile: Middle or second of the three quartiles that divide a ranked data set into four equal parts. About 50% of the values in the data set are smaller and about 50% are larger than the second quartile. The second quartile is the same as the *median.*

Selection Error: The error that occurs because the sampling frame is not representative of the population.

Significance Level: The pre-specified probability of a Type I error below which the null hypothesis is considered to be so rare as to be implausible.

Significant: When the probability of obtaining a statistical value is below the significance level, the statistic is said to be *statistically significant.*

Simple Event: An event that contains one and only one outcome of an experiment. It is also called an *elementary event.*

Simple Linear Regression: A regression model with one dependent and one independent variable that assumes a straight-line relationship.

Simple Random Sample: A sample chosen in such a way that each element of the population has the same probability of being included in the sample.

Sixtieth Percentile: The sixtieth percentile is larger than 60% of the scores (and smaller than 40%).

Skewed: A skewed distribution is not symmetric. That is, it has different shapes on each side of the median. The right-tailed skewness means the skew is positive whereas if the skewness is left-tailed, the skew is negative. The skewness can be positive, zero, negative, or undefined.

Skewed-to-the-Left Histogram: A histogram with a longer tail on the left side.

Skewed-to-the-Right Histogram: A histogram with a longer tail on the right side.

Skewness: Skewness is the degree of asymmetry or departure symmetry of a distribution. Of the frequency curve of a distribution has a longer tail to the right of the central maximum than to the left, the distribution is said to be skewed to the right or to have positive skewness. Of the reverse is true, it is called skewed to the left or to have negative skewness.

Slope: The coefficient of x in a regression model that gives the change in y for a change of one unit in x.

Small Samples: The samples of site lesser than 30 are called small samples.

SSB: The sum of squares between samples. Also called the sum of squares of the factor or treatment.

SSE (Error Sum of Squares): The sum of the squared differences between the actual and predicted values of y. It is the portion of the SST that is not explained by the regression model.

SSR (Regression Sum of Squares): The portion of the SST that is explained by the regression model.

SST: The total sum of squares given by the sum of SSB and SSW.

SST (Total Sum of Squares): The sum of the squared differences between actual y value and $\bar{y}$.

SSW: The sum of squares within samples. Also called the *sum of squares of errors*.

Standard Deviation: A measure of spread that is given by the positive square root of the variance.

Standard Deviation of $\bar{x}$: The standard deviation of the sampling distribution of $\bar{x}$, denoted by $\sigma_{\bar{x}}$, is equal to $\sigma/\sqrt{n}$ when $n/N \leq 0.05$.

Standard Deviation of a Discrete Random Variable: A measure of spread for the probability distribution of a discrete random variable.

Standard Deviation of Errors: A measure of spread for the random errors.

Standard Deviation of $\hat{p}$: The standard deviation of the sampling distribution of $\hat{p}$, denoted by $\sigma_{\hat{p}}$, is equal to $\sigma/\sqrt{n}$ when $n/N \leq 0.05$.

Standard Error: The standard deviation of the sampling distribution for any given statistic.

Standard Error of Mean: The standard deviation of the sampling distribution of the mean.

Standard Normal Distribution: The normal distribution with $\mu = 0$ and $\sigma = 1$. The units of the standard normal distribution are denoted by *z*.

Statistic: A summary measure calculated for sample data.

Statistics: Statistics deals with scientific methods for collecting, organising, summarising, presenting and analysing data, as well as drawing valid conclusions and making reasonable decisions based on such analysis.

Statistical Hypothesis: Assumptions or guesses made which may or may not be true, are called statistical hypotheses and in general are statements about the probability distributions of the populations.

Stem-and-Leaf Display: A display of data in which each value is divided into two portions, a stem and a leaf.

Stratified Random Sampling: The sampling technique under which the population is divided into different strata and a sample is chosen from each stratum.

Stratum: A subgroup of the population whose members are identical with regard to the possession of a characteristic.

Subjective Probability: The probability assigned to an event based on the information and judgment of a person.

Sure Event: An event that is certain to occur.

Survey: Collecting data on the elements of a population or sample.

Symmetric: A symmetric distribution has the same shape on each side of the median. The normal distribution is an example of a symmetric distribution. Compare *skewed.*

Symmetric Histogram: A histogram that is identical on both sides of its central point.

Systematic Random Sampling: Sampling method used to choose a sample by selecting every k^{th} unit from the list.

Target Population: The collection of all subjects of interest.

Target Value: A value that a product is expected to posses. Most often this value is different from what a single unit actually does exhibit. For a 9 volt transistor battery the target value is 9 volts.

Test of Homogeneity: A test of the null hypothesis that the proportions of elements that belong to different groups in two (or more) populations are similar.

Tests of Hypothesis: Procedures, which will enable to decide whether to accept or reject hypothesis or to determine whether observed samples differ significantly from expected results are called tests of hypothesis; tests of significance, or rules of decision.

Test of Independence: A test of the null hypothesis that attributes of a population is not related.

Test Statistic: The value of *z* or *t* calculated for a sample statistic such as the sample mean or the sample proportion.

Third Quartile: Third of the three quartiles that divide a ranked data set into four equal parts. About 75% of the values in a data set are smaller than the value of the third quartile and about 25% are larger. It is the median of the values that are greater than the median of the whole data set.

Tree Diagram: A diagram in which each outcome of an experiment is represented by a branch of a tree.

Trimmed Mean: The k% trimmed mean is obtained by dropping k% of the smallest values and k% of the largest values from the given data and then calculating the mean of the remaining $(100 - 2k)$% of the values.

Two-Tailed Test: A two-tailed test considers whether the null hypothesis might be wrong in either direction; that is, it allows the possibility that the true parameter might be either above or below the value of the null hypothesis. Compare *one-tailed test.*

Type I Error: An error that occurs when a true null hypothesis is rejected.

Type II Error: An error that occurs when a false null hypothesis is not rejected.

Unbiased Estimator: Of the mean of the sampling distribution of a statistic equals to the corresponding population parameters, the statistic is called an unbiased estimator of the parameters, and otherwise it is called a biased estimator.

Uniform or Rectangular Histogram: A histogram with the same frequency for all classes.

Unimodal Distribution: A distribution that has only one mode.

Union of Two Events: All outcomes that belong either to one or to both events.

Upper Inner Fence: The value in a data set that is 1.5 × IQR above the third quartile.

Upper Outer Fence: The value in a data set that is 3.0 × IQR above the third quartile.

Upper Quartile: The 75th *percentile.* The observation that is greater than or equal to 75% of the observations and less than 25% of the observations. Sometimes designated by Q_3.

Variable: A characteristic, trait, attribute, or measurement that can take on different values. A variable must vary, having at least one value for some observations and another value for other observations.

Variables, Factors, or Parameters: These words are used synonymously to indicate the controllable factors in an experiment. In the case of a plastic molding experiment, molding temperature, injection pressure, set time, etc., are factors.

Variance: The typical or average squared error. For a population, the sum of squared errors is divided by n the number of observations. More often, interest is in the sample estimate of the variance in which case the sum of squared errors is divided by $n - 1$.

That is, $S^2 = \dfrac{\sum (x_i - \bar{x})^2}{n-1}$

Venn Diagram: A picture that represents a sample space or certain events.

❑❑❑

Answers to Numerical Problems

Numerical values given as answers are rounded off and hence the readers may find in some cases their answers differing from the given values in the second or third decimal place.

Chapter 2 [24]

	Males		*Females*		
Year	*Permanent*	*Temporary*	*Permanent*	*Temporary*	*Total*
1985	1400	300	100	200	2000
1986	1900	100	650	150	2800

[25] Sexwise percentage of Coffee Drinkers in Town A and Town B.

	Town A			*Town B*		
	Males	*Females*	*Total*	*Males*	*Females*	*Total*
Coffee Drinkers	40	5	45	25	15	40
Non-Coffee Drinkers	20	35	55	30	30	60
Total	60	40	100	55	45	100

[27] Distribution of employees of a sugar mill according to sex, marital status and trade union membership.

Member-ship	*Males*			*Females*			*Total*	
	Married	*Unmarried*	*Total*	*Married*	*Unmarried*	*Total*	*Married*	*Unmarried*
Members	240	260	500	12	88	100	252	348
Non-Members	60	40	100	8	92	100	68	132
Total	300	300	600	20	180	200	320	480

Chapter 3

[13] 150.89 lakh ha.

[14] 29.34 per cent

[15] mean = 0.34 mm., mode = .30, .31 mm

[16] (*i*) 40.06 yrs. (*ii*) 40.24 yrs. (*iii*) 41.56 yrs.

[17] (*i*) 24.84 yrs. (*ii*) 24.82 yrs. (*iii*) 24.86 yrs. (*iv*) 27.04 yrs. (*v*) 25.59 yrs. (*vi*) 28.78 yrs.

[18] 674.28 crores

[19] Rs. 4.44 per kg.

[20] 24 days

[21] A.M. = 132.62 lbs., Mode = 125 lbs., 135 lbs., Median = 135 lbs.

[22] 30 per cent

[23] A.M. = Rs. 165.17, Median = Rs. 99, Mode = Rs. 75. Median is the best representative of the series.

[24] Median = 12.15, Mode = 11.35.

[25] Total bonus = Rs. 1940, Av. bonus = Rs. 77.60

[26] Mode = 38.636 yrs., Median = 39.986 yrs., Q_1 = 33.98 yrs., Q_3 = 47.05 yrs. The curve is unsymmetrical.

[27] Rs. 67.92, No. of workers having monthly income between 60 and 72 is 58 (round figure).

[28] (*a*) H.M. = 40 m.p.h. (*b*) 3.71 per cent

[29] 9

[30] 16.21 yrs.

[31] No. of students = 52, Percentage of students = 27.37.

[32] H.M. = 28.23, Obs. are 240 and 15.

[33] Median = 29, Mode = 32.78, A.M. not possible.

[34] Mode = 6.17, P_{75} = 18.5

[35] Rs. 252.78.

[36] $a = 8$, $b = 7$

[37] Mode = 28.0

[38] G.M. = 29.16.

[39] Median = 31.04, Q_1 = 18.125, Q_3 = 44.43

[40] Median = 47.0

[41] (15–20), $f_1 = 64$, f_2, (20–30), $f_2 = 51$, mode = 26.55

[42] $\overline{X}_c$ = Rs. 1047.59 per month.

[43] $x = 10$.

[45] 80% males and 20% females.

Chapter 4

[14] (*i*) 49.3–131.4 Mn. lbs. (*ii*) M.D. = 22.80 Mn. lbs.

(*iii*) σ^2 = 731.76, C.V. = 31.67

[15] M.D. = 1.29, $\sigma^2 = 2.16$

[16] (*i*) Q.D. = 11.82. (*ii*) M.D. Rs. = 11.51 (*iii*) σ = 13.09

[17] $C.V_A = 26.59\%$, $C.V_B = 43.89\%$, Shooter *A* is more consistent.

[18] $\sigma_{12} = 22.96$

[19] (*i*) Q.D. = 4.26 yrs. (*ii*) M.D. = 5.44 yrs. (*iii*) 23.47 per cent
(*iv*) No. of teachers = 25 (round figure)

[20] $\overline{X}$ = Rs. 74.05, σ_p = Rs. 12.21

[21] $C.V_A = 123.93\%$, $C.V_B = 109.17\%$, Team *B* is more consistent.

[22] σ = 5.24 cm.

[23] $s^2 = 1486.9$

[24] Correct mean = 39.9, Correct S.D. = 5.0

[25] σ = 1.61

[26] $\sigma_p = 6.076$.

[27] (*i*) $\overline{X}_A$ = 68.57 lbs., $\overline{X}_B$ = 71.0 lbs, Company B has higher tearing weight.
(*ii*) $S_A^2 = 40.68$, $S_B^2 = 76.52$., Company *B* is more variable in quality.

[28] A.M. = 2.20, C.V. = 25.54 per cent.

[29] Interval: 0–10 10–20 20–30 30–40 40–50 50–60 60–70
Frequency: 10 15 25 25 10 10 5

[30] Average = 160.71, S.D. = 11.64.

[31] Mean = 55.0, S.D. = 12.0

[32] Range = 15, S.D. = 4.38, C.V. = 7.14.

[33] $\overline{X}_{123} = 16.0$, $\sigma_{123} = 7.19$

[35] $C.V_A = 3.33\%$, $C.V_B = 2.5\%$. Factory A has greater variation.

[36] Range = 32, coeff. of range = 0.24

[37]

	Lamp A	*Lamp B*	
	Av. Life	1016.67 (hrs)	940.00 (hrs)
S.D.	234.52 (hrs)	200.00 (hrs)	
C.V.	23.07%	21.28%	

Average life of Lamp A is more than B. But there is more variability and less consistency in the length of life of bulbs A than B.

Chapter 5

[4] *A*: 1, 2, 4, 5, 7, 8, 10, 11, *B*: 2, 4, 6, 8, 10, 12
C: 1, 3, 5, 7, 9, 11

(*a*) $A \cap B$ = *2, 4, 8, 10;* $P(A \cap B) = \frac{1}{3}$

(*b*) $A \cup \overline{C}$ = 1, 2, 4, 5, 6, 7, 8, 10, 11, 12; $P(A \cup \overline{C}) = 5/6$

(*c*) $A \cup B \cup \overline{C} = A \cup \overline{C}$; $P(A \cup B \cup \overline{C}) = 5/6$

(*d*) $\overline{A} \cap B$ = 6,12; $P(\overline{A} \cap B) = 1/6$

(*e*) $A \cap B \cup C$ = 1, 2, 3, 4, 5, 7, 8, 9, 10, 11; $P(A \cap B \cup C) = 5/6$

[5] $P(E_1) = 1/2$; $P(E_2) = 1/3$; $P(E_3) = 1/4$; $P(E_4) = 7/36$ $P(E_1 \cap E_2) = 1/6$;
$P(E_1 \cup E_2) = 2/3$; $P(E_2 \cup E_3 \cup E_4) = 5/9$

[6] (*i*) 0.0158 (*ii*) 0.00046 (*iii*) 0.0291

[7] 0.393

[8] (*a*) 2/15 (*b*) 13/30 (*c*) 8/13

[9] (*i*) 1/5 (*ii*) 2/3 (*iii*) 4/11

[10] 5/396

[11] 5/42

[12] (*i*) 56/143 (*ii*) 421/429

[13] 3/4

[14] (*i*) 1/9 (*ii*) 2/9 (*iii*) 2/3

[15] 1/13

[16] 3/125

[17] 0.2

[18] 2/9

[19] 78/115

[20] 3/28

[21] *P* (All graduates) = 1/64; *P* (At least one graduate) = 37/64

[22] 3/8

[23] (*a*) 768/3125 (*b*) $(4/5)^6$

[24] 0.8645

[25] (*a*) 1/35 (*b*) 2/7 (*c*) 24/35

[26] 14/45

[27] (*i*) 3/4 (*ii*) 1/5

[28] 1/3

[29] 1/36

[30] 1/18

[31] (*a*) 21/31 (*c*) Not independent (*d*) (*i*) No (*ii*) yes

[32] (*a*) 0.42 (*b*) 0.60 (*d*) independent

[33] 1/6

[34] (*a*) (*i*) $A \cap B$ (*ii*) $A \cap B \cap C$ (*iii*) $A \cap B \cap C$ (*iv*) $A \cup B \cup C$
(*v*) $(A \cap B) \cup (A \cap C) \cup (B \cap C) \cup (A \cap B \cap C)$ (*b*) (*i*) 42/625 (*iii*) 207/625

[35] (*a*) (*i*) 0.559 (*ii*) 0.427 (*b*) (*i*) 0.3679 (*ii*) 0.2642

[36] 0.4

[37] 5/12

[38] (*i*) 0.648 (*ii*) 0.484

[39] (*i*) 15/64 (*ii*) 160/729 (*iii*) $1-1/6^6$ (*iv*) 13/729

[40] (i) $\frac{2}{77}$ (ii) $\frac{3}{11}$ (iii) $\frac{54}{77}$

[41] $P(A|B) = \frac{3}{4}$, $P(A \cup B) = \frac{7}{12}$, $P(\bar{A} \cap \bar{B}) = \frac{5}{12}$

[42] (a) $\frac{6}{7}$ (b) $\frac{3}{5}$

[43] $\frac{17}{20}$

[44] (a) $\frac{4}{10}$ (b) $\frac{13}{40}$ (c) $\frac{27}{40}$ (d) $\frac{9}{16}$ (e) $\frac{11}{50}$

[45] (i) $\frac{2}{5}$ (ii) $\frac{4}{15}$ (iii) $\frac{1}{5}$ (iv) $\frac{13}{15}$

[46] $\frac{2}{5}$

[47] (i) 0.04 (ii) 0.42 (iii) 0.54

[48] (a) $\frac{1}{12}$ i.e. (iii) (b) $\frac{7}{13}$ i.e. (i)

Chapter 6

[18] 1/3

[19] Answer is correct

[20] (i) 15/64 (ii) 11/32 (iii) 3/32

[21] (i) 0.98 (ii) 0.9998

[22] $\mu = 50$, $\sigma = 10$

[23] $n = 11$

[24] (i) 95 (ii) Almost none (iii) Almost none.

[25] More workers are on low wages, variation in wages is moderate.

[26] $S_k = -0.05$ (Bowley's formula).

[27] $\mu_1 = 3$, $\mu_2 = 15$, $\mu_3 = -86$

[29] (i) $\frac{1}{2}$ (ii) 5/16 (iii) $\frac{1}{2}$

[30] (i) 189 (ii) 58 (iii) 42

[31] $N(17.5, 1.19)$

[32] (i) 0.276 (ii) 0.041 (iii) $(3/5)^6$ (iv) $(2/5)^6$

[33]

30–60	60–90	90–120	120–150	150–180	180–210
5	10	17	16	10	2

$S_k = 0.026$

[34] (i) 15.87 (ii) 2.28 (iii) 49.71

[35] S.D. = 8.0

[40] 75.09 per cent

[41] (a) (i) 0.1446 (ii) 0.476 (iii) 0.3793 (b) 37.18

[42] −0.30

[43] 0.008

[44] 38.0

[45] Mean = 200, S.D. = 40.0

[46] Corrected $m'_1 = 8.91$, $m'_2 = 96.03$, $m'_3 = 1207.975$

[47] 0.16

[48] (*b*) 13 (*c*) 135.486

[49] (*i*) Rs 225.80 (*ii*) 174.20

[50] (*i*) 0.9500042 (*ii*) 0.9500042

[51] $y = 11$

[52] 9/8

[53] Rs 6107.14

[54]

x:	0	1	2	3	4
f:	30	59	44	15	2

[55] (*i*) 6687 persons (*ii*) Rs 6376

[56] (*a*)

p (x) :	0	1	2	3;
	$\frac{1}{8}$	$\frac{3}{8}$	$\frac{3}{8}$	$\frac{1}{8}$

E(x) = 1.5; V (x) = 0.75

(*b*) (*i*) 0.3 (*ii*) $\frac{2}{9}$

[57] (*a*) (*i*) 50 (*ii*) 577

[58] $E(x) = 5.5$, $E(x^2) = 46.5$, $E(2x + 1)^2 = 209$

[59] K = 0.1, E(x) = 0.8, V(x) = 2.16

[60] $K = \frac{3}{4}$, $E(x) = 3$.

[61]

x:	0	1	2	3	4
f:	122	61	15	2	0

[62] Poisson model; Prob. = 0.08

[63] $K = 2;\ P\left(\frac{1}{2} < x \le \frac{3}{2}\right) = \frac{3}{4};\ E(x) = 1$

[64] $E(x + y) = 96;\ E(x).\ E(y) = \frac{8687}{4}$

Chapter 7

[14] No. of persons $\hat{X} = 4651$, Var ($\bar{X}$) = 0.103

[15] $\bar{x}_{st} = 11.90$, Var ($\bar{x}_{st}$) = 0.7917

[19] $E(\bar{x}) = 61 = \mu;\ V(\bar{x}) = \frac{53}{2} = \frac{\sigma^2}{2}$

[21] $n = 16$, S.E. of $P = \frac{\sqrt{3}}{16}$

[23] Sampling Distribution

$\bar{x}$:	6	7	8	9	10	11	12
Prob. :	$\frac{1}{10}$	$\frac{1}{10}$	$\frac{2}{10}$	$\frac{2}{10}$	$\frac{2}{10}$	$\frac{1}{10}$	$\frac{1}{10}$

$E(\bar{x}) = 9$

[24] $\bar{x} = \frac{132}{30} = 4.4 = \mu.$

Chapter 8

[6] $F_{.05\,(10.\,5)} = 4.74, \quad F_{.95,\,(5.10)} = 0.211$

[9] (*a*) 2.878 (*b*) 2.179 (*c*) 1.753 (*d*) 1.372 (*e*) 0.05

[10] (*a*) 21.026 (*b*) 28.83 (*c*) 32.00 (*d*) 21.026 (*e*) 22.307

[13] (*a*) 6.63 (*b*) 3.00 (*c*) 2.36 (*d*) 3.89 (*e*) 2.46 (*f*) 0.99

Chapter 9

[34] Coeff. of reproducibility = 0.96

Chapter 10

[19] (*a*) 2.069 (*b*) 2.763 (*c*) 1.96 (*d*) 1.645 (*e*) 1.753

[20] $t = 0.566$, old view not rejected

[21] $t = 0.51$, Av. yield of 30 q/ha. accepted

[22] $Z = 0.431$, claim not refuted.

[23] $Z = 4.82$, unequal proportion ascertained at $\alpha = .05$

[24] $t = 0.27$, mean yields equal

[25] $t = 4.336$, significant difference at $\alpha = .05$

[26] $P = 0.02$

[27] $Z = 0.45$, equality asserted at $\alpha = .05$

[28] $t = 1.09$, performance is at par for $\alpha = .05$

[29] $t = 1.47$, $t^* = 2.12$, no one is superior.

[30] $Z = 7.51$, significant decrease affirmed at $P = .05$

[31] $Z = 1.15$, not inferior at $P = .05$

[32] $t = 3.21$, income exceeds.

[33] $t = 0.748$, non-significant increase at $\alpha = .05$

[34] $t = 1.70$, drugs at par at 5% level.

[35] (*a*) $Z = 8.69$, Av. wages not equal (*b*) U.L. = 0.3635, L.L. = 0.3445

[36] $t = 1.78$, diets equally effective.

[37] $t = -1.846$, machine is not defective.

[39] $Z = 7.071$ claim is correct

[40] $t = 0.277$, doing job correctly, C.I. = 0.9272

[41] $Z = -2.66$, sample is not likely belong to the given population at $\alpha = 0.01$

[42] Testing $H_0 : P_1 = P_2$ by Z test.
$Z = 2.01$, Reject H_0 at $\alpha = 0.05$. It confirms light colour paper yield better response.

[43] $Z = 2.50$, sample does not belong to the postulated population.

[44] $t = 3.90$, Reject H_0 i.e. $\mu_1 = \mu_2$, Average consumption of two brands significantly differ at $\alpha = 0.05$.

[45] $Z = 2.21$, Sale increases significantly after advertisement.

[46] $t = 1.724$, Sample can be regarded from the population with mean 3.25. Lower limit = 3.23, Upper limit = 3.57

[47] $t = 2.00$, Sample can be regarded from the assumed population at $\alpha = 0.01$

[48] $Z = 1.82$, Difference is not significant at $\alpha = 0.05$

[50] Assuming $\sigma_1^2 \neq \sigma_2^2$, $t = 0.497$, $t^* = 2.18$, $t < t^*$, the two means are not different at $\alpha = 0.05$.

Chapter 11

[8] (*i*) 2.59 (*ii*) 0.41 (*iii*) 3.23 m (*iv*) 0.31 (*v*) 2.16 (*vi*) 12.592 (*vii*) 3.841

[9] $F = 4.287$, variances unequal at $\alpha = .05$

[10] $\chi^2 = 17.16$, fit for use.

[11] $\chi^2 = 44.12$, Data have not come from a normal population.

[12] $\chi^2 = 3.20$, fr. dist. follows Poisson's dist.

[13] $\chi^2 = 0.74$, hypotherical ratio acceptable.

[14] $\chi^2 = 46.35$, Univ. edu. influenced by specialisation in school

[15] $\chi^2 = 2.30$, expected ratio supported at $\alpha = .05$

[16] $\chi^2 = 0.167$, condition not dependent on the sex of the child.

[17] $\chi^2 = 5.98$, result is related to sex.

[18] $\chi^2 = 0.88$, claim of coaching school acceptable.

[19] $F = 14.27$, av. yields during three years differ significantly

[20] $F = 2.66$, populations have equal variability at $\alpha = .05$

[22] $F = 2.14$, populations have equal variance at $\alpha = .05$

[23] $\chi^2 = 20.89$, condition of children affected.

[24] $\chi^2 = 3.57$, accidents are uniformly distributed.

[25] $\chi^2 = 0.539$, Poisson's dist. fits to the data.

[26] $F = 8.14$, strains differ significantly.

[27] $\chi^2 = 0.49$, independent

[28] $\chi^2 = 7.16$, male and female births are equally possible.

[29] $t = 9.73$, mean salaries not equal.

[30] $\chi^2 = 1.44$, data are consistent.

[31] $F = 1.467$, variation in the two samples is not significant.

[32] $\chi^2 = 8.89$, skilled fathers have intelligent boys.

[33] $\chi^2 = 3.345$, data follow Poisson distribution.

[34] $\chi^2 = 5.85$, accept H_0: $\sigma^2 = 125$

[35] $\chi^2 = 5.732$, C = 0.045, no significant association.

[36] $F = 4.0$, Reject H_0 at $\alpha = 0.05$.

[37] $\chi^2 = 8.00$, The die is unbiased.

[38] χ^2 = 15.238, communities are not independent in the matter of tea taking.

[39] χ^2 = 9.48, the vaccine is effective

[40] χ^2 = 113.74, drug is effective.

[41] Testing $H_0 : \sigma_1^2 = \sigma_2^2$ vs. $H_1 : \sigma_1^2 > \sigma_2^2$, F = 2.25, Variance of Brand A is not more than Brand B.

[42] Theoretical frequencies: 122, 61, 15, 2.5, 0.5

[43] χ^2 = 19.86, Education achievement is dependent on sex.

[44] χ^2 = 243.58, There is a relation between TV ownership and level of income.

[45] Lower limit = 7.1648, upper limit = 7.6352

Chapter 12

[26] ANOVA

Source	*d.f.*	*S.S.*	*M.S.*	*F-value*
Weeks	2	261.77	130.88	16.72*
T	2	38.77	19.38	2.48
H	1	53.38	53.38	6.82
T × H	2	52.40	26.20	3.35
Error	8	62.62	7.83	
Total	15	468.94		

* Sig. at $\alpha = 0.05$

[27] ANOVA

Source	*d.f.*	*S.S.*	*M.S.*	*F-value*
Varieties	4	0.47	0.12	0.50 NS
Error	20	4.85	0.24	
Total	24	5.32		

NS – Non-significant

[28] ANOVA

Source	*d.f.*	*S.S.*	*M.S.*	*F-value*
Rows	3	11.25	3.75	1.00
Columns	3	5.25	1.75	0.47
Treatments	3	214.75	71.58	19.09*
Error	6	22.50	3.75	
Total	15	253.75		

* Sig. at $\alpha = 0.05$

[29] ANOVA

Source	*d.f.*	*S.S.*	*M.S.*	*F-value*
Blocks	3	18.00	6.00	3.61 NS
Treats.	2	8.00	4.00	2.40 NS
Error	6	10.00	1.67	
Total	11	36.00		

NS – Non-significant

[30] ANOVA

Source	*d.f.*	*S.S.*	*M.S.*	*F-value*
Machines	4	35.20	8.80	1.24 NS
Operators	3	53.80	17.93	2.52 NS
Error	12	85.20	7.10	
Total	19	174.20		

NS – Non-significant

[31] ANOVA

Source	*d.f.*	*S.S.*	*M.S.*	*F-value*
Treats.	2	4.02	2.01	1.07 NS
Error	10	18.75	1.88	
Total	12	22.77		

NS – Non-significant

Note : Data was analysed after dividing each value by 100, as the test remains unaffected.

[32] ANOVA

Source	*d.f.*	*S.S.*	*M.S.*	*F-value*
Rows	4	23.6	5.90	0.94
Columns	4	3.2	0.80	0.12
Treats.	4	387.6	96.90	15.38*
Error	12	75.6	6.30	
Total	24	490.0		

* Sig. at $\alpha = 0.05$

[33] ANOVA

Source	d.f.	S.S.	M.S.	F-value
Makes	2	63.33	31.66	5.43
Error	12	70.00	5.83	
Total	14	133.33		

* Sig. at $\alpha = 0.05$

[34] ANOVA

Source	d.f.	S.S.	M.S.	F-value
Salesmen	3	17.00	5.67	3.40
Methods	2	18.00	9.00	5.38*
Error	6	10.00	1.67	
Total	11	45.00		

* Sig. at $\alpha = 0.05$

Chapter 13

[9] $D_n = 0.136$, die is imperfect.

[10] (*i*) $f(u) = 0.183$, samples have come from the same lot. (*ii*) Prob > .05, samples have come from the same lot. (*iii*) $r = 6$, samples have come from the same lot.

[11] $r = 13$, The numbers are in random order.

[12] (*a*) P $(X \leq 4) = 0.377$, samples have come from identical populations
(*b*) $T^+ = 19$, same conclusion as in part (*a*).

[13] $r_1 = 4$; $r_2 = 4$, coin is unbiased.

[14] (*i*) $q = 1.796$, Students belonged to identical populations. (*ii*) $H = 2.04$, same result as in (*i*).

[15] $F = 3.8$, drugs have no effect.

Chapter 14

[5] Q = 0.50

[6] Data are consistent.

[7] Date are consistent.

[8] Data are inconsistent.

[9] $Q_B = -0.72$, $Q_G = -0.61$

[10] Q = – 0.53

[11] Q = 0.69, Coaching is useful.

[12] 48 and 2

[13] $Q_A = -0.27$, $Q_B = -0.28$. Low degree negative association.

[14] Data are inconsistent, since ab = – 1

[15] (*ABC*) = 293 but given that (*ABC*) = 297, report is incorrect.

[16] $O_F = 0.7$. Frenchmen are more associated with their own music than German, since $Q_G = 0.47$

[17] $Q = -0.56$.

Chapter 15

[20] $r = 1.173$, $t = 0.43$, nonsignificant correlation.

[21] (*a*) $\hat{Y} = 0.35X + 0.8788$ (*b*) $\hat{Y} = 1.054$ (*c*) $t = 1.64$, regression coefficient is nonsignificant.

[22] 0.918

[23] (*a*) $\hat{Y} = 0.04X + 3.673$ (*b*) $t = 0.58$, regression coefficient is nonsignificant (*c*) t = 1.04, a is nonsignificant (d) $\hat{Y} = 5.67$ Lakhs tonne

[24] 0.416

[25] 0.785, there is concordance.

[26] $r = 0.742$ and $r_s = 0.735$. The rank correlation does not use the actual values.

[27] $\hat{Y} = -0.469X + 53.497$

[28] $r = 0.735$, $\overline{X} = 2.565$, $Y = 9.522$

[29] $r = 0.943$, yes, Minimum score $\hat{X} = 14.07$

[30] (*a*) (*i*) $\hat{Y} = 186.8$ and $\hat{X} = 32.0$ (*ii*) $r = 0.49$

(*b*) $\hat{Y} = 0.653X + 21.7$ and $\hat{X} = 0.27Y + 26.675$

[31] $r = 0.95$, $\hat{Y} = 0.95X + 7.25$, $\hat{X} = 0.95\ Y - 6.4$

[32] $\hat{Y} = 0.8X + 12$ and $\hat{X} = 0.45Y + 1$

[33] $\hat{Y} = 0.61X + 15.1$, $\hat{X} = 1.36Y - 5.2$

[34] -1

[35] $\hat{Y} = 5.0 + 3.25X$

[36] $r_s = 0.738$

[37] 0.939

[38] $S_x^2 = 9.0$, $S_{xy} = 9.0$

[39] (*i*) 2 units/year (*ii*) 7 yrs (*iii*) 42 units

[40] $\hat{Y} = 0.56X + 1.25$ (*i*) Rs 12450 (*ii*) Rs 560 with an increase of 100 building permits.

[41] $n = 10$, $\sigma_x = 3$, $b_{YX} = 4/3$, $b_{XY} = \frac{3}{16}$

[42] $y = 2035\ e^{-1.7495}$

[43] $r_s = 0.747$

[45] $b_{YX} = \frac{4}{5}; b_{XY} = \frac{5}{9}; r = \frac{2}{3}$

[46] $r = 0.03$ without adjustment for tied ranks and $r = 0$ after adjustment for tied ranks.

[47] (*i*) $\overline{X} = 8$, $\overline{Y} = 0$; (*ii*) $b_{YX} = \frac{4}{5}, b_{XY} = \frac{9}{20}$ and (*iii*) $r = 0.60$

[48] $r = 0.87$ and regression equation of rating (y) on experience (x) is $\hat{Y} = 69.7 + 1.13X$

[49] (*a*) $\rho = 0$ and $\rho = \pm 1$ when two lines of regression intersect at 90° and 180° respectively.
(*b*) $r = 0.80$

[50] $r = 0.948$; value of r for new set will also be 0.948.

[51] $Y = -1 + 3.55 X - 0.27 X^2$

Chapter 16

[9] (*i*) $\hat{Y} = 3446.41 - 2.247X_1 - 0.1515X_2 - 0.0349X_3$ (*ii*) Partial regression coefficients are nonsignificant (*iii*) β_3 is nonsignificant (*iv*) $\hat{Y} = 3029.5$ (*v*) $R^2 = 0.0745$, X_1, X_2, X_3 are poor regressors (*vi*) $R = 0.27$

[10] (*i*) $\hat{Y} = 9.828X_1 + 3.127X_2 - 1901.73$ (*ii*) $\hat{Y}$ = Rs.749.58 (*iii*) β_1 and β_2 are nonsignificant (*iv*) $r_{YX_2X_1} = 0.449$

[11] $r_{13.2} = 0.98$

[12] $R_{1.23} = \sqrt{2r}/\sqrt{1+r}, r_{12.3} = r(1-2r)/(1-r^2)$

[13] $R_{1.23} = 0.67$ and $r_{31.2} = 0.51$

[14] Regression line is, $x_1 = 0.3\, x_2 + 0.2\, x_3 + 24$ and $\hat{x}_1 = 51.6$

[15] (*i*) $r_{12.3} = 0.53$ (*ii*) $b_{12.3} = 0.31875$ (*iii*) $b_{21.3} = 0.8813$

[16] (*a*) $r_{12.3} = 0.6673$ and $R_{1.23} = 0.8561$
(*b*) $1 - r_{12}^2 - r_{13}^2 - r_{23}^2 + 2r_{12}r_{13}r_{23} = -0232 < 0$. Hence correlation coefficients are inconsistent.

Chapter 17

[17] (*i*) $Y_{1972} = 196$ (*ii*) $Y_c = 148.17 + 3.835X$; $Y_{1972} = 198.025$ (*iii*) $Y_{1972} = 198$

[18] $Y_c = 15.325 - 0.169X$

[19] $Y_c = 358.575 + 27.55X$; $Y_{1980} = 661.625$

[21] S.I: 99.65, 108.96, 95.22, 96.17

[22] S.I: 39.5, 63.3, 99.2, 113.9, 129.8, 148.3

[24] S.I: 69.42, 78.24,84.66, 167.68

[25] $Y_c = 10 + 1.08X$

[26] $Y_{1976} = 218.6$

[27] $Y_c = 14.312 + 1.84X + 0.114X^2$ with 1941 as origin. $Y_{1971} = 20.858$.

[28] S.I: 100.03, 109.54, 103.14, 87.28

[29] Log Y = 1.9704 + 1.544X with 1968 as origin; $Y_{1972} = 387.3$

[30] 3-yearly moving averages: 7.00, 9.33, 10.67, 11.00 9.67, 10.00, 11.00, 14.00, 16.33, 16.67, 15.33, 13.00, 13.33.

[32] S.I: 104.9, 97.5, 90.2, 112.2, 112.2, 114.7, 119.5, 92.7, 82.9, 78.1, 87.8, 107.3

[33] 300, 500, 500, 400, 500, 550

[34] $\hat{Y} = 3.82\, X + 69.33$ (with 1984 as origin and X units = 1 yr.)

[36] 6.857, 10.857, 14.857, 18.857, 22.857, 26.857, 30.857 and $\hat{Y}_{1988} = 34.857$

[37] $\hat{Y} = 33.60 (1.013)^X$ (with 1941 as base and X units = 1 *yr.*)
Trend values : 22.80, 25.95, 29.53, 33.60, 38.23, 43.50, 49.50;
$Y_{1981} = 56.32$

[39] 44.19, 20.32, 30.38 and 36.27

[40] Taking $x = \frac{1}{2}$ year, 87–88 = x_0, $\hat{Y} = 113 + 7.69X$, $Y_{1993} = 197.59$

[41] (*i*) $\hat{Y} = 133.86 + 16.107X$; $\hat{Y}_{2000} = 214.395$

[42]

Summer	Rainy	Winter	using average for seasonals
93.127	95.202	111.682	

[43] (*a*) Trend line is, $y = 186 - 11.7\,x$
Trend values : 232.8, 221.1, 209.4, 197.7, 186, 174.3, 162.6, 150.9, 139.2
Short term fluctuations ;
– 0.8, 4.9, 10.6, – 17.7, 4, – 6.3, – 0.6, 1.1, 4.8

[44]

Q_1	Q_2	Q_3	Q_4
63.1	64.8	62.9	63.5

[45] (*i*) Equation of the line, $\hat{Y} = 89.0 + 2.0\,X$
Trend values : 83, 85, 87, 89, 91, 93, 95
(*ii*) Monthly increase = $\frac{1}{6}$

Chapter 18

[14] 127.85
[15] 139.81
[16] 66.84, 70.05, 74.33, 86.10, 94.65, 100, 98.40, 103.21, 106.42, 147.06, 156.68, 171.66
[17] Group CPI: (*a*) 184.30 (*b*) 235.98 (*c*) 277.79 (*d*) 280.29 (*e*) 289.40;
General CPI = 253.55
[18] 100, 109.8 107.28, 108.83, 111.54, 105.24, 106.05
[19] Indices to the base 1967: 101.5, 104.5, 86.4, 95.5, 107.92, 143.25, 179.54, 171.90, 142.30, 159.48.
[20] Real income indices: 100, 106.20, 104.74, 74.92, 70.86, 51.04, 48.73, 45.08, Actually the wages have reduced.
[21] Laspeyre's index = 86.02, Paasche's index = 81.25
[22] 188.00 104.25, 104.08, 93.14, 103.16, 102.34
[23] 115.76
[24] Rises are: Food — 420, Fuel — 210, Rent — 175, Misc. — 350
[25] Paasche's Formula, CPI = 170.94
[26] 131.90
[27] 138.53
[29] Missing figure = 4.0
[30] $L_{71.80} = 103.8334$, $P_{71.80} = 104.2330$
$F_{71.80} = 104.0330$

[31] The worker is a looser by Rs 50.

[32] $I_p = 240$, $I_q = 80$, $I_p \times I_q = 192$.

[33] $L_{01} = 126.84$, $P_{01} = 125.00$, $L_{10} = 80.00$, $P_{10} = 78.84$ $Q_{01} = 100.633$. These figures satisfy both the tests.

[34] Fisher's $P_{01} = 104.03$, $P_{10} = 96.12$, $\therefore P_{01} \times P_{10} = 1$, $Q_{01} = 127.3250$, $V_{01} = 132.46$, $P_{01}\ Q_{01} = 132.\ 4562$. $\therefore P_{01}\ Q_{01} = V_{01}$. Both the tests are satisfied.

[35] $I_{01} = 128.75$, with new weights, $I_{01} = 129.\ 34$, Increase is 0.59%

[36] Fisher's $P_{01} = 131.75$, $P_{10} = 75.90$, $Q_{01} = 99.392$, Holds the tests.

[37] (*i*) 170.30% (*ii*) Rs 2554.50

[38] $L_{01} = 221.98$; $P_{01} = 216.30$

Chapter 19

[15]

x	y	Δy	$\Delta^2 y$	$\Delta^3 y$	$\Delta^4 y$	$\Delta^5 y$
0	2					
		6				
2	8		26			
		32		42		
4	40		68		10	
		100		52		–8
6	140		120		2	
		220		54		
8	360		174			
		394				
10	754					

[16] By Newton's backward formula, $y_{1972} = 18.20$

[17] By Newton-Gregory forward formula, $y_{45} = 47.87$, Percentage of students = 25.19

[18] By Newton's forward formula, No. of workers = 53

[19] 1.03 lakhs

[20] (*i*) By *N—G* backward formula, $l_{45} = 299$

(*ii*) By *N—G* forward formula, $l_{25} = 497$

(*iii*) By Gauss forward formula, $l_{35} = 391$

[21] By Lagrange's formula, $\log_{10} 130 = 2.1139$

[22] y_{15} = Rs 207.50

[23] (*b*) $y_3 = 4.79$

[24] $f(1.4) = 1.56$, $f(2.0) = 3.00$

[25] (*i*) 4.06 (*ii*) 4.06

[26] $\Gamma 1.7 = 0.9232$

[27] 1.835

[28] 13.34°

[29] (*i*) y_{38} = Rs 38.35, (*ii*) y_{24} = Rs 25.30

[30] 32
[31] y_{1972} = Rs. 24.38 crore, y_{1975} = Rs. 34.78 crore
[32] $y_{2.1} = 0.123$, $y_{2.4} = 0.0904$
[33] y_{22} = 27.85 yrs.
[34] By Lagrange's formula, $P(7)$ = 15.67 lbs.
[35] y_{17} = Rs. 11.36
[36] 135
[37] $f(x) = 1 + x + x^2$ and $f(4) = 21$
[38] (*i*) $f(2.5) = 15.625$ (*ii*) 14.015 (*iii*) Least square estimate is better than estimate by interpolation method.

Chapter 20

[6] Payoff Table

Event	ACTS		
	Travel by aeroplane	*Travel by train*	*Travel by car*
Money saving	0	400	300
Time saving	14	0	8
Enjoyment	1	4	10

[8] (*a*) EMV_{Ho} = 30,500, EMV_{SA} = 37,250, EMV_{FA} = 36,450 (*c*) EPVI = 50
[9] Stock semi-automatic machines.
[10] Act A_2 is inadmissible; EP A_1 = 34.5, Act A_1 has maximum expected payoff.
[11] A_3 has minimum EOL.
[12] (*a*) Payoff Table (Cash receipt)

	Tomato	*Pea*	*Cauliflower*	*Prob.*
Little	1,00,000	1,20,000	2,40,000	0.4
Good	1,25,000	1,60,000	4,00,000	0.6

(*b*) Cauliflower has maximum EMVI.
(*c*) Cauliflower (*d*) Cauliflower.

[13]

	Hot snacks stall	*Exp.profit*	*Ice cream & cold drink stall*	*Exp. profit*
Warm	3,000 × .4	Rs. 1,200	18,000 × .4	Rs. 7,200
Cold & Rainy	15,000 × .6	Rs. 9,000	3,000 × .6	Rs. 1,800
Total		Rs. 10,200		Rs. 9,000

He is advised to run the hot snack stall as the expected profit for it is more than ice cream and cold drink shop.

[14]

	Opportunity Loss Table		
	I	II	III
Team x wins	Rs. 0	100	400
Team y wins	Rs. 400	300	0

Gift article	Expected opportunity loss
I	Rs. 80
II	Rs. 140
III	Rs. 320

Buy Type I since EOL is lowest.

[15] EMV : A B C
19.4 12.5 13.0; Select A with highest ΣMV.
Σ Max. payoff × Prob. = 32, EVPI = 32 – 19.4 = 12.6

[16] (*a*) EVV : A_1 A_2 A_3
412.5 455.0 417.5 ; Select A_2

(*b*) (*i*) Maximin payoff = 3000; Choose P_3

(*ii*) Minimax payoff = 3000, Select P_3

(*iii*) $E(P_1) = 3833.33$, $E(P_2) = 3166.66$, $E(P_3) = 3000$. $E(P_1)$ is maximum. So best strategy is P_1.

[19] Maximum EMV is 4000 for the act expand 100 units. So best act is expand 100 units.

[20] (*i*) $E(a_1) = 14.5$, $E(a_2) = 11.5$, $E(a_3) = 18.0$, $E(a_4) = 21.5$. $E(a_4)$ is maximum, so best action is a_4.

(*ii*) Maximin payoff = 15, Best action is a_4.

(*iii*) Minimax payoff = 21, Best action is a_3.

(*iv*) $H_1 = 15$, $H_2 = 15$, $H_3 = 16.5$, & $H_4 = 22.5$. Since for a_4, H is maximum, the best action is a_4.

[22] Regret table

	E_1	E_2	E_3
A_1	0	5	15
A_2	10	0	10
A_3	30	15	0

	A_1	A_2	A_3
EOL :	8	6	12

Optimum action is A_2

[23] (*i*) Maximax payoff = 30; Best alternative is A.

(*ii*) Maximin payoff = 15; D is the best alternative.

(*iii*) Regret table

	A	*B*	*C*	*D*
P	20	15	7	0
Q	15	16	15	0
R	0	3	9	0
S	0	8	11	15
Col.Max.	20	16	15	15

Minimum regret is 15 for C and D both. Therefore, select either Act C or Act D.

Chapter 21

[13] U.C.L.$_{P}'$ = 0.1779, L.C.L$_{P}'$ =0.1295

[14] U.C.L. = 0.111, L.C.L. = 0.025

[15] U.C.L. = 35.37, L.C.L. = 7.57, Process is not in S.Q.C.

[16] (*i*) U.C.L. = 1034.3, L.C.L. = 965.7. Process is not in S.Q.C. (*ii*) *U.C.L.*$_{\bar{x}}$ = 1322.42, L.C.L.$_{\bar{x}}$ = 504.66, *C.L.* $\bar{x}$ = 913.79, Process is under S.Q.C. U.C.L.$_{R}$ = 1118.92, L.C.L.$_{R}$ = 0, C.L.$_{R}$ = 4990.33. Process is in S.Q.C.

[17] U.C.L. = 25.22, L.C.L. = 2.78, C.L. = 14, Process is under S.Q.C.

[18] (*ii*) *U.C.L.* $\bar{x}$ = 20.49, *L.C.L.* $\bar{x}$ = 11.91, *C.L.* $\bar{x}$ = 16.2, Process is under S.Q.C., U.C.L$_{R}$ = 15.61, L.C.L$_{R}$ = 0, C.L.$_{R}$ = 7.4, Process is under S.Q.C.

[19] U.C.L $\bar{x}$ = 46.90, L.C.L $\bar{x}$ = 41.50, C.L. $\bar{x}$ = 44.2,
Process is not under S.Q.C. U.C.L$_{R}$ = 11.22, L.C.L.$_{R}$ = 0, C.L.$_{R}$ = 5.6, Process is under S.Q.C.

[21] U.C.L. $\bar{x}$ = 33.57, L.C.L $\bar{x}$ = 32.63, C.L. $\bar{x}$ = 33.1; U.C.L. σ = 0.79, L.C.L. σ = 0.13. C.L. = 0.46.

[22] (*i*) σ = 0.00144 (*ii*) U.C.L. $\bar{x}$ = 3.13, L.C.L. $\bar{x}$ = 3.12, C.L. $\bar{x}$ = 3.126 (*iii*) U.C.L.$_{R}$ = 0.018, L.C.L.$_{R}$ = 0, C.L.$_{R}$ = 0.009 (*iv*) Within the limits 3.1303 and 3.1216.

Chapter 23

[12] 39.38, 39.54, 39.33, 38.84, 38.30, 37.88, 38.58, 37.94, 38.71, 38.39

[14] 8.4, 7.40, 7.90, 9.62, 11.30, 12.60, 12.87, 14.17, 18.96, 23.92

[15] 7.82, 10.06, 11.35, 11.06, 11.30, 9.57, 11.30, 10.43, 11.44, 14.48, 13.49, 14.64, 16.08, 14.01

Chapter 24

[9] (*i*) C.D.R (*X*) = 36.36‰, C.D.R (*Y*) = 8.20‰. (*ii*) S$_{T}$.D.R (*X*) = 36.36, S$_{T}$.D.R (*Y*) = 8.50, Town *Y* has superior health conditions.

[10] 51.08‰

[11]

Age	l_x	d_x	q_x	p_x	L_x	T_x	e_x^0
72	4,412	688	0.1559	0.8441	4,068	34,097	7.73
73	3.724	523	0.1404	0.8596	3,462	30,029	8.06
74	3,201	642	0.2006	0.7994	2,880	26,567	8.30

[12] GRR = 1.235 per woman; NRR = 0.903 per woman

[13] G.F.R = 177.71, ASFR (‰): 69.97, 256.99, 274.01, 220.97, 151.97, 83.93

[14] S_T.D.R. (I) = 6.382, S_T.D.R. (II) = 5.00

[15] GRR = 2.145 per woman

[16]

Age	l_x	d_x	p_x	q_x	L_x	T_x	e_x^0
4	98,000	500	0.9947	0.0053	94,750	48,50,300	51.06
5	94,500	400	0.9958	0.0042	94.300	47,50,500	50.32

[17] NRR = 1.149 per woman

[18] GRR = 2.148 per woman

[19] S_T.D.R (A) = 13, S_T.D.R (B) = 15, Locality A is better for health.

[20] C.D.R (A) = 23.11, C.D.R (B) = 22.80

For Standard Population A, S_T.D.R (A) = 23.11, S_T.D.R (B) = 23.89

Index of Topics

O

P

Q

T